ANCESTRAL TRAILS

THE COMPLETE GUIDE TO BRITISH GENEALOGY AND FAMILY HISTORY

SECOND EDITION

MARK HERBER

FOREWORD BY
JOHN TITFORD

GENEALOGICAL PUBLISHING Co., Inc.

Originally published by Sutton Publishing Limited
Phoenix Mill, Thrupp, Stroud, Gloucestershire, England GL5 2BU
in association with the Society of Genealogists
14 Charterhouse Buildings, Goswell Road, London, England EC1M 7BA

First Edition 1997
Second Edition 2004

Second Edition published in the U.S.A., 2006,
by arrangement with Sutton Publishing Limited
by Genealogical Publishing Co., Inc.
3600 Clipper Mill Road, Suite 260
Baltimore, Maryland 21211-1953

ISBN-13: 978-0-8063-1771-7
ISBN-10: 0-8063-1771-X
Library of Congress Catalogue Card Number 2006927330
Made in the United States of America

Cover illustrations: left, group photograph at the marriage of Frederick Eagles and Jessie Law in 1926
(author's collection); right, The Story Teller, 1890 (courtesy of Hastings Museum and Art Gallery).

CONTENTS

CONTENTS

LIST OF ILLUSTRATIONS

FOREWORD TO THE
SECOND EDITION

The closing decades of a century would seem to be a time of particular inspiration for authors and editors of genealogical reference works. So it was in the 1880s and 1890s, and then again in the 1990s, at which time Mark Herber's *Ancestral Trails* first saw the light of day.

My foreword to the original edition of 1997 opened with the phrase "Genealogy has come of age". We might now say, as the twenty-first century is upon us, that *Ancestral Trails*, too, has come of age. Winner of the Library Association's prestigious McColvin Medal for an outstanding work of reference, used and recommended by genealogists far and wide, it has been granted the ultimate accolade of being widely referred to simply as "Herber", in the style of other major genealogical reference books such as "Marshall" and "Whitmore", as I was bold enough to hope would be the case.

A book like this doesn't maintain its pre-eminence in the field by resting on its laurels, however. The subject with which it deals has become more of a moving target in recent years than it ever was before, and the author's sure aim and steady hand have been much in evidence as he has meticulously updated and expanded his original work. An increasing amount of material of relevance to family historians is being made available in print, on microform, on CD-ROM and on the Internet; fresh finding aids appear and older ones become redundant; record repositories, libraries, family history societies and other interest groups appear afresh on the scene, separate from or merge with others, or change their names. None of this has escaped the notice of the author of *Ancestral Trails*, and this welcome new edition, to which the phrase "bigger and better" hardly does justice, is testimony to the continuing careful attention to detail which characterised the first edition.

Ancestral Trails remains the essential guide to an area of research which, as the author points out in his opening sentence, is so complex and yet so fascinating precisely because it "involves the study of many subjects". Exhaustive but not exhausting, this is a book to be read, dipped into and enjoyed, as well as one to be referred to by way of its copious index. Above all, it is anchored in reality by the author's use of material from his own family history research, as he guides us through the sources of information we will need to consult and the processes we will need to follow.

The growing number of people interested in British family history are well served by *Ancestral Trails*. Amateurs and professionals alike can trust its accuracy and have confidence in the breadth of its coverage, enjoy the fine range of illustrations provided, and use the detailed appendices and bibliography as a guide to further sources of information and inspiration.

A book of this kind appears only once in each generation. Long may it, and the subject with which it deals, continue to prosper!

John Titford

Chairman of Examiners, Institute of Heraldic and Genealogical Studies
Former Chairman, Society of Genealogists' Publications Committee and the Federation of Family History
Societies' Education Committee
Member of Council, Association of Genealogists and Researchers in Archives

Higham, Derbyshire
November 2003

FOREWORD TO THE
FIRST EDITION

Genealogy has come of age. Once the preserve of a handful of enthusiastic amateurs and a mere smattering of professionals, it now offers countless hours of enjoyment and fascination to those who like a leisure pursuit offering some degree of intellectual challenge, and a means of making a living to a not inconsiderable army of record agents and paid researchers.

We might choose to think of genealogy as the pursuit of ancestry and the compilation of pedigrees. In the event Mark Herber's book goes beyond this: his is the complete guide to British genealogy *and family history*. We can make a quite genuine, if contentious, distinction here: family historians are keen to move beyond the constraints of mere pedigree-making and to arrive at an understanding of their ancestors within the broader context of time and place. Little wonder that demographers and local and social historians are increasingly keen to open up lines of communication with family historians, given the ample opportunities for mutually beneficial relationships to be established involving these and other disciplines.

Professional and amateur family historians often fail to understand or to appreciate each other, alas, though each group benefits from the work of the other. What is certain, however, is that amateurs in the field are increasingly becoming professional in their standards, whether or not they are paid for what they do. In other words, many family historians are keen to learn, to educate themselves in the mysteries of their craft; they know that the greater their understanding of the subject in all its breadth and depth, the greater the chance of solving seemingly intractable problems.

Family historians educate themselves in different ways. Many progress by way of self-instruction and experience, others follow a correspondence course or attend lectures and seminars provided by family history societies or other organisations. Some are content to learn at their own pace, seeking no validation of the level of knowledge and competence they have achieved, while others prefer to move through a series of graded examinations which lead to approved qualifications. All need a comprehensive and accurate body of information concerning their subject – and now, with the publication of Mark Herber's book, that is exactly what is available to them.

Genealogy, unlike its grand relation, heraldry, has long suffered from the lack of printed handbooks (textbooks, if you prefer) which cover the subject across its range and in a systematic way. Stacey Grimaldi's pioneering book, *Origines Genealogicae: Or the Sources whence English Genealogies may be Traced from the Conquest to the Present Time*, published in 1828, was a start, at least. This century has seen the publication of a number of user-friendly general guides such as *In Search of Ancestry* by Gerald Hamilton-Edwards, *Introducing Genealogy* by Arthur J. Willis and the three volumes of *Genealogical Research in England and Wales* by David E. Gardner and Frank Smith, which is painstakingly thorough in many of the areas it chooses to cover.

Ancestral Trails follows in this tradition but goes beyond its predecessors and is comprehensive in its coverage in a way that they never even claimed to be. Family historians are now exceptionally well served when it comes to compact yet detailed guides to specific topics or groups of records, compiled by the indefatigable Jeremy Gibson and others, but only now, with the publication of *Ancestral Trails*, is there a textbook which spans the world of genealogy and family history in all its rich diversity, written by a practitioner for practitioners. Family historians deserve no less.

In years to come *Ancestral Trails* may be referred to simply as "Herber", in the style of "Marshall" and "Whitmore". That would be the ultimate accolade, and richly deserved.

John Titford
Chairman of Examiners, Institute of Heraldic and Genealogical Studies
Chairman, Federation of Family History Societies' Education Sub-Committee
Series editor, Society of Genealogists' My Ancestors . . . *publications*

Higham, Derbyshire
June 1997

ACKNOWLEDGEMENTS
AND ABBREVIATIONS

Many people have helped me in producing the original and new editions of this book. John Titford has kept me supplied with documents and information about particular records and some of my ancestors' families. I must also thank my relatives, particularly Jack Bulleid, Jeff Russell, Ros Dunning, Dave Morecombe, Carol O'Neill and Frank Radford, who provided invaluable help in the form of photographs, documents and their own research into our mutual family trees. I have also received useful comments from Miriam Scott, Geoff Stone and Charles Tucker, for which I am grateful. Dr John Keen was also kind to inform me of the full text of the inscription on the tombstone of my ancestor James Chapman (see chapter 8). My greatest thanks go to Kay Lovick and Karen Poole, who typed much of the draft of the first edition, and to Colleen Keck, who endured me for the six years that it took to write it (and the months that I have taken to prepare this new edition).

My thanks also to the staff of libraries and record offices that I used, particularly Guildhall Library, the Society of Genealogists, Devon Record Office, Essex Record Office, Bedford Record Office, the Family Records Centre, London Metropolitan Archives and the National Archives. Thanks are also due to those people who have made the hobby much easier for everyone, by transcribing and indexing documents, or producing books for researchers. For example, Cliff Webb, Jeremy Gibson and Anthony Camp, MBE, have made great contributions to the hobby. All genealogists owe them an enormous debt.

The designs of the map, the birth, marriage and death certificates, the application forms and the census returns at illustrations 9–20, 89 and 113 (and illustrations 75 and 76, and the information contained in illustrations 21–23) are Crown copyright and included by kind permission of the Controller of HMSO. The following individuals and organisations have also kindly permitted the reproduction and inclusion of illustrations: the Church of Jesus Christ of Latter-Day Saints (illustrations 21–23 and 37–39); Essex Record Office (25 and 83); the Institute of Heraldic and Genealogical Studies (26); Devon Record Office and the ministers of Dunsford, Sandford and Winkleigh (27, 30, 33, 34, 36, 72 and 84–88); Vestry House Museum and the PCC of Walthamstow, St Mary (31); Guildhall Library, Corporation of London (35, 42, 55, 62, 68, 69, 71 and 115); Jeremy Gibson and the Federation of Family History Societies (49); the Religious Society of Friends (62); Bedford Record Office (63, 64 and 132); Harry Margary (69); the Ordnance Survey and David & Charles (Publishers) Ltd (70); the British Library Newspaper Library (79 and 80); J.B. Hayward & Sons (100); Lloyds of London and Guildhall Library, Corporation of London (116); the House of Lords Record Office (121); and the Naval and Military Press (101). Illustration 78 is from an Australian newspaper, but I have not been able to identify the paper or any copyright owner.

Books to which I refer in the text, by author's name and a number, for example "Steel (29)", are listed in numerical order in the bibliography. Most of these books are held at the Society of Genealogists, reference libraries or family history society libraries and many can be obtained from local libraries by inter-library loan. The study of family history involves cross-referencing many different sources of material. For example, civil registration certificates help you to use the census records (and vice-versa). Each chapter of this book therefore includes many references to other chapters. I have consequently used "(# chapter 8)" to indicate that you should also refer to the noted chapter for further information. The following abbreviations are also used throughout this book:

CRO	County Record Office
FFHS	Federation of Family History Societies
FHS	family history society
FRC	Family Records Centre
g.g.g. grandfather (etc.)	great great great grandfather (etc.)
IGI*	International Genealogical Index
IHGS	Institute of Heraldic and Genealogical Studies
LDS	Church of Jesus Christ of Latter-Day Saints
PRO	Public Record Office (now The National Archives)
SoG	Society of Genealogists
TNA	The National Archives

As far as practical, information in this book is correct as at November 2003. Any errors are my own and suggested corrections to the text will be gratefully received.

Finally, I have read many complimentary reviews of *Ancestral Trails* (and readers' comments) in journals, newspapers and on the Internet. I would therefore like to thank everyone who has used and enjoyed *Ancestral Trails*. I hope that this new edition will also be enjoyed by family historians and that it will help many people in the search for their ancestors.

*International Genealogical Index and *Ancestral File* are registered trademarks of the Church of Jesus Christ of Latter-Day Saints. *FamilySearch* is a trademark of Intellectual Reserve, Inc.

INTRODUCTION

The research of family history involves the study of many subjects. The starting point is genealogy, that is the study of individuals' descent and relationships. Genealogical research reveals facts such as names, dates and places. It answers questions such as "Who were your great grandparents?" and "When were they born?" The study of genealogy has always been important because of the inheritance of property or titles (most people in this country have seen a family tree of our monarchs). Religious books (such as the Bible) and ancient histories (such as the *Anglo-Saxon Chronicle*) include detailed ancestries of those people who appear in the history. The Bible tells how all people are descended from Adam and Eve, and the *Anglo-Saxon Chronicle* records the lineage of the Saxon kings back to the god Woden.

Your own family tree may soon become a vast document with many generations of ancestors and many lines of cousins. Even if you investigate only your ancestors, the number of people on the family tree becomes extremely large. The number of ancestors in a generation doubles every time you step back a generation (although marriages between cousins may reduce the number of individual ancestors). You have four grandparents and eight great grandparents, but if you go back seven generations, you will have 128 ancestors (g.g.g.g.g. grandparents) in that generation. If you go back ten generations, there are 1,024 ancestors in that generation. Go back twenty generations and you could in theory find 1,048,576 ancestors in that generation. However, that would take you back to the middle ages and you are unlikely to find many ancestors of that time (because of the lack of records) unless you have links with royal, noble or landowning families.

Your family tree, with names, dates and places, will be of interest in itself. You may also find links with famous people, or with nobility or royalty. Wagner (31) notes that the 64 g.g.g.g. grandparents of the late Queen Mother included dukes, earls, country gentlemen, clergy, the landlord of an inn, a plumber and a toymaker. Your ancestry could show a similar range of people. Do not be put off the idea of researching your ancestry simply because you believe that your ancestors were poor and would not have been recorded. The poor can be as interesting as the rich and the majority of people living in Britain since the late 16th century were noted in at least one type of document. My family were fairly average, yet I have located my ancestors in nearly every type of English record described in this book. You should also not be deterred from research by reason of your surname being of foreign origin or because you know that many of your ancestors came from abroad. Foreign research can be difficult, but it is not impossible nor necessarily more difficult than British research.

Family history has many aspects other than genealogy. What were your ancestors really like, what did they look like, what did they do, how were they affected by great historical events and how did they live from day to day? Family history includes the research of all these matters. This entails obtaining old photographs, finding out about your ancestors' occupations, visiting places and finding out what those places were like in earlier days. If you have some special interest, this can be researched. For example, you could investigate the effect on your ancestors of a war or a recession in the economy. You may have specific reasons for undertaking research. I wanted to find out whether I really was of German descent and, if so, whether Herber was the German name or an anglicised version of my family's original name. You may have heard a story that your family is descended from royalty or from a famous historical figure and you might wish to establish whether there truly is such a link. It is for you to decide exactly what research you wish to undertake and how far you wish to pursue it.

Tracing your family history is a time-consuming and interesting hobby. It can be frustrating, but it can also be very exciting. It is particularly suitable for those who enjoy historical detective work; sorting new information, analysing clues and deciding the next step to take. As with most research, luck also plays an important part. One piece of information can start you off on a lengthy piece of research and you may find it easy to trace many generations within a few hours if, for example, you find a register for a parish where your ancestors lived for centuries. If you find a link with a family that possessed a title or substantial property, one of the published works containing genealogies of the nobility or gentry will take you back several centuries. Such links are surprisingly common.

The records available in England and Wales are extensive for the period after 1800 and on most lines of ancestry you may have little difficulty in tracing your family tree back to the late 18th century. You may encounter problems. For example, you may find that your great grandfather was a foundling and that no one knew his parentage. Other problems may also arise, but if you continue your research and collect more information, you may be able to take the next step back in your family tree. For the period before the late 18th century, you may face greater problems. The main source of information is parish registers and, with luck, you can trace your family tree back to the 16th or 17th century. However, missing registers, unrecorded movements of people between parishes and other difficulties may bring you to a halt. If you are looking for the baptism of your ancestor John Smith in a certain parish in a certain year, yet find that three John Smiths were baptised in that year, your progress on that ancestral line will come to a halt unless you can ascertain which John is your ancestor. For the period before the mid-16th century, it is very difficult to progress further unless you have found a link with a family that held property or a title, or which otherwise merited an entry in the relatively few records available. An advantage of researching many ancestral lines is that although you may be disappointed on some lines, your research of others may continue to be successful.

Always research backwards in time. Do not pick someone in the 18th century who had your surname and try to trace all that person's descendants, hoping to find that they include yourself. This would be time-consuming and would probably fail. Fortunately, people are now no longer so intent on proving a particular descent. In Victorian England, many wealthy people commissioned genealogists to research and prove their descent (usually incorrectly) from titled families (who had a coat of arms) so that they could claim the same right. Fortunately, this is now less important to most people, but it is not an unknown motive and you must still beware of the genealogist who boasts of his illustrious ancestors.

There is a general book on family history that I would recommend to anyone commencing research. *Discovering your Family History* by Steel (29) was originally published in conjunction with a BBC television series presented by Gordon Honeycombe. The programme and book dealt not only with tracing a family tree but also with investigating the social and economic aspects of family history. Gordon Honeycombe was principally interested in whether a family legend about his Honeycombe ancestors was true. The book is a fine example of why people become intrigued by family history, but also illustrates the many sources of information available to build up a family history. The book shows how (by collecting old photographs, maps or engravings and consulting local history books) one can recreate an ancestor's life. The books that I recommend for specific aspects of family history or genealogical research are noted in the relevant chapters.

While researching my family tree, I realised that there was no sufficiently detailed and up to date general work available that described genealogical records and guided researchers to the extensive published sources or to the many detailed books dealing with specific aspects of genealogical research, such as records of the Royal Marines or records of the 17th-century hearth tax. I hope that the publication of *Ancestral Trails* in October 1997 filled that gap by guiding researchers to the vast range of sources, reference works and finding aids (and passing on my own experience of the records), but also linking the many sources together, to ensure that researchers could use material found in one source to assist a search in other sources.

Family history research has developed since 1997, but the basic principles of research (and most of the materials used by researchers) remain the same. Some developments are of a minor nature, such as new indexes, books and some changes to the names and addresses of certain archives. However, some developments are significant, for example, the release of further records and the increasing amount of material available on computer disk and the Internet.

Important new material continues to be deposited at archives, including records of men who served in the armed forces in the First World War, records of merchant seamen from 1918 to 1972 and the 1901 census. More material is also being transcribed, indexed or published and archives' catalogues and indexes are being improved. Many family historians, perhaps the majority, now use a computer. Family history programs, such as *Family Tree Maker*, enable the results of research to be input on a computer. Millions of names and an enormous amount of data about ancestors and family members (as well as scanned documents) can be organised in files on computer disks and found quickly and efficiently. Family historians, archivists, librarians, authors and publishers are taking advantage of the benefits offered by computers and digital technology to undertake more research and index or publish an increasing amount of source material.

Desktop publishing has made it cheaper and easier to publish a wide range of material in books or on microfiche. Within only seven years, the SoG has published 38 volumes that contain indexes to thousands of apprentices of the London livery companies. Family history societies continue to publish many transcripts of parish registers, census indexes and monumental inscriptions. An increasing number of facsimile reprints of 18th-century poll books, 19th-century commercial directories and other rare books have also been produced. Purchasing some of these essential reference works can save researchers many trips to libraries or record offices.

The advent of publishing on computer disk has substantially increased the amount of material that is easily accessible in archives or which can be purchased by researchers for use on home computers. For example, the complete, indexed transcript of the 1881 census of England and Wales can be purchased on CD-ROM or reviewed at the SoG, LDS family history centres and many local record offices. Naval & Military Press has produced a CD-ROM of *Soldiers Died in the Great War*. This is searchable by name (an improvement over the original volumes that lacked indexes). Many parish registers, original census returns and 19th-century town and county directories are also being published on CD-ROM.

It is important to find out what material is in print. Hampson (249), Perkins (263) and Raymond (265–267) list British genealogical books, fiche and CD-ROM that are available from family history and record societies, commercial publishers and archives. Many can be purchased from the FFHS and TNA bookshops (the web pages of their online bookshops are noted in Appendix XI). Researchers should also obtain catalogues from publishers of family or local history books, or review the catalogues on their web pages. Appendix XI includes the web addresses of Sutton Publishing, Genealogical Publishing Co., Phillimore & Co. and Naval & Military Press. It also includes the sites of smaller publishers, such as Francis Boutle Publishers (who publish Fleet Register transcripts and material about First World War soldiers), Stuart Tamblin (criminal register indexes), Alan Godfrey (reprints of Ordnance Survey maps), Nick Vine Hall (microfiche directories) and MM Publications (microfiche directories, army and navy lists).

Most important original genealogical records can be seen at the National Archives (TNA), until recently called the Public Record Office, the Family Records Centre and at County Record Offices. In addition, an enormous amount of source material has been transcribed, indexed and published and there are many published histories of places and research guides for particular types of records. Indeed, there are so many published works that assist family historians that I can refer to only a selection of them in this book. Thousands more are listed in genealogical bibliographies (# chapter 11) and held at libraries and archives including the SoG, TNA, the Institute of Heraldic and Genealogical Studies, the British Library and other reference libraries such as Guildhall Library and the Bodleian Library. You can also obtain many of them through the inter-library loan system. Local record offices, FHS libraries and family history centres also hold collections of published material.

Mullins (260) is an important bibliography for family historians. It lists the publications up to 1982 of national record societies, including the British Record Society, the Harleian Society, the Public Record Office/HMSO, the Royal Commission on Historical Manuscripts (RCHM) and the Catholic Record Society but also local record societies such as Surrey Record Society. Mullins' work has been continued by I. Mortimer and C. Kitching on the RCHM web site (# appendix XI). References in this book to Mullins (260) therefore include this online continuation.

The Internet is a great asset to family historians. It improves the efficiency of our research and our communication with archives and other researchers. Most archives, libraries and family history societies have their own web pages on the Internet, with details of opening hours, membership and publications. The important web sites for family historians are listed in appendix XI. Many others, for example, of family history societies, are listed in the annual *FLHH* (5). Many archives and libraries have increasingly detailed online catalogues of their holdings. You can communicate by e-mail almost instantaneously with other relatives or researchers, anywhere in the world, or with your FHS (about membership, lectures and its publications). You can communicate with archives to request particular information or documents (or to reserve a seat for your visit). You can also join newsgroups of people with common interests.

The Internet also provides an increasing number of indexes and transcripts of source material at our fingertips. Organisations and individuals are rapidly expanding the transcribed or scanned material on their web pages, for example parish register and census transcripts, civil registration indexes, as well as researchers' own family trees and research notes. Most of these web pages can be searched quickly, easily and (in many cases) cheaply or for free. Even sites that require payment may work out cheaper for researchers if account is taken of savings in time and travel expenses.

Four sources of information on the Internet are of particular note. The IGI is the most important index to baptisms and marriages, but you no longer need to travel to a record office or LDS family history centre to use it. You can use your home computer to access the IGI and the 1881 census index on the LDS *FamilySearch* web site. Second, the ScotlandsPeople web site enables researchers to carry out searches from home (for a fee) in various indexes of Scottish material: civil registration records, the 1891 and 1901 censuses, and baptisms and marriages from church registers before 1855 (and then order copies of relevant documents). The web site of TNA includes its information leaflets and catalogues. These assist researchers to prepare their research before visiting Kew. TNA has also made important resources available online, including the complete 1901 census of England and Wales (with indexes) and PCC wills. Indexes to part of the collections at the SoG can also be consulted at the web site of English Origins. The site already includes extensive indexes to marriage licence records and wills, large parts of Boyd's marriage index as well as Cliff Webb's indexes of apprentices of the London livery companies.

The number of web sites of interest to family historians is increasing very rapidly. For example, as I make the last few amendments to this introduction and the appendices of this book (having finalised the text of all 30 chapters), I discover two new important web sites (# appendix XI for their web addresses). The first is a pay-per-view web site, The National Archivist, which features indexes of certain records held at TNA (at present an index to divorces 1858–1903, indexes to the death duty registers 1796–1903 and an index to births, marriages and deaths at sea 1854–90). The second is the Roll of Honour web site. This site has details of over 600 war memorials in England and the names of the men and women commemorated on them.

A warning is unfortunately appropriate about CD-ROM and Internet material. First, the data on computer disks is likely to degrade, perhaps within 20 years. New developments may also make floppy disks and the CD-ROM redundant within only a few years. Second, manuscript records can be difficult to read and so any transcription work is subject to error. However, many web sites and CD-ROM incorporate transcripts that are of poor quality, having been produced cheaply abroad (or by inexperienced transcribers) and not checked. The transcript and index of the 1901 census (available online for a fee) is a wonderful finding-aid but it contains many obvious transcription errors. Ancestry sells a number of disks that include its transcripts of parish registers and will indexes (previously published in books) and the Pallot indexes. The data is also available on Ancestry's web site. However, the transcripts contain many errors, even omitting whole pages of some of the transcribed books.

None of this changes the fundamental approach to genealogical research. A family historian must still carry out research by moving back in time, searching for evidence in original source material for a genealogical link between a person and his or her parents. However, all these changes make our work easier, quicker, more successful and therefore more enjoyable.

This new edition has been substantially expanded so as to describe the new sources available for family historians. I have also taken the opportunity to add more detailed information on certain sources, particularly for education, the armed forces, trades and professions. The changes in family history research since 1997 have been substantial and exciting. Changes over the next few years are likely to be just as important. For example, TNA is placing more material and indexes on its web site. The number of county indexes to parish registers continues to increase (and many of these are being added to the FFHS web site *FamilyHistoryOnline*). The transcription and indexing of census records continue, with many of the original census returns as well as the transcripts and indexes being made available on CD-ROM or online.

In general, we have many advantages over genealogists in the past, for example increased access to records, published material and indexes. However, future generations of family historians face new challenges. People move around the country or abroad, to work, study or live, with far greater ease and regularity than ever before. Many more people marry abroad (perhaps on a Caribbean island), or marry and have children while working abroad for a year or two, perhaps in the United States, Australia or the Middle East. Our descendants may have great difficulty tracing those movements and the records of births, marriages and deaths.

New social structures also present a challenge to family historians. A traditional family tree shows a man and wife, with several children and perhaps an illegitimate child (most usually because of a straying husband). Births out of wedlock no longer bear the stigma that they did years ago. More and more people marry two or three times or live (without marrying) in long term relationships and have children by one or more partners. It is difficult to present these relationships in a family tree that is intelligible to anyone other than the compiler. More importantly, many children grow up without one of their parents and have little (if any) contact with that parent's relatives. When those children decide, later in life, to investigate their family tree, they may start with very little information about one side of the family and not have the benefit of many of their older relatives' recollections.

After years of campaigning, it is possible that older records of civil registration of births, marriages and deaths will soon be opened for public viewing, probably as online digital images. However, the government is also proposing to limit researchers' access to civil registration records that relate to living people. The proposals are too detailed to be described or examined here in any depth. However, the suggestion that addresses and occupations of people noted on a birth or marriage certificate, 20, 50 or 99 years ago, should be kept secret (except to proven family members) in order to protect people's rights to privacy is, in my opinion, completely unjustified. Have you ever heard anyone refuse to disclose what their address or occupation was 15 or 20 years ago? There are some compelling reasons to limit access to such information on certificates of the last five or ten years. There is no good reason to impose further limitations (except to create jobs for the civil servants who would administer the system). If the government proceeds with its plans, there is no doubt that the task of tracing ancestors and relatives is going to become more difficult.

Important issues also arise with the role of new technology in the reproductive process. The first in vitro fertilisation baby was born in 1978. Between 1991 and 2002, nearly 18,000 children were born in the United Kingdom as a result of the donation of sperm, eggs or embryos. Most of those children do not know (and may never know) the true identity of one or both of their natural parents. Even when they reach maturity, they may have no idea that they were born as a result of such a process. In that case, their descendants will also not know and will not discover it from civil registration or any other public records. Technology has undoubtedly answered the prayers of many people who want children but it will also cause many problems for genealogists in the future.

Chapter 1

AN INTRODUCTION TO GENEALOGICAL RESEARCH

WHO ARE YOU LOOKING FOR?

The choice is yours. I investigate all my lines of ancestry, searching for as many ancestors as possible, but also for some collateral lines of cousins. Some people only investigate the ancestry of their father, his father and so on. If you have a rare surname it is worthwhile investigating that name, collecting as much information on the family as possible. I collect all the information that I can about the Herber family in England. If you have a rare or interesting surname, you might wish to join or form a "one-name society" (# chapter 11).

Some people study a particular ancestral family, for example one of their great grandfathers, his wife and their children. They research their lives, the history of that time, both locally and nationally, and try to recreate the family's life from history books and museums. Your ancestors may have been involved in (or affected by) great historical events and it is important to keep these in mind when studying your ancestry. Setting your ancestors in their historical background is an important part of family history. If a family emigrated to or from this country, why did they do so? Your parents or grandparents may have lived through events such as the Great Depression or the General Strike. How were they affected by those events? What did they do during the two world wars?

RELATIONSHIPS

Everyone should know what is meant by the terms father, mother, grandfather, great grandmother or aunt or uncle. A great aunt or uncle, sometimes called a grand aunt or uncle, is a sister or brother of your grandparent. A great great aunt (or great grand aunt) is a sister of a great grandparent. You should also know the meaning of terms such as stepfather, half-brother or stepsister. If Tom's mother dies and his father John marries Eleanor, then Eleanor becomes Tom's stepmother. If Eleanor already has children (William and Frederick) they and Tom would be stepbrothers. The "step" indicates that there is no blood relationship, but only a relationship by marriage. If John (Tom's father) and his new wife Eleanor then had a child (Jane), she would be the half-sister of Tom, William and Frederick. They would be her half-brothers. The "half" indicates that they have only one parent in common.

Relationships between cousins are more complex. Cousins are people who share a common ancestor. The different types of cousins, and other relationships, are illustrated in the diagram below. The children of two siblings are "first" cousins of each other. The children of two first cousins are "second" cousins of each other, and so on. The children of your parents' brothers and sisters are therefore your first cousins. Your children, and your first cousins' children, will be second cousins of each other. The important point is how many generations intervene between you, your cousin and the common ancestor. You are first cousins if you have a common grandparent and second cousins if you have a common great grandparent.

If you and a cousin are not of the same generation, this is indicated by adding a number and the word "removed" to describe the relationship, so that someone may be your "first cousin twice removed". You must work out how many intervening generations there are between the common ancestor and yourself (let us say one) and between the common ancestor and the cousin (let us say three). The smallest of those numbers describes whether you are first, second, third (and so on) cousins. The difference in generations between you and your cousin (indicated by "once removed", "twice removed" and so on) is the difference between the two numbers of generations that you calculated (in this case two). The word "removed" is generally only used to express relationships down a family tree. Thus, in the following diagram, John (the child of my second cousin) is my second cousin once removed. However, John should not refer to me as his second cousin once removed but as his parent's second cousin.

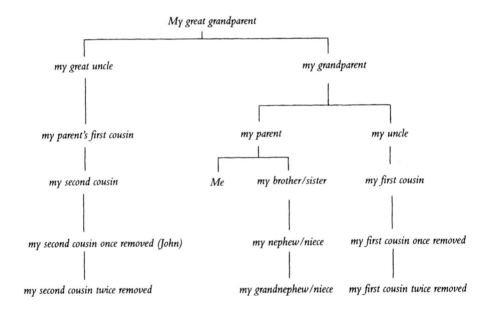

HOW FAR WILL YOU GET?

Many people claim descent from a monarch, a noble, or someone who fought at the battle of Hastings in 1066. Such claims are often untrue. Very few people can prove a descent in the male line from someone alive in 1066. Many people cannot trace any ancestors before the 17th century, and some people can get no further back than the 18th or 19th century on certain ancestral lines. On one line of ancestry I could not, for many years, trace back any further than a great grandfather who was born in about 1875. Even now, that line has only been traced back to

1790. In contrast, I have traced some of my Devon and Bedfordshire ancestors back to the 16th century. The success that you have in tracing your family tree will depend upon many factors including your persistence, the organisation of your records and your ability to think around a problem to find alternative sources of information. However, the four main factors are probably status, record, name and continuity.

Status

Position in the social structure is important when studying family history. It is far easier to trace prominent families than others. If you are descended from nobility, a part of your family tree may have already been researched or published. Professionals such as clergymen, lawyers and army officers are usually far easier to trace than ancestors who were labourers. Fortunately, many families have risen and fallen in social status over time and there were many marriages between families of different classes or wealth. You may well find that you are descended, through female ancestors or through younger sons, from a noble family, or descended from a family that is well recorded for some other reason. Having traced such a link, your continued progress back in time will become easier.

Record

British records are very well preserved compared to those of other countries. Most parish registers (recording baptisms, marriages and burials) survive from the 17th century onwards (and some extend back to 1538). Most types of records have suffered some loss or destruction over the years, and losses unfortunately continue, for example in fires such as that at Norwich Central Library in 1994. However, the only major losses of records this century have been the loss of many Irish records in 1922, the destruction of original wills of Devon, Cornwall and Somerset at Exeter in 1942 (some copies fortunately survived) and the destruction (also during the Second World War) of many parish registers (particularly of London churches) and of the personnel records of many soldiers who fought in the First World War. Consequently, documents are available for research of most British ancestors, although some families may be difficult to research because of the loss of a parish register or the loss of other particular records. If your ancestors originated abroad, it may be more difficult to trace your family tree.

Name

Surnames generally became hereditary in England in the 13th and 14th centuries. People are often fascinated by the meaning of surnames. Most surnames arose from a place of origin or landmark (Wood, Field, Hill, York or London), an occupation (Smith, Miller, Cook, Baker, Butcher or Carpenter), a personal relationship (Johnson, Watson, Wilson, Williamson or names with the prefix "Mac" or "Mc" in Scotland) or a nickname from a physical characteristic (Short, Wise, Redhead, Strong). Unfortunately, surnames came into use so long ago that the original meaning of a surname is unlikely to assist your ancestral research. For example, your surname may be Cook and it could be that one of your ancestors was so named because he was a cook. However, that will not help your research because the "naming" probably took place in medieval times, many other people were also named Cook in this way and they probably have absolutely no relationship to you. A surname may assist your research if it is particularly distinctive or if it evidences a link with a certain area of Britain or the ancestor's foreign origin. Thus about 99 per cent of references that I have found in the 16th to 18th centuries to the name Bulleid (or variants such as Bulled,

Bulhead or Bullied) are from Devon. If you trace your ancestry back to someone named Bulleid in the 19th century, you can be fairly certain that his or her ancestors came from Devon.

Tracing your ancestry is much easier if you have a rare name. There may even be a one-name society for the name. Relatives or other people with that surname can be easily contacted and requested to assist. A rare name is of great assistance if your ancestors moved around the country, or if you are searching for particular events. You may know that your great grandfather, Henry Smith, was born in about 1870, but there may be 50 Henry Smiths born around that period. In contrast, all the registers of births, marriages and deaths since 1837 in England and Wales contain references to only three men named William Herber; my great grandfather (named William Henry Herber), a brother of my grandfather (William Edward Herber) and my father (William Leslie Herber).

There are many books concerning surnames. McKinley (46) is an excellent general summary of the origin of surnames and of the difficulties of researching these origins. Reaney (47) is also a detailed examination of the origin of surnames. Titford (51) is a profusely-illustrated guide to discovering the origin and meaning of British surnames that takes account of the extensive surname databases now available to assist researchers and the possibilities offered for the future by DNA research. You can also consult Hanks & Hodges (43) or Reaney & Wilson (48). Jewish, Scottish, Welsh and Irish names are considered further below (# chapters 13 and 29). When surnames came into use in Scotland, many people adopted the name of the clan chief, even though there may have been no blood link between them. Similar considerations apply to Ireland. Names are a particular problem in researching Welsh ancestry, as discussed in chapter 29.

Surnames changed over the years for many reasons. Anyone can change their surname and many people did so by way of formal documentation. The procedures for these changes of name, and surviving records of the changes, are considered in chapter 5. Spelling of surnames also altered over the centuries by usage. The name Bulhead gradually became Bulleid, Bullied or Bulled. Changes were particularly common in the case of foreign names, which were gradually anglicised. Thus the name Beauchamp often changed to Beacham. Informal or unintended changes of name also occurred because, until the late 19th century, most people were illiterate and the spelling of a surname was not important. The research problems caused by incorrect spelling are considered in chapter 4. Your ancestor's surname may also have changed because one official, recording information about your family, was replaced by an official who spelt that family's name in a different way to his predecessor. In the 18th century my ancestor Ann Voisey, her brother and her sister all married in Sandford in Devon at about the same time and were named Voisey in the marriage register. Many years earlier, however, another vicar had recorded their surname, at their baptisms, as Veysey or Vesey. If you take account of the Devon accent, and the fact that most people could not spell (or even write), you can see how easily this sort of thing happened. Therefore, before you can find the meaning of your surname, you must find the earliest known version of the name and consider that spelling, rather than its modern variations.

During your research, particularly in 16th- and 17th-century documents, you may come across someone using an alias (or "als"), which means "also known as", such as John Holloway alias Thompson. It is not always clear why people used an alias. However, it was not uncommon for a man to take an alias if he married a girl from a family which had an illustrious name but no male heirs to continue that name. Oliver Cromwell was often referred to as "alias Williams" because his ancestor (surnamed Williams) had adopted the surname Cromwell in the 16th century from his uncle, Henry VIII's minister, Thomas Cromwell.

Cresswell (39), Hanks & Hodges (44), Withycombe (53) and Smith (49) are useful works on the history and origin of Christian names. Until this century most children were given quite common names such as John, William, James, Elizabeth or Mary, and a rare Christian name therefore makes it much easier to find relevant records. Two of my female ancestors were named Arminella and Sybilla. Having found their marriages, it proved relatively easy to find their baptisms. Names may also indicate the religious views of parents. A 17th-century couple with daughters named Charity, Faith or Hope are likely to have been Puritans.

It was very common, especially before 1800, for the parents' Christian names to be passed on to their children, often the first son and daughter. This can be a clue to baptisms that are missing from parish registers. The parish register of Dunsford in Devon records the baptism of children of my ancestors Thomas and Elizabeth Sercombe in the period 1736 to 1748: three sons (including a Thomas) and three daughters (none of them named Elizabeth). The marriage of Thomas and Elizabeth was not recorded in the Dunsford register. I suspected that they had probably also had a daughter named Elizabeth, but that she had been baptised elsewhere. I therefore searched the registers of nearby parishes and, in the register of Bridford, I found the marriage of Thomas Sercombe and Elizabeth Parr taking place in 1726 and four elder children (including an Elizabeth) being baptised between 1726 and 1735. It was also quite common for children to be christened with a family surname (perhaps the mother's or a grandmother's maiden surname). George Keates and Ann Leaver were my g.g.g. grandparents. Their eldest son, John Josiah Keates, had a daughter named Agnes Louisa Sophia Keates. Agnes married George Thompson and one of their sons was named Clark William Leaver Thompson, even though Clark was born about 50 years after the death of our mutual ancestor (Ann Leaver) who had borne Leaver as a surname.

Continuity
This refers to the continuation of a family for several generations in one place or in one trade. Research in parish registers is much easier if an ancestral family remained in the same parish for more than one generation. Some families remained in a parish for centuries, so that tracing a line of ancestry back to the 16th or 17th century may be quite easy. However, if your ancestors moved from parish to parish, tracing them can be very difficult unless there is some indication of where they were before each move. Continuity in the same trade is also helpful. Some of my ancestral families carried on the same trades (such as shoemakers or butchers) for a number of generations. This continuity can constitute important evidence of relationships and may lead you to particular records of an occupation (# chapter 22).

PURE CHANCE

Luck may play a part in your research. Thus any index of names is worth checking, just in case something interesting turns up. I once picked up an index of the names of people whose wills had been proved in a particular London court between 1841 and 1858, with no thought that any of my ancestors would be listed. But there, listed in 1852, was the will of a widow named Susannah Eagles. I had not previously been able to find any trace of my g.g.g.g. grandparents, James and Susannah Eagles, after the baptism of their seventh child in 1811. This was my ancestor. Susannah's will recorded that she left all her goods (furniture, clothes, silver spoons and kettles) to my g.g.g. grandfather Joseph Eagles and two other relatives.

HAS IT BEEN DONE BEFORE?

You should enquire whether anyone has already researched any part of your family tree, and perhaps even published their work. As a first step, ask close relatives whether they know of anyone researching any part of the family tree. An uncle, aunt or cousin may have researched their ancestry (which would include some of your ancestors) and their collection of material about your common ancestors may be invaluable. Your ancestors may also have been researched by other people, and a book may have been published about one of your ancestral families, or published pedigrees may include some of your ancestors. Pedigrees or other genealogical material on the Internet may also include your ancestors. You should also search for unpublished material. Someone may have undertaken some research and be holding relevant papers. Alternatively, those papers may have been deposited in an archive. You should never rely without question upon another researcher's work. Their work can be of great assistance, but you should check it as far as possible (and compare it to your own research) to ensure that it is accurate.

PUBLISHED RESEARCH

Many pedigrees are contained in works such as *Burke's Peerage* and *Debrett's Peerage*. Illustration 1 is the entry from the 1890 edition of *Debrett's Peerage* (1012) for the family of the 10th Earl of Chesterfield. Important information can also be found in books such as *Who's Who* or biographical dictionaries. This information can be relevant to anyone's family tree, not merely the ancestors of the aristocracy, the rich and the famous. These sources are considered in detail in chapter 26. Pedigrees were also produced as a result of the visitations by Heralds, in the 16th and 17th centuries (# chapter 26), who reviewed men's right to bear coats of arms. Many of the visitations have been published, such as that for Nottinghamshire of 1662–64 in Squibb (1060).

Many other collections of pedigrees have been published. Some were based on the Heralds' visitations but extended by information in wills, parish registers or families' own records, such as *Pedigrees of the Families in the County of Sussex* of 1830 by Berry (36). Pedigrees of many families were also published later in the 19th century, for example in *Pedigrees of the County Families of England, Lancashire* by Foster (42) from which illustration 2, a pedigree of the Cross family of Red Star and Cottam in Lancashire, has been taken. F.A. Crisp produced an important series of pedigrees, up to the early 20th century, in 18 volumes of the *Visitation of England and Wales*, 10 further volumes entitled *Visitation of England and Wales: Notes* (40) and six volumes of the *Visitation of Ireland* (41). Pedigrees also appear in many other published works, for example in local histories such as Ormerod's history of Cheshire (195) or in studies of particular families. One of my ancestors was Ann Bater of Chawleigh in Devon. Bowerman (37) is an extremely useful book about the Bater families of Devon, which included my ancestors and many cousins. The Society of Genealogists (SoG), which is described in chapter 11, holds a large collection of published pedigrees and family histories.

There are four important indexes to pedigrees that have been published in Britain. These should be consulted, particularly for rare surnames, when you commence your research and whenever you discover another ancestral family surname that you wish to research. Marshall (45) is an index to surnames (in four editions from 1879 to 1903) noting any pedigrees, from a large variety of works, that included at least three generations in the male line. I was descended from Eliza Cass, born in Walthamstow in Essex in 1804. Her family had appeared in Walthamstow in about 1795. Marshall's entry for Cass was:

CHESTERFIELD, EARL OF. (Scudamore-Stanhope.)

From God and the king.

EDWYN FRANCIS SCUDAMORE-STANHOPE, 10th Earl and a Baronet; *b.* March 15th, 1854; *s.* 1887; ed. at Eton, and at Brasenose Coll., Oxford (B.A. 1877); Bar. Inner Temple 1880; is a J.P. and a D.L. for Herefordshire; formerly Capt. 4th Batn. The King's (Shropshire L.I.).

Patron of three livings,—Ballingham V., Bolstone R., Holme Lacy V., Herefordshire.

Arms,—Quarterly: 1st and 4th quarterly, ermine and gules, *Stanhope*; 2nd and 3rd gules, three stirrups with buckles and straps or, *Scudamore*. **Crests,**—1st, A tower azure, thereon a demi-lion rampant or, ducally crowned gules, holding between his paws a grenade fired proper; 2nd, out of a ducal coronet or, a bear's paw sable proper.

Supporters,—*Dexter*, a wolf ducally crowned or; *sinister*, a talbot ermine.

Seat,—Holme Lacy, Hereford. *Residence,*—19A, Mount Street, Grosvenor Square, W. *Clubs,*—Brooks's, Bachelors', Turf, Travellers'.

BROTHERS LIVING.

Hon. HENRY ATHOLE, *R.N.*, *b.* May, 1855; became Lieut. 1879. *Club,*—Naval and Military.

Hon. Claude Dormer, *b.* 1857.   *Hon.* Chandos, *b.* 1859.

Hon. Evelyn Theodore, *b.* 1862; ed. at Wellington Coll.; is Lieut. King's Royal Rifle Corps, and attached to Army Service Corps with rank of Capt.: *m.* 1888, Julia Dasha, dau. of J. Gerald Potter, Esq., of 2, Ennismore Gardens, S.W., and has issue living, Edward Henry, *b.* 1889.

Hon. Charles Hay, *b.* 1864; ed. at New Coll., Oxford (B.A. 1888).

UNCLES LIVING. (*Raised to rank of Earls' sons* 1884).

Rev. the Hon. Berkeley Lionel, *b.* 1824; ed. at Oxford (B.A. All Souls' Coll. 1845, M.A. 1851); is Archdeacon of Hereford, R. of Byford, and a J.P. for Herefordshire: *m.* 1858, Caroline Sarah, dau. of John Arkwright, Esq., and has issue living, *Rev.* Lionel, *b.* 1861; ed. at Harrow and at New Coll., Oxford (B.A. 1884, M.A. 1880); is Curate of Holy Trinity, Weymouth,—Mary. *Residence,*—Byford Rectory, near Hereford. *Club,*—Arthur's.

Rev. the Hon. William Pitt, *b.* 1827; ed. at Brasenose Coll., Oxford (B.A. 1849, M.A. 1851); is V. of Holme Lacy. *Residence,*—Holme Lacy Vicarage, near Hereford. *Club,*—University and Public Schools.

WIDOWS LIVING OF EIGHTH AND NINTH EARLS.

AGNES (*Countess of Chesterfield*)), dau. of James Payne, Esq., of Manchester: *m.* 1882, as his 3rd wife, the 8th Earl, who *d.* 1883. *Residence,*—

DOROTHEA (*Countess of Chesterfield*), dau. of Sir Adam Hay, 7th Bart.: *m.* 1851, the 9th Earl, who *d.* 1887. *Residence,*—

COLLATERAL BRANCH LIVING.

James, eldest son of the late Hon. Alexander Stanhope, 12th son of 1st Earl of Chesterfield, was created Earl Stanhope [see E. Stanhope].

PREDECESSORS.—Sir John Stanhope, Knt., married twice; from the el. son of his 2nd marriage the Earl of Harrington descends; his el. son by his 1st wife [1] *Sir* PHILIP, *K.B.*; a zealous supporter of the royal cause during the Civil Wars, was cr. *Baron Stanhope* of Shelford, co. Northampton (peerage of England) 1616, and *Earl of Chesterfield* (peerage of England) 1628; he *m.* twice, and his son by his 2nd wife was father of the 1st Earl Stanhope, *d.* 1656; and was *s.* by his grandson [2] PHILIP, 2nd Earl; *d.* 1714; *s.* by his son [3] PHILIP, 3rd Earl; *d.* 1726; *s.* by his son [4] PHILIP DORMER, *K.G.*, 4th Earl, known as the "celebrated Lord Chesterfield"; was Ambassador to Holland 1728, Lord Steward of the Household 1730, a Member of the Cabinet 1744, and Lord Lieut. of Ireland 1745; *d. s. p.* 1773; *s.* by his kinsman [5] PHILIP, *K.G.*, 5th Earl, heir male in the 4th generation of the Hon. Arthur, M.P., 11th son of 1st Earl; was Master of the Horse; *d.* 1815: *s.* by his son [6] GEORGE, 6th Earl; *d.* 1866; *s.* by his son [7] GEORGE PHILIP CECIL, 7th Earl; sat as M.P. for Nottinghamshire S. (*C*) 1860-6; *d.* unmarried 1871; *s.* by his cousin (8) GEORGE PHILIP, 8th Earl, *b.* 1822; *d.* 1883; *s.* by his cousin [9] HENRY EDWYN CHANDOS Scudamore-Stanhope, 9th Earl, *b.* 1821: *m.* 1851, Dorothea, dau. of Sir Adam Hay, 7th Bart.; *d.* 1887; *s.* by his son [10] EDWYN FRANCIS SCUDAMORE-STANHOPE, 10th Earl and present peer.

₊₊* [1] *Adm.* HENRY EDWYN Stanhope, great-great-grandson of the Hon. Arthur Stanhope, M.P., 11th son of the 1st Earl, was cr. a Bart. 1807; *d.* 1814; *s.* by his son [2] *Sir* EDWYN FRANCIS, 2nd Bart.; *b.* 1793; assumed in 1826 by royal license the additional surname and arms of Scudamore: *m.* 1820, Mary, dau. of Thomas Dowell, Esq., of Parker's Well, co. Devon; *d.* 1874; *s.* by his son [3] *Sir* HENRY EDWYN CHANDOS, 3rd Bart., who in 1883 as 9th Earl of Chesterfield.

1. Pedigree of the 10th Earl of Chesterfield from Debrett's Peerage *1890*

Pedigree of Cross, of Red Star and Cottam.

JOHN CROSS, son of Richard Crosse, of Liverpool, died seised of lands in Goosnargh, 17 Car. I, and this family has been settled in Barton and Goosnargh, near Preston, ever since, and has held considerable property there. John Cross, the nephew of Richard Cross, of Myerscough House, near Barton, was the founder of Bilsboro' School in 1710.

Henry Cross, of Barton, inn burgess of Preston, at the guilds=JOAN, daughter of Henry Hall, of 1702 and 1722, married 1691, and died 1728 / of Wood Plumpton.

WILLIAM CROSS, of Barton, inn burgess of Preston, =ELLEN, daughter of George Beesley, 3rd son, born 1702, and died 1783. / of Beesley and Ingolhead.

2. GEORGE, born 1738.

4. WILLIAM, born 1754.

3. JOHN CROSS, Esq., of Preston and Cottam, born 1742. dep. prothonotary, ob. 1799.=DOROTHEA, daughter of Richard Assheton, of Preston, Esq., and granddaughter and one ot the representatives of Edmund Assheton, of Preston, Esq., Guild Mayor 1722, 3rd son of Richard Assheton, Esq., of Downham and Cuerdale.

HENRY CROSS, born 1736, whose descendants now possess Myerscough House, near Barton.

WILLIAM CROSS, Esq., of Red Scar and Cottam, only son, born 1771, dep. prothonotary, J.P. and D.L. for co. Lancaster, married 24 June, 1813. ob. 4 June, 1827.=ELLEN, daughter and co-heiress of Edward Chaffers, Esq., of Everton and Liverpool, by Ellen, his wife, daughter of E. Molyneux, Esq., of Liverpool.

RICHARD ASSHETON CROSS, Esq., of Eccle Riggs, Broughton-in-Furness, co. Lancaster, J.P. and D.L. for that co., and J.P. for Cheshire, and chairman of Lancaster quarter sessions, B.A., M.P. for Preston, 1857 and 1859, and for south-west Lancaster in 1868; born 30 May, 1823, married 4 May, 1852.=GEORGINA, 3rd daughter of Thomas Lyon, Esq., of Appleton Hall, co. Chester, and Eliza his wife, daughter of George Clayton, Esq., o Lostock Hall, near Preston.

JOHN EDWARD CROSS, in holy orders, M.A., F.R.A.S., F.G.S., J.P., for Parts of Lindsey, vicar of Appleby, near Brigg, co. Lincoln, married 22 June, 1854, Elizabeth, daughter of Sir Phipps Hornby, G.C.B., Rear-Admiral of the United Kingdom.

WILLIAM ASSHETON CROSS, Esq., F.R.A.S. of Red Scar and Cottam, co. Lancaster, J.P., D.L., Col. 1st Royal Lancaster Militia, born 19 January, 1818, married 19 Aug. 1846.=KATHARINE MATILDA, 4th daughter of Charles Winn, Esq., of Nostell Priory, co. York.

HENRY ASSHETON CROSS, born 1826, of Christ Church, Oxford, died unmarried. ELLEN, married to Rev. W. Hornby, of St. Michael's-on-Wyre, Garstang, and is deceased (see that family).

ANNE HARRIET, died young.

THOMAS RICHARD CROSS, born 23 April, 1853.
WILLIAM HENRY CROSS, born 22 August, 1856.
JOHN EDWARD CROSS, born 5 September, 1858.

CHARLES FRANCIS CROSS, born 22 September, 1860.
GEORGIANA HARRIET.
MARY DOROTHEA.

MARGARET LUCY.
ELLEN PRISCILLA.
CECILY SOPHIA.
DIANA BEATRICE ANNIE.

WILLIAM CROSS, born 27 November, 1850.
CHARLES HENRY CROSS, born 18 May, 1852.
KATHERINE ELLEN.
HARRIET ESTHER.

2. Pedigree of the family of Cross, of Red Star and Cottam in Lancashire

Cass. Burke's Landed Gentry, 3,4,5. Burke's Visitation of Seats and Arms, i.38. Burke's Heraldic Illustrations, 142. Howard's Visitation of England and Wales, i.114. East Barnet, by F.C. Cass, Part i.120. Burke's Family Records, 145.

I have not yet obtained any evidence that these pedigrees of Cass families are relevant to my (rather poor) ancestors from Walthamstow, but this should not deter you from making similar searches. You may at least obtain important clues. One of the sources noted by Marshall was *East Barnet* by Cass (38), which included a pedigree for a Cass family (landowners in Barnet) who originated in Yorkshire, including a William Cass who came to London in the 18th century. Interestingly, however, the pedigree recorded that at least three of William's children were born or buried at Walthamstow around 1790. This family therefore merited further investigation.

Marshall's work was continued by others. British pedigrees that were published from 1900 to 1950 are indexed in Whitmore (52), those published from 1950 to 1975 are indexed in Barrow (35) and those published from 1975 to 1980 are indexed in Thomson (50). Together, the works by Marshall, Whitmore, Barrow and Thomson list the majority of pedigrees published in England up to 1980. However, neither Marshall nor Whitmore indexed *Burke's Peerage*, *Debrett's Peerage*, the *Complete Peerage*, the *Complete Baronetage*, Walford's *County Families* or works such as the *Dictionary of National Biography* (all considered further in chapter 26). These works should therefore also be reviewed.

The extensive genealogical resources on the Internet include researchers' pedigrees, collections of material relating to particular names and researchers' enquiries about particular names or records. The Internet is an increasingly useful resource for family historians and is reviewed further in chapter 11. In brief, you may find a short, but helpful reference on a researcher's web site to one of your ancestors. However, you may be fortunate and find hundreds of pages of genealogical information, produced by another researcher, concerning one of your ancestral families.

Published information should always be checked against original records so that you are satisfied as to its authenticity. Many pedigrees were researched, especially in the 19th century, for people who paid for this service. The pedigrees were then printed and made available to the client's friends and family. Consequently, inconvenient facts may have been ignored. For example, an illegitimacy may appear in a printed pedigree as a legitimate birth. Dates or the status and names of people may also have been changed.

UNPUBLISHED RESEARCH

You should also investigate whether any other genealogists are currently researching a family tree that includes your ancestors. This is more likely than you might think. Chapter 11 contains more information about the following five sources that may assist you:

a. The SoG. Copies of family histories are deposited by members and the SoG journal, *Genealogists' Magazine*, includes lists of members' interests. Members also deposit their "birth briefs" (showing their known ancestors) and many of their working papers with the SoG. The birth briefs (about 6,300 of them with about 94,000 names) are indexed. These papers may include information relating to your own ancestors

b. Family history societies throughout Britain publish members' interests in their journals and on their web sites. Family history societies will be very important to you for their publications, indexes and for assistance in your research. You should consider joining at least one society

c. "One-name" studies (research of a particular surname) are undertaken by societies or individuals. If one of your ancestral surnames, especially a rare name, is being researched, you should contact the researcher or society

d. The monthly journals *Family Tree Magazine*, *Practical Family History* and *Family History Monthly* list readers' interests and enquiries

e. Genealogical directories list the interests of family historians from all over the country and abroad

Unpublished research should be checked thoroughly. Some years ago, a researcher deposited at the SoG some notes and a family tree concerning my ancestors, the Charnock (or Chernock) family of Eversholt in Bedfordshire. My ancestor James Charnock was baptised in 1610, the son of Robert and Alice Charnock, but he is also shown on the researcher's tree as having been buried in 1612. This is incorrect. The Eversholt parish register does record a James Charnock being buried in 1612 (so the researcher no doubt assumed that this was the infant James). However, the James Charnock who was buried was in fact the grandfather of the infant James. This is proved by a will of the James Charnock who was buried in 1612 and also the will of Robert Charnock (who died in 1638), leaving property to his son James. You should therefore always check other people's research. We all make mistakes.

STARTING YOUR RESEARCH

Ancestral Trails is designed to help researchers through all stages of British genealogical research but an annual volume, *The Family and Local History Handbook* (*FLHH*) by Blatchford (5), is also an indispensable reference work. It includes the addresses, telephone numbers and web sites of British and Irish record offices, archives, libraries, family history centres, family history societies, record societies, local history societies, museums, civil registrars, land registry offices and probate registries. It also includes lists of archives and family history societies in many other countries, as well as lists of individuals and organisations offering research services. With this copy of *Ancestral Trails* and the *FLHH*, you are ready to start the search for your ancestors.

CHAPTER 2

PERSONAL RECOLLECTIONS AND MEMORABILIA

Recording your relatives' memories of the family is a vital part of genealogical research. Most people remember their parents, grandparents, brothers, sisters, nephews, nieces, uncles, aunts and some cousins. If you commence your research when you are young, a surviving grandparent or a great aunt will be of great help. If your grandparent can remember his or her own grandparents, you can obtain information about four generations of your ancestors before you review any records.

Before you question your relatives, there are two important steps to be taken. The first is to write a short account of your own life. A family tree is not only for you, but also for your descendants. They will want to know about you, in the same way that you want to know about your ancestors. Start with the important events in your life; your birth and marriage (and the births and marriages of your children) and include details of your education, qualifications, employment, clubs and hobbies. You can later expand this into a narrative account, an autobiography. You may not consider this document very interesting, but your descendants will want this information and you may be the only source for some of it.

The second step is to draw up a provisional family tree (detailed guidelines for drawing family trees are provided below) containing any information that you already have about your ancestors and relatives. You may be surprised at how much you know, such as the names, occupations and dates of birth of your parents, brothers, sisters, nephews and nieces. You may also know the names of your grandparents, uncles, aunts and many of your cousins. If you are unsure as to whether some details are correct, you can start in pencil and use ink when you know that the information is correct, or perhaps mark the uncertain information with question marks. You can show this family tree to the relatives who are featured on it, so that they can check that it is correct and add whatever information they can. As soon as the tree becomes large and complex, you can split it up, firstly between your mother's family and your father's family. You can subsequently prepare a tree for each of your grandparents' families and (as your research progresses) a tree for each of your great grandparents' families. You should also prepare a diagram that includes only your ancestors (an example is in appendix IV), showing how many generations and how far back in time you have researched.

You should also obtain copies of any birth, marriage or death certificates (your own and those of your parents and grandparents) that are already held by family members (obtaining documents from relatives is considered below). These are the basic blocks from which you build a family tree. You may also need these records later in your research, since you may have to prove to certain organisations that you are descended from a particular person in order to gain access to records (concerning that ancestor) that are not available to everyone.

You should then request information from your relatives. In particular, grandmothers and aunts usually know a great deal about a family. My grandmother had an amazing knowledge about her family and that of my grandfather. She recalled many relatives' dates of birth, jobs, addresses and the names of their spouses and children. This personal knowledge of people and events will save you hours of research in record offices and you will also obtain important clues which assist you later in obtaining other information from public records. The information that you obtain from relatives can be either remarkably accurate or remarkably inaccurate and so it should always be corroborated from other sources. People have faulty memories and they may even lie. They may forget that a grandparent had been married twice, or they may know that a certain relative was illegitimate (by your great grandmother and another man), yet tell you that the person was the son of your great grandmother and your great grandfather. Problems such as this can usually be resolved only by comparing the information obtained from various sources.

One of my ancestors came from Germany to England in the 19th century. A relative told me that he had then changed his surname from Herbacht (or a similar name) to Herber because he wanted to appear to be English and also avoid the problem of people spelling his name incorrectly. However, this seemed unlikely, since the name Herber sounds Germanic rather than English and causes many problems for people attempting to spell it. I discovered that the ancestor who emigrated from Germany was my g.g. grandfather Bernard Herber. He was born in Schwanheim in Germany and came to England sometime before 1851. Schwanheim records showed that Bernard had been baptised as Bernard Johann Herbert (not Herber) on 12 October 1823, son of Wilhelm Herbert, a farmer. The name Herbert is not particularly common in Germany although it is of German origin. It appears that Bernard Herbert arrived in England and changed his surname to a German name (Herber) that was not used by anyone else in England at the time. I do not know why he did this, but at least the story that was told to me about a change of name was correct.

It is important to remember that information passes down the generations in a haphazard manner. Certain information was passed from a parent to one child but not to others. The youngest daughter of a family was often the main conduit for information (or documents and photographs) to the next generation, because she was usually the last child who lived at home with the parents. In turn, she may have passed that information and documentation to only some of her own children. Your second, third or more remote cousins will therefore probably have much information (and many photographs and documents) about your mutual ancestors which is not known by your immediate family. Since Herber is a rare name in Britain, I consulted the records of births, marriages and deaths in England and Wales since 1837 (# chapter 5) and obtained birth and marriage certificates of some people named Herber. I also used telephone directories to contact people named Herber who appeared to be related to me. I discovered that my ancestor, Bernard Herber, married in 1852. Two of his sons (William and Frederick) survived infancy and had large families. I do not know why it happened but the families then lost contact with each other. The descendants of my great grandfather (William) were not aware that he had a brother. Frederick's family did not know William and his family, but they had some very useful information about our mutual ancestor.

It is vital to speak to as many relatives as possible. Most people enjoy talking about their family and so it may be easy to obtain much information from relatives before you consult any records. Most people underestimate their knowledge of the family and it is amazing how memories can be activated by a little information. One of my aunts remembered her grandmother but not (she said) that grandmother's brothers or sister. I knew that the sister (Ann) had taken to her bed when her husband died, and stayed there until she died about 20 years later. I mentioned this and my aunt then remembered visiting her. However, you should be cautious and compare relatives' recollections because they may only believe that they remember something (because you suggested it). People also remember faces better than names. Photographs are therefore useful for activating memories. If you have photographs of family groups, for example at a wedding, ask as many relatives as possible to identify all the people who appear in them (before you state who you think they are). You can then compare and corroborate the relatives' identifications. You should also ask relatives about the people who do not appear in group photographs. This can be illuminating. A relative may recall that uncle Tom was not at the wedding because his ship was at sea or because he was abroad with the army.

Memories are selective. People forget the information that genealogists consider to be vital, but remember stories that you may consider unimportant. However, any anecdote can later turn out to be significant. One of my aunts did not know the name of her grandfather (my ancestor William Henry Herber) because he was always referred to as "grandfather". However, she did remember being told that his job had been to drive a horse-drawn bus from Shepherds Bush to Richmond. Another relative then remembered that the bus company was Thomas Tilling & Co. Ltd. One of my grandfather's brothers did not know his mother's maiden surname, yet he recalled many wonderful stories about his early life with his parents, his brothers and his sister. The number of those stories that you note down is a matter for you to decide, but they could be important later. The research of names, dates, occupations and places is only part of the family historian's work. Other memories are also important since they illustrate the daily lives of your ancestors and place them in their true social and historical context.

It is almost definite that, during your research, you will come across skeletons in the family closet. My family was no exception. I discovered adultery, desertion, illegitimacy, drunkenness and a case of bigamy. You may discover similar matters, for example that a great grandmother was not married to your great grandfather. However, no one should be embarrassed or ashamed about being illegitimate or having illegitimacies in the family. King William I (the Conqueror) was illegitimate and most later English kings had some illegitimate children (Henry I had at least 20 and Charles II had at least 16). Many illustrious families are descended from these bastards. Some information that you obtain may not be welcome to certain family members and you must take care to whom you reveal such information. If you discover that an elderly relative's father was illegitimate, is it really necessary to tell that relative, or anybody else, of the illegitimacy? If you are uncertain as to how a person might react, you should keep the information to yourself unless there is a compelling reason to do otherwise. Similar problems arise if an ancestor was in prison. Any surviving children of that person may not know about the episode and, if the parent kept the matter quiet, you should perhaps do the same.

QUESTIONNAIRES

Many of your relatives may live far away or you may have insufficient time to visit everyone. Some researchers therefore prepare a questionnaire for relatives to complete. You should first ascertain whether a relative is willing to help and only then send such a document. You should ask for full names, occupations, dates and places of birth and marriage of that relative and his or her spouse, children or grandchildren. You should also ask for similar details about that relative's parents, siblings, grandparents, aunts and uncles if they are also your blood relatives. You can then turn to more specific topics. Ask where your relatives and ancestors went to school or where they went on holiday (which was often to see other relatives). Other questions could relate to family legends, the location of any family Bible, or the location of documents such as birth, death or marriage certificates, family photographs, wills, medals, newspaper cuttings or letters. You can also ask the relative about specific people. For example, you might ask an aunt to answer the following questions about her grandfather (your great grandfather):

a. What was his full name? Did he have a nickname?
b. When and how did he die? Where was he buried or cremated?
c. What was the name of his wife, when did she die and where was she buried or cremated?
d. When and where were they married? Did either of them marry twice?
e. Where did they live?
f. What were their children's names, who did they marry and where do (or did) they live? If they have died, when did they die, and where were they buried?
g. What was your grandfather's job? Where was he employed? Did he fight in any wars?
h. Where and when was your grandfather born? Did he have an accent?
i. Do you know the name of any schools or colleges that he attended?
j. Did he attend any church? If so, what denomination and where was it?
k. Do you have his birth, marriage or death certificates, a will, or employment records?
l. Do you have any photographs of him or can you remember what he looked like?
m. Which other relatives may have information about your grandfather?

More detailed lists of questions that you can put to relatives, with guidance on interview techniques, are included in Howarth (65) and Thompson (89). If the relative completes the questionnaire, you can ask further questions by a telephone call or at a meeting. It is preferable to meet relatives and discuss the family history with them. A relative may know more about family members by way of interesting anecdotes rather than genealogical facts. For example, a relative is more likely to remember that her grandfather was a tailor who spoke with a Yorkshire accent than she is to know his date of death. At a meeting, you can obtain an indication of dates, and narrow down the records to be searched, by asking questions such as "Was your grandfather alive when you married?" A great aunt may not remember the exact dates of birth of her brothers and sisters, but she will remember them in order of their ages. This type of information is easier to obtain at a meeting. Some researchers tape record (or video) interviews with their relatives. However, the presence of a tape recorder or video camera may inhibit conversation, especially if there are scandalous matters to discuss. You should never record a discussion secretly. You should ask to take photographs of relatives to add to your collection. Other relatives may like to see up to date photographs of family members whom they may not have seen for years. You should leave your telephone number and address with the relative. Once you have stirred memories, the relative might remember more information or recall where some important documents are located.

There are a number of points to remember when interviewing relatives, especially the elderly. First, it is important that relatives feel at ease in providing information to you, that they see you as a serious researcher (not just looking for family gossip) and understand that they have a vital role to play in the research. Show the relative the work that you have done, copies of documents that you have obtained and point out the gaps in your knowledge which they might help you with.

Second, you must ensure that the relative does not think that you are a treasure-hunter, trying to persuade him or her to give you family heirlooms. If your grandfather's medals are kept by his sister, who is to have them when she dies? Any genealogist would like to possess such items but she may be planning to sell them or to leave them to another relative. The important point is to know where such items are held and that they are safe. It is not vital to possess them yourself. Items may be given to you (as the family historian) but you should never press for such gifts. Thirdly, you will be asking what may be considered as personal questions. Older relatives may not like to reveal when they were born or what their father did for a living. If they obviously do not wish to give you certain information, do not press them to do so. That will simply upset them and make further help unlikely. Finally, if a relative tells you something in confidence (for example, that another relative went to prison, or had an illegitimate child), you should respect that confidence and refuse to disclose the information to others. If you also obtain the information from another source, for example from a record office, you may disclose the information to others who have a valid interest but, if people ask how you found out, you should specify the public source, not the confidential one.

Family legends can be helpful and often contain an element of truth, but they are usually inaccurate and much time can be wasted in trying to prove them. Many families have a story of a female ancestor being seduced by the local squire, with the son being sent to an expensive school but never able to claim his inheritance. You should be sceptical about such stories (since they are rarely true) and carry out research on the basis of facts and the evidence that you locate. Do not waste time trying to prove a story that is not based on any evidence.

If you are attempting to trace relatives, you could advertise in a local newspaper for the area in which they (or your mutual ancestor) last lived. This can elicit a great response. However, it can be very difficult to trace living people. The increase in people's mobility in the 19th and 20th centuries has been very great, especially since the Second World War, and forwarding addresses are often lost or only known to other cousins who have in turn died or moved. Chapter 28 of this book and Rogers (1137) will hopefully assist you in tracing relatives with whom your family have lost touch. The National Archives (TNA) has also issued two leaflets (# appendix VI) to help researchers trace missing persons. The Department of Social Security keeps records of people's addresses, but will not help genealogists. The DSS will only assist for "welfare purposes", for example notifying a relative of a death in the family. In those cases, the DSS will not disclose a person's address but may pass on a letter (to the last address shown in their records) if you provide the missing relative's name, age and the last address known to you. The letter to the relative should be stamped and your covering letter should be addressed to the DSS, Contributions Agency, Special Section A, Longbenton, Newcastle upon Tyne, NE98 1YX.

The Office for National Statistics (ONS) does operates a search service, named Traceline, that family historians can use to locate relatives with whom they have lost touch. Traceline will not assist former spouses find each other or become involved in cases involving adoption. Application forms and details of the fees charged can be obtained from Traceline, PO Box 106, Southport PR8 2WA (telephone 0151 471 4811). Traceline uses National Health records and you need to provide the person's name, date of birth (or approximate age) and last known address. You will be informed if the person has been found in the records (and is still living) in which case Traceline will then forward a letter to that person.

There are two further, important, points about enquiries of your relatives. Firstly, if relatives are interested in your work, ensure that you send them a copy of the family tree, especially to thank them for their time. Secondly, you should not delay your research. As time passes, old documents or photographs are lost or destroyed, people's memories fail and relatives die or move away. I started researching my family tree when I was 19, but I soon became interested in other things. By the time that I recommenced research, a few years later, my grandmother (my last surviving grandparent) had died, as had some great aunts and uncles to whom I had never even spoken. Although my grandmother had helped me enormously in my research, I know that she had much further information that would have helped my work. The moral is "don't delay, start today".

PHOTOGRAPHS

One of the most fascinating aspects of family history research is obtaining old photographs. Most people now have cameras and large collections of photographs of their family, friends, weddings, holidays or other special events. This is a relatively recent phenomenon since, in the 19th and early 20th centuries, the expense of amateur photography generally made it a pastime of only wealthy or middle-class families. Despite this, you should be able to find many photographs evidencing your family history. From the late 19th century, people could have their photograph taken fairly cheaply at professional photographers' studios, and sitting for photographs became very popular among people of all classes by the end of the century. Many families also employed a photographer to record important events such as weddings. Professional photographers (and

3. *Group photograph at the marriage of Frederick Eagles and Jessie Law in 1926*

many amateurs) produced thousands of other photographs that may be relevant to your family history. Street scenes, old buildings, ships, and craftsmen or agricultural labourers at their work were favourite subjects.

It is fascinating to find out what ancestors looked like. When I started my research, one of my grandparents was still alive and my family had photographs of all my grandparents and of one great grandparent. I now have photographs of seven of my great grandparents, four great great grandparents and a photograph of one g.g.g. grandparent (George Keates, 1805–70). One of the most useful photographs that I obtained was of the wedding, in 1926, of my grandparents Frederick Eagles and Jessie Law (*see* illustration 3). This picture includes three of my great grandparents, two of my great great grandmothers and many of my grandparents' aunts, uncles, brothers and sisters. Photographs bring a family tree to life and also help people's memories. Relatives may not know the name of a person in a photograph, but they may know that he was, for example, your grandfather's uncle.

Photographs pass between generations in a variety of ways and you may be surprised at the number of old photographs in your relatives' possession. The earliest photograph that my family had of my grandfather, Henry John Herber, was from 1933, when he was 45 years old. Fortunately, cousins in England had two other photographs of him (one when he was aged 18 and another when he was serving in the First World War). Furthermore, descendants of my grandfather's brother, Arthur Herber (who emigrated to Canada in 1913) had a collection of photographs taken in about 1915. These included my grandfather (*see* illustration 7), his brother William Edward Herber who was killed in the First World War (illustration 6), his sister, his other brothers, and their parents, William Henry Herber (illustration 4) and Alice Amelia Keates (illustration 5). A cousin in Australia even had a photograph of George Keates (who died in 1870), the grandfather of my great grandmother, Alice Amelia Keates. Relatives may give you their photographs for your collection. If they wish to keep the originals, you should arrange for copies to be made. Most photographic shops can make a negative (and then further prints) from an old photograph at a reasonable cost. Alternatively, you can scan photographs into a file on your computer (# chapter 3).

In chapter 11, we shall consider the archives from which you may be able to obtain other useful photographs, showing the houses in which your ancestors lived, the churches in which they were married, or the buildings in which they worked. Archives may also hold group photographs (of soldiers, policemen, fire brigades, school classes or sports teams) which may include your ancestors. From the late 19th century, photographs of people were often made into postcards to be sent to friends or relatives. Postcards were also made from photographs of local buildings of note, or the local high street. Many of these survive in photograph and postcard collections and may be useful to illustrate your family history.

You should also collect photographs that record your ancestors' way of life and the area in which they lived. There are many books that contain selected photographs from the 19th and early 20th centuries, mostly dealing with particular counties, cities, towns or activities. The "Victorian and Edwardian" series of books published by Batsford, the "In Old Photographs" series by Sutton Publishing and the "Archive Photographs" series by Chalford Publishing are especially useful. A selection of these are listed in the bibliography for this chapter. If your ancestors lived in a town or city, there is probably at least one book available that reproduces old photographs or postcards of that place, some of which may be directly relevant to your family history. Copies of the photographs can then be obtained from the archive that holds them. If

4. *William Henry Herber (1860–1923)*   5. *Alice Amelia Keates (1863–1951)*

your ancestor lived in the countryside, a book of photographs from the relevant county or area may include photographs of your ancestor's village, or a farm that he owned or on which he worked. Some books contain photographs selected from specialist collections, or from the work of particular photographers. For example, in the late 19th and early 20th centuries Frank Meadow Sutcliffe took many photographs of Whitby in Yorkshire and nearby villages (particularly their fishing communities). The displays of his work at the Sutcliffe Gallery in Whitby, and three books by Shaw (82–84) containing selections of his work, are therefore a vital source for anyone whose ancestors originated from that area. The Batsford series noted above includes books on particular aspects of life such as farming, canals and ships. Other specialist books may also assist. If your ancestor drove a particular type of locomotive, bus or tram, a photograph of that type should be added to your collection. Books of photographs may illustrate particular jobs. For instance, if your ancestor worked on canals in southern England, Denney (58) will be an invaluable source of photographs about that ancestor's life.

During your research, you may take many photographs yourself. My photograph collection includes my own photographs of relatives and my ancestors' houses, churches, villages and gravestones. Gravestones (# chapter 8) are an important source for family history. When you locate stones, you should both transcribe and take photographs of the inscriptions, since many are becoming illegible. Steel & Taylor (28) and Pols (80) describe the methods of collecting, annotating and storing photographs relating to family history and also advise on copying, restoring and dating those photographs. Information is provided to assist your searches in local or national photograph collections (# chapter 11). For example, a photograph of an ancestor's shop may be held in a local collection, perhaps featuring your ancestor standing outside. Oliver (78) is also very useful, describing how to locate and collect photographs to illustrate the local history of your ancestor's city, town or village.

You will probably obtain some photographs that do not identify the person or the place that is featured. Steel & Taylor (28), Drake & Finnegan (14) and Pols (79) and (80) assist the dating and identification of photographs. Useful information is provided about the different types of photographs, the styles of clothes worn by people and their hairstyles between about 1840 and 1920, as well as the props or backdrops used by photographic studios (photographs of ancestors in military uniform are a specialist topic, dealt with in chapter 20 below). Drake & Finnegan (14) includes a useful section on postcards and particularly the methods of dating them from information such as the picture featured on the card, the postage stamp, the postmark, the printing process and the manufacturer. If you obtain photographs of people who cannot be identified, you should not assume that they are your relatives. Firstly, they may not be blood relatives but only related by marriage (perhaps the brothers or sisters of an uncle's wife). If photographs are provided to you by a cousin, they will probably include many people who are only related to you (if at all) by marriage, rather than by blood. Secondly, many photographs will include people who are not related to you at all. They may be an ancestor's friends or neighbours. However, these people should not be ignored. When researching your family history, it is important to find out as much as possible about an ancestor and his or her life. The man who lived next door to your ancestor may have been far more important to him than a brother who lived 100 miles away. Thirdly, if you are lucky enough to find an old family photograph album, it is important to note that it was a common practice to include photographs or postcards of famous people. This does not mean that your ancestors knew, or were related to, those people. If the album includes a photograph of a famous actor, it is likely that your ancestor merely saw that actor in a play, or received a postcard from someone else who had seen the play. The same point applies to photographs of large country houses. Your ancestor is more likely to have worked in that house (or visited it) rather than owned it.

OTHER MEMORABILIA

Relatives may hold many documents that will assist you. They may have their own (or other relatives') birth, marriage or death certificates (# chapter 5). My grandmother had her birth and marriage certificates and her mother's death certificate. Obtaining copies of these from your relatives (rather than from archives) will save you much time and money. They may also have ancestors' wills, memorial cards (noting a place and date of burial) or certificates of baptism. Professional certificates (for example recording someone's qualification as a lawyer), wedding invitations, apprentice records, letters, postcards, identity cards or ration books from the Second World War, insurance policies or other financial documents may also have been retained by your family. Relatives may have kept old newspaper articles which concern family members (such as obituaries or notes of funerals and weddings) or which report on events in which they were involved (such as local disasters or crimes). Books that belonged to your ancestors may have inscriptions, perhaps from other relatives or from friends, schools or religious organisations. The following are examples of documents that I obtained from my relatives:

6. William Edward Herber (1892–1916)   *7. Henry John Herber (1889–1958)*

a. A certificate, under the Factory and Workshop Act 1901, attaching a copy of my grandmother's birth certificate, which had been obtained in order to prove that she was old enough to be given certain employment

b. A certificate from London County Council releasing my grandfather from school attendance in 1916 (when he was 13) enabling him to obtain employment (and attaching a letter as to his character from his headmaster)

c. A certificate evidencing the discharge of Charles Richard Garner (a brother of my great grandmother) from the army in March 1919 because of his war wounds. This noted the units in which Charles had served and the medals that had been awarded to him

d. A deed of change of name of one of my great aunts and a copy of the entry in the *London Gazette* advertising that change

e. My father's certificate of Second World War service (and related papers) from the Royal Navy, noting the ships on which he had served

f. An obituary, from an Australian newspaper, of a brother of my great grandmother

g. A sketchbook kept by my ancestor John Josiah Keates from 1887 to 1897 containing his drawings of many buildings (mostly demolished many years ago), including his home in Leyton, a Norfolk cottage in which his wife had been born and his father's business premises on Wapping High Street, London

Some families are lucky enough to have a family Bible in which an ancestor has written the dates of births, baptisms, marriages or deaths of family members. This information should be checked from other records. In particular, you should check the date of publication of the Bible so that you know what information was written from memory and what information was likely to have been written in the Bible contemporaneously (since that is more reliable). A family Bible could have been handed down to your cousins, rather than to your immediate family, so enquiries of all your relatives are worthwhile. Most family Bibles have unfortunately been lost or destroyed. Some can be found in secondhand bookshops, but your chances of finding a long-lost family Bible are very small. However, an index to family Bible inscriptions, described in Gibson & Hampson (158) and in *Genealogists' Magazine* (March 1995), is being produced by Rena King.

Other items of interest may be obtained. Relatives may hold medals that were awarded to your ancestors for military service. Medals can assist research of an ancestor's military career since the rims of many medals were inscribed with the name, rank, number and regiment of the person to whom the medal was awarded. Some items held by your family may be of interest even though they do not provide any genealogical information. One of my cousins has a set of spurs which belonged to my grandfather when he was in the artillery in the First World War. My grandfather also worked for many years as a leather goods repairer and my father still has some of my grandfather's tools. These items may not help to trace your ancestors but they do add a human aspect to the names, dates and places that appear on your family tree.

CHAPTER 3

ORGANISATION OF YOUR RESEARCH MATERIAL

Family historians collect a great deal of information and documentation and it is vital to arrange notes and documents in a clear and logical manner. Lack of organisation hinders further research, particularly the ability to progress by comparing different sources of information.

TAKING NOTES AND FILING

Your notes must be clear and legible. It is important that your notes distinguish between facts that you extract from records (with a note of the source that you consulted) and your analysis of the information (which may change as you obtain more data). Information that you obtain should be recorded in the form in which it appears in the book, index or archived document. If the original wording is unclear in a manuscript source, you should record this uncertainty in your note, by placing square brackets and question marks around that wording. If you review indexes or documents but fail to locate the information for which you are searching, you should note the source that you consulted and the information that you failed to find, to avoid duplicating searches later.

An efficient filing system is vital. It is also important to take care of the documents that you obtain and ensure that your work is preserved. Organisation and filing is easy if you only investigate one ancestral line, but the more lines (or collateral lines of cousins) that you research, the more difficult the task becomes. There are many ways of organising your material. My own method is described below, but it could no doubt be improved, particularly by the use of a genealogical computer program. My first file contains the large family trees (known as pedigrees), showing all known relatives (and brief details about them) and a separate diagram showing all my known ancestors. Other records and notes are divided between loose-leaf files for different family names. Thus I have a file for the Herber family and a file for my mother's family (named Eagles). As your research progresses back in time, you become aware of more ancestors' surnames and further files can be opened. This division is not perfect. Information about my grandmother (Jessie Law) is contained in the Law family file. She married Frederick Eagles and became a member of his family. She also had close links with her mother's family (named Sheppard) and also the family of her stepfather Arthur Francis. Family files therefore necessarily contain many cross-references.

In each family file, I include pedigrees containing the names of all known members of that family and their descendants. This includes people with different surnames (because of daughters' marriages) and that often justifies creating a separate file. The family trees include only brief information, such as occupations and the date and place of baptisms, births, marriages, deaths or burials. If you have many people of the same name, code numbers can be used to differentiate them, such as John Keates I, John Keates II and so on. I then include a summary of the steps taken in researching that family, recording how I linked each generation to the previous generation. This is important since a file of notes or copies of genealogical documents is extremely confusing to anyone other than the researcher.

A family file contains, for each family member, a curriculum vitae (CV) that includes any information obtained relating to that person (with a note of the source). A CV for one person also refers to other family members. Thus the CV for a great grandmother includes the dates of her childrens' births or baptisms and perhaps their dates of marriage if she was still alive at that time. Each CV also includes notes on people's occupations, addresses, literacy, whether I have photographs of the person, and a list of all documents in which the person is mentioned. At any time, I can review an ancestor's CV and see what further research is required. If a search of particular records is unsuccessful, that fact is recorded in a CV. For example, if I was informed of the approximate date and place of birth of a relative, I would note that information and the informant. If I then undertook a search without success, I would note that, for example, "No birth recorded for John Wilson in Hackney, in civil registration records of 1890 to 1899", and note the date of my search. I type each CV on my computer. As I obtain more information about an ancestor, I can easily add it to the CV without having to rewrite the whole document (as might be necessary with a manuscript CV). Some people use a card index to record information about each of their ancestors or relatives. The cards (usually 5 in. × 3 in.) are available from stationers. The May 1995 edition of *Essex Family Historian* (221) contains useful articles about two researchers' methods of record-keeping using such cards. Many researchers use computer programs to store the data that they collect (with cross-references to files of the documents that they obtain). Computers (and software designed for genealogists) are considered below but they are designed to work like files of papers with the added advantage of better cross-referencing between each ancestor's record and the capability of sorting and editing data.

In each family file, I include copies of the source documents and information, for example copies of birth, marriage or death certificates, entries from church registers, and a photocopy or manuscript or typed note of the entry for a family in a census (with an exact reference of where the entry appears in the census returns). Copies of other documents relating to the family, such as wills, maps of villages or towns, copies of directory entries and court records, are also inserted in the file. In the case of other sources, I note the name, author and publication date of the book, or a description of the register, index, web site or list that contains the information (and where it is located and when I reviewed it). Any original documents must be properly cared for. I use A4-size plastic holders (available from stationers) into which documents slip but remain visible. Photographs are kept in a separate album, with labels noting the source of the photograph or (for copies) identifying the person holding the original. You may know who the people are in photographs, or what event is portrayed, but your descendants may not. Each photograph's label must therefore state who appears in it (particularly important for group photographs), the approximate date or event (if known) and who identified the people in the photograph. Photographs of churches or other buildings should also be kept in albums, cross-referenced to family files, and clearly identified as to subject matter, source and date. Original documents and photographs must be preserved for future generations. Keep them away from heat and direct sunlight. Ensure that they are not stored in damp conditions and only handle them when necessary. You should make copies for security (or scan originals into your computer) and use only the copies in your day to day research. More detailed advice on caring for original documents is provided in articles in the 2000 and 2001 editions of the *FLHH* (5).

I have a separate research file (with sections for each family), listing information that is still required, and noting further research tasks, such as records to be searched or people to contact. I can review a family file and identify the further information that I would like to obtain. I also copy from the family file (into the research file) any information that I already have which may assist in finding the material required.

It is sometimes useful to draw up documents that relate to all families within your family tree. I was interested in the effect of the First World War on my ancestors and their families. I therefore prepared a schedule of all relatives known to have taken part in the war and noted the military units in which they served and whether they survived, died or were wounded. Similar schedules can be drawn up for your relatives' service in the Second World War, or your ancestors' longevity, religion, family size or occupations. Once you have your information properly sorted, it is important to keep it that way. At any time, you will have a large amount of unsorted information (or documents that you have recently obtained). However, you should try to keep this unsorted material to a minimum, by updating your files as soon as possible. This will assist you to take the next step in your research.

FAMILY TREES AND PEDIGREES

Lynskey (101) is a comprehensive guide to drawing family trees, so this section is only a brief review. Large and complex family trees (or pedigrees) are impressive, but time-consuming to prepare and they require regular amendment. It is easier to prepare a family tree in small sections so that each section is easily updated (only amending large trees at convenient intervals). If you are providing copies of the family tree to relatives, they will usually only be interested in the part that is relevant to them (your father's brother will not be interested in your mother's ancestry) and a family tree in small sections is more suitable for this purpose.

Different types of family tree can be prepared. A tree showing only your ancestors, known as a total descent chart, birth-brief or pedigree chart, is particularly interesting, especially to other researchers. If it shows your parents, grandparents, great grandparents and your 16 great great grandparents, it is called a *seize quartiers*. If it also shows one more generation (your 32 g.g.g. grandparents) it is called a *trente-deux quartiers*. These pedigrees only include your ancestors, not their brothers, sisters or other relatives. A *seize quartiers* of my grandmother, Bessie Maud Symes, is in appendix IV. Husbands appear in pedigree charts above their wives and women are (in all family trees) given their maiden name and not their married name. Pedigree charts are designed to show ancestry and so the information included in them should be limited to an ancestor's name, occupation, date and place of baptism (or birth), marriage and burial (or death). Pedigree chart forms that you can complete as your research proceeds, are available from the SoG or from your FHS. Some have space for perhaps 15 generations. However, since the number of ancestors in a generation doubles each generation back in time, the charts become unmanageably large and are best limited to your 32 g.g.g. grandparents. Separate pedigrees can be prepared for each of those 32 ancestors. The space available for each ancestor in a pedigree chart reduces as you go back through the generations. Pedigree charts are therefore sometimes prepared in the form of concentric circles. Your name is in the centre circle; your parents' names in each half of the next circle, your four grandparents' names in the quarters of the next circle and so on. The space for names and information therefore expands each time you step back a generation. However, this method also exaggerates the gaps in your knowledge. If you cannot identify the parents (and therefore any earlier ancestors) of one of your grandparents, one whole quarter of the circle remains annoyingly blank.

Since many other people are also descended from your ancestors, your pedigree charts should be deposited with the SoG or an FHS, so that other researchers can review them for mutual ancestors and exchange information with you. You should not underestimate the likelihood of other people researching the same ancestral lines as you, or the amount of information that researchers can exchange. Eight of my cousins are researching their family trees. One of those cousins and I have mutual ancestors who were born in the late 19th century. The other cousins are more distantly related, our mutual ancestors living in the 17th or 18th century. Each of us had information about our ancestors that the others did not.

There are also different types of family tree to show family groups as well as descents. You may prepare a tree showing all known descendants of a certain ancestor (even if you start from an ancestor who lived recently, this tree may be very large). You might prepare family trees showing only the descent through one or more male lines, or trees showing all relatives with the same surname. Some people prepare a family tree of their close relatives and attach photographs of those people, perhaps illustrating a family likeness passing down the generations. You can also draw a tree of two or three families, showing the links between them. If your ancestors and those families stayed in a small village for many years, there may have been a large number of intermarriages.

Appendix V includes some extracts from my family tree but (for reasons of space) these do not follow all of the advice set out below. You may therefore find it useful to study the family trees included in the collections of pedigrees noted above in order to make your family trees clear and interesting for those people who will be studying them. The pedigrees that you prepare are for your descendants' and relatives' benefit as well as for yours. It is therefore important that a tree is comprehensible and legible (you should always use black ink so that photocopies are of better quality). When drawing family trees, an = sign or m. (for married) is placed between two spouses. A line descending from that sign then divides into a horizontal line from which you draw lines that descend to each child of the marriage (as in the diagram below). Twins can be shown by a further division of a single descending line (as shown for Ann and Grace below). The couple's children should run from left to right across the page with the eldest on the left and the others appearing in order of their dates of birth:

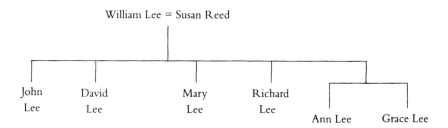

If someone (such as John in the next example) has married twice, his two spouses should appear upon either side of his entry and the marriage signs should be annotated with the figures (1) and (2), with vertical lines (to the children of each marriage) only descending from the marriage sign that is between their actual parents, as follows:

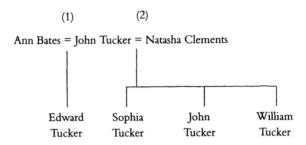

If a pedigree shows many generations (and many cousins of your ancestors), you should draw it so that people of the same generation appear in the same horizontal position across the page. You should also avoid allowing a line that shows someone's descent to cross other lines of descent since this causes confusion. Only brief information, such as people's occupations and the dates and places of their baptism, birth, marriage, death or burial should be included on pedigrees. If someone is interested in a particular ancestor, you can provide a copy of the ancestor's CV. Good, concise entries for people could be in the following form:

James Peterson	=	Margaret Berry
born 12 Jan. 1834, Exeter		born 23 Jun. 1836, Exeter
died 18 Aug. 1878, Exeter		died 5 Nov. 1901, Weymouth
carpenter		seamstress

The date and place of the marriage of a couple should be noted just above the equals sign between their names. Illegitimate children are shown by dotted, zigzag or broken lines descending from the known parent or parents, as follows:

Joanna Smith	Jane Brown	Peter Baker – Ann Williams
:	<	|
:	<	|
:	<	|
John Smith	John Brown	Richard Williams

Another method of recording relationships, used in works such as *Burke's Peerage* (# chapter 26), is the "narrative indented pedigree". This a narrative with indented paragraphs and different styles of numbers to differentiate between generations, as in the following example:

John Smith who married Joanna Christie in 1793 leaving issue:
1. John Smith, born 1794

2. James Smith, born 1796, married Ann Stone in 1820 leaving issue:
   (i) Ann Smith, born 1821, died 1825
   (ii) James Smith, born 1823
   (iii) Mary Smith, born 1825, married Edward Fox in 1851 leaving issue:
      (a) Andrew Fox, born 1853
      (b) Catherine Fox, born 1855
   (iv) Peter Smith, born 1827
3. Ann Smith, born 1798, married William Tucker in 1825.

This form of pedigree commences with the earliest known ancestor and his wife. Their children are then listed, usually in order of their dates of birth. The entry for each child is numbered and indented (from their parents' entry) to indicate that they are a different generation. Any children of that second generation are treated similarly; their entries are indented from their parents' entry and a different style of numbers is used. Some biographical details (dates of birth, marriage and death, and perhaps occupations) are noted for each person. The above example is clear, even though one has to jump between generations when reading through the pedigree. The method is more complex (and difficult to follow) the more generations and collateral lines that you include. For example, if the James Smith born in 1796 had fathered six children (and they all married and had children), his descendants could cover many pages of text before the pedigree returned to James's younger siblings and their descendants. Despite this drawback, the narrative indented pedigree is commonly used and illustration 134 is an extract from *Burke's Landed Gentry* of 1843, with such a pedigree for the family of Fanshawe of Fanshawe Gate, Derbyshire. If you prepare a pedigree in this form, you could try a different layout, first listing any children who left no issue, then listing the children who left issue (dealing with them only briefly) and lastly note your ancestor, his or her spouse and children, since that leads into the next generation of your ancestors.

ABBREVIATIONS

Abbreviations are very important in genealogical research. It is very time consuming to repeatedly write the words "born" and "married" or the names of counties. It is therefore usual to employ abbreviations. The Chapman county codes are three-letter abbreviations for each pre-1974 British county (by which many genealogical records are still arranged). For example, Norfolk is NFK. The codes (listed in appendix III) are used in family history books, journals and indexes. If you have to write a long county name such as Nottinghamshire a few times, the benefit of these codes quickly becomes apparent. Many other abbreviations are used in genealogy, but they must be used with care since they can lead to confusion. For example, the letter "b" in a book or record could mean born, baptised or buried. You must therefore make sure which of these was intended by the writer and ensure that you clearly differentiate between them in your own notes. You should use "b" only for "born", but use "bp", "bap" or "bapt" for baptisms and "bur" for burials. If you use abbreviations that are particular to your work, such as "S" to indicate the surname Saunders, you must ensure that every document in which this abbreviation is used includes a note as to its meaning. You know that it means Saunders, but other people may not. Commonly used abbreviations include:

bachelor	bach.	licence	lic.
daughter	dau.	married	m. or marr.
died	d.	monumental inscription	MI.
died childless	dsp. or osp.	son	s.
grandfather	g.f.	spinster	spin.
grandmother	g.m.	unmarried	unm.
great grandfather	g.g.f.	widow	wid.
great grandmother	g.g.m.	widower	wdr.
infant	inf.	wife	w.

COMPUTERS AND GENEALOGY

Computers are playing an increasing part in genealogy because they are designed to store, process and communicate information and, as the author D. Hawgood has noted, "the essence of family history is storing, processing and communicating information about people, their families, and events".

Genealogical information comes from many sources, but searching the original sources and extracting relevant information is time-consuming. Indexes are therefore important to genealogists since they enable information to be found and extracted more efficiently. Computers make indexing a much quicker task, and so the number of indexes of source material is increasing rapidly. A computer also allows information to be searched, or sorted into a different listing. For example, a researcher can extract from the civil registration records all the entries for deaths of people surnamed Herber and sort them into chronological order or into Christian name order. Three lists (one each of births, marriages and deaths) for the Eagles family in Warwickshire during a certain period could be combined into one list and then sorted into chronological order. Indexes can also be prepared that collate information from many different sources. A word processor program makes amending and editing documents easy. It allows you to insert additional text anywhere in a document and print a new copy. Amending family trees is, in principle, no different. You can spend hours producing large complex family trees by hand, calculating how much space to leave for each generation, or for each child of the family. If you then discover that a child of the family got married and had 10 children, how do you fit this new family into the tree without starting again? A computer with a suitable program can be the answer.

The introduction of voice-activation systems (allowing you to dictate text into a computer with little need to make corrections) and high quality scanners (allowing reproduction of documents or their conversion into computer text) speeds up the transcription, abstraction and indexing of the source material used by genealogists. The vast amount of material that can be contained on one CD-ROM makes more source material available at reasonable prices and so an increasing number of books, records and indexes are becoming available on disk or CD-ROM. A large selection of genealogical software and CD-ROMs can be obtained from S&N Genealogy Supplies of West Wing, Manor Farm, Chilmark, Salisbury, Wiltshire SP3 5AF, TWR Computing of Clapstile Farm, Alpheton, Sudbury, Suffolk CO10 9BN and Back to Roots of 16 Arrowsmith Drive, Stonehouse, Gloucestershire GL10 2QR. Each of these has a web site catalogue and advertises in journals such as *Family Tree Magazine*.

Hawgood (98) and (99) are excellent introductions to the use of computers in family history, describing how computers work, what equipment is needed, how to create and use databases, how to extract data from the Internet or CD-ROM as well as reviewing some genealogical computer programs. The packages for genealogists include *Family Tree Maker*, *Generations*, *The Master Genealogist*, *WinGenea*, *Brothers Keeper*, *Personal Ancestral File*, *Custodian II* and *Family Origins*.

Two computer journals are produced for genealogists and are particularly useful for reviews of new genealogical software: *Computers in Genealogy* (95) is published by the SoG and *Genealogical Computing* is published by Ancestry Publishing (PO Box 476, Salt Lake City, Utah 84110, USA). *Family Tree Magazine* (2) is a monthly journal (# chapter 11) which also includes information on computers in genealogy. An article by T. Rix in June 2000 advised on choosing a computer for family history, K. Priestley advised in September 2002 on protecting a computer against viruses and D. Greenhalgh described in December 2001 how to use mailing lists. New versions of software for family historians are also regularly reviewed in *Family Tree Magazine*. For example, articles in September 1997 by N. Bayley and in June 2000 by E. Probert reviewed programs available for genealogists who use Microsoft Windows™. Many articles review the genealogical material available on the Internet.

TIME

Genealogy is time-consuming and so it is vital to prepare properly for visits to relatives, libraries and archives. Published lists of archives (# chapter 11) such as Mortimer (259) note archives' opening times and the requirements for obtaining readers' tickets or reserving a seat. You should obtain and read any leaflets or published guides produced by an archive or consult its web site. These will describe the records that it holds and the catalogues and indexes available for researchers. You should decide, before a visit, exactly which records you wish to see, and list the points that you wish to research. This list may change during a visit to a record office if you find important information, but deciding beforehand upon a priority list of items to research saves precious time at a record office.

PUBLICATION OF YOUR RESEARCH

You should deposit copies of your family tree and research papers with the SoG, an FHS or a local record office. This allows other genealogists to consult your research for mutual ancestors and it safeguards against accidental destruction of your (perhaps unique) research. You should also consider publication of your work, at least amongst your interested relatives. Titford (105) is a practical guide to writing and publishing your family history, and reference can also be made to Fitzhugh (97) or Meadley (103). These all advise on choosing a theme for a book, how to include background information about places or history in order to put facts about your ancestors into context, and how you should present both facts and families' oral traditions (whether or not they are true). A published family history should include pedigrees, maps, photographs, drawings or other illustrations to assist a reader. An index is also necessary, including the names of people and places appearing in the text. A person's entry should include important events in his or her life, such as:

Brown, John, 5, 6, 8, 11; shoemaker, 13; married Faith White, 15; emigrated to New Zealand, 17; children, 18, 20, 22; died, 25.

Indexing is extremely important, particularly if you decide, later in your research, to transcribe or publish any of the original records that are reviewed in later chapters. Hunnisett (100) is a detailed guide to indexing, dealing with matters such as the different forms of indexes, the indexing of names that are spelt in different ways in records and the use of cross-references. The technical side of writing and publishing must also be considered. Titford (105) and Drake & Finnegan (14) deal with publishing the results of family or local history research, including choosing an audience, the form of publication (book, journal or newspaper), copyright, design and layout, paper size, typeface, illustrations, binding, approaching publishers or publishing and distributing the work yourself. A useful article by D. Hawgood on the cost and procedure of publishing your work appears in *Family Tree Magazine* (February 1995). Publishing material on computer disk is described by J. Leach in *Family Tree Magazine* (January 2002).

The best way to learn how to write an interesting and informative family history is to read a few examples, perhaps at the SoG or an FHS library. A good example is *The Titford Family 1547–1947* by John Titford (106). Importantly, a published family history must combine two essential (but often contradictory) requirements: fact and interest. You should not embroider a family history to make it more interesting, but you should not omit important facts merely because you think them too dull.

Many family historians place the results of their research on their own web pages (# chapter 11). It is worth searching the Internet for any of this work that may relate to your own ancestry. Christian (96) is a guide to publishing genealogical material on the Internet, advising as to the equipment and software required, designing the web site, creating files and incorporating them (and scanned images) into the site. C. Searl described the types of scanners available in *Family Tree Magazine* (June 1999).

A warning is necessary about using personal information that you obtain during your research, particularly if you make it available to other people. The Data Protection Acts 1994 and 1998 were introduced because computer data can be communicated and misused so easily. Anyone storing information about living people (extended by the 1998 act from computer data to manual records) may have to register with the Data Protection Commissioner. They may also have to notify the commissioner of the data held, comply with certain principles set out in the legislation and allow people access to the data held about them. A detailed review of the legislation by D. Lambert appears in *Family Tree Magazine* (February 2000). Many family historians are exempt from the legislation because they keep data about living persons only for "domestic purposes" and do not disclose it to third parties. Others will be exempt from some of the legislation's provisions if they do not use a computer. However, researchers who keep data about living persons for other purposes (for example while undertaking research for fees), or disclose it to other people (for example publishing research on a web site) are probably caught by the legislation.

CHAPTER 4

GENERAL PROBLEMS ENCOUNTERED BY RESEARCHERS

The problems that arise with particular types of records containing genealogical information are dealt with in later chapters. This chapter reviews some of the general problems that arise when searching for, or using, records. For example, you are certain that your grandfather was born in 1890 in Oxford, but you cannot locate his birth certificate. Why is this? You may find a document which (an index tells you) refers to your ancestor, but the document is meaningless to you since it is not in modern English. How can you find out what it says? Dates can pose another problem. For example, a child is recorded as baptised in June 1689 but buried in February 1689. How is this possible?

SPELLING

Many problems are caused by the incorrect spelling of names in records, particularly if a name contains silent letters. A person who is researching the Knott family must also search records for Nott. I am researching the Symes family but also have to search for Syms, Sims, Simms, Simes and Cymes. Some letters sound similar and may have been transcribed incorrectly, so that "m" was written as "n" (or vice versa) and "p" was written as "b". You must consider all likely variations (and even some unlikely variations) when searching records or indexes. Two different spellings of a name, such as Knott and Nott, or Sims and Simms, can appear many pages apart in an index (or even in different volumes of an index). Unsuccessful searches of indexes or records are most commonly caused by spelling or clerical errors. One of the sons of my ancestor Bernard Herber was named Frederick Burnot Herber. I spent hours searching for his birth in civil registration records until, by chance, I found the entry for Frederick Burnot *Heber*.

A registrar, priest or official (whose spelling might have been poor) would write down the name that he heard. The person providing information to the official was often illiterate and therefore unable to correct any mistake. We have already noted the different spellings used by officials recording the baptism and marriage of my ancestor Ann Voisey. For many years, spelling was not important, so little attention was paid to it. If the name of Joanna Knott was spelt as Joan Nott in a parish register, it was unlikely to cause any problems later. Differences in spelling also arose from different British accents. Therefore, you should also look for any entries for a name spelt as it sounds. You should also say the name while holding your nose and note any variations. Foreign names gave clerks and registrars particular difficulty and the names of foreign ancestors often changed because local people had so much difficulty in saying or writing the true name. You should consider a wide range of alternative spellings when reviewing records for foreign ancestors. Titford (30) is a detailed guide to overcoming problems caused by names, particularly by reason of changes in ancestors' surnames or because of incorrect spelling or indexing of names in civil registration and census records.

CHRISTIAN NAMES

A Christian name that was recorded for an ancestor may not have been the name used by him later in life. My grandfather, Henry John Herber, was known to most relatives and friends as Jack Herber. When asking relatives for information about ancestors or relatives, you should always check this point. If relatives tell you about aunt Lou, you should ask whether her name was really Louise, Louisa or Lucy, because that is the name by which she will be recorded in official documents. Similarly, you should ask whether great uncle Bert was named Albert, Robert, Herbert, Bertram or really just Bert. It is also important to look out for variations of names such as Susan/Susanna, Mary/Maria, or Joan/Joanna.

Most people today have two or more Christian names. The fashion of giving a child two Christian names started in the 18th century and became widespread in the 19th century. This makes it easier to find a particular person, especially if the ancestor's surname was fairly common. However, searches in records may still not be straightforward. Documents may not include all the person's Christian names. An ancestor may also have preferred to use the second of the Christian names chosen by his parents. The brother of one of my great great grandmothers was baptised William James Chapman but, as an adult, he was known (and appears in many records) as James Chapman or James William Chapman.

HANDWRITING AND LANGUAGE

Illustration 54 is a copy of the 1867 will of George Keates, my g.g.g. grandfather, written out by a court clerk in 1871. Even this relatively recent document seems almost indecipherable at first sight and shows that handwriting can cause problems even when the author was writing in modern English. As you start using older documents, such as parish registers and court or property records, the problems become more acute, and you will need specialist books on handwriting, Latin and on words that are no longer used. Some letters cause particular difficulty. An "s" (especially the first in "ss") was often written like "f" and the letters "th" were often written as "y". Therefore, in an old document, what looks like "confefed to ye" actually reads "confessed to the". McLaughlin (116) and Barrett & Iredale (107) are useful introductions to old handwriting, but the most comprehensive work is Wright (124), which contains 30 plates of alphabets or documents in handwriting from the 11th to 17th centuries. Illustration 8 shows many of the different forms of letters used in the 16th and 17th centuries, as reproduced from plates in Wright. Other detailed books on handwriting are Munby (120), Grieve (112), Buck (108) and Gardner & Smith (18). Grieve (112) includes illustrations of many old records with translations and explanations of the styles and abbreviations used. Buck (108) contains detailed alphabets of the forms of letters from 1550 to 1650.

Old handwriting can be fairly easy to decipher. You should study a complete document, identify the words that are obvious or which you know must appear on the page (the names of months or the words baptised, married, buried, son, wife and daughter) and note how the writer structured the letters. You can then build up an alphabet of letters in the style of that writer.

8. *Letters of the alphabet: handwriting styles of the 16th and 17th centuries*

If you then compare any indecipherable word or letters to this alphabet, you should be able to identify them. Alternatively, you can try to find the indecipherable word elsewhere in the document since in that instance it may be identifiable from its context. Numbers can also be difficult to decipher. The figures 7 and 1 can be very similar to each other, as can 5, 6 and 8. You should take particular care with any abbreviations used in documents. You should copy abbreviations exactly as they appear. You can subsequently review the whole document at your leisure in order to ascertain the true meaning of the abbreviation, rather than just guessing what the complete word should be. Any transcript of the document that you include in your research files should include the abbreviation and (in square brackets) the full word that you believe it represents.

You will come across many unfamiliar words during your research, including legal terms or words that are no longer used. Many of these are noted in later chapters, but some terms that are often found in the documents that you will be reviewing are:

Yeoman	(generally) a man who cultivated his own land
Husbandman	(generally) a man who cultivated land that he rented
Indenture	a written agreement between two or more people, usually in two identical parts, each signed by one of the parties
Journeyman	a man who hired out his services to an employer by the day
Coparceners	co-heirs
Moiety	a half, usually a half-share of a deceased's estate
Demesne	land of the manor that was retained by the lord of the manor
Affidavit	a written statement made on oath
Recognizance	an obligation (for example to attend court on a certain day), usually set out in a document, specifying a financial penalty for failure to comply
Relict	widow
Intestate	a person who dies without leaving a valid will
Conveyance	the transfer of land or buildings from one person to another (or a document that evidences the transfer)

If you are uncertain as to the meaning of a word, you should consult a good dictionary. The full version of the *Oxford English Dictionary* is extremely useful for obsolete words or for the old meanings of words that are still used. Alternatively, Richardson (25) has sections on many aspects of genealogy and local history, including the terminology used in the law, property and agriculture. You will also find it helpful to have a law dictionary, particularly when reviewing the courts' records (# chapters 24 and 25) or property records (# chapter 27). Mozley & Whiteley's law dictionary, for example the ninth edition by Saunders (121), is usually sufficient, although you may have to turn to the more detailed *Stroud's Judicial Dictionary* (5th edition in five volumes) or *Oxford English Dictionary* for some words. Many words had a different meaning in previous centuries, or were used with less exactness than they are now (words also had different meanings in different parts of Britain). For example, the term husbandman might be used for an agricultural labourer who was employed by a landowner rather than for a man who worked on land that he rented. More importantly, the term father was often applied to a man who was really a father-in-law or stepfather (the terms mother, son, daughter, brother or sister might be used in the same way). A girl recorded as a daughter might have been a daughter-in-law and a brother might have been only a stepbrother or brother-in-law. The term cousin was often used merely to denote a relative (however remote) and perhaps someone related only by marriage.

PLACE NAMES

Many places in Britain have the same (or similar) names. For example, there are villages named Brampton in Norfolk, Suffolk and Cumbria (and probably in many other counties). In addition, when British people colonised much of North America and Australasia, they named many places after British towns or villages. If a British person is recorded as born in London, it is likely that he was born in London, England, rather than London in Ontario, Canada, but you should be aware of other possibilities. Is a reference to Yarmouth referring to Yarmouth in the Isle of Wight or to Great Yarmouth in Norfolk? One researcher noted that an ancestor was recorded as born in Gibraltar. This turned out not to be the Gibraltar at the southern tip of Spain, but a village in Lincolnshire; there are also many other places named Gibraltar in England, for example in Bedfordshire, Kent and Suffolk.

You may find a document that indicates that your ancestor lived in a parish or hamlet that you have never heard of. How do you ascertain in which county you should search for other records? Places are listed (with descriptions) in topographical dictionaries such as those produced by Samuel Lewis in the 19th century for each of England, Wales, Scotland and Ireland (# chapter 16). Smith (169) is a list of English parishes and hamlets, extracted from Lewis' work, from which you can quickly ascertain the parish or parishes in which you should continue research. Thus Winkley or Winkleigh is noted as a parish in Devon (about six miles south west of Chulmleigh) located in the Archdeaconry of Barnstaple and the Diocese of Exeter. Gatcomb is a parish in the Isle of Wight and Gatcombe is a hamlet in the parish of Colyton in Devon.

LATIN

Most medieval documents and many 16th- and 17th-century records (such as early parish registers and court records) were prepared in Latin. Some legal records were written in Latin until the early 18th century. English words were often used as well as Latin, but you may require help from someone able to read Latin in order to deal with such records. If you locate a Latin document, you should copy it in full, since reviewing it at your leisure with the aid of a dictionary is easier than doing so at a record office. McLaughlin (117) and Barrett & Iredale (107) are good introductions to reading and translating Latin records. Morris (118) and Gardner & Smith (18) also provide the Latin versions of most names, places, occupations, months or other words regularly found in the records that you will be using. Parish registers in Latin are fairly easy to use (since the parish clerk may have known little more Latin than you) and because the text is usually limited to names, dates and a few words such as the Latin for son, daughter, baptised, married or buried. Many names and words are easily recognised. As examples, here are the Latin versions of some Christian names:

Andrew:	Andreas	John:	Johannes
Charles:	Carolus	Mary:	Maria
Henry:	Henricus	Ralph:	Radelphus
James:	Jacobus	William:	Gulielmus or Willelmus

Latin words had different forms so that, for example, the Latin for Richard might appear as Ricardus (when he was the subject of the phrase) but as Ricardi in the genitive (possessive) form, perhaps when talking about Richard's horse. Abbreviations were also commonly used in Latin text. Clerks abbreviated common names and words and indicated that letters had been omitted by a horizontal line over the next letter. Ricardus might therefore be written as Ricus, with a line over the u. Some other Latin words that are regularly found in records are listed below, but they may appear with different endings because of their different forms:

bastard	:	illegitimus	mother	:	mater
born	:	natus	month	:	mensis
buried	:	sepultat	parish	:	parochia
daughter	:	filia	son	:	filius
day	:	dies	widow	:	vidua
died	:	mortuus	wife	:	uxor
father	:	pater	year	:	annus
marriage	:	matrimonium		

More complex documents, especially court rolls or property records, require more detailed analysis and more knowledge of Latin, but you should be able to use these types of records with a little practice and the assistance of textbooks such as Stuart (1130) and Gooder (111). You should also obtain a good Latin dictionary or word-list, such as Latham (114) which lists about 20,000 Latin words (and their meanings) or Martin (115), which has extensive lists of the Latin forms of English surnames, Christian names and place names.

Roman numerals are still used today, but appear regularly in older records. Latin numbers were represented by one or more letters. The figure one was represented by I, i or j, the figure five by V and 10 by X. The letter L represented 50, C was 100, D was 500 and M was 1,000. The number represented by the letters is ascertained by adding the figures for each letter (so that XI is 11), except where a letter in the sequence precedes a letter representing a larger figure (as in IX). In that case, the smaller figure is subtracted from the following figure; so that IX is nine and XIX is 19. Roman numerals sometimes appear rather strange. For example, the number three may appear as iii, but it might look like iiy, with each vertical stroke joined at the bottom, the third vertical stroke descending further downwards (as a j) and with some ink dots having flaked off. The figure four (represented by iiii or iv) causes similar problems. The iiii may look like iiy.

DATES

Dates before 1752 can cause confusion. From about 1190 until 1 January 1752 the Julian calendar was used in England and each year began officially on Lady Day (25 March) rather than on 1 January. Therefore, the year 1739 began on 25 March but ended on 24 March of the year that we would now call 1740. Consequently, dates in January, February and most of March 1739 that are noted in old records were actually later than, for example, 1 April 1739. An act of Parliament, Lord Chesterfield's Act of 1751, replaced this calendar by the Gregorian calendar which was already used in Scotland and most of Europe. The year 1751 commenced (as in previous years) on 25 March, but ended on 31 December 1751 so that 1752 and subsequent years then started on 1 January. (To confuse matters further, the year in Saxon and Norman times had begun on 25 December rather than 25 March or 1 January.)

Books or documents written since 1752 often apply the new style of calendar (a year from January to December) when referring to dates in years before 1752. A reference to February 1710 may be in the old style, that is the penultimate month of the year 1710 (that commenced on 25 March 1710). Alternatively, it may be a date in the new style, referring to the February that was the penultimate month of the year that started in March 1709. You should therefore always indicate in notes whether a date is old style (OS) or new style (NS), or note a date in both ways to avoid uncertainty in the future. Dates can therefore be written as 1 February 1739/40 to show that the date was in February 1739 in the old style but February 1740 in the new style. To confuse matters further, some people before 1752 (such as Samuel Pepys) considered that the year began on 1 January (rather than on 25 March) and they often noted dates, in records prior to 1752, in the form 10 January 1730/1 or 1730–1.

The Julian calendar was also 11 days out of step with the Gregorian calendar. When it was 18 May in Scotland, it was only 7 May in England. In order to bring England into line with Europe and Scotland, 11 dates (3–13 September) were omitted from September 1752 in England (so that 14 September 1752 followed 2 September). Christmas Day remained as 25 December, even though the true anniversary of the Christmas that had been celebrated in England in previous years was now 6 January. Banks also ignored the shorter year and continued with a full year of 365 days, so that their financial year ended on 5 April 1753 (11 days after 25 March) and has continued to do so in every year since then.

You can calculate whether a particular date was a Monday, Tuesday or some other day of the week by using perpetual calendars, which are included in Webb (123) and Fitzhugh (15). A table gives a code for the year that you are researching and you then apply the calendar with that code. The calendar will show that, for example, 21 March 1913 was a Friday. Many records refer to events by reference to Easter, such as "on the twenty-third day after Easter". The date of Easter varies each year, but can be found in tables in Webb (123) or Cheney (110). Medieval documents often record events by reference to feast or saints' days, such as St Swithin's Day (15 July). These are listed by Richardson (25) and Webb (123).

REGNAL YEARS

Early parish registers, manorial and legal records use regnal years, for example referring to the "second year in the reign of King Charles" (or "2 Charles I" in shorthand). The regnal year begins on a monarch's date of accession and on subsequent anniversaries, except in the reign of King John, whose regnal years were calculated from Ascension Day. The commencement dates of the reigns of English and British monarchs are listed in appendix VIII, so that you can calculate the dates of each regnal year. Thus a reference to the year "25 George III" is the 25th year of the reign of King George III, which ran from 25 October 1784 to 24 October 1785. The reign of King Charles II was deemed to have commenced when his father, Charles I, was executed in 1649, so that the first year in which King Charles II actually sat on the throne (1660) was described as "12 Charles II". Acts of Parliament were for many years designated not by a name and year as they are now (such as the Marriage Act 1949), but by the regnal year and a chapter number, that is whether it was the first, second or a later act of Parliament (or chapter) in the regnal year. Therefore, the act "26 Geo.II, c.33" (Lord Hardwicke's Marriage Act) was the 33rd act of Parliament in the 26th year of the reign of King George II.

It is important to keep general historical dates, or dates of national importance, in mind. For example, a child born in 1805 or 1806 and baptised Horatio was undoubtedly named after Lord Nelson because of his victory at Trafalgar in 1805. If one of your London ancestors died in 1563 or 1665, you should note that London suffered terrible plagues in those years (killing about 24 per cent and 17 per cent of the population respectively).

MONEY, WEIGHTS AND MEASUREMENTS

Many records refer to money. Parish records note payments to the poor, wills contain legacies and property records may note the value of property. These figures may be meaningless to you because of inflation. Was a legacy of £10 in 1750 a generous gift or an insult? An increasing number of people will also not recall British currency or coins other than the decimal system of pounds and pence. Chapman (109) reviews money and coins in England since Saxon times. In brief, before 1971 a pound sterling (indicated by £ or l) was divided into 20 shillings. A shilling (or s.) consisted of 12 pennies or pence (indicated by d.). Most records that you review will use this monetary system, but may possibly refer to other coins or units of account; a farthing was a quarter of a penny, a florin was two shillings, a crown was five shillings and a guinea was 21 shillings. In medieval England a groat was a coin worth four pennies and a mark (there was no coin, it was just a measure of value) was 13 shillings and four pence.

Munby (119) reviews the value of money but notes that there is no absolute answer to the question "How much is the £10 that my ancestor earned in 1750 now worth?" This is because the change in prices and values varies depending upon whether you are considering the value of property, the cost of bread, or some other item (and is also affected by the relative value of wages). However, a rough answer can be obtained by ascertaining what the money could purchase at the time. If a labourer received six shillings a week in 1810, the value of this wage can be found by reviewing the weekly cost of rent and food. Many indexes of the cost of living over the years have been prepared. Munby reproduces some of these but also notes the qualifications that should be taken into account when using them. Any summary of changes in value over time can only be approximate (and figures are unreliable if taken out of the context of the index in which they appear), so reference should be made to Munby (119) and the sources that he notes. However, a few figures are set out below (from different indexes in Munby) for the average daily wage (in pence) of agricultural workers in southern England, to give a general idea of monetary values from 1450 to 1800:

Years	Average daily wage (pence)
1450–1520	4
1560	7
1590	8
1620	10
1640–1680	11
1740	12
1800	13

Weights and measurements have also changed since medieval times and the terms used in old records for distances, areas or weights may be very different to those now used. Measurements of distance and land area are considered in chapter 15 and Chapman (109) reviews the historical units of weights and measures, showing how some (such as the pound weight) have varied over time, or varied depending on what was being weighed.

SOURCES OF FAMILY HISTORY

The following chapters review the particular types of records that are available for the study of family history. This is the only practical way of describing them in detail, but it does not adequately reflect the research process. You will not finish using one type of record before moving on to the next type. Research should be advanced on all fronts, since successful research in one type of record allows you to use other records, but there is always more to do in the records with which you started. Information obtained from records located later in your research will help you return, for more information, to the records with which you started. Furthermore, the most effective method of research is to combine and compare the different sources of material (# chapter 10). When looking at any document, you should ask yourself "how did I get to this point?" and "where can this document, in turn, take me?"

CHAPTER 5

CIVIL REGISTRATION OF BIRTHS, MARRIAGES AND DEATHS

On 1 July 1837 a civil registration system for births, marriages and deaths was introduced in England and Wales. Registration was undertaken by civil registrars who reported to the Registrar General at the General Register Office (GRO) in London, now part of the Office for National Statistics (ONS). Copies of anyone's birth, marriage or death certificates can be obtained by the public (for examples see illustrations 13, 14 and 15) although, as noted in the introduction, the government is considering significant restrictions on the availability of records from the last 100 years. Civil registration records are vital to family historians because of the genealogical information that they include.

THE REGISTRATION SYSTEM

Nissel (130) describes the history of the GRO, the operation of the civil registration system and the population and health statistics that have been produced since 1837. England and Wales were divided in 1837 into 619 registration districts (reorganised into 623 districts in 1851). Each district originally covered the same area as a poor law union of parishes (# chapter 18) and was the responsibility of a superintendent registrar. Each district was divided into sub-districts which were the responsibility of local registrars.

From 1 July 1837 all births and deaths had to be reported to a local registrar, who in turn reported them to the superintendent registrar of the registration district. The superintendent registrar retained his own records but copied them, every three months, to the Registrar General at the GRO. Marriages also had to be registered. A marriage certificate (retained by the married couple) and two registers are completed at Church of England weddings. One register of the marriages is kept by the church. When the other register has been filled with entries (sometimes many years after some of the weddings took place) it is sent by the minister to the superintendent registrar of the registration district in which the church is situated. However, every three months the minister must also prepare a further copy, from his register, of any entries of marriages taking place during that last quarter and send that copy directly to the Registrar General.

Between 1754 and 1837 marriages had to take place in a parish church of the Church of England in order to be valid (the only exceptions were ceremonies in accordance with Quaker or Jewish rites). The acts of Parliament of 1836 and 1837 that established the civil registration system also provided that marriages would be valid if they took place either as a civil ceremony before a local registrar in a civil registry office or in the presence of a civil registrar (or, from 1898, certain authorised persons) in buildings used for Roman Catholic or non-conformist worship and registered for the celebration of marriages. These civil and non-conformist marriages were subject to the system, described above, regarding the keeping of marriage registers and so similar registers were retained by a church but also sent to the Registrar General and superintendent registrars.

OBTAINING CERTIFICATES

The original registers that record births, marriages and deaths cannot be inspected by the public, but the GRO has national indexes, for each of births, marriages and deaths, most of which are divided into periods of three months. These quarterly volumes list the names, in alphabetical order, of the people who were born, who married or who died. You may obtain a certificate that includes a copy of the register entry of any birth, marriage or death, if you can locate it in an index. The indexes can be searched at a number of archives and libraries but also on certain web sites. However, certificates of entries can only be obtained from the GRO.

The Family Records Centre
Birth, marriage and death certificates are most easily obtained by visiting the GRO search room on the ground floor of the Family Records Centre (FRC) at 1 Myddelton Street, London EC1R 1UW. The map at illustration 9 shows its location and public transport services. The FRC telephone number is 020 8392 5300 but there is a dedicated number (0870 243 7788) for enquiries about the GRO search room and civil registration certificates. The searchroom is open Monday, Wednesday and Friday (9 a.m. to 5 p.m.), Tuesday (10 a.m. to 7 p.m.), Thursday (9 a.m. to 7 p.m.), and Saturday (9.30 a.m. to 5 p.m.), except on bank or public holidays. The basement at the FRC contains a refreshment room with lockers for your belongings. The first floor of the building is occupied by the National Archives, also known as TNA (# chapters 6 and 11) which provides access to census records, wills and non-conformist registers (discussed below).

There is no charge for searching the GRO indexes. Having found a relevant index entry, you then order a copy of the certificate by completing a form using the information obtained from the index and pay a fee. If it is difficult for you to go to the FRC in person, there are other methods of finding index entries or obtaining certificates, although these methods are also subject to the problems (discussed later) that apply to searches in the indexes at the FRC. Firstly, you can apply for certificates by post from the General Register Office, PO Box 2, Southport, Merseyside PR8 2JD (telephone 0151 471 4800 for general enquiries; 0151 471 4816 to order certificates). Application forms are available from the same address or can be downloaded from the GRO web site (# appendix XI). If you have already found the index reference of a birth, marriage or death, you include that reference on the form. If you do not have the index reference, you can request a search of the GRO indexes to be undertaken. You should specify as closely as possible the date and place of the relevant event (and ONS staff will search up to five years of the indexes). Over half the fee is forfeited if the search is unsuccessful. Unfortunately, the cost of postal applications (even with the index reference) is about twice the cost of applications made in person. Requests for certificates from ONS can now also be placed online, by UK residents using a credit or debit card, via the GRO web site.

There is another alternative. You may live near one of the many record offices or libraries which hold microfilm or microfiche copies of all, or part, of the GRO indexes. For example, the SoG has microfiche copies of the birth, marriage and death indexes for 1837 to 1925 and York

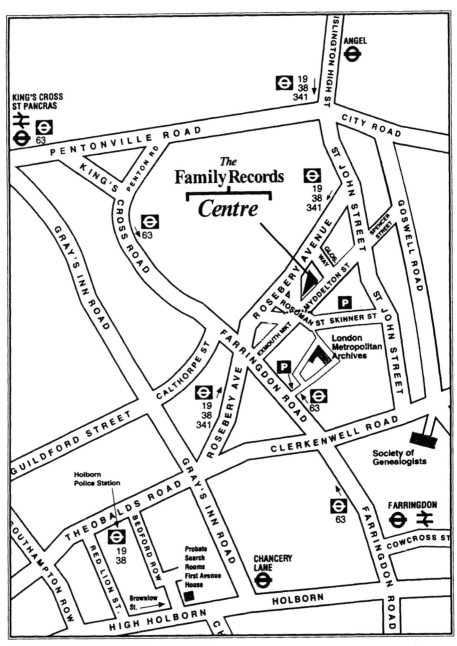

9. *The location of the Family Records Centre, the Society of Genealogists, First Avenue House and the London Metropolitan Archives*

Central Library holds the indexes for 1837 to 1946. Many family history societies (# chapter 11) have also purchased microfiche copies of the indexes (the Essex Society for Family History has copies for 1837 to 1950). Joining your local society may therefore allow you easier access to this information. Details of local holdings of GRO indexes are contained in Gibson (128) and Wood (135), or you can contact your local FHS or record office to ascertain the extent of the indexes that they presently hold. In addition, the Mormons, or LDS (# chapter 11), also have microfilm copies of the GRO indexes which can be consulted at the many family history centres that they operate in Britain. The GRO also sells microfiche copies of the indexes to the public (the indexes of 1837 to 1980 are on over 21,000 fiche) but they are extremely expensive.

The GRO indexes can also be searched online (although certificates can only be obtained from the GRO offices at the FRC or Southport). The complete GRO indexes to births, marriages and deaths in England and Wales since 1837 can be viewed at the web site of Family Research Link (# appendix XI). The procedure for searching these online indexes and the fees payable are noted below. There is an alternative online source that is free. Volunteers are transcribing the GRO index entries that are at least 100 years old into a fully searchable database. This database is on the FreeBMD web pages (# appendix XI). At present, the site includes over 58 million entries from the GRO indexes of 1837 to 1902 (of an estimated 100 million for those years) and the database should be complete by early 2005.

Another alternative is to visit the office of the superintendent registrar of the registration district in which the birth, marriage or death took place, or apply to him by post for a search to be undertaken in his records and for a certificate to be provided. The addresses and telephone numbers of superintendent registrars are listed in the annual editions of the *FLHH* (5). A fee may be payable in order to make a personal search in superintendent registrars' indexes (and an appointment may be necessary). Since there are over 600 registration districts in England and Wales, this option is only realistic if you know the registration district in which the birth, marriage or death occurred. It is impractical to search a superintendent registrar's records to find a birth, marriage or death that took place in a large city (such as London) which was divided into many registration districts. Other problems arise when researching at these local offices. If you discover that your ancestors moved between registration districts, you then have to go to another office, or to the FRC in London, to continue your research. There may not be a composite index to the records held by a superintendent registrar, but only an index for each sub-district, or each church, within the registration district. You may therefore have to search many indexes. Superintendent registrars should hold the registers (dating back to 1837) for the areas that are presently within their district. However, the boundaries of districts and sub-districts have changed over the years so that the early registers for areas that have been moved between registration districts could be held by the registrar of either its present or its previous district. The GRO indexes and superintendent registrars' indexes also have different systems of reference numbers (which you need to order certificates). When recording index entries, you should note whether a reference is from a superintendent registrar's index or from the GRO indexes.

Research at a superintendent registrar's office may pay off if you are researching ancestors from a particular country district or town. Furthermore, a few entries were no doubt omitted from the returns made by superintendent registrars or by church ministers to the Registrar General in London. If you cannot find entries in the GRO indexes, this is most likely due to incorrect spelling or (especially before 1875) non-registration, but an entry that is truly missing from the GRO indexes might be found in a superintendent registrar's records.

FORMS AND FEES

The forms for ordering certificates at the FRC are a red form (CAS 51) for birth certificates (see illustrations 10 and 11), a green form (CAS 53) for marriage certificates (illustration 12) and a grey form (CAS 52) for death certificates. The fee for a certificate is £7 if you apply in person at the FRC. You can collect certificates or ask that they be posted to you. They will be ready for collection, or posted, four working days after you order them. The fee for a certificate from a superintendent registrar is also £7. Postal applications (to Southport) are made with different forms and cost £8.50 if you supply the index entry or £11.50 if you request a search of the indexes. Postal applications take about two weeks.

THE GRO INDEXES

The major difficulty in obtaining civil registration certificates is finding the correct index entry. To put into perspective your search for the record of a birth that took place in about 1838, you should bear in mind that the indexes for the first year of registration alone contain 463,000 entries of births and the annual number of registrations has increased substantially since then, partly because of the growing population but also because the registration system became increasingly effective and complete. During 1896 about 915,000 births, 242,700 marriages and 526,700 deaths were registered. By 1998 the GRO records included about 246 million births, marriages and deaths in England and Wales since 1837 and there are now about 7,500 volumes of indexes. You must therefore prepare thoroughly before a search, especially if you are looking for a fairly common name.

The GRO indexes at the FRC are contained in large typescript or manuscript volumes (although microfiche copies for 1837–1984 are also available for researchers who are disabled and the indexes since 1984 can also be accessed on computer terminals). There are separate indexes for births, marriages and deaths, the volumes being coloured red, green and black respectively. Each index is arranged by year, but divided (until 1983) into quarters ending on the last day of March, June, September and December. Each quarterly index contains an alphabetical list, by surname and then Christian name, of the people who were reported during that quarter as having been born or having died (marriages are considered below). The index for some quarters is divided into volumes, for example there may be separate volumes for surnames beginning A to D, another for E to H and so on. The date of the report of a birth or death to the registrar determines the quarterly index in which that entry appears, and this report could take place weeks after a birth. The indexes since 1984 have not been divided into quarters, but entries are in alphabetical order for a full year and the index notes the month of registration of each entry.

For each named person, the GRO index states the name of the registration district in which the birth or death occurred and gives references for the area, volume and page (which enable an entry to be found by ONS staff in the original registers). This is the entry for my great grandfather's birth in the quarter ending September 1860:

Herber, William Henry   W. Ham   4a 37

Write these details on an application form, together with your own personal details and the reason why you require the certificate (for example "family history"). Since the September quarter of 1911, the mother's maiden name has also been included in the birth index. A typical entry for a birth is therefore:

Application for Full Birth Certificate   CAS 51

USE THIS FORM ONLY TO ORDER CERTIFICATES THROUGH THE PUBLIC SEARCH ROOM

PLEASE COMPLETE SECTIONS A-E IN BLOCK CAPITALS
BEFORE TAKING YOUR APPLICATION TO THE TILLS

A **HOW MANY COPIES** DO YOU REQUIRE ▶ ☐
(extra certificates are £6.50 each)

TICK THE APPROPRIATE BOXES FOR QUESTIONS 1-3

1 ○ **POSTED** within 4 working days, first class post £6.50

2 ○ **COLLECTION** after 11am on the fourth working day
£6.50 (on production of your receipt)

3 ○ **24 HOURS** for a fee of £22.50 (COLLECTION)

4 **Are you applying for your own certificate?** ....

If not please state your relationship to the person whom the
certificate relates ....

5 **Explain your reasons for wanting a certificate**
....

For purposes of detection and prevention of crime, information relating to this application may be passed on to other Government departments or law enforcement agencies	Entry No.
	Taken out by
	for office use only

Birth details

Please note that details supplied in section B will NOT be checked against the entry to which section C refers. If you are unsure that you have found the correct entry see the back of this form.

B

Surname at Birth	
Forenames	
Date of Birth	
Place of Birth	
Father's Surname	
Father's Forenames	
Mother's Maiden Surname	
Mother's Forenames	

APPLICANT DETAILS

E

NAME	
ADDRESS	
SIGNATURE	
TEL. No	DATE

PLEASE REFER TO THE RED INDEX BOOKS TO COMPLETE THIS SECTION

C

1837 - 1983	YEAR	QUARTER	DISTRICT		VOL	PAGE.(Number following VOL)
1984 - 1992	YEAR	DISTRICT		REG	VOL	PAGE.(Number following VOL)
1993 ONWARDS	YEAR	DISTRICT Name and No.		REG No.	ENT No.	DOR

IMPORTANT
DO NOT FORGET TO REPEAT THE NAME
AND THE INDEX DETAILS BELOW
(SEE SECTIONS B+C)

D

SURNAME AT BIRTH	FORENAMES

1837 - 1983	YEAR	QUARTER	DISTRICT		VOL	PAGE.(Number following VOL)
1984 - 1992	YEAR	DISTRICT		REG	VOL	PAGE.(Number following VOL)
1993 ONWARDS	YEAR	DISTRICT Name and No.		REG No.	ENT No.	DOR

B0345 7/00

10. *Application form for birth certificate (GRO, Family Records Centre)*

11. *Reverse of application form for birth certificate (GRO, Family Records Centre)*

| Herber, Mark D. | Eagles | Surrey S.E. | 5g 1051 |

I was born in August 1959 and this entry is in the volume for the quarter ending September 1959. Eagles was my mother's maiden name. Surrey S.E. (that is South East) is the registration district in which I was born. The code 5g refers to one of the areas into which registration districts were grouped and also the volume number of the original registers in which the entry is included. The last number, 1051, is the volume's page number on which the entry appears.

Marriages are indexed in the quarter in which they took place (rather than when they were reported). There is an index entry for each spouse. If you know both spouses' names, search for the rarest surname first. Having found a likely entry, you should check the index for the same quarter for the other name. If you find it you must ensure that the same volume and page number references are given for both entries. The index entries for the marriage of my great great grandparents Bernard Herber and Emily Clements, in the volume for the quarter ending in September 1852, were:

Application for Marriage Certificate CAS 53

USE THIS FORM ONLY TO ORDER CERTIFICATES THROUGH THE PUBLIC SEARCH ROOM

PLEASE COMPLETE SECTIONS A-E IN BLOCK CAPITALS
BEFORE TAKING YOUR APPLICATION TO THE TILLS

HOW MANY COPIES DO YOU REQUIRE ▶ ☐
(extra certificates are £6.50 each)

TICK THE APPROPRIATE BOXES FOR QUESTIONS 1-3

1 ○ **POSTED** within **4** working days, first class post £6.50

2 ○ **COLLECTION** after 11am on the fourth working day £6.50 (on production of your receipt)

3 ○ **24 HOURS** for a fee of **£22.50** (COLLECTION)

4 Are you applying for your own certificate? ....

   If not please state your relationship to the person whom the certificate relates ....

5 Explain your reasons for wanting a certificate
   ....

For purposes of detection and prevention of crime, information relating to this application may be passed on to other Government departments or law enforcement agencies

| Entry No. |
| Taken out by |

for office use only

Please note that details supplied in section B will always be checked against the entry to which section C refers. If you are unsure that you have found the correct entry see the back of this form.

Marriage details

	SURNAME	FORENAMES
Man		
Woman		

APPLICANT DETAILS

NAME

ADDRESS

SIGNATURE

TEL. No   DATE

You should ensure that the reference you quote from the the indexes in section C refers to both parties quoted in section B. The fact that the same reference appears against both parties' names does not, however, necessarily mean that they married each other.

PLEASE REFER TO THE GREEN INDEX BOOKS TO COMPLETE THIS SECTION

1837 - 1983	YEAR	QUARTER	DISTRICT		VOL.	PAGE.(No. following VOL)
1984 - 1993	YEAR	DISTRICT		REG	VOL.	PAGE.(No. following VOL)
1994 ONWARDS	YEAR	DISTRICT Name and No.	MTH	PAGE No.	ENT No.	SOURCE CODE

IMPORTANT
DO NOT FORGET TO REPEAT THE NAME
AND THE INDEX DETAILS BELOW
(SEE SECTIONS B+C)

	SURNAME	FORENAMES
Man		
Woman		

1837 - 1983	YEAR	QUARTER	DISTRICT		VOL.	PAGE.(No. following VOL)
1984 - 1993	YEAR	DISTRICT		REG	VOL.	PAGE.(No. following VOL)
1994 ONWARDS	YEAR	DISTRICT Name and No.	MTH	PAGE No.	ENT No.	SOURCE CODE

B0347 7/00

12. Application form for marriage certificate (GRO, Family Records Centre)

Clements, Emily	Whitechapel	1c 760
Herber, Bernhard	Whitechapel	1c 760

From the March quarter of 1912, the marriage index entry for one spouse also records the other spouse's surname, making entries easier to find. The two entries for the marriage of my grandparents Frederick Eagles and Jessie Law, in the September quarter of 1926, were:

Eagles, Frederick Charles	Law	Hackney	1b 892
Law, Jessie Amelia	Eagles	Hackney	1b 892

Deaths were registered in the registration district where they occurred (not necessarily where the deceased lived or was buried). From the March quarter of 1866 until the March quarter of 1969, the death indexes specify the deceased's age at death (or rather the age stated by the person reporting the death to the registrar). This information can assist the identification of the correct entry in the index but it is often unreliable since the informant (often a doctor, friend or child of the deceased) might not know the deceased's true age. From the June quarter of 1969 the death indexes provide the deceased's date of birth, but this may also be unreliable. The entry in the March quarter of 1924 for my great grandfather's death was:

Herber, William H.	Hammersmith	63	1a 382

The name of a registration district may be unfamiliar because registration districts took the names of the local poor law unions. Two maps published by the IHGS in Canterbury (# chapter 11), show the approximate location of each registration district. One map covers the period 1837–51 and the other covers 1852–1946. The area code in the index entry, such as VII or 5b, may also assist. These codes are for areas into which registration districts were grouped (either a county, part of a county or parts of several neighbouring counties). The codes used from 1837 to 1851 and from 1852 to 1946 are listed in appendix I. The codes used in entries since 1946 are listed in Newport (129). Thus, the code 1c, in the 1852 index entry noted for the marriage of Bernard Herber, would indicate (if you did not know the location of Whitechapel registration district) that the event took place in London or Middlesex. Newport (129) provides an alphabetical list of all registration districts in England and Wales (and an alphabetical list of districts in each county), noting the codes of the area in which a registration district was included from 1837 to 1989. Registration districts are also listed alphabetically in Wiggins (134), specifying the county in which a district was located and the names of adjacent districts and sub-districts.

Some researchers have extracted from the GRO indexes (for some or all years since 1837) all the references that they can find to a particular surname (or its variants). The SoG has a large collection of these one-name lists that have been deposited by members. The surnames included in the lists, with a note of the years and events (births, marriages or deaths) that they cover, are catalogued in Fogg (126). For example, there are lists of all births, marriages and deaths from 1837 to 1989 for people surnamed Ship. These lists are of great assistance to other people researching families with the same name, and can save hours of searching in the GRO indexes.

When searching the indexes, it is easy to make invalid assumptions and choose an entry (and obtain a certificate) for someone who is not related to you but had the same name as your ancestor. It is therefore vital to ensure that any certificates relate to your ancestors and not to unrelated people. When ordering certificates, you may request a cross-check that assists to ensure that you have identified a correct entry. This checking system is considered below.

CERTIFICATES

Birth, marriage and death certificates include a photocopy of the original entry in the registers (as in illustration 14) or a copy of the entry written out by GRO staff (as in illustration 13). Transcription mistakes do occur. Both I and a cousin obtained the same marriage certificate, but an address was stated correctly as Mundford Road on one certificate and incorrectly as Standford Road on the other. Birth certificates (such as that for my great grandfather William Henry Herber at illustration 13) should include:

a   the date and place of birth (in some cases, usually multiple births, the time of birth)
b. the name of the child
c. the name and occupation of the father
d. the name and maiden name (or previous married name) of the mother
e. the signature (or mark), name and address of the informant (usually a parent)

A marriage certificate, such as that for the marriage of my great grandparents William Henry Herber and Alice Amelia Keates (at illustration 14) states:

a. where and when the marriage took place
b. the names and ages of the spouses
c. their places of residence
d. the spouses' occupations and "conditions" (bachelor, widower, spinster or widow)
e. the names and occupations of their fathers
f. whether the marriage took place after banns or by a marriage licence
g. the signatures (or marks) of the spouses and of two witnesses

The ages given are often incorrect (particularly if women were marrying younger men) so you should take this into account when subsequently searching for the spouses' births. A certificate may merely state that a person is of "full age" or a "minor". Minor means under 21, and the true age could be as low as 16 or (before 1929) as low as 14 for boys or 12 for girls (although marriages at such ages were very rare). Full age means only that a spouse was 21 or older. If the age is stated as 21, this might mean that the spouse was actually 21 years old, but it often merely indicated that the spouse was 21 or over, that is of full age.

If the father of a spouse was dead, this should be noted in the register entry (but was often omitted). If a spouse was illegitimate, a father's name may have been invented just to insert in the marriage record. Widows who remarried were usually identified in a marriage register (and therefore in the index), by their previous married name rather than their maiden name. However, a maiden name can be ascertained from the father's surname. My g.g.g. grandparents Sarah Boxall and John Clements married in 1834. John died in 1847 and Sarah then married Henry Coles in 1848, as Sarah Clements, a widow. However, the certificate for the second

13. *Birth certificate of William Henry Herber, 1860 (GRO, Family Records Centre)*

marriage recorded her father as Thomas Boxall. Any descendants of Sarah and Henry Coles who obtained this certificate would therefore see that she was a widow when she married Henry and that her maiden name was Boxall and not Clements (the surname of her first husband).

The residences given for spouses on a marriage certificate may only be the name of a village or town, but are often specific addresses. The addresses were sometimes very close (or perhaps even next door) to each other. This does not necessarily mean that your ancestor married the girl next door. The church required at least one of the spouses to have been resident in a parish for a minimum of four weeks before the marriage could take place in a parish church. One or both of the couple sometimes took up temporary residence in a parish so that they could marry in that parish church. An address may therefore be only an accommodation address. Furthermore, banns (considered below) had to be read in the church in which the marriage was to take place, but also in the other spouse's parish church. The couple had to pay for both sets of banns, so if a non-resident spouse gave an address that was in the parish of marriage, the couple saved the cost of a second set of banns.

Witnesses at weddings were often the spouses' relatives. The marriage of my great grandmother Alice Amelia Keates to William Henry Herber (*see* illustration 14) was witnessed by Alice's father, John Josiah Keates, and by her sister Harriett Keates. On the 1862 marriage certificate of my g.g. grandparents Joseph James Eagles and Elizabeth Ann Truby, one of the witnesses was an Elizabeth Lewis. I later discovered that she was Elizabeth Ann Truby's mother and she appeared to have married, or taken the surname of, Samuel Lewis, the man that she was then living with. The actual signatures of spouses and witnesses appear in the original church register and in the superintendent registrar's records of marriages, but not in the copies (made by ministers) sent to the Registrar General in London. In some cases, a signature may be important evidence (particularly to confirm that you have correctly identified a marriage as that of your ancestor) so that you need to see the actual signature, rather than the GRO copy. In that case, you should apply to the relevant superintendent registrar for the marriage certificate.

Death certificates (such as that for my ancestor Susannah Eagles at illustration 15) are sometimes thought to be of little use to genealogists, but this is not true. Death certificates state:

a. the name of the deceased and the date and place of death
b. the cause of death (very unreliable on earlier certificates)
c. the age or (from June 1969) the date of birth of the deceased
d. the deceased's occupation
e. the signature (or mark), name and address of the informant

If a married woman or widow died, the certificate may name her husband. If the deceased was a young child, the child's father may be named. Informants may be described as "present at death" or "in attendance". However, the words in attendance did not necessarily mean that an informant was present at the death. They usually indicate that the informant was generally caring for the dying person, or was head of the household in which the death took place. You may sometimes find a death certificate for a child but no birth certificate, because the death took place before the parents had registered the birth. Deaths of stillborn children did not have to be registered until 1874. Deaths could only be registered under a name if a body was identified. If the body was not identified, the death was registered as "unknown" or "unidentified" with an estimated age. These deaths appear in the index at the end of a volume for the quarter.

14. *Marriage certificate of William Henry Herber and Alice Amelia Keates, 1886 (GRO, Family Records Centre)*

SEARCHING THE RECORDS

A typical course of research in the GRO records would be as follows:

a. Your grandfather's birth certificate gives his date of birth, his father's name and his mother's maiden name. You need to find the record of the marriage of your grandfather's parents. Starting at the date of your grandfather's birth, work back through the indexes (searching for the rarer surname first), find both names in the index, with the same registration district and reference numbers and then order the marriage certificate.

b. If you have no luck, review the marriage indexes for a few years after your grandfather's birth date, since a high percentage of brides were already pregnant when a marriage took place and a marriage sometimes took place only after the birth of the first child. Remember also to watch for incorrect spellings as these are far more likely to cause difficulty than any other reason. It is also worth checking the names of your grandfather's parents from birth certificates of his brothers and sisters (if you have these already or can find them in the GRO records) since a small spelling error in the names on your grandfather's birth certificate could be the reason why you cannot find the marriage. If you still cannot find a marriage certificate, you should remember that marriages (and also births and deaths) could have taken place in Scotland, elsewhere in the British Isles or possibly abroad. Records of these events are considered later. It is of course also possible that your ancestors did not marry.

c. Having found the marriage certificate, you then need the birth certificates of the two spouses (your great grandparents). The marriage certificate gives the date of their marriage, their reported ages and their fathers' names. Assume that the spouse's age is correctly stated on the marriage certificate, then turn to the index of births for the relevant year, check each quarter, identify the entry in the index and order the birth certificate. When you receive that certificate, you should check that the name given for the spouse's father is the same as the name given on the marriage certificate.

d. The spouse's age may have been given incorrectly on the marriage certificate, so if you cannot find the birth, you should also search a few years either side of the year that you checked in step (c) in order to locate the correct entry.

e. Having obtained the birth certificate of one of the spouses, you can return to step (a) above and repeat the process to find the marriage of that ancestor's parents.

If you are looking for the birth, marriage or death of someone with a rare surname, and you know the approximate date and place of the event, finding an index entry may be easy. If the surname is common, such as Jones or Williams, you may have a long search.

As noted above, the GRO indexes to births, marriages and deaths since 1837 can be viewed at the Family Research Link web site. When you first use the site, you have to register, specify a password and download a special viewer ("DjVu") in order to use indexes. Scanned images of the GRO index volumes up to 1983 are in folders and files that you search online in the same way as the original registers, that is working backwards or forwards through quarterly volumes. To find an entry, you first click on births, marriages or deaths, then choose the decade, then a year and then a quarter. You then choose a file containing the range of surnames that includes the name for which you are searching. There is an alternative search mechanism by which you

15. *Death certificate of Susannah Eagles, 1851 (GRO, Family Records Centre)*

specify a range of dates and the first three letters of a surname. This produces a list of relevant files that you can then view. The indexes since 1984 are in the form of a database that you search by name, year and registration district (but also, for example, by a mother's maiden surname). The search techniques are described in more detail by J. Cavell in *Family Tree Magazine* (April 2003). The site works on a "pay-per-view" basis with credit or debit cards. The minimum charge is £5, which allows you to view 50 pages of the indexes or results from the post-1983 database. The more you pay, the less each page or result costs (so £25 allows you to see 300 pages). The system can therefore be expensive to use but you can undertake research from your home and this may save travelling time and costs (and particularly benefit people who cannot travel with ease).

The transcribed GRO indexes for 1837–1902 on the FreeBMD web site, also noted above, form a database. You can therefore search a range of quarters or years for a particular name, or extract all entries for a particular surname. This database (although subject to transcription error) is therefore not only free but can be easier to use than the original GRO indexes or the online images at the Family Research Link web site.

MISSING ENTRIES

Nearly all deaths were registered because from 1837 burial was only permitted on the production of a death (or coroner's) certificate, which confirmed that civil authorities had been informed of the death. The system was thought to be effective for the registration of marriages. However, Foster (127) reveals defects in the GRO indexes of 19th-century marriages, due mainly to errors by clerks who compiled the national indexes from copies of registers submitted by the clergy. They omitted to copy some marriages into the national indexes (perhaps 5% of marriages in some years). In other cases, the clerks could not read a clergyman's writing and so the spouses' names have been copied into the GRO indexes incorrectly (making it difficult to find some marriages). The solution to the problem is to collect together the superintendent registrars' registers and create a new national index to them but such an enormous project is unlikely to proceed in the near future. Researchers who cannot find a marriage in the GRO indexes will, despite the difficulties noted above, have to search indexes at superintendent registrars' offices.

Many births were also not recorded during the early years of civil registration. Parents were only legally obliged to inform a registrar of the details of a birth if the registrar demanded them. It is estimated that in some parts of England (particularly Surrey, Sussex, Essex, Shropshire and Middlesex), up to 15 per cent of births were not registered between 1837 and 1875. Many people did not know about the law, or thought that a child's baptism, recorded in a church register (# chapter 7), was a legal alternative to registration. If you cannot find a birth entry, you should search church registers for a baptism.

The position improved from 1875 when the Births and Deaths Act 1874 imposed a duty upon those present at a birth or death to report it to a registrar. There were fines for non-registration and penalties for late registration (that is more than 42 days after a birth). Despite this, some births and deaths since 1875 have not been recorded. Furthermore, in order to avoid paying a late registration penalty, some parents reported a later (incorrect) date of birth for a child. My great grandmother, Bessie Jane Garner, celebrated her birthday in July, even though her birth certificate states that she was born in October 1881. It is possible that she did not know her true date of birth (and so celebrated it in the wrong month), but another explanation is that Bessie was actually born in July 1881 but her parents failed to register the birth until October 1881, and so they told the registrar that Bessie had been born in October (rather than July) in order to avoid paying a late registration penalty.

You may also have difficulty finding a record of your ancestor's birth because it may not have been registered under the name that he or she later used. One of my relatives appeared in the 19th-century census records as Anna Keates or Anna P. Keates. A search for her birth certificate under this name failed because she was born Priscilla Anna Keates. Nicknames can also cause great difficulties. My grandfather was known as Jack, but his name was actually Henry John Herber. In some cases, only the surname and sex of a child is recorded in the birth indexes and certificates (for example "Harrison, male") since the parents may not, at the date of registration, have decided upon a Christian name for the child. When a name was later chosen by the parents, they may have forgotten (or not bothered) to tell the registrar. Foundlings appear in the birth indexes, without names, listed after the letter Z.

ILLEGITIMACY

During the period 1837 to 1965 about 5 per cent of births were of illegitimate children. It is therefore very likely that you will find an illegitimacy in your family tree. Fathers' names rarely appear on birth certificates of illegitimate children. Between 1837 and 1875, if the mother informed a registrar of an illegitimate child's birth and also stated the father's name, the registrar could record him as the father. From 1875 a man could only be named as the father of an illegitimate child on the birth certificate if he consented and was also present when the birth was registered. The space for the father's name is therefore blank on the birth certificates of most illegitimate children. If a father is not named on a certificate, that does not prevent further research of that ancestral line since he might be named in parish or poor law union records (# chapter 18) or in courts' records (# chapters 24 and 25).

If an illegitimate ancestor used the mother's surname, but you cannot find the birth under that name, it is possible that the birth was registered under the father's surname. The father may have agreed to this even though the couple were not married. On some occasions, an unmarried mother (let us say Mary Jones) might appear before a registrar to register a birth but pretend to the registrar that she was married and give the father's name (for example John Smith), calling herself a "Mrs Mary Smith, formerly Mary Jones". I am not aware that registrars ever required proof of the parents' marriage when a birth was registered. Since registration sub-districts were quite large areas (so registrars could not know everyone) an unmarried mother might feel safe in making a false statement such as this. It is therefore worth searching against the surname of any man whom the child's mother later married, or that she ever lived with, or perhaps even with whom she shared an address (for example, two servants in the same house).

THE IMPORTANCE OF DEATH CERTIFICATES

Some family historians do not bother to obtain death certificates of their ancestors (or other relatives) under the misapprehension that they do not assist tracing a family tree. This is a mistake. Dates of death assist searches for records of a will or administration (# chapter 12) which provide information about an ancestor's relatives or property. Addresses on death certificates assist searches in the census records. Ascertaining the exact place of death from a death certificate also assists in locating an ancestor's place of burial and any gravestone which may provide further information.

The informant named on a death certificate is often the deceased's spouse or a doctor (especially since 1874 when doctors' certificates were first required by registrars before the issue of death certificates). However, the informant was sometimes another relative of the deceased who lived at a different address. Locating brothers, sisters or children of your ancestors can therefore become much easier. Illustration 15 is the 1851 death certificate of my ancestor Susannah Eagles, the widow of James Eagles. The informant, Agnes Eagles, was the wife of one of Susannah's grandsons. The address given on the certificate enabled me to find the family in census records. Agnes reported Susannah's age as 84, so this certificate is also a good example of how the civil registration system, although only introduced in 1837, can take you back to the 18th century. Susannah was born, according to the certificate, in or about 1767, but she is still recorded by the system.

Death certificates should also record whether a coroner's inquest took place, for example if the death was a sudden one. In such cases, you can search for inquest records (# chapter 25), or a local newspaper report (# chapter 17) of the death or inquest. The cause of death may add to the family history in other ways. Your ancestor may have died in an epidemic, such as the cholera epidemic of 1839.

Death certificates can be difficult to find if you do not know when or where an ancestor died. Searches in the indexes may consequently produce a number of possible entries. In these cases, other records that are considered later may narrow down the dates and area to be searched. For example, you can search the census records to find families in 1841 and then every 10 years up to 1901. If you find a husband and wife in the census of 1851 but only the wife (recorded as a widow) in 1861, you know that the husband died between 1851 and 1861.

CERTIFICATES RELATING TO ANCESTORS' FAMILIES

Tracing an ancestors' brothers and sisters is important. For example, it may be difficult to find a great grandparent's birth certificate. Obtaining the birth certificate of a brother or sister of that great grandparent may make it easier to find your great grandparent's birth certificate. This is especially so if your ancestor had a common name such as John Jones, but he had a sibling with a rare Christian name, whose birth is easier to locate. If there were many children in a family, obtaining all their birth certificates provides you with information as to where the family lived and the father's occupation throughout that period. Your ancestor may have been born a few years before civil registration commenced in 1837. We shall see in chapter 7 that a baptism record will usually not reveal a mother's maiden name but only record the baptism of a child of, for example, William and Ann Wilson. In such cases, obtaining a birth certificate for a younger brother or sister, born after 1837, should reveal the mother's maiden name (assuming that all the children had the same mother). This can be checked by locating the marriage of that Ann to William Wilson, in a parish register, on a date that precedes the birth or baptism of your ancestor.

It is important to establish whether all the children of a family had the same mother. For example, your great grandfather James might have been an eldest child and the census records (# chapter 6) might reveal that he had six brothers and sisters. Childbearing caused many women's deaths and James' mother may have died shortly after his birth, or after the birth of a later child. His father may have remarried and raised further children. The death of an ancestor's mother when that ancestor was a child, followed by life with a stepmother and half-brothers and sisters, was very common, and can be very important to your family history. My Keates ancestors are a good example of this. My g.g.g. grandparents George and Ann Keates had a son, my ancestor John Josiah Keates in 1836, two daughters (Mathilda and Sarah) and four other sons, George, William, Ebenezer and Jesse. However, Ann Keates died in 1855. George then married Anna Unwin and had three further children, Emma, Alice and Flora, all born more than 20 years after their eldest half-brother, John Josiah.

Addresses on civil registration certificates are important. Addresses help you undertake searches in census records. It is therefore useful to obtain birth certificates of your ancestors' siblings (and any other certificates for your ancestors' families), especially for dates close to census years, so that you can search those addresses in the census. The buildings at addresses given on certificates may still exist and you can visit them to take photographs or enquire whether archives hold photographs of a building as it was at the relevant date. As your research progresses towards 1837 and you turn to parish records, addresses are useful in order to find the correct parish (particularly in cities) in which to search the records.

OTHER PROBLEMS

You may find it very difficult to locate certain certificates because of the problems already considered, particularly the number of index entries for common surnames. You must not merely guess which is the relevant entry. You should obtain other information in order to narrow the time period or area for your search, or to prove that an index entry or certificate is indeed the correct one. Difficulties in finding civil registration records are often caused by poor handwriting and incorrect indexing of the original records. The surname Milton in bad handwriting in the register may be mistakenly indexed under Wilton or Hilton. If you have difficulty in locating an entry, search the indexes for such variations.

You may find an entry for your ancestor's name, but that birth, marriage or death may have taken place far from the family home. Do not ignore such an entry. Your ancestor may have been a sailor from Plymouth who married or died in another English port. Your ancestor (whose family lived in London) may have been born almost anywhere in Britain during the Second World War if his expectant mother had been evacuated from the city.

Your ancestor may not be found in the civil registration records because he was not born in England or Wales. You can use the census records to ascertain his birthplace. People moved around in previous centuries much more than is popularly believed. Your ancestor may have had an English name, but he could have been born in Scotland, Ireland, the Channel Islands, the Isle of Man or abroad. Records of these areas are considered in later chapters.

THE CHECKING PROCEDURE

When applying for birth, marriage or death certificates at the FRC, you can ask (on the reverse of the application form, *see* illustration 11) for a check to be made by GRO staff to assist in ensuring that you have requested the correct certificate. This procedure is important if you are searching for the birth, marriage or death of someone with a common name, especially if there are a number of index entries that could be the person for whom you are searching.

For example, your great grandfather may have been named Thomas Cross and been born in about 1885 or 1886. The index may include two children named Thomas Cross who were born in that period but you cannot tell which is the correct entry. If you have the marriage certificate of your Thomas Cross, this should reveal the name of his father, perhaps John Cross. The application form for the birth certificate allows you to direct that Thomas' birth certificate should only be produced to you if the father's name on that certificate is recorded as John Cross. If this is not the case (if you have chosen the incorrect entry from the index) the certificate is not provided and you receive a partial refund. Similar checks can be made in respect of marriage certificates. You can state that you only require the marriage certificate of Thomas Cross if the name of his wife is Mary, or if the name of his father is John Cross. If the indexes contain many possible references to your ancestor's birth, you can check one reference in the manner noted above and add the other references to a reference checking sheet (obtained from the cashiers' desk). A fee is payable for each reference that you wish to be checked.

However, the checking procedure should be used with care. If you specify the particulars that you require to be checked in a register entry, and those particulars turn out to be incorrect, the form is returned to you with the particulars marked "no" or "n/s" (not stated). Therefore, if you specify the name of the person's father, that name may be marked "no", but you will not know the name that actually appears in the register for that index entry. If you request the birth certificate of Thomas Cross only on condition that the father's name is John Cross, but the father's name in the register is William John Cross, you will not receive a certificate and you will not know exactly why. Therefore, if you can afford it, it is preferable to order each certificate that could relate to your ancestor since you can then review each one before deciding which, if any, is the correct one. The checking procedure also allows you to check whether a death certificate for which you are applying is the correct one by reference to a man's occupation. However, as people often changed occupations and some trades could be described in many different ways, it is not advisable to use occupations in the checking procedure.

ADDITIONAL RECORDS OF CIVIL REGISTRATION

The GRO holds some further registers and indexes which may contain the birth, marriage or death for which you are searching. The indexes of these registers are listed in appendix II and special application forms must be used to obtain certificates of the register entries. The most important of these records are the births, marriages and deaths of British citizens overseas as registered at HM Consulates from 1 July 1849; the deaths of those serving in the armed forces during the two world wars; the births and deaths of people at sea since 1 July 1837; and the births, marriages and deaths (other than during the two world wars) recorded by the armed forces in various registers, some dating from 1761. The indexes to these registers are also available on fiche at the SoG and the National Archives (TNA). The military and marine registers are considered further in chapters 20 and 21. The registers of foreign events are reviewed in chapter 30. All of these records are described in detail, with illustrations of typical certificates, in Colwell (125). Other records of births, baptisms, marriages and burials of British people abroad, but held by Guildhall Library, TNA or in the India Office collections at the British Library, are also described in chapter 30.

These GRO indexes and registers (and certificates of entries) generally contain similar information to the indexes and certificates of births, marriages and deaths considered above. As an example, William Sheppard, a brother of my great grandmother Sarah Ann Sheppard, was killed in the First World War. His death appears in the index entitled "First World War Deaths (Army) 1914 to 1921 – other ranks". He was a private in the Royal Welch Fusiliers. William Herber, my grandfather's brother, who served in the Royal Fusiliers (City of London) Regiment, was also killed and is in the same index. The index entries are:

Name	Rank	No.	Unit	Year	Volume	Page
Sheppard; William J.,	Pte	27046	R.W.F.	1917	I 29	27
Herber; William E.,	Pte	7875	R.F.L.R.	1916	I 82	10

Indexes of some civil registration records of Scotland and Northern Ireland (# chapter 29) can also be seen in the "Scottish Link" area of the GRO search room at the FRC. Two computer terminals provide a direct link to Scottish GRO indexes in Edinburgh of births, marriages and deaths (since 1855), divorces (since 1984) and adoptions (from 1930) and also to indexes of Scottish census returns and parish registers. Time can be booked on one terminal (the other is "first come, first served"). The fee for using them is £4 per half-hour (by purchasing a card from a vending machine). Certificates can then be ordered by completing a form (stocks of these are held near the terminals) and sending it to Edinburgh with the fee. A third computer terminal, which is free to use, permits you to search the index of births registered in Northern Ireland from 1922 to 1993. In order to obtain a certificate, an application must be sent to Belfast with the fee.

ADOPTION

Until 1927 there was no formal adoption process, although the term adoption was often applied to what we call guardianship or fostering. This did not entail a legal, or formal, change of name for a child, but the child would usually use the guardians' or foster parents' surname. Because guardianship and fostering were primarily private arrangements, it is extremely difficult to locate relevant records, even if any were prepared and have survived. Some records of charities (or organisations such as Dr Barnardo's) have survived and are considered in chapter 18. It is estimated that about 300,000 children passed through Barnardo's since it was founded in 1845.

The legal process of adoption was introduced in 1927. The GRO holds the Adopted Children's Register which records legal adoptions under the Adoption Acts since 1 January 1927. A special form (CAS 54) has to be completed to obtain a certificate of a register entry. The index to this register (which can be consulted at the FRC) gives the adopted name of the child and the date of adoption. A certificate provides the register entry which was made by the Registrar General after a court made an adoption order. It gives the court's name, the date of the order, the date of the child's birth and the names, occupation and address of the adoptive parents. The country and place of the child's birth are shown from 1950 and 1959 respectively. The register and certificates do not reveal the child's name prior to the adoption.

Most people know if they have been adopted and usually have a copy of their adoption certificate. An adopted person aged over 18, if not aware of the names of his true parents, may apply for this information to be released to him after a course of counselling, described in Rogers (132), on the problems of taking this course of action. Access to adoption papers can be granted to others, such as an adopted person's children, but an application to court has to be made (and an applicant should obtain legal advice on the procedure). Even with information from a birth certificate, an adopted person (or his descendants) may find it difficult to research the family tree. An address given on a birth certificate may be a hospital or a temporary address of the mother. Many adopted children were illegitimate and it may be difficult to discover the father's name. The child's mother may have died since the adoption, or perhaps remarried, and so be difficult to trace (or she may not wish to be traced). Furthermore, many adoption records have not survived and those that have may be held by any one of many different public or private agencies, social services departments of local authorities or archives. Stafford (133) is a detailed guide to British and Irish fostering and adoption agencies with notes on the survival and location of agencies' records. An article by the same author about adoption and its records (dealing particularly with the difficulties of research) appears in *Genealogists' Magazine* (December 1995).

CHANGE OF NAME

Changes of name are not generally recorded by the civil registration system but the system did record some changes of Christian name. More importantly, although changes of name (particularly foreign names) occurred at all times, formal changes of name are most common in the last 200 years and therefore very likely to cause you problems when searching civil registration records.

Firstly, the Christian name of a child given on a birth certificate can be changed within 12 months of the birth being registered if the child has not been baptised with the registered name. This procedure is rarely used and should not cause you any difficulty in tracing an entry since the record of the birth should be indexed under both names.

At common law, a name is merely the label by which a person is generally known. I could start calling myself John Smith and it would be quite legal (unless it was for a fraudulent purpose). No legal formality or advertisement is now required to change your name. However, between 1939 and 1945 British subjects could only change their names if they published, 21 days beforehand, a notice of the proposed change in the *London Gazette* (# chapter 17), or in the Scottish or Irish equivalents of that journal. Illustration 76 includes such a notice.

However, if I wanted some proof that I had changed my name from that appearing on my birth certificate, I could execute a document known as a deed poll, that is a deed formally evidencing an intent to use a new name. These deeds can be lodged at court so that there is a permanent record of the change. Since 1903 the enrolment of deeds has taken place after an application to the High Court of Justice. The deeds are kept in books and those books more than three years old are deposited at TNA (# chapter 11) in series J 18. Before 1903 deed polls were enrolled in the Close Rolls (# chapter 27) which are also held at TNA. From 1914 it was necessary, in order to enroll the deed at court, to advertise the change of name in the *London Gazette*. Such an entry, from 1941, is also included in illustration 76.

Names could also be changed by Royal Licence or by private act of Parliament, although these procedures were rarely used. Records of Royal Licences are at TNA and described in TNA legal records leaflet 32. Private acts of Parliament are at the House of Lords Records Office (# chapter 11). Phillimore & Fry (131) index the new and discarded names of people who used the licence or parliamentary procedures from 1760 to 1901 to change their name, as well as some who used deed polls. The source of information is also recorded, usually an advertisement of the change in the *London Gazette* or *The Times* newspaper.

THE PROHIBITED DEGREES

Two of my great grandparents were first cousins. The marriage of first cousins is not unusual and has been legal since the 16th century. However, marriages between people who were related in some other ways (known as the prohibited degrees) were forbidden by acts of Parliament and ecclesiastical law. A marriage between two people within a prohibited degree required (and still requires) a private act of Parliament authorising that marriage. The prohibited degrees have varied over time, but are explained in detail in Chapman & Litton (362). The present position is set out in the Marriage Act 1949, as amended in 1986, but for most of the period that you will be researching, the relevant rules (reached in about 1560 and confirmed by church laws, known as Canons, in 1604) were listed in the Book of Common Prayer of 1662. The prohibitions prevented someone marrying his or her:

(a) brother or sister (or their spouse);

(b) parent, grandparent, aunt, uncle, child or grandchild (or their spouse);

(c) niece or nephew (or their spouse);

(d) spouse's child, grandchild, parent, aunt, uncle or grandparent.

Statutes of 1907 and 1921 made an exception to the prohibition at (a) above, allowing people to marry the spouse of their brother or sister, if that brother or sister had died. Some further exceptions were made in 1931, 1949 and 1986 so that, for example, a man was allowed to marry his deceased wife's niece, aunt or widowed mother.

FINALLY

There are two further points worth noting. Firstly, you will see references to short birth certificates. These cost £7, but they only certify the date of a person's birth in a particular registration district. They omit the important genealogical information, such as parentage, for which you will be searching.

Secondly, when searching for a particular index entry, you may see other entries which appear relevant to your family. You may be searching for an ancestor's birth in a registration district and find other people with the same surname born in that district. It may be worth noting these entries for future reference since they may be births, marriages or deaths of relatives. For example, I was searching in Hackney registration district for the death, in about 1917, of my ancestor Joseph James Eagles. During the search, I found an entry for the death in Hackney in 1915 of Charles F. Eagles, aged 0. Since Joseph's son was named Charles Frederick Eagles and his son (my grandfather) was Frederick Charles Eagles (and both were from Hackney), I suspected that this infant Charles F. Eagles was related and so obtained the certificate. The child, Charles Frederick Eagles, was the son of Richard Charles Eagles who was another son of Joseph James Eagles.

CHAPTER 6

CENSUS RETURNS

A census has taken place in England and Wales every 10 years since 1801, except in 1941 when a census was taken in only a few places. Each census since 1841 listed the names of people in a place on census night and recorded some details about them.

In 1801, 1811, 1821 and 1831, the government wanted to know the number of people in each area (and their sex and age groups) but not their names, so only statistics were sent to the central authorities by the local census enumerators (and most of those returns were subsequently destroyed). The surviving statistical summaries are of little genealogical value. However, some enumerators also listed the names of householders (and occasionally their families). A few of these lists survive in parish records and are considered below.

From 1841 to 1901 the names of people in each household were included in the records collected centrally, together with some information about each person. The census returns of England and Wales for 1841, 1851, 1861, 1871, 1881, 1891 and 1901 are public records and a vital genealogical source. Many surname indexes to these returns have been prepared and so it is becoming much easier to locate your ancestors in the records. Census records after 1901 are confidential for 100 years and no searches can be made in them. The 1911 census is therefore closed to the public until January 2012. Census records of Scotland, Ireland and the rest of the British Isles are considered in chapter 29.

WHERE TO SEE THE CENSUS RECORDS

The enumerators' manuscript records of the censuses of 1841 to 1891 can be consulted by the public on microfilm. The 1891 census is also available on microfiche. These records are held by the National Archives (TNA) at its search room (telephone 0208 392 5300) on the first floor of the FRC at 1 Myddelton Street, London EC1R 1UW (# chapter 5). Its opening hours are the same as those for the GRO search room. Access to the census records is free and copies of entries can be obtained for a small charge. TNA also sells microfiche copies of the census returns. This is considered below.

Scanned pages of the 1901 census of England and Wales, with a transcript and name indexes, are available on the web site of the 1901 census online service (# appendix XI). Searches can be made online for the names of people or places. Access to the site is possible from dedicated terminals at the FRC and TNA at Kew (# chapter 11) but also from computers anywhere. There is no charge to use the online indexes but researchers can only see the census pages and transcript on a "pay-per-view" basis. Microfilm and fiche copies of the 1901 census (but not including the transcript or name indexes) can also be seen at TNA at Kew and the fiche version can be viewed at the FRC.

Microfilm copies of the census records of 1841 to 1901 can also be ordered and viewed, for a fee, at LDS family history centres (# chapter 11) and the Hyde Park family history centre also has many of these films permanently in stock. In addition, the SoG holds many of the census returns of 1841 to 1861 and 1891 on microfilm. These are listed in Churchill (138) and recent acquisitions are noted in the SoG library catalogue (# chapter 11). Many CROs and libraries also have microfilm or fiche copies of some of the census records (usually for the county or area that the CRO or library serves). Gibson & Hampson (140) list their holdings of the census returns of 1841–91 and *Family Tree Magazine* (August 2002) lists the CROs, libraries and other archives holding microform copies of parts of the 1901 census. You should contact the CRO or library before your visit, since it may be necessary to obtain a reader's ticket or reserve the use of a microfilm reader.

An increasing number of census returns are also becoming available, on CD-ROM or the Internet, from commercial suppliers noted below. The disks cost between £30 and £50 per county per census year and the Internet sites are "pay-per-view" or accessible only to subscribers. However, these options are ideal for people who cannot easily attend the FRC, other archives or libraries (or for people who wish to browse through census returns, at their leisure, at home).

OTHER SOURCES AT THE FRC

The search room of TNA at the FRC is the most convenient place to study census records because all the returns can be seen there (in some format) and there are many finding aids (for places and addresses) and a good collection of surname indexes. In addition, it takes only a short time to walk downstairs at the FRC in order to use the GRO search room and, furthermore, the search room of TNA also holds other records for family historians. These are reviewed in later chapters but they include computer terminals with the databases *FamilySearch*, the British Isles Vital Records Index and the National Burial Index (principally baptisms, marriages and burials from church registers), a database of trade directories and microfilm or fiche copies of:

a. wills and related records from the Prerogative Court of Canterbury up to 1858
b. the National Probate Calendar for 1858 to 1943
c. death duty registers of 1796 to 1857
d. non-conformist and non-parochial registers (for example of Methodists, Baptists, Quakers and some hospitals and prisons) from the 17th to 19th centuries, and
e. some registers of baptisms, births, marriages, deaths and burials of Britons abroad.

ORGANISATION OF THE CENSUS RECORDS

The census returns are lists of people but arranged by place, then street, then building, as shown in illustration 17. Therefore, in order to find an ancestor, you need to know where he lived (and find that place in the returns) or you must search all the records for a particular area. The difficulties of searching for ancestors in the census have been reduced substantially by the enormous number of indexes that have been produced to the names of people appearing in each census (with references to the places in the returns where they can be found). In addition to the online transcript and index of the 1901 census, the 1881 census has also been transcribed and indexed in full and most of the 1851 census has been indexed.

There are an increasing number of indexes to the censuses of 1841, 1861, 1871 and 1891. However, for large parts of these records, it is still necessary to undertake the traditional search procedure, that is obtain an address from civil registration certificates or other records, then find that address in the census. The census indexes for these years (and 1851) that have been prepared cover particular counties, cities or parishes and so you need some general indication of where your ancestors lived in order to know which index to consult. Furthermore, your ancestor may be in an area covered by an index but omitted from that index because of transcription errors. Therefore, it is important to know how the census returns are arranged and what information they contain. This enables you to make searches in the returns and analyse the information obtained from them.

The Registrar General was responsible for the 1841 and later censuses. The administrative unit for the collection of census data was the registration district, also used for the administration of civil registration. The census returns are therefore arranged by registration district (and sub-districts). You may know in which district your ancestors lived from civil registration certificates you have obtained. Each sub-district covered a number of civil parishes and was also divided into enumeration districts. The census information was collected, in each enumeration district, by an enumerator.

Higgs (142) is a detailed review of how censuses were taken in the 19th century. Enumerators distributed forms (or schedules) to the head of each household, who completed them by listing all people in the household on census night. The form would be completed by an enumerator if the householder was illiterate or failed to complete the form for some other reason. People in charge of military barracks, prisons, hospitals, ships, workhouses or boarding schools had to complete lengthy schedules of the soldiers, sailors, the sick, children or other residents. The enumerators copied the information from the householders' schedules into books and completed tables to calculate the number of people in each enumeration district. The enumerators' books were retained and are the records that are available to the public (the householders' schedules of 1841 to 1901 were destroyed).

An enumerator's book commences with a description of the area covered by the enumeration district. There were spaces at the top of each page of the books for enumerators to note the administrative areas in which households were located. These areas varied for each census year. For example, in 1841 there were spaces for the enumerator to insert the name of the city or borough and the name of the parish or township. By 1871 there were spaces (inter alia) for the names of the civil parish or township, the city or municipal borough, the town, village or hamlet and the parliamentary borough.

Parishes are discussed in detail in chapter 7, but it is useful to know a little about them when consulting census records. England has been divided since medieval times into ecclesiastical parishes, each with its own parish church. People worshipped at the parish church but many parishes were very large and so chapels (sometimes called chapels of ease) were built to serve parishioners who lived far from the parish church. The parish authorities also dealt with many administrative matters such as poor relief and the repair of highways. Some ecclesiastical parishes were too large for these purposes and so were divided into chapelries or townships, centred on the chapels. The townships undertook much of the local administration and many became established as civil parishes. From 1871 those ecclesiastical parishes that had not been divided into chapelries or townships also became deemed to be civil parishes for purposes of civil administration. Ecclesiastical parishes have continued in existence but remain important only for religious affairs. The ecclesiastical or civil parish is usually noted at the top of each page of census returns. If you know the ecclesiastical parish in which a family lived, but you need to know the civil parish and registration district in which that parish appears in the census, you can refer to a reference book (*List of Ecclesiastical Parishes*) at the FRC. For each ecclesiastical parish (or hamlet in that parish), the book notes the relevant civil parish, and also gives further information about the place, such as the poor law union in which it was located.

INFORMATION RECORDED IN CENSUS RETURNS

The census returns are in manuscript and the enumerator's handwriting can be difficult to read. The quality of the microfilm photography is not always perfect and the microfilm is also a negative (so that you will see white writing on a black background), which makes the records more difficult to read. Some returns have also been damaged and a few returns are missing, such as some 1841 returns for Kensington and Paddington in London.

Illustration 16 is an extract from the 1841 census of Hainford in Norfolk, including the family of my ancestor Henry Chapman. The address or location of the householder's property is noted, but this may only be approximate, such as James Street or even just the name of a village or hamlet (such as Waterloo in illustration 16). The returns list the names of the persons resident in each property, starting with the head of the household, on the night of 6 June 1841. Enumerators were instructed to include only one forename for each person. The returns then specify a person's sex and age. The age of a person aged over 15 was usually (but not always) rounded down to the nearest five years. A man who gave his age as 43 should therefore have been recorded as only 40. The returns also state an individual's occupation (if any). The final column states whether a person was born in the same county as that in which he was living at the time of the census. In this column you will see yes or no (or more usually y or n), but often the abbreviation NK, that is, not known. Birthplaces outside England or Wales were indicated by an S for Scotland, an I for Ireland or an F for "foreign parts".

The 1841 census returns do not state the relationship between the people in a household. These relationships can often be inferred but you should not make assumptions about the relationships without other evidence. A man and woman of the same surname, living together and both aged about 60, may not be husband and wife, but a brother and sister. The rounding down of ages can make the relationships very uncertain. If John Smith (noted as aged 50) is living with Jane Smith (noted as aged 30) this could be a widowed father John (truly aged 54) with his daughter Jane (truly aged 30) or it could be a husband (truly aged 50) with a young wife (truly aged 34). The entry for the family of my ancestor Emily Clements, in Wanstead, Essex, in 1841 is:

Name	Age: Male	Age: Female	Trade	Born in same county
John Clements	37		Fishmonger	Yes
Sarah Clements		32		No
William Clements	12			Yes
Emily Clements		5		Yes
Frances Clements·		2		Yes
Henry Clements	5 mths			Yes

I originally assumed that this was a father, mother and their four children. However, William Clements was actually John's son by a previous marriage to a girl named Frances. Frances died in

PLACE	HOUSES		NAMES of each Person who abode therein the preceding Night	AGE and SEX		PROFESSION, TRADE, EMPLOYMENT, or of INDEPENDENT MEANS	Where Born	
	Uninhabited or Building	Inhabited		Males	Females		Whether Born in same County	Whether Born in Scotland, Ireland or Foreign Parts
			James D°	1			yes	
			Lucy D°		80		yes	
			Rhoda Burton		5		yes	
Water Coo		1	*Robert Gage*	70		*Butcher*	yes	
			George Lovell	11			yes	
do		1	*Martin Druit*	26		*Carpenter*	yes	
do		1	*Julia D°*		25		yes	
			John Brown	30		*Ag. Lab.*	yes	
			Hannah D°		30		yes	
do		1	*Michael Anne*	60		*Ag. Lab.*	yes	
			Francis Smithson	20		*Ag. Lab.*	yes	
			Esther D°		25		yes	
			Eleanor D°		6		yes	
		1	*William D°*	1			yes	
do		1	*Henry Stephens*	20		*Ag. Lab.*	yes	
			Susan D°		25		yes	
			George D°	9			yes	
			Henry D°		2		yes	
			Jeremiah D°	6			yes	
			Martha D°		4		yes	
			Alice D°		2		yes	
			Charlotte D°		1		yes	
			Thomas Stephens	70			yes	
		1	*William Druit*	30		*Weaver Silk*	yes	
			Judith D°		30		yes	
TOTAL in Page 13	9	6		11	14	1		

16. *Extract from census returns, 1841 (TNA, HO 107/783/8)*

17. *Extract from census returns, 1851 (TNA. HO 107/1547)*

18. *Extract from census returns, 1881 (T.N.A., RG 11/1726)*

1833 and John married Sarah Boxall in 1834. William was therefore a stepson of Sarah and a half-brother of Emily, Frances and Henry.

The authorities obviously wished to avoid double-counting people in the census. The returns therefore only recorded family groups to the extent that members of a family were actually present in the same household on census night. No information should have been recorded about family members who were away from home that night. A family that you locate in the census records may therefore be incomplete.

The censuses of 1851 to 1881 were taken on the nights of 30 March 1851, 7 April 1861, 2 April 1871 and 3 April 1881. These provide more information than in 1841, including the actual age and place of birth of each person. Illustrations 17 and 18 are pages from the censuses of 1851 and 1881 that include my ancestors. The returns also state each adult's condition (that is whether they were unmarried, married or widowed), a person's occupation (children were often noted as scholars) and, importantly, the relationship of each person to the head of the household. The 1851 and 1861 returns specify whether people were blind, deaf or "idiot" and the 1871 and 1881 returns note whether a person was "blind, deaf, imbecile, idiot or lunatic". From 1851 people's ages were not rounded down (as in 1841) although the ages given for people (or even their names and places of birth) may still be inaccurate, since the head of the household may have provided incorrect information to the enumerator. An entry may note more than one forename for a person, but not all forenames were necessarily included. The recorded place of birth was usually a town, parish or city but sometimes just a county. If the person was born outside England or Wales, only the country of birth may be identified. Thus my ancestor Bernard Herber's birthplace was recorded in 1851 (# illustration 17) as Germany (the 1861 census fortunately specified Schwanheim in Germany). The information recorded in the census returns of 1851–81 can be seen from a simplified version of the entry in 1851 for the household of my ancestor George Keates in Wapping High Street, London:

Name	Relationship	Condition	Age	Occupation	Where born
George Keates	Head	Mar	41	Blockmaker	SUR, Rotherhithe
Ann do.	Wife	Mar	41		KENT, Dartford
John Josiah do.	Son		13	Apprentice	SUR, Rotherhithe
William Tho. do.	Son		12	Scholar	Limehouse
George Alb. do.	Son		10	Scholar	St George
Ebenezer James do	Son		8	Scholar	St George
Jesse do.	Son		4		Wapping

The 1891 census was taken on the night of 5 April. In addition to the information contained in earlier returns, this census recorded the number of rooms (if less than five) occupied by a family and notes whether a working person was an employer, an employee, or neither of these (the latter appears to have been used for the self-employed). The extract shown in illustration 19 records the family of my ancestor Richard Rice in Exwick near Exeter. Richard and most of his children were noted as employed. His wife Bessie, a laundress (probably working from home), seems to have been self-employed.

The 1901 census was taken on the night of 31 March 1901. Illustration 20 is a page from this census recording my great grandfather William Herber in Shepherds Bush, London with his family (including my grandfather Henry John Herber, aged 12). This census recorded the same

19. *Extract from census returns, 1891 (TNA, RG 12/1682)*

20. Extract from census returns, 1901 (TNA, RG 13/40)

information as in 1891 except that regarding employment status. The 1901 census noted whether a person was an employer, a worker or worked on his or her own account (and whether he or she worked at home). For those people resident in England or Wales but born in Scotland or Ireland, the returns should record the Scottish or Irish counties in which they were born. However, the returns often note only Scotland or Ireland without specifying the county.

There are many manuscript marks on the returns. Enumerators drew two diagonal strokes after the name of the last person in each building and one diagonal stroke after the name of the last person in each household within a building. There are also many manuscript ticks, or other marks, which were made by officials who counted the entries in order to compile statistics. Many abbreviations were also used: M or Mar for a married person, Unm for an unmarried person and W for a widow or widower. Other common abbreviations are F.S. (female servant), M.S. (male servant), App (apprentice), Dom (domestic servant) and Ag. Lab (agricultural labourer). Hey (23) notes the difference (not always applied in the census) between farm servants and agricultural labourers. Servants tended to be single, live on a farm and be paid by provision of their board, lodging and wages; labourers usually lived in cottages on the estate or in a nearby village and were paid a weekly wage or a piece-rate for casual work.

GENERAL PROBLEMS

Searching for your ancestors in a census can be very difficult. The enumerators' handwriting was often poor, and searching for a family in the large number of records that cover any area is a lengthy process. Even searching for a short time is tiring for your eyes so that you can easily miss one important entry in the hundreds of pages that you might have to scan.

If you know that your ancestors lived in a particular village or hamlet, it is easy to undertake a search of the area and so you will not need an exact address in order to find a family. The whole village (and surrounding countryside) can be searched for the family and other relatives. In large cities, especially London (which had millions of inhabitants), a blanket search of an area is difficult or impossible. It is therefore important to find addresses of city ancestors so as to find a family in the returns. People also moved accommodation frequently, so that an address that you have for a family (perhaps from a birth certificate) may not have been their address on census night. A move by your ancestors of even a short distance may frustrate your search.

Indexes to the surnames of people listed in each census are extremely important (and are sometimes the only realistic method of finding a family in the returns). However, if you know the address (or just the street name) where a family lived at about the date of a census, that address or street should obviously be the first for which you search. Addresses can be obtained from family records (such as letters or postcards), or from birth, marriage or death certificates. Addresses can also be obtained from other records such as probate records, trade directories, electoral registers, rate books and cemetery records. Directories (# chapter 9) are particularly useful for finding the addresses of tradesmen or well-off private individuals (especially in large cities or towns). Electoral registers (# chapter 17) also included the addresses of many voters and included more and more adult males as the franchise was extended during the 19th century. An alternative for earlier years is to use the records of poor law rates (# chapter 18), which may note addresses of persons assessed for the rate. However, the poor rate was often paid by landlords, so that many tenants were not listed.

Care must be taken in using census records to expand a family tree or to commence searches in other records. The information contained in a census may be incorrect. The ages given are often inaccurate. Women often gave lower ages, especially if they were married to younger men. The age of children may be exaggerated because the parents were telling a farmer or other employer (and therefore told an enumerator) that their son was 15 (even though he was only 12), so that he could earn better wages. Places of birth recorded in a census can be unreliable. A person may not have known where he was born or he may just have assumed that he was born in the place that he remembered as a child. The birthplace stated in the census was often a large town or city near to the actual place of birth, which was perhaps only a village or hamlet. The recorded relationship of a person to the head of household is often inaccurate, sometimes because of the wide meaning given to terms such as "in-law", but also because of honest mistake or deliberate lie. Illegitimate children of a daughter of a family were often treated as younger children of the child's grandparents. It is therefore vital to corroborate the information contained in census records with other source material.

SEARCH PROCEDURE: FINDING THE MICROFILM

At the search room at the FRC you must first decide what material you want to review:

a. the 1901 census: if so, choose one of the dedicated terminals for the 1901 census online service (described below) or a microfiche reader (with an orange marker card)
b. the 1881 census index on CD-ROM: if so, choose one of the computer terminals containing the family history databases or a microfiche reader
c. other census indexes: if so, choose a computer terminal containing the family history databases or a microfiche reader as appropriate
d. the microfiche copy of the 1891 census returns: if so, choose a microfiche reader, or
e. microfilm copies of the census returns of 1841–91: if so, choose a microfilm reader, note its number and collect the plastic box with that number from a shelf near the microfilm cabinets.

If you have decided to look at census returns on microfilm or fiche, you must then find the correct microfilm (or fiche), for which you will need the series number and piece number for the census records of the street or area that you wish to search. Each year of the census records has a series number. The returns of 1841 and 1851 are both in series HO 107 and the returns for 1861, 1871, 1881, 1891 and 1901 are in series RG 9, RG 10, RG 11, RG 12 and RG 13 respectively. Each census is divided between piece numbers. A piece consists of a few hundred pages of census returns (and each page is numbered). A microfilm or fiche might cover one, two or more pieces, but a substantial piece may be divided between two rolls of microfilm or between a number of fiches.

There are many indexes and other aids in the search room for locating the piece number of a place that you wish to search. TNA indexes for each census year are in books of a particular colour. Those for 1841 are green. If you wish to search the 1841 returns for a particular town or village, you can find the name of the town or village in the 1841 Place Name Index. Each place is given a number which is highlighted in yellow. This is the number of a page in the 1841 Reference Book to which you then turn. Each page lists the places covered by one or more piece numbers. The place that you wish to search will appear on that page, under one or more piece numbers. The places listed are parishes, hundreds (which were groups of parishes), registration districts and sub-districts. Therefore, if you wished to search the 1841 census records (HO 107) for Wanstead in Essex, the 1841 Reference Book would show that this parish was in the registration district of West Ham, in the sub-district of Leyton. It would also show that the piece number that includes Wanstead is 323, so the full reference for the piece including Wanstead is HO 107/323.

For each of the 1851 and later censuses, you consult the Place Name Index for that year, but the number obtained from it is the number of the registration district that included the place that you wish to search (not a page number in the Reference Book). You turn to that numbered district in the Reference Book for that year. This lists the sub-districts and parishes included in the registration district, with the piece numbers covering each place, so you can note the piece number that includes the place that you wish to search. You then collect the microfilm (or, for 1891, either a film or fiche) from self-service cabinets, placing the numbered plastic box for your microfilm reader in its place (so that you can return a film to the correct place). Take the film to your reader and commence your search. If you are using fiche, replace the fiche that you require with the orange marker card from your fiche reader. The microfilm and fiche readers are easy to use but there is also a leaflet describing how to operate them or the staff will assist.

If you are searching for an address taken from a civil registration certificate, that certificate will note the registration district and sub-district in which you must search so you can turn immediately to that district and sub-district in a Reference Book for the relevant year and find the piece number for your chosen area. The piece numbers for each registration district in England and Wales are also listed, for each census from 1851 to 1891, in Rosier (147). For example, the registration district of Exeter was covered by pieces HO 107/1868 to 1869 in 1851 and by RG 9/1393 to 1399 in 1861. Rosier (147) also notes the piece numbers covering each county in 1841.

SEARCH PROCEDURE: FINDING A PLACE ON THE FILM

TNA Reference Books list the places covered by a piece, but also tell you where a place can be found within a piece. Each piece consists of several enumerators' books (each covering an enumeration district). Enumeration districts varied in size and the number of people who were recorded. In rural areas they tended to cover a larger area (but fewer people) than in towns or cities. A parish might be divided into several enumeration districts, but an enumeration district sometimes covered more than one parish. The enumeration districts are numbered and that number is noted on the front page of each enumerator's book. Hainford in Norfolk was included in piece RG 12/1517 in 1891. The Reference Book notes that this piece includes:

Enumeration district number	Parishes
1	Catton
2	Rackheath & Beeston St Andrew
3	Crostwick & Frettenham
4	Drayton & Hellesdon
5	Hainford & Spixworth

The 1841 census returns are arranged differently from those of 1851 to 1901. Each piece contains a number of books and each book contains the returns for one or more enumeration districts. It is the book number that is important, not the enumeration district number. Book numbers appear on the front page of each book and also on an identification strip that was photographed at the side or bottom of each microfilmed page of the 1841 returns. Thus book one of piece HO 107/783 is indicated by the mark 783/1 (and book five is 783/5). It is important to differentiate between books and enumeration districts. For example, the 1841 census of Hainford in Norfolk appears in book eight (but enumeration district five) of piece HO 107/783. The books and parishes are listed in the 1841 Reference Book as follows:

Book number	Parishes
1	Attlebridge
2	Beeston St Andrew
3	Catton
4–5	Crostwick & Drayton
6	Felthorpe
7	Frettenham
8	Hainford

Each book in the 1841 census has its own folio numbers (a folio is a leaf of paper with text on each side), commencing with folio 1 marked on the top right hand corner of the first page (that is folio 1 recto; the other side is folio 1 verso). The next book started again at folio 1. From 1851 folio numbers run through each entire piece (rather than periodically starting again at folio 1). For example, in illustration 17, the folio number is the figure 517 in the top right hand corner. If more than one microfilm was needed to photograph a piece, the microfilm box notes the folios on each film reel (for example one box may be marked folios 1–365 and a second box marked folios 366–end). Each page of the returns within an enumerator's book (for all census years), also had a page number. Thus, in illustration 17 the page number (12) is at the top centre of the page. In illustrations 18 and 19, it is in the top right hand corner.

Although the code and numbering systems sound confusing, you will quickly become used to them. In brief, your ancestors should appear on a page in the census returns. That page will have a page number and a folio number. It will appear in a numbered enumeration district (and also, in the 1841 returns, in a numbered book) which is included in a numbered piece of census records for a particular year (indicated by a series number). For example, the full reference for the entry (set out above) for the Clements family in Wanstead in the 1841 returns is series HO 107, piece 323, book 21 (enumeration district seven), folio 20.

FINDING A FAMILY

There are three main methods of finding your ancestor's family in the census if no surname index appears to be available. The method to be used depends on where they lived and the information already available to you.

a. If they lived in a large town or city and you have their address, first find the reference for the registration district, sub-district and parish, then use a street index (see below) to find the folio numbers of the records in which that street appears.

b. If your ancestors lived in, or near, a small town or village, you should find the reference for that place (registration district, sub-district and parish) and search for the family in the returns for that place. It should not take you very long to find them in an area that had only a small population.

c. If your ancestor's family lived in a large town or city (but you have no address) or somewhere within a large rural area, the search is more difficult. A general search in many returns, perhaps covering thousands of people, is one option (considered below), but should be avoided if possible. Check again whether there are any surname indexes for the area or whether you have any information to narrow the area to be searched, for example the name of a parish or street.

STREET INDEXES

There are TNA street indexes for London and other large towns and cities (generally those with a population of over 40,000), for most census years. The Place Name Index indicates whether there is a street index for a place. If you know the name of the street in which your ancestors lived (from civil registration certificates or other sources), you can turn immediately to that street index. That will note the piece reference covering the street that you wish to find, but also tell you where you should search on a film, by noting the enumeration district or districts in which a street appears, or folio numbers for the street or each part of it. The following is an extract from the 1871 street index for the registration district of Holborn in London:

Street	Numbers	Piece No	Folios
Goswell Road	1–23 odd	RG10/420	61–62
	25–71 odd	RG10/381	59–61
	2–18 even	RG10/420	59–61
	20–22 even	RG10/408	48
	24–42 even	RG10/408	29–32
	72–98 even	RG10/396	24–26

This shows how addresses in a street, especially on a major road that formed a boundary between a number of enumeration districts (as was the case here), can be in different districts (and therefore on different films). Street indexes also include lists of workhouses, inns, schools, prisons or ships and a note of their location in the returns. Lumas (144) describes some further finding aids for London street names.

RECORDING YOUR SEARCHES

When you find a family or person for whom you are searching, you should record all relevant details from the census. Note the names of the registration district, sub-district, city, town, village and parish. Record the piece number (and book number in 1841), the enumeration district number, the folio and page numbers and, from the left hand column on the page, the schedule number for the household. You should then note the address, the names of all members of the household (and all information in the return about those people) and preferably any other households in the same building. You should record any visitors or lodgers since they were often related to the family. TNA sells blank forms, in the format of the census returns, on which your search results can be inserted. If your search is unsuccessful, you should also record that failure, so that you do not repeat unsuccessful searches.

Copies of pages from the census returns can be ordered at the FRC or TNA. For this service, you will require the piece number (and for 1841 only, the book number), the folio number and the page number. There are also self-service microfilm and fiche copiers in the searchroom. These operate with cash or rechargeable copy cards that can be purchased at the service desk. The cards are inserted in the machine attached to the microfilm copier and the credit on the card reduces as you make copies. The cards can be topped up in value at the service desk or by inserting coins into the copier's cash box.

USING SEARCH RESULTS

Having found your ancestor's family at a certain address in one census year, it is worth searching the returns of other years to see if the family was in the same house, street or village at an earlier or later date. When you find a family, you will discover the names, ages, occupations and (from 1851) the places of birth of all the family members. Other relatives may also be living with the family, especially mothers-in-law or brothers or sisters of the mother or father, but perhaps a grandparent, grandchild, nephew or niece. Cousins from "the country" may be living with families in cities, having moved in order to find work or perhaps visit their relatives.

You can use these details to search for the birth certificates of brothers and sisters of your ancestor. This may assist you in finding the family in an earlier census. For example, you may find your ancestor's family in the 1881 census at 1 Smith Street, Hackney, in London. If three children of the family were aged 15, 12 and 9 respectively (and all recorded as born in Hackney), yet the family was not in Smith Street in the 1871 census, the birth certificates of the children aged 12 and 9 will give you another address (or addresses) in Hackney, at which the family were living in about 1869 and 1872. You can then search for these addresses in the 1871 census. If that 1881 census had stated that the same children were born in Birmingham, their birth certificates would reveal addresses for which you can search in the 1871 census of Birmingham.

If you find your ancestors living in a small town or village in one census year, a search of the remainder of that village or area, in the same and earlier census records, is often rewarding. You may find other families with the same surname and it is worth noting them, because they may be relatives. Referring back to civil registration records or to parish registers (# chapter 7) may then enable you to establish a relationship between the households. I was searching for my ancestor Richard Rice and his father William in the 1851 census of the area around Ide in Devon. While searching, I noted entries concerning four families surnamed Rice in the nearby village of Dunsford. I then found William Rice and his family in Ide. The census stated that William had been born in Dunsford. The Dunsford parish register showed that the four Rice families in Dunsford were closely related to my ancestors.

The census records are also a great source of sociological information. You will often find two, three or more families sharing a house. You should record the families with which your ancestors shared a house; or note the names and occupations of your ancestors' neighbours so that you can build up a picture of the area in which your ancestors lived. A house may also have been the husband's shop or business premises. If your ancestors were wealthy, some servants, employees or apprentices may have lived with them. If your ancestor was a servant or apprentice, the census may therefore provide you with information about his employers.

GENERAL SEARCHES

If you do not know an address at which to search for a family, or if you cannot locate the family in the census at known addresses, a general or blanket search may be required. This may be easy if you know that the family lived in a small town or village. If you only know the name of a county or city, a search will be very time-consuming, if not impossible. Before you search a large area, check again whether the county or area has been indexed by surname for that census year. The availability of surname indexes (considered below) has greatly reduced the number of occasions when searches of large areas are necessary.

If you have no option but to undertake a general search (especially of a large city) you should first decide upon a proper methodology, in order to ensure that you do not miss any streets or areas. Very few contemporary maps showing the extent of enumeration districts have survived. Therefore, you should first obtain another contemporary map of the area, perhaps an Ordnance Survey map (# chapter 15). From TNA Reference Books you should then work out which piece numbers and enumeration districts are included in the area that you wish to search. If it is an urban area, you should list the streets in the area and, using street indexes, draw the approximate boundaries of the enumeration district on to a photocopy of your contemporary map. You can then turn to a film containing one of those districts. You should read the enumerator's description of his district (so that you are certain of the extent of the area covered) and then search through the returns. After noting the result of your search, you can search the second enumeration district and so on. In this way, you always know exactly what area has been covered and what searches remain to be undertaken.

PURCHASING CENSUS RETURNS

The census returns are being released on CD-ROM, arranged in the same way as the microfilms at the FRC. Any page that includes an entry of interest can be printed out or copied to another computer file. The disks (or sets of disks for larger counties) generally cover one county in one census year. The three principal suppliers of such disks are S&N Genealogy Supplies (# chapter 3), Archive CD Books of 5 Commercial Street, Cinderford, Gloucestershire GL14 2RP and Stepping Stones of PO Box 295, York YO31 1YS. The catalogues of these organisations are available on their web sites (# appendix XI) and lists of their new releases appear in regular advertisements in *Family Tree Magazine*. The disks generally include an index to parishes and hamlets, from which you can move directly to the relevant pages of the returns. The disks produced by S&N Genealogy Supplies also include the relevant parts of TNA Reference Books and any available street indexes. To date, S&N Genealogy Supplies has concentrated on releases of the 1841, 1871 and 1891 censuses, Archive CD Books has concentrated on the 1861 census and Stepping Stones has concentrated on 1841. However, the number of counties and years covered by each of these suppliers is increasing so rapidly that most (if not all) English counties will be available for each census year between 1841 and 1891 by late 2004. S&N Genealogy Supplies has also produced disks of the 1901 census of London, Lancashire and Yorkshire and intends to release the 1901 returns for other counties in due course.

Microfiche copies of the 1891 census of England and Wales can be purchased from The Reprographic Ordering Department, The National Archives, Ruskin Avenue, Kew, Surrey, TW9 4DU. However, the census is on over 15,000 fiche (each fiche contains about 100 census pages) and so you must specify the piece numbers for the areas that you require. These can be identified from the 1891 census Reference Book, which is also sold on microfiche. TNA will tell you how many fiche cover a piece (and the cost). The minimum unit that can be purchased is a registration sub-district, which usually consists of three fiche and costs £7.80 (plus postage). Street indexes to the 1891 census of London are also sold on microfiche. TNA also sells microfiche copies of the Reference Books for other census years (at £3 each). In addition, TNA will prepare and sell (in response to specific requests), microfiche copies of whole pieces from the censuses of 1841 to 1881, but these are more expensive.

CENSUS SURNAME INDEXES

It is usually very easy to find a family in the census returns if they have been indexed. Many surname indexes have been produced by family history societies and individuals. Most indexes list people's names (but sometimes only surnames) and their ages, alphabetically for each parish or for the whole county, with the piece and folio number of the census returns in which you will find them.

Census indexes, as with any transcription of original records, do include errors and so you should always check the original returns to ensure that an index or transcription is correct. The name of your ancestor may have been indexed or transcribed incorrectly, for example as John Budge instead of John Bridge. If so, you may not find him and assume, incorrectly, that he was not living on census night in the area covered by the index. The online transcription of the 1901 census (reviewed below) contains many errors. I found three brothers in Essex, who had been born in Wapping but in two cases, the transcript recorded the birthplace as "Dapping", even though Wapping is fairly clear in the original returns. My ancestor Joseph Eagles was noted in the 1901 returns as a boot maker but the transcript records him as a "boal maker" (whatever that is). The index included three men named William Herber. Two of them were my grandfather's father and brother. The mystery third man lived in Poplar in East London. Checking the original return revealed a transcription error; he was clearly recorded as William Hebber, not Herber. A descendant of William Hebber who searches for him in the index is unlikely to find him. The 1901 census transcript and index are fantastic finding aids that permit you to find most ancestors in any part of the country in a few minutes but they have not been checked sufficiently. To overcome this problem, you should search for as many variations of a name as you can. If that fails, you may have to revert to the traditional search method for the census; finding an ancestor's address and locating that in the returns. The 1881 census index also contains errors. For example, Sutherland in Scotland has been incorrectly transcribed as Sunderland (in County Durham) in thousands of entries. An article about reported mistakes in the 1881 index, by S. Lumas, appears in *Family Tree Magazine* (June 1999).

The censuses of 1881 and 1901 have been transcribed and indexed for all parts of Great Britain and it is therefore easy to find most people on census night in both years. Both indexes are considered in more detail below but the 1881 census index for Britain is on both microfiche and CD-ROM (and is one of the databases on computer terminals at the FRC). It can also be consulted on the *FamilySearch* web site (# appendix XI). The transcript and index for the 1901 census of England, Wales, Isle of Man and the Channel Islands can be viewed online (from any computer or from FRC and TNA terminals) and researchers can call up images of the census returns.

The SoG, FRC, TNA, Guildhall Library, CROs and FHS libraries hold the 1881 census index and collections of indexes for other census years. The majority of the 1851 census has been indexed and there are an increasing number of indexes to parts of the censuses of 1841, 1861, 1871 and 1891. Census indexes are in book form, on microfiche, on CD-ROM or available on the Internet and many can be purchased from individuals, commercial organisations or the FHS for the relevant county or area. In the past, most census indexes were booklets that covered a few parishes and so you had to search many indexes in order to find an ancestor whom you believed to be in a particular county or city on census night. More recent indexes, particularly on CD-ROM or the Internet, tend to cover a whole county. This makes it much easier to find an ancestor. Examples of CD-ROM indexes are the Buckinghamshire FHS transcript and index of the 1851 census of Buckinghamshire, the Gloucestershire FHS transcript and index of the 1851 census of Gloucestershire and Oxfordshire FHS indexes to the 1861, 1871 and 1891 census records of Oxfordshire. There are also CD-ROM indexes for the 1851 and 1891 censuses of Dorset (produced by Somerset and Dorset FHS), the 1851 census of Cornwall (produced by Cornwall Business Systems in Redruth) and the 1851 census of Wiltshire (by Wiltshire 1851 Census Productions in Cirencester). S&N Genealogy Supplies is also issuing CD-ROM indexes to some of the census records that, as noted above, it has reproduced on disk. As the indexing projects proceed, so new versions of the CD-ROM indexes are released. For example, version three of the index of the 1891 census of London now includes about 1,300,000 entries. Similar indexes for Lancashire and Yorkshire presently contain over 300,000 entries and 368,000 entries respectively. Smaller but expanding indexes are available for other counties and other years, for example that for the 1861 census of London presently contains about 270,000 entries. Expanded editions of each of these indexes should be issued at regular intervals.

There are hundreds of indexes in book or microfiche form (usually a series of booklets or fiche for each county). Most FHS publications are listed in Hampson (249) or Perkins (263). Indexes that can be purchased on CD-ROM are listed in Raymond (267). Most census indexes, including many that have not been published (and the places where they can be viewed), are listed by county in Gibson & Hampson (141). For example, Nottinghamshire FHS has indexed the whole county by surname for each of the 1841 to 1891 censuses. Lincolnshire FHS has produced indexes for the whole of the 1871 census of Lincolnshire. Another commercial index deserves mention. Clive Ayton is indexing the 1871 census of London (pieces RG 10/1–794) and undertakes name searches in the index for a fee. By 2002, he had indexed 141 pieces, covering over 500,000 people and published the indexes for 31 pieces.

In addition to the online 1901 census, some other census transcripts and indexes are being placed on the Internet. Volunteers are transcribing the 1891 census of Devon, Cornwall and Warwickshire (and the 1841 census of Cornwall) and completed parts are being placed on the FreeCEN web site. Other web sites levy a charge for use of the indexes they feature. Some census indexes are available on the FFHS "pay-per-view" web site *FamilyHistoryOnline* (# chapter 11 and appendix XI), including complete indexes for the censuses of Cornwall (in 1841, 1861 and 1871), Derbyshire (1891) and Northamptonshire (1851). The S&N Genealogy Supplies' indexes noted above (and some others) can be consulted, on a subscription basis, at *The Genealogist* web site (# appendix XI). Some of these indexes are complete, for example, the index for Herefordshire in 1891. Others are incomplete but rapidly expanding. Thus the index for the 1891 census of Kent presently has only 22,000 entries but the index for Lancashire in 1891 has over 600,000 entries. Some smaller indexes can also be found on web sites dedicated to particular parishes. The best way to find these is through GENUKI (# chapter 11).

The SoG has the largest collection of census indexes in Britain and this collection is continually expanding. The indexes are listed in its catalogue but those in the collection by late 1997 are also listed in Churchill (138) and some recent additions are listed in Gibson & Hampson (141). The search room at the FRC also holds many census indexes; the Place Name Index notes whether there is a surname index at the FRC for any place, so you should check this when you are searching for the piece number for a place. The FRC also has separate lists, for each census year, of those parishes covered by its collection of indexes.

THE 1881 CENSUS INDEX

The 1881 census returns of Great Britain, the Isle of Man, the Channel Islands and the Royal Navy have been transcribed in full, indexed and published on microfiche and CD-ROM by the LDS (the Genealogical Society of Utah) and family history societies. The transcript and index are also available on the LDS *FamilySearch* web site. It is therefore easy to find most people who were recorded in this census. In particular, the index makes it easy to find people away from home on census night (such as soldiers or travelling salesmen) and those, such as Gypsies, who had no settled home. Some researchers prefer the fiche version of the index and some prefer the CD-ROM or online versions. The CD-ROM has a number of advantages, including its low price and the fact that it fits on only 24 disks (in comparison to thousands of fiche). The online version can be consulted without charge but the fiche version also has advantages and it can be reviewed at many archives. The 1881 index is also best understood by first considering the fiche version.

The fiche version of the transcript and index is divided into sections for each pre-1974 county of England, Wales and Scotland, and for the Isle of Man, Channel Islands and the Royal Navy returns. There is also a national index, listing all people alphabetically by surname and Christian name and a national list of all ships recorded in the returns. The index is available at LDS family history centres, the SoG, Guildhall Library and many other archives and FHS libraries. The microfiche version of the 1881 transcript and index can be purchased from the FFHS Finance Officer, 1 Tenterk Close, Bleadon, Weston-Super-Mare, Somerset, BS24 0PJ (the CD-ROM version can be purchased from the LDS Distribution Centre, 399 Garretts Green Lane, Garretts Green, Birmingham B33 0UH).

All census indexes are useful, but the 1881 index is particularly useful for two reasons. Firstly, the index includes all information from the census, rather than just peoples' names and relevant folio numbers. Secondly, each part of the 1881 index covers a whole county, whereas many other indexes are of surnames in a particular parish, so that you may have to search many indexes.

The microfiche version of the 1881 census index for each British county (and for each of the returns of the Royal Navy, Jersey, Guernsey and the Isle of Man) is divided into the following seven sections. In each section, most of the information in the census returns is sorted and listed by a different criterion. The fiches of each section have different coloured headers:

a. as enumerated – yellow
b. surname index – pink
c. census place index – orange
d. birthplace index – green

e. miscellaneous and various notes – brown
f. list of vessels/ships – brown
g. list of institutions – brown

The **as enumerated section** is a transcript of the census returns. Each page on the fiche notes the piece, folio and page numbers covered. Each person is then listed in the order that they appear in the original returns (together with the information noted about them in the census). In columns to the right of the entry for each person appear TNA references (the piece, folio and page numbers) where you will find that person in the original returns and the LDS film reference (which you will need to order the films at LDS family history centres). There is also a column headed "notes". A mark in this column means that you should refer to the miscellaneous notes section of the index (see below). Illustration 21 shows a page from the as enumerated section of the index for Essex, including the family of Ebenezer Keates, a brother of my ancestor John Josiah Keates. In order to use this section, you find the fiche that includes the piece, folio and page numbers that you obtain from other sections of the index (such as the surname index). This transcript is much easier and quicker to use than the microfilm census returns but you must beware of transcription errors, so all entries should be checked against the original returns.

The **surname index** lists all people in the county on census night, but sorted in alphabetical order of surname, then Christian name, then age. Most of the other information provided by the census returns is then noted for each person (age, sex, relationship to head of household, marital condition and occupation). A column then notes the census place in which they resided on census night (but not the actual address), and the place where each person was born. The name of the head of the household in which the person lived is also noted in a column in this index. There is also a column headed notes which may refer you to the miscellaneous notes section of the index. Illustration 22 is a typical page from this index, showing all those surnamed Keates in Essex. The index notes the piece number, folio and page upon which each person appears, so that you can turn to the as enumerated section or original returns for full information about the person, household and neighbours. If you are searching for a particular person, this surname index is ideal for locating him if he was in the county on census night. Illustration 22 also confirms the importance of checking different spellings of names. This page of the index does not include my g.g. grandfather John Josiah Keates or his family. They do appear in the index for Essex, but a few pages later, with the surname Keats, because the surname was spelt incorrectly in the original returns. Some names have also been incorrectly transcribed from the original returns so, as with any transcript or index, you should check for variations of names.

The **census place index** lists people in alphabetical order of surname. Individuals of each surname are then sorted by the names of places in which they lived, so that people surnamed Hodge living in a particular census place in 1881 are listed together. They are then sorted in order of their Christian names and then by age. This section is useful for finding all those people with the same surname who lived in a census place (perhaps a town such as Crediton) on census night. However, you should note that a census place might be only part of the area that you wish to search (Exeter was divided into places such as Exeter St David and Exeter St Thomas).

The **birthplace index** lists everyone in the census of the county, alphabetically by surname but then (for each surname) sorted by their birthplace (as recorded in the census) and only then by forename and age. It is useful for tracing what happened to brothers and sisters of your ancestors, although it remains difficult to find the married daughters or sisters of your ancestor, unless you

Leyton Low

1881 CENSUS—AS ENUMERATED, COUNTY: ESSEX , 1727 153 39 PAGE: 03450

CENSUS PLACE	HOUSEHOLD ADDRESS	SURNAME	FORENAME	RELATIONSHIP TO HEAD	MARITAL CONDITION	AGE	SEX	OCCUPATION	WHERE BORN CO	WHERE BORN PARISH	PRO PIECE	FOLIO	REF	G.S.U. FILM
Leyton Low	Leyton Rd Or Nr //	DIXON	William J.	Head	M	34	M	Boot Maker Emp	MID	Bethnal Green	1727	153	39	1341115
Leyton Low	Leyton Rd Or Nr	DIXON	Mary A.	Wife	M	34	F		WIL	Milton	1727	153	39	1341115
Leyton Low	Leyton Rd Or Nr //	LAKE	Mary	Serv	U	16	F	Servant Domest	NFK	Grimston	1727	153	39	1341115
Leyton Low	Leyton Rd Or Nr	BARRON	Robert	Head	M	37	M	Grocer	SUR	Rotherhithe	1727	153	39	1341115
Leyton Low	Leyton Rd Or Nr	BARRON	Sophia	Wife	M	39	F		SUR	Rotherhithe	1727	153	39	1341115
Leyton Low	Leyton Rd Or Nr	BARRON	Clara	Daur		9	F	Scholar	ESS	Leyton	1727	153	39	1341115
Leyton Low	Leyton Rd Or Nr	BARRON	Bertram	Son		6	M	Scholar	ESS	Leyton	1727	153	39	1341115
Leyton Low	Leyton Rd Or Nr	BARRON	Walter	Son		4	M		ESS	Leyton	1727	153	39	1341115
Leyton Low	Leyton Rd Or Nr	BARRON	Charles	Son		1	M		ESS	Leyton	1727	153	39	1341115
Leyton Low	Leyton Rd Or Nr	TREE	Sophia	Moll	W	77	F	Formerley Mar	MID	St Pancras	1727	153	39	1341115
Leyton Low	Leyton Rd Or Nr //	UNINHABITED									1727	153	39	1341115
Leyton Low	Leyton Rd Or Nr //	MASKELL	Richard	Head	M	43	M	Draper Emp 1	ESS	Tillingham	1727	153	39	1341115
Leyton Low	Leyton Rd Or Nr	MASKELL	Emma S.	Wife	M	40	F		ESS	Tillingham	1727	153	39	1341115
Leyton Low	Leyton Rd Or Nr	MASKELL	Selina M.	Daur		12	F	Scholar	KEN	Forest Hill	1727	153	39	1341115
Leyton Low	Leyton Rd Or Nr	MASKELL	Emma S.	Daur		6	F	Scholar	ESS	Leyton	1727	153	39	1341115
Leyton Low	Leyton Rd Or Nr //	LAWRENCE	Mabel J.	Serv			F	Drapers Assist	KEN	Canterbury	1727	135	39	1341115
Leyton Low	Leyton Rd Or Nr	FASCAM	Emma F.	Serv		25	F	Grocer	ESS	Leyton	1727	153	39	1341115
Leyton Low	Leyton Rd Or Nr	FASCAM	William	Wife	M	37			MID	New	1727	153	39	1341115
Leyton Low	Leyton Rd Or Nr	FASCAM	Esther	Son		13	M	Scholar	ESS	Leyton	1727	153	39	1341115
Leyton Low	Leyton Rd Or Nr	RUTTY	Fredk. W.	Son		11	M	Scholar	ESS	Leyton	1727	153	39	1341115
Leyton Low	Leyton Rd Or Nr	RUTTY	Thos.	Head	M	33	M	Ironmonger	MID	Shoreditch	1727	153	39	1341115
Leyton Low	Leyton Rd Or Nr	RUTTY	Samuel		M	32			ESS	St Lukes	1727	153	39	1341115
Leyton Low	Leyton Rd Or Nr	RUTTY	Harriet						ESS	Leyton	1727	153	39	1341115
Leyton Low	Leyton Rd Or Nr //	UNINHABITED	Harriet	Daur			F				1727	153	39	1341115
Leyton Low	Leyton Rd Or Nr //	BARDSLEY	John I.	Head	M	54	M	Vendor Of Milk	MID	St Pancras	1727	153	39	1341115
Leyton Low	Leyton Rd Or Nr	BARDSLEY	Rebecca M.	Wife	M	52	F		MID	Marylebone	1727	153	39	1341115
Leyton Low	Leyton Rd Or Nr	BARDSLEY	John F.	Son	U	21	M	Assists His Fa	SUR	Croydon	1727	153	39	1341115
Leyton Low	Leyton Rd Or Nr	KEATES	Lillian M.	Daur		12	F		SUR	Banstead	1727	153	39	1341115
Leyton Low	Leyton Rd Or Nr	KEATES	Ebenezer I.	Head	M	34	M	Builder Employ	MID	St Georges East	1727	153	39	1341115
Leyton Low	Leyton Rd Or Nr	KEATES	Isabel	Wife	M	34	F		ESS	Mile End	1727	153	39	1341115
Leyton Low	Leyton Rd Or Nr	KEATES	George E.	Son		11	M	Scholar	ESS	Leyton	1727	153	39	1341115
Leyton Low	Leyton Rd Or Nr	KEATES	Anna F.	Daur		10	F	Scholar	ESS	Leyton	1727	153	39	1341115
Leyton Low	Leyton Rd Or Nr //	UNINHABITED	Chas I.	Son		7	M	Scholar	ESS	Leyton	1727	153	39	1341115
Leyton Low	Leyton Rd Or Nr		John N.	Son		4	M		ESS	Leyton	1727	153	39	1341115
Leyton Low	Leyton Rd Or Nr		Frank A.	Son		1	M		ESS	Leyton	1727	153	39	1341115
Leyton Low	7 High St	STRATFORD	William	Head	M	43	M	Engineer And	KEN	Dartford	1727	153	40	1341115
Leyton Low	7 High St	STRATFORD	Sarah	Wife	M	51	F		KEN	Town Malling	1727	153	40	1341115
Leyton Low	6 High St //	TAYLOR	Sarah	Head	W	41	F	Laundress	ESS	Colchester	1727	153	40	1341115
Leyton Low	5 High St	COOK	George	Head	U	44	M	Labourer	MID	Westminster	1727	153	40	1341115
Leyton Low	Leyton Rd Or Nr //	GILL	Henry M.	Head	M	34	M	Fish Monger	MID	Clerkenwell	1727	164	41	1341115
Leyton Low	Leyton Rd Or Nr	HANCOCK	George	Wife	M	24	F	Dressmaker	ESS	Maldon	1727	164	41	1341115
Leyton Low	Leyton Rd Or Nr	HANCOCK	Emma	Son		2	M		MID	Clerkenwell	1727	164	41	1341115
Leyton Low	Leyton Rd Or Nr	HANCOCK	George E.	Head	M	12	M	Scholar	ESS	Leyton	1727	164	41	1341115
Leyton Low	Leyton Rd Or Nr	BURLEIGH	William F.	Head	M	36	M	Labourer	ESS	Leyton	1727	164	41	1341115
Leyton Low	Leyton Rd Or Nr	BURLEIGH	Thos.	Head	M	36	M		SUF	Haverhill	1727	164	41	1341115
Leyton Low	Leyton Rd Or Nr	BURLEIGH	Ellen	Daur	L		F		SUF	Keddington	1727	164	41	1341115
Leyton Low	Leyton Rd Or Nr	BURLEIGH	Mabel	Daur		3	F	Scholar	SUR	Peckham	1727	164	41	1341115
Leyton Low	Leyton Rd Or Nr	BURLEIGH	John	Son		2	M	Scholar	SUR	Peckham	1727	164	41	1341115

M = MARRIED   U = UNMARRIED   W = WIDOWED
D = DIVORCED   O = OTHER

M = MONTHS   W = WEEKS   d = DAYS
+ = GREATER THAN   < = LESS THAN

* = SEE ORIGINAL CENSUS FOR FULL DATA
R = SEE MISCELLANEOUS NOTES

21. 1881 census index, "as enumerated" section, showing the family of Ebenezer Keates in Low Leyton, Essex (The Genealogical Society of Utah)

KEARSEY

1881 CENSUS-SURNAME INDEX, COUNTY: ESSEX

, Louisa

PAGE: 05680

SURNAME	FORENAME	AGE	S/X	RELATION-SHIP TO HEAD	MARITAL CONDITION	CENSUS PLACE	OCCUPATION	NAME OF HEAD	CO	WHERE BORN PARISH	NOTE	PIECE (FOLIO)	PAGE	G.S.U. FILM NUMBER
KEARSEY	Louisa	4	F	Daur	-	West Ham	...	KEARSEY, Jacob	ESS	Wigbrough		1713	56	1341489
KEARSEY	Mary A.	57	F	Wife	M	West Ham	...	KEARSEY, Thomas	ESS	Fingerhoe		1713	56	1341489
KEARSEY	Samuel	49	M	Head	M	Thundersley	Farm Bailiff	Self	ESS	Thunderley		1744	43	1341426
KEARSEY	Thomas	60	M	Head	M	West Ham	Labourer	Self	ESS	Tingham		1713	56	1341489
KEARSON	James W.	14	M	Bord	U	Dagenham	Under Groom D		LEC	...		1745	31	1341428
KEARTLAND	John	23	M	Sldr		Colchester St	Soldier	I. INFANTRY CAMP	IRE	...	*	1789	78	1341432
KEARY	Ada	6	F	Daur	U	West Ham	Scholar	KEARY, Frederick	ESS	West Ham		1786	24	1341407
KEARY	Anne Maria	3	F	Vist	U	West Ham	...	SACH, George Tho.	ESS	West Ham		1717	128	1341489
KEARY	Bertie W.	8m	M	GSon		Great Totham	...	EVE, Chas. Walter	ESS	Gt. Totham		1777	13	1341424
KEARY	Charles	19	M	Bord	U	West Ham	Railway Clerk	MANT, John	ESS	Sticatford		1777	13	1341408
KEARY	Christine E.	28	F	Wife	M	Walthamstow		KEARY, Lionel	MID	Islington		1734	92	1341416
KEARY	Christine E.	4	F	Daur		Walthamstow		KEARY, Lionel	MID	Clacton		1734	92	1341416
KEARY	Eliza	51	F	Wife	M	Chipping Ongar	Engine Driver's	KEARY, George	ESS	Saffron Walden		1761	37	1341410
KEARY	Ellen	29	F	SDau	W	Great Totham	Barmaid	EVE, Chas. Walter	ESS	Gt. Totham		1777	13	1341424
KEARY	Frederick	30	M	Head	M	West Ham	Tailor	Self	ESS	Colchester		1786	127	1341407
KEARY	George	54	M	Head	M	Chipping Ongar	Engine Driver	Self	ESS	Birch		1761	37	1341410
KEARY	George	21	M	Lodg	U	Brentwood	Railway Clerk	Self	ESS	Colchester		1741	1	1341423
KEARY	George	11	M	Son		West Ham	Scholar	KEARY, Frederick	ESS	West Ham		1786	127	1341407
KEARY	Hannah	2m	M	Daur		West Ham	...	KEARY, Frederick	ESS	West Ham		1786	127	1341407
KEARY	Harriet	42	F	Wife	M	West Ham	...	KEARY, Frederick	SUF	Ipswich		1786	129	1341407
KEARY	Irene	6	M	Son		Walthamstow	Scholar	KEARY, Lionel	MID	Hackney		1734	92	1341416
KEARY	John	34	M	Head	M	Walthamstow	Clerk	Self	SUF	Ipswich		1739	92	1341407
KEARY	Lionel B.	2	M	Son		Walthamstow		KEARY, Lionel	MID	Hackney		1753	92	1341416
KEARY	Rachel	12	F	Daur		West Ham	Scholar	KEARY, Frederick	MID	Hackney		1786	127	1341407
KEARY	Robert S.	9m	M	Son		West Ham	...	KEARY, Frederick	ESS	West Ham		1786	16	1341407
KEATE	Edward	44	M	Head	M	Prittlewell	Colonel N.M.	Self	MID	London	*	1749	54	1341426
KEATE	Margaret F.	37	F	Wife	M	Prittlewell	Wife	KEATE, Edward	MID	London		1749	54	1341426
KEATE	M.K. Emma	14	F	Daur	U	Prittlewell	Daughter	KEATE, Edward	HAL	...		1749	54	1341426
KEATES	Alice D.	17	F	Serv	U	Layton	Genl Serv Dom	ASHCROFT, Henry	MID	Wapping		1725	6	1341416
KEATES	Alice H.	21	F	Daur	U	Layton	Scholar	KEATES, Anna	ESS	Walthamstow		1725	163	1341415
KEATES	Alice I.	2	F	Daur		Layton	Scholar	KEATES, Obadiah	ESS	Bow		1743	37	1341416
KEATES	Anna P.	17	F	Head	M	Layton	Income From Ho	Self	MID	London		1725	163	1341415
KEATES	Chas. I.	14	M	Son	U	Layton Low	Scholar	KEATES, Ebenezer I.	MID	London		1727	163	1341415
KEATES	Ebenezer I.	8	M	Son		Layton Low	Scholar	KEATES, Ebenezer I.	CAM	...		1727	163	1341415
KEATES	Emma	34	M	Head	M	West Ham	Builder Emplot	Self	MID	Wapping		1725	41	1341415
KEATES	Flora A.	19	F	Daur		Layton	Schoolmistress	KEATES, Anna	MID	London		1725	163	1341415
KEATES	Frank A.	1	M	Son		Layton Low		KEATES, Ebenezer I.	ESS	Layton		1727	163	1341415
KEATES	George E.	11	M	Son	U	Layton Low	Scholar	KEATES, Ebenezer	ESS	Mile End		1727	183	1341415
KEATES	Isabel	38	F	Wife	M	Layton Low		KEATES, Ebenezer	MID	St Georges East		1727	163	1341415
KEATES	Jesse	6	M	Lodg		Layton Low	Scholar	NORRIS, Mary A.	MID	Shadwell		1727	117	1341415
KEATES	John H.	33	M	Son		Layton Low	Carpenter	KEATES, Ebenezer	CAM	...		1727	163	1341415
KEATES	Louisa	22	F	Wife	M	Layton	Box Maker At	KEATES, Obadiah		...		1743	163	1341416
KEATES	Obadiah	24	M	Head	M	West Ham	Fitters Labour	Self	ESS	Rhodwell		1743	37	1341416
KEATES	Sarah	29	F	Wife	M	Layton	Carpenter	KEATES, William	ESS	Millwall		1725	112	1341414
KEATES	Thomas	2m	M	Son		Layton		KEATES, William	ESS	Epping		1725	112	1341414
KEATES	William	42	M	Head	M	West Ham	Carpenter (Hat	Self	MID	Limehouse		1725	112	1341414
KEATEY	John	29	M	Asst	U	West Ham	Drapers Assist	BOND, Samuel	KEN	Deptford		1768	164	1341410
KEATING	Ann	44	F	Wife	M	West Ham		KEATING, Edward	IRE	...		1717	110	1341489

* SEE ORIGINAL CENSUS FOR FULL DATA.
o = MONTHS w = WEEKS d = DAYS
> = GREATER THAN < = LESS THAN

M = MARRIED   U = UNMARRIED   W = WIDOWED   D = DIVORCED   O = OTHER

= SEE MISCELLANEOUS NOTES

22. 1881 census – surname index for Essex – the Keates family (The Genealogical Society of Utah)

know their married names. Illustration 23 is an extract from the birthplace index for Devon. This lists some of those people surnamed Rice who were recorded as born in Devon (including some born in Exeter, some in Exwick and other places, alphabetically, through to Ideford). After the list of all those people surnamed Rice who were born in Devon, the index lists those born in other counties and then those born abroad. For each person, most of the other information from the census is then set out. The information that is not included (such as occupations and other members of the household), can be obtained by referring to the as enumerated section or the original returns. The birthplace index is useful if you are trying to locate brothers and sisters of your ancestor, particularly if all the siblings were born in the same parish. In illustration 23 you will see (noted as born in Ide) my g.g. grandfather Richard Rice aged 45 (living in Exeter, St Thomas). This index enabled me to find his brothers William, aged 49 (at Crediton) and John, aged 36 (at Heavitree). Before the 1881 index was produced, if brothers and sisters had moved away from home, you would have had to consult many indexes or undertake a blanket search of the county (and perhaps other counties) in order to find them. Now it is easy to find siblings with the same surname. Even if they moved outside the county of birth, you can quickly check other county indexes (or the national index, reviewed below) to find people of that surname who are recorded as born in your ancestor's county and parish.

The limitation of the birthplace index is that the birthplace in the original returns may not be exact (perhaps only Ireland or London) and the index cannot improve upon this lack of information. I used the Essex birthplace index to find people surnamed Law who were born in Walthamstow. I turned to the list of those surnamed Law and then to that part of the list for those born in "Essex, Walthamstow". There was only one entry and it seemed that three family members were missing. However, they were in the index. The problem arose because they were living in Walthamstow on census night and so their birthplace was only recorded, in the census, as "Walthamstow", rather than "Essex, Walthamstow" (enumerators often omitted the county name). However, when the 1881 census index was being prepared, this meant that the computer (which sorted the information) did not place these births in the Essex section, but only in the section for those people whose county of birth was unknown or not specified. Remember also that someone's birthplace may be incorrectly stated in the census. In the extract at illustration 23, my g.g. grandfather Richard Rice is recorded as having been born in Ide, but I discovered that he was baptised in 1835 in the neighbouring parish of Doddiscombsleigh. Richard spent most of his childhood in Ide, and he probably just assumed that he had been born there. It is worth noting that, in the 1851 census, when Richard was young and his father was informing the enumerator of his childrens' birthplaces, Doddiscombsleigh was recorded rather than Ide.

Three sections of the 1881 census index have microfiche with brown headers. One is a list of ships and vessels (in alphabetical order) giving a ship's name and a few notes such as the ship's number (# chapter 21), home port, census place (a port or harbour), the name of its master and its location in the census records. The second section is a list of institutions such as schools, prisons, workhouses and hospitals, noting their location in the census records. Institutions are therefore very easy to find in the 1881 census. The miscellaneous notes section is an alphabetical list of those persons against whom a mark was made in the notes column in other sections of the index. Each person to whom a note applies is listed in order of surname, then Christian name, age and census place. The note appears in a further column (usually that the person was recorded in the census as blind, deaf, an idiot, lunatic or imbecile).

RICE

1881 CENSUS-BIRTHPLACE INDEX, COUNTY: DEVONSHIRE

, DEV Exwick

PAGE: 08735

23. 1881 census – birthplace index for Devon – the Rice family (The Genealogical Society of Utah)

The microfiche **national index** lists all people recorded in the census, but with only some of the information from the census. There are two lists. The first lists all people in alphabetical order of surname, then forename and then age. The second is sorted by surname, then birthplace, then forename and then by age. The national index can be used in exactly the same way as the county indexes, reviewed above, to find people if you do not know in which county they were residing on census night.

USING THE MICROFICHE 1881 CENSUS INDEX: AN EXAMPLE

Richard Rice (baptised in 1835 in Doddiscombsleigh) was the son of William Rice and Ann Bater. Richard had five brothers and sisters: William baptised in 1832 in Dunchideock, Martha baptised in 1838 in Ide, and George, John and Robert born in Ide in 1841, 1845 and 1851 respectively. I discovered that Martha married a man named William Soper, but I could not find Richard's brothers William and John in the 1861 or later censuses until I used the 1881 census index. The birthplace index included John Rice, noted as born in Ide, aged 36 and married, as the head of a household in Heavitree. The as enumerated section for Heavitree (and original returns) revealed that, by 1881, John had five children: William aged 13, Martha aged 12, Frederick aged 5 and Edith aged 3 (all born in Ide) and a son John, aged 1 month (born in Heavitree). I then searched the 1891 census of Heavitree. John and his family were living in the same street and I obtained the name of a further child, who had been born after the 1881 census. The birthplace index (in illustration 23) also included an entry for William Rice, who was married, aged 49, head of a household in Crediton and who had given his birthplace as Ide. I had little doubt (but needed further evidence) that this was Richard's brother William, baptised in 1832 in Dunchideock. The as enumerated section of the 1881 index for Crediton and the original returns, included the following entry. The different birthplaces of the children (all in Devon) reveal that the family had moved at least five times in 16 years. It is not surprising that I had lost track of William.

Address	Name			Age		Occupation	Where born
Tolleys	William Rice	Head	Mar	49	M	Ag.Lab	Ide
	Mary Ann Rice	Wife	Mar	41	F		Exeter
	John Rice	Son	Un	16	M	Ag.Lab	Dunsford
	Mary Ann Rice	Dau	Un	15	F	Servant	North Bovey
	Alice Rice	Dau		12	F	Scholar	Heavitree
	Harry Rice	Son		10	M	Scholar	Exeter
	Rebecca Rice	Dau		8	F	Scholar	Woolfardisworthy
	Lucy Rice	Dau		6	F	Scholar	Woolfardisworthy
	Albert Rice	Son		3 mo	M		Exeter

I noted above that my Richard and William's sister, Martha, had married William Soper. I obtained the 1862 marriage certificate of William Rice to Mary Ann. This revealed that the father of William Rice (as with my Richard Rice) was named William Rice. It also revealed that William's bride, Mary Ann, had the surname Soper. Importantly, the witnesses to the marriage were William and Martha Soper. All this supported the identification of this William Rice of Crediton as my ancestor Richard's brother.

THE 1881 CENSUS INDEX ON CD-ROM

The transcript and index of the 1881 census has also been produced on 24 CD-ROM. A further disk contains a user's guide and "Resource File Viewer" (the software enabling your computer to read the data) which is easy to install by putting the disk into the CD-ROM drive and following instructions that appear on the computer screen. Eight disks contain a national index to the people in the census (thus the first disk covers surnames commencing with A and B). The other 16 disks contain the census transcript, arranged in eight regions: "Greater London", "East Anglia", "Midlands", "Southwestern" "North Central", "Northern Borders & miscellany", "Wales & Monmouth" and "Scotland". The titles chosen for these regions are rather odd, for example Hampshire and Sussex are on the Greater London region disks, but you quickly become used to this. You can start a search with the national index disks or turn to the disks for the region in which you are interested.

The national index (as with the fiche version) includes all people recorded in the census, but with only some of the census information. It is used to discover the region in which an ancestor lived. You type the person's details into the search screen boxes; a surname, a forename and (if you wish) a year of birth (or range of years) and the country or county of birth. Unfortunately, wild cards (to cover slight variations in spelling) cannot be used in name searches in this national index. The search engine searches for the spelling that you insert, but also retrieves those spellings on its own lists of synonyms (for example Weatherby and Wetherby or John and Jn.). Many people's names were spelt incorrectly in the original returns and so you should search for variations of a name.

The search produces a list of all entries for people of the requested name with their relationship to the head of their household, approximate year of birth (calculated from the person's age noted in the census), place of birth and the place in which they resided on census night. My search of the national index for the surnames Bulleid and Bullied produced 50 entries, including:

BULLEID, John   Head   [birth year] 1850   [birth] Devo.   [place] Devo.

If you place the cursor on a person's name and choose the command "Locate individual" (or just double click on a person's name) a box appears specifying the regional disk which includes that person. When you insert that disk, the entry for the person (and his or her household) appears automatically. This is an abbreviated entry, for example omitting people's occupations, but all the information appears if you click on the "More details" command on the tool bar. You then have the address, census place, PRO (which is now TNA) film reference and LDS Family History Library film reference and the full entry for the person's household. In this case, the regional disk produced this entry for John Bulleid and his household:

Dwelling: Sturstone Farm   **Census Place: Inwardleigh, Devon**
Source: FHL Film 1341535   **PRO reference: RG 11 piece 2223 folio 106 page 3**

	Marr	Age	Sex	Rel	Occup	Birthplace
John BULLEID	U	31	M	Head	Farmer 100 Acres	Winkley, Dev.
Elizabeth BULLEID	W	74	F	Mother	Annuitant	Winkley, Dev.
Charles REECE		11	M	Farm Servant		Hatherleigh, Dev.

Any entries of interest can be printed out or saved as Rich Text Files, which can be converted (with suitable software) into data that can be input into family history computer programs. You can also view neighbouring households by clicking on the "Neighbours" tab and scrolling up or down the screen.

You can also start a search for a person on the regional disks. Name searches on regional disks can utilise the symbol "?" as a wild card (to represent any single letter). This is useful for silent letters or for letters that might be misheard or incorrectly transcribed. It should assist you retrieve all relevant entries for a name. A search request produces a list of entries in the same way as the national index, but a second, lower, window also appears on screen. As you scroll down the list of entries, the lower window shows you abbreviated details (without occupations) of the household of each person on the list. Again, clicking on the "More details" command will bring up the full details of the whole household. This information can be printed out or saved to disk. More information about using the 1881 census index on CD-ROM, in particular making searches with wild cards and extracting or editing data, is provided by B. Tyrwhitt-Drake and J. Hanson in *Family Tree Magazine* (July and October 1999).

The data from the 1881 census index for Bedfordshire, Berkshire and Buckinghamshire has been issued, with different search engines from those on the LDS disks, on three CD-ROM entitled *Mapping and Analysis of Census Households* (MACH). The disks can be purchased from Drake Software Associates, 1 Wychwood Rise, Great Missenden, Buckinghamshire HP16 0HB or from TWR Computing.

THE 1881 CENSUS INDEX ON *FAMILYSEARCH*

The 1881 census index for England, Wales, the Channel Islands, the Isle of Man and the Royal Navy has also been placed on the LDS *FamilySearch* web site (# appendix XI). This site is particularly useful to genealogists for its extensive index (known as the International Genealogical Index, or IGI) of baptism, marriage and other records. This index, the web site and search procedures are therefore described in detail in chapters 7 and 11 below. However, you can also use the site to search the online version of the 1881 census index. In brief, the site's home page allows you to search all the databases available, a selection of them or just the 1881 census. The search screen is similar to that for searches on the regional disks of the CD-ROM version. Searches are made in the same way except that wildcard symbols cannot be used and the format of search results is rather different. If you were searching for a John Smith in Essex, a typical result would be:

John Smith – 1881 British census/Essex
Head   Gender: Male   Birth <1840>   Hornchurch, Essex, England

The year 1840 is John's year of birth (calculated from the age noted for him in the census). Hornchurch is his recorded place of birth. If a search result appears to be the person for whom you are searching, you can click on that person's name. His or her "individual record" appears on screen, including all the information for that person from the 1881 census transcript and a button marked "household". If you click on that button, a transcript of the census entry for the complete household appears on the screen. The data from searches can be printed out or copied to other computer files.

THE 1851 CENSUS INDEX: DEVON, NORFOLK AND WARWICKSHIRE

The LDS have also produced a complete transcript and index of the 1851 census for Devon, Norfolk and Warwickshire on microfiche and CD-ROM. The fiche for each county are in similar form to the 1881 microfiche indexes and used in the same way. They can be seen at the SoG, LDS family history centres and many other archives and libraries. They can also be purchased from the FFHS Finance Officer (at the address noted above for the 1881 index).

The CD-ROM can be purchased from the LDS distribution centre (also noted above). It combines the indexes for the three counties into one database and is accompanied by a detailed manual that explains how to use the disk and conduct searches. You may search for an individual by surname and incorporate "wild cards" into that name (? for one letter and * for more than one letter). Thus a search for the name CH?RNOCK produces entries for anyone named Charnock and Chernock. You can also filter (that is limit the ambit of) those searches by adding a person's forename, approximate year of birth, birthplace or census place. A search produces a list of persons of that name, their relationship to the head of household, place and approximate year of birth, and the census place, as follows:

Name	Relationship	Born	Birthplace	Census place
Bulleid, Thomas	Head	1782	Winkleigh-DEV	Winkleigh

Having found a person for whom you are searching, you click on the name and that person's household appears on the screen, with people's occupations and the PRO (now TNA) and Family History Library microfilm references. Neighbouring households can also be called up on screen. Household entries can be printed out or saved to disk as a text file. The CD-ROM also contains an alphabetical list of all surnames featured in the index. This helps you look for unexpected variations or incorrect spellings of a surname. If you find such a name in this list, that you think may be a person for whom you are searching, you click on it and all the entries for people with that name are brought up on screen. If one of those entries is of interest, you can click on it to bring up the entry for the person's household.

THE 1901 CENSUS

There are about 1.5 million pages, with 32 million names, in the 1901 census returns of England and Wales. A transcript of the census (with name and place indexes) can be searched on the web site of the 1901 census online service. Researchers can also see scanned images of the census returns. The web site can be accessed from computers anywhere (or from dedicated terminals at the FRC or TNA at Kew). Access to the indexes is free but the transcript and original census pages can only be accessed on a "pay-per-view" basis (50p and 75p respectively). Payment is made by credit card or by vouchers that can be purchased at the FRC and TNA bookshops, libraries or your FHS. Microfiche copies of the original census returns can also be seen at Kew and the FRC, with reference books, street indexes and other finding aids that enable researchers to find addresses or places in the returns. Many CROs and libraries (listed in *Family Tree Magazine* in August 2002) also hold microfiche copies of the returns for the area that they serve.

The standard of transcription (and consequently indexing) can be criticised but the 1901 online service is a marvellous tool for family historians. On the first occasion that I used it from

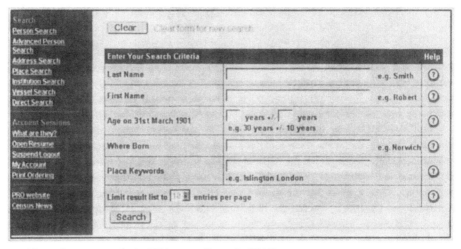

24. *The search request screen for the 1901 census online service (TNA)*

the FRC terminals, I found the entries (and printed out copies of the returns) for 21 families or individuals that were of interest to me within less than three hours. Some people were not easy to find but even they were located by varying my search requests. Three of the people I found were in wholly unexpected places. If it were not for this transcript and index to the complete census, I would probably never have found them.

The search request screen (illustration 24) lists the index search options: a person search, an advanced person search, an address search, a place search, an institution search, a vessel search or (if you already know the piece, folio and page number that you wish to see) a direct search. Searching the indexes is free. Charges only apply if you request part of the transcript or an image from the original returns to be brought up on screen.

A person search is very easy. You can search by surname or by forename and complete the search request screen boxes accordingly. You can insert a surname such as Herber (without completing any other boxes) then click on the search button. A list of all people in the transcript surnamed Herber appears on screen with entries in this form:

Name	Age	Where born	Admin. County	Civil parish	Occupation
William Herber	40	Essex, Wanstead	London	Hammersmith	. . . Driver

In this case, a transcriber had been unable to read the first word of William's occupation (it was in fact Stage) and so some dots had been inserted in its place. You can click on a person's name to see a transcript of the full entry for that person (a charge of 50 pence is made for this). If you click on a symbol at the left of the person's name, this brings to the screen the page from the original returns on which the person appears (a charge of 75 pence is made for this). You can then request a print of that page. The FRC has laser printers in which you insert your copying charge card. A screen by the printer lists the items (with researchers' seat numbers) that are ready to print. You touch the screen where your request is noted, then touch the print button on the screen and a copy of the census page is printed out. Illustration 20 is the image that I printed after finding William Herber. You can also pay for an even higher quality image to be sent to you. If you are searching from your own computer, you can print out the image or copy it into another file. In each online session, the first time you request something that incurs a fee, a box appears asking how you wish to pay. You can insert credit or debit card details (there is a minimum charge of £5 per session for using such cards) or you can insert the two numbers that appear on the vouchers you purchase. When you have used the credit available on a voucher, the screen asks you to insert details of another voucher. You then continue your research.

When an image of a census page is on your screen, you can increase its size so as to read it more easily. You may also wish to look at other pages in the same piece. For example, your ancestor's household may be partly on one page and partly on another or you may be studying a long schedule for a ship or institution. You may also want to see entries for your ancestor's neighbours. You navigate between pages by using the "next" or "previous" buttons that appear below the census image. Each further page you look at results in a further charge.

Herber is a rare name and so searches are easy. However, it is the type of name that might be spelled in many ways (or transcribed incorrectly) so you may need to search using various spellings, for example Symes and Syms, Keates and Keats, Shepherd and Sheppard. If you are searching for common names, you must refine or vary your search requests, in order to locate an ancestor. The key to success with the 1901 online service is to start with a broad search and then refine it.

The search request screen allows you to refine a surname search by a person's forename, gender, age (plus or minus a number of years), birthplace and also "place keyword". The last item allows you to limit searches to people living, on census night, in a particular county, city, town or parish. You can use wildcards for some of these items. The underscore symbol (_) is used to represent one letter and the asterisk symbol (*) for more than one letter. A search for the surname HERBE* will thus produce results for people with the surnames Herber, Herbert and Herberger. You can vary forenames but any search should retrieve common abbreviations; thus a search for William should produce entries where the person is named in the census as "Wm". Searching for people with common surnames can be difficult but distinctive forenames help. Law is a common surname but my great grandfather's forename was Horace and so I found him very easily. The person search also permits a search by someone's forename alone rather than the surname. This is useful if your ancestor had a rare forename such as Tryphena. For these searches, you must also complete the boxes for the person's age (plus or minus a number of years) and birthplace.

Refining a search request by specifying a person's place of birth or using keywords for the census place in which an ancestor may be found must be undertaken carefully. You may need to search using various place names, abbreviations or wildcards. For example, John Smith's birthplace may have been noted in the census as a specific village, town or city in Yorkshire. However, the enumerator may have noted Yorks, or Yks instead of Yorkshire. In that case, if you use the keyword "Yorkshire" when searching for John, he will be omitted from the results. If your John Smith was born in a city, such as York or Sheffield, the enumerator may have noted only this as the birthplace, omitting reference to Yorkshire. Your John Smith would again be omitted from the results of a search for John Smith born in Yorkshire. If a search produces too many entries, return to the search request screen and limit the ambit of the search by adding more information. Alternatively, you can try an "Advanced Person Search", the request screen for which permits searches by someone's occupation, middle name, exact address, marital status or relationship (for example a son) to the person in whose household they lived. Caution is necessary because occupations could be described in many ways and transcription errors may cause problems (as in the case noted above of boot maker being transcribed as boal maker).

You can also make other types of searches. If you know an address for your ancestor at about the time of the census, such as 23 Wellington Street, Exeter, you can use the address search. However, if this does not locate your ancestor, remember that some house numbers were omitted from the census returns and that the numbering of streets often changed. 23 Wellington Street may have become 45 Wellington Street. Institution searches are easy but a variety of search requests may be necessary because the names of some institutions, particularly schools and colleges, varied over the years. Over 70,000 people were recorded on naval or merchant vessels, coastal boats and barges in 1901. They can usually be found by the person search but if you know the name of the boat or ship you can try a vessel search. You may need to try alternative names (such as Marie and Maria) or use wild cards in a ship's name to cover transcription errors or mistakes by the enumerator. If you know the reference, for example RG 13, piece 352, folio 128, page 8, for the census page you wish to view (perhaps as a result of previous use of the index) you can request the image through the direct search option.

As with the 1881 census index, a great advantage of the 1901 index is that you can find people who would be very difficult, if not impossible, to find with conventional methods of searching. Many people lived in crowded areas of cities, such as the East End of London, moving regularly between lodging houses (or even "doss" or "sponging" houses). The census enumerators missed some of these people but most were recorded and the 1901 census index makes it relatively easy to find them. Thousands of people were in institutions such as workhouses and therefore very difficult to find. Other people moved around, particularly to find work. Many of these moves, particularly short term moves, are not recorded in civil registration records, directories or other records. Again, the 1901 census index makes it very easy to find many of these people.

My great grandfather Charles Frederick Eagles was a piano maker who married Bessie Garner in 1900. He was born, married and died in Hackney (and had six children who were born in Hackney). However, Charles and Bessie were not in Hackney on census night 1901. Fortunately, it took me only a few minutes with the 1901 census index to find them in Plumstead, Kent. Charles Keates was a brother of my great grandmother Alice. I knew that Charles was a policeman who had been born in Leytonstone in Essex and lived most of his life in Leyton or Leytonstone. Again, I found him in minutes, serving as a policeman but stationed at the Royal Naval College in Greenwich. I also found my g.g.g.grandfather Charles Timms in Hackney Union workhouse (# illustration 89). I would never have found these three people in the 1901 census by conventional searches. I would have had to search many indexes as they were produced over a period of years. The time and costs would have been substantial. I was happy to pay just a few pounds to locate these ancestors and relatives so quickly.

Paying to see the census images or transcript can become expensive. Your ancestor may have lived in a village of a few hundred people (perhaps 25 pages of names). It is worth searching all the census pages for such a place for other relatives, for example married daughters or sisters of your ancestor. The 1901 online service charges you for each page. If you cannot find a person in a particular area (and fear that the problem is due to transcription error) so that it is necessary to search each page for that area, doing so with the 1901 online service will be very expensive. In these cases, you should use microform copies of the census, not the online service.

OTHER ONLINE CENSUS RECORDS

TNA was planning to make digital images of the 1891 (and possibly earlier) census returns available online but has now chosen to license other organisations to do this. Ancestry.com is publishing images from the 1891 census, with transcriptions and indexes, on its subscription web site (# appendix XI). The present coverage is unclear from the site's introductory pages (at least until you pay your subscription) but announcements have been made that the images for London, Oxfordshire and Dorset, with surname indexes, are now available.

MISSING FROM HOME

Don't assume that the records show complete families. A teenage son or daughter may have lived away from the family home, perhaps working nearby as a domestic servant or as a farm servant (and living-in) at a large house or on a farm. One in eight girls and women were in domestic service in 1871. Schools and inns also had domestic staff. My great grandmother Alice Amelia Keates, then aged 17, was not at home with her family in Leyton in the 1881 census but I found her working as a domestic servant in the household of a Mr Ashcroft, fairly close to her parents' house.

Men may have been away from home because they were serving with the army or navy elsewhere in Britain or abroad. A family member may have been in an institution such as a prison, hospital, boarding-school, or workhouse. Over 569,000 people were in such institutions on census night in 1841, out of a population in England and Wales of 15.9 million. There were 295,856 people in workhouses in 1841 (and 126,488 in 1851). A surprisingly large number of people were in prison on census night, so these records should not be ignored. An interesting article, "Prisons and Census Returns" by C.J. Parry, appears in *Genealogists' Magazine* (December 1990). Almost 24,000 people were in prison on census night in 1861 and over 166,000 people spent some time in prison in 1849 alone. In the 1861 census, prisoners were only identified by initials. A typical entry from Pentonville Prison is:

G.E.	prisoner	Unmarried	53	Miner	Somerset, Bath

In the 1851 census many returns for prisons also contain only initials instead of the full name of the prisoner. However, full names are included in some returns such as those for the Middlesex House of Correction at Tothill Fields. The 702 prisoners included:

Catherine Barrett	prisoner	Un	28	Dressmaker	Middlesex, Marylebone

The convict hulk *Warrior* at Woolwich held 426 prisoners. Surnames were listed with the initial of the Christian name:

J. Bowyer	Convict	Mar.	55	Solicitor	Sussex, Petworth

Mr Parry also considers hospitals in an article in *Family Tree Magazine* (April 1987). He shows that the London Hospital in Whitechapel Road in 1851 had 389 residents on census night; that is 88 officers, staff or servants and 301 patients. Many of these people had been born far away; in Lancashire, Wales and Ireland.

Many people also lived in army barracks: officers and soldiers, their wives and children, as well as officers' servants, cooks, cleaners and other staff. If your ancestor was a seaman, it may be very difficult to find him in census records, other than in 1861 (see below), 1881 or 1901, unless he was on shore-leave at the time. The 1841 census only records the numbers of men on board each Royal Navy or merchant ship. Names were collected from British ships from 1851. If ships were at sea at the time of the 1851 and later censuses, they generally should have been included in the census but the organisation of this was very complex, especially for ships which were away from home for a long time. Higgs (142) and (143) describes the system and the types of ship that were included. Shipping on rivers, in ports or in territorial waters on census night was generally included at the end of the return for the registration district in which the port, river or coast lay. From 1861 British shipping on the high seas and in foreign ports was enumerated in separate schedules at the end of that year's returns (that is, in pieces at the end of series RG 9, RG 10 etc). The FRC search room has an index to the names of the ships in each census, noting each ship's location (for example Bristol or at sea) and the piece number for the return. Your first step (if searching the 1851, 1871 or 1891 censuses), is therefore to find the ship on which your ancestor was serving (# chapter 21). You can then find the ship (and your ancestor).

The 1881 and 1901 census indexes make it easy to find an ancestor on board a ship in those censuses. For the 1861 census the Mormons have produced a microfiche index (a copy is at the FRC) to the names of all people who were on merchant or naval ships (whether at sea or in port). The index lists about 120,000 people alphabetically by surname and then Christian name. The index also records each person's age, sex, marital status, occupation and place of birth, the name of the ship on which the person was travelling or working, as well as the piece and folio numbers where the ship can be found in the returns.

Some people are truly missing from census returns, since the enumerators did not locate all residents in their areas. Some front doors and some travelling families were missed. Even in 1991 the census enumerators probably missed about 2 per cent of the population of Great Britain – about one million people. The problem was no doubt greater in the 19th century.

OTHER PROBLEMS

Finding a family in successive censuses shows how the reported ages and birthplaces of people varied. Rogers (26) refers to a study showing that the places of birth given in the 1851 and 1861 censuses, for the same people, were different in 15 per cent of cases. You should therefore find and compare all census entries for a particular person. The place of birth of my ancestor Sarah Boxall, in three successive censuses, was recorded as Doctors Commons (near St Paul's Cathedral in London), Stanmore and Middlesex. Many people did not know where they were born and therefore guessed. In the 1881 census my great grandfather Charles Symes gave his birthplace as Topsham, Devon. This was not a bad guess as Charles had spent most of his life in Topsham, but he was actually born in Devonport.

Another important factor was the Poor Law (# chapter 18). If a man had no work and required poor relief, the responsibility for giving that relief, whether outdoor relief (clothes and money) or indoor relief (the workhouse) lay with the person's parish of legal settlement (and later the Poor Law Union including that parish). A person could not always obtain a settlement in a parish merely by living or working there. Migrants (particularly those who had only recently arrived in an area) might therefore tell a census enumerator that their birthplace was the place where they were then living and working, fearing lest they should be removed from their new home for admitting that they had been born elsewhere.

Another problem that arises when searching the census is that addresses that you discover for your ancestors may not have existed (at least in the same name) by the time of the next census. This is a particular problem in London and other towns or cities that expanded rapidly in Victorian times. For example, a row of cottages on a main road might originally be named Smith Terrace, but later numbered as part of that road, becoming, say, 102 to 108 Cambridge Road. Reference books at the FRC and TNA list some of the different names that have been given to roads and streets. For example, there is the 1912 edition of a list of streets and places then in the administrative county of London, recording the alterations in street names since 1856 (including street names that were abolished) and noting the parishes, metropolitan boroughs and electoral divisions in which the streets were located.

POPULATION: 1200–1901

The population figures contained in the census records are useful for your family history. For each enumeration district the returns include the number of people and the number of inhabited and uninhabited houses. Tables in the census Reference Books also contain population figures for each registration district, sub-district, parish or township (the statistics were also published in parliamentary papers). You can therefore ascertain how the population increased or decreased in the village, town or city in which your ancestors lived. The table below sets out, to the nearest thousand, the population recorded in each census of England and Wales (in column A) and of Scotland (column B) from 1801 to 1901. Some people were omitted from the census, so column C sets out the estimate by Mathias (145) of the population (in millions) of England, Wales and Scotland. Column D notes the population of Ireland from the Irish censuses of 1821 to 1901.

Year	A (thous.)	B (thous.)	C (millions)	D (thous.)
1901	32,528	4,472	37.09	4,459
1891	29,003	4,026	33.12	4,705
1881	25,974	3,736	29.79	5,175
1871	22,712	3,360	26.16	5,412
1861	20,066	3,062	23.19	5,799
1851	17,928	2,889	20.88	6,552
1841	15,914	2,620	18.55	8,175
1831	13,897	2,364	16.37	7,767
1821	12,000	2,092	14.21	6,802
1811	10,164	1,806	12.15	–
1801	8,893	1,608	10.69	–

This table shows the enormous increase in the British population during the 19th century and, conversely, the dramatic fall in the Irish population because of famines (and consequent emigration). The startling population growth in England, particularly in the 19th century, can be illustrated by figures for Surrey (including those parts of the county now in London).

Year	Population
1801	268,000
1821	399,000
1851	683,000
1871	1,091,000
1891	1,731,000
1931	2,400,000

Further research of your family tree may take you back to the 18th century or earlier. The approximate population of England (excluding Monmouth) from 1200 to 1751, as estimated by Finlay (157), is set out below. You will see how epidemics (such as the Black Death) and harvest failures caused the population to fall during the 14th century.

Year	Population (millions)
1751	6.1
1701	5.4
1651	5.5
1601	4.0
1551	3.1
1500	2 to 2.5
1300	4.0
1200	1.5 to 2.5

CENSUS PROBLEMS AND FURTHER RESEARCH

The entries for families in successive census records often resemble a jigsaw puzzle and they must be carefully analysed, and compared with other records. The 1851 census entry for the family of my ancestor Sophia Chapman, in Hainford, Norfolk, is set out below. It is straightforward, provides substantial information about a family and also suggests further enquiries that could be made. I had already found Sophia in the 1861 census in London (giving her birthplace as Hainford) and I had obtained her 1838 birth certificate (recording her parents as Henry Chapman and Susan Chapman, formerly Climpson).

Name	Relationship	Condition	Age	Occupation	Where born
Henry Chapman	Head	Mar.	45	Ag. Lab	Hainford, Norfolk
Susan Chapman	Wife	Mar.	39		do.
George Chapman	Son	Unm.	18	Silk weaver	do.
Jeremiah Chapman	Son	Unm.	16	Blacksmith	do.
Sophia Chapman	Dau		12		do.
Charlotte Chapman	Dau		10		do.
Mary Chapman	Dau		8		do.
Emily Chapman	Dau		6		do.
Harriet Chapman	Dau		4		do.
Louisa Chapman	Dau		2		do.
Mary Climpson	Moth.-in-law	Wid.	79	Pauper	Horstead, Norfolk

It was clearly important to search the census records of Hainford for other years in order to obtain more information about the family, but this entry suggested some further enquiries:

a. The entry revealed seven of Sophia's siblings, all born in Hainford. I therefore searched the Hainford parish register to obtain records of their baptisms.

b. Both Henry Chapman and Susan Climpson were recorded as born in Hainford. I searched the Hainford parish register and found their marriage and baptisms.

c. Mary Climpson (Susan's mother) was aged 79 in 1851. I could not find her in the 1861 census, so she had probably died by that year. I searched the GRO death indexes from 1851 and obtained her death certificate, which also named her deceased husband as Isaachar Climpson. Mary Climpson was also noted in the 1851 census as a pauper, so it was worth searching for her in poor law records (# chapter 18).

d. Mary Climpson was noted as born in Horstead. I searched the Horstead parish register and found the baptisms of Mary and two siblings and their parents' marriage.

CENSUS RECORDS – A JIGSAW PUZZLE

Census records are not always straightforward. The entries for the family of my great grandfather Horace Law, from the 1841, 1851, 1871 and 1881 censuses of Walthamstow (I could not find a relevant entry in the 1861 returns), are set out below. I already had Horace's 1874 birth certificate and the 1859 certificate of the marriage (in Walthamstow) of his parents, Thomas Law and Amelia Bateman. The marriage certificate showed that Thomas was born in about 1830 and that his father was James Law. Walthamstow parish registers also recorded that a James Law had married an Eliza Cass in 1827.

1881 Census	St James Street, Lilly Yard				
Amelia Law	Head	Widow	49		Upminster
Arthur Law	Son	Unm	15	Bookbinder	Walthamstow
Albert Law	Son		10		Walthamstow
Horace Law	Son		7		Walthamstow

1871 Census	St James Park, Marsh Street				
Thomas Law	Head	Mar	40	Labourer	Walthamstow
Amelia Law	Wife		39		Upminster
William J. Law	Son		10	Scholar	Walthamstow
Arthur Law	Son		6	Scholar	Walthamstow
Thomas H. Law	Son		4	Scholar	Walthamstow
Albert Law	Son		7 ms	Scholar	Walthamstow
William Hammond	Lodger	Mar	55	Labourer	Walthamstow
Mary A. Hammond	Wife		46		Upminster

1851 Census	Ormes Row				
William Hammond	Head	Mar	37	Labourer	Shoreditch
Eliza Hammond	Wife		45	Laundress	Walthamstow
Sarah Law	Dau	Unm	23	Laundress	Walthamstow

William Hammond	Son		15	Scholar	Walthamstow
Mary Law	Granddau		2		Walthamstow
Thomas Law	Grandson		1		Walthamstow

[Thomas Law aged 23, an unmarried labourer born in Walthamstow, was lodging nearby.]

1841 Census	**Ormes Row**			**Born in County**
William Hammond		20	Labourer	N
Eliza Hammond		30		Y
William Hammond		5		Y
Sarah Law		13		Y
Thomas Law		12		Y

I speculated that the following events had occurred. James Law and Eliza Cass married in 1827 and had two children, Sarah and Thomas (my ancestor) who appear, aged 13 and 12, in the 1841 entry. James Law died and his widow Eliza married William Hammond. William and Eliza had a son, William, in about 1836. Sarah Law had two illegitimate children (Mary and Thomas) and they were noted in 1851 as William Hammond's grandchildren, although they were really his step-grandchildren. My ancestor Thomas Law married Amelia Bateman in 1859. Eliza Hammond (née Cass) died between 1851 and 1871. The William Hammond in the 1871 census, lodging with Thomas, was possibly the widower (now remarried) of Eliza (although the birthplaces and ages did not match). I had to corroborate the information (and my guesses) from other sources, but I prepared a speculative family tree:

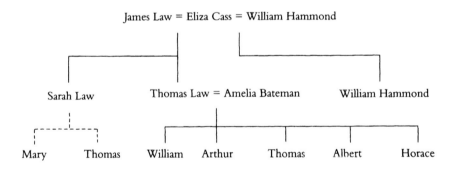

Many further enquiries were required to check whether or not this was correct. Among other items I had to find the Law and Hammond families in the 1861 census; I had to search the parish register of Walthamstow for the baptisms of Thomas and Sarah Law, the burial of James Law, the remarriage of Eliza Law (née Cass) to William Hammond, and the baptism of William Hammond; and I had to find civil registration records (or parish register entries) for the death of Eliza Hammond (previously Law, née Cass), the marriage of William Hammond to Mary, and the births or baptisms of Mary and Thomas Law.

In the Walthamstow parish records, I found the baptisms of Thomas and Sarah Law and the burial of James Law as well as records of some other children (who died young, so were not recorded in a census) of James and Eliza Law, and of William and Eliza Hammond. I also obtained the birth certificate of Mary Law (the illegitimate daughter of Sarah Law). I could not find the marriage of Eliza and William Hammond, but I did locate them in Marsh Street, Walthamstow in the 1861 census:

William Hammond	Head	Mar.	45	Ag.Lab	Shoreditch, Middlesex
Eliza Hammond	Wife	Mar.	53		Walthamstow
Elizabeth Gurney	Granddaughter		5		Walthamstow

Eliza Hammond had therefore survived until at least 1861. The age given for William Hammond in this census also matched the age of the William who appeared in the 1871 census but, because of the different birthplaces, it remained unclear whether these entries were the same person. This entry also raised further questions. Who was the Elizabeth Gurney who was born in about 1856? Was she a granddaughter of William, or Eliza, or of both of them? It was possible that Eliza's daughter (Sarah Law) had married a man named Gurney and that Elizabeth Gurney was their daughter, but there were other possibilities. I had to turn back to the GRO birth records of 1855 to 1856 to find Elizabeth's parents. As you can see, the search never ends.

THE CENSUSES OF 1801 TO 1831

Censuses were also taken on 10 March 1801, 27 May 1811, 28 May 1821 and 30 May 1831. The enumerators recorded the number of people in each parish, the number of houses, some information on people's occupations and some other statistics. Fortunately, some enumerators also made lists of names. Over 750 parish listings of names survive for these censuses (mostly in CROs) and the parishes are listed in Chapman (137) and Gibson & Medlycott (139). Most of the records only list the heads of households, but about 80 list all inhabitants. Some of these census listings have been transcribed and published. For example, East of London FHS has published booklets containing the censuses of Hackney in 1811 and 1821 and Poplar in 1821 and 1831. The surviving census listings from 1801 to 1831 for Essex parishes (and a few earlier parish listings) have been published on microfiche by Essex FHS.

One surviving list is the 1831 census of Upminster in Essex. Illustration 25 is an extract showing the names of some heads of households together with some other details, including the number of males and females in each household and whether they were employed in trade, agriculture or manufacture. A further page (not illustrated) gave more information, such as how many males in the household were aged 20 or more. If your ancestor was a householder in such a return, the other unnamed occupants may be identifiable from parish records (# chapters 7 and 18) but this is not always the case. The individuals may not have been family members. They may have been relatives from outside the parish, friends of the family, lodgers, or perhaps family members who were not recorded in the parish register. In illustration 25, my ancestor Benjamin Bateman, an agricultural labourer, is listed as the head of a household of three males and three females. The parish register showed that, by May 1831, he and his wife Ann had two sons and a daughter. The identity of the third female was a mystery. The parents of Benjamin and Ann (and Benjamin's known siblings) were dead. The female could have been a child of Benjamin and Ann (who had not been baptised) or one of Ann's sisters but possibly a lodger or friend.

25. *Extract from 1831 census of Upminster, Essex (Essex Record Office, D/P 117/18/6)*

EARLIER CENSUSES

Many earlier returns or lists of population also survive, for example in tax records (# chapter 23). Other lists of population were made and surviving lists are noted in Chapman (137) and in Gibson & Medlycott (139). For example, the Corporation of London Record Office holds indexed lists of the names of the population, in 1695, of 80 out of the 97 parishes within the walls of the City of London (containing about 60,000 names) and 13 parishes outside the walls (a further 54,000 names). An earlier survey, of 1638, is held at Lambeth Palace Library and lists the householders in 93 City parishes. The SoG has published an indexed transcript of this list (available in book form and on microfiche). TNA also holds a list, from 1640, of the "principal inhabitants" of the City of London and an indexed version has been published.

As we will see in chapter 18, many lists of inhabitants survive in parish records (listing poor law ratepayers, or recipients of poor relief). Some of my ancestors lived in the village of Sandford in Devon, between about 1600 and 1880. Devon Record Office holds, with the Sandford parish records, a volume of lists (prepared by the vicar of Sandford) of the names of the entire population of Sandford in 1790, 1793 and 1800 and also lists of householders' names (with the numbers of people in each household) in 1775 and 1783. These documents were of great assistance to me when researching my Sandford ancestors in the parish registers.

CHAPTER 7

PARISH REGISTERS

Church of England parish registers record baptisms, marriages and burials, sometimes as early as 1538. They are the prime source of information for genealogists in the period up to 1837, but they are also an important source for the period since 1837. From 1598 copies of entries from many parish registers were also prepared by parish priests and sent to bishops or archdeacons. These copies are known as bishops' transcripts. Catholic priests also kept registers of baptisms, marriages and burials. From the 17th century Protestant groups such as Baptists also developed independently of the Church of England; these non-conformists also kept their own registers. Catholic and Protestant non-conformist records are reviewed in chapter 13, but most of this chapter also applies to their registers.

THE PARISH

Since medieval times an ecclesiastical parish has been that area committed to the charge of a clergyman, at the parish church, who was responsible for the "cure" of the souls of the people living within the parish. Until the early 19th century there were approximately 12,000 Church of England (or Anglican) parishes in England and Wales. These parishes are often called ancient parishes to distinguish them from the many new parishes that have been created since about 1830. The parish clergyman (often called a priest, parson or the incumbent) could be a vicar or rector (a distinction important for purposes of tithes, see chapter 15). Many clergymen were responsible for more than one parish (and received payments, or stipends, for each of them) but perhaps visited some of them only sporadically. In those cases the clergyman was required to appoint and pay a curate or chaplain to perform his duties during his absence.

Tate (532) is an excellent account of parish administration and records, and of life and work in the parish. The parish landowners paid tithes (an ecclesiastical tax) to the parish incumbent for his support and for the upkeep of the parish church. Administration of the parish was undertaken by a council (known as a vestry) and by parish officials (# chapter 18) such as the churchwardens and overseers. In the 16th and 17th centuries many administrative functions (such as highway repairs) passed from the manorial courts (# chapter 27) to the parishes. The parish also became responsible for care of the sick and the poor. During the 19th century responsibility for most secular matters was in turn passed from parishes to central government or to county or borough councils. Parishes varied greatly in both the number of their population and in the area of land they covered. Therefore, a chapel of ease (or chapelry) was often built in larger parishes to allow parishioners to attend worship at a church that was not too far from their homes. In the 19th century the growing population (and changes in population distribution) resulted in the Church of England building more churches and creating many new parishes by dividing up some existing ancient parishes. Chapels of ease often became the parish churches of these new parishes.

The ecclesiastical parish must be distinguished from a township (or vill) and from the civil parish (which was confirmed in 1889 as the lowest level of local, secular, government). Ecclesiastical parishes and townships were both medieval in origin. In rural parts of southern England, ecclesiastical parishes tended to cover the same area as one township but, in the north, parishes tended to cover a number of townships (the parish of Kendal in Westmorland contained 25 townships). Because of their size, many northern ecclesiastical parishes were unable properly to administer matters such as poor relief and so these civil functions were often delegated, from the 17th century, to the townships. Townships became known as civil parishes and their role was formalised in the 19th century. Therefore, the boundaries of ecclesiastical and civil parishes (the old townships) often coincided in rural areas of southern England but a northern ecclesiastical parish might cover many civil parishes. A hundred (or wapentake in northern England) was a group of adjoining parishes. Some records, principally records of tax (# chapter 23), that list the inhabitants of parishes, are organised by hundreds. You should therefore discover the name of the hundred that included each ancestor's parish, from gazetteers or maps (# chapters 15 and 16) since this will assist searches for these records. Winchester (177) provides more detailed information on parishes, townships and hundreds.

Even the smaller counties had many parishes and people often moved between parishes and counties. This causes problems in using parish records. The following table sets out the approximate number of ancient parishes in certain counties:

Cornwall	206	Norfolk	691
Durham	113	Oxfordshire	280
Kent	408	Somerset	482
Lancashire	62	Surrey	140
Lincolnshire	630	Wiltshire	304

The number of parish records to be searched can be enormous. If your only information is that an ancestor was born in Norfolk in about 1810, the records of 691 parishes might have to be searched, although the process has been made much easier by the production of county-wide indexes of parish register entries. Large towns and cities were also divided into a number of parishes, each with their own church and registers. In the 17th century there were 101 parishes in the City of London, 35 in Norwich and 19 in Exeter. This is a large amount of documentation to review, making it difficult and time-consuming to search for an ancestor from a city. If your ancestors lived for two centuries in a small village in the countryside, the relevant documentation is much reduced. However, if my ancestors in Hainford (a small village in Norfolk) walked only three miles in various directions they could reach about 12 other parishes. Norwich itself, with its 35 churches, was only seven miles away. This factor must be remembered if you discover that a parish register does not include all the baptisms, marriages or burials that you expect for a family. The position became more complex from the 17th century as other religious groups, such as Baptists, Independents and Quakers (and later Catholics), felt sufficiently secure from persecution to found their own chapels and start recording baptisms, marriages and burials for their congregations, who might live in a number of different Anglican parishes.

The IHGS (# chapter 11) has published extremely useful maps for each pre-1974 county of England and Wales showing the approximate boundaries of ancient parishes (and any new parishes created up to about 1832) and noting the commencement dates of surviving parish registers. There is one map for the City of London and one map for each county except Lincolnshire (two maps) and Yorkshire (four maps). Illustration 26 is the IHGS map for Bedfordshire, at a reduced scale. You should buy the maps for each county in which you are researching your ancestors. They are particularly valuable when considering which parish registers to search. The IHGS maps for all English, Welsh and Scottish counties are available together (but in a reduced size) in *The Phillimore Atlas and Index of Parish Registers* (165) which also includes topographical county maps of 1834.

Anglican parishes were grouped into dioceses and archdeaconries (# chapter 12). The bishop and archdeacon also held or received records relating to a parish and its inhabitants (including their wills until 1858) and the IHGS maps also show the diocese and archdeaconry for each parish. From the Reformation until the mid-19th century England was divided into the 22 dioceses listed below (there are now 42). There were also four dioceses in Wales (there are now six) and the diocese of Sodor and Man (the Isle of Man).

Bath & Wells	Exeter	Oxford
Bristol	Gloucester	Peterborough
Canterbury	Hereford	Rochester
Carlisle	Lichfield	Salisbury
Chester	Lincoln	Winchester
Chichester	London	Worcester
Durham	Norwich	York
Ely		

In addition to the ancient parishes, many Anglican parishes were founded later, mostly during the 19th century, especially in London and other expanding towns and cities. As the population grew or moved, some larger parishes were divided into smaller parishes and a few parishes were amalgamated with others. When researching parish registers for the period since 1832 it is therefore important to ascertain whether new parishes were formed in your ancestors' district since those new parishes are not shown on the IHGS maps. Many of these new parishes are listed in the volumes of the *National Index of Parish Registers* (151) and similar works (considered below). You should ascertain the name of the "mother" parish, out of which "daughter" parishes were formed, and then search the records of all those parishes.

PARISH REGISTERS

In 1538 King Henry VIII's Vicar-General, Thomas Cromwell, ordered that each parish priest should keep registers of the baptisms, marriages and burials taking place in his parish. Church registers have been maintained ever since (except from 1653 to 1660, when registration was usually undertaken by civil officers confusingly named "Parish Registers"). But parish registers should not only be used for the period prior to 1837, when civil registration was introduced. They are also an extremely helpful source for the period after 1837, particularly up to 1875 (that is the period when many births were omitted from the civil registration system). Even if a birth was registered, a baptism record may be easier to find than the civil record of birth. It generally provides the same information (except the mother's maiden surname) and you will save the fees payable for civil registration certificates. The information contained in church records of marriages since 1837 is the same as that provided by the civil registration system.

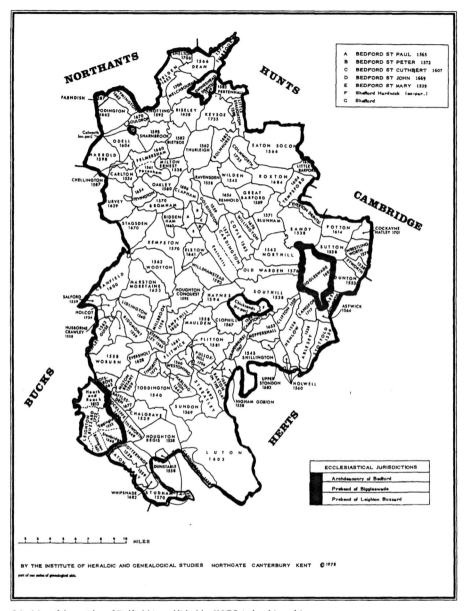

26. Map of the parishes of Bedfordshire published by IHGS (reduced in scale)

Illustration 27 shows an extract from an 18th-century parish register from Dunsford in Devon. This shows the marriages of my ancestors Richard Crump and Elizabeth Sercombe, and my ancestors John Rice and Elizabeth Hill. Illustration 31 is an example of a page from a 19th-century parish register, which shows the baptism of Sarah Law, a daughter of my ancestors James and Eliza Law, on 25 November 1827, at St Mary's Walthamstow, Essex.

Few parishes have surviving registers that are complete since 1538. Despite the 1538 order, many parishes did not start to keep registers until some years later. Many early registers have also been lost or destroyed. In 1598 it was ordered that registers should henceforth be kept on parchment because the paper in the books that had been used since 1538 was of poor quality and many entries were already illegible. The order stated that existing entries in registers were to be copied on to parchment, *especially* the entries for the period since Queen Elizabeth's accession in 1558. Unfortunately, some priests therefore decided to copy only those entries made since 1558 and many registers therefore survive only from that year. In some parishes copying was not undertaken at all, often because earlier registers were already lost, destroyed or illegible. Later registers also suffered from fire, theft, damp or loss. In particular, there are gaps in many registers during the period of the English Civil War and the subsequent Commonwealth and Protectorate.

Fortunately most parish registers since the late 16th century have survived and most registers up to the 19th century (and many later registers) have been deposited in diocesan archives, usually CROs, or equivalent archives in metropolitan areas (# chapter 11 and appendix VII). Furthermore, in 1992 the Church of England required all parish registers of baptisms and burials containing entries that are 150 years old or more to be closed and (in most cases) deposited in a record office. This does not apply to a church's copy of marriage registers since 1837, but most of these have also been deposited. Consequently, most old parish registers are now in CROs. Most of these are available to the public only on microfilm or microfiche, in order to prevent further damage to the originals. Some CROs, such as Norfolk and Essex, also sell microfiche copies of registers. This is extremely useful for researchers who have a microfiche reader and who live far from the relevant archive.

Some registers remain with incumbents at parish churches. The name and address of the vicar or rector of a parish can be found in *Crockford's Clerical Directory* (# chapter 22) at a local library. You should request an appointment for access (in writing, with an SAE) and you may be supervised while viewing the registers, since some people have been known to deface registers or tear out pages. You may be charged a fee for inspecting registers or for a copy of an entry. If no fee is charged, a donation to the church is a nice gesture.

Burn (154) and Cox (156) review the evolution of English parish registers since the 16th century, and the circumstances in which many have been lost or destroyed, and they include many examples of baptism, marriage and burial entries to illustrate the fascinating information noted by the clergy.

A family historian must find out what registers survive for the area in which his ancestors lived, where those registers are now, and what copies and indexes can be consulted. The best way to do this is to consult volumes of the *National Index of Parish Registers* (151), or *NIPR*, published by the SoG. These volumes describe the location of surviving parish registers up to at least 1837 (and for many parishes up to this century). Each volume of the *NIPR* covers one or more counties and should be used in conjunction with the IHGS county maps noted above. The *NIPR* lists the dates of surviving parish registers, bishop's transcripts, printed copies and indexes

No 29

Richard Crump —— of [the] Parish of Dunsford, in the County
of Devon —— and Elizabeth Sercomb of the [ ] were
same Parish, Spinster
Married in this [Church] by [Banns]
this twenty seventh Day of October —— in the Year One Thousand Seven Hundred
and Sixty —— by me Joshua Hole —— [Curate]
This Marriage was { Richard Crump
Solemnized between Us{ The Mark of + Elizabeth Sercomb.
In the { The Mark of X Thomas Sercomb
Presence of{ Thomas Brooking

No 30

John Rice —— of [the] Parish of Dunsford, in the County
of Devon —— and Elizabeth Hill of the [ ] were
same Parish, Spinster
Married in this [Church] by [Banns]
this tenth Day of November —— in the Year One Thousand Seven Hundred
and Sixty —— by me Joshua Hole —— [Curate]
This Marriage was { the mark of + John Rice
Solemnized between Us{ the Mark of + Elizabeth Hill.
In the { Arthur Rugge
Presence of{ Thomas Brooking

27. Parish register of Dunsford in Devon: the marriages of Richard Crump and Elizabeth Sercombe and of John Rice and Elizabeth Hill in October/November 1760 (Devon Record Office)

to the entries (and states which archives hold those documents). The *NIPR* volumes also provide information about Catholic and Protestant non-conformist churches. The *NIPR* is a valuable work of reference (although some volumes are now a little out of date). If the *NIPR* states that a register is at a CRO, it will almost definitely still be there. If a register is stated to be held by an incumbent, your first enquiry should still be to the CRO for the county in which the parish is situated in case the registers have been deposited since the *NIPR* volume was published. The law on access to registers held by incumbents is also set out in Volume 1 of the *NIPR* although the fees have been increased. Volume 1 of the *NIPR* describes parish registers and other genealogical sources before 1837. Volumes 2 and 3 deal with non-conformist, Catholic and Jewish genealogy and volumes 12 to 15 describe genealogical sources for Scotland, Wales, the Channel Islands and Isle of Man. The volumes that list parish registers, copies and indexes for English counties are:

Vol. 4   South East England; Kent, Surrey and Sussex, replaced in part by vol. 4 part 1 Surrey
Vol. 5   Gloucestershire, Herefordshire, Oxfordshire, Shropshire, Warwickshire and
          Worcestershire, replaced in part by vol. 5 part 1 Shropshire
Vol. 6   Part 1 Staffordshire; part 2 Nottinghamshire; part 3 Leicestershire and Rutland; part 4
          Lincolnshire; part 5 Derbyshire
Vol. 7   Part 1 Suffolk; part 2 Cambridgeshire; part 3 Norfolk
Vol. 8   Part 1 Berkshire; part 2 Wiltshire; part 3 Somerset; part 4 Cornwall; part 5 Devon;
          part 6 Hampshire and Isle of Wight; part 6 (*sic*) Dorset
Vol. 9   Part 1 Bedfordshire and Huntingdonshire; part 2 Northamptonshire; part 3
          Buckinghamshire; part 4 Essex; part 5 London and Middlesex; part 6 Hertfordshire
Vol. 10   Part 1 Cheshire; part 2 Lancashire; part 3 Cumberland & Westmorland
Vol. 11   Part 1 Durham and Northumberland; part 2 Yorkshire (York and the North and East
          Ridings); part 3 Yorkshire (West Riding)

Volumes 4 and 5 are now quite old and only replaced in part by new volumes for Surrey and Shropshire. You should therefore also look at other sources: Harnden (160) for Herefordshire, Harris (161) for Oxfordshire, Watkin & Saul (173) for Warwickshire (except Birmingham) and Wright (178) or a North West Kent FHS booklet (153) for Kent. Researchers should also consult CRO's catalogues (or published lists) for their holdings of registers, copies and indexes. Anyone searching for ancestors in Kent parish registers should therefore review the catalogues of the principal archives of Kent in Maidstone and Canterbury (# appendix VII).

Those genealogists with London ancestors (that is living in areas that are now considered to be in London) may need to review a number of the *NIPR* volumes. London south of the Thames is covered in the *NIPR* volumes for Surrey and Kent while those parts of London that were formerly in Essex (for example West Ham, Walthamstow and Wanstead) are covered by the Essex volume. For the City of London and Middlesex, you should turn to the London and Middlesex volume of the *NIPR* (which includes parishes created up to 1837) and obtain the IHGS maps for both the City of London and Middlesex. Parishes created since 1837 can be ascertained from archives' catalogues of their collections of registers and the booklets noted below. Most City of London and Middlesex registers are held by Guildhall Library and the London Metropolitan Archives (LMA), but some are at other archives, such as Westminster, or remain with incumbents. Bishops' transcripts for London are at Guildhall Library, LMA and Lambeth Palace Library. Guildhall Library publishes lists of its collections of City of London parish registers

(148), Greater London parish registers (149) and non-conformist, Roman Catholic, Jewish and burial ground registers (307). Harris (162) lists the registers deposited at LMA.

The library of the SoG holds many copies of registers on microfilm and fiche, as well as the best collection in Britain of transcripts and indexes. The collection continues to expand but it is estimated to include registers or transcripts (full or partial) for about two-thirds of the approximately 12,000 ancient parishes of England and Wales. The best way of ascertaining whether a copy, transcript or index of a register is at the SoG is to consult the library's computer catalogue. The SoG published a list of its collection as at December 1994 in a booklet (152). This has been superseded for English counties by a series of booklets entitled *County Sources at the Society of Genealogists*, by N. Taylor, such as the volume for Cornwall and Devon (170), the volume for London and Middlesex (171a) or that for Cheshire, Lancashire and the Isle of Man (171). The booklets are regularly updated and list parish registers, transcripts and indexes as well as transcripts or indexes of monumental inscriptions (# chapter 8), non-conformist registers (# chapter 13) and marriage licence records (# chapter 14). The booklets can also be consulted on the SoG web site.

PARISH REGISTER ENTRIES

A parish register contains the names of people, the dates when they were baptised, married or buried (or when banns were called), and the names of some of their relatives (for example the parents of children who were baptised or perhaps the husband of a woman who was buried). However, a register may also record whether spouses were widows or widowers, as well as the occupation and place of residence of those people marrying, being buried or having their children baptised. After 1754 marriage registers should include the signatures or marks of the spouses and witnesses (who were often the spouses' parents or other relatives). You may also find that your ancestor acted as a witness at other people's weddings in the parish. If he ceased to act as a witness, this may be evidence of his death or his movement away from the parish. Many parish register transcripts (considered below) do not specify the witnesses at weddings, so reference should be made to the original registers. Transcripts often also omit the entries for marriage banns, despite the importance, noted below, of these entries. Remember also that early registers may be in Latin (# chapter 4).

BAPTISMS

From 1538 to 1812, typical parish register entries for baptisms were in the following forms:

Baptised 1698 April 6th Samuel, son of Nicholas Bulhead
Baptised 1764 April 23rd Susanna, daughter of John and Joan Bullied

Registers of the 16th and 17th centuries were often written in Latin and can be difficult to read. A baptism entry in early registers may only record the date and the names of the child and father. The extract at illustration 28, from the published register of Leyland in Lancashire by White (176), includes baptisms of August 1694 to June 1695. These entries do not record the mother's name except in the two cases where the child was illegitimate. The mother's Christian name appeared increasingly as time passed, as in the 18th-century entries in illustration 30. This is a

Christenings, 1695.   91

Jennet, ye D. of Ralph Cross, of Leyland ... ... Aug. 19
Ann, ye D. of Edmund Piccop, of Heapey... ... ... Sept. 2
Andrew, ye S. of Andrew Stones, of Leyland ... ... Oct. 9
Ann, ye D. of Ralph Whittle, of Whittle ... ... „ 18
Jane, ye D. of George Moonk, of Leyland ... ... „ 28
Lucia,[1] ye D. of Sr Charles Hoghton, Bnt ... ... „ 29
Elizabeth, ye D. of Mr. William Shurd, of Clayton H. Nov. 6
Alice, ye D. of William Jackson ye youngest, of
    Cuerden ... ... Dec. 16
Richard, ye S. of Michael Southworth, of Wheelton ... „ 16
George, ye S. of James Eastham, & ... ... „ 19
John, ye S. of Andrew Cooper, both of Euxton ... ... „ 19
Elizabeth, ye D. of John Stopford, of Leyland ... ... „ 19
Henry, ye S. of Oliver Garstang, of Whittle ... ... „ 23
Jennet, ye D. of Thomas Croft, of Whittle ... ... „ 30
James, ye S. of Robert Charnock, of Charnock Richard[2] Jan. 13
John, ye S. of William Hesketh, of Leyland ... ... „ 13
B. William, ye bastard child of Mary Tinsley, of
    Euxton ... ... „ 21
John, the S. of Robt. Turner, Junr, of Leyland ... ... ffeb. 10
Margaret, ye D. of Thurstan Litherland, of Whittle ... „ 24
Ellen, ye D. of John Parker, of Leyland ... ... Mar. 3
Charles, ye S. of Thomas Nowel, of Leyland ... ... „ 6
Elizabeth, ye D. of Ralph Eves, of Kuerden ... ... „ 17
William, ye S. of John Hawworth, of Whittle ... ... „ 24
B. Jane, ye D. of Jennet Stephenson, of Whittle ... „ 24

1695 Y'nings.[3]

Richard, ye S. of James Hall, of Euxton ... ... Mar. 31
Edward, ye S. of John Blackledge, of Heapy ... ... „ 31
Alexander, ye S. of Robert Baron, of Euxton ... ... Ap. 7
John, ye S. of John Beardsworth, of ffarington ... ... „ 7
William, ye S. Thomas Ditchfield, of Leyland ... ... „ 28
Elizabeth, ye D. of Andrew Waterworth, of Exton ... „ 28
Margaret, ye D. of Richard Waring, of Leyland ... May 14
Dorothy, ye D. of Richard Lever, of Leyland ... ... „ 14
John, ye S. of William Ugnall, of Wheelton ... ... June 2
Alexander, ye S. of Robert Hindle, of Keurden ... „ 3
Henery, ye S. of Richard Whittle, of ffarington... ... „ 5
Robert, ye S. of Robert Waring, of Leyland ... ... „ 16

[1] She was married Feb. 6, 1721-2, to Thomas Lutwidge, Esq.
[2] In Standish parish.
[3] The transcript is signed by Vicar and Churchwardens.

28. *Transcript of the parish register of Leyland in Lancashire (Record Society of Lancashire and Cheshire)*

Jan. 27   Robert Whittel, B., & Elizabeth Hart, S., both of Harrow, co. Midd. L.A.C.

Jan. 30   John Trebilcock, of St Collomb Major, co. Cornwall, B., & Frances Sargent, of Alderton, co. Wilts, S.   Fac. Lic.

Feb. 14   Thomas Willis, of St Clement Danes, co. Midd., B., & Margaret Hyde, of this parish, S.   L.A.C.

1743.

April 5   Joseph Peiarce, of Eaton, co. Bucks, B., & Mary Ann Leader, of Staines, co. Midd., S.   Fac. Lic.

April 7   Robert Duncombe, of St Gregory by St Paul, London, B., & Elizabeth Barlow, of this parish, S.   L.A.C.

April 7   Joseph Wild, W., & Mary Downs, S.

April 10   William Wood, B., & Sarah Sowerby, W.

April 11   Edward Baker, B., & Margaret Ainsley, S.

May 16   John Bimson, B., & Ann Stone, S.

May 16   Richard Willis, B., & Sarah Norton, S.

May 18   John Aynge, B., & Susanna Fowke, S., both of St James, Westm^r. Fac. Lic.

May 20   Anthony Stewart, of St Margaret, Westm^r, B., & Elizabeth Archbould, of this parish, S.   L.B.L.

May 22   Thomas Paris, W., & Ann Sommons, S.

May 25   Charles Nicholas Jenty, of St Ann, Westm^r, B., & Hannah Anderson, of this parish, S.   L.B.L.

May 31   James Chauvel, B., & Mary Barrat, W., both of St James, Westm^r. L.A.C.

June 13   William Watkins, W., & Ann Smith, W.

June 13   Thomas Llewellin, B., & Elizabeth Rand, S., both of St Mary le Bone, co. Midd. L.A.C.

June 21   Edward Williams, B., & Ann Simmonds, S.

June 21   Barnabas Eveleigh Leigh, of Shorwell, co. Southampton, B., & Catherine Clarke, of Bobbington, co. Essex, S.   L.B.L.

June 21   William Oates, B., & Margaret Preston, S., both of Hampton, co. Midd. Fac. Lic.

June 23   Matthew Mills, of St Nicholas Acon, London, B., & Cornelia Soulogre, of St Ann, Westminster, S.   L.A.C.

June 30   James Brown, B., & Elizabeth Bennet, S., both of St Martin in the Fields. Fac. Lic.

July 1   Ely Leach, B., & Sarah Chamberlayn, S.

July 4   Edward Jones, of Walton upon Thames, co. Surrey, B., & Elizabeth Hawson, of this parish, S.   Fac. Lic.

July 7   John Cruton, of St Andrew, Holborn, co. Midd., W., & Frances Keene, of this parish, W.   L.B.L.

July 14   Cornelius Vanderstop, W., & Dorothy Davies, W.   Fac. Lic.

July 17   Robert Davies, B., & Mary Girdler, W.

July 18   Samuel Pendered, B., & Ann Godwin, S.

July 19   John Barker, B., & Dorothy Little, S.   L.A.C.

July 23   Robert Oldisworth, B., & Mary Daniel, S., both of the Liberty of the Rolls, London. Fac. Lic.

July 24   James Ward, of St Giles in the Fields, W., & Martha Ryalton, of this parish, W.   L.B.L.

July 24   William Catherwood, B., & Susanna Groves, S.

July 28   John Ellis, B., & Elizabeth Wise, S.

July 30   Thomas Lewis, W., & Jane Evans, W.

Aug. 7   Robert Frew, B., & Isabella Sims, S.

Aug. 7   Henry Bromley, B., & Margaret Downs, S.

Aug. 9   Thomas Oxlee, of St Giles in the Fields, W., & Alice Wilkinson, of Paddington, co. Midd., W.   L.B.L.

29. *Transcript of the marriage register of St George Hanover Square (Harleian Society)*

page, for baptisms in 1769, from the parish register of Sandford in Devon. It includes the baptism on 17 September 1769 of my ancestor Ann Vesey. In the period 1780 to 1812 some registers also included the mother's maiden name or perhaps her previous married name. The baptism entries for my ancestors Henry Chapman and Susan Climpson (or Climson) in the parish register of Hainford in Norfolk are:

> Henry son of James Chapman and Curtis his wife (late Wright) baptised February 2, 1806
> Susan daughter of Issachar Climson and Mary his wife (late Pinchen, spinster) was born Thursday September 26, 1811 and privately baptised September 29, 1811 and admitted into the church

You may be lucky enough to have ancestors who are recorded in "Dade registers" from many parishes in Yorkshire and Nottinghamshire between 1770 and 1812. The clergyman William Dade persuaded many of his colleagues to record the mother's maiden name in a baptismal entry. Even more usefully, these registers sometimes record the parentage of both the father and mother of the child being baptised (so three generations are recorded in one entry of baptism) and their place of birth or residence. R. Bellingham describes these important registers in *Ancestors* (August/September 2003).

Baptisms of two or more brothers and sisters sometimes took place on the same day. The parish register of Winkleigh in Devon records the twins of my g.g.g.g. grandparents being baptised in 1802:

> April 11th: James and Elizabeth; twins of Isaac and Susanna Stanlake

Baptism on the same day does not, however, necessarily mean that the children were twins. Although most children were baptised shortly after birth, this was not always the case and it was common practice to have more than one child baptised at the same time. Until this century children were born to most couples at regular intervals (my g.g. grandparents John Josiah Keates and Sophia Chapman had 16 children in 28 years) so the parents may not have arranged the baptism of one child before another was born. The parish register may give a date of birth, as well as the date of baptism. The following extract is from the parish register of St Mary, Rotherhithe. It shows the baptisms of my g.g.g. grandfather, George Keates, his sister and one of his brothers, all baptised on the same day (18 August 1811):

Ann, daughter of John and Catherine Keates	20 (days old)
George, son of John and Catherine Keates	born 6th April 1808
William, son of John and Catherine Keates	born 9th April 1806

Most children were baptised and most of the ceremonies took place a few days, or weeks, after the child's birth. However, many children were baptised later (in the example above, William Keates was five years old) and these baptisms can be difficult to find. Some people were only baptised as adults, some very late in life. This was often because their parents (perhaps Catholics or non-conformists) had not had them baptised as children but they decided that they wanted to be baptised before they died. A minister often noted "adult" against the entry or recorded a person's age, as in this example from the register of Kelvedon in Essex:

BAPTISMS A.D. 1769

Ann D. of Mr John Read & Ann his wife }
John S. of Jacob & Ann Greenslade } May 17.
Jemmy S. of James & Agness Morgain — 28.
Thomazin D. of Thomas & Thomazin Wright 29.
John S. of John & Mary Roach — June 6.
John S. of Mary Lee (a Base Child) — 6
James S. of James & Margaret Sargent — 10.
Elizabeth D. of James & Elizabeth Bradford July 2.
John S. of William & Mary Corkram — 4
Mary D. of William & Mary Clifton — 16.
Betty D. of John & Elizabeth Jarman — 18.
Mary D. of John & Susanna Herding — 19
John S. of John & Elizabeth Wright Augst 7.
Elizabeth D. of William & Grace Gregory — 20.
Mary D. of Philip & Mary Mare 20.
Zacharias S. of John & Hannah Martin, Sept 12.
John Son of Sir John Davie Baronet and } 13.
   Catharine his Lady —
Ann D. of John & Mary Vesey 17.
John S. of John & Mary Tozer 17
Charity D. of Michael & Ann Towell — Octr 8.
Elizabeth D. of Francis & Joan Yard — 22.
Jenny D. of George & Sarah Tribble 31.
Mary D. of Mr Richard & Mary Read Novr 27.
Robt S. of Robt & Mary Baker 28.
Betty D. of John & Rose Strong Decr 10.
Walter S. of Thomas & Mary Daw — 24.
Christian D. of Peter & Mary Leash 26.

William Barter Chaplain.

30. Register of baptisms in the parish of Sandford in 1769, including that of Ann, daughter of John and Mary Vesey (or Voisey) (Devon Record Office)

115

Elizabeth Barns, an adult of 73 years was baptised 29th June 1727.

However, it is unknown how many adult baptisms appear without any age noted (and so appear to be baptisms of children). In the months before the introduction of civil registration on 1 July 1837, there was an increase in the number of baptisms, especially of older children and adults. This may have been due to a popular belief that the law introducing civil registration also required anyone born before July 1837 to have been baptised. For example, the registers of St Leonard's Shoreditch in London contain hundreds of baptisms (of infants, children and adults) in June 1837. If you cannot find an ancestor's baptism in the late 18th or early 19th centuries, you should search for an adult baptism in registers of 1836 and 1837.

A statute of 1812, known as Rose's Act, required parish incumbents to use specially printed registers, with baptisms, marriages and burials in separate books. These printed registers are much easier to read than earlier registers. The act required detailed information to be recorded. In addition to the date of baptism and the child's name, Rose's Act required the register to include the names of the parents, their abode, the father's quality, trade or profession and the name of the officiating clergyman. Illustration 31 shows the page of a register in this statutory form; it includes the 1827 baptism of Sarah Law in Walthamstow. Another example is the baptism record of my g.g. grandmother Emily Mary Clements at St Mary, Wanstead, in Essex in 1837:

Baptised April 16th; Born August 25th (1836)	Emily Mary daughter of	John & Sarah	Clements	Wanstead	Fishmonger	Wm Gilly Rector

Baptisms should have taken place in church, but private baptisms (that is, baptisms at the parents' home or elsewhere, such as that of Susan Climpson noted above) were sometimes permitted, usually if a child was too ill to be brought to church. From 1603 parish registers were supposed to record both public and private baptisms, but this was not always done. If private baptisms were recorded, you may see a note "P" (also used for pauper baptisms) or "Priv." against the entry, or a statement that a child was privately or "half" baptised. From 1812 the registration of private baptisms appears to have improved. If a child was privately baptised, he or she should have been "received" or "admitted" into the church by a later ceremony, the date of which may be noted in the register (usually in a marginal note).

It was common for there to be more than one man in a parish with the same name, let us say John Bull. The two men could have been a father and son, or cousins, but they were not necessarily related to each other. This can cause problems. If the register notes that John Bull was married or was buried, which of the two men is this? It is especially confusing if both men were fathering children in the same period. The position may be clear if the incumbent has noted the name of the mother of each child, or if he differentiated between the two men by referring to them as John Bull senior and John Bull junior (or perhaps elder or younger). If the incumbent ceased to use this identification, this may indicate that one of the men had died or left the parish.

Page 214.						

BAPTISMS solemnized in the Parish of *St Mary Walthamstow*
in the County of *Essex* in the Year 18*27*

When Baptized.	Child's Christian Name.	Parents Name. Christian.	Surname.	Abode.	Quality, Trade, or Profession.	By whom the Ceremony was performed.
1827. Nov No. 1705.	Edward of	William & Esther	Eaton	Chapel End		Mr Terrington
Novr 25th Samuel No. 1706.	Samuel	John and Elizabeth	Young	Clay Street	Husband man	Mr Wilson
Novr 25th No. 1707.	Sarah	James and Eliza	Law	Hale End	Husband man	Mr Wilson
Decr 2^d No. 1708.	John	John and Martha	Law	Clay Street	Husband man	Mr Terrington
Decr 2^d No. 1709.	John	John Bevan and Sarah Ann Dandy	Bevan - Dandy	From the Workhouse		Mr Terrington
Decr 2 No. 1710.	Maria Elizabeth	John Pekin and Maria Spencer	Pekin Spencer	From the Workhouse		Mr Terrington
Decr 9th No. 1711.	William Setten	Thomas and Elizabeth	Clark	Marsh Street	Coachman	Benjⁿ Nicol
Decr 9th No. 1712.	Richard Joseph	Charles and Susannah	Woollard	Chapel End	Husband man	Benjⁿ Nicol

31. *Walthamstow parish register, including the baptism of Sarah Law in 1827 (Vestry House Museum)*

117

People often needed proof of their age or of the fact that they had been baptised (or married). Accordingly, clergymen sometimes provided certificates confirming that entries had been made in the parish registers. For example, if John Hunter died, his son William might need a certificate confirming that he had been baptised the son of John Hunter, in order to inherit John's property. A certificate of baptism is shown in illustration 32. Similar certificates were issued to confirm that marriages had taken place, or that a man had been buried, for example to support widows' applications for army pensions.

INFANT MORTALITY

Large families were very common in the 18th and 19th centuries. There are families of 12 or 13 children in my family tree (and one family of 16 children) but the rate of infant mortality was extremely high. Many children were stillborn or died before they could be baptised so that no record of them may exist. Of those children who were baptised, many did not reach adult age. My ancestors Benjamin and Mary Bateman had five children between 1782 and 1795, but four died in infancy, leaving my g.g.g. grandfather Benjamin Bateman as the sole survivor. Rogers (26) suggests that, in the late 18th century, half the children born in large towns died before they reached the age of 5. In London half the children died before the age of 3. Consequently, many children were given the same name to ensure that one of them carried on a family name. My ancestor James Eagles had seven sons, four of whom had James as a Christian name. Ironically, they all survived to become adults.

ILLEGITIMACY

The baptism of my ancestor Ann Simpson in Vange, Essex, in 1803 was recorded as:

27 February Ann the illegitimate daughter of Mary Simpson, widow, baptised.

Similar entries for two illegitimate children, baptised in 1694, can be seen in illustration 28, from the published transcript of the register of Leyland, Lancashire. Illegitimate children were noted in registers by various descriptions, including "base born", "bastard", "son of the people" or "begotten in adultery". Some ministers noted the father's name or added other comments to baptism records of illegitimate children as in these entries from Morden and Wimbledon:

Ann, dau. of Joan Money, and J. Bayley supposed father, begotten in fornication: bap. 15 Mar. 1654
Johan, the daughter of an Harlot, was baptiz'd Nov. 7, 1579

If the baptism of an ancestor records that he or she was illegitimate, and only the mother's name is given, you may never discover the father's name. However, other parish or court records (# chapters 18, 24 and 25) may fill the gap. In the case of my ancestor Ann Simpson, I could not locate any such records. However, her mother Mary Simpson married Charles Howlet on 20 May 1803, only 12 weeks after Ann's baptism, and it is therefore possible that he was Ann's father.

CERTIFICATE OF BAPTISM,

Performed within Six Calendar Months after Registry of Birth, pursuant to the Act of 6 & 7 GULIELMI IV, c. 86.

I *John Pye Smith* of *Homerton*, in the County of *Middlesex*, do hereby certify, That I have this day baptised, by the name of *Mary,* —— a female child produced to me by daughter of *himself* and *Mary his wife,* at the ~~son~~ of *Alfred Le Mare* and declared by the said *Alfred le Mare* to have been born at *Hackney*, in the County of *Middlesex* on the *Twenty Second* day of *December.* 1844.

Witness my hand ~~this~~ on the *Sixteenth* day of *March*, 18 45, *John Pye Smith.*

N.B. This Certificate must be delivered by the Minister who shall have performed the rite of Baptism, immediately after the Baptism, whenever the same shall be then demanded, (on payment of the Fee of One Shilling, which he shall be therefore entitled to receive,) to the Person preceding the Baptismal Name to be given; and such Person must deliver this Certificate within Seven Days next after such Baptism to the Registrar or Superintendent Registrar in whose custody the Register of the Birth of the Child may then happen to be, to the intent that such Baptismal Name may be inserted in such Register.

32. Certificate of baptism of Mary Le Mare on 16 March 1845

BURIALS

The recording of burials also improved between 1538 and 1837. Early registers may only name the deceased and record the date of burial. This causes difficulty if there were two or more people of the same name in a parish. Fortunately, further information may be noted, such as the name of the husband of a married woman who died, or the name of the father (or even both parents) of a child who died. Illustration 33 shows a page from the register of Sandford in Devon recording the burial of Ann (daughter of John and Mary Vesey) on 25 October 1768 (John and Mary had another daughter named Ann, my ancestor, in 1769). A burial register may also record the deceased's age, occupation, abode or even the cause of death. The deceased's occupation is noted in this example from Winkleigh in Devon:

Buried 1741 January 24th   Samuel Bulleid the butcher

Burial entries may note how a person died. References to plague were common, sometimes as a note "p" or "pest" in the registers. These examples of deaths caused by the plague are from the registers of Darley Dale, Derbyshire in 1558 and St John's, Peterborough in 1606:

1558. Alice Stafford dyed of the plague and was buryed 14th April (Darley Dale)
1606. Dec. 16. Henry Renoulds was buryed. Henry came from London, where he dwelt, sicke of the plague and being receyved by William Browne, died in his house. The said William soon after fell sicke of the plague and died and so did his sonne, his daughter and his servant: only his wife and her maid escaped with sores (St John's, Peterborough)

Here are some more examples of entries that note the cause of death. John Gotnell, in the last example, was one of Monmouth's rebels and sentenced to death at the Bloody Assizes by Judge Jeffreys.

John Fitzwilliams, servant to Sir Edward Dymocke, Knight, slayne in a tavern, buried 14 February 1610 (St Gregory by St Pauls, London)
1720, buried Jane Cressop, who was killed by the coloquintada, or bitter apple, which she took to procure an abortion (St Alkmund's, Derby)
Dame Whittingham, murthered by her husband, bur. 17 April 1604 (All Saints, Newcastle)
1604, August 29. Lawrence Wilcox and John Carter, killed in the colepitt (Walsall)
1722, 30 August. Buried James Graham, a felon, he was hanged the same morning just after baptism (St Mary-le-Bow, Durham)
1685, July 9. Buried John Gotnell, executed for treason against His Majesty (Taunton).

Many burials went unrecorded in times of civil rebellion or during visitations of the plague, for example in Plymouth in 1626 or London in 1593, 1603, 1625 and 1665. Omissions of burials were most common if a parish priest was also struck down. Registers include many anonymous corpses. If a body was found in a country area or washed ashore in a coastal parish, the local residents might have no clue as to the person's identity and so registers note many burials of unidentified travellers, soldiers or sailors. You may therefore never find a burial entry for your ancestor.

Burials AD: 1768.

Ann Dau: of Samuel Underhill March 30.
Agness Southcott Wid.ʳ — — April 2.
Richard Son of Will.ᵐ & Sarah Stoneman — 23.
Roger Son of Peter & Sarah Snow — 25.
Elizabeth Challocombe — — May 31.
William Stevens — — June 1.
Joseph Bezant — — 6
Widow Ewings — 10
Joseph Davis — — July 15.
Elizabeth Wife of John Ridge — 21.
Mary Wife of Samuel Taylor juⁿ 25.
Mary Wife of John Bragg juⁿ Aug. 4.
Will.ᵐ Pierce — — Sep.ᵗ 25.
Betty D: of John & Hannah Martin Oc.ᵗ 5.
Daniel S. of John & Margaret Norrish — 6.
William S. of John & Hannah Martin — 16
Ann D: of John & Mary Vesey — 25
Thomas S. of Thomas & Joan Smale — 27.
Elizabeth Hawkins Nov: 2.
Mary D: of John & Hannah Martin — 9.
Mary D: of Thomas & Joan Smale — 9.
Thomas S. of William & Cecil Harvey De.ᵉ 4
John Herding — — 28.

William Barter Chaplain

James Hawkins} Church
Abraham Lane } Wardens

33. *Register of burials in the parish of Sandford in 1768, including Ann Vesey's elder sister Ann (Devon Record Office)*

Rose's Act of 1812 required printed registers to be used for burials, to be completed with the deceased's name, abode, date of burial and age. The entry for the burial of my ancestor Susanna Stanlake in Winkleigh in 1819 reads:

Susanna Stanlake   Winkleigh   October 8th   58   John Clyft, Vicar

Burial entries may be accompanied by the word poor or the letter p. This indicates that the deceased was a pauper, and that the funeral was paid for by the parish, in which case other parish records may record poor relief being granted to the person. A marginal note such as "aff." or "A" refers to an affidavit being sworn that wool was used for the burial shroud. Records of poor relief and these affidavits are considered in chapter 18.

The word mortuary or mort was sometimes added in the margin of a burial entry. In medieval times a lord of the manor (# chapter 27) was entitled to a deceased's best animal (a lord's right of heriot). A manor's customs sometimes entitled the parish priest to receive a deceased's second best animal or article of clothing. An act of 1529 provided for monetary payments to replace the clergyman's right (where the custom survived) and exempted the goods of anyone who had not been a householder. No payment was due if the deceased's movable goods were worth less than £30. The fee payable on larger estates increased on a sliding scale from 3s. 4d. (payable on estates worth £30) up to 10s. or 10s. 6d. (on estates worth over £40). The note "mort" indicates that payment was made. Entries for mortuaries may be more detailed. Tate (532) notes an example from the register of Ampthill in Bedfordshire. The rector Edward Rowse had noted:

That on the 1st of May 1713, I received [from] Mrs Carleton widow the full sum of ten shillings for a mortuary, becoming due upon the death of Rowland Carleton, esq. her husband, he dying possessed of goods to the value of more than forty pounds.

The records of burials in parish registers are important. If a burial entry specifies the age of the deceased this will assist you in finding the record of the person's baptism. A date of burial may assist the location of a will of the deceased in probate court records (# chapter 12). Furthermore, if you are looking for the baptism of your ancestor (let us say John Harris) in about 1730 in a certain parish, but find one child of that name baptised in 1729 and one in 1731 (of different parentage), the burial register may show that one of them died in infancy, so that your ancestor is likely to be the other John Harris.

MARRIAGES AND BANNS

From 1538 to 1754, a marriage was usually recorded in the following manner:

1697 June 15th   Nicholas Bulhead and Damaris Daw were married

Additional information might be given, such as the groom's occupation, the name of the bride's father and whether the marriage was after banns or by the authority of a marriage licence (# chapter 14). An extract from a register in Latin (of Winkleigh in Devon) is shown in illustration 34. This records marriages in 1606; the fourth entry is for the marriage on 16 June of my ancestors John Bulhead and Armynell Jeffery. The entries are easier to decipher after some study of Latin and old handwriting.

34. *Winkleigh parish register of 1606, including the marriage of John Bulhead and Arminell Jeffery on 16 June (Devon Record Office)*

Marriages can be difficult to locate in parish registers. Weddings commonly took place in the bride's parish rather than in the groom's parish. However, your ancestors could have married in another parish nearby, or perhaps in the nearest city or market town. Records of marriages can be particularly difficult to locate in the period up to 25 March 1754. This is the date upon which Hardwicke's Marriage Act of 1753 came into force in England and Wales. The objective of the act was to prevent irregular, clandestine or runaway marriages. Until 1754 marriage ceremonies that did not comply with church rules (such as those relating to banns, licences and the spouses' residence) were irregular but nevertheless legally valid. Many marriages did not take place in the parish church of either the groom or the spouse, and sometimes not even in a parish church (but in marriage houses or even prisons such as the Fleet in London). It was not even essential for a ceremony to take place (since the exchange of vows by the couple was sufficient under English law). Many clergy were prepared to conduct irregular marriages. Even in prisons there were clergymen, imprisoned for debt and therefore in need of the money, who would conduct a wedding ceremony for a fee (usually less than that charged by church officials for calling banns or issuing a marriage licence). It was easy for couples to get married almost anywhere. Clandestine weddings often involved minors (people under the age of 21) or heiresses whose parents opposed the marriage (or were not even aware of it). More information about marriage licences and clandestine or irregular marriages is contained in chapter 14. However, in brief, marriage licences could be obtained from many different church authorities, and a marriage was often celebrated in a church or chapel close to the church registry that issued the licence. If a couple came from a village or villages in the countryside, you may find that their marriage took place in the nearest city or town in which a church official was issuing licences.

Hardwicke's Act required a marriage to be performed in the parish church of one of the spouses (or in certain designated chapels) by an Anglican clergyman, in the presence of at least two witnesses, and only after the publication of banns or by the authority of a valid marriage licence. The only exemptions were for marriages in accordance with Jewish or Quaker ceremonies. Other non-conformist and civil marriage ceremonies only became legal again in 1837 when civil registration was introduced. Under Hardwicke's Act, minors had to obtain their parents' or guardians' consent in order to marry but, until 1929, the law still allowed boys as young as 14 and girls as young as 12, to be legally married with that consent.

Until 1754 the entries in parish registers for marriages, baptisms and burials were often mixed up in one chronological sequence. Another common arrangement was for the entries for each year to be set out in three sections (perhaps a list of the baptisms, then a list of marriages and then a list of burials) followed by the next year's entries. The arrangement was a matter for the incumbent. Hardwicke's Marriage Act provided that, from 1754, the records of marriages and banns had to be kept separate from the registers recording baptisms and burials. From 1754 marriage registers were usually (but not always) books of printed forms that the clergyman could complete (*see* illustration 27). Marriage entries in parish registers before 1754 were usually limited to the date and the names of the spouses but Hardwicke's Act also required clergymen to record further information. Entries after 25 March 1754 should therefore record the spouses' parishes of residence, their status (bachelor, spinster, widow or widower), whether the marriage was by banns or licence, and the groom's occupation. Most spouses were stated to be "of this parish" or "otp", but this did not necessarily mean much since the legal requirement for this description was only three weeks' residence in the parish. Someone who had only recently moved to the parish might also be described as a sojourner. Registers after 1754 should include the signatures or marks of the spouses, two witnesses and the clergyman. The witnesses often included the churchwarden or parish clerk (in these cases the same signature appears in many entries) but witnesses were often the spouses' relatives. Thus the entry (*see* illustration 27) for the marriage of Richard Crump and Elizabeth Sercombe was witnessed by Thomas Sercombe. From 1754 the incumbent might keep one register for marriages and one register for banns, but they were often recorded in different parts of the same register. You might also find that a register has entries that combine the banns and the marriage, such as the entry for the first marriage of my ancestor John Keates (or Keats) at St Dunstan, Stepney, in 1796:

> Banns of marriage between John Keats and Sarah Anderson were published on August the 7th, 14th and 21st. John Keats of this parish, and hamlet of Poplar, bachelor, and Sarah Anderson of this parish and same hamlet, spinster, were married in this church by banns this 22nd day of August 1796 by me . . .

The signatures of John, Sarah and the witnesses then followed (including the signature of William Keates, who was probably John's brother). The rector who officiated at the wedding wrote John's surname as Keats, but John signed as Keates. However, you should not assume that someone who signed their name could necessarily write anything else. The information that was recorded in marriage registers improved further when a new form of marriage register was introduced (for civil registration) in 1837. From that year a civil registration certificate of marriage and the parish register entry will be the same, except that the parish register (and superintendent registrar's copy) include the actual signature or mark of each spouse or witness whereas the copy register in the GRO records will only be a transcript and not include original signatures or marks.

Banns are considered further in chapter 14, but a banns register may help you find a marriage that took place in another parish. Illustration 35 shows typical entries from a 19th-century banns register, including an entry for Bernhard Herber and Emily Clements. The calling of banns in both parishes was required by law from 1823 and sometimes took place in earlier years. If your ancestor was baptised, had children and was then buried in one parish, but you cannot find his marriage, you should check the banns book. His spouse may have originated from another parish and the couple may have married there. However, if the banns were also called in the groom's parish, the banns book may disclose where the wedding took place. For example, my ancestor Richard Bater was baptised in Chawleigh in Devon and so were his children. His marriage took place in 1793 in Sandford but banns were called in both Chawleigh and Sandford. Entries in the banns book of each parish noted the home parish of each spouse. Illustration 36 shows the entry from Sandford for Ann Voisey "of this parish" and Richard Bater "of Chawleigh". The Chawleigh banns book notes Richard Bater as "of this parish" and Ann Voisey as "of Sandford".

THE ENGLISH CIVIL WAR

Many gaps occur in registers at the time of the English Civil War and the Commonwealth. From 1642 some incumbents fled or were ejected from their parishes. Many children were not baptised and some were only baptised when the priest returned, sometimes as late as 1660. Between 1653 and 1660, responsibility for the registers was taken out of the hands of the church and given to a local official (the Parish Register) who was elected by parish ratepayers and whose appointment

35. *Extract from banns book of Holy Trinity Minories, London, 1852: the entry for the banns for Bernhard Herber and Emily Clements (Guildhall Library, Ms 9946/5)*

No. 41.

Banns of Marriage between Richard Bater of Chawleigh Batchelor & Ann Voisey of this Parish Spinster ‒ ‒ ‒ ‒ ‒ ‒ ‒ ‒ ‒ ‒ ‒ ‒ ‒ were published on the three Sundays underwritten:

That is to say, On Sunday, the tenth of March 1793 by me Geo: Bent Chaplain

On Sunday, the seventeenth of March 1793 by me Geo: Bent Chaplain

On Sunday, the twenty fourth of March 1793 by me Geo: Bent Chaplain.

No. 42.

Banns of Marriage between George Voisey of this Parish Batchelor & Ann Pine of this Parish Spinster ‒ ‒ ‒ ‒ ‒ ‒ ‒ ‒ ‒ ‒ ‒ ‒ were published on the three Sundays underwritten:

that is to say, On Sunday, the twelfth of May 1793 by me Geo: Bent Chaplain

On Sunday, the nineteenth of May 1793 by me Geo: Bent Chaplain.

On Sunday, the twenty sixth of May 1793 by Samuel Hart Minister.

36. *Extract from banns book of the parish of Sandford in 1793, recording the calling of banns for Richard Bater of Chawleigh and Ann Voisey of Sandford (Devon Record Office)*

was approved by local magistrates. He registered births (rather than baptisms), marriages and deaths (rather than burials). Many Parish Registers started their own books to record these events but few of these books survive. However, the Parish Register was often the former parish clerk (because no one else was available who could read or write) and he often merely carried on making entries in the church register. The survival of the registers in these cases is somewhat better, but many are missing.

From 1653 to 1660 only civil marriages, conducted by a Justice of the Peace, were legally valid and marriages were not supposed to be conducted in church. A document known as the "publication of intention to marry" would be posted in the market place or in the church porch for three weeks before the civil ceremony. Few parish registers note these civil marriages but the publications of intention were sometimes recorded. The parish register of Winkleigh in Devon does contain records of marriages for this period. This is a typical entry:

1653, 26th February; the contract of marriage was had and made between Richard Seward, the son of John Seward of Drustenton and Thomazine Summer the daughter of John Summer of Winkleigh and publication made according to the act [the] three Lords Days following. 25th March Richard Seward and Thomazine Summer were married.

After the restoration of Charles II in 1660, these Commonwealth marriages were recognised by the church as valid and they were sometimes retrospectively recorded in a parish register. Furthermore, some clergy had remained at their churches and continued to secretly conduct baptisms and marriages, often only retrospectively recording the events in 1660.

We return to parish registers later in this chapter, but we must now consider bishops' transcripts and modern transcripts of parish registers. We shall then consider the IGI and other indexes, which usually provide a more convenient method of starting research in parish records.

BISHOPS' TRANSCRIPTS

Most parishes were required, from 1598, to prepare an annual list of the baptisms, marriages and burials that had taken place in that year and send it to the bishop (or sometimes, for example in Suffolk, to an archdeacon) who had authority over that parish. This list had to be provided within a month after Easter or, in later years, within a month after Lady Day (25 March). From 1813 the lists had to be prepared within two months of the end of the calendar year and be submitted by 1 June. The lists are known as bishops' transcripts or register bills, and contain similar information to the parish registers. Early transcripts consist of folded (or rolled) parchment or paper, so great care is necessary if you review these at an archive. Later transcripts are generally on printed forms, usually bound into books, and very similar in form to the later parish registers.

A few bishops required transcripts before 1598, but in some dioceses the transcripts do not commence until later (1731 in Dorset and 1760 in Durham). Few transcripts survive from before 1800 for Essex, the City of London and Middlesex. Certain parishes, known as "peculiars" (# chapter 12), only had to provide transcripts from 1 January 1813, although some volunteered transcripts before this. Not all parishes made the necessary returns. Some did so every two or three years instead of annually. Bishops' transcripts for many parishes cease around 1837, when civil registration commenced, and those for other parishes rarely extend beyond the mid-19th century. There are no transcripts from 1649 (the establishment of the Commonwealth) until the restoration of Charles II in 1660 although some transcripts covering this period were prepared after 1660 and then sent to the bishop.

Many transcripts have been lost or destroyed. However, surviving transcripts may cover periods of time for which the parish registers are missing. Published copies of registers therefore often include some entries from bishops' transcripts to cover periods for which the parish register is not available. Where the transcripts and registers cover the same periods, the two sources may contain considerable differences in spelling, names, dates and even as to the entries included or omitted. In some cases, even though the bishops' transcripts were meant to be a copy of the register entries, it is almost as if two people in the parish maintained separate registers. Additional information may be included in either the transcripts or in the registers. Transcripts may contain less information because an incumbent did not bother to include all information from the parish register. He may also have copied entries incorrectly. A transcript may be better than the register because an incumbent took the opportunity to correct or make additions to the register entries. You should therefore check both sources and compare the entries.

Surviving bishops' transcripts are usually held by CROs. However, the seat of the bishop of a diocese may have been in a different county from that in which the parish was located. Transcripts can therefore be in the CRO for either the county in which the bishop resided or the county that included the parish. It may be obvious which diocese was responsible for the parish in which you are interested, but this is not always the case. Essex was in the diocese of London and many church records for Essex are consequently held in London archives. Northumberland formed part of the diocese of Durham. Transcripts for peculiars may be in a number of locations. For example, many parishes in West Kent, such as Chevening and Chiddingstone, formed part of the Archbishop of Canterbury's peculiar of the deanery of Shoreham. The bishops' transcripts were therefore sent to the Archbishop and are now held in Lambeth Palace Library. Gibson (367) specifies the location of surviving bishops' transcripts (and any known copies of those transcripts that have been lost). Surviving transcripts are also listed in the *NIPR* volumes (151), in similar works such as Harris (161) and in CROs' catalogues.

PARISH REGISTER TRANSCRIPTS

All counties have some parishes for which the registers (or bishops' transcripts) have been transcribed but the best example is Bedfordshire. All its surviving parish registers for the period up to 1812 have been transcribed, indexed and published by Bedfordshire County Council in 80 volumes (except for the registers of the parish of Haynes that were privately printed). Copies are held at Bedford Record Office and the SoG and can be purchased.

Many other parish registers have been transcribed (and in many cases published in books, on microfiche, CD-ROM or the Internet). The principal bodies who have published registers are the Parish Register Society, the Harleian Society, Phillimore & Co. (which published 237 volumes of marriage registers of about 1,200 parishes up to 1812 or 1837) and family history societies. Registers have also been published by county parish register societies such as those of Buckinghamshire, Shropshire, Surrey and Northumberland & Durham. These four societies have ceased to publish material but others continue. Yorkshire Parish Register Society has published over 150 volumes of registers and Lancashire Parish Register Society has also published over 150 volumes of registers (as well as many registers on fiche and CD-ROM). Some county record and archaeological societies have also published registers, including the Thoresby Society, the Banbury Historical Society, the Devon & Cornwall Record Society and the Cumberland and Westmorland Antiquarian & Archaeological Society. Illustration 28 is an example of a page from a published register transcript. It includes baptisms of 1694 and 1695 from the register of Leyland in Lancashire of 1653 to 1710, published by the Record Society of Lancashire and Cheshire in White (176). Illustration 29 is a page of marriage entries of January 1742/3 to August 1743, from the marriage register of St George Hanover Square, London of 1725 to 1787, published by the Harleian Society in Chapman (155).

There has been an explosion in publishing on microfiche and CD-ROM. Three of the best-served counties are Kent, Lancashire and Oxfordshire because of the many transcripts published by Kent FHS, Lancashire Parish Register Society, Lancashire FHS and Oxfordshire FHS. However, Surrey, Warwickshire, Staffordshire and Worcestershire are also well-served by the fiche publications of West Surrey FHS, East Surrey FHS and the Birmingham & Midland Society for Genealogy & Heraldry (covering Staffordshire, Warwickshire and Worcestershire). Most of Phillimore's volumes of marriage registers and many other transcripts, such as those of the Parish Register Society and Surrey Parish Register Society, have been reproduced on CD-ROM by S&N Genealogy Supplies (# chapter 3) and are listed on its web site. Register transcripts reproduced by Archive CD Books are listed on its web site and the registers transcribed and published on disk by the Parish Register Transcription Society (enquiries to S. Tanner, 50 Silvester Road, Cowplain, Waterlooville, Hampshire PO8 8TL) are regularly listed in *Family Tree Magazine*. Many transcripts of registers have also been published on the Internet.

There are also a vast number of parish register transcripts and indexes that have not been published. Most of these have been produced by individuals and deposited at the SoG, CROs or in FHS libraries. For example, LMA (# chapter 11) has a good collection of transcripts and indexes of London registers. Two of the most important series of unpublished transcripts are those by C.R. Webb and W.H. Challen. Webb's transcripts concentrate on parishes in the City of London and have been deposited at Guildhall Library and the SoG. Challen's transcripts concentrate on parishes in the City of London, Middlesex and Sussex, with a few from other counties. The parishes covered by Challen (and the years covered) are listed in McIntyre (166). Challen's transcripts were deposited at Guildhall Library and can be seen on microfilm. Copies of parts of his work were also deposited at the SoG and at the British and Bodleian Libraries.

Transcripts of parish registers are listed in the *NIPR* volumes and in some other lists. The registers published by the Harleian Society and many county record societies are listed in Mullins (260). The parishes (and years) covered by Phillimore's marriage register transcripts are listed by Rosier (168). Many FHS publications in book form, microfiche and CD-ROM are listed in Hampson (249), Perkins (263) and Raymond (267) respectively.

The best collection of parish register transcripts is at the SoG and listed in its catalogue and the *County Sources* booklets noted above. Collections of transcripts are also held at CROs, reference libraries and FHS libraries and so their catalogues should also be reviewed. The Mormons have also microfilmed many parish registers and transcripts. The films are listed in the Family History Library catalogue (# chapter 11) and can be ordered for viewing at LDS family history centres. The Hyde Park family history centre, at 64–68 Exhibition Road, London SW7 2PA (telephone 020 7589 8561), keeps a large stock of the LDS microfilms for viewing on its premises. These are listed (with the many other records included on the films) in a separate catalogue at the centre, described in chapter 11.

Raymond (167a) lists, by English and Welsh county, many of the web sites which include transcripts or indexes of parish registers. For example, this work tells you the web site at which you can find a transcript (with indexes) to baptisms (1714–70) and marriages (1713–54) of Carhampton in Somerset. In order to find other sites, you should:

i.   look at FHS sites, for example the Northumberland & Durham FHS web site includes transcripts of baptisms, marriages and burials from 86 Durham parishes,

ii.   search for a place name, leading you to a site on which someone has placed material concerning that place; for example a web site for Wirksworth, Derbyshire includes transcripts of the registers of 1608–1837 with 70,000 baptisms, marriages and burials, or

iii.   search on the GENUKI web site (# chapter 11). Examples of register transcripts that can be accessed on GENUKI pages include some volumes of Phillimore's marriage registers for Hampshire, and the "Joiner marriage index", covering many parishes in Northumberland, Durham and Yorkshire.

Transcripts must be used with caution. Original registers should always be consulted, in addition to transcripts, because of the possibility of transcription errors. For example, I was searching for the marriage of my ancestors William and Susannah Pinchen which I believed took place in about 1770 in (or near) the parish of Horstead in Norfolk. The Phillimore transcript of Horstead marriages listed, on 4 August 1767, a marriage of William Pinchar and Susannah Deane. This was an error. The original register recorded the names William Pinchen and Susannah Dearie. Errors such as this are carried over into CD-ROM or microfiche copies of any published register and into any indexes (see below) which relied on the transcript. Errors are especially prevalent in transcripts, published on CD-ROM, that incorporate recent transcription work (as opposed to fascimiles of older books). Some of this transcription work is being undertaken abroad and is not being carefully checked, if at all, by organisations publishing the disks. When using a transcript of a register, you should also read the introduction to check exactly what it covers. Is it based on all surviving registers, or only part of them? Are any periods excluded? Is it only a copy of the bishops' transcripts? Is it a compilation of the registers and bishops' transcripts? Was it transcribed from the registers or was it transcribed from another transcript (so that it is two transcriptions away from the original entries)?

THE INTERNATIONAL GENEALOGICAL INDEX (IGI)

It can be extremely difficult to trace a family in parish registers if they moved between parishes. In rural areas there might have been 20 or more parishes within a day's walk of your ancestor's parish. Families and individuals moved around such an area with surprising frequency and the family that remained in one village for hundreds of years is probably the exception rather than the rule. The easiest method of commencing a search for your ancestors in parish (or non-conformist) registers, or to locate a family who moved between parishes, is to use the IGI. This index (which is available on microfiche, CD-ROM and the Internet) contains entries for over 320 million people from Britain, Ireland, the United States and about 70 other countries.

The entries in the IGI are principally of baptisms, but there are also many marriages. Most entries in the English section have been extracted from parish (or non-conformist) registers or bishops' transcripts, but also certain other sources. There are also some other events. Some births are recorded, usually extracted from registers of the Baptist Church (which baptised adults and so often recorded the birth dates of its members' children) or from registers of the period 1653 to 1660, when registers should have included the births of children rather than baptisms. It must be stressed that the IGI is only a finding aid. People who construct family trees using only information from the IGI are wasting their time. The IGI is a marvellous tool, but it is only an index (and an incomplete one) that may lead you to parish registers that record your ancestors. The IGI is not a substitute for research in parish registers.

The IGI has been compiled by the Genealogical Society of Utah, which was established by the Mormons (or LDS). Their interest in genealogy arises from their desire to posthumously baptise their ancestors and other people (the people named in the IGI) into the Mormon faith. Genealogists are indebted to the Mormons for their work on, and accumulation of, genealogical records. They have hundreds of libraries, called family history centres (# chapter 11) around the world. There are about 70 family history centres in Britain, listed in the *FLHH* (5), such as those in London, Liverpool, Glasgow, Norwich, Bristol and Leicester. The LDS allow the public free access to them, although small fees may be charged to order and view certain records.

New (and expanded) editions of the IGI are produced every few years. It is available at family history centres, the SoG and (that part covering Britain) at the FRC, TNA, Guildhall Library, some CROs and libraries. Many family history societies also hold copies of part of the IGI. The most recent microfiche edition of the IGI (of 1992) includes about 187 million entries, of which about 58 million entries are for England and Wales. It was substantially expanded compared to the previous edition (1988). However, some entries contained in the 1988 edition of the IGI were not included in the 1992 edition because the Mormon ceremonies in respect of those names had not been completed. If possible, you should therefore check both the 1988 and 1992 editions. Illustration 37 shows a page from the 1992 edition of the IGI.

The IGI is also available as part of *FamilySearch*, accessed from any computer on the *FamilySearch* web site or as a CD-ROM, which can be consulted at the SoG, FRC and LDS family history centres. The IGI included in *FamilySearch* is in two parts. First, there is a 1993 edition of the IGI (not available on fiche). This includes about 14 million entries (from around the world) that do not appear in the 1992 microfiche edition. There is also an IGI addendum (version 4) issued in 2000 that includes a further 120 million entries. In addition to the IGI, *FamilySearch* includes *Ancestral File* (considered below), the LDS Family History Library catalogue, the 1881 census index, an index to Scottish parish registers (# chapter 29), the Canadian 1881 census index and US census, death and military indexes (# chapter 30).

The majority of information in earlier editions of the IGI was extracted from sources such as parish registers, but there was a major change in 1992. More reliance was placed on information that was deposited with the LDS (known as compiled records) consisting of LDS members' recollections of their relatives, or information from family bibles, letters and other documents. More care must therefore be taken when using the IGI as an introduction to parish registers since an entry that you find may not have been taken from a register. More information about the entries for compiled records (mostly noted in the IGI as "pre-1970") is provided by E.L. Nichols in *Genealogists' Magazine* (September and December 1993).

Many parishes are not covered by the IGI and the coverage of different counties varies considerably. For example, the 1988 edition of the IGI included baptisms from about 100 of the 482 parishes of Somerset and about 150 of the 509 parishes of Suffolk. Furthermore, only some years of a parish register may be included. You can check whether a parish may be covered by

EAGLE, JOSEPH JA

COUNTRY: ENGLAND   COUNTY: LONDON

PAGE 46,921

AS OF MAR 1992

NAME	FATHER / MOTHER or SPOUSE or RELATIVE	T/C	EVENT DATE	TOWN, PARISH
EAGLE, JOSEPH JAMES		M C	23OCT1808	SHOREDITCH, SAINT LEONARDS
EAGLES, JOSEPH JAMES	JAMES EAGLES/SUSANNA	M C	11NOV1855	NOTTING HILL, SAINT JOHN THE EVANGELIST
EAGLE, JOSEPH JAMES ROYALE	JAMES EAGLE/SARAH ANN	M C	15AUG1802	LONDON, SAINT LEONARD EASTCHEAP
EAGLE, JOSEPH JOHN BARTHOLOMEW	JOSEPH EAGLE/MERCY	M C	24APR1803	WANDSWORTH, ALL SAINTS
EAGLE, JOSEPH WILLIAM	WILLIAM EAGLE/HANNAH	M C	07MAY1609	LONDON, SAINT DIONIS BACKCHURCH
EAGLES, JOYCE	JOHN NESTONE	F C	07MAY1609	LONDON, SAINT DIONIS BACKCHURCH
EAGLE, KATH.	THO. EAGLE	F C	31JUL1612	LONDON, SAINT GILES CRIPPLEGATE
EGLES, KATHERIN	THOMAS LEESE	W M	24JUN1594	LONDON, SAINT MARY MOUNTHAW
EAGLE, LOUISA	FRANCIS EAGLE/MARY	F C	28DEC1806	SHOREDITCH, SAINT LEONARDS
EAGLES, LOUISA	JAMES BUSBY	W M	29JAN1821	WESTMINSTER, SAINT JAMES
EAGLE, LOUISA	JOHN EAGLE/LOUISA	F C	13APR1856	SHOREDITCH, SAINT LEONARDS
EAGLE, LOUISA EMILY	ELIJAH EAGLE/LOUISA SUSANNA WHITE	F B	25JUL1872	ISLINGTON, 13 DEVONSHIRE ST.
EAGLE, LOUISA EMILY	ELIJAH EAGLE/LOUISA SUSANNA	W M	20JUL1897	CAMBERWELL
EAGLES, LOUISA SUSANNAH	PHILIP EDWARD FALKNER	F C	06FEB1832	SHOREDITCH, SAINT LEONARDS
EAGLE, LUCY	JOSEPH JAMES EAGLES/LOUISA	F C	03JUN1810	FINSBURY, SAINT LUKE OLD STREET
EAGLES, LUCY ANN.I	DANIEL EAGLE/LUCY	F C	12FEB1865	SHOREDITCH, SAINT LEONARDS
EAGLE, LYDIA	JOSEPH EAGLES/ELIZABETH ANN	F C	27JUL1838	CHELSEA, SAINT LUKE
EAGLES, MARGARET	WILLIAM EAGLE/SARAH	F C	01JUL1618	WESTMINSTER, SAINT MARGARET
EAGLES, MARGARET	JOHN FRYE	W M	01JUL1618	WESTMINSTER, SAINT MARGARET
EAGLE, MARGARET a	JAMES NITINGALE	U M	25JAN1670	LONDON, SAINT KATHERINE BY THE TOWER
EAGLE, MARGARET	WILLIAM EAGLE/MARGARET	F C	24AUG1806	SOUTHWARK, SAINT SAVIOUR
EGLESE, MARGARET	EDWARD EGL'SE/JANE	F C	17JUN1827	SHORDITCH, SAINT LEONARDS
EGLES, MARGARETT	WILLIAM DRURY	U M	27NOV1705	LONDON, SAINT KATHERINE BY THE TOWER
EGLES, MARGERY	JOHN GRIFFIN	U M	07OCT1591	WESTMINSTER, SAINT CLEMENT DANES
EAGLE, MARIA	WILLIAM EAGLE/MARIA	F C	31MAR1802	SOUTHWARK, SAINT SAVIOUR
EAGLE, MARIA	SAMUEL BENJAMIN HOLMES	U M	12AUG1832	SHOREDITCH, SAINT LEONARDS
EAGLES, MARIA	EDWARD EAGLES/MARY	F C	19JUN1836	BETHNAL GREEN, SAINT MATTHEW
EAGLE, MARIA	BENJAMIN EAGLES/MARIA	F C	09DEC1849	BATTERSEA, SAINT MARY
EGLES, MARIA	JAMES COOLEY	W M	09JAN1882	ISLEWORTH
EAGLES, MARIA ANN	CHARLES EAGLES/SARAH	F C	29APR1827	LONDON, ST. BOTOLPH WI
EAGLES, MARIA ANN	MICHAEL KEILY	U M	1849	OF
EAGLES, MARIA ELIZABETH	WILLIAM EAGLES/MARY NIGHTINGALE	F C	13MAY1866	LONDON, SAINT STEPHAN
EAGLES, MARIE	SAMUEL EAGLE/MARTHE	F C	24DEC1257	SPITALFIELD DE LA PATENT FRENCH HUGUENOT
EAGLE, MARKE	ANN BRIGGS	H M	18NOV1658	STEPNEY, ST. DUNSTANS
EAGLES, MARY	EAGLES/	F C	09OCT1587	LONDON, SAINT BOTOLPH
EAGLES, MARY	THOMAS EAGLES/	F C	30JAN1594	LONDON, SAINT MARY WOOLNOTH
EAGLES, MARY	THOMAS EAGLES/	F C	25SEP1596	LONDON, ST. BENET FINK
EAGLES, MARY	THEODORE EAGLES/	F C	03JUL1617	WESTMINSTER, SAINT MARGARET
EAGLES, MARY	THOMAS EAGLES/	F C	AUG1625	WESTMINSTER, SAINT MARGARET

F.: MULT CHRISTENING   B: BIRTH   C: CHRISTENING
B: BIRTH OR CHRISTENING   F: FIRST KNOWN CHILD
A.: BIRTH   M.: MARRIAGE   D.: DEATH OR BURIAL   N.: CENSUS   W: WILL

A= ENTRY ALTERED FROM SOURCE; #,3,>=RELATIVES NAMED IN SOURCE. SEE "SYMBOLS" IN INSTRUCTIONS.

37. A page from the IGI, London and Middlesex page 46,921 (Church of Jesus Christ of Latter-Day Saints)

the IGI (and if so, for what periods) by consulting the *Parish and Vital Records List* (*PVRL*), last published in January 1994, which appears on a series of fiche with the IGI. The *PVRL* is divided into sections for each country (those for England and Wales are divided into county sections). For each county, there is a list of the registers (and the approximate periods) which have been filmed by the LDS as part of their extraction programme. For each record listed in the *PVRL*, there are also "printout", "project" and "source" numbers which can be used to order computer printouts or microfilm copies of the material, for example, a transcript of the baptisms extracted from a particular parish register. Full details of this system are provided in the introduction of the *PVRL*.

Unfortunately, it is unclear which parish registers (and for what years) are actually indexed in the IGI. The parish listings in the *PVRL* include records that have been filmed by the LDS but only parts of those may have been included in the IGI. The Family History Library catalogue included in *FamilySearch* also has parish listings but again these are of LDS films and not necessarily what has been indexed in the IGI. Therefore, having used the IGI, you cannot be certain what parish registers (or years) you have searched or what registers (or years) you still need to search. Because of the uncertainty as to the IGI's content, recent volumes of the *NIPR* omit any reference to a particular parish being included in the IGI.

An original parish register may also not have been the source used for the IGI. The source may have been the bishop's transcripts or a published copy of a register. Most published registers do not include entries after 1812 or 1837, and many are incomplete for earlier years. If you find that the IGI records a family in one parish for many years after, for example, 1732, but that it has no entries for the family (in that parish) before that date, it may be because the earlier period was not included in the source that is indexed in the IGI. Similarly, if you search the IGI for a baptism of a John Garner in a certain parish in about 1812, and find only one (in 1811), you must not assume that it is the correct baptism. The IGI may only contain baptisms in that parish up to 1812. The parish register may have recorded another John Garner being baptised in 1813, which is not included in the IGI. A few researchers, not realising the limitations of the IGI, find an entry in it and decide that it must be their ancestor because it is the only likely entry. This is rather foolish. The IGI contains less than half of the parish register entries of baptisms and marriages in England and Wales up to 1837 and in some counties the percentage is as low as 10% or 20%. For some counties, the coverage of parish register entries is much better in certain county indexes noted below.

ENTRIES IN THE IGI

The IGI can be used on microfiche, CD-ROM or the Internet. The fiche version has fewer entries but it has some advantages. You can scan many pages to consider spelling variations or to spot families in other parishes. Using the fiche version also gives you a clear understanding of the entries and the way in which the index operates which, in turn, will help you use the CD-ROM or Internet versions more effectively.

The IGI is divided into series of microfiche for each country, each fiche containing entries for about 16,000 to 17,000 people. The indexes for England and Scotland are divided between each pre-1974 county. The series of fiche for Wales includes Monmouthshire. Because of the Welsh system of names (such as Owen ap Evan being a son of Evan ap Madoc), there are two indexes, each divided into pre-1974 counties, one listing entries by surname, and the other listing entries by forename or "given name" (# chapter 29). The IGI also includes separate fiche for each of Ireland, the Channel Islands and the Isle of Man (and two fiche for "Great Britain", one for "Births at Sea" and 27 fiche headed "England/County Unknown").

The format of the microfiche version of the IGI can be seen from illustration 37. The entries for each English or Scottish county are in alphabetical order by surname (including some variations, so that Eagle and Eagles are intermixed) and then by Christian name of the person who was baptised or married. A marriage is indexed under both spouses' names. Entries for people with the same name are listed in chronological order (whether the event was a baptism or marriage and whichever parish the events took place in). In each county section, the first few entries are those where only Christian names, not surnames, are known; for example recording that Agnes, a child of John and Mary, was baptised in 1659. The IGI usually indexes names as they were spelt in the parish register or other source. Therefore, an entry will be in the IGI under the Latin form of the name if this is how it appears in a register. If the name was abbreviated in the source (eg. Wm for William or Thos for Thomas) the IGI lists the entry under Wm or Thos respectively. If you are searching for William Keates, entries for both William and Wm must therefore be checked.

Each fiche of the index includes about 460 pages (and each page has up to 60 entries of baptisms, marriages or other events). Illustration 37 is page 46,921 for England (from the London and Middlesex section) of the 1992 edition. The first entry is the baptism of my ancestor Joseph James Eagles. The name of the person indexed is followed by the names of the parents (in the case of a baptism) or the spouse (in the case of a marriage). Joseph's parents are recorded as James and Susanna Eagles. The next column indicates the sex of the child who was baptised or the person getting married and the next column indicates the type of event. Most entries are indicated as C (christening) or M (marriage), but you will also find B (birth), A (adult christening) and certain other codes (noted at the bottom of each page of the IGI). Although marriages are indicated in the IGI by an M, the same couple may be recorded in another event of the same date and noted as S (spouse). This is usually because the same marriage was extracted twice, once from a parish register and once from a series of transcripts (such as Phillimore's marriages). The next two columns in the IGI specify the date of the event and the name of the parish (or non-conformist chapel) in which the event took place. If a year is given in the form "<1800>" in the date column, that means that it is an estimate. Dates up to 1752 have been converted into new style in the IGI, so that a baptism dated 1 February 1712 in the IGI will be found in an original register at 1 February 1711.

Some IGI entries merely record an unspecified relationship between two people and a year. In these cases, the indexed names are marked by a sign "a" (indicating "relative"). An entry marked with the sign ">" indicates that more information about the person or his family is available (to direct descendants) by contacting Special Services, Temple Department, 50 East North Temple Street, Salt Lake City, Utah, USA. The symbol "#" indicates that the original record lists other relatives (such as a marriage entry naming parents of a spouse). Another note that appears in the IGI is "infant", which means that the indexer believed that the baptised child also died as an infant.

There are five further columns of information in the IGI. Three columns, headed B, E and S respectively, record the dates of Mormon ceremonies. The final two columns note the batch or film number and the serial sheet number, which direct you to the source material held by the LDS, which can be ordered and viewed at family history centres. Most input to the IGI was obtained from indexing projects (such as lists of all baptisms from a parish register) and the batch numbers for these extracted records generally start with C, E, J, K, M and P or 725, 744, 745 or 754. Some information (family group records) was provided by individuals who had undertaken genealogical research. The batch numbers for these generally start with F, or do not include any letters but do include 0, 1, 2 or 3 as the third digit. Any information from family group records should of course be corroborated by your own research in other sources.

The IGI is a finding aid and is not meant to replace use of the original sources. It is essential to check IGI entries against parish registers. You may think that you have found an ancestor's baptism in the IGI, but the parish register (or the register of a nearby parish) may reveal that he or she was buried as a child. The IGI may contain transcription errors, or a parish register may contain extra information such as occupations or dates of birth. The IGI includes the baptism of one of my ancestors in Sandford, Devon, by this entry:

Betsy Hodge. Richard Hodge/Grace F[emale] C[hristening] 25 Dec 1832

but the Sandford parish register also discloses her date of birth and her father's occupation:

Born November 3rd 1832, baptised December 25th 1832; Betsy, daughter of Richard and Grace Hodge. Sandford. Labourer.

In marriage entries, if one of the spouses was from another parish, the name of that parish may be recorded in the parish register but not in the IGI. The parish register may also name the witnesses and state whether a marriage was by licence or after banns, whereas the IGI does not do so. For example the IGI contained this entry:

Richard Hodge Elizabeth Daw M[arriage] Sandford 8 July 1834

The Sandford register showed that Richard was from Bampton and the marriage was by licence:

Richard Hodge of Bampton parish [and] Elizabeth Daw spinster by licence, 8th July 1834 . . . witnesses Wm. Partridge: Elizabeth Hodge

A parish register may give other clues as to someone's origin. My ancestors Isaac Stanlake and Susanna Bulleid married in Winkleigh in 1795. The IGI included the 1768 baptism in Winkleigh of an Isaac Stanlake. I believed that this might be my ancestor. The entry was:

March 7th : Isaac, son of Robert and Grace Stanlake

The IGI did not include the marriage of Robert and Grace. Fortunately, the entry in the Winkleigh parish register for the 1763 baptism of Isaac's elder brother was more informative:

July 5th : Robert, son of Robert and Grace Stanlake of Ashreigney

The words "of Ashreigney" did not appear in the IGI entry for Robert's baptism, nor did the IGI include entries from the register of that neighbouring parish of Ashreigney. I turned to the

Ashreigney register and found the marriage of Robert Stanlake and Grace Isaac in 1758. However, I also found the burial in Ashreigney (in June 1771) of the Isaac who had been baptised in Winkleigh in 1768. He could not have been my ancestor, but the Ashreigney register also contained the baptism of another child of Robert and Grace named Isaac, in October 1771, who appeared to be my ancestor. None of this would have been possible using only the IGI.

The IGI is most helpful in locating families that moved between counties or between different parishes as shown by the following example. The census records for Wapping in London included my g.g. grandfather John Josiah Keates, his younger brothers and sisters, and their parents George and Ann Keates. John Josiah was recorded as born in about 1835 in Rotherhithe. The birth certificates of his younger brothers and sisters recorded the mother's maiden name as Ann Leaver. The parish registers of St Mary Rotherhithe recorded baptisms of many Keates children but there was no record of John Josiah's baptism, or the marriage of his parents. The IGI recorded the marriage of George Keates and Ann Leaver in 1834 at St James Bermondsey, only a short distance from Rotherhithe, and the baptism of John Josiah Keates on 25 September 1836 at an Independent Chapel in Old Gravel Lane, St George in the East. Without the IGI, the search for John Josiah's baptism would have been extremely difficult because of the enormous number of parishes and non-conformist chapels in London.

Microfiche copies of the 1992 IGI can be purchased by the public. This is extremely useful if you have many ancestors in one county, if you live far from a library holding the IGI and if you own or have access to a microfiche reader. The cost works out to only about 10 pence per fiche. Free copies of the *PVRL* are also provided. Orders must be sent to the Family History Department in Utah. Forms can be obtained from the LDS Distribution Centre in Birmingham (# chapter 6). These note the number of fiche for each county (or country) and the cost.

We can now turn to the version of the IGI that appears on the *FamilySearch* CD-ROM. The information for each entry in this version of the IGI is the same as in the microfiche version. The CD-ROM version allows the information to be read on-screen, sorted into different orders, printed out in hard copy or copied on to your own computer disks for later use.

Nichols (167) and Hawgood (163) are detailed booklets on how to use the IGI on CD-ROM (and the other material on *FamilySearch*), with many illustrations of what appears on the computer screen and how to use the commands and functions to find or sort relevant information. Searching the IGI on disk is easy. You insert the disks for the IGI or for the addendum into the computer. You then choose the region (for example "British Isles") in which you wish to search. You then choose the type of search that you wish to make. You can search for an individual's birth, baptism or marriage or for the children of named persons (a parent search, described below). You type in a person's surname and have the option to add a forename and start date (for example for entries after 1750) to the search request. You can add further filters to narrow down the search, for example a search in only one or more counties. You can search for entries by exact spellings of names or use the similar spelling retrieval option (which retrieves those similar surnames, such as Eagle and Eagles, that are mixed together in the microfiche version). However, you may still have to search for other variations (as you would search other surnames on the fiche) to ensure that all possibilities are covered. The CD-ROM version of the IGI retrieves similar and abbreviated Christian names. Thus a search for William Smith also retrieves entries for Wm Smith, Willm Smith and Will Smith. Entries are not sorted by middle Christian names; thus an entry for John Robert Hodge would not be retrieved by searching for Robert Hodge. The search results brought up on screen consist of a list with the full name of each person, the type of event (for example baptism or marriage), the place, the year and the name of one relative (usually the father, mother or spouse). You can highlight an entry of interest, press "enter", and the full IGI entry appears on screen. Pressing "enter" again brings up the LDS microfilm and source details. You can obtain a description of those source documents (for example an original parish register or a published or unpublished transcript) from the Family History Library catalogue that is included on the *FamilySearch* CD-ROM. You can then order the microfilm of the source at family history centres.

A parent search is very similar and a great help if your ancestors' children were baptised in different places. It is much quicker than scanning the microfiche version for any children with parents of particular names. You type in the name of one or both parents, for example requesting a search for all children of John and Mary Harvey baptised in England (or restrict the search to one or more counties). The entries produced by the search will be for the children of all couples of that name and not just your ancestors and so the results of this type of search must be used with caution.

Entries found as a result of searches can be printed out or copied into other computer files. Downloading and editing data from the CD-ROM version of the IGI is described in great detail in Hawgood (163) and an article "Downloading, Editing and Using Data from the IGI on CD-ROM" (and a supplemental item) in *Essex Family Historian* (221) of May 1994 and August 1995. The author, Mr Goring, explains how he transferred 4,700 IGI entries on to disks for his one-name study. He could then review, sort and analyse the information at leisure.

FamilySearch also includes *Ancestral File*, an LDS database of over 40 million entries from pedigrees submitted by researchers. You select the surname that interests you (and add forenames and approximate birth dates if you wish). The search produces a list of persons on the database of that name, with their country (or US state) of birth and the name of a relative (for example a father or spouse). You can then request the display of a pedigree or family group of anyone of interest and then either print the information or copy it to a disk for loading into your own computer.

The IGI and *Ancestral File* can also be accessed on the *FamilySearch* web site. Using *FamilySearch* online is similar to using the CD-ROM. You can choose the "ancestor search" (a search of both the IGI and *Ancestral File*) or a "custom search" (the IGI only). The two search pages are very similar, illustration 38 is that for the custom search. For either search, you can type in the surname of the person for whom you are searching and see what records are produced. You can also refine the search by adding a forename, the name of a spouse or one (or both) parents, the type of event, year, range of years, country or county. A list of matches is produced and you can then call up a person's individual record, which includes the full information from the IGI entry. An ancestor search for James Charnock produced 37 results. Illustration 39 is the first page of results, some from the IGI and some from *Ancestral File*, the fourth entry telling me that *Ancestral File* included a James Charnock of Leyland in Lancashire who was born or baptised in about 1553. Clicking on his name brought his individual record to the screen, noting his parents William Charnock and Elizabeth Cansfield. Clicking on the pedigree tab produced a brief pedigree of the family, and clicking on the family tab produced a list of 14 children of William and Elizabeth who had been located by the researcher who had submitted this pedigree. Hawgood (164) describes how to copy and edit such data.

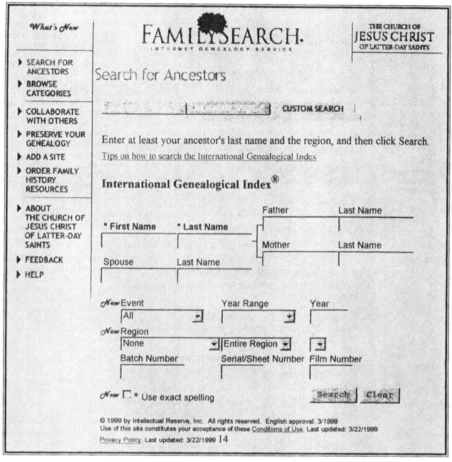

38. FamilySearch, *the search page for the IGI (Reprinted by permission. Copyright © 2000 by Intellectual Reserve, Inc.)*

THE BRITISH ISLES VITAL RECORDS INDEX

The LDS *Vital Records Index: British Isles* (BVRI) supplements the IGI. The second edition (of 2001) can be purchased on 16 CD-ROM from the LDS Distribution Centre. It can also be seen at family history centres, the SoG, FRC and many other archives and libraries. The BVRI is an index to about 10 million births or baptisms and two million marriages in the British Isles from 1538 to 1888, few of which appear in the IGI. They are principally from English, Welsh and Scottish parish registers, but also include extracts from the following records:

1. Irish civil registration indexes of births 1865–74 and Protestant marriages 1847–64,
2. Irish Quaker births and marriages 1850–75,
3. births noted in the Protestant Dissenters' Registry at Dr Williams' Library and the Wesleyan Methodist Registry (# chapter 13).

139

What's New

FAMILYSEARCH.
INTERNET GENEALOGY SERVICE

THE CHURCH OF
JESUS CHRIST
OF LATTER-DAY SAINTS

- SEARCH FOR ANCESTORS
- BROWSE CATEGORIES
- COLLABORATE WITH OTHERS
- PRESERVE YOUR GENEALOGY
- ADD A SITE
- ORDER FAMILY HISTORY RESOURCES
- ABOUT THE CHURCH OF JESUS CHRIST OF LATTER-DAY SAINTS
- FEEDBACK
- HELP

Search for Ancestors

You searched for: James Charnock   [refine search]
Exact Spelling: Off

Results: All Sources (37 matches)

1. James CHARNOCK - Ancestral File
Gender: M Birth/Christening: 1845 Wheeling, , Virginia

2. James CHARNOCK - Ancestral File
Gender: M Birth/Christening: 1785 <Elswick>

3. James CHARNOCK - Ancestral File
Gender: M Birth/Christening: 1702

4. James CHARNOCK - Ancestral File
Gender: M Birth/Christening: Abt 1553 Of Leyland, Lancashire, England

5. James Nixon CHARNOCK - Ancestral File
Gender: M Birth/Christening: 4 Jun 1824 Wheeling, Ohio, West Virginia

6. James CHARNOCK - Ancestral File
Gender: M Birth/Christening: Abt 1604 Fulwood, Preston, Lancashire, England

7. James CHARNACK - International Genealogical Index/BI
Gender: M Christening: 5 Nov 1771 Bradford, Yorkshire, England

8. James CHARNOCK - International Genealogical Index/BI
Gender: M Christening: 14 Oct 1806 Southworth Hall-Rc, Southworth, Lancashire, England

9. James CHARNOCK - International Genealogical Index/BI
Gender: M Birth: 6 Dec 1806 Ormskirk, Lancashire, England

10. James CHARNOCK - International Genealogical Index/BI
Gender: M Birth: 6 Dec 1806 Ormskirk, Lancashire, England

11. James Worrall CHARNOCK - International Genealogical Index/BI
Gender: M Christening: 31 Aug 1804 Wigan, Lancashire, England

12. James CHARNOCK - International Genealogical Index/BI
Gender: M Christening: 3 Mar 1837 Zion Methodist New Connexion, Ovenden, Yorkshire, England

Sources Searched
Matches were found only in the sources listed below. Click on a source to see more matches for that source.

- Ancestral File (6)
- IGI/British Isles (25+)
- IGI/North America (2)
- IGI/Southwest Pacific (1)
- IGI/World Misc. (3)

39. FamilySearch; using "Ancestor Search", the results of a search for James Charnock (Reprinted by permission. Copyright © 2000 by Intellectual Reserve, Inc.)

Unfortunately, as with the IGI, it is uncertain what parish registers (and for what years) are included in the BVRI. The disks include parish listings but these are lists of what has been filmed by the LDS, not necessarily what is included in the BVRI. For example, the list includes 16 Bedfordshire parishes but the notes to the BVRI say that extracts have only been taken from eight (unspecified) parishes. Despite this, the BVRI is a useful finding-aid. For example, it includes 677 marriages of people named Keates or Keats and 743 Charnock baptisms or births.

Searching the BVRI is easy. If you are using it on your own computer, you first load the viewing software (the Resource File Viewer) from a disk provided with the BVRI. You then insert the disk for the family name and the type of event that you wish to search (for example, disc one is for births and baptisms of people with surnames commencing with the letter A) and choose a baptism/birth search or a marriage search. You then type a person's surname and forename in boxes on the search request screen. You can choose to see entries with that exact spelling or with any names linked together (as in the IGI). A wild card "?" can be used instead of any one letter, so that your search covers name variations. The search can also be filtered by year (or range of years), country or by county. The search produces a list of people in the top part of the screen, with the year and type of event, the county in which it was recorded and the names of relatives (a father and mother or a spouse). Clicking an entry of interest produces the full index entry (in the same form as the IGI) in the lower part of the screen with the LDS microfilm and source details. Entries of interest can be printed out. Data can also be copied into other computer files and B. Tyrwhitt-Drake provides guidance on this in *Family Tree Magazine* (January 1999). You may also carry out a "parent search", by inserting the names of one or both parents. This produces entries for all children in the database with parents of those names.

As with the IGI and any other index, having found relevant entries, it is essential to turn to the original records in order to check the accuracy of the index and extract any further information that the original source may include.

If your ancestors moved between parishes, your first step should be to search in the registers of neighbouring parishes. The second option is to use the IGI and BVRI. However, these are not the only indexes of parish register entries. Some other indexes may also assist your search.

BOYD'S MARRIAGE INDEX

Percival Boyd compiled an index of marriage entries from many English parish registers. It is especially useful if a marriage did not take place in the parish (or county) in which you expect to find it. Parental disapproval or an obvious pregnancy often led to a marriage taking place elsewhere. The index includes only marriages, but it therefore supplements the IGI which concentrates on baptisms. The SoG holds the 534 original typescript volumes and the public may view them on microfilm. Much of the index is also included on the English Origins web site (see below). Guildhall Library holds a microfiche copy of the complete index and some other archives have copies of the sections covering their own counties. Boyd's index records the spouses' names, the name of the parish and the year of marriage. Marriages are indexed by the names of both the groom and bride (except as noted below) so you may search for either name. The index recorded the marriage in Brampton, Norfolk in 1802 of my ancestors Isaacher (or Issacher) Climpson and Mary Pinchen:

1802 Climpson, Issacher   Mary Pinchen   Brampton.

The index consists of three series. The main series is divided into sections for each of the 16 counties covered. The "first miscellaneous" and "second miscellaneous" series are not divided between counties. Each series (or each county within the main series) is then divided into sections, usually covering periods of 25 years. Some volumes are divided into separate lists of grooms and brides. The main and second miscellaneous series cover 1538 to 1837. The first miscellaneous series only covers 1538 to 1775. The section for 1701 to 1725 in this section only indexes grooms' names, while the section for 1726 to 1750 only indexes the grooms' names that commence with the letters A to M.

Some counties are not included in Boyd's index. For other counties, only certain parishes (or some registers of a parish) are included, but the index includes part of the registers of about 4,300 English parishes and it is estimated to contain about 7 million names, that is about 15 per cent of all English marriages from 1538 to 1837. Boyd also used some bishops' transcripts, banns registers and marriage licences (in the latter case, two parish names may be given since a licence may have named two churches in which the marriage could take place). A list of all the parishes (and dates of registers) included in the index is contained in an SoG booklet (150). This also includes lists for certain parts of the index (for Gloucestershire, Cambridgeshire and Oxfordshire) that were added after Boyd's death and lists for further separate indexes for Northumberland and Huntingdonshire. The SoG booklet also includes a useful section on the abbreviations used in Boyd's index for Christian names (such as Jas for James) and his method of indexing surnames. For example, surnames commencing with the letters Kn are indexed under N, those commencing Ph under F and those commencing Wr under R. Volumes of the *NIPR* (151) also note, for each parish, the years of marriage entries included by Boyd.

It is essential to check the original parish registers. Boyd only noted the year of marriage and the names of the parish and spouses, and more information is to be found in the registers. Furthermore, the sources used by Boyd were usually published transcripts of registers. Therefore, his index is sometimes two transcriptions away from an original register.

Most of Boyd's index has been added to the SoG material on the English Origins web site (# appendix XI) and the remainder of the index will be added soon. English Origins is a pay-per-view site (although SoG members have some free access time) which is described in chapter 11.

THE NATIONAL BURIAL INDEX

The National Burial Index for England and Wales has been created to complement the IGI and Boyd's marriage index. The FFHS has organised the project and family history societies contribute the entries. The index records burials from parish, nonconformist or cemetery registers and bishops' transcripts from the period 1538–2000. It includes the deceased's name and age (if recorded in the source material) and the date and place of burial as in the following examples:

29 Jul 1639	Mary CHARNOCKE	Beds	Eversholt, St John the Baptist
5 Dec 1847	James EAGLES [Age] 5	Worcs	Badsey, St James

The index is being made available to researchers on CD-ROM at regular intervals. The first edition (on two disks) was issued in 2001 and included 5.4 million entries, predominantly from

1813–37. It can be purchased from FFHS (Publications) Limited, 15/16 Chesham Industrial Centre, Bury, Lancashire BL9 6EN. The disks include a list of the places and years covered (and this information is included in recent volumes of the *NIPR*). There are some entries from over 4,400 English and Welsh parishes (of varying periods) but the coverage varies between areas of the country. There are only 1,030 entries from Dorset but over one million from Yorkshire. Entries are included from only four Welsh counties and there are no entries for Cornwall, Cumberland, Devon, Nottinghamshire, Sussex or Westmorland.

The disks are easy to use. One contains the installation program and burial entries of 1538–1825; the other contains burials of 1826–2000. Notes with the disks explain installation and search procedures. Searches for a particular forename and surname include alternative spellings regarded by the program as equivalent (a list of these is revealed by clicking the "variants list" button) or you can choose an "exact spellings only" search. Wild cards can also be used. A question mark in the name means any letter (thus "Her?er" would search for Herber, Herder, etc). An asterisk represents any number of letters (so that "Her*er" would also search for Herberger). The ambit of a search can be limited by specifying the county, place, year or years. Results of searches can be printed out or copied into other computer files.

As with any index, it is vital to look at the source material for any entry of interest since there may have been transcription errors. The original entry might also note further information, for example the cause of death or the deceased's occupation, residence or relationship to another named person.

COUNTY INDEXES

Many other indexes to parish registers have been compiled. They are usually county wide, but some indexes cover the registers of a particular city or part of a county. Many are incomplete in time periods and in the coverage of parishes. Marriage indexes are listed in Gibson & Hampson (141) and baptism and burial indexes are listed in Gibson & Hampson (158). Indexes are usually held by an FHS or by individual researchers (and only rarely by CROs), so you should write to the relevant FHS or individual for more information. A fee may be charged for searches in the indexes. One example is the Oxfordshire marriage index, which is complete for 1538 to 1837. A copy of this index is available on microfilm at the SoG. Herefordshire FHS has two marriage indexes, one for the period before 1754, containing over 47,000 marriages (that is over 95 per cent of marriages in surviving pre-1754 registers), and another for marriages from 1754 to 1837, which includes all marriages in the surviving registers of that period. The Surrey marriage index covers 1538 to 1837 for 139 of the 146 ancient parishes of Surrey (as well as records of a few churches founded after 1812) but can presently only be searched by the grooms' names. Devon FHS has marriage indexes which are complete for surviving Devon registers of 1754 to 1837. Buckinghamshire FHS has a database to all of the 171,000 marriages in Buckinghamshire parish registers of 1538–1837.

Cambridgeshire FHS has compiled a baptism index for 1801 to 1837, covering all surviving Cambridgeshire registers for that period. Gibson & Hampson (141) note other baptism indexes, for example for the city of Oxford 1800–1837. Cambridgeshire FHS has a county burial index for 1801 to 1837, with over 97,000 entries. Hampshire FHS has a complete burial index for 1813–37 (and the index back to 1538 already has 500,000 entries). Cornwall FHS has a complete burial index for Cornwall 1813–37. There are microfiche indexes, by Hanson & Stevens (159) and Webb (174), to over 115,000 burials in 97 City of London parishes from 1813 to about 1853. The Birmingham & Midland Society for Genealogy and Heraldry has an almost complete index for burials in Staffordshire from 1538 to 1837. Other burial indexes are listed in Gibson & Hampson (158). Some of these county indexes can be purchased. The Oxfordshire marriage index and the burial indexes for London by Hanson, Stevens and Webb are available on fiche. Cheshire FHS has released a CD-ROM containing the Bertram Merrell index of about 100,000 Cheshire marriages of 1750–1837 and the Hartley Jones index of marriages of 1580–1850 in 11 parishes in the Wirral. Other CD-ROM indexes include a Gloucestershire burial index for 1813–51 produced by Gloucestershire FHS, a Berkshire FHS index to 210,000 burials in Berkshire parish registers and an index to 100,000 Norfolk marriages between 1813 and 1837 that is available from Norfolk FHS. Bedfordshire FHS has published a surname index on CD-ROM to all the published transcripts of Bedfordshire registers up to 1812.

Boyd's index of deaths in London and Middlesex, known as *Boyd's London Burials*, indexes over 250,000 entries (but only of adult males) from burial registers of London churches and cemeteries from 1538 to 1853. The index is held at the SoG and a microfilm copy is at Guildhall Library. The index omits many parishes and periods of years, but you may be lucky and find relevant entries. The index entries are similar to those in Boyd's marriage index, that is usually the name, the year of burial and the parish, but sometimes also the age of the deceased.

THE FAMILY HISTORY ONLINE WEB SITE

The FFHS (# chapter 11) has launched an extensive "pay-per-view" web site, *FamilyHistoryOnline* (# appendix XI), which brings together indexes and transcription work of many of its member societies. The site includes census indexes and monumental inscriptions but the entries are predominantly from English and Welsh parish registers, including many entries from the National Burial Index. The name indexes can be consulted for free and then payment (a few pence per entry) is by pre-paid voucher or credit card. By September 2003, the site included 13.6 million records from 35 English or Welsh counties. The site's contents are listed on its introductory pages. Although there is, as yet, no material for some counties, others are strongly represented. For example, the Suffolk material includes two burial indexes (with over 630,000 entries), a baptism index (of over 130,000 entries) and a marriage index (of 23,500 entries).

THE PALLOT MARRIAGE AND BAPTISM INDEXES

The Pallot marriage index is a card index covering the period 1780 to 1837, with entries for about 1,800,000 spouses mainly from London and Middlesex parishes but also other counties. The index is stated to include 98 per cent of marriages in that period from 101 of the 103 parishes of the City of London. Most entries for areas outside London (including marriages from 159 parishes of Cornwall, 45 parishes of Bedfordshire and 22 Essex parishes) were taken from published copies of parish registers. There is also a Pallot baptism index, but much of it was destroyed by fire and only about 200,000 entries survive. The Pallot indexes were started in 1818 and therefore include some entries from a few parish registers that have since been lost or destroyed. For example, the marriage registers of Christchurch, Southwark, for 1671–1792 were destroyed during the Second World War, but the entries from 1781 onwards are included in the Pallot marriage index. The indexes are owned by Achievements Limited (at the same address as

IHGS) and searches are undertaken for a fee. The *Phillimore Atlas* (165) lists the parishes and dates covered by the index, but a more detailed guide can be obtained from Achievements.

The two indexes are also available on CD-ROM from Ancestry.com and on its subscription web site (# appendix XI). Entries for marriages note the names of the bride and groom, the year of marriage and the parish. Baptism entries note the name of the child (or adult) baptised, the names of the parents, the parish and the year. Each entry in these indexes has a hyperlink to an image (on the Ancestry.com web site) of the original index card, which often includes more information than the index, for example the names of witnesses. Some of the writing on the card images is very difficult or impossible to read. This may explain why many index entries on the disks appear to have been typed incorrectly. For example, the marriage index disk includes surnames such as Eaeds, Wsaver, Kinght, Llanos and Chwichill, or incomplete names (such as "Bu---age"). Despite the errors, the CD-ROM and online indexes are a useful finding aid.

BOYD'S INHABITANTS OF LONDON

Boyd's *Inhabitants of London* (or *Citizens of London*) consists of 238 volumes that record the families of about 60,000 London residents from the 15th to 19th centuries (particularly the 17th century). These volumes are indexed in 27 further volumes. The original volumes are held by the SoG, and there is also a microfilm copy of the indexes at Guildhall Library. Boyd attempted to include, for each person in the index, a date of baptism (or birth) and burial (or death), parentage, livery company (# chapter 22) and details of any marriage and children. For example, the index contains six entries for the surname Eagles, including:

1636 & 1658 Edw(ard)   [Livery Company]   Coop(er)   Mary Powell 27876

Entry 27876 includes detailed information on Edward Eagles, his admission to the Coopers' Company, his marriage in 1636 to Mary Powell, his burial in 1658 and his will, which referred to his wife, his mother, six brothers and sisters, three brothers-in-law and a niece.

ELUSIVE ENTRIES

Many published studies suggest that parochial registration was relatively accurate in the early 18th century, less accurate from about 1780, virtually collapsed from about 1795 to 1820, but then improved. Finlay believes that this view is in need of revision. Registration of burials was relatively effective. Studies in particular parishes also suggest a high level of registration of baptisms. A study of the parish register and 1851 census of Colyton in Devon shows that 79.1 per cent of the residents who claimed to have been born in Colyton were recorded as baptised in the parish church, 6.3 per cent were recorded in Colyton's non-conformist registers and 7.5 per cent were recorded as baptised in the registers of neighbouring parishes. Only 7.2 per cent of residents claiming a Colyton birthplace could not be traced and this might have been due to people not knowing their true place of birth rather than omissions from the parish register.

However, entries that you expect to see may not appear in parish registers, or at least in the register for the parish where you expect it to be. There are several reasons for this. For example, you may find a marriage of ancestors in one parish, and then only find the baptisms of the second and later children of the couple. It was very common for a mother to return to her parents' home (in a nearby parish) for the birth of at least the first child, who was then baptised in that parish. Alternatively, a man from one parish might marry and live for a time in his bride's parish and the first children might be baptised there. The family then later returned to reside (and later children would be baptised) in the father's parish. In these cases, the IGI, county indexes or searches of the records of neighbouring parishes, may solve the problem.

There are many other reasons for entries to be missing from parish registers. Entries were sometimes originally noted in rough books and then copied into the registers. Errors or omissions occurred during this copying. Some rough books survive for a few parishes and are held by CROs. They may be more accurate than the parish register. Entries were sometimes made on loose sheets of paper and only later bound together. You should look for gaps in the dates noted in the register, since such gaps may indicate that pages are missing from the register. If an incumbent made notes of baptisms (especially when visiting homes for private baptisms) with the intention of writing them up later in the register, the loss of one or more slips of paper could mean that a register entry was never made. The incumbent may have only made entries in the register once a week, and forgotten some of the baptisms or burials that he had conducted (particularly if he was elderly). Many entries might be omitted if an incumbent died without writing up the register (especially if a new incumbent did not arrive for some time). The neighbouring parish incumbent, who possibly conducted burials in the meantime, might not have bothered to make entries. A clergyman might also have recorded an event incorrectly, noting a mother's name as Mary rather than Margaret.

One reason for missing entries, especially baptisms, was the Stamp Duty Act of 1783, which levied duty of 3d. until 1794 on each parish register entry of baptism, marriage or burial. Paupers were exempt and so it is possible that, to avoid paying the duty, the number of people who declared themselves to be paupers rose substantially and many clergymen (resenting having to act as tax collectors) were willing to incorrectly record parents as paupers. Many parents also avoided payment by not baptising their children. From 1783 to 1794 the note P against an entry in the register denotes a pauper, whilst the note Pd 3d denotes payment of the duty. If you cannot locate an ancestor's baptism in the period 1783 to 1794, it is worth reviewing the registers after 1794 in case the child was only baptised after the tax was withdrawn. A similar statute of 1695 had a similar effect on the recording of baptisms, marriages and burials until it was repealed in 1706. That act is considered further in chapter 23 because it resulted in other useful documents being produced. However, you should review registers for the period after 1706 if you cannot find a baptism that you expect to find between 1695 and 1706.

Marriages were generally well recorded but can be difficult to find. Irregular and clandestine marriages are considered further in chapter 14, but records of marriages can be elusive for another reason. In the 17th and 18th centuries the average ages at which men and women married were about 26 and 24 respectively. However, when searching for a marriage, you should remember that it was legal until 1929 for boys to marry at 14 and girls as young as 12. Marriages at such low ages were rare but they may appear in your family tree.

Most burials were recorded, except during some epidemics or if a clergyman was too ill to preside over a burial, in which case the burial would go ahead and possibly be unrecorded. Most corpses were buried where the death took place and so you may find it difficult to trace the burial of an ancestor who was a soldier or sailor or who travelled around the country and died while away from home. Certain people could not, in theory, be buried in the parish churchyard (and so would not appear in a burial register); these included heretics, suicides, people who had not been baptised and those who had been excommunicated. However, many exceptions were made, especially by tolerant incumbents who were willing to turn a blind eye. Tate (532) notes some examples, such as the case of Andreas Symock, buried in Somerset, in respect of whom the incumbent wrote (in Latin): "This excommunicate was buried in the northern corner of the churchyard, but by what person or persons I know not."

CHURCH OF ENGLAND NON-PAROCHIAL REGISTERS

Baptisms, marriages and burials conducted by clergymen of the established church did not always take place in parish churches. From the 16th century these events could be recorded in non-parochial registers, such as those of cathedrals, workhouses, the Inns of Court or hospitals (such as the Royal Hospital at Chelsea). The term "non-parochial" also applies to records of Anglican communities abroad (# chapter 30). The term is sometimes applied to religious bodies outside the Church of England. However, these are more properly designated as non-conformist and are dealt with in chapter 13, together with Catholics, Jews and the foreign churches that became established in England.

You can ascertain what non-parochial registers have survived (and where they are held) from the *NIPR* (151), similar published works, or CRO catalogues. For example, Guildhall Library holds the registers of St Paul's Cathedral, Bridewell Chapel, the Royal Hospital of St Katherine by the Tower, Aske's Hospital Chapel (in Hoxton) and Geffery's Almshouses Chapel in Hackney. LMA holds a register of the Middlesex Hospital. Many non-parochial registers were surrendered to the Registrar General and are now held by TNA at the FRC (with non-conformist registers in series RG 4 to RG 8 – see chapter 13). These include:

a. registers of the Rolls Chapel, Chancery Lane (1736–1892)
b. registers of the Dockyard Church, Sheerness, Kent (1688–1960)
c. birth, marriage and death registers of Greenwich Hospital (1705–1864)
d. Chelsea Royal Hospital registers from 1691 (to 1812 for baptisms, 1765 for marriages and 1856 for burials)
e. baptism and burial registers of the Foundling Hospital, London (1741–1838)
f. baptism registers of the British Lying-In Hospital, Holborn, London (1749–1830)
g. Westminster Penitentiary registers of baptisms (1816–71) and burials (1817–53)
h. the Fleet marriage registers (# chapter 14)

ELUSIVE MARRIAGES

It is particularly difficult to find marriages in the period 1780–1837. There are a number of reasons for this. People's mobility increased at this time. Depression in the earlier years of the period led to people migrating in order to find work. The wars with France (and the resulting economic resurgence) also led to increased industrialisation (and therefore more migration) and to movements of males serving in the armed forces.

My ancestor John Keates and a William Keates (who appeared to be his brother) each had children baptised at St Mary, Rotherhithe between 1799 and 1813. Both John and William worked in the shipyards as mast and block makers. John married Sarah Anderson at St Dunstan, Stepney, in 1796 (with William Keates as a witness). A child Sarah was born and the mother

Sarah was buried in 1799 in Rotherhithe. John then had four children between 1804 and 1811 (but all were baptised at Rotherhithe on two days in 1811). Their mother was named Catherine. William and Eleanor Keates had seven children baptised in Rotherhithe between 1800 and 1813, some on the same days as the baptisms of the children of John and Catherine. No marriages for John (to Catherine) or William (to Eleanor) appeared in the Rotherhithe registers.

Where should I search? Rotherhithe was in Surrey but is now in London. The next parish to the east was Deptford in Kent. Just across the Thames lay Wapping, Poplar, Stepney and Limehouse in Middlesex. It was only a few miles to the City of London and much of Essex. I tried the IGI and Boyd's marriage index for London and Middlesex, Surrey, Kent and Essex, with no success. I then started searching the IGI and Boyd's index for other counties, especially those with large ports or dockyards. Finding nothing, I started searching registers of the parishes that were close to Rotherhithe (particularly those not covered by the IGI or Boyd's marriage index) such as Bermondsey, Deptford and (across the river) Wapping, Limehouse and Stepney. I also tried the Pallot index and the county marriage indexes for Essex, West Kent and Surrey, again without success. However, reviewing the lists of parishes covered by the indexes, I could now list those parishes near Rotherhithe that were not covered by any of these indexes. It was still a large number, but searching these registers was a practical task. If the marriages took place, they were most likely to have been celebrated in the following years: John and Catherine between 1799 and 1811 (the year when their four children were baptised), and William and Eleanor between 1795 and 1803 (when their second son was baptised). I started with the remaining seven Surrey parish registers at LMA. In the register of St Mary, Lambeth, I found the marriage in April 1799 of William Keates and Eleanor Hemersley. The signature of William was exactly the same as the signature of the William Keates who had been a witness in 1796 to the marriage of John Keates. I then started (and continue) to search the registers of parishes in the City of London, Middlesex, Essex and Kent that were not covered in the indexes. I also reviewed the BVRI and many indexes of marriage licences (# chapter 14).

I have still not found the marriage of John and Catherine Keates. It is possible that they never married. However, there are still a few registers of parishes in or around London that I have not reviewed. It is also possible that the marriage took place in a parish that I had already searched or which was covered by an index already consulted, but the entry had been missed, or mistranscribed by the indexer. The marriage could have taken place in another English county, but in a parish not covered by the IGI, the BVRI or Boyd. It could have taken place abroad – perhaps John Keates had (since it was wartime) temporarily worked in a shipyard abroad (such as Gibraltar) and met his bride Catherine there. There are a number of other possibilities and so my search continues.

CHAPTER 8

CHURCHYARDS AND CEMETERIES

Parish churches, churchyards and cemeteries are an important source for genealogists, because they contain memorials to our ancestors and relatives (and cemeteries' burial records provide similar information to parish burial registers). Wealthy people were often buried inside churches, or in the vaults, and were commemorated by memorials, such as sculptured effigies, monumental brasses and carved tombs. Other people were usually buried in churchyards (and later cemeteries) and their resting place was often recorded by an inscribed memorial. Few churchyard memorials were erected before the 17th century, and those that were tended to be made of wood and so have not survived. However, stone has generally been used for memorials since the late 17th century and many have survived, so that it is not uncommon to find headstones dating from the late 17th or early 18th centuries with legible inscriptions.

GRAVESTONES

Illustration 40 shows a gravestone in the churchyard at Lansallos, near Polperro in Cornwall. Most gravestones have a memorial inscription (often abbreviated as "MI") which usually records the name and age of the deceased and the date of death. The Lansallos stone records the death of two children of Reginold and Ann Barrett: William who died on 7 March 1793, aged only 17 days, and a daughter Jenny, who died on 5 August 1801 aged six. Similar gravestones should survive for your ancestors and their families. For example, the gravestone of my ancestor James Chapman, at Hainford in Norfolk, has the inscription:

In memory of James Chapman who died
3rd of August 1830 aged 77
Here the [illegible] cease from troubling,
the [illegible] at rest

The partly illegible inscription was actually from the book of Job:

40. A gravestone in Lansallos churchyard, Cornwall

> There the wicked cease from troubling;
> There the weary be at rest.

Memorial inscriptions may also note a deceased's occupation or place of origin or include information about other relatives, perhaps the names of husbands, wives or children. Inscriptions confirm family relationships and corroborate information obtained from civil registration certificates, census records and parish registers. They may reveal the married names of daughters or sisters of your ancestors and may record two, three or more generations of a family. The inscriptions from two adjacent headstones in the churchyard of St Michael & All Saints, Alphington, Devon are:

> (1) In loving memory of John Rice, died 6th June 1864 aged 60 years also
> Catherine Rice, wife of the above died 10th November 1886 and Eliza
> Blanchford daughter of the above died 2nd February 1906 aged 70
> (2) In loving memory of Walter Mortimer Rice who departed this life
> September 5th 1887 aged 21 years, also of John Rice father of the
> above died September 30th 1909 aged 69 years and of Sarah the
> beloved wife of John Rice died April 27th 1920.

The John Rice recorded in the second inscription was a son of the John and Catherine Rice commemorated in the first inscription. The two inscriptions therefore provide information about three generations, including the married name of a daughter of John and Catherine. A preliminary tree (subject to corroboration from other sources) would be:

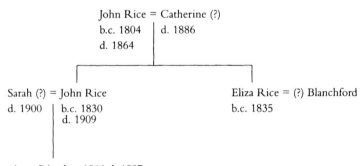

Unfortunately, many headstones (even from the 19th or 20th centuries) are now illegible and of course many families could not afford any monument in memory of those who died. Many corpses (particularly of paupers who were buried by a parish or poor law union) were placed in large common graves without any stone recording their names. Even if headstones were erected, they may no longer exist. At Topsham cemetery in Devon, I located the burial plot of some of my ancestors and relatives from the period 1850 to 1930, but the headstones had been removed and broken up. However, there were registers of burials (considered below).

The condition of churchyards and cemeteries varies enormously. Some churchyards have been carefully tended for centuries. The parish churchyard at Dunsford in Devon contains about 30 headstones relating to the Sercombe family and most of the stones were easy to read. Even if a churchyard is overgrown, such as the old churchyard at Hainford in Norfolk, many of the headstones may have survived and still be legible, as in the case of the 1830 headstone of my ancestor James Chapman. Sadly, however, many churchyards (especially in cities) have been built over or suffered from the effects of the weather, pollution and vandalism. For example, the churchyard of St Pancras Old Church in London contains only a few weather-beaten and generally illegible gravestones of the many that once stood around this important and ancient church. Therefore, even if you find your ancestors' burial ground, it may be difficult to find any memorials to them. A churchyard may be overgrown and the gravestones covered in ivy or lichen. The stonework may have crumbled, rendering the inscription illegible. Stones may have been moved (often repositioned around the churchyard wall or piled in corners of the churchyard) or removed from the churchyard altogether and broken up. The recording of memorial inscriptions has therefore always been very important.

Groups of volunteers, particularly family history societies and the Women's Institute, have transcribed the names, dates and ages from surviving headstones in many parish churchyards. The transcripts may be held either at the church itself, in FHS libraries, at CROs or at the SoG. The SoG has an enormous collection of MI transcripts, for example 28 volumes of Cornish MIs donated by Cornwall FHS and 20 volumes of Gloucestershire MIs from Gloucestershire FHS. The collection is listed in the SoG catalogue and, for each English county, in the SoG's *County Sources* booklets (# chapter 7). The collections relating to Wales, Scotland, Ireland, the Channel Islands and overseas are listed in the SoG catalogue or (as at 1997) in Collins & Morton (186). Many collections of MIs have been published, particularly by family history societies. These are listed in Raymond's county volumes of genealogical bibliographies, such as those for Devon (446) and Lancashire (447). One example includes the MIs (on microfiche) for St Helen & St Giles, Rainham and for St Mary & St Peter, Wennington in Essex, by East of London FHS (180). Another example is a booklet (179) by the RAF Swanton Morley FHS, of the MIs at St Margaret's, Worthing in Norfolk, containing not only transcripts of the inscriptions, but also sketches of the surviving gravestones. Earlier published collections of MIs are discussed below. There are also some county indexes of MIs, held by individuals or family history societies, listed in Gibson & Hampson (158). For example, Wiltshire FHS has produced a microfiche transcript of all surviving MIs in the county, and Gloucestershire FHS and Herefordshire FHS (which have ongoing projects to index all the MIs in those counties) have published indexes on CD-ROM to about 65,000 and 51,000 of them respectively. An increasing number of MI transcripts can be found on the Internet and the sites are listed in Raymond (196a). An important project, the National Index of Memorial Inscriptions (NAOMI), has also commenced. It is intended to record all surviving MIs, starting with Norfolk, and make them accessible on the Internet.

You must take great care with gravestones and transcripts (or indexes) of inscriptions. As time passes, the stones become more difficult to read. A recent transcript of the MIs at Sandford in Devon recorded that the inscription on a headstone for Daniel Hodge stated that he was aged 19 when he died. However, the parish registers, census returns and civil registration records showed, conclusively, that he was 39 when he died. The mistake in the transcript probably arose because the headstone was becoming illegible. The booklet *Rayment's Notes on Recording Monumental Inscriptions*, revised by Pattinson (196), describes how to decipher and record MIs, how to undertake surveys of burial grounds and produce records of the MIs and a plan of their location. White (200) also provides detailed guidance for recording MIs. If you are recording an inscription, you should note what you can from the stone, leave spaces for those parts you cannot read and identify (in your note) those parts of the inscription which are unclear. You should also photograph the church and any relevant gravestones to supplement your notes. Background information on the history of a church should also be obtained: booklets are available about most British churches and there are many books containing professional photographs of churches, such as Hibbert's (190) excellent work on London's churches.

If you find an ancestor's gravestone, you should make a careful search of the area around it for stones relating to other ancestors or relatives, since members of a family were often buried in the same plot in a churchyard (or perhaps in adjacent plots). You should treat the information on a headstone (especially ages) with some care. For example, a stone may refer to two or more people and it may only have been placed there on the death of the last person, perhaps many years after the death of the first person buried in the plot (by which time that person's age at death had been forgotten). A stone may also say "in loving memory of X" even though "X" was actually buried elsewhere, because some stones were intended to commemorate the deceased rather than mark the place of burial. In these cases, any information on a memorial as to the date, place or circumstances of death may be unreliable.

LOST MEMORIALS

Many burial grounds, especially in cities, were built over many years ago, but the memorial inscriptions may have survived. When permission was granted for the removal of stones, the local authority often made copies of the inscriptions, retained original transcripts and deposited copies with the Registrar General. Transcripts of inscriptions from about 170 of these burial grounds are now held at TNA in series RG 37. The burial grounds, the covering dates of the inscriptions and the piece numbers of the transcripts are listed in the series list for RG 37 and in articles by Watts & Watts in *Genealogists' Magazine* (September 1978 and June 1979).

Even if you have carefully searched a churchyard for memorials, it is always worth reviewing any surveys that have been made of that churchyard, even if they are quite recent. I carefully searched the churchyard at Hainford in Norfolk, but a transcript of MIs for Hainford, held at the SoG (with a plan showing the headstones' location) showed that either I had missed three important headstones, or that those MIs had become illegible (or that the stones had been removed) between the date of the survey and my visit. Since so many monuments have already been lost, it is fortunate that local historians and antiquaries have been recording MIs in churchyards for many years. Their published or manuscript works, some dating from the 18th century, are usually held in the SoG, CROs or libraries. In 1820 and 1821, the antiquary Sir Thomas Phillips directed his assistant to copy many epitaphs in Wiltshire churches and churchyards. The collection was published in 1822, has been reprinted in Sherlock (197) and includes hundreds of inscriptions that were subsequently destroyed. The work of many other antiquaries has been published, such as the collection of MIs by Cansick (182), recorded around 1870 from tombs and gravestones in Middlesex churchyards (such as St Pancras and Kentish Town) and also some MIs from Highgate cemetery. Many of the stones from which these inscriptions were taken no longer survive. Some of my ancestors lived at Hockliffe in Bedfordshire. Around 1900 an antiquary recorded MIs at many Bedfordshire churches and his manuscript notes are at the SoG. They include MIs for my ancestors Thomas and Elizabeth Gillman and their eldest son Michael. However, a further survey taken just after the Second World War did not include the MIs for Thomas or Elizabeth, no doubt because their memorials were by then illegible. The old survey was therefore the only remaining record of my ancestors' memorials.

Any local histories, particularly histories of your ancestors' church, should also be reviewed for any MIs, since some of these may have disappeared years ago and been omitted from recent surveys. For example, many epitaphs (principally from tombs of the gentry or famous people) appear in the volumes of *Magna Britannia* by Lysons, such as the two volumes for Devon (438) or in other county histories such as the three-volume history of Cheshire by Ormerod (195).

CHURCH INTERIORS

Memorials inside churches may be sculptured tombs, inscribed stones, brass memorials or plaques and are usually in better condition than the stones outside. These memorials usually commemorate local landowners, other families of wealth or note, or men who died in wars. You should remember to look for memorial stones in the church floor (now often covered by carpets). Cathedrals have an enormous number of memorials, either inside the cathedral, in chapels within the building, in adjacent burial grounds or in the cloisters.

Sculptured tombs, effigies and brass memorials survive from the middle ages and many were erected as late as the 19th century. They often feature the deceased's coat of arms (# chapter 26) and perhaps record other members of the deceased's family. Illustration 41 is an example of a brass memorial in the parish church of Chipping Campden. Brass memorials generally commemorate the wealthier classes: nobility, knights, other landowners, clergy and merchants. Chapman (183) is a good general description, and Macklin (194) is a more detailed study (both with many illustrations), of the types of memorial brasses that survive in cathedrals, churches and abbeys. Stephenson (198) is a detailed list of surviving monumental brasses, to which Giuseppi & Griffin (188) is a supplement. Brasses are listed by county and parish, with the names of those featured and a description of the brass. A typical entry from Bedfordshire is:

41. *Monumental brass in the parish church of Chipping Campden*

Husborne Crawley; John Carter, [died] 1600 aged 67 in civil dress and wife Agnes, dau. of Thos. Tayler of Lidlington, with two sons; John and Thos. and 6 daughters; Dorothy, Mary, Lucy, Penelope, Susan, Alice.

Thousands of surviving monumental brasses are also listed, by county and then church, in Le Strange (193) and Macklin (194). These works also list published county surveys and lists of surviving brasses. Works on brasses in a county, such as Stephenson (199) for Surrey or Davis (187) for Gloucestershire, are useful because they provide more illustrations and detailed information on the brasses and brief biographies of the people featured in them. The Monumental Brass Society has also published a number of volumes that list and describe surviving brasses, such as that for Bedfordshire by Lack, Stuchfield & Whittemore (192). Sadly, many thousands of brasses have been lost or destroyed and many have been moved into museums and private collections. Details of these may be found, as in the case of MIs, in older published local histories or in collections of antiquaries' papers at record offices. Brass rubbings, which appear in many collections, are copies of monumental brasses, usually made by rubbing a pencil over paper held over a brass. Clayton (184) is a detailed illustrated work on brass rubbings, listing the thousands in the collection at the Victoria & Albert Museum, featuring many brasses that have been lost since the brass rubbings were made.

FINDING YOUR ANCESTOR'S BURIAL GROUND

If a parish register records the burial of your ancestor in the churchyard, any surviving headstone should be in that churchyard. If your ancestor's burial does not appear in the parish register, you must find a record of the death or burial and find the church or cemetery in which the burial took place. A death certificate does not indicate the place or date of burial, but relatives may hold memorial and funeral cards, or burial plot deeds (discussed below). You should also ask relatives about the location of ancestors' graves. Photographs may include memorial inscriptions. I have a photograph of my great grandmother placing flowers on the grave of her daughter (my great aunt) Dorothy Law, who died in the flu epidemic of 1918. If relatives do not know where an ancestor was buried, you should search first in churchyards or cemeteries close to where he or she lived at the time of death. You should also check any cemeteries near to where your ancestor lived previously, since he or his parents may have purchased a burial plot at a cemetery near that home, then moved away from the area but may still have been buried in the plot. Searches should also be made at non-conformist burial grounds (# chapter 13). The records of many of these are at TNA or at CROs. For example, Bunhill Fields in London was established in 1665 and about 120,000 burials took place up to 1854. TNA holds its burial registers for 1713 to 1854 (in series RG 4 at the FRC) and Guildhall Library holds some records of MIs.

CEMETERIES

By the early 19th century many parish churchyards, especially in London and other cities, were already full (and a health hazard). Private companies were therefore formed to establish and operate cemeteries. The first urban cemetery in England (the Rosary Cemetery in Norwich) was established in 1819. The first burial was in 1821. It permitted the burial of any person, of any religion, who could pay the fee. A transcript of the burial registers of the Rosary for 1821–37 (in series RG 4 at the FRC) has been published in Hamlin (189), with the MIs that date from the period 1821 to 1986.

Many other cemeteries were opened in the next few years. Two cemeteries were opened in Manchester (in 1821 and 1824) and one in Liverpool in 1825. London cemeteries were opened at Kensal Green in 1832, Norwood (1837), Highgate (1839), Brompton (1840), Abney Park (1840) and Tower Hamlets (1841). Municipal authorities also opened cemeteries, usually on the outskirts of towns or cities where land was cheap, for example in Southampton (1845) and Leeds (1846). By 1850 thousands of people were being buried in the new cemeteries and the number of burials in urban churchyards declined. Private companies continued to establish cemeteries until the 1850s, for example the enormous cemetery for Londoners at Brookwood in Surrey. However, legislation between 1852 and 1857 established Burial Boards across the country and these public authorities then provided the majority of new cemeteries that were required, such as the City of London cemetery at Little Ilford and a cemetery at Toxteth in Liverpool (both opened in 1856). The board cemeteries also provided cheap burials for the working classes. Brooks (181) includes a gazetteer of Victorian and Edwardian cemeteries. There are also some books about particular cemeteries, usually providing a history of the cemetery, notes about famous people buried there and information about surviving records. An example is Joyce (191) about Abney Park cemetery in Stoke Newington, London. The majority of people are now cremated, but cremation only became legal in 1884 and was, until recently, a relatively rare method of disposing of corpses. There were only three cremations in Britain in 1885. Even by 1947 only 10 per cent of the dead were cremated.

It can be very difficult to locate an ancestor's place of burial in London and other large cities if it did not take place in the parish churchyard (and is not therefore recorded in a parish register). Death certificates do not record a place of burial, although it is likely to have taken place close to the place (and within a few days of) the death. The records of burials in cemeteries may be in a number of places, so the first step is to ascertain the location of cemeteries near the place of death. There is no exhaustive national list of cemeteries, but many of them are listed in the *FLHH* (5) and there are some published lists of burial grounds in particular areas (which may also note the location of their burial records). Wolfston (201) lists the burial places for the inhabitants of Greater London (other than parish churches) including military, Roman Catholic and Jewish burial grounds (and also notes the dates and location of burial registers). Cemeteries may also be found on maps or (if they are still open) in telephone directories, usually listed under the relevant local authority. When I was searching for the burial of my g.g. grandfather John Josiah Keates (who lived in Leyton and Leytonstone), maps revealed that in addition to parish churchyards, there were, within a short distance, the City of London cemetery (at Ilford), West Ham cemetery, Manor Park cemetery, Queen's Road cemetery (in Walthamstow) and a Roman Catholic cemetery.

Cemeteries kept registers of burials, but also other records such as grave and plot books. Cremations should also be recorded in a register (and perhaps by a plaque). Records of cemetery burials are very important since many gravestones have been removed or destroyed (and because many people could not afford headstones). Cemetery records are usually held in CROs, local authority archives, or (if a cemetery is still in use) at the cemetery office. Some cemeteries provided copies of burial register entries to the diocesan registrar and these copies are usually in CROs. Cemetery registers record the name, date of death, date of burial or cremation, and sometimes the age, address and occupation of the deceased. If a cemetery is still operating and

No.	Date of Burial	Name of Person Buried	Description, Avocation, and Situation of Persons Buried	Sex and Age	District in which the Death is Registered	From what Parish Removed	Situation of Grave Square	Situation of Grave Number	No. of Grave	Description of Interment	Consecrated or Unconsecrated Ground	Ceremony performed by
177952	1901 Oct. 17	James Cotterell	106 Northampton Buildings	Male - aged	Clerkenwell Holloway Middlesex	St Mary	365	9232	25399	4th Class Common interment	Unconsecrated	J. Christie
177953	1901 Oct. 17	William Peter Davies	at Old Street Finsbury	Male 4 days	Finsbury Middlesex	St Luke	365	9260	251400	4th Class Common interment	Unconsecrated	J. Christie
177954	1901 Oct. 17	Lilian Ward	61 Shup Lane Hackney	Fem. 2 mnth	South Met Hackney Middlesex	St John	375	4029	251401	2nd Class Common interment	Consecrated	J. Christie
177955	1901 Oct. 17	Maud East	56 Levoy Street St Lukes	Fem. 1 year	Finsbury Middlesex	St Luke	375	4052	251402	3rd Class Common interment	Consecrated	J. Christie
177956	1901 Oct. 17	Jane Terrell	27 Shaynmour St St Lukes	Fem. 2 years	Hampstead Middlesex	Hampstead	375	4051	251403	1st Class Common interment	Consecrated	J. Christie
177957	1901 Oct. 17	George David Baker	17 Labyrth Street Leyton	Male 1 mnth	North Leyton Essex	Leyton	358	8952	251404	4th Class Uncommon interment	Unconsecrated	F. Moulton
177958	1901 Oct. 17	Mary Ann Bacon	97 Crystal Palace Rd Camberwell	Fem. 83 years	Camberwell Surrey	St Giles	304	5795	767	3rd Class Private interment	Consecrated	J. Christie
177959	1901 Oct. 18	Elizabeth Mary Brett - Ruggden	56 Two Shut Finsbury	Fem. 2 mnth	Shoreditch Middlesex	St Leonard	365	9243	251405	1st Class Common interment	Consecrated	J. Christie
177960	1901 Oct. 18	Sarah Hebrett	17 Bayworth Street St Lukes	Fem. 28 years	St Matthew Green London	of St Lukes	365	9247	251406	2nd Class Common interment	Unconsecrated	J. Christie
177961	1901 Oct. 18	Rebecca Mary Jones	7 Ashling Lane City	Fem. 71 years	St Brides City	St Bridgets Brides	365	9247	251407	2nd Class Common interment	Unconsecrated	J. Christie
177962	1901 Oct. 18	Rosa Clayton	Gray Shopland	Fem. 7 years	Saint Saviour Surrey	St Saviour	375	6052	251408	2nd Class Common interment	Unconsecrated	J. Christie
177963	1901 Oct. 18	John Josiah Keates	11 Claude Road Leyton	Male 6 mnth	North Leyton Essex	Leyton	126	8547	NIL	3rd Class Private interment	Unconsecrated	J. Sinkins
177964	1901 Oct. 18	Emma Mackett	99 Fisher Street	Fem.	St Matthew Green	St Matthew	195	6723	2010	3rd Class Common interment	Consecrated	J. Christie

42. Extract from the register of interments at the City of London Cemetery, Little Ilford, Essex showing the burial of John Josiah Keates on 18 October 1901 (Guildhall Library)

holds its own records, you should telephone first to enquire whether a search in the records can be made for you in response to a written enquiry and, if so, whether there is a fee. Hours of searching will be saved if you know the date of death or burial (even an approximate date) because the register entries are usually chronological and rarely indexed. John Josiah Keates died in 1901 and I found his burial in the records of the City of London cemetery at Ilford. A microfilm copy of the register of interments for 1856 to 1915 is held at Guildhall Library. The extract in illustration 42, including the burial of John Josiah Keates on 18 October 1901, gives his address, age and the location and number of his grave.

A grave or burial plot number enables you to find a grave on a cemetery plan. You can also check the names of those who were buried near your ancestor (they may be relatives). In addition to the burial register, a cemetery's records often include a grave book, listing who is buried in each grave, so that the authority or company would know whether a grave was full. A deceased's grave number should appear in the burial register. You can then turn to the grave book. Having located the number of John Josiah Keates' grave at the City of London cemetery, I was able to make further enquiries about him and his wife Sophia (who died on 10 May 1899). The grave book was still at the cemetery, but an officer helpfully found the records for me. Sophia had been buried, in the same grave, on 15 May 1899. The grave book also recorded three other burials in the plot (but no gravestone):

13th March 1876; Albert John Keates aged 14
3rd October 1876; Thomas Julius Keates aged 8 months
28th April 1882; Thomas Leaver Keates aged 2 years.

These were three of the sons of John Josiah and Sophia. Until consulting this grave book, I had been unaware of Thomas Julius Keates. Although I had known of the child Albert John Keates, I had not known what had happened to him after the 1871 census.

Many families purchased a private grave for family burials over a period of time. The family received a burial plot deed (evidencing their right to the plot), which was produced to the cemetery when another burial was required. These deeds often survive in family papers and include the plot number, so that you can search in the cemetery grave book to discover who is buried in the plot. A cemetery may also hold plot records, stating who purchased the plot and paid the burial fees, although this was often a firm of undertakers (or the information may be confidential). Some burial plot deeds have documents annexed, listing the burials in the plot. I have a deed for the City of London and Tower Hamlets' cemetery on Bow Road in London, granting an exclusive right of burial, in private grave number 2325, to Mary Hamilton Eastey of Stepney. Attached to the deed are cemetery company receipts for fees paid for three burials in the grave: David George Eastey (aged 4) in 1865, Mary herself (aged 86) in 1882 and a further unnamed person in 1889. You may find similar papers for your family.

WAR MEMORIALS AND CEMETERIES

The Commonwealth War Graves Commission (# chapter 20) cares for the enormous cemeteries that exist abroad for those who died in the two world wars and maintains registers of the burials in those cemeteries. Cemeteries located near army camps in Britain should also be researched. The brother of one of my great grandmothers, who was wounded and brought back from France

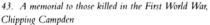

43. *A memorial to those killed in the First World War,*
Chipping Campden

44. *Roll of honour for the two world wars in the parish*
church of Chipping Campden

during the First World War, died at the army base at Shorncliffe in Kent and is buried in the camp's cemetery.

Many war memorials were erected in Britain to honour those who died in wars, listing the men's names and sometimes their regiment, ship or squadron. More information about war memorials is included in chapter 20 but they can be seen in most villages, towns and cities, usually in churches or churchyards, on village greens or by public buildings (such as railway stations). Illustrations 43 and 44 are examples at Chipping Campden. Illustration 43 is a memorial in the High Street, listing the men of Chipping Campden who died in the First World War; illustration 44 is a roll of honour, for both world wars, in the parish church. Most memorials commemorate local residents (or company employees) who died, but some are national memorials. For example, memorials at Chatham, Portsmouth and Plymouth record the names of the 25,563 men of the Royal Navy who died at sea in the First World War, specifying their rank and the name of their ship. These three memorials (and three others at Lee-on-the-Solent, Lowestoft and Liverpool) also list the names and ranks of the 46,012 men and women of the Royal Navy who died at sea during the Second World War.

CHAPTER 9

DIRECTORIES

COMMERCIAL DIRECTORIES

In later chapters, we shall consider specialist directories, lists and registers of the legal and medical professions, army and navy officers and the clergy. However, many commercial and trade directories (the forerunners of telephone directories) were also published. Directories were first published for cities and large towns around 1800, and a few decades later for small towns or rural areas. However, there were earlier directories for London. A directory of London merchants was published in 1677 and London directories were published annually from 1734. The number of directories increased enormously during the 19th century. Some covered a county (or a number of counties), a city or even the whole of London. Others covered a few towns (perhaps a particular industrial area) or parts of London. The publication of directories continued until the 1970s when they were superseded by telephone directories.

Directories were originally aimed at commercial travellers and usually contained general descriptions of a city, town or village and its communications (stagecoach and railway connections). An entry for a place then listed its churches, schools, inns, Justices of the Peace, other prominent residents, farmers, shopkeepers and other traders. Advertisements from tradesmen were often included. Illustration 48 is a typical entry for a town (Hatherleigh in Devon) from a county directory of 1830. Directories of the 19th century are especially useful for finding the addresses of people who had their own business. This assists searches in the census records. Entries in directories of successive years may evidence changes of address or even change of business. A typical entry for a trader (taken from a London directory of 1856) is:

7 Grace's Alley, Wellclose Square; Bernhard Herber; carver and gilder

Similar entries for my ancestor Bernard Herber appeared in London directories each year up to 1864. From 1865 to 1868, there were entries for Bernard as the publican at the George Tavern on New Road, St George's East. These directory entries are the only records that I have found concerning Bernard's time as a publican. London directories also include many entries for my g.g. grandfather Joseph James Eagles, a boot and shoe repairer (who lived from 1843 to 1918). There are also entries for his father Joseph James Eagles, his grandfather James Eagles (both bootmakers), his great-uncle John Abraham Eagles (a shopkeeper) and John Abraham's two sons, George (a silversmith) and John Thomas Eagles (a smelling bottle manufacturer).

In addition to entries for trades and businesses, directories included some private residents. Early directories included only the wealthier (or otherwise notable) private residents. West (463) shows that a typical directory of the early 19th century listed only about 6 per cent of the population of the area covered by the directory. However, as the 19th century progressed, commercial directories not only became more comprehensive in their coverage of businesses, but also began to include the names and addresses of more private residents, whether or not they were wealthy or prominent. Directories with householders' names and addresses also assisted the proper direction of post, and the Post Office's own directories became increasingly important during the 19th century. Illustration 46 is an extract from *Kelly's Directory* for Leyton in Essex, 1894–5, and includes Ebenezer Keates, a brother of my ancestor John Josiah Keates, living at 1 Claremont Road, Leyton. It can be seen that, by this time, directories were almost complete lists of the heads of households in residential areas.

By 1850, the directories of cities and large towns (but also counties, considered below) were large volumes (with thousands of names) and usually divided into the following sections:

a. commercial: general alphabetical listings of all traders
b. trades: alphabetical lists for particular trades or businesses
c. streets: lists of tradesmen and residents, arranged by street
d. court: listing wealthier residents, local government and court officials or dignitaries and (in London) central government officials

A typical alphabetical commercial listing for a town might appear as follows:

Chapman, John;	baker,	25 High Street
Chapman, Henry;	mason,	3 Albert Road
Clements, William	carpenter,	18 Market Road

Illustration 45 is a page from the commercial section of the *Post Office Directory* of London for 1848 (205). It lists four men named Charnock: Richard Charnock, a barrister at 5 King's Bench Walk, Temple, William Charnock, a painter of 20 Albion Terrace, Wandsworth Road and solicitors Richard Stephen Charnock and John Charnock, in partnership at 44 Paternoster Row in the City of London. The trades classification would repeat these entries, but the entries would be sorted by trade, with all the bakers appearing under the heading Bakers and so on. The streets section of a directory (as shown in illustration 46) would list some (or in later years most) of the heads of household in each street, usually in numerical order of the houses in which they lived, down one side of the street and then down the other side. Some people (particularly a shopkeeper or other trader) may therefore appear in more than one section of a directory. A butcher might appear in the list of butchers in the trades section, but also in the general listing in the commercial section. He might also appear in the streets section, listed with other shopkeepers or residents in his street. A prosperous businessman might also appear in the directory's court section if he held some local office, perhaps that of Justice of the Peace, or if he was a member of a town council.

This organisation of directories is helpful if you are trying to find your ancestors before or after a move, or trying to find out about the sale of a business to or from your ancestors. If an ancestor appears in a commercial directory for many years as a baker at 25 High Street and then does not appear in, let us say, the 1879 directory, it is worthwhile looking in the streets section for 1879 to see who is then living there. Is it another baker, who had perhaps purchased the business from your ancestor? Is it a different type of business? Had your ancestor died, or did he move to another part of town (or to another town or city)? If he only moved to another part of the city or town, you can probably still find him, at his new address, in the alphabetical list in the commercial section of the directory.

Chapman Thomas, sen. dairy, 179 Tottenham court road
Chapman ThomasHenry,surgeon,16Lr.Seymourst.Portm.sq
Chapman Thomas M. teadealer & grocer, 13 Gray's inn lane
Chapman Thory, stockbroker, Stock exchange
Chapman Wm. baker, 19 Bermondsey new road
Chapman Wm. beer retailer, 1 Macclesfield st. north,Cityrd
Chapman Wm. boot & shoe wareho. 62 Mount st. Lambeth
Chapman Wm. boot&shoemaker, 6 Woburn ct. Bloomsbury
Chapman Wm. carver & gilder,3Manorpl.Grangerd.Brandsy
Chapman Wm.chair&sofamaker,31Norfolk st.Middlsx.hosptl
Chapman Wm. chairmaker, 21 Old Boswell court, Strand
Chapman Wm. coal merchant, Union wharf, 68 Wapping wall, & 2 New London street, City
Chapman Wm. dentist, 81 Albert street, Mornington cres
Chapman Wm. fruiterer, 71 Friar street, Blackfriars road
Chapman Wm. fruiterer, 46 Long lane Bermondsey
Chapman Wm. coal dlr.& beer retailer, 1 & 2 New st.Cloth fr
Chapman Wm. nurseryman & grape grower, South Lambeth (South side)
Chapman Wm. plumber, 19 Charterhouse st. Charter ho. sq
Chapman Wm. professor of languages, 1 Albion place, Upper Kennington lane
Chapman Wm. Ship P. H. 67 Sun street, Bishopsgate
Chapman Wm. surgeon, 10 Nottingham st. Marylebone
Chapman Wm. surveyor of taxes,3 Church pl. Covent garden
Chapman Wm. tobacconist, New cross, Deptford
Chapman Wm. wheelwright, 36 New street mews,Dorset sq
ChapmanWm.jun.wine&spirit mer.4 Pancras la.Bucklrsbry
Chapman Wm. Alexander, pawnbroker,35High st.Kensingtn
ChapmanWm.Chas.Dyers Arms P.H.56Long alley,Finsbry
Chapman Wm. Cotton, corn merchant, 2 New London street
Chapman Wm. Hen. bougie ma. 81 York pl. Waterloo road
Chapman Wm. Henry,ship biscuit baker & potato salesman, 21 Mill lane, Tooley street
Chapman Lewis, flatting mills, 6 Ball court, Giltspur st
Chapman's Universal Salve & Pill Depôt, 5 Swallow place
Chappel Wm. carpenter, 61 Warren street, Fitzroy square
Chappell John & Co. stationers &news agents,31 Lombard st
Chappell Benjamin, smith, White's row, Whitechapel
Chappell Charles, carpenter, 4 Foley street, Portland place
Chappell Emily (Mrs.), music & musical instrument seller to her Majesty, 50 New Bond street
Chappell Fred. jun.stock br. 4 Bank chmb. &stock exchange
Chappell Frederick O. stockbroker, 15 Angel court, Bank
Chappell Fred. Patey, sol. & parlmnty. agnt. 25Golden sq
Chappell George, baker, 3 William street, Lisson grove
Chappell Geo. Swan & Horse Shoe P.H. 63 Gray's inn lane
Chappell Henry, locksmith, 51 Leader street, Chelsea
Chappell James, boot maker, 36 Long acre
Chappell James, boot maker, 388 Strand
Chappell John, baker, 60 Flagon row, Deptford
Chappell John, brush manuf. & warehouseman, 129 Long acre
Chappell John, cabinet maker, High street, Deptford
Chappell John, porkman, 56 Skinner street, Snowhill
Chappell John, poulterer, 26 Great hall, Hungerford mrkt
Chappell John, stationer & bookseller, 146 Minories
Chappell John Cramer, surgeon, 14 George st. Hanover sq
Chappell John Wm. solicitor, 10 Wyndham pl. Bryanstone st
Chappell Mary (Mrs.), pork butcher, 76 Fore st. Cripplegate
Chappell Mary (Mrs.),straw bonnet ma.17Gt.Smith st. Watm
Chappell Robert, stockbroker, see Austin & Chappell
Chappell Samuel, butcher, 59 Wood street, Cheapside
Chappell Sarah (Mrs.), plumber, 28 Walbrook
Chappell Thos. Baisard, sup: registrar, Mount st. Brkly. sq
Chappell Thomas, bedstead mak. 17 Gt. Smith st. Westmnr
Chappell William, butcher, 6 Farringdon market
Chappell William, music sellr.see Cramer, Beale & Chappell
Chappell William, tailor, 27 Tottenham pl. Tottenham ct. rd
Chappellsmith John, stationer & booksllr. 18 Dean st. Watm
Chappelow & Potch, bridle cutters, wholes. harness makers, saddlers, ironmongers & leather sellers, 196 Long acre
Chappelow Wm. jun. military wholesale & export saddler, bridle cutter & warehouseman, 107 Jermyn street
Chappenden John Wm. tobacconist, 2 City rd. Finsbury sq
Chapple Wm. & James, leather & glove manf. 15 Staining la
Chapple Edward, grocer & oilman, 1 Ranelagh ter. Pimlico
Chapple James, confectioner, Triangle, Kensington
Chapple John, confectioner,19 Cross street, Newington butts
Chapple John, dyer, 9 Gibson street, Waterloo road
Chapple John, solicitor, 35 King street, Cheapside
Chapple John, trunkmaker, 31 Piccadilly
Chapple Thomas, linendraper, 5 Borough road
Chapple William, tailor, 9 East street, Red Lion square
Chapple William, trunkmaker, 14 High Holborn
Chapple William, jun. trunkmaker, 17 King William st. City

Chappuis François, engine turner,3 Corporation row,Clknwl
Chapter House, 68 St. Paul's churchyard
Chapter House Record Office, Poet's corner, Old Palace yd
Chapuy Louis, perfumer, 23 Litchfield street, Soho
Chard Wm. & Edward, navy agents, 3 Clifford's inn, Fleet st
Chard Charles Thos. White Hart P.H. 18 Abchurch lane
Chard James, china warehouse, 9 Up. Seymour st. Euston sq
Chard Thomas, smith, &c. 2 Great Sutton st. Clerkenwell
Chardin William Alfred, printer, Mare street, Hackney
Chardle Charles Matthews, coffee rooms, 6 Old st.St. Luke's
Charle George, working jeweller, 84 Long lane,Bermondsey
Charing Cross Hospital (John Robertson, hon. sec.), Agar street, West Strand
Chark Willm., cowkeeper, 1 Wilmot st. Bethnal green road
Charker Edward & Henry, butchers, 26 Brewer st.Golden sq
Charleroy & Erquelinnes Railway Office,31 Golden square
Charles & Fox, merchants, 161 Upper Thames street
Charles Andrew, baker, 198 Bishopsgate street without
Charles Edmund, veterinary surgeon, 26 Clarges street
Charles Francis, oilman, 55 Great Ormond street, Queen sq
Charles James, merchant & agent, 1 WhiteLion st.Birchin la
Charles John, fishmonger, 15 Park side, Knightsbridge
Charles John, perfumer, 240 Wapping High street
Charles Joseph, tailor, 171 Fleet street
Charles Mary (Mrs.),strawhatma.5 Carthusian st.Chtrho.sq
Charles Richard, basket maker, 23 Bury street,Bloomsbury
Charles Richard, clothier, 12 Queen's buildgs.Knightsbridge
Charles Robert, soap maker, see Paton & Charles
Charles Robert, tailor, 9 Little Chester street, Pimlico
Charles Robert, jun. soap maker, see Paton & Charles
Charles Samuel, bricklayer, 21 Dalgleish st. Comcl. rd. east
Charles Thomas, fishmonger, 9 Arabella row, Pimlico
Charles Thos. Wm. law stationer, 12 Took's ct. Chancery la.
Charles Wm. bricklayer, 2 Lower Trinity st. Rotherhithe
Charles Wm. hairdresser, 36 Earl st. west, Edgeware road
Charles Wm.Geo.& Co.impt.of forgn.goods,58tBenets pl.Cty
Charles Wm. David, grocer, 19 Elizabeth pl. Balls pond rd
Charlesworth John Barff, barrister, 2 Tanfield court,Temple
Charlesworth Wm. tobacconist, 108 Union street, Borough
Charleston & Watson,coalfactors & ship & insurance brokers, 26 St. Mary at hill
Charlett Henry, tailor, 4 Eldon street, Finsbury
Charlier Henry, wine merchant, 48 Fenchurch street
Charlotte Street School (George D. Dermott, surgeon), Charlotte street, Bloomsbury
Charlton & Easton, grocers & teamen, 48 Charing cross
Charlton Cha. H.solicitor,see Leany,Howard,Charlton & Co
Charlton Charlotte (Mrs.), rope maker, 2 Brook st. Ratcliff
Charlton Edwin, sec. to AlbionInsuranceCo. New Bridge st
Charlton Edward Wm. physician, 21 Albion st. Hyde park
Charlton Geo. baker, 23 Marylebone street, Piccadilly
Charlton Geo. painting brush manuf. 175 Bermondsey st.
Charlton Henry,corn & coal dealer, 146Praed st. Paddington
Charlton Henry, paperhanger, 56 Regent st. Horseferry rd
Charlton Hubert, working jeweller,36 Coldbath sq. Clnkwl
Charlton Isabella (Miss), milliner, 16 Princes st. Cavend. sq
Charlton James, watchma. & jewelr. 15 Holywell st. Strand
Charlton John, tobacconist, 15 King's row, Pentonville
Charlton Richard, haberdasher, 40 Great Marylebone street
Charlton Richard Arkwright, accountant, 14 Bucklersbury
CharltonSarah(Mrs.), hearth stonema.22Union st.Lmbth. wt
Charlwood Geo. seedsman, &c. 14 Tavistock row,Covent gdn. & 20 Villiers street, Strand
Charlwood William, cloth factor, 38 Coleman street, City
Charman Wm. manufacturing jeweller, 63 Berwick st. Soho
Charnley & Abraham, wine&spirit mers. 21 Harp la.Tower st
Charnley Thos. Catherine Wheel P.H.11Church st.Kensington
Charnock Rich. Stphn.&John, solicitors, 44 Paternoster row
Charnock Richard, barrister, 3 King's Bench walk, Temple
Charnock Wm. painter, &c. 20 Albion ter. Wandsworthroad
Charrett William, baker, 46 Church rd. Commercial rd. east
Charrington, Head & Co. brewers, Mile end road
Charrington John & Co. coal merchants, 178 Fenchurch st. & 56 Lower Shadwell
Charrington Harry, coal merchant, 18 Upper Thames st
Charrott Richard, dairyman, 9 Crescent place, Burton cresct
Chart John, tailor, 30 Dean street, Soho
Chart MaryAnn(Mrs.),milliner,11 Monmouth pl.OldKent rd
Charter John, boot & shoe maker, 14 Little Saffron hill
Charter Sarah (Mrs.), lodging house, 87 Norton st. Fitzy. sq
Charter House, Charterhouse square
Chartered Gas Light Co. (Charles Earls, secretary),10 New Bridge st. Blackfriars ; Horseferry road, Westminster ; (works, Brick lane,St. Luke's) ; wharf,7 Macclesfield street south, City road ; Curtain road, Shoreditch
Charters, Holland & Newson, coach makers,30 New Bond st

45. Extract from the Post Office Directory of London, 1848

162 Lambert Mrs
164 Stewart Mrs
166 Fairham Mrs. shirt & collar dresser
168 Quick George
170 Ingram Aug. wine mrchnt
174 Wall James
176 Aukett Henry (Garth)
178 Burley Thomas
180 Bryant Wm. Hy.(Caldy)

Claremont road, from 4 Iddesleigh ter. Grove Green rd.
[Letters through Leytonstone.]
SOUTH SIDE.
THE GROVE:
1 Bartlett William Frederick
2 Prendergast James
3 Bailey William
4 Thompson Mrs
5 Riches William
6 Collar John T
7 Jones Misses
NORTH SIDE.
HALSBURY TERRACE:
1 Cohen Alfred John
2 Saywell Mrs
3 Bear Charles
4 Pitt John
5 Dodds George T. printer
6 Holmes Fk. Geo. decorator
WEST SIDE.
LIME GROVE TERRACE:
1 Pollard J. A
2 Green Walter
3 Churchward William
4 Cook John

5 Drake Herbert Joseph
6 Lawrence Mrs
7 Bailey William H
8 Burgess John
9 Smith John
10 Watson Philip
12 Webber Richard
13 Martin Henry James
14 Wisby Thomas
MARY ANN TERRACE:
10 Le-Bosquet John
9 Brigden Frederick
8 Carnaby Joseph
7 Bluett Henry James
6 Moddrel Mrs
5 Cumming William
4 Taylor Charles
2 Gilbert Geo. Hy. musician
1 Adams Richard J

5 Rush Spencer
3 Pitt Thomas
2 Blake Patrick H. A
1 Keates Ebenezer
NORTH SIDE.
HAMILTON TERRACE:
1 Price Robert
2 Turner Robert
3 Hughes Frank
4 Costick Joseph

Grove Green road, from Leyton road, Leyton to Fillebrook rd. Leytonstone.

[On West Side to 13. Claremont terrace & on East Side to Union road are in Leyton Postal District.]
WEST SIDE.
CLAREMONT TERRACE:
1 Dipple John
2 Nixon William Guy
3 Kinsey Mrs
3 Kinsey Miss D. teacher of music
4 Snowdown Robert
5 Harland Frederick William
6 Lloyd Archibald
7 Holdgate Robert
9 Brown Edward James
10 Loake Thomas
11 Young Thomas Robert W
12 Rose Frederick Walter
13 Titsink John
14 Day Percy
15 Furneaux Samuel
16 Kelly Herbert William
17 Ross John Butchart
18 Castle Albert Edward (Holmleigh)
19 Hughes Mrs
20 Seward John James
21 Stead John Christopher
22 Durrant James
23 Saltmarch Thomas
24 Clifton George
25 Pepper Dennis
26 Tween Walter
27 Sharp Mrs
28 Leppard Miss
29 Ensor George Lewis
30 Madell Frank Townsend
31 Barrett James
32 Fraser Walter Thomas
35 Moger Charles
36 Gross Philip
37 Pracy Henry Charles
76 Forbes Frank
78 Thompson Henry George
82 Heughebaert Edmond
86 Kern James John
88 MacLaren William
90 Waymout Henry James
92 Currie William Henry
94 Jarrett James
96 Morris Mrs
100 Waghorn William
106 Smyth Charles, surgeon
108 Kurtz William. baker
....here is Francis road...
The Northcote P.H. Harvey Sidney Smith
HARVEY VILLAS:
1 James Mrs
2 Farley Frederick
3 Hughes John Henry

Gidney Frederick, stone mason

......here is Elm road......

Parrott Mrs. Mary, general shop (Elm stores)
BROAD OAK VILLAS:
1 Search Mrs
2 Leserve George
3 Loudon John
ELLEN'S TERRACE:
1 Anderson Ernest Frederick
2 Osborne George Edward

46. Extract from Kelly's Directory of Leyton, 1894/5

London is the subject of many directories, but there were also many for provincial cities, towns and counties, the first being published in the late 18th century. A directory of Birmingham was published in 1763 and the first county directory (for Hampshire) was published in 1784. Some national directories were also published, such as the five volume *Universal British Directory 1793–1798*. It includes entries for about 16,000 cities, towns or villages, listing the local "principal inhabitants" including the gentry, clergy and businessmen. Within a few years, the number of county directories was growing rapidly. Pigot & Co. commenced publishing county directories in the early 19th century. Illustration 48 shows the entry for Hatherleigh in Devon, from Pigot's 1830 directory (202). Samuel Bulleid, a cousin of my Bulleid ancestors, appears under "shopkeepers and traders" as a butcher. In 1845, Kelly & Co. commenced publishing the Post Office Directories of provincial towns and counties, such as the 1864 directory for Buckinghamshire (209). By 1850 there were directories covering most British cities and counties.

Directories could be out of date, usually by about a year, by the time they were published. Furthermore, some publishers merely repeated information from previous years' directories (or even other publishers' directories) without checking whether it was still correct. When researching my Keates ancestors, who were mast and blockmakers in London, I found the following entry in the commercial section of the 1851 *Post Office Directory*:

George Keates – mast and blockmaker – 203 Wapping High Street

This was my g.g.g. grandfather, who ran the business with his sons (including my ancestor John Josiah Keates). However, a search of this address in the 1851 census showed that another family was then living there. The Keates family had already moved. Fortunately, it was easy to find them. They had only moved to another building in the same road (329 Wapping High Street) and later directories recorded the family business at this new address. The commercial section of the *Post Office Directory* for each year from 1863 to 1871 contained this entry:

George Keates – 329 Wapping High Street – mast and blockmaker

Census records and civil registration certificates showed that John Josiah Keates, his wife Sophia, their children (and two of John Josiah's brothers) lived and worked at these premises while George Keates (with his second wife and younger children) lived in Walthamstow. My great grandmother, Alice Amelia Keates, was born at 329 Wapping High Street in 1863. Although directories up to 1871 continued to include the Keates' business at this address, the census of April 1871 recorded the building as uninhabited. John Josiah and his family had by then moved to Leytonstone. It was not clear from the census whether the building was still used for the business. George Keates had died in December 1870 and in his will, he bequeathed the mast and blockmaking business to John Josiah. I suspect therefore that the business was continuing in 1871 but that, by this time, the family was better off and no one had to live at the premises. The George Keates entry in the 1871 directory may be explained by the directory being out of date. However, it is also possible that his business name was retained (because of customer loyalty) even though the business was now run by John Josiah.

Many directories also included advertisements for local trades and businesses. Illustration 47 is an example of a page of advertisements from Kelly's *Post Office Directory* of 1864 for Buckinghamshire (209). The adverts are for Edward Hayes, an engineer of Stony Stratford, E. &

47. Advertisements from the Post Office Directory of Buckinghamshire, *1864*

H. Roberts, iron-founders of Stony Stratford, and Barrows & Carmichael, engineers of Banbury, Oxfordshire. Your own ancestors' advertisements may well appear.

A directory's descriptions of cities, towns or large villages (small villages were generally ignored until the late 19th century) can be very useful. The entry for Hatherleigh in Devon (illustration 48) from *Pigot's Directory* of 1830 is not complimentary, describing it as an "inconsiderable" market town and the houses as mostly of "mean appearance". However, it provides useful details about Hatherleigh, such as local industries, the number of inhabitants in 1821, the name of the Lord of the manor and the fact that he held a manorial court (# chapter 27). The town's charitable institutions (a school and five almshouses) are also mentioned. All this information can lead you to further records of your ancestors. Did they appear before the manorial court? Did they attend the school or live in the almshouses? As another example, White's 1845 directory of Norfolk (214) includes a detailed entry for Hainford (or Haynford) near Norwich. My Chapman ancestors lived in Hainford in the 18th and 19th centuries. They are not listed in the entry, but the description of the village is:

Haynford, 6½ miles north of Norwich, is a large straggling village, occupied partly by weavers and having in its parish 570 souls and 1,755 acres of land. The Hall is the seat of the Rev. W.A.W. Keppel and the Rev. H.N. Astley has an estate here, but the greater part of the soil belongs to Robert Marsham, esq., the patron of the church (All Saints) . . . Here is a National School, attended by about 80 children. The poor have £30 a year from the owners of the new [enclosed land]. . . In 1693, Thomas Bulwer left £200 to the poor, which was laid out in land . . . [and] land was also left [to the poor] by John Sporle in 1677 and by Mr. Bolts and comprises altogether about 66 acres (with eight cottages), let for £84 a year. Of this income, £2 is paid to the rector, £2 to the poor communicants and the residue is divided equally among the poor parishioners.

Another type of directory should be mentioned here. Peers, baronets and the gentry are well recorded in works such as *Burke's Peerage* and *Kelly's Handbook to the Titled, Official and Landed Classes* (# chapter 26). However, other directories of the landed and wealthier classes were regularly published in the 19th and 20th centuries, aimed at wealthy people who needed lists of government offices, theatres, and other private residents. Two of the most useful only covered London. *Webster's Royal Red Book, Incorporating Boyle's Court Guide*, for example the edition of January 1928 (207), was published under various titles from 1792 and the *Royal Blue Book*, such as the 1939 edition (206), was published from 1841. Both recorded names and addresses, in alphabetical, trade and street listings, of the better-off private residents and the businesses that such people might frequent. Thus the 1928 edition of *Webster's Royal Red Book* listed only two London window cleaners, one in Eaton Place and one in Grosvenor Square. Similar volumes covered provincial counties in Britain. For example, there was a *Royal Red Book* for Yorkshire and *Deacon's Court Guide and County Blue Book* for counties such as Devon and Yorkshire.

LOCATION OF DIRECTORIES

The first London directory was published in 1677. The second was published in 1734 by Henry Kent. His company then published a London directory annually until 1828. Other London directories include those published by Holden from 1799 and by Pigot from 1822. The *Post*

Directory. **Devonshire.**

HATHERLEIGH,

IS an inconsiderable market-town and parish, in the hundred of Black Torrington ; 201 miles from London, 29 from Exeter, 12 from Torrington, and 8 from Oakhampton ; situated on a branch of the river Torridge, near its confluence with the Oke. The houses are for the most part of mean appearance, being built of what is provincially called 'cob.' The inhabitants are chiefly employed in agriculture, the working some excellent free-stone quarries, and the manufacture of serges ; the latter occupation was at one time much more beneficial to the town than at the present period. Hatherleigh is governed by a portrieve, chosen annually, with two constables and tith-ing-men, &c. at the manorial court, held under Joseph Oldham Laug, Esq. the lord of the manor ; a hundred court is also held occasionally, for the recovery of debts under 40s. The church possesses nothing to attract particular notice ; the living is a vicarage, in the possession of the Rev. G. C. Glascott. Here are five alms-houses and a small free-school, which are the only charitable institutions to be named in the town. The market-day is Tuesday ; and there are considerable cattle-fairs on the 21st of May, the 22nd of June, the 4th of September, and the 8th November. The number of inhabitants in Hatherleigh parish, by the returns for 1821, was 1,499.

POST OFFICE, John Turner, *Post Master.*—Letters from LONDON, &c. arrive every morning at six, and are despatched every evening at a quarter before eight.

NOBILITY, GENTRY AND CLERGY.

Burdon John Dennis, esq. Burdon house]Hatherleigh
CardewLieut. John Trevanion,R.N.
Clinton the Right Hon.Lord Heanson, Satchville
Glascott Rev.Geo.C. Vicarage house
Laffer Lieut.Nathl.R.N.Hatherleigh
Mallet Hugh, esq. Ash
Morris Wm. C. esq. Fishley house
Oldham Mrs. Hatherleigh
Veale James Harris, esq. Passaford

ACADEMIES AND SCHOOLS.

Cowle Fanny (day)
FREE SCHOOL, Robt. Rice, master
Jay James (boarding)   [day]
Larkworthy Mary Ann(boarding &
Lisle James (& land surveyor)

PROFESSIONAL PERSONS.

Day James, surgeon
Fisher John, surgeon
Wivell Nathaniel, attorney

INNS AND PUBLIC HOUSES.

George & Dragon (posting house)
    William Couch
London Inn, Vincent Bird
New Inn, James Hancock

SHOPKEEPERS & TRADERS.

Aggett Thomas, butcher
Baddaford William, hatter
Balkwell Elizabeth, corn miller
Bews John, turner
Bolt William, wheelwright
Braund John, watch maker

Bullied Samuel, butcher
Burridge William, hatter
Chasty Robert, watch maker
Chudley John, draper, grocer, &c.
Chudley John,joiner & cabinet mkr
Clarke Abraham, baker
Dart Robert, smith   [maker
Edward John, smith and edge-tool
Edward William, smith
Edward William, shoemaker
Edwards Edward, carpenter
Essery James, painter & glazier
Facey James, butcher
Ford Edmund, cooper
Glanville William, currier
Hooper John, stone mason
Hooper William, stone mason
Jewell John, maltster
Kemp William, carpenter
Lisle James, land surveyor
Lock Thomas, tailor
Luxton John, wheelwright
Madge Ann,miliner & dress maker
Madge John, boot & shoe maker
Martin John, saddler
Morcombe George, tailor
Northcott John,boot & shoe maker
Northcott Wm. boot & shoe maker
Palmer Christr. tailor, draper, &c.
Pearse George, serge manufacturer
    and liquor dealer
Pearse Henry, butcher
Pearse Robert, maltster
Pederick William, smith
Rice John, boot & shoe maker
Rice Robert, draper & grocer

Saunders Richard, farrier
Short John Smale, fire office agent
Smale George, hatter
Smale John, cooper
Stuckley Elizbth. draper & grocer
Trenaman John, stone mason
Tucker Arthur, butcher
Vanstone Samuel, painter & glazier
Westlake William, wheelwright
WEST OF ENGLAND FIRE OFFICE,
    John Smale Short, agent
White William, saddler

COACHES.

All call at the George and Dragon.
To BARNSTAPLE, the *North Devon* (from Plymouth) everyTuesday,Thursday and Saturday afternoon at three ; goes through Torrington & Bideford.
To BIDEFORD, the *Torridge Express* (from Exeter) every Monday, Wednesday and Friday afternoon at three ; goes through Torrington.
To EXETER, the*Torridge Express* (from Bideford) every Tuesday, Thursday and Saturday at twelve ; goes thro'Crediton.
To PLYMOUTH, the*North Devon* (from Barnstaple) every Monday, Wednesday and Friday at one; goes through Oakhampton and Tavistock.

CARRIERS.

To BARNSTAPLE, Jno. Bowman, every Friday—and James King, from the London Inn, every Saturday ; goes through Torrington and Bideford.
To EXETER, Thos. Durant's *Waggon,* every Wednesday.
To PLYMOUTH, John Bowman and James King, every Tuesday.

HOLSWORTHY,

IS a small market-town, in a parish of its name, in the hundred of Black Torrington ; 214 miles from London, 42 from Exeter, 19 from Bideford, and 16 from Torrington ; situated near to the small river Deer, and within about half a mile of a branch of the Bude canal. It is a place much reduced in trade since the introduction of machinery, prior to which the humbler classes could well support themselves by hand-spinning ; but the hum of the revolving wheel is now no longer heard in their habitations.

The places of worship are, the parish church, dedicated to St. Peter and St. Paul ; and a meeting-house for the Wesleyan methodists. The living of Holsworthy is a rectory, of which the Rev. Roger Kingdon is the patron and incumbent. The Earl of Stanhope is lord of the manor, and holds a court leet annually, when a portrieve is nominated for the government of the town. The land surrounding this place is generally of good quality, principally in tillage. The market-days are Wednesday and Saturday ; and there are several others, for cattle, during the year. The fairs are, April 27th (a large one for horned cattle), and July 9th and two following days, for cattle, horses, and various commodities. By the census for 1821, the population of the parish of Holsworthy amounted to 1,440 persons.

POST OFFICE, Lucy Perrers, *Post Mistress.*—Letters from LONDON, &c. arrive every morning at half-past nine, and are despatched every afternoon at half-past four.—Letters from the western parts arrive every afternoon at half-past four, and are despatched every morning at half-past nine.

GENTRY AND CLERGY.

Allin Wm. esq. Thouborough
Cann Hugh, esq. Herdwick
Coham Mrs. Elizabeth, Holsworthy
Edgecumbe Rev. J. Thornbury
Hart Rev. Samuel, Holsworthy
Hawkey Lewis, esq. Tackbeer
King Capt.Henry, R.N. Holsworthy
Kingdon Rev. Roger, Holsworthy
Kingdon Rev. Thomas Hockin (magistrate) Bridgerale vicarage

Mayricks the Misses, Holsworthy
RouseRev.Oliver,Tedcott parsonage
Vowler John, esq. Furze
Vowler John, sen. esq. Parnacott
Wilcox Rev. Geo. Milton parsonage

ACADEMIES & SCHOOLS.

Friend Arthur, boys' day
Friend Walter, boys' day
Sceddon Florence, boarding & day

PROFESSIONAL PERSONS.

Cann Hugh, attorney

Cock Richard, attorney, Way
Cory Samuel, surgeon
Hearle Stephen, surgeon
Kelly BenedictusMarwood, attorney
Kingdon Charles, attorney
Vine William, surgeon

INNS AND PUBLIC HOUSES.

Crown & Sceptre, Jas. Penwarden
Globe, Walter Dobell
King's Arms, David Mill
New Inn, Richard Hoskin

213

48. *Extract from the Devon section of* Pigot's Directory, 1830

166

Office London Directory was published from 1800 by various publishers, most notably by Kelly & Co. from 1837. Directories were also published for the London suburbs: by Holden and then Underhill from 1799 to 1822, by Pigot in 1827 and 1828, and by Watkins in 1852. The *Post Office London Suburban Directory* was first published in 1860. The best list of London directories is Atkins (208). This is a very detailed work, describing the origin and development of directories (with many illustrations of the layout of different directories), followed by a list of London directories from 1677 to 1977, the different editions of each and the archives which hold copies.

Provincial directories of England and Wales published before 1856 are catalogued in Norton (211) and those published from 1850 to 1950 are listed in Shaw & Tipper (212). The number of provincial directories is very substantial, particularly after 1850. Shaw & Tipper (212) list over 2,200 entries for different directories, 284 published by Kelly alone. The 2,200 entries actually constitute almost 18,000 volumes if one takes account of different editions of each directory. The works of Norton and Shaw & Tipper also specify where copies of these directories are held but such location lists are often out of date, as archives' collections of directories continue to grow. The entry in Shaw & Tipper (212) for *Kelly's Directory of Bedfordshire* illustrates the large number of directories available. There were 18 editions of this directory between 1854 and 1940. Copies of all of them are held at Guildhall Library and at University Library, Cambridge, and all except two editions are at Bedford Central Library. The SoG has copies of nine editions between 1864 and 1931, Buckinghamshire County Library in Aylesbury has copies of all editions from 1890 to 1940.

Guildhall Library in London possesses the largest collection of London directories, but it also has a large collection of provincial directories. This collection has been substantially enlarged by the donation of the collection of directories previously held by Kelly's Directories. Much of the library's collection is available on microfilm and there is a microfilm copier available for public use. The SoG also has a very substantial collection of British, Irish and foreign directories, both originals and reprints (books, fiche and computer disks). The collection is listed in the library catalogue and (as at 1995) in Newington-Irving (210). CROs and some local libraries also usually hold good collections for the area that they serve.

A substantial number of directories have been reprinted in book form, on microfiche, CD-ROM or the Internet and so are becoming more widely available. Michael Winton publishes reprints of various directories, such as the *Universal British Directory 1793–1798*, *Kelly's Post Office Directory of London 1846* and some of Pigot's county directories of 1828 to 1830, for example Pigot's 1830 directory (204) for Bedfordshire, Cambridgeshire, Lincolnshire, Huntingdonshire and Northamptonshire. Brooks, Davies & Co. publish a large number of directories on microfiche, including many of Pigot's provincial directories for 1823/4 and Slaters' provincial directories for 1850. A selection of directories have also been published on microfiche by the SoG. These include sections of *Pigot's Directory* of 1830 for many English counties, such as Devon (202) and Norfolk (203). N. Vine Hall in Australia has reproduced a very extensive selection of British directories on microfiche (listed on his web site). By Spring 2003, he had reprinted more than 450 directories, for example those of Devon by Holden, Pigot, White, Slater or Kelly for 1805, 1823, 1830, 1844, 1850, 1852, 1889, 1890, 1910 and 1923. Microfiche reprints are also available from other commercial suppliers, such as MM Publications and Original Indexes, or from family history societies. These are listed in the publishers' or societies' own catalogues, in Raymond (266) or Perkins (263).

The number of directories available on CD-ROM, some with scanned images of the directory, some with a transcript of its text, has also multiplied. Many are listed in Raymond (267). Back to Roots (# chapter 3) and Stepping Stones (# chapter 6) produce many CD-ROMs containing scanned images of directories, for example the Cumberland section of *Pigot's Directory 1834*, the commercial and trades sections of *The Post Office London Directory 1865* and the sections for trades and private residents of *Kelly's Directory of Cornwall 1919*. These disks have a list of contents from which you can navigate to the pages for a particular town or village, a list of people in a particular trade or the list of private residents. Having found a page with an entry of interest, you can also print it out or copy it to another computer file. Hundreds of similar disks, such as *Pigot's Directory of London 1825/6*, *Kelly's Directory of London 1848* and *Kelly's Directory of Lancashire 1895* are produced by Archive CD Books (and listed on its web site).

Very few directories included an index to the people they listed. Therefore, those CD-ROMs that combine scanned images of the directory with a personal name search function are even more useful. Many disks of this type are available from S&N Genealogy Supplies (# chapter 3) and listed on its web site, including disks for the Devon and Somerset sections of *Pigot's Directory 1844* and *Slater's Directory of Lancashire 1855*. It is worth noting, however, that the name search function on disks of this type does not always work satisfactorily. The directory text has been subjected to optical character recognition (OCR), but the text of some directories is so small that present OCR technology cannot always read it correctly. For example, I used the search function on one of these disks (*Pigot's Directory 1844* for Devon), to find people surnamed Bulleid. No entries were found. However, three men with this surname do appear in the directory.

Some disks include both scanned and digital versions of a directory, permitting effective personal name searches (subject to transcription errors). One example is a CD-ROM of the Berkshire, Buckinghamshire and Oxfordshire sections of *Pigot's Directory* of 1830 produced by Drake Software Associates (# chapter 6). The disk includes about 13,000 people. A search for the surname Timms (or Tims) produced eight entries in this form:

Forename	Surname	Occupation	Address	Town	County	Page
John	TIMMS	Boot & shoemaker	Ock St	Abingdon	BRK	3

I could then call up a facsimile of the directory page on which the entry appeared (and print a copy).

Avero Publications of 20 Great North Road, Newcastle upon Tyne NE2 4PS is publishing a series of five CD-ROMs entitled *The Biography Database 1680–1830* that include transcripts (but not scanned images) of many directories. The disks can also be seen at the SoG and reference libraries. The first disk includes many 18th-century directories; 52 for London, 13 for Birmingham, eight for Newcastle upon Tyne and a few others, as well as book subscription lists and notices of births, marriages, deaths, bankruptcies and appointments from *Gentleman's Magazine* (# chapter 17). The disk contains about 900,000 names (about 300,000 from British trade directories) and can be searched by name, occupation or address. The second disk in the series includes similar material (although many of the directories are of American towns or cities) but there are trade directories of the late 18th century for London, Bristol, Manchester and other British cities containing about 300,000 names. The contents of the third disk are principally Welsh, Scottish and American directories (# chapters 29 and 30) but also four English directories.

Fascimiles or transcripts of directories can also be consulted on the Internet. The best way to find these transcripts is through GENUKI (# chapter 11) or in the lists of web sites in Raymond (268). At present, most of these online copies are only parts of directories, for example for a particular town. However, some complete directories can be viewed at the web site of the Digital Library of Historical Directories (# appendix XI). This is a lottery-funded project to place a selection of trade directories online, with name and place indexes (from which you can bring up any relevant page of the directory). The number of directories is gradually increasing – for example, the site presently includes *Kelly's Directory of Berkshire 1877* and *Pigot's National Commercial Directory 1835* (covering Derbyshire, Lincolnshire and a number of other counties).

TELEPHONE DIRECTORIES

For the 20th century you may find Post Office telephone directories helpful. If you have an unusual name, telephone directories may assist you to find cousins. Very few people in this country are called Herber and so I located many cousins by a few telephone calls. The first telephone directory dates from 1880 and lists about 300 people in London. Use of the telephone developed quickly, especially for trade and business, and if you are researching a family business in the early years of this century, you can find business addresses of your ancestors by consulting old telephone directories.

The British Telecom Archives, at Holborn Telephone Exchange (3rd floor), 268–270 High Holborn, London WC1 7EE, include an almost complete set of London and provincial telephone directories from 1880 to 1984 which are listed on the archive's web site and can be viewed on microfilm. An appointment must be made to consult these (by telephoning first on 020 7492 8792). Guildhall Library holds some telephone directories for London from 1881 to 1918 and most of them for the period since 1920. Many local libraries and CROs also have collections of recent (or sometimes older) telephone directories for the areas that they serve. The SoG has a large collection of recent telephone directories, mostly on microfiche, and these are listed in Newington-Irving (210). Three Victorian telephone directories, of 1884 and 1885, from London and the south of England have been reprinted in Thomas (213).

Contemporary British Telecom telephone listings can be searched online at the BT web site or (combined with information from electoral registers) on CD-ROM. The 1999 edition of *UK Info Disk 4.1* contained the address and telephone number (from 1998 or 1999) of over 47 million residents of the United Kingdom, Ireland, the Channel Islands and Isle of Man. The SoG has a copy of this disk and later versions from 2000 and 2001.

CHAPTER 10

COMBINING SOURCES
OF INFORMATION

The sources of information described in previous chapters may enable you to trace your ancestry back as far as the 16th century. However, many problems will arise during the course of your research and these may prevent you finding a record of a certain event. For example, you may locate a family in the census records of 1861 to 1901, yet be unable to find them in the 1841 or 1851 censuses. You may become stuck at some point in the 19th century (perhaps because you cannot locate a great grandfather's birth certificate) or in the 17th or 18th centuries (unable to find your ancestors in parish registers). In order to make progress, it is therefore vital to combine different sources of information. Chapter 28 summarises the sources available to locate migrant families, that is those families who moved between parishes (or counties), since they cause particular problems. This chapter provides examples of how the combination of source material is essential at all stages of your research.

Information obtained from one type of record usually leads you to other records so that you can progress your research. Birth, marriage or death certificates, directories and cemetery records reveal addresses which assist searches in the census returns. In turn, census returns give the ages and birthplaces of your ancestors or other relatives. This information can be used to obtain other civil registration certificates, or to search parish registers for baptisms, marriages and burials, especially in the late 18th and early 19th centuries. Information from parish records allows further searches to be made in the GRO records. For example, you can search in GRO records for marriages and deaths (that took place after 1837) of those people whose baptisms are recorded in parish registers. Parish registers after 1837 may include entries for events that you cannot find in civil registration records. Census records give clues as to approximate places and dates of death for ancestors, thus helping you to find burial records. A burial record or death certificate may lead you to a memorial inscription or a will (# chapter 12) which may provide much useful genealogical information.

Corroboration of evidence is also vital. You must always ensure that you are researching your ancestors, rather than people of the same name who are not truly related to you. Civil registration records can confirm the relationships indicated by census records. Wills can also prove (or disprove) the relationships that are evidenced by civil registration records, parish registers or census records. For example, we shall see below that census records and the death certificate of my ancestor Richard Hodge of Sandford in Devon indicated that he was born in Sandford in about 1799. The Sandford parish register contained the baptism of a Richard Hodge in 1799 (the son of John and Hannah Hodge), and baptisms of his siblings named William, Ann, Hannah and Betty. It was fortunate that, before I spent too much time on the ancestry of that Richard Hodge, I discovered the will of a Richard Hodge who had died in a neighbouring parish in 1834. In that will, Richard Hodge left gifts for his brother William and sisters, Ann, Hannah and Betty: therefore the Richard who was baptised in Sandford in 1799 was clearly the Richard who had died in 1834 and not my ancestor who survived until 1861. If I had only considered parish registers, rather than other sources, I would have followed a false trail.

This chapter is therefore intended to illustrate the importance of combining the sources of information that we have already reviewed. The same principles can then be applied to the further sources of genealogical information considered in later chapters. Two examples follow. The first shows how the combination of source material can not only extend the family tree, but can also assist the location of elusive births, baptisms or marriages. The second example shows how a family tree that is based on civil registration, census and parish records can be proved to be correct by a will. After these examples, there are descriptions (or CVs) of two of my ancestors. Each account shows how information can be drawn from a number of sources to build up a picture of a person's life, but also illustrate the gaps that remain in a researcher's knowledge, and the further research that can be undertaken.

THE HODGE AND STANLAKE FAMILIES

My great grandmother Bessie Ann Rice was born in Exwick, near Exeter, in 1867. Her birth certificate recorded that she was the daughter of Richard Rice and his wife Bessey, formerly Hodge. The 1871, 1881 and 1891 censuses of Exwick recorded Bessie Ann Rice at home with her parents and her brothers and sisters. I searched the 1861 census of Exwick (before the birth of Bessie Ann) and again located Richard and Bessey Rice. All these census records stated that Richard's wife Bessey (née Hodge) was born in Sandford, Devon and the recorded ages indicated that she was born in about 1832, so that no birth certificate could be obtained for her. Living with the Rice family in Exwick in 1861 was Bessey's brother, Richard Hodge, who was also recorded as born in Sandford, in about 1839.

I found the certificate of the 1857 marriage (in Exeter) of Richard Rice and Bessey Hodge, recording Bessey's father as Richard Hodge, a labourer. Since the Hodge family came from Sandford, I turned to the Sandford census records. In the 1851 census, I found Bessey Hodge, with a brother William, and their parents Richard and Grace Hodge. Richard Hodge was an agricultural labourer. Bessey's brother Richard was not with the family, but there was a Richard Hodge, a farm servant aged 12, living with another household in Sandford. The 1851 census also recorded some teenagers, Thomas, John and Mary Ann Hodge, working as servants on farms in Sandford. I then turned to the 1841 census. This also recorded Bessey Hodge with her parents Richard and Grace. The household also included children named Thomas, Mary Ann and Richard, who appeared to be Bessey's brothers and sister (the position was uncertain because relationships were not recorded). The brother Richard was no doubt the same Richard who was living with his sister Bessey (and her husband Richard Rice) in Exwick in 1861. As noted above, Thomas, Mary Ann and Richard Hodge had all been included in the 1851 census of Sandford, but in other households. These relationships could be confirmed from civil registration records and parish registers. At this point in my research, I drew up a preliminary family tree.

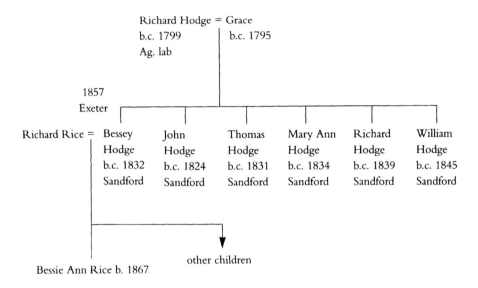

The Sandford parish register recorded the 1832 baptism of Bessey Hodge (my g.g. grandmother) and also the baptisms of John, Thomas, Richard and Mary Ann Hodge. In each case, their parents were recorded as Richard and Grace Hodge. I also found baptisms of two other sons of Richard and Grace (both named James), who had not appeared in the census. The first James had probably died young. The second (baptised in 1827) may have died before the 1841 census, or he may have been living away from home. My next step was to ascertain the maiden name of Grace Hodge. There was no birth certificate for her daughter Bessey (because she was born before 1837) so I obtained the birth certificate of her younger brother, Richard (born in 1839). I was assuming that Richard and Bessey had the same mother (but confirmed this later from other records). The certificate recorded Grace's maiden name as Stanlake.

I had already found Richard and Grace Hodge in the 1841 and 1851 censuses of Sandford. I now searched the 1861 census and again located them (all their children had left home). I then searched the 1871 census. There was no entry for Richard Hodge, but Grace (recorded as a widow) was still living in Sandford, sharing a home with her brother James Stanlake and her sister, Elizabeth Smale (who was married to John Smale). Grace, James and Elizabeth were all recorded as born in Winkleigh, Devon. I knew that Richard Hodge had died after the census of April 1861, so I turned to civil registration records and found the certificate for his death in late 1861.

There was no record of a marriage at Sandford between Richard Hodge and Grace Stanlake, but the census had recorded that Grace was born in Winkleigh. The IGI for Devon and the Winkleigh parish register included a marriage at Winkleigh in 1817 of Richard Hodge and Grace Stanlake. Richard was recorded as a sojourner and one of the witnesses was Isaac Stanlake. The Winkleigh register also recorded baptisms, in 1817 and 1819, of Elizabeth and Grace, two other children of Richard and Grace Hodge. The position was therefore:

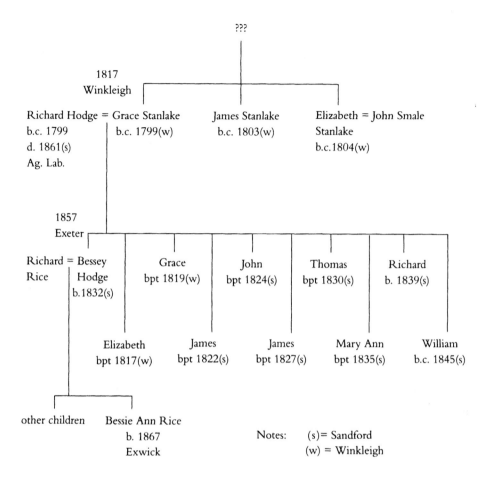

The 1851 and 1861 census records had recorded that Richard Hodge was born in Sandford and the ages given for him (and stated on his death certificate), indicated that he was born in about 1799. The Sandford parish register recorded the baptism of a Richard Hodge in 1799, the son of John and Hannah Hodge. At first, I assumed that this was my ancestor Richard Hodge. The Sandford register also recorded the baptisms of four siblings of this Richard (William, Betty, Ann and Hannah) in the period 1789 to 1795. However, I later discovered a will of a Richard Hodge who died in 1834 in the nearby village of Stockleigh English. In his will, this Richard named his brother (William) and his three sisters (Betty, Ann and Hannah). The testator Richard Hodge was clearly the Richard who had been baptised in Sandford in 1799. That baptism entry did not relate to my ancestor Richard Hodge. I therefore had to find the true origin of my ancestor Richard Hodge and find out why (and from where) he had appeared in Winkleigh in 1817.

The Stanlake family was much easier to research. The Winkleigh parish register recorded the baptism of my ancestor Grace Stanlake in 1795, the baptisms of six of her brothers and sisters and the marriage of their parents, Isaac Stanlake (an agricultural worker) and Susanna Bulleid, in 1795. Isaac survived until 1846 and appeared in the 1841 census of Winkleigh and in civil registration records (his death certificate recording that he died aged 79). The parish register recorded that his wife Susanna had been buried in Winkleigh in 1819.

This is only a simple example, in summary form, but it does show how the combination of civil registration certificates, census records, the IGI and parish registers should be used together to extend your family tree. Importantly, it also shows how corroboration of information should always be obtained from other sources.

THE EAGLES AND GILLMAN FAMILIES

My g.g.g. grandfather Joseph James Eagles was baptised at St Leonard's, Shoreditch, in London, in 1808. He was a son of James and Susan (or Susannah) Eagles. Joseph James had a brother (John Abraham Eagles) who was baptised at St Luke, Old Street, Finsbury, London, in 1794. Six other siblings were baptised at St Leonard's, Shoreditch, between 1797 and 1811. The St Leonard's baptism registers recorded that James Eagles was a shoemaker living in Hoxton Old Town.

I could not locate a record of the marriage of James and Susannah. I searched the registers of St Leonard's, Shoreditch and St Luke, Old Street, the IGI for London (and a few other counties) as well as Boyd's marriage index, the Pallot Index (which covers most parishes of London and Middlesex from 1780 to 1812) and marriage indexes for Surrey, Essex and West Kent. There was no relevant entry and so I therefore started searching the registers of parishes that were not covered by those indexes. I searched parts of the 1841 census records of Hoxton and Shoreditch for James and Susannah, but I could not find them. I also searched many London parish registers up to 1837 for their burials, but without success. I reviewed the first 10 years of the GRO death indexes (that is up to 1847), but found no entries for either James or Susannah Eagles. I therefore suspected that they had died before 1837 and that their burials were recorded in one of the many parish registers of London or Middlesex. Although I continued my research, it was clearly going to be difficult to trace this line of ancestry back any further using only the records noted in previous chapters.

We shall review wills in chapter 12. Only a minority of people left wills, so I did not expect to find any wills for the Eagles family. However, wills are such an important source of genealogical information (particularly for confirming relationships) that searches for wills should always be made. Wills for the period up to January 1858 are held in many different record offices. I started the search, but actually found the will of Susannah Eagles by chance at Guildhall Library. Susannah died, a widow, in December 1851 (I subsequently discovered that she was over 80 years old). I should have considered the possibility of Susannah (or James) living to such an age and should have searched a few more years of the GRO death indexes rather than stopping at 1847. In any event, knowing Susannah's date of death, I could obtain her death certificate. This certificate and her will each provided an address at which I could search for her in the 1851 census. I found her in Clerkenwell, living with her grandson John Thomas Eagles. Her place of birth was merely stated to be Bedfordshire (unfortunately without the name of a parish).

I could, however, turn to Bedfordshire parish registers. All Bedfordshire registers up to 1812 have been transcribed and published (and the IGI also has fairly complete coverage of baptisms and marriages for this period). The IGI for Bedfordshire included the marriage of James Eagles and "Susan" Gillman in Hockliffe, Bedfordshire, in November 1787, and also recorded their son

William being baptised in Hockliffe in April 1792. These were very likely to be my ancestors James and Susannah. The parish register of Hockliffe confirmed these IGI entries, but neither the IGI nor the Hockliffe register contained any later entries for James and Susan Eagles or any other children. The register did contain many entries for the Gillman family, including the baptism of Susan in 1769 (a daughter of Thomas and Elizabeth Gillman). They appeared to be the Thomas Gillman and Elizabeth Read who were married in Hockliffe in 1763. Susan Gillman had a number of brothers and sisters, one of whom married by licence. That marriage licence (# chapter 14) stated that Thomas Gillman was a cordwainer (shoemaker).

Were the James Eagles and Susan Gillman who married in Hockliffe in 1787 my ancestors? Although I knew that my ancestor Susannah originated from Bedfordshire, I had no information that corroborated the identification of this couple as my ancestors, although there was some circumstantial evidence. The dates obtained from the records (the baptism of William in 1792 in Hockliffe, then the baptism of a son John Abraham in 1794 in St Luke) suggested a move by James and Susan Eagles from Hockliffe to London in about 1792 or 1793. Such a move would explain why I could not find any Bedfordshire entries for the couple after 1792. There was also the shoemaker link. My ancestor James Eagles was a shoemaker, as was Thomas Gillman who appeared to be his father-in-law. Had James Eagles worked for Thomas Gillman and married his daughter? How could I prove that the James Eagles and Susan Gillman who married in Hockliffe in 1787 were my ancestors who lived in London from 1794?

The proof was obtained from the will of Thomas, the father of Susan Gillman. Wills are vitally important for corroborating information that is obtained from civil registration, census and parish records. As a first step, I reviewed the Hockliffe register of burials and found a transcript (made in about 1900) of inscriptions from gravestones in Hockliffe churchyard. These recorded that Thomas Gillman was buried in 1823 in Hockliffe. I then found Thomas's will (# chapter 12) in records of the probate court of the Archbishop of Canterbury. Thomas had fortunately made a detailed will, referring to all his children, including:

My daughter Susan, the wife of James Eagles of Hoxton, co. Middlesex.

This proved the link. Some researchers might say that I was being over cautious in looking for further evidence that the James and Susan Eagles of Hockliffe were indeed my ancestors who were living in Hoxton a few years later. However, the example of Richard Hodge, noted above, is a warning as to how easy it is to assume that a parish register entry relates to one of your ancestors when it truly relates to someone else. The chances of the 1799 baptism of Richard Hodge not being the baptism of my ancestor must have been extremely small, but I could easily have spent years researching the ancestry of people who were not related to me. Therefore, it is always worthwhile looking for other evidence to corroborate a link. You should be looking for other documents concerning your ancestors (such as wills) in any event, so you are not undertaking extra or unnecessary work, but rather cross-checking all the information that you obtain from different sources to ensure that it supports the research that you have already undertaken and your conclusions. If evidence from one source does not fit in with evidence from other sources, you must consider whether you have made a mistake in your research. Have you made an assumption that is not supported by the evidence? You should check all the evidence carefully, but also obtain other evidence to corroborate your findings and conclusions.

BERNARD HERBER OR HERBERT

We can now review how evidence of an ancestor's life can be built up from the records considered in previous chapters (with a few entries taken from records that we shall consider later). This section deals with my g.g. grandfather Bernard Herber, who was baptised in 1823. I did not know anything about him (not even his name) when I started my research. The following section deals with my ancestor Thomas Gillman, of Hockliffe in Bedfordshire, who was born about 80 years before Bernard. The sources of information for these men's lives are quite different and it is interesting to note that I actually know more about Thomas than I do about Bernard.

1823 October 12   Bernard Johann Herbert was baptised in Schwanheim, near Frankfurt-am-Main, the son of a farmer Wilhelm Herbert and his wife Margaretha Safran. The Schwanheim registers recorded that Wilhelm Herbert was a Catholic and that Margaretha was the daughter of Jost Safran and his wife Anna Maria Schlaud.

1823 to 1851   At some point prior to April 1851, Bernard emigrated to England and from then appears in most records with the surname Herber.

1851 April   Bernard Herber was recorded in the census at 4 Ship Alley, Wellclose Square, St George in the East, London. Many other Germans were living in the area. Bernard was recorded as aged 28, born in Germany and unmarried. His occupation was gilder and he was one of two men at that address employed by the head of the household, Jacob Safran, a carpenter who was also born in Germany. Since the surname of Bernard's mother was Safran, it seems likely that Jacob and Bernard were related.

1852 September 6   Bernard Herber married Emily Clements (after banns) at the church of Holy Trinity near the Tower of London. Emily, a daughter of John Clements, was born in Wanstead, Essex. Bernard was a gilder and his father's name was given as Wilhelm Herber, a farmer. Bernard signed his name and Jacob Safran was a witness.

1853 July   A son Jacob (no doubt named after Jacob Safran) was born to Bernard and Emily (now living at 7 Grace's Alley, Wellclose Square). Jacob Herber died later in 1853.

1856 to 1860   Bernard Herber seems to have had his own business, appearing in the *Post Office London Directory* (*POLD*) for each of these years as a carver and gilder at 7 Graces Alley. Bernard and Emily also had another son (Frederick Burnot Herber), who was born in 1856 in Wanstead.

1860   Bernard and Emily Herber's third son, William Henry Herber (my great grandfather) was born in Wanstead. Bernard was recorded on the birth certificate as a gilder master.

1861 April   Bernard was recorded in the census (at 7 Graces Alley) as a gilder, who was married, aged 37 and born in Schwanheim, Germany. Bernard's wife Emily and their sons Frederick and William were recorded in the census as living in a house in Voluntary Place, Wanstead. It is presently impossible to tell whether Bernard and Emily had separated, or whether Bernard merely spent many nights at his business premises in Graces Alley.

1861 to 1864   During these years Bernard Herber was recorded in the *POLD* as a carver and gilder, at 7 Graces Alley. However, in the 1865 *POLD*, 7 Graces Alley was stated to be occupied by a firm of carvers and gilders named Spalding & Dawsons.

1865 to 1869   Bernard appeared in the *POLD* as a publican at the George Tavern, at 8 New Road, St George's in the East, in succession to the previous publican, Mr G. Gaze. Later London directories do not include any reference to Bernard.

1871 April   In the census Emily and her sons Frederick and William Herber were living at 3 Martha Cottages, Walthamstow, with Emily's sister and a lodger. Emily was noted as a gilder's wife. Bernard has not yet been found in this census.

1879   Bernard and Emily's son, Frederick Burnot Herber, married Jane Williams in Shoreditch. Their first son, also named Frederick Burnot Herber, was born in 1880.

1881 April   In the census Bernard and Emily's son, William Herber, was recorded as employed at a bakery on Leyton High Road. Emily Herber was recorded as a laundress at 2 Shernhall Street, Walthamstow. She was also recorded as a widow, so Bernard had evidently died by this date. No record of his death has been found in the GRO indexes and no record of any will or administration has been located. Emily gave her age as 39 (although she was really 44). With Emily in the house was a lodger, John Phillips, a gardener aged 36.

1884   Emily Herber, then living at 3 Raglan Cottages, Walthamstow, was remarried by licence to John Phillips in Shoreditch. No subsequent trace of her has yet been found.

1886   William Henry Herber, a baker, married Alice Amelia Keates in Leyton. William's father was recorded as Frederick Bernard Herber, carver & gilder, deceased.

I have therefore managed to build up a brief picture of Bernard's life. You can hopefully do better with your 19th-century ancestors. Importantly, the preparation of documents such as this illustrates the gaps in your knowledge and the further research that you can undertake. In the case of Bernard Herber, there are many sources (considered in later chapters) that I have yet to consult, for example, records of Bernard's emigration from Germany. Rates and electoral records may also contain useful information. Business or property records may include information about Bernard's business as a carver and gilder, and as a publican.

THOMAS GILLMAN

My g.g.g.g. grandfather Thomas Gillman was a cordwainer. He lived for most of his life in Hockliffe, Bedfordshire and appears to have become wealthy because he was able to purchase some properties. All the events noted below took place at Hockliffe unless otherwise stated.

1740 May 20   Thomas Gillman was baptised at Barton le Clay, Bedfordshire, the son of William Gillman (a shoemaker) and Susan Hull.

1763 September 11   Thomas Gillman married Elizabeth Read (a daughter of Michael Read, a dairyman and Elizabeth Hannell) at Hockliffe. Thomas and Elizabeth signed their names and Elizabeth's father, Michael Read, was a witness. In this year, a boy named William Fisher was apprenticed to Thomas, who was recorded as a cordwainer of Hockliffe.

1764 September   Elizabeth, a daughter of Thomas and Elizabeth, was baptised.

1766 January 12   Thomas's daughter Susan was buried (there is no baptism record).

1768 February 21   Thomas's son William was buried (there is no baptism record). During the course of 1768, a boy named Joseph Innard commenced his apprenticeship with Thomas.

1769, 1772 and 1773   Thomas's children Susan (my ancestor), Rebecca and Thomas were baptised.

1774 October 20   Thomas was noted, in a poll book, as the owner of one property and the occupier of two other properties in Hockliffe.

1775 and 1777   Thomas's sons William and Michael were baptised. Thomas insured his shop and business with the Sun Insurance Company for £400.

1779 September   Thomas's father-in-law, Michael Read, died. Michael had appointed Thomas as a trustee and overseer to his estate and left £20 for his daughter, Thomas's wife Elizabeth.

1780 February 29   Thomas's son James was baptised.

1781   Thomas acted as surety in support of an application for a marriage licence for Sarah Gurney and John Walker. Their relationship (if any) to Thomas is unknown. Thomas's brothers-in-law, Michael and James Read, were the witnesses at the marriage in Hockliffe.

1782 January   Thomas's brother-in-law, James Read, a butcher of Hockliffe, died. Thomas was appointed as one of the executors of James's will (and received a share of James's estate).

1782 September   Thomas's son Abraham was baptised (but buried in April 1783). Thomas was also a witness at the marriage in Hockliffe of his brother-in-law, Michael Read.

1784 December 30   Thomas's daughter Elizabeth married William Waterfield, a cordwainer. Thomas acted as surety for the application for the marriage licence. William and Elizabeth subsequently moved to Dunstable and started a family.

1787 November 29   Thomas's daughter Susan married James Eagles. Their son William was born in 1792 and the family later moved to Hoxton in Middlesex.

1790 October 6   Thomas's daughter Rebecca gave birth to an illegitimate daughter, Elizabeth Dover Gillman. The child was buried in 1792 and Rebecca later married George Harley of Hadley in Hertfordshire (a son James was baptised in Hockliffe in 1801).

1792 November 8 Thomas's father, William Gillman, was buried in Hockliffe.

1797 July 3 Thomas's son William married Rebecca Partridge. The couple moved to Flitton-with-Silsoe in Bedfordshire and raised a family.

1798 Land tax records show Thomas Gillman as the owner and occupier of property in Hockliffe. His land tax was assessed at 7s. 6d.

1800 Thomas's mother-in-law, Elizabeth Read, died in Hockliffe. Thomas was appointed as one of the executors of her will. Thomas's wife Elizabeth received £40 and a share of her mother's household goods, furniture, plate, linen and jewellery.

1804 Thomas's brother-in-law, Abraham Read, a dairyman, died in Hockliffe. Thomas was appointed as one of the guardians of Abraham's three children.

1806 September Thomas's wife, Elizabeth, died and was buried at Hockliffe. The inscription on her memorial stone (now illegible) was transcribed in about 1900.

1810 Thomas's son Michael married and started a family in Hockliffe. His descendants remained in Hockliffe, running a grocery business, until the late 19th century.

1816 December 25 Thomas executed his will, dividing his property between two of his sons (Michael and William), his three daughters (Rebecca Harley, Elizabeth Waterfield and Susan Eagles), and some of his grandchildren. Thomas appointed Thomas Waterfield of Dunstable (his grandson) and William Millard of Hockliffe as his executors.

1819 December 29 Thomas executed a codicil to his will, dealing with six cottages in Hockliffe (all tenanted) that he had recently purchased (jointly with his son Michael) from Robert Nixon of Woburn and John Elliott of Dunstable.

1820 March Thomas was recorded in a poll book as the owner of property in Hockliffe. He voted for the Marquis of Tavistock and Sir John Osborn in an election for Members of Parliament for Bedfordshire.

1823 July Thomas died and was buried at Hockliffe. The inscription on his gravestone was recorded in 1900. His will was proved in the Prerogative Court of Canterbury.

I am sure that many other sources for Thomas Gillman await discovery, and a schedule or CV such as this helps to direct me to other possible avenues of research. I should be able to find more records concerning Thomas's properties in Hockliffe (perhaps property deeds or tax records). I can perhaps find out exactly which properties he owned in Hockliffe and locate them on maps and plans. The properties may still survive. Papers relating to the Read family (that is, his wife's family) may also disclose more about Thomas, his business and properties.

CHAPTER 11

ARCHIVES, LIBRARIES AND FAMILY HISTORY SOCIETIES

The GRO and FRC and many of the genealogical resources held there have been described in previous chapters. The wills and non-conformist registers at the FRC are reviewed in chapters 12 and 13. Brief mention has also been made of CROs and TNA at Kew. This chapter contains more information about these archives and others that hold records concerning your ancestors (the archives of Scotland, Wales, Ireland, the Channel Islands and Isle of Man are described in chapter 29). This chapter also describes the organisations that can assist you to make progress in your research. The SoG and family history societies help you to contact other researchers (who may be researching the same families as you) and they also hold valuable sources of information. You can also obtain assistance from genealogical journals and professional researchers The Internet is an increasingly important source for genealogists and so is also discussed in this chapter.

ARCHIVES AND LIBRARIES

This section describes the principal archives, record offices and libraries that you may visit in the course of your research. You may have only limited time available to spend at archives and so it is essential to organise your searches before each visit. What records do you wish to see, where are they and how will you find them? The first step is to ascertain which archives hold the relevant records and ensure that you know each archive's rules and the organisation of its records. A number of books list British record offices. The most important are noted below and addresses of CROs are listed in appendix VII. The annual *FLHH* (5) lists addresses, telephone numbers and web sites of British and Irish record offices, libraries, family history centres, museums and family history, record and local history societies. A detailed list of CROs and other archives, the ARCHON directory, can also be seen on the HMC web site (# appendix XI). Gibson & Peskett (248) provide town or city maps (noting local car parks, train and bus stations) with the location, address and telephone numbers of record offices. Cole & Church (241) is more detailed, providing archives' and libraries' addresses, telephone numbers, opening hours, a brief description of their holdings and publications, conditions of study (such as the need for a ticket or to book a seat) and copying facilities. Mortimer (259) also lists archives' addresses and telephone numbers. These often change, so you should consult the most recent edition of any of these lists.

Documents concerning any place (and its inhabitants) may be fairly scattered. For example, records for a town in Essex could be held in archives in Essex, London or other counties. Many useful records have been accumulated over the years by families that own (or used to own) land.

A family collection may be held in one archive yet relate to its holdings of land (and its tenants) in many different counties. As discussed below, even if the records you require are held in the county to which they relate, they may not be at the main county archive, but at a local archive or library. You must therefore decide which records you wish to see and then ascertain their location. Many published lists (noting locations) are available for specific types of records. These are noted in the relevant chapters of this book and you should review any such lists before commencing your research so that you do not waste time by travelling to the wrong record office. There are also about 2,300 museums in Britain, in which displays and exhibits may assist the research of your family history. Some museums also hold records that may assist your research. For example, the National Maritime Museum (# chapter 21) holds some records of merchant ships and their crews. Other museums with useful archives are dealt with in the appropriate chapters of this book.

Two series of booklets are worthy of special note. The SoG publishes a series entitled *My Ancestor Was . . .*, describing the records available for soldiers, merchant seamen, migrants, manorial tenants and non-conformist religious groups. The FFHS "Gibson Guides" are also excellent booklets by Jeremy Gibson (and sometimes others) which review particular types of records and describe the location of the surviving documents for each county. These guides deal with records such as pre-1841 census returns (# chapter 6), hearth tax records, poor law union records, electoral registers, poll books, militia lists and coroners' records. Extracts from the Gibson guides to hearth tax records (890) and to land and window tax records (892), showing the useful information that these guides contain, are shown in illustration 49. You should also purchase Gibson & Hampson (158), which lists about 1,000 specialist indexes for genealogists that are held by CROs, family history societies, libraries and individuals, including many indexes of MIs, newspapers and parish, occupational and court records.

Information about archives and genealogical sources is also available on the Internet, providing access to millions of other computer users and the information available on their web sites. It is important to note that the vast majority of archive and library catalogues and indexes are not on the Internet (and will not be for many years). Some archives have extensive online catalogues, for example TNA, the British Library Newspaper Library, the National Maritime Museum, Lambeth Palace Library, the CROs for Essex and Durham and the LDS Family History Library. However, others have few, if any, online finding aids.

Two important web sites permit online searches of catalogues or records at a number of archives. The National Register of Archives, described below, brings together thousands of unpublished catalogues of business and personal papers held at archives throughout the British Isles. Another good starting point for research is the web site (# appendix XI) of Access to Archives (A2A) which features online catalogues for an inceasing number of British archives, including many catalogues of Quarter Sessions records (# chapter 25). By September 2003, this database included about 4.7 million entries from 326 archives and libraries. Searches for documents (by keyword, date or range of dates) can be made in all the catalogues, in those of one archive or in those of a particular region. Searches can therefore be made for a person, a parish, another place name or a particular institution (such as a non-conformist chapel).

The National Archives
The National Archives (TNA) was formed on 1 April 2003 when the Public Record Office (PRO) was merged with the Historical Manuscripts Commission (see below). The PRO was

BEDFORDSHIRE

Publication

Hearth Tax 1670M (wrongly described as 1671L) [P.R.O. E.179/72/301] (9,500) in Beds. Hist. Record Soc. 16, 1934, as Appx. (pp. 65-159) to 'The Rural Population of Bedfordshire 1671-1921'. Lydia M. Marshall; reprinted 1990. Includes exempt poor and empty houses. Indexed. Accompanying article mainly comparison of C17 and C19 population, no apparent comment on or comparison with other HT records.

Public Record Office [E.179]

Free and Voluntary Present, 1661-2
County [2436] (1,250), parchment roll, arrears [243/7] (100), paper sheets.

Hearth Tax (Assessments and returns)

1662M. County (72/297/4) (5,000), Stodden and Willey hds. missing. Some ms. badly decayed; entries badly faded in parts; modern list of parishes and ms nos.

1663L. Westoning [2436] (1,000). Paper Constables' returns, those exempt.

1664M. County (243/14/4) (5,000). Some decay repaired, variable legibility, some fading. Notes against entries relate to 1662M. Modern description and contents list.

1665L&M. County (72/298) (1,000). Variations. Valuable notes on reasons for not paying, i.e. in prison, no distress to be taken. Dated 12 April 1666.

(1666). Stodden, Clifton, Barford, Wixhamtree hds. [2439] (5,000). Paper, repaired, bound. Annotated Flitt, Manshead, Biggleswade, Redbornstoke hds. [243/10] (2,500). Paper book, repaired, annotated VG

1670M . County (72/293/01) (9,500) *Published*
1671L(2). County (72/302) (9,500) Badly decayed, otherwise legibility adequate.

(Arrears)
1664L. County [37/01] (30). Latin
1683-4. Miscellaneous [358].

Subsidies
(1660). Wixhamtree, Clifton, Biggleswade hds. [72/295] (400).
1661. Manshead hd. (72/297) (900) Parts badly faded, variable legibility
(1673). Barford, Stodden, Willey hds. (72/306) (500) Poor legibility

Association Oath Rolls, 1695-6 [C.213]
[2] County. [3] Bedford

Bedfordshire Record Office, Bedford

Hearth Tax
1665. Part of Manshead hd. Billington, Houghton Regis, Toddington, Harlington, Tottenhoe, Milton Bryan, Woburn [AD 3350 pp. 15-18] c.1683. Northill, incl. the hamlets of Ickwell, Over or Upper Caldecote, Nether or Lower Caldecote, Thorncote, Hatch, Brook End, Beeston [HY 823]

Poll Tax
1689-90. Renhold [PO 14 p.19-20] Copy CAMPOP
1694. Aspley Guise [HW 41]

Aids:
1693. Cranfield [LL 7/3]; Maulden [LL 7/4]

Ship Money:
1677. Renhold [PO 14 p.8]. Copie [ABPW 1684/20]

Weekes' Tax:
1707, 1715. Renhold [PO 14 p.40]

Certainty Money:
1712. Houghton Conquest [RAG24]

Land Tax: 1697, 1706. Renhold [PO 14 p.39]

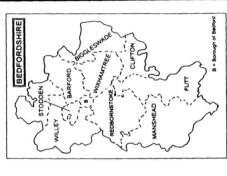

BEDFORDSHIRE

Land Tax

Bedfordshire Record Office, Bedford:

1) Pre-1780: Manshead Hundred, 1750, complete [F.89].
a few isolated LTAs as below.

2) 1780-1832: 1783 complete (except Bedford) [HA.14/5];
1782-83 Bedford (town) [BOR B.F/16/1-2];
1797-1832 [QDLI], NC.

3) Post-1832: variable coverage according to Hundred, arranged by place [LX series for long runs; isolated returns have ref's. as below].

LTAs are arranged by place.

Hundreds (for 1783, 1797-1832, see above).
Barford: 1) Great Barford, 1720, 1740, 1750, 1753, 1759 [FN 1253-4];
Renhold, 1697, 1706, 1717 [PO 14].
2) Renhold, 1782 [PO 14].
3) 1930-49, SY, MP.
Great Barford, 1901 [X 290/338];
Ravensden, 1841, 1865-6 [X 85/140-2];
Wilden, 1838 [P 106/28/2].
Biggleswade: 1) Biggleswade parish, 1765 [RI 1/3].
Old Warden, 1770 [PE 195].
3) 1915-49, MY, MP.
Biggleswade parish, 1841 [X 440/718];
Potton, 1690 [LX 83];
Sandy, 1691 [LX 91a];
Tempsford, 1869, 1874, 1884-5 [WY 911].
Clifton: 3) 1915-49, SY, MP
Flitt: 1) Silsoe, 1750 [L 26/35].
3) 1857-1946, MY, MP.
Manshead: 1) 1750, NC [F 89].
3) 1834-1946, MY, MP.
Redbornstoke: 1) Ampthill, 1725, 1739-41
[R 4/319-20, Duke of Bedford estates];
Houghton Conquest, 1725 [R 4/318];
Maulden, 1765-9 [P 31/28/4].
3) 1842-1949, MY, MP
Stodden: 1) Bolnhurst, 1750 [Fac 172];
Keysoe, 1765, 1767 [C 1722-3].
3) 1930-49, MY, MP.
Willey: 1) Felmersham, 1757 [V 292]; Radwell in Felmersham, 1764 [V 293];
Podington, 1737, 1739, 1748, 1783 [OR 1752-7];
Thurleigh, 1765, 1767 [C 1722-3].
2) Podington, 1764-5 [OR 1760-1], 1787 [OR 949], 1769 [OR 1764].
3) 1930-49, MY, MP.
Farndish, 1883-97, SY [OR 950];
Podington, 1882-93, SY [OR 950].
Wixamtree: 3) 1912-49, SY [LX 77].
Northill, 1902 [LX 77].

Bedford (town): 2) 1782-3, 1797-1832.
3) 1930-49, SY, SP.

Public Record Office, Kew:
Whole County, 1798 [IR.23/1] (see page 9).

Window Tax

Bedfordshire Record Office, Bedford:
Keysoe, 1731 [P 48/28/1].
Great Barford, 1750-57 [FN 1253, 1255].
Old Warden, 1770 [PE 196].

---

49. Extracts from Gibson guides to hearth tax, land tax and window tax records

established in 1838 to preserve the government's and law courts' records and other national archives. Most of these records are open to the public 30 years after the end of the year in which they were created, although some are closed for longer (thus census records are closed for 100 years). TNA therefore holds a wealth of information for family historians. Despite the change of name, you will continue to see many references to the PRO for some time. For example, the online catalogue of TNA is still called PROCAT and many of its information leaflets will continue to refer to the PRO until reprints are prepared. In particular, the web site of TNA is under construction and so presently forms a gateway to the separate PRO and HMC web sites (# appendix XI) which contain the useful guides, catalogues and information leaflets required by researchers. It is intended to merge the PRO web site into the web site of TNA. Consequently, I have referred in this book to information, indexes and documents appearing on the web site of TNA even though, as at November 2003, they are still on the PRO web site.

TNA is located at Ruskin Avenue, Kew, Richmond, Surrey TW9 4DU (telephone 020 8392 5200). It is open Monday to Saturday from 9.30 a.m. (10 a.m. on Tuesdays) to 5 p.m. (7 p.m. on Tuesdays and Thursdays). It is closed on bank holidays and for the first two full weeks in December. Researchers must have a reader's ticket (issued at reception on production of identification). The ticket's barcode can be read by the turnstiles and by the computer which is used to order documents. The bookshop of TNA stocks many books on family history and on particular types of records. The web site of TNA includes general information about TNA, an online bookshop, an online catalogue (PROCAT) described below and information leaflets about services at TNA and many of the documents that it holds.

We have already noted that microfilm copies of the census records can be seen at the search room of TNA at the FRC. Some wills and other probate records (# chapter 12) as well as non-conformist registers (# chapter 13) are also available on microfilm in that search room. The amount of material held at Kew is enormous. For example, the Admiralty records include over 17,000 volumes of ships' musters (# chapter 21) for the period 1688–1808 (and further volumes cover the 19th century). In the War Office records there are 13,300 volumes of muster books and paylists for units of the British army covering the 18th and 19th centuries. Since very few of the millions of documents available are indexed by the names of those people recorded in them, it is vital to prepare thoroughly for a visit to TNA in order to make the best use of your time and locate your ancestors in the records. The records that will assist research of your family history are so substantial that they can only be briefly described in the following chapters, but they are reviewed in detail in Bevan (239), an illustrated guide to sources at TNA, and in works (noted in later chapters) which review particular records, such as army and navy records. In addition to the census returns, the records at TNA that are most useful to genealogists (and reviewed in later chapters) are:

a. Army, navy, air force, Royal Marine and merchant navy records
b. Non-conformist and non-parochial registers of baptisms, marriages and burials
c. PCC wills and administrations and Inland Revenue death duty registers
d. Records of legal proceedings
e. Taxation returns and assessments
f. Apprenticeship books
g. Records of property
h. Records of railways and some other business records

An increasing number of the records at TNA are on microfilm and in these cases the terminal on which you order documents directs you to the microfilm reading room where you take the film from self-service drawers.

The prospect of searching for ancestors noted in the millions of documents at TNA may be daunting but it is actually quite easy. In order to see a document, you need its reference number (called a piece number). Researchers can find the piece numbers of documents from PROCAT (the online catalogue) and many other lists, indexes and finding aids.

PROCAT is an online database of over nine million document references. You can search this catalogue, to find material of interest, by keywords (such as "County Courts"), by TNA reference (to obtain a detailed breakdown of a series of documents) or even, for some series, by a person's name. The introduction of PROCAT has changed the method of searching for documents at TNA. However, many older finding aids are still useful and so are described here as well. Until recently, the key finding aids were detailed lists (known as class lists) of the records in each series (formerly named a class), with introductory notes about the documents, their purpose and the department or court that produced or collected them. Illustration 50 is a page from a list describing the Fleet marriage registers in pieces 231 to 238B of class (now series) RG 7. It shows that piece RG 7/235 is a register of the minister Walter Wyatt for June 1747 to June 1749. You could then order that piece. Similarly, series WO 12 contains muster lists and pay books of the British army, arranged by regiment or unit and by date. The list for the series tells you what each piece contains. Having found the piece number for a regiment (and dates) in which you are interested, you can then order the document.

Many of the old class lists have been incorporated into PROCAT, permitting online searches by keywords of the lists and descriptions. However, some of the introductory notes and descriptions of documents on PROCAT are shorter than the text in the old class lists. Therefore, you will probably find useful information about documents (additional to that on PROCAT) in the enormous collection of old paper class lists (known as the Standard Set of lists) that are in about 1,100 green files shelved in 22 bays around the research enquiries room. This is the only copy of the lists that is updated. Importantly, some volumes contain indexes (many of them to people's names) and detailed notes on various types of documents, many of which have not yet been incorporated into PROCAT.

Some other old finding aids remain useful. The three-volume *Guide to the Contents of the Public Record Office* (228) is out of date in many respects but remains useful for its descriptions of legal records, the courts and government departments. You can also consult the *Current Guide* (234) which is in several loose-leaf volumes in the research enquiries room at TNA (it was also published on microfiche until 1998). It contains administrative histories of government departments and the courts, lists for each series (briefly describing the documents in each piece) and a very good index. PROCAT is an excellent online catalogue that can be used at TNA or from your home computer but the *Current Guide* remains a handy reference work. You can browse through the lists, looking for material of interest or read the descriptions of the records, government departments or the courts. The index also refers you to descriptions of the records as well as to specific pieces that appear relevant to your search. As Bevan (239) advises, you should search for documents in both PROCAT and the *Current Guide* since a search in one may produce references that are not revealed by the other. Keyword searches on PROCAT are not always successful because of problems (such as those caused by abbreviations) noted below. In such cases, the index to the *Current Guide* may be more helpful. PROCAT is likely to produce

Reference				RG 7

RG 7	Date	Officiating Ministers	Index	Remarks
231*	1746 Dec.- 1749 Dec.	Tarrant, Dare, Deneveu, Symson, Wyatt, etc.	-	Transcribed in in no.172. Baptisms †
232*	1747 Jan.- 1749 Dec.	Wyatt, Symson, Tarrant, Deneveu	In no. 276 (Sec- tion 102)	Baptisms †
233	1747 Jan.- 1750 Dec.	Wyatt, Symson, Tarrant, Deneveu, Crawford	-	-
	1747 Mar.- 1754 Mar.	-	-	See no.230
	1747 May- 1747 June	-	-	See no.15
234*	1747 June- 1749 June	Wyatt, Symson, Dare, Deneveu, Tarrant	-	Baptisms †
235*	1747 June- 1749 June	Wyatt	In volume	Wyatt's register of marriages 'At home'
236*	1747 July- 1748 Oct.	Tarrant (?Townsend), Crawford	-	Baptisms †
237	1747 July- 1749 Dec.	Symson, Tarrant, Crawford Deneveu, Dare	-	Baptisms †
238A	1747 Aug.- 1749 Mar.	Dare, Tarrant, Deneveu, Symson, etc.	In no.276 (unnum- bered section, 1747- 1749)	Baptisms †
238B	1747 Sept.- 1748 July	Dare, Wyatt, Tarrant	-	Baptisms †
	1747 Sept.- 1749 Sept; 1752 Dec.	-	-	See no.221
	1747 Sept.- 1750 Sept.	-	-	See no.144
	1747 Sept.- 1753 Apr.	-	-	See no.181
	1748 Apr. 1748 Dec.	-	-	See no.178

* For Fleet marriage entries relating to Sussex, South-West Kent
and South-East Surrey see volumes 91C and 91D in Press B in the
Long Room

† Occasional Baptismal entries only

50. A page from the list for series RG 7 at TNA, describing pieces 231 to 238

references that cannot be found from the index to the *Current Guide*, for example because of new accessions or because of the addition of name indexes to PROCAT that are not included in the *Current Guide*.

TNA also holds many indexes, calendars and other finding aids (manuscript, typescript, published or unpublished) that have not yet been incorporated into PROCAT. Some are in the research enquiries room but others, especially for the voluminous records of the courts, are in the map room. In particular, many finding aids have been published in the volumes of *Public Record Office Lists & Indexes* and by the List and Index Society. Copies of these are at TNA, the SoG and some reference libraries. For example, many volumes of *Lists & Indexes* list the parties to litigation (and the subject of the disputes) in the Court of Chancery (# chapter 24). The List and Index Society volumes 265–267 list TNA holdings of non-conformist registers (# chapter 13) and volumes 68 and 83 list tithe maps (# chapter 15) for most English and Welsh parishes. There are also many manuscript indexes or calendars of the personal and place names featured in documents at TNA. Most of these are not included in PROCAT (although PROCAT features name indexes to some documents that have not been published elsewhere). These lists, calendars and indexes are therefore noted in later chapters of this book.

TNA has produced many information leaflets (listed in appendix VI). There are general information leaflets (on matters such as copyright and ordering copies of documents) and over 240 domestic, military, legal and overseas records leaflets that describe particular types of records. For example, if your ancestor was a Royal Marine, you should refer to military records leaflets 45–48 which describe the most useful records available and give TNA reference numbers. The leaflets are available at Kew and on the web site of TNA. The online versions of the leaflets include links to the online catalogue; whenever they refer to a series of documents, you can click on the link to move directly to their description in PROCAT. TNA also produces "source sheets" that list references to records that are relevant to particular areas of study. For example, source sheet 7 lists the documents that include information on the General Strike of 1926 and sheets 10 and 16 list the sources for the Zulu war and for suffragettes.

TNA produces an extremely useful bi-monthly magazine, *Ancestors* (215), for those people researching their ancestors at TNA. In addition to regular updates as to the services, catalogues and indexes available at TNA, *Ancestors* also includes detailed, illustrated, articles on the records at TNA that will assist family historians, such as military, naval and court records.

All documents at TNA have a reference number (thus census records have references such as RG 10/547). Each document's reference starts with a department code of up to four letters. This indicates the government department or court of law that produced or collected the records. Examples include HO (Home Office), RG (Registrar General), ADM (Admiralty) or WO (War Office). The reference then contains two or three sets of figures. The first figures indicate the type of document (the series). The second figures (sometimes combined with a third set of figures or some letters) indicate the particular item within that series (the piece number). For example, series WO 12 consists of muster books and paylists of the British Army. Piece 3179 in that series consists of muster books and paylists of the 14th Regiment of Foot from 1861 to 1862. The complete reference for this volume of documents is WO 12/3179 and this is the number that you use to order it. Brief descriptions of each series of records are contained in PROCAT and the *Current Guide* (234). For example, the description for series ADM 10 is:

Officers' services; indexes & miscellaneous 1660–1851 15 vols. Indexes to officers' services; abstracts of captains' services 1660–1741; journal of Admiral Rooke 1700–1702; list of commissions of captains and lieutenants registered at the Navy Board 1730–1818; schedule of the accounts, entry books, correspondence, etc. for the service of prisoners of war 1796 to 1816.

Some piece numbers include more than two sets of figures. For example, series C 2 (some records of litigation in the Court of Chancery) is subdivided by monarch's reign, then by bundle and then item, so that a piece number may be C 2/CHASI/B42/10. In such cases, the full piece number that you need to order the document is provided by PROCAT or other finding aids.

The ground floor at TNA has a bookshop, restaurant and cloakroom. You cannot take bags, pens or more than 10 sheets of loose paper into the reading rooms. Having obtained a reader's ticket, you go through the turnstiles to the first floor. This contains the research enquiries room, the document reading room (including a section where you order copies of documents), the library (which has a huge collection of published material) and the microfilm reading room which has microfilm and fiche readers and printers (and terminals for the 1901 online census service). The map and large document reading room (the map room) is on the second floor, with its own reprographic room. Unless you are only going to look at records on microform, you should first go to the service counter in the document reading room and request a seat. Some seats are reserved for researchers using dictation machines, laptop computers or cameras.

You should then go to the research enquiries room. This contains the PROCAT screens, the *Current Guide*, the Standard Set of lists and many other indexes and finding aids. Searching for documents and ordering them through PROCAT is easy. PROCAT contains over nine million entries arranged in levels (department, series, piece and also items within a piece), each with a description. The PROCAT search engine allows you to search all these descriptions by key words (and a range of dates). The descriptions are also cross-referenced to the online versions of TNA information leaflets. Therefore, if a search on PROCAT takes you to series C 2 (records of the Court of Chancery) it also offers a link by which you can bring the relevant leaflet to your screen. At the screen (or from your home computer), you click on "Catalogue and Document Ordering". You can then use the catalogue but you must log on as a registered reader, with your TNA reader's ticket number, if you wish to order documents or save your searches (for future research). Once logged on, you can click on "Quick Order" to order documents (if you already know their references and have a seat number) or you can browse the catalogue and make searches with key words. Browsing is useful if you know, from published guides or TNA leaflets, that a particular series of documents is likely to refer to your ancestor. You can read the descriptions of various pieces to see how the documents are arranged and which, from their descriptions, are likely to be worth ordering for a detailed review.

Searches on PROCAT are most effective with keywords for places or subjects rather than people's names, because PROCAT is primarily a description of the documents rather than an index of the people recorded in them. You will therefore primarily be searching for types of documents in which you have some prospect of finding an ancestor. However, PROCAT does include some peoples' names and so searches for an ancestor may also be successful. You can search for more than one keyword by using a linking word in capitals; thus OR, for example "attorney OR solicitor" or limit the ambit of a search by using AND (requiring results to have both words) for example "Herber AND Mark". You can also filter searches by a range of years or by department, for example limiting searches to records of the War Office (WO). Detailed guidance on using PROCAT for searches is provided by Bevan (239) but remember that a search will only succeed if the keyword you use is in the description. Your ancestors will be mentioned in many documents but rarely in the catalogue descriptions of those documents. There were also many ways to describe some things. Army regiments (# chapter 20) had various names and numbers over the years (and many abbreviations might be used) and so searches should be made with a number of different keywords.

When you have found documents that you wish to review, you can order them on the same screen. You may have up to three documents on order at any one time. In some cases, a message on the screen will tell you that the documents are on microfilm or fiche in which case you go to the microfilm reading room, choose a microfilm or fiche reader and collect the film or fiche from the self service drawers. In other cases, a screen message tells you that the document has been ordered for you (unless it is being used or is temporarily unfit for production) and states whether it will be produced to you at the counter in the document reading room or in the map room. Documents are produced in about 30 minutes. You can check whether your documents have arrived at one of the counters by swiping your reader's ticket through the "order status terminals". When a document is noted as having arrived, you ask for it at the counter by its reference number. Accompanying the document will be a repository slip that you will need if you later leave the document with the copying department. You can then also order another document so that documents are being collected for you from storage while you work on others. Documents for use the same day must be ordered before 4 p.m. on Monday, Wednesday and Friday or before 4.30 p.m on Tuesdays and Thursdays. Documents can be ordered on Saturdays from 9.30 a.m until 12 noon and from 1.30 p.m to 2.30 p.m. When you have finished with documents, they must be returned to the service counter. If you know the piece numbers of items that you wish to see, an order for three documents can be made in advance by telephone (020 8392 5200) or by e-mail, so that they are ready for you upon your arrival at Kew.

Maps and large documents are reviewed in the map room. TNA holds thousands of maps, for example in the records of the courts, the Ministry of Agriculture and the Crown Estates, but many maps have been extracted from other classes and stored and catalogued separately. There are also some series that consist predominantly of maps, such as the tithe and enclosure maps (# chapter 15). HMSO has published a catalogue (231) of about 4,200 maps and plans of the British Isles at TNA that date from 1410 to 1860. There is a section for general maps of Britain and then separate sections for each county. Each county section has a general section and then entries for each place for which maps are held, describing each plan and noting its reference. Thus, the entry for Eversholt in Bedfordshire reveals that TNA holds a map of 1808 which notes the names of fields and landowners. Similar catalogues have been published for Europe, America and Africa. There are also card indexes to uncatalogued maps. The map catalogues and other finding aids are described in TNA domestic records leaflet 36.

The microfilm reading room has rows of microfilm and fiche readers (each with markers that you place in the self-service storage drawers when you take a film or fiche), printers that work with cash or rechargeable cards as well as terminals for the 1901 census online service. There are also some drawers containing card indexes. A chart on the wall lists the series or pieces that are held on film or fiche and notes their locations in the storage drawers. For example, the Fleet Registers (# chapter 14) in series RG 7 are in row 4, drawer 64 and army service records (# chapter 20) in WO 364 are in row 11, drawers 50–135.

Photocopies and photographic copies of documents can be ordered. When reviewing a piece (whether loose pages or bound volumes), you insert slips of paper marked "LH only" (left hand page only) or "RH only" at the pages to be copied. For a sequence of pages, you insert slips marked with "LH" or "RH" and "start" or "end" at the beginning and end of the section required. You take the piece to the reprographic room. There is a "while you wait" and a same day copying service but copies can also be posted to you or collected on a later visit. Copies of maps are ordered from the reprographic room adjacent to the map room. Researchers can make photographic copies of documents with their own cameras. It is necessary to register in the reprographic room and sign a copyright declaration form. Flash photography and tripods cannot be used. TNA staff will also undertake research for you in certain records (such as First World War medal rolls, wills and non-conformist registers). Details of the records and the fees are available from the Reader Services Department.

Some records at TNA are being input into databases and added to PROCAT although it will be some years before these are complete. Work has commenced on indexes to the map collections (# chapter 15) and to the tax records of 1188–1689 in series E 179 (# chapter 23). An index to some civil court proceedings of the 16th to 19th centuries, from the records of the Courts of Chancery, Exchequer, Star Chamber and Requests (# chapter 24) is in operation and gradually being expanded. PROCAT will clearly become more and more effective as a finding aid and index over the next few years.

Digital images of many documents at TNA are also being made available online, through the DocumentsOnline section of its web site. At present, the most important documents available are PCC wills (# chapter 12).

The British Library

The British Library is located at 96 Euston Road, London NW1 2DB (telephone 020 7412 7000). The Oriental and India Office Collections (an essential source if your ancestors served in India, see chapter 30) are also located in this building (telephone 020 7412 7873). The library's web site includes information about its collections, catalogues and indexes and there is an online catalogue to its collection of about 12 million books and journals. The library holds millions of manuscripts but, as it is also one of the British copyright libraries, it is entitled to receive a copy of every work published in Britain. It therefore holds a copy of almost every book, journal or pamphlet ever published in Britain (and many from abroad). Most genealogists will not need to use the British Library until their researches are very advanced, since most published material is held at the SoG, TNA, CROs or reference libraries. However, some sources (particularly manuscripts) are available only at the British Library. Researchers must obtain a reader's ticket, available to those people aged 21 and over (who show that they need access to material that is not easily available elsewhere) on production of proof of identity and two colour passport photographs. A written reference is required in order to use the Manuscripts Department's collections.

The Printed Books Department holds some books on open shelves, but most must be ordered from storage. There is a *General Catalogue of Printed Books* in 366 volumes (but also on CD-ROM) for acquisitions up to 1975 and a microfiche *Current Index* for later material. The catalogues generally index books by the name of the author or editor, but works relating to an area may also be indexed under the name of the town, parish or county. Printed family histories, including diaries and memoirs, are indexed by surname. The library holds most published parish registers. It also holds London newspapers up to 1801. Other newspapers are held at the British Library Newspaper Library at Colindale, London NW9 (# chapter 17). The Manuscripts Department holds many collections of family archives and antiquaries' papers, including many pedigrees, the most useful being the Cotton and Harleian collections (and the collections of Additional Manuscripts and Additional Charters). Most of the manuscript collections are catalogued and calendared, in published volumes, such as (217), which catalogues manuscripts acquired between 1861 and 1875. This includes thousands of useful records such as manorial court rolls and lists of tenants (# chapter 27), title deeds to property and the correspondence and papers of families or individuals such as Warren Hastings. One example from the manuscripts collection is a casebook kept by a Justice of the Peace in Dorset from 1614 to 1635, which has also been published in Bettey (962), recording the cases that the Justice heard, including examinations of paupers, victims of crimes and witnesses.

Maps held by the British Library are summarised in Wallis (407) and listed in detail in the Library's *Catalogue of Maps, Charts and Plans* and its supplement (for acquisitions up to 1974) or in the *Catalogue of Cartographic Materials* for subsequent acquisitions.

Other copyright libraries
Other libraries, which may be more convenient for your research, are also entitled to receive a copy of all works published in Britain. These are the Bodleian Library in Oxford, Cambridge University Library, the National Library of Wales, the Scottish National Library and the Library of Trinity College, Dublin. The Bodleian Library's holdings and catalogues are described by S. Tomlinson in *Genealogists' Magazine* (December 1987). It is the library of Oxford University but also the second largest public library in Britain, holding about six million books and thousands of manuscripts, such as families' archives (including records of their property holdings). The Bodleian also holds thousands of useful published works such as county histories, parish registers, and army and navy lists.

County Record Offices
Each English county and many metropolitan districts have established record offices for the county's or district's records. These archives are the major repositories of civil records for each county or metropolitan district. In this book they are referred to as County Record Offices (or CROs), but it is important to remember that many of them are for the archives of an area that is now a metropolitan district. There is an archive for each London borough as well as the London Metropolitan Archives (LMA) at 40 Northampton Road, London EC1R 0HB (its location is shown on the map at illustration 9), which holds many records for the whole of Greater London.

The addresses of most CROs and some other important archives (as well as area record offices in Wales and Scotland) are listed in appendix VII. Telephone numbers often change, so they are not listed but can be obtained from the *FLHH* (5), Cole & Church (241), the ARCHON web pages and Mortimer (259). However, in addition there are many other archives (such as city and borough archives or local studies libraries). For example, if you are interested in records of Bedfordshire, you may have to visit not only Bedford Record Office (# appendix VII), but also the Bedford Council archives and Bedford and Luton museums. These are not listed in appendix VII but are noted in the *FLHH* (5), Cole & Church (241) and Mortimer (259).

CROs usually hold the records of the local courts, schools and Boards of Guardians (who administered the poor law from 1834), but also electoral registers, poll books, taxation and militia records, business records and many documents concerning property. Most CROs hold those parts of the IGI and census returns for the county or other area which they serve. Most CROs also act as diocesan record offices and therefore hold church records such as parish registers, other parish records, bishop's transcripts, wills, other probate records, marriage licence records, church court records and tithe documentation. CROs also have large collections of local history books (such as publications of local record societies), engravings, maps and photographs. Publications of local record or history societies, such as the Bedfordshire Historical Record Society and the Devon & Cornwall Record Society, are very important. Every county has one or more societies that transcribe and publish useful material from county records. Many copies of their volumes are also held at the SoG and numerous examples are noted below. These should, in the case of each type of record, be your first point of research since even if the transcribed records do not mention your ancestors, they are a useful introduction to the type of records that you may wish to review. Lists of publications of many societies are contained in Mullins (260).

Many CROs produce books or leaflets describing the records they hold and how to locate and use them. A good example is the booklet for Essex (222), which describes the services available at Essex Record Office in Chelmsford (and its branch offices) and lists the archive's holdings in some detail. There are also many older but still useful guides, such as Hull (254) for Kent records and the guide to Bedford Record Office (227). You should always review any such guides. Even less detailed guides, such as those for Norfolk Record Office (226) or Devon Record Office (220), are essential reading before your first visit to a CRO. Guides to local sources and archives, such as *West Kent Sources* (153), have also been produced by family history societies. All record offices have slightly different methods of indexing or cataloguing their records. You can save valuable research time by reviewing these guides to discover what records are available, how they are arranged or catalogued, how to find and use the records, and whether they are indexed. CROs usually have many unpublished name indexes (manuscript, typescript or computer databases) to their holdings of records. It is important to establish what indexes are available, since these can save much time by directing you to important records of your ancestors. The indexes are usually listed in a CRO's published guide to its holdings and some are also listed by county in Gibson & Hampson (141) and (158). For example, the latter reveals that Bedford Record Office has indexes (albeit incomplete) to Methodist baptisms for the 19th and 20th centuries, and burials in Bedfordshire towns after 1812.

Proof of identity is required at CROs (and sometimes a reader's ticket). Pencil must normally be used and cameras, tape-recorders and typewriters are often not permitted, although laptop computers usually are. Most CROs provide photocopying services and can recommend local photographers who can photograph records that cannot be photocopied. Some record offices are also able to undertake a limited amount of research for you. Details of the service and fees can be obtained from each CRO. A CRO may also have details of local researchers who will undertake research for a fee.

Many surviving records that you might expect to find in CROs are in fact held at other local record offices or libraries. During my research, I wished to consult parish registers for parts of south-west Essex. Most are at Essex Record Office but some of the relevant registers (and other important local records), are held at Vestry House Museum in Walthamstow. When researching the Keates family in Rotherhithe, I found only a few records at LMA relating to the parish and poor law administration of St Mary, Rotherhithe – the majority were at Southwark Local Studies Library. Similarly, while LMA holds the parish registers of Putney (as well as churchwardens' accounts for the 17th and 18th centuries), other parish records can be found elsewhere. Battersea

Library holds Putney vestry minutes and poor rate records, and Surrey Record Office holds Putney land tax records and the tithe map. London has many archives and local studies libraries that hold useful records about our London ancestors. Silverthorne (270) is a directory of London archives and libraries. Marcan (257) also describes the local history archives and libraries of Greater London and their publications. Other large cities or metropolitan areas also have a number of archives, most listed in the *FLHH* (5), Cole & Church (241) and Mortimer (259).

In addition to CROs, there are also some regional archives such as the National Library of Wales and the National Archives and National Library of Scotland (all described in chapter 29) and the West Country Studies Library (WCSL) in Castle Street, Exeter EX4 3PQ (telephone 01392 384216, see appendix XI for its web site). If your ancestors lived in Cornwall, Devon, Somerset or Dorset, the records held by WCSL will be of great assistance. WCSL holds not only the collections (particularly parish register transcripts) of the Devon & Cornwall Record Society, but also microfilms of the census returns for the West Country, local history books, newspapers, electoral records and photographs as well as much other relevant material. It is therefore important that you enquire about all local archives that might hold relevant records. You should not merely assume that all surviving records are held at a CRO.

Guildhall Library, City of London
Guildhall Library in Aldermanbury, London EC2P 2EJ (telephone 020 7606 3030, see appendix XI for its web site) is an important archive for anyone with London ancestors, but it also has much to interest other researchers. The collections relating to genealogy are described in Harvey (250). No reader's ticket is required and the library is open from Monday to Saturday. The library's enormous collections for the City of London include parish registers, other City parish records (such as rate books and churchwardens' accounts), wills, marriage licence records, maps and plans, directories and local history books. The collections also include apprenticeship and freedom records of the City livery companies (# chapter 22) and records of property (# chapter 27) owned by the church, schools and livery companies.

The library's collections of parish, non-conformist and burial ground registers are listed in its booklets (148), (149) and (307). The collections also include the baptism, marriage and burial registers of many Anglican communities abroad (# chapter 30) that were subject to the jurisdiction of the Bishop of London. The manuscript collections are also listed by Bullock-Anderson (240). A wide range of other material is held including the Lloyd's Marine collection (# chapter 21) and poll books and registers of electors (# chapter 17) for many areas of Britain, which are listed in a booklet (465). The substantial microfiche collection includes copies of the IGI, the 1881 census index, national indexes of wills from 1858 to 1935 (# chapter 12), *British Trials* (# chapter 25), FHS publications and Boyd's marriage index. There are also microfilm copies of Boyd's *London Burials*, *The Times* newspaper, Lloyd's shipping list, and lists of officers and soldiers who died in the First World War. *FamilySearch* and an index to *The Times* newspaper are also held on CD-ROM. The enormous printed books collection, to which there is a computerised catalogue, includes general books on genealogy, surnames, heraldry, and peerages, as well as published parish registers, biographical dictionaries, university and school registers (# chapter 19), the *London Gazette* (# chapter 17) and county histories (# chapter 16). Much of the collection is on open shelves (those books on "closed access" are produced from storage in a few minutes) and include copies of the vast majority of published works referred to in this book. Guildhall Library also has an extensive collection of maps, prints, photographs and engravings of

London. About 20,000 of these images are included in the library's database "Collage" and can be seen on terminals at the library or on the library's Collage web site.

Corporation of London Record Office

CLRO is also located at Guildhall in London (telephone 020 7606 3030) and holds the archives of the City of London's governing bodies since medieval times. Many other British cities and boroughs have their own archives, which are similar to CROs and listed in the works noted above. However, CLRO probably has the richest collections of material of any city or borough archive. Its collections are described in Deadman & Scudder (244). They include the usual local authority archives recording civic administration, but they date from the 11th century and are enhanced by the importance of London and of those people who lived and worked there over the centuries. The most useful records are the records of 500,000 freemen of the City of London from 1681 to 1940 (# chapter 17). CLRO also holds many property records (concerning land in many counties), records of the proceedings of City government, its finances and records of the City law courts from medieval times, London militia records from the 17th century and records of some charities, schools, prisons, markets and hospitals.

Borthwick Institute of Historical Research

The Borthwick Institute is a department of the University of York, at St Anthony's Hall, Peasholme Green, York, YO1 2PW (telephone 01904 642315 and see appendix XI for its web site), which also acts as the registry for the diocese and province of York. It holds many records of the Archbishops of York, including wills, marriage licence records, parish registers, bishops' transcripts and church court records. Since the ecclesiastical province of York extended over most of northern England, the Institute's records are of interest to many researchers. The Institute is open from Monday to Friday (but an appointment should be made). Its holdings of genealogical sources are described in Webb (273). The Institute has also published detailed guides, such as Smith (271), to its holdings of parish records and other ecclesiastical and family archives.

The Parliamentary Archives (House of Lords Record Office)

The House of Lords Record Office, also called the Parliamentary Archives, is located at the House of Lords, London SW1A 0PW (telephone 020 7219 3074). Opening times and other general information are noted on its web site. The archive's main purpose is to serve both Houses of Parliament and preserve their archives but it holds many records of interest to family historians which are reviewed by A. Camp in *Family Tree Magazine* (July 2001), in Bond (922) and in later chapters of this book. They include biographical material about MPs (# chapter 22), records of legal proceedings before the House of Lords (chapter 24), peerage claims (chapter 26), the Protestation returns (chapter 23) and private acts of Parliament concerning name changes, estates and naturalisation (chapters 5, 24 and 30). HLRO also holds a database of witnesses at committee hearings on local acts of Parliament (# chapter 22). Useful information is also contained in Parliamentary Papers, that is thousands of official reports presented to Parliament about topics such as charities, education, mines, prisons and the poor law. Many have appendices that contain witnesses' evidence or useful lists of names. For example, a report on London prisons in 1819 lists about 850 men and women committed to Bridewell in 1815, 1816 and 1817 as "disorderly persons", with their ages and sentences. Parliamentary Papers and the subject indexes available are described in more detail by S. Fowler in the 2001 edition of the *FLHH* (5).

Lambeth Palace Library
The library of the Archbishop of Canterbury at Lambeth Palace, London SE1 7JU (telephone 020 7898 1400) is open to the public (opening times and other information are noted on the library's web site). It is the principal record office for the Church of England and includes the archives of the Archbishops of Canterbury and of the Province of Canterbury, but also many family papers (for example of the Earls of Shrewsbury). The documents of interest to genealogists include marriage licence records (# chapter 14), estate records (# chapter 27) and records of the Court of Arches (# chapter 24).

Royal Commission on Historical Manuscripts (RCHM)
The RCHM (also known as the Historical Manuscripts Commission) does not hold any archives but it has published many detailed reports on records held in archives or private collections (# chapter 27). In April 2003, RCHM and the PRO merged to form the National Archives and the reading room of RCHM will open, on 8 December 2003, at the premises of TNA at Kew.

The RCHM web site (# appendix XI), which will be merged into the web site of TNA in due course, includes a database named ARCHON, of archival sources and projects, with links to hundreds of archives and libraries (and the addresses of many others) that hold archives relating to Britain or British people. Each entry lists the records held by the archive, extracted from the catalogues and lists held by RCHM and noted below. RCHM holds two other important finding aids. The Manorial Documents Register (# chapter 27) is a card index to manorial records. The parts for Wales, Norfolk, Yorkshire and Hampshire have been converted into a database that can be consulted on the RCHM web site. The National Register of Archives (# chapter 22) is a database which catalogues many records held in CROs, libraries, museums, business archives and private collections. It can be consulted from terminals at RCHM or through the RCHM web site. The database incorporates 43,000 unpublished lists and catalogues of manuscript collections obtained by RCHM from those archives. Searches are made through indexes, containing about 150,000 references of personal names, places and the names or type of business.

The personal names index refers to the personal papers of about 35,000 individuals of note (such as those people listed in the *Dictionary of National Biography*). Thus it reveals that most of the papers of the Duke of Wellington are at Southampton University Library while those of Admiral Nelson are at the National Maritime Museum. The business index can be used to locate surviving archives of over 26,000 businesses, such as solicitors' firms, shipbuilders and publishers. The entries give the business name, describe the records held (for example, receipt books 1750–77) and note the archive holding them and a number referring to one of that archive's catalogues held by RCHM. The third index (to organisations) refers to the bodies that created records, such as law courts, police authorities or professional bodies.

Other libraries
Local, university and specialist libraries are listed in the *FLHH* (5). Local libraries usually hold a selection of books on genealogy and local history. Most libraries use the Dewey decimal classification system, and family history and genealogy are in class 929. Local history books (# chapter 16) are in class 942 and are useful because they describe an area's industry, agriculture, schools, churches and prominent residents.

Public libraries hold many sources that may assist family historians. The FAMILIA web site is a directory of libraries' holdings of genealogical material, such as the GRO or census indexes, the IGI, directories, poll books and electoral registers. You can therefore discover the holdings of some of the libraries near your home, or the libraries that hold material concerning your ancestors' place of residence. Searches can be made by type of material (such as poll books) and by county or place.

Many libraries also have collections of old photographs relating to the area, usually including local buildings, people of note and group photographs (perhaps the local fire brigade). Local libraries usually hold books which reproduce old photographs of the area (particularly of local buildings). These books reveal what a place was like in the 19th century and note the sources of the photographs (so that you can search in those archives for further photographs). Many libraries also hold copies of local maps, published local or county histories, parish registers, school registers, commercial directories, reference books on peerages (or works such as the *Dictionary of National Biography*) and publications of county record societies. Some libraries also have copies of local newspapers and electoral registers.

Specialist archives

There are many specialist archives which you may wish to visit. These are dealt with in later chapters. For example, non-conformist denominations such as the Quakers and Methodists have substantial archives (# chapter 13). Some military records are held in museums (# chapters 20 and 21).

Photographic archives

The importance of photographs of your ancestors, the houses in which they lived or the shops that they owned, was briefly considered in chapter 2. It is also helpful to obtain photographs that illustrate an ancestor's way of life. Photography started in the early 19th century but photographs are rare before about 1855. Photography then boomed and photographs of buildings, views or special events became fairly common. Photography of individual people also became widespread by about 1870. West (463) notes that there were 633 photographic studios in Birmingham alone between 1842 and 1914 (and probably thousands of amateur photographers). Unfortunately, many old photographs have not survived and the subject matter of surviving photographs (especially a person's name) is often not identified.

Photograph collections are held at CROs, libraries and many other archives. Thousands of surviving photographs provide views of streets, towns and villages, even work-places and shops. Churches and ships were also popular subjects for early photographers. Some of the most important collections are described below. Eakins (245) is a guide to about 1,100 UK photograph collections with archives' addresses (as at 1985), terms of access and indexed lists of the general subject matter of each collection. The entries for collections are grouped by their main subject matter, for example "military history", "local history and geography" (including collections about particular places) and "transport" (including collections about sailing ships, railways, harbours and aircraft). Wall (272) is a similar directory of about 1,600 collections, but also a little out of date as to the location of collections.

The Hulton Getty Collection, based at Unique House, 21–31 Woodfield Road, London W9, was founded in 1944 as the Hulton Picture Library, an archive for the journal *Picture Post* which was published from 1937 to 1957. As the archive grew it gradually incorporated other collections, including many older photographs. It is now Europe's largest photographic archive, containing approximately 12 million photographs, many dating from the late 19th and early 20th centuries. Selected photographs from the collection have been published. Weightman (90) and Sackett (269) contain selections of photographs of London from the collection. *The People's War* by Gardiner (247), illustrates life in Britain during the Second World War and Keen (70) is a portrait of Britain from 1880 to 1919.

The National Monuments Record at Kemble Drive, Swindon (telephone 01793 414600) holds over six million photographs of Britain. Most feature views or buildings (many of which no longer exist), taken during and after the Second World War, but there is also much earlier material. The archive also has a reference library of over 30,000 books and journals on local history and buildings. The records and photographs are being incorporated into a database so that you can search for information by the name of a parish. Copies of photographs, maps or other material in the collection can be purchased (details are on the NMR web site). The NMR is also placing its photographs of listed buildings online on the Images of England web site. There is also a London search room, at 55 Blandford Street, W1 (telephone 020 7208 8200), which holds material on London but also provides researchers in London with access to the records at Swindon. Unfortunately, this office is due to close in March 2004.

The LMA photograph collection is an essential source if your ancestors lived in London. It contains over 350,000 photographs of Greater London, mostly showing buildings and monuments (particularly schools, churches, hospitals, housing, pubs and Second World War bomb damage). There is a detailed index and copies of the photographs can be purchased. Guildhall Library also has a collection of about 100,000 photographs and prints of London. The London Transport Museum has over 100,000 photographs concerning London's public transport.

CROs and other local archives usually have large collections of photographs of the areas they serve. For example, the Hammersmith and Fulham local history centre has a collection of about 60,000 photographs; a selection of them are reproduced in Farrell & Bayliss (61). A selection of the London borough of Hackney's collection of photographs has been published in Mander & Golden (75), illustrating life in Hackney (in particular housing, businesses and noteworthy buildings) since the mid-19th century. The planning and building departments of local authorities often retain photograph collections of local buildings from recent years. Enquiries can also be made to see if photographs are held of buildings that have now been demolished. Museums are considered further below, but they often hold many photographs of local buildings and people.

Collections of military photographs are considered in more detail in chapters 20 and 21, but many military museums have large collections of photographs, perhaps featuring your ancestors who served in the armed forces, but at least illustrating the uniform that an ancestor would have worn. The Imperial War Museum has about two million photographs, many dating from the First World War and the National Maritime Museum has over 750,000 photographs.

The Rural History Centre at Reading University, Whiteknights Park, Reading (telephone 0118 3788660), holds approximately 750,000 photographs (as well as a substantial collection of exhibits and documents relating to rural life). The Victoria & Albert Museum's department of prints, drawings and photographs has about 300,000 prints and photographs, particularly illustrating daily life in Victorian times. TNA holds many photographs, described in TNA general information leaflet 36, mostly in records of bodies such as the War Office and the RAF. In particular, series INF 9 is a collection of about 13,000 photographs taken throughout Britain in the 1930s. The series list specifies the places covered. The India Office collections at the British Library (# chapter 30) include over 250,000 photographs of India under British rule. Oliver (78) notes other large photographic collections of interest to local historians, for example those at Birmingham Central Library (180,000 items), Aberdeen University (40,000 items in the Wilson Collection) and the Public Record Office of Northern Ireland in Belfast (100,000 items). Other institutions (such as the police, fire brigade or lifeboat service) and clubs (particularly sports clubs) often have useful photographs. Most universities and schools have collections of photographs of the pupils and teaching staff.

Two commercial photographic archives are worthy of mention. Firstly, Saul & Markwell (27) recommend "Railprint", an archive of over 100,000 historical photographs of Britain (not merely railways). A catalogue can be obtained from Railprint, 302 Holdenhurst Road, Bournemouth. Secondly, there is the Francis Frith collection of Victorian photographs. Francis Frith (1822–98) was one of the great pioneers of photography and he and his assistants took thousands of photographs in Britain and abroad, including almost every British village, town and city, and sold them to the public. About 60,000 negatives survive from Frith's business, relating to over 2,000 British towns or villages. Most are held, with other photographs, in the Francis Frith collection which now includes about 375,000 photographs. Wherever in Britain your ancestors lived and whatever their jobs, there is probably a photograph in the collection that will be relevant to your family history. About 50,000 of these can be viewed on the Francis Frith collection web site (from which prints can also be ordered). Enquiries can also be addressed to The Francis Frith Collection, Frith Barn, Teffont, near Salisbury, Wiltshire SP3 5QP (telephone 01722 716376) which is producing a series of volumes of photographs in the collection. The first volume of *Frith's Photographic Directory, Great Britain and Ireland* includes about 3,500 of Frith's photographs of British towns, cities and villages that can also be printed out from an accompanying CD-ROM. Other selections of Frith's work have been published, for example in Jay (68), Wilson (91) and in West (274), which includes some of Frith's photographs of ships, harbours and fishing villages.

Paintings

It is possible that portraits were painted of your ancestors, particularly if they were peers, gentry, famous for some reason or (especially in Victorian times) if they were from a wealthy family, perhaps from industry and commerce, and wished to impress their friends and business colleagues. You should ask relatives whether they remember any family portraits. The National Portrait Gallery in London holds about 8,000 portraits (including some photographs) to which Yung (276) is an illustrated catalogue. Portraits are also held in many other art galleries or collections accessible to the public. About 5,000 of them, from medieval times to 1900, are listed in Ormond & Rogers (1052).

Museums

Museums can assist your research through their collections of archives and photographs (the archive collections of museums such as the National Maritime Museum and the National Army Museum are considered below). However, museums are also useful to family historians for other reasons. There are museums in Britain for almost every interest or activity, including local history, transport, historical costume, industries or religion, while regimental and other military museums illustrate the life of army and navy ancestors.

HMSO has published seven books (for the Museums and Galleries Commission) covering the regions of England as well as one book for each of Wales, Scotland and Ireland, listing museums and describing many of their exhibits and the archives they hold. Examples of these books are Olding (261) for London and Wilson (275) for south-west England. If you are interested in a particular area of the country, works such as these will tell you about the local history museums. If you are interested in a particular activity or aspect of life, it is worthwhile consulting each volume to ascertain the specialist museums around the country that may be of assistance to you. Alternatively, Richardson (25) provides a useful list of museums by specialisation (for example agriculture, costume and transport).

Buying and selling photographs, deeds, wills and other genealogical material
Many types of documents refer to our ancestors. Certificates of civil registration or church baptisms have already been noted. Many more are reviewed in later chapters, including wills, apprenticeship indentures, certificates of qualifications or service, property deeds, commercial ledgers, diaries, letters, rent schedules and court documents. Many of these have been deposited in archives but a great number are held privately, perhaps by a member of the family they concern but in some cases by someone who collects such material. Most documents, photographs and medals survive because there is an active market for them. They are not lost forever and so old photographs, family Bibles, medals and documents of interest to family historians can be found in secondhand bookshops, auctions or on market stalls. Title deeds proved ownership of property, but were discarded when no longer of use, for example when title to the property was registered (# chapter 15). Unfortunately, groups of such documents often become split up and are lost to those people who would be most interested in them. Single documents are therefore more common than bundles of related records. For example, I purchased a deed of June 1871 concerning the settlement (or trust) of Mr and Mrs Royds. It named many members of the Royds family (as trustees and beneficiaries) and also referred to family property and to a marriage settlement of 1841. Many people helpfully advertise such finds, for example in *Family Tree Magazine*.

When manuscript dealers or auction houses sell this material, they often produce catalogues that describe the documents, sometimes noting the names of people mentioned in them. Consequently, even if a document concerning your ancestors was sold years ago, perhaps to another dealer or collector, a record of it may survive in a catalogue. The documents recorded in catalogues were reviewed in 14 articles by J. Titford in *Family Tree Magazine* (2000–2003), with many examples from a selection of catalogues, including this apprenticeship indenture:

Essex, Elandon, 5 June 1756. George Prentice apprenticed to John Burr, blacksmith. Printed vellum document, 6″ × 8″, with manuscript insertions. Signed and sealed by George Prentice the elder and John Burr.

The SoG has a collection of catalogues issued by James Coleman who dealt (1859–1911) in books, wills, pedigrees, marriage settlements, property deeds and other manuscripts. The catalogues note brief details of items and the parties' names (and there is a card index of about 50,000 names). Catalogues of auctioneers and dealers who specialise in medals are also useful. Your ancestor's medals may have been sold years ago but they may appear in a catalogue, perhaps with a photograph.

FAMILY HISTORY SOCIETIES AND PERIODICALS

Society of Genealogists

The Society of Genealogists (SoG) is located at 14 Charterhouse Buildings, Goswell Road, London EC1M 7BA (telephone 020 7251 8799) near to Barbican and Farringdon underground stations (as indicated on the map at illustration 9). The SoG library holds the best collection of genealogical information in Britain. Members have free use of the library and non-members can use the library for an hourly fee. The SoG is generally open from Tuesday to Saturday from 10.00 a.m. to 6.00 p.m. (8.00 p.m. on Thursdays). It has a bookshop and also organises many lectures on genealogical research and family history.

Members receive a quarterly journal, *Genealogists' Magazine* (3), which contains articles on records and other aspects of genealogy and also lists of new material added to the library. The SoG also publishes *Computers in Genealogy* (95) and many booklets which describe the SoG's collections (and are noted in the relevant chapters of this book), for example census indexes, parish registers, MIs, directories and poll books. The SoG also publishes many records and indexes in book form and on microfiche. SoG members receive a 20% discount on its publications and on the fees for its lectures.

The SoG web site includes membership details, a general description of the SoG's collections, some articles from *Computers in Genealogy* and copies of the SoG *County Sources* booklets (# chapter 7) which list the SoG's holdings of parish registers, MIs and marriage licence records. The SoG has two free electronic mailing lists. One provides a news service for all genealogists about the SoG (for example about publications and lectures). The other, for members only, provides an opportunity to submit queries and comments (an e-mail conference facility) which are posted to all subscribers to the list in full or in digest form. Details of the mailing lists are noted in the SoG's journals.

The ground floor at the SoG includes a bookshop, cloakroom and lecture theatre. The library is arranged over the lower ground floor (the Lower library) and the first and second floors (the Middle and Upper libraries). A guide to the location of material is available at reception. The principal book collections and many unpublished transcripts of parish registers, MIs and wills are in the Middle and Upper libraries. The Upper library includes an enormous collection of family histories and works on the armed forces, professions and schools. The Lower library has computers, microfilm and fiche readers and printers (and parts of the manuscript, document and special collections). Many books in the collection are on open shelves. These are arranged by English county (or in sections for each of Wales, Scotland, Ireland and many foreign countries) or by subject matter (such as works on the navy). The sources are so extensive that they are only briefly summarised here (although many are noted throughout this book).

The SoG collections are catalogued on computer. The OPAC (On Line Public Access Catalogue) terminals on each floor of the library are easy to use, with instructions available at each terminal. Researchers can search the catalogue by the author or title of specific works, or by subject matter (for example, "Bedfordshire-registers") and then scroll through the list of results to find the item required (and its reference details, format and location in the library). The microfilm sources at the SoG include copies of parish and non-conformist registers, census records, directories, the GRO indexes of births, marriages and deaths in England and Wales (1837–1925), indexes of births, marriages and deaths in Scotland (1855–1920), the actual Scottish registers for 1855, indexes of wills of England and Wales (# chapter 12), marriage licence records, and Quaker registers from the 17th century to 1837. The microfiche collection includes the IGI for the whole world, indexes to baptisms and marriages in Scottish registers (1553–1854) as well as thousands of British and Irish parish registers and census indexes. There are many resources on CD-ROM, such as *FamilySearch*, which includes the IGI and *Ancestral File*, the LDS 1881 census index, the BVRI and (described below) Griffith's Valuation of Ireland 1848–64, Palmer's index to *The Times* 1790–1905 and *Biography Database 1680–1830*. The book and document collections include many copies of parish or non-conformist registers, Boyd's marriage index, Boyd's index of London burials, Boyd's *Citizens of London*, census indexes, MIs (from about 8,500 burial grounds), maps, local history books, birth briefs of many members (to which there is an index) and some card indexes of surnames. Other sources in the library include:

a. *Genealogists' Magazine* (since 1925), other genealogical and family history societies' journals and many copies of *Gentleman's Magazine* (# chapter 17)
b. publications of the British Record Society, the Harleian and other record societies
c. Army and navy lists from the 18th to 20th centuries, law and medical directories, clergy lists and directories or other works on many other professions and trades
d. published registers of schools and universities
e. marriage licence records, wills and also indexes to wills held at various archives
f. poll books and electoral registers
g. reference books such as county histories, *Burke's Peerage* or works on royal families
h. directories (including many for Scotland, Wales, Ireland and abroad)
i. family histories (published and unpublished) and manuscript pedigrees
j. the *Apprentices Index* for the period 1710 to 1774
k. records (such as pedigrees) donated by members (for about 15,000 surnames)

The SoG holds some unique collections of material (in addition to Boyd's indexes noted above) which are described by S. Gibbons in the 2001 edition of the *FLHH* (5). The Bernau card index (available on microfilm) refers to about four million people in the records of the Courts of Chancery and Exchequer between 1350 and 1800 (# chapter 24). The Great Card Index (now available to researchers on 605 microfilms) consists of over 3.5 million slips, arranged alphabetically by name, referring to a vast range of sources, including parish registers, MIs, marriage licence records, court proceedings, wills and newspapers. The contents and arrangement of the index are described by P. Loveridge in *Genealogists' Magazine* (March 2003). It is a lucky dip but it can be of great help. I was researching the family of Charnock (or Chernock) and found that the index included many entries for the family from parish registers as well as references to court actions involving disputes over wills and property. The Civil Service "evidence of age" records (# chapter 22) and Crisp's collection of wills and bonds are also important sources. The family document collections include thousands of pedigrees, wills, parish register extracts and similar material, arranged by surname, with a separate section (filed by county then parish) for extensive material relating to particular places. The Whitmore collection includes 61 volumes of pedigrees and notes on various families. The Holworthy collection consists of seven boxes of notes on armorial families and will abstracts. The Fawcett index is a collection of published and unpublished material about clergymen from the 12th to the early 20th century. There are also collections relating to particular counties that include parish register extracts, MIs, wills, deeds, marriage licences and pedigrees. For example, there is the Campling collection (for Norfolk and Suffolk), the Snell collection (for Berkshire), the Rogers bequest (for Cornwall), the Glencross collection (Cornwall and Devon), the Whitehead collection (East Anglia), the Dwelly Index (principally West Country), the Macleod papers (Scotland), the Percy-Smith index (India), the Colyer Fergusson and Mordy collections (Jewish) and the Smith collection (West Indies).

Indexes of important collections at the SoG are also available on the English Origins web site. Those presently available on the site are noted in other chapters of this book but they include:

a. Most of Boyd's marriage index (# chapter 7)
b. Bank of England will abstracts index 1717–1845 (# chapter 12)
c. Prerogative Court of Canterbury wills index 1750–1800 (# chapter 12)
d. Archdeaconry Court of London wills index 1700–1807 (# chapter 12)
e. Vicar General marriage licence allegations index 1694–1850 (# chapter 14)
f. Faculty Office marriage licence allegations index 1701–1850 (# chapter 14)
g. City of London Livery Company apprenticeship indexes (# chapter 22)

A surname search is free. The result notes the number of matches in each type of record. You then pay an access fee to see up to 150 entries. SoG members have a free access period of 7 days in each quarter (from any computer). Searches can also be made without charge from terminals in the SoG library. Copies of some documents referred to in the indexes can be ordered online for a further fee.

The SoG is the best place to deposit copies of your research papers for the benefit of other researchers and future generations. S. Fowler provides guidance on the deposit of material, including that on computer disk, in *Genealogists' Magazine* (December 1999). For those who cannot visit the SoG library, staff will undertake research and copy documents (for fees) in parts of the collections, as described by E. Churchill in *Genealogists' Magazine* (March 2002).

Family history societies
Family history societies promote and assist the study of genealogy and family history in a particular county, city, area or district. There are about 200 societies in Britain. For example, there are societies for Devon, for each of East and West Surrey and for many areas in London. They are listed, with contact details, in the *FLHH* (5). There are also many local history societies (# chapter 16) and many societies for particular interests, occupations or religious views, such as the Catholic FHS, the Quaker FHS and the Anglo-German FHS. These are also listed in the *FLHH* (5). Most societies publish a quarterly journal for members (with articles about local records and members' interests) as well as publishing genealogical material relating to their area. They also exchange journals with other societies. The annual subscription for membership of a family history society is about £10. You should consider joining the FHS for any area in which your ancestors lived for a few generations as it will assist you to discover the location of records and archives, and meet other researchers who may be able to help you solve problems encountered in your research, or who may be researching the same lines of ancestry as you.

Family history societies usually have substantial libraries of local sources, such as copies of parish registers, MIs, local histories and directories. Many societies have also prepared indexes to parish registers, census records or other material that may assist your research. For example, Devon FHS has produced a surname index for the 1851 census of Devon and indexes to Devon marriages from 1754 to 1837. Family history societies also publish a large amount of other source material in books or on microfiche or CD-ROM, including MIs, parish register transcripts, maps, and indexes to wills. Details are available from each society or in the booklets noted below. Some societies also operate schemes to assist research, especially for those people who cannot easily attend at certain archives. The Essex Society for Family History operates a scheme, at very reasonable cost, to obtain civil registration certificates and extracts from the census returns.

Most family history societies have web sites, listed in the *FLHH* (5), with details of membership, publications and lectures. Some societies also include some transcribed material and indexes on their web pages. For example, Northumberland & Durham FHS includes many transcripts of parish registers and MIs. The web sites of GENUKI and the FFHS (see below) also have links to FHS web sites.

Most British family history societies (as well as some in Australia, Canada, New Zealand and the United States) are members of the Federation of Family History Societies (FFHS). The FFHS publishes the journal *Family History News and Digest* (225) twice a year in which societies describe their activities and publications. The digest also summarises hundreds of articles from the journals of member societies, which can be of interest to all genealogists. The societies that are members of the FFHS are listed in each issue of its digest (with up to date names and addresses of membership secretaries). Enquiries can also be directed to Maggie Loughran, FFHS Administrator, PO Box 2425, Coventry CV5 6YX (telephone 07041 492032). FFHS (Publications) Ltd, of Units 15–16, Chesham Business Centre, Oram Street, Bury BL9 6EN, publishes many booklets on particular aspects of research, such as the Gibson Guides, which are listed on the FFHS web site (and most are noted in this book). The book and fiche publications of family history societies that are members of the FFHS are listed in Hampson (249) and Perkins (263) respectively. FFHS Publications also operates an extensive online bookshop (# appendix XI) that incorporates GENfair, from which you can purchase the publications of the FFHS, many family history societies and some commercial publishers and suppliers.

The FFHS "pay-per-view" web site *FamilyHistoryOnline* (# appendix XI) brings together indexes and transcription work of its member societies. The site includes indexes to parts of the English and Welsh census, many indexes to parish registers and MIs, including many entries from the National Burial Index. The name indexes can be consulted for free and then payment (a few pence per entry) is by credit card or by pre-paid voucher, purchased from FFHS Publications or the FFHS online bookshop. By September 2003, the site included 14.6 million records from 36 English or Welsh counties. The contents of the site are listed on its introductory pages. Although there is, as yet, no material for some counties, there are thousands of entries for others. The Suffolk material includes two burial indexes (with over 680,000 entries), a baptism index (over 120,000 entries) and two marriage indexes (with 66,000 entries). The material for Cornwall includes indexes to over 260,000 MIs, 940,000 baptisms and 350,000 marriages and burials, transcripts and indexes to the 1841, 1861 and 1871 censuses of Cornwall and partial transcripts and indexes for other years.

LDS (Mormon) family history centres
The Church of Jesus Christ of Latter-Day Saints (LDS) – the Mormons – have made a great contribution to genealogy through the Genealogical Society of Utah which gathers records to

assist people tracing their ancestry. The IGI is the most important finding aid for pre-1837 records and the Family History Library in Salt Lake City, Utah is the largest in the world. It holds copies of records from most countries, principally on two million microfilms and 500,000 fiche that can be ordered by the public for viewing at LDS family history centres. The library also has about 250,000 books (many of them also available on film or fiche).

The Hyde Park family history centre, at 64/68 Exhibition Road, South Kensington, London SW7 2PA (telephone 020 7589 8561) is open from Monday to Saturday. The addresses and telephone numbers of about 70 other family history centres in Britain are listed in the *FLHH* (5) and on the LDS church and *FamilySearch* web sites. However, the opening hours of some are limited, so it is advisable to telephone before visiting (particularly on Saturdays) to make an appointment and book a microfilm reader or computer. Each family history centre holds the IGI on microfiche for the whole world, *FamilySearch* (incorporating the IGI and *Ancestral File*, see chapter 7) on CD-ROM and many books and microfilm records. A vast amount of other microfilmed material (such as parish registers, census records, civil registration indexes and wills) can be ordered from the Family History Library in Salt Lake City for viewing at family history centres. The library's holdings are listed (with their microfilm or fiche numbers) in a catalogue, available on the *FamilySearch* web site and on fiche or CD-ROM at each family history centre, the SoG and some libraries. The fiche version of the catalogue is arranged by country, county, then parish. The CD-ROM version can also be purchased from the LDS Distribution Centre, 399 Garretts Green Lane, Garretts Green, Birmingham B33 0UH. It contains the same information as the fiche version but as a database so that it is easy to search for all the records held concerning any place.

As noted in chapter 7, the Hyde Park family history centre has a large collection of microfilms of the holdings of the Family History Library available permanently at its premises. The contents of the 43,000 films presently available are listed by country, state, county, city, town or parish, in a separate catalogue at the centre. They include parish registers, MIs and census, probate and poor law records. Although the films may include nothing about one parish in which you are interested, they may include both the parish registers and extensive parts of the parish officers' records (# chapter 18) of poor relief and the related matters of settlement and apprenticeship. The films are particularly useful, to researchers in or near London, for the extensive records of Scotland, Ireland and foreign countries that they contain. For example, they include indexes to Irish births, marriages and deaths of 1865–1959 (# chapter 29) and many civil registration and parish records from Jamaica (# chapter 30).

Institute of Heraldic and Genealogical Studies
The IHGS, of 79–82 Northgate, Canterbury, Kent, CT1 1BA, was founded to further research and provide training in genealogy. It provides residential and correspondence courses on all aspects of family history, genealogy and heraldry. It also publishes maps (noted earlier) showing civil registration districts and parish boundaries and a quarterly journal *Family History* (223) which includes transcripts of records and other useful articles. The IHGS holds, for Achievements Limited, the Pallot indexes (1780–1837) and the IHGS library has a large collection of books and genealogical material including a Catholic marriage index (# chapter 13), an East Sussex baptisms index for 1700 to 1812, the East Kent 1851 census index, and the Andrews' Index of Britons dying overseas (principally in the 19th and 20th centuries).

Other journals
There are some other genealogical journals. The best is *Family Tree Magazine* (2), published monthly and available from some newsagents, FHS bookshops or directly from the publishers at 61 Great Whyte, Ramsey, Huntingdon, Cambridgeshire PE17 1HL. Back numbers (since November 1984) can be reviewed at the SoG or FHS libraries and can be purchased on microfiche. The magazine contains articles of general interest, but also specialised articles, for example on particular trades or research problems. It reviews new books, newly published source material and has a monthly article entitled "Questions and Answers" in which readers' questions (the answers to which may be of interest to other readers) are printed together with answers researched by Jean Cole. The magazine also contains lists of readers' enquiries (and the names of families that they are researching) and adverts from people offering research services.

The journal *Ancestors* (215), noted above, is an excellent journal about sources at TNA. The journals *Practical Family History* (4) and *Family History Monthly* (224), as well as a new journal, *Your Family Tree*, are also useful aids to family historians, including articles on genealogical records, surnames and new publications as well as readers' enquiries.

Some genealogical journals that were produced in the late 19th and early 20th centuries are held by the SoG and described by Wagner (31). These contain important material: family histories, pedigrees, extracts of records such as parish registers, wills, marriage licences, deeds and MIs, as well as general articles on genealogy and heraldry. In some cases, they reproduce material that has since been lost (such as MIs and some wills). The most important of these journals are:

a. *Collectanea Topographica et Genealogica*; 8 volumes published (1834–43)
b. *Topographer and Genealogist*; 3 volumes published (1846–58)
c. *The Ancestor*; 12 volumes published (1902–5)
d. *The Genealogist*; 44 volumes published (1877–1921)
e. *Miscellanea Genealogica et Heraldica*; 31 volumes published (1868–1938)
f. *Herald and Genealogist*; 8 volumes published (1863–74)
g. *The Genealogical Magazine*; 7 volumes published (1897–1904)

Most of these journals have their own indexes, usually for each volume, but new consolidated indexes for the journals listed at (a) to (e) above have been produced by Raymond (264). These indexes have sections listing places and family names, then listing references in the journals to material (concerning those names and places) such as parish register extracts, wills, MIs, obituaries and family histories.

One-name studies or societies
Thousands of families are the subject of "one-name studies", by societies or individuals, who try to collect all available information on people with that surname. Notices also appear in journals and periodicals from people researching particular names. Many of the researchers are members of the Guild of One-Name Studies (GOONS). You can find out if a particular surname is being researched by a Guild member by writing to the Registrar of the Guild at Box G at the SoG's address. Alternatively, the Guild's published register (235) and its web site list the surnames and variations (about 7,000 of them) that are being researched, by members, with each member's name and address. If you are considering undertaking a one-name study and joining the Guild,

you should be aware of the workload that is involved (for example the minimum requirements for records that you should have used, and the obligations of liaising with other researchers). Information on these points can be obtained from the Guild's web site.

The Internet has made it much easier to find out whether other people are studying a particular surname but also made it easier for the results of that research to be shared. A number of researchers have placed the results of their one-name studies on their own web sites, thus making the information available for anyone interested in that family. This is considered further below.

A warning is unfortunately necessary in respect of letters offering books in the style of *The World Book of Herbers* or whatever your surname happens to be. These books are usually linked to an organisation named Halberts. I received typical letters in 1991 and 1995, offering me information (for a fee) on a "unique coat of arms which was granted to an early Herber" and a book, apparently including an "international Herber directory" and articles such as "How the old and distinguished Herber family got its name and what the Herber name means". You may receive similar offers. These books are little more than lists of names and addresses extracted from sources such as telephone directories. The genealogical value of these books is illustrated by the fact that one letter was addressed to me as "Ms" Mark Herber, no doubt because the organisation sending it out simply took my name from a mailing list that contains the same mistake.

Common interests and contacts

Genealogists are always looking for other people who are researching the same ancestral lines, so advertising your own enquiries can be very productive. *Genealogists' Magazine, Family Tree Magazine*, FHS journals and the other magazines noted above have sections in which you can list your interests. Annual registers of members' interests are also produced by most family history societies or included on FHS web sites. When I listed in the Devon FHS journal some surnames that I was researching in Devon, I received letters from two other members (who turned out to be cousins) who were also researching the surnames Bulleid and Rice. They each had an enormous amount of information relevant to my family tree, much of which would have taken me years to collect and some might never have come to my attention.

Family Tree Magazine also has a column entitled "Can you help?" (inviting readers to respond directly to those posing questions), a feature "Pass it on" (in which readers notify others of useful information or of their discovery of family Bibles, photographs or documents that other researchers might want) and readers' adverts for connections with other families or one-name studies. Whenever you write to an individual or organisation for the first time (and in some cases on every occasion), you should enclose a stamped addressed envelope. If you write to someone abroad, you should send an addressed envelope and sufficient international reply coupons (available from post offices) with which your correspondent can buy stamps for a reply.

Genealogical information on the Internet

The Internet is an international network of computers that can communicate with each other. It is easy for any computer user to obtain access to the Internet. Computer users can send electronic mail (e-mail) to other users on the net, or consult the many pages of information that organisations and individuals make available from their computers. Hawgood (251) describes how to search for this information. At present, using the Internet for genealogy is similar to visiting a new library that has not yet purchased most of the books that people want to read (and which has only a few of the pages of some other books). You can find many archives' catalogues on the Internet as well as some digital images, transcripts or indexes of records but nothing like the vast amount of material held in genealogical libraries or CROs. You may also find a transcript of certain years of a parish register or of part of a trade or commercial directory (for example covering one or two towns) but not the parts for the rest of a county. However, to put the matter in perspective, there was very little genealogical material on the Internet five years ago and the amount of data and the number of sites are growing daily.

Some useful web sites have already been noted. The 1901 census online service, the Online catalogue of TNA (PROCAT), the National Register of Archives and the web sites of English Origins and *FamilySearch* are just five examples of the wonderful finding aids or data collections now available to family historians. Other sites are reviewed later in this book. For example, the DocumentsOnline service of TNA (# chapter 12) features digital images of over one million wills. Cheshire Record Office's web site includes an index to 70,000 wills and other probate documents that it holds. The web site of the Commonwealth War Graves Commission permits online searches of burial or memorial registers to 1.7 million British and Irish men who died in the two world wars. The most important web site addresses are included in the first part of appendix XI. The second part of that appendix notes a few sites of relevance to particular topics. Many other sites are listed in Raymond (268), (1214) and (1215). New web sites of interest and useful information that is added to existing sites are reviewed regularly in *Family Tree Magazine* and other family history journals.

As noted above, the Internet makes it easy for any researcher, but especially someone who is undertaking a one-name study, to share that information by creating his or her own web site. For example, the "Sterry worldwide pages", edited by Robert Sterry, include a large amount of information about people with the surname Sterry or its variants, including transcripts of many records. Researchers who are descended from one of the Sercombe families of Devon are very fortunate. Daniel Morgan has prepared hundreds of pages of transcripts of records (wills, parish registers, MIs, directory entries as well as civil registration, census and other records) that refer to people with this surname (including my ancestors from Dunsford and Bridford). Mr Morgan has made these transcripts available to other researchers on a Sercombe web site, together with a detailed Sercombe pedigree, prepared from the records. Thousands of researchers' pedigrees can be found in *Ancestral File* (in *FamilySearch*) as noted above. The largest online collection of pedigree data is probably *WorldConnect* (# appendix XI) which lists about 250 million names. This site and other online pedigree databases are reviewed by P. Christian in *Ancestors* (April/May 2003).

There are a number of methods of finding genealogical information on the Internet. You can use web directories (such as the genealogy page of Yahoo UK), mailing lists, search engines (through which you can search for names and places) such as Google, and also gateways (collections of links to other web sites). All of these are described in more detail in Christian (8) and (9). The two best gateways for British genealogical research are the web sites of Cyndi Howell and GENUKI.

Cyndi's list is a continually updated gateway to genealogy web sites. It presently has links to about 120,000 sites, arranged by geographical and subject categories (such as England, Belgium, marriages, newspapers and Quakers). The list of sites has also been published in book form (the second edition in 2001 listing 70,000 web sites). The majority of sites relate to North American material but many deal with records in Britain and other countries.

GENUKI is the most important web site for genealogical material for those researching British and Irish ancestry. GENUKI is a gateway to other sites, maintained by individuals, archives and family history societies. However, it also includes thousands of pages of information about each British and Irish county or about particular parishes together with extensive transcripts and indexes of source material. The site is arranged by county, city, town and parish (so that you can turn to pages that are likely to be of interest) and also lists of topics, such as cemeteries, schools and military history. There is also a search facility (described below). The transcripts and indexes include civil registration records, census returns, parish registers, MIs, wills and trade directories. Hawgood (252) is a guide to using GENUKI but here are a few examples of the material on GENUKI that I have found of interest:

a. a transcript of the 1851 census of Bedford Prison
b. an index of British men who served in the Shanghai Police (1900–45)
c. abstracts of wills proved in the Consistory Court of London (1629–34)
d. abstracts of hundreds of wills from Berkshire and Herefordshire
e. lists of prisoners in gaols in Gloucester in 1850 and 1851
f. transcripts of five volumes of Phillimore's Hampshire marriage registers
g. parts of Pigot's 1830 directory of Gloucestershire
h. admissions to Devon County Lunatic Asylum 1880–81, and
i. a list of over 1,600 men who fought at Trafalgar in 1805

The GENUKI site includes a search facility so that you can search for names and places recorded in the thousands of GENUKI web pages. For example, a search for the name Charnock resulted in 103 "hits". Some of these were for Charnock Richard or Heath Charnock in Lancashire but about 50 were for members of the Charnock family. A few hits took me to FHS web pages that included the names of other researchers who were interested in this family. Others took me to census, parish register and will abstracts, directories, a memorial in the churchyard of Lee in Kent, two inscriptions on a war memorial in Slaidburn and a history of an Essex family named Smyth (into which Agnes Charnock of Lancashire had married in the 16th century). You cannot build a family tree from this material – it is still a "lucky dip" – but searching GENUKI can alert you to important material that you might not otherwise find.

One other web site should be mentioned here, that is the site of Ancestry.com, the largest commercial collection of genealogical data on the Internet. The site claims to feature over 2,000 databases with about 500 million names, some of which can be consulted for free but most can only be used by paying a subscription. Many of the databases are of American material, such as US census indexes, lists of immigrants arriving in America (# chapter 30), US newspaper indexes and US births, baptisms, marriages, deaths and burials. Others are useful to British researchers but similar information can, in some cases, be accessed elsewhere for free (for example in books or on CD-ROM at libraries) such as a Cambridge University alumni database for 1261–1900.

Genealogical directories
The *Genealogical Research Directory* (*GRD*) by Johnson & Sainty (256), published annually since 1982, lists the interests of researchers from all over the world. It lists surnames being researched, the area, time period and the names and addresses of the researchers. You can pay for your interests to be inserted so that other researchers can contact you. The 2003 edition of the *GRD*,

containing about 90,000 research interests and the addresses of hundreds of record offices and genealogical societies around the world, can be purchased from Mrs E. Simpson, 2 Stella Grove, Tollerton, Nottinghamshire NG12 4EY. The 2004 edition will be available in May 2004. Editions of the *GRD* are held at the SoG and some archives and libraries. It is worth reviewing old editions to see who in recent years has been researching the families in which you are interested. The research queries from old editions of the *GRD* can also be purchased on two CD-ROM. However, you must remember that people advertising their interests some years ago may have ceased to have any interest in the subject or may have died.

The British Isles Genealogical Register (*Big R*) is a similar list of researcher's interests that is published by the FFHS (and can be purchased from the FFHS or your FHS). The *Big R* was published on microfiche in 1994 and 1997 and on both fiche and CD-ROM in 2000 (when it listed 155,000 notices about surnames being researched in British records). A new edition should be published shortly.

Professional genealogists

Advertisements appear in *Genealogists' Magazine, Family Tree Magazine, Ancestors,* the *FLHH* (5) and FHS journals from those people offering to undertake genealogical research for payment. Help can be provided for most research but it can be expensive and, in my view, it takes most of the fun out of the hobby. Experts may be essential, however, for certain enquiries. Many expert and specialist researchers are members of the Association of Genealogists and Researchers in Archives (AGRA). A list of members can be obtained from AGRA at 29 Badgers Close, Horsham, West Sussex, RH12 5RU or from AGRA's web site. AGRA attempts to ensure a high standard of competence and expertise among its members. There are similar organisations in Scotland and Ireland.

However, many researchers advertising their services may have no formal qualifications in genealogical research, and those with such qualifications may be no better at their work than those without. Many researchers are excellent but you should preferably work on the basis of personal recommendations and keep a close eye on costs since (unless your enquiry is for a particular civil registration certificate, census entry or will to be located) the cost may be calculated by reference to the time spent by the researcher rather than on the basis of results. A good use of local or professional genealogists is to request them to find particular information which you are fairly certain is in a particular place, but which is difficult for you to obtain in person. You may obtain a useful entry from the IGI, or from Boyd's marriage index but find that the parish register is in a record office many miles from your home. In that case, a professional can quickly and easily locate the full entry for you.

CHAPTER 12

WILLS AND
ADMINISTRATIONS

A will is a document that sets out a person's wishes as to the disposal of his or her property after death (for example leaving money, land or shares to his widow or to his children). Until this century, most people had little property and so did not bother to make a will. You may believe that most of your ancestors were in this category, so that wills are irrelevant to your family history. That would be a mistake. Wills were made by the rich and by professionals, but also by many people who were not wealthy (such as shopkeepers, farmers and labourers). I have 17th- and 18th-century ancestors, including farmers, a shoemaker and two butchers, who left wills. An ancestor's will should describe the property that he owned and reveal the names (and perhaps addresses) of his family, other relatives and friends. Some wills even pre-date parish registers.

Wills are particularly important because they were prepared with the intention of acknowledging or confirming relationships. The will of Thomas Gillman of Hockliffe, Bedfordshire confirmed that my ancestors James and Susannah Eagles of Hoxton were indeed Thomas's son-in-law and daughter (# chapter 10). Wills may evidence many relationships. Emma Keates, a half-sister of my g.g. grandfather John Josiah Keates, died in 1948 and named 15 relatives in her will. My g.g.g. grandfather George Keates died in 1870. In his will (illustration 54) he named his wife, his eldest son and his maid. He also identified two of his properties and his shares in the Walthamstow Joint Stock Association, the Essex Building Society and the Sussex Land Company. My ancestor Michael Read died in 1779 in Hockliffe. In his will, he appointed his wife Elizabeth and his youngest son Abraham as his executors and then left gifts to:

> my eldest son William Read . . . my second son Michael Read . . . my eldest daughter Elizabeth, wife of Thomas Gillman . . . my third son George Read . . . my fourth son James Read . . . my fifth son Thomas Read . . . my sixth son John Read . . . my daughter Rebecca, wife of John Partridge . . . my daughter Massella (wife) of William Cumberland.

After the Norman Conquest, interests in real property (that is land and buildings) descended automatically to the deceased's heir. An heir was usually a man's eldest surviving son (the principle of primogeniture) but there were different customs in some areas of England, such as "borough English" (inheritance by the youngest son) or, in Kent, "gavelkind" (inheritance by all sons in equal shares). A man could not ignore these rules and direct that his land should be inherited by, for example, his second son rather than his first. A testator could choose who should inherit his personal property, such as money, tools or furniture (and, later, leasehold interests in land), but ecclesiastical law provided that at least one-third of a man's personal property should pass to his widow (as her dower) and one-third should pass to his children.

Property owners wished to avoid this prohibition upon choosing who should inherit their land. They therefore began transferring the land, during their lifetime, to trustees who would hold it in accordance with the owner's instructions which were set out by the landowner in a deed or, as he approached death, in his will. For example, a testator could stipulate that "the land at West Court is to be held upon my death for the use and benefit of my second son Richard if he shall survive me and, if not, for my fourth son, John". The Statute of Uses of 1535 (# chapter 27) prohibited land being transferred in this way. However, the Statute of Wills of 1540 allowed most real property to be devised (the legal term for a gift of real property) by owners to relatives or friends of their own choosing rather than to the heir stipulated by the law. This applied to all land from 1661. A gift of personal property (also known as personalty) was termed a bequest, so that a testator therefore devised his real property and bequeathed his personal property. A will dealt with real property and a testament bequeathed personal property. In England, a will and a testament could be contained in the same document and the terms will and testament gradually came to have the same meaning, the term will being most popular.

An executor or executors (a woman was an executrix) were appointed by the deceased in his will to administer and distribute his estate after his death. Executors had to apply to a court, which would have to be satisfied that the will was valid and that it was the deceased's "final will and testament". This process was known as proving a will. The court then issued a document, called a grant of probate (illustration 51), that permitted the executors to effect the will's terms. A testator could change the terms of his will by executing a completely new will (in substitution of an earlier will), or by executing a codicil (that is a written amendment to a will). In most wills, you will see the words: "I hereby revoke all wills and testamentary dispositions previously made by me and declare this to be my last will." Any earlier wills were of no effect from the date of execution of a will containing these words. They do not necessarily mean that the deceased had prepared an earlier will. You should not therefore assume that any will, containing this wording, included dramatic changes from an earlier document. It was simply standard wording inserted by lawyers to ensure that the will was accepted (unless and until a later will was executed) as the testator's final word. A codicil was in similar form to a will, but it confirmed that an earlier will remained effective subject to the amendments in the codicil. A testator could prepare as many codicils as he wished and these should have been proved at the same time as the will.

The Statute of Wills of 1540 allowed males from the age of 14 and females from the age of 12 to make a will or testament (these ages were raised to 21 by the Wills Act 1837). However, valid wills could not be made by lunatics, prisoners, traitors, heretics or slaves. Furthermore, while wills of unmarried women and widows were fairly common, wills for married women before 1882 are very rare. Married women could not, by law, own property until the Married Women's Property Act 1882. Before this, they and their possessions were treated as possessions of the husband and they could only make valid wills with their husbands' consent.

It is possible that you will come across a nuncupative will. The deceased may not have left a written will but he may (knowing that he was near death) have made an oral declaration of his last wishes. If a court was satisfied that the deceased had made a declaration in the terms alleged (proved by the sworn evidence of people who heard the declaration), the court would record the deceased's declaration as a nuncupative will and grant probate, authorising the distribution of the estate in accordance with those wishes. Nuncupative wills were common in parishes where few people, except perhaps the clergyman, could write and perhaps no one was available, as someone

ON the *10th* day of *January* 18*71*
the Will with Codicil thereto of

George Keates

formerly of

but late of *Wallwood Farm Leyton in the county*
of Essex Auctioneer

deceased, who died on the *14th* day of *December* 18*70*
at *Leyton aforesaid*

was proved in the Principal Registry of Her Majesty's Court of Probate, by the Oaths
of *John Josiah Keates of Leyton aforesaid*
Surveyor the Son and Anna Keates
of Wallwood Farm aforesaid Widow the
Relict of the said Deceased two

one of the
Execut**ors** named in the **said Will** they having been first sworn duly to
administer, power being reserved of granting Probate of the said Will and to *Edward*
Unwin

the other Execut**or** named in the **said Will**

the other Executor having
renounced the Probate and Execution of the said Will

Effects under £ *1500*

R. *Leaseholds*

51. Grant of probate for the will of George Keates, 1871 (Principal Registry of Family Division)

approached death, to write out a will. Nuncupative wills naturally resulted in many arguments and court disputes and the Wills Act of 1837 made such wills invalid except in the case of declarations by members of the armed forces who died in action.

English and Welsh grants of probate, wills and codicils are public records, mostly now held at First Avenue House in London (see below), TNA and CROs. Executors retained a copy of the will so that they could administer the estate in accordance with its terms and so copies of wills have also been retained in family papers or in collections of deeds relating to a property.

INTESTACY AND ADMINISTRATION

If a person died intestate (that is without leaving a will), an application could be made to a court for the appointment of one or more administrators, to administer the deceased's estate and divide it among the beneficiaries. Administrators were usually the deceased's next of kin (a widow, child or brother), but his creditors were sometimes appointed. The records of appointment by the court, known as letters of administration (or admons) are public records, but they contain far less information than wills.

The administration vested legal title to the deceased's property, such as land, or money in a bank account, in those to whom the property would be passed. Since medieval times, the law has stipulated who should receive the estate of someone who died intestate (thus a widow was entitled to one-third of her husband's estate). The Statute of Distributions of 1670 confirmed this and also provided that the residue of an estate was to be divided equally between the deceased's children. If he had no wife or children, the estate passed to his parents, or (if they were dead), it was divided equally between his siblings. The division of intestates' estates is now governed by the Administration of Estates Act 1925 (as amended) which applies similar rules. John Abraham Eagles, a brother of my g.g.g. grandfather, died in 1859. The letters of administration that were granted in respect of his estate are shown in illustration 52. Letters of administration could be granted in other cases. For example, the deceased might have left a valid will, but without naming any executors. Alternatively, a testator might appoint executors who died before the testator or who refused to act. In these cases, a court granted letters of administration "with will" or "with will annexed". Administrators were appointed by the court and they dealt with the estate in accordance with the terms of the will.

Many of our ancestors did not own land, shares or similar property. Their few belongings (work tools, furniture, money and clothes) were left with the widow or widower, or were divided between the children, the exact division often depending on who wanted what, or who arrived at the deceased's house first. Most of my recent ancestors came from the working or lower middle classes, and so few of them appear in the records of wills and administrations. Furthermore, a deceased may have left a will (but few assets) and if there was no dispute as to who should benefit, the will may not have been proved in order to save the cost of applying to court for probate. Wills that were not proved have rarely survived, but some remain in family papers. These points should not prevent you searching for wills. You should make thorough searches, since many of your ancestors may have left wills. Even if they did not, other relations may have done so, and referred to your ancestors. For example, an ancestor's brother (or perhaps a brother-in-law) may have left a will with gifts for your ancestor or his children. The wills of unmarried siblings of your ancestors can be particularly useful as they often list many relatives.

ON the *13th* day of *April* 185*9*,

Letters of Administration of all and singular the personal Estate and Effects

of *John Abraham Eagles*

~~formerly of~~

and late of *No. 10. Lambs Place Kingsland Road in the parish of West Hackney in the County of Middlesex Fancy Shop Keeper* deceased,

who died on the *23rd* day of *March* 18*59*,

at *No. 10. Lambs Place afpresaid a Widower*

were granted at the Principal Registry of Her Majesty's Court of Probate

to *George Eagles of No. 1. Hooper Street Clerkenwell in the same County & Silvermounter one of*

the *natural and lawful children* of the

said deceased, having been\first sworn duly to administer

~~(add, in case of renunciation)~~

~~the~~

~~and next of Kin of the said deceased, having first renounced~~

under £ *100*

x/. JB

52. *Letters of administration for the estate of John Abraham Eagles, 1859 (Principal Registry of Family Division)*

WILLS AND ADMINISTRATIONS SINCE 1858

Before 1858 grants of probate and letters of administration were dealt with by the ecclesiastical courts. The civil Court of Chancery had jurisdiction over the validity and interpretation of wills. These courts are considered below. The Probate Act 1857 provided that from 12 January 1858 jurisdiction over wills and administrations should be transferred from ecclesiastical courts and the Court of Chancery to a new civil Court of Probate (and its probate registries in London and across the country). These probate registries have continued their work ever since although the courts of which they form part have been reorganised. The Court of Probate was merged into the Probate, Divorce and Admiralty Division of the High Court of Justice in 1875. This division became the Family Division in 1970 and contentious probate matters (but not the proving of wills) were transferred to the Chancery Division of the High Court.

Finding the records

Since 1858 applications for grants of probate or letters of administration have been made at either the Principal Probate Registry in London, now called the Principal Registry of the Family Division (PPR), or at a district probate registry. The PPR has a search room at First Avenue House, 42–49 High Holborn, London WC1V 6NP (telephone 020 7947 6000). Its location is shown on the map at illustration 9. If an application for probate or administration was made at a district registry, that registry kept the original will or letters of administration, made a copy in a register and also sent a copy to the PPR. The PPR therefore holds originals or copies of all wills and administrations for England and Wales since 1858. They are all indexed in the National Probate Calendar and searches at the PPR are therefore very easy (and free of charge). The searchroom is open from 10.00 a.m. to 4.30 p.m., Monday to Friday. The National Probate Calendar consists of typescript, annual, volumes up to 1992 (some with important manuscript annotations), microfiche indexes for 1993–98 and a computer index for 1996 to date. The annual volumes list the names of the deceased in alphabetical order. If you know when someone died, you find the volume for that year (or the following year) and search for the entry. Between 1858 and 1870 administrations and wills were listed separately, or sometimes in separate volumes. Between 1858 and 1876, the volumes have appendices listing those Scottish and Irish wills and admons for which a grant of probate was also obtained in England. This process, known as resealing, was necessary if, for example, a deceased Irish landowner also owned a house in London.

A district probate registry should have calendars of the grants in that registry (and some registries have copies of the National Probate Calendar). The address and telephone numbers of local probate registries are listed in the *FLHH* (5). However, the originals (and register copies) of old wills at district registries (and often the older calendars) may have been moved, usually to CROs, so you should check the availability of records before you visit a district registry. The National Probate Calendar for 1858–1943 is also available on microfilm or fiche at other archives and libraries, listed in Gibson (291). For example, the FRC, Guildhall Library and many CROs hold microfiche copies for 1858–1943 and the SoG has a microfilm copy for 1858–1930. The fiche copy was made from a district probate registry's copy of the National Probate Calendar and so does not include the manuscript annotations that appear in the copy at First Avenue House. *Family Tree Magazine* (March 2003) reviews a project to issue the National Probate Calendar on CD-ROM. However, it will take up to seven disks (which are quite expensive) to include just one year's entries in the calendar. Most researchers will therefore prefer to use the original calendars (or fiche copies), without charge, as noted above.

Calendar entries

The calendars note the deceased's name, date of death, where and when the will was proved (or where and when the letters of administration were granted), the names of the executors or administrators and the value of the deceased's estate (considered in more detail below). The calendars often specify the occupations of the deceased, executors or administrators. From 1858 to 1892 the addresses of executors or administrators were given and, if they were related to the deceased, this relationship was usually described. Illustration 53 is a page from the National Probate Calendar of 1859, including the grant of probate for the estate of John Bulleid, yeoman of Winkleigh in Devon, to his brother William Bulleid, yeoman. My g.g.g. grandfather George Keates died in 1870. The grant of probate and his will are shown in illustrations 51 and 54. The entry in the 1871 calendar, which led me to these records, was:

Keates, George: 10 January 1871 Effects under £1,500
The Will of George Keates, late of Wallwood Farm, Leyton in the County of Essex, Auctioneer, who died 14th December 1870 at Leyton was proved at the Principal Registry by John Josiah Keates of Leyton, Surveyor, the son and Anna Keates of Wallwood Farm, widow, the Relict, two of the executors.

Having located an entry in the National Probate Calendar at First Avenue House, you complete a form and take it (with the calendar) to a registry officer. The fee to see a will, grant of probate or admon is £5 and you can take notes (in pencil) from the documents. If you want to look at copies of probate records that are over 100 years old, no fee is payable if you first obtain a Literary Enquirer's Permit, valid for one year, by written application to the Probate Department Manager at First Avenue House. Copies of wills, grants of probate and admons can be purchased for £5 each. You should also ask whether there are any other records on the file (these have rarely been kept, but there may be affidavits or perhaps powers of attorney). You pay the fees at the cashier's desk. Photocopies of the documents can be posted to you or collected within about a week. Unfortunately, most of the records are actually stored in another building, so if you merely wish to see a document, it can take between one and three hours for it to be retrieved. Postal applications can also be made for copy documents or for searches to be made in the PPR calendars, but must be sent to York Probate Sub-Registry, Postal Searches and Copies Department, Duncombe Place, York YO1 7EA (telephone 01904 624210). Applications must specify a deceased's full name, last known address and date of death (if known). Detailed information about making applications can be obtained from the Probate Service's web site. A fee of £5 (by cheque payable to H.M. Paymaster General) pays for a search of four years of the calendars and a copy of the will or admon if it is located. Further years of the calendars will be searched for an additional fee. The Mormons have filmed the PPR wills of 1858–1925 and the microfilms can be ordered and viewed at LDS family history centres.

In order to find a calendar entry, the important date is that of the grant of probate or letters of administration. This could be some months after the death. Letters of administration for Anna, the widow of my g.g.g. grandfather George Keates, were not granted until June 1913 even though she died in February 1911. Therefore, you should always check the calendars for a few years after the date of death. If your ancestor died abroad, a will may nevertheless have been proved in this country if he or she had land or other property here. In those cases, the delay between the date of death and date of probate could be substantial.

WILLS. 1859.

Turner of Sheffield aforesaid Metal Caster and John Marsden of the same place Razor Blade Grinder the Executors.

BULLEID John.

Effects under £800.

30 March.   The Will of John Bulleid late of Winkleigh in the County of **Devon** Yeoman deceased who died 6 February 1859 at Staddon in the Parish of Winkleigh aforesaid was proved at **Exeter** by the oath of William Bulleid of Winkleigh aforesaid Yeoman the Brother and the sole Executor.

BULLEN Benjamin.

Effects under £100.

22 August.   The Will with a Codicil of Benjamin Bullen late of East Dereham in the County of **Norfolk** Gentleman deceased who died 4 July 1859 at East Dereham aforesaid was proved at **Norwich** by the oath of Thomas Ayers the younger of Great Yarmouth in the said County Photographic Artist the Grandson and one of the Executors.

BULLEN David.

Effects under £800.

28 May.   The Will of David Bullen late of Melling in the County of **Lancaster** Farmer deceased who died 2 April 1859 at Melling aforesaid was proved at **Liverpool** by the oaths of Thomas Bullen of 5 and 7 Hardy-street Liverpool Cowkeeper and John Bullen of Ince Blundell near Great Crosby in the said County Farmer the Brothers and the Executors.

BULLEN Joseph.

Effects under £50.
Savings Bank.

1 September.   The Will of Joseph Bullen late of the City of **Hereford** Innkeeper a Depositor in the Hereford Bank for Savings deceased who died 23 August 1859 at the said City was proved at **Hereford** by the oath of Elizabeth Lloyd of the Parish of All Saints in the said City Widow the Sister and the sole Executrix.

BULLER William.

Effects under £3,000.

21 March.   The Will of William Buller late of Hanwell in the County of **Oxford** Farmer deceased who died 28 February 1859 at Hanwell aforesaid was proved at **Oxford** by the oath of William Buller of Hanwell aforesaid Farmer the Son and the sole Executor.

BULLEY William.

Effects under £9,000.

13 April.   Letters of Administration (with the Will annexed) of the Personal estate and effects of William Bulley formerly of " The Angel " Inn in the City of **Oxford** and late of

53. A page from the National Probate Calendar of 1859 (Principal Registry of Family Division)

The calendars usually note the value of the deceased's estate. This value, analysed by Rubinstein & Duman in the journal *The Local Historian* (299) and by A. Camp in *Family Tree Magazine* (November and December 2001), is the gross figure, that is an estate's value before payment of debts or funeral expenses. Until 1881 the figure was often expressed as "effects under £1,500" (as in the case of George Keates noted above) but exact figures should have been given from 1881. Until 1898 the noted value was for personal estate only. The value of real property (land or buildings) was excluded unless it was freehold property which had been leased to a tenant for a fixed term of years. From 1898 real property was included in valuations unless it was settled, that is subject to a settlement or trust (# chapter 27). In brief, settlement was the process by which the owner (or settlor) transferred property to trustees to hold for the benefit of a succession of beneficiaries, for example the settlor's wife for her life, then his eldest son (for his life) and then his grandchildren. If the deceased only had a life interest in the property and it had already been directed that someone else would receive the property following his death, that life interest would constitute settled property. From 1926 settled real property was also valued (by a separate figure) if the property ceased to be subject to a settlement as a result of the death. It was omitted if it remained subject to the settlement.

The grant of probate

A grant of probate may tell you little more than the calendar. It can be seen that the wording of the grant of probate for the estate of George Keates (illustration 51) is extremely similar to the calendar entry, except that the grant reveals that George's estate included leaseholds. However, it is worthwhile obtaining a copy of the grant since it may contain further useful information or there may be mistakes in the calendar.

Contents of a will

George Keates executed his will in 1867. When probate was granted, court clerks copied the will into a register. It is the registers that are usually copied for you. Illustration 54 is a register copy of George's will. The contents of a typical will can be described by extracts from George's will. It commences with the name, address and occupation of the testator: "This is the last will and testament of me, George Keates of Wallwood Farm House in the parish of St Mary, Leyton (Essex), Auctioneer." After some suitable wording about eternal life and the mercy of God, a will usually continues with the appointment of executors: "I hereby appoint my son John Josiah Keates together with Edward Unwin, printer of Bucklersbury and my beloved wife Anna Keates to be my executors and trustees for the carrying out of this my will." If, as in this case, a will established a trust that required future administration and distribution of property, trustees (often the executors) were also appointed. A will then deals with the payment of debts and funeral expenses: "I desire first, after the payment of all my just debts and funeral expenses, that the sum of £400 be paid to the trustees of Miss Mead to clear off a mortgage on property at Walthamstow." A will then provides for distribution of the estate. It was usual to provide first for the spouse, then for children and then other relatives, friends or possibly employees. This could be done by specific bequests of property or money, or by a general gift of property to a group of people. George Keates made specific bequests to his son John Josiah and his maid:

(I give) to my son John Josiah . . . one half of my business as Mast and Block maker together with one half of the stock in trade and all implements used in carrying out the business, for his own use and benefit absolutely. I further give to Emily Irving my maid servant five pounds.

This is the last Will and Testament

of mee George Keates of Wallwood Farm House in the Parish of St
Mary Leyton in the County of Essex Auctioneer I hereby declare my hope
for eternal life to be through the Mercy of God in Christ Jesus my Lord to
Whose Glory I desire to devote the remainder of my days I hereby appoint my
son John Josiah Keates together with Edward Lewin Printer of Buckhurstow
and my beloved wife Anna Keates to be my Executors and Trustees for
the carrying out of this my Will I desire first after the payment of all my just
debts and funeral expenses that the sum of four hundred pounds sterling be paid
to the trustees of Miss Mead to clear of a mortgage on property at Walthamstow
I further will that all my real and personal estate both leasehold and freehold
together with all monies found in my possession at the time of my decease and
all my shares in the Walthamstow Joint Stock Association the Eclipse a
Building Society and the Oxford Land Company and all my household
furniture plate jewelery books pictures horses chaise carts and all my other
property not otherwise disposed of by this my Will shall be for the use and
benefit of my beloved wife Anna Keates and my children until the youngest
surviving child shall be 21 years of age and that my w.. shall in no wise
transfer any power she may have under this Will to any future husband she
may marry but that her own writ alone shall be a sufficient discharge to
the trustees for any monies she may be entitled to receive upon this my
Will I further will that upon my youngest surviving child arriving at the
age of twenty one years then if my beloved wife is not living all my property
shall then be divided between my then surviving children but should any
of my children die and leave issue then that portion that would have come
to their parent shall be equally divided between his or her surviving or
children I also will that my trustees if they be mutualy agreed dispose of
any portion of my property for the purpose of paying of of any incumbrance
that may remain upon any of my property I further give to my son John
Josiah Keates one half of my business as Mast and Block Maker or
together with one half of the stock in trade and all implements used in
carrying out the business for his own use and benefit absolutely And I
further will that upon my property realizing the sum of two hundred per
annum to be paid to my beloved wife exclusive of property tax or income
derived from Mellows Retreat the which property I sold to her father
Henry Fisher Lewin and his wife Anna Lewin for their joint lives to
revert to my wife Anna Keates at their death and to her children after her
death I further will that after paying my beloved wife 200 per year as
afore directed then it shall be lawful for my trustees to divide amongst
all my surviving children any sum that may remain annualy I further
give to each of my children the sum of ten pounds each to be paid as soon
as convenient after my death Also I give to my trustees the sum of fifty
pounds to be divided between them I further give to Emily Irving my
Maid servant five pounds I declare this to be the last Will and Testament
of me In witness whereof I this day have set my hand 21 day of July
1867 ————— George Keates ————— And acknowledged in due to be
this last Will and Testament in the presence of us present at the same time
and subscribed by us in the presence of the said testator and each other ————
J. Rowlett, May Villa, Church Road, Leyton ——————
W. McFinlay, Finlay Villa, Church Road, Leyton —

In Her Majesty's Court of Probate   The Principal Registry
In the Goods of George Keates deceased.

54. The will of George Keates, 1867 (Principal Registry of Family Division)

George then directed that all his other property should be placed into trust, for his wife Anna and his children, until the youngest child was 21:

> I further will that all my real and personal estate both leasehold and freehold together with all monies found in my possession at the time of my decease and all my shares in the Walthamstow Joint Stock Association, the Essex Building Society and the Sussex Land Company and all my household furniture, plate, jewellery, books, pictures, horses, chaise carts and all my other property not otherwise disposed of by this my Will shall be for the use and benefit of my beloved wife Anna Keates and my children until the youngest surviving child shall be 21 years of age . . . I further will that upon my youngest surviving child arriving at the age of 21 years then, if my beloved wife be not living my property shall be divided between my surviving children.

The will was dated 27 July 1867, signed by George and witnessed. The copy of the will that I obtained did not show the real signatures of George Keates or the witnesses, because this was the copy made in the register by the court clerk when the will was proved. The clerk also noted, in the register, the details of the grant of probate:

> Proved 10th January 1871 by the oaths of John Josiah Keates the son and Anna Keates widow, the relict, two of the executors to whom admon was granted, power reserved of making the like grant to Edward Unwin the other executor.

A testator's financial position may have changed substantially after he executed his will so that at his death the value of his estate may not have been sufficient for the executors to carry out all his wishes. The contents of a will may also contain surprises, for example little being left to an eldest son. However, the family business or estate may already have been transferred to (or settled upon) him, so that a will only had to deal with smaller items of property and legacies for the testator's widow and other children.

Letters of administration

Letters of administration contain far less information than wills. The deceased's name, address, occupation and the date and place of the death are specified. The name, address and occupation of the administrator will be noted, as well as his or her relationship to the deceased and the value of the estate. The identity of beneficiaries is not revealed but may be disclosed in death duty registers (considered below). Letters of administration were granted in 1859 (see illustration 52) for the estate of John Abraham Eagles of Hackney, Middlesex, a brother of my ancestor Joseph James Eagles. The grant was to John's son, George Eagles:

> On the 13th day of April 1859 Letters of Administration of all . . . the personal estate and effects of John Abraham Eagles late of No. 10 Lambs Place, Kingsland Road in the parish of West Hackney . . . Middlesex, Fancy Shop Keeper who died on the 23rd day of March 1859 at No 10 Lambs Place, a widower, were granted at the Principal Registry of Her Majesty's Court of Probate to George Eagles of No. 1 Hooper Street, Clerkenwell in the same county, Silver-mounter, one of the natural and lawful children of the said deceased, he having been first sworn duly to administer. Effects under £100.

A summary of this grant appears in the PPR calendars. This example shows that letters of administration, although less useful than most wills, can nevertheless provide useful information about your ancestor and assist in tracing other family members.

Further information about estates since 1858 can be found in the records of law suits over contested wills, or disputes over the administration of estates. For example, executors may have applied for probate of a will, only for other members of a family to allege that the will had been revoked by a later will, or amended by a codicil. Alternatively, beneficiaries may have alleged that executors or administrators had sold part of the estate too cheaply, or divided the estate (or proceeds) incorrectly. Records of such disputes are at TNA in the records of the Court of Probate, or the Probate or Chancery Divisions of the High Court of Justice (# chapter 24).

WILLS AND ADMINISTRATIONS BEFORE 1858

Locating wills and administrations before 1858 is more difficult. Before 12 January 1858 the proving of wills and the grant of administrations was undertaken by the ecclesiastical courts (# chapter 24). It is therefore necessary, in order to locate wills, to have some knowledge of the system of these courts, even though most surviving wills are now in civil archives such as TNA or a CRO. Guides by Camp (280), Gibson & Churchill (291), Newington-Irving (297) and Scott (300) will assist your search.

Jurisdiction of the courts
The parish was described in chapter 7. A group of parishes formed a deanery (administered by a rural dean) and a number of deaneries were grouped into an archdeaconry (administered by an archdeacon). A diocese, that is the area within a bishop's jurisdiction, consisted of a number of archdeaconries. Each diocese belonged to one of the two ecclesiastical provinces of York (which had jurisdiction in Northumberland, Westmorland, Cheshire, Cumberland, Durham, Yorkshire, Lancashire and Nottinghamshire) or Canterbury (which had jurisdiction over the other English counties and over Wales). The archdeaconry and diocese to which each parish belonged are shown on the IHGS county maps.

If a man's property lay entirely within one archdeaconry, his will was generally proved in that archdeacon's court. However, if he also owned property or goods elsewhere, to the value of £5 or more (known as *bona notabilia* or "considerable goods"), the archdeaconry court would generally not have jurisdiction. In those cases, a superior church court (of a bishop or archbishop) dealt with probate. If a deceased's property was in more than one archdeaconry (but all in the same diocese) his will was proved in the bishop's court (called a Consistory Court). However, an exception to this arises because the Archbishops of Canterbury and York were also the bishops of the dioceses of Canterbury and York. The bishops' courts for these dioceses were named the "Court of Commissary General" and the "Exchequer Court of York" respectively. The Archbishop of York also had a Chancery Court of York that dealt with the wills of clergy within York diocese. During some periods, an archdeacon might decide not to exercise his jurisdiction, so that all wills would have to be proved in the bishop's court. There were also periods of inhibition, when a bishop was undertaking a visitation to an archdeaconry. During a visitation, the archdeacon's court would be closed and all legal business was conducted in the bishop's court. A bishop's court was generally called a Commissary Court when it was exercising the jurisdiction that had not been exercised by an archdeacon.

If the deceased held *bona notabilia* in more than one diocese, the will was proved in one of the two archbishops' prerogative courts. The Archbishop of York's court was the Prerogative Court of York (PCY), established in 1577. In addition to its prerogative jurisdiction, the PCY appears to have acted in some cases where a testator's property was all within the diocese of York (that is, the Exchequer Court's jurisdiction). The Prerogative Court of Canterbury (PCC), was the court that had jurisdiction if a testator had property in more than one diocese within the province of Canterbury. It was located at Doctors Commons, near St Paul's Cathedral in London, but it also had some regional offices. If the deceased owned property in the provinces both of Canterbury and York, his will had to be proved in the PCC, which was the senior of the two prerogative courts. The PCC also proved the wills of English and Welsh property owners who died in Scotland, Ireland or abroad. It also had sole testamentary jurisdiction (and so proved all wills in England and Wales) during the Commonwealth period (1653–60) when it was called the Court of Probate of Wills and Granting Administrations. The only exceptions in this period were that a few wills continued to be proved in some courts of Yorkshire peculiars (considered below).

Because court jurisdiction depended upon the location of property, a will may not necessarily have been proved in the area where your ancestor lived or where his death took place. It is therefore sometimes necessary to search the records of a number of courts for the areas in which an ancestor may have had property. As one example, government stock (or gilts) were held and administered by the Bank of England in London. Any person who possessed gilts therefore had property located in London (as well as any property in other places) so that on his death an application for probate was usually made to the PCC. From 1812 the Bank of England only recognised PCC grants of probate or admons, so that applications for probate or administration had to be made to the PCC. However, a further difficulty is that some people, especially the wealthy, arranged for wills to be proved in a higher court than necessary (particularly in the PCC). Furthermore, if the executors lived in an area other than where the property was located, they might have had the will proved in a higher court than necessary if that was more convenient for them. The PCC became more popular as time passed and searches for wills after 1800, wherever your British ancestor died, should not exclude PCC records.

Another problem arises because of areas known as peculiars. These are identified on the IHGS county maps and listed for each county in Gibson & Churchill (291). Peculiars were parishes that were situated in one archdeaconry or diocese but subject to the jurisdiction of another archdeacon or bishop, some other religious or lay authority (such as the Dean and Chapter of cathedrals, for example Westminster and York) or even a local lord of the manor (# chapter 27). Until 1858 most peculiars had their own courts for the granting of probate (or dealing with other matters in the jurisdiction of the church courts). Thus the court of the Dean and Chapter of York dealt with probates of many residents of the parishes that were peculiars of the Dean and Chapter. If your ancestor owned property in a peculiar, his will may have been proved in the peculiar court (if his property was only within that peculiar), or in a court of higher jurisdiction, if he also held land in that court's jurisdiction. There were also some other courts which could grant probate for wills of the residents of certain areas. One example is the Court of Husting in the City of London (which proved wills until the late 17th century). Two other examples (in Exeter) are the Court of the Mayor of Exeter and the King's Customary Court, both of which proved wills from the 13th century until about 1600. Similar courts were held in other cities and boroughs.

The terms of wills and administrations before 1858

Probate documents before 1858 were little different to those produced since 1858. Wills were in similar terms, although the handwriting and language become more difficult as you research further back in time. Grants of probate and admons were also in similar form, although they were usually more verbose than the documents produced in the civil courts since 1858. Illustration 55 shows the will of my ancestor Susannah Eagles which was proved in the Commissary Court of the Bishop of London in 1851. Illustration 56 is an example of letters of administration granted in 1764 (by an official acting for the Bishop of Lichfield) to Margaret Hide, to administer the estate of her late husband Samuel Hide of Glossop in Derbyshire.

Wills and admons are invaluable for information about your ancestors' trades or standards of living. Part of the will of Susannah Eagles, which she executed in July 1850, is as follows:

> This is the last will and testament of I, Susannah Eagles of No.8 Queen Street, Percival Street in the Parish of St James, Clerkenwell in the County of Middlesex, widow.
> I give and bequeath to my daughter Amelia Day, wife of Joseph Day of No.5 Essex Street in the Parish of St Matthew, Bethnal Green all my wearing apparel, two gold rings, one silver tablespoon marked J.S.E., six teaspoons, sugar tongs, one pair of silver spectacles, coal scuttle, tea caddy, best set of china, large blanket, feather pillow and feather bed.
> I give and bequeath to my grandson John Thomas Eagles my best carpet, copper tea kettle, five mahogany chairs, all my books . . . and large silver tablespoon marked T.C.
> I give to my son Joseph James Eagles one silver table spoon, one pair of silver salt spoons and mustard spoon marked J.S.E, one pair of silver spectacles and all the rest and remainder of my property to be divided between my two children and grandson (Amelia, Joseph and John aforesaid) share and share alike and I appoint my son Joseph James Eagles and my grandson John Thomas Eagles to be executors of this my will.

Apart from the amusing gifts of spectacles, this will was a mine of information. Susannah was the widow of James Eagles. The initials J.S.E. may have been his, but who was T.C.? Since Susannah's father was Thomas Gillman, was this a clerk's error for T.G.? The will also revealed what had happened to Amelia, a daughter of James and Susannah (of whom I had no record after her baptism in 1811). She had married Joseph Day and (because the will provided an address), I was able to find them in the census of Bethnal Green.

Probate disputes

Records of probate disputes can provide very useful genealogical details, but also interesting information about your ancestor's life. Actions in ecclesiastical and civil courts (including those in respect of wills and administrations until 1858) are reviewed in chapter 24. However, in brief, the ecclesiastical courts had jurisdiction over the personal estate of the deceased and the carrying out, by executors and administrators, of their functions and duties. If there was any dispute as to the progress of the probate or administration, that dispute was dealt with by the church court that had probate jurisdiction. The civil Court of Chancery had jurisdiction over disputes about the inheritance of real property and the validity or interpretation of wills. If a will devised real property, it was the Court of Chancery which enforced the gift (if necessary) and not the ecclesiastical court. A party to litigation could appeal from bishops' courts: in the province of Canterbury to the Court of Arches of the Archbishop of Canterbury or, in the province of York,

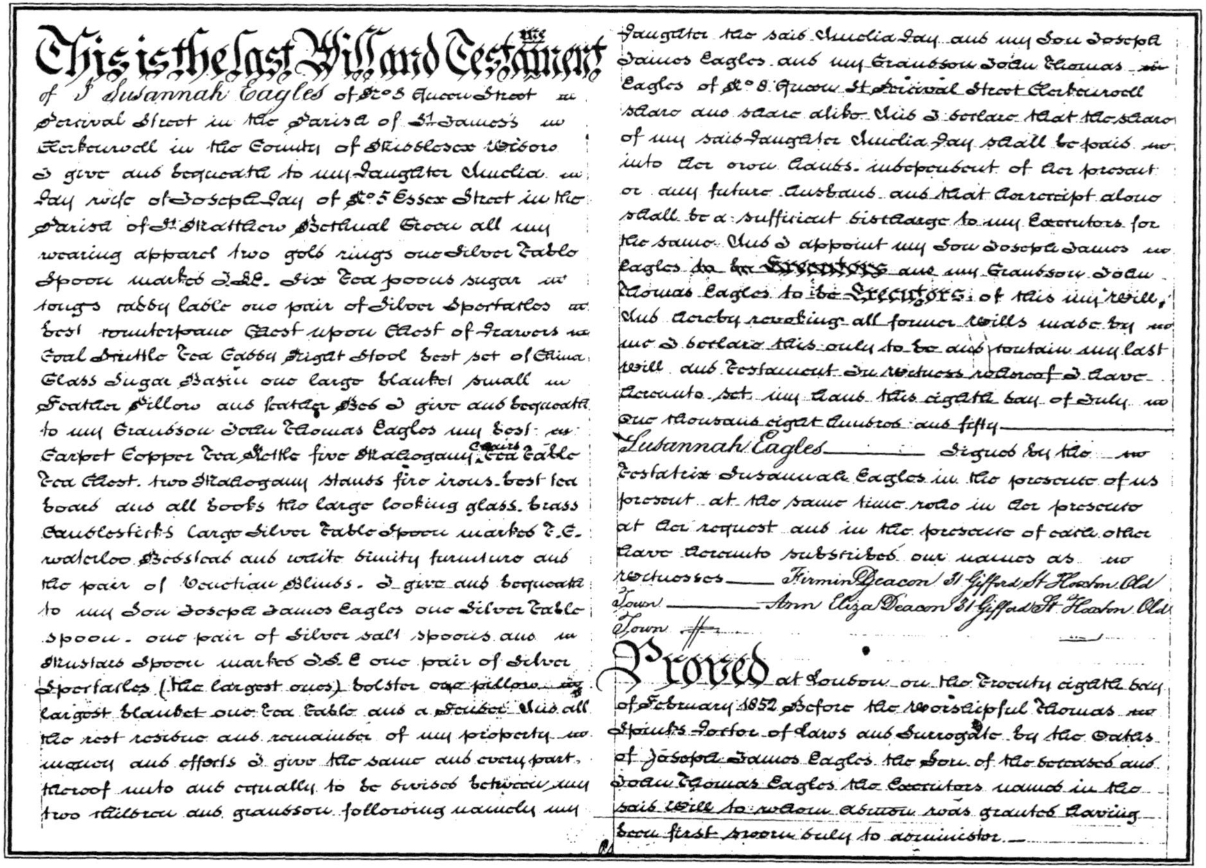

This is the last Will and Testament of me Susannah Eagles of No 8 Queen Street Percival Street in the Parish of St James's Clerkenwell in the County of Middlesex Widow

I give and bequeath to my Daughter Amelia Day wife of Joseph Day of No 5 Essex Street in the Parish of St Matthew Bethnal Green all my wearing apparel two gold rings one Silver Table Spoon marked I.E.L. Six Tea spoons sugar tongs [illegible] table one pair of Silver Spectacles best counterpane Chest upon Chest of Drawers Coal Scuttle Tea Caddy Night Stool best set of China Glass Sugar Basin one large blanket small Feather Pillow and feather Bed I give and bequeath to my Grandson John Thomas Eagles my best Carpet Copper Tea Kettle five Mahogany Chairs Tea table Tea Chest two Mahogany Stands fire irons best tea board and all books the large looking glass brass Candlesticks large Silver Table Spoon marked T.E. waterloo Bedstead and white dimity furniture and the pair of Venetian Blinds. I give and bequeath to my Son Joseph James Eagles one Silver Table spoon one pair of Silver salt spoons and Mustard Spoon marked I.S.E one pair of Silver Spectacles (the largest ones) bolster one pillow largest blanket one tea table and a fender. And all the rest residue and remainder of my property money and effects I give the same and every part thereof unto and equally to be divided between my two children and grandson following namely my daughter the said Amelia Day and my Son Joseph James Eagles and my Grandson John Thomas Eagles of No 8 Queen St Percival Street Clerkenwell share and share alike. And I declare that the share of my said daughter Amelia Day shall be paid into her own hands independent of her present or any future husband and that her receipt alone shall be a sufficient discharge to my Executors for the same. And I appoint my Son Joseph James Eagles to be Executors and my Grandson John Thomas Eagles to be Executors of this my will, And hereby revoking all former Wills made by me I declare this only to be and contain my last Will and Testament In witness whereof I have hereunto set my hand this eighth day of July one thousand eight hundred and fifty

Susannah Eagles — Signed by the Testatrix Susannah Eagles in the presence of us present at the same time who in her presence at her request and in the presence of each other have hereunto subscribed our names as witnesses — Firmin Deacon 31 Gifford St Hoxton Old Town — Ann Eliza Deacon 31 Gifford St Hoxton Old Town

Proved at London on the twenty eighth day of February 1852 before the Worshipful Thomas Spinks Doctor of Laws and Surrogate by the Oaths of Joseph James Eagles the Son of the deceased and John Thomas Eagles the Executors named in the said Will to whom Admon was granted having been first sworn duly to administer.

55. *The will of Susannah Eagles, 1850, London Commissary Court (Guildhall Library, Ms. 9171/98)*

56. *Letters of administration for the estate of Samuel Hide (1764)*

to the Chancery Court of York. From those courts, or from the archbishops' courts (the PCC, PCY and Exchequer Court of York), appeals could be made to the High Court of Delegates until 1834. From 1834 appeals were made to the Judicial Committee of the Privy Council. Many ecclesiastical courts were situated at Doctors Commons in London. In addition to the PCC, the registries of the courts of the Bishops of London and Winchester and the Archdeacons of London, Middlesex, Surrey and Rochester were grouped in Doctors Commons, together with the offices of the proctors and attornies who practised in the courts. Cox (364) provides a fine description of these courts and examples of some of the cases that they heard.

The location of records
The records of the High Court of Delegates, the Judicial Committee of the Privy Council and the Court of Arches are considered further in chapter 24. However, in brief, the records of the High Court of Delegates from 1538 to 1834 and the records of the Judicial Committee of the Privy Council are at TNA. Records of the Court of Arches are at Lambeth Palace Library. Wills which were proved (and admons granted) in the PCY or Exchequer Court of York (or which

were subject to litigation in the Chancery Court of York) are at the Borthwick Institute of Historical Research. TNA holds wills proved in the PCC (the earliest dated 1383) and records of administrations (the earliest dated 1559). The registered copies of wills are in series PROB 11 and copies are available online; original wills are in PROB 10 and administrations are in PROB 6 (PROB 6 and 11 can also be seen on microfilm at the search room of TNA at the FRC). TNA at Kew holds records of litigation in the PCC, many of the cases being indexed by the names of the deceased and by names of plaintiffs (that is, those starting actions).

Most wills which were proved in the bishops', archdeacons' or peculiar courts (and admons from those courts) are held in CROs, since they usually act as diocesan record offices, and are generally available to the public on microfilm. These courts' records of litigation concerning wills and administrations are also held in CROs. Your first task is to ascertain which CRO holds records for your ancestor's area. In most cases, an ancestor's will should be held in the CRO for the county presently covering the area in which he lived. However, the jurisdiction of dioceses or archdeaconries did not coincide with county boundaries. Probate records of the church courts are therefore sometimes held in the CRO for the county in which the seat of the bishop or archdeacon was located. For example, the probate records for Derbyshire and Staffordshire are held at a record office in Lichfield, the records for Surrey (for both the Commissary Court of the Bishop of Winchester and the Archdeaconry Court of Surrey) are at the London Metropolitan Archives, those for Rutland are at Northampton Record Office and those for Cambridgeshire are in Cambridge University Library. For each English county, Gibson & Churchill (291) list the relevant church courts (bishops' and archdeacons' courts as well as peculiars) and the present location of those courts' records. Welsh probate records are also dealt with by Gibson & Churchill (291) and in chapter 29 below.

The position in London and Middlesex (and for those parts of other counties now in London) is especially complex, and you should search the records for all the major courts. Most wills proved before 1858 are in the records of the PCC or in the archives listed below, but large parts of what is now London were formerly in Surrey, Kent or Essex. For ancestors who lived in those areas, you should also search the records of the courts having jurisdiction in those areas:

a. Guildhall Library: records of the Commissary Court of London (London Division), the Archdeaconry Court of London, the peculiar court of St Katherine by the Tower and the peculiar court of the Dean and Chapter of St Paul's Cathedral

b. London Metropolitan Archives: records of the Consistory Court of London and the Archdeaconry Court of Middlesex

c. Westminster City Archives: records of the Dean and Chapter of Westminster

d. Lambeth Palace Library: records of the Archbishop of Canterbury's peculiars of the Deanery of the Arches and of Croydon (with jurisdiction in parts of Kent, Surrey and Middlesex)

e. CLRO: records of the Court of Husting of the City of London

Finding the will or administration

An index to the names of the deceased, whose wills and administrations were the subject of disputes in the High Court of Delegates, was published in volumes 11 and 12 (new series) of the journal *The Genealogist*. Houston (941) is an index to cases heard in the Court of Arches from 1660 to 1913 which indicates, for each case, the subject of the dispute. Many cases up to 1858 concerned wills or administrations and Houston also provides references, for each case, to the surviving records of the court (# chapter 24). Indexes to records of the PCC and of courts of York province are considered below.

Most of the wills and admons at CROs, from the bishops', archdeacons' and peculiar courts, are indexed. Published and manuscript indexes are listed, by county, in Gibson & Churchill (291). Many indexes have been published in volumes of the British Record Society (BRS) and copies of these volumes are held at the SoG, TNA and CROs. The SoG has a very large collection of published and unpublished indexes to wills and these are listed in Newington-Irving (297). As an example of the available published indexes, wills and administrations of Bedfordshire are indexed in two BRS volumes by Cirket (283) and (284). Index entries usually give the testator's name, parish (sometimes an occupation) and the year in which the will was proved (or the administration was granted) as in the following examples for the wills of my ancestors Michael and William Read:

Name	Parish	Occupation	Year/Ref.
Read, Mich.	Hockliffe	dairyman	1779/36
Read, Wm.	Hockliffe	dairyman	1728/94

The references permit you to order a copy of the will at the relevant CRO.

There are many other published indexes. For example, Hampshire Record Office has published a microfiche index of the wills that it holds for 1571 to 1858. Cheshire Record Office has published (and placed on its web site) a 10-volume index (279) to the wills that it holds that were proved in the Consistory Court of Chester from 1492 to 1857. Copies of most of the wills can be ordered for a small charge. The online genealogical database of Gloucestershire Record Office includes an index of all wills proved at Gloucester from 1541 to 1858 and Bristol Record Office's web site includes an index of wills proved at Bristol from 1793 to 1858. There are four BRS volumes and a CD-ROM produced by Lincolnshire Archives that index most of the wills and administrations from Lincoln Consistory Court, the Archdeaconry Court of Stow and some of the peculiar courts in Lincolnshire. Wills proved in the Archdeaconry Court of London are indexed up to 1700 (with administrations) in BRS volumes 89 and 98 and from 1700 to 1807 in Webb (303a). Family history societies are also producing useful indexes of wills, such as Webb (303), for the records of the Archdeaconry Court of Surrey from 1752 to 1858.

If there is no published index, you should use the CRO's own indexes. These may be typescript, manuscript or card indexes. Some old indexes contain only a name and a year of probate (or admon), so that it may be difficult to identify correct entries. For example, Guildhall Library holds the registers of wills and admons of the Commissary Court of London (London Division). Published indexes of these records extend to only 1700 and there are presently only manuscript indexes to records of 1701 to 1858. It can be difficult to find the will of a London ancestor because of the large number of church courts (noted above), in addition to the PCC. However, David Wright of 71 Island Wall, Whitstable, Kent CT5 1EL, has compiled an index to the wills and administrations of 1750–1858 in the courts (listed at (a) to (d) above) that had jurisdiction in London and Middlesex. The index has over 60,000 entries and can be consulted for a small fee.

The records of probate material for York province (and published indexes) are rather complex. The records are at the Borthwick Institute and described in Gibson & Churchill (291), Chapman

(926) and Smith (271). Indexes for PCY, Exchequer Court and Chancery Court wills and admons prior to 1688 have been published by the Yorkshire Archaeological Society. The Borthwick Institute has typescript or manuscript indexes for 1688–1858. However, the wills proved in one court were often filed at a different court (and many of the published indexes have incorrect titles as to the courts they cover) and so great care is necessary when working with these records.

PCC wills

The importance of PCC wills justifies a detailed description of the arrangement of the records and of the indexes and finding aids. Registered copies of PCC wills are in series PROB 11, on microfilm at the FRC and TNA at Kew. The PCC will registers for most years had names such as Rowe or Langley. These were the names of PCC clerks or of the first testator recorded in a register. Registers were divided into quires (bundles of 16 pages). Until recently, researchers had to use many different indexes and calendars in order to find a registered PCC will in PROB 11. However, digital images of all those wills (that is over one million) are being made available by TNA, with a full name index, in the DocumentsOnline section of its web site. By November 2003, all wills for 1610–1858 could be seen online and almost all of those from 1383 to 1609. The remaining wills should be available by the end of 2003.

Searches of the index on DocumentsOnline are easy and free. You type a surname (and, if you wish, a forename) in the search request boxes. You can also limit a search to a range of years, county, other place or testator's occupation. You press the "go" button and a list of results is produced. Searches pick up a variety of spellings, similar to a requested name, but you can also use an asterisk as a wildcard so as to obtain results for various spellings of a name (thus Ch*rnock produces results for both Charnock and Chernock). You can also require only exact matches by putting quotation marks around a name. Although I had already found the PCC will of my ancestor Thomas Gillman of Hockliffe, Bedfordshire, the index entry that you obtain if you search for Gillman, Thomas and Hockliffe is:

Thomas Gillman, cordwainer of Hockliffe   07 November 1823   PROB 11/1677

My search request, for the surname Bulleid in the period 1610–1858, produced five results including:

John Bulleid, yeoman of Maryansleigh, Devon   06 February 1629   PROB 11/155

For £3 payable by debit or credit card, you can then download a copy of the will. TNA may soon waive the £3 charge for wills ordered by researchers at Kew or the FRC but there will be a small printing charge. You can also choose to view some details of the will, including the number of pages and the name of the PCC register (in PROB 11) and the quire numbers in which the will is included; for example "Register Langley, quire numbers 52–114". As noted, a quire is a bundle, within a register, of 16 pages and so this reference is only telling you that the will is somewhere within about 1,000 pages of one PROB 11 register. You cannot therefore realistically use the reference to find the will yourself in PROB 11 at the FRC or at Kew.

As an alternative to the online service for PCC wills, you can use a number of published and unpublished indexes to find (and copy) the will in the relevant piece in PROB 11. This traditional method of searching is still necessary for PCC administrations, reviewed below. You may also choose this route to save the online charge of £3 per will or because you want a good photographic copy of the will rather than a digital image. There are published indexes to PCC wills of 1383–1800 (including administrations with wills annexed). These indexes are listed in appendix IX and reviewed below. A calendar of PCC wills and administrations for 1853–57 (and a separate volume for January 1858) is at the FRC, TNA and SoG. It is also included on the microfiche copies of the PPR calendars, noted above. Illustration 57 is a page from the calendar of 1853–57, listing wills proved in that period for testators surnamed Eade to Eagles.

For wills (and administrations with wills annexed) in PROB 11 for the years not covered by published indexes (that is 1800–52), you can use the annual manuscript calendars in series PROB 12 which are on open shelves at the FRC. These calendars cover both wills and admons but they are incomplete (up to 10% of entries may have been omitted). The entries for each year are arranged by the first letter of the deceased's surname, and then in the order that applications were submitted to the PCC. Therefore, all surnames starting with S for both wills and admons are mixed up in one list. You may therefore have to search many pages to find your ancestor. Entries for soldiers and sailors (except officers) who died at sea or overseas from 1800 to 1852 are listed separately, either at the end of the section for each letter or at the end of each volume of the calendars. The entry from the manuscript calendars for the will of Thomas Gillman of Hockliffe, proved in 1823, is:

Gillman,   Thomas   Bedford   Nov(ember)   629

The number 629 is the quire number, within the bundles for 1823, in which the registered copy of the will is included. Having found the entry for Thomas Gillman, I turned to the series list for the registered wills in PROB 11. This showed that the registers for 1823 are pieces PROB 11/1665 (for quires 1–50) to PROB 11/1679 (for quires 691–725). Piece PROB 11/1677 included quire 629. I found the relevant microfilm, searched for quire 629 (this number is written on the top right of the first page of the quire) and located the registered copy of Thomas Gillman's will. Copies of wills can be ordered, or you can make copies on microfilm copying machines.

Most of the published indexes to PCC wills (or admons with wills annexed) of 1383–1700 note the name and parish of the deceased, the year of probate, the name of the PROB 11 register in which the will appears and the quire number. The PROB 11 series list at the FRC or TNA notes that a named register for a particular year is in, for example, PROB 11/121. You take the microfilm of that piece to a microfilm reader, find the quire specified by the published index and look through it to find the will. The pages also have stamped folio numbers to assist you to order a copy or make one on the self-service microfilm copiers. Some published indexes do not specify the register name but record the year of probate and a folio number. In these cases, the PROB 11 series list tells you the piece that covers that year (and you can turn to the folio noted in the index). The calendars of 1853–57 and 1858 note the month and year of probate and the folio. The PROB 11 series list tells you which piece includes that month and year.

An alphabetical index to PCC registered wills (and also admons, see below) of 1700–49 has been prepared from the manuscript calendars in PROB 12. It can be seen at the FRC, SoG and TNA (or purchased on microfiche). The index notes a testator's name, the month and year of probate, the county of residence (or Scotland, Ireland or "Pts" for foreign parts), the piece

WILLS PROVED IN THE PREROGATIVE COURT OF CANTERBURY.

From 1st January 1853 to 31st December 1857.

E.

					Reference to Registered Will.
EADE	William Aislabie Esq.	Middlesex.	July	1853.	530
EADEN	John.	Cambridge.	June	1853.	450
EADES	Catherine Waterman.	Middx. Special Administration (with Will).	September	1854.	673
EADES	Francis Esq. Retired Brevet Lieut.-Colonel East India Company's Service.	Gloucester.	March	1857.	188
EADSON	Elizabeth.	Bath.	April	1857.	286
EAGLE	Catherine.	Oxford.	June	1854.	448
EAGLE	Charles.	London.	September	1856.	890
EAGLE	Francis King Esq.	Suffolk.	August	1856.	621
EAGLE	Robert.	Middx.	August	1854.	605
EAGLE	William.	Middx.	August	1853.	683
EAGLE	William.	Suffolk and London.	December	1854.	905
EAGLEMAN	Robert "Victoria and Albert."	Southampton. (G.C.)	November	1855.	912
EAGLES	The Reverend John.	Gloucester.	January	1856.	25
EAGLES	Joseph.	Worcester.	October	1856.	754

(1.)

57. *A page from the calendar of wills and administrations in the Prerogative Court of Canterbury 1853–57 (TNA, PROB 12/276)*

number in PROB 11 and the quire number (called a "sig" number in the index) in which the will can be found. If you found the following entry, you would take the microfilm of PROB 11/524, turn to quire 228 and search the 16 pages for John Balderston's will:

Balderston, John   1711 Nov. Norfolk   PROB 11/524, sig 228

The SoG has a card index (prepared from some old manuscript calendars in series PROB 13) of the PCC registered wills of 1750–1800. The index has about 330,000 entries. A typescript version has been published in book and fiche form in Camp (281) and is included on the English Origins web site. It notes a testator's name, county of residence, year (and month) of probate and a quire number. Typical entries for the surname Bateman are:

Year	Forename		County		Quire
1785	John, Esq	Admon with will	Northampton	March	119
1793	John	Will	Essex	July	353
1774	Mary	Will	Kent	October	359
1763	Miles	Will	Pts (foreign parts)	February	45

The PROB 11 series list tells you which piece includes the register for that period. You then turn to the relevant quire on the microfilm and search the quire's 16 pages for the will.

All the above refers to PCC registered wills in PROB 11, that is those copied into registers by the PCC clerks. The original wills (from which the copies were made) are held by TNA at Kew in series PROB 10. There are various finding-aids to assist your search in these records (in case you want to see your ancestor's signature). Having found a correct reference, an original will has to be ordered a few days in advance of your visit.

Some entries in PCC will indexes note "by sentence" or "by decree" which means that there was litigation about a deceased's estate. If so, there may be other records concerning your ancestor, such as court pleadings, statements of witnesses and probate accounts (# chapter 24).

PCC administrations

PCC administrations were recorded in court orders (or acts), listed in Act books in series PROB 6 (on microfilm at the FRC). They date from 1559 and entries up to 1732 (except for 1651–60) are in Latin. There is one Act book for each year and they are listed in the PROB 6 series list. For example, PROB 6/183 is the Act book for 1807. Illustration 58 is part of a page from this book with acts for the estates of three deceased. Thus, on 26 February, letters of administration were granted over the estate of William Anderson, a seaman on HMS *Centurion*, to his cousin William Jennings. By the fourth act on the page (not included in the illustration), letters of administration were granted for the estate of Nicholas Barnardi (of St Andrew Holborn but recently residing in Italy) to his uncle Peter Barnardi, guardian of the minor Joseph Barnardi (the only son of Nicholas). No Act books survive from before 1559 but a few other records refer to admons of 1535–59 (an index in PROB 45, acts of court books in PROB 29/1–10 and some administrators' bonds in PROB 51).

Appendix IX lists published indexes to PCC administrations of 1559–1660, 1701–49 and 1853–58. The Act books up to 1660 are arranged in monthly sections. Published indexes list the deceased and note the year and month in which an admon was granted and usually the quire

58. *Part of a page from an Act book of the Prerogative Court of Canterbury, showing three administrations in February 1807 (TNA, PROB 6/183)*

number (confusingly, this is often noted as a "folio" number) in that year's Act book in which you will find the act. The PROB 6 series list tells you the piece number for that year's Act book. You then take the microfilm for that piece, turn to the specified month and quire and search its 16 pages for the admon. If the index does not record the quire number, you have to search through all the quires for that month. One Act book in this period is not covered by published indexes. During the English Civil War, the PCC sat in both London and Oxford. Only one Act book from Oxford survives (in PROB 6/234, for January 1643 to April 1644) but it has its own index.

Finding administrations in the period 1661 to 1852 is more difficult. From 1661 to 1718, the Act books have a section for each month. From 1719, the PCC divided its business between five registry "seats", each dealing with a part of England or Wales. The seats were designated "Registrar", "Surrey", "Middlesex", "London" and "Welsh". The counties in each seat are listed in Bevan (239) and the PROB 6 series list. The estates of those living or dying abroad or dying at sea were dealt with by the Registrar's seat. From 1719 to 1743, Act books are arranged by month and then subdivided by registry seat. Some Act books have more than one 12-month sequence (sometimes up to four). Admons in June may therefore appear in up to four sections of an Act book. Act books of 1744 to 1858 are arranged by seat, then month. Unfortunately, the Act books' sections are not marked with the registry seat but with the names of the registry clerks. A finding-aid is on the FRC shelves, listing the clerks' names for each year (so that you can identify the correct section of an Act book).

The index to wills and admons of 1701–49, noted above, lists the names of the deceased with an "A" in the case of admons, then notes the year, month, county (or country) of residence and the piece reference, for example PROB 6/122. You take the microfilm for that piece, ascertain the relevant registry seat for the deceased's county or country from the sources noted above, then search the Act book's sections (up to four of them) for the month noted in the index. You also have to search each of those monthly sections for your ancestor's admon.

The British Record Society is preparing an index to PCC admons of 1661–1700 and A. Camp is indexing admons of 1750–1800 (about 170,000 of them) from an SoG card index (prepared from old PROB 13 calendars, noted above). Until these are available, in order to find admons of 1661–1700 and 1750–1852, you must search the annual PROB 12 manuscript calendars (described above for PCC wills). The calendars record a deceased's name, county or country, and either a "folio" (but really a quire) number for the Act book of that year or the month of the grant, as in illustration 59 which is a page from the PROB 12 calendar listing admons of 1836. Remember that names are only in order of their first letter and that there are separate sections for some soldiers and sailors. Admons of 1853 to January 1858 are listed in the calendars of PCC wills and administrations for 1853–57 and 1858, noted above, at the FRC, TNA and SoG (and included on microfiche copies of the National Probate Calendar). These note the deceased's county (or country) and the month of the grant. Having found your ancestor in the PROB 12 manuscript calendars or in the printed calendars (of 1853–58), you obtain the piece reference for the Act book of the relevant year from the PROB 6 series list. If the calendar gives a folio (quire) number, the search is easy. If it only indicates the month, you must ascertain the relevant registry seat for the deceased's county or country from the finding aids noted above. You then have to search the Act book for the sections for the relevant month and registry seat. Finally, you have to search those sections in order to find the admon.

Some other records of PCC wills and administrations are at TNA at Kew. Probate Act books are in series PROB 8. These record the fact that a grant of probate was made in respect of a testator and also note the names and residence of the executors. In some cases, there was a limited grant of probate or administration (that is, over only part of the deceased's estate). Limited probates of 1800–58 are in series PROB 9. Limited administrations up to 1810 are in the PROB 6 Act books but for 1810–58 are in separate Act books in series PROB 7 which are at TNA and (on microfilm) at the FRC. Some applications for grants of letters of administration, providing dates of death and the signature of the proposed administrator, are held in series PROB 14. The administrator may have had to submit a bond (see below) and these are in series PROB 46, 51 and 54. Information on the beneficiaries of the estate may be noted in death duty registers from 1796 (considered below). An inventory of the deceased's possessions (described below) may also survive.

Administrations 1836

K

Kinchin	William	Berks	Jan
Kilsby	William	Midx	Jan
Kettle	George	Kent	Jan
Kirkman	Henry	Midx	Feb
Knight	William	Essex	Feb
	Admon of Goods unadm.d Former Grant Oct.r 1834.		
King	Henry	Berks	Feb
Knowles	Olivia	Kent	Feb
King	Sarah Sturgess	Bedford	Feb
Knapp formerly Lush	Sophia	Midx	Feb
Knowles	Richard	Leic.r	Mar
Keates	Charlotte	Surry	Mar
Koster formerly Sapte Barber formerly Kavanagh	Mary Antoinette Amelia p.ts / Ann Sarah Essex Admon of Goods unadm.d Former Grant April 1827.		Mar / Mar
Klingender	Frederick Charles Louis	Midx	Mar
Kendall formerly Harding	Mary Ann	Lond	Mar

59. A page from the calendar of wills and administrations in the Prerogative Court of Canterbury, listing administrations of 1836 (TNA, PROB 12)

Abstracts of wills and administrations

Many abstracts of the wills proved in the church courts have been published, and these works are listed in Gibson & Churchill (291). Thus Evans (288) includes abstracts of almost 900 wills from 1630 to 1635 that were proved in the Archdeaconry Court of Sudbury in Suffolk. Abstracts of wills proved in the Court of Husting of the City of London are contained in Sharpe (301). Volumes such as this should always be reviewed prior to consulting the original wills so that you can avoid problems caused by language or handwriting, but also because they are usually indexed, not only by the testator's names, but often by the names of beneficiaries, witnesses and tenants of property. This is the only realistic method of finding ancestors who were noted in wills in these capacities.

Researchers with Essex ancestors are particularly fortunate as a result of the work of F.G. Emmison who produced 12 volumes of abstracts of over 10,000 wills, proved from 1558 to 1603, held in Essex Record Office. Thus one volume, Emmison (287), contains abstracts of 971 wills from 1597 to 1603 from the courts of three archdeaconries: Essex, Colchester and Middlesex (Essex and Hertfordshire jurisdiction). Each volume is indexed by place but also by the names of testators, beneficiaries, witnesses and other people named in the wills. Abstracts of many of the early wills proved in the PCC have also been published, usually by county record societies (selecting those PCC wills relating to their county). Thus McGregor (295), published by Bedfordshire Historical Record Society, has abstracts of 132 PCC wills, from 1383 to 1548, executed by Bedfordshire residents or dealing with Bedfordshire property (with all names and places indexed).

A few examples of pre-1858 wills or administrations of my ancestors (two of them butchers), will emphasise the enormous value of these documents and illustrate how many testators were very ordinary people. The first example is an abstract of letters of administration granted in the Archdeaconry Court of Barnstaple for the estate of John Bulhead, who died in 1645:

Administration of the goods of John Bulhead of Winkleigh, granted to Thomas Bulhead, his son, 21 March 1645.
Bond of Thomas Bulhead of Winkleigh, butcher and Thomas Jeffreye of the same, butcher, in £16. Condition that Thomas shall administer the goods of John Bulhead, his father. Signature of Thos. "Buled". Witnesses: Wm Baker, George Bray.
Inventory by Tho. Jefferye & Hen. Weyvell 5 March 1645. Sum £8. 7s. 4d

John's son and grandson were both butchers in Winkleigh (and both named Thomas Bulhead). The grandson Thomas died in 1702 leaving a will of which an abstract survives:

Will of Thomas Bulhead of Winkleigh, butcher. Dated 31 October 1702.
To James Bulhead, my son, the white nosed nag.
Nicolas Bulhead, my son £20.
Samuel Bulhead, son of Nicolas Bulhead, my grandson, £15 and if he die before he comes of age, £10 of the said money to be paid to John Bulhead, son of Nicolas Bulhead, and the residue to Nicolas Bulhead, their father.
Residue to Grace Bulhead, my wife, and John Bulhead, my son and Samuel Bulhead, my son, executors. Signed. Witnesses; Richard Bullhead (mark), Agnes Hill, Thomas Weekes.
Proved 9 Jan 1702. Inventory 11 Nov 1702 by George Letheren, Richard Bulhead and Christopher Weekes. Farm stock and household goods. His estate, inn houses and ground £93. Sum £269. 6s. 10d

Both of these examples refer to an inventory, which was a list of the deceased's movable goods. These lists were commonly prepared until about 1750, and they are considered below. In some wills of the same period, a deceased might appoint two or three overseers. These were usually close friends or relatives whose responsibility was to ensure that the executors carried out their duties correctly.

Probate Inventories

In the period 1530–1750, many courts required an inventory to be filed when probate or letters of administration had been granted. An inventory was a list of the deceased's movable goods, prepared by appraisors or inventors (two, three or four local men, usually relatives or friends). Many inventories survive in CROs (or at TNA for PCC wills and admons) and some are indexed. About 40,000 PCC inventories from 1417 to 1858 (mostly for 1661 to 1720) are at TNA in series PROB 2 to 5, 31, 32 and 37. These series, and the name indexes to most of them, are described in detail in Cox (285). For example, List and Index Society volumes 85–86, 149 and 221 index the deceaseds' names for most of the inventories in series PROB 3–5. List and Index Society volume 204 indexes the PCC filed exhibits in PROB 32. There are also some indexes to the inventories of particular counties. Holman & Herridge (294) indexes the probate inventories of residents of Surrey that are in the PROB series noted above (as well as inventories from the lower ecclesiastical courts, held in CROs, which had jurisdiction in Surrey). Indexes to inventories held in CROs are listed in Gibson & Churchill (291).

Inventories provide an excellent insight into an ancestor's life and status. They list items such as furniture, clothes, tools, farm animals (and their approximate values). West (463) includes a good study of inventories, with a glossary of unusual words used in inventories to describe items. Gibson & Churchill (291) list, by county, published collections of inventories. Steer (302) is a collection of 248 inventories from Essex between 1635 and 1749, with a detailed analysis of the items, such as furniture, farming stock and tools, that they list. Another published example is Havinden (293), containing transcripts of 259 inventories from 16th-century Oxfordshire, from which the following is an example:

[the goods of] Nicholas Coates, of Chadlington, husbandman [the deceased] taken 17th February 1584/5, by Robert Launder, John Loonchpray and Thomas Robbyns.

	£	s.	d.
2 Oxen	3	0	0
3 horses	3	0	0
Corn in the barne and in the fyld	3	6	8

Other probate records of the church courts

The Probate Act books of the PCC were noted above. The Probate Act books (or registers) of other church courts have often survived. These have entries for each probate granted and should include the deceased's name, occupation, the date of the grant of probate and the executors' names. In the case of administrations, there may be an Admon Act book, naming the administrators and noting the date of death of the intestate. If the court granted letters of administration "with will annexed", the terms of the will may also be noted in the Act book.

Church court records may contain other relevant documents. In some cases the court required executors or administrators to provide a bond to the court as a guarantee that they would carry out their duties correctly. A bond was usually in a sum equal to, or double, the amount of the estate to be administered. Bonds contain little genealogical information and were in similar form to the bonds given for marriage licences (# chapter 14). If the deceased left young children, a court could appoint guardians, who also might have to provide a bond. Someone with an interest in the estate of a deceased, such as a widow or creditor, could prevent probate of a will being granted without his or her knowledge, by entering a *caveat* (a warning notice) at court. No probate would be granted without the person who filed the caveat being given the opportunity to be heard. This procedure could be used if, for example, a widow suspected that another relative had custody of an old will of her deceased husband which she believed to have been revoked. Caveats may be noted in act books or in separate caveat books. Act books also include renunciations. If executors or administrators did not wish to act, they could renounce their rights and request a court to appoint successors. A typical entry for a renunciation would be:

I, Joanna Read of Newtown, widow and relict of Henry Read of Newtown, do hereby renounce all my right, interest and claim in the administration of the goods of the said Henry Read and desire that the administration be granted to William Read of Exeter, brother of the said Henry Read.

Litigation sometimes arose, perhaps from a dispute over the validity of a will or over acts of the executors or administrators. These testamentary suits were usually brought by a creditor of the estate (or a disappointed relative) against the executors or administrators. The records of the proceedings may include affidavits or other documents concerning the testator, his family and property. Good descriptions of ecclesiastical court cases, mostly from the north of England, are contained in Addy (919). Ecclesiastical court records are considered further in chapter 24 so, in this chapter, we shall only consider an example from my family tree to illustrate the type of information that may be revealed. Transcripts survive (the original records have been lost) describing litigation over the estate of Samuel Bulleid (a cousin of my ancestor John Bulleid) who died in 1781 in Winkleigh in Devon. His will has been lost but the notes reveal that Samuel's brother George acted as executor. William Stoneman claimed that he had been a creditor of Samuel. George had to provide an inventory of Samuel's goods to the court with an account of the distribution of the estate. The account revealed that Samuel had left legacies to his sisters and most of his property to George, and that Samuel's widow Agnes had been married previously. The notes also recorded a claim made against Agnes. She had been administratrix of the estate of her first husband, Richard Dart (and stepmother to Richard's children by his previous marriage). A guardian of one of her stepchildren tried taking control, from Agnes, of the continuing administration of Richard Dart's estate. The guardian made various allegations against Agnes, for example that she (and Samuel Bulleid) had purchased land cheaply from Dart's estate and that she had extracted unjustified expenses from the estate's cash funds. Agnes denied the allegations, producing property valuations and reasons for the expenses. The outcome of the dispute is unknown because the original records are lost.

Wills that were not proved
A will may not have been located after the testator's death. He may have lost it, or deposited it somewhere, moved on and not left a forwarding address. Many wills were not proved because

they were invalid or because they were subsequently replaced by another will, and a court case may have been fought to establish whether or not the will was valid. If a will was invalid, letters of administration were usually granted. Some church courts' archives include some unproved wills. You should also note that, until 1858, there was no need for those wills that dealt only with real property, that is land, to be proved in the courts and so they could have been kept with other family papers or perhaps kept with title deeds to a property.

Wills that have been destroyed

A great loss of probate records occurred during the Second World War when the probate registry of Exeter was destroyed, together with many wills, admons and other probate records of the church courts of Devon, Cornwall and Somerset, dating from the 16th to 19th centuries. Fortunately, wills and admons since 1858 survived at the PPR in London. Some indexes of the lost wills up to 1858 survive (and have been published in part), although they do not cover all courts or time periods. Furthermore, many of the wills proved from 1812 to 1857 had been copied by the Estate Duty Office for the purposes of collecting death duty. Copies of these have been provided to the relevant CROs. Some information can also be obtained from the death duty registers for 1796 to 1811 (see below). Some abstracts had also been made, for example by Miss Moger and Sir Oswyn Murray, of the Devon wills that were subsequently lost. These abstracts are held at Devon Record Office and at the West Country Studies Library in Exeter. A few other wills survive in family archives or in collections of title deeds for property.

Turning to the lost wills of Somerset, many wills, copies, transcripts or abstracts have been located. Sir Mervyn Medlycott produced an index to about 15,000 wills that survived in 320 archives or collections. David Hawkings has also produced indexes to about 13,000 copies of Somerset wills for the period 1812–57 that were made by the Estate Duty Office (and held by TNA). There is also a further index to about 2,400 Estate Duty Office wills and administrations for the period 1805–11. These indexes can be purchased from Harry Galloway Publishing, The Cottage, Manor Terrace, Paignton, Devon TQ3 3RQ.

Death duty registers

Various duties were imposed on estates from 1796. These taxes had different names but are known generally as death or estate duties. In the years after 1796 the exemptions from death duties were reduced and inflation brought more and more estates above the taxable level. It is estimated that only about 25 per cent of wills and admons were recorded in the registers up to 1805, but the figure was about 75 per cent from 1805 to 1815 and later almost 100 per cent.

Legacy duty was introduced as a tax on deceased's estates in 1796. The tax was levied on legacies and on the residue of personal estate valued above £20. There were exemptions for that part of the estate that passed to the deceased's close relatives (spouse, children, parents and grandparents) but the exemptions were restricted in 1805 to the deceased's spouse and parents and from 1815 to the spouse. Legacy duty was also subsequently imposed on the proceeds of sale of any real property that had formed part of a deceased's estate. Further taxes were imposed on estates during the 19th century. Estates worth over £100 became liable (from 1853 to 1949) to succession duty. This applied to any type of property that was transferred at death. Probate duty (later called estate duty) was also charged on all personal property passing upon the occasion of someone's death. All these duties were replaced by capital transfer tax in 1975.

The Estate Duty Office (later merged into the Inland Revenue) made abstracts of wills and administrations and then calculated the tax payable. The registers containing these abstracts (consisting of about 8,000 volumes) are known as the death duty registers and cover the period 1796–1903. They are held by TNA in series IR 26 and the registers up to 1857 are also on microfilm at the FRC and SoG. Those for 1904 to 1931 were destroyed and a few registers are missing. There are also indexes on microfilm, up to 1903, at the FRC (in series IR 27). The wills and administrations noted in the registers are from all the probate courts of England and Wales (although incomplete for some years) but only concern those estates large enough to attract death duty. From 1812 copies of all wills and administrations had to be lodged at the Estate Duty Office, but the registers prepared by the office continued to record only those estates that were subject to duty. The office's copies of wills and administrations were generally destroyed (since the important information was contained in the registers), except for those for Devon, Cornwall and Somerset, which were sent to the relevant CROs.

The death duty registers in series IR 26 of 1796 to 1903 are most conveniently seen (up to 1858) on microfilm at the FRC. You must give TNA at Kew about one week's notice in order to see the later registers. The registers (and years covered) are:

PCC wills	1796–1811	Will and admon registers	1882–1894
PCC admons	1796–1857	Reversionary registers	1812–1852
Country court wills	1796–1811	Succession duty registers	1853–1894
Country court admons	1812–1857	Succession duty arrears	1853–1894
Will registers	1812–1881	Estate duty registers	1894–1903
Intestate registers	1858–1881		

These registers provide supplementary information about the estates of the deceased. The entries are in columns across the register pages. The information in the columns varied over the years and is reviewed in detail in Cox (285), TNA domestic records leaflets 57 and 58 and an FRC leaflet. An entry usually recorded the deceased's name (addresses and occupations are sometimes given), the probate court, the date the will was made, the dates of death, probate or administration, the name, occupation and residence of executors and administrators, important extracts from the will, the beneficiaries' names (and their relationship to the deceased), a description of the property or the fraction of the estate to which a beneficiary was entitled, the value of the legacy or share, the rate and amount of duty and the date of payment. Importantly, the death duty registers often identify those beneficiaries who were not named in wills (for example if the testator left property to "all my sons") and also the beneficiaries in administrations (which letters of administration do not do). This can be particularly helpful for ascertaining the married names of daughters. A testator, John Clements, may have left property to "my daughter Jane", but the death duty registers may reveal the beneficiary as Jane Dale. It is then easier to find her marriage. The relationship of a beneficiary to the deceased was noted in the registers by codes (for example "GG child" meant the deceased's great grandchild), which are set out in TNA leaflets. The registers may also include other useful notes, for example that a beneficiary named in a will had died before the testator.

The indexes in IR 27 note the names of the deceased, the executors or administrators, and the probate court and therefore constitute a national index to all wills and admons that attracted duty since 1796. The series list for IR 27 tells you which index should be consulted for particular years (and its piece number). For the period 1796–1811, the indexes in IR 27 are divided into three groups. Firstly, there is a PCC wills index for 1796–1811 (IR 27/1–16). This is divided into sections for each year, with testators then indexed, not in true alphabetical order of surname, but with entries in order of the first letter of a name and then sub-divided by the first vowel used in that name. Therefore, the names Carpenter, Clark and Chapman all appear under CA. The second index (IR 27/17–20) is for PCC administrations, covering 1796–1811 (and also, in IR 27/21–66, the years up to 1857). The volumes of this index each cover a number of years, with entries for testators arranged in the same manner as the PCC wills index. The third index (IR 27/67–93) is for country courts for 1796–1811. This covers both wills and admons in the PCY, diocesan, archdeaconry and peculiar courts, but each volume contains entries for more than one court and year. The entries for testators are arranged in the same manner as the other indexes.

There are also three indexes for the period 1812–57. There is the PCC administrations index, noted above, which covers the period 1796–1857. Secondly, there is one index (IR 27/140–323) to all PCC and country court wills (for 1812–57) listing all wills that attracted duty and were proved each year in each court. Thirdly, there is an index (IR 27/94–139) for country court administrations (for 1812–57). The index of wills is divided into years and for each year there are four parts (covering names starting with A–D, E–J, K–R and S–Z respectively). From 1812 the indexes are arranged so that entries for testators are grouped according to the particular range of letters at the start of the testator's name, for example, all testators with surnames commencing with three letters within the range HOG to HON. Series IR 27 also contains indexes for the period since 1858, when the civil courts had jurisdiction. The PPR calendars of wills and administrations at First Avenue House are easier to use for finding wills or admons but the death duty registers may provide you with further information, for example about beneficiaries.

A typical entry in an index in IR 27 is that for my ancestor Thomas Gillman, whose will was proved in the PCC in 1823. Piece IR 27/185 is shown in the IR 27 series list as the index covering 1823 for PCC and country court wills, for surnames beginning E–J. In IR 27/185, under GIL, was the following entry (the register and folio numbers refer you to the entry in the relevant death duty register in IR 26):

Testator	Executors	Court	Register	Folio
Gillman, Thomas	Thos. Waterfield, Dunstable, Beds	P.C	4	955

This referred me to Register 4, folio 955 of the relevant piece in IR 26. The IR 26 series list noted that the registers of wills proved from 1812 to 1881 are in piece numbers IR 26/535 to 3292, and that the register for 1823 (for deceased's surnames starting with E–G) commenced at piece IR 26/953. Folio 955 was in piece IR 26/956. I quickly found the entry for Thomas Gillman on the microfilm that included this piece. The entry named the beneficiaries (and also noted the provisions of the will relating to each). They included Thomas's daughter Susan (as Susan Eagles of Hoxton, Middlesex). Although this information was already known to me from Thomas's will, the registers would have been of great help to me if Thomas's will had referred to her only as Susan, or if he had died intestate.

Beneficiaries

Searching lists of wills and administrations for a deceased's surname is relatively easy. However, one of the most beneficial results of finding a relevant will is the confirmation of relationships between people with different surnames. We have noted the importance of the will of Thomas Gillman (confirming that James Eagles and Susannah Gillman, of Hockliffe, were my ancestors James and Susannah Eagles of Hoxton, Middlesex). John Bulleid of Winkleigh (a cousin of my Bulleid ancestors) died in August 1820. He left gifts to his daughter Mary Snell and his sisters Jane Brealy (or Brayley) and Ann Brock. A descendant of Mary, Jane or Ann might not know their maiden name and therefore have no reason to look at Bulleid wills. Fortunately, there are some indexes to the beneficiaries in wills.

Firstly, as noted above, many volumes of abstracts of wills from the church courts have been published. These are usually well indexed by names of testators, witnesses and beneficiaries. Any volumes for the church courts with jurisdiction in your ancestor's county should be reviewed. Secondly, there are some published indexes to beneficiaries' names. For example, Nicholson & Readdie (298) indexes the names, stated relationships and occupations of people noted in wills proved in the Consistory Court of the Bishop of Durham 1787–91. A typical entry is that for the will proved on 5 June 1788 of Elizabeth Whitehead, widow of Morpeth:

> Late husband Joshua Whitehead; son Henry Whitehead; daughter Jane Archbold; granddaughters Elizabeth Ware and Henrietta Ware; friend Stephen Watson [of] North Seaton, Northumberland, esq. Witnesses: John English. Edw. Lawson.

Thirdly, some archives, family history societies and individuals hold indexes to some of the people named in wills. These indexes are listed in Gibson & Hampson (158). For example, the West Country Studies Library in Exeter holds the Burnett-Morris Index, a slip index arranged by surname, that includes many entries for beneficiaries named in wills. I found a reference to Arminell Bulhead, named in a 1/10 will of William Pike of Winkleigh as his servant. My previous knowledge of Arminell (my ancestor's sister) was limited to the dates of her baptism and burial. Only the index could have alerted me to this further information.

Mrs J. Ackers of Scorton in Lancashire has produced an index (a copy is at the SoG) of people mentioned in the wills of reputed Lancashire Catholics of the 17th and 18th centuries. The index lists over 21,500 people mentioned in 1,748 wills or letters of administration, including 42 members of the Charnock family; 20 of them in the six Charnock wills covered by the index, but 22 of them in wills of people with other surnames (relatives, neighbours and friends). An Essex wills beneficiaries index is also being collated by Mrs Thora Broughton. Articles about this index appear in *Family Tree Magazine* (December 1993) and *Essex Family Historian* (May 1995). Mrs Broughton is indexing the beneficiaries, executors and trustees (with surnames different to the testator) in wills at Essex Record Office which were proved before 1858. By 2002 the index covered all such wills for the period 1657–1858. Details of the index (and the fees for searches) can be obtained by sending an SAE to Mrs Broughton at 43, Pertwee Drive, Chelmsford, Essex CM2 8DY. Similar indexes are being prepared for other counties (including Hampshire and Wiltshire).

Stock registers
More information about a deceased's estate or beneficiaries may be obtained from sources similar to the death duty registers. The SoG holds registers of abstracts of wills, dating from 1717 to 1845, which were used by the Bank of England in respect of bequests of government stocks. The registers can be seen on microfilm and are described in detail by A. Camp in *Family Tree Magazine* (May 2000). If your ancestor held such stocks at death, these registers should include an

abstract of the relevant part of the will (or a note of the administration), details of the stock held and information about the beneficiary who was entitled to receive that stock. An index to the 139 volumes of registers for 1807–45, containing about 31,000 abstracts, has been published by the SoG in book form (277) and on microfiche. A microfiche index to the volumes of 1717 to 1807 (containing another 30,000 abstracts) is also available at the SoG. Both indexes are included on the English Origins web site.

The SoG also holds 270 volumes of the Great Western Railway stockholders' probate registers (for the period 1835–1932). These record, in chronological order, the transfer of the company's stock, usually on a stockholder's death. They note the name and address of the stockholder, the date of death, the name of the person to whom the stock was transferred and a description of the document supporting the transfer (a will or death certificate). The registers, containing perhaps 175,000 entries, are described by F. Hardy in *Genealogists' Magazine* (March 2003). They are not available for public consultation but Mr Hardy is preparing an index to all the names appearing in the registers (it presently covers the first five volumes) and copies of pages from the registers can be provided for a fee.

The Courts of Orphans
These courts are described in detail by Carlton (282). In the City of London and a few other cities or boroughs, the corporation supervised the administration of the estates of the city or borough freemen (# chapter 17) who had died leaving children who were called orphans (even though their mothers might still be alive) who had not yet attained their majority, that is, the age of 21 (or 18 for a girl who had married a man aged over 21). During the middle ages, a borough court often granted the custody of an orphan (and the orphan's property) to a guardian, who was usually a friend or relative of the deceased. The guardian agreed to look after the orphan (and his inheritance) until he attained the age of 21. In the 16th and 17th centuries, 19 English boroughs or cities (including Bristol, Worcester, Exeter and Hull) established or revived Courts of Orphans to review these arrangements.

When a freeman died, his executor was required to file at court an inventory of the dead man's estate, so that the court would be able to check that orphans were not being swindled and their inheritances were not being dissipated. The inventory was usually prepared by four independent appraisers. In most boroughs it was customary to divide a freeman's net personal estate into three parts: one third for his widow, one third divided equally among his children and one third that could be bequeathed by the deceased as he wished. The executor would either promise the court to keep the orphan's portion himself and pay it over when the orphan came of age, or he could pay it to the borough chamberlain to be invested during the term of the minority.

The courts of orphans declined in the 17th century, principally because most of their role was assumed by the Court of Chancery (# chapter 24). This court had national powers of enforcement and was therefore more effective than the borough courts, whose jurisdiction effectively extended only as far as the city or borough boundaries. The financial position of the City of London (and many boroughs) also became precarious in the late 17th century, so that handing over an orphan's inheritance to the chamberlain was not always safe. Orphans' courts were therefore little used after the 17th century. A few records of the Courts of Orphans survive; those for the City of London, Bristol and Exeter are listed in Carlton (282). For example, over 230 inventories from the 16th and 17th centuries survive in the records of the Court of Orphans at Exeter. Records of the Court of Orphans in London (including about 2,000 inventories) are held by CLRO. A useful article by Carlton about the administration and records of the London Court of Orphans, from the 13th to the 17th centuries, appears in the journal *Guildhall Miscellany* for October 1971 (278).

Locating wills and administrations before 1858: a summary
If you are searching for a pre-1858 will, you should consult the following indexes:

    a. TNA DocumentsOnline for PCC wills 1383–1858
    b. Alternatively, published indexes to PCC wills (1383–1800 and 1853–58) or manuscript calendars (1801–52)
    c. Published indexes to PCC administrations (up to 1660, 1701–49 and 1853–58)
    d. TNA manuscript calendars of PCC administrations (1661–1700 and 1750–1852)
    e. Estate Duty Office indexes, at the FRC and TNA, to wills and admons (1796–1858)
    f. Indexes (published and unpublished) to wills and admons proved in the Archbishop of York's courts (up to 1858)
    g. Published indexes to records of bishops' and archdeacons' courts
    h. Indexes held at CROs to records of bishops' and archdeacons' courts
    i. Indexes of beneficiaries and published abstracts of wills

Advertisements
Executors and administrators were concerned to ensure that they paid all the deceased's valid debts before they distributed his estate to the beneficiaries. In some cases, they might also wish to ensure that all potential beneficiaries were aware of the death and the possibility of an inheritance. Thus, in recent times, if a testator appointed a friend (or an institution such as a bank) as executor, but bequeathed his property to "all my children" or "all my nephews and nieces", the bank might not be certain who (or where) they all were. To protect themselves, executors and administrators advertised in the *London Gazette* or national newspapers (# chapter 17) for creditors of the estate and for potential beneficiaries. Illustration 76 includes an example of such a notice in the *London Gazette* of 4 November 1941.

Dormant funds in court
Finally, many people believe that there are vast sums of money waiting to be claimed by long-lost heirs. This is an exaggeration, but the courts do hold sums of money (most of them quite small), principally for missing heirs of deceased persons. This money is administered by the Court Funds Office (22 Kingsway, London WC2B 6LE) and there is a database to these dormant funds (referring to over 27,000 estates) that can be consulted by the public. A leaflet on the Probate Service web site (# appendix XI) and TNA legal records leaflet 21 describe the procedure to be followed if you believe that you may be entitled to any of these funds. You can also research whether there were dormant funds in earlier times that concerned your ancestors' estates (but which were subsequently distributed) to relatives. Newspapers (# chapter 17) included advertisements requesting lost heirs of a deceased to come forward and a number of lists of deceaseds' names were published in the 19th and early 20th centuries, such as *Dougal's Index Register to Next of Kin* (available in reference libraries).

CHAPTER 13

CATHOLIC, NON-CONFORMIST AND JEWISH RECORDS

From the Reformation until the 19th century, most people were members of the Church of England and are recorded in its parish registers. However, some were members of religious bodies operating independently of the established Church. This includes non-conformists (that is groups of Protestant dissenters such as Baptists or Methodists), Catholics, Jews and followers of foreign churches that were established in Britain. Although the term non-conformist generally applies to Protestant groups, I shall use it to refer to all denominations (including Catholics and Jews) that were independent of the Church of England, since much information applies to all these groups.

Non-conformists' births, marriages and deaths since 1837 are recorded in civil registration records (as well as in their own records) and so research of these events is straightforward. However, research before 1837 is more difficult and this chapter therefore concentrates on that period. If you know that your ancestors were non-conformists (or if you suspect that they were because they do not appear in Anglican registers), you need to ascertain the religious body to which they belonged (or discover which non-conformist groups had chapels in your ancestors' area) and then locate any surviving registers. It is sometimes not obvious that a family was non-conformist. They may have been members of a non-conformist group for only a short time, so that only a few entries for the family are missing from the Anglican registers. Some of my ancestors appear sporadically in non-conformist records. The baptism of John Josiah Keates, the second marriage of his father (George Keates) and the marriage of Thomas Law and Amelia Bateman took place in Independent and Baptist chapels. One important point to watch for is the appearance of your ancestors' marriages since 1754 in Anglican parish registers, but not their baptisms or burials. This is indicative of non-conformist families having weddings (in conformance with Hardwicke's Marriage Act) in their parish church, but celebrating baptisms (and burying their dead) at their own chapels.

NON-CONFORMISM SINCE THE REFORMATION

Until the 16th century English Christians were members of the Catholic (that is, universal) church, owing allegiance to the Pope in Rome. However, England became a Protestant country under Henry VIII (who declared himself Supreme Head of the English Church) and during his reign and those of Edward VI and Elizabeth followers of the old church who continued to be obedient to Rome became known as Roman Catholics.

Religious toleration is a recent phenomenon in England. Catholics and Jews were not emancipated until the 19th century and people were burnt at the stake for their religious beliefs as late as 1611. Attendance at Anglican church services was compulsory until 1689. A "recusant" (that is refuser) who did not attend could be brought before the courts and fined (or have his lands seized). Prior to about 1640 only foreign churches (such as those of the Huguenots) were allowed some toleration by the State (and the established Church) and so the registers of foreign churches are the only non-conformist registers to survive from that period. During the Commonwealth non-conformists enjoyed a large degree of freedom. Many Anglican parish clergy were replaced by Presbyterian or Independent preachers (considered below), the church courts were temporarily abolished and registration of births, marriages and deaths became a civil, rather than a religious, function until 1660. This encouraged some non-conformists to keep their own registers (the earliest registers of the Quakers commence in 1656).

Further legislation discriminating against non-conformists was introduced after the restoration of Charles II in 1660. Many Presbyterian ministers were ejected from their parishes and the Conventicle Act 1664 prohibited them from setting up their own chapels or holding open air meetings in, or near, a town. Fines were imposed on those holding (or even attending) religious services other than at Anglican churches. However, non-conformism gathered strength and legislation permitting dissent from the established Church gradually followed. The Declaration of Indulgence of 1672 allowed Protestant non-conformists to apply for licences for meeting houses and their teachers. However, many non-conformists still thought it too risky to keep registers that revealed their members' names. Even if a register was kept, it was often held by a minister who conducted services at many chapels (and he might keep it until his death) and many of these registers have been lost.

Parliament forced Charles II to withdraw the Declaration of Indulgence in 1673 and passed further legislation, including the Test Act (# chapter 23) designed to suppress non-conformism. James II, who came to the throne in 1685, espoused Catholicism but was ousted by the Glorious Revolution of 1688/9 by the Protestant William of Orange and Mary Stuart. From that time, Protestant non-conformism spread rapidly, principally because of the Act of Toleration of 1689, which effectively allowed freedom of worship to most people (other than Catholics). If Protestant dissenters swore an oath (Quakers could make a declaration in similar terms) of allegiance to the Crown and of belief in the Holy Trinity, they were no longer compelled to attend their parish church. The act also permitted dissenters to obtain licences, from the church courts or Justices of the Peace, for the establishment of chapels. The continued persecution of Catholics (and their eventual emancipation) is dealt with below, but it is important to note that Protestant non-conformists also faced discrimination for many years after 1689. They could not enter Oxford or Cambridge universities or hold government offices.

NON-CONFORMIST REGISTERS – AN INTRODUCTION

Although some non-conformist groups kept registers of births, baptisms, marriages, burials or deaths from the late 17th century, there are many chapels (founded in the 17th or 18th centuries) for which no registers were made (or survive) until much later, perhaps the late 18th century. Many non-conformists may therefore not be recorded in any surviving register. However, most marriages after 1754 had to take place in Anglican churches and some dissenters' baptisms, marriages or burials are recorded in earlier Anglican registers. Furthermore, between 1695 and

1705 Anglican clergy were required by the Marriage Duty Act (# chapter 23) to register the births of any children in their parish who were not baptised (that is, mainly non-conformists). Although this act was widely ignored, you may find non-conformist ancestors recorded in this manner.

Many non-conformists were buried in Anglican parish churchyards but it was only from 1880 that non-conformist ceremonies were permitted at these burials. Many non-conformists therefore established their own burial grounds; Bunhill Fields, for example, was the main burial ground for non-conformists living in or near London. Burials took place from about 1665 until 1854. Burial registers survive from 1713 and are held by TNA. In more recent times non-conformists were generally buried in cemeteries rather than in Anglican churchyards.

Protestant non-conformist genealogy and Roman Catholic and Jewish genealogy are reviewed in volumes 2 and 3 of the NIPR (151). These volumes describe the beliefs, history, organisation and records of each religious movement, and include detailed bibliographies. Mullett (343) is a good general work on the records and beliefs of Protestant non-conformist groups. Shorney (350) is a guide to Protestant non-conformist and Catholic records at TNA and summarises the early history of non-conformism (and the State's attempts to suppress it). The existence of non-conformist or Catholic churches and chapels (and surviving registers) can be ascertained from the county volumes of the NIPR (151), similar published works (# chapter 7) or the specialist works noted below for each non-conformist group. Welsh non-conformist registers are listed in Ifans (1184).

It is also worth noting the "Census of accommodation and attendance at worship", popularly known as the Religious census, taken on 30 March 1851. This was a voluntary census of places of worship. It is held at TNA in series HO 129, provides a useful list of the churches in your ancestors' district and it is described, with references for further reading, in TNA domestic records leaflet 85. Some churches and chapels were omitted but for each one listed, the census notes its denomination, address, the date of its foundation and the size of the congregation. The census has been transcribed and published for some counties, for example Hampshire and Surrey. Ede & Virgoe (322) is a transcript of the Norfolk returns, which also describes the background to the census and the responses of different denominations.

The Non-Parochial Register Act of 1840 requested all non-conformist groups or foreign churches in England and Wales (except Jews) to surrender to the Registrar General any of their registers that contained entries for the period before 1837. The surrendered registers are now held by TNA in series RG 4 to 6. Not all registers were surrendered, particularly those of Catholics, and a further collection was therefore made in 1857 (these are in series RG 4 and 8). These series include about 9,000 registers, mainly of Protestant congregations (Baptists, Congregationalists, Huguenots, Methodists, Presbyterians and Quakers), but also some Catholic registers and non-parochial registers (# chapter 7) such as the Greenwich and Chelsea Hospital registers. All these are available on microfilm at the searchroom of TNA at the FRC. Microfilm copies of the registers in RG 4 and 5 are also in the microfilm reading room at TNA. List and Index Society volumes 265–267 list the registers in RG 4, 6 and 8, arranged by county and place, noting the chapels' names (or location of a Friends' meeting), the years covered and the events recorded (baptisms, births, marriages, deaths or burials). Series RG 5 contains certificates of births or baptisms that were recorded in the Protestant Dissenters Registry at Dr Williams' Library and at the Metropolitan Wesleyan Registry (described below). Searches for registers of a church or chapel in a particular place can also be made on PROCAT.

There are many transcripts and indexes to the registers and some have been published. Large collections of these are held at the FRC and SoG. The SoG's collection is listed in its catalogue or (for English counties) in the *NIPR* and *County sources* volumes (# chapter 7). The IGI includes baptisms from many registers in RG 4 (but not those of Catholics). The BVRI includes births recorded (in RG 5) at the Protestant Dissenters Registry (1767–1837) and Metropolitan Wesleyan Registry (1822–38).

Registers dating from after 1857 and those registers that were not surrendered are still held by ministers at the churches and chapels, or have been deposited in archives of each non-conformist group (noted below) or in CROs. These registers are listed in the county volumes of the *NIPR* or the detailed works on each denomination noted below. Some transcripts are held at the SoG.

ROMAN CATHOLICS

The separation of the Church of England from Rome was completed in 1559 with the Acts of Supremacy and Uniformity, completing the process started by Henry VIII. Most bishops and many priests were ejected from their posts and celebration of a Catholic mass was forbidden. Catholics (often known as papists) were persecuted until the Catholic Relief Acts of the late 18th and early 19th centuries. Catholic priests were sometimes jailed or even executed and Catholics were denied the vote and barred from most official posts They also suffered extra taxation and there were periodic enforcements of acts requiring Catholics to take various oaths (with fines levied on those who refused). Despite the persecution, many Catholics remained loyal to their faith, particularly in northern England, and many men went to the continent, trained as priests and returned to England on a mission to reconvert the English to Catholicism. The number of Catholics was substantially increased from the late 18th century by refugees fleeing from the French Revolution and by immigrants from Ireland. For example, by 1840 the Catholic population of Liverpool was about 80,000. Volume 3 of the *NIPR* (151) provides excellent background material for the study of Catholic family history and describes the surviving records. Gandy (326) is a detailed bibliography, arranged by county, of published works and articles on Catholics. Sources for Catholics from 1559 to 1791 are described in the October 1993 edition of *Recusant History* (308) and many published works about Catholics are also listed by M. Gandy in *Family Tree Magazine* (August 1996).

The Catholic Record Society has published much information relating to Catholics, extracted from church court records, lists of recusants and other documentation. Its publications are listed on its web site and those published up to 1989 are listed in Gooch & Allison (328). In particular, they include much material on the education abroad of Catholics (especially priests). The society's journal *Recusant History* (308) is published twice each year and concentrates on historical and religious information but it includes articles on Catholic families, records and priests. The contents of each journal up to 1989 are listed in Gooch & Allison (328). *Catholic Archives* (305), the journal of the Catholic Archives Society, published annually since 1981, includes reviews of archives' holdings of material relating to the Catholic Church and its members. The Society for the English Catholic Ancestor also publishes a journal on Catholic family history, named *ECA Journal* or, since 1989, *Catholic Ancestor*. Researchers with Catholic ancestors in Essex should also refer to the journal *Essex Recusant*, copies of which are at the SoG, since this includes family histories, recusant records and other material on Essex Catholics, particularly from Essex Quarter Sessions.

Some Catholics were baptised, married or buried in Anglican churches and therefore appear in parish registers. A parish priest often noted the word papist or recusant in such entries. The births of Catholics may also be recorded from 1695 to 1706 (because they were dissenters) in lists prepared pursuant to the Marriage Duty Act 1695 (# chapter 23). However, many Catholics were not recorded in Anglican registers, either because a Catholic family refused to attend an Anglican church, or because the Anglican incumbent refused to conduct baptism, marriage or burial ceremonies for papists. Catholics were generally buried in the parish churchyard (there was usually nowhere else for burials to take place) but the register may not record them. Many Catholics were buried at night, so that their friends or family could conduct a secret Catholic service. A few night burials are recorded in registers, for example in North Elmham, Norfolk:

1642. Rose, the wife of Robert Lunford was buried the 23 of December, she was a recusant papist, she was buried in the night without the church ceremonies.

A register of births held at the College of Arms records about 220 births (mainly of Catholics and Jews) from the 18th century. The surnames are listed in volume 3 of the *NIPR* (151).

Many Catholics were baptised or married (usually secretly) by their own priests. A Catholic priest did not have a parish to serve (until after 1900) but established a "mission", which was either an unofficial chapel or the location of a priest who served as many Catholics as he could. Although the Catholic Church ordered its priests to keep registers of baptisms and marriages from 1563, very few early Catholic registers have survived. Many priests did not keep registers because of the fear of persecution if the registers fell into the wrong hands. Some priests prepared registers but retained them with their personal papers and so many have been lost. Furthermore, Catholic priests often moved over large areas of the country and so their registers may have entries, for example, for both London and Yorkshire. It can be difficult to find entries for a Catholic family that was served by an itinerant priest. Spouses who had a Catholic marriage ceremony, rather than an Anglican ceremony, were often prosecuted in the church courts (# chapter 24) for taking part in a clandestine ceremony or for fornication (that is, sex without a valid marriage). Church court records may therefore record Catholic marriages which do not appear in surviving registers. Some embassies of foreign Catholic countries (such as Sardinia) had their own chapels in which English Catholics could worship and some baptisms and marriages appear in these chapel registers.

From 1754 to 1837, most Catholics complied with Hardwicke's Marriage Act and married in Anglican churches to ensure that the marriage was valid under English law. However, many couples also had a Catholic marriage ceremony (which might be recorded in a Catholic register). It was only following the Catholic Relief Acts of 1778 and 1791 that a Catholic chapel could be legally registered as a place of worship and that Catholics felt it safe to keep registers which identified them. Many churches were built and Catholic cemeteries were also established in the 19th century. The Catholic Church could also officially organise itself by permanent missions, although Catholic dioceses were not established until 1850 and Catholic parishes were only established in the 20th century. Catholics are recorded by the civil registration system from 1837 and marriages in a Catholic church were permitted (in the presence of a civil registrar) if the church obtained authorisation under the civil registration acts. An alternative source for records of marriages after 1837 is the Catholic marriage index (with about 30,000 entries, mainly for 1837 to 1880) which is held by IHGS on behalf of the Catholic FHS.

Gandy (324) lists by county the known Catholic missions from 1700 to 1880 and their surviving registers and copies (similar information, but sometimes out of date, is included in the county volumes of the *NIPR*). Gandy (325) is a companion volume of maps of Catholic parishes, dioceses and archdioceses in Britain as they were in about 1950. Gandy has also reprinted a 1907 work by Kelly (334) which has notes (including dates of foundation and priests' names) for each Catholic mission in England. Many Catholic registers have been published by the Catholic Record Society and these (and other published copies) are listed in Gandy (324) and Gooch & Allison (328). For example, the society's volume 35 (306) includes indexed transcripts of Catholic registers of Little Blake Street Chapel in York (1771–1838) and of Newcastle upon Tyne (1765–1824). Volume 36 by Trappes-Lomax (352) includes registers of Lee House Chapel, Thornley in Lancashire (1752–1841) and of Ribchester, Lancashire (1783–1837). Volume 15, by Smith (351) includes six Lancashire registers. Illustration 60 is a page of the transcript of one of those registers, for baptisms at Cottam (1783–1834). If there is no published copy of a register, the location of the original (if it survives) can be ascertained from Gandy (324) or the *NIPR*. Only a few Catholic registers were deposited with the Registrar General in 1840 and 1857. Some registers have been deposited in record offices. Many transcripts of Catholic registers, including those produced by the Catholic FHS, are held at the Catholic Central Library, Lancing Street, London NW1 (telephone 020 7383 4333) and listed (with some of the library's other material) by M. Gandy in *Family Tree Magazine* (April 1998). Some registers remain with priests at Catholic churches. Details of the present Catholic priests can be obtained from the *Catholic Directory*. You should write to the priest, requesting an appointment to see the registers, but he is not obliged to grant access. Catholic registers are similar to Anglican registers but are more likely to be in Latin. In addition, baptism registers may note the names of godparents or sponsors (and perhaps their relationship to the child). For example, this baptism appears in the register of Nut Hill and Bredon, Yorkshire:

1802. Ann daughter of John and Jane Wade of the parish of Burstwick born September the 28 and baptized October 3, Godfather George Wade (grandfather of the girl), Godmother Ann Wade (her aunt) by me Joseph Swinburn

The sacrament of confirmation perfects baptism. It was administered in England by a bishop (or some missionary priests), usually to a child aged between seven and 12, although often for older people. Some Catholic registers list those who were confirmed but there are also registers of confirmations in Catholic archives, some of which have been published. Bishop Leyburn's confirmation register of 1687, in Hilton (331), and indexed in Ackers & Ackers (312), lists almost 19,000 Catholics in Staffordshire, Lancashire, Yorkshire and seven other English counties. Egan (323) is a transcript of a bishop's register of thousands of confirmations in the Midlands and East Anglia from 1768 to 1816.

Catholic burial grounds could only be established legally from 1852 but Catholics had purchased their own burial grounds from the early 19th century and some of these were adjacent to Catholic chapels. Some earlier Catholic burial grounds are also noted in volume 3 of the *NIPR*. Catholic cemeteries in London are listed in Wolfston (201).

Until the rise of Protestant non-conformism in the 17th century, Catholics formed the majority of recusants. They were often summoned to appear before the church courts or the Justices at Quarter Sessions (and so may appear in their records) and were fined, excommunicated or had their land seized for refusing to attend their parish church. Excommunication meant that

REGISTERS OF COTTAM

FIRST BOOK.
1783
A register of ye baptised at Cottam
by ye Revd John Lund of Cotham.

Catharine Valentine born November 7th and bptz^d the same day, daughter of James and Catharine **Valentine**

John Hull son of George **Houle** and Alice **Singleton** his wife Baptized ye 18 of Decem^r, 1783. Sponsors, John Singleton and Agnes Adkinson

1784
March. Margret **Kirk** daughter of Cuthbert and his wife Mary
. . . . . . baptized ye 19 of March, 1784. Sponsors, John Miller and Mary Fearclough

April 28. John Kitchen son of John **Kitchen** and Jane **Hubershaw** his wife baptized ye 2^d of May. Sponsors, William Hubbershaw and Alice Ireland

July 9. Jennet Haydock Daughter of Robt **Haydock** and Mary **Fiddler** his wife was born July 9 and baptized the same day. Sponsores, Jo^s Fiddler and Eliz. Haydock

July 26. Thomas Parker son of Richard **Parker** and Ann his wife was born July 26 and Baptized the same day. Sponsors, Jo^s Fiddler and Ann Dewhurst

Augt 30. John Turner son of John **Turner** and Margery **Smith** his wife was born August 30 and baptized the same day. Sponsors, James Smith and Mary Turner

Sepr 26. Isabel Sheperd Daughter of Rob: **Shepherd** and Catharine **Haythornwhite** his wife was born Sepr 26 and baptized the same day. Godfather and Godmother, Robt Haythornwhite and Elizabeth Valentine

Oc^br 3. John James Johnson son of Richd **Johnson** and Elizabeth **Barrow** his wife was born October the 3^d and baptized the same day. Godfather, Mr James Maudesley. Godmother, Ann Adamson

Oct^br 18. Ann Smith Daughter of Tho. **Smith** and Mary **Kirk** his wife was born the 17 of October and baptized the following day. God Father, William Smith. god Mother, Mary Ferclough

1785
January 12th, 1785. Magaret Billington Daughter of James **Billington** and Elizabeth **Goodear** Conjuges was born the 12 of Jan: and baptized the same day. Sponsors, Joseph Miller and Mary Miller

Feb: 11. Thomas Ireland son of William **Ireland** and Elce **Adamson,** Conjuges, was born ye 11 of Feb: and Baptiz'd the same day. Sponsors, Henery Adamson and Sara Ireland

Feb: 16. Francis Turnur son of Richd **Turnur** and Margret **Billington** his lawfull wife was born february 16th and Baptiz'd the same day. Sponsors, John Wilson and Mary Turnor

Feb: 27. Thomas Fiswick son of William **Fiswick** and Hellen **Billington,** Conjuges, was born the 26 of february and Bapz^d the 27. Godfather, John Livesey and Mary Turnor

March 17th. Catharine Akers daughter of William **Acres** and Alice

60. *Extract from the published transcript of the Catholic register of baptisms for Cottam, Lancashire*
(Catholic Record Society)

a recusant would not be buried in the parish churchyard and his will might not be proved by a church court. In addition, the fines for recusants were increased to £20 a month from 1581 and were levied by a sheriff (the Crown's chief officer in a county) and so names of recusants appear in central government records. Convictions, fines and forfeitures from 1581 to 1592 are noted in the Pipe Rolls (# chapter 27) in series E 372 at TNA, and from 1592 there are Recusant Rolls (*rotuli recusancium*) which were annual returns (described in detail in volume 3 of the *NIPR*) listing recusants and their fines. They survive for most of the period up to 1691 at TNA (in series E 376 and E 377) and are mostly in Latin. The entries are arranged by county and note the fine levied or the land that was forfeited to the Crown. The recusant rolls of 1592–6 have been translated and published. An example is Bowler (314), which contains abstracts of the rolls for 1594/5 and 1595/6, providing records of convictions, fines, the rentals obtained for seized lands and details of seized chattels. Accounts for rent due to the Crown (for land that had been seized and then re-let) give the name of the new tenant, the rent, the name of the recusant from whom the land was seized and details of the property and the new lease (such as the date and term). A typical conviction for recusancy in 1594/5 is recorded (in summary) as:

Grace Marshe, wife of John Marshe, lately of Rewe, Devon, gent. owes total fine of £60 . . . for not attending church for divine service for two months . . . including £20 for not complying after conviction . . .

Other documents that list recusants or papists can be found in various records at TNA, described in TNA domestic records leaflet 66, for example seizures of land by sheriffs are recorded in E 379. Inventories of many Catholics' possessions from 1642 to 1660 are in State Papers in series SP 28. Oaths of allegiance by Catholics from 1778 to 1857 are in courts' records (# chapter 24), for example in series E 169, CP 37 and C 214. Catholics often arranged for their wills (and deeds to their property) to be enrolled on the Close Rolls (# chapter 27) in series C 54 and lists of these have been published in volumes 1 and 2 (new series) of *The Genealogist*. The House of Lords Records Office, CROs and Lambeth Palace Library hold some further lists of papists, compiled in 1680, 1705/6, 1767 and 1780, which include names, ages and sometimes occupations. The estates of many Catholics were also forfeited after the Jacobite risings of 1715 and 1745 (# chapters 24 and 29). From 1715 to 1791 Catholics were required to register their estates by a certificate lodged with the Clerk of the Peace at Quarter Sessions. Surviving records are in CROs and some have been published. Thus Hudleston (332) includes recusants' certificates for estates in county Durham for 1717–78. The certificates note recusants' property and liabilities, but also provide genealogical information, as in this example:

25 April 1717. Ann Cockson of Old Elvitt in the parish of St Oswalds, co. Durham . . . One tenement in Elvitt in my possession . . . I am interested in the remainder of a term of 40 years granted by the Dean and Chapter of Durham . . . from 19 March 1697 under the yearly rent of 5 shillings . . . Several tenements, lands and two mills at Colepigghill in the parish of Lanchester . . . wherein I am interested during the term of my life (so long as I continue as the widow of George Cockson my late husband) on condition . . . I maintain my two daughters Elizabeth and Ann . . .
[Details of properties let to tenants by George Cockson.]
Payments and allowances . . . A yearly payment of £5 to Thomas Cockson for his life.

Discrimination and persecution caused many Catholic men to seek education abroad from the 17th to early 19th centuries and some of them returned to England as priests or missionaries. The most popular schools and colleges were those established specifically for British students such as the English Colleges at Rome, Madrid, Valladolid, Lisbon and Seville. Registers with biographies of students (and other material about the colleges) have been published by the Catholic Record Society.

Your ancestors may also be featured in biographical dictionaries of Catholics. Gillow (327) is a dictionary of priests, martyrs, nobles, authors, soldiers, politicians and other eminent Catholics since 1534. It includes biographies of four members of the Charnock family. John Charnock was executed in 1586 for his role in Babington's plot to release Mary, Queen of Scots. Robert Charnock was a 16th century priest. Thomas Charnock was a Captain in the Royalist Army in the Civil War and Robert Charnock was executed at Tyburn in 1695 for plotting to assassinate King William III. Many other members of the family are mentioned in these biographies. Kirk (335) contains hundreds of biographies of Catholics of the 18th century, including many people omitted by Gillow.

PROTESTANT DISSENTERS

Protestant non-conformists also suffered discrimination for many years. Many were recusants and were included on the rolls noted above. Protestant dissenting groups were initially prohibited from establishing chapels. This disability was removed by the Declaration of Indulgence 1672, on condition that the chapels were registered. About 4,000 houses were registered for non-conformist worship in 1672 and 1673. The records are in the State Papers at TNA (and abstracts of the registrations have been published) noting the occupier of each house and the religious group using it. Further persecution followed this temporary respite but the Act of Toleration 1689 again permitted the establishment of non-conformist chapels and meeting houses if they were registered with the bishop, archdeacon or Justices of the Peace for the area. This registration system remained in force until 1852. The records (registers, licences and certificates) are in CROs and describe the meeting-houses, note any occupiers of the buildings and sometimes note the denomination of the group or include signatures of their leading members. Chandler (317) describes the surviving records of 1,780 chapels and meeting houses in Wiltshire. This entry, for a meeting-house in Devizes in 1771, is typical:

> The dwellinghouse of Martha Phillips widow, situated in the New Port, St John's parish. [Signatures of] Edward Bayly, John Filkes and Thomas Neeves, housekeepers in Devizes.

From 1754 to 1837 Protestant dissenters (except Quakers) could only be legally married in an Anglican parish church. Many non-conformists also had their children baptised in the Anglican Church so that matters such as inheritance were more easily proved. However, many dissenters were not recorded at all in Anglican registers. Non-conformist groups usually compiled their own registers of baptisms, births, marriages or deaths and many non-conformist groups also had their own burial grounds and burial registers. Many chapels did not have their own registers, but were served by itinerant ministers on a circuit (perhaps of many chapels). You may therefore need to find the name of the minister (and the names of other places where he conducted services) so that you can find the register. Most surviving registers for the period up to 1837 of the

Congregationalists, and some of the registers of the Baptists, Methodists, Presbyterians and Unitarians, were surrendered in 1840 or 1857 and are now held by TNA (and can be seen on microfilm at the FRC) in series RG 4, 5 and 8. Quaker registers are in RG 6. Illustration 61 shows a page from a Wesleyan Methodist register, for the Clitheroe circuit in Lancashire, recording births and baptisms from February 1807 to January 1809. Some microfilm copies are also held at CROs. Other surviving registers have been deposited at CROs or are still held by congregations. Some registers include lists of members of a congregation, details of a chapel's financial affairs or minutes of meetings. Some examples are provided by Shorney (350).

Non-conformist ministers were often lax in keeping registers. Consequently, in 1742 a General Register of Births of Children of Protestant Dissenters was set up at Dr Williams's Library. This library was established in Red Cross Street in 1729 to house the records collected by Dr Williams, and is now at 14 Gordon Square, London WC1. A total of 48,975 births were registered (some were retrospective entries, dating back to 1716) until the register was closed in 1837. Parents paid a small fee to have the date and place of birth of their child (and their own names) recorded. Parents had to provide the registry with two certificates (from the local incumbent, a midwife or from witnesses) verifying that a child had been born. The birth was noted in the register, one certificate was filed, and the other was returned to the parents endorsed with a note that the birth had been registered. From 1828 the filed certificates became the main record and the register was merely a calendar to the certificates. Most entries in the register relate to the three main denominations of non-conformists: the Baptists, the English Presbyterians (including Unitarians) and Independents (also known as Congregationalists). However, the register was also used by Scottish parents living in England and by English parents living abroad (including Florence Nightingale's parents who were in Italy when she was born). The volumes of the register are held by TNA in RG 4/4658–65 (with indexes in RG 4/4666–73) and RG 4/4674–76. The certificates are in RG 5. The entries are not included in the IGI, but (in addition to the old surname indexes) new surname indexes are being prepared (arranged by the county of birth) and the certificates in RG 5 appear to be included in the BVRI.

Dr Williams's Library has an enormous collection of material (including that formerly held by the Congregational Library) on non-conformist movements, chapels and congregations. The library's collections include general histories of each non-conformist group, published and manuscript histories of particular chapels, non-conformist journals and information on non-conformist ministers. Twinn (353) lists the published and manuscript histories of Protestant non-conformist congregations and chapels held by the library as at 1973, including articles in journals of the Baptist, Congregational, Presbyterian, Unitarian and Wesleyan historical societies. The John Rylands Library at the University of Manchester (Deansgate, Manchester M3 3EH) has substantial Methodist archives (described below) but also much material for other Protestant groups. We shall now deal with the records of each group.

Independents and Congregationalists
Separatists, dissenters with similar views to the Puritans, began meeting in the mid-16th century. Their leaders were persecuted by the State (and the established Church) and many were exiled, a number moving to Holland. In the 17th century the movement adopted the name Independent and began to found chapels in England. The movement gathered strength during the Civil War (Oliver Cromwell was an Independent) and many Independent preachers temporarily replaced Anglican clergymen in parishes during the Commonwealth period. With the restoration of

61. A page from a Wesleyan Methodist register of births and baptisms recorded on the Clitheroe circuit 1807–09 (TNA, RG 4/814)

Charles II, many Independents and other dissenters left the established Church, many Independant incumbents were ejected from their new parishes, and a few more Independent chapels were founded (usually in people's houses). Many chapels were built in the 18th century (when the movement had about 60,000 followers) particularly as a result of the Act of Toleration 1689. In the early 19th century most Independents began to call themselves Congregationalists. Most Congregational chapels merged with the Presbyterians in 1972 to form the United Reform Church, but some chapels decided not to join and remained independent.

Clifford (319) and Mullett (343) provide brief histories of the movement. Clifford also lists all known Congregational or Independent chapels for the period before 1850 and the location of their surviving registers. Most of these only commence in the late 18th or 19th centuries and are held by TNA in series RG 4 and 8. CROs often have microfilm copies of these registers as well as some original baptism and burial registers that were not surrendered to the Registrar General. From 1754 to 1837 Independents had to marry in Anglican churches, and from 1837 to 1898 a civil registrar had to be present at weddings in Independent chapels. Independents' registers are in similar form to Anglican registers. This is the baptism, of my g.g. grandfather John Josiah Keates, recorded in 1836 at an Independent chapel in Old Gravel Lane, St George in the East, Middlesex:

Sept. 25. John Josiah Keates, son of George Keates & Ann his wife;
St George in the East, master blockmaker, born June 21 1835

Minutes of chapel administrative meetings often include the names of members of the congregation. Many such records have been deposited at Dr Williams's Library or at CROs. Some chapels have retained their records, together with later registers of baptisms and burials. In those cases, you should contact the chapel for further information. The United Reformed Church Historical Society of 86 Tavistock Place, London WC1, also holds some archive material and can provide information on the location of archives.

Presbyterians

The Presbyterian church became the established church in Scotland by the early 17th century. In England and Wales the Presbyterian movement began within the Church of England as a puritan movement, in favour of abolishing many rituals of the established Church. During the English Civil War the Presbyterian movement gathered strength and it became the established form of the Church in England in 1647. Following the Restoration in 1660, many Presbyterian clergy were ejected from their parishes and Presbyterians were subject to discriminatory legislation. The Act of Toleration of 1689 allowed freedom of worship to Protestants and led to the establishment of meeting houses and burial grounds. By the early 18th century there were over 600 Presbyterian congregations with almost 180,000 members. In the early 19th century the Scottish Presbyterians also founded some churches in England. By this time, most English Presbyterian congregations had become known as Unitarians (that is, because they did not believe in the Trinity of Father, Son and Holy Spirit) and so these new churches were known as the Presbyterian Church of England. This merged with the Congregational Union of Churches in 1972 to form the United Reformed Church.

Detailed histories of the Presbyterian movement are provided by Mullett (343) and Ruston (348) which also lists surviving registers. Most Presbyterian and Unitarian registers were deposited with the Registrar General in 1840 and so are now on microfilm at the FRC (and many entries from these are in the IGI). Some registers are held by the United Reformed Church Historical Society (noted above). From 1860 the details of each Unitarian congregation, with the name and address of each minister, were included in the Unitarian Year Book which appeared under various names listed by Ruston (348). Minute books and other records of congregations (such as membership lists from the early 19th century) are generally held by CROs, Dr Williams's Library or the United Reformed Church Historical Society. Some minute books and other records are still held by congregations. Information about these records (and possibly access to them) may be obtained by written application to the relevant church secretary. Ruston (348) also lists the Presbyterian and Unitarian journals that include birth, marriage and death notices (some dating from the late 18th century).

Quakers

The Religious Society of Friends (whose members are known as Quakers) was founded in the 17th century by George Fox. Quakers suffered persecution for their beliefs for many years. For example, they were often fined, imprisoned or even transported for refusing to take oaths, serve in the armed forces, attend Anglican church services, or pay tithes to their parish clergyman. Despite this, the Society had a large following and in 1682 William Penn founded Pennsylvania in North America as a Quaker state.

Quakers generally only used figures for the days and months, since they objected to names of pagan origin such as Thursday (named after the Norse god of war). A date was therefore expressed as the 7th day of the 12th month. However, until the calendar change in 1752, the first month of the year was March and not January. Therefore a 1739 entry for the second month (often indicated by "2 mo") was for April 1739, not February 1739. Until 1751 the names September, October, November and December could be used because they were not pagan, but simply meant the seventh, eighth, ninth and tenth months of the year (which they then were). These months might be written as 7ber, 8ber and so on. However, after 1751 September was no longer the seventh month in the year (but the ninth) so the term 9th month had to be used. The same point applied to October, November and December.

The Society's affairs were regulated at meetings which are described in detail in Milligan & Thomas (340). In addition to local meetings for worship, the Quaker congregations (or perhaps two or three congregations in a district) met for business matters at Preparative Meetings and sent representatives to district Monthly Meetings (or, in London, to a Two-Weeks meeting). There were 151 of these meetings in 1694 (reducing to 108 meetings by 1800). These meetings sent representatives to Quarterly Meetings. These originally covered areas approximating to each county but some were amalgamated so there were only 29 such meetings by 1800, listed in Milligan & Thomas (340). They in turn sent representatives to Yearly Meetings in London which considered general aspects of the Society's affairs. Until 1896 men and women attended separate meetings (and a separate Women's Yearly Meeting continued until 1905). During the 18th century there were also Northern, Bristol and Western Circular Yearly Meetings. Minutes were drawn up of all these meetings.

The Society of Friends' library is at Friends' House, 173–177 Euston Road, London NW1 2BJ (telephone 020 7663 1135). The library's opening times and other information is noted on its web site. It holds lists of representatives at the Yearly Meetings since 1668 and records of sufferings. Many Quakers were prosecuted and imprisoned for their refusal to attend Anglican services, to take oaths of allegiance (they believed that all men were equal) or to pay tithes or church rates. Over 450 friends died in prison in the 17th century. Cases of persecution were recorded in books of sufferings at Monthly, Quarterly and Yearly Meetings. A separate Meeting was established in the late 17th century to consider the persecution suffered by friends all over the country. Minutes of this Meeting date from 1676. Returns were copied up at the Yearly Meeting into the great book of suffering covering 1659 to 1856, which has been indexed up to 1791. Information was also sent to the Yearly Meeting by way of answers to Queries from 1682. The questions varied over time but included requests for the names of friends who had died in the previous 12 months. Many published works about the persecution of Quakers are listed by Milligan & Thomas (340).

Since Quakers refused the offices of the Anglican church, they were generally not recorded in parish registers. They therefore established their own registration system for births (since they did not practise baptism), marriages and burials. Meetings were ordered from 1656 to keep registers and some surviving registers do commence around that date. A clerk at a Monthly Meeting registered the births, marriages and burials that were reported to him and some meetings also produced their own certificates of birth and marriage (usually including witnesses' signatures). Importantly, Quakers had to obtain permission to marry from their Monthly Meeting and so the minutes also record these requests. Following the couple's declarations of intention, a check was made that they were free to marry. Thus minutes of the Two-Weeks Meeting in London in 1705 record the following request:

At a two weeks meeting held at Devonshire House, London the 12th of the 9th month 1705 . . . Jeremiah Beal of St Johns Wapping, grocer, son of Thomas Beal of Wretton in Norfolk, yeoman, deceased and Sarah Plumley, daughter of John Plumley of London, merchant, proposed their intentions of taking each other in marriage. The man has no parents living. The maid's father being present gave his consent. It is referred to Silvanus Grove and Lascells Metcalfe to make enquiry and receive information concerning them and report to this meeting.

At a two weeks meeting held at Devonshire House, London the 28th of the 9th month 1705 . . . Jeremiah Beal and Sarah Plumley the second time proposed their intentions of taking each other in marriage and were passed with the meetings' consent.

Marriage ceremonies consisted of declarations by the couple. No priest was present but the adults present at the meeting signed a certificate as witnesses. English law treated Quaker marriages as valid. Quakers were exempt from Hardwicke's Marriage Act and continued celebrating marriages in their own manner rather than in an Anglican church. In the early years of the movement, many Quakers were buried in parish churchyards, although some preferred to be buried elsewhere (perhaps in an orchard). However, many Anglican clergymen refused to bury Quakers in the parish churchyard and so they established their own burial grounds. By the end of the 17th century most Quaker meeting houses had burial grounds and a burial register. Gravestones were rarely erected.

The Quaker registers of births, marriages and burials from 1656 to 30 June 1837 were surrendered to the Registrar General in 1840. A few further registers were surrendered in 1857 and all 1,620 registers are held by TNA in series RG 6 and listed in List and Index Society volume 267. They contain about 250,000 births, 40,000 marriages and 300,000 burials. A very few registers were not surrendered and these are in CROs or at Friends' House library. After 1837 the Quakers (though subject to civil registration) continued to record births, marriages and burials (later deaths) but they established a new recording system (described in volume 2 of the *NIPR*). These registers record births (until 1959), deaths (until 1961) and they still record marriages. Many of these post-1837 registers are also held by TNA. If your ancestors were Quakers, these records may be easier to use than civil registration records.

Before depositing their pre-July 1837 registers, the Quakers prepared indexes (or digests) in duplicate for each Quarterly Meeting. Digests were also prepared for the later (retained) registers. The areas covered by Quarterly Meetings did not coincide exactly with county boundaries and by 1840 some Quarterly Meetings also covered more than one county, so you may have to search a number of digests to find a particular entry. One set of digests was retained by the Quarterly Meetings (and some of these have been deposited at CROs). The other set of digests is held (together with many post-June 1837 registers) at Friends' House library. Microfilm copies of the digests can be viewed (or purchased) at the library and also seen at the SoG. Many CROs hold microfilm copies of the Quaker digests for their area up to 1837. The digests provide references to the full entries in the Monthly Meeting registers, but also some of the information from the registers. For births, they give the date, the child's and parents' names, and the parents' residence and occupations. For marriages, they give the date, the spouses' names, residences and occupations and also the names of the spouses' parents (but not the witnesses' names). For burials, they give the deceased's name, age, residence, occupation and place of burial (and often the names of the deceased's parents). The Quaker FHS is preparing a database of the digest entries. Alphabetical printouts of births, marriages and burials for Essex and Suffolk Quarterly Meetings are available at Friends' House library and the SoG.

Friends' House holds much other useful material, described in Milligan & Thomas (340), including many minutes of meetings. Minutes and other Quaker records are also held at local meeting houses, although some records (or copies) have been deposited at CROs (thus Guildhall Library holds a copy of the minutes of the London Two-Weeks Meeting). Minutes of Monthly Meetings deal with membership, discipline, marriage, finance, property, apprenticeship, education and care for the poor. Friends in need of poor relief were unlikely to be helped by parish officials, so they usually had to rely on their brethren's charity. Records of Quakers' wills are also included in the minutes of some meetings. Friends moving between Monthly Meetings often carried a certificate to present to their new meeting (or certificates were sent from Meeting to Meeting). These certificates were similar to parish settlement certificates (# chapter 18), and made it easier for families to move in search of work. A Quaker's Meeting would recommend him to his new Meeting and confirm that he was of sober habits and free of debt. If the migrant fell into want within three years, his old Meeting would support him so that he and his family did not become a burden on his new Meeting. Many certificates have survived and some Meetings kept books of copies of certificates. Illustration 62 (from a certificate book of the London Two-Weeks Meeting) is a certificate of 15 February 1773 which recommends Isaac Sargent to the Monthly Meeting in Chippenham, Wiltshire, and it is signed by many friends of the London Meeting. Monthly Meetings also considered whether a member's conduct (drunkenness, bankruptcy or absence from worship) should result in disownment. The minutes record decisions and the relevant facts. However, a disowned friend was not barred from the Meetings for worship and he or she might later be reinstated. A friend could appeal against such decisions to the Quarterly Meetings. Many Meetings also kept registers of members from the early 19th century.

Isaac Sargent

From our Two Weeks Meeting held in London this 15th Day of the 2nd Month 1773. To the Monthly Meeting of Friends in Chippenham, Wilts.

Dear Friends / Our Friend Isaac Sargent being removed within the Compass of your Meeting, hath applied for our Certificate.

We can therefore inform you that due Enquiry hath been made concerning him, and do not find but that he was of sober & orderly Life, and Conversation, clear of Debt, and Marriage Engagements here — We recommend him to divine Protection, and your christian Care, and are with affectionate Regard,

Your loving Friends

Signed in, and on behalf
of our said Meeting by —

Jos. Travis
John Townsend
Sam. Brady
William Tittell
Jos. Carr
Sam. West jun.
Abel Howard
Simon Bailey
Jacob Agar

Wm. Storrs Fry
Robt. Webb
Zach. Cockfield
Tho. Corbyn
Jacob Hagen
John Hill
John Eliot
Claude Gay
Abr. Gray
John Wallis
Joseph Row
Thos. Talwin
Thos. Roake
Robt. Bell
Edw. Neale
Saml. West
Rich. Smith
Danl. Mildred
David Barclay

62. *Quaker certificate of 1773, recommending Isaac Sargent to the meeting of Friends in Chippenham, Wiltshire (Guildhall Library)*

Some Quaker records have been published. For example, the minute book of 1686–1704 of the men's meeting in Bristol has been published in Mortimer (342). The minute book for 1669 to 1719 for the Monthly Meeting of Gainsborough in Lincolnshire has been published in Brace (315). In addition to approvals of proposed weddings, the Gainsborough minutes contain much other useful material of which the following are a few summarised entries:

At a Monthly Meeting held the 10 day of the xth month 1671:
The case of Joseph Cooper of Haxey, who was marryed by a priest was brought before Friends & it was by the Meeting desired that Christopher Edwards, John Ury & Robert Everatt should speak to him, to reprove him for so doing & to exhort him . . . that he may be recovered to Truth . . .
At a Monthly Meeting held the 9th day of the 8th month 1672:
It is concluded . . . that Rebekah the daughter of Christopher Codd deceased be disposed of unto William West of Gate Burton [as] an apprentice [for] ten years . . . and that there be paid unto William West, in consideration of his keeping Rebekah, the sum of 7 pounds 10 shillings . . .
At a Monthly Meeting held the 13th day of the 7th month 1676:
Thomas Wresle & Henry Hudson spoke to Mary Parnell concerning her intended marriage with Hezekia Browne who was not a professor of the truth . . . she resolved to marry him . . . and the Meeting concluded that the intended marriage is contrary to Truth and Friends can [only] condemn it.

The Quakers founded many schools and some are listed in Milligan & Thomas (340). Admissions books or other records listing pupils or teachers, some dating from the 18th century, survive for many of these schools and are at Friends' House. Other sources at Friends' House include Quaker journals dating from 1701 (including birth and marriage notices) and a typescript dictionary of Quaker biography with about 25,000 entries. Obituaries and death notices of Quakers were published from 1813 in *The Annual Monitor and Memorandum Book*, renamed as *The Annual Monitor* in 1841. Entries up to 1892 (about 20,000 of them) are indexed in Green (329). Typescript indexes at Friends' House library extend this work up to 1920. The Quaker Family History Society publishes a journal *Quaker Connections*. Many histories of Quaker meetings have also been published, such as Leimdorfer (337), an illustrated history of the Quakers of Sidcot in Somerset. This lists all known members of the meeting (with biographies of noteworthy members) and describes the meeting-houses and schools with many extracts from the meeting's records, for example concerning payments to the poor.

Baptists
The Baptist movement began in the 17th century. Mullett (343) provides an introduction to Baptist records and beliefs. Breed (316) reviews surviving Baptist records and their location, with a useful bibliography. Baptist congregations were not regulated by a central organisation (each Baptist chapel was self-governing), although there were various associations between them. By 1660 there were about 240 congregations. The Baptist movement split in the 17th century between the General Baptists and Particular Baptists (who believed that only a chosen few, and not all believers, would achieve paradise). The General Baptists split in the 18th century between the Old Connection (later named the Unitarians) and the New Connection, who merged in 1891 with the Particular Baptists.

Baptists recorded the births of children and the baptism of adults, because they believed that only believers should be baptised (and only adults were able to make such a decision). Since Baptists baptised adults, and not children, you should take care in assessing the age of the baptised ancestor. You should search for other evidence of the ancestor's age, perhaps his baptism as a child in Anglican registers, or his age being recorded when he was buried. Most birth, baptism, death and burial registers of the Baptists up to 1837 were surrendered to the Registrar General and are held by TNA in series RG 4 and 8. Breed (316) lists these registers (and covering dates) and the copy registers held at the SoG. The entries in registers in RG 4 (but not RG 8) are in the IGI. Few Baptist records survive from before 1688. There are many 18th-century registers of baptisms, births and burials, but very few marriages were recorded before 1754. After 1754 Baptists had to marry in Anglican churches and so should be recorded in their registers. Baptist marriages became legal again in 1837 (if a civil registrar was in attendance). Many Baptist burial grounds were opened in the late 18th and early 19th centuries and many burial registers are held by TNA. Some pre-1837 registers were not surrendered. These (and post-1837 registers) are held at CROs, churches, archives of Baptist associations and Baptist Theological Colleges, or at the following archives:

a. Regent's Park College, Pusey Street, Oxford (including registers previously held at Baptist Church House in London)
b. The Strict Baptist Historical Society's library, Dunstable Baptist Chapel, St Mary's Gate, Dunstable, Bedfordshire
c. The Gospel Standard Baptist Library, 5 Hove Park Gardens, Hove, East Sussex

The registers and other Baptist church records held at the archives at (b) and (c) above are listed (with covering dates) in Breed (316). Many other Baptist records are at CROs or at chapels. Some records are also held by the Baptist Historical Society, details of which are on its web site. Minutes of some Baptist assemblies survive from the 17th century, including the names of those attending. These contain much information on the movement generally but also about particular congregations. The Church minute books of Baptist congregations deal with matters of theology and doctrine, but also with membership, finance and charity. Some minutes include lists of members, their addresses or even the dates of members' baptisms. Congregations had to finance their church, so that donations may be recorded in the minutes or accounts. Some chapels also provided charity for members and so the minutes may therefore note persons' names (and sums of money) for both donations and expenditure. Minutes also record disciplinary cases against members (many for drunkenness or fornication) that were heard by chapel meetings. Proceedings often resulted in a person's expulsion from the congregation. Many church minute books are held at the archives listed at (a) to (c) above and some examples from Baptist minutes are provided in Mullett (343).

Sources of information for Baptist ministers are listed by Breed (316). Baptist churches and ministers are also listed in the *Baptist Handbook*, published annually from 1861 (renamed the *Baptist Union Directory* in 1972). The *Baptist Magazine* commenced publication in 1809 and many copies are held at the British Newspaper Library at Colindale (# chapter 17) or at the archives listed above. Many histories of Baptist churches are held at Dr Williams's Library and by the Baptist Historical Society and the Strict Baptist Historical Society (the details of which are on its web site).

Methodists

The Methodist movement was founded in 1740 by John Wesley, Charles Wesley and George Whitefield. Followers of the movement organised societies which met at members' houses, but gradually established preaching houses or chapels throughout Britain. The movement split into many different groups in the 18th and 19th centuries, including the Methodist New Connexion, the Primitive Methodists, the Bible Christians, the United Methodist Free Churches and the Countess of Huntingdon's Connection. The Methodist New Connexion, the United Methodist Free Churches and the Bible Christians combined in 1857 to form the United Methodist Church. The Wesleyan Methodists, the Primitive Methodists and the United Methodist Church combined to form the Methodist Church in 1932. Leary (336), Mullett (343) and volume 2 of the *NIPR* (151) describe the organisation and beliefs of the different Methodist groups and contain useful bibliographies.

Few Methodist registers survive for the 18th century. Until about 1795 baptisms (and a few marriages before 1754) were generally recorded in chapel registers (or in circuit registers) by preachers who attended upon a number of congregations. Few of these records have survived. In 1818 a Methodist General Registry (also known as the Metropolitan Wesleyan Registry) was established in London to record births and baptisms centrally. Parents had to submit two original baptism certificates (one being returned to them). Some entries were recorded retrospectively back to 1773 and about 10,000 entries were made up to 1838 when the register was closed. The volumes of the register (and an index) are held by TNA in series RG 4. The certificates submitted by parents are in RG 5. The entries are not included in the IGI but the certificates are indexed in the BVRI. Many other Methodist registers for the period up to 1837 are also in RG 4, some are at CROs and some are held locally. As an example, a page from the register of baptisms and births, recorded on the Clitheroe circuit in Lancashire from 1807 to 1809 (from RG 4) is at illustration 61. From the late 18th century some Methodist burial grounds also kept registers. Some of these are held by TNA (and copies are at the SoG) and they are listed by county, with covering dates, in Leary (336). The registers held in CROs are listed in the county volumes of the *NIPR*. Baptism and burial registers since 1837 are mostly at CROs, but some are still at chapels. From 1837 marriages could again take place in Methodist chapels but, until 1898 a civil registrar had to attend (and record the marriage) and the Methodists do not appear to have kept their own records of these marriages. Registers of marriages since 1898 are at chapels or CROs.

The Methodist movement developed a nationwide structure of government. Congregations (or Societies) were grouped in local circuits to which ministers were appointed. Each circuit associated with other circuits in a district and the district representatives held quarterly meetings. There was also a national Annual Methodist Conference which dealt with the movement's most important business. Minutes of the conference and of districts' quarterly meetings dealt mainly with theological matters. Circuit records include financial and administrative matters but also references to many followers of the movement. Societies' or chapels' records note payments (such as pew rents) from the congregation or expenditure on the chapel. Minutes of meetings and other records are held at chapels or CROs, but many are held (with other Methodist records, especially magazines and newspapers) at the Methodist Archives and Research Centre, John Rylands Library, University of Manchester, Deansgate, Manchester. This library is presently closed for refurbishment but should re-open in 2005. Leary (336) and volume 2 of the *NIPR* (151) list many Methodist magazines and newspapers, from the late 18th and early 19th centuries. These include useful genealogical material, particularly members' biographies and obituaries. Examples of newspapers are the *Watchman*, published from 1835 to 1863 and the *Methodist Recorder* published from 1861. Magazines include *Methodist Magazine* published from 1798 to 1821 and the *Wesleyan Magazine* (1822 to 1932). Further information on Methodism may be obtained from the Wesley Historical Society or the Museum of Methodism at Wesley's Chapel, City Road, London.

The Mormons

The Church of Jesus Christ of Latter-Day Saints (LDS), more commonly known as the Mormon Church, was founded in New York State in 1830. Missionaries were sent to Britain and by 1851 there were over 30,000 church members and 220 meeting places in England. More than 110,000 English people joined the church in the 19th century, although many converts emigrated to the United States and the number of members in England declined to less than 3,000 by 1890. A. Camp describes the history of the Mormon Church in England and its records in *Family Tree Magazine* (August 1998). Most records are in the Family History Library in Salt Lake City but can be ordered for viewing on microfilm at LDS family history centres. Branch membership books include the dates of members' birth, baptism into the church, death, emigration or leaving the church. There are some indexes of members in the earlier years and registers of emigration (and the LDS has produced a CD-ROM index of Mormon immigrants to the USA 1840–90).

OTHER ENGLISH NON-CONFORMISTS

There were many other smaller non-conformist groups who kept their own registers (most of which are now at TNA). For example, the Moravians developed in the mid-18th century and there were about 25 congregations by 1800. The earliest Moravian register, for a chapel in Fetter Lane in London, commences in 1741. Registers usually record births (rather than baptisms), burials and some marriages. Most registers were surrendered to the Registrar General. Volume 2 of the *NIPR* (151) provides a detailed history of the Moravian movement, a list of Moravian registers at TNA and details of other surviving records of congregations, such as lists of members and minutes of meetings of the church elders.

The Inghamites, who had similar beliefs to the Methodists, had a number of chapels, particularly in Yorkshire and Lancashire. TNA holds the registers of eight chapels and this denomination is described, with transcripts of some of their records, in Oates (343a). The Swedenborgians (or the New Church) developed in the late 18th century. By 1851 they had about 50 places of worship with about 5,000 people in attendance. Their registers are held by TNA but copies were retained and are held at the church's headquarters. Details of the movement are provided in volume 2 of the *NIPR* (151), which also reviews the surviving records of smaller movements, such as the Sandemanians, the Universalists, the Catholic Apostolic Church (or Irvingites) and the Plymouth Brethren.

THE SALVATION ARMY

The Salvation Army (perhaps best known to most people for its social work) is a denomination that had its roots in Methodism. William Booth, often considered as the founder of the movement, was originally a Methodist preacher. The Army began life in 1865 as a Christian mission in poorer parts of Britain. Its members preached, undertook social or medical work, and assisted in fostering, adoption and emigration schemes. By 1878 there were 50 missions, or stations, in Britain and the Army also opened hospitals and homes for the aged (as well as missions abroad).

Wiggins (354) is a guide to the movement's work and records. Salvationists should be recorded in civil registration records but the Army's records may add a great deal to your knowledge of an ancestor's work. Records may be held at a local Army centre (listed in telephone directories), at the Army's United Kingdom territorial headquarters at 101 Newington Causeway, London SE1 6BU (telephone 020 7367 4500) or at its International Heritage Centre at 101 Queen Victoria Street, London EC4P 4EP (telephone 020 7332 0101). The Army keeps registers of the dedication of children (a ceremony that is similar to baptism), marriages, burials, the swearing in of soldiers and the commissioning of officers who were full-time, paid, ministers. These registers include dates and places of birth, addresses (and sometimes the names of a person's parents). Examples of these records are included in Wiggins (354). The Army's yearbook (published annually since 1906) includes information on officers. A few surviving records of fostering and adoption are held at the Army's Social Services Headquarters at Newington Causeway.

HUGUENOTS

The Huguenots were Protestants, mostly from France, who fled from civil war and religious persecution in the 16th and 17th centuries. Many arrived in England after the massacre of over 100,000 Huguenots in France in 1572. Other groups followed, particularly after 1685 when Louis XIV revoked the Edict of Nantes (which had granted religious freedom to French Protestants). About 45,000 Huguenots settled in Britain in the late 17th century alone, mainly around Spitalfields and Soho in London, but also in Bristol, Southampton, Canterbury and Norwich. By 1700, there were 23 Huguenot churches in London alone. Currer-Briggs & Gambier (321) describe the persecution of the Huguenots and the early settlements in England. Gwynn (330) is a detailed study of the Huguenots from the 16th to 18th centuries, reviewing their settlement in England, their trades, crafts, churches and their gradual assimilation into the English population.

Huguenot congregations kept registers of baptisms, marriages and burials (most are now held by TNA in series RG 4) and other records, such as those concerning poor relief and charities. Many Huguenots were also recorded in Anglican or non-conformist registers. Particular care should be taken to look for alternative spellings (or anglicisation) of Huguenot names, for example the name Batteleur being written as Butler. Many Huguenot records have been published by the Huguenot Society (# appendix XI for its web site), principally in 59 volumes of its "Quarto" series, listed in Mullins (260). They include church registers, certificates of naturalisation (# chapter 30) and lists of aliens. For example, Scouloudi (349) lists Huguenots and other "strangers" in London between 1593 and 1639. The lists, some extracted from State Papers Domestic at TNA (# chapter 22), were made in response to concern about the increasing number of alien craftsmen (and fear that they were damaging the livelihood of indigenous workers). This is a typical entry from returns in 1593:

Giles Bonchier and Mary his wife, French, he born in Ponwey in Normandy, she in Honfleur. Button maker, one daughter English born of 13 years, one French maidservant, dwelt in England 30 years, denizen, of the French Church. Keeps two English apprentices, sets no English person to work, dwells in the parish of St Anne, Blackfriars.

A surname index to volumes 1–40 of the Quarto publications has been published by the Society of Australian Genealogists. The Huguenot Society has also published about 120 issues of its journal, the *Proceedings*, which also includes much useful material, together with a master name and place index to issues up to 1998.

The Huguenot Library, which also holds extensive archives, is held at University College, Gower Street, London WC1E 6BT (telephone 020 7380 7094). Readers should make an appointment to visit the library but its catalogue is available online (# appendix XI). Its holdings include many manuscript records (such as the records of committees established from 1687 to administer funds collected for the relief of refugees) and Huguenot pedigrees prepared by members of the society. Some other Huguenot records (including records of relief for refugees) are at Guildhall Library. Many Huguenots are included in further lists, for 1618 to 1688, of foreigners resident in England, contained in the State Papers Domestic and published in Cooper (320). Lart (335a) is a collection of the pedigrees of many Huguenot families, in most cases back to the 16th century, but often earlier.

FOREIGN CHURCHES

Many other Protestant and Catholic groups, described in volumes 2 and 3 of the *NIPR* (151), also fled to England from Europe, because of persecution or for economic reasons, and founded their own churches. They include the Dutch Church in Austin Friars in the City of London (the registers of which commence in 1559), the churches of Dutch communities in Norwich and Colchester, and a Swiss church, which opened in 1775 in Moor Street, Soho, London (its register for 1762–1839 is held by TNA). At least a dozen German churches were founded in London between the 17th and early 19th centuries (about 30,000 Germans came to London between 1820 and 1860 alone). These churches and their registers are described by S. Pearl in *Family Tree Magazine* (December 1989, February 1990 and June 1990). Their registers were often written in German and although some are held at TNA, others are held by local record offices or remain at the churches. Some of the registers have been indexed by L. Metzner for the Anglo-German FHS (# chapter 30).

JEWS

Jews were banished from England (or killed) by King Edward I in 1290. They were only legally allowed to return in 1655 (although some arrived earlier) but discrimination against Jews continued. Although synagogues were opened from about 1690, Jews were not allowed to own land until 1728, to become barristers until 1833, to vote until 1835, obtain military commissions until 1846 or enter Oxford or Cambridge universities until after 1871. Lindsay (338) contains a useful introductory history to the Jews in Britain. Reference should also be made to the section on Jewish genealogy, by E.R. Samuel, in volume 3 of the *NIPR* (151) and Joseph (332a) is an introduction to Jewish genealogy with detailed bibliographies for many aspects of Jewish family history. Useful articles on Jewish genealogy also appear in *Family Tree Magazine* (July and August 1990). All of these note published transcripts of records that may assist your research. *Avotaynu:*

The International Review of Jewish Genealogy (304) has been published quarterly since 1985. It includes articles on the holdings of archives around the world, on particular records (such as US visa records) on Jewish names and on the history of Jewish settlement in particular countries. Avotaynu has also published a guide to genealogical sources held in Israel. The Jewish Genealogical Society of Great Britain (see appendix XI for its web site) was formed in 1992 and publishes a quarterly journal *Shemot* (309).

There were two main groups of Jews in England from the 17th century: Sephardic Jews (who came mainly from Portugal, Spain or Italy) and Ashkenazi Jews (mainly from Germany or Eastern Europe). Ross (347) estimates that there were only about 600 Jews in England in the late 17th century and only about 3,500 in the early 18th century. Despite discrimination, the number of Jews in Britain gradually increased. By 1800 there were perhaps 30,000 Jews in England, over half of them in London. Other 18th-century settlements were in Bristol (a synagogue was built in 1786) and Exeter. By 1870 there were about 60,000 Jews in Britain and, after 1880, persecution of Jews in eastern Europe resulted in further immigration, so that the Jewish population amounted to about 250,000 by 1921, including large communities in cities such as Birmingham, Leeds and Manchester.

Jewish surnames are considered in Joseph (332a) and Kaganoff (333). Many Jewish names were anglicised, or changed entirely, when families arrived in Britain. The majority of these name changes are not officially recorded, but changes may be evidenced in denization and naturalisation records (# chapter 30), by which aliens obtained the rights of British subjects. The naturalisation of Jews is also considered by Ross (347). For Jews who arrived in Britain before 1901, changes of names may be found in Phillimore & Fry (131). Researching Jewish ancestry can be difficult since many records are in Hebrew. They also refer to the Jewish calendar, which is described in Webb (123). The Jewish year begins on variable dates in autumn and is generally about 3,760 years (in numbers) ahead of the British year, so it is usually correct to deduct 3,760 from the year given in Jewish records. The recorded events may also be different from other British records. The circumcision of boys (eight days after birth) may be recorded instead of births. Circumcision (*brit milah*) records were kept by the circumciser (the *mohel*) and can be hard to find. Jews were exempt from Hardwicke's Marriage Act and so Jewish marriages could be solemnised in synagogues. A wedding was not always recorded in synagogue registers, but synagogues kept a duplicate of the *Ketubah* (marriage contract). A typical *Ketubah* appears as an illustration in Joseph (332a). Many marriages of wealthy Jewish families were also reported in journals such as *Gentleman's Magazine* (# chapter 17) or in newspapers such as the *Jewish Chronicle*. From 1837 Jewish marriages were recorded by the civil registration system (synagogues copied their registers to the Registrar General).

There are now about 400 synagogues in Britain. Since 1896 lists of synagogues and Jewish cemeteries have been included in the *Jewish Year Book* (published annually by Jewish Chronicle Publications). Volume 3 of the *NIPR* lists the synagogues established in Britain before 1838. London synagogues are described (with many illustrations) in Lindsay (338) and Jewish cemeteries in London (and their registers) are listed in Wolfston (201). Some synagogues' registers have been published, such as the marriage registers of the Spanish and Portuguese Synagogue of London for 1687 to 1837 and the burial registers of the Bevis Marks congregation for 1733 to 1918. In the 17th and 18th centuries some Jewish people were also recorded in Anglican parish registers. The Jews were not requested to surrender their pre-1837 registers to the Registrar General in the 19th century. Most synagogues therefore retain their registers and a request for access to the registers should be made to the synagogue.

Synagogue records may also include minute books of the synagogue council and lists of founder members, seatholders or benefactors. Some early registers of synagogues are now held in the archive office of the Court of the Chief Rabbi, London Beth Din, Adler House, 735 High Road, Finchley, London N12 0US. No research facilities are available, so research must be conducted by post, for small fees. The registers and other records that are held include those (then in two buildings at Tavistock Square), listed in an article in *Family Tree Magazine* (July 1992). In addition to registers of some defunct congregations and closed burial grounds, the records include marriage authorisations since 1845 (including over 240,000 issued since 1880) and over 350,000 burial authorisations issued since 1896. Many of these note a person's place of birth (this may not be recorded in any other surviving records). The Anglo-Jewish archives (formerly at University College, London) have provided a large collection of material to the SoG and to the Parkes Library at the University of Southampton (to which there is a published guide). The collections at the SoG, noted by Joseph (332a), include the Colyer-Fergusson collection (containing many pedigrees of Jewish families, MIs, wills and newspaper cuttings) and the Hyamson collection of Jewish pedigrees and lists.

The most important Jewish newspaper for genealogists is the *Jewish Chronicle* which was published from November 1841 to May 1842 and since October 1844. Copies are held at the British Newspaper Library at Colindale (# chapter 17) and many Jewish archives. It includes obituaries and reports of births, marriages and deaths. The Jewish Museum, at 129–131 Albert Street, Camden Town, London NW1, holds an extensive library of Jewish reference books, genealogical manuscripts and family histories (and copies of the *Jewish Chronicle*). The Jewish Historical Society of 33 Seymour Place, London WC1, publishes records in its series of *Transactions* and *Miscellanies*, copies of which are at the SoG. For example, volume 22 of the *Transactions* (310) lists Jewish apprentices and masters from 1710 to 1733, extracted from the apprenticeship books at TNA (# chapter 22) and lists denizations and naturalisations of Jews from 1609 to 1799 (# chapter 30). There are many other published works on the Jewish community in Britain. One of particular note is the *British Jewry Book of Honour* by Adler (596). This lists 50,000 Jewish men (with hundreds of photographs) who fought in the armed forces of Britain and the Empire in the First World War. It includes the names and addresses of the 2,500 men who died and lists those who received gallantry medals or were mentioned in despatches.

Records of immigration into Britain are considered in chapter 30, but researchers should consult the following records at TNA: (a) records of denizations and naturalisations; (b) certificates of aliens entering Britain (1836–52) and (c) ships' passenger lists from 1890. Clapsaddle (318) also recommends the records of the Jews' Temporary Shelter (founded in 1885) and the Jewish Refugee Committee (founded in 1933) for information on Jews arriving in Britain since the late 19th century. The records of the Jewish Refugee Committee list over 400,000 Jews fleeing from Nazi persecution, giving dates and place of birth, nationality, profession, home address, date of arrival and address in Britain. Access to these materials is restricted to the people who are the subjects of the files or their next of kin. An index to the records of the Poor Jews Temporary Shelter, Leman Street, Whitechapel in London of 1896 to 1914, with about 43,000 names, can be accessed on the Internet. The Mormons hold microfilm copies of all those records of German, Polish and Hungarian synagogues that survived the Second World War and these may be seen at LDS family history centres.

Although Jews were banished from England in 1290, many records survive of the Jewish community in the 13th century. Civil litigation between Jews and Christians was heard in the Exchequer of the Jews and there are also many records of the taxes on Jewish residents. The plea rolls of the Exchequer of the Jews have been published by the Selden Society and the Jewish Historical Society, for example in Rigg (346). Useful articles on Jews in England in the 13th century, lists of those paying taxes, those accused of coinage offences, or appearing in the Patent Rolls (# chapter 27), are included in volume 32 of the *Transactions* of the Jewish Historical Society. Unfortunately, it has not been possible to prove anyone's ancestry back to this medieval Jewish community.

CHAPTER 14

MARRIAGE AND DIVORCE

MARRIAGE LICENCES AND BANNS

Banns are notices, proclaimed in church, of a couple's intention to marry. This publicity gives people the chance to declare any reason why that couple cannot marry. The church has required banns to be called since 1215 but they were rarely recorded until the 18th century. Banns are called in the church in which a couple are to marry on three Sundays before the wedding takes place. If one of the spouses was from another parish, banns should also have been called (since 1823) in the church of that other parish. This sometimes happened in earlier years. Marriage by licence was introduced in the 14th century. A marriage licence authorised a wedding without banns being proclaimed. Since there was no need to wait for the proclamations, a marriage could take place on the day on which the licence was obtained, or more usually the following day. Ecclesiastical and secular laws on marriage since medieval times were complex, but they are reviewed in detail by Chapman & Litton (362).

Hardwicke's Marriage Act of 1753 confirmed ecclesiastical law by requiring that all marriages after 25 March 1754 (except those of Quakers and Jews) had to follow banns or be authorised by a licence. Marriage entries in parish registers since 1754 (and marriage certificates since 1837) should state whether a marriage was by licence or banns. The act also required the calling of banns to be recorded in the parish register, although some incumbents had already been recording banns for some years. From 1837 marriages could also take place before civil registrars or in chapels licensed under the Civil Registration Acts. The law permitted the superintendent registrar to issue a certificate (similar to an Anglican licence) authorising marriages (without banns) in licensed places of worship. The written declarations of the couple were open to the public for 21 days before any such marriage.

THE BANNS REGISTER

Banns may be recorded in the marriage register or in a separate banns register. The entries for banns might be recorded alone or on printed forms for dual entries, that is, also recording a marriage (usually the same couple's wedding, but sometimes that of another couple). Guildhall Library holds the banns register for the parish of Holy Trinity Minories in London. Illustration 35 is an extract, recording the calling of banns (on 15, 22 and 29 August 1852) for the marriage on 19 September of Bernard Herber and Emily Clements.

Banns registers are useful since, like marriage registers, they may note the spouses' places of residence (and they sometimes record residences when the marriage register does not). A spouse who had recently arrived in a parish might be recorded as a sojourner or "of this parish" in the marriage entry, but the entries for the banns (recorded a few weeks earlier) may state the place from which that spouse had migrated. A banns book may also assist if your ancestor did not marry in his home parish. Since banns should have been proclaimed in the home parishes of both spouses (from 1823, but sometimes earlier), the banns register for an ancestor's parish may include the banns for his wedding taking place elsewhere. Although the place of marriage is rarely noted, the other spouse's home parish should be specified (and is the first place to search). My ancestors Richard Bater of Chawleigh and Ann Voisey of Sandford married in Sandford in 1793. Banns were called in both parishes and both banns registers noted the parish of the non-resident spouse. Illustration 36 shows the entry from the Sandford register. In illustration 35 the first entry is for the banns for the marriage of Esau Collins and Honor Sheppard. The remark "not married in this church" is unhelpful as to where (or even whether) the couple married, but Honor Sheppard's abode was noted as Harrington in Somerset, so a researcher could search for the marriage in that parish.

The parish churchwardens usually arranged the calling of banns. Hardwicke's Marriage Act required intending spouses to give the parish a written notice that banns should be published. This requirement was often waived (since so many people were illiterate), but some notices survive in parish records. However, the Marriage Act 1822 required that, from 1 September 1822, an intending couple should submit an affidavit to the churchwardens that stated the couple's names, abodes (and for how long they had lived there) and whether they were occupiers or lodgers. The affidavit also had to state whether they were of full age and if not, had to provide the name of the parent or guardian who was consenting to the marriage. An article about these affidavits, with examples from the parish records of Princes Risborough in Buckinghamshire, appears in *Genealogists' Magazine* (September 1983). It is unfortunate for genealogists that this requirement for affidavits was repealed in March 1823.

MARRIAGE LICENCES

A couple, or their families, might wish to avoid waiting at least three weeks (for the calling of banns) before a wedding could take place, or wish to avoid the publicity of banns. The couple might be away from home (thus making it difficult to arrange banns in their home parish) or they might wish to marry quickly because the bride was pregnant or because the groom was going abroad with the army or navy. In such cases the couple could obtain a marriage licence and avoid the need for banns. Most people were married by banns, mainly because licences cost more money than banns, but many who could afford it therefore preferred to be married by licence (as a status symbol) rather than by banns.

There were two types of marriage licence. A special licence allowed a marriage to take place anywhere. These licences could only be granted by the Archbishop of Canterbury or his officials and are very rare. A common licence usually named one or two parishes where the marriage could take place, since the church required the marriage to take place in the parish in which one of the couple lived. This restriction was often ignored by the church officials and parish clergy so that, in practice, common licences could often be used at churches other than those named in a licence. Common licences could be issued by archbishops, bishops, some archdeacons, ministers in some parishes (usually peculiars) or by their "surrogates" (that is clergymen or officials entitled to act on their behalf). Deans and chapters (such as the Dean and Chapter of St Paul's Cathedral) could also grant licences for marriages in their peculiars. A common licence could generally be obtained from the church official who had jurisdiction over (a) the parish in which the couple wished to marry, and (b) over the place in which both bride and groom were resident (from 1640 at least one of them should actually have lived in that official's jurisdiction for at least one month). Despite this requirement, one or both of the couple might simply take up temporary residence in a parish in which they wished to marry and these temporary residents usually had little difficulty in obtaining a licence. Hardwicke's Marriage Act of 1753 reiterated ecclesiastical law by providing that marriages by licence should take place in the parish in which one of the spouses had his or her "usual abode" for four weeks before the grant of the licence. This period was reduced to 15 days in 1823.

Marriage licence jurisdictions (which were similar to probate jurisdictions) are described in Gibson (367). A licence obtained from an archdeacon who had authority to grant licences (such as the Archdeacon of Norfolk) permitted the marriage of a couple who resided in the archdeaconry to take place in any parish in that archdeaconry. A licence obtained from a bishop or his officers (such as the bishop's chancellor at a diocesan registry) allowed a couple residing in his diocese to marry in any parish in that diocese. If the bride and groom lived in different dioceses, a licence had to be obtained from the Archbishop (of Canterbury or York) who had jurisdiction over both dioceses. These licences were known as Vicar-General licences because they were issued by the Archbishops' Vicar-Generals. If the couple lived in different ecclesiastical provinces (one in the Province of Canterbury and one in York Province) an application had to be made to the Master of Faculties of the Archbishop of Canterbury. These licences were known as Faculty Office licences.

A marriage licence was provided to the couple being married and handed by them to the minister performing the marriage ceremony and so has usually been lost. Some licences were retained by families or by the ministers officiating at weddings but they usually note only the spouses' names and the date and place of the wedding. However, one of the couple (usually the groom) had to apply for the licence at the appropriate church official's registry by submitting an allegation, a sworn statement that there was no impediment to the marriage taking place (for example an existing marriage). An allegation usually states the names, ages, occupations and places of residence of the bride and groom, whether they were single or widowed, and where the marriage was to take place. If one or both of the couple were minors, the allegation should have named the parent or guardian who was consenting to the marriage. Bonds may also have been submitted until the need for these was abolished in 1823. Bonds were sworn statements, containing assurances by a couple's friends or relatives (and often the groom), that they knew of no impediment to the marriage, confirming that the couple would marry in a specified church, and also stating the amount of money by which they were bound (and which they might forfeit if the licence was not complied with). Most allegations and bonds were in standard form. My widowed g.g. grandmother Emily Herber, married John Phillips on 13 March 1884, by a licence obtained from the Bishop of London. The allegation, sworn the day before, is at Guildhall Library and states:

Diocese of London . . . 12th March, 1884 . . . appeared JOHN PHILLIPS of the new parish of St John Hoxton . . . a bachelor of the age of 21 years and upwards and prayed a licence for the solemnisation of matrimony in the said new parish church of St John Hoxton between him and Emily Herber of the parish of Walthamstow, Essex a widow

And made oath that he believeth that there is no impediment of kindred or alliance, or of any other lawful cause, nor any suit commenced in any ecclesiastical court to bar or hinder . . . the said matrimony . . .

AND he further made oath that he hath had his usual place of abode within the said parish of St John Hoxton for the fifteen days last past.

This marriage took place after the requirement for bonds was abolished. A bond was required for the marriage by licence in 1784 of Elizabeth Gillman (a sister of my ancestor Susannah Gillman) and William Waterfield. The allegation and bond are shown in illustrations 63 and 64. My ancestor Thomas Gillman (Elizabeth's father) was a party to the bond, promising to "save harmless" the church officials (that is agreeing to indemnify them against any financial loss) in the event that the marriage would breach any ecclesiastical law:

Know all men by these presents that William Waterfield of the parish of Hockliffe in the County of Bedford, cordwainer and Thomas Gillman of the parish of Hockliffe, cordwainer, are held and firmly bound to Richard Shepherd, Commissary of the Archdeaconry of Bedford in (the sum) of one hundred pounds to be paid to the said Richard Shepherd dated the 27th December 1784 . . .

The condition of this obligation is such that if hereafter there shall not appear any lawful let or impediment by reason of any pre-contract entered into before 27th December 1784, consanguinity, affinity or any other lawful means whatsoever but that William Waterfield batchelor of the age of 22 years and Elizabeth Gillman of the parish of Hockliffe spinster of the age of 20 years may lawfully solemnise marriage together . . . and if the said marriage shall be openly solemnised in the church or chapel, in the licence specified, between the hours appointed in the Constitutions Ecclesiastical . . . and according to the form of the Book of Common Prayer . . . and if William Waterfield and Thomas Gillman do save harmless the said Richard Shepherd (and his officers) . . . then this obligation shall be void. Signed W. Waterfield; Thomas Gillman.

A marriage licence, bond or allegation does not prove that a couple married. My ancestors Thomas Bulhead and Grace Gibbons of Winkleigh in Devon obtained a marriage licence in 1670 and later had children in the same village. However, I cannot find a record of the marriage. It is possible that it took place and that I will one day find the marriage record. It is also possible that Thomas and Grace did not have a ceremony. Similarly, the only record that has yet been discovered of the marriage of William Shakespeare and Ann Hathaway (their first child was baptised in May 1583) is a bond, in the registry of the Bishop of Worcester, as security for the bishop to issue a marriage licence in November 1582.

We noted above that a statute of 1822 required an affidavit to be sworn (until March 1823) if a couple wanted banns to be called. The act imposed similar provisions, from 1 September 1822, for the issue of marriage licences. It is unfortunate for genealogists that this provision was also repealed in March 1823. For seven months, every intending spouse (who required a licence) had to swear an affidavit as to his or her own age, marital status and belief as to the age and marital status of the person they intended to marry. If either of the couple were under 21, they had to swear that the minor's parents or guardian had consented (and exhibit a written and witnessed consent). Importantly, the couple's ages had to be proved by exhibiting copies of baptism entries

Dec: 27 1784

ON which Day appeared Perfonally *William Waterfield* of the Parifh of *Hockliffe* in the County of *Bedford* and Diocefs of *Lincoln* and being Sworn on the Holy Evangelift Alledged and made Oath as follows: That he is of the Age *of Twenty five years and intends to marry with Elizabeth Gilman of the Parish of Hockliffe aforesaid Spinster of the Age of Twenty years.*

Not knowing or believing any lawful Let or Impediment by reafon of any Precontract entered into before the 25th Day of *March*, 1754. Confanguinity, Affinity, or any other Caufe whatfoever, to hinder the faid intended Marriage. AND he prayed a Licence to folemnize the faid Marriage in the Church of *Hockliffe* aforefaid, in which faid Parifh of *Hockliffe* the faid *Elizabeth Gilman* hath had *her* ufual Abode for the fpace of four Weeks laft paft.

THE faid *William Waterfield* was }
Sworn the Day and Year firft above written
before me }

Wm Jeffreys Surrogate.

63. Allegation of 1784 for marriage licence for William Waterfield and Elizabeth Gillman (Bedford Record Office)

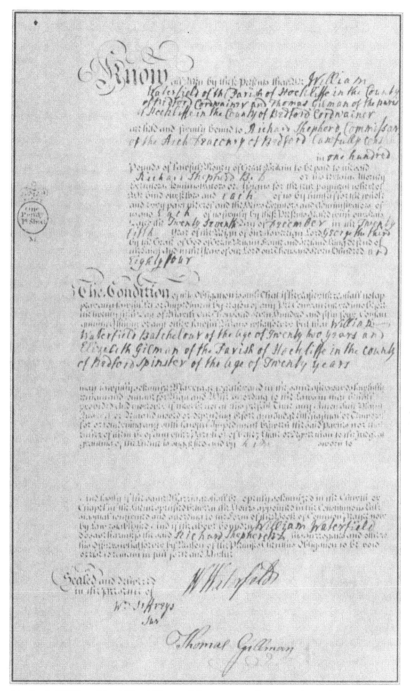

64. Bond of William Waterfield and Thomas Gillman in 1784 for marriage licence for William
Waterfield and Elizabeth Gillman (Bedford Record Office)

from parish registers (certified as true copies by the incumbent). If there had been no baptism (or if the entry or register could not be found), an intending spouse had to procure a certificate (as to their age) provided by someone (usually a parent) who had known them for a long time. If your ancestors married by licence between 1 September 1822 and 26 March 1823, an allegation for the licence will provide a great deal of genealogical information.

THE LOCATION OF MARRIAGE LICENCE RECORDS

Allegations and bonds were retained by church officials. Most of the bishops', archdeacons' and peculiars' records are held at diocesan record offices (usually CROs). The records of licences issued by the two archbishops' officials are at Lambeth Palace Library or the Borthwick Institute of Historical Research. Gibson (367) notes the location of surviving marriage licence allegations and bonds, and provides, for the two archbishops' offices and for each county, a list of published and unpublished calendars and indexes. Most of the published works have been produced by the Harleian Society, the British Record Society, family history or local record societies and the SoG. If there is no published index, the relevant archive usually has a manuscript, typescript or card index to its marriage licence records. The SoG has a large collection of calendars and indexes to marriage licence records listed for English counties in its *County sources* booklets (# chapter 7) and for Wales in its booklet (356). In addition, about 20,000 marriage licences of the 18th and 19th centuries (mainly from London parishes) were collected by F.A. Crisp. The originals are held at the SoG and IHGS and abstracts (and an index) to the collection are at the SoG.

As with probate records, the number of ecclesiastical jurisdictions can make it difficult to find the record of a marriage licence in certain counties but in others a search is straightforward. There were few peculiars in Suffolk, so most parishes were in the jurisdiction of the Archdeaconry of Suffolk or the Archdeaconry of Sudbury as described in Gibson (367) and on the IHGS county maps. The archdeaconries' records are at Suffolk Record Office. There are manuscript or typescript indexes to the Archdeaconry of Suffolk allegations and bonds (and published indexes for some years). Bannerman & Bannerman (359) is an indexed calendar of the Archdeaconry of Sudbury marriage licence records of 1683–1839, from which this is a typical entry:

4 October 1761. Thos. Mudd of Lavenham, single man, 21 years & Mary Ruffle of Thorpe, 20 years, single woman (father Ambrose Ruffle) at Thorpe. Bondsman Rich. Mudd.

However, as with grants of probate, an ancestor could have applied to a higher court for a marriage licence. Suffolk residents could apply to officials of the Diocese of Norwich or the Archbishop of Canterbury. As another example, Hampshire was in the Diocese of Winchester. The Bishop of Winchester's records of marriage allegations and bonds, including records of the many Hampshire peculiars, are in Hampshire Record Office in Winchester. Most of the records from 1607 to 1837 have been published, those from 1689 to 1837 in Harleian Society volumes by Moens (373) and two supplements, by A. Willis, in *Genealogists' Magazine* (June and September 1962).

Family history societies are also producing indexes to marriage licence records. Wiltshire FHS has indexed the records of the Bishop of Salisbury (covering most of Berkshire and Wiltshire) and the Dean of Salisbury (parts of Wiltshire and Dorset) from about 1615. Cumbria FHS has published indexed calendars in Singleton (377) to marriage licence records of 1668 to 1752 from the Diocese of Carlisle (that had jurisdiction in much of Cumberland and Westmorland).

It can be very difficult to find a record of an ancestor's marriage licence if he or she lived in London (which is considered below) but fortunately, the position in Yorkshire and other places within the jurisdiction of the Archbishop of York is not as complex as for probate records. Most of Yorkshire was in the Diocese of York (although part was in the Archdeaconry of Richmond which, in turn, was in the Diocese of Chester). Marriage licence records of York Diocese, of peculiars of the Dean and Chapter of York, and of the Archbishop of York (for his peculiars or for couples from different dioceses within the Northern Province) are at the Borthwick Institute. The institute has published indexes by Newsome & Newsome (375) and Chilman (362a) to the marriage licence records of the Archbishop of York (which survive from 1660). These indexes, in 11 volumes, cover 1660 to 1839. In the 19th century W. Paver made some abstracts and indexes of earlier licence records, dating from as early as 1567 but which are now lost. Paver's work was published by the Yorkshire Archaeological Society and the couples' names are in Boyd's marriage index. The Borthwick Institute has also published an index, in Newsome & Newsome (374), to the marriage licence records of 1613–1839 of the Dean and Chapter of York (which included some parishes in Lancashire and Nottinghamshire).

The records of licences issued by officials of the Archbishop of Canterbury are especially important because they are so substantial and relate to people from all over Britain. Lambeth Palace Library holds the surviving allegations and bonds for both Faculty Office and Vicar-General licences. The allegations were bound in volumes. Faculty Office allegations survive from 1632–50 and since 1660 (with a further 730 allegations from 1543–49 and 1567–75). The Vicar-General allegations survive from 1660. Copies of the Faculty Office and Vicar-General allegations up to 1851 are also available on microfilm at the SoG. The bonds filed in support of the allegations were not bound into volumes and many have therefore been lost. The original finding-aids to the Faculty Office and Vicar-General allegations and bonds were manuscript calendars that provide, in chronological order, the spouse's names (their surnames only for Vicar-General licences) and the date of issue of the licence. Some examples from the calendar of Faculty Office licences for June 1789 are:

June 1st	Boddy, Francis	&	Field, Charlotte
2nd	Carlisle, William	&	Scarborough, Ann
2nd	Jennings, David	&	Greene, Sarah
5th	John Drummond, esq.	&	Hester Cholmondeley (Special licence)

Indexes have been prepared from most of these calendars and published, so the best finding aid for each period is noted below. If you find a relevant index entry, you do not need to consult the manuscript calendars because the licence's date and the parties' names enable you to find the allegation at Lambeth Palace Library or on microfilm at the SoG.

Vicar General licences

1660–1694   Indexed transcript of calendars (but with addition of parties' abodes and intended place of marriage) in Harleian Society volumes 23, 30, 31, 33 and 34.

1694–1850   Indexes prepared from the manuscript calendars, with dates of licences and spouses' surnames, published as books and on fiche by the SoG (357) and searchable on the English Origins web site.

1851 to date   Manuscript calendars at Lambeth Palace Library with dates of licences and spouses' surnames.

Faculty Office licences

16th century   Indexed list of surviving allegations published in Harleian Society volume 24.

1632–1714   Indexed transcript of calendars published in British Record Society volume 33.

1701–1850   Indexes prepared from the manuscript calendars, with date of licences and spouses' surnames and forenames (or initials), published on fiche by the SoG and searchable on the English Origins web site.

1851 to date   Manuscript calendars at Lambeth Palace Library with dates of licences and spouses' surnames and forenames (or initials).

LONDON

As in the case of probate records, the jurisdictions in London and Middlesex for the issue of marriage licences (and the location of surviving records) are not straightforward. Details are provided in Gibson (367). Both the City of London and Middlesex were in the Diocese of London. The diocesan records are at Guildhall Library and LMA. British Record Society volumes 62 and 66 index the allegations of 1597–1700 and more details of many of these allegations (the intended place of marriage and names of parents consenting to the marriage) are noted in abstracts of the allegations in Harleian Society volumes 25–26 and Foster (366). These volumes also include abstracts of a few surviving earlier allegations of 1520–97. For the period since 1700, there are manuscript calendars or typescript indexes, listed in Gibson (367), at Guildhall Library and the SoG. The Archdeacon of London and the Dean and Chapter of St Paul's Cathedral also had jurisdiction over certain London parishes. These records are at Guildhall Library. Marriage licences could also be issued by officials of the Archdeacon of Middlesex, the Royal Peculiar of St Katherine by the Tower, the Peculiar of the Deanery of the Arches and the Peculiar of the Dean and Chapter of Westminster (these records are held at Guildhall Library, Lambeth Palace Library, LMA and Westminster Archives). Finding aids for these records are listed in Gibson (367). Furthermore, Surrey and Kent extended to the south bank of the Thames, so that places such as Southwark, Lambeth and Deptford were generally in other ecclesiastical jurisdictions. Therefore, marriage licences for ancestors who lived in these places could be issued by the Bishop of Winchester's Commissary Court for the Archdeaconry of Surrey, the Peculiar Deanery of Croydon (which included parishes such as Putney and Wimbledon) or the Diocese of Rochester (which covered west Kent). Finally, both the Faculty Office and the Vicar-General of the Archbishop of Canterbury had offices at Doctors' Commons, near St Paul's Cathedral, and so many Londoners applied to these offices for their marriage licences (whether for reasons of status or convenience) even if a licence from such high authority was not necessary to authorise the marriage. All these records may therefore have to be searched in order to find an ancestor's marriage licence.

IRREGULAR AND CLANDESTINE MARRIAGES

The church originally regarded the validity of a marriage as being established by the exchange of wedding vows, expressed in the present tense, between two people who were free to marry each other. However, in 1200 the Archbishop of Canterbury declared that marriages in his province should be solemnised before a priest and congregation. The calling of banns was instituted in 1215 and further rules and restrictions were gradually introduced. Ecclesiastical law concerning the validity of marriages was set out in the canons of 1604, which codified earlier church rules. These specified that marriages had to take place in the parish church of one of the spouses, after banns or after a valid marriage licence had been issued. The church also required people under the age of 21 to obtain the consent of their parents or guardians in order to marry. Marriages should have been celebrated during the canonical hours of 8 a.m. to noon and not during the closed seasons, which were (a) from Advent to the Octave of Epiphany, (b) from Septuagesima to the Octave of Easter, and (c) from Rogation Sunday to Trinity Sunday. If these canons were not complied with, the marriage was deemed invalid by the church.

However, until Hardwicke's Marriage Act of 1753, a marriage was valid under English common law if each spouse had merely expressed (to the other) an unconditional consent to the union. Vows could be exchanged by a boy as young as 14 and a girl as young as 12. This was a binding contract that courts would enforce. No particular words were necessary. There was no need for a clergyman to perform a ceremony or for witnesses to be present (although vows were commonly exchanged in the presence of witnesses, to avoid disputes in the future over whether or not a marriage contract had been entered into). Furthermore, despite the legal validity of marriage contracts without a church ceremony, most people married in church because that is what their church desired, and what their family and friends expected. It was only from 1754 that Hardwicke's Marriage Act required most marriages to be in accordance with the canons of the church in order to be valid under English law. Before 1754 many marriages were valid under English common law but did not comply with ecclesiastical law, and are known as irregular or clandestine marriages. Benton (360) and Outhwaite (376) are fascinating studies of irregular and clandestine marriages. Stone (379) is a detailed study of marriage and divorce from 1530 to 1987. Two companion volumes of source material, *Uncertain Unions* and *Broken Lives*, have also been published together in Stone (378).

Marriages that took place away from the home parishes of the spouses (but after banns or licence) are usually termed irregular, as are those marriages that took place in the home parish of one of the spouses, but without banns or licence. Marriages were also irregular if they were performed by clergy at an improper time. The term clandestine is usually applied to irregular weddings that also had an element of secrecy about them (that is, marriages away from the parties' homes and without either banns or a valid marriage licence). Secrecy might be desirable for many reasons. A man might be marrying an heiress without her parents' consent, but a clandestine ceremony allowed the couple to present a *fait accompli*. Apprentices might wish to marry before the expiry of their seven-year term (# chapter 22) and so married clandestinely in order to keep secret the breach of their articles. Many widows were left money by their husbands on condition that they did not remarry. A clandestine ceremony allowed widows to obtain a new husband yet keep their first husband's money. Men who had deserted their wife and who were remarrying bigamously preferred a clandestine ceremony to a public one (even if they were miles from home). A couple within the prohibited degrees could also marry by a clandestine ceremony with little fear of detection. Clandestine marriages could take place almost immediately. This appealed to sailors or soldiers going abroad or to pregnant women (or to anyone in an advanced state of drunkenness or passion).

Many clergymen were willing to conduct irregular or clandestine ceremonies for a suitable fee. The church authorities sometimes took action in the church courts against priests who ignored the canons when conducting ceremonies or granting licences. However, court action was sporadic (and half-hearted) compared to the extent of abuses, and couples could easily obtain marriage licences from many surrogates without complying with the rules as to residence in the parish in which they were to marry. Stone (379) notes that, in 1752, there were 31 surrogates of the Bishop of Worcester (within an area approximating to the county of Worcestershire) who had authority to issue marriage licences. Many surrogates were more interested in the fees payable to them for issuing licences than in the truth of applicants' statements as to their residence or age.

The number of irregular and clandestine marriages was enormous and certain churches were important centres of the trade. The Tower of London's chapel was a clandestine marriage centre as early as 1630 and almost half of all London weddings took place at Holy Trinity Minories or at St James Duke's Place between 1676 and 1683. In the 1740s, over half of all London weddings took place in the environs of the Fleet Prison, with many others conducted at May Fair Chapel. Other clandestine centres in London included St Pancras, St Botolph Aldgate, St Katherine by the Tower and St Dunstan, Stepney. Some of the clandestine marriage centres arose from ancient privileges. For example, the incumbents of St James Duke's Place claimed to be exempt from control of the church authorities (and so able to marry whomever they wished) because the Lord Mayor and citizens of London were the Lords of the manor and had the right to appoint the incumbent. Holy Trinity Minories was originally the chapel of Crown land at Aldgate in London that had been taken from the Priory of Holy Trinity. The parishioners, rather than church officials, had the right to appoint the incumbent and he could therefore ignore the church canons (and concentrate on raising income from issuing licences and conducting weddings).

The Marriage Duty Acts of 1694 and 1695 required that places "pretending to be exempt from the visitation of the bishop of the diocese" (that is, the centres of the irregular and clandestine marriage trade) should only conduct marriages after the calling of banns or the obtaining of a licence. A clergyman who ignored this requirement could be fined £100. However, the incumbents of many London marriage centres were then given the right by the Bishop of London to issue (as his surrogates) the marriage licences required by the couples. In other cases licences were obtained by couples from the offices of other church officials in London (such as the Vicar-General or Faculty Office of the Archbishop of Canterbury), even though such licences were not required if both spouses lived in the Diocese of London. An unforeseen result of the Marriage Duty Acts was that other marriage centres also became popular, because the acts appeared to validate a marriage that took place away from the couple's home parishes so long as a marriage licence was obtained (and licences were easy to obtain). Furthermore, while the £100 fine caused a decline in clandestine or irregular marriages at some churches, there were many clergymen who were not perturbed by a fine (such as those already imprisoned for debt). The Fleet Prison (considered below) therefore became important from this time as a clandestine marriage centre. The Revd Alexander Keith also ignored the legislation. His May Fair Chapel was built in 1729, close to the parish church of St George Hanover Square. He conducted hundreds of irregular marriages at the chapel until he was excommunicated in 1742 and imprisoned in the Fleet (where he died in 1758). However, Keith had also established a small chapel in a house in Mayfair and appointed curates who continued to conduct marriages on his behalf until 1754.

Although the majority of marriages at London marriage centres were of couples from London (or from counties close to London), many of the spouses came from other parts of Britain. Some examples from the Fleet registers are noted below, and the registers of Keith's May Fair Chapel in Armytage (358) include the following entries:

27 Jan 1746   John Butler of Woburn, and Lydia Lovelace of Great Marlow, Buckinghamshire

8 Nov 1748   Joseph Stokes of St Mary Steps, Exeter and Margaret Wrightson of East Putford, Devon

19 May 1751   George Myon and Bridget Young of Gloucester

Irregular marriage was not limited to London. Many parish registers include a high proportion of marriages taking place by licence, often of couples who were not resident in the parish. These parishes were often near the seat of a bishop (or surrogate) who could issue marriage licences. Elusive marriages may therefore be found at, or near, these centres. As examples, Benton (360) draws attention to St Nicholas (in Rochester in Kent), to Holy Trinity (in Stratford-upon-Avon) and to the parish churches in the city of Oxford. The ease with which couples could arrange an irregular or clandestine ceremony can make it very difficult to find a pre-1754 marriage, even in rural areas. Stone (379) notes that from 1661 to 1690 at Colyton in Devon, the proportion of "missing" marriages is 68 per cent (that is, baptisms of children but with no marriage of the parents being recorded in the parish register). Stone also notes the effect of an incumbent being appointed as a surrogate. In the parish of Fledborough in Nottinghamshire, only 11 marriages took place between 1712 and 1730. The incumbent became a surrogate in 1730 and then issued many licences. Between 1730 and 1754 there were 490 marriages in the parish, only 15 of those couples residing in the village.

Most irregular or clandestine marriages appear in the registers of the church or chapel in which they took place and may be found in the same manner as regular marriages. It may be more difficult to find a marriage if it took place at one of the major centres, such as the Fleet, St James Duke's Place or Holy Trinity Minories. Many registers of clandestine marriages no longer survive (and many such marriages were not recorded). Some registers of Holy Trinity Minories (most entries from 1649–58 and 1663–76) are missing as are the registers of St James Duke's Place for 1668–79. Perhaps 30,000 weddings took place at these churches in these periods alone. Many Fleet registers are also missing. Benton (360) lists the location (and any transcripts and indexes) of the surviving registers up to 1754 of the more important marriage centres in London. The registers for St Pancras, St James Duke's Place, St Dunstan Stepney, St Benet Paul's Wharf, St Gregory by St Paul, Holy Trinity Minories, St Katherine by the Tower, St Botolph Aldgate and St Mary Magdalen are at Guildhall Library or LMA (and many of these marriages are included in Boyd's marriage index). The East of London FHS has published microfiche indexes to the registers of Holy Trinity Minories from 1676 to 1754. The surviving registers from 1664 to 1837 for St James Duke's Place have been published by Phillimore. TNA at Kew holds the surviving Fleet marriage registers in series RG 7 (and piece PROB 18/50), except for one register held at the Bodleian Library. Most of the registers for the King's Bench Prison and the Mint at Southwark have been lost, but some are at TNA (also in RG 7). The surviving marriage registers of Keith's May Fair Chapel (held at the church of St George Hanover Square and at TNA in RG 7) have been published in Armytage (358) and are included in Boyd's marriage index.

THE FLEET REGISTERS

The Fleet prison was established in the 12th century and by the 17th century it was used to hold debtors or those in contempt of court. It became the most well known centre for clandestine marriages. As a prison, the Fleet was (or was claimed to be) outside the jurisdiction of the church. Anyone could visit the prison and the inmates usually included some clergy who were willing to marry anyone in the prison chapel for a fee. The prison wardens took a share of the profit.

The earliest documentary evidence of a marriage in the Fleet's chapel is for a ceremony in 1613 but marriages undoubtedly took place earlier. The registers of the Fleet only commence in the late 17th century, so the records of many early marriages are missing. The number of marriages in the chapel gradually increased and the government tried to end this abuse. A statute of 1711 imposed fines on prison keepers for allowing marriages (without banns or licence) to take place in prison chapels. However, the clandestine marriage trade simply moved elsewhere. There were too many debtors for the Fleet prison to hold and many were permitted to reside in the area outside the prison known as the Rules or Liberties of the Fleet (a congested, lawless area bounded by Ludgate Hill, Farringdon Street, Old Bailey and Fleet Lane). Many indebted clergy lived in the Rules and many other disgraced or crooked clergymen (or charlatans pretending to be clergy) sheltered there, relatively safe from the authorities. Chapels were set up just outside the walls of the Fleet, often in taverns, and the marriage trade continued. Burn (361) provides short biographies of the ministers who performed wedding ceremonies at the Fleet or in the Rules, and also of some men who kept the marriage houses and taverns or who kept registers of the marriages conducted there. Fleet marriages are also reviewed in articles in *Family Tree Magazine* (March and April 2000).

During the 1740s up to 6,600 marriages a year were taking place in the Fleet, out of an annual average of about 47,000 marriages in England. Many different types of people (both rich and poor) married in the Fleet (farmers, mariners, gentlemen, craftsmen, labourers and soldiers). It was not merely a marriage centre for criminals and the poor. The entries in the registers and notebooks were in similar form to parish registers as can be seen from illustration 65, a page from the register in piece RG 7/116, with entries from 1 to 3 May 1731. Indeed, many Fleet registers are superior to pre-1754 parish registers, since many entries note the parish of each spouse and the man's occupation. In illustration 65, three grooms are cordwainers, one a skinner, one a sailor and one a drayman (the other was noted as a gentleman). Most Fleet marriages (as at other London marriage centres) were of couples living in London or nearby counties, but many entries concern people from all over England (and sometimes the rest of Britain). Most of the spouses in illustration 65 are noted as being from London or Middlesex parishes, but Thomas Goodman was from Greenwich in Kent and John Rouse was from Cambridge. Piece RG 7/98 is a Fleet register with entries from 1726–51. It includes these entries from December 1726:

11th. George Pope, weaver of Crediton in Devonshire & Temperance Courtenay of Colebrook in Devonshire; batchelor and spinster
14th. Robert Hutson, seafaring man of Scarborough, Yorkshire & Mary O'Brian, widow

Unlike Anglican parishes (or other clandestine centres), there were many ministers conducting ceremonies at the Fleet at any time. Stone (379) estimates that there were between 70 and 100 ministers working in the Fleet between 1700 and 1753. There were also many clerks who made money by recording the ceremonies. Therefore, although many of the Fleet records have been

May 1731 2313

1 James Hinchley of St Martins in the Fields Cordwainer Bat & Mercy Smith of the same Spins — W.

2 John Cox Cordwainer & Ann Thomas both of St Andrews Holborn Bat & Wid — W.

2 Thomas Bloome Gent & Anna Mariah Griffitts both of St Mary yₑ Born Bat & Spins — W.

2 John Hatterway of St Gyles's Cripplegate Drayman Bat & Mary Clifford of the same Wid — W.

2 William Hitchcock Skinner & Katharine Phipps both of St Johns Westmr Bat & Spins — W.

2 Thomas Goodman of Greenwich in Kent Sayler Bat & Patience Bird of St Clements Dean Wid — W.

3 John Rouse of Great St Marys Cambridge Cordwainer Bat & Francis Barnsley of St Gyles's Cripplegate Spins W.

65. A page from a Fleet marriage register, 1731 (TNA, piece RG 7/116)

lost, about 290 registers and about 540 notebooks survive, recording approximately 250,000 marriages. The registers and notebooks overlap not only in time, but some marriages appear in more than one register or notebook. Most of the Fleet registers remain untranscribed, unindexed and underused, but there are some transcripts and indexes (and a few registers have their own indexes). TNA and SoG hold an indexed transcript, by Hale (368), to about 6,700 Fleet marriages of people from Sussex, south-west Kent or south-east Surrey. Three volumes by Herber (369) contain indexed transcripts of the Fleet registers and notebooks in RG 7/3, 44, 87, 95, 118, 162, 163, 190, 293, 294, 403 and 563, recording about 3,500 marriages and further volumes are being prepared. Certain entries from the Fleet registers are also included in Burn (361). The Fleet registers must be used with caution. A few entries are forgeries (another good source of income for the clergy and clerks of the Fleet). Some marriages were backdated so that, for example, a marriage would pre-date a child's birth. Some entries were wholly fictitious but created so that one person (usually poor), could claim to have married another person (perhaps a wealthy heiress). Some entries were later erased or altered, perhaps after payment from the distressed parents of an heiress who had made a hasty marriage to a fortune-seeker, or of the eldest son of a wealthy family who had married an "unsuitable" girl. Details of certain forgeries are contained in Outhwaite (376) and Lloyd (371).

Most marriage certificates supplied by Fleet ministers or clerks to the couples have been lost but some are in Admiralty records at TNA and family papers at CROs. Illustration 66 is an example from Admiralty records, recording a marriage on 24 March 1738/9 by the minister Thomas Rider of a sailor, Charles Rice to a widow, Elizabeth Gray of St Botolph Bishopsgate. The Fleet ministers often used printed forms, bearing the royal coat of arms, for the certificates that they issued. They also rarely referred to the Fleet as the place of marriage, preferring to specify the parish in which the marriage house was located, in this case St Sepulchres.

THE END OF CLANDESTINE MARRIAGES

The clandestine and irregular marriage trade was brought to an end by Hardwicke's Marriage Act. The act required all marriages (except Jewish or Quaker ceremonies) to take place in the parish church of one of the spouses, during canonical hours, after banns or with a licence (in which case one of the spouses had to have resided in the parish for four weeks). The act required marriage registers to be kept, with signatures or marks of the parties and witnesses. Marriages that did not comply with these provisions were void and ministers conducting such marriages were guilty of a felony and liable to transportation. Some clandestine marriages still took place. The incumbent of the Savoy Chapel in London claimed to be exempt from Hardwicke's Act and conducted irregular marriages for over 1,500 couples in 1754 and 1755. He was convicted and sentenced to transportation.

The legal uncertainties surrounding marriage, particularly the validity of marriage contracts, resulted in many court cases (# chapter 24). Legal disputes about marriage were generally dealt with by the church courts until the mid-19th century. However, from the late 17th century the civil courts heard an increasing number of actions for breach of promise and we shall see below that, from about the same time, a cuckolded husband was able to sue his wife's lover for damages (usually in the Court of King's Bench) for what was known as "criminal conversation". The Court of Common Pleas also heard some matrimonial cases, such as widows' claims for dower from their deceased husbands' estates.

66. *A marriage certificate from the Fleet, 1738/9 (TNA, ADM 106/3026)*

BORDER MARRIAGES

Another important area for irregular or clandestine marriages was near the border between England and Scotland. Until 1949 the only formality required by Scottish law for a valid marriage was that mutual declarations of consent were made by the parties before witnesses. Marriage centres such as Gretna Green and Lamberton Toll in Scotland were therefore a convenient destination for eloping English couples. After March 1754 English couples could still go to Scotland or the Channel Islands, to which Hardwicke's Act did not apply. The use of Gretna Green by English couples was substantial until 1856, when such marriages were declared invalid under English law unless the couple had been resident in Scotland for three weeks. Irregular marriages in Scotland are reviewed in volume 12 of the *NIPR* (151) and an interesting account of irregular border marriages, with details of those conducting ceremonies and some couples marrying there, was written by M. Fowle Smith under the pseudonym "Claverhouse" (363). Some registers and other records from Gretna Green are held by IHGS. Other surviving registers of irregular border marriages (and their location) are listed in an index by R. Nicholson available from the National Archives of Scotland (# chapter 29) or on its web site.

MARRIAGE SETTLEMENTS

Members of wealthy families often entered into marriage settlements. A father might transfer land or personal property to his son (or to his daughter and her husband) to ensure that they had sufficient income. Settlement deeds provide information about a family's property as well as genealogical information. Property records are considered further in chapter 27, but many deeds of settlement have survived in family archives, often deposited at CROs. Many deeds are also held by the British Library manuscripts department and transcripts of some of these were included in articles by G.W. Watson in volumes 33 to 37 of the journal *The Genealogist* (# chapter 11). Many marriage settlements were also collected by F.A. Crisp and abstracts are in volume XI of *Fragmenta Genealogica* by Crisp (365). The following is a typical example:

Indenture made 30 April 1703 between
(1) William Richards of Fressingfield, co. Suffolk, gent and his son Daniel Richards of Mendham, and (2) George Reed of Sutton, co. Suffolk, gent and Mary Reed, spinster, his daughter; In consideration of the intended marriage of Daniel Richards and Mary Reed; William Richards grants unto George Reed [property described] in Wetheringsett, co. Suffolk to the use [in trust for] the said Daniel and Mary and their issue. . . .

BREAKDOWN OF MARRIAGE

It is estimated that one-third of marriages in England now end in divorce. However, divorce was difficult to obtain (and very expensive) until this century. Indeed, until 1857, divorce as we understand it (giving each party the right to remarry) could only be obtained by a private act of Parliament. Copies of these acts are held at the House of Lords Record Office. A bill had to pass through the House of Lords (a committee of which heard the evidence) and then through the House of Commons. By 1857 there had been only 318 such divorces. Adultery had to be proved and a husband often took separate proceedings in the civil courts for damages against the wife's lover, for trespass and criminal conversation. Divorce was particularly difficult for women to obtain (there were only four successful petitions before 1857).

Until 1857 only the ecclesiastical courts had jurisdiction to assist spouses who could not use the parliamentary procedure. The church courts could annul a marriage (by a decree of nullity), declaring that the marriage had never been valid. This allowed one or both spouses to marry again. A common ground of these applications was that one of the spouses had entered into a prior contract of marriage with a third party (thus making the second marriage bigamous). Other grounds were non-consummation, lunacy or that the marriage had been incestuous. From 1754 another ground for applications was that one or both spouses had been under 21 at the time of the marriage and that parental consent had not been given. Before 1857 the church courts could also grant a decree of separation *a mensa et thoro* (from bed and board). This decree did not allow the parties to remarry, but it released them from the obligation to cohabit as man and wife. A spouse had to prove that the other had been guilty of adultery or life-threatening cruelty. Even by the 1840s only about 40 cases of separation or annulment came before the church courts of England each year.

The most common remedy for an unhappy marriage was desertion by one party or separation by agreement. However, the church did not recognise the right of a spouse to leave the other. In particular, if a husband deserted, his wife and children were likely to become dependent on parish relief. The church courts therefore prosecuted many deserting husbands (and sometimes a wife). However, in most cases, a deserting husband was soon far away and starting a new life (often in the army or navy). Remarriage constituted the offence of bigamy (punishable as a felony by civil courts), but it happened anyway. In some cases, if a spouse left home and was not heard of for seven years, he or she was presumed dead and the other spouse could remarry (at least church courts in practice rarely prosecuted for bigamy after a seven-year absence).

Horstman (370) is a detailed study of separation and divorce proceedings from 1670 to 1900. Detailed information is also provided by Stone (379) and examples of matrimonial disputes from the ecclesiastical courts are included in Cox (364). The procedure and records of the church courts are considered further in chapter 24. However, there was one church court of particular importance for matrimonial affairs. As noted in chapter 12 (in respect of probate disputes), appeals from a church court of first instance were made, in the province of Canterbury, to the Court of Arches. The records of this court survive from about 1660 (there are only a few earlier records) at Lambeth Palace Library. Houston (941) is an index to cases heard by the court from 1660 to 1913, listing about 10,400 actions, with the parties' names and the subject of the dispute. About 1,400 of the cases concerned separation, nullity or other matrimonial claims. Thus Ellen Charnock of London took separation proceedings against her husband John Charnock because of his cruelty. The court gave judgment in 1673 and Houston notes the volume and folio references to the court's act books, the parties' pleadings and the depositions of witnesses. The process books of the court include copies of the orders made in the court of first instance (and much of the evidence). Some cases in the Court of Arches are described in detail in Stone (378), but he also refers to records from the lower church courts and to contemporary pamphlets about the cases, thus providing a fascinating account of marriage (and marriage breakdown), as well as providing a useful review of court procedures in matrimonial disputes.

Another method of separation, described in Stone (379), was the custom of wife-selling. Some husbands sold their wives in public (usually in markets), believing this to be a legal method of bringing a marriage (and its rights and obligations) to an end. Such transactions (usually involving a sale to the wife's lover) were rare but are recorded as taking place as late as 1900. The practice had no legal basis and was often a collusive device (between a husband, wife and her lover) for a separation, which (because of the publicity) protected a husband from future liability for his wife's debts and protected a purchaser from a later action by the husband for damages for criminal conversation. Menefee (372) is a detailed study of wife-selling, listing 387 cases of sales (with references to source material) from the 16th century up to about 1900, including many that are recorded in church court proceedings.

DIVORCE

From 1 January 1858 a divorce could be granted by the new civil Court for Divorce and Matrimonial Causes. Husbands could obtain divorce because of a wife's adultery. However, until 1925, a wife had to prove not only her husband's adultery but also that the adultery had been aggravated by his cruelty or certain other offences. Divorce actions were commenced by a petition and, if successful, resulted in a decree absolute that brought the marriage to an end. The new court sat in London. It was merged into the Probate, Divorce and Admiralty Division of the Supreme Court of Judicature in 1873 (# chapter 24) and, without Admiralty cases, became the Family Division in 1970. Divorce petitions could also be heard at county assizes (# chapter 25) and, from 1873, by the Supreme Court's District Registries around the country.

In 1937, the grounds for divorce were extended to include adultery, cruelty, desertion by one party of the other for three years, insanity (at the time of marriage) and refusal by one party to consummate the marriage. The availability of civil divorce reduced the need to use other separation procedures and there were about 150 divorces a year by 1860 (and about 800 a year by 1914). The number of divorces then increased dramatically (mainly as a result of further legislation making divorce more easily obtainable). By 1939 there were about 8,000 divorces each year (and over 20,000 a year by 1950). The Principal Registry of the Family Division at First Avenue House in London (# chapter 12) keeps a record of successful divorce actions. It has indexed registers of decrees nisi and absolute granted in England and Wales since 1858. The records are closed to the public but officials conduct searches on receipt of a fee and completed application form, available at the registry.

Series J 78 at TNA contains 42 volumes of indexes to the parties in divorce petitions since 1858, whether or not a case succeeded. The indexes can also be seen on microfilm at the FRC and were reviewed by A. Camp in *Family Tree Magazine* (February 2002). TNA also holds files for divorce actions of 1858–1927, whether or not they succeeded, in series J 77 at Kew. Series J 77 also includes files for the divorce actions of 1928–37 that were dealt with by the Principal Registry in London. All these are included in the J 78 indexes. The district registry case files of 1928–37 were destroyed and are not included in the J 78 indexes (so the only surviving documents for these cases are the decrees at the Principal Registry). Most files of divorce actions since 1938 have been destroyed but a few sample cases from 1938–54 are in series J 77 (and further sample cases up to the 1960s will soon be added). Principal Registry cases of 1938–59 are included in the J 78 indexes. The closed Principal Registry and TNA files may be examined only if permission is obtained from the Principal Registry.

Information about marital breakdown may also be obtained from magistrates courts' records (# chapter 25), generally held at CROs. From 1878, if a man was convicted of a serious assault on his wife, she could apply to a magistrate for a separation and maintenance order. From 1886, husbands who deserted their wives and failed to support their children could also be ordered to pay a weekly sum by way of maintenance. Bevan (239) notes that 10,000 orders were being made each year by 1900.

MEDIA SOURCES

Newspapers (# chapter 17) reported many separation and divorce actions (and suits for criminal conversation) and may provide more information about a couple's family or the facts and allegations of a case. Newspapers have always reported scandalous and titillating matters, so that criminal conversation trials (or any cases involving allegations of adultery) became increasingly common in newspapers and journals in the late 18th and 19th centuries. *The Times* carried reports of the progress in Parliament of private bills requesting divorce. It also published reports of divorce cases in the civil courts from 1858. Some reports were brief, as in the case of Weare v. Weare and Harvey reported in *The Times* of 15 May 1862:

> The marriage took place in 1846; cohabitation continued until last year and there were seven children. The petitioner was a carpenter at Pimlico. In September last, Mrs Weare went to Gravesend and lived there with an engineer named Harvey, who had formerly

lodged at her husband's home. Her husband discovered her misconduct and separated from her. Decree nisi granted with costs against the co-respondent.

Some reports were much longer, and included details of the alleged adultery, the couple's life and the names of witnesses to the events that evidenced the matrimonial breakdown. These cases are included in the indexes to *The Times* (# chapter 17). A separate index to the divorce cases or private bills that were reported in *The Times* from 1788 to 1910 (indexing the names of the spouses and any co-respondent who was named for adultery) has been produced by About Archives on microfiche (355) and in book form. Copies are at the SoG and Guildhall Library.

CHAPTER 15

MAPS, LAND REGISTRATION AND PROPERTY RECORDS

MAPS

The IHGS maps of civil registration districts, parishes and probate jurisdictions have already been noted. Other maps are also invaluable research aids. Hindle (389) is an excellent study of the history of maps in England and Wales, including town plans, county, estate, enclosure, transport and tithe maps, and the Ordnance Survey maps of the 19th and 20th centuries. Hindle provides detailed bibliographies of published maps and of published catalogues of the maps held in archives. Wallis (407) contains essays by various authors on the types of maps available for Britain before 1900 (each essay having a useful bibliography).

If your ancestors lived in a city, a street map of that city will be essential. If they lived in a small village or town, a map of the area should be obtained, since this will show your ancestors' village, its communications and the nearest towns and cities. In particular, you should obtain copies of maps of towns, cities or rural areas at the approximate date of the records that you are reviewing, for example, street maps of towns or cities at the time of each census. This is because many places have changed dramatically over the years. Some of my ancestors were farm labourers in Upminster, Hornchurch and Walthamstow in Essex in the period around 1800. Illustration 68 shows an extract of a 1794 map of London and the Thames, covering the district of those villages. Walthamstow was not large enough to be mentioned and Hornchurch was a village surrounded by countryside. Deptford and Greenwich appear far from London and even places such as Stepney, Islington and Hackney were at the edge of London's urban area. Maps such as this are therefore essential in order to place your ancestors in their true historical setting.

Maps are held at TNA, CROs and libraries. Thus LMA has over 10,000 maps of London from the 16th to 20th centuries. Maps are listed in archives' catalogues or in published lists, such as that for Essex Record Office by Emmison (385). Wallis (407) provides a summary of the map collections of over 360 archives in England, Wales, Scotland and Ireland, including CROs, city archives, university and college libraries and some business archives. For example, the libraries of Oxford and Cambridge colleges hold many useful maps, dealing particularly with the large estates that the colleges once owned.

The enormous collections of maps at TNA, and the catalogues or finding aids for those maps, were noted in chapter 11. Many of these maps remain in the series of documents to which the maps or plans were originally annexed. TNA domestic records leaflet 36 contains a brief description of the series that consist largely or entirely of maps. A few examples are the Admiralty charts (in series ADM 1), estate surveys and enclosure awards relating to property of

Greenwich Hospital (ADM 79), enclosure awards (enrolled on the Close Rolls in C 54), tithe files and maps (series IR 18, 29 and 30), Ordnance Survey plans and maps (department codes OS and ZOS) and about 15,000 First World War plans or maps (series WO 153). These examples illustrate the wide range of maps and plans available. The British Library's collection of maps and the available catalogues were also noted in chapter 11. For example, the library has the most complete collection of original Ordnance Survey maps, but also many topographical maps, fire insurance plans (reviewed below) and about 1,000 estate maps (# chapter 27).

County maps

The earliest useful maps began to appear in Elizabethan times, and they depict counties. They show the location of towns, large villages, forests (and sometimes roads) and reveal old place names. Thus a 1594 map of Surrey shows Rotherhithe as Rodruth. Harley (388) describes the history and development of county maps. The most famous of the early county map-makers were John Speed and Christopher Saxton. Saxton's county maps of England and Wales of the late 16th century are reproduced in Ravenhill (398). More detailed county maps began to appear in the 18th and early 19th centuries. For example, Emanuel Bowen produced a series of county maps around 1760 and John and Christopher Greenwood published maps of 38 counties, at a scale of one inch to the mile, between 1817 and 1834. Another series of English county maps, by Thomas Moule, were published in 1830 and have been reproduced in Moule (396). Other old county maps have also been reproduced, such as Donn's 1765 map of Devon, which has been reprinted in Ravenhill (399). Lists of many county maps are provided by Hindle (389) and West (462). Thus Hindle notes that large scale maps of Bedfordshire were produced by Gordon (in 1736), Jefferys (1765), Greenwood (1826) and Bryant (1826). There are a number of other bibliographies and catalogues of county maps, many of them listed in Harley (388) and Hindle (389).

Town plans

If your ancestors lived in towns or cities, street maps are especially useful. In some places the layout of streets has changed relatively little in the last two centuries, but in many other places, the present layout of streets would be unrecognisable to an 18th- or 19th-century ancestor. Many streets, particularly small alleys, have disappeared under urban renewal schemes or after the Blitz in places such as London, Plymouth or Coventry. Old street maps are also useful because they feature the old names of streets. They also show the contemporary local public buildings and communications. An 1820 plan of Nottingham shows 4 parish churches, 17 chapels, 3 workhouses, 10 schools, 15 almshouses or hospitals, a lunatic asylum, the house of correction, and the town and county halls (both of which had gaols). It is very helpful to know of the existence (and location) of these buildings.

Ordnance Survey maps (considered below) date from the 19th century and include many detailed town plans. However, town plans were first produced in the late 16th century and many (particularly of London) were being produced by the 18th century. The production of urban plans grew rapidly in the early 19th century when many were produced for provincial towns and cities, especially the expanding northern industrial towns such as Manchester. Care must be exercised in using any town plan that was commercially produced. Some plans incorporated proposed redevelopments as though they had been completed, whereas they might not have been undertaken as shown on the plan (or even at all). Hindle (389) provides a useful analysis of town

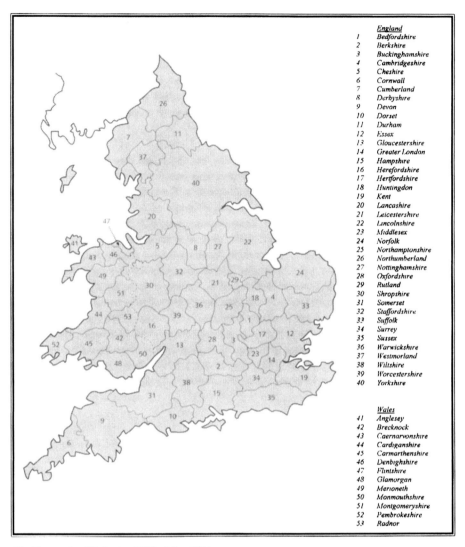

England	
1	Bedfordshire
2	Berkshire
3	Buckinghamshire
4	Cambridgeshire
5	Cheshire
6	Cornwall
7	Cumberland
8	Derbyshire
9	Devon
10	Dorset
11	Durham
12	Essex
13	Gloucestershire
14	Greater London
15	Hampshire
16	Herefordshire
17	Hertfordshire
18	Huntingdon
19	Kent
20	Lancashire
21	Leicestershire
22	Lincolnshire
23	Middlesex
24	Norfolk
25	Northamptonshire
26	Northumberland
27	Nottinghamshire
28	Oxfordshire
29	Rutland
30	Shropshire
31	Somerset
32	Staffordshire
33	Suffolk
34	Surrey
35	Sussex
36	Warwickshire
37	Westmorland
38	Wiltshire
39	Worcestershire
40	Yorkshire

Wales	
41	Anglesey
42	Brecknock
43	Caernarvonshire
44	Cardiganshire
45	Carmarthenshire
46	Denbighshire
47	Flintshire
48	Glamorgan
49	Merioneth
50	Monmouthshire
51	Montgomeryshire
52	Pembrokeshire
53	Radnor

67. The counties of England and Wales before 1974

plans, with examples and bibliographies. A list of town plans from about 1600 to 1900 (although incomplete), including Ordnance Survey and fire insurance plans, is provided by West (463). There are detailed listings of plans for some towns and cities. Hindle (389) catalogues the published lists of plans of Bristol, Chichester, Manchester, Leeds, Norwich, Portsmouth and Southampton. Many plans of London were published, some of which contained great detail. London plans, for the periods 1553–1850 and 1851–1900, are catalogued in chronological order by Howgego (391) and Hyde (392) respectively. Each work lists over 400 maps and plans, the various editions of each and the archives holding copies, principally Guildhall Library, LMA and

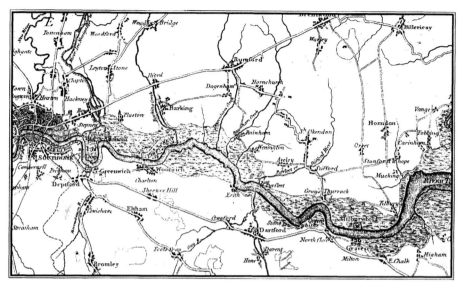

68. Map of London and the Thames, from Boydell's History of the River Thames, 1794

the British Library. In addition, there are many maps of parishes, wards or other areas within London. These are usually well catalogued at the relevant archives. Hyde (392) also analyses the different types of London plans, including those showing poverty in different areas of London.

The most famous maps illustrating poverty in Britain were those produced by Charles Booth's enquiry into the condition of the London working class. The enquiry of Booth and his investigators began in 1886 and culminated in the publication in 1903 of *Life and Labour of the London Poor* in 17 volumes with 12 colour-coded street maps. The seven codes ran from yellow ("Upper-middle and upper classes. Wealthy") down to dark blue ("Very poor, casual. Chronic want") and black ("Lowest class. Vicious, semi-criminal"). You can assess the type of neighbourhood in which your London ancestors lived from these important maps, which have been reprinted by the London Topographical Society. The London School of Economics holds 449 of the survey notebooks, which were completed by investigators as they walked the streets and interviewed local residents. The notebooks record the conditions in which families lived but note only a few peoples' names. They can be viewed, by appointment, at the Archives Department, London School of Economics, 10 Portugal Street, London WC2A 2HD (telephone 020 7955 7223). The maps and a few notebooks can be seen on the Charles Booth Online Archive, which is part of the LSE web site.

Books that reproduce collections of maps and plans for particular cities or areas may include many maps that are difficult to find in archives, or which are useful to have at hand during your research. Examples of these collections are Barker & Jackson (384) on London maps and Stuart (403) on Plymouth maps before 1800. Many individual town and city maps have also been reprinted. During my investigations in London, I have found *The A to Z of Victorian London* (394) particularly useful. This is a reprint by Harry Margary of an atlas of London and its suburbs that was originally published by G.W. Bacon in 1888. In the same series is *The A to Z of Regency*

London (395), which reproduces a map of London prepared by Horwood (revised to 1813 by Faden). Illustration 69 shows part of this map depicting part of Clerkenwell, including Queen Street, Compton Street, Goswell Street and Hooper Street, where some of my ancestors lived and worked from about 1830 to 1860. Margary has also reprinted some earlier London maps: *The A to Z of Elizabethan London* reprints a 1562 map of London and *The A to Z of Georgian London* reprints Rocque's 1746 plan of the City of London, Westminster and Southwark.

Parochial Assessment Maps

A parish levied rates to finance its expenditure on matters such as poor relief (# chapter 18). Properties were assessed for a rate, but usually by parish officials rather than surveyors, so the rateable values were rarely uniform. Some parish maps were prepared in the late 18th and early 19th centuries to assist the parish officials in ensuring that properties were not omitted from the assessments. These parochial assessment maps cover both urban and rural parishes, but they are most useful for towns and cities because rural areas are generally well covered by tithe maps (see below). A statute of 1834 established Boards of Guardians and a central Poor Law Commission in order to administer the relief of the poor. Parish officials then levied poor rates in the parishes on behalf of the Guardians. The Parochial Assessments Act of 1836 required that all rates should be levied on the net annual value of a property and authorised the Poor Law Commissioners to carry out parish surveys and prepare valuations to assist the assessments. Consequently, at about the same time as tithe maps were being created, further parochial assessment maps were produced. Many of these dealt with urban areas (rarely covered by tithe maps) and the maps were accompanied by reference books containing the valuations. A useful article on these maps, by R. Hyde, appears in the journal *Guildhall Studies in London History* of April 1976 (380). By 1843 valuations and surveys had been carried out in about 4,000 parishes. Although the standard of some maps was not high, others were extremely detailed, for example those of City of London parishes. Most of the maps survive in CROs, Guildhall Library or local studies libraries.

The Ordnance Survey

The Pathfinder series of modern Ordnance Survey maps of Britain (at a scale of 2½ inches to the mile) are particularly useful for rural areas, showing the names and position of farms (and some of these farm names have remained the same for centuries). However, because towns, roads and the countryside have changed so much over the period that you will be researching, old Ordnance Survey maps should also be obtained. The British Library holds the best collection of Ordnance Survey maps. Its holdings of printed maps and plans are listed in *The British Museum Catalogue of Printed Maps, Charts and Plans* (published in 15 volumes in 1967). However, most of the maps or plans that genealogists require have been republished or are available at TNA, at CROs or local libraries, and their collections should be consulted first.

The first Ordnance Survey work (covering Kent) was published in 1801. The first series (the Old Series) of one inch to the mile maps (and revised versions) were published between 1805 and 1873. A complete set of the 110 sheets covering England, Wales and the Isle of Man is held at TNA (and many are in CROs). The later versions of this series have been reprinted on 97 sheets (with railways added) by David & Charles of Brunel House, Forde Close, Newton Abbot, Devon TQ12 2DW. Illustration 70 is an extract from sheet 83, showing Crediton in Devon and, to the north, the village of Sandford, where many of my ancestors lived between 1600 and 1870. The earliest versions of the first series have also been published in book form, in eight volumes by Margary (381).

69. Extract from Horwood's map of London, revised to 1813 by Faden

70. *Extract from the first edition of an Ordnance Survey map*

As Britain was changing rapidly, survey work began around 1840 for a new edition of one inch Ordnance Survey maps, divided into 360 sheets, although publication only commenced in about 1870. TNA also holds a set of this series. Between 1903 and 1913 the Ordnance Survey published a third, updated, series of one inch maps, again on 360 sheets. Later editions were also produced and details of these are contained in Hindle (389). In addition to these one inch maps, maps of larger scale were also produced. Surveys commenced in 1840 for a series of maps at a scale of 6 inches to the mile. From 1853 there were further surveys for maps of the whole country at 25 inches to the mile (and 6 inch to the mile maps were then produced by reduction from these 25 inch maps). These large scale maps were produced for most of England and Wales by 1900 and there were some revised editions. Hindle (389) lists the publication dates of 6 inch and 25 inch maps for each county of England and Wales between 1854 and 1923.

The Ordnance Survey also produced town plans, some at scales of up to 126 inches to one mile (that is, 1:500). These are also reviewed by Hindle (389). Oliver (397) describes the history of the Ordnance Survey and the details (the types of boundaries, names, paths, churches, railways and other items) that were included on each scale of Ordnance Survey map. Oliver also provides a list of towns (all those mapped at 1:2,500 or larger, with a selection of those mapped at 1:10,560), stating the dates of surveys and the scales of maps available. The listing of counties contains details of all maps at 1:10,560 or larger, but also all pre-1841 maps. The Ordnance Survey maps for a particular area can usually be seen at CROs or other local archives. Illustration 71 is an extract from one of the Ordnance Survey 25 inch to the mile maps of London, held at Guildhall Library, covering an area just to the north and east of the Tower of London and the Royal Mint and showing part of St George in the East and Wapping. In the centre is the London & Blackwall Railway, which ran into Fenchurch Street station. Just to the south of the railway is Wellclose Square, from which ran Grace's Alley and Ship Alley. My g.g. grandfather Bernard Herber worked in Ship Alley at the time of the 1851 census and he had his own business at 7 Grace's Alley from about 1853 to 1864. Each house or building is marked and churches, schools, hospitals, public houses and many other buildings are also noted.

If you need a 19th-century town plan, you should first ascertain whether the town or city is covered by Godfrey's reprint of 19th-century Ordnance Survey maps. Alan Godfrey has reprinted over 1,000 Ordnance Survey maps of London and many other cities and towns (listed on the Alan Godfrey web site and available from bookshops and record offices). These include reprints of the 25 inch to the mile maps of most of London (but reduced to about 14 inches to the mile) at different time periods (for example Lower Clapton in 1868, 1894 and 1913). Other reprints by Godfrey cover towns and cities throughout Britain and include some larger scale Ordnance Survey maps, for example 13 plans of central London reproduced at 1:1,760 (about one yard to a mile). All these maps are especially useful when you are reviewing census records. It is often possible to mark on the map the exact buildings in which your ancestors lived, worked or prayed, by obtaining addresses and then, by careful analysis of the directories and census returns, applying those numbers to the marked buildings in the street.

Fire insurance plans
Early insurance records are considered in chapter 23. However, in order to assess potential liabilities, fire insurance companies commissioned the production of town plans from the 18th century. These plans are described in an essay by G. Rowley in Wallis (407) and many of them are held by the British and Guildhall libraries. The most important of these plans are those

71. *Extract from an Ordnance Survey map, showing part of St George in the East and the southern part of Whitechapel in 1873 (Guildhall Library)*

produced by Charles Goad. The British Library holds his initial series of 73 volumes, issued between 1885 and 1896. These include 21 volumes for London, but also plans of 37 other cities and towns, mostly at a scale of one inch to 40 feet. They specify the use of a property and (by codes) the number of storeys and the building materials. House numbers are often given (sometimes with schedules of occupiers). Later revisions of the plans are held in CROs.

Public utility maps and plans

Hindle (389) has a useful chapter on transport maps. From the 17th century many maps and plans were produced showing roads, canals (or schemes to build them) and, later, railways. The plans often provide details of the surrounding land and landowners. Schemes for roads, canals, docks or railways had to be authorised by private acts of Parliament. After 1792 the promoters of canal schemes had to submit detailed plans to Parliament showing the proposed works, usually with detailed notes about the affected land and landowners. This requirement was extended to other public utility schemes (and to railways in 1837). These plans may have been lodged at the House of Lords' Record Office and, from 1837, duplicates of scheme maps also had to be deposited with the Clerk of the Peace and so may be in Quarter Sessions' records (# chapter 25) in CROs. Many of these plans and documents are also held at TNA, the British Library or reference libraries.

Parishes were responsible from the 16th century for the upkeep of roads (# chapter 18). However, the failure of parishes to maintain roads (particularly important highways) led to the formation of turnpike trusts from about 1700. A local act of Parliament would authorise a trust to improve or build a road and then levy tolls from road users to pay for the construction and maintenance costs. Wright (408) is an illustrated guide to turnpike roads, including a map of the network of turnpikes in about 1750. There were about 15,000 miles of turnpike roads across the country by 1772 and about 22,000 miles by 1838. From 1835 parishes were authorised to combine in groups to establish Highway Boards, to upkeep roads more efficiently, and from this time the turnpike trusts were gradually replaced by these boards or by committees of the new civil local authorities. The records of many turnpike trusts and Highway Boards survive in CROs, including many maps, plans and agreements between parishes and local landowners.

Tithe maps and awards

Tithe apportionment maps were prepared for most parishes between 1838 and 1854. These maps are particularly useful for those studying the census records of 1841 and 1851, in building an accurate picture of places during that period. Tithe records may also provide information about the property in which your ancestors lived or the land that they worked upon. Tithes were originally a payment of one-tenth of the land's produce (every tenth cow or one-tenth of its milk or the corn produced in a field) to a monastery, or later to the Church for the support of the parish incumbent. Great tithes (crops and timber) were payable to the parish rector and small tithes (for example new born animals and wool) were payable to the vicar of a parish. Some tithe rate books, recording payments or arrears, survive in parish records at CROs. When the monasteries were dissolved, their rights to receive tithes were often obtained by laymen to whom the monastery land was sold or granted. The Church's rights to receive tithes were also bought and sold, so that by the 19th century many tithes had to be paid by parishioners to local landowners rather than to the Church. In the 17th and 18th centuries tithes were often converted by agreement into cash payments. As the real value of cash reduced with inflation, the incumbent or other tithe-owner often tried to revert to the one-tenth payment in kind. This resulted in many court actions, the records of which provide useful information about land in the parish. The tithe system also discouraged farmers from spending money on agricultural improvements, since the tithe-owner took one-tenth of the extra produce. Quakers and other non-conformists objected to paying a tax to the Church of England. Farmers objected to paying a tax which was not levied on industry or most urban areas. Reform was therefore necessary.

Tithes were converted under the Tithe Commutation Act of 1836 into an annual rent on land (a tithe rent charge) that varied with the market price of cereals (to take account of inflation). The tithe rent charge was later replaced, under the Tithe Act 1936, by annuities payable for 60 years by landowners to the government (the tithe-owners were compensated with income from government stock). Evans (386) is a detailed study of tithes, the political movement for reform and the act. Kain & Prince (393) provide a detailed examination, with many illustrations, of the surveys, maps and agreements that were produced as a result of the act. It provided for the appointment of tithe commissioners to oversee or arrange the conversion of tithes to a rent charge. In some areas, commissioners reviewed and approved (by a tithe agreement) the voluntary arrangements to commute tithes that were made between landowners and tithe-owners. If landowners and tithe-owners could not agree terms, the commissioners calculated a new tithe rent charge which was then imposed. A survey was undertaken of each tithe district (usually a parish, but often a township in larger parishes) to calculate the apportionment between landowners of either the agreed rent charge, or the rent charge calculated by the commissioners. The commissioners obtained evidence about the tithes that had been paid previously and included this in their reports, together with information about disputes between landowners as to how the new charge should be apportioned between them. Their decision was incorporated into a tithe award. These documents include much information about land, especially where there were disputes over the tithe charge.

The surveys and agreements resulted in detailed maps and records being produced from 1838 to 1854 for those areas where tithes survived (that is, for about 11,800 parishes or townships, or about three quarters of the land area of England and Wales). The coverage varies from county to county. If there were no tithes in the area to be commuted, this was often because of 18th-century enclosure, and so it is more likely that such land was the subject of enclosure maps (considered below). Harley (388) estimates that about 98 per cent of Devon and Cornwall are covered by tithe surveys, but only about 35 per cent of Bedfordshire. Each field, house or garden should have been shown (and numbered) on a map of the parish or township (old maps were sometimes used to save the cost of a new survey). Tithe apportionment schedules, annexed to the maps, describe each parcel of land, name the owners and occupiers and specify the rent charge payable. The maps and schedules are useful for showing exactly where people lived (or owned property) in a village or surrounding countryside.

Three copies of tithe maps and schedules were produced for each tithe district in which commutation of tithes was necessary. The parish copies were kept with other parish records (and so many have been lost) but surviving copies are in CROs. Copies for the bishop were sent to the diocesan registry (and are usually now in CROs). A third set of copies were sent to the Tithe Redemption Commission and are now at TNA. The tithe apportionments are in series IR 29 and the maps are in IR 30. The series lists for IR 29 and IR 30 have been published by the List and Index Society. Although the tithe maps and apportionments are in different series, a map and the apportionment for a particular tithe district have the same piece numbers (just different series numbers) and they can be found very easily since, in the series lists, English (then Welsh) counties are arranged alphabetically and, within each county, the tithe districts are in alphabetical order. I wished to review the tithe records for Winkleigh in Devon. Each county has a number (for example Devon is 9) and each tithe district in a county is also given a number. Winkleigh was tithe district 452. These two numbers together form a piece number, so that the tithe map for Winkleigh is piece IR 30/9/452 and the tithe apportionment is piece IR 29/9/452.

The apportionments are on microfilm and can be viewed on readers in the map room at TNA. The maps (some of them are enormous) are also produced in the map room (but many are also on microfiche). A copy of the tithe map for Winkleigh was also held by Devon Record Office and an extract is shown in illustration 72. Each plot of land has a number. The tithe apportionment is a lengthy and detailed document. The recital gives total acreages in Winkleigh of arable land, pasture, meadows, woodland and commons. It also records the amount of the tithe charge and who was entitled to receive it. Detailed schedules then follow,

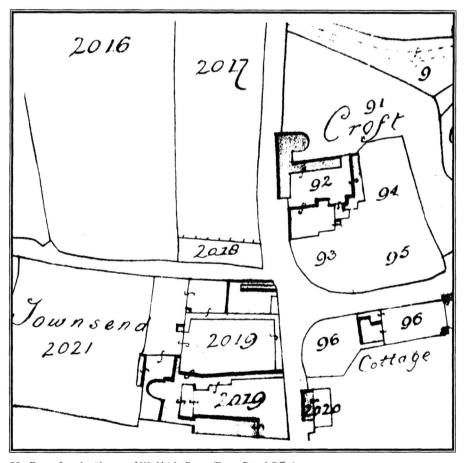

72. Extract from the tithe map of Winkleigh, Devon (Devon Record Office)

with the names of landowners, occupiers, farms and fields, the number (used on the tithe map) for each plot of land, its acreage and cultivation and the amount of the tithe charge for that plot. These schedules gave me much information about the Bulleid family. Thomas Bulleid owned two houses with gardens in the village and also occupied a house and a cooper's shop (which were owned by Robert Luxton). John Bulleid farmed over 69 acres (many of the fields were named) at Taw Green farm (the land was also owned by Robert Luxton). William Bulleid was the occupier of Herdwick farm (57 acres) which was owned by John Hearle Tremayne. John Bulleid also occupied Stabdon farm (Stabdon features in Bulleid wills back to the early 18th century), consisting of over 280 acres, which was also owned by Mr Tremayne. Illustration 73 shows a page from the apportionment, including the entry for William Bulleid at Herdwick and part of the entry for John Bulleid at Stabdon farm. TNA also holds almost 15,000 tithe files for 1836 to 1870 in series IR 18. Some files include minutes of meetings at which local witnesses gave evidence about local farming practices and how tithes had been paid in the past. They also contain the commission's surviving working papers, such as the commissioners' reports on their visits to parishes, their review of agreements and the draft awards that they prepared. A few other documents held by TNA are described in TNA domestic records leaflet 41. The holdings of TNA of tithe maps and related documents are also reviewed in Foot (387).

As another example of tithe records, Essex Record Office holds a copy of the tithe map and apportionment for Wanstead in Essex. My g.g. grandmother Emily Clements was born in this village in 1834, the daughter of John Clements, a fishmonger. The apportionment schedule included the entries noted below, showing that John Clements occupied two cottages (one owned by Thomas Barker and one owned by William Coggar). The tithe map showed that buildings numbered 71 and 72 were in the centre of the village. Since John was a fishmonger, it is likely that one cottage was the family home and the other was a shop.

Landowners	Occupiers	Plan numbers	Name & Description of land and premises
Thomas Barker	John Clements	72	Cottage & yard
William Coggar	John Clements and		
	Thomas Green	71	Two cottages

Land measurements

The tithe records (and other property records noted below) include terms for the measurement of land that will be unfamiliar to many researchers. The measures used since medieval times are explained in Richardson (25) and Chapman (109). Importantly, some measures varied in different parts of Britain. Thus, a hide (used in the Domesday Survey of 1086), also known as a carucate or ploughland, was the area of land that a team of oxen could plough in a year, and that would be sufficient to support a peasant family. This varied (because of soil quality) from 60 acres up to 180 acres. As the practice of buying, selling and leasing land became established, so units of measurement became more standard across the country. An acre was originally the area of land that a team of oxen could plough in a morning but it became standardised in most of England (by about 1300) at 4,840 square yards. However, an acre was about 6,100 square yards in Scotland and 7,840 square yards in Ireland. Some other land measurements (when they became standardised) are as follows:

LANDOWNERS.	OCCUPIERS.	No.	NAME AND DESCRIPTION OF LANDS AND PREMISES.	STATE OF CULTIVATION.	Quantities in Statute Measure.			Amount of Rent-Charge apportioned upon the several Lands, and to whom payable.						REMARKS.
					A.	R.	P.	Payable to Vicar. £ s. d.			Payable to Appropriators. £ s. d.			
			GERRYDOWN. (contd.)	*Brought Forward* .	122	3	33	2	1	11	1	7	4	
John Hearle Tremayne, Esq. (continued)	Walter Heywood (continued)	1669	Three Acres	Arable	3	0	5	0	2	6	0	8	6	
		1670	North Gerry Down Hill ..	Arable	3	0	34	0	1	6	0	5	0	
		1671	Part Do.	Timber & Coppice	0	2	20	0	0	1				
		1739	South Gerry Down Hill	Arable	3	2	36	0	2	0	0	6	8	
		1740	Part Do.	Timber and Coppice ..	1	0	15	0	0	1				
		1741	Woodley	Meadow	2	2	38	0	6	6				
		1742	Part Do.	Timber and Coppice ..	0	3	13	0	0	1				
		1743	Garden	..	0	0	22	0	0	6				
		1744	Garden	..	0	0	32	0	0	9				
		1745	House, Barton, &c.	..	0	2	25							
		1746	Green	Meadow	1	0	12	0	3	9				
					140	1	5	2	19	8	2	7	6	
	George Packer	1902	Lower Budehill Moor	Coarse Pasture & Arable	8	2	30	0	1	7	0	1	4	
		1903	Brake	Coarse Pasture & Furze	6	0	4	0	1	8				
		1904	Three Acres	Coarse Pasture & Arable	3	3	13	0	1	2	0	1	0	
		1905	New Moor	Coarse Pasture........	5	0	3	0	1	1				
		1906	Great Beacon	Arable & Coarse Pasture	14	0	18	0	3	5	0	2	10	
		1907	Budehill Moor	Coarse Pasture ..	8	0	18	0	1	8				
		1908	Turnip Close	Arable & Coarse Pasture	7	0	37	0	2	1	0	3	1	
		1909	Quarryclose	Do. ..	4	2	24	0	1	4	0	2	0	
		1910	New Close	Do. ..	6	1	12	0	2	6	0	4	4	
		2093	Birds Orchard	Orchard	0	1	21	0	0	10				
		2094	Liverpark Orchard	Orchard	0	3	23	0	2	0				
		2095	Little Liverpark	Coarse Pasture & Arable	0	2	2	0	0	4	0	0	5	
		2096	Western Close	Meadow	4	2	30	0	10	10				
		2097	Higher Orchard	Orchard & Garden ..	0	2	16	0	2	2				
		2098	House, Barton, &c.	Part Garden	0	2	17	0	0	3				
		2099	Kitchen Orchard	Orchard	0	1	26	0	1	3				
		2100	Lower Orchard	Orchard	1	0	3	0	2	11				
		2101	Hophay	Timber and Coppice ..	0	0	18							
		2102	Long Meadow	Coarse Meadow	0	3	6	0	1	5				
		2103	Nursery	Garden and Orchard ..	0	1	29	0	0	6				
		2104	Great Liverpark	Coarse Pasture	0	3	37	0	0	5				
		2105	Middle Meadow	Do. ..	2	3	0	0	1	11				
		2106	Long Meadow	Coarse Meadow	0	2	39	0	1	3				
		2107	Higher Meadow	Meadow	1	1	0	0	4	7				
		2108	Meadow Orchard	Orchard	0	1	26	0	1	2				
		2109	Kitchen Close	Arable	4	2	18	0	5	6	0	13	11	
		2110	Home Close	Arable	7	0	36	0	7	11	1	0	4	
		2111	Lower Ground Hill	Arable	6	2	10	0	6	11	0	18	1	
		2112	Higher Ground Hill	Arable	6	3	15	0	3	1	0	10	4	
		2151	Higher Broomclose	Arable	6	1	17	0	6	10	0	17	4	
		2152	Lower Broomclose	Arable	4	3	36	0	5	4	0	13	5	
		2153	Ley	Arable	7	3	32	0	8	5	1	1	8	
		2154	Tongue Meadow	Arable occasionally ..	0	2	24	0	1	1	0	1	2	
		2155	Fern Close	Arable	7	0	13	0	4	5	0	14	11	
		2194	Lower Meadow	Coarse Pasture	4	1	15	0	2	6				
					137	0	38	5	0	4	7	6	2	
	William Bulleid	2113	Backer Plot	Coarse Pasture & Arable	1	0	35	0	0	9	0	0	11	
		2114	Western Great Close ..	Arable	4	3	1	0	3	6	0	10	2	
		2115	Eastern Great Close	Arable	5	2	18	0	3	1	0	10	5	
		2116	Coarse Plot	Coarse Pasture & Arable	1	0	22	0	0	5	0	0	4	
		2117	Western Beaconclose	Do. ..	3	2	36	0	1	8	0	5	5	
		2118	Eastern Beaconclose	Do. ..	3	3	35	0	1	7	0	2	10	
		2119	Beacon Hill	Do. ..	3	0	8	0	1	1	0	1	1	
		2120	Little Herdwick Moor	Do. ..	2	1	35	0	0	9	0	0	11	
		2121	Great Do. Do.	Do. ..	4	3	38	0	1	8	0	2	4	
		2122	Splat	Arable	1	0	18	0	2	6	0	8	9	
		2126	Furze Close	Arable	6	3	25	0	3	8	0	12	6	
		2127	Mowhay Plot	Orchard and Garden ..	0	1	16	0	0	8				
		2128	Grove	Pasture......	0	1	15	0	0	3				
		2129	Part Do.	Timber	0	0	33							
		2143	Kitchen Close	Arable occasionally	2	3				1	0	4	3	
		2144	House, Barton, &c., &c.	..	0	2		0	0	2				
		2145	Back Orchard	Orchard	0	0	37	0	0	9				
		2146	Little Close	Arable	1	2	13	0	1	10	0	4	9	
		2147	Great Orchard	Orchard	1	0	34	0	3	3				
		2148	Orchard Hill	Arable occasionally	1	3	32	0	4	1	0	4	6	
		2149	Pond Hill	Meadow	1	2	0	0	4	3				
		2160	Long Meadow	Meadow	1	1	26	0	4	6				
		2161	Crump	Arable	2	0	32	0	3	4	0	6	3	
		2162	Backer Meadow	Meadow	0	2	32	0	1	7				
		2163	Little Plot	Coarse Pasture	0	0	8							
					57	0	17	2	9	11	3	15	6	
		2122	Two Acres	Coarse Pasture & Arable	2	0	37	0	0	8	0	0	9	
		2123	Stony Close	Do. ..	2	2	35	0	0	10	0	1	0	
		2124	Long Close	Do. ..	3	1	27	0	1	2	0	2	0	
		LIFTON. 2130	House, Barton, Road, Out-houses, &c.	..	1	2	11							
		2131	Garden	..	0	0	30	0	0	5				
		2132	Court Plot	Arable	2	1	23	0	1	5	0	4	5	
		2133	Orchard	..	3	2	25	0	1	2				
		2134	Brake	Arable and Furze	6	0	33	0	1	2	0	2	5	
		2135	Path Field	Arable & Coarse Pasture	4	0	1	0	1	7	0	2	5	
		2136	Lower Field	Arable	3	3	2	0	1	7	0	2	9	
					27	1	31	0	9	9	0	15	6	
	John Bulleid	2354	Dagger Plot	Nursery	0	0	25	0	0	2				
		2355	Long Moor	Coarse Pasture & Arable	13	1	15	0	4	2	0	2	7	
		STABDON. 2356	Great Blackaton	Do. ..	9	0	36	0	3	1	0	4	9	
		2357	Lower Blackaton	Do. ..	8	2	21	0	3	1	0	3	3	
		2358	Little Blackaton	Do. ..	4	3	4	0	2	2	0	3	3	
		2359	New Take	Do. ..	2	1	29	0	1	2	0	1	0	
				Carried Forward ..	40	2	10	0	14	3	0	15	0	

73. *Extract from the 1846 tithe apportionment of Winkleigh, Devon (TNA, IR 29/9/452)*

1 rod (or pole or perch)	= 16½ feet (5½ yards)
1 furlong	= 40 rods (220 yards)
1 English mile	= 8 furlongs (1,760 yards)
1 rood	= an area of 40 square rods
1 English acre	= an area 40 rods long by 4 rods wide (that is 4 roods or 4,840 square yards)
1 square mile	= 640 acres

Enclosure maps and awards

Until the 18th century much of England consisted of open fields that were farmed by a system of crop rotation. Farmers had strips in each field and also rights over the common pasture, meadows, heath and woodland. Common land is not, as often thought, owned by the public as a body. It is land that was held privately (originally by the Lord of a manor) but over which people had "rights of common" (for example to pasture their animals). The system of open fields, strips and commons was complex and encouraged uneconomic smallholdings. Enclosure (often spelt inclosure) was therefore undertaken. This involved pieces of land in different ownership being swapped and amalgamated, but also involved the division of common land between those who had previously enjoyed rights over it. The new larger fields were then enclosed, with hedges or ditches dividing the land of different owners or occupiers. Between 1700 and 1900 about 7 million acres of land were enclosed, consisting of about 4.5 million acres of open arable fields and about 2.5 million acres of common land and waste (that is, marshland or moors).

At first, enclosure was often carried out by private agreement between a lord and his tenants. Many agreements (with maps) have survived, often in landowners' estate papers (# chapter 27). Landowners sometimes took advantage of the enclosure process to claim (for their sole use) land which had long been considered common land. Land was also enclosed by acts of Parliament, especially during the late 18th and early 19th centuries. About 15,000 private enclosure acts were passed by Parliament between 1760 and 1797 alone. These acts (with maps annexed) were often only printed privately and so may now only be available in the House of Lords' Record Office, although some copies are held at the British, Bodleian or other libraries. The acts usually provided for the appointment of a commission to survey the land, review the holdings and rights of landowners, and then divide up the land by an enclosure award. The enclosure awards and maps were usually lodged with the Clerk of the Peace (and are now in CROs) or enrolled at court (mostly now held at TNA). Documents enrolled at court are considered in chapters 24 and 27, but the series at TNA which contain enrolled enclosure agreements for the 18th and 19th centuries include C 54, CP 40, CP 43, E 13, E 159 and KB 122. The agreements are listed by county and place in *The 27th Annual Report of the Deputy Keeper of the Public Records*. Other enclosure awards at TNA are in records of Crown lands (series CRES 6), the Duchy of Lancaster (DL 41 and 45) and the Palatinates of Chester and Durham (CHES 38 and DURH 4 and 26).

Between 1801 and 1845 general enclosure acts were passed by Parliament and enclosure awards were made pursuant to these acts and then lodged with the Clerk of the Peace or enrolled at court. The General Enclosure Act 1801 did not obviate the need for private acts of Parliament, but simplified their passage by providing model clauses which they could include (and most acts after this date therefore refer to the 1801 act). The General Enclosure Act 1836 allowed the enclosure of open arable fields (extended in 1840 to other types of land), without the need for an act of Parliament but by an award of appointed commissioners, if two thirds of those interested in the land (in number and value of the land) agreed. Commissioners then redivided the land between those previously owning strips, or having rights of common. If seven-eighths of the landowners (in number and value) agreed, they could redivide the land themselves, without appointing commissioners. Awards since 1836 (with maps) were usually lodged with the Clerk of the Peace. The General Enclosure Act 1845 established a standing Enclosure Commission. When enclosure of land was proposed, the Commission held a local enquiry and made recommendations to the House of Commons. If the enclosure was approved, it was effected by the Commission. Three copies of enclosure awards (with maps) were produced. One copy was for the parish. One was retained by the Enclosure Commissioners (now held at TNA in series MAF 1). Copies were usually also lodged with the Clerk of the Peace.

Surviving enclosure awards and maps usually note the names of the new owners of the land. If only common land was enclosed and divided, the award and map will only concern that land but, if a large amount of land was being redivided, the award and map might cover most land in the parish. The extent of enclosure varied considerably between counties. Harley (388) notes that there was very little parliamentary enclosure in Devon, Cornwall and Kent but that about 44 per cent of common fields in Bedfordshire were enclosed by these procedures.

Tate (405) is a detailed description of open field farming since medieval times, the enclosure process, parliamentary procedures and the work of the Enclosure Commission. Hollowell (390) is a detailed, illustrated guide to the procedures and records of enclosure. Tate (404) reviews parliamentary enclosure and lists, for each county, enclosure acts and awards pursuant to private acts of Parliament or the General Enclosure Acts of 1836 and 1845. Tate also notes whether a map or plan survives (although many maps have been discovered since this work was published in 1978). Thus, Tate notes that enclosure was undertaken by a private act of Parliament of 1797 at Chalgrave in Bedfordshire, resulting in an enclosure award of 1800, the documents being held at Bedford Record Office. Since some of my ancestors farmed land at Chalgrave, I could turn to these records to see if the family were involved. There are also many studies on particular counties, listed in West (462), reviewing (and often listing) the enclosure awards, acts and maps for that county. For example, abstracts of about 200 enclosure awards and agreements of Wiltshire are contained in Sandell (400). Each abstract notes the names of landowners and commissioners (and usually the Lord of the manor and the surveyor) and describes the land concerned.

LAND REGISTRATION AND OTHER PROPERTY DOCUMENTATION

For centuries ownership of land was proved (and still is in some cases) by a succession of documents known as title deeds, such as conveyances, wills and trust deeds. Many of these records survive in CROs or other collections and are reviewed below and in chapter 27. We shall first consider the modern system of registration of the title to land.

Land registration
Registries for deeds of title to land were opened between 1704 and 1735 in Middlesex and Yorkshire (and are considered below). A national system of voluntary registration of title to land in England and Wales was established in 1862, allowing title to land to be proved by an entry in a

register. From 1899 certain areas became subject to compulsory registration of title but even then the title was usually only registered when a property changed hands. The areas subject to compulsory registration were slowly extended and the majority of land in England and Wales is now registered. The Land Registration Act 1988 opened certain records of the Land Registry to public inspection. The register describes a property (usually by reference to a plan), records the names of the property owners since the date of first registration and notes the rights that the property has, or to which it is subject (such as a right of way). The register also includes details of mortgages, such as the name of a bank (but not the amount owing or the purchase price).

Most properties have only been registered in the last 50 years. Most of our ancestors' houses were demolished years before registration commenced and are therefore not included in the register. Even if your ancestor's property has survived and the title has been registered, the register is unlikely to mention him, since it only records the names of owners since first registration, let us say in 1920. As time passes, the register will become increasingly useful to genealogists, since each title will include more owners. A genealogist in the year 2050 may find a list of owners for the previous 100 or even 188 years. Even now, you may find useful information. I bought a house in Wimbledon in 1988. This was built in about 1870 but the title was first registered only in 1979. Only the three owners since 1979 were therefore noted. However, the register refers to a conveyance of 1869 (of a much larger area of land upon which many houses were to be built) between the vendor (the British Land Company Limited) and the purchaser (William Foice), who was probably also the subsequent developer. This information would be of interest to descendants of Mr Foice.

Full information on searching the register can be obtained from HM Land Registry at Lincoln's Inn Fields, London WC2A 3PH (telephone 020 7917 8888). Applications (which cost £4) are made to District Land Registries. Searches must be undertaken by reference to the present address of a property and the title number. Searches by the name of owners (whether past or present) are not possible. Forms for postal applications for searches are available at District Land Registries, but personal inspection (at the registries) of the register of titles is also possible. A property's title number can usually be ascertained by searching the Official Index Map. The property address should be sufficient to identify the title number. The fee for this service is also £4.

The deeds registries of Middlesex and Yorkshire are reviewed in an article by Sheppard & Belcher (401) in the *Journal of the Society of Archivists* (April 1980). The objective of the registries was to make it easier for landowners to prove their title to land, thus making it easier to use land as security for raising capital. The Middlesex Registry was established in 1708 for the voluntary registration of deeds or wills that affected the title to land in Middlesex that was freehold or held by a lease of over 21 years. The Middlesex register covered the City of Westminster and Middlesex parishes such as Holborn and Stepney, but not the City of London. The registry was superseded by the national system of land registration and no deeds were registered in the Middlesex Registry after 1938. Deeds were brought to the registry with a memorial, which was a document summarising the deed, including the date, the names and abodes of the parties, the witnesses' names and a description of the property (and sometimes of the transaction). The registrar checked that the memorial was accurate, endorsed the deed with a certificate and date of registration and returned the deed to the owner. The memorials were bound into rolls and also copied into a register, with a note of the date of registration. The registers for 1709 to 1938 (containing over 2.5 million registrations) and many memorials (except those for 1838–90 which were destroyed) are at LMA, which produces a leaflet on the use of the records. There are annual indexes of names of the vendor or landlord of the property for 1709–1919 and one index for 1920–38.

Deeds registries were established for the West, East and North Ridings of Yorkshire in 1704, 1707 and 1735 respectively and operated until about 1970. Sheppard & Belcher (401) provide detailed information on their operation. The procedure was similar to that in Middlesex, but the nature of the transaction was rarely noted. Separate books were kept to record some court judgments and enclosure awards that affected the property, but also deeds of bargain and sale (a form of conveyance considered in chapter 27). From 1885 the memorials themselves were bound in volumes rather than copied into registers. The registers and memorials (with over two million registrations) are in record offices at Northallerton, Beverley and Wakefield (# appendix VII).

There was an even earlier registry for about 95,000 acres of the Fens in East Anglia that had been drained (and became known as the Bedford Level). All conveyances (except leases of seven years or less) were entered in a register. The deeds registry, established in 1663, functioned until 1920. The 132 volumes of the register are held at Cambridge Record Office.

Title deeds and related property documentation
Old title deeds of property are often still held by families, especially if the land is unregistered. The deeds are proof of title to the property. The Law of Property Act 1925 provided that, when selling property, a seller generally only had to prove title to the land during the previous thirty-year period and this has now been reduced to only 15 years. Many older records became unnecessary to prove title and were destroyed, but many were saved and are in CROs or other archives. If land has been registered, so that the deeds became unnecessary, they may still be held by families or in archives, although many have been destroyed. There were many types of property deeds. A deed could simply transfer the freehold of property from one person to another. It could transfer land to trustees to hold for a series of beneficiaries or it could provide for a lease of the property from one person (a landlord) to another person (a tenant) for a specified period. If a family held an estate for many years, a series of deeds describing the dealings in the land, or parts of it, can tell you much about the family. Title deeds and other property records can be very complex and are considered in chapter 27. Deeds could get lost and so many were enrolled, for example on the Close Rolls, or with the Clerk of the Peace for the county. Enrolled deeds are at TNA and CROs and are also reviewed in chapter 27.

If your ancestor owned or occupied a farm or other business property (particularly in the 19th and 20th centuries), you should search for auction or sale catalogues. Farms being sold by auction could be described in great detail in sale catalogues (and more briefly in newspaper articles notifying the public of the sale). Many of these survive in CROs.

The return of owners of land 1873
These returns, also known as the Modern Domesday, were the result of a survey to ascertain the number of owners of land of one acre or more in the United Kingdom (except London). The returns were compiled from rates records. The returns for England and Wales were published by HMSO in 1874 as *Return of Owners of Land, 1873*. Returns for Scotland and Ireland were also published by HMSO in 1874 and 1876. Copies of the papers are available on CD-ROM. In addition, the returns for each county of England and Wales have been reprinted on microfiche by MM Publications and the returns for many counties, such as those for Devon (382), are also available on microfiche from Mrs R.A. Cleaver, 17 Lane End Drive, Knaphill, Woking, Surrey,

GU21 2QQ. The returns for Middlesex (383), Surrey and Cornwall have been reprinted in booklets by West Surrey FHS.

The returns list owners' surnames in alphabetical order. They also give the owner's address (usually just the town, village or area in a city), the area of land (acres, rods and poles) that he owned and its estimated rental value (but not the land's location). Typical entries in the Devon returns are:

Name of Owner	Address of Owner	Extent of lands			Estimated rental	
		A	R	P	£	s
Bulleid, Samuel.	Hatherleigh	8	2	–	75	2
Bulleid, Thomas.	Hatherleigh	23	–	38	52	6
Bullen, J.B.T.T.	Marshwood	1	–	3	3	10

The survey established that almost 270,000 people (or organisations such as railway companies, charities and schools) owned an acre or more of land. For Devon alone, about 9,740 names are given (although this is out of an approximate population of 602,000). The returns are therefore of principal use to descendants of the landowners, but are also useful to other researchers, since they reveal the names of the landowners in the county, and enable searches to be made for that family's records (often held in CROs).

Inland Revenue valuations and surveys
The Finance Act 1910 imposed a tax on the profits made from sales of property in England and Wales if that profit arose from amenities provided at public expense (such as roads or drainage). The act also provided for property to be valued so that tax could be assessed. Although the tax was withdrawn in 1920, the Inland Revenue had by then undertaken surveys and valuations of most houses and property. The records describe (and value) each property and list the name of owners (the person holding the freehold or a lease with more than 50 years unexpired) and tenants (but not necessarily the actual occupiers of the property). Most of the records are held by TNA in series IR 58 and IR 121 to 135. The legislation and valuation process are described in Short (402) and TNA domestic records leaflet 46.

England and Wales were divided into 14 divisions, each consisting of a number of Valuation Districts. The 118 Valuation Districts were subdivided into smaller units, Income Tax parishes (ITP), each of which covered one or more civil parishes. The divisions are shown on maps in Short (402) and Foot (387). Each property was allocated a unique assessment (or hereditament) number within the ITP in which it was located. These numbers (and the boundaries of each hereditament) appear on the Valuation Office maps (in IR 121–135) which contain 55,000 Ordnance Survey maps, varying in scale between 1:2,500 and 1:500. For example, IR 121 contains plans from the London district and IR 124 holds those for the south-eastern district. The hereditament number can be easily extracted from a map if, for example, your ancestors lived on an isolated farm. If they lived in a house in an urban street, a map will show hereditament numbers for each house, but you may not know which is your ancestors' house (because the house numbers in a street are not shown on the map). You may only be able to note the range of hereditament numbers for houses in that street. Foot (387) is a detailed guide to locating the correct documents, with lists of the district valuation offices and TNA references for the maps of each district.

With the hereditament number (or a range of numbers), you can then refer to the 95,000 volumes of fieldbooks in series IR 58. The series list shows how the fieldbooks are arranged alphabetically by valuation office district and, within each district, in alphabetical order of ITP names. Within each ITP, the documents are arranged with hereditament numbers in numerical order, so that you can use the series list to find the correct fieldbook (within the ITP) that includes the hereditament number that you obtained from a map. The fieldbooks (with four pages for each hereditament), name the property owner and any tenant (but not necessarily the occupier), give details of any tenancy, the floor area, condition and use of the property, the number of rooms and the valuation. Unfortunately, in some cases, the fieldbooks do not include the property details, but refer to Form 4 (which was completed by landowners with detailed information about a property). Most of these forms have not survived in government records, but some landowners retained copies. In addition, valuation (or Domesday) books were also prepared at an intermediate stage of the valuation process, with information from owners, occupiers and rates lists. These sometimes included a detailed description of the property for each hereditament number, the address, and named the occupiers, owners and tenants. They are generally held in CROs, except those for the City of London and Westminster. Those for the City and Paddington are at TNA, but the others for Westminster were destroyed.

Short (402) and TNA domestic records leaflet 46 note some other defects in the material. Some fieldbooks and valuation books, for example those for the Isle of Wight and part of Sussex, were destroyed during the Second World War. Land owned by the Crown or statutory companies (such as railway companies) was exempt from the tax and so this land was usually the last to be valued. In some cases, these valuations had not taken place by the time the legislation was repealed so that no records of these properties survive. Many of these statutory companies built or owned houses (for their employees) or commercial buildings that they leased to other firms or individuals. In either case, your ancestors may have lived or worked in premises that are not included in the records.

The National Farm Survey 1941–43
If your family were farmers in or around the period 1941–43, useful information about their farm can be obtained from the records of the National Farm Survey, which are reviewed in detail, with illustrations, in Foot (387). These do not contain any genealogical information but, in brief, all farms of five acres or more were surveyed (that is, about 300,000 farms). The records of individual farms are in series MAF 32 at TNA, noting the farmer's name, whether he was the owner or tenant (and any owner's name), the rent payable, the other terms of occupation, the conditions on the farm, details of crops, livestock and the number of farm workers. Maps were produced of each farm (and are held in series MAF 73).

CHAPTER 16

LOCAL AND SOCIAL
HISTORY

Most places have changed substantially over the years and so the study of local and social history is important in order to obtain a true picture of our ancestors' lives. The population of Britain has multiplied in recent centuries and the growth of cities and towns (transforming many rural areas) makes it difficult to picture those places 100 or 200 years ago. The changes in some areas are now in reverse. Many valleys in South Wales no longer have any heavy industry or mines and would be unrecognisable to 19th-century coalminers.

Family historians must take account of these changes. For example, if your ancestors lived in Wimbledon in about 1700, you must remember that Wimbledon has changed dramatically. It is now a London suburb but in 1700 it was a village considered to be some distance from London. Life in Wimbledon in 1700 was very similar to life in other English villages. The housing conditions varied from the comfortable homes of the wealthy to the almost uninhabitable cottages of the poor. In 1700 one could walk from the centre of Wimbledon to farmland or forests. One must now drive for 30 minutes. Some changes are more recent. A description of Walthamstow in 1848, from Evans (60), is set out below. Walthamstow has changed a great deal, but this description explains why my ancestor George Keates (with a flourishing business) bought a villa in Walthamstow in about 1857.

> The largest and handsomest suburban village near the metropolis [London], delightfully situated in the vale of the River Lea . . . surrounded by beautiful and romantic woodland scenery, containing many large and handsome villas . . . mostly occupied by wealthy merchants and others who have their place of business in London.

Local and social history is important for establishing the conditions in which your ancestors lived and their way of life. If your ancestor was a coalminer in Wales, it is important to learn about coalmining in that area. If he was a farm labourer, a study of local history may reveal the names of landowners for whom he worked and lead you to estate records which mention your ancestor, or record his wages or the location of his cottage. A study of local and social history may also reveal other sources of records that will help your research, or provide you with information about matters such as local trade, communications, customs or epidemics.

Many of the sources reviewed in other chapters of this book are helpful in studying local history. Dunning (421) shows how to build up a history of a village, using parish registers, maps, monumental inscriptions, rate books, tax records, wills and inventories. Hey (24) and Friar (16) are dictionaries of local history, each with over 2,000 detailed entries on items such as place names, local government, plagues, agriculture and fairs. However, the best way to start is to find any published material.

COUNTY HISTORIES

The *Victoria History of the Counties of England* (*VCH*) is a particularly useful source for local history. Not all counties are yet covered in full (so that other county histories may have to be used) but over 200 volumes have already been published (for example nine for Essex and eight for Lancashire) and further volumes are being prepared. For each county that is covered, the *VCH* consists of two parts (each of one or more volumes). The first part is a general description of the history and geography of a county, including the relevant part of the Domesday book. The second part is a detailed historical and topographical account of each parish in the county, including information about local landowning families (and their pedigrees), important buildings, manors, schools, hospitals and charities. The second part has only been completed for a few counties (and has not yet been commenced for some counties).

For example, the *VCH* for Bedfordshire (410) consists of three volumes and an index. The first part describes the county's political, economic and social history (including industries and agriculture). An account is then given of the religious houses and hospitals of the county, with details of the properties that were owned by these institutions. A history of education in Bedfordshire is also included, describing the county's medieval and reformation schools (such as Bedford Grammar School, founded in the 16th century) and listing the public elementary schools founded before 1902. Thus it is noted that an elementary school was founded in Chalgrave in 1844, providing education for 118 children. Educational records are reviewed in chapter 19 below, but these lists are useful for identifying schools that your ancestors may have attended. The second part of the *VCH* for Bedfordshire (part of volume 2 and all volume 3) provides an account of each parish in the county, describing the church (including interesting memorials), chapels, manor houses or other buildings of note (such as almshouses). This is followed by notes on the parish registers, charities, place names and the families of the Lords of the manor (or manors) in the parish. Detailed references to source material are provided. Although the *VCH* concentrates on landowners and other people of note (rarely mentioning other people), the historical and descriptive material on each parish will assist any researcher.

Many other county histories, similar in content to the *VCH*, have been published since the 18th century, for example Ormerod's history of Cheshire (195), Lysons' histories of Devon (438) and Middlesex (439) and histories of Lancashire, Leicestershire and Kent by the antiquarians Baines, Nichols and Hasted respectively. These works are available in reference libraries. The authors' working papers may have been deposited in a CRO or library (particularly the British Library) and sometimes include his notes of original documents, from parish or town archives, that have since been lost or destroyed. There are also many modern county histories. An excellent example is a history of Bedfordshire by Godber (429) with over 200 photographs or illustrations. It deals with all aspects of life in the county: the manors, churches, farming, law and order, towns and transport. It has references to thousands of documents, articles in local history journals and other publications. It is essential reference for anyone whose ancestors came from Bedfordshire.

PLACES AND PLACE NAMES

A good modern gazetteer (such as Bartholomew's) is useful for information on place names, roads and topography, but earlier gazetteers should also be reviewed. The *Topographical Dictionary of England* by Samuel Lewis was first published in 1831 (and has been reprinted by GPC). There were also later editions, such as the 5th edition of 1844 (437), and similar volumes for Scotland, Wales and Ireland. All the volumes are also available on CD-ROM. They contain descriptions of places with information on local institutions or markets. A typical entry, for Winkleigh (or Winkley) in Devon, is:

> A parish in the union of Torrington, hundred of Winkley, South Molton division . . . 6½ miles from Chulmleigh; containing 1650 inhabitants. The parish forms a distinct hundred, to which it gives [its] name; the new road from Torrington to Exeter passes through it, and the scenery is agreeably enlivened with the grounds of Winkley Court. A fair for cattle is held on the Monday after July 7th; and courts leet and baron annually. The living is a vicarage, valued at £21. 8. 9; net income, £215; patrons and appropriators, the Dean and Chapter of Exeter. There is an endowed almshouse, called Gidley's, for widows.

Place names are also worthy of study. How did your ancestor's village obtain its name and what does it mean? Ekwall (424) lists English place names, notes documents in which a name first appears and provides meanings if these are known. Reaney (449) is also a general work on place names. The English Place Names Society has also published volumes dealing with place names in many counties, showing the Celtic, Anglo-Saxon, Latin, Scandinavian and French influences upon those names.

OTHER LOCAL HISTORIES

Many other guides to counties or areas are available in bookshops or local libraries. Even brief guides provide useful information about an ancestor's town or village, perhaps including photographs of the church and notes on important monuments or historical events. Shire Publications produce a series of county guides, such as Stanier (455) for Devon, with entries for towns, villages and important buildings, that include useful historical information.

You should ascertain whether any local histories have been written about the city, town or village in which your ancestors lived. These histories first appeared in the 16th century. One of the most famous is John Stow's *Survey of London* (456) of 1598 (reprinted in modern editions). Stow described the history of the city and many of its buildings, particularly its churches (and their monuments), as well as its famous inhabitants since medieval times. Many modern works on cities, towns and villages (or rural areas) combine a useful historical description with copies of maps, documents, photographs and engravings. Farrar (427) is a detailed history of Bedford, with illustrations of buildings or noteworthy people and extracts from Bedford's records, such as parish registers, memorial inscriptions, property deeds, letters, diaries, accounts and gaol records. Many local studies are published by Phillimore, such as the volumes on Chagford by Hayter-Hames (432) and Teignmouth by Trump (459). Another useful series, by Historical Publications Limited, includes *Soho Past* by Tames (458) and *Islington Past* by Richardson (450). Even small towns, villages or their churches have often been the subject of studies by local historians. Examples are *Ide* (a village near Exeter) by Rowland (453) and *The Church of St Mary, Walthamstow* by Reaney (448). Books such as these tell you much about life in a town or village (or about the history of a church, its clergy and parishioners) but also include old maps, photographs and references to documents (in archives or private collections). You are very fortunate if your ancestor's parish is the subject of a detailed study such as Bishop (417) on St Ive, near Liskeard in Cornwall. This contains over 600 photographs (of many buildings and hundreds of people), newspaper clippings and other memorabilia about the parish and its inhabitants.

The London Encyclopaedia by Weinreb & Hibbert (461) is an essential guide to the history of London and its environs. It contains about 5,000 alphabetical entries for London people, streets, buildings (churches, theatres, inns, livery company halls, prisons and hospitals), organisations (societies, clubs and livery companies), businesses (such as the Stock Exchange and Lloyd's) and important events. It includes about 500 prints, drawings and photographs as well as indexed references to about 10,000 people. An interesting example of the variety of local history books available is *An Illustrated Guide to London 1800* by Borer (419), published in 1988 (but written as if for visitors to London in 1800). It describes well known buildings (with many illustrations) as well as London's churches, shops, trade, commerce, entertainment and crime in 1800. Borer notes that London had 112 Anglican churches, 58 Anglican chapels attached to institutions or private homes, 12 Catholic chapels, 19 foreign Protestant chapels (German, French, Swiss and others), 6 Quaker meeting-houses, 6 synagogues and 133 other non-conformist chapels.

ONE-PLACE GENEALOGICAL STUDIES

There are a growing number of studies of the people (and their families) of particular places, in which researchers collect information about a place, its records and the people who lived there. These studies are described by Hawgood (431) with a list of studies being undertaken by individuals and local history societies (and notes of their contact details, web sites and publications). Published one-place studies include that of St Ive in Cornwall, by Bishop (417), noted above. One of the most substantial studies is that of Wirksworth in Derbyshire, by J. Palmer (much of the information being available on his web site through GENUKI).

If you are considering undertaking such a study, perhaps because some of your ancestors lived for centuries in the same village, published guides such as those by Gibson (that list records by county and parish), will be of great assistance. The process of finding records for particular places is similar to the search for named ancestors except that you will rely more often on place name indexes if these are available (for example for courts' records, see chapter 24). A CRO or local studies or reference library should have an enormous amount of information, both published and unpublished, typescript or manuscript, about any place and its inhabitants. The web sites or online catalogues of TNA, RCHM, GENUKI, Cyndi's List and Access to Archives are also invaluable for one-place studies.

OTHER SOURCES FOR LOCAL HISTORY

Many places have local history museums or libraries and these are listed in the *FLHH* (5). For example, some of my ancestors lived in Topsham in Devon. A visit to the Topsham Museum gave me a feel for the life they led through its displays of old maps, photographs, artefacts and a model of Topsham in about 1900. The Southwark local studies library held much useful information, including parish records, engravings and maps for Rotherhithe, where my Keates ancestors lived around 1810.

It is sometimes difficult to find out what information is available. Searching library shelves and catalogues is a good starting point and Anderson (411) is a catalogue of about 14,000 local history and topographical works published up to 1880. Reading the bibliographies of local history books will also lead you to other sources (published or manuscript). Genealogical bibliographies have also been produced, listing the books which may be of use to those researching a family in a particular county. Genealogical bibliographies have been produced by S. Raymond for many counties, including Norfolk (443), London and Middlesex (444), Buckinghamshire (445), Devon (446), Lancashire (447) and also for Cheshire, Cornwall, Cumberland/Westmorland, Dorset, Gloucestershire, Hampshire, Lancashire, Lincolnshire, Oxfordshire, Somerset, Suffolk and Wiltshire. For each county, Raymond lists county histories, published family histories, pedigrees and parish registers, newspapers, and articles in journals on local history and records. These bibliographies lead you to a wealth of material, much of which you might otherwise never find. Webb (460) describes many of the published and manuscript records of London and Middlesex and Marcan (257) is a local history directory for Greater London, listing archives, museums, local history societies and their publications.

One of the most productive methods of finding new sources for ancestors is to review catalogues of CROs for the places in which your ancestors lived. You will probably be surprised at the large amount of material that survives for any place, including parish records, property and estate records, school records or perhaps the archives of charities, local businesses, friendly societies and sports teams. Another important source is the National Register of Archives (# chapters 11 and 22). This is a database of manuscript collections, held in thousands of archives or other collections, which can be searched by place name through the RCHM web site. It can lead you to material held in archives that you might not otherwise search. For example, property records for land in one county may be held with the papers, of a family that previously owned the land, in the CRO of another county.

Photographic archives and published books of photographs were considered in chapter 11. Even if you cannot find photographs of your ancestors' home, you may find photographs of similar buildings. Calder (420) illustrates rich and poor people's homes (both indoors and outdoors) in Victorian and Edwardian times. Published collections of photographs also illustrate other aspects of daily life in the 19th century. Thus Spence (87) is a collection of photographs of railways and railway travel. For earlier scenes of your ancestor's village, town or city (particularly buildings of note, such as churches), you must rely on engravings and paintings. These scenes are unlikely to be totally realistic, since engravers and painters tended to present an idealistic view of an area and living conditions. Few engravings (except those by Gustave Doré) truly show the poverty that so many people suffered. Illustration 74 is an engraving of the parish church at St Mary Rotherhithe in 1809 (two years before my ancestor George Keates was baptised there). Similar engravings can be obtained of castles, large houses or public buildings. Libraries and CROs usually hold selections of engravings or books of reproductions. A good example for London and its environs is Shepherd (454) originally published in 1829, containing almost 200 engravings of churches and other important London buildings in the early 19th century.

The publications of county or local record societies were noted in chapter 11. In addition, local history societies publish important material on an area, its history and inhabitants. For example, the East London History Society publishes an annual journal, *East London Record* (409). Other examples are *Devon and Cornwall Notes & Queries* and *Bedfordshire Magazine*. Journals such as these have often been published for many years and collections of them are held at the SoG or CROs. They include articles of interest on local history, trade, religion, or even specific families. Useful articles on source material also appear in the *Local Historian*, the quarterly journal of the British Association for Local History. There are also many national societies for particular

74. *St Mary's Rotherhithe from an engraving published in 1809*

historical interests. The *FLHH* (5) lists local history societies and also national societies concerned with agriculture, industrial history, costume, military affairs and transport.

If there are no books available on the history of your ancestors' town or village, you should concentrate on primary sources, most of which are described in this book. West's *Village Records* (462) and *Town Records* (463) will also assist. These review the types of records available to prepare a local history (from Anglo-Saxon times to the 19th century) of villages, towns or cities. Other excellent books on the study of local history are Hoskins (434), Hey (23) and Edwards (423), which particularly assist research of the social, economic and population histories of villages, towns or cities using documents such as parish registers and manorial records. Following the lines of research they suggest, one can obtain more information about local housing, farming, trades or employment, the mobility of population and health. Maps are of great importance and a collection of maps of an area, covering a period of time, will show the growth of towns and cities far better than any description. Hey (23) notes that Barrow grew from a single house into a fishing village (of about 300 people) by about 1840 and into a town (of 40,000 people) by about 1870. This is vitally important if your ancestors lived in Barrow at that time. As Hey points out, the expansion of towns and cities, especially during the Victorian period, resulted in many villages being engulfed by an expanding town or city. The rural township of Everton had only 499 inhabitants in 1801, but it had almost 110,000 inhabitants (and had become part of Liverpool) by 1881. In cases such as this, you should study the reasons for the expansion (perhaps the founding of a particular industry, or the arrival of the railway). If your ancestors migrated to such a town, you may be able to obtain an idea of why they arrived and from where they came.

Expansion was particularly marked around London. London maps show that, as late as 1801, only a relatively small area had been built up even though the population had already reached 865,000. Population growth was then very rapid. By 1901 London's population was over 4.5 million and many country towns and villages, such as Leyton in Essex, had become London suburbs. Hey notes that between 1881 and 1891 Leyton suffered the most rapid population growth in England (133.3 per cent). Hey also notes that Hampstead was transformed between 1801 and 1901 from a country village into a high class London suburb, with a population that grew from 4,343 to 82,329 and the number of inhabited houses rising from 691 to 11,359. This type of information is available from many sources, including census returns. You should not ignore the general information available from the census. You may find a family living at the same address in two or more successive censuses but it is dangerous to assume that nothing had really changed: in fact your ancestor's life and surroundings may have changed dramatically.

Even if you cannot find any books on your ancestors' town or village, an understanding of their way of life can be obtained from works on similar villages or towns. Two works are particularly useful. Richard Gough's *The History of Myddle*, edited by Hey (433), is a history written in 1701 and 1702 about the parish and many of the families living there. Blythe (418) contains recollections, covering the late 19th and early 20th centuries, of inhabitants of the village of Akenfield in Suffolk. Edwards (423) is a general guide to rural life and the records evidencing it (particularly useful if your ancestors were farmers). Bettey (416) is a guide to the sources available for a study of life in the parish since Saxon times. Girouard (428) describes, with many illustrations, life in English country houses or castles since the middle ages, which is useful whether your ancestors owned such a house or worked in one.

SOCIAL HISTORY

Studies of national or regional trends are also important. Hey (23) reviews many studies on aspects of life in the Tudor, Stuart and Hanoverian periods. For example, it was rare for more than one married couple to live together in the same house. Men generally married between the ages of 27 and 29 (and women at about 26) and between one in four and one in six people never married. Hey also notes that about one third of children died before the age of 10 and that, of the rural population aged between 15 and 24 from the 15th and 19th centuries, about 60 per cent were farm servants. It is interesting to compare these figures to your ancestors' families. Many of the children of my ancestral families in Devon worked as farm servants in the late 18th and early 19th centuries. It therefore appears that this was fairly typical for the rural population of England rather than evidence of particularly poor families.

Hey also considers epidemics and harvest failures from the 16th to 18th centuries. When researching your ancestry, it is important to keep these matters in mind (and especially that conditions varied greatly around the country). The bubonic plague was particularly serious in towns and, in 1563, killed one in five Londoners. Bubonic plague appears to have struck Chesterfield in 1586 and 1587 because of the vast increase in the number of burials. Evidence of epidemics (which often followed harvest failures) may be important to your family history. My ancestor John Keates (aged 61) was buried in July 1832 on the same day as a William Keates (aged 72) who appeared to be his brother. They both lived in Rotherhithe. The chance of two elderly brothers being buried on the same day is very small unless they both perished in a fire or accident. The answer appears to be an epidemic. The parish vestry minutes (# chapter 18) of February 1832 recorded great concern about cholera (which was affecting many parts of the country) and the establishment of a hospital was suggested. A book about this cholera epidemic revealed that Rotherhithe was the first area in London to be affected. Places such as Rotherhithe (on the banks of the River Thames and having many shipbuilding yards) were especially prone to cholera and it therefore appears likely that both John and William caught the disease, probably drinking the same infected water at their place of work or at home.

Drake & Finnegan (14) advise on the use of diaries, autobiographies and letters in local and family history, emphasising the care that is required in analysing them. It is unlikely that your ancestors wrote autobiographies or diaries, but other people's work evidences the way of life of many different types of people and so is relevant to anyone's family history. From the 17th century, an increasing number of people wrote diaries or detailed letters that provide much information about their life. Most were the work of famous people, the wealthier classes or clergymen, but some were prepared by ordinary men and women. The most famous diarist is perhaps Samuel Pepys, whose record of life in London from 1659 to 1669 describes the plague, the Great Fire and other important events, but also refers to many ordinary Londoners. The original diary is held at Magdalene College, Cambridge, but has been published in various editions, the best being the complete transcription, with extensive notes and index, in 11 volumes, by Latham & Matthews (436). Many men who fought as officers or soldiers in the Napoleonic, Crimean and other wars kept diaries. These provide an insight into the life of any ancestors who fought in those wars. There are many diaries (some of which have been published) of 19th-century farmers, factory workers, agricultural labourers, army or navy officers, seamen and household servants. Batts (414) is a catalogue of over 3,000 British manuscript diaries of the 19th century (indexed by author, subject and region or place) such as the diary of 1834–83 kept by James Hirst, a weaver of Huddersfield in Yorkshire (held at Huddersfield Central Library).

Diaries of clergymen are useful since they include much information about their parishioners or congregations. Many have been published, such as the diary of James Woodforde (held at the Bodleian Library), covering 1758 to 1802. Woodforde attended Oxford University and was later a curate in various Somerset parishes and then parson of Weston Longeville in Norfolk. His diary was published in five volumes by Oxford University Press (1924–31) and lengthy extracts are contained in Beresford (415), including many references to his friends and parishioners, and details of his travels. These extracts illustrate the value of diaries to the descendants of both the diarist and the people mentioned in the diaries:

1785 [in Weston Longeville] April 12. I buried poor old widow Pully this afternoon, aged 80 years. My servant William Coleman was out all evening . . . came home in liquor; behaved very rudely and most impudently to me . . . Mr Peachman called about 7 o'clock and paid me for 4 acres of turnips at 30s. per acre.

April 13. I got up between 5 and 6 o'clock this morning. Had Will [Coleman] before me as soon as possible, paid him his wages [details given] and dismissed him before 8 o'clock.

April 14. Will is now at work in the garden at Mr Cary's. I wish he might do well and better than he did here.

Occupational records are considered in chapter 22, but general information can also be obtained about an ancestor's work. For example, my great grandfather was a baker in East London in the late 19th century. There are many books and other material about the work of bakers in earlier centuries, such as the 1991 edition of *East London Record* (409) which included an article on bakers in the 19th century in East London. If your ancestor was a farmer, Edwards (422) describes the sources available for the study of farming through the centuries. Similar works are available on soldiers, seamen, farm labourers, textile workers and shoemakers. Shire Publications publish over 500 invaluable booklets, dealing with many trades or aspects of life, such as *The Victorian Farmer* by Eveleigh (426), *The Victorian Domestic Servant* by May (440), *Baking and Bakeries* by Muller (441) and *Shoemaking* by Swann (457). A catalogue of titles can be obtained from Shire at Cromwell House, Church Street, Princes Risborough, Buckinghamshire HP27 9AJ or viewed on its web site.

Many people wish to research the history of a particular house. Most of our ancestors' homes were demolished long ago, but many old buildings survive (from large country houses to small cottages) especially in rural areas. Harvey (430) and Barratt (413) are guides to sources for the history of houses and Elton, Harrison & Wark (425) is a guide to undertaking research about country houses (and their estates). Most of the records that contain information about houses have already been considered (photographs, tithe and Ordnance Survey maps, land registry records, census records, directories, inventories, auction catalogues and engravings) or are reviewed in later chapters (title deeds, rate books, land tax records, insurance records and manorial records). Larger houses may be described in the *VCH*, or in published works on local architecture (such as the volumes of the *Survey of London*). The archives of families that owned large houses may include useful material about a house and the lifestyle of its owners, such as plans, surveys, accounts (for example for building works, food, or servants' wages), sale particulars or correspondence.

As a final example of the importance of local and social history, let us consider the Christmas festival. Much of our Christmas celebration originates in Victorian times. How did our ancestors celebrate Christmas? Baker (412) is a history of Christmas traditions, demonstrating the recent origin of our present depiction of Father Christmas, but showing also the older rituals such as mumming (old folk plays in costume) and the great importance, until the 19th century, of Twelfth Night – the night before Epiphany, 6 January. A work such as this is invaluable for what it tells us about our ancestors' Christmas – a very different affair from our modern commercial festival.

CHAPTER 17

NEWSPAPERS AND ELECTIONS

NEWSPAPERS AND JOURNALS

An enormous number of newspapers and journals have been published since the 17th century and Lake (490) is an illustrated account of the development of the British press. Newspapers and journals contain a vast amount of information about our ancestors, but they are underused as a genealogical source because there are few indexes to their contents and researchers usually do not know whether any particular newspaper mentions their ancestors.

Journals

The *London Gazette* (originally named the *Oxford Gazette*) has been published since 1665. It was published twice weekly at first but subsequently every weekday. It contains official court and government announcements, such as appointments in the government, church and armed forces, grants of peerages, medal awards, naturalisations, changes of name and notices of bankruptcies (about 2,000 a year by 1850) or companies' liquidations. Complete sets of the *Gazette* are at Guildhall Library, TNA (in series ZJ 1), the British Library, Birmingham Public Library and the Bodleian and Cambridge University libraries. There are also some incomplete runs, for example in libraries in Edinburgh and Newcastle. Editions of the *London Gazette* are being made available online (# appendix XI). At present, the editions from 1914–20 and 1939–48 are available but others from the 20th century are being added to the web site.

The *Gazette* included indexes (originally half-yearly but now quarterly) from 1787, divided into subject matter (such as army promotions) each with alphabetical surname lists. There are also some indexes to specific subjects or certain periods, which are particularly useful for the years before the general indexes commence in 1787. These include indexes to bankrupts 1772–93 and dissolution of partnerships 1785–1811. Over 19,000 entries about Londoners from issues of the *Gazette* of 1665 to 1700, extracted by R. Hall, are held at the SoG. There are also some published collections of items from the *Gazette*, relating to particular counties (such as some booklets of extracts concerning Devon), copies of which are at the SoG.

Illustration 75 shows extracts from the *Gazette* of 26 January 1788, reporting the appointments of Thomas Keate as the Queen's surgeon, the Revd James Jones as Archdeacon of Hereford and William Stapleton as cornet in the 15th Regiment of Light Dragoons. There are also announcements concerning the bankruptcy of Michael Hubert of Liverpool and Mark Allegre Bennett of Bloomsbury, London. Creditors of John Johnson of Newton cum Larton, Cheshire and of William Dymock of Oxford Street, London were requested to present proof of debts that were due to them. There is also an advertisement seeking Abraham Green (a son of Abraham Green of Ipswich). Illustration 76 shows extracts from a 1941 edition of the *Gazette*,

Numb. 12958.   [35]

The London Gazette.

Published by Authority.

From Tuesday January 22, to Saturday January 26, 1788.

Whitehall, January 26.

THE King has been pleased to present the Reverend James Jones, Doctor in Divinity, to the Archdeaconry of Hereford, void by the Promotion of the Right Reverend Doctor John Harley to the Bishoprick of Hereford.

The Queen's Palace, January 26.

The Queen has been pleased to appoint Doctor James Ford to be Her Majesty's Physician In Extraordinary.

And also to appoint Mr. Thomas Keate to be Her Majesty's Surgeon in Extraordinary.

Whereas a Commission of Bankrupt is awarded and issued forth against Michael Hubert, of Liverpool, in the County of Lancaster, Dealer and Chapman, and he being declared a Bankrupt is hereby required to surrender himself to the Commissioners in the said Commission named, or the major Part of them, on the 14th and 15th Days of February next, and on the 8th Day of March following, at Eleven of the Clock in the Forenoon, on each of the said Days, at the King's Arms, in Water-street, in Liverpool in the said County, and make a full Discovery and Disclosure of his Estate and Effects; when and where the Creditors are to come prepared to prove their Debts, and at the Second Sitting to chuse Assignees, and at the last Sitting the said Bankrupt is required to finish his Examination, and the Creditors are to assent to or dissent from the Allowance of his Certificate. All Persons indebted to the said Bankrupt, or that have any of his Effects, are not to pay or deliver the same but to whom the Commissioners shall appoint, but give Notice to John Culcheth, of Liverpool.

Pursuant to a Decree of the High Court of Chancery, made in a Cause the Allix and another against Scott and others, the Creditors of John Johnson, late of Newton cum Larton, in the County of Chester, Esq; deceased, are to come in and prove their Debts before Alexander Popham, Esq; one of the Masters of the said Court, at his Chambers in Symond's-inn, Chancery-lane, London, on or before the 15th of February next, or in Default thereof they will be peremptorily excluded the Benefit of the said Decree.

Pursuant to a Decree of the High Court of Chancery, made In a Cause wherein Harriet Margaret Dymock, an Infant, and others are Plaintiffs, and Richard Atkinson and others are Defendants, the Creditors of William Dymock, late of Oxford-street, in the Parish of St. Mary-le-bone, in the County of Middlesex, Coach-master, deceased, are to come in and prove their Debts before Alexander Popham, Esq; one of the Masters of the said Court, at his Chambers in Symond's-inn, Chancery-lane, London, on or before the 22d Day of February next, or in Default thereof they will peremptorily be excluded the Benefit of the said Decree.

War-Office, January 26, 1788.

15th Regiment of (Light) Dragoons, William Stapleton, Gent. is appointed to be Cornet; vice William Aylett.

16th Regiment of (Light) Dragoons, Lieutenant John Bailey, from the Half Pay of the late 19th Dragoons, to be Lieutenant, vice Patrick Maxwell.

THE Partnership of Andrew Primerose and John Manhall, Linen-drapers, of Putney, Surrey, is this Day dissolved by mutual Consent. Witness our Hands,

Andrew Primerose.
John Manhall.

IF Abraham Green, Son of Abraham Green, formerly of Ipswich, in the County of Suffolk, Peruke-maker, and Ann his Wife, lately deceased, will apply to Mr. John Girling, of Ipswich, he will hear of something to his Advantage; or if any Person or Persons will give Information respecting the said Abraham Green (the Son) to the said John Girling, he will reward them for their Trouble.

TO be peremptorily sold, pursuant to a Decree of the High Court of Chancery, before Alexander Popham, Esq; one of the Masters of the said Court, at his Chambers in Symond's-inn, Chancery-lane, London, on Friday the 15th of February next, between Five and Six in the Afternoon, in One Lot, the Manor of Highlands, with the Royalties and Appurtenances, situate in the Parish of Sutton Athone, in the County of Kent, with the Quit Rents thereof, together with two Farms in the same Parish in the Occupation of William Chapman and Thomas Hardstone; also a Piece of Wood Land and Cottage and Garden in the Occupation of Henry Rixon, late Part of the Estate of John Calcraft, late of Ingress, in the County of Kent, Esq; deceased, of the yearly Value of 101 l. or thereabouts. Particulars whereof may be had at the said Master's Chambers.

THE Commissioners in a Commission of Bankrupt awarded and issued forth against Mark Allegre Bennett (Partner with Charles Heaven) late of Great Russell-street, Bloombury, in the County of Middlesex, Merchants, Dealers, Chapmen and Copartners, intend to meet on the 4th Day of March next, at Ten of the Clock in the Forenoon, at Guildhall, London, (by further Adjournment from the 22d of January instant) to take the last Examination of the said Bankrupt; when and where he is required to surrender himself, and make a full Discovery and Disclosure of his Estate and Effects, and finish his Examination; and the Creditors, who have not already proved their Debts, are to come prepared to prove the same, and, with those who have proved their Debts, are to assent to or dissent from the Allowance of the said Bankrupt's Certificate.

75. Extracts from the London Gazette *(number 12958), 26 January 1788*

including a notice of change of name (of my great aunt Maud Louisa Law) and a notice from executors of Thomas Dickson of Weybridge, Surrey, requiring creditors of the estate to submit claims. *Gazette* entries for awards of medals, liquidations and bankruptcies are considered in later chapters.

Gentleman's Magazine, published monthly from 1731 to 1868, contains notices of births, marriages and deaths, and announcements of bankrupts and military and clerical appointments. Entries refer to the upper classes but also to middle class families or other persons of note. There were long obituary notices of prominent people, especially clergymen or military officers, and even poor people were mentioned if they lived to a great age or if there was something of special note in their lives. For example, the death notices include many criminals who were executed at Tyburn. TNA, the British Library and the SoG hold complete (or almost complete) runs of *Gentleman's Magazine* (and there are also copies in many reference libraries). Copies for 1731–50 (and the *Annual Register*, see below, for 1758–78) can be viewed on the web site of the Internet Library of Early English Journals. The notices and news items usually only summarised newspaper reports and so, if you find a relevant entry, you should search contemporary newspapers (considered below) for a more detailed report. Entries in the July 1782 edition of *Gentleman's Magazine* include:

Marriages: July 19. At Lynn, Norfolk; Thomas Allen, esq. to Miss Jones, daughter of the Reverend Mr Jones of Navenby.

John Fiott, esq. to Miss Harriot Lee, second daughter of the late William Lee, esq. of Totteridge Park and granddaughter of the late L.C.J. Lee.

Deaths: At Fareham, Hampshire, aged 102, Henry Molding. He served in Queen Anne's wars and had plied the passage-boat from Fareham to Portsmouth for 60 years.

At Brockhill House, near Exeter, Richard Boyer, esq.; formerly an officer under the late Duke of Cumberland at the battle of Culloden.

At Ware, Mr Keys, formerly a farmer at Enfield Highway; where his house was broke open a few years ago by a gang of villains, whom he shot at, and who dangerously wounded his servant.

June 19. Captain Jos. Richards, commander of the "Sea-Horse", in the service of the Hudson's Bay Company.

News items: Wednesday 24 July. At Maidstone assizes, Charles Storey, labourer, was capitally convicted of the robbery and murder of Henry Perkins, journeyman papermaker, late of Chartham in Kent, on May 22, in the parish of Thannington, near Canterbury.

The last item is an extract from a very long account, providing details of the murder and of Storey's trial. It recorded that Storey was under 18 years old, originally from Norfolk, the youngest of 12 children and employed as a waggoner's mate by Mr Sarkey at Milton, near Chartham. Henry Perkins was married with two children and employed by Mr Leeds Payne. However, any of this information could be incorrect. Newspapers have always contained mistakes and the problem was worse in earlier years when informants were often illiterate and it was difficult for publishers to check that reports were true.

Each volume of *Gentleman's Magazine* is indexed and there are also cumulative indexes to surnames (sometimes with initials) for 1731 to 1786 and 1786 to 1810. A complete index to the full names of people recorded in the notices of births, marriages, deaths, bankruptcies and

The London Gazette

Published by Authority

Registered as a newspaper	*.*	For Table of Contents see last page

---

TUESDAY, 4 NOVEMBER, 1941

NOTICE is hereby given that I, MAUD LOUISA LAW Spinster of 17 Theydon Road, Clapton, London E.5, natural born British subject intend after the expiration of twenty-one days from the date of publication of this notice to assume the name of Maud Louisa Francis in lieu of and in substitution for my present name of Maud Louisa Law.—Dated this 31st day of October 1941.

(135)   M. L. LAW.

NOTICE is hereby given that by deed dated the 25th day of October 1941 duly executed and attested and enrolled in the Central Office of the Supreme Court of Judicature on the 28th day of October 1941 Harry Weightman of 16 Cow Pasture Lane, Sutton-in-Ashfield in the county of Nottingham abandoned the surname of Weightman and adopted the surname of WARING.—Dated this 31st day of October 1941.

HIBBERT and SON, 45, Westgate, Mansfield, (162) Notts, Solicitors for the said Harry Waring.

THOMAS DICKSON, Deceased.
Pursuant to the Trustee Act, 1925, Section 27.
NOTICE is hereby given, that all creditors and other persons having any debts, claims or demands against the estate of Thomas Dickson late of Elgin Lodge, Weybridge, in the county of Surrey (who died on the 4th day of July, 1941, and whose Will was proved by the Public Trustee and Constance May Dickson the executors therein named, in the Principal Registry of the Probate Division of His Majesty's High Court of Justice, on the 27th day of October, 1941), are hereby required to send particulars in writing of their debts, claims or demands to me, the undersigned, as Solicitor to the said executors on or before the 10th day of January 1942. And notice is hereby given, that at the expiration of that time the said executors will proceed to distribute the assets of the said testator among the parties entitled thereto, having regard only to the debts, claims and demands of which they shall then have had notice; and that they will not be liable for the assets or any part thereof so distributed to any person or persons of whose debt, claim, or demand they shall not then have had notice.—Dated this 30th day of October, 1941.

R. L. MASON, 61, Carey Street, Lincoln's Inn, (167) London, W.C.2, Solicitor to the said Executors.

THE BANKRUPTCY ACTS, 1914 AND 1926.

RECEIVING ORDERS.

No. 551. ALEXANDER, Lamuel Harold, 34, North End House, West Kensington, W.14. BUYER (Fruit and Vegetable), formerly 19, Glyn Mansions, Kensington, W.14. Court—HIGH COURT OF JUSTICE. Date of Filing Petition—Oct. 24, 1941. No. of Matter—239 of 1941. Date of Receiving Order—Oct. 24, 1941. No. of Receiving Order—142. Whether Debtor's or Creditor's Petition—Debtor's.

No. 552. FAWKES, Mrs. J. G., lately carrying on business at " The Rutland Court Hotel," 63, 64, 65, Lancaster Gate, London, W.2. HOTEL PROPRIETRESS. Present whereabouts unknown. Court—HIGH COURT OF JUSTICE. Date of Filing Petition—April 12, 1940. No. of Matter—174 of 1940. Date of Receiving Order —Oct. 24, 1941. No. of Receiving Order—141. Whether Debtor's or Creditor's Petition—Creditor's. Act of Bankruptcy Proved in Creditor's Petition—Section 1-1 (H.), Bankruptcy Act, 1914.

FIRST MEETINGS AND PUBLIC EXAMINATIONS.

ALEXANDER, Lamuel Harold, 34, North End House, West Kensington, W.14. BUYER (Fruit and Vegetable), formerly 19, Glyn Mansions, Kensington, W.14. Court—HIGH COURT OF JUSTICE. No. of Matter—239 of 1941. Date of First Meeting—Nov. 13, 1941. 11 a.m. Place —Bankruptcy Buildings, Carey Street, London, W.C.2. Date of Public Examination—Nov. 26, 1941. 11 a.m. Place—Bankruptcy Buildings, Carey Street, London, W.C.2.

---

76. *Extracts from the* London Gazette *(number 35335), 4 November 1941*

appointments is held in the LDS Family History Library in Salt Lake City. It is unfortunately not available on microfilm. For those unable to visit the library, there are some other (partial) indexes available. Farrar (481) indexes the obituary notices from 1731 to 1780. Most of these are for the upper classes, such as "Richard Hare, a brewer and justice of the peace for Middlesex" in 1776, but many other people also appear, such as "John Elware, executed at Tyburn" in 1741. Nangle (493) indexes obituary notices from 1781 to 1819 and Guildhall Library has a manuscript index to obituary notices up to 1855. Musgrave's *Obituary* (471) indexes many deaths in the 16th to 18th centuries, some from notices in *Gentleman's Magazine*, but also from other contemporary journals, such as *London Magazine*. Fry (482) indexes the marriages reported from 1731 to 1768. Typical entries are:

1731 Jan 8	Acland, Richard	Portugal, merchant
	Burrell, Miss	dau. of Peter Burrell; MP Haslemere
1756 Jan 13	Charnock, John	of the Inner Temple
	Boothby, Miss	of Leyton, Essex

The *Biography Database 1680–1830*, a series of CD-ROM that is searchable by peoples' names, was noted above (# chapter 9). In addition to directories, it also includes notices of births, marriages, deaths, bankruptcies and appointments from *Gentleman's Magazine*. The first two disks include notices from 1731–50 and 1751–70 respectively. The first disk also includes about 1,500 book subscription lists dating from 1680–1830.

The *Illustrated London News*, published weekly since 1847, included international news, reports of notable events in Britain, extracts from the *Gazette*, advertisements and engravings. Thus edition 721, for 30 December 1854, included reports on the Crimean War, the loss of the troop-ship *Charlotte* off the African coast, some obituaries (particularly of officers killed in the war), birth, marriage and death notices, military appointments (extracted from the *Gazette*), a report on the cholera epidemic of 1854, reports on plays at London theatres and a description of Ponteland church in Northumberland. The edition of 8 October 1898 featured a photograph of eight officers (with their names and regiments) who had been wounded at the battle of Omdurman. The edition of 6 March 1915 included photographs of 10 men who had been awarded the Military Cross.

The *Graphic* was another illustrated journal that commenced publication in the 19th century and includes material of interest to family historians. For example, the edition of 24 March 1900 included photographs of eight soldiers who had distinguished themselves in the war in South Africa. The edition of 23 June 1900 included photographs of 16 officers who had died in the conflict. The Illustrated London News Picture Library, 20 Upper Ground, London SE1 9PF (telephone 020 7805 5585), described by E. Hart in *Genealogists' Magazine* (September 2000), holds collections of the *Illustrated London News*, *The Graphic* and some other illustrated newspapers, with indexes of subject matters and famous people.

The *Annual Register* was first published in 1758. It also contained birth, marriage and death notices but generally only for well-known people. There are also many other journals which may assist your research of the religion or occupation of your ancestor. Examples include *Methodist Magazine*, first published in 1798, *Baptist Magazine*, first published in 1809, *Hairdresser's Journal* (from 1863) and *Boot and Shoe Maker* (from 1878). Copies of most of these journals are held at the British Library Newspaper Library at Colindale (described below).

National newspapers

A few newspapers and newsletters (usually published weekly) appeared in the early 17th century, but for many years they had to be licensed, were sometimes censored and included little information of interest to genealogists. The first English daily newspaper, the *Daily Courant*, commenced publication in 1702. Stamp duty was levied on newspapers from 1712, making them more expensive. Despite this, newspapers proliferated in the 18th century (although many were short-lived) and by 1785 eight morning papers were being published in London. In the 18th century national newspapers gradually began to include information that assists family historians. The gentry began to appear by name, for example in birth, marriage and death notices. By the end of the 18th century newspapers also began to mention poorer people, usually because of the crimes that they had committed or suffered.

The Times was first published in 1785 (but named *The Daily Universal Register* until 1788). Copies (on microfilm) are held at the Newspaper Library at Colindale, Guildhall Library and many other libraries. It carried very few notices of births, marriages or deaths until the 19th century and they concentrated on the rich or famous. Illustration 77 is an extract from an 1871 edition of the paper. The SoG and Guildhall Library have separate microfilm copies of the birth, marriage and death notices, to which there are manuscript surname indexes (on microfilm), each index covering a period of six months. There are also two series of general indexes to *The Times* (in quarterly volumes). These are *Palmer's Index*, covering 1791 to 1941 and the *Official Index to The Times*, covering 1785 to 1790 and 1906 to date. These index the obituary and bankruptcy notices, criminal trials, civil court actions, fires, highway robberies, inquests, knighthoods, meetings of creditors, shipping news, other news reports and a few of the birth, marriage and death notices. Thus *The Official Index* (467) for January to March 1915 includes many entries of genealogical interest, such as:

Lumb, Capt. F.G.E.,	awarded Military Cross Feb.19 [page] 4, [column] e.
Mackenzie, Capt. F.O.,	killed in action Mar 8 [page] 4, [column] d.
Urwick, Mr William H.,	Will. Jan 21 [page] 11, [column] c.

Palmer's quarterly indexes for 1791 to 1905 have been reprinted and are also available on CD-ROM at the SoG and reference libraries. *The Official Index to The Times* for 1906–80 is also available on CD-ROM, for example at TNA. For example, the reprint of *Palmer's Index* (468) for 1790 to 1795 includes Palmer's quarterly index for 1 October to 31 December 1790. Each entry has a reference in the form "8 o 11 e" (which means "8th October, page 11, fifth column"). A few examples of the index entries reveal the importance of the material to family historians:

Bankruptcies		**Births**	
Boardman, Giles	8d 2a	Lovelace, Mrs, of a son	29n 3b
Civil actions		**Highway robberies**	
Freeman v. Lockier	11n 3c	of Mr & Mrs Craughton near Epsom	2o 4b
Fires		**Inquests**	
at Barnstaple	11n 4b	on Mr Ashwin, killed in a riot	19a 3c
at Rotherhithe	15o 2c	Eliz. Beal murdered by her mother	8j 3c
Criminal trials		**Marriages**	
Seymour, Ann, for stealing	10d 4b	Baddeley, Dr to Miss C. Brackenbury	2d 3d
Time, Edward, for burglary	29o 3c	Charnock, Mr to Miss Parish	1o 3d

Deaths		**Ship news**	
Anderson, Mr J	15a 3d	Loss of the "Tigris"	23d 3d

Digital versions of many editions of *The Times* from 1785 to 1985, searchable by names, places, subjects and other keywords, are being placed on the web site of *The Times* Digital Archive. This is presently only available, on subscription, to certain libraries and other institutions but was reviewed by J. Reid in *Family Tree Magazine* (May 2003). Present technology is only partially effective in digitising and indexing the small print used in newspapers, so projects such as this do not yet replace the indexes noted above. However, the technology (and therefore indexes) will no doubt improve.

Other national newspapers also contain items of genealogical interest, although the lack of indexes makes it difficult to find items about particular people. Four articles by C. Nicholson in *Genealogists' Magazine* (March to December 1929) review the important items that appear in early English national newspapers, including obituary, marriage and birth notices, advertisements for missing relatives, or notices from masters about runaway apprentices and from men whose wives had eloped with other men. Nicholson's examples include:

From *The Protestant Intelligence* of 10 February 1679:

Nathanael Tetcomb, an apprentice to Edward Wilkins, a hatmaker in . . . Southwark, has been gone from his Master these three months. He is a tall young man, having black hair, in a brown cloth suit. Whoever brings this lad to his master shall, as a reward, have 20 shillings.

From the *Original Weekly Journal* in 1737:

Last Wednesday, Mr Abraham Butterfield, a merchant and Mrs Rebecca Fielder, two wealthy and agreeable Quakers, were married at the Park Meeting House, in Southwark, before a numerous assembly, after which a very elegant dinner was provided for [their] relations and friends at the White Lion Tavern in Talbot Court, Gracechurch Street.

From the *Flying Post* of 24 September 1700:

On 30th August 1700, Deborah the wife of Mr Richard Latchfield, solicitor in Chancery, whose house is in Chichester Rents in Chancery Lane, did rob her husband of all his household goods . . . and ran away with another man, whose name is unknown. If any person shall harbour Deborah Latchfield, lately called Deborah Alaman, widow of Samuel Alaman, who lived in Mitre Court in Fleet Street and kept Sam's Coffee House there . . . they shall be prosecuted . . . and if any person do apprehend the said Deborah and bring her to her husband, or discover his goods, they shall have 10 shillings reward.

From *The Post* in 1704:

John Nolson and Mary Nolson his sister, born at Knottingley near Pontefract, Yorkshire, who came away from thence near 30 years ago, and are supposed to be about London (if living) are desired to come to Mr Thomas Whitehead, at the sign of the Sugar Loaf in Long Lane, where they may hear of a near relation, who hath some money for them.

If you know the dates of ancestors' marriages or deaths, more recent newspapers may assist. *The Times* and *Daily Telegraph* have lists of births, marriages and engagements. Some national daily newspapers continue to include obituaries of notable people.

BIRTHS.

On the 28th Jan., at Geneva, the wife of JOHN BURY, Esq., of a son.

On the 29th Jan., the wife of the Rev. T. ARTHUR CURTIES, New bold Pacey, Warwickshire, of a daughter.

On the 30th Jan., at La Fontaine, St. Helier's, Jersey, the wife of EDWARD PERCY HICKS, Esq., 42d Royal Highlanders, of a son.

On the 31st Jan., at Edinburgh, the wife of G. A. BALLARD, Esq., of twin daughters.

- On the 31st ult., the wife of the Rev. JAMES BURY, of Sudbrooke near Lincoln, of twin boys.

On the 1st Feb., at 37, Grove-park, Liverpool, the wife of G. M. POWER, Esq., of a daughter.

On the 1st Feb., at Castle-street, Hereford, the wife of Capt.THOMAS PROTHERO NEWALL, Adjutant 1st Administrative Battalion Herefordshire Rifle Volunteers, of a son.

On the 1st Feb., at The Laund, near Lancaster, the wife of R. A. CLARKE, Esq., of a daughter.

On the 2d Feb., at 5, Berkeley-gardens, Campden-hill, the wife of W. F. KEMP, Esq., of a son.

On the 2d Feb., at Feering House, Kelvedon, Essex, the wife of HARRIS HILLS, of a daughter.

On the 3d Feb., at Draycot Lodge, Tolworth, Surbiton, Surrey, the wife of STANLEY SLOCOMBE, of a son.

On the 3d Feb., at Potter's-bar, Herts, the wife of I. STEVEN PRICE, Esq., of a son.

On the 3d Feb., at Arborfield, Reading, the wife of the Rev WYNDHAM C. H. HUGHES D'AETH, of a son.

On the 3d Feb., at the College, Glasgow, the wife of GEORGE G RAMSAY, of a son.

On the 3d Feb., at The Thorn, Chesham, Bucks, the wife of Captain HARDY, late 18th Hussars, of a son.

On the 3d Feb., at Clutha Villa, Downs-road, Clapton, the wife of JOHN POTTER, of a daughter.

On the 4th Feb., at 43, Kensington-park-gardens, W., the wife of HENRY ALEXR. HAIG, Esq., of a daughter.

On the 4th Feb., at 111, Connaught-terrace, Hyde-park, W., the wife of EDWARD A. JONES, Esq., of a son.

At 24, Park-lane, Hon. Mrs. ELLIOT, of a son.

MARRIAGES.

On the 3d Feb., at St. George's, Hanover-square, by the Rev. J. C Gregory, assisted by the Rev. M. Rainsford, HENRY NEVIL SHERBROOKE, Esq., late of the 43d Light Infantry, second son of Henry Sherbrooke, Esq., of Oxton, Notts, to the Lady HARRIE ALICE CURZON, only child of the Earl and Countess Howe.

On the 23d Jan., at Algiers, by H.M.'s British Consul, HENRY ROBERT WILLIAM MILES, Esq., to ISABELLA ANNIE, only surviving daughter of the late C. D. LEEVIN, Esq.

On the 30th ult., at the Registrar's-office, Amptbill-square, London ALFRED WILLIAM PALMER, fifth son of the Rev. Ellis Palmer, vicar Hanley, Staffordshire, to ROSE HUGHES, youngest daughter of the late William Hughes.

On the 1st Feb., at the parish church, Welton, after banns, by the Rev. W. Williamson, vicar, JOHN, only son of JAMES CONEY, of Welton, to ELEANOR, second daughter of the late ROBERT CONEY, of Faldingworth. No cards.

On the 1st Feb., at the parish church, Beeston, Notts, by the Rev J. C. Jones, assisted by the Rev. T. J. Oldrini, FREDERIC ORTON M.D., of Hornsey, to CLARA, daughter of the late G. WHITE, Esq., surgeon, Nottingham.

On the 1st Feb., at Trinity Church, Paddington, by the Rev. W. F Walker, GEORGE EDWARD, eldest son of the late GEORGE STOKES Esq., of 2, Porchester-gardens, Bayswater, to ANNA MARIA, only daughter of HENRY LE PATOUREL, Captain South Glocester Militia.

On the 1st Feb., at Edgbaston Parish Church, by the Rev. George Lea, the Rev. FREDERICK THOMAS SWINBURN, vicar of Acock's Green, to JULIA SOPHIA, only surviving daughter of WILLIAM GEORGE POSTANS, Esq., George-road, Edgbaston.

On the 2d Feb., at All Saints' Church, Notting-hill, by the Rev Alfred Newby, rector of Little Gransden, uncle of the bride, assisted by the Rev. John Light, incumbent of All Saints, HENRY BAYLY GARLING, Esq., Southborough Hall, near Tunbridge-Wells, to MARIAN, youngest daughter of T. CAUTLEY NEWBY, Esq., Talbot road, Westbourne-park, Bayswater. No cards.

On the 2d Feb., at St. Jude's, Wolverhampton, by the Rev. S. C Adam, CHARLES H. BROOKING, Esq., M.D., of Brixham, Devon, to LAURA, daughter of the late ALFRED PUDDICOMBE, Esq., of More tonhampstead, Devon. No cards.

On the 2d Feb., at St. Peter's Church, St. Alban's, by the Rev. H. N Dudding, THOS. GODDARD, jun., to ELIZABETH, youngest daughter of T. COX, Esq., of St. Alban's. No cards.

On the 2d Feb., at St. Mary's Catholic Church, Cadogan-terrace Sloane-street, JOHN JAMES HEATH SAINT, of the Inner Temple, barrister-at-law, only son of the Rev. J. J. Saint, of Groombridge Place Kent, to SARAH, youngest daughter of ANDREW LYNCH FRENCH Esq., of Lynch's Estates, St. Kitt's, West Indies, and niece of Lieut. Gen. French, of 17, Belgrave-road, Eccleston-square.

77. *Births and marriages of January and February 1871 announced in* The Times

The location of national newspapers

London newspapers from 1603 to 1800 are in the Burney Collection at the British Library in London and can be viewed on microfilm. The British Library also holds the Thomason Collection which covers the Civil War and Commonwealth period. London newspapers since 1800 (as well as a microfilm copy of the Burney Collection), other British national newspapers and local newspapers (considered below) are held at the British Library Newspaper Library, at Colindale Avenue, Colindale, London NW9 5HE (telephone 020 7412 7353), close to Colindale underground station. It is open Monday to Saturday from 10 a.m. to 5 p.m., but it is advisable to reserve a seat in advance. You will need a British Library reader's ticket or a Newspaper Library annual or day pass (the latter is available on production of proof of identity). The newspapers are available for inspection in large bound volumes or on microfilm. Copies of pages or articles can be ordered or, if the newspaper is on microfilm, copies can be made on self-service microfilm printers. The staff at Colindale can also undertake searches (for a fee) if you know the date and location of an event that might have been reported.

The collection at Colindale consists of over 500,000 volumes and 300,000 microfilm reels of British and Irish newspapers and journals (and of some overseas countries), which are listed in a computerised catalogue, which can also be accessed on the library's web site (# appendix XI). Colindale also holds some indexes to particular newspapers (such as the indexes to *The Times*) and a large collection of books about newspapers. Microfilm copies of many runs of newspapers can also be purchased (prices are listed in catalogues available at Colindale). Digital versions of a few editions of selected newspapers (for example the *Daily News* from 1851, 1856, 1886, 1900 and 1918), are being placed on the library's web site. The database can be searched by name, place, subject and date. As noted above, digitisation of newsprint is not completely effective and so such database searches presently miss many relevant articles or references in the newspapers.

The Bodleian Library in Oxford also holds many early newspapers. The National Library of Scotland and the National Library of Wales have large collections of Scottish and Welsh papers (# chapter 29). The India Office collections at the British Library (# chapter 30) include a fine collection of English language newspapers from India from about 1780. Copies of many of these are also held at Colindale.

Local newspapers

Provincial newspapers were first published in the early 18th century. The *Norwich Post* commenced publication in 1701 and was followed by papers such as the *Post Boy* in Bristol and the Exeter *Post Man* (both in 1704), the Newcastle *Gazette* (1710), the *York Courant* (1715), the Plymouth *Weekly Journal* (1718) and the *Liverpool Advertiser* (1756). However, even by 1800 there were only about 100 provincial papers and they concentrated on national or international news rather than local news. The great growth in the number of local newspapers came with the reduction of stamp duty on newspapers in 1836 and its abolition in 1855. For example, in Devon, local newspapers began publication in Torquay (in 1839), Sidmouth (1849), Dartmouth (1853) and Totnes (1860). At this time, local newspapers also began including more local news.

A local newspaper may contain an obituary of an ancestor or relative who held a local office or was wealthy or well known in the community. However, you should treat information in obituaries with some care. Information as to the deceased's place of birth and early life, which was provided to a newspaper by his children or friends, may be unreliable. Illustration 78 is the obituary of John Herbert Keates (a brother of my great grandmother Alice Amelia Keates) who died in Australia in 1959. This obituary provides limited genealogical information (omitting the names of his widow and children, his age, place of birth and the date when he emigrated to Australia), but it does provide information that would be very difficult to obtain from other records. Local newspapers also contain notices or photographs of weddings. The 1945 marriage of one of my great uncles (on leave from the 8th Army) was featured (with a photograph) in a local newspaper. Marriage announcements appeared in local newspapers from the late 18th century, generally recording local weddings (particularly of wealthier families) but often reporting marriages elsewhere if they were of local interest (for example a local landowner marrying in London). Many births and deaths of local residents were also recorded (illustration 79 includes examples from an 1870 edition of *Trewman's Exeter Flying Post*), although birth notices often omitted the child's name. Announcements may add little to the information that you already have, but they may help you find a marriage that took place elsewhere in Britain. The extracts in illustration 79 announce marriages (of Devon residents) in Bath, Weymouth and London.

Local newspaper reports may refer to your ancestors if they were involved in notable events, such as fires, epidemics and mining or shipping disasters. You may find only a summary news item, but possibly a detailed report of the event and the people involved. Newspaper reports of criminal trials (in cases of murder, theft, fire or riots) are of great value. If someone died, or was killed, the newspaper may report on the inquest. Local papers also carried lists (and sometimes photographs) of local men who were killed in wars or who were awarded medals. An example of a valuable newspaper report concerns my great grandfather, Charles Richard Symes. Relatives told me that Charles died of blood poisoning following an accident when he was working on a ship. His burial at Topsham in Devon was recorded on 13 July 1913. At Colindale, I located the weekly newspaper *Trewman's Exeter Flying Post* for 12 July 1913. This included two items:

Fatal Finger Injury. Charles Symes, 58, of Topsham, mate of the steam barge Sirdar, who injured his finger while unloading stone at Exmouth dock last month, died in Exeter Hospital this week from poisoning. At the inquest on Thursday a verdict of accidental death was returned.

Obituary
JOHN HERBERT KEATES

The Anglican Church Mission lost a most valuable honorary helper by the death of Mr. John Herbert Keates, who died on 30th June, 1959.

Mr. Keates was an accomplished wood-carver and cabinet craftsman. He worked for over 18 years at the Brisbane General Hospital in the Works Department and was highly respected by all other tradesmen.

Mr. Keates was truly a Man of God, honest and thorough in all his dealings. A devoted husband and father — he leaves a wife and two married sons and a daughter to mourn his loss. Mr. Keates was also an organist of the first quality, and for more than 20 years, Sunday by Sunday, accompanied Canon W. P. B. Miles or Canon G. Neale to two or more Church Mission centres to play the organ for the services. His valuable honorary services are greatly missed. In his spare time he made Altars, Prayer Desks, Fonts, Hymn Boards, Missal Stands, and innumerable articles for any centre where they were needed. One of his last efforts was to make a set of altar furnishings for a church in Melanesia. These beautifully finished articles, the work of a true and devout craftsman, will remain a monument to his generous and devoted service.

May he rest in peace.

78. Extract from an Australian newspaper with the obituary of John Herbert Keates

OTTERY ST. MARY.—The Ottery St. Mary petty session was held on Thursday before C. J. Cornish and J. B. Lousada, Esqrs., when Roland Cheese, of Rockbeare, was fined 40s., including costs, for poaching on lands occupied by Mr. James Trickey, of Rockbeare. He had been previously convicted.—Hake and Son, for having deficient weights in their possessions at their coal store at the Ottery Road Railway Station, were fined 40s., including expenses.—William Selley, mason, of Sidmouth, for creating a disturbance, was fined 40s., including costs.—Charles Haggerty, hawker, was fined 5s., with costs, for an intemperate freak at Sidmouth.—The victuallers' licenses in the district were renewed, excepting those of Thomas Cole, of the Greyhound Inn, Fenny bridge, whose license is suspended during the trial of a poaching case against him; and Richard Wilson, of the Halfway House, Aylesbeare. Wilson's application was opposed by Rebecca Selick, of Aylesbeare-hill, and she brought neighbours to support her statement as to the character of the Halfway House, and the Bench refused the license. George Dorey, the only beer house keeper in Rockbeare, applied for a spirit license. The applicant produced a numerously signed memorial from the parishioners of Rockbeare. Superintendent Dore opposed the application, and succeeded in establishing the fact that the house applicant lived in was not suited for a licensed house. Application refused. Mr. W. H. Godfrey, on applying for his renewal, was opposed by Superintendent Dore on the ground that the tenement rated was not one tenement. Mr. Jeffery supported the application, and demanded to see the rate book. The overseer for some time refused; but Mr. Jeffery argued that every ratepayer was entitled to inspect the rate book, and had the same produced to the magistrates, when it was found that applicant's tenement appeared on the books as one tenement. Application granted.—[The Bishop of Oxford (on visit to his venerable father-in-law, Sir J. J. Coleridge) preached to a full congregation on Sunday in Ottery Church in aid of the funds of the parish schools. The collection amounted to £16 7s. 8d.—[A man named Coombes, a labourer, living at Ottery town, has cut his throat to such an extent that there is no hope of his recovery. A slight quarrel is said to be the reason for the rash act.

BIRTHS.
September 5, at Lansdown-place, Plymouth, the wife of J. Russell Hicks, Esq., a daughter.
September 3, at the Royal Marine Barracks, Stonehouse, the wife of Lieut.-Col. T. V. Cooke, a daughter.
September 1, at Western-road, Launceston, the wife of Mr. John Langman, a son.
September 1, at Bickleigh Rectory, Tiverton, the wife of the Rev. R. B. Carew, a son.
August 30, at Watcombe, the wife of F. A. Cranning, Esq., a son.
August 30, at Croydon, the wife of Mr. James Phillips, a daughter.
August 27, at Ranscombe, near Chudleigh, the wife of Mr. S. L. Bennett, a son.
August 27, at Bowood, the Marchioness of Lansdowne, a daughter.
July 4, at Melbourne, Australia, the wife of Mr. M. A. Alexandra, a daughter.

MARRIAGES.
September 4, at Exeter, William Walter Harn, of Chagford, to Dorcas, eldest daughter of Mr. W. Carter, of Bicton.
September 1, at Walcot Church, Bath, Colonel W. P. Radcliffe, C.B., to Isabel, daughter of the late Hon. P. B. Le Blaquiere.
August 31, at St. Mary's Church, Weymouth, by the Rev. J. Ground, Frederick Edwin Harrisonn, eldest son of the Rev. F. Nebbs, Kilburn, London, to Frances Caroline Annie, youngest daughter of Major Barbor, late 8th Bengal Light Cavalry.
August 29, at St. Michael's Church, Great Torrington, by the Rev. S. Buckland, Henry Barr to Harriet Hughes.
August 29, at Chulmleigh, Thomas Alfred Head, of Bath, to Maria Susan, third daughter of Mr. Jas. Derr, The Cottage, Chulmleigh.
August 29, at East Budleigh, Mr. Edwin Potbury, of Washington City, United States, to Mary Vickary, niece of Mr. W. White, of Victoria Lodge, Budleigh Salterton.
August 29, at the Wesleyan Chapel, Liverpool-road, London, Mr. John Edrn, of Exeter, to Mrs. Ann Jarman, late of Bickleigh, near Tiverton.
August 28, at Castle-street Chapel, Mr. J. Redlen, of Heavitree, to Miss M. A. Baker, of Ottery St. Mary.
August 27, at Ilfracombe parish church, by the Rev. J. M. Chanter, vicar, George S. Bascom, Esq., to Ida, eldest daughter of H. Sarsfield Bascom, Esq., of Demerara.
August 18, at St. Paul's Church, Chariton, Kent, Christopher G. Millman, Esq., J.P., of Dawlish, to Caroline Lydia, daughter of the late Lieutenant-Colonel Read, Deputy-Quartermaster-General, Madras.

DEATHS.
September 5, at Cheeke-street, Exeter, after a lingering illness, Richard Lang, aged 44.
September 4, at Maine Villa, Westward Ho! (the residence of her father), the wife of Mr. Thomas Goaman, of Bideford, aged 33.
September 3, at St. Mary Arches-street, Mr. John P. Westlake, aged 61.
September 3, at Plymouth, Sarah, widow of Vice-Admiral Monday, aged 77.
September 3, at Plymouth, of consumption, Mr. Samuel Berr, of H.M. Customs, aged 32.
September 3, at York-place, Plymouth, Agnes, wife of Mr. Samuel Watters, aged 28.
September 2, at the Rock Hotel, Horrabridge, after a lingering illness, Mr. L. Shillibeer, aged 26.
September 2, at Westleigh, near Bideford, the wife of Mr. James Ryan, late of the 17th Lancers, aged 40.
September 1, at Teignmouth, Edward Bowles Pripp, Esq., formerly of Westbury-on-Trim, Bristol, aged 53.
September 1, at No. 5, Eldon-place, Mrs. Elizabeth Richards, relict of Mr. William Richards, aged 82.
August 31, at Bampton-street, Tiverton, Mr. Henry Skinner.
August 31, the wife of Mr. W. Willcocks, of Pengelley Farm, Exminster, suddenly, by breaking a blood-vessel.
August 31, at Bedford-place, Tavistock, Jane, wife of J. Grant, Esq., retired paymaster R.N., aged 66.
August 30, at Sidmouth, Richard Campion, Esq., of Denmark-hill, Camberwell.
August 30, at Longfleet, Poole, Emma, the wife of Wm. Lewis Cockram Adey, Esq., aged 48.
August 30, at Clifton, Bristol, Lionel Oliver Rigg, Esq., aged 77.
August 29, at Corringa, Torquay, Hamilton Campbell, infant son of George Maconchy, Esq.
August 28, at Northiawton, Elizabeth, wife of Mr. John Sampson, aged 48.
August 25, at Blackheath, Powderham, Annie Mortimer, daughter of Mr. Fred. Pitts, aged 6 months.
At Radford, Dawlish, the wife of Mr. T. W. Clutsam.
At Kenton, Charlotte, the daughter of Mr. Knott, aged 18.

79. *Extracts from* Trewman's Exeter Flying Post, *7 September 1870*

Topsham. A slight accident which occurred to Charles R. Symes on June 28th ended fatally at the Royal Devon and Exeter Hospital on Tuesday. The deceased, who was well known and respected in Topsham, was a naval pensioner, acting as mate on the steam barge Sirdar, which belongs to Messrs Hooper and Cooke of Exmouth . . . the crew were unloading stone at Exmouth Dock when Symes knocked his little finger. He thought little of it . . . he continued at work until last Saturday when he complained of feeling very ill. Mrs Symes and a neighbour applied poultices, but the patient being no better on Sunday, Dr. Macpherson was called in and he ordered immediate removal to hospital, where the patient succumbed to blood poisoning. The case is very sad, the breadwinner of the family being so suddenly taken away and much sympathy is felt for the widow and her three daughters and a son.

In addition to the account of Charles's accident and death, this report noted facts which allowed further research into his life. I already knew that Charles was a naval pensioner, but I could now look for records of the inquest, for his service as mate on the barge *Sirdar*, and for any surviving records of his employers, Hooper & Cooke. As another example, a researcher, Alan Poole, found that his grandmother's first husband was killed in a train crash in Essex in 1905. Mr Poole's article in the *Essex Family Historian* (November 1993) notes that a local newspaper included a detailed account of the accident and coroner's inquest, listing the names of 10 people who were killed, the 50 people who were injured and the names of many passengers, witnesses or railway staff. The newspaper also reported many people's ages, occupations and residences.

If your ancestors ran a shop or business, you may find advertisements for the shop or business in local newspapers. Late 19th-century newspapers included advertisements from coal merchants, fishmongers, butchers, tailors and many others. Illustration 79 includes examples from *Trewman's Exeter Flying Post* of 7 September 1870, such as adverts for Mr E. Trowt (a grocer and tea dealer); Paul Collings (a hay, straw and corn merchant) and W. Mortimer and Son (stockbrokers). There is also an advert from John Milford, a decorator of Thorverton in Devon. There will also be notices of bankruptcies, sales of farms or businesses, and police notices for the apprehension of criminals. If your relatives emigrated by ship, you may find an advertisement for the sailing in the local newspaper of the port of departure. There may also be detailed reports of local council meetings. There are usually detailed news items about criminal court cases which involved local people, naming criminals, victims and witnesses. Court proceedings are considered further in chapters 24 and 25, but illustration 79 includes a report from *Trewman's Exeter Flying Post* of cases before the justices at Ottery St Mary in Devon. Roland Chown of Rockbeare was convicted of poaching from land owned by James Trickey. William Selley, a mason of Sidmouth, was fined for creating a disturbance. Thomas Cole's application for renewal of a victualler's licence for the Greyhound Inn at Fennybridge was dismissed. Illustration 80 consists of extracts from reports in *Trewman's Exeter Flying Post* of 20 March 1845 of court sessions of the Justices at Exeter. The reports refer to many cases, including:

Edward Drewe, 16, was indicted for stealing a pair of boots, value 6s, the property of James Buckingham . . . the case was clear and being again convicted [Drewe had only just been released from gaol for a previous offence] he was sentenced to transportation for seven years.

Adeline Harris, 34, a "fille de joie", occupying apartments in North Street, was indicted for stealing . . . from . . . Abraham Cleeve, a gold watch . . . the jury pronounced a verdict of acquittal.

EXETER CITY GENERAL SESSIONS.

A General Sessions for the City and County of the City of Exeter commenced on the morning of Saturday last, at the Guildhall, where the Learned Recorder *Francis Newman Rogers, Esq.*, Barrister-at-Law, arrived at 10 o'clock, in the State Carriage of, and accompanied by *Wm. Denis Moore, Esq.*, High-Sheriff of Exeter. There was also with them *Edwin Force, Esq.*, Under-Sheriff; and these were met at the entrance and preceded to the Bench, by *Edward Woolmer, Esq.*, Mayor; *P. Miller, J. Harris, S. Kingdon, H. Hooper, T. P. Barham, Esqrs.*, Justices.

GRAND JURY.—*Richard Halswell Dewdney, Esq.*, was sworn as Foreman; and the following, with him, formed the Grand Jury:—*Bartholomew Dickes, James Luke Knight, George Du Chemin, Robert Browne, Wm. Tracr, George Tucker, Wm. Davis, Doherty Smith, Robert Harvey, Wm. Cuthbertson, Wm. Kerswell Mogridge, George Curzon, John Phillips Chas. Manley, Ambrose Jarvis, John Butler Fitzgerald, Wm. Wreford, James Templeton, Thomas Pitt, Edward Hawkins.*

The Proclamation against Vice and Immorality was read by *John Gidley, Esq.*, Town Clerk; and this done,

The Recorder proceeded to deliver

THE CHARGE,

Saying, Gentlemen of the Grand Inquest, the Calendar at the present Sessions contains the names of fourteen prisoners, a number somewhat exceeding the average of later years, but still not equal, certainly, to the average of former years. Gentlemen, There is no case among these but what is of the usual and ordinary description of offences, nor is there any requiring observation on my part. But at the same time I take the opportunity of saying to you that should any difficulty present itself in the course of your inquiries, and you will be so good as make this known to me, I shall be most happy to afford you every assistance in my power. At present, however, and viewing the cases as I do, it does appear to me that it would be an absolute waste of time to detain gentlemen of your good sense and experience here in the discussion of subjects of the most trite or common place kind.

TRIAL OF PRISONERS.

Edward Drewe, 16, was indicted for stealing, on the 18th of January last, in the market place, a pair of boots, value 6s., the property of James Buckingham, who had a stall there with boots and shoes exposed for sale. The youthful prisoner, at the time of the commission of this act, had just been liberated from the city gaol, where he had undergone the punishment of the law, for felony. The case was clear, and being again convicted,—as also that it was evident there was no hope by any milder method of producing reformation in the prisoner,—he was sentenced to transportation for seven years.

John Rogers, 17, was indicted for stealing, on the 23rd of Feb last, a £5. promissory note, four sovereigns, one half-sovereign, and 2s., the monies of his master John Blackmore, of Stepcote hill, in this city. The particulars of this case appeared in our paper last week. The prisoner, some time in the service of Mr Blackmore, was sent with a parcel in which this money was inclosed, to his mistress, at Dawlish. Instead, however, of going there he set out for Plymouth,—opening the parcel, and converting the money to his own use. He made a statement that he had been impelled to make use of a portion of the money in consequence of not having sufficient to provide food; an assertion completely negatived by the fact that, apart from this money, the sum of 3s. 10d. was given to him for his day's maintenance. And the jury finding him guilty,—the Recorder said, that offences by servants against their masters must be visited with severe punishment; he, therefore, sentenced him to be transported seven years.

John Hoare, 15, and *John Knott*, 17, were indicted for feloniously breaking and entering the dwelling house of James Stoneman, in St. Sidwells, on the 12th of February last, and stealing 2 lbs. weight of fish; a pack of cards, value 6d; and other articles; and being found guilty, were sentenced to be severally imprisoned for the term of six calendar months, and during that time kept to hard labour.

James Trick, 16, was indicted for stealing on the 2nd of March inst., a sovereign, 10s. in silver, a sixpence and four penny silver coin, the monies of John Thomas, of Paul-street. Trick had come to Exeter from Bearferris, in order to ascertain the fate of Wm. Ellis, of the same age, tried and convicted of felony at the Devon County Sessions,—whom he calls his brother; and was lodging at John Thomas's, a dealer in cider, &c., in Paul-street. On the morning of Sunday the 2nd, John Thomas left home about 7 o'clock, to attend service at a Wesleyan Meeting House, leaving the money in question in his bed room; and shortly after his return Trick came down stairs and left the house. By and by the money was missed,—the police informed,—and search made after Trick, who in the mean time, in his rambles, had dined at Hopper's eating house, South street, where he regaled himself with half-a-duck, besides *et ceteras*, and changed the sovereign. The jury returned a verdict of guilty, and the prisoner was sentenced to be imprisoned and kept to hard labour two calendar months.

Leah Richards, 22,—who was attired in mourning,—was indicted for stealing on the 18th of January, from her furnished lodgings on Stepcote hill, a blanket, value 2s., the property of Matthew Lucas. There was also a second charge of a similar nature against her; and being found guilty, the Recorder observed that he was sorry to be obliged to say this was a description of offence that prevailed to a considerable extent in this city, and must be met with punishment. He, therefore, sentenced her to be imprisoned six weeks, and kept to hard labour.

Elizabeth Jenkins, 24, pleaded guilty to a charge of stealing on the 22nd of Jan. last, a blanket, value 2s. 6d., the property of George Loray. This, like the former, was a case of robbing furnished lodgings; and the Recorder addressing the prisoner in similar terms, sentenced her also to imprisonment and hard labour for six weeks.

Adeline Harrison, 31, a *fille de joie*, occupying apartments in North-street, was indicted for stealing on the night of the 8th of March, from the person of Abraham Cleave, a gold watch value £5, and chain value £2, his property. The prosecutor in this case was subjected to a most rigid cross examination, and it appeared that about midnight on Saturday the 8th inst., he entered the apartments occupied by the prisoner. He had drank freely, but knew what he was about. While there, however, he was robbed by some one of the watch and chain. Harrison stoutly denied having committed the robbery; and the jury pronounced a verdict of acquittal.

DEVON AND EXETER ASSIZES.

Mr. Justice Coleridge, one of the Judges on the Western Circuit arrived in this city between two and three o'clock on Monday afternoon, from Ottery, having reached his residence at that place from Dorchester, on Saturday night. The Learned Judge was met near Heavitree Bridge, by Edward Simcoe Drewe, Esq., High Sheriff of Devon; Mark Kennaway, Esq., Under-Sheriff; and Frederick Leigh, Esq., County Clerk, in the splendid state, and private carriages of the much beloved and universally respected High Sheriff. In order to give the most public evidence of the estimation in which this worthy gentleman is held, and furnish proof of the opinion entertained concerning him by his tenantry and all with whom he has connection, there were also assembled on this occasion a body of yeomanry on horseback, of near ninety in number. There were, likewise, a troop of javelin men, the majority of whom were from Mr. Drewe's estates;—trumpeters and officers, in a handsome uniform.

Mr. Justice Coleridge presided at NISI PRIUS, where was presented the following

CAUSE LIST.

Plaintiff's Att.	*Plaintiffs.*	*Defendants.*	*Defendant's Att.*
E. Smith	Atkinson	v Stacey & ano.	Barron.
Walker & Co..	E. o Egremont (s.j.)	v Isaac	Gillard.
Sims	Doe d Egremont (s.j.)	v Courtney ..	Riccard & Son
Brown	The Queen ..	v Sleeman (wd)	Pattison.
Bulteel	Nuttle, Pauper, (s.j.)	v Cornish	Walford.
Pearce	Glanville	v Hawkey	Fox.
Watts & Whidborne	Wilking	v Brock......	T. Sanders.
Head	Jennings & ano.	v Sanders	Gould.
A. Rooker	Whiddon, Extx.	v Wakeham ..	Bayly.
Same	Whiddon	v Same	Same.
Square	Holman, Esq...	v White......	Lavers.
Palmer, F. & P.	Johnson & ano.	v Phillips	Gem & Co.
Bridgman & L.	Commins (s.j.)	v Willesford ..	Willesford & T.
Foot	Plymouth Dock Water Works Comp. (s.j.)	v Scott & ano.	Whiteford & Co
Tucker	Sawdye	v Ireland	Fryer.
Davie	Wood	v Webber & an	Rodham.
Aberdein	Wood	v Hewett	Bowerman.
Appleyard	Daykin (s.j.)..	v Cornish	Edwards & B.
H. Elsworthy ..	Jackman	v France	Poole & Gamlen
Rowcliffe & Son	Cutcliffe & ano	v Brownridge &c.	Glubb.
Sumpter	Doe d. Dayman	v Moore	J. Rooker.
Little & Co. ..	Doe d. Molesworth.	v Sleeman	Pattison.
Elliott........	Barrett	v Oliver......	Evans Clerrtn.
Tanner	Maunder......	v Wivell	In Person.
Same	Northcote	v Same	Same.
Watts & W. ..	Doe d. Wilking	v Brock	Sanders.
Geare & Co. ..	Glass	v Cowd	J. H. Terrell.
Edwards & B..	Cornish	v Daykins	Appleyard.
Little & Hearle	Symons	v Stone	Hunt.
Brown	The Queen....	v Sleeman (r.e.)	Pattison.
CITY OF EXETER.			
H. W. Hooper.	Sobey	v Burdon & wf.	Wreford.
T. Flood......	Tanner	v Moore Extx.	Hooper.
Paul	Ware	v Ridge the yr.	Drake.

NISI PRIUS COURT—TUESDAY.

Atkinson v. Stacey & another.—Mr. Cockburn and Mr. Barstow conducted the plaintiff's case, and Mr. M. Smith appeared for the defendant.

This was an action of trespass brought by the plaintiff, who was now the proprietor of some Marl Pits near Plympton, against the defendant, who formerly occupied the Pits; they having put in a distress to recover £45 alleged to be due for two years' premium on an endowment received by a deed between Stacey and a person named Dixon, in December, 1841. Dixon having parted with his interest to the plaintiff.

The pleadings were extremely complicated and much discussion took place upon them; a verdict was entered for the plaintiff for 40s. damages, and, as we understood, both parties had leave to move.

The Queen v. Sleeman.—Mr. Rowe and Mr. Cornish were the Counsel for the plaintiff, and Mr. Greenwood and Mr. Merivale appeared for the defendant.

This was an indictment against the defendant who was the Churchwarden of Clawton, for having altered a poor rate of the parish. As soon as the case for the prosecution had closed,

Mr. Justice Coleridge interposed saying he had not heard the other side, but from the appearance of the facts already before the Court, he thought the alteration might have been done in ignorance. No man ought to alter a document of that kind; but it was very possible that there had not been the slightest intention to do anything fraudulently. The defendant might have considered it a rough way of doing himself justice. He (the learned Judge) thought the matter might be so arranged that neither party should have a triumph.

Mr. Rowe had recommended this course in order that the parish might be restored to peace.

A Juror was therefore withdrawn.

WEDNESDAY.—*Glanville v. Hawkey.*—Mr. Rowe appeared for the plaintiff.

This was an undefended action upon a bond. Verdict for the plaintiff, for the amount claimed.

Wilking v. Brock.—Mr. Barstow appeared for the plaintiff, and Mr. Cockburn and Mr. Elliott for the defendant.

This was an undefended action of debt. Verdict for the plaintiff, for the amount sought to be recovered.

Jennings & another v. Sanders.—Mr. Crowder and Mr. M. Smith appeared for the plaintiffs.

From the evidence it appeared that the plaintiffs had been carriers between this City and London, and the defendant was their agent at Honiton, where it was his duty to receive goods to be forwarded by the plaintiffs' waggons, and the action was brought to recover a sum of between £18 & £19, being a balance of account between the parties. In January, 1844, the book keeper of the plaintiffs went over to Honiton and had an interview with the defendant, when a balance was struck between them of £19. The cause was undefended. Verdict for the plaintiff, for £19, with execution in a fortnight.

Wood v. Webber & Bloomfield.—Mr. Sergeant Kinglake was Counsel for the plaintiff.

This was an action brought to recover the sum of £100 upon a promissory note, dated 11th February, 1840. Evidence was given of the signatures of the defendants, and the cause being undefended, a Verdict was returned for the plaintiff, for £100 principal, and £5 for interest, with execution in a fortnight.

The number of PRISONERS was 66, and the Grand Jury having promptly returned a bill, the Court proceeded to

THEIR TRIAL.

Wm. Smith, and *Thomas Smith*, who had been admitted to bail, were charged with maliciously wounding Richard Westlake, with intent to do some bodily harm; and being found guilty, were sentenced to be severally imprisoned three calendar months, and kept to hard labour.

John Ware, 19, was charged with having, on the 31st of Dec last, at Hampton, stolen a bundle of straw, value 6d., the property of John Trewey Parlam; and being found guilty, was sentenced to be imprisoned six calendar months, and kept to hard labour.

Joseph Lamacraft, 26, was charged with having on the 8th of March inst., at Broadclist, stolen two faggots and a half of wood, the property of John Loosemore: and being found guilty, was sentenced to be imprisoned one month, to hard labour.

Richard Hawking, was found guilty, and sentenced to 6 months imprisonment, and hard labour.

Thomas Wallis, 28, and *John Jones*, 26, charged with uttering in Jan. last, counterfeit coin, at Braunton:—No Bill.

George King, 24, and *John Williams*, 17, charged with stealing on the night of the 16th of Feb., various articles from the larder attached to the dwelling house of Admiral John Wight, at Dawlish;—No Bill.

Thomas Edmonds, 25, charged with having on the 12th inst., at Sherford, stolen two hempen sacks, the property of Nicholas Pitts,—was acquitted.

CITY ASSIZES.

WEDNESDAY—(this day)—This morning at 9 o'Clock, Mr. Justice Erle took his seat at the Crown Bar, and the case of *Isaac Taylor*, 20, as the principal; and *John Sambo*, 21, and *James Jackson*, 27, as accessories in the manslaughter of Charles Diddick, otherwise Derrick, on the 27th of January last, in Hoopern Fields, St. David, in this City, was called on. Of this case the particulars were fully reported by us at the time the Coroner's inquest on the body of Derrick was taken. It will, therefore, suffice to say briefly, that some dispute having taken place, the parties went to these fields to fight for half a sovereign, when Derrick received such injuries that he expired in the Hospital, to which he had been taken. The Jury found the whole of the prisoners Guilty, and they were sentenced severally to be imprisoned in the gaol, one calendar month.

Richard Parish, was indicted for having on the 7th of March instant, at the parish of St. John, in this City, maliciously cut and wounded Henry Bailey Poole. The particulars of this case appeared in our paper last week; and the jury finding the prisoner Guilty, the Judge pointed out the enormity as well as the un-English character of the crime, and told the prisoner that but for two extenuating circumstances which had come out in his favour, he should have felt it his duty to pass upon him the sentence of transportation for a very long period. The first of these was, that at his coming to his own house he found the prosecutor there, where he had no business. He ordered him to leave, which the other did not attend to. He then proceeded to do that which a man under such circumstances might lawfully do, and that was to cause him to quit the premises; and then came the second extenuating circumstance, which was that the prosecutor struck him; a fight ensued, and in the course of this, unfortunately for himself he did that which he need not to have done,—he made use of a dangerous weapon, and the injury charged ensued. Still, extenuated as his offence was in consequence of these circumstances, it was one of a very serious nature, and must be severely punished whenever the commission of it was clearly proved, the sentence of the Court therefore is that you Richard Parish be imprisoned for the term of Two Years, and that during that time you be kept to hard labour.

The Judge is now proceeding with the County Cases.

Yesterday (Tuesday) a boy about 13 or 14 years of age, offered for sale at Mr. Silverston's, Fore-street, two bowls of silver spoons, and a portion of the handle of a spoon, which he said he found on the ballast quay. Mr. S., however, suspecting he had dishonestly come by it, sent to the station house, and Woolcott went down, and searching the lad, found in his pocket the handle of a spoon, marked in cipher "M. A. H." He gave his name as Roger Henry Hill, and says his friends live at the bottom of the Friars. Wolcott took him into custody, and he is remanded for a week. The pieces of silver are in possession of the police at the station house.

SHEEP STEALING.—On the night of Monday last, a Hog Sheep, the property of Mr. W. Muggleton, maltster, Honiton's Clist, was stolen from the field in which it was feeding. The entrails were left, and the skin torn into a great number of pieces, as if to prevent it from being sworn to. There is evidence the animal was killed by a person used to killing sheep.

CONVICTS.—On the evening of the 11th instant, John Thomas, 31, convicted at the recent Devon General Sessions of robbery at Brixton, and sentenced to transportation for ten years. Charles Blackmore, 25, for robbery at Ottery, and transported for the like period. Charles Westcott, 18, for robbery at Kenton. Thomas Mullins, 22, for robbery at Woodbury. Amos Honeywell, 32, for robbery at Cornworthy. John Eveleigh, 22, for robbery at Devonport; James Clark, 32, for robbery at Uffculm; and Sarah Collins, 51, for robbery at Devonport,—all convicted at the same Sessions, and severally sentenced to transportation for seven years,—were removed from the Devon County Gaol, and sent,—per railway,—to the prison for the reception of convicts in London.

INCENDIARISM.—On Thursday, 6th inst., a thatched outhouse in the occupation of Mr. I. Baker, Bovey Tracey, was maliciously set fire to, and but for prompt discovery the consequences would have been most disastrous. A reward of £50 has been offered by the West of England Insurance Company, in whose office the property was insured.——On Thursday last, a shed near the way side at Huxham, near Mr. J. Hayward's, was set on fire, but fortunately soon extinguished.

INSOLVENT DEBTORS.—William John Law, Esq., one of her Majesty's Commissioners for the Relief of Insolvent Debtors, will hold Courts at the Guildhall, and Castle of Exeter, for this purpose on Saturday next, the 22nd inst.

80. *Reports of court proceedings in* Trewman's Exeter Flying Post, *20 March 1845*

Convicts . . . John Thomas 31, convicted at the recent Devon General Sessions of robbery at Brixton and sentenced to transportation for ten years . . . Charles Blackmore, 25, for robbery at Ottery . . . [and six others] . . . were removed from the Devon County Gaol and sent [by] railway, to the prison for the reception of convicts in London.

The location of local newspapers

The first task is to ascertain what local papers were published and where surviving copies are held. Copies of most local newspapers can be found at the Newspaper Library at Colindale. Local studies libraries and CROs also hold large collections of newspapers (many on microfilm). Local newspapers are listed (by county, cities and major towns) in Gibson, Langston & Smith (484), with the covering dates of surviving issues and the archives in which they are held. West (463) also has a useful list of about 4,000 local newspapers from 1690 to 1981 for about 450 towns and cities. Even a town such as Ludlow in Shropshire had four local newspapers between 1840 and 1912. Another useful finding aid for newspapers from 1620 to 1919 is the *Times Tercentenary Handlist* (469). This has two sections. One lists the names and dates of local newspapers in London and its suburbs; the other deals with the provincial press, with a general listing for 1701 to 1799 and then annual lists. Crane & Kaye (477) and Cranfield (478) also list many English local newspapers of the 17th and 18th centuries.

There are also bibliographies of local newspapers for particular counties, which may provide more detailed listings. For example, Smith (495) is a guide to Devon's local newspapers and the location of surviving copies. The British Library has also produced some county bibliographies of British local newspapers. The volume for Kent by Bergess, Riddell & Whyman (472) is very detailed, with sections for major towns and areas of Kent, an index of titles (and places) and a list of the locations of surviving newspapers (and archives' addresses). For example, in the entry for Dover, it notes that issues 1 to 174 (from 1887 to 1890) of the *Dover Times* are held at Dover Library (but also at Colindale). Kent newspapers are held at 118 different archives (of which 87 are in Kent). This shows how finding local newspapers may not be straightforward. The British Library has produced similar volumes for Durham, Northumberland, Nottingham, Derbyshire, Wiltshire, Cornwall and Devon. The published reports of the British Library "Newsplan" project are also helpful. These reports compare the British Library's holdings of local newspapers with the collections available in local archives. For example, the report for the East Midlands in Gordon (486) covers eight counties. The available reports are listed in Gibson, Langston & Smith (484) but cover the south-west of England, the "Northern region", the north west, Yorkshire and Humberside, the East Midlands, the West Midlands, the London and south eastern region and Wales (reports have also been published for Scotland and Ireland).

To illustrate the variety of local newspapers available, here is part of the entry from Gibson, Langston & Smith (484) for Tiverton in Devon (although the newspapers' names varied, over the period, from those noted below). There were also county-wide newspapers, listed in the same work, that dealt with events in Tiverton and so might be useful to anyone researching a Tiverton family:

Tiverton Gazette 1858–1920 & later (Colindale and Tiverton Museum)
Tiverton Times 1865–84 (Colindale and West Country Studies Library)
Tiverton News 1875–95, 1898–1920 & later (Colindale) and 1893–1920 & later (Tiverton Museum)
Tiverton Journal 1898–1916 (Colindale).

Because of the volume of newspaper material covering even one town, you should always check, before commencing your reading, whether any name indexes have been prepared. The library holding the collection that you are reviewing may hold (or should know of) any such indexes. The SoG has a few indexes, such as an index to the *Hull Times* for 1857 to 1927. Gibson, Langston & Smith (484) list some indexes of personal names (usually limited to the notices of births, marriages, deaths and obituaries) held at archives and some indexes are also listed in Gibson & Hampson (158). Some indexes are available on the Internet. For example, the Newspaper Detectives' web site includes indexes to the *Surrey Advertiser* for 1864–76. Some archives also have subject indexes which may assist.

POLL BOOKS AND ELECTORAL REGISTERS

Poll books list the men who voted in parliamentary elections and the candidates for whom they voted. This was public knowledge because men voted in public until the secret ballot was introduced in 1872. Electoral registers were introduced in 1832 and list all those people who were entitled to vote in parliamentary elections. Burgess or freemens' rolls listed the freemen of a city or borough (considered below). The freemen were often entitled to vote for the parliamentary representatives of the borough (or city) as well as for members of the city or borough corporation. From 1889, when elected county councils were introduced, electoral registers were also prepared for those elections.

Poll books
England has been divided into parliamentary constituencies since medieval times. Until 1832 each English county was a constituency and returned two members to Parliament (except for Yorkshire which returned four members from 1821). Welsh counties had one MP each. Most English boroughs had two MPs, while most Welsh boroughs shared an MP with another borough. Until 1832 most boroughs were in southern England, but the Reform Act of 1832 (and later statutes) gave the new industrial towns of the north and midlands fairer representation. Most counties were divided into two or more constituencies and the number of MPs for each county was varied so as to better reflect population distribution. Further redistributions of seats took place in the late 19th and 20th centuries. Gibson & Rogers (485) include maps of England and Wales showing boroughs and county representation both before and after 1832 (and list the years of general elections from 1715 to 1874).

Until the late 19th century, the qualification for voting in parliamentary elections was generally linked to ownership of land and only a minority of men had the right to vote. From 1429 the qualification in the counties was ownership, by men aged 21 or over, of freehold land with an annual value (that is the value to the owner if he leased it to a tenant) of 40 shillings or more. In cities and boroughs the right to vote depended on local custom. In some boroughs, all householders (known as potwallopers) had the right to vote but, in others, only a few people, perhaps freemen, had the franchise.

Poll books for county and borough seats list the names of electors, their parish of residence and how they voted. Poll books may also state an elector's exact address and (if different) the address of the property that gave him the right to vote. Within a poll book, the list of electors may be arranged by parish, ward, hundred or township. Poll books are extremely rare for the period prior to 1696, when Parliament made sheriffs responsible for recording the poll in county elections. An act of 1711 required poll books to be deposited with the Clerk of the Peace and so many poll books survive for elections after this date. In 1872 the secret ballot was introduced so that documents recording how men voted could no longer be prepared. The last general election for which true poll books exist is therefore that of 1868. Illustration 81 shows an extract from the poll book for the election in November 1868 in the southern division of Norfolk, listing the electors in Framingham, Frettenham and Hainford. The poll was for two members of Parliament and there were three candidates (although four was usual): Edward Howes, Clare Sewell Read and Henry Lombard Hudson. Their initials appear at the top of the columns. The horizontal lines in the columns indicate how each elector cast his votes. A voter at this time could vote for two candidates. The front page of the poll book recorded that Read and Howes were successful.

The location of surviving poll books for each county and borough (held at the SoG, CROs, the British Library, Guildhall Library or other libraries) can be ascertained from Gibson & Rogers (485). The collection held by the SoG as at 1995 is listed by Newington-Irving (210) and recent acquisitions are noted in the library catalogue. The collection at Guildhall Library, listed in the booklet (465), covers many areas of Britain and not just London (for example, pollbooks for county elections in Bedfordshire for 1705, 1807, 1820, 1831 and 1859 and a pollbook for Bedford in 1790). Large collections of poll books are also held by the British Library and the Institute of Historical Research at Senate House, University of London. The SoG has reproduced some poll books on microfiche. Some poll books (such as those for the City of London in 1768 and for Suffolk in 1710 and 1790) have been reprinted by S.A. and M.J. Raymond of 6 Russet Avenue, Exeter EX1 3QB, and others have been reprinted by family history societies (such as the 1775 poll book for Surrey reprinted by West Surrey FHS). A few poll books have also been reproduced on CD-ROM and are listed in Raymond (267).

Electoral registers
Electoral registers specify entitlement to vote (you could only vote if the register included your name) and not who voted or how votes were actually cast. Electoral registers for national elections have been compiled every year since 1832 (except 1916–17 and 1940–44). From 1832 electoral registers had to be deposited with the Clerk of the Peace (# chapter 25) and most registers are now held in CROs, the British Library and local libraries. A few are held at TNA, the SoG and Guildhall Library. Archives' holdings of electoral registers, arranged by county, are listed in Gibson & Rogers (483) except for most of the British Library's collection, which is listed in Cheffins (474).

The franchise for elections to Parliament was extended in 1832, 1867 and 1884. In 1832 the vote in the boroughs was given to a wider range of those men having an interest in property, including all male householders (so including tenants) of land worth at least £10 per year. In the counties the franchise was granted to the owners of property worth at least £10. This increased the electorate to almost one million men. In 1867 the electorate was increased to about 2.5 million. All male owners of real property worth £5 or more were enfranchised in the counties, together with those who occupied land and paid rent of £50 or more per year. In the boroughs, all owners of dwelling-houses and most occupiers, who paid rent of £10 or more per year, were given the vote. In 1884 the county franchise was widened (to approximately the same extent as in the boroughs), so that the majority of male householders over 21 were entitled to vote (although Gibson & Rogers (483) estimate that, even by 1911, only about 60 per cent of adult

SOUTH NORFOLK ELECTION.

THE POLL

FOR

TWO KNIGHTS TO SERVE IN PARLIAMENT

FOR THE

Southern Division of the County of Norfolk,

TAKEN NOVEMBER 24TH, 1868,

WITH A

COMPLETE REGISTER OF THE ELECTORS;

INCLUDING DOUBLE ENTRIES, WHICH ARE SPECIALLY MARKED.

PREPARED FROM THE CONSERVATIVE AGENT'S RETURNS.

CANDIDATES:

CLARE SEWELL READ, ESQ...... 3097
EDWARD HOWES, ESQ............. 3055
HENRY LOMBARD HUDSON, ESQ. 1679

NORWICH:
MATCHETT AND STEVENSON, "NORFOLK CHRONICLE" OFFICE,
MARKET PLACE.

Noah Thomas
Pratt James Worsley
Sparkes Robert
Steel Edward, Great Yarmouth
Weaver Robert Miller, Magdalen-road, Norwich

£13 RATED OCCUPIERS.

Archer Robert
Barton James, Stenton Strawless
Gilham William
Gilham Robert Edward
Harvey George
Melton James
Neale James Frederick, Norwich
Plummer Michael
Reed James
Wright William
Wenkling William

Framingham Earl.

Barker Thomas
Blyth Benjamin
Brewster Charles David Ker.
Goodwin Benjamin, Poringland
Greeves Henry, Norwich
Leader Thomas, 7, Mincing-lane, London (r East Wrexham)
Plummer Charles Taylor, Night-cap-lane, Norwich
Shalders Charles, Yelverton
Stacey Henry, Beccles, Suffolk
Wright Walter, junior, No. 5, All Saints' Green, Norwich

£13 RATED OCCUPIERS.

Loly William Greenfield
Matthews Henry
Nobbs William Peter, Norwich
Alpington and Sething)
Spruce Jonathan
Trower Alfred, Yelverton

Framingham Pigot.

Alexander David
Barker Thomas
Christie James Henry Brooke
Christie George Henry
Dey John
Ewing Robert
Fitzgerald William Robert
Gilbert William, Pitt-street, Norwich
Clansell's without, Norwich
Gilbert Smith, Berry, Elm-terrace, St.
Gilbert Keeve Smith, Pitt-street, Norwich
Gillingwater William
Hawkes Daniel
Hawkes John
Meadham Wace Lockett, Norwich
Thorpe St. Andrew, Mattishall, and Hockering)
Nunn William
Plane William Henry
Read Charles
Robinson William Henry, Norwich
Spink John, junior
Thetford William, Trowse Newton

Wilkinson West Thomas
Wilkinson Pinchomham
Winter James, Norwich (r Drayton)
Young John (r Kelhelton)

£13 RATED OCCUPIERS.

Frettenham.

Culling William
Drew Robert
Hawkes John, junior
Holmes William
Mark Robert
Sherman Robert
Youngs William

Hinde Ephriam Willin
Joby William
Reed Robert
Scottow William Wright
Shirley Rev. James

£13 RATED OCCUPIERS.

Hainford.

Bennington Charles
Rassborough William

Banks Thomas, 46, Butter-market, Ipswich
Berrell James, Magdalen-street, Norwich (r Catton)
Cornell John, Ringsfield
Pinkey Hugh, Stenton Strawless
Foster Sir William, Bart, St. Giles'-street, Norwich
Fryer Jeremiah, Frettenham
Golding Robert
Golding William
Green Charles, Gunthorpe
Heylett John, Hindolveston
Hines John
Keppel William Arnold
Keppel Frederick Charles
Kitton George, St. Peter per Mountergate, Norwich
Lockett James Charles
Lockett Samuel
Loftus George William Ferrars, Esq., Breccon Ash (r Brome Ash)
Middleton Edmund Plane, Hindringham
Pointer George Edmund, Lowestoft
Pooley Thomas, Northwold
Robert William
Self Thomas, Lowestoft
Sexton William
Shirley Horatio Henry, 14, Lower Berkeley-street, Portman-square, London
Smith Benjamin, Cricket-hill, Norwich
Tillz Thomas Ransom, North Walsham
Warren Daniel William (d e Great Ellingham)

£12 RATED OCCUPIERS.

Amiss John, Horsted
Barton Frederic William
Brook Frederic
Chapman James
Orono Jonathan
Roberts Charles Stephen Wright

---

81. Extract from the poll book for the 1868 election in South Norfolk

males appeared in the registers). In 1918 the franchise for men was extended to all those aged 21 normally resident in the constituency. Women did not obtain the vote in national elections until 1918, when it was limited to those over 30 who were householders, or the wives of householders. It was only in 1928 that the vote was granted to women over 21.

Until 1918 electoral registers listed the names of electors, their address and the nature of their qualification to vote in the constituency (for example "freehold house and land"). Many 19th-century registers contained separate lists for property owners and occupiers, so that all sections of a register should be checked. For much of the 19th century, the registers list the names of electors in alphabetical order, but the expansion of the electorate led to more and more registers being compiled in order of electoral wards, then streets and then by house numbers. This format became standard in 1918 when entitlement to vote was extended to all men normally resident in a constituency (and qualifying property became irrelevant). Registers since 1918 are so large that it is almost essential to know your ancestors' address in order to find them.

Illustration 82 shows an extract (listing voters in the parish of Hainford) from the electoral register for the eastern division of Norfolk, compiled for any election of members of Parliament that was to take place between November 1885 and 1 January 1887. Jeremiah Chapman, a brother of my ancestor Sophia Chapman, is listed as a voter living in the hamlet of Waterloo. As another example, the electoral register for the northern division of Devon for 1874 is divided into polling districts and then parishes. The polling district of Dolton included the parish of Winkleigh and the list of voters for that parish included John Bulleid, whose abode was recorded as the village of Inwardleigh. His qualification for voting was noted as ownership of freehold houses and gardens in Lower Town, Winkleigh.

Electoral registers are also useful for tracing families after the 1901 census. Having located a family at a particular address, you can check later electoral registers to ascertain how long the family remained there. You will then know approximately when the family moved, even if you do not know where they moved to. The date noted on an electoral register is usually the date when it came into force. This date (usually 1 January) was generally about five months after the qualifying date (usually 31 July), that is the date on which a voter had to establish his right to vote (for example the date on which he owned a certain property). You should remember that many electors might die, move or sell that property between these two dates.

LOCAL ELECTIONS

Poll books and registers were also prepared for local elections. Until the 19th century parish affairs were administered by a council known as a vestry (# chapter 18). In some places a vestry was a group of the wealthier residents but, in others, any ratepayer had the right to attend and vote at vestry meetings. Reference should therefore be made to the lists of ratepayers held with parish records (# chapter 18). Cities and boroughs were governed by corporations or city councils, usually elected (until the 19th century) by the freemen.

Freemen

From medieval times most cities or corporate towns were governed or controlled by a body of men known as freemen, those men who had been granted the freedom of the city or borough and had a number of rights and privileges. These privileges depended on local custom and the city's (or borough's) charter, but usually included an exclusive right to vote in elections for the

1885-6.

EASTERN DIVISION OF NORFOLK.

INT FAITH'S Polling District (District N.)

PARISH OF HAYNFORD.

OWNERSHIP VOTERS.

No.	Name of each Voter at full length, the Surname being first.	Place of Abode.	Nature of Qualification.	Description of Qualifying Property.
N 31	Brown William	Haynford hall	Freehold house and land	The hall
N 35	Cory James	Haynford	Freehold blacksmith's shop & land	Near the Maid's Head
*	Denny George James	Northwold	Freehold house and land	Waterloo
N 36	Golden Robert	Haynford	Copyhold house and land	Chequers street
°	Green Charles	Sharrington	Freehold house and land	William Fiddy, tenant
N 37	Haylett John	Haynford	Copyhold cottages and land	On the Spixworth road
N 38	Howlett Horatio	Haynford	Freehold & copyhold house & land	Frettenham road
N 39	Huson John	Haynford	Freehold house and land	Waterloo
N 40	Keppel Edward George	Shorncliffe camp, Kent	Freehold houses and land	In occupation of James Pearce, Thomas Sexton, Benjamin Smith, and others
{ °	Keppel William Arnold Walpole	Lexham hall, Norfolk	Freehold cottages	Near the hall
{ *	Kitton George	Surrey road, Norwich	Mortgagee in possession of copyhold cottages	Next the Norwich road
N 11	Laws Samuel	Haynford	Freehold house and land	Newton road
{ *	Matthews John	Brooke	Freehold houses and land	Waterloo
{ *	May George	Unthank's road, Norwich	Freehold house and land	Cross road
{ *	Middleton Edmund Plane	Hindringham	Freehold house and land	Haynford lodge
N 42	Middleton Frank Edward	Haynford	Freehold globe land	Dumb's lane
°	Parkerson Jude	Gladstone street Norwich	Freehold & copyhold cottages & land	Near the Chequers
N 43	Springall Elijah	Haynford	Copyhold cottages and land	Near the Maid's Head inn
N 11	Tills Thomas Ransom	Haynford	Copyhold house and land	Norwich road
N 15	Woodcock Peter	Haynford	Freehold & copyhold house & land	Burgate's hill

OCCUPATION VOTERS (other than Lodgers.)

No.	Name of each Voter at full length, the Surname being first.	Place of Abode.	Nature of Qualification.	Description of Qualifying Property.
N 46	Arthurton Robert	Haynford	Land and tenement	The Chequers
N 47	Algate Horace	Haynford	Dwelling-house	Waterloo
N 48	Burton William	Haynford	Dwelling-house	Waterloo
N 19	Bean John	Haynford	Dwelling-house	Waterloo
N 50	Bowen Alfred	Haynford	Dwelling-house	Waterloo
N 51	Bowen Samuel	Haynford	Dwelling-house	Waterloo
N 52	Breese Walter	Haynford	Dwelling-house	Waterloo
N 53	Burton Walter	Haynford	Dwelling-house	Waterloo
N 51	Barnard William	Haynford	Dwelling-house	Cross road
N 55	Bunn Henry	Haynford	Land and tenement	Cross road
N 56	Bloom James	Haynford	Dwelling-house	Near the hall
N 57	Bean George	Haynford	Dwelling-house	Near the Chequers
N 58	Barnard William	Haynford	Dwelling-house	Dumb's lane
N 59	Bird Edward	Haynford	Dwelling-house	Frettenham road
N 60	Burton John	Haynford	Dwelling-house	Waterloo
N 61	Bowman Robert	Haynford	Dwelling-house	Near the hall
N 62	Bowen John	Haynford	Dwelling-house	Near the Chequers
N 63	Buck John	Haynford	Dwelling-house	Farm house near the Chequers
N 61	Bowen George	Haynford	Dwelling-house	Waterloo
N 65	Burton James	Haynford	Dwelling-house	The Carr
N 66	Crome Stephen	Haynford	Dwelling-house	Cross road
N 67	Crome James	Haynford	Dwelling-house	Dumb's lane
N 68	Clerk Luke	Haynford	Dwelling-house	Near the hall
N 69	Coleman Charles	Haynford	Dwelling-house	Near the hall
N 70	Curson James	Haynford	Dwelling-house	Near the Chequers
N 71	Curson Robert	Haynford	Dwelling-house	Near the Chequers
N 72	Crane Charles	Haynford	Dwelling-house	Near the Church lane
N 73	Chapman Jeremiah	Haynford	Dwelling-house	Waterloo
N 71	Coman Robert John	Haynford	Land and tenement	Near the hall

82. *Extract for the parish of Haynford from the electoral register for the eastern division of the county of Norfolk for November 1885 to 1 January 1887*

city or borough council (and also for the city's or borough's members of Parliament) and also an exclusive right to carry on a craft or trade in the city or borough.

Useful information about freemen can be obtained from registers or rolls of freemen. The freemen were usually members of one of the city or borough guilds or livery companies (# chapter 22). Indeed, an application for the freedom of the City of London could only be made, until 1835, after a man had obtained the freedom of a livery company. A man became a freeman of a guild or livery company (and usually, in turn, a freeman of a city or borough) in three principal ways: by patrimony (that is born to a freeman after that father's own admission); by servitude (by serving an apprenticeship to a freeman), or by redemption (purchasing his admission). In addition, a few people were granted honorary freedom because of some worthy deed (thus Nelson and Churchill were granted honorary freedom of the City of London). It is important to distinguish between the freedom of a city or borough on the one hand and the freedom of a livery company or craft guild on the other. While the methods of admission were almost the same and most men were freemen of both their company/guild and their city or borough, there were important differences, and men were not always freemen of both. The freedom of a city or borough gave the right to vote and membership of a particular guild or company, let us say the Bakers' Company, gave a man the right to carry on the trade of baking within the company's jurisdiction. Importantly, you may find two sets of records for your freeman ancestor: the city or borough records as well as guild or livery company records.

By the late 18th century the freemen's exclusive trading rights were often being ignored by other traders and it was becoming more difficult to enforce their rights through the courts. The exclusive right of freemen to trade or practise a craft was abolished by the Municipal Corporations Act 1835 (except in the City of London, where exclusive rights remained until 1856). The Reform Act of 1832 gave the parliamentary vote to £10 householders in cities and boroughs (whether or not they were freemen) and the restriction of the franchise to freemen in elections for municipal councils was also abolished in 1867. The right of corporations to grant freedom by redemption was also abolished by the 1835 act, except in the City of London (where the Corporation tried to make the freedom more attractive by reducing the cost of purchasing it and by abolishing the need for applicants to be freemen of a livery company).

The City of London has been governed since medieval times by the Corporation of the City of London, that is the Mayor and Commonalty and Citizens. The bodies governing the City consisted of the Lord Mayor, the aldermen, the Common Council, Common Hall and the freemen. Common Hall was an assembly, originally of all freemen but restricted from about 1475 to liverymen (the senior freemen in each City livery company). Doolittle (480) estimates that there were about 4,000 liverymen in 1625 and up to 8,000 in the 18th century. It was the liverymen (rather than all freemen) who had the right, until 1867, to elect the City's members of Parliament. The freemen in each ward elected representatives (about 230 of them in the 17th and 18th centuries) to sit on Common Council (which in turn elected or nominated a City Chamberlain and other officials). Common Council had extensive legislative and financial powers and so the City was, for centuries, one of the most democratic institutions in Britain. There were also 26 aldermen (one for each City ward) who were elected for life by the freemen. Each year one alderman was chosen (by Common Hall) to act as Lord Mayor.

Freedom records of the City of London are especially important because they include many people from outside the City and also many men who were not professionals or craftsmen. M.T. Medlycott notes, in *Genealogists' Magazine* (June 1977), that few freemen actually lived in the

City; many more lived in the rest of London or in places such as Lambeth or Southwark. Some lived in the Home Counties or even as far away as Liverpool or Bristol. Medlycott also discovered that many shopkeepers, mariners (and even labourers) obtained the freedom of the City. These records can therefore be relevant for all researchers.

Records of freemen

Records of towns and cities often include lists of their freemen, some lists dating back to the 13th century. Freemen rolls usually record names, dates of admission and perhaps a man's trade and parentage. Lists of freemen have been published for towns or cities such as Exeter in Rowe & Jackson (494), Gloucester in Jurica (489), Newcastle upon Tyne in Hope Dodds (487) and Hunter Blair (488), York in Collins (475) and (476) and Llantrisant, Wales in Davies (479). The freemen's rolls of York for 1272–1759, transcribed in Collins (475) and (476), list about 36,500 freemen with their occupations (and the names of their fathers if they were admitted as freemen by patrimony). Typical entries for freemen admitted by patrimony are:

1671/2	Thomas Maskall, merchant, son of John Maskall, grocer.
1758	William Clark, bricklayer, son of Samuel Clark, translator.

Records of freemen of the City of London were kept from 1275. The surviving records (held at CLRO) concern about 500,000 men between 1681 and 1940 (and a few earlier records also survive). There were 1,564 admissions to the freedom of the City in 1704 alone (of which 1,274 were by apprenticeship). The records are described in Deadman & Scudder (244) and in detail, with illustrations, in Aldous (470). There are freedom admission papers from 1681 to 1940 (except for a few gaps), arranged in monthly bundles. The information in these papers varies according to their date and the method by which the freeman obtained admission. Early orders for admission by redemption usually note only a man's name and date of admission. Later orders may provide a freeman's age, trade, residence or father's name. Early papers concerning admission by patrimony provide the freeman's name, livery company and his father's name. Later records give a freeman's age and place of birth (and sometimes the date of admission of his father). Papers for admissions by servitude generally consist of a man's apprenticeship indenture (endorsed with a note of his admission to the freedom), providing the apprentice's name, master's name and livery company, the date of binding as well as the father's name, occupation and residence. Some later papers note the applicant's date of admission to a livery company and his master's trade. Sometimes there is no indenture, but a certificate (usually from the applicant's livery company or old master) certifying the completion of the apprenticeship or the admission to the freedom of the company. The freedom admission papers are indexed in 14 volumes of alphabets (entries being arranged by a period of years then by the first letter of the freeman's surname) with the month of admission. From 1784 to the present there are also freedom books or registers (also known as declaration books) which provide the exact date of admission (often omitted from the freedom papers).

There are other important types of City of London freedom records. The apprentices of freemen had one year, from the start of their apprenticeship, to enrol their apprenticeship indenture with the City Chamberlain. If they did not do so, they had to pay a higher fee if they subsequently applied for freedom of the City. CLRO holds apprenticeship enrolment books for 1786 to 1974. These registers (to which there are alphabets of apprentice's surnames) provide brief details of the apprenticeship. Secondly, freemen were permitted from 1750 to employ non-freemen or "strangers" in the City if they obtained a licence. Licences for 1750 to 1845 are held at CLRO with alphabets or indexes for some periods. Boyd's *Inhabitants of London* (# chapter 7) is another useful finding aid for London freemen and their families.

Some further records of freemen held at CLRO are listed in Aldous (470). Former soldiers or sailors often found it difficult to find employment or make a living after their discharge. Various statutes therefore enabled former servicemen, as "King's freemen", to exercise a trade in certain towns or cities despite any local laws or regulations preventing them from doing so. Records of about 4,000 such men from 1750 to 1820 survive at CLRO (with a slip index). They include men's army or naval discharge papers, certificates of service and baptism or marriage certificates.

Extension of the franchise for local elections

The franchise in rural and urban areas was gradually extended and local government was reformed. The Municipal Corporations Act 1835 extended the franchise for local elections to men who, for example, paid the poor rate. We shall also see in chapter 18 how responsibility for relief of the poor was passed from parish vestries to Boards of Guardians, who were elected by ratepayers. Women who had the necessary property qualification and who paid rates could also vote in local elections from 1869.

County Councils were established in 1889 and the vote at County Council elections was given to all those who already had the vote in county parliamentary elections. The Local Government Act of 1894 established District Councils in rural and urban areas (except for London, where similar councils were only established in 1899) and parliamentary electors (generally all ratepayers) could vote for these councils. By 1918 the franchise for men (and women over 30) for all local elections had been extended to all those who had been resident for six months in the relevant place.

County or borough rate books were prepared from the latter part of the 19th century, when a right to vote usually depended upon payment of rates (and was therefore often wider than the parliamentary franchise). The rate books are normally held in local authority archives, CROs or reference libraries. They list ratepayers' names and sometimes addresses. However, the lists of the occupiers of properties (and sometimes an owner, if this was a different person) are arranged by the address of the property and the volumes are rarely indexed, so that searching for a family who lived in a city or large town can be extremely difficult unless you know the street in which the family lived. As more and more people paid rates, these lists became increasingly large, so that many have sadly been destroyed. Some local authorities have only retained a selection. CROs and local archives can inform you of the lists that survive. A few indexes have been prepared for rate books. Vestry House Museum holds rate books for Leyton, with a card index, covering the late 19th century. The index recorded my ancestor George Keates (and subsequently his widow) owning a large number of properties in the area during this period.

CHAPTER 18

PARISH AND TOWN RECORDS

The clergyman and parish officers created many records (as well as the parish registers) in the course of their administration of parish affairs. *The Parish Chest* by Tate (532) is a detailed review of the records of parish administration (including poor relief, charities, the maintenance of highways and law and order). The parish chest itself was a strong wooden box in which the parish kept alms for the poor, the church silver and the parish records.

Most surviving parish records have been deposited in the CRO for the county in which the parish is located. They are therefore generally easy to find and listed in archives' catalogues and finding aids. Many CROs also publish lists of their holdings of parish records, either included in their general guides (# chapter 11) such as the guide to Kent archives by Hull (254) or in lists dealing specifically with parish records, such as *Parish Poor Law Records in Devon* by Devon Record Office (500). Extensive records have survived for some parishes, including minutes of meetings of parish officials, apprenticeship records, rate books, poor relief expenditure books and papers about settlement and bastardy. However, many records have been lost or destroyed, so that few papers survive for some parishes. Consequently, the records of a parish may not survive for the period in which you are interested (or include any records of the type for which you are searching). The variation between parishes as to the amount of surviving documentation is illustrated by summaries of entries, from Hull (254), for the records of two Kent parishes:

Milton Regis: Churchwardens' rates and accounts, 1607–1909; Overseers' rates and accounts, 1671–1839; settlement papers, 1691–1830; apprenticeship indentures, 1704–1800; surveyors' rates, 1860–62 and surveyors' accounts, 1771–1862.

Norton: Overseers' accounts, 1842–48.

Parish records of London and Middlesex are more difficult to find. Most records of City of London parishes are at Guildhall Library. Many documents for parishes in Middlesex and for those London parishes that were previously in Essex, Kent and Surrey are at LMA or City of Westminster Archives Centre, but many are in local archives such as Southwark Local Studies Library, Vestry House Museum in Walthamstow or Hackney Archives. Webb (175) lists the surviving parish records for each Middlesex parish and notes their location. Many parish records have been filmed by the Mormons so that microfilms can be ordered from Salt Lake City to view at LDS family history centres. This may be more convenient for you, if you live near a centre, than travelling to the relevant CRO. The parish records that have been filmed are listed in the catalogue of the Family History Library. The Hyde Park family history centre holds copies of thousands of the LDS films on a permanent basis. For example, the centre's films include the following material for Coleshill, Berkshire (as well as the parish registers for 1557–1812):

Churchwardens' accounts, 1656–77; vestry minutes, 1693–1779; overseers' accounts, 1735–66 and 1848–74; settlement and removal records, 1759–1803; apprenticeship indentures, 1763–68; bastardy papers, 1771–95; poor rates, 1835–86.

Justices of the Peace (# chapter 25), usually wealthy local landowners, were closely involved in parish affairs. They reviewed complaints from the poor that they were being refused poor relief by a parish and complaints from one parish that a pauper should be the responsibility of another parish. The Justices approved the placing, by parish officials, of pauper children as apprentices to local farmers or tradesmen. If your ancestor was illegitimate, the father may not be named in the parish register or other surviving parish records, but the Justices may have questioned the mother as to the father's identity and recorded the examination. Justices' records may also include a complaint brought against the father (by the mother or parish officials) requiring him to pay maintenance for the child. Books and accounts of parish officers were also regularly examined and approved by Justices. The Justices' records should therefore also be consulted for information about parish affairs.

Most parish records are not indexed and so locating your ancestors in them can be a lengthy task and, because of the loss of records, often a matter of luck. Some indexes are available, many of them listed in Gibson & Hampson (158). Some CROs hold unpublished indexes of the people appearing in a selection of parish and Justices' records and many family history societies are indexing the parish records for their area. For example, Holland (521) is a calendar and index on CD-ROM to thousands of settlement examinations, removal orders, bastardy bonds and similar documents that survive for Surrey parishes. Bedfordshire FHS has published a surname index to the people named in those parish records at Bedford Record Office (dating from 1622 to 1834) which concern apprenticeship, bastardy, and settlement or removal of paupers. Bedford Record Office also holds a card index to the people named in the settlement papers and bastardy bonds contained in the Justices' Quarter Sessions rolls of 1714–1835. London & North Middlesex FHS has published a microfiche index (503) to people who were subjected to settlement examinations in the parish of St James, Clerkenwell, London, between 1778 and 1851. Any such index should always be your first source. You can later concentrate your efforts on records that are not indexed.

THE VESTRY, THE CHURCHWARDENS AND THE OVERSEERS OF THE POOR

In medieval times the manor and the manorial courts (# chapter 27) were the most important institutions for the administration of local affairs and justice. However, from the 16th century, as the manorial courts declined in importance, the ecclesiastical parish became the principal administrative unit. The parish became responsible for the care of the poor and sick, for the maintenance of parish roads and for levying a rate to finance this expenditure. Parish administration was the responsibility of a parish council (the vestry) and the Justices of the Peace.

Some vestries developed as early as the 14th century. There were two types. An open vestry consisted of all male ratepayers. Any ratepayer could attend meetings of an open vestry and vote, although in practice these vestries were dominated by the leading residents of the parish. In many parishes (particularly more populous parishes in which open vestries were unwieldly) administration was undertaken by a select vestry. The select vestries in some parishes were committees established by open vestries in the 16th or 17th centuries but, in other parishes, select vestries were established by order of a bishop, or by act of Parliament. The parish minister was often the chairman. A select vestry usually consisted of 12, but perhaps 16 or 24 ratepayers (usually the wealthier parishioners) who filled vacancies on the vestry by appointing new members of their own choice. Minutes of vestry meetings were recorded in vestry books and some of these books survive from as early as the 16th century. They cover matters such as care of the poor, repairs to the church, charities, schools and (later) the parish water supply, housing, sanitation, police and grants to assist paupers' emigration. Many names appear in vestry minutes and examples of entries are given below. Some vestry minutes have been published, such as those for Wimbledon in the late 18th century in Cowe (511). Vestries remained important until the 19th century when responsibility for the poor was transferred (in 1834) to Poor Law Guardians and many other duties were transferred to new civil local authorities. Vestries were finally replaced in 1894 by parish councils which took over their remaining duties and records.

Vestries gradually obtained the right to raise money by levying various rates on parish householders. Thus rates were authorised by statutes of 1530/1 (for the building or repair of bridges), 1531/2 (for the construction of gaols), 1597/8 (for poor relief) and 1654 (for the repair of highways). It was inefficient to levy a number of rates (often for small amounts) to pay for different types of expenditure and so by the 18th century most rates were amalgamated with the larger poor rate. The poor rate continued to be collected after 1834, when responsibility for the poor was transferred to Boards of Guardians (in charge of unions of parishes), but the money raised was handed over by the parish to the Guardians. Some other church rates (for example for maintenance of the church) continued until 1868, when the right of the church to levy compulsory rates was abolished.

The office of churchwarden came into existence in medieval times. Two churchwardens (the guardians of the parish church) were usually elected for a year by the vicar and parishioners (but in some places by the vestry). Sometimes the wealthier parishioners acted in rotation. Churchwardens were principally concerned with the upkeep of the church, administration of parish charities, managing church property and arranging the baptism of foundling children or the burials of strangers who died in the parish. The churchwardens might allocate a church pew to a family in consideration of a payment to church funds. The churchwardens could also summon (or present) parishioners to the church courts (# chapter 24) for many offences (such as failing to attend church, libel or blasphemy). The vestry could levy a church rate from parish householders to pay the churchwardens' expenses.

From 1572 two members of the vestry were elected annually to act as Overseers of the Poor and their duties (and records) are considered below. There were also other parish officers, such as the constable and the waywardens (also discussed below), who produced records of the expenditure incurred in performing their duties. In the event of a dispute as to parish officers' accounts or expenses, or as to the level of rates levied by the vestry, the Justices of the Peace could be called upon, by parishioners or parish officers, to resolve the matter.

RELIEF OF THE POOR

Records of poor relief provide evidence of relationships and information about our ancestors' lives. In medieval times the church was considered to have moral responsibility for the poor and the religious houses distributed alms to paupers. After the monasteries were suppressed by Henry VIII, a statute of 1536 made the parish responsible for the care of its poor, and the office of overseer of the poor was created in 1572. It was intended that expenditure on poor relief should be funded by voluntary donations from the parishioners. However, this voluntary system did not produce sufficient income and an act of 1597/8 therefore authorised overseers to levy a poor rate on parish householders to finance the expenditure on the poor. These provisions were consolidated and reinforced in the Poor Law Act of 1601, which remained in force until 1834. From 1601 to 1834 the system of poor relief consisted of the levying of a poor rate, and the distribution (by the overseers) of the income to needy parishioners (whether their poverty was caused by sickness, unemployment or old age) or to pay for paupers' medical treatment. The children of poor families could be bound out as apprentices (usually to local farmers or tradesmen) and provision was also made for orphans and foundlings.

In the 17th and 18th centuries poor relief was generally in the form of outdoor relief, that is the provision of money, food, clothing or other goods to paupers who continued living in their own cottages or in relatives' homes. The able-bodied poor were sometimes given work. Women often nursed the sick or undertook laundry work and men might work on repairing parish roads or bridges. A system of indoor relief (in workhouses) originated in the 18th century and early workhouses were principally intended for the sick, the elderly and orphans. However, the Poor Law Amendment Act of 1834 substantially changed the system of poor relief. Parishes were grouped into approximately 600 Unions and the act transferred responsibility for the poor from the parish to Boards of Guardians (elected by ratepayers) for each union. The 1834 act also replaced outdoor relief for the able-bodied poor by compulsory indoor relief in workhouses. The workhouse system remained in place until the 20th century and is considered below.

Until 1834 the expenditure on the poor (whether in money or in kind) was set out in the vestry minutes, in overseers' accounts or in a poor book. These may record expenditure in great detail, including the pauper's name and the amount and purpose of the payment. The money might have been for a pauper's rent, or food, or paid to a widow to nurse someone who was sick or used to purchase clothing which was given to the pauper. The vestry minutes of Wimbledon, in Cowe (511), contain many entries for the distribution of clothes and money:

26th December 1751 Jo. Lucas, 2 shirts; Widow Bowen's girl, a gown, petticoat, 1 pair of shoes and stockings; Widow Brown, 1 shilling; Widow Goose, 2 shifts, shoes and stockings.

Overseers' accounts of Hornchurch (in Essex) record the following payments in March 1789:

Paid widow Bateman for nursing Thomas Patten	15 shillings
Relieved Thomas Patten in the small pox	£1 and 5 shillings

Illustration 83 shows an extract from an overseers' accounts book, recording expenditure in Hornchurch by the overseer Mr Alexander, which was approved at a vestry meeting on 3 May 1790. The accounts record payments to the elderly men and widows of the parish, or to sick people (who were therefore unable to work) such as a payment of six shillings and six pence to my ancestor Benjamin Bateman, who was suffering from smallpox. There were payments for many other items, such as a butcher's bill and for a coroner's inquest on "the body" of Mary Ford. Other interesting entries include:

83. Extract from the overseers' accounts of 3 May 1790 from Hornchurch, Essex (Essex Record Office, D/P 117/18/6)

5th July 1790:

Paid Dame Smythers for laying [childbirth] the wife of Bateman;	5s.

9th December 1793;

Paid for apparel for B. Bateman's daughter;	14s. 6d

7th July 1794;

Paid for the fees and coffin for Phipps' child buried at Rainham;	11s. 4d.

The entry for 5 July 1790 records the birth of a child of Benjamin Bateman and his wife Mary, yet the child's baptism did not appear in the parish register (although the baptisms of five other children were recorded). The entry for 9 December 1793 also referred to a daughter of Benjamin and Mary (possibly the child born in 1790). Overseers accounts may also record the parentage of illegitimate children. The Hornchurch accounts of 11 June 1805 stated:

Cash received (from) George Gooch to exonerate him from a bastard child liable to be born on the body of Jane Pavitt	£10

Some overseers' accounts have been published, for example those for 1767 to 1806 for the parish of Hooton Pagnell in Yorkshire, in Whiting (535). This work provides a good example of how the life of a poor family can be recreated from overseers' records. John Newton appears regularly in the accounts from April 1781, in entries such as "to Jn Newton of Barnbro, for relief 10s 6d". In addition, John's rent was also paid on some occasions, such as on 11 February 1783: "to Thos. Lister for rent of Jn. Newton £2. 1s". Further payments of rent were made in 1784, and further payments of relief (and gifts of coal for the family's fire) were made in 1785. By spring 1786 John was still receiving relief, but the overseers had further reason to include his family in their records – the death of his wife and child:

May 17	To John Newton for relief.	4s.
May 26	To Ann Godfrey nursing Newton's wife	3s. 9d
May 29	To Ann Godfrey nursing Newton's wife	4s. 8d
June 1	To John Newton for relief	3s. 6d
June 2	To John Machan: 2 coffins for Newton's wife and child	10s. 6d

Poor rates were usually levied annually (but sometimes more often) and the income was recorded in poor rate books. These list parish householders who were not paupers (whether landowners, farmers, tradesmen or labourers) and the amount paid, which depended on the value of the property that they owned or occupied. The payment therefore indicates your ancestor's wealth. The overseers' poor rate book for Wanstead in Essex for 1845 is at Essex Record Office and includes an entry for my ancestor John Clements:

Occupier	Owner	Property	Situation	Gross Rental	Rateable value
John Clements	Thomas Barker	Cottage	Wanstead Village	10 shillings	5 shillings

An ancestor's appearance in, or disappearance from, the poor rate books also helps ascertain the timing of his moves between parishes. The parish records of rates and expenditure therefore mention the wealthy as well as paupers or the sick and they may significantly augment the information that you obtain about your ancestors from parish registers.

SETTLEMENT

The Poor Law Act of 1601 provided for relief to be granted to paupers only in their parish of legal settlement. This restriction was intended to prevent an influx of poor labourers into those parishes where there was temporary work (perhaps a harvest), but which were already burdened for most of the year with many paupers. Sickness, unemployment or the death of a family's breadwinner could occur at any time, and so every family faced the possibility of poverty and reliance on the parish to avoid starvation. It was therefore vital for people to ensure that they had a legal settlement in the parish in which they lived. The 1601 act provided that a person was legally settled in a parish after he or she had lived there for one month. However, this allowed migrant workers or vagrants to move to a new parish and quickly obtain the right to receive poor relief from their new community. This was a great burden on some parishes and so the Poor Relief Act of 1662, usually called the Settlement Act (and later amending acts), provided that a newcomer to a parish only acquired a legal right to settlement in a parish (and entitlement to relief from that parish) if that person was:

a. someone who held public office in the parish, or paid the parish rate
b. someone who rented property in the parish worth over £10 per annum
c. an unmarried person who had worked in the parish for one year
d. a woman who had married a man of the parish
e. a legitimate child, aged under 7, whose father lived in the parish
f. a child who was illegitimate and born in the parish
g. a person who was apprenticed to a master in the parish, or
h. a person resident in the parish for 40 days after having given the parish authorities prior written notice of his intention to do so

The rules were often strictly enforced. People might be forcibly ejected from a parish if they were not legally settled there and they became (or were likely to become) a liability to the parish. The parish officials or Justices of the Peace could examine newcomers, on oath, as to their place of settlement. Settlement examinations include much information, such as people's place of birth, their employment or apprenticeship and the places in which they lived over a period of time. Surviving records of examinations can be found in parish records or in the Justices' records (# chapter 25) and an example is shown in illustration 84. Elizabeth Brewer was residing in Sandford in Devon and was examined by the Justices on 15 July 1809. She said that she had been born in Sandford and apprenticed to Richard Kelland of Sandford until she was 21. She then worked as a servant for Henry Chown of Exminster and later for Robert Norrish of Sandford. Parish records of examinations may appear in the vestry minutes. The vestry minutes of Wimbledon of 3 January 1773, in Cowe (511), record the case of Mary Stone. She was born and brought up in Wimbledon, but had moved to Merton to work and a year later she returned to Wimbledon and fell into need:

Whereas the case of Mary Stone concerning her settlement came before this Vestry: it appears upon her examination on oath that she served the two Miss Pearsons at Merton for

Devon. } THE Examination of *Elizabeth Brewer* ———— now refiding in
to wit, } the Parifh of *Sandford* ————— in the faid County *Singlewoman*
————taken on Oath this *15* day of *July* ——— 180*9* ————
before *me one* ———— of his Majefty's Juftices of the Peace in and for the
faid County, touching her laft legal place of Settlement.
Who faith that he was Born in the Parifh of *Sandford in the said county*

which was her Fathers legal place of settlement as she
heard and believes. that she was bound apprentice by the
Churchwardens and Overseers of the Poor of the said Parish
to Richard Kelland of the same parish yeoman until she
should attain the age of Twenty one years served out her
time and then went into the Parish of Exminster in the said
county and hired herself with one Henry Chown of that parish
yeoman for a year at the wages of Three pounds & Ten
Shillings served him Two years under that hiring and after
living about at different places she went back into the
Parish of Sandford aforesaid and hired herself with one
Robert Norrish of that parish yeoman for a year at
the wages of Four pounds served out the year and received
her wages and continued to live with him in Sandford
aforesaid about Half a year after, since which she has
not lived as a covenant Servant for a year at any place
nor done any other Act whereby to gain a settlement.

The mark
Taken on Oath   *Elizabeth ✗ Brewer*
before me

R. Whipkisley Tuckfield

84. *Examination of Elizabeth Brewer in Sandford, July 1809 (Devon Record Office)*

one year and received wages for the same, it is the opinion of this vestry that she is a parishioner of Merton and the officers are to take her before some J.P.s and take out an order of removal and convey her to Merton as the law directs in such case.

Although few settlement examinations survive for some parishes, there are extensive collections for other parishes, particularly in cities that attracted people from the countryside. About 30,000 settlement examinations survive in the parish records of St Martins-in-the-Fields in London from 1708–95 and an index to those of 1750–75 (referring to those people examined but also their relatives, employers and the parish officers) has been published. Examinations were sometimes recorded in settlement examination books, such as those for Mitcham in Surrey for 1753 to 1825. The entries of 1784–1814 have been published in Berryman (507). The following is a typical entry:

Susan Starr. 15 Jan. 1785. She is about 21 years of age, born in Esher. About 6 years ago, she hired herself for one year to John Prior, a farmer at Walton upon Thames . . . and served the said year. She has two children by John Prior, namely John aged near 4 years, born in Walton and Lydia, about 15 months, born in Mitcham and neither of them born in wedlock. [Susan Starr was removed to Walton 19 Jan. 1785]

The Justices issued a removal order if they were satisfied that a person or family needed (or were likely to need) relief, but had no right to settlement in the parish. A removal order directed that a person or family be returned to their parish of legal settlement. An example is shown in illustration 85. The churchwardens and overseers of St Thomas in Devon had complained to Justices that Richard and Ann Sercombe had come to St Thomas without a settlement certificate (see below) and had become a liability to the parish. After an examination, the Justices decided that the Sercombes' lawful place of settlement was Dunsford and ordered that they be sent back to Dunsford and that the authorities of Dunsford should provide for them. The family would be escorted by the constable to the parish boundary. The Justices also issued passes, which recorded a pauper's parish of legal settlement and required the constables of parishes on the route to conduct the pauper towards that parish. The family would be passed to the constable of the neighbouring parish, who would in turn take them to the next boundary (and so on until the family reached their destination). At that point, the paupers might receive relief, but the receiving parish might deny liability and apply to court for another removal order. The courts gave rulings if two parishes disputed liability for a pauper and the records of the Justices and the assizes (# chapter 25) include many such disputes, with both parishes employing lawyers to argue that the other parish was liable.

The difficulty of obtaining a legal settlement, the fear (if one moved) of your old parish denying liability for you, and the distrust of parish officers (and parishioners) towards any newcomers who might need relief in the future, combined to make it difficult for people to move in search of work. The Settlement Act of 1697 therefore allowed overseers to give settlement certificates to parishioners who were moving to another parish, certifying that the person or family would be accepted back in the event that they subsequently required relief. This system allowed some mobility since a receiving parish would allow migrants with a settlement certificate to stay, knowing that they could be returned to their old parish if they required relief. Newcomers usually had to file their certificates with the officials of their new parish so that those

85. Removal order in respect of Richard and Ann Sercombe from St Thomas to Dunsford, Devon in 1821 (Devon Record Office)

officials could prove their case against the home parish if the migrants became a liability. Some indexes of settlement certificates have been published. An example is McLaughlin (525), which indexes the certificates (and settlement examinations and removal orders) in the parish records of Iver in Buckinghamshire. These record people arriving in Iver from other Buckinghamshire parishes, but also from other counties such as Middlesex, Devon and Surrey.

An illegitimate child obtained a legal settlement in his or her parish of birth (and was likely to become a charge on the poor rates in the future). The overseers therefore often removed migrant single women, who were pregnant, to a neighbouring parish before the birth. This practice was curtailed by an act of 1732/3 that prohibited removals of women during pregnancy and during the first month after childbirth. A further act of 1743/4 provided that an illegitimate child's parish of settlement should be the mother's parish of settlement (and not where the birth occurred). It therefore no longer mattered, as regards a child's settlement rights, if a woman was allowed to stay in a parish for her confinement. An act of 1794/5 also reduced much of the harm of the Settlement Acts by prohibiting the removal of paupers unless they actually required relief. Removals could no longer be justified merely because parish officials feared that someone might require relief in the future. The act also allowed the Justices to suspend removal orders against sick people.

The Settlement Act of 1697 also provided for badging the poor. Paupers had to wear a large badge on the right shoulder of their outermost garment, featuring the letter P together with the first letter of the name of their parish. The penalty for failing to comply with this provision was a loss of poor relief, or being whipped and committed to hard labour at a house of correction (a prison). This provision remained in force until 1810, although it was often not enforced and an act of 1781/2 exempted those paupers who were of orderly behaviour.

The Settlement Acts (or statutes of similar effect) remained in force after 1834. From that year paupers requiring relief generally had to enter a workhouse (for the Union in which their parish was located) and this is considered below. However, migrant paupers could still be denied entry to a workhouse and removed by a Board of Guardians to the Union that was legally responsible for them. Settlement examinations from 1834 should therefore be found in Unions' records reviewed below. Gibson & Rogers (515) estimate that about 15,000 people were still being removed each year in the early 20th century until Poor Law Unions were abolished in 1930. The system may seem unfair and cruel, but the surviving records evidence family relationships and our ancestors' movements between parishes.

PARISH APPRENTICES

Many people learned a trade by the system of apprenticeship (# chapter 22). However, from 1601 parish officers (and later Guardians of the Poor) were also empowered to arrange apprenticeships for orphans and for paupers' children, since this relieved the parish of the cost of supporting the child. Children were usually apprenticed to masters, such as farmers, tradesmen or factory owners, in the parish, but in some cases the masters lived miles from a child's home. Children were apprenticed from the age of seven and often against the will of their parents (if they were still alive). Many apprenticeships were purportedly for the children to learn the trades of husbandry or housewifery, but the children were, in effect, a cheap supply of labour for masters who needed agricultural or factory workers and domestic servants. The children had little protection from ill-treatment or overwork and the conditions were often little better than slavery.

The parish overseers and the master signed two copies of an indenture, which was approved and signed by the Justices of the Peace, by which the master agreed to feed and clothe the child and teach him or her the trade specified, usually in return for a small sum of money. Most apprenticeships were for a term of seven years, but parish apprenticeships usually continued until the child was aged 21 (or 24 for boys before 1768). Apprentices were not allowed to marry without their master's consent. Overseers often looked for masters in neighbouring parishes since, after 40 days of apprenticeship, the child obtained a right of settlement in that new parish and thus relieved his home parish of liability to relieve him in the future. Some examples of decisions about apprenticeships are contained in the Wimbledon vestry minutes in Cowe (511):

4 Feb. 1753. Ann Lanchester to be bound out apprentice to William Draycutt, Old Street, St Luke's, London, victualler, who keeps the sign of the Cart and Horses.

16 June 1751. Jo. Boulter to be bound apprentice to Henry Parkhurst, fisherman of Kingston; Parkhurst having agreed, in consideration of £6 paid to him . . . to (keep) him in clothes during his apprenticeship and to give him a new suit at its expiration . . . as the parish are to be at no other expense it is agreed to give £6 upon the above conditions, but this is to be no precedent.

Surviving indentures for pauper apprentices can be found in parish records at CROs. Illustration 86 shows an indenture of 6 June 1744 from the parish of Winkleigh in Devon by which my ancestor John Bulleid was apprenticed to Thomas Bulleid of Croft. John was baptised in 1736 and his father died in 1742, leaving a widow and six children. Samuel (John's elder brother), was apprenticed by the parish in 1742 and John and his sister Martha were apprenticed on the same day in 1744 but to different households. John was perhaps fortunate in being apprenticed to a relative (Thomas Bulleid was a cousin) but his indenture bound him to work in husbandry until he reached the age of 24. Indentures also name the Justices, churchwardens, overseers and the master. The document in illustration 86 (the copy kept by the parish) is signed by Thomas Bulleid and by the Justices. Another copy (kept by Thomas Bulleid) would have been signed by the overseers and churchwardens. These indentures therefore evidence the poor and the rich. You may find a series of indentures in which your ancestor was the master to whom several children were apprenticed. Your ancestor might have been a magistrate, overseer or churchwarden and these records may include his signature or allow you to establish when he held office. Many indentures have been lost, but extensive collections survive for some parishes in CROs (and a few others are in collections such as that at the SoG). The apprenticeship records for Winkleigh and Dunsford in Devon each included about 20 indentures that concerned my ancestors or their families (either as apprentices or as the churchwardens or overseers).

Apprenticeship indentures also illustrate that official records never tell the whole story. My ancestor George Rice of Dunsford had a niece, Eliza Rice. The Dunsford apprentice records include an indenture by which Eliza was apprenticed in housewifery in 1827, until her 21st birthday, to a Dunsford farmer named Jonathan May. Attached to the indenture is a further deed of 1835 stating that Jonathan died on 17 July 1835 and that Eliza would therefore serve Walter May, Jonathan's executor, for the residue of the apprenticeship term. However, Jonathan May was in fact murdered. Harrison (983) describes it as "the county's most famous crime of murder and a serious miscarriage of justice". One man was hanged for the murder but another, Edmund Galley (who was probably innocent) was transported to Australia and only pardoned and released 43 years later.

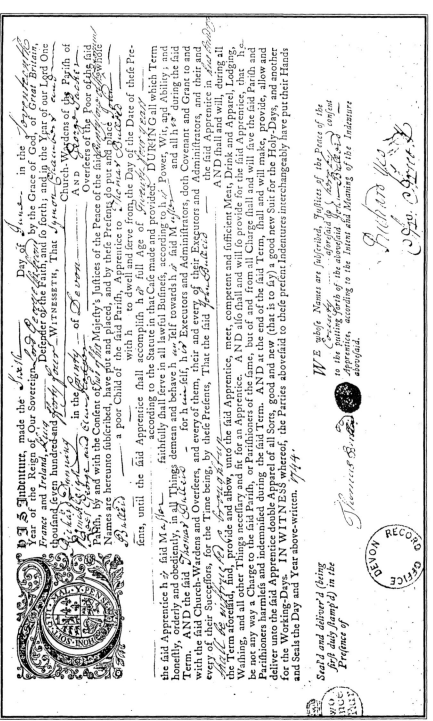

86. *Apprenticeship indenture of John Bulleid, June 1744 (Devon Record Office)*

ILLEGITIMACY

Between 1837 and 1965 about 4 per cent to 7 per cent of children were illegitimate. The figure in earlier years was probably lower (about 2 per cent in the early 18th century) but you are very likely to find illegitimacies in your family tree. It was common in earlier centuries for a couple to marry only after a girl became pregnant (or even after she had borne a child). The identity of parents in these cases is usually clear (the child was regarded as legitimate and usually took the father's surname). However, if your ancestor was born to an unmarried woman, the parish register may not identify the father. Typical entries for baptisms of illegitimate children were:

John, base son of Ann Smith
William, son of Mary Ferguson, baseborn, by Richard Clark

If a father is not named in a parish register, other records may assist. Parish overseers wanted to know a father's identity so that he could be made liable for a child's maintenance. Neighbours and other villagers in the 16th to 19th centuries usually knew who the father was, and so parentage was often recorded in parish or Justice's records. A statute of 1610 provided that mothers of bastards could be sent to a house of correction for up to a year and, in the 17th and 18th centuries, they were often whipped. An unmarried couple who produced a child might be coerced to marry (by their parents or the parish officials), or the father might be persuaded to pay maintenance for the child. Voluntary payments by a father to the mother will not be recorded in the parish documents, but voluntary payments by the father to the parish officials were often noted. An example of a lump sum payment, recorded in the overseers' accounts of Hornchurch, was noted above. The parish records may also include bonds of indemnification or bastardy bonds, by which a father agreed to pay any future expenses of the parish. Illustration 87 shows a bond of indemnification from Dunsford. My ancestor, Mary Hill of Dunsford, was widowed in 1741 but bore an illegitimate child, George Hill, in February 1753. The father (George Furze of Dunsford) agreed in the bond to pay the overseers a weekly sum and also indemnify the parish officers for any costs of maintenance for the child. Christopher Furze, Thomas Furze and Mary's brother (William Holman) also executed the deed (and joined in George's obligation), binding themselves in the sum of £40.

An act of 1576 empowered Justices to examine the circumstances of the birth of an illegitimate child who was (or was likely to become) chargeable to the parish and order the father, by a bastardy order, to pay maintenance. If a father refused either to marry the woman or pay maintenance, an application could then be made to the Justices for a maintenance order. A woman or her family might apply, prove the child's paternity and obtain a maintenance order. If they did not apply, cases could be brought by the parish officers, in order to prevent the cost of a child's upkeep falling on the parish. A woman would be examined on oath as to the father's identity. Women often refused to identify the father and so an act of 1732/3 required that a woman who was pregnant with a bastard child should declare herself as pregnant and declare the name of the father. A man who was accused on oath as being the father could be committed to gaol until he provided security to indemnify the parish against its expense. A father might be ordered to pay the mother, or the parish, a lump sum or a series of maintenance payments. The records of bastardy examinations and orders may therefore identify the father of an illegitimate child.

Illustration 88 shows a bastardy order of 3 January 1809. Ann Rice (the sister of my ancestor George Rice) had at least four illegitimate children in Dunsford between 1799 and 1808. On

87. Bond of indemnification of 1753 from the parish records of Dunsford, Devon (Devon Record Office)

88. *Bastardy order from the parish records of Dunsford, Devon in respect of two children of Ann Rice, 3 January 1809 (Devon Record Office)*

6 November 1808 her twin illegitimate children William and Elizabeth Rice were baptised and the Dunsford churchwardens and overseers applied to the Justices for a bastardy order. The order records that the twins were born on 11 October 1808 and were likely to become a charge to the parish. Richard Orchard was alleged to be the father and was brought before the Justices but he "hath not showed any sufficient cause why he should not be deemed the reputed father of the said bastard children" and the court therefore ordered Richard to pay the parish for Ann's lying-in and for the maintenance of the children.

Parish officials were particularly concerned if a single pregnant woman arrived from outside the parish since both she and the child could become a liability for the parish (because there was no local father to be made liable). Consequently, parish officials might send a pregnant unmarried woman back to her own parish of settlement, until this was forbidden in 1732/3. An act of 1743/4 provided that a bastard only gained a right of settlement in the mother's legal place of settlement and the mother could no longer be moved until a month after the birth. She could still be punished by a public whipping.

WORKHOUSES

Towns and cities that had a number of parishes found it easier to provide for poor relief if the parishes worked together, because town or city parishes were usually very small in area, so that inhabitants might move between parishes even if they only moved a short distance. In the 17th century the authorities also concluded that certain people (often called "the idle poor") had to be dissuaded from living off the parish. These factors led to the establishment of workhouses. Early workhouses were primarily used to accommodate the sick, aged and orphaned poor, instead of the parish paying for their rent and food. A statute of 1695/6 authorised the building of a workhouse in Bristol (to serve its 19 parishes) and similar statutes were passed for workhouses to be built in places such as Exeter, Hereford, Gloucester, Plymouth and Norwich. Some rural parishes also built workhouses (such as Thaxted in Essex in 1711 and Eaton Socon in Bedfordshire in 1719).

An act of 1723 allowed churchwardens and overseers (with the consent of the majority of the parishioners) to establish workhouses. The act also allowed overseers to refuse relief to paupers who refused to enter the workhouse. This was known as the workhouse test. The test was rarely enforced in the 18th and early 19th centuries, but it became the central tenet of the poor law after 1834. The 1723 act also permitted parishes to combine to establish workhouses (with the cost shared by all the parishes), if they were too small to support their own workhouses. Gilbert's Act of 1782 permitted parishes to join together in voluntary unions to administer the poor law and employ paid guardians at the union's workhouse. Unions of parishes therefore began to appear, especially in urban areas which could be better served by one large authority than four or five small ones. There were about 70 voluntary Gilbert Unions by 1834.

THE POOR LAW AFTER 1834

By the early 19th century poor relief was becoming increasingly expensive. However, many people also believed that the system encouraged people to avoid work (and live on parish relief) and allowed employers to pay low wages (since the parish ensured that workers and their families did not starve). Substantial changes to the poor law were therefore introduced by the Poor Law

Amendment Act of 1834. All parishes were compelled to amalgamate into unions, each of which had an elected Board of Guardians to administer poor relief. The guardians were elected by those who paid the parish poor rates, which continued to be collected by parish overseers (but for the union rather than the parish) until 1865. In that year the parish poor rates were replaced by a union rate, which was also collected by the overseers until their office was abolished in 1925.

Each union was divided into districts, each with a relieving officer who considered the circumstances of anyone applying for relief. The 1834 act also required guardians and relieving officers to apply the workhouse test. The able-bodied poor were no longer given outdoor relief, but were admitted to a workhouse. Workhouse conditions varied from humane and clean (and possibly better than many paupers' homes) to institutions that were little better than prisons. Outdoor relief could still be granted to the old, the sick, or to widows with dependent children. The guardians of some unions (in areas of high unemployment) continued to grant out-relief to paupers whom they considered to be the deserving poor. In some other areas, the provision of out-relief had to continue temporarily until a workhouse was built (but all unions had workhouses by about 1865).

The Boards of Guardians reported to the Poor Law Commission in London (renamed the Poor Law Board in 1847 and the Local Government Board in 1871). In 1919 the boards became part of the Ministry of Health. Much of the need for the poor law and workhouses was removed by the introduction of old age pensions and unemployment insurance in 1908 and 1911, and poor law administration was transferred from the unions to local authorities in 1930. The Boards of Guardians were then abolished. However, many of the workhouses continued to operate until the final abolition of the poor law in 1948 and some were subsequently converted into hospitals or asylums. The modern welfare system dates from the National Assistance Act of 1948 but few of its records are available to the public.

RECORDS OF POOR LAW UNIONS AND THE COMMISSIONERS

Most people discover that an ancestor was in a workhouse because it is noted on his or her death certificate or because the ancestor is located in a workhouse on census night, usually through searching census indexes (particularly those of 1851, 1881 and 1901). I found my g.g.g.grandfather Charles Timms (with almost 1,500 other inmates) in the Hackney Union workhouse in London in the 1901 census (illustration 89). In these cases it is easy to turn to the workhouse or other union records noted below. In order to find other ancestors in union records, you must first ascertain the union in which his parish was located. The organisation of unions (and the areas covered by each) did change. For example, in 1834, the City of London was divided into three unions: the City of London, East London and West London Unions, but all three were merged into the City of London Union in 1869. Gibson & Youngs (518) is a gazetteer of England and Wales, listing the places in each union. Since the poor law unions were also utilised for the civil registration and census systems, this gazetteer is also helpful for research in those records.

Poor law documents since 1834 are held in the guardians' records (in CROs) or at TNA in the records of the Poor Law Commission and successor bodies. Three volumes by Gibson & Rogers (515–517) are guides to poor law unions of England and Wales, describing the surviving records of each union (and any relevant papers for the union in the Commissioners' records), their covering dates and location. Each volume is arranged by county, then by union (although a

LIST of all PERSONS who SLEPT or ABODE in this INSTITUTION on the NIGHT of SUNDAY, MARCH 31st, 1901.

No.	NAME and SURNAME	RELATION to Head of Family, or Position in the Institution	CONDITION as to Marriage	AGE last Birthday		PROFESSION or OCCUPATION.	Employer, Worker, or Own Account.	If Working at Home.	WHERE BORN.	(1) Deaf and Dumb (2) Blind (3) Lunatic, Imbecile, Feeble-minded
				Males	Females					
1	Benjamin Saunderson	Pauper	Wid.	59		— Marine	Worker	—	London, Spitalfields	
2	John Gowley	"	"	55		Butcher	own account	Altham	Islington	
3	William Ellwood	"	Wid.	69		Shepherd	Unmarried		Hants, Stoc	Pension
4	Charles Furman	"	"	74		General Labourer	"		Russia, Watorth	
5	Thomas Jappurdon	"	"	83		Shoemaker	"		Kent, Canterbury	
6	Charles Thomason	"	"	81		—	"		London, Marylebone	
7	John Thomas	"	S	84		Boatman	—		St George E	
8	Thomas R. P. Taylor	"	Wid.	81		House Steward? Paris	—		Suffolk, Ipswich	
9	Charles Juper	"	"	77		Waiter	—		Sussex, South Overton	
10	Samuel Thompson	"	M.	65		Man of Lens	—		London, Southwark	war
11	Daniel Taylor	"	M.	60		General Labourer	—		Hanover, Birmingham	war
12	Charles Thomas	"	Wid.	68		Bricklayer	—		London, Paddington	
13	James Taylor	"	"	77		General Labourer	—		Sussex, West Lewes	
14	Samuel Jreybuy	"	"	77		Sailor Merchant OS	25		Sussex, Rayleigh	
15	Robert Jury	"	M.	71		Lodging House Keeper	own account	Altham	West India	
16	Isaac Tuthell	"	S	34		General Labourer	Worker		London, Hackney	
17	Samuel Hanbury	"	Wid.	60		Boot? Collator	—		City of	
18	Richard Taylor	"	Wid.	69		Street Porter/Box?	—		Holborn	
19	Henry J Taylor	"	"	64		Street Porter/Box?	own account	Altham	Bethnal Green	
20	Thomas Taylor	"	"	78		General Labourer	Unmarried		Holborn	
21	Alfred Thomas	"	M.	48		Sailor	—		St Pancras	
22	William Tophey	"	Wid.	70		Fiddler	—		Colchester	
23	Henry Taylor	"	S	48		Sailor	—		" Hackney	
24	Thomas Taylor	"	M.	58		General Labourer	—		Sussex, Blatten	Sea-going
25	James Ho. Lewis	"	S	36			—		London, Millwall	

Total of Males and of Females........ 25

union might cross county boundaries), with maps showing the area covered by each union. Importantly, records of paupers since Gilbert's Act of 1782 (allowing the combination of parishes into unions) until 1834, may be held in the post-1834 union's records rather than in the parish records, so you should search both groups of records at archives.

The administration of workhouses and the conditions experienced by inmates are considered in three articles by J. Lodey in *Family Tree Magazine* (January to June 1986). The law relating to the operation and administration of workhouses (and the relief granted inside) is set out in detail in Holdsworth (520). Workhouses kept registers of births, baptisms, deaths and burials that took place in the institution. These are particularly important between 1837 and 1875 (when the civil registration system omitted many people). Any recorded events should have been reported to the local registrar (and so appear in civil registration records) but some births and deaths are only recorded in the workhouse registers. Workhouse admission and discharge registers from 1834 are usually in CROs. Most registers note the name, age, occupation, marital status, parish of settlement, religion and perhaps a physical description of each pauper who was admitted, as well as dates of admission and discharge. The reason why relief was granted should also be noted. Since the person providing this information was usually the pauper, he or she might lie to ensure that relief was granted (and so be admitted to the workhouse). Information such as place of birth and recent residence may therefore be untrue. The registers are rarely indexed, but indoor relief lists should have been compiled (from the registers) every six months, listing the names of paupers who had been admitted, their date of birth and the amount of time that they spent in the workhouse. These lists are easier to search than the registers.

Some workhouse records have been indexed by family history societies. Nottinghamshire FHS has produced an index (499) to admissions at Nottingham Union workhouse 1856–58 (and indexes for 1858–69 are also available on microfiche). It is no surprise that the index shows an increase in workhouse admissions in winter but it also illustrates how some people moved in and out of workhouses on a regular basis. Thomas Rawson is noted as having been admitted on 27 December 1856 (aged 65), 9 November 1857 and 17 August and 3 November 1858. The descendants of Thomas would be able to locate useful information about his occupation, health, address and other personal circumstances from the admission and discharge registers and other workhouse records.

The relieving officers for each district reviewed people's claims for relief. They sent many paupers to the workhouse, but granted outdoor relief (usually money) to people who were not obliged to enter a workhouse (usually those who were ill for only a short time). Surviving papers of relieving officers (out-relief lists or relief order books) may note a pauper's name, the amount of money and the reasons for payment (and possibly the pauper's address and the names of any dependants). The detail of workhouse and relieving officers' records is illustrated in Rumbelow (530). In the records for St Marylebone, St Pancras and other areas of London, Rumbelow traced the periods spent in workhouses by a grandmother, mother and daughter over a period of 40 years from 1880. Although some records are missing, the detailed documents that survive provide a good picture of where people lived, their poverty and their state of health.

A union's records should also include guardians' correspondence and minutes of meetings, which mention many paupers. There are also workhouse expenditure books, rate books and workhouse registers of offences (and punishments) of inmates. A punishment book of Foleshill Union workhouse for 1864–1900, transcribed in Castle & Wishart (509), is a fascinating example. It records that William Rowney, Thomas Cox and William Flanagan each received 12 strokes with a birch rod on 13 December 1870 for having been "disobedient and insolent to the Governess". Ann Paxton received only bread and water for 24 hours as punishment for having used obscene language on 8 May 1889. Some inmates were punished a number of times. George Richards was taken before a magistrate and imprisoned for 21 days for threatening Henry Hammersley (another inmate) on 20 May 1864. Richards assaulted the inmate George Twigger on 29 April 1867 and was sentenced by a magistrate to another 21 days in prison with hard labour. Richards was imprisoned twice more (in 1875 and 1877) for assaults or for damaging workhouse property.

The guardians also became responsible for binding children as apprentices (although the minimum age for such a child was raised to 9 in 1847), so that the guardians' records include lists of apprentices and their masters. K. Thompson reviewed the Leicester Poor Law Union's register of apprentices in the 2001 edition of the FLHH (5). It records 476 apprentices between 1844 and 1927, noting each child's age, the names and residence of the parents, the name, trade and residence of the master as well as the date and term of the apprenticeship. Records also concern assisted emigration of paupers to the colonies (# chapter 30). The guardians often paid families to emigrate (by paying travelling costs and providing a cash sum for food and the expense of setting up home elsewhere) since this relieved the union of the future expense of caring for a poor family.

Union documents also include smallpox vaccination records. There were serious smallpox epidemics in Britain in 1837–40 and 1870–72. Vaccination was provided by the guardians from 1840 and was compulsory for infants from 1853 to 1948. Vaccination certificates were given to the parents and these often noted the child's age and place of birth. Vaccination registers were kept from 1862 to 1948, noting a child's name and sometimes age (or date and place of birth) and the father's name and occupation. Older registers often survive in CROs, but later registers may still be held in hospitals' archives. However, only those records older than 50 years are open to public inspection.

Your ancestor may have been employed at a workhouse, perhaps as the master, or as a schoolmaster, porter, cook or nurse. The masters are usually named in directories. The names of other employees can be found in the census records but also in the guardians' and Commissioners' records. Series MH 9 at TNA contains registers, from about 1834 to 1921, of paid officers (including masters, clerks and nurses) of English and Welsh unions, arranged by county and then union. The registers note salaries and dates of appointment, resignation or dismissal. Series MH 19 contains appointment registers for staff of Boards of Guardians for 1834 to 1850. The records of the Poor Law Commission (and successor bodies) at TNA, in series MH 12, include over 16,000 volumes from 1834 to about 1900 (sometimes up to 1909). They consist mainly of the Commissioners' correspondence with the Boards of Guardians, covering matters such as the appointment of staff (including applications and references), the examination of paupers, vaccination, guardians' accounts (including copies of out-relief lists) and financial assistance for paupers' emigration. This correspondence includes the names of many paupers. There are subject indexes in series MH 15 (but no indexes to names or places). Most correspondence since 1900 was destroyed in the Second World War, but some files survive in series MH 68.

In order to find a union's records, you should first turn to the booklets by Gibson (515–518). For example, if your ancestors lived in the poor law union of Okehampton in Devon, the entry in Gibson's work tells you that the guardians' records at Devon Record Office include guardians' minutes (1836–1927), minutes of the guardians' assessment committee (1862–1927) and outdoor relief lists (1853–1914). The relevant correspondence files (between the guardians and Commissioners) for 1834–1900 are in pieces MH 12/2394 to 2416 at TNA and staff registers for 1837–1921 are in piece MH 9/12. More detailed information may be contained in the published guides of CROs or in their catalogues. Thus the guide to Bedford Record Office (227) provides detailed lists of the surviving records for each union. A shortened version of the entry for the Bedford Poor Law Union is:

Administration: Minutes 1835–1930 (37 vols); committee records 1835–1928 (15 vols); letter books 1835–1919 (33 vols); financial registers 1837–1928 (50 vols) including accounts for clothing, special diets, etc.

Relief: Indoor lists 1836–1929 (96 vols); outdoor lists 1875–1920 (49 vols); relief order books 1874–1920 (41 vols); medical officer's reports 1892–1909 (4 vols); application and report books 1875–1920 (85 vols).

Workhouse: Admission and discharge registers 1835–1927 (50 vols); weekly returns 1892–1910 (9 vols); master's reports 1842–43 and 1873–1928 (37 vols); medical relief 1870–1914 (15 vols); registers of births, deaths, inmates' property, pauper lunatics, school attendance, apprentices 1838–1930 (30 vols); punishment book 1896–1912 (1 vol); visitors' books 1836–1914 (22 vols); chaplain's journal 1887–97.

FOUNDLINGS AND ORPHANS

Unwanted children (perhaps children of paupers or single mothers) were often abandoned in places such as the church porch or in a market place. The churchwardens arranged the baptism of these foundlings. They were often named after the saint of the parish church (perhaps Mary or Peter) with a surname after the place (such as Porch or Lane) or the parish where they were found. Most of these children were illegitimate and you are most unlikely to discover their parents' names. A foundling might be fortunate and be brought up by another family as their own child. Most foundlings were cared for by the parish, that is put out to nurses and later apprenticed to a local farmer or tradesman.

Captain Thomas Coram was horrified that children were abandoned on the streets of London and left to die. He established the Foundling Hospital in London in 1741 to look after foundlings (with branch hospitals in other towns in later years). Thousands of children were left with the hospital and the hospital generally placed them with foster mothers in rural areas. Many died in infancy, but children who survived to the age of eight were apprenticed to farmers, factory owners or the Royal Navy. Some records of the Foundling Hospital are held by LMA and its baptism and burial registers are at the FRC in series RG 4. Admission registers from 1794 are held by the Thomas Coram Foundation at 40 Brunswick Square, London WC1, but access is restricted (and impossible if records are less than 150 years old) and fees are charged. Anyone considering making an enquiry should review an article in the spring 1990 edition of *Cockney Ancestor* (218) about the procedure and difficulties. The records of children reclaimed by their parents are described by A. Camp in *Family Tree Magazine* (June 2000) and articles on the Foundling Hospital also appear in *Family Tree Magazine* (May/June 1986) and *Genealogists' Magazine* (March 2002).

Many other organisations were dedicated to the care of children. One of the most famous was Dr Barnardo's. Dr Barnardo founded his first home for orphans and destitute children in Stepney in 1867 and homes were soon established across the country. The last home closed in 1981, by which time about 300,000 children had been assisted. Many of the children were orphans or illegitimate, but some were sent to Barnardo's because of their parents' poverty, or because a widowed parent could not cope. Many of the children were subsequently fostered and thousands were sent by Barnardo's (and other organisations) to Australia, Canada and other parts of the British Empire to start new lives (# chapter 30). Barnardo's kept detailed records from 1867, including admission registers that note the reasons for a child's admission. The records are held at Liverpool University, but can only be searched by postal application to the After-Care Department, Barnardo's, Tanners Lane, Barkingside, Essex IG6 1QG. The records are confidential for 100 years (except to the now adult children, their next of kin or with their consent). Each child admitted by Barnardo's was photographed and Barnardo's still holds its enormous photographic archive, which is reviewed in *Family Tree Magazine* (August 1995). This includes many photographs of life in Barnardo's homes.

OTHER PARISH RECORDS: CHURCHWARDENS' ACCOUNTS

Churchwardens' accounts list expenditure for church ceremonies or work on church buildings (such as the purchase of wine for communion, or items such as bellropes), rather than genealogical information, but the accounts commonly record payments to carpenters and stonemasons for work on the church. Cox (512) is a detailed analysis of churchwardens' accounts of the 14th to 17th centuries, with many examples of the types of entries that they include. Early churchwardens' accounts noted burials, especially those inside a church. These are especially useful where they pre-date parish registers or where a burial register has been lost. Land owned by the church was often leased to parishioners and the tenants and their rents may be noted in churchwardens' accounts. Some accounts have been published, such as those for Hooton Pagnell in Yorkshire for 1767–1820 in Whiting (535), those for Chipping Campden, Gloucestershire for 1626–1907 in Bishop (508) and those for Shillington, Northill and Clifton in Bedfordshire in the late 16th century, in Farmiloe & Nixseamen (514). The Northill accounts include the following payments:

1573.	To John Totnam for mending the bells	12d.
1580.	Paid to John Careles the smythe for making new great bell clapper	12s.

The money required for this work was levied by a church rate from parish householders. Ratepayers may be listed in the accounts. The Northill accounts of 1573 record the names of 28 men of the parish who paid a levy. By the 19th century, church rate books had become fairly complete lists of the names of heads of households in a parish (and also noted the street in which people lived). They can be used with early street plans and directories to locate an ancestor's home. Churchwardens' accounts, rate books and many other parish records also note the names of the churchwardens and these may include your ancestors.

HIGHWAYS

In medieval times liability for the maintenance of highways lay with the owners of the adjoining land. A Lord of a manor passed on his obligations to his tenants and enforced the obligations through the manorial courts (# chapter 27). The Highway Act 1555 transferred responsibility for the maintenance of most roads and highways to parishes. Able-bodied men were required to provide their labour or pay someone to work on their behalf. Surveyors of highways (or waywardens) were appointed by the parishioners to supervise the work. A man who refused to work could be fined by the Justices at Quarter Sessions. The labour obligations were often commuted into a money payment and from 1654 the vestry was empowered to levy a highway rate to pay for the upkeep of highways, to pay the waywardens or surveyors and to pay those providing materials and labour.

Details of the rate, payments and expenses may be noted in vestry minutes or in highways' accounts. Some accounts have been published, such as those for Hooton Pagnell in Yorkshire for 1767–1819, in Whiting (535). From November 1792 to October 1793 these record many payments to Abraham Haigh for his labour (at about four or five shillings per week) and payments to Richard Newsom for gravel. Names of the surveyors who were appointed each year usually appear in vestry minutes or in the accounts. The office of surveyor of highways continued until the Highway Act 1835 (or later in some places) when responsibility for highways was transferred to the new civil local authorities. The establishment of turnpike trusts to build important roads was noted in chapter 15. Records of turnpike trusts in CROs cover the building and upkeep of highways, noting payments to labourers for work or to merchants for materials. A minute book for 1711–54 of the trustees of the Portsmouth and Sheet Turnpike Trust, published in Albert & Harvey (505), includes annual accounts of the trust's surveyors. These note various payments, for example in 1720–21:

Paid Jno. Smith bricklayer	£2 5s. 0d.
Paid Thos. Allnutt for cartage	£3 5s. 0d.
Paid Jno. Starks bringing gravel to Portsbridge	7s. 3d.
Paid Jno. Fatchen labourer, repairing the lane at Corsham, 4 days at 15d. per day	5s. 0d.

AFFIDAVITS OF WOOL

The Burial in Woollen Acts of 1666–80 required that the dead (except plague victims) should be buried in shrouds made of pure wool. Furthermore, an affidavit (a statement on oath) had to be sworn before a Justice of the Peace (usually by a relative of the deceased or some other credible person) confirming that the body had been buried in wool. A penalty of £5 should have been levied if other material was used. The affidavits were given to the incumbent and he might write the word affidavit (or a note A or Aff) against burial entries in the parish register. Many poor families could not afford a woollen shroud and these burials may be noted in the register as "naked". Some affidavits survive and examples are reproduced in Yurdan (33). In many parishes the affidavits were copied into registers and these may survive even if the affidavits have been lost. Notes of the burials, affidavits and fees paid may appear in churchwardens' accounts or vestry minutes. The text of the affidavits varied but a simple, short version might be:

John Clements maketh oath that the body of Ann Clements of this parish, which was buried on [date] was not wrapped in anything but what was made of sheeps' wool only.

An article, by S. Tomlinson, about the operation of the acts in Oxfordshire (and surviving records, including over 1,000 affidavits) appears in *Oxfordshire Family Historian* (Summer 1982). The legislation remained in force until 1814 but was generally ignored after about 1770. The statutes also required overseers of the poor to compile annual lists of people who had been buried in wool but this requirement was generally ignored and few lists survive in parish records.

THE PARISH CONSTABLE

In the middle ages the constable was an officer of the manor, appointed by the manorial court (# chapter 27). However, the post of constable continued despite the decline of the manorial system and in many places the constable became a parish official (usually appointed by the vestry and supervised by the Justices and churchwardens). The constable was responsible for maintaining law and order in the parish or manor, arresting those committing crimes and bringing them before the courts. He was also responsible for removing vagrants or paupers (who had no right of settlement in the parish), supervising alehouses, destroying vermin and organising ballots, from 1757, for men of the parish to serve in the local militia (# chapter 20). The Parish Constables Act 1842 required constables to be appointed by the Justices and surviving records of appointments should be held with records of the Clerk of the Peace. County police forces were established from 1839 and gradually replaced parish constables.

The constable's expenditure was sometimes paid by the levy of a constable's rate from parish householders or, from 1778, it could be paid out of the poor rates. Constables' accounts may survive in parish records in CROs. Most entries record the type of expenditure and the amount but the names of villagers may also be included, such as men receiving payments for the destruction of vermin, for work on the parish walls or otherwise assisting the constable. Some accounts of constables have been published, such as the constables' books for 1691–1836 from Wiggington in Oxfordshire, in Price (528), and those for the parish of Hooton Pagnell in Yorkshire for 1767–1818, in Whiting (535), from which typical entries are:

| 1801 | Aug 14 | Paid Wm Shaw for mole catching | £2. 2s |
| 1801 | Oct 18 | Paid [for] Francis Laurence inquest | £1. 4s |

In some places, constables remained officers of manorial courts until the 1842 act. Constables' names and records of their work may be found in manorial records (# chapter 27) and some have been published. Accounts of the constables of Manchester of 1612–47 and 1743–76, transcribed in Earwaker (513), include these entries from 1619–20:

Paid for bringing Tho Potter to Lancaster [for trial at the assizes] for wounding Anne Erlom	20s.
Paid for meat for Tho Harrison and George Hunter in the dungeon	3d.
Paid for hue & cry that came from Ashton-under-Lyne after Edward Hudson for killing a man the 21 of June	8d.
Paid for carrying a cripple Anne Taylor to Cheetham Hill	12d.
Paid for a passe & whippinge John Hyde of Barnseley & bringing him to the Constables of Newtown	9d.

CHURCH SEATING PLANS

Until the 17th century attendance at church was compulsory, and surviving church seating plans show the names of adults in the parish and also indicate their status. As pews were introduced into churches, many people had particular places to sit, often because they had paid to install the pews. Church seating plans recorded parishioners' rights to sit in certain church pews for life, a period of years or in perpetuity. Some plans date from the late 16th century but most are later. Records of pew rents, that is the money paid by people for their rights, also survive in CROs and include important genealogical information. Examples from Devizes, Calne and Melksham, published by Wiltshire FHS (504), include this entry from Calne in 1774:

> Jane Gale, widow of John Gale, blacksmith, deceased, was possessed of one pew under the North gallery stairs, which seat was purchased (from) Thomas Harwood & Ann his wife, which pew Jane Gale widow gave (to) Rebecca Bowman daughter of John Bowman.

EASTER BOOKS AND COMMUNICANTS LISTS

Communicants' lists recorded the members of the Church of England. Each communicant was meant, by custom, to offer two pence to the incumbent at Easter and these Easter dues were listed in Easter books. Further details of Easter books are contained in two articles by Wright (536) in the journal *Local Population Studies* (spring and autumn 1989). These list surviving Easter books, for example those of Ludlow in Shropshire for 1717–1835. Furthermore, in addition to the tithes payable to the church in respect of crops and animal produce (# chapter 15), a priest had a right to a personal tithe, which was calculated according to a person's wages or the profits of his craft or trade. Personal tithes were usually collected at the same time as the Easter offering. Since the amount of offerings and tithes varied from person to person, some church officers prepared lists of the sums due from parishioners (or the sums received). The few surviving records up to 1800 that name parishioners are listed by Gibson & Medlycott (139). Examples from Norfolk (held at Norfolk Record Office) include those for the parishes of Catfield (1632), St Etheldreda, Norwich (1686–93) and Great Melton (1729–40).

CHURCH BRIEFS

Church briefs, also known as King's briefs, were Letters Patent from the monarch authorising money to be collected in churches for charitable purposes. Briefs were usually intended to assist people in other parishes (most commonly following a fire). Records of briefs include lists of parishioners and the amounts paid. Thus Guildhall Library holds records of money received from parishes in London and 30 counties in England and Wales for the rebuilding of St Paul's Cathedral after the Great Fire of London. Other briefs are in CROs, usually in the records of a parish that received money, but occasionally in the records of a parish that made a collection. Bewes (507a) is a detailed study of briefs, including a list of known briefs from the period 1642–1828.

THE PROTESTATION RETURNS

The Protestation returns are lists of people, arranged by parish, who took an oath in 1641/2. They are national, rather than parish, records and are considered with other records of oaths (and certain tax assessments) in chapter 23. However, they are most useful if studied in combination with the parish registers and other parish records.

OTHER LISTS OF NAMES

Some other church records include lists of names. For example, a census was undertaken in the diocese of Stafford in 1532/3. It lists about 51,000 names and is held in Lichfield Record Office. There was a survey of communicants in the diocese of Canterbury in 1565 and the records for about 40 parishes include names, about eight of which list the whole population of those parishes. In 1676 the Bishop Compton census took place. This was predominantly a statistical survey, but lists of names survive for 19 parishes. In the 1680s a census was undertaken in the diocese of St Asaph in Wales, listing householders' names from many parishes. Details of all these records are contained in Gibson & Medlycott (139).

PARISH MAGAZINES

Parish magazines were published (usually monthly or quarterly) from the late 19th century, principally to inform parishioners about church services or special events in the parish. They include much information of interest to family historians, such as lists of baptisms, marriages and burials, obituaries, lists of those attending parish events, profiles of the vicar (or other parishioners), or accounts of weddings with lists of guests' names. Collections of parish magazines are held in many local libraries and a useful article, by Z. Wade, with examples of entries from a Surrey parish magazine, appears in *Family Tree Magazine* (May/June 1986).

CHARITIES

Until the late 19th century most charities were of a local nature, that is limited to the parish or town in which the benefactor lived, and usually administered by parish officials. Many examples of parish charities and benefactors are provided by Tate (532). Charities were typically intended to assist the poor, to pay for the upkeep of the church, provide a school or almshouses (charity cottages for needy families), or pay masters to train apprentices. The most common method of establishing a charity was by a gift of money, shares, or land in the benefactor's will (although many gifts were also made by lifetime deeds of settlement). If a charitable fund was for the benefit of the poor, the income might be used to supply clothing, fuel or cash payments to paupers. Charitable bequests were also commonly made to hospitals or guilds (# chapter 22), such as the London livery companies, which in turn assisted the poor by providing medical care, almshouses, food, clothing or cash to those in need.

Directories often note local charities in the descriptions of towns or villages. Thus the entry for Haynford in the 1845 directory of Norfolk by White (214) noted that 66 acres of land were held for the poor and the rent obtained from that property was divided between the poor parishioners. The entry also noted the names of the three benefactors, including John Sporle in 1677 and Thomas Bulwer in 1693. The directory also recorded that, at the nearby village of Sprowston, Catherine and Ann Corbet had left six cottages for the benefit of the poor and at Felthorpe it was recorded that in 1687 William Brereton had left two houses and two acres of land for the residence of poor aged widows. The notes about charities in directories were usually a summary of the detailed information contained in the 32 volumes of *Reports of the Commission for Inquiring Concerning Charities* (502). These reports (published 1819–40) were intended to record all charities in the country. Copies are held in Guildhall Library and many reference libraries. The entries are arranged by county, then hundred, then parish. They do not record who received benefits from a charity but they do include detailed information about the benefactor, his will (or deed of settlement) and the charity's trustees, property or income. Volume 10 of the reports includes a survey of charities in Dunsford in Devon, of which the following is an extract:

> **Preston's Gift**: Robert Preston, by will dated 19th July 1763, directed that £25 should be retained in the hands of his executors, and placed at interest, and the interest employed for the keeping of three poor children of the parish of Dunsford at school in or near the said parish, until his grandson, John May, should become entitled to the possession of his lands, called "Farrants" by virtue of his will (upon attaining the age of 24 years) . . . at which time the said £25 should be paid into the hands of his said grandson and that he and his representatives should from thenceforth, for the term of 70 years, continue the same at interest and employ that interest for the schooling of three poor children.

Sections of the commission's reports were republished. Thus *The Endowed Charities of the City of London* (498) reprints the entries for the City. A detailed entry about property is considered in chapter 27 below, but a brief entry is:

> Edward Heylin, by a codicil to his will, dated 5th November 1795, gave to the minister and churchwardens of [the parish of St Michael Bassishaw] the sum of £52 10s, upon trust, to apply the interest in purchasing two sixpenny loaves each Sunday for two poor men or women who should attend divine service . . . with this sum was purchased £101 18s 10d of three per cent Consols in the names of Gabriel Leeky, the Rev John Moore and Daniel Waldron; the dividends of £3 1s per annum are added to the bread fund.

Parish records often include the original deed or will by which someone established a charity and set out its aims. The records may also include letters, accounts and lists of those who benefited (perhaps details of the poor who received money or lived in the almshouses, or the children who were sent to school or apprenticed). Vestry minutes may also record charitable bequests. The Wimbledon vestry minutes in Cowe (511) for 24 July 1748 note that:

> A legacy of £100 given by the will of Mrs Ann Lordell, late of this parish, to ten poor families of the parish, was distributed by direction of William Hanger esq, her executor . . . to the following parishioners each being paid £10; Ja. Adams, Ri. Lowick, Jo. Beacham, Ri. Cobham, Ri. Stevens, Ri. English, Fra. Trevour, Ri. Till, Ro. Maybank, L. Fenton.

From 1812 the Clerk of the Peace usually kept the records of charitable trusts, noting the names of trustees and the charity's objects, investments and income. Many of these records are in CROs. The Charity Commission was established on a permanent basis in 1853 and the Commissioners have been responsible for the supervision of charities since that time.

HOSPITALS

Much useful information about hospitals and their records is provided by Bourne & Chicken (779), together with information about the medical professions (# chapter 22). Prescott (527) is a detailed account of hospitals and almshouses up to 1640, which concentrates on the architecture of the buildings, but also includes information on the work of early hospitals and their few surviving records (such as charters). Many early hospitals were monastic or charitable foundations. By the end of the 13th century, about 500 hospitals (for example St Bartholomews in Smithfield in London) had been established in England and, since leprosy was widespread in England in the 12th and 13th centuries, there were also many leprosy hospitals (or lazar houses) which segregated lepers from the rest of the community. Private individuals also founded hospitals, often by their wills, or founded charities to establish hospitals for the poor. By 1547 there were between 700 and 800 hospitals in England and although many were closed upon the dissolution of the monasteries, many more were established in the following century. Prescott (527) includes a list of many of the hospitals and almshouses founded before 1640, with details of the founder (whether an individual or a religious body). As examples, the almshouses in Cheriton Fitzpaine in Devon (to accommodate six paupers) were founded in 1594 by Andrew Scott, and the hospital of St John the Baptist in Ludlow in Shropshire was founded in about 1220 by Peter Undergod, a burgess of Ludlow. The few surviving records of these institutions (few survive from before the Reformation) are held by TNA, LMA or CROs.

Further hospitals, many of which still survive, were founded in the 18th century, including Westminster Hospital, Guy's Hospital and the Middlesex Hospital in London (in 1719, 1724 and 1745 respectively), Addenbrooke's Hospital in Cambridge (in 1719), the Radcliffe Infirmary in Oxford (in 1770) and the Manchester Infirmary in 1755. Some parishes also founded hospitals, usually in the same building as the workhouse. Lying-in hospitals (for women about to give birth) were established in the 18th century in London and other cities.

Many hospital records (especially clinical records) have been destroyed and administrative records are closed to the public for 30 years (and patients' records are closed for 100 years). However, many hospital registers (particularly recording burials) and some other records are held by CROs. TNA and the Wellcome Institute are collaborating in the Hospital Records Database, that catalogues the records of more than 1,000 hospitals since 1600 and can be searched, by name of the hospital, through the web site of TNA. The database lists the records available for each hospital, their covering dates, the archive holding them and some of the finding aids available. TNA holds (in series RG 8, on microfilm at the FRC) the baptism registers for the British Lying-in Hospital at Holborn from 1749–1868 (about 30,000 baptisms) and the entries are included in the IGI. Many entries are for the poor or for the wives of soldiers and sailors. The admission records for 1749–1868 are also in series RG 8, listing women's names and ages, their husbands' names, occupations and parish of settlement and the names of the children (and dates of birth and baptism). Some later registers record the place of marriage of the parents. LMA holds a copy of the baptism register of Middlesex Hospital, many records of St Thomas's, Guy's and Charing Cross Hospitals as well as records of about 150 other hospitals, many of them outside London. They are listed by J. Foster in *Genealogists' Magazine* (September 1992) and in Webb (533a), which is a list of London hospital records held at various archives, including baptism or burial records, admissions registers, clinical records, staff registers and minute books. A few hospitals keep their older records. Thus St Barthomew's Hospital in London has its own archives department (and some of its records have been published), including admissions registers (1818–1917) and clinical casenotes

(1826–1920). Other hospitals with their own record offices include St George's in London, Addenbrooke's Hospital in Cambridge and the Manchester Royal Infirmary.

Until the early 19th century hospitals for the mentally ill were either private establishments or charitable hospitals. A statute of 1828 permitted Justices of the Peace to build asylums (financed from the rates) and Justices were required to provide suitable accommodation for pauper lunatics from 1845. This duty was transferred to county councils in 1888. Records concerning asylums may therefore be in Quarter Sessions' or county council records. An institution's records may, however, still be held at the institution itself or in the archives of the National Health Service which became responsible for asylums in 1948. Surviving asylum records are usually closed for 100 years. Other records of lunatics may be found in court records (# chapters 24 and 25) or from 1842 in the records of the Lunacy Commission and successor bodies. The records held at TNA are listed in Bevan (239) and TNA domestic records leaflet 105. They include petitions in the Court of Chancery (in series C 211 and 217), some returns of lunatics in asylums or prisons (in MH 51), workhouse and asylums' returns of inmates of 1834–1909 (in MH 12) and the Lunacy Commissioners' registers of asylum admissions since 1846 (in MH 94). Some hospitals' records of lunatics can also be located on the Hospital Records Database.

PARLIAMENTARY COMMITTEES

The English Civil War disrupted the administration of counties, particularly in the areas controlled by Parliament. The Parliamentary leaders established County Committees, the main tasks of which were to levy troops, raise money to pay those men (and feed them) and deal with petitions from people affected by the war. The few records of County Committees that have survived are in CROs or in private papers (some are noted in the National Register of Archives). One example is an order book of the Staffordshire County Committee for 1643–45, which has been published in Pennington & Roots (526). It includes information on local administration during the war as in these examples:

a) a dispute over rent between Nicholas Hurt and Mrs Brett of Dimsdale,
b) John Gratrix (a soldier under Captain Gough) was accused of killing a man but released upon the captain undertaking to bring him back to answer the case, and
c) Mr Goring was to go to Norton Farm and take all of Mrs Sneads' cheese (leaving only such quantity as was necessary for the family) and deliver it to the commissary.

COUNTY COUNCILS

Most administrative duties of parishes and Justices of the Peace have now been transferred to central or local government. The relief of the poor was transferred to Boards of Guardians in 1834 and most other civil duties of parishes and the Justices were transferred to County Councils (or County Boroughs) which were established in 1888. Further duties (such as education, housing and the fire service) have also been passed to the councils (or various other local government bodies). County Council records are gradually being deposited in CROs and include council minute books and administrative files. CRO catalogues of council documents are worth reviewing in case they contain something relevant to your family history. For example, your ancestor may have been elected to the council (so that his work can be traced in council or committee minutes). In addition council decisions may have affected your ancestors. A redevelopment scheme (for roads or housing) may have been carried out in the area where your ancestors lived. Importantly, council records include many documents that pre-date 1888. We shall consider property records in chapter 27, but local authorities are substantial landowners and their archives often include property deeds that date back some centuries and may refer to your ancestors.

CIVIC RECORDS

Cities, boroughs and towns were divided into parishes and so your ancestors may appear in the parish records considered above. However, in addition, boroughs and cities produced many records that will not be found in a rural parish. A borough (the term developed from the Anglo-Saxon *burh*, meaning a fortified town) usually had the right to elect members of Parliament and many boroughs and cities had charters of rights and liberties dating from Saxon or medieval times. They were given a legal or corporate identity, acted through the name of the Mayor and the Council and they could own land and hold their own borough courts. The Municipal Corporations Act 1835 provided for many of these (and a number of other towns) to become municipal boroughs, with elected councils, carrying out the tasks of local government.

West (463) is an excellent description of English towns and the extensive archives of borough administration that survive in CROs or city and town libraries. Council meetings were recorded in minutes. Boroughs levied rates from residents to finance expenditure and lists of those who paid rates have often survived. Records of expenditure may include the names of corporation employees (boroughs had many officials, clerks and workmen), those who provided goods or services (such as building materials) or note payments to the poor. Boroughs usually had their own civil and criminal courts (# chapters 24 and 25) and many of their records date back to medieval times. Many borough and city archives hold extensive property records (# chapter 27), often recording relationships as well as details of an ancestor's property. Medieval towns also supported guilds (or gilds), that is associations of craftsmen or tradesmen who often took a substantial role in local administration.

Many town or borough records have been published. Examples are the town books of Lewes in Sussex for 1542–1901 (in three volumes by Sussex Record Society), the register of the Mayor and Burgesses of Reading in Berkshire for 1431–1654 (transcribed in four volumes by J. Guilding), the civic records of York for 1461–1590, in two volumes by Attreed (506) and in nine volumes published by the Yorkshire Archaeological Society, and Oxford Council acts for 1583–1752 (in five volumes by OUP and Oxford Historical Society). These illustrate all aspects of municipal affairs. The civic records of York (known as the "House Books") refer to many disputes between citizens. Attreed (506) includes entries about a dispute between Richard Knaresborough and Richard Beleby in 1487. Knaresborough was arrested by the sheriffs 'at the suit of Beleby'. He then appeared before the Mayor and bound himself (in the sum of £40) to keep the peace towards Beleby. Typical entries from the York House Books of 1588–90, in Sutton (531) include these concerning poor relief in May 1590:

It is agreed that Robert Sawghell, sonne of Thomas Sawghell, deceased, shall be apprentice with John Wilson, joyner, from Pentecost next for ten years, and the said master to have 13s. 4d. out of the common chamber.

Margaret Wright being old and poore shall have 3d. weekly.

Nicolas Shippert, a poore boy, is put apprentice to Roger Spinkes, tapiter, for 10 years.

Also it is agreed that Thomas Barton, a childe in the custody of Margret Forest in Alholles parishe in Northstrete, shall have 2d. weekly.

The volume of Oxford Council acts of 1626–65 by Hobson & Salter (519) records the admission of freemen of the borough (# chapter 17) and the election or appointment of aldermen, bailiffs, chamberlains and other officials. The following extracts are typical of these important records:

21 Sept. 1630: Richard Jones, maltster, is admitted free for 40s since he was born in the City and has lived as servant to Mr Alderman Smyth for eight or nine years.

22 Mar. 1659: Thomas Hallam is to have a new lease of a small tenement on the town wall by Exeter College, formerly rented to Dr Prideaux.

14 Nov. 1659: The Mayor and his brethren are to contract with Mr Tillier, for the use of his house at the North Gate, for a guardhouse for the foot soldiers now in the City.

The following examples, from three other published works also illustrate the importance of town records. Watkin (533) provides abstracts of many of the pre-Reformation records of Dartmouth in Devon, such as records of the proceedings of the Mayor's Court from the 15th century, with the names of many people involved in civil and criminal suits. There are also abstracts of the borough property records from the 12th to 16th centuries, for example:

January 1391: John Deneband of Dertemouth and Alexander Juyl lend twenty pounds to William Lange, son of Nicholas Lange of Dertemouth in order that Walter Pollard and Isabella his wife may bring an action in the right of Isabella to recover (from) Ranulf Juyl and Johanna his wife a place in Dertemouth between the tenement of William Taillor.

May 1391: William Monnfort of Dertemouth and Alice his wife granted to John Monnfort the elder of Dertemouth, Ralph Sechevyle and Ralph Parys, chaplain, a tenement in Waymouth . . . which tenement John Corp and Elizabeth his wife, mother of the said Alice, now wife of William Monnfort held for [term and other details].

Weinstock (534) is a transcript of the minute book of the borough council of Weymouth and Melcombe Regis for 1625–60. It records the election or appointment of the mayor and other borough officials, the levying of rates, council expenditure, licences for traders, admissions of freemen, apprenticeships, property dealings, and court cases. Thus:

4th Feb. 1647: It was agreed . . . that Mr Richard Harrison shall have a new lease of the shop that he now hath, for one and twenty years at the old rent. The same day Mr Abraham Day (upon his request) had leave to [carry on] the trade of a clothier in the towne.

2nd July 1649: Erasmus Holland, son of John Holland of Tickleton in Dorset, clothworker, by indenture dated 18 May 1649, bound apprentice unto Stephen Edwards of this towne, shoemaker, to serve for 7 years.

1st Sept. 1651: Edmond Speare was admitted a Freeman.

21st Sept. 1615: Mr George Pley was elected Mayor: Mr William Holmes and Mr John Swetnam were elected Bailiffs for the year.

City or borough records are usually far better preserved than those of rural parishes (and there was usually more going on in cities that was worth recording). Documents from the medieval period consequently survive in surprising numbers. The financial records of cities and boroughs from this early period include many names of our ancestors. Rowe & Draisey (529) include a transcript of the accounts of the receivers of the City of Exeter for 1304–06 and 1339–53 (the original accounts continue up to 1835). The receivers' role was to collect rents and other monies due to the city, but also to record the city's expenditure (for example on building works and the wages of city officials and workmen). For example, in the year 1349 to 1350, they note:

Rent Deficits:	A plot of Walter Gyffard next to the North Gate	6d
	A tenement which William Cogan held between the city walls	1d
Allowances:	To Alexander Oldeston for the work of the bridge	31s 2d

These early records tell us much about ancestors' lives and business affairs but they rarely note relationships. However, the all-important proof of your descent from someone noted in these old city records may be available in other documents, for example property records (# chapter 27).

CHAPTER 19

EDUCATION

The records of schools and universities include genealogical information such as a child's parentage, date of birth and place of origin. Chapman (551) is a detailed survey of British education and relevant records. The administration of the education system since the 19th century is also described by Riden (451). Horn (560) is a good illustrated work on the lives of children at elementary schools in the 19th and early 20th centuries and May (564) is a brief illustrated guide to Victorian schools. TNA domestic records leaflets 65 and 67 and Morton (566) describe the classes of records at TNA that relate to the foundation of schools, colleges and universities, or to the government's role in the provision and administration of education.

SCHOOLS

We keep many of our own (or our children's) school records, such as reports, examination certificates or awards. Your relatives may hold similar records about your ancestors in the 19th or 20th centuries (or perhaps photographs of an ancestor with other pupils). For example, my grandmother had a letter of 1916 that contained a character reference for my grandfather from his headmaster. Relatives may also hold school attendance medals or a child's school books, inscribed with a name and date, or a note of the prize-giving at which a book was awarded. A statute of 1876 provided for some pupils to be given a school leaving certificate (for example if they left school before the statutory leaving age). My grandmother had such a certificate that had been issued to my grandfather in 1916. If you discover the name of a school or college which your ancestor attended, you can also investigate whether any school records survive. Many schools and colleges have archives that include registers, log books and admission records (considered below), or photographs of pupils (usually in groups). Similar material has been deposited in CROs, libraries or education department archives.

Some schools were founded in Britain during the Anglo-Saxon period (most of them linked to monasteries or cathedrals) and the number of schools slowly increased in medieval times. The Guilds and many private benefactors also established schools, some of them now famous, such as Mercers' School (a grammar school founded in 1542 by the Mercers' Company of the City of London). A useful list by county of some older schools is contained in Richardson (25). By the mid-16th century there were about 300 grammar schools in existence and the number continued to increase. For example, by the early 17th century there were grammar schools in Devon at Ashburton, Crediton, Ottery St Mary, Great Torrington, Plymouth, Tavistock, Tiverton, Dartmouth, Colyton, Barnstaple, Chudleigh, Honiton, Okehampton and Totnes. Most places at these early grammar schools were for fee-payers, but some local boys were educated for free. Many of these schools later became known as public schools, because they were able to attract pupils from a wide area. These schools were almost exclusively for boys; it was not until the 19th century that similar schools were established for girls.

Some elementary schools were established by the church for young children in the 16th century (the classes were often held in the parish church), but few records survive from before the 19th century. The church also began to regulate schoolteachers (many teachers were clergymen) in order to influence what was taught and prevent the promulgation of views contrary to the teaching of the Church. A canon of 1603 required schoolteachers to be licensed by a bishop (# chapters 22 and 24) but from the late 17th century some non-conformists were permitted to teach and Jews and Quakers were permitted to establish their own schools. Charity schools, primarily for the children (both boys and girls) of poor families, also developed in the late 17th century. Many were sponsored by the Society for Promoting Christian Knowledge (SPCK). For example, there were about 50 charity schools in London by 1704 and four in Exeter by 1712. In the late 18th century children in some workhouses also began to receive basic education, and after the Poor Law Amendment Act of 1834 district schools were established to teach children in workhouses. Records of workhouse schools are usually held with other poor law union records. Sunday schools were first established in the late 18th century and flourished in the 19th century. Despite this gradual increase in educational facilities, the majority of people remained illiterate.

The number of schools increased principally because of support from the church and charities. From about 1810 the Anglican "National Society for Promoting the Education of the Poor in the Principles of the Established Church" and the "British and Foreign School Society" (which was primarily supported by non-conformists) were particularly active in providing elementary schools for boys and girls. By 1851 there were about 17,000 "National' and 1,500 "British" schools. There were also some teacher training colleges (the Church of England established 22 training colleges by 1845). Other religious groups, notably the Catholics, Baptists and Methodists, also established their own schools. Dame schools (so named because many of the teachers were old women) also became important in the 19th century, but the standard of education at these schools varied enormously. Ragged schools, which provided free schooling for very poor children, were also founded from about 1820 (and there were over 600 of them by 1870).

The government also assisted in providing schools. Grants were made to the National and British Schools from 1833 (and school inspections began a few years later). The Elementary Education Act of 1870 divided England and Wales into school districts, each with elected school boards. A board had to establish schools at public expense if there were insufficient voluntary schools in their area. However, poor parents were discouraged from sending their children to school since many of these board schools charged fees (even if it was only one penny a week per child) and a family lost the wage that a child could otherwise earn. Acts of 1876 and 1880 prohibited the employment of children under 10 years old and children up to 13 (subject to some exemptions) were required to attend school. However, it was only in 1891 that further government funding made it possible to provide free elementary schooling for all children. Secondary education remained dominated by public and grammar schools, although these accepted a few poor children (by way of scholarships). In 1902 (1904 in London) the school boards were replaced by the education authorities of county councils, which were given the power to provide or fund secondary education as well as elementary schooling (a few school boards were providing secondary education from around 1880). The number of grant-aided secondary schools then expanded rapidly. They had about 190,000 pupils by 1914 and the minimum school leaving age was increased to 14 in 1918 and to 15 in 1947. The government also provided for teacher training. At first, apprentices (aged 13 and above) worked as pupil-teachers for five years in an elementary school, and took examinations set by government inspectors. By the early 20th century most pupil-teachers remained at school until the age of 18, and then went to a training college (or served for a year as a student teacher before taking up a teaching post).

SCHOOL RECORDS

Census records include lists of staff (and pupils if they boarded at the school) with ages and places of birth. Information about schools, particularly special events (such as school excursions or charitable fund-raising events) may also be reported in local newspapers. The minutes and reports of school boards or county council education departments are held in CROs or local authorities' own archives. These records rarely mention children by name, and so you need to find the records of particular schools.

If you do not know the school that your ancestor attended, the first step is to find the names and addresses of the schools in the area in which he lived. This may be easy if he lived in a village with only one or two local schools, but more difficult if he lived in a town or city within easy reach of many schools. Commercial directories list schools from the mid-19th century, sometimes in the description of towns, cities or villages, but also in the trade or commercial sections. CRO catalogues, the Victoria county histories and old town maps are also very useful. Having found one or more schools which your ancestor may have attended, you can then search for any surviving school records. These may still be held by the schools themselves or by the body that originally supported them (such as the Church of England or the Society of Friends). However, they may also have been deposited in local authority archives or at CROs. Thus Guildhall Library holds records of some schools founded by City of London charities or by the London livery companies, such as Aske's Hospital School (founded by the Haberdashers' Company). Records of non-conformist schools may have been deposited with the particular group's archives or historical society, at a CRO or at Dr Williams' Library.

The public and grammar schools kept lists of their pupils (and some of these records survive from medieval times). When financial support was offered by the government during the 19th century, many other schools commenced preparing records that evidenced the education that they were providing (and justified the government grants). From about 1880 (but sometimes as early as 1862) school admission registers were kept with information such as admission and leaving dates for each child, the names and addresses of the parents and the ages of the children. The amount of information available from such records can be very great. Colwell (12) includes a three-generation family tree of 11 people (including nine pupils) constructed merely from the register of admissions to an elementary school in Westmorland.

Many of the larger, famous, schools (but also some smaller schools) have published registers of their students. For example, there is a published register for Wolverhampton Grammar School (for 1515–1920) and seven published registers for Winchester College, for 1653–1946. Published school registers often include the age of students entering a school, the name and address of their parents, and perhaps information about students' later careers. For example, Boreham (548) is the register for 1838–1938 for Highgate school in north London. A typical entry is:

Walter Meacock Wilkinson [of] Hornsey Lane; [born] 28th Sept. 1834. Left April 1851. Solicitor. For 40 years Clerk to the magistrates of the Borough of Kingston-on-Thames. Died 23rd Sept. 1903.

The registers of Merchant Taylors' School for 1562–1874 have been published in Robinson (567) and later editions of this school's register cover the period up to 1934. Illustration 90 is a page including students admitted in January 1830, noting the date of birth of each boy, his parents' names, and his father's occupation and residence. Footnotes describe some pupils' subsequent careers. As a further example, the registers and school lists of Eton have been published for 1441–1698 in Sterry (571), for 1698–1752 in Austen-Leigh (545), for 1753–90 in Austen-Leigh (546) and for 1791–1877 in Stapylton (570). The first three of these works list pupils alphabetically and record a pupil's date and place of birth, his parentage and often his later career (perhaps his university and his trade or profession). A typical entry, from Austen-Leigh (546), is that for Edward Bullock, which also illustrates how families in British colonies often sent their children to schools in Britain:

> 1782–1784. Bullock, Edward; son of Edward Bullock of Jamaica, barrister; shared room at dame Naylor's with Arthur Wesley; married in August 1796, Dorothy, dau. of Thomas Harrison, attorney-general of Jamaica; father of Edward Bullock, common serjeant 1850–5.

Stapylton (570) includes Eton school lists for every third year of the period 1791–1877 (with varying amounts of biographical information about the pupils). Although generally shorter, these entries are also useful, such as the following from the school list for 1847:

> Luxmoore, John Nicholl. Son of the Dean of St Asaph. Trinity College Cambridge; thrown from his horse and killed at Cambridge.
> Marshall, William Julius. Captain in West Suffolk Militia. Lives in London.

There are published registers for many other famous British public schools, such as Harrow, Wellington, Durham, Aldenham, Rossall, Sherborne and Rugby. Registers may be available in a number of editions, covering different periods, and some including pupils from as early as the 16th century. You should check all editions because one may feature only a short entry for a pupil but later editions may include more information about the boy's subsequent career. The entries for pupils vary considerably, as illustrated by these three entries from the third edition of Durham School's register, in Burbridge (550). It should also be noted that none of these entries appeared in the fifth edition of the register, in Baty & Gedye (547), which only covered pupils at the school from 1907 to 1991.

> Rackett, Roger: King's scholar 1577.
> Walton, John: King's scholar 1678: son of John Walton, cordiner [cordwainer]. Bapt. at St Nich. Feb. 5, 1664/5.
> Powell, Samuel Hopper: son of Samuel Powell and nephew of Thos. Hopper of Durham. Born at Paddington, Derbyshire 1804; entered January 1813; left June 1824 . . . admitted Trinity College, Cambridge 1824 . . . B.A. 1829, M.A. 1832 . . . lived at Ripon; J.P. for Yorkshire (North and West Ridings). Died 1901.

There are some published registers for lesser-known schools. For example, Darch & Tween (552) is the register of Chigwell School in Essex up to 1907. Most of the entries post-date 1800 because many of that school's records have been lost, but the school was actually founded in 1629

240   *Merchant Taylors' School Register.*

William Grain,[1] b. 2 Nov. 1818, s. of *William* and *Priscilla*,
Notary Public, Nicholas Lane.
John Henry Grain,[2] b. 1 Jan. 1820, s. of *William* and
Priscilla, Notary Public, Nicholas Lane.

1830.

Jan.
Richard Atwood Glass,[3] b. 3 July, 1820, s. of *Francis* and
Mary, Blackwell Hall, Aldermanbury.
Joseph Burgess Spencer, b. 7 Dec. 1815, s. of *Edward* and
Elizabeth, deal merchant, Billiter Street.
Charles James Spencer, b. 16 April, 1819, s. of *Edward*
and *Elizabeth*, deal merchant, Billiter Street.
Robert Twyford Mills,[4] b. 12 July, 1819, s. of *Joseph*
Langley and *Ann Cecilia*, D.D. Army Chaplain, Canada.
George Hopcroft, b. 24 Mar. 1818, s. of *Robert* and
Elizabeth, iron founder, Seward Street.
Alexander Lee, b. 10 Aug. 1817, s. of *Alexander* and *Ann*,
surgeon, Southwark.
Joseph Richardson, b. 14 Jan. 1817, s. of *James* and
Frances, clothier, Wapping.
Henry John Hall, b. 26 Jan. 1821, s. of *Henry J.* and *Ann*,
Lieutenant R.N. Bow Road.
Joseph Edward Fisher, b. 19 Sep. 1819, s. of *Edward* and
Mary Ann, Carver Street, Leadenhall Street.
Henry Court,[5] b. 9 Oct. 1820, s. of *Charles Thomas* and
Mary Ann, gentleman, Old Kent Road.
George Carter, b. 8 Mar. 1817, s. of *Aaron* and *Frances*,
Vintner, Borough.
Thomas Fry, b. 8 June, 1815, s. of *William* and *Eliza*
Sybilla, gentleman, Croydon.
Fred. Aug. Harold France, b. 24 Mar. 1818, s. of *Harold*
and *Charlotte*, Lieutenant, Eastcheap.
John William Henry Pownall,[6] b. 14 Oct. 1817, s. of
Thomas and *Lucy Ann*, Lieut. R.N. Camden Place.
Robert Hague, b. 24 Mar. 1821, s. of *John* and *Jane*,
engineer, Cable Street.
Feb.
George Scotland,[7] b. 11 April, 1815, s. of *George* and *Sarah*,
barrister, Harpur Street.

---

[1] *W. Grain*, Notary Public, 1841.   Master of the Scriveners' Company, 1859.
[2] *J. H. Grain*, Attorney and Notary Public. M. of the Scriveners' Comp. 1864.
[3] *R. A. Glass*, afterwards of King's Coll. London; C.E.   Constructor of the first
Atlantic Telegraph.   Knighted, 1866.   M.P. for Bewdley.   Died 1873.
[4] *R. T. Mills*, of Magd. Coll. Oxf. B.A. 1842, M.A. 1844.   V. of Halse, co. Som.
1845.   Died 1878.
[5] *H. Court*, Deputy Controller, National Debt Office.
[6] *J. W. H. Pownall*, entered H. E. I. C. Army (Bengal), served in the China War of
1842.   Died 1844.
[7] *G. Scotland* (son of Sir George S.) of St. John's Coll. Oxf. B.A. 1840.   In Holy
Orders.   Dead.

90. A page from a published register of Merchant Taylor's School, recording admissions in January 1830

and one early pupil was William Penn, who founded Pennsylvania. Devon FHS has published the admissions register of the Bishop Blackall Episcopal Charity School in Exeter for 1839–55 (539). This includes the child's date of birth or baptism, the parents' names and place of residence and sometimes a father's occupation, as in this example:

> Heacock, William; [born] 6 July 1836 [baptised] 1837 [parents] George & Elizabeth, St James (Exeter), tile cutter.

There are also many published school histories. These may mention your ancestor (or at least tell you much about his or her school) but some also include lists of pupils or biographies of those who subsequently became noteworthy.

The school registers of Britain and Ireland published up to 1963 are listed in Jacobs (563). Copies of most published school registers are held by the SoG and reference libraries. A SoG booklet (543) lists its collection as at 1 October 1996 of published and unpublished records of schools, universities and colleges. Published registers and histories of many London schools are listed in Raymond (850) and in Webb (573), which also lists many other surviving records of London schools, such as admissions registers, log books and punishment books (and the archives in which they are held). Other school records are listed in CRO catalogues.

School log books contain general information about the school and teachers, the number of children attending, notes of punishments, health, school inspections and important events (but name only a few individual children). Some schools kept separate registers of children's results in examinations or of their punishments (with names, ages, dates and offences). Correspondence files may also survive, perhaps including letters from parents providing reasons for a child's absence from school. Hackney Archives in London holds log books for three local schools, including the log book of 1874–94 for Tottenham Road Primary School. It is likely that my great grandfather Charles Frederick Eagles and his brothers and sisters attended this school since they lived only a few doors away. The log book was written up every week (and some extracts are set out below). It only names a few children but it often mentions teachers and the school inspectors who visited. The number of children attending each week is recorded and there are references to epidemics, discipline problems and the subjects of school lessons. A log book is therefore useful for background material if your ancestor was a pupil or teacher at the school:

> February 15th 1875: Mr Cope returned to his duties. I cautioned the boys against the bad practice of stone-throwing.
> February 22nd 1875: School attendances very poor owing to the severity of the weather. The Reverend Mr Finch visited the school.
> April 19th 1875: Admitted 8 boys from the infant school. Removed the names of 4 boys who had not attended for 3 weeks and whose absence could not be accounted for. Received a visit from the Drill Inspector Mr Sheffield. He drilled the 1st class.
> July 19th 1875: Average number (of children) on register   248.1
>   Highest daily attendance   226
>   Lowest daily attendance   127
> April 10th 1876: A youth named Freckleton, who has been recommended by the head teacher of High Street Stoke Newington School, has applied to be employed here as a candidate (teacher). He has worked 2 days and appears to be very satisfactory.

An interesting article about the school log book for Stokeinteignhead appears in *Devon Family Historian* (August 1991), with examples of entries that refer to particular children:

28 April 1882: Thomas, Alfred and Harriett Payne; forbidden to attend school; fever having broken out in the vicinity of their home.

1 April 1887: William and George Rendell absent. Potato planting.

6 November 1889: Lucy Derges and Ernest Martin died from measles.

24 June 1892: Clara Buck moved to Colchester.

Some log books have been published by county record or family history societies. Oxfordshire Record Society has published the log book of Whitchurch school of 1868–93 in Horn (561). Coventry FHS has published the log book of Hawkesbury school for 1885–1908 in Brannigan & Brannigan (549). A log book may contain much information about a particular child. For example, the Whitchurch school log book notes that Charles Barrett was absent because of illness on 19 November 1880 and for a week in early January 1884. He was punished on 12 January 1883 for playing truant and punished again on 6 June for refusing to do his lessons. He was sent home on 4 June 1884, with his brother John and two other children, for refusing to bring their school money. Five other children named Barrett (probably Charles' siblings or cousins) were also noted in this log book.

UNIVERSITY REGISTERS

Until the 19th century Oxford and Cambridge were the only two universities in England. Some of the Oxford and Cambridge colleges were established in medieval times (for example, Peterhouse College at Cambridge was founded in 1280). Extensive records of students have survived (together with many other records about the colleges). The student registers are particularly useful. Many of them have been published and are reviewed, with examples of the biographical entries for students, by J. Titford in *Family Tree Magazine* (January and April 1998). Jacobs (563) is a catalogue of registers and other lists of students at Oxford and Cambridge Universities that were published up to 1963. Those held by the SoG are listed in its catalogue; those acquired up to 1996 are listed in its booklet (543).

Alumni Oxonienses by Foster (556) is an alphabetical register, in four volumes, of students at Oxford University between 1500 and 1714, with the student's name, college and dates of entry and degree. Some entries give the name and occupation of the student's father or even details of the student's later career or death. Four further volumes by Foster (557) provide the same information for Oxford students from 1715 to 1886. A typical early entry is:

Bullied, John; pleb. Exeter Coll. Matric. 2 April 1652; BA 12 Oct 1654.

Illustration 91 shows extracts from two pages of *Alumni Oxoniensis 1500–1714*, including the students named Charnock and Chernock. Most of them came from Lancashire families but the others (from Bedfordshire, London, Warwickshire and Worcestershire) were also descended from the Lancashire Charnocks. They include Robert Chernocke who was executed in 1695/6 for plotting to assassinate William III. *Alumni Oxoniensis* is available in reference libraries and has also been reproduced on CD-ROM by Archive CD Books.

Jersey, thence to Nantwich, and finally returned to London, born at Shepton Mallet 2 Feb., 1619, died 24 April, 1707, aged 87. See Munk's *Roll*, i. 390; *Ath.* iv. 752; *Hearne*, ii. 17; & *D.N.B.*

Charleton, William, of HART HALL in and before 1568. See Foster's *Inns of Court Reg.*

Charlton, William, of MAGDALEN HALL in or before 1572.

Charlton, William, y.s. Job, of Ludford, co. Hereford, equitis. ST. EDMUND HALL, matric. 30 March, 1666, aged 14; bar.-at-law, Lincoln's Inn, 1674, probably M.P. Ludlow 1685, until his death before June same year, brother of Francis and Gilbert same date. See Foster's *Judges and Barristers.*

Charlwood, John, of BRASENOSE COLL.; B.A. 16 Jan., 1569-70, M.A. 14 March, 1572-3. vicar of Hambledon, Hants, 1576. See Foster's *Index Ecclesiasticus.* [2]

Charman, Richard, of Sussex, pleb. BRASENOSE COLL., matric. 9 Feb., 1593-4, aged 15 (called CHARMER in *Mat. Reg.*); B.A. 25 Feb., 1597-8.

Charman, Stephen; B.A. from BALLIOL COLL. 17 March, 1626-7, M.A. 11 April, 1633, rector of Hemsworth, Yorks, 1637, ejected for nonconformity 1662, died 1667, father of the next named. See Foster's *Index Ecclesiasticus & Calamy*, iii. 437.

Charman, Stephen, s. Stephen, of Hemsworth, co. York, minister. NEW INN HALL, matric. 14 Nov., 1661, aged 18; B.A. 1 April, 1671, M.A. 5 July, 1671, rector of Liddiard Tregoze, Wilts, 1692. See Foster's *Index Ecclesiasticus.*

Charnley, William, s. John, of Carlisle, Cumberland, p.p. QUEEN'S COLL., matric. 14 May, 1696, aged 17; B.A. 1701, M.A. 1704, vicar of Brayton, Yorks, 1727.

Charnock. See also CHERNOCK, page 266.

Charnocke, Edward, of co. Lancaster, arm. TRINITY COLL., matric.-entry under date 3 April, 1579, aged 13. [10]

Charnock, Hugh (Chernocke or Carnock) B.A. of Cambridge 1511, incorp. 15 June, 1514; M.A. from BRASENOSE COLL. 21 June, 1514, B.D. (sup. 24 July) 1523, canon of Hereford 1529, until his death in 1550. See *Le Neve*, i. 525.

Charnoke, Hugh, B.A. 5 Feb., 1531-2, ? fellow of BRASENOSE COLL. in and before 1565.

Charnocke, James, of BRASENOSE COLL.; B.A. 15 June, 1544, M.A. (sup. 10 Oct.) 1562, rector of Aston Sandford, Bucks, 1554. See Foster's *Index Ecclesiasticus.*

Charnoke, James, B.A. 21 Jan., 1558-9, M.A. 1 Dec., 1562; fellow BRASENOSE COLL. in and before 1565, proctor 1568, B.C.L. 27 May, 1569.

Charnocke, John, of CHRIST CHURCH 1567; B.A. 26 Jan., 1570-1. [15]

Charnock, Robert, the conspirator, of TRINITY COLL. 1680. See CHERNOCK.

Charnocke, Roger; scholar CORPUS CHRISTI COLL. 1563, from Lancashire, fellow 1566, B.A. 15 Oct., 1568, M.A. 14 June, 1572, inventory at Oxford 18 Feb., 1577.

Charnock, Roger, s. Roger, of London, arm. MAGDALEN HALL, matric. 31 Jan., 1639-40, aged 15.

Charnock, Stephen, s. Richard, an attorney or solicitor; B.A. from EMANUEL COLL., Cambridge, 1645, incorp. as M.A. 19 Nov., 1652, proctor 1654, fellow NEW COLL. 1650, a preacher and author, died in Whitechapel 27 July, 1680, aged 52, buried in St. Stephen's, Walbrook, 30th. See *Burrows*; *Ath.*, iii. 1,234; *Fasti*, ii. 173; *Calamy*, i. 208; & *D.N.B.*

Charnoke, Thomas; Dominican; B.D. 15 June, 1528, D.D. 8 April, 1530. [20]

Charoll, John Chrysostom du; incorp. M.A. of Avignon by decree of convocation 9 June, 1684 (*Cat. Grads.*), a daily chaplain in Chapel Royal for 7 or 8 years. See *Fasti*, ii. 395.

Cheltenham, Thomas (Cheltnam), Benedictine; B.Can.L. 15 June, 1507, one of these names bishop of Sidon, preb. of St. Paul's 1553. See Foster's *Index Ecclesiasticus.* [20]

Chempes, James de, orator of the most Christian King of France; M.A. Dijon, incorp. 25 Aug., 1624. See *Fasti*, i. 419.

Chenell, John. See CHEYNELL, page 269.

Cherington, Joseph, paup. MERTON COLL., subscribed 17 July, 1686.

Cherite, Humfry (Chayrite), Benedictine; B.D. 1 July, 1535, D.D. 29 July, 1538.

Cheryte, William, M.A.; B.D. (sup. 14 June) 1512.

Cheriton, Charles, of Devon, pleb. GLOUCESTER HALL, matric. 13 Oct., 1598, aged 18 (called CHARINGTON in *Mat. Reg.*); B.A. from CORPUS CHRISTI COLL. 28 June, 1604; M.A. from GLOUCESTER HALL 27 June, 1607. [26]

Cheriton, Clement, 'subscribed' 23 April, 1613, B.A. from GLOUCESTER HALL 24 Nov., 1615, M.A. 10 June, 1618.

Cheriton, Mathew, of Devon, pleb. [GLOUCESTER HALL, matric. 23 Oct., 1601, aged 15; B.A. 10 June, 1608, M.A. 9 May, 1611.

Chernock. See also CHARNOCK, page 264.

Chernooke, (Sir) Boteler, s. Pinsent, of Holcutt, Beds, baronet. MERTON COLL., matric. 5 Feb., 1713-14, aged 17; 4th baronet, M.P. Bedford Nov., 1740-7, died in 1756. [30]

Chernooke, Francis, s. Robert, of Warwick (city), gent. TRINITY COLL., matric. 29 Oct., 1675, aged 16 (called CHARNOCKE in *Mat. Reg.*); of Wedgenook Park, co. Warwick, brother of Robert 1680, and father of Robert 1710.

Chernooke, Robert, s. Robert, of co. Warwick, gent. TRINITY COLL., matric. 27 May, 1680, aged 16; demy MAGDALEN COLL. 1680-6, B.A. 4 Feb., 1683-4, M.A. 1686, fellow (by royal mandate) 1686, and vice-president (by royal mandate) 1688, turned papist, and on the accession of the Prince of Orange he turned (Jacobite) conspirator, and was dubbed captain by the banished king; for plotting the assassination of William III. he was executed 18 March, 1695-6. See *Blomam*, vi. 27; & *D.N.B.*

Chernock, Robert, s. Francis, of Wedgenock Park, co. Worcester, gent. BALLIOL COLL., matric. 8 July, 1710, aged 17, B.A. 1714; M.A. from ALL SOULS' COLL. 27 Jan., 1717-18. See CHARNOCK & Foster's *Index Ecclesiasticus.*

Chernooke, St. John, 1s. J., arm. PEMBROKE COLL., matric. 13 Dec., 1658; of the Inner Temple 1660, as son and heir of St. John, of Hulcote, Beds, esq. See Foster's *Inns of Court Reg.*

Chernook, Villiers, s. V(illiers), of Holcutt, Beds, bart. EXETER COLL., matric. 2 June, 1701, aged 17.

Cherrett. See also CHERITE. [36]

Cherrett, William, s. Tho., of Corf Mullen, Dorset, p.p. NEW INN HALL, matric. 20 Nov., 1668, aged 16; B.A. 1672.

Cherrieholme, John, s. Tho., of Wakefield, Yorks, p.p. UNIVERSITY COLL., matric. 31 March, 1671, aged 16; B.A. 1674, M.A. 1677, rector of Morestead 1679, and of Stoke Bishop, Hants, 1699. See Foster's *Index Ecclesiasticus.*

Cherry, Antony, s. Samuel, of Great Bookham, Surrey, sac. QUEEN'S COLL., matric. 2 March, 1637-8, aged 16; B.A. 14 Oct., 1641, Pauline Exhibitioner 1637-43. See *St. Paul's School Reg.*, 39.

Cherry, Charles, 'cler. fil.' NEW INN HALL, matric. 10 March, 1656-7; vicar of East Lulworth, Dorset, 1662, and of Combe Keynes 1672. See Foster's *Index Ecclesiasticus.* [40]

Cherry, Francis, s. William, of Maidenhead, Berks, arm. ST. EDMUND HALL, matric. 6 April, 1682, aged 16; of Shottesbrooke Park, Berks, entered the Middle Temple 1681, a nonjuror and patron of some of the most eminent of the nonjuring party, died 23 Sept., 1713. See Foster's *Inns of Court Reg.; Hearne*, iii. 337; 503; & *D,N,B.*

Foster extended his work on Oxford students in *Oxford Men 1880–1892* (558), including biographical entries for students but also many photographs, particularly of college sports teams. Foster also produced *Oxford Men and their Colleges* (559), which provided supplemental information about students and biographies of the masters, fellows and other staff of Oxford colleges since medieval times. Foster's *Alumni Oxoniensis* did not cover students before 1500 and his work was not entirely complete for the period up to 1567. You should therefore also consult works by Emden (553) and (554), which are biographical registers of Oxford students up to 1500 and 1501–40 respectively, providing detailed biographies, with sources, such as that for Hugh Charnock:

> Charnock, Hugh. Brasenose College, fellow, admitted c. 1531–2; in 1535 . . . rented room in Exeter College (Exeter College Rectors' Accounts). B.A. admitted 5 Feb 1532 . . . M.A. by 1535–6. Ordained deacon 23 Nov 1550 . . . Curate at Milton Keynes, Bucks in 1550; rector of Milton Keynes 1565 till death. Buried 20 Mar 1584.

The registers of many individual Oxford colleges, including the period since 1892 (the last year covered by Foster's works), have also been published. The SoG holds copies of many of these, such as the registers for Brasenose College (537) which included seven members of the Charnock or Chernock family between 1511 and 1579 including these three admissions (the abbreviations are explained in the register's introduction):

> 1556. Charnock, James (Lancs.) B.A. 21 Jan. 1558/9; Fellow (Founders) 25 Oct. 1559; M.A. 1 Dec. 1562; Proctor; res. Fell. 23 July 1568; B.C.L. 27 May; readm. 30 Sept. 1569.
> 1556. Charnock, Robert (Lancs.)
> 1579. Charnock, Edward (Lancs.) Matr. Arm. Trinity 3 Apr. 1579; died 5 Aug. 1581. On a brass fastened to the buttress of the steeple of St Mary the Virgin, Oxon, he is described as of Brasenose.

These entries illustrate the different amounts of information available about students. The last entry also illustrates why family members may seem to disappear. Someone researching the Charnock family in Lancashire parish registers will find Edward's baptism and wonder what became of him. This entry reveals that he was sent to study at Oxford but died there before he completed his studies.

Women were not admitted to Oxford University until the 19th century and so few appear in Foster's *Alumni Oxoniensis*. However, the colleges for women have published their registers, for example that of Somerville College for 1879–1971.

University and college calendars are another important published source. They were published annually and included information about the institution (such as the names of officers, professors and other teachers), scholarships, fees, examinations and admission procedures. Most calendars also listed students, graduates and sometimes examination results. *The Oxford University Calendar 1847* (541) lists the students then in each college, students' examination results back to 1807, students who had obtained scholarships and all current members of the university (basically those with degrees who were still alive). The 1947 calendar (542) contains similar information except that the class and honours lists only go back to 1940. The lists of graduates in these calendars make it easy to locate ancestors and relatives at Oxford University since 1892 (the final year covered by Foster's works).

The registers of Cambridge University have also been published and copies are held at the SoG and reference libraries. *Alumni Cantabrigiensis*, in 10 volumes, by Venn & Venn (572) covers students (and teachers) at Cambridge from the late 13th century up to 1900. Students' ages, their fathers' names and other biographical or family information are noted in similar form to the entries in Foster's *Alumni Oxoniensis*. They include 11 members of the Charnock or Chernock families (in some cases students who attended colleges at both Oxford and Cambridge). A typical entry from *Alumni Cantabrigiensis* for the late 19th century is:

> Eagles, Edwin Mortimer, Admitted sizar at St John's, Sept 12 1891. Son of James, coal merchant, of Buckhurst Hill, Essex. Born Dec 23, 1872 Bethnal Green, London. Matric. Michaelmas 1891; BA 1894, MA 1898, Senior Physics Master, Central Foundation School, Cowper Street, London EC, 1894–1902 and Head of Science Dept. Willesden Polytechnic. Headmaster, Enfield Grammar School, Middlesex 1909, retired 1934. (Schoolmasters' Year Book 1933)

A database of the entries in *Alumni Cantabrigiensis* has been produced by Ancestry.com and can be consulted on CD-ROM or on its subscription web site. Further information about Cambridge students in medieval times became available after publication of Venn's work so, for students before 1500, you should also consult Emden (555), which provides biographies in similar form to those in his works for Oxford.

More information about students also appears in published registers of individual Cambridge colleges. For example, the men admitted to Trinity College from 1546 to 1900 are listed in Rouse Ball & Venn (568), compiled from various records including the college registers, account books and university matriculation lists. Typical entries, from 1659 and 1779, are:

> Ardern, Henry. Of Cheshire. Pensioner on Westminster Election, May 10, 1659. Tutor, Mr Duport. Scholar, 1659; matriculated, 1660; B.A. 1662–3. Migrated to Peterhouse. Thence, M.A. 1666; Fellow there.
> May, William. Son of Rose May of Spanish Town, Jamaica. School, Westminster (Dr Smith). Age 17. Pensioner on Westminster Election, June 2, 1779. Tutors Mr Collier and Mr Atwood. Did not matriculate or graduate.

Admission registers of St John's College, Cambridge for 1629–1802 have been published, with additional biographical material from various sources, in Mayor (565) and Scott (569). Illustration 92 is a page from Mayor's work, for students admitted from December 1663 to March 1663/4. They were from all parts of the country (for example Shropshire and Lincolnshire) and their fathers were not all members of the upper classes but included a farmer, a shoemaker and a tailor.

Women were also excluded from Cambridge University until the 19th century and so few appear in *Alumni Cantabrigiensis*. The best sources of information on female students are therefore the published registers of individual colleges, such as that for Girton College for 1869–1946.

Your ancestors and relatives may also be found in the Cambridge University calendars, such as that of 1928–29 (538), which contain similar information to the Oxford calendars. Importantly, they list graduates of the university after 1900, the last year covered by *Alumni Cantabrigiensis*.

The published registers of the other universities and colleges of England and Wales are listed and described by J. Titford in *Family Tree Magazine* (June and August 1998). The University of Durham was founded in 1832, the University of London in 1836 and further universities were

(11) Thomas Mason, of Houghton in Spring, Durham, son of Marmaduke Mason; bred at Northallerton (Mr Smelt) for 5 years; admitted sizar for Mr Webster, tutor and surety Mr Rayne, 18 Dec. aet. 20.

(12) William Eaton, of Litleport, Cambs, son of William Eaton, 5 farmer (*firmarii*); bred at Little Rattin (Wratting) (Mr Burwell) for 1 year; admitted sizar for his tutor and surety Mr Broughton, 23 Dec. aet. 17.

166¾

(13) Richard Andrews, of Salop, son of Roger Andrews, shoemaker (*fabri calcearii*); school, Shrewsbury (Mr Chaloner) for 1 10 year; admitted sizar for Mr Armstrong, tutor and surety Mr Walthall, 13 Jan. aet. 16.

(14) John Bennet, of Salop, son of John Bennet, clothier (*pannificis*); school, Shrewsbury (Mr Chaloner) for 1 year; admitted sizar for his tutor and surety Mr Walthall, 13 Jan. aet. 18. 15

(15) Richard Lister, of Atsham (Atcham), Salop, son of Robert Lister, 'yeoman'; bred at Shrewsbury (Mr Piggot) for 2 years; admitted sizar for his tutor and surety Mr Peck, 4 Febr. aet. 20.

(16) Thomas Thislwait, of Stamford, Lincolnshire, son of Thomas Thislwait, saddler (*ephippiarii*); bred at Stamford (Mr Shalcros) for 20 2 years; admitted sizar for Mr Yorke, tutor and surety Mr Rayne, 6 Febr. aet. 17.

(17) Thomas Dickinson, co. Cambs, son of Thomas Dickinson; bred at Cambridge (Mr Griffith) for 3 years; admitted sizar for Mr Charlton, tutor Mr Peck, 8 Febr. aet. 16. 25

(18) Samuel Bray, of Islington, Middlesex, son of Thomas Bray, tailor (*vestiarii*); bred at Islington (Mr Lovejoy); admitted sizar for Mr Cooke, tutor and surety Mr Crouch, 19 Febr. aet. 17.

(19) Antony Elletson, of Furnesfell, Lancashire, son of Robert Elletson; bred at Sedbergh (Mr Fell) for 2 years 'aut paulo minus'; 30 admitted pensioner, tutor and surety Mr Watson, 23 Febr. aet. 18.

(20) Laurence Elletson, of Furnesfell, Lancashire, son of Robert Elletson; bred at Sedbergh (Mr Fell); admitted pensioner, tutor Mr Watson, 23 Febr. aet. 17.

(21) Francis Cope, of St Olave's, Surrey, son of Thomas Cope, 35 deceased; school, St Paul's (Mr Crumholme) for 4 years; admitted pensioner, under Mr Watson, 25 Febr. aet. 18.

(22) Samuel Crowbrow, of Repton, Derbyshire, son of Hasting Crowbrow; bred at Repton; admitted sizar for Mr Pilkington, tutor Mr Peck, 27 Febr. aet. past 17. 40

(23) John Sanford, of Broadclist, Devon, son of Humfrey Sanford; bred at Broadclist (Mr Coplston) for 4 years; admitted sizar for Mr Thurlin, tutor and surety Mr Peck, 2 March, aet. 16.

92. A page from the published register of admissions to St John's College, Cambridge recording admissions from December 1663 to March 1663/4

established in the late 19th and early 20th centuries. Admissions registers or lists of graduates of many of these universities have been published, for example, the University of Exeter register for 1893–1962 (540). There are also published registers of many colleges of the University of London. The annual calendars of that university, such as that for 1927–28 (544), list students at each college and those who had previously graduated (and were still living in 1927). Many of the registers of modern universities merely list students' names (with subjects and dates of graduation). However, you can at least discover from them whether an ancestor or relative went to university, the subject he or she studied (and explain the gap in their lives between school and work). Attendance at a university, perhaps Exeter, can explain why an ancestor from Birmingham is found working in Devon in later life.

SPECIALIST SCHOOLS AND COLLEGES

A number of schools and colleges catering to special educational needs were established from the early 19th century. J. Titford reviewed the published sources for some of these in *Family Tree Magazine* (June and December 1998). If your ancestor appears in these institutions' records, that will direct you to records of particular occupations. For example, Haileybury College was established in 1805 as a school for boys intending to work as civil servants of the East India Company (# chapters 20 and 30). A college was also established at Addiscombe for boys who were intended by their parents for a military career with the EIC. If your ancestor appears in the early registers of one of these colleges, the records of the British in India are a likely source of further information about him.

Alternatively, you may discover that your ancestor had a career in medicine, dentistry, law, the military, the church or that he later worked as a scientist or mining engineer. Again, there were specialist colleges for these professions. In particular, you should look at the records and published registers of certain colleges in London, for example the medical schools of Guy's or St Thomas' Hospitals, the Royal College of Science or the Royal School of Mines. Those training for the law are easily located in the records of the Inns of Court and Inns of Chancery (# chapter 22). Men who aimed to be an officer in the army could attend the Royal Military College at Sandhurst or the Royal Military Academy at Woolwich (# chapter 20). Those who desired a career in the church, whether the Church of England or one of the many dissenting groups, could attend various theological colleges. These are listed in the annual clergy lists of the Church of England (# chapter 22), in yearbooks of the non-conformist churches or in the detailed works on each dissenting group (# chapter 13). J. Titford described the published lists of theological college students in *Family Tree Magazine* (December 1998 and February 1999).

EDUCATION ABROAD

From the 16th to 19th centuries many Catholics were not permitted to attend British universities and therefore studied abroad, usually in France, Spain and Italy. Some relevant records have been published by the Catholic Record Society (# chapter 13). Many other English people, particularly those studying medicine, also attended Scottish universities (# chapter 29) or studied abroad, for example at Leyden in Holland. Innes Smith (562) is a biographical dictionary of English-speaking students (English, Welsh, Scottish, Irish and others) who studied medicine at Leyden from 1575 to 1875. British students will also be found in the records of other schools, colleges and universities around Europe. Foreign records (# chapter 30) may therefore also contain references to your ancestor's education.

CHAPTER 20

RECORDS OF THE ARMY, ROYAL MARINES AND ROYAL AIR FORCE

Many family historians find that an ancestor who served in the armed forces or at sea is of special interest. Military and marine records provide interesting information about an ancestor's life and any wars in which he took part, but also include vital genealogical material. This chapter reviews the records of the army, the militia, the Royal Marines, colonial troops and the Royal Air Force. Chapter 21 reviews the records of the Royal Navy and the merchant navy.

Ancestors who served in the armed forces may be difficult to find in the sources already described. A military ancestor may rarely appear at home in census returns. His marriage (and his children's births) could have taken place anywhere in Britain (or its empire). For example, the parish register of Barnstaple in Devon records this marriage in 1803:

John Jackson of Wallton, Norfolk, 28th Regiment of Foot & Catherine Larkin of this parish.

If John and Catherine returned to John's home in Norfolk to raise a family, their descendants may have difficulty finding this Devon marriage. Deaths can also be difficult to find, since a soldier or sailor may have died on service abroad or at sea (or perhaps in port or army barracks in Britain but far from his home). Even if you locate an ancestor in census, civil registration or parish records, you may have little information about his military service.

Your family may hold some useful records (medals, photographs or letters) but many military records survive in archives. Most army records before 1921 are held in War Office records (code WO) at TNA. There are also many published works on the armed forces and those noted in this chapter (and chapter 21) are available at the SoG or reference libraries. Many can also be purchased from the Naval & Military Press (NMP) at PO Box 61, Dallington, Heathfield, East Sussex TN21 9ZS. The NMP catalogue (also on its web site, see appendix XI) is full of useful reference works, including histories of wars or particular military units, lists of casualties and recipients of medals.

THE ARMY

Before the English Civil War, England and Wales had no standing army but troops were raised as required for particular wars. Soldiers were organised in infantry regiments (divided into battalions and companies) and cavalry regiments (divided into squadrons). The artillery was divided into batteries. Units on active service were formed into brigades, divisions, corps or armies. After the union of 1707, the British army also included Scottish regiments and, in the 18th and 19th centuries, many colonial regiments. Soldiers' names first appear in records of the English Civil War, but only a few documents survive. The names of some officers (and a few soldiers) are contained in muster rolls and pay lists at TNA (in series E 315 and pieces SP 28/120–5). Peacock (664) lists many officers of both civil war armies. Some other published and manuscript sources (principally dealing with officers) are noted in TNA military records leaflet 3 and by M. Bennett in *Genealogists' Magazine* (December 1996).

More records are available from about 1660 but it is only from the early 18th century that substantial records survive. These records are reviewed by Watts & Watts (685) and Fowler & Spencer (627). Infantry and cavalry regiments were originally named after their commanding officer but by the 18th century they had a number and description, such as the 23rd Foot (the Royal Welch Fusiliers) and the 4th Dragoons. The cavalry consisted of regiments of Hussars, Dragoons, Dragoon Guards and Lancers as well as the Life Guards and Royal Horse Guards. The infantry consisted of regiments of Foot Guards (five of them by 1915) and about 100 other regiments. There was a major reorganisation in 1881 when many regiments were merged and most became linked to a county (although many already had county names). For example the 48th and 58th Foot were merged to form the Northamptonshire Regiment. Brereton (601), Hallows (639) and Swinson (678) provide brief histories of each British army regiment, noting any changes of name or number as well as each unit's battle honours. In addition, the regular army included the Royal Artillery (founded in 1716), the Royal Horse Artillery (founded in 1793), the Royal Engineers and a number of other service corps. Furthermore, militia forces had existed since Saxon times and there were many volunteer units. An ancestor may also have served in the army of the East India Company, in the Indian army, or in colonial regiments. All these units are considered below.

Roper (670) is a detailed study of the administrative records of the British Army from 1660 to 1964 that are held at TNA. These records, of the War Office, the Board of Ordnance, the Adjutant General, the Quartermaster General, the Paymaster General and Military Intelligence, include useful background material for researchers with army ancestors. The documents also include the names of many soldiers and civilians. Many of the most important classes (and finding aids) are noted below. The other administrative records described by Roper (670) may assist researchers but few are indexed and it is difficult to locate an ancestor in them unless he was an officer or you know that he worked (whether as a soldier or civilian) in a particular department.

Ascertaining your ancestor's regiment
Unless your ancestor was an officer, you are unlikely to make much progress in the records unless you know the regiment in which he served. Most records were not kept centrally, but by the regiments, and that is how the papers are archived. Your relatives may know the regiment in which an ancestor served or they may hold documents specifying his unit. For example, one of my cousins had a discharge certificate of 1919 for Charles Richard Garner, a brother of my great grandmother. This document (shown in illustration 93) identifies Charles's regiment and the medals awarded to him. Photographs may reveal an ancestor's unit, or where and when he served. Swinnerton (677) and a chapter by D.J. Barnes in Steel & Taylor (28) will assist you in dating photographs of ancestors in military uniform and identifying the military unit. You might also discover an ancestor's regiment from his medals (see below). Medal rolls at TNA (some of which have been published) usually specify the recipient's regiment.

93. *Certificate of discharge of Charles Richard Garner from the army in March 1919*

The sources described in previous chapters may also record a man's unit. Civil registration certificates may only note an ancestor as a "soldier", but may specify his regiment. The GRO records of deaths during the Boer War and the two world wars also reveal a man's unit. Wills often reveal men's regiments (the calendars of wills and administrations since 1858 include many soldiers who died in the two world wars). Census indexes can be used to find men in army camps in Britain on census night. Census records may also assist if your military ancestor was at home and described, for example, as "pensioner – 40th Regiment of Foot". Annoyingly, a more common description is simply "soldier" or "army pensioner". However, census records may help (even if the entry does not specify a man's unit) because they may lead you to certificates of births in Britain or abroad. My ancestor William Rice had a cousin, John Radford, who served in the army. The census recorded John as an army pensioner but revealed that John's children were born in England, Ireland, Corfu, Trinidad and Jamaica. John's descendant, Frank Radford, obtained their birth certificates. John's regiment was revealed in an English birth certificate:

When & where born	Name	Sex	Name of father	Name of mother	Father's Occupation
28th January 1868; Whitestone	James	Boy	John Radford the younger	Margaret Radford formerly Moriarty	Pensioner, late serjeant in 14th Foot

Entries may also be found in the GRO index of births and baptisms (in Britain and abroad) contained in army regimental registers. These cover 1761 to 1924. The names are indexed in one alphabetical sequence for the entire period and the index (and any certificate obtained) records the father's regiment. If an entry for one child is found, it is worth checking the index for siblings. Examples from the index are:

Surname	Name	Place	Year	Regiment	Vol	Page
Bullen	Martha H	Malta	1880	R(oyal) E(ngineers)	664	251
Bulleck	Mary A	Liverpool	1810	2nd D(ra)g(oo)ns	231	7

Frank Radford obtained a certificate for an entry from the register of the 1st battalion, 14th Regiment of Foot, which recorded the following event in Jamaica:

Date of birth	Place/date of baptism	Christian name of child	Parents' names	Father's Rank
October 27th 1861	Newcastle, Jamaica 22nd Dec. 1861	Francis Patrick Joseph	John & Margaret Radford	Serjt.

GRO also holds regimental registers of marriages and burials but, unfortunately, only parts of these registers have been indexed (and the incomplete index cannot be searched by the public). Applications can, however, be made for GRO officials to search the index (and the unindexed registers) for any relevant marriage or burial entries. Army chaplains at the army's foreign stations also kept registers of baptisms, marriages and burials. These registers (known as the chaplains' returns) cover 1796 to 1880 and are held by GRO, but the indexes to them only provide names, places and the year, so that a certificate must be obtained to ascertain a man's unit. GRO also holds indexes to the army's registers of births, marriages and deaths for 1881 to 1955 for men serving abroad.

TNA holds registers of the Chelsea Royal Hospital in series RG 4 (# chapter 7) and some regimental registers of baptisms, marriages and burials in series WO 68, 69 and 156. These are listed in Fowler & Spencer (627) and Bevan (239). Soldiers may also have married or baptised their children in a church at (or near) their garrison abroad. Records of the British abroad are considered in chapter 30, but many other records of baptisms, births, marriages, deaths and burials of British people living abroad are held at the GRO, TNA, Guildhall Library and in the India Office collections at the British Library. They include registers of garrison chapels, for example for the Cape of Good Hope garrison (1795–1803) and Gibraltar (1807–12). Registers at TNA and Guildhall Library are listed in Yeo (1342) and those held by GRO are listed in Watts & Watts (685). Some garrison records are still held locally. Watts & Watts (685) note that registers of Holy Trinity, Quebec (1768–1800), and the Quebec Protestant chaplaincy (1797–1800 and 1817–26) are in the Public Archives in Canada (# chapter 30) and that the Military (or King's) Chapel at Gibraltar has registers of baptisms, marriages and burials dating from the late 18th century. The archives of Australia, Canada and New Zealand hold some other records relating to British army units that were stationed there. Deserters were listed in local newspapers and British soldiers who were discharged and started a new life in those colonies may be found in their militia records.

If census returns show that a soldier's child was born abroad, there is another method of discovering the man's regiment. TNA holds "monthly returns" for 1759 to 1865, in series WO 17 and 73, which note regiments' locations each month. The stations of army units were also listed in the *United Service Journal and Naval and Military Magazine* (later named *Colburn's United Service Magazine*) which was published monthly from 1829. Thus the July 1860 edition (694) lists units' stations on 28 June 1860. For example, the 6th Dragoons were in Bombay and the 2nd Battalion of the 10th Regiment of Foot was in the Cape of Good Hope. If a child was born in Gibraltar in June 1860, the journal tells you that five infantry battalions were there on 28 June: the 2nd Battalions of the 6th, 7th and 8th Foot, the 1st Battalion of the 25th Foot and the single battalion of the 100th Foot. This means only five sets of regimental muster rolls (see below) at TNA need to be searched (although you should also check the May and July lists, in case any other units were stationed in Gibraltar around June 1860).

Having discovered your ancestor's unit and approximate period of service, you can find out more about the campaigns in which his regiment took part. There are many regimental histories which provide detailed information on where regiments served and in which battles they fought. White (688) is a bibliography of British regimental histories published up to about 1965 (or a little later in an NMP reprint of 1993). Hallows (639) also lists some published regimental histories. Information can also be obtained from regimental museums and your local library should have a range of books on particular wars. TNA also holds many army operational records.

Those for 1660 to 1913 are described in TNA military records leaflets 23–25. The records of the two world wars are considered below.

Officers

Commissioned officer ranks included lieutenant, captain, major, lieutenant-colonel, colonel and general. Much information about officers is included in the regimental records reviewed below (such as muster rolls), that concern rank and file soldiers. However, there are some sources that deal exclusively with officers. Research of officers is also relatively easy because most of them appear in published lists, which lead you to a regiment's records at TNA.

Official army lists have been published in a number of overlapping series: a list of 1740, annual lists from 1754 to 1878 and from 1951 to date, monthly lists from 1798 to 1939 and quarterly or half-yearly lists from 1879 to 1950. Most of the lists are arranged by regiment but they are usually indexed. They list all serving officers, their dates of commission or promotion and sometimes details of their earlier careers. Illustration 94 shows a typical page from the army list of October 1855, recording the officers of the 9th to 14th Regiments of Foot. Having located an ancestor in one list, you can review earlier and later lists to obtain more information on his career. Reference should also be made to the unofficial *Hart's Army Lists*, which were produced quarterly from 1839 (and also annually from 1840) up to 1915, because they include much information about officers' careers that is not included in the official lists. Illustration 95 is a page from *Hart's Army List for 1863* (641) listing officers of the 16th (The Queen's) Regiment of Lancers, with the dates on which each was promoted through various ranks and footnotes for some officers, noting battles in which they served or medals awarded to them. The entry and footnote for Lieutenant Arthur Alexander Wilkie is a good example of the extensive information provided by Hart's lists. Wilkie had served for nine years, being promoted to lieutenant on 29 June 1855. The absence of a letter P by that date in his entry means that he had not purchased the commission (explained below). The footnote states that:

> Lieut. Wilkie served with the 38th Regt. [of Foot] at the siege and fall of Sebastopol from 23rd July 1855 (Medal and Clasp, and Turkish Medal). Served in the Indian campaign from Nov. 1857, including the battle of Cawnpore, capture of Meangunge, siege and capture of Lucknow, affairs of Barree and Nugger (Medal and Clasp).

Army lists and *Hart's Army Lists* are at TNA (on open shelves) and many are held by the SoG. NMP has reprinted *Hart's Army Lists* for 1840, 1860, 1885 and 1906. MM Publications has also published some of the army lists and *Hart's Army Lists* on microfiche. TNA also holds manuscript army lists from 1702 to 1823 (in series WO 64 and 65) with an index (in the research enquiries room) to the manuscript lists up to 1765 noting, for each officer, the lists in which he appears. Further published material about officers serving in the First World War is considered below, but the *Service of Military Officers* (587) records the service details of officers who appeared in the army list of 1919 or who were then on retired pay (that is, most officers who survived the First World War). The entries note an officer's rank, regiment and medals, perhaps the theatres of war or campaigns (often before 1914) in which he fought and (if he was mentioned in despatches) the date of entries in the *London Gazette* (considered further below).

TNA and the SoG hold some published works that list officers who were commissioned from 1661 to 1727 (prepared from the State Papers and various other records at TNA) and

94. Extract from The Army List, October 1855

156　　　16th (*The Queen's*) *Regiment of Lancers.*　　[Head Quarters, Sheffield.

"TALAVERA" "FUENTES D'ONOR" "SALAMANCA" "VITTORIA" "NIVE" "PENINSULA" "WATERLOO" "BHURTPORE" "AFFGHANISTAN" "GHUZNEE" "MAHARAJPORE" "ALIWAL" "SOBRAON."

Years' Serv.		
53		Colonel.—**Hon.** Sir Edward Cust,[1] KCH. *Cor.* 15 Mar. 10; *Lt.* P 27 Dec. 10; *Capt.*
Full Pay.	Half Pay.	P 9 Dec. 13; *Maj.* P 24 Oct. 21; *Lt.Col.* P 26 Dec. 26; *Col.* 23 Nov. 41; *Maj.Gen.* 11 Nov. 51; *Lt.Gen.* 14 May 50; *Col.* 16th Lancers, 9 Apr. 59.
16	0	Lieut.Colonel.—William Thomas Dickson, Cornet, P 23 Apr. 47; *Lieut.* P 25 Feb. 48; *Capt.* P 25 Apr. 51; *Major,* P 19 May 54; *Bt.Lt.Col.* 26 Oct. 58; *Lt.Col.,* P 3 Oct. 62.
16	0	Majors.—Thomas Woollaston White, *Cornet,* P 7 May 47; *Lieut.* P 7 Apr. 48; *Capt.* P 23 Sept. 51; *Major,* P 2 Nov. 55.
15	0	Lancelot Halton, *Cornet,* P 25 Feb. 48; *Lieut.* P 13 April 49; *Capt.* P 12 Oct. 52; *Major,* P 3 Oct. 62.

		CAPTAINS.	CORNET.	LIEUT.	CAPTAIN.	BREV.MAJ.	BT.LT.COL.
14	0	David Barclay	P 13 April 49	P 2 Apr. 50	P 11 Oct. 53		
24	0	Patrick Dynon[3]	29 May 39	16 June 42	14 Sept. 55		
9	0	Hugh D'Arcy P. Burnell	P 14 July 54	14 Sept. 55	P 30 July 58		
9	0	Go. Wm. Hutton Riddell	P 21 July 54	P 2 Nov. 55	P 24 Dec. 58		
7	0	Thomas Boyce	26 Feb. 56	P 15 May 57	P 17 June 59		
7	0	Frederick Stoodley......	14 Mar. 56	27 Nov. 57	P 30 Apr. 61		
7	0	Arthur John Armstrong	P 3 June 56	P 11 Dec. 57	P 29 July 62		
6	0	Arthur Gooch..........	P 10 Apr. 57	P 30 July 58	P 3 Oct. 62		
		LIEUTENANTS.					
5	0	R. Fielding Morrison[4] ..	P 30 Mar. 58	P 24 Dec. 58			
5	0	Thomas Francis Agg....	27 Oct. 58	P 17 June 59			
7	0	Henry Clement Wilkinson[5]	15 Feb. 56	P 5 Aug. 59			
4	0	George James Gilbard ..	18 Jan. 59	P 22 Feb. 61			
4	0	William John Wauchope.	P 7 Oct. 59	P 30 Apr. 61			
3	0	Wm. Alex. Battine,[6] *Adj.*	14 Feb. 60	P 29 July 62			
9	0	Arthur Alexander Wilkie[7]	6 June 54	29 June 55			
3	0	C.Carrington Churchward	P 16 Mar. 60	P 2 Sept. 62			
2	0	Robert Thirkill Maillard .	P 12 Mar. 61	P 3 Oct. 62			
		CORNETS.					
2	0	Hans Sloane Stanley	P 25 June 61				
2	0	Ion Turner	P 27 Sept. 61				
1	0	William Erskine ..	P 7 Jan. 62				
1	0	Godfrey Clem. K. Baldwin	P 18 Mar. 62				
1	0	David George Sandeman	P 3 Oct. 62				
1	0	Alex. Baring Bingham ..	P 9 Dec. 62				
1	0	Richard Tomkinson	P 9 Dec. 62				
1	0	VC Henry Michel Jones[8]	P 19 Dec. 62				

4 Lieut. Morrison (late a Captain in the 51st F.) served with the 19th Regt. in the Eastern Campaign up to 28th Oct. 1854, including the battle of Alma and siege of Sebastopol (Medal and two Clasps and Turkish Medal).

5 Lieut. Wilkinson served with the 95th Regt. in the Indian Campaign of 1858, and was present at the siege and capture of Awah, siege assault and capture of Kotah, battle of Kota-kaseria, general action resulting in the capture of Gwalior, assault and capture of Rowa, siege and capture of Pouree, battle of Beejapore, and affair of Koondry (Medal and Clasp).

10 Riding Master Brown served with the 16th Lancers during the campaign in Affghanistan, under Lord Keane, in 1839, including the siege and capture of Ghuznee (Medal).

1	0	Paymaster.—Thomas Dynon, 22 April 62.
3	0	Adjutant.—Lieut. Wm. Alex. Battine,[6] 5 Sept. 62.
6	0	Riding Master.—Thomas Brown,[10] 7 Sept. 58; Cornet, 20 Dec. 57.
3	0	Quarter Master.—James Fuller,[9] 18 May 60.
18	0	Surgeon.—William Ker Park, 6 Oct. 54; Assist.Surg. 31 Oct. 45.
8	0	Assist.Surgeon.—Charles Alexander Innes,[11] MD. 14 March 55.
15	0	Veterinary Surgeon.—Francis Frederick Collins, 8 Dec. 48; 1st *Class*, 26 Nov. 61.

Scarlet—*Facings* Blue.—*Agents*, Messrs. Cox & Co.　　[*Returned from Bengal*, 26 *Dec.* 1846.]

1 Sir Edward Cust joined the Duke of Wellington's army prior to the advance from Portugal in 1811, and continued with it up to the cantonments on the Adour in 1813, having been present with the 16th Light Dragoons at the battles of Fuentes d'Onor, and with the 14th Dragoons at the battles of Salamanca, Vittoria, the Pyrenees, Nivelle, and Nive, investment of Ciudad Rodrigo, siege of Badajoz, and generally in all the affairs of that period, until he quitted the Duke's army on promotion. He has received the War Medal with seven Clasps.

3 Capt. Dynon served with the 16th Lancers during the campaign in Affghanistan under Lord Keane, including the siege and capture of Ghuznee (Medal). He served also at the battle of Maharajpore (Medal), 9th Dec. 1843; and in the campaign on the Sutlej in 1846, including the battles of Buddiwal, Aliwal, and Sobraon (Medal and Clasps).

6 Lieut. Battine, as a Lieut. in the Bengal Army, served with the Persian expeditionary force from January to June 1857, and was present at the bombardment and capture of Mohumrah (Medal). Served in Bengal with Havelock's column, on the Staff of that General, and was present in the several actions leading to and ending in the relief of the Residency at Lucknow on 25th Sept. 1857; also during the subsequent defence as a D.A.Q.M. Gen. to the force until its final relief by Lord Clyde on 24th Nov. 1857 (Medal and Clasp).

7 Lieut. Wilkie served with the 38th Regt. at the siege and fall of Sebastopol from 23rd July 1855 (Medal and Clasp, and Turkish Medal). Served in the Indian campaign from Nov. 1857, including the battle of Cawnpore, capture of Meangunge, siege and capture of Lucknow, affairs of Barree and Nugger (Medal and Clasp).

8 Cornet Jones (formerly a Captain in the 7th Fusiliers) served the Eastern Campaign of 1854-55, including the battle of Ghuznee (severely wounded while carrying the colors), sortie on 9th May, attack and capture of the Quarries on the 7th June (wounded), and assault of the Redan on 8th September—dangerously wounded, mentioned in despatches (Medal with two Clasps, Victoria Cross, Knight of the Legion of Honor, and Turkish Medal).

9 Quarter Master Fuller served with the 16th Lancers at the battle of Maharajpore on 29th Dec. 1843 (Medal). Also the Sutlej campaign of 1846 including the battles of Buddiwal, Aliwal, and Sobraon (Medal and Clasp).

11 Doctor Innes served with the R. Artillery in the Crimea from 26th May 1855, was present at the bombardments of 18th June and 8th Sept., also with the expedition to Kertch (Medal and Clasp and Turkish Medal). Served with the 52nd Lt. Inf. during the Indian Mutiny in 1857, and was in medical charge of the Regt. during part of the siege assault and capture of Delhi (Medal and Clasp).

95. Officers of the 16th (The Queen's) Regiment of Lancers, from Hart's Army List for 1863

artillery, engineer and medical officers who served from the 17th to 20th centuries. Dalton (616) is an indexed collection of army lists and commission registers from 1661 to 1714 and Dalton (617) is an indexed account of regiments, officers and their careers from 1714 to 1727. Askwith (598) lists artillery officers from 1716 to 1862 (and some up to 1899), with their ranks, dates of promotions and other notes (for example dates of death). Some information pre-dates 1716 for officers serving in that year (thus Albert Borgard is noted as having been promoted to major in April 1702). Morgan (661) provides similar information for artillery officers from 1862 to 1914. Francis Roberts is recorded as born on 5 March 1843, becoming a gentleman cadet on 1 July 1861, lieutenant on 17 December 1862, captain (17 November 1875), major (1 November 1882) and lieutenant-colonel (2 February 1890). He served in India from September 1863 to May 1866 and died at Southsea on 1 September 1904. Connolly & Edwards (613) provide detailed information on the careers (and some dates and places of death) of Royal Engineer officers from 1660 to 1898 (and engineer officers in Indian, Irish or other units). Edward Harvey is noted as becoming a lieutenant on 22 December 1859, with subsequent promotions up to his appointment as lieutenant-colonel in October 1887 and his retirement on 30 October 1892. His war service is recorded as Looshai (1871–72), Jowaki (1877–78) and Afghanistan (1879–80). Peterkin & Johnston (666) list officers in the army medical service from 1660 to 1898 and Drew (620) lists medical officers from 1898 to 1960. Both works note men's dates and places of birth, education, ranks, medals and dates of promotions, retirement and death.

Some published lists of officers, describing their military service, concentrate on a particular war, campaign or battle. Hall (637) is a biographical dictionary of about 3,000 British officers who were killed or wounded in the Peninsula War of 1808–14, based on information in the *London Gazette*, army lists as well as manuscript records such as regimental musters, pension records and officers' service records at TNA. Entries note an officer's promotions, medals, the battles in which he served and some useful genealogical material. For example, Captain Andrew Brown of the 79th Foot is noted as born in Edinburgh on 6 January 1766, married to Ann Dixon on 26 August 1794 at St Mary's, Dover and having two children prior to her death. He then married Mary Balfour on 10 September 1803 in the parish of Templemore in Londonderry by whom he had two more children.

Lummis & Wynn (653) is a biographical register of the 2,000 officers and men of the five cavalry regiments in the Light Brigade during the Crimean War of 1854–56, many of whom took part in the famous charge at Balaclava. The entries were compiled from various sources at TNA including medal rolls and regimental muster rolls. There are detailed entries for officers (and some other ranks), including their dates of birth, parents' names, promotions, the campaigns or battles in which they served, the medals they received and the date (and place) of their death or burial. Mackinnon & Shadbolt (655) describe the role of British officers who served in the Anglo-Zulu war of 1879 and include photographs and detailed biographies (including education, military career and parents' and wives' names) of the 62 army and navy officers who died. Dooner (619) is a biographical dictionary of officers who died in the Boer War of 1899–1902. This is one of the shorter entries:

Capt. Ralph Nevile Fane, 4th Batt. North Staffordshire Regt., died of pneumonia at Wynberg, Cape Colony May 27th, 1900. He was the younger son of Col. Francis Fane, of Fulbeck, was 30 years of age, and educated at Wellington . . . 1884–6. He was appointed

Lieut. 1889 and promoted Capt. 1894. His battalion was embodied Jan. 1900, and Capt. Fane volunteering for active service, proceeded with it to South Africa in March and served with it till his death.

The next step is to review an officer's service records. Records of officers who served after 1922 are held by the Ministry of Defence, but earlier records are at TNA. Returns of serving officers were prepared in 1809/10, 1829 and from 1870 to 1872 (all held in series WO 25). Each regiment and corps also made returns (known as Services of Officers on the Active List) from 1829 to 1913 (but sometimes as early as 1764). These regimental lists of officers are in series WO 25 and WO 76 and usually note an officer's rank, career details, date and place of birth, age at commission and the campaigns in which he fought. The date and place of an officer's marriage, the name of his wife and children (with ages or dates of birth) may also be given. Incomplete indexes to these returns are in the research enquiries room at TNA. Alphabetical returns of retired officers, made in 1828 and 1847, are in WO 25. They record a man's regiment, promotions, age, date of commission and details of his marriage and children. Reports of officers' marriages from 1830 to 1882 are also in WO 25 (because they needed their colonels' permission to wed), providing the bride's name and the place and date of marriage. Commissioned officers also had to submit a baptism certificate and many of these survive in WO 42.

Until 1871 officers could purchase commissions (up to the rank of colonel), although the number who did so varied between regiments (more officers purchased commissions in the cavalry or foot guards than in other units). Having discovered an ancestor's date of commission from the above sources, you can turn to the Commander-in-Chiefs' memoranda of 1793 to 1870 (in series WO 31) which include letters of application to purchase and sell commissions. Examples are included in Hamilton-Edwards (640). Some other commission registers and related records from 1660 to 1858 are described in Fowler & Spencer (627). Appointments and promotions of officers were also announced in the *London Gazette* (# chapter 17 and illustration 75) and in the *United Service Journal and Naval and Military Magazine*.

There are some additional service records for officers of the Royal Artillery in series WO 54/684 for 1727–51 and WO 76 for 1771–1914 and service records of artillery officers are in WO 25/3913–20 for 1796–1922. Commission books and warrants for commissions for both services are in WO 54.

At the start of the First World War, there were about 15,000 army officers. Between 1914 and 1918, another 235,000 were granted commissions. Some records survive for most of these officers but the files of officers who continued to serve after 1922 are still held by the MOD. Most service records of officers who served in the First World War were destroyed in the Blitz but files of correspondence survive for about 217,000 of them in series WO 339 and WO 374 at TNA. The files of some men who transferred into the RAF (and some RFC officers) are in series AIR 76 (see below). Some files in WO 339 and 374 include little more than a note of the date of a man's death, but many contain detailed records, including an officer's application for a commission, his attestation papers (if he was promoted from the ranks), statements of services and correspondence. The documents are described in detail, with illustrations, in Spencer (676). Series WO 374 contains files in alphabetical order of about 77,800 officers, primarily those with a temporary commission or those commissioned into the Territorial Army. Series WO 339 contains files of about 140,000 officers, arranged by their personal identification or "long" numbers. The series can be searched by men's names on PROCAT. Alternatively, officers' numbers can be found in an alphabetical index (in series WO 338) in the microfilm reading room. The WO 339 series list tells you the piece that includes the records for that number.

Officers were not entitled to pensions on retirement until 1871. Before that, retiring officers either sold their commissions or received half-pay, which was similar to a retainer and paid to men who remained available for future service. Many records of officers on half-pay since about 1730 are in series WO 23–25, but also in the Paymaster General's papers (series PMG 3–14). Thus alphabetical registers of officers on half-pay from 1858 to 1894 are in pieces WO 23/68–75 and half-pay registers for 1737 to 1921 (alphabetical from 1841) are in PMG 4. Half-pay records should include the date of an officer's death, and the date and place of payments (which therefore reveal officers' movements after retirement). The records of army pensions are complex, but reviewed in TNA military records leaflets 6 and 15, Fowler & Spencer (627) and Watts & Watts (685). From 1708 widows of officers killed on active service could claim a pension. Widows' applications from 1760 to 1818 are in series WO 25 and registers of widows receiving pensions from 1815 to 1892 are in WO 23. The pieces (and some indexes) are listed in the leaflets, which also review the records of allowances paid to deceased officers' children (or other dependants). Miscellaneous certificates (in WO 42) include some widows' pension applications of 1755 to 1908, sometimes attaching baptism, birth, marriage or death certificates. Pensions for wounded officers were introduced in 1812 (and available to officers who were wounded before 1812) and registers of these pensions are in series WO 23 and PMG 9 and 42. Widows, children and other dependent relatives of officers who served in the First World War could claim pensions, sometimes many years after the war. The applications are in PMG 43–47 (some are also in PIN 26 and 82).

The Royal Military Academy at Woolwich was founded in 1741 to train artillery and engineer officers. The academy was merged (in 1947) into the Royal Military College, which was founded in 1800 and moved to Sandhurst in 1812. Registers of cadets from about 1790 are available at Sandhurst and many applications for entry include baptism certificates.

Other ranks

Until this century other ranks (privates or non-commissioned officers such as corporals or sergeants) were usually the poorer men in society, including many criminals. Most men enlisted voluntarily (the minimum age being 18 from 1780). Enlistment was for life (if they did not die in battle, from wounds or disease), but in practice was for 21 years (reduced to 12 in 1871), when men were usually discharged with a pension. Many soldiers were discharged early (when wars ended or because of ill-health). If you have identified an ancestor's regiment from the sources noted above, the next step is to consult the records at TNA. If you have not identified his unit, there are some records at TNA that may reveal this. TNA holds service records for men discharged in or before 1920 (although records for 1914 to 1920 are considered separately below). The Ministry of Defence holds records of soldiers serving since 1921 and the Royal Artillery keeps many of its own later records at the Royal Artillery Manning & Record Office, Imphal Barracks, York.

The most useful records at TNA for the period up to 1913 (other than medal rolls which are considered below) are those in the following nine categories. However, they are incomplete (for example, a regiment's muster rolls may only cover certain years). The covering years of the surviving papers in these classes, for each unit, are listed by Watts & Watts (685). In order to use most of these records, it is vital to have identified an ancestor's unit, since only some of them are sorted by surname and few indexes are available.

(1) Attestation and discharge papers (or "soldiers' documents") 1760–1913   A recruit completed an attestation form when he enlisted and received discharge papers when he left. These survive in series WO 97 for most men who were discharged to pension or (from 1883) who purchased their discharge or completed a term of limited engagement. They do not survive for soldiers who were killed in service. They are arranged by year of discharge and then:

a. from 1760 to 1854 (in pieces WO 97/1–1271) and 1855 to 1872 (WO 97/1272–1721) by regiment (then alphabetically by surname)
b. from 1873 to 1882 (WO 97/1722–2171) by "group" (cavalry, artillery, engineers, foot guards, infantry or miscellaneous corps), then by surname
c. from 1883 to 1900 (WO 97/2172–4231) and 1900 to 1913 (WO 97/4232–6322) alphabetically by surname (whatever unit a man served in)

There are also two supplemental sequences, each arranged alphabetically by surname, for 1834–99 (pieces WO 97/6355–93) and 1900–13 (WO 97/6323–54). The records of 1760–1854 are best consulted by using the index to names noted below. For other years, the series list (also published in List and Index Society volume 201) tells you which piece to search. For example, men discharged from the infantry between 1873 and 1882, with surnames commencing with the letters Till to Tom, are included in piece WO 97/2122.

The soldiers' documents usually note a soldier's place of birth, age, date of enlistment, previous occupation, physical description and a summary of his army career (and from 1883, his next of kin). Piece WO 97/1435 contains attestation and discharge papers for the 14th Regiment of Foot. Illustrations 96 and 97 are the first two pages of papers for John Radford who was discharged to pension in 1867. Another page noted that John was born in Whitestone in Devon and enlisted in June 1846, when he was 17 years and 10 months old (that is, under age). The pages in the illustrations record that John was promoted to corporal in January 1854 and serjeant in June 1854. He served 21 years and 20 days, including one year in the Crimea, one year in Malta, 17 months in the Ionian Isles and over 4 years in the West Indies. John was described as 38 years and 10 months old, 5 feet 5 inches high, with light brown hair and hazel eyes. John's conduct was "very good" and he received the Crimean medal (for his part at the battle of Sebastopol), the Turkish War Medal and a medal (and a gratuity of £5) for good conduct and long service.

The soldiers' documents of 1760 to 1854 in pieces WO 97/1–1271 are on microfilm. An index to the soldiers' names in these records (about 170,000 men), can be consulted online through PROCAT. This index notes a man's regiment, birthplace, age at discharge and years of enlistment and discharge, as in this example for Thomas Charnock of the 25th Foot:

Name	Birthplace	Enlistment Date	Discharge Date	Discharge Age	Regiment & WO 97 piece no
Charnock, Thomas	Croston, Lancs.	1806	1824	36	F25 443

The soldiers' documents of 1855–72 in WO 97 are arranged by regiment, then by soldiers' surnames. However, Ms S. Davis of 18 Manor Road, East Molesey, Surrey KT8 9JX holds an index to these men which can be consulted for a fee. Some additional service records are in WO

86511. *Chatham 12 Sept 67* W. O. Form 83.

HER MAJESTY'S OF *Foot* 1/14th REG.

Whereof *General Sir W. Hood K.C.B, K.H.* is Colonel.

[Place and Date] *Chatham* 30th *August* 1867.

PROCEEDINGS OF A REGIMENTAL BOARD, held this day, in conformity to the Articles of War, for the purpose of verifying and recording the Services, Conduct, Character, and cause of Discharge of No. *2476 Serjeant John Radford* of the Regiment above-mentioned.

President.
Capt a. a. Le Mesurier. 1/14 Regt

Capt P. G. Gilling 1/22 Regt Members. *Capt R. Furneaux 2/14 Regt*

THE BOARD having examined and compared the Regimental Records, the Soldier's Book, and such other Documents as appeared to them to be necessary, report that after making every deduction required by Her Majesty's Regulations, the Service up to this day, which he is entitled to reckon, amounts to *21* years, *XX 20* days, as shown by the detailed Statement on the 2nd page; during which period he served abroad *7 7/12* years, viz. :

at _____, years,

in *Crimea 1* years;

Ionian Isles 1st 12 years West Indies 4 7/2 years ,

and further, that his DISCHARGE is proposed in consequence of *Free to Pension*

[Here state whether—Completion of period, at his own request, or as unfit for further Service.]

as an indulgence and by authority dated Adjutant Generals Office Dublin 12 August 1867.

With regard to the CHARACTER and CONDUCT of *No 2476 Sergt John Radford*, the Board have to report that upon reference to the Defaulter's Book, and by the Parole testimony that has been given, it appears that *they*

[Insert opposite—the man's Character, the number of Good Conduct Badges in his possession, and all Badges of Merit, or gallant conduct in the Field, conferred upon him.]

have been very good he was when promoted Sergt in possession of 1 G.C. Badge and would had he not been promoted Serge Some now been in possession of 4 G.C.B also Crimean Medal with Clasp for Sebastopol Turkish War Medal & Medal for Good Conduct and Long Service

[Insert the number of times his Name appears in the Defaulter's Book, and that he has been tried by Court Martial.

The charge, finding, and sentence, on each occasion, is to be recorded on a separate sheet, which is to accompany the Discharge Documents.

If never tried or entered in the Defaulter's Book, state so.]

his name appears 6 times in the Regt Defaulters Book and he has never been tried by Court Martial

[If this man received Wounds, &c., in action, or other Injuries in or by the Service, although not invalided on account thereof, state here the nature of the wound, or injuries, and when and where he received the same, and if any Court of Enquiry was held, (as is required) state or annex the result.]

He has never been wounded in action

96. *Extract from the discharge papers of John Radford of the 14th Foot, 1867 (TNA, WO 97/1435)*

Nº 2476 Sergeant John Radford being asked to what date he has been paid, answered that his Account is balanced up to the latest period required by the Regulations ; and being further asked whether he has any claim on the Regiment for Arrears of PAY, ALLOWANCES, or CLOTHING, answered that he has received all just demands, from his entry into the Service up to the ___30th august 1867___ and in confirmation therefore, affixes his signature hereto.

I acknowledge this to be true. _John Radford_

Witness _illegible_

Commanding the Company to which he belongs.

THE Board have ascertained that _Nº 2476 Sergeant John Radford_ Soldier's Book is correctly balanced, and signed by the Officer Commanding his Company, and they declare, that they have impartially inquired into, and faithfully reported upon, all the matters brought before them, in accordance with the Regulations and Instructions issued by Her Majesty's Orders.

illegible Capt 1/14 President.

illegible } Members.

Detailed Statement of the Services of _Nº 2476 Sergt John Radford_

Regiment	Promotions, Reductions, &c.	Rank	Period of Service in each Rank		Amount of Service towards G. C. Pay and Pension		Amount of Service towards completion of limited engagement	
			From	To	Years	Days	Years	Days
1/14th		Private	1 June 1846	8 Aug 1846	under	age		
		"	11 Aug 1846	31 Dec 1853	7	143	7	143
	Good Conduct pay at 1 2 April 1862							
	Promoted Corporal	Corporal	1 Jan 1854	13 June 1854		164		164
	"	Sergeant	14 June 1854	30 Aug 1867	13	78	13	78
	Granted a Silver Medal with Gratuity of £5.0.0 for long Service & Good Conduct							

Further Service from the _31 August_ to the _17 Sept 67_ when finally discharged

Total of the foregoing Statement .. .. .. 21 | 20 | 21 | 20 | 18 | 18 | Total Service allowed to reckon to the day of final discharge .. 21 | 38 | 21 | 38

I have carefully examined the Proceedings of this Board in all its details and I find them in every respect correct.

Commanding _illegible Betts_

97. _Another page from the discharge papers of John Radford in 1867 (TNA, WO 97/1435)_

121 (also on microfilm), including certificates of service for men awarded Chelsea out-pensions (1787–1813) and general registers of discharge (1871–84). The names of the men in these documents are gradually being added to the index of WO 97.

(2) Muster rolls and pay lists   These records are arranged by unit and generally cover 1760 to 1898 but they date back to 1708 for some units. Most of the records up to 1878 are in series WO 12, but those for the artillery, engineers and other corps are in WO 10, 11, 14 and 15. The muster rolls are quarterly, each usually recording three monthly musters. They note a unit's location and list officers' and soldiers' names, ranks, pay, dates of enlistment, discharge or death, punishments, time spent in hospital or other absences from the unit. Some rolls since 1795 note a soldier's place of birth and age on enlistment. The rolls provide a month by month account of men's army service. Having found an ancestor in one roll, you can review the regiment's earlier and later rolls for more information. The last muster in which a man appears should give a reason for the end of his service (such as death or discharge to pension). Series WO 16 contains the musters of 1878 to 1898 for all regiments and corps, but they are arranged by regimental district, so that it is more difficult to locate the correct rolls. The information recorded was similar to that in earlier rolls although the format was different.

Knowing that John Radford served in the 14th Foot, it was easy to find him in the muster rolls. Piece WO 12/3179 included rolls of 1861 to 1862 for the 1st Battalion of the 14th Foot (then in Jamaica). Illustration 98 shows an extract from the roll for 1 April to 30 June 1861. This shows that John Radford spent 14 days in hospital. Other entries in the roll note that Serjeant Richard Martin was in hospital for 69 days and then invalided back to England. Serjeant Christopher Leithbridge had been arrested and tried on 30 April but "forgiven", although his offence is not stated.

In 1806, a return was prepared, arranged by regiment, of all NCOs and men in the army on 24 June who were liable to serve abroad. The return, in pieces WO 25/871–1120, noted each man's name, date of enlistment and any other regiment in which he had served. Indexes to the regiments' returns are being published by Chambers (609).

(3) Description books   These survive from 1795 to 1900 (with some as early as 1756) and most are in pieces WO 25/266–688 or in series WO 67. They are arranged by regiment (then alphabetically by initial letter of men's surnames) and noted (to assist searches for deserters) a recruit's age, place of birth and enlistment, trade and physical description.

(4) Casualty lists and returns   Series WO 25 contains the *Muster Master General's Index of Casualties* for 1797 to 1817, which includes deserters and is arranged by regiment. Casualty lists for 1809 to 1910, arranged by campaign, then regiment, are also in WO 25 and 32, noting a man's name, rank, birthplace, trade, next of kin (and including some men's wills). The casualty rolls for some wars or campaigns have been published including the Crimean War roll in Cook & Cook (614), the roll for the Indian Mutiny in Tavender (679) and the roll for the Zulu and Basuto wars 1877–79 in Tavender (680). The Boer War casualty roll is in series WO 108 and has been published in two volumes, one for the Natal Field Force (589) and one for the South African Field Force (590). Entries are arranged in periods of a few months, then by regiment, and note names, dates and the type of casualty (dead, missing, captured or seriously injured), for example Lieutenant C. Blewitt of the 1st Battalion of the Rifle Brigade, who was killed on 17 September 1901.

98. *Extract from pay list of the 14th Foot, 1861 (TNA, WO 12/3179)*

(5) Records of pensioners   Soldiers were entitled to pensions for wounds (or for completing an agreed term of service) from the 17th century. The Royal Hospital at Chelsea was opened for invalid pensioners in 1692. It was responsible for all army pensioners (other than officers), who therefore became known as Chelsea pensioners, although only some men lived at Chelsea. Most men lived at home (and were known as out-pensioners) and received a monetary pension.

The soldiers' documents in WO 97 noted above evidence a man's entitlement to pension, but many other pension records survive and are reviewed in Bevan (239) and TNA military records leaflets 6 and 15. There are admission books for out-pensioners, which note a man's age, birthplace, regiment, rank, length of service and physical description. The books are in two series (WO 116 and 117) for medical pensions from 1715 to 1913 (WO 116) and for long service pensions from 1823 to 1913, with some to 1920 (in WO 117, on microfilm). Entries are chronological (by the date of a man's discharge and examination for a pension) so you therefore need to know the approximate date of a man's discharge from the army in order to find records of his admission to a pension. For the period 1806–38 this date may be found in an index (for series WO 120) noted below. Examples of entries from the books are contained in Watts & Watts (685) and Fowler & Spencer (627). Series WO 23 includes many records of in-pensioners at the Royal Hospital, for example muster rolls (1702–89 and 1864–65) in WO 23/124–132, a list of in-pensioners (1795–1813) in WO 23/134, and an alphabetical register (1837–72) in WO 23/146. There are also chronological admission books for in-pensioners (1824–1917) in WO 23/162–180 and an index of in-pensioners (1858–1933) in WO 23/173. These records note a man's name, regiment, age, rate of pension, date of admission to pension and brief details of his army service. TNA also holds the hospital's records of baptisms, marriages and burials (# chapter 7).

Each regiment also kept registers of men who were discharged to pension. These are in two sequences in series WO 120. The first sequence covers 1715 to 1843. The documents are arranged in six date bands and (within a band) by regiment. Entries for men of each regiment are chronological by date of discharge to pension, and note a soldier's age, rate of pension, place of birth, physical description and a brief record of his service. Beckett (600) is an index to the regimental registers in pieces 20 to 30, that is, for pensions awarded to men of nearly all regiments from 1806 to 1838. The index is at the SoG and TNA (and can also be purchased on microfiche from Manchester and Lancashire FHS) and gives a soldier's name, year of discharge, age, regiment and birthplace. It includes Thomas Gillman of Hockliffe (a brother of my ancestor Susan Gillman), aged 37, who was discharged to pension in 1815 from the 103rd Foot. The second sequence of regimental registers in WO 120 covers pensions paid from 1814 to 1854 (and some up to 1857). Entries up to 1845 are arranged by pension rate and later entries are chronological.

In 1842 the War Office established a district system for payment of out-pensions. Series WO 22 contains quarterly pension returns for 1842 to 1862 (up to 1883 for pensions paid to men who had moved overseas). The returns are arranged by the district where a pension was paid. The districts (about 100 in Britain and Ireland) are listed in Watts & Watts (685). The records are easy to use if you know the name of any place where a soldier lived after his discharge, because there are only two or three volumes for most districts. They note a soldier's regiment and changes rather than pension payments (such as a man becoming a pensioner, a change in his pension rate, his moves between districts, or his death). Some examples of entries appear in an article by R. Oliver in *Genealogists' Magazine* (June 1984).

(6) Records of deserters   The harsh army discipline and poor conditions caused many soldiers to desert. Registers of deserters from 1799 to 1852 are in series WO 25 (each piece covering a few years and different regiments) noting a man's age, description and the dates and places of enlistment and desertion. The pieces and their covering dates are noted by Bevan (239). Deserters were also listed in local newspapers and in the *Police Gazette* (TNA holds copies for 1828–45 in series HO 75). Manchester & Lancashire FHS has produced a CD-ROM index to the deserters (over 36,000 men) listed in the *Police Gazette* from 1828 to 1840. This lists each man's name, regiment, age, birthplace, occupation at enlistment and the date of the *Police Gazette* notice. The index reveals that in 1837 the authorities were searching for William Charnock of the 7th Fusiliers, aged 22, noted as born in Charnock in Lancashire, who had been a labourer when he enlisted.

(7) Records of courts martial   Army discipline was enforced by a regiment's officers but also by army courts (staffed by officers) known as courts martial. If your ancestor was reduced in rank or noted (in muster rolls) as in prison, he may have faced a court martial and the records may include an account of the offence and trial. TNA military records leaflets 22 and 75 describe the different types of courts martial, their powers and surviving records, which date from about 1688 to the 20th century and are in series WO 71, 72 and 81 to 93. Most records are closed for 75 years after the date of the last entry, although lists of death sentences during the Second World War are available in WO 93. Trials of officers from 1806 to 1904 are indexed in WO 93/1B. The records of courts martial during the First World War are reviewed further below.

(8) Registers of soldiers purchasing their early discharge   These date from 1817 to 1870, are arranged by regiment and are in pieces WO 25/3845–3893.

(9) Household Cavalry service records   The service records of other ranks of the 1st Life Guards (1801–1920), the 2nd Life Guards (1799–1919), the Royal Horse Guards (1805–1919) and the Household Battalion (1916–19) are held at TNA in series WO 400. These records are arranged by regiment, then period (of about 50 years) and then alphabetically by men's names. The range of names covered by each piece is noted on PROCAT.

Royal Engineers, the Royal Artillery and other corps
Men of the Royal Engineers (and its predecessors, the Corps of Engineers and the Royal Corps of Sappers and Miners) are recorded in soldiers' documents (in WO 97), muster books from 1816 to 1878 (in WO 11), and description books (WO 54). Royal Artillery musters and pay books (since about 1760) are in series WO 10 and 16, description books are in WO 54, 67 and 69, records of service from 1756 are in WO 69, soldiers' documents (1760–1882) are in WO 97 and admission books for pensions (1833–1913) are in WO 116. Similar records survive for the Royal Corps of Signals, the Royal Waggon Corps, the Army Service Corps and the Medical Corps. The covering dates and piece numbers are listed in Watts & Watts (685) and Fowler & Spencer (676).

OTHER RANKS, THE FIRST WORLD WAR

Researching ancestors who served in the First World War can be difficult because many records were destroyed in the Second World War and because there were so many units (about 1,700 infantry battalions and 4,000 other units) and so many soldiers (about 8 million men and women). Thousands of men volunteered to serve. However, casualties were so high that conscription was introduced in January 1916 for all men aged 18–41 who were single or widowers (without dependants), except those who were unfit for service or who undertook indispensable civil work. Conscription was extended to married men in May 1916.

The surviving records of non-commissioned officers and other ranks who served in the war (and up to 1920) are at TNA. The location of pay lists and muster rolls is not known, but service records for soldiers whose service ended (by discharge or death) between 1914 and 1920 were collected from regiments and corps. Many were destroyed in a fire during the Second World War and only about 30 per cent survived in 33,000 boxes (that is, for about two million soldiers). They are known as the "burnt" documents and relate to soldiers who died and those who survived to be demobilised. They include men who joined the army during the First World War but also many who were serving before August 1914, in some cases since the 1890s. They do not include service records of men who continued to serve after 1920 or those who served in the Household Cavalry (their records are in series WO 400) or the Foot Guards regiments (their records are still held by the regiments). The records are on microfilm in series WO 363 in alphabetical order of men's surnames then forenames (although some records were filed or filmed out of sequence). About 5,000 service records that were noted to be out of sequence were extracted and filmed as a second alphabetical sequence. The WO 363 series list notes the range of names that appear on each film (which you find in self-service cabinets in the microfilm reading room). There are over 29,000 reels of film, almost 3,500 of them for men with surnames beginning with the letter S, 562 reels for men named Smith which include service records of about 1,500 men named John Smith. Consequently, finding a man with a common name is not easy. All the films (and those of WO 364 noted below) can also be seen at LDS family history centres. It is unclear how these service records were arranged at the time of the fire and so it is also unknown whether those destroyed were predominantly of certain regiments or corps rather than others. The service records of my grandfather Henry John Herber and two of his brothers have not survived but you may be luckier.

Further service records of First World War soldiers, known as the "unburnt" documents, were collated from service records held by the Ministry of Pensions. They are in series WO 364, on over 4,000 microfilms in self-service cabinets in the microfilm reading room. They concern about 750,000 soldiers, primarily those awarded a pension, including regular soldiers who were discharged at the end of their term of service or men discharged on medical grounds. They do not include men killed in action (who had no dependants) or men who were demobilised after the war (since they were generally not entitled to a pension). The principal sequence is in pieces WO 364/1–4912 but there are three further sequences in WO 364/4913–15, 5000–5802 and 5803–4. Each sequence is arranged alphabetically (although a few documents are out of sequence), by surname then forename. The WO 364 series list notes the range of names in each piece. Thus WO 364/740 is part of the main sequence and covers William Cole to Frederick Coleman. Some of the men recorded in WO 364 also appear in WO 363.

Spencer (676) reviews the records in WO 363 and 364 in detail, with illustrations of the types of documents that they include. Most men's files include an attestation form. Illustration 99 is the attestation on 12 December 1915 (from WO 363) of my great grandfather's brother, Richard Charles Eagles, from Hackney in London. His file included a report, prepared on his enlistment, noting his wife's name and address and his children's names and dates (and places) of birth. The

99. *Attestation of Richard Charles Eagles on 12 December 1915 (TNA, WO 363/E4/647)*

file also included his certificate of demobilisation in 1919 after his service in the 30th Battalion, the London Regiment. A man's files may include other forms such as a medical history sheet (noting vaccinations and admissions to, or discharges from, hospital), a casualty form (noting casualties, promotions, a service description and next of kin), a statement as to disability (any medical complaints on demobilisation) and a regimental conduct sheet (for offences that led to disciplinary action).

Unless you find your ancestor in these service records, it is vital to ascertain the unit in which he served if you wish to research his service during the First World War. The unit may be recorded in family archives (such as discharge or death certificates, memorial plaques and letters). If not, the best method of identifying the unit is to search the Commonwealth War Graves Commission (CWGC) records and the medal rolls considered below. Most soldiers were entitled to campaign medals (and many men received gallantry awards). However, not all men are included in the rolls and a man with a common surname may be difficult to identify, as noted above for the name John Smith. Even if you know an ancestor's number, this rarely identifies his unit. Soldiers were not given unique numbers until 1920. In 1914 men were given numbers by their battalion so that many men in different battalions had the same number; also men often changed number if they transferred between units. Another problem is that many units (particularly infantry) had a number of names (some unofficial). These are listed by Holding (644). For example, the 18th Battalion of the Durham Light Infantry was known as the Durham Pals. Research is even more difficult if an ancestor served in a corps such as the Army Service Corps, the Medical Corps or the Royal Artillery, since there were about 100 different types of corps (and about 4,000 different companies or other units). It is essential to ascertain the type of unit in order to start your research. If service records, CWGC records and medal rolls do not include your ancestor, the following sources may identify his unit:

a. photographs (revealing badges, uniforms and medals)
b. casualty lists, war memorials and regimental rolls of honour
c. local newspapers (featuring obituaries or articles on local heroes)
d. pension records
e. electoral roll absentee voter lists

Holding (644) explains how to identify a man's unit (or a theatre of war in which he fought) from photographs, letters and postcards. Even if his unit cannot be identified from a photograph, it may narrow the area of search because of the soldier's badges, insignia, chevrons or equipment (such as belts). For example, illustration 7 is a photograph of my grandfather Henry John Herber in his First World War uniform. The badge on his right arm shows that he was a saddler in a mounted unit and the inverted chevron on his lower left arm is a stripe for two years' service or good conduct. His cap badge is that of the Royal Artillery. Swinnerton (677) also describes how to identify a First World War soldier's unit from badges, medals or photographs. Other detailed works on soldiers' uniforms, badges, buttons and insignia are listed by Holding (644).

From 1918 servicemen were permitted to register to vote in their home constituency. The first two issues of absent voter lists, dated 15 October 1918 and 15 April 1919, are important since most men were not demobilised until 1919. The lists usually give a man's name, home address, unit, rank and number and they are held at CROs or local libraries. Holding (644) gives examples from Bedford including:

Stanton, Geoffrey J.G.	Goldington Road	55190 P(riva)te, 1st Manchester
Fenn, James Mills	8 St Cuthbert's St	S/4125635 Pte, 2/3rd Field Bakery, A(rmy)
		S(ervice) C(orps)

Pensions were granted for service in the First World War to disabled or invalid officers and men as well as to dependants of the deceased. If a soldier survived the war and received a war pension, you may find his records in series WO 364 (reviewed above). Some records of pensions paid to soldiers, sailors and their relatives from 1914 are also in series PMG 4, 9 and 42–47. Series PIN 26 also contains over 22,000 personal files (the men's names can be searched on PROCAT). The dates of these records and the types of pensions are listed in Bevan (239) and in TNA military records leaflet 15.

Servicewomen

The heavy casualties of the First World War persuaded the army to permit women to enlist (although not for combat roles). About 57,000 women served with the Women's Army Auxiliary Corps (WAAC) which was formed in 1917, renamed as Queen Mary's Auxiliary Army Corps in 1918 and disbanded in 1920. About 10,000 women transferred to the Women's Royal Air Force when it was created in 1918 and their service records are in AIR 80 (see below). Incomplete nominal rolls of the WAAC are at TNA in WO 162/16 and WO 162/62. Many WAAC service records were destroyed in the Blitz, but about 9,000 women's records survived and are arranged alphabetically on microfilm in series WO 398. Women also played a vital part in the army's medical services and nurses' records are described below.

Records since 1920

Records of officers who served after 1922 and other ranks who served after 1920 are held by the Ministry of Defence. Information from the records is only released to the next of kin (or to others with the next of kin's consent). Applications must be made in writing to the Army Personnel Centre, Historical Disclosures, Mailpoint 400, Kentigern House, 65 Brown Street, Glasgow G2 8EX (telephone 0141 224 3030). A fee of £25 is charged for each name searched. If a man's records survive, the MOD will provide his number, date of enlistment, regiment (or regiments), date of discharge and list any medals awarded to him.

The MOD also has an enormous archive of personnel records of about 1.9 million civilians who have worked for the military or related organisations over the last 80 years. Information can be provided to those employees or their next of kin, as described in *Family Tree Magazine* (March 2003). Requests should be addressed to I. Todd, DSDC, Llangennech, Llanelli, Carmarthenshire SA14 8YP.

First World War casualties

The GRO registers of deaths have already been noted. TNA also holds (in RG 35/45–69) French and Belgian death certificates for British soldiers who died away from the immediate war zone (for example in hospitals). After the war about 1,150,000 memorial brass plaques (with scrolls) were issued to the next of kin of those who died, recording the deceased's name, rank and number. A relative may hold one for your ancestor.

Approximately 750,000 British soldiers were killed in the war or died from wounds or illness. Most of these men appear in published casualty lists. A volume entitled *Officers Died in the Great*

War (581) lists the names of about 39,000 officers and 80 volumes of *Soldiers Died in the Great War* (588) list about 667,000 other ranks. Men are listed alphabetically, but only within each battalion (of a regiment) or each corps. Entries note each man's rank, number, place of birth, place of enlistment and (if different) residence, date of death and the theatre of war in which the death occurred. Most entries state "France and Flanders", Italy or Egypt (which included Palestine, Syria and Libya). Copies of these volumes are held at the Imperial War Museum, TNA, the SoG and reference libraries. The volume for officers has been superseded by a 1988 reprint by J.B. Hayward (with over 1,600 new entries and a section of over 1,400 European officers of the Indian Army). Another useful source for officers who died in the war is *The Cross of Sacrifice* by Jarvis & Jarvis (649), the first volume of which lists officers who served in British, Indian and East African regiments and corps. Volume 3 lists officers who died serving in Commonwealth or Colonial units. The entries note each officer's rank, decorations, date of death, unit and place of burial (usually from registers of the Commonwealth War Graves Commission, considered below).

My great uncle, William Edward Herber was killed in the First World War. The GRO register of *War Deaths 1914–1921 (other ranks)* records his death in 1916. He was a private, number 7875, in the Royal Fusiliers (City of London Regiment). William is also listed in *Soldiers Died in the Great War*. He was in the regiment's 11th battalion and the entry (in illustration 100) is:

Herber, William Edward, b[orn] Stratford, e[nlisted] Hammersmith, [place of residence] Shepherd's Bush [number] 7875, P[riva]te, k[illed] in a[ction], F[rance] & F[landers] 26/9/16, formerly [number] 3815, Middlesex Regiment.

William and many others in the 11th Battalion had been transferred from the Middlesex Regiment (men who had completed training were often transferred to units that needed men to fill gaps in the ranks). The casualty list for the 11th Battalion was a reminder of how many men might be killed in one day during the war. The battalion suffered horrific casualties on 1 July 1916 and 26 September 1916 (when William died). Military histories record that on 26 September the 11th Royal Fusiliers played a significant part in the capture of Thiepval and I later discovered that William's name appears on the Thiepval Memorial in France.

The 80 volumes of *Soldiers Died in the Great War* and the volume for officers have been converted by NMP into two databases on a CD-ROM which can be purchased or consulted at the SoG, TNA and many archives or libraries. A key advantage of the disk over the printed volumes is that it is no longer necessary to know a man's regiment. It is much easier to find a man in two databases (if you do not know his unit) than it is to find him in hundreds of alphabetical listings for each battalion or corps. You can search for a man in each database by his full name or just his surname but the records include many men of the same name. If you find a number of men with the same name, you will need other evidence in order to establish which is your ancestor or relative. R. Goring reviews the CD-ROM and provides guidance on undertaking searches in *Family Tree Magazine* (November 1999).

Illustration 101 is a typical search result from the CD-ROM, showing the death of Alexander Luke of the 19th Battalion, the King's (Liverpool Regiment). You can also extract all entries for a particular surname. For example, I found 26 entries for men with my mother's surname, Eagles. You should note that the disk contains transcription errors (although some were corrected on version 1.1 of the disk). William Edward Herber appears on the disk as William Edward Herbert.

Hart, Archer Frederick Charles, b. Tooting, e. Tooting (Balham), 51766, Pte., k. in a., F. & F., 17/2/17, formerly 6911, Middx. Regt.

Hart, Thomas Benjamin, b. Hornsey, e. Highgate (Hornsey), 8538, Pte., k. in a., F. & F., 26/6/16.

Hart, William Claude, b. Kingscliffe, e. Golchester (West Ham), 8607, Pte., k. in a., F. & F., 18/1/16.

Harvey, Herbert, b. Isleham, e. Newmarket (Isleham), 40148, Pte., k. in a., F. & F., 10/8/17.

Harvey, James Harold, b. Islington, e. Whitehall (Islington), 75047, Pte., d. of w., F. & F., 24/3/18, formerly 42013, 99th T.R. Battn.

Hawkes, Thomas, b. Kingston, e. Surbiton (Kingston), 66996, Pte., k. in a., F. & F., 10/8/17, formerly 9965, E. Surrey Regt.

Hawkins, George Frederick, b. Ealing, e. Hounslow (Ealing), 7880, Pte., k. in a., F. & F., 22/12/15, formerly Middx. Regt.

Hayes, William, b. St. Andrew's, Dublin, e. Dublin (Dublin), L/100286, Pte., k. in a., F. & F., 29/9/18, formerly L/6134, R. Berks Regt.

Hayley, William John, e. Deptford (Rotherhithe), 12426, Pte., k. in a., F. & F., 29/10/17.

Hazell, Frederick William, b. Lambeth, e. Hounslow (Brixton), L/3566, C.S.M., k. in a., F. & F., 10/8/17.

Heads, Richard William, b. Shoreditch, e. Finsbury Barracks (Hoxton), SR/8266, Pte., k. in a., F. & F., 26/9/16.

Heath, Bernard, b. Raunds, Northants, e. Northampton (Northampton), 78811, Pte., k. in a., F. & F., 18/9/18, formerly 37073, E. Surrey Regt.

Heath, Joseph, b. Loughton, Staffs, e. Aldershot (Stoke-on-Trent), 79682, Pte., d. of w., F. & F., 31/8/18, formerly S/4/109838, A.S.C.

Hedgcock, Bertram, b. Ealing, e. Ealing (Ealing), 51714, Pte., k. in a., F. & F., 14/3/17, formerly 29251, K.R.R.C.

Hedges, William, b. St. Pancras, e. Holborn (Holborn), 7596, Pte., k. in a., F. & F., 25/10/16, formerly 3486, Middx. Regt.

Herber, William Edward, b. Stratford, e. Hammersmith (Shepherd's Bush), 7875, Pte., k. in a., F. & F., 26/9/16, formerly 3815, Middx. Regt.

Hern, Harry, b. St. Luke's, Leicester, e. Mill Hill (Market Harborough), 11888, Pte., k. in a., F. & F., 26/9/16.

Hewish, Thomas William, b. Clerkenwell, e. Holborn (Clerkenwell), 11984, Pte., k. in a., F. & F., 26/9/16.

Hewlett, Montague William, b. Kentish Town, e. Tonbridge (Tonbridge), 51752, Cpl., d., F. & F., 24/6/18, formerly 15609, R.W. Kent Regt.

Heywood, Arthur Percival, b. Unsworth, e. Bury (Unsworth), 8120, Pte., k. in a., F. & F., 1/7/16, formerly 4092, Middx. Regt.

Heywood, William, b. Weston-super-Mare, e. Bargoed (Bargoed), 8747, Pte., k. in a., F. & F., 26/9/16.

Higgins, Reginald Percy, b. Kennington, e. Camberwell (Tooting), 8134, L/Cpl., d. of w., F. & F., 25/2/17, formerly 4033, Middx. Regt.

Highley, Cecil Frank, b. Willesden, e. Finsbury Barracks (Balham), 26927, Pte., k. in a., F. & F., 23/10/17.

100. *Extract from* Soldiers Died in the Great War 1914–1919 *including William Edward Herber*

101. A typical search result from Soldiers Died in the Great War *on CD-ROM, from NMP, showing the death of Alexander Luke of the 19th Battalion, King's (Liverpool Regiment)*

Any entries that you extract from the disk should always be compared to the entries in the 81 published volumes.

The *National Roll of the Great War* (580) was an unofficial roll of honour of men and women who died and those who survived, providing service details and addresses of servicemen (or their next of kin) and war workers. Most of the information was obtained from the men (or women) or their families. Only 14 volumes were published, but they include about 150,000 people from places such as London, Southampton, Leeds, Manchester and Bedford. Copies are held at the Imperial War Museum and the SoG. Entries in each volume are in alphabetical order. NMP has reprinted the 14 volumes and published an extra volume containing an index to all the entries. A typical entry for a deceased soldier (from volume 12) is:

Eagles, R.E: 8th Middlesex Regiment. He was called up from the Reserve in August 1914 and quickly drafted to France, where he took part in the retreat from Mons and the battles of Ypres and Givenchy. He died gloriously on the field of battle at Hill 60 on April 30th, 1915 and was entitled to the Mons Star, and the General Service and Victory medals. 9 Farrar Street, Kempston, Bedford.

The Roll of Honour by Ruvigny (671) is another unofficial work providing details of about 25,000 men (from all branches of the armed forces) who were killed. Photographic portraits are included for about 7,000 men. Some entries are very short (perhaps just a name, unit and date and place of death), but many entries are very detailed (usually provided by the next of kin). A typical entry is that for George Sawyer Eagles:

> Private no. 24231. 1st battalion, the Buffs [East Kent Regiment], son of Alfred George Eagles of Holly Cottages, Wheat Ash Road, Addlestone, Surrey by his wife Harriett Jane, dau. of George Turner. Born Addlestone 10 September 1898. Educated St. James' Church of England School, Weybridge; employed at Lang's Propellor Works; enlisted 22 May 1917; trained at Dover; served . . . in France and Flanders from 29 September; died at the General Hospital, Camiers on 1 December 1917 from wounds received 20 November. Unmarried.

The Bond of Sacrifice by Clutterbuck (611) was intended to be a biographical record, with photographic portraits, of all British officers who died in the war. The project was defeated by the enormous number of casualties. Only two volumes, for August 1914 to June 1915, were published. As noted in chapter 13, the *British Jewry Book of Honour* by Adler (596) also includes many photographs of the 2,500 Jewish men who died fighting for Britain in the First World War.

Schools and colleges also published rolls of honour. A memorial volume for George Watson's Boys' College in Edinburgh (579) includes biographies of over 3,100 former pupils of the school who served in the war. It includes photographs of most of the 590 men who died. Illustration 102 is one of the pages of portraits. Harrow, Rugby, Stonyhurst, Downside, Tonbridge, Dulwich College and many other schools also issued memorial volumes with portraits of the deceased. Published school registers (# chapter 19) also included lists of their pupils or former pupils who had served or died in the war.

Commercial, professional and other organisations also commemorated the men who served or died. Examples of these memorial volumes (some with photographs) include those produced by Lloyds Bank, Cambridge University Press, the City of Manchester, the National Union of Teachers, Yorkshire Rugby Football Union and the Institution of Electrical Engineers. Solicitors and articled clerks (trainee solicitors) who served in the war were commemorated in a Law Society volume (584). It includes this biography for Frederick Gamble Barrett (who survived):

> Admitted January 1913, practising with Ernest Bevir & Son, of Devereux Chambers, Temple. Joined January 31, 1915 as 2nd Lieut, 21st Batt, London Regt, promoted Lieut. Jan. 1916, seconded to 181st Trench Mortar Battery July 1916 . . . served in France June 1916 to Nov. 1916, at Salonica Nov. 1916 to Aug. 1917 and in Palestine Aug. 1917 to July 1919.

Holding (645) is a directory of sources, arranged by English county then regiment, which list men who served in the war. It also lists the sources that cover the whole country, Scotland, Wales, Ireland or Jersey. Many of the sources are rolls of honour, similar to the examples noted above, published by schools, local government or professional, commercial and sporting organisations. Some rolls were not published but can be found in archives. For example, the Midland Railway Company roll of honour is at TNA (in piece RAIL 491/1259). For each regiment or corps, Holding (645) lists a selection of regimental, battalion or corps histories that have been published and also notes whether the regimental museum or local CRO holds any original records that may assist researchers. For example, the museum of the Foot Guard

102. *A page from the memorial volume for the First World War of former pupils of George Watson's Boys' College, Edinburgh*

regiments (at Wellington Barracks, London) holds the service records of men who served in those regiments since 1914. The museum may be able to assist men's next of kin (in response to written enquiries). Most other regiments do not hold any records of First World War officers or soldiers but some are in CROs. For example, recruiting books listing about 100,000 men are held at the Surrey History Centre in Woking (# appendix VII) and Somerset Record Office in Taunton has a list of Taunton residents who served in the war (with their service details).

Local newspapers are another useful source. Many carried reports on the circumstances of a local man's death or his receipt of a medal (perhaps including a photograph of the soldier and the name and address of his wife or parents). Newspaper reports have been used in many books on First World War soldiers. Some of these provide biographies of men named on a war memorial of a particular town or village. For example, Thorpe (683) is a study of the men of both world wars who are commemorated on the memorial at Wooburn, Buckinghamshire. The biographies include substantial genealogical information but also photographs and documents from each man's family or local sources. The "Pals" series of histories may also assist you. The Pals Battalions were formed from groups of friends or men who worked together and who volunteered to serve together in the war. Maddocks (656) is a history of the four Liverpool Pals Battalions, the 17th, 18th, 19th and 20th Battalions of The King's (Liverpool Regiment). There are similar "Pals" volumes, available from NMP, for another 32 battalions raised in Leeds, Barnsley, Manchester, Salford, Accrington, Sheffield, Hull, Tyneside and Birmingham. They describe each unit's part in the war and include photographs of some of the men, letters, diaries, and other documents from local archives or from soldiers' families. Some include lists of all the men who served or who were awarded gallantry medals.

First World War medical records
Holding (644) describes how wounded soldiers were moved away from the front line and treated at dressing stations or hospitals in France or England. These treated about 2½ million wounded men (many men were wounded more than once). All treatment points kept admission books for the sick or wounded, noting a man's name, rank, unit, number, date and the reason for admission. Record cards were kept for patients, and operations were noted in hospital log books. A sample of about 5–10 per cent of the records (about 2,000 boxes) survive at TNA in series MH 106. Holding (644) lists the hospitals and covering dates of these records. Medical units serving overseas also prepared war diaries (reviewed below), which are in series WO 95. Many of these listed the men who died whilst in their care. However, there are no indexes to these deaths and finding your ancestor in them would be extremely difficult.

First World War courts martial and executions
Courts martial records were noted above. Most sentences they imposed were periods of imprisonment or hard labour. However, conditions in the First World War were horrendous. Men were so affected by shellshock and trench warfare that the incidence of drunkenness, mutiny, desertion or mental illness (rarely recognised as such) increased. Registers of courts martial during the First World War are in pieces WO 86/62–86 (for District Courts Martial) and WO 90/6–8 and WO 213/2–26 (for more serious cases before Field General Courts Martial). Some other courts martial records are in WO 71 and death sentences are noted in WO 93/42–45.

Oram (663) lists over 3,000 soldiers who were sentenced to death by military courts between 1914 and 1924, with TNA references to the courts martial records. About 90% of the death sentences were commuted to other punishments, such as penal servitude, but 361 executions proceeded. These men were omitted from *Soldiers Died in the Great War*. For example, Private Edward Tanner, aged 33, of the 1st Battalion, the Wiltshire Regiment was found guilty of deserting in Flanders in 1914. He was executed on 27 October 1914 (recorded in WO 213/2 and WO 71/389). Over 2,000 British and Commonwealth soldiers were charged with mutiny in the period 1914–20 and almost 90% were convicted. The men are listed in Putkowski (668), with the punishments they received, references to the courts martial registers and a fascinating introduction about mutinies and army discipline. For example, 19 soldiers of the 12th Battalion, the South Wales Borderers were charged with mutiny in France in December 1916 and 17 of them, including Privates S. Kelly and T. Hale, were convicted and sentenced to periods of hard labour. Another mutiny occurred at Etaples in 1917 and 54 men were court-martialled for various offences (four for mutiny). These four were convicted; three were imprisoned and Corporal Jesse Short of the 26th Battalion, Northumberland Fusiliers was shot. An index to military courts' records has also been produced on CD-ROM by S. Tamblin (listed with his other indexes on the web site of Family History Indexes). This covers army courts martial from 1879 as well as trials of navy and air force personnel. It includes references for each man to the records in series WO 71 and 93 for soldiers, AIR 18 for airmen and ADM 1, 116, 156 and 167 for naval personnel.

Conscription and objectors
Following the introduction of conscription in 1916, men could appeal against their call-up to Military Service Tribunals. Appeals were made on the grounds of health, conscientious objection, the need to support relatives or the importance of a man's occupation (many applications for exemption were made by employers). The men, employers or army could appeal further, to a County Appeal Tribunal. About 16,500 men obtained exemption certificates from tribunals but many applications failed. Most tribunal records were destroyed, but some survive in CROs. The records of the Middlesex Appeals Tribunal (at TNA) and the Lothian and Peebles Tribunal (in the National Archives of Scotland) were retained as samples. The Middlesex records are in series MH 47, with a card index to about 12,000 names, and were reviewed by D. Hawkings in *Genealogists' Magazine* (December 1998). Some tribunal cases were reported in local newspapers. Slocombe (673) contains details of many cases heard by Military Service Tribunals in Wiltshire, including 683 cases in surviving records of the Calne Tribunal and about 900 other cases reported in newspapers. Thus John Williams Paradice of Trowbridge, a Great Western Railway porter, aged 38, appealed in March 1916. He stated that his widowed mother was dependent on him and that he had varicose veins and rheumatism. His appeal was dismissed. Walter Cox of Stert, aged 24, also appealed in 1916. He was employed by his mother (he was the only son) to farm the family's 60 acres. He was granted an absolute exemption (probably because of the country's need for food at this time).

Records of military actions during the First World War
If you wish to research the actions of specific units, you should first learn about the various fronts and campaigns. Brown (606) is a good general history of the war, based on photographs, letters and diaries held at the Imperial War Museum. Brown (605) uses similar sources to describe the

battles in France and Flanders. The official history of the war, in 21 volumes published from 1927 to 1949 by HMSO (reprinted by NMP), is available in reference libraries. Sixteen volumes describe the conflict in France and Flanders and others deal with the war in Italy, Africa and at Gallipoli. Many other works are available. Enser (621) is a detailed bibliography listing about 4,000 works, on all aspects of the war, arranged by subject. An enormous amount of material on the war is held at TNA. Beckett (599a) describes those sources for all aspects of the military conduct of the war, intelligence, government decision-making, conscription, food supply and other home front issues.

The British Army in France was divided into armies, each consisting of two or more corps. Each corps had a number of divisions and supporting troops (cavalry, artillery, medical corps and engineers) and a division had two or more brigades, each with three or four infantry battalions. Because of the size of the armies, general histories rarely mention smaller units. They record that a particular division took part in a battle, without specifying the battalions, so you must ascertain the division, corps or army in which an ancestor's battalion served. This is noted (with a detailed account of a unit's part in the war) in most regimental histories, listed in White (688). Alternatively, Gould (636) notes the theatres of war in which British cavalry, infantry and machine-gun units served. Thus it records that the 11th Battalion of the Royal Fusiliers, in which William Herber fought, served in France and Flanders from July 1915 and the 4th Battalion of the Norfolk Regiment served at Gallipoli, then in Egypt, Palestine and Syria. James (648) gives detailed information on the location of cavalry regiments and infantry battalions (extracted from regimental histories, orders of battle or war diaries) in August 1914 (or the date of formation), then listing their movements and final disposition in November 1918. The entry for the 11th Royal Fusiliers is:

Formed at Hounslow, 6th September 1914; to Colchester in 54th Brigade, 18th Division . . . May 1915. Salisbury Plain . . . July 1915 to France . . . on 11th November 1918 in 54th Brigade, 18th Division in France, near Le Cateau.

More detailed information is contained in *The Order of Battle of Divisions* by Becke (599). This lists (for each year) the battalions or other units in each division, corps or army in a theatre of war. Becke also lists the battles in which a division took part. Part 1 deals with the army divisions that existed in 1914; part 2 deals with territorial and yeomanry divisions; part 3 covers divisions that were raised from 1914; part 4 deals with corps (such as the Tank Corps), and part 5 deals with divisions of Empire or Dominion troops. Thus part 1 includes the 2nd Division, listing its commanding officers (and the actions in which it took part) and the infantry battalions, cavalry, artillery batteries and other units (such as engineers) that were in the division (as at August 1914, September 1915, June 1916, June 1917 and March 1918). There are also notes on the dates of units' formation and movements to France. Becke identifies 12 infantry battalions in the 2nd Division in June 1916 as well as units such as the 16th Field Artillery battery, the 5th Company of Field Engineers and the 100th Field Ambulance. Becke's work is thus a useful source of information about the service of ancestors who were in corps such as the artillery or engineers, since these units are not covered in the works by Gould and James noted above. Further information can also be obtained from the General Headquarters Orders of Battle of the British Armies in France at TNA in series WO 95, which describe the organisation of the British Army in France, showing (approximately monthly) the units that were serving in each army, corps or division.

You can then refer to the war diaries. Since 1907 each infantry battalion on active duty (and larger units such as divisions) as well as smaller corps, kept daily diaries with a detailed account of the unit's activities. They often mention officers (particularly those killed or wounded) but rarely name other ranks. The diaries can, however, give you a good idea of your ancestor's activities. Useful information about a battalion may also be found in its division's war diary. Over 10,000 diaries are in series WO 95, arranged according to the order of battle noted above (that is, by army, then corps, then division). In order to find a unit's war diary, you can search the WO 95 series list for references to the unit. You can also search PROCAT (remembering that units might be recorded by different names or abbreviations) to find the unit's diaries for various periods, or when it was serving in different theatres of war. Spencer (676) includes illustrations of pages from the war diary of the 7th Battalion, the Queen's Royal West Surrey Regiment. These recorded that 2nd Lieutenant H. A'Bear joined the battalion in January 1917 (having been promoted from the ranks and attended cadet school at GHQ). He was promoted to Acting Captain, in charge of A Company but was killed on 10 July 1917 by a shell that landed on the company's headquarters.

TNA also holds trench maps (which assist when reading war diaries) showing the complex trench systems and countryside in which operations took place. Trench maps of the Western Front are in series WO 297. Those for other theatres, such as Gallipoli and Italy, are in WO 298, 300–303 and 369. The Imperial War Museum also holds a collection of trench maps. The use of trench maps, in conjunction with war diaries, allows you to recreate your ancestor's life in the trenches. To assist such work, 175 trench maps from the Imperial War Museum collection, covering most of the Western Front, have been reproduced on CD-ROM by NMP. About 12,500 other British army maps from the Great War are in series WO 153. These maps and the collection of trench maps at TNA are described, with illustrations, by G. Beech in *Ancestors* (June/July 2002).

The Commonweath War Graves Commission and war memorials
The Commonwealth War Graves Commission (CWGC) maintains the graves or memorials to those men of the Imperial forces who died in the First World War (about 1.1 million) and the Second World War (about 580,000). The CWGC has registers for each cemetery (and all casualties are recorded in a computer database) which include information from each man's headstone and details of some men's next of kin. Many bodies could not be identified (or found), so memorials were erected to those men and there are similar registers for each memorial.

Hundreds of the CWGC cemetery and memorial registers were published in *The War Graves of the British Empire*. For example, volumes 14–19 of the published memorial registers contain the CWGC register for the Thiepval Memorial, listing 73,077 men who died on that part of the front and whose bodies were not found. The register of the Highland cemetery at Le Cateau is in volume 12 (591) for French cemeteries with maps showing the location of the cemetery and the plots that it contains. There are alphabetical lists of the deceased (noting each grave's location in the cemetery by plot, row and grave number). A typical entry from the Highland cemetery register is:

Ballard, Pte. Thomas Harold, 14320. 3rd Bn. Royal Fusiliers. Killed in action 17th Oct. 1918. Age 21. Son of Thomas and Eliza Ballard of White House, Ninfield, Battle, Sussex. Plot III. Row E. Grave 19.

If you do not know where a man was buried you will find it impossible to find him in the hundreds of published registers. However, the CWGC registers and indexes can be consulted on a database, *The Debt of Honour*, on the CWGC web site. This database includes about 1.7 million Commonwealth servicemen and women who were casualties in the two world wars and were buried in (or commemorated on) over 23,000 cemeteries or memorials around the world. The database also includes the entries from the Civilian Roll of Honour (the original of which is on display in Westminster Abbey) that lists over 66,400 Commonwealth civilians who were killed in the Second World War. As noted, my grandfather's brother, William Edward Herber, was killed in 1916. My father's half-brother also died in service during the Second World War. The entries for these men in *The Debt of Honour* are:

In memory of William Edward Herber, Private 7875, 11th Bn., Royal Fusiliers who died on Tuesday, 26th September 1916.
Thiepval Memorial, Somme, France. Pier and Face 8 C 9A and 16A.

In memory of Donald Henry Herber, Sapper 2030344, 582 Army Field Coy. Royal Engineers who died on Thursday, 19th September 1940. Age 24. Son of Henry John and Florence Jessie Herber of Westminster, London.
Northfleet Cemetery, Kent; grave reference Sec. C. Grave 24.

The CWGC allows free access to the database and it is very easy to use. The registers include many men with the same name (for example 11 men named Thomas William Green). It is therefore vital, for common names, to insert as much information as possible in the search request screen boxes (such as the man's unit, if known). If there is a known grave, the CWGC may be able to provide a photograph of the gravestone. You should write to the Records & Enquiries Section of the CWGC at 2 Marlow Road, Maidenhead, Berkshire SL6 7DX (telephone 01628 634221). There is a small fee (and additional donations are always welcome).

There are many war memorials in Britain to commemorate those who died (# chapter 8 and illustrations 43 and 44), particularly on village greens or in churches. These were usually erected shortly after the First World War and more names were added after 1945. A memorial outside St Matthew's Church in Clapton in London records the names of Joseph and William Sheppard, two brothers of my great grandmother. There are also memorials at places such as railway stations, commemorating the railway employees who served and died. If your ancestor is named on such a memorial, you should photograph the memorial (with a close-up of the names) to add to your file. The Imperial War Museum and RCHM are preparing a National Inventory of War Memorials (NIWM), recording the location of all war memorials in Britain, whether monuments or tablets and plaques in churches or other public buildings. The archive includes a record of about 45,000 memorials (of the 54,000 estimated to survive in Britain). It does not record the names on memorials, but those names are being listed by some family history societies and individuals. For example, West Surrey FHS has produced a microfiche index to the names of over 35,000 men and women who died in the two world wars and who are commemorated on war memorials and rolls of honour in Surrey. Transcriptions of the names on war memorials also appear on hundreds of web sites and those sites concerning English or Welsh memorials are listed in two volumes by Raymond (668a). The SoG's collection of MIs (# chapter 8) includes a large number copied from war memorials.

THE SECOND WORLD WAR

Soldiers' service records for the Second World War are only released by the Ministry of Defence to veterans or to the next of kin of deceased soldiers, but casualty records are available. The GRO registers of Second World War deaths and the CWGC records were noted above. TNA also holds a roll of honour (in series WO 304), listing over 171,000 officers and men who died between September 1939 and December 1946, including many who died of their wounds or sickness after the end of the war. It consists of two lists, one in alphabetical order of surname and one arranged by regiment. The roll notes each man or woman's rank, army service number, regiment or corps, date of death and place of birth, residence and death (codes indicate the regiment or unit, rank and places of birth, domicile and death). The roll is being published, with codes replaced by unit and place names, in a series of 10 volumes, each with a name index. The first four, by Devereux & Sacker (618), are available. Volume 1 includes the cavalry regiments, Yeomanry, Royal Armoured Corps, Royal Tank Regiment and the Brigade of Guards. A typical entry is that for George Abbots of the Welsh Guards.

Guardsman [no.] 4191572. Born Staffordshire, [domicile] Denbighshire. Died North Africa 12/4/43.

NMP has published a database of the complete roll of honour on CD-ROM, reviewed by R. Goring in *Family Tree Magazine* (October 2001). The search screen for the database is similar to that for the CD-ROM of *Soldiers Died in the Great War*. It is possible to search not only by a person's name but also by regiment or unit, date of death or gallantry medal. A search may lead to many entries, brief details of which are listed, so that you can choose any worth viewing in full or printing out.

Schools, colleges and commercial organisations published memorial volumes to the men and women who served or died in the Second World War. For example, The Commercial Bank of Scotland memorial volume (592) lists all of its employees who served (and photographs of employees who died), as in the following example:

HUTTON, George H. Sergeant, Royal Scots Fusiliers. [Branch] Grassmarket, Edinburgh.

A book of remembrance and roll of honour for Mill Hill School, by Brett-James (602), includes biographies of former pupils who served in the war and photographs of those who died. Dulwich College, Wellington College and many other schools produced similar volumes.

There are many books about the war from which you can obtain information on campaigns, regiments, aircraft, ships or life on the home front. Liddell Hart (652) is a good general work and Gardiner (247) is a collection of photographs of life in Britain during the war. Enser (622) and (623) are detailed bibliographies for all aspects of the war, listing books by subject (such as the Battle of Britain, the Home Guard or nurses). In addition, TNA holds millions of documents, described by Cantwell (607), about military operations and life on the home front. Army operational records are also described in TNA military records leaflets 68. In particular, monthly returns of army units are in series WO 73. Orders of battle (in WO 212) have been published by HMSO. The war diaries of army units are in WO 165–179, 215, 218 and 257, arranged by theatre of war and then by orders of battle. Researchers must sign a confidentiality undertaking relating to any personal information contained in the diaries.

Records of militia and similar units are considered below but the Second World War resulted in the creation of the most famous British units of amateur soldiers. The Home Guard was founded in 1939 and by 1943 almost 1.8 million men were serving with it. Most surviving Home Guard records, such as attestation and service records, are held by the Ministry of Defence, but some are in CROs. A list of Home Guard officers in 1944 is at TNA in series WO 199. TNA also holds some operational records and war diaries of the Home Guard in PREM 3 and WO 166. Histories of some units are in series WO 199. Officers of the Home Guard are included in the *Home Guard Lists* of 1941 to 1944 (in similar form to army lists) in the library at TNA. Whittaker (689) contains the Orders of Battle for Home Guard units in November 1944, with the date of a unit's formation and the name of its commanding officer.

Service Voters' Registers were compiled in 1945 to permit servicemen and women to vote in the General Election in the constituency of their home address. Some registers survive in local record offices or local authority archives. They include a person's name, address, unit and number but are not indexed by name, so a home address must be known in order to find a serviceman and ascertain the unit in which he served.

MEDALS

Medals were instituted in the early 19th century for officers and other ranks, although senior officers sometimes received decorations at earlier dates for particular battles. There were three types of medal: for campaigns (or particular battles), for good conduct (or long service) and for gallantry. If your family have an ancestor's medal, it can be identified by consulting published books on medals such as Purves (667), Abbott & Tamplin (594) or Joslin (650), which deals with 184 gallantry, campaign or other medals, providing details of the battles and campaigns, some of the regiments involved and some of the recipients of medals. An ancestor's medals may have been lost (or sold by a soldier or his family many years ago) but many medals can be found in specialist shops or markets. Some dealers offer a search service for medals and an article on these services appears in *Family Tree Magazine* (February 1996).

Information about many medals awarded to soldiers since 1919 is held at the Army Medals Office, Ministry of Defence, Government Buildings, Worcester Road, Droitwich, Worcestershire WR9 8AU. Written applications should include as much information as possible and an SAE.

The first campaign medal to be issued was the Waterloo Medal of 1815, which was awarded to all men who took part in the battle (or their next of kin). A medal roll at TNA, in piece MINT 16/112 (a published version is available from NMP) lists the regiments in the battle and the names and ranks of officers and men who received the medal. Recipients of other campaign medals up to 1912 are listed on medal rolls on microfilm in series WO 100 at TNA, arranged by campaign (or battle) then regiment, rank and surname. The rolls for the Crimean War 1854–55 (about 7,000 pages in pieces WO 100/22–34) have been reproduced on a CD-ROM reviewed in *Family Tree Magazine* (August 2003). Most of the rolls are listed by S. Dymond in *Family Tree Magazine* (March 1996). They include a roll for the Military General Service Medal and medals for the Crimean War, the Indian mutiny, campaigns in Egypt (1882) and Sudan (1896) and the Boer War (1899–1902). Many of these medal rolls have been published and copies are at the SoG and TNA. For example, Mullen (662) is the roll for the Military General Service Medal, about 25,000 of which were issued in 1847 to those men (still living) who had served in the wars with the French from 1793 to 1815. The roll is arranged by regiment. Another example, Everson (624), is the roll for the 1853 South Africa medal, which was awarded to soldiers who fought in wars in Southern Africa from 1834, but also to men of the Royal Navy, Royal Marines and some local units. The lists are transcribed from the army medal rolls in WO 100 or the navy and marines' rolls (# chapter 21) in series ADM 171. The Ashanti Star was awarded to about 2,500 men who took part in a campaign in 1895 to capture the King of Ashanti in West Africa. The roll of recipients, in WO 100/79, has been published in McInnes & Fraser (659) with additional biographical information about the men from campaign reports, service records and newspaper articles.

Campaign medal rolls for the First World War are in over 3,200 volumes in series WO 329 and described in TNA military records leaflet 76. The principal campaign medals were as follows:

a. 1914 Star (or Mons Star) for men serving from August to November 1914
b. 1914–1915 Star for men who served up to 31 December 1915 but who had not received the 1914 Star
c. British War Medal for soldiers who served overseas from 1914 to 1918
d. Victory Medal for soldiers serving in an overseas theatre of war
e. Territorial Force War Medal
f. Silver War Badge

The 1914–1915 Star awarded to Private T. Cooke of the Worcestershire Regiment and the British War and Victory medals awarded to Private L. Cheeseman of the 16th Battalion of the Royal Fusiliers are shown in illustration 103. The men's names, regiments and numbers are inscribed on the medal rims. A copy of the Army Medal Office's card index for the First World War (for recipients of these six medals and for men who were mentioned in despatches) is held on about 10,000 microfiche at TNA (series WO 372). The index cards are in alphabetical order of surname, then forename or initials. You are given the fiche (each with up to 360 cards) that includes the surname that you wish to search. Each card notes a man's rank, medals, unit and the Army Medal Office references (a number and page) for the rolls in series WO 329. The card in WO 372 for my grandfather, Henry John Herber, confirmed that he served as a gunner in the Royal Field Artillery and received the Victory and British War Medals (both awards having the reference page 34473 of roll RFA/272B). Piece WO 329/1 is the medal roll key (a volume in the microfilm reading room) which, for each regiment or unit, gives a volume number for these medal office references. You can then find that regiment and volume in the WO 329 series list and order the relevant piece from WO 329. Illustrations in Spencer (676) show the typical layout of cards in WO 372 and a sample page from the medal rolls in WO 329.

Privates and NCOs received long service and good conduct medals. Rolls of awards from 1831 to 1953 are at TNA in series WO 102. The Meritorious Service Medal (MSM) was awarded from 1846 to selected NCOs to reward long service. A roll of awards up to 1919 is in WO 101. Some recipients of these medals also received annuities, a register of which (for 1846–79) is in piece WO 23/84. Rolls for later awards of all these medals are held by the MOD. Between 1916 and 1928, the MSM was also awarded to warrant officers, NCOs and other ranks in the army, navy, RFC and RAF as a reward for meritorious service. The awards were announced in the *London Gazette* and the 27,500 recipients are listed in McInnes (657).

103. First World War medals: the British War Medal, the Victory Medal and the 1914–15 Star

Records of campaign medals awarded during the Second World War are held at the Army Medals Office. If you locate a relative's medals for this war, they can be identified from published works on medals, such as Joslin (650). The campaign medals of WW2 were:

a. 1939–45 Star, awarded for six months service between 1939 and 1945

b. War Medal 1939–45, awarded for service of at least 28 days between 1939 and 1945

c. Africa Star, for service in North or East Africa 1940–3

d. Pacific Star, for service in Hong Kong, China or Malaya 1941–5

e. Burma Star, for service in Burma, Bengal or Assam 1941–5 and China or Malaya 1942–5

f. Italy Star, for service in Italy, Greece and Yugoslavia 1943–5

g. France and Germany Star, for service in France, Belgium, Netherlands and Germany 1944–5

h. Air Crew Europe Star, for operational flying over the UK and Europe 1939–44

i. Atlantic Star, for six months service in the Atlantic, home waters or on convoys to Russia

j. The Defence Medal for three years service in the UK or one year overseas

Gallantry medals were first awarded during the Crimean War and the awards are reviewed in Abbot & Tamplin (594). Rolls of recipients of gallantry medals (noting regiments and ranks) are at TNA in series WO 146 for the Distinguished Conduct Medal (DCM), in WO 98, WO 32 and CAB 106 for the Victoria Cross (VC), and in WO 32 for the Distinguished Service Order (DSO). Awards of gallantry medals were also announced in the *London Gazette* and many lists of recipients have been published.

The DCM was instituted in 1855 for army NCOs and privates (there were also some awards to air force and naval personnel). Recipients of the DCM up to 1909 are listed in Abbot (595). For example, Private Edward Battle of the 66th Foot received the DCM for gallantry at the battle of Maiwand in 1880. From 1881 a bar was awarded to recipients for subsequent gallantry. Awards of bars before 1914 are listed in Abbot & Tamplin (594). Walker (684) lists awards of the DCM from 1914 to 1920, to British and Commonwealth troops (over 25,000 men), extracted from *London Gazette* citations. Entries note the *Gazette's* date, a man's rank, regiment, number and sometimes the theatre of war and his battalion or company, for example J.W. Scott (of 459 Battery, Royal Field Artillery), W. Hendersen (8th Battalion, Gordon Highlanders) and Charles Richard Garner (my great grandmother's brother), who was then in the Royal Engineers:

32790   Cpl. (Acting. Serjeant) Garner, C.R.   6.2.18.

Published booklets for each regiment or corps reproduce the DCM citations from the *Gazette* (and the date of the *Gazette* entry). A typical citation, dated 15 March 1916, in the booklet for the King's Shropshire Light Infantry (577) is:

9159. Sjt. T. Barrett 1st Battalion. For conspicuous gallantry during and after a gas attack. He went across 60 yards of open ground within close range of the enemy, to bring back a man who had been incapacitated.

Almost 2,000 men received the DCM in the Second World War. The awards were announced in the *London Gazette*. Brown (604) lists the recipients from 1939 to 1992 with the text of original recommendations for the award, prepared by units shortly after the act of courage. These provide much more detail than the citations in the *Gazette* (to which a cross-reference is also provided).

The DSO was instituted in 1886 for junior officers (in all services) and extended in 1943 to merchant navy and Home Guard officers. Over 1,700 awards of the DSO were made before 1914, over 9,000 during the First World War and about 5,000 between 1920 and 1945. Awards were noted in the *Gazette* and in a register in WO 390 (arranged by date). Recipients up to 1920 are listed, with biographical details, in Creagh & Humphris (615).

The Victoria Cross was instituted for all ranks and services in 1856. Awards were announced in the *Gazette*. About 1,160 men received the VC up to 1920 and are listed in Creagh & Humphris (615), with the *Gazette* entries, photographs (and biographies) of many recipients and accounts of the acts that resulted in awards. *The Register of the Victoria Cross* (585) includes photographs and brief biographical details of the 1,348 recipients of the medal up to 1981. Detailed biographies of the men who were awarded the VC from 1914 to 1918 are contained in a series of volumes, *VCs of the First World War*, including *The Somme* and *The Road to Victory 1918* by Gliddon (633) and (634). Laffin (651) contains biographies of the 106 men of the British armed forces who were awarded the VC during the Second World War. The Military Historical Society also holds detailed biographical information about each recipient of the VC.

The Military Cross was instituted in January 1915 for officers below the rank of captain and also warrant officers (sergeant majors). Bars were awarded for subsequent acts of bravery. Over 37,000 medals (and about 3,000 bars) were awarded up to 1920 and announced in the *London Gazette*. Copies of the *Gazette*, with manuscript annotations as to the date and place of the action for which the Military Cross was awarded are in pieces WO 389/1–8, with indexes in WO 389/9–24. Webb (686) lists awards to warrant officers up to 1920 (and all recipients of bars) with each man's rank, unit, date of award and the date of the *Gazette* citation. A further 11,000 awards were made between 1921 and 1945, with about 500 bars.

The Military Medal was instituted in 1916 for army NCOs and other ranks (there were also some awards to naval and air force personnel). The roll for the Military Medal will soon be transferred into series WO 326 at TNA (a card index of recipients, on microfilm, is already available). Awards were recorded in the *Gazette*. Over 115,000 awards were made during the First World War. Almost 16,000 awards were made between 1919 and 1945 and a list of recipients since 1919 has been published. The Conspicuous Gallantry Medal and the Distinguished Service Medal were instituted for Royal Marines (and naval personnel) and are considered in chapter 21.

Gallantry awards to all ranks were listed in the *London Gazette*. Until 1941, announcements were usually arranged by award, so it can be difficult to find an entry without knowing the type of award and approximate date (the *Gazette*'s lists of awards during the First World War were enormous). TNA holds quarterly indexes to the *Gazette*'s entries of 1914–21 for the DCM, MM and MSM. Each quarter's index lists men's names in alphabetical order with a page number. The series list at TNA for the *Gazette* (ZJ 1) tells you the month (and TNA piece number) of the issue of the *Gazette* that includes that page. The *Gazette* also printed despatches of commanding officers (in the field or at sea) that mentioned men's courageous acts. At first, the despatches only noted officers but the practice was extended to other ranks. Sadly, "mentions" in the *Gazette* during the two world wars usually gave only a man's name, and rarely describe his act. TNA has microfiche card indexes to these mentions (which are used in the same way as the quarterly indexes to medal awards). Men who were mentioned in despatches since 1914 were also awarded a bronze oak leaf (to be worn on one of their campaign medals). Over 141,000 mentions were gazetted during the First World War, and during the Second, over 12,000 mentions were gazetted in 1942 alone.

Awards for gallantry in the Second World War were announced in the *London Gazette* and recommendations for those awards are on microfilm at TNA in series WO 373 arranged by theatre of war and then in date order.

You might also investigate whether your ancestor received any medal or award from a foreign country. For example, many British servicemen received medals from the White Russian government during the British intervention in the Russian civil war (1918–20). The recipients of these awards (army, marine, navy and air force personnel) are listed in Brough (603), which also lists British servicemen who are buried in Russia. Thus Lieutenant T.F. Aitchison of the RAF was awarded the medal of St Stanislaus and Private Anthony Lewis of the 9th Battalion, the

Royal Warwickshire Regiment, is buried in Baku British Military Cemetery (having died of malaria in July 1919). Lists of the recipients of other foreign awards, such as the Croix de Guerre and Legion d'Honneur, are in series WO 388 and in the *London Gazette*.

PRISONERS OF WAR

The information available about prisoners of war is very incomplete. TNA holds some lists (in series ADM 103) of British prisoners held in France between 1793 and 1815 and other sources are noted in Bevan (239). About 180,000 British men were taken prisoner during the First World War. Deaths of prisoners of war in enemy territory were notified to the British authorities and should appear in the GRO death indexes. The names of nearly all British and Commonwealth officers (army, air force or Royal Naval Division) who were taken prisoner in the First World War (about 8,700 men) are recorded in a published list (578), copies of which are at the SoG and TNA. Entries are arranged by unit (with dates of capture and release) but indexed.

Some of the First World War medal entitlement cards in WO 372 indicate that a man was taken prisoner by the letters "P of W" but not all prisoners can be identified in this way. A few thousand reports by men as to their capture and treatment in captivity are in WO 161/95–100 (with name indexes in WO 161/101). A. Bowgen describes these records in *Ancestors* (February/March 2002).

British servicemen who died in captivity during the Second World War should appear in the GRO registers of war deaths (# chapter 5). TNA also holds substantial records for prisoners of war in the Second World War (described in TNA military records leaflet 19), but there are no comprehensive lists of prisoners and the records are in many series. For example, lists of British and Dominion airmen held prisoner in Germany in 1944 and 1945 are in AIR 20/2336, AIR 40/263–281 and AIR 40/1448–91. A list of Royal Marines held in German POW camps between 1939 and 1945 is in ADM 201/111 and some lists of naval personnel in German POW camps are in files in ADM 1 and 116. HMSO published some rolls of prisoners in 1945 and these have been reprinted. One of these (582) is an alphabetical list of about 107,000 officers and men of the British Army who were captured by the Germans, noting each man's name, rank, number and unit, as well as the camp in which he was confined. A similar volume (583) lists captured men who served in the RAF, the navy and merchant marine (as well as men who served in the Australian, Canadian, New Zealand and South African air forces). For example, W.G. Hodge (a greaser on the merchant ship *Cymbeline*) was a prisoner in Marlag POW camp. These volumes were prepared from a number of sources, including incomplete lists of British prisoners of war held by the Germans and Italians which are at TNA in series WO 392. Some other lists of prisoners from each branch of the armed forces are listed in Bevan (239).

The Japanese took about 50,000 British and 140,000 Imperial, Dominion and American servicemen prisoner during the Second World War of whom about 60,000 died (12,000 of them British). The Japanese also detained about 130,000 British civilians of whom 14,000 died. Series WO 345 is a card index of about 57,000 British, Indian and Australian prisoners held by the Japanese. The cards include a prisoner's name, rank, date of birth, parent's names, unit, date (and place) of capture. There are also registers of prisoners held in Singapore (in WO 367) and an alphabetical list of prisoners held in Japan (or in Japanese-occupied territories) in WO 392/23–26. Japanese prison camps are listed by G. Thompson in *Family Tree Magazine*

(November 1999) who also reviews the WO 345 card index and WO 367 registers in detail (and notes some other surviving records and published diaries of prisoners held by the Japanese).

Records of prisoners of war and civilian internees were kept during both world wars by national branches of the Red Cross. The records are now held centrally by the Archives Division and Research Service, International Committee of the Red Cross, 19 Avenue de la Paix, Geneva CH 1202. Searches are made in the records for an hourly fee in response to written enquiries that note a person's full name and nationality (and if possible information such as regiment or date of birth).

ARMY NURSES

TNA military records leaflet 55 describes the history of army nursing services and the available records. Until the Crimean War army medical services were provided by regimental medical officers and orderlies. The inadequacies of this service became apparent in the Crimean War and the Army Hospital Corps (later the Royal Army Medical Corps) was created and female nurses were recruited in the 1860s into an Army Nursing Service (ANS). Medical and nursing services expanded and Queen Alexandra's Imperial Military Nursing Service (QAIMNS) was established (in place of the ANS) in 1902. The Territorial Force Nursing Service (TFNS) was also formed in 1908 to support the Territorial Army. TNA holds only a few records of early military nurses, for example some lists of nurses serving in the Crimea and rolls in WO 100 for the South Africa medal. Service records do not survive for the ANS. However, service records (including enlistment and discharge papers and correspondence) of over 15,000 nurses in QAIMNS and TFNS up to 1922 survive in two alphabetical sequences in series WO 399. These include some nurses who served between 1922 and 1939. Some pension records for QAIMNS are in PMG 34/1–5 and PMG 42/1–12. Nurses also received the First World War service medals noted above and so can be found in the rolls and card index in WO 329 and 372.

INDEXES

Many people or organisations have compiled specialist indexes containing information on those who served in the armed forces. An example is the Turner index of all NCOs and soldiers (about 200,000 names) for the April to June quarter of 1861 (extracted from muster rolls and paylists). The index gives names, ranks, numbers and regiments. Details of this index and many others are contained in Gibson & Hampson (158). B. Oldham has compiled an index of over 100,000 men of the British Army who served in the Crimean War. This index is described in *Ancestors* (June/July 2003).

MILITIA RECORDS

The Home Guard was noted above, but local defence forces (known as militia) have been levied since Anglo-Saxon times and records survive from the 16th century. Many muster rolls, listing adult men available for military service, survive for the period 1522–1640 and they (and the archives holding them) are listed in Gibson & Dell (631). Most of the records are held by TNA, CROs or the British Library. The holdings of TNA are in Exchequer Papers or State Papers Domestic. The amount of surviving documentation varies from county to county but there are usually good collections for 1522, 1539, 1542, 1569 and 1624. Most rolls are arranged by hundred, then parish, and list the able-bodied men who were called (or liable to be called) to arms. A man's income determined what arms or armour he had to provide, and so the rolls may indicate either his income or the arms. Gibson & Dell (631) list the rolls that have been published, such as some Bedfordshire rolls in Lutt (654) and a Devon muster roll of 1569 (with about 18,000 names) in Howard & Stoate (647). The rolls are a useful addition to parish registers. The registers of Winkleigh in Devon include the Bulleid or Bulhead family back to John Bulhead who married in 1582. The registers only commence in 1569, so John's parents are not recorded, but the 1569 muster roll includes Henry Bullhead (an archer) of Winkleigh. Was he John's father?

The Militia Act of 1757 established militia regiments for each county and required each parish to provide a number of able-bodied men, aged between 18 and 50 (reduced to 45 in 1762) for militia training. There were not enough volunteers so men were conscripted into the militia by a ballot system. Lists of suitably aged men were prepared. Clergy, teachers, seamen, apprentices, magistrates, peers (and men with infirmities) were excused service, but an act of 1758 required all men of the relevant age (even those excused service) to be listed. If a man was chosen in the ballot but was unwilling to serve, he had to find (and usually pay) a substitute to serve in his place. From 1757 to 1831 most militia ballot lists noted men's names and whether they had any infirmities (for example noting them as lame or blind). From 1758 most lists also noted a man's occupation; from 1802 the number of his children (and whether they were aged over or under 14) and, from 1806, a man's age. A man's previous service in the militia, or in the volunteers or yeomanry (discussed below) may also have been noted. The system was organised by the Lords Lieutenant of each county, Justices of the Peace and parish constables. Surviving lists are at CROs (usually in the Lord Lieutenant's or Justices' papers). Militia regiments' records are considered below.

Militia units served in Britain or Ireland but not overseas. Men had to serve for three years (for five years after 1786). In peacetime the men spent just a few weeks a year at military camps but, during a war, they were on duty for much of the year and their unit might serve anywhere in Britain. This may explain a man's marriage many miles from his home. For example, the parish registers of Barnstaple in Devon, note these marriages in 1797:

7th Feb. John House of the Surrey Cavalry, of Chiswick & Grace Hill.
14th Dec. James Hayward, militia man of St Edmunds, Salisbury & Mary Blake.

During the French wars of 1793–1815, some other auxiliary troops, known as yeomanry (which were cavalry), volunteers or fencible infantry or cavalry were raised in each county. Fencibles were regular troops, but only for home defence. The men were volunteers but were usually paid. By 1800 there were about 110,000 men in such units and by 1805 about 330,000. Records of these militia and volunteer units are considered below. Legislation of 1798 and 1803 also required men to be listed for the organisation of further reserve forces, called the *Posse Comitatus* (in 1798) and the *Levée en Masse* (in 1803/4). Lists were prepared of the able-bodied men in each parish aged between 15 and 60 (17 and 55 in 1803) who were not already serving in the militia. They were not required to join the militia but (if the French invaded) they were to assist the military (for example by evacuating civilians). Separate schedules were prepared of men who were bakers or millers or who owned barges or wagons. The schedules of 1803 were very detailed, noting men's names, occupations and infirmities, and dividing them into four classes which indicated a man's marital status, his age (or age group) and the number of children he had aged under 10 years. The schedules also noted the number of men and women in a household (and the names of women, children and the aged who would have to be evacuated). Many returns have not survived but the Buckinghamshire returns of 1798 list 27,000 men (and can be purchased on a computer disk) and the lists of 1803 for Bedfordshire have been published in Lutt (654).

Most volunteer units were disbanded after the French wars, but the yeomanry regiments remained in existence throughout the 19th century (about 15,000 men were serving in them in 1838), often helping to curb local disorder. Conscription into the militia continued, but was generally hated and sometimes led to rioting. The militia ballot was therefore suspended in 1829 and no lists were made (or ballots held) after 1831. The militia was then recruited only from volunteers. An invasion scare in 1859 caused many men to volunteer for local defence. The Rifle Volunteers were formed in 1860 and almost 120,000 men enlisted by October 1860. Westlake (687) lists, by county, each unit of the Rifle Volunteers and its subsequent history. In 1881 the militia and volunteer units became linked (usually as third or fourth militia or volunteer battalions) to the regular army regiments (the yeomanry remained separate). Thus the various Rifle Volunteer Corps raised in Bedfordshire in 1860 were re-designated as the 3rd Volunteer Battalion (and the Hertfordshire militia became the 4th Volunteer Battalion) of the Bedfordshire Regiment. Spencer (675) lists these changes. From 1881 the records of volunteers and militia are usually held with the records of the regiment concerned (usually at TNA). The Imperial Yeomanry was formed in 1899 because of the need for mounted infantry to serve in South Africa and about 39,000 men (many from the yeomanry but some with no military training) had been raised by 1902. The Special Reserve (also known as the Territorials) was formed in 1908 and the volunteer battalions were transferred into this new force, but kept their regimental name and link. For example, the 3rd and 4th Volunteer Battalions of the Bedfordshire Regiment were amalgamated as the 5th Battalion, the Bedfordshire Regiment, but then formed part of the Territorials. The Special Reserve was merged with the yeomanry in 1921 to form the Territorial Army. Over 700,000 men enlisted with the Territorials during the First World War. Almost 700 territorial infantry battalions were formed and many of them served in France. Territorial units also served alongside regular army units during the Second World War.

Steppler (676a) is a history of the British volunteer soldier since the 18th century, with a useful bibliography (and detailed information on militia and volunteer units in Rutland and Leicestershire). Gibson & Medlycott (632) list, by county, the location of surviving militia records for 1757 to 1856 and any indexes or published lists of the militiamen. Most records are held at TNA or CROs, though some are in the British Library. Published militia lists include a selection from Bedfordshire in Lutt (654) and a *levée en masse* list for Exeter in 1803, in Hoskins (646). This contains over 3,100 names. Typical entries from the parishes of Holy Trinity and Allhallows on the Walls are:

Name	Description		Remarks
John Bullied	Officer of Customs	[Class] 4 [between 17 and 55]	–
William Syms	Salesman	[Age] 52	Infirm

In addition to the ballot lists (of those eligible for militia service), there are also muster rolls and other records of the men who actually served. Spencer (675) describes the holdings at TNA of records of militia or similar units since 1757. The War Office published some lists of militia officers from 1794 (copies are at TNA) and officers of the militia and rifle volunteers appear in the army lists from 1865. The British and Bodleian libraries also hold some lists of militia officers (for 1780–1825) which are reviewed in Hamilton-Edwards (640). Appointments of militia officers were recorded in the *London Gazette*. Some lists of officers' commissions and returns of officers' service for 1780 to 1840 are in Home Office correspondence (in series HO 50) and some records of commissions are in the military entry books for 1758–1855 (in HO 51). A few birth and baptism certificates of the children of militia officers are in WO 32.

Muster books and pay lists of militia regiments are at TNA, arranged by county, in series WO 13 (1780–1878) and WO 68 (1859–1925). Indexes to the militia muster books of 1781–82 in WO 13 have been produced on fiche and computer disk by L. Hore and S. Tamblin for most English and Welsh counties. These note each man's name, rank and company, the dates of musters he attended (and whether he was chosen by ballot or was a substitute). The indexes produced to date include about 23,000 men. Attestation papers of militiamen (1769–1915) are in series WO 96 and 97, arranged by regiment, then alphabetically by surname. Series WO 68 also contains monthly returns (of the location of militia regiments) and some regiments' enrolment books, with recruits' names, places of birth and attestation, physical descriptions, dates of promotions and previous military service. The series also contains some registers of militamen's marriages and the baptism of their children, casualty books for 1759–1925 (including records of desertions and discharges) and some courts martial records. Records of pension payments to militiamen between 1817 and 1927 are in series PMG 13 and registers of militiamen who became out-pensioners of Chelsea Hospital up to 1913 are in WO 116.

Some militia records are at CROs, so if TNA does not have a unit's records, you should try the CRO for the unit's county. The Honourable Artillery Company (the senior regiment in the Territorial Army) has for centuries been the City of London militia unit. Its archives (at Armoury House, City Road, London EC1) are described in Gibson & Medlycott (632) and include rolls of members from 1611 (complete from 1682). Guildhall Library holds annual printed lists of members from 1775.

Spencer (675) lists the few surviving records at TNA of the volunteers (1794–1813), the fencibles, the yeomanry (1804–1921), Imperial Yeomanry (1899–1903) and the Rifle Volunteers (1859–1908). For example, officers are listed in the army lists and there are some muster rolls and pay lists in series WO 13. Attestation and discharge papers of officers and men of the Imperial Yeomanry are in WO 128, arranged by their service numbers. A man's number can be found in seven books in WO 129, each of which lists men by the initial letter of their surnames and then in order of their service numbers. Most of the men served in South Africa and so were awarded the Queen's South Africa Medal, the rolls for which are in series WO 100 (arranged by battalion then company). Some records of these units are also at CROs. Thus Leicester Record Office holds regimental registers for the Leicestershire Yeomanry (1849–79), some records of officers' services in the yeomanry and a volunteer battalion of the Leicestershire Regiment (1860–1916) and muster rolls of rifle volunteers (1860 and 1880–86).

Some records of the formation and administration of the Special Reserve, or Territorials, are at TNA. The service records of Territorials who served in the First World War are included in the army service records in series WO 363 and 364 (or WO 339 and 374 for officers). Long service and good conduct in the Territorials was recognised by the Territorial Force Efficiency Medal of 1908–21 and the Territorial Efficiency Medal 1921–30, to which there are microfiche card indexes in the microfilm reading room at TNA.

OTHER SOURCES FOR ARMY ANCESTORS

The National Army Museum at Royal Hospital Road, Chelsea, London SW3 4HT (telephone 020 7730 0717) is described below. It holds records of the money owed to soldiers who died in service between 1901 and 1960. These note a man's name, rank, regiment, number, the date (and place and cause) of death, details of money owed, to whom it was paid (usually the next-of-kin) and often the payee's address. The records for all officers and for soldiers who died between 1901 and 1914 and between 1929 and 1960 are in the museum's reading room. The records for soldiers who died between 1914 and 1929 will be available soon. The museum cannot answer enquiries about an individual's records and it is not possible to take copies because of the volumes' bindings.

The Society for Army Historical Research (based at the National Army Museum) has published a quarterly journal since 1921 on the history of the British Army. There is an index to the journal up to 1962. Most libraries have a variety of books containing useful information on wars in which an ancestor served. Fabb (625) is a collection of army photographs from before the First World War, recording uniforms and soldiers' daily life. Regimental museums (considered below) hold some regimental records, photographs and medals. Many soldiers' diaries, letters and memoirs are held at the Imperial War Museum, Lambeth Road, London SE1 6HZ (noted in more detail below). The telephone number of the museum is 020 7416 5000 (its Department of Printed Books is on 020 7416 5344 and its Department of Documents is on 020 7416 5221). Its photographic library (visits by appointment only) holds millions of photographs relating to the two world wars.

INDIAN, COLONIAL AND OTHER FOREIGN REGIMENTS

The East India Company (EIC) controlled most of India until 1858 (when the Crown took direct control) and administered it through three presidencies: Bengal, Madras and Bombay. Although British Army units were stationed in India, most of the military forces serving there were the EIC's own armies (one for each presidency), with regiments of British men, but also Indian (or sepoy) regiments led by British officers. In 1861 the British troops became part of the British Army (and so their records are at TNA) and the sepoy troops formed the Indian Army (with British officers), controlled by the Viceroy.

TNA holds lists of officers of European regiments in the EIC armies for 1796–1841 (in series WO 25). Officers in the Indian Army (on 1 November 1871) are listed in service registers in WO 74. There are also some pension records of officers and other ranks in WO 23 and 25. Other records of EIC and Indian Army troops up to 1947 (with many other records of British India) are held at the British Library in its India Office collections. The military records in the India Office collections are considered in this section, but the other records are described in chapter 30. Thus officers, soldiers and their families are recorded in ecclesiastical returns of baptisms, marriages and burials in India, in wills and in regiments' registers of births, marriages and deaths.

Baxter (1257) and Moir (1306) review the records in the India Office collections and Farrington (1281) is a detailed list of the military records, including operational records, army lists, muster and medal rolls, casualty lists and discharge papers. They consist of about 45,000 files and 2,000 boxes, from the 18th to 20th centuries, for the EIC armies, the Indian Army up to 1947 and the Indian Navy. Published lists of EIC army officers, many with detailed biographies are held in the India Office collections and at the SoG. These are listed in Baxter (1257). Thus Hodson (642) provides biographies of Bengal army officers from 1758 to 1834. A typical entry is:

GILLIES, Daniel (died 1802) Captain 10th Native Infantry. Cadet 1781. Ensign 14 Sept. 1781. Lieutenant 22 June 1783. Captain 21 Feb. 1801. Died Calcutta 1 December 1802. Services; Lieutenant 15th battalion Sepoys in July 1787. Fourth Mysore War; Seringapatam. Will dated 30 Nov. 1802; proved 3 Dec. 1802.

Another example is *War Services of Officers of the Bengal Army* by Anderson (597), a biographical dictionary of that army's officers (including artillery, engineer and medical officers) serving in January 1861. The biographies include notes on the officers' roles during the Indian Mutiny and other campaigns (in India or elsewhere) as in this example:

Captain A.H. Campbell, P.H., late 9th Native Infantry.
Ensign, 25 Aug 1841. Lieut. 1 Jan 1845. Captain, 23 Nov 1856.
Service. Captain Campbell served in the Crimea as Assistant Adjutant-General of Division in the Turkish contingent, from October 1855 till the end of the war. Obtained 4th Class of the Order of the Medjidie. Served as Major of Brigade at Allahabad, and engaged at Munseeta on 5th January 1858 under Brigadier W. Campbell. Mentioned in Despatch 22nd January 1858. Commanded the 8th Irregular Cavalry during the campaign in Oude in 1858, 1859. Present at capture of town and fort of Sandee, 24th October 1858. Medal.

The India Office collections include many service records, reviewed in detail by Farrington (1281), of officers and soldiers serving in India. Officers' careers can be traced in the indexed service army lists, dating from about 1839 to 1859 (but with details of service prior to 1839), for each of the three presidencies. There are also some manuscript and published army lists, listed by Baxter (1257), for each presidency army. For example, there are manuscript lists for the Madras army from 1759 to 1846 and published lists for 1804 and 1810–95. The careers of army officers can be also traced in the *East India Register and Directory* which was published each year from 1803, or in succeeding directories and Indian Army lists up to 1947 (# chapter 30). Copies are also held at the SoG, and some are available on microfiche from MM Publications. These directories and registers include lists of officers of the EIC and Indian armies in similar form to the British army lists noted above. For example, the 1819 *East India Register* (1242) lists officers of each army unit, such as the 41 British officers of the 7th Regiment of Native Infantry of the Bengal Presidency (see illustration 147). The *Indian Army List*, for example that of January 1931 (1249) lists the officers of each unit and is indexed. The National Army Museum holds Hodson's card index to British officers who served in the EIC or Indian armies (as well as maritime officers and EIC civil servants). Officers of Indian Army units who were killed in the First World War are listed in volume 1 of *The Cross of Sacrifice* by Jarvis & Jarvis (649).

Appointments of officers in the 17th and 18th centuries may be found in the EIC Court minutes (that is, minutes of the EIC's governing body) or in correspondence files listed by Baxter (1257). There are cadet papers (1789–1860) which are men's applications for commissions in the EIC armies. They are indexed and give details of the applicant's parents and education and many have baptism or birth certificates or letters of recommendation attached. Many cadets were educated or trained in England at the Royal Military Academy at Woolwich (1798–1808), the

Addiscombe Military Seminary (1809–61) or the Royal Engineers' Institution at Chatham (1815–62). The India Office collections include those institutions' records of EIC cadets. The Addiscombe records include registers that note a cadet's date of birth or baptism. Baxter (1257) also reviews the records of military funds and pensions for officers and their dependants. For example there are indexed lists of pensioners and payment books for the Lord Clive Fund which was established in 1770 to provide benefits for retired officers, other ranks and widows.

British private soldiers in the EIC armies were recruited in Britain from the 17th century. A permanent recruiting and training depot was established in 1801 at Newport in the Isle of Wight, moving to Chatham in Kent in 1815 and Warley in Essex in 1843. The India Office collections include registers of recruits (or depot registers) from about 1801 to 1860, giving a recruit's age, birthplace, marital status, date and place of enlistment, former employment, physical description and date and ship of embarkation. There are also embarkation lists of men leaving for India between 1753 and 1861, arranged by year, then ship, providing a recruit's name, age on enlistment, residence and previous occupation (they also list a few wives and children who accompanied their husbands to India). There are also muster rolls and casualty returns of NCOs and other ranks for the Bengal army (1716–1861), the Madras army (1762–1861) and the Bombay army (1708–1865). From the early 19th century these rolls specify each soldier's county of origin or (in the Bengal and Madras rolls) his town or parish. There are also registers of European soldiers in each army from the late 18th century that record a man's place of origin and date of arrival in India. Pension funds were also established, such as the Lord Clive Fund noted above. There are many records in the India Office collections relating to the Indian medical and nursing services, including annual lists of surgeons from 1787 and registers of nurses from 1882.

Officers and men of the EIC armies and the British Army in India received many of the medals discussed above (such as the Victoria Cross and DCM) but also campaign, long service and good conduct medals specifically for service in India. Most awards were recorded in the Bengal, Bombay and Madras army lists (and later in the *Indian Army List*) and in medal rolls in the India Office collections. There are some published casualty and medal rolls. Farrington (626) is the casualty roll for the second Afghan War of 1878–80, listing about 3,000 British and Indian officers and men who were killed or wounded. The Army of India Medal was instituted in 1851 and granted to surviving British and Indian officers and men of the British or EIC armies, navy or marines who had been engaged in specified battles between 1799 and 1826. The original roll is in the India Office collections and a copy is at TNA (in series WO 100). The British recipients are listed in Gould & Douglas-Morris (635) with notes on some of the men's careers and the other awards that they received.

Many colonial regiments were raised in the 18th and 19th centuries, particularly in Canada and South Africa, often including former members of the British army. Some foreign regiments were also raised to fight for Britain, such as troops from Hesse who fought in North America from 1776, and the King's German Legion (formed from the disbanded Hanoverian army) which fought during the Napoleonic wars. Many men from these units later settled in Britain or its colonies and many of the units' records are at TNA (in the same series as British army regiments). Perkins (665) is a detailed bibliography (also available on CD-ROM from NMP) of published regimental and other unit histories for troops of the British Empire and Commonwealth from 1758 to 1993, including the EIC and Indian armies, foreign troops and colonial regiments.

THE ROYAL MARINES

A regiment of soldiers was formed in 1665 specifically to serve on ships. This was replaced in 1698 by two regiments of troops called marines and further regiments were raised (and later disbanded) in the early 18th century. The marines became a permanent force in 1755, when 5,000 men were raised (in 50 companies) under the control of the Admiralty. The marine companies were divided into divisions based at Chatham, Plymouth, Portsmouth and (from 1805 to 1869) at Woolwich. The marines were renamed the Royal Marines in 1802 and marine artillery companies were formed in 1804.

Royal Marine records, most of which are at TNA in Admiralty records (code ADM), are similar to army records and described in detail in Thomas (682) and TNA military records leaflets 45 and 48. Each marine division kept its own records. A list of all marines is being prepared (to be held at TNA when complete). This will enable researchers to find marine ancestors in the records very easily. In the meantime, you need to know in which division's records to search. The survival rate of records varies between divisions. For example attestations survive from 1790 for Chatham, from 1804 for Plymouth and Portsmouth, but only from 1839 for Woolwich and from 1861 for the marine artillery. Thomas (682) and the leaflets of TNA list the types of records available, the covering years and the piece numbers for each division. Importantly, each division kept registers of births, marriages and deaths of marines and their families. The Chatham registers (in series ADM 183) cover 1830–1913, the Plymouth registers (ADM 184) cover 1862–1920 and the Woolwich registers (ADM 81) cover 1822–69. The Portsmouth registers (ADM 185) cover 1869–81 but record only marriages. Registers of the marine artillery (in ADM 6 and 193) cover 1810–53 and 1866–1921.

Marine officers were included in the army lists from 1740, the navy lists (# chapter 21) from 1814 and in *Hart's Army List* from 1840. Service details up to December 1916 (including medal awards) of marine officers who served in the First World War are included in *The Naval Who's Who* (703). Obituaries of marine officers are contained in the Royal Marines' magazine, *The Globe and Laurel*. Detailed service records of marine officers from 1793 to 1925 are at TNA in series ADM 196, but they are incomplete before 1837. An index to these records up to 1883 is in piece ADM 313/110 (and a copy is in the research enquiries room). The records of 1883–1925 have their own indexes. Commissions and promotions of marine officers were recorded in the *London Gazette* and, from 1703 to 1814, in registers in series ADM 6. Royal warrants of commissions are in volumes of military entry books in series SP 44 (1679–1782) and HO 51 (1782–92). There are also many records of marine officers on half-pay and retired pay from 1758, principally in series ADM 6. Information about officers serving after 1925 can be obtained by application to the Commandant General, Royal Marines, Ministry of Defence, Main Building, Whitehall, London SW1A 2HB.

Throughout his period of service a marine usually remained in the company in which he had enlisted and most companies remained in the same division. The companies and divisions are listed in Thomas (682) and the leaflets of TNA. Attestation forms of marines, including a marine's age, birthplace, trade and physical description, cover the period from 1790 (but later for some divisions) up to 1869 (for the Woolwich division), 1900 for Plymouth, 1912 for Chatham and 1923 for Portsmouth and the marine artillery and engineers. They are in about 3,600 pieces in series ADM 157, arranged by division, then company, then date (sometimes the date of enlistment but often the date of discharge). The easiest way to find most men is to use a card index (in the research enquiries room at TNA) to these attestations. However, this covers only about 660 pieces (that is some of the marines who served in the 19th century). If your ancestor is not included in this index, you can also find his company number and division from the casualty roll for the First World War or from the published register of deaths in the Second World War (both described below).

There are also description books in series ADM 158 (arranged by division, then company and then the initial letter of a man's surname). These date from 1755 for Chatham (but later for other divisions), up to 1940 giving the date of a marine's attestation (and much other information from the attestations) but also recording promotions and casualties. Series ADM 96 contains effective and subsistence lists for 1688 to 1837, which are companies' pay lists.

From 1884 each marine was given a number by his division and records of service were introduced and filed under this number in series ADM 159, with indexes in ADM 313. They note a man's date (and place) of birth, trade, religion, date (and place) of enlistment, physical description and service record (including his conduct and promotions). These numbers were also applied retrospectively (and in some cases numbers had been used informally for some years) so that the records of service cover many marines serving since about 1850. Thomas (682) includes an illustration of a typical service record for a marine, from 1867 to 1888, listing his periods of service in the Portsmouth division and his duty on six ships. Registers are closed for 75 years after the date of the last entry made in them but records of marines in the closed records can be obtained from the Ministry of Defence, Royal Marines Drafting and Record Office, Centurion Building, HMS *Sultan*, Grange Road, Gosport, Hampshire, PO13 9XA, on the same terms as post-1920 army records.

Pensions for marines were organised similarly to those for the Royal Navy (# chapter 21) and most records are in series ADM 165 and 166. Registers of marine officers receiving pensions from the Royal Hospital at Greenwich between 1862 and 1908 are in ADM 201. There are also some records of pensions paid to marines' widows and families (and some marines' wills), the relevant pieces being listed in Thomas (682). Medals awarded to Royal Marines are listed in the Royal Navy medal rolls in series ADM 171 (# chapter 21). Good conduct medal rolls from 1849 to 1894 are in ADM 201. The naval long service medals that could be awarded to Royal Marines are reviewed, with lists of recipients, in Douglas-Morris (716). Marines also received the gallantry medals considered above. Courts martial records of marines for the 18th and 19th centuries are in series ADM 1 and 194. A marine may also be found in pay lists of Royal Navy ships (# chapter 21), but you need to know the ship's name in order to find those lists. If you do locate a marine on a ship, the navy records (ships' logs, pay lists and muster rolls) may note his place of birth and tell you about a ship's voyages and the battles in which it took part.

War diaries for marine units in the First World War are in series ADM 116 and 137. Those for the Second World War are in ADM 202. There are many casualty lists of marines in the Admiralty's records, dating from the mid-19th century (listed in TNA military records leaflet 48) such as registers of deaths in ships 1893–1956 in ADM 104/102–121. Some of these records are indexed. Marine deaths in the two world wars are included in the CWGC *Debt of Honour* database. In addition, there is a war graves roll for 1914–19 in series ADM 242, arranged alphabetically by marines' names, noting men's rank, service number, date and place of birth, unit or ship's name and cause of death. This roll of over 6,000 marines has been published by the Royal Marines Historical Society (593). It includes details of burials and memorials from the CWGC records. A typical entry is:

Name	Rank	No.	Death	Ship/Unit	Place	Burial
Eagles, George	Cpl.	Ply. 16006	13.7.15	Ply. Bn.	Gallipoli	MR 4

Thus George Eagles was a corporal, number 16006 of the Plymouth division, who was killed at Gallipoli on 13 July 1915. The MR 4 in the final column refers you to the cemetery memorial register (which includes the plot, row and grave number). Marine officers killed in the First World War are also listed in volume 2 of *The Cross of Sacrifice* by Jarvis & Jarvis (649). A register of the 4,000 marines who died between 1939 and 1945 has also been published by the Royal Marines Historical Society (576), providing information in similar form to the First World War register. Background information on the life and uniforms of marines can be obtained at the Royal Marines Museum (considered below).

AIR FORCE RECORDS

The Royal Air Force (RAF) was formed in 1918 by the amalgamation of the army's Royal Flying Corps (RFC) which was founded in 1912 and the Royal Naval Air Service (RNAS) which was established in 1914. This section covers the records of all three services but also records of those serving in the Fleet Air Arm (created in 1924 and controlled by the Admiralty from 1937), the Women's Royal Air Force (WRAF) and its successor, the Women's Auxiliary Air Force (WAAF). Most of the records of these services that are open to the public are at TNA and described in detail in Spencer (674) and Fowler (629). The former work is more up to date and so includes more personnel records. The latter includes more information on operational records. Air force records rarely note genealogical information except some next of kin and dates and places of birth which are probably known to the researcher already. Research in air force records is therefore primarily to find out more about an ancestor's life, perhaps his part in the Battle of Britain.

The titles of ranks of officers, NCOs and other airforce personnel were very different from army and navy ranks, and schedules of these ranks are set out in Spencer (674). Since 1914 the air services have been organised into squadrons, which were grouped into wings (and in the Second World War into groups). By late 1918, the RAF had 188 squadrons. Halley (638) lists all RAF squadrons from 1918 to 1988 and notes where each squadron was stationed during those years, the aircraft that it operated and the campaigns in which it took part. By 1918 the RAF had over 22,000 aircraft, 27,000 officers and 264,000 other ranks. This shows how important it is to remember that most men in the air services were not pilots, but ground staff such as engineers and mechanics. The WRAF was founded in 1918 and had over 25,000 servicewomen by the armistice. It was disbanded in 1920 (although resurrected in 1939, see below).

RFC and RNAS officers were included in the army and navy lists up to 1918. Monthly lists of RAF officers were prepared from 1918 and copies are at the SoG and TNA. They have sections for the Air Ministry, each station and each squadron, listing their aircraft and officers (and their dates of posting to a unit). The volumes are indexed, so officers are easily found in each list and their careers can be traced. For the years 1939–54, copies of the Confidential Air List are in series AIR 10. The lists for 1918 and 1940 have been reprinted and are available from NMP. The Royal Air Force College at Cranwell opened in 1920 to train RAF officers and a list of graduates from 1920 to 1952 has been published. More details of training and specialist units are contained in Fowler (629).

McInnes & Webb (660) is a detailed biographical dictionary (with notes of medal awards and many photographs) of the approximately 1,400 warrant officers, NCOs and other men who joined the RFC before the First World War. They generally acted as ground crew, but many flew planes, or acted as observers or gunners. One of the shorter entries is that for T.C. Lock:

Enlisted 6 June 1908, formerly 11257 Private Worcs. Regt. Transferred to RFC on 2 May 1914. As air mechanic (2nd class) with No. 4 Squadron served in France from 9 Sept. 1914 and earned 1914 Star and bar. Promoted Sergeant (carpenter) 3 Sept. 1917 and retained that rank and trade in April 1918 RAF muster roll. Awarded RAF long service and good conduct medal 6 June 1926.

The GRO registers of First World War deaths (# chapter 5) and the CWGC *Debt of Honour* database include many RAF and RFC personnel. Volumes 1 and 2 of *The Cross of Sacrifice* by Jarvis & Jarvis (649) include RFC, RNAS and RAF officers who died in the war, and volume 4 lists NCOs and other ranks of the RFC and RAF who died. Williamson (690) is a roll of honour for the RFC and RAF, listing about 8,000 airmen who died in the war (with biographical information such as a man's rank, squadron and date of death). It also lists all those entries from the CWGC register of the Arras Memorial (that is, about 1,000 names) commemorating airmen with no known grave. Most of these entries note a pilot's age and the next of kin's name and address. The RAF Museum holds an incomplete set of casualty cards for the RFC and RNAS, noting the cause of the casualty, the type of aircraft and some next of kin names. The Imperial War Museum also has a roll of honour for RFC and RNAS personnel killed during the war.

An official history of the role of the RFC, RNAS and RAF in the First World War, *The War in the Air, Being the Story of the Part Played in the Great War by the Royal Air Force* by W. Raleigh and H.A. Jones, was published in six volumes (1922–37) and has been reprinted by NMP. An article by N. Hurst in *Family Tree Magazine* (May 1992) lists published sources for pilots' careers, decorations and histories of the war in the air. The RNAS is described, with lists of background material for the service, its aircraft and pilots, by N. Hurst in *Family Tree Magazine* (January 1994). Most of its records are in Admiralty documents at TNA.

Many useful records are held by TNA and described in Fowler (629) and Spencer (674). Most records of military aviation at TNA up to 1918 are in series AIR 1. These were mostly collated by the Air Historical Branch (AHB) of the Air Ministry. The series list for AIR 1 gives a piece number but also the AHB reference (for example 4/26/6) and all the numbers must be used when ordering these documents. AIR 1 includes a muster roll of all ranks serving in the RAF on its formation on 1 April 1918, a few units' nominal rolls, weekly lists of the locations of RFC, RNAS and RAF units in 1917 and 1918 and pilots' combat reports. In order to use TNA records successfully, you must ascertain the squadron in which a pilot served. There are no complete muster lists after 1918 and other ranks, such as ground crew, are difficult to find in the records unless there was a special reason for them to be mentioned, such as an award of a medal or court martial. RAF courts martial records are in pieces AIR 2/1A–3 and AIR 43/1. An index prepared by E. Wilson and J. Partington to 6,000 RAF other ranks noted in TNA records is at TNA, noting each man's service number, job, rank, unit and a document reference.

In 1915, the RFC began issuing regular communiques, for internal consumption, that described the corps' main activities on the Western Front. They included notes of fights with enemy aircraft, bombing raids and losses of planes or pilots. Edited versions of RFC and RAF communiques of 1915–18 have been published. This extract is from the volume for 1915–16 by Cole (612):

> May 29th 1916. Capt E.W. Parrett, 29 Sqn, while patrolling over Ypres salient in a De Havilland was shot down during a combat in the air with two hostile machines. Capt Parrett had a bullet wound in the head. His machine fell close behind our own lines near St Eloi. One of the German machines was seen to come down a few minutes later out of control.

Service records of most RFC, RNAS and RAF personnel up to 1919 are at TNA. In most cases, they note a man's date and place of birth, next of kin, date of enlistment, dates of promotions, postings and some other service details. Files for RFC officers who ceased service before the formation of the RAF in April 1918 are included in army officers' service records in series WO 339 and 374. Records of some RFC other ranks are in WO 363 and 364. Records of RNAS officers and ratings who ceased service before April 1918 are held with records of naval personnel (# chapter 21) in series ADM 196 and 273 (officers) and ADM 188 (ratings).

Records of about 26,000 officers of the RAF who ceased service before 1920 are on microfilm in series AIR 76. These note men's postings, next of kin, medals and date of death. The records of airmen and NCOs who transferred from the RFC and RNAS into the RAF or enlisted from 1918 to the early 1920s (but did not serve in the Second World War) are in series AIR 79. There is an index in AIR 78 for about 329,000 airmen but this includes those who continued serving after 1919 and whose records are not in AIR 79 because they have been retained by the MOD. Service records of officers who served with the WRAF from 1918 until it was disbanded in 1920 have not survived but the records of some other ranks are in series AIR 80, arranged alphabetically.

Examples of the types of documents that appear in all these service files are included in Spencer (674) and in an article by P. Elliott in *Genealogists' Magazine* (March 2002). Illustration 104 is the service record from AIR 76/158 for R.S. Fear who had joined the RFC in August 1917 from the 5th battalion of the Worcestershire Regiment. His next of kin was noted as his sister, Miss A. Fear of 6 Kensington Square, London (Williamson's roll of honour, noted above, records that Fear was a Second Lieutenant serving with 15 Squadron). Fear is noted as having received instruction at Reading and then served at Brooklands. It seems that Fear was originally reported as killed in action on 1 March 1918 but the record was later amended to note that he had in fact been wounded on 5 March and subsequently died of his wounds. Some First World War medical records survive from hospitals and casualty clearing stations and these are included in the records in MH 106. There are no name indexes and so it is difficult to find a man in them but the pieces and covering dates are listed by Spencer (674).

D. Barnes of Burnley in Lancashire is compiling a biographical register of British and Commonwealth airmen who served in the RFC, RNAS and RAF during the First World War from service records, the RAF muster of 1 April 1918, medal rolls, casualty lists, the CWGC registers and other sources. Barnes describes this project in the 2002 edition of the *FLHH* (5).

Service records of most men and women who served after 1919 (including those of the RAF Nursing Service, established in 1919) are held by the RAF Personnel Management Agency, PMA(CS)2a2(RAF), RAF Innsworth, Gloucester GL3 1EZ, who may release information to next of kin on the same terms as post-1920 army service records.

104. *Service record of 2nd Lieutenant R. S. Fear with the Royal Flying Corps from 1917 until his death in March 1918 (TNA, AIR 76/158)*

RAF operational records from 1919 up to about 1960 are at TNA and described in TNA military records leaflet 60, Spencer (674) and Fowler (629). In 1936 the RAF was reorganised into four Commands: Bomber, Coastal, Fighter and Training. Their records are in series AIR 14, 15, 16 and 32 respectively. The Fleet Air Arm was formed as a separate service in 1924 and from 1937 was controlled by the Admiralty. Service records of Fleet Air Arm personnel are held by the Navy Records Centre of the Ministry of Defence (# chapter 21). The records are released on the same conditions as post-1920 army records.

A new women's air service, the Women's Auxiliary Air Force (WAAF), was formed in 1939 and over 180,000 women were serving by 1943. Most records of the WAAF are included with those of the units with which they served (such as the records of stations in series AIR 28) but personnel records are still held by the RAF Personnel Management Agency, noted above. The service reverted to the name Women's Royal Air Force in 1949. Fowler (629) describes other commands that existed for certain periods.

By the end of the Second World War, the RAF had over one million personnel, 9,200 aircraft, 460 squadrons and 1,200 airfields. Halley (638) provides a brief history of each squadron during the war, noting the aircraft it used and its stations. Richards & Saunders (669) is a detailed history of RAF operations in the Second World War, including lists of senior officers and organisation tables (such as the squadrons in each group and command) at particular dates during the war. Further information on the RAF and the Fleet Air Arm is held by the Department of Archives and Aviation Records at the Royal Air Force Museum at Hendon (noted below). The museum has a card index of every RAF aircraft and many photographs. There are also many published books of photographs of RAF aircraft (usually available at local libraries).

In 1928, the RAF introduced an operations record book (Ops Book or ORB) consisting of form 541 (for statistics and other data) and form 540 for a narrative of the unit's activities. Fowler (629) includes illustrations of these forms. ORBs for units' Second World War activities are in series AIR 24, 25, 27 and 28, for commands, groups, squadrons and stations respectively. Squadron ORBs include details of pilots' sorties and often note that a pilot and aircraft did not return. A selection of aircrews' flying log books are held in series AIR 4. Many operational records of Fleet Air Arm squadrons, similar to the ORBs of the RAF, are in series ADM 207. Other operational records are reviewed by Fowler (629).

Most RAF war dead of the Second World War are recorded in a GRO index and register (# chapter 5), which notes names, ranks, service numbers and units but also in the CWGC *Debt of Honour* database. Some lists of casualties are in series AIR 20 at TNA and losses of aircrew or aircraft are also noted in squadron or station ORBs. About 50,000 men (and about 9,000 aircraft) of RAF Bomber Command were lost in the war (of about 125,000 men who served). Details of the lost aircraft (in chronological order), their squadrons, the names of the crew and the circumstances (if known) of each loss in the period 1939 to 1945 have been published in six volumes by Chorley (610). The information has been extracted from ORBs, Ministry of Defence records of aircraft losses, the CWGC cemetery registers and lists of prisoners of war. The first volume covers losses in 1939 and 1940. For example, it records the loss on 24 September 1940 of a Blenheim of 139 Squadron operating from Horsham St Faith in Norfolk. It was shot down while operating over the English Channel. All three crew members (Squadron Leader M.F. Hendry and Sergeants P.M. Davidson and V. Arrowsmith) were killed and are commemorated on a memorial at Runnymede. The six volumes do not have name indexes, but an entry is easy to find once the airman's death is located in the GRO indexes of RAF Second

World War deaths or in CWGC records. The men and aircraft of Bomber Command lost in the war are also listed on a CD-ROM produced by K. Fletcher and reviewed in *Family Tree Magazine* (February 2003).

Fighter Command lost fewer men than Bomber Command during the war but its losses were also heavy and the bravery of its pilots can be said to have saved Britain in 1940. Three volumes by Franks (630) list the lost aircraft and crew of Fighter Command with information, similar to that provided by Chorley for Bomber Command, extracted principally from ORBs in series AIR 27 and casualty records in AIR 16. (Similar volumes are being published that list the lost aircraft and crew of Coastal Command.) K. Fletcher has produced a CD-ROM of the men and aircraft of Fighter Command lost in the war (similar to his work for Bomber Command, noted above). Wynn (692a) is a detailed biographical dictionary, with many photographs, of the 2,917 pilots and aircrew of Fighter Command (of whom 544 were killed) who served between July and October 1940 in the Battle of Britain.

Fowler (629) lists the records of aircrew who were captured during the Second World War. In particular, a list in piece AIR 20/2336 lists all RAF prisoners held in Germany in 1944/5 with their ranks, service numbers and the camps in which they were held. This list has been transcribed and included in the volumes by Chorley (610), together with lists of airmen interned in neutral countries extracted from reports in series WO 208.

Medals

Personnel who served in the RFC and RAF in the First World War were awarded the same campaign medals as army personnel (for example the British War Medal and Victory Medal) and awards are listed in the medal rolls in WO 329 and on the index cards in WO 372. Airmen were also eligible for army gallantry medals and some awards are listed in published works, such as Walker (684) for the DCM. RNAS personnel received naval decorations (# chapter 21) and the medal rolls are in series ADM 171.

Four gallantry medals were instituted in 1918 specifically for the air services: the Distinguished Flying Cross, the Distinguished Flying Medal, the Air Force Cross and the Air Force Medal. Aviators were also eligible for those medals (such as the Victoria Cross and DSO) that were awarded to all servicemen. In addition, eligibility for the Conspicuous Gallantry Medal was extended in 1942 to RAF personnel. Between 1918 and 1945 there were about 4,300 awards of the Air Force Cross, 470 awards of the Air Force Medal, 22,500 awards of the DFC and about 6,800 awards of the DFM. About 100 awards of the CGM were made between 1942 and 1945. Recommendations for awards during the First World War are in series AIR 1 and for 1919–38 in AIR 2. RAF medal rolls for the Second World War are not available, but awards were noted in the *London Gazette* and sometimes in squadrons' operations record books. Tavender (681) lists each recipient of the DFM from 1918 to 1982 with his number, rank, squadron and the *Gazette* citation describing the act of courage that led to the award. This is one of the shorter entries:

FLETCHER, John Laurence. 564192 Sergeant
LG 26 March 1940. Sergeant Fletcher was the captain of one of the aircraft which attacked the seaplane base at Sylt on the night of 19/20 March 1940. He set the highest example of gallantry by successfully attacking the hangars and slipway at a height which brought him and his crew up against the full force of the anti-aircraft fire of this heavily defended base.

The Meritorious Service Medal was awarded to those serving with the RFC, RNAS and RAF from 1916 to 1928. The recipients are listed in McInnes (658). The RAF still holds records of the RAF Long Service and Good Conduct Medal (instituted in 1919 for other ranks after 18 years of exemplary service) and the RAF Meritorious Service Medal (awarded from 1918 to 1928). Information about these awards (and other medals awarded more recently to RAF personnel) is available from the RAF Personnel Management Agency.

Information about medals or awards since 1939 to Fleet Air Arm personnel is available because it was controlled by the Admiralty which, in 1939, began compiling a card index, the "Naval Secretary's Honours and Awards Index" for all its personnel. The index noted a man's name and rank, the ship or unit in which he was serving, the award, the reason for the award and the date of the *London Gazette* announcement. This index therefore includes the medals noted above, medals awarded to naval personnel and some other honours or medals, but also notes whether a man received a commendation or a mention in dispatches. The information from this index has been published in volumes known as "Seedie's lists", of which there is one volume (586) for awards to Fleet Air Arm personnel from 1939 to 1969. It is arranged by ship or air station, then date of announcement and then alphabetically, but has a name index. For example, the *London Gazette* of 30 May 1944 announced the destruction of three U-boats (U 472, U 366 and U 973) by airmen in Swordfish aircraft from the carrier HMS *Chaser*, escorting a convoy to Russia. Lieutenant Edwin Bennett and five others were awarded the DSC. Three men received the DSM and six were mentioned in dispatches.

Fowler (629) reviews the RAF records at TNA for the period 1945–63, including the RAF's role in the Berlin airlift, Suez and the Korean War. RAF uniforms, badges and insignia, as well as pilots' training, are described in Wilson (691).

MILITARY MUSEUMS

Military museums may provide useful information. If you know that your ancestor served in a regiment at a certain period, a regimental museum may have photographs or paintings of the uniforms worn at the time and the museum exhibits may reveal where a regiment was stationed and the campaigns or battles in which it fought. Museums are particularly useful for campaign histories, photographs and newspaper reports. They also hold published histories of the regiment (but you should be able to obtain these from libraries). Research can also be undertaken at the Imperial War Museum, the National Army Museum, the Royal Air Force Museum, the Royal Marines Museum or at the Fleet Air Arm Museum. The Royal Naval Museum at Portsmouth (# chapter 21) holds much material on the navy, but is also useful for research of the marines.

Most British regiments and corps have their own museums which usually hold some records (but rarely personnel records), photographs, uniforms or other relevant material. There are also museums for the other branches of the armed forces (and for special forces such as the Airborne Forces Museum at Aldershot). The address, telephone number, opening times (and a brief description of the collections) of these museums are listed in Wise (692). The Army Museum Ogilby Trust, of 2 St Thomas Centre, Southgate Street, Winchester, Hampshire, SO23 9EF (telephone 01962 841416), can also provide information on the location of military museums (and the few regimental records that they hold – most museums have passed their records to CROs). Even if museums have retained records, they usually have few staff and so generally cannot undertake research. Access to the records is usually by appointment only.

The National Army Museum (noted above) does not hold soldiers' service records but does hold material such as army lists, regimental histories, books on particular wars or campaigns and papers of famous soldiers (the details of which can be found in the National Register of Archives). It has displays of uniforms, badges, medals, weapons and photographs that portray the history of the British army and soldiers' daily life. The museum holds 40,000 books and 500,000 photographs (as well as drawings and films) providing background information on wars and military life. As noted above, the museum also holds records for 1901 to 1960 of money owed to soldiers who died in service. The museum is open nearly every day of the year. The reading room is open from Tuesdays to Saturdays. Access is by a ticket obtained in advance, the forms being available by sending an SAE to the museum's department of printed books.

The Imperial War Museum (open most days of the year) is dedicated to military operations since 1914. It has displays of aircraft, tanks, uniforms, photographs and other military items. S. Patterson described the resources in the museum's reference departments (which can be visited by appointment) in *Family History News and Digest* (April 1998). The Department of Printed Books holds over 100,000 books as well as thousands of maps, periodicals and pamphlets. These include copies of the CWGC registers, published medal rolls, army, navy and air force lists, memorial volumes (to the deceased of both world wars), regimental histories and regimental or other units' journals. The Department of Documents holds many private diaries, collections of letters and other personal papers of men and officers, indexed by unit. The photographic library (holding about 100,000 photographs for the First World War and about five million for the Second) can be visited by appointment. Copies of photographs can be purchased. Sample photographs from the museum's collection can be seen on its web site. The National Inventory of War Memorials (noted above) is also housed at the museum.

The Royal Marines Museum at Eastney Barracks, Southsea, Portsmouth (open daily), has a collection of about 6,000 medals, as well as uniforms and other displays on the marines' history, and a large (indexed) collection of photographs and other records of marines.

The Royal Air Force Museum is open daily at Grahame Park Way, Hendon, London NW9 5LL (telephone 020 8205 2266). The museum has some aircraft and also galleries of photographs, uniforms and equipment which are described on its web site. Its department of research and information services has extensive collections of records of the history of military aviation, including senior officers' papers and some aircrews' logbooks, as well as about 250,000 photographs, principally of aircraft and airfields. The reading room is open from Monday to Friday by appointment. Researchers with ancestors who served in the Fleet Air Arm should visit the Fleet Air Arm Museum at the Royal Naval Air Station, Yeovilton, Somerset BA22 8HT (telephone 01935 840565).

THE EFFECT OF WAR

A family history is not merely a collection of names, dates and places, but illustrates the effect of great historical events on everyday life. In addition to family members serving in the armed forces, you may find that the family was affected in other ways. One of my relatives in Guernsey was deported by the Germans to a detention centre in Germany, together with many other residents of the Channel Islands. During the Second World War, many people were evacuated from their homes in London and other cities. My father and his brothers were evacuated to Sussex, and his mother and sister were evacuated to Wales. Unfortunately, it is often impossible to trace records of individuals being evacuated, but LMA produces a leaflet about evacuation from London and the surviving records (mostly dealing with administration rather than with individual evacuees). Samways (672) contains an almost contemporaneous account of the evacuation of children, some mothers and handicapped people from London, with many illustrations and a description of surviving records (such as council minutes).

The First World War had a devastating effect on many families. About one million men died and twice as many were wounded. This is illustrated by most family trees. My grandfather Henry John Herber served in the Royal Artillery on the Western Front. His elder brother Phillip was on non-combatant duties at Aldershot (because of illness). Their brother William was killed on the Somme in 1916. The youngest brother, James, served in the navy. Another brother, Arthur Stanley Herber, had emigrated to Montreal in 1913 but joined the Canadian army and returned to serve in France. He was wounded, captured but exchanged. He convalesced in a London hospital and married one of the nurses who tended him. My grandmother, Jessie Amelia Law, was only eight years old when the war broke out but her sister Dorothy died in the great flu epidemic which swept Europe at the end of the war. Their mother, Sarah Ann Sheppard, had two brothers (William and Joseph Sheppard) who served in the Royal Welch Fusiliers. Both were killed. My grandfather Frederick Charles Eagles left school in 1916, aged 13, to take up employment, which was very common for teenagers during the war. His mother had four brothers, all of whom served in the army. Two of them (George and William Garner) were killed and one (Thomas Garner) was badly gassed. The fourth brother, Charles Richard Garner, was badly wounded, but he was awarded the Military Medal and the Distinguished Conduct Medal.

CHAPTER 21

RECORDS OF SHIPPING
AND SEAMEN

Britain has a long history of maritime exploration, conquest and trade. Many of our ancestors were sailors in the merchant marine or Royal Navy, or worked in dockyards and ports. For many years Britain had the strongest navy in the world and Linebaugh (996) estimates that, during the course of 1721 alone, over 20,000 British men worked as crew on merchant ships. Over 400,000 men served in the Royal Navy or reserves in the First World War. It is therefore very likely that some of your ancestors were seamen.

Many of the records already considered (such as family archives and civil registration or census records) may reveal that an ancestor was a seaman. For example, my father has papers from his Second World War service in the Royal Navy, listing the ships on which he served. Similar papers may be held by your relatives. Civil registration certificates and photographs showed that my great grandfather, Charles Symes of Topsham in Devon, served in the Royal Navy and later as a merchant seaman. The 1881 census recorded that Charles was serving on HMS *Tenedos*. Charles died in 1913, following an accident on the merchant ship *Sirdar* on which he then served. The accident and inquest were reported in a newspaper (# chapter 17). Charles's father (Robert Symes), his uncle (John Symes), his grandfather (Richard Symes) and his great uncle (John Symes) were also recorded as mariners in civil registration, census and parish records. These were the starting points for my research in Royal Navy and merchant shipping records.

Most of the important records of naval or merchant seamen, reviewed below, are at TNA, the National Maritime Museum or Guildhall Library but other archives also hold large collections. There is also an enormous amount of published material at those institutions, the SoG and reference libraries. The maritime sources at the SoG are listed in Hailey (726). Due to the great interest in naval history, there is a growing amount of information about ships and seamen on the Internet. For example, pages on the GENUKI web site list men who served at the Battle of Trafalgar.

THE ROYAL NAVY

We have already noted some records of Royal Navy ancestors, such as the GRO registers of naval deaths during the two world wars and census records (listing the crews on ships in British ports and later on all British ships). The wills of seamen who died at sea, or abroad, were proved in the Prerogative Court of Canterbury and later in the Principal Probate Registry. However, most records of officers and sailors of the Royal Navy (and employees at naval dockyards) are held in Admiralty (ADM) records at TNA and described in Pappalardo (739a) and Rodger (740).

In general, TNA holds records of naval officers and ratings only up to about 1923. Enquiries about men who served between 1923 and 1938 should be directed to the Ministry of Defence,

Navy Records Centre, DR 2a (Navy Search), Room 31, Bourne Avenue, Hayes, Middlesex UB3 1RF (telephone 020 8573 3831). Enquiries about men who served after 1938 should be directed to the Ministry of Defence, Pay, Pensions, Personnel, Administration (PPPA), Centurion Building, Grange Road, Gosport, Hampshire PO13 9XA (telephone 023 9270 2174). These offices deal with enquiries on the same terms as those for post-1920 army records, noted above.

The records at TNA are voluminous but difficult to use because information about an ancestor may be contained in many types of records (in many series), often sorted only by ships' names or by men's naval rank and rarely indexed by surname.

Officers are easily located in published lists and biographical dictionaries. These identify the ships on which they served. Many officers' service records can also be located, without too much difficulty, in the records at TNA. Ratings who joined the navy since 1853 are also easily located in the service records at TNA. However, a rating who served before 1853 is difficult to trace unless you know the name of a ship on which he served. Census indexes, civil registration records or parish registers may assist. For example, the parish registers of ports (and the Fleet registers) include many sailors' marriages and the man's ship is sometimes recorded. The 1881 census index recorded that Charles Symes was serving on the ship HMS *Tenedos*. The census listed the 195 men on board that ship on census night, when it was at sea near Antigua. I then located published information relating to the ship. Colledge (712) and Manning & Walker (734) list all Royal Navy warships (about 13,000 of them) and Colledge (713) lists about 11,000 other naval ships. Certain popular names were given to a succession of ships and these works list each ship bearing a name and describe what happened to it and any battle honours that it earned. Lyon (731) also lists and describes naval ships from 1688 to 1860, with plans or pictures of ships of most classes. HMS *Tenedos* was the name of four ships. The first was a warship built in 1812, which became a convict hulk in 1843 and was broken up in Bermuda in 1875. The second (upon which Charles Symes served in 1881) was a corvette built at Devonport in 1870 and sold in 1887, having earned the battle honour "Zulu War 1879". Further information on particular ships can be obtained from the National Maritime Museum (considered below).

Officers

The many different ranks of naval officers and their responsibilities are described in Pappalardo (739a) and Rodger (740). Officers might be commissioned officers (such as admirals, commodores, captains, lieutenants and commanders) or warrant officers, who headed specialised branches of a ship's company (including the master, surgeon, boatswain, carpenter, gunner, purser and engineer). Many warrant officer ranks were upgraded in the 19th century to commissioned officer rank.

You should commence research of officers in published sources. Officers commissioned between 1660 and 1814 are listed in Syrett & DiNardo (743), which is based on navy lists of officers (considered below), TNA records, the *London Gazette* and published obituaries. It lists over 15,000 officers, noting men's ranks, dates of commissions and promotions (with references to the source material) and includes much post-1814 information for officers commissioned by that year. Thus, Joseph Symes (probably not related to my Symes ancestors) is recorded as serving at the battle of Trafalgar in 1805. He became a lieutenant in 1808, a commander in 1810 and a captain in 1812. He retired in 1846 and died in 1856.

You should then refer to the navy lists (although information about officers alive in 1823 or 1845 may be found more quickly in the works by Marshall and O'Byrne noted below). Steele's

Navy List was first published in 1782 and superseded in 1814 by the annual official *Navy List*. A few other official and unofficial lists of naval officers were also published between 1700 and 1782. Each *Navy List* contains lists of officers (either alphabetically or by seniority but usually indexed) and most of them provide cross references (for each officer) to separate entries for each ship, listing the names and ranks of the officers on that ship. The lists include all commissioned officers but also many warrant officers, such as surgeons, pursers and (in later lists) mates, boatswains, chief engineers and midshipmen. The lists are on open shelves at TNA, except for those issued during the two world wars, which are on microfilm in series ADM 177. Most lists are also at the SoG and some have been reproduced on microfiche by MM Publications. A typical entry in the alphabetical section of the *Navy List 1881* is:

Where serving	Name	Rank	Seniority
486	Hume, Charles R.P.	L(ieutenant)	13 Nov 1878

The number 486 refers to the entry for the ship (or port or station) on which Lieutenant Hume was serving, providing details of his ship and a list of its commissioned and warrant officers. In this case, 486 was HMS *Tenedos*, upon which Charles Symes was serving in 1881. Illustration 105 shows an extract from the *Navy List April 1884* (704), including the entries for ships such as HMS *Temeraire*, HMS *Tenedos* and HMS *Terrible*.

There are some other useful published works. O'Byrne (739) is a detailed biographical dictionary, published in 1849 (but also available as a reprint from NMP or on fiche or CD-ROM), which was intended to include all naval officers with the rank of lieutenant or above who were alive in 1845 (that is about 5,000 men). O'Byrne also included about 600 officers who had died but who had appeared in *The Navy List 1845*. The entries are in alphabetical order, and include personal details and service histories for each officer. As an example, a shortened version of the entry for Lieutenant Grosvenor Bunster is set out below. Much of the information was obtained by correspondence with the officers themselves and some entries in O'Byrne's original manuscript (held by the British Library manuscripts department) are more detailed than in the published work:

Grosvenor Bunster entered the Navy on 18 April 1806 on board the "Monarch" . . . under Captain Richard Lee . . . with Hood's squadron at the capture, on 25 September, off Rochefort of four French frigates . . . attained the rating of Midshipman on 8 June 1807, continuing with Captain Lee until 1812, was employed in . . . escorting the Royal Family of Portugal to Brazil and in the expedition to the Walcheren in August 1809. In January 1812, he joined "La Hogue" (under) Captain Capel . . . and transferred to the "Aboukir" in January 1813 . . . in August of the same year he became attached, as Acting Second Master, to the "Caledonia", flagship of Sir Edward Pellew . . . and was present on 5 November 1813 and 13 February 1814 in two actions with the French fleet off Toulon. From September 1814 until February 1815, Mr Bunster served on the "Prince Frederick" at Plymouth. He obtained his commission on 8 February 1815 but has not since been afloat. Lieutenant Bunster is married and has issue.

Charnock (711) contains detailed biographies of many naval officers from 1660 to the late 18th century. Campbell (709) describes naval actions up to 1779, including much information about

479 SYLVIA, 4. S. Surveying Vessel.

865 (695) Tons. 690 (150) H.P.

Surveying Vessel, South America.

Captain	Henry H. Dyke	10 Mar 82
Lieutenant	Casper J. Baker	4 Nov 82
	Arthur M. Field	16 Mar 82
	(W) Arthur Havergal	19 Dec 81
	Henry B. Anson	4 Apr 82
Staff-Surg.	William D. Wodsworth	
Paymaster	Henry Marsh	16 Mar 82
Chief Eng.	Samuel J. Bock	24 Dec 81
Sub.-Lieut.	Wyndham Richardson	15 Mar 82
Engineer	William J. Brown	13 Dec 81
Boatswain	James May	4 Jan 81

Commissioned at Sheerness, 16th March 1883.

---

481 TAMAR, 2. Iron S. Troop Ship.

4650 (1813) Tons. 2500 (500) H.P.

Devonport.

Nav. Lieut.	Charles Heyward	19 Mar 84
Chief Eng.	George H. Weeks	30 May 82
Boatswain	James Jones	19 Mar 84
Carpenter	John J. T. Honey	18 Aug 83

(Borne in 'India.')

---

482 TAY, 3. Double S. Iron Gun-Boat. 363 Tons. 400 H.P.

Devonport.

Engineer	John Muir	1 Oct 83
Gunner	John Endicott	3 Mar 84

(Borne in 'India.')

---

483 TEAZER, 4. Double S. Composite Gun-Vessel.

603 (464) Tons. 490 (110) H.P.

Chatham.

---

484 TEES, 3. Double S. Iron Gun-Boat. 363 Tons. 320 H.P.

Portsmouth.

The Engineer and Gunner of 'Spey' have charge of this Gun-Boat.

---

485 TEMERAIRE, 8. Double S. Iron Armour-plated Barbette Ship.

8540 Tons. 7520 H.P.

Mediterranean.

Will shortly be recommissioned on Mediterranean Station, when Officers marked ‡ *will be reappointed.*

Captain	Horace D. Lascelles	18 Jan 82
Commander	Francis C. B. Simpson	
Lieutenant	(G) Francis C. B. Simpson	
	Edward A. Richmond	5 Jan 84
	William A. L. Q. Henriques	5 Jan 84
	John Gibbings	8 May 79
	Norman G. Macalister	19 Mar 83
Beauchamp St. J. Mowbray		22 Nov 82
		25 Nov 82
Staff Comm.	Harry H. Stileman	13 Nov 83
	John Edwards	31 Dec 81
Capt. Mar.Art.	Alexander Allen (R.)	
Lieut. Mar.	Frederick White	10 June 82
Chaplain	Rev. William S. Harris	M.A.
Fleet Surg.	Robert Nelson	12 Aug 81
Paymaster	Alfred Whiffin	9 June 80
Chief Eng.	James G. Barrow	9 May 80
Nav. Instr.	James McCarthy	6 June 83
Sub.-Lieut.	Montague E. Browning	
	Harry S. Bolders	23 Jan 84
	Horace E. P. Cross	1 Jan 81
Surgeon	William Tait, M.B.	1 Jan 84
Assist. Paym.	Henry S. Baskerville	1 Jan 81

Engineer	William Scott	1 Jan 81
	John A. Cawley	1 Jan 81
	Robert B. Frison	1 Jan 81
(For Chap., Surg., and Nav. Instr.)		
Assist. Eng.	John A. H. Hicks	8 Jan 83
	William Milton	30 Aug 80
Gunner	Thomas Hawkins	1 Jan 81
Boatswain	Charles Dagnall	13 Dec 81
	Walter E. Milgate	11 Jan 80
	John Connelly	1 Sept 81
Carpenter	Charles Wyatt	1 Jan 81
Midshipman	Cecil P. Wilkinson	13 Mar 80
	Anthony D. Gurney	13 Mar 80
	Frank B. C. Bayne	1 Jan 81
	Stewart R. Forster	29 Aug 81
Naval Cadet	John C. Soady	24 Sept 83
	Arthur H. Walsh	10 Jan 83
	George E. B. Petch	10 Jan 83
	George H. Cave	10 Jan 83
	Maurice Woollcombe	24 July 85
	Guy L. Schleler	4 Jan 84
	Henry W. Armstrong	4 Jan 84
Clerk	Francis M. W. B. Barnes	1 Jan 81
	George A. Koe	1 Jan 81
	Frederick Trelohan	15 May 83

Recommissioned at Malta, 1st January 1881.

† *Lent to 'Lord to' for special service.*

The following Officers have been appointed to the 'Alexandra,' as additional for appointment to 'Temeraire' when recommissioned.

Captain	Compton E. Domville	1 Apr 84
Lieutenant	Ewen Crawford	1 Apr 84
	Frank Finnimore	1 Apr 84
	George A. Ballard	15 Mar 84
Nav. Lieut.	William J. N. Baird	1 Apr 84
Paymaster	Norcott D'E. Roberts	1 Apr 84
Asst. Paym.	Lewis le Bran	1 Apr 84
Gunner	Patrick Sweeney	1 Apr 84
Boatswain	George Trice	1 Apr 84
Carpenter	William J. Cousins	1 Apr 84
Clerk	Gover H. Miall	1 Apr 84

---

486 TENEDOS, 12. S. Corvette.

1760 (1175) Tons. 2030 (350) H.P.

North America and West Indies.

Captain	Edmund C. Drummond	
Lieutenant	(G) Bryan J. H. Adamson	8 Jan 84
	(W) Thomas Y. Greet	13 Nov 82
	John A. M. Fraser	1 Nov 82
	Arthur H. D. Raven	
	Hill	1 Nov 82
Chapl. and Nav. Instr.	Rev. James Dick	M.A. 3 Feb 83

---

490 TERROR, 8. Iron.

Floating Battery.

Armour-plated.

1844 (1971) Tons.

(Late Screw; Machinery removed.)

Bermuda.

Captain	John P. C. Grant	1 Mar 84
Lieutenant	Henry Crawford	15 Aug 81
	John H. Ellis	1 Apr 84
Staff Comm.	Edmund Hickson	22 Feb 84
Surgeon	Anthony Kidd	5 Jan 83
Paym.	Robert L. Tymott	20 July 81
Assist. Paym.	Thomas W. May	14 June 83
Boatswain	Thomas Woollacott	19 Aug 81

Officers borne for various services.

Inspr. of Machy.	John H. Heffernan	30 Oct 83
	William L. Wishart	23 Nov 82
Engineer	George Twohy	27 Nov 83
Boatswain		

(For Bermuda Yard.)

(For 'Irresistible.')

	Edwin C. Collins	12 June 82
Captain Mar.	Charles B. G. Dick	28 Jan 84
Lieut. Mar.	Richard K. W. R. Clowell	6 Apr 81
	Roland M. Byne	12 Mar 84

For service at Bermuda.

Recommissioned at Bermuda, 1st January 1880.

---

105. Extract from The Navy List, April 1884

senior naval officers. Marshall (736) contains biographies for many naval officers of the late 18th and early 19th centuries. Marshall only included officers of the ranks of commander or captain and above (whereas O'Byrne also included lieutenants) but Marshall included officers on the Admiralty list of 1823 and so included many officers who had died before O'Byrne prepared his work. A typical entry from Marshall for a junior officer (entries for senior officers are much longer) is that for William Blight:

> Son of a respectable warrant officer in the navy . . . obtained the rank of lieutenant April 15th 1803 and employed as an agent of transports at Palermo during the latter part of the war. His next appointment was Oct. 4th 1819; first lieutenant of the "Queen Charlotte", flagship of Sir George Campbell, at Portsmouth, where he continued until the death of that officer, when he obtained a commander's commission . . . Feb. 12th 1821. From this period, he remained on half-pay until May 31st 1828, when he was appointed second captain of the "Britannia", bearing the flag of the Earl of Northesk, at Plymouth, where he continued in that ship and the "St Vincent", during the remainder of his lordship's command, a period of nearly two years. His promotion to the rank of captain took place July 22nd 1830. This officer's brother, Emanuel, is a lieutenant in the Royal Navy.

The *Naval Who's Who 1917* (703) notes service details (and medal awards) of officers then alive, including war service records up to 1916. The entry for Lieutenant J.G. Nicolas is:

> Commended for service in action during the operations in Gallipoli (April 1915–January 1916); he was in command of H.M.S. "Chelmer" and was twice wounded during the landing operations of 6th and 7th August 1915 but refused to give up his duty of directing gunfire until no longer able to stand; awarded the DSC [*London Gazette* 14 March 1916].

The *Naval Chronicle* was a monthly journal, published from 1799 to 1818, which included naval news (for example news of battles) but also notices of births, marriages, deaths and obituaries of naval officers and their families. The birth, marriage and death notices are indexed in Hurst (728). Promotions and appointments of naval officers were also announced in the *London Gazette* and, from 1829, in the monthly *United Service Journal and Naval and Military Magazine*, later named *Colburn's United Service Magazine* (# chapter 20) which also gives the year of a man's first commission). Examples of appointments from the July 1860 edition (694) are:

Commanders:	Edward H. Howard (1857) to "Mohawk"
Lieutenants:	C.G. McGrigor (1846), J.B. Grove (1854) and F.H. Blair (1859) to "Colossus"
Masters:	W.H. Crane (1846) to "Colossus"
Chief Engineers:	Robert Roughton (1856) to "Bulldog"

The publications of the Navy Records Society are another useful published source. The society has published over 140 volumes of material about the Royal Navy, most referring to naval officers (and some to other ranks). For example, Toogood & Brassey (746) is an index to the six volumes of *James' Naval History*, including over 4,000 naval officers mentioned in that work, such as Midshipman James Forbishly who was wounded at the battle of Camperdown when serving on HMS *Montague*. Lavery (730) reviews shipboard life and organisation from 1731 to 1815, providing information on the daily life of naval ancestors with examples of documents that refer to many officers and ratings.

You must then turn to the naval records at TNA. The King, through his council, managed the affairs of the navy until 1546 when they were delegated to the Lord Admiral. Until 1660 relevant papers are in Privy Council, Exchequer, or Admiralty records (or in the State Papers Domestic) at TNA and include the names of some officers. From about 1660 the records are mostly in Admiralty Papers but until 1832 the Royal Navy was administered by both the Admiralty and the Navy Board so that some records are duplicated. In 1832 the Navy Board was abolished and the Admiralty took sole control of naval affairs.

Naval records at TNA (particularly the service records of officers and records of pensions) are in many series, records of a particular type may be divided between series (thus records of officers' appointments from 1790 to 1850 are in at least six different series) and a bewildering number of pieces, most of them overlapping in dates. Some types of documents survive only for short periods or for certain ranks. Rodger (740) provides detailed tables for 32 important types of documentation, noting the piece numbers (and covering dates) of the records that survive for various ranks. Pappalardo (739a) is an illustrated review of the records, with detailed advice on how researchers can find their way through the various series. Pappalardo's work is especially useful for its analysis of the digests and indexes of 1793–1858 in series ADM 12. These digests and indexes (to subjects, ships and men's names) are the principal finding-aids for the voluminous correspondence, records and minute books of the Admiralty in series ADM 1–3 and the Navy Board in ADM 106. This correspondence may refer to any officer or rating and any subject (for example a man's commission, service, wound, death, pension or family). Anyone with naval ancestors should read Pappalardo's analysis and search the records in ADM 1–3 and 106, for references to their ancestor's service or ship, so as to add material to that found in the other important naval records, which are summarised below.

A good source of information for officers is the collection of lieutenants' passing certificates at TNA, evidencing their passing of an oral examination (introduced in 1677) to qualify for their first commission. Surviving certificates cover 1691–1832 and 1854–1902. The certificates are in three sequences, overlapping in dates, in pieces ADM 6/86–118, ADM 13/88–101 and 207–238. The Navy Board copies are in ADM 107/1–63. They are arranged alphabetically (or indexed) and the List and Index Society has published an overall name index to the documents (in its volumes 289–90). The certificates usually include the applicant's age, the names of any ships on which he had served and the period he had served in the navy. From 1789 the Navy Board copies include a baptismal certificate which had to be produced to prove the applicant's age. There are also a number of series of passing certificates and service records for midshipmen, masters, gunners, boatswains and others, the dates and piece numbers (and availability of indexes) being listed by Pappalardo (739a).

Many registers of commissioned and warrant officers' services are on microfilm in series ADM 196, mostly beginning around 1840, but some dating from the late 18th century. Rodger (740) and the ADM 196 series list note the ranks of officer included in each register (and the covering dates). The registers name the ships on which an officer served and dates of appointments. Some later records include dates of birth, marriage and death, names of parents or wives or notes on a man's character. The registers extend to 1923 (and note the deaths of retired officers as late as 1960). There is an incomplete card index to the registers in the microfilm reading room and also indexes for individual registers in pieces ADM 196/7, 26–28, 33 and 57. TNA military records leaflet 30 explains how to convert the references in these indexes to the registers' piece references. TNA military records leaflet 79 provides more detail about officers' service records (and indexes) of 1893–1923. In particular, service records of many officers who served in the First World War are in pieces ADM 196/117–124 (to which there is an index in the microfilm reading room) and ADM 196/152 (which has its own index). Many service records of warrant officers who joined the navy from 1903 to 1931 are in pieces ADM 196/156–159 (partially indexed in ADM 196/163) and in ADM 196/131–136,164–165 and 174 (most of which have their own indexes). Some other service registers survive, such as those for engineers for 1839–79 in series ADM 29 (a new index to this series is reviewed below) and for surgeons in ADM 104. These are listed by Pappalardo (739a).

There are also two censuses of serving and retired officers for 1817 and 1846 (in ADM 9, with name indexes in ADM 10). Officers were required to complete forms, noting their ages and service details (ranks, ships and the relevant dates). The censuses are sadly incomplete because some officers failed to complete forms. Lists of naval officers and men who took an oath of allegiance to Charles II in 1660 are in piece C 215/6 and lists of officers who took an oath in support of William III in 1696 are in C 213.

TNA has recently received further service records, from the Ministry of Defence, of naval officers who served in or after the First World War. These are being placed in ADM 340. The first few batches in the series are for officers born before 1900. These are arranged alphabetically by men's names. They also include records for some officers in the Royal Naval Reserve and the Royal Naval Volunteer Reserve, described below.

TNA also holds the muster rolls of ships (considered below) since the late 17th century. These note the names and ages of men on each ship, and other details such as place of residence or birth. TNA also holds (in ADM 50–55) over 60,000 logs and journals of captains and masters of naval ships, dating from the 17th to 20th centuries. They may provide useful information about a ship's voyage.

Many documents evidence an officer's commissions. Until 1860 an officer received a new commission whenever he joined a new ship. Records of commissions from 1695 to 1849 are in series ADM 6 (mostly in chronological registers) and there are some partial indexes in the research enquiries room. Officers' appointments and promotions were also recorded in the *London Gazette*. Succession books list the officers appointed to each ship and are in various series listed by Pappalardo (739a) and Rodger (740). Thus one of the books of engineers has entries for each ship, listing the men appointed as each ship's engineer over a period of time. Many books have name indexes to men and ships. Much correspondence (with applications, lists, registers and related documents) relating to officers' commissions, promotions and appointments also survive at TNA. The relevant series are described by Pappalardo (739a).

Officers (and naval ratings) often had to prove their rank and the duration of their naval service in order to qualify for commissions, promotion, pensions and the admission of their children into Greenwich Hospital School. Certificates recording a man's service were therefore provided by the navy pay office to support such applications. Many of these certificates, dating from about 1802 to 1894, are in series ADM 29. Although they cover officers, warrant officers and ratings, the series is misleadingly entitled "Admiralty: officers' service records". Rodger (740) lists the piece numbers and covering dates of surviving certificates for each rank. For example, pieces ADM 29/3–6, 23–24 and 121 are volumes of entry books of certificates of service from 1817 to 1873 for boatswains, gunners and carpenters (each with an index). Two overall, but unreliable, indexes in ADM 29/97–104 have been replaced by a new index to the service records in ADM 29, compiled by B. Pappalardo, and reviewed in *Ancestors* (August/September 2003). It is searchable on PROCAT and notes over 55,000 men's names, age on joining the navy and on discharge (and, in some cases, rank, date and place of birth) as well as the ADM 29 document reference.

There are full-pay registers for commissioned and warrant officers for 1795–1905 in series ADM 24 and, for warrant officers for 1847–94 in ADM 22). Half-pay registers for 1693–1924 are in ADM 18, ADM 25 and PMG 15. Half-pay registers note the amounts paid to an officer at times when he was not on active service with a ship but sometimes also note his address. All these pay registers (and some indexes) are described by Pappalardo (739a).

From 1733, the Admiralty provided training for potential officers at the Royal Naval Academy (renamed in 1806 as the Royal Naval College) and also, from 1857, on training ships such as HMS *Britannia*. There are various records of the cadets, scattered between many series but reviewed by Pappalardo (739a).

More information about a naval officer is available if he played a prominent part in a battle, or if he was court-martialled, killed or wounded. Officers might be mentioned in despatches or in senior officers' or Admiralty correspondence. Wills of commissioned and warrant officers from 1830 to 1860 (with applications for back pay) are in series ADM 45 to which there is a card index. Rodger (740) lists the classes containing casualty lists of officers. Volume 2 of *The Cross of Sacrifice* by Jarvis & Jarvis (649) lists naval officers who died in the First World War. A card index of these officers is also in pieces ADM 242/1–50. Many records of courts martial survive at TNA and are described below. These records include much information about an officer's service career.

If an officer was wounded and had to leave active service, he had to petition for a pension. The petitions (describing an officer's service career and the action in which he was wounded) are in many pieces, listed in Rodger (740) and TNA military records leaflets 60–61. For example, pension records of flag officers, captains, commanders and lieutenants for wounds between 1832 and 1835 are in piece ADM 6/222, but some are also in ADM 23/22 and 23. Some officers received pensions from the Royal Greenwich Hospital and registers of these pensions, for 1704–1846, are in ADM 73 and those for 1814–1961 are in ADM 22, ADM 165 and PMG 71. Officers' widows were also entitled to payments from the Admiralty, the Chatham Chest (later combined with pensions from the Royal Greenwich Hospital) or the Compassionate Fund (later named the Compassionate List). The records are contained in many different pieces, but these (and the years and ranks covered by each) are listed by Rodger (740) and TNA leaflets. For example, records of Admiralty pensions for widows of flag officers, captains, commanders and lieutenants are in piece ADM 22/50 (for 1832–35), but also in ADM 23/29 (for 1834–37). About 760 applications for pensions from officers' widows (from 1846 to 1865) are in series ADM 1 and are named promiscuous (i.e. miscellaneous) letters. These include certificates of baptism and marriage provided by parish incumbents, or declarations by the widows as to the members of their family, their late husband's career and their income. A microfiche index to these records is available from East of London FHS. From 1862 officers had to submit marriage certificates to the Admiralty so that their wives would later be eligible for a pension and a few of these certificates survive for 1806–66 in pieces ADM 13/70–71, to which there is a card index (and a published version of the index has been produced by S. Tamblin) and for 1866–1902 in

ADM 13/186–192. Many sons of officers entered the school of Greenwich Hospital. The school's records (particularly application papers for entry), dating from 1728, are in series ADM 73 and the hospital's registers of baptisms, marriages and burials of 1705–1864 are in RG 4/1669–77 and RG 8/16–18.

Ratings
Research of an ancestor who was a naval rating can be difficult if he joined the navy before 1853. This is because ratings were recruited to a particular ship (and recorded in its musters or pay lists) and the navy did not keep central records of ratings. It is therefore important to discover the name of a ship on which he served. A sailor's ship may be recorded in civil registration or census records, wills, parish registers, letters, diaries, photographs, medal rolls, Trinity House petitions (see below) or pension records. Ratings might be volunteers but could (until 1815) have been press-ganged into service.

Seamen who joined the navy between 1853 and 1923 (and who were discharged or who died in or before 1929) are fairly easy to trace in the records at TNA because there is an overall index to them. The records of men who served in the Royal Navy after 1923 (unless they had left or died by 1929) are still held by the Ministry of Defence. Information about them is available on the same terms as post-1920 army records, by writing to the addresses noted above for officers' records.

If you already know the ship upon which an ancestor served, you can immediately turn to that ship's muster rolls for the relevant date. Ships' muster rolls are at TNA in overlapping sequences in series ADM 36–39 and 41 covering the period 1667–1878 (although few survive from before 1740). Similar documents (record and establishment books of 1857–73 and ships' ledgers of 1872–84) are in ADM 115 and 117. Series ADM 102 also contains some miscellaneous musters from 1740 to 1880 for naval hospitals in Britain and for naval stations abroad such as Gibraltar. The muster rolls are not in alphabetical or date order but are found by searching for a ship's name on PROCAT. The musters recorded a man's presence on a ship (so that his wages could be calculated) and recorded the issue to him of clothing, tobacco and other items. Musters were sent by the ship to the navy pay office which arranged the payment of the crew. There were two main types of musters: monthly musters and general musters. A "monthly" muster usually covered a period of two months and recorded musters that took place each week, listing the men on board (or elsewhere but still on the ship's complement) at the muster date. General musters covered a period of 12 months. The musters for a year were usually bound together, so that many ship's muster rolls consist of one general muster and six "monthly" musters. Each muster notes the number of men on board and usually the ship's location. There are then lists of the names of officers, ratings, servants, marines or others, with columns that indicate a man's presence or absence at each muster, and provide some other information about him. Musters usually give the date when a man joined the ship and (from about 1764) his place of birth and his age at the time of joining the ship. The first muster roll of a ship in which a seaman is listed should name any ship from which he had transferred. The last muster roll in which he appears may name the ship to which he transferred if he remained in the navy.

John Syms (or Symes) of Topsham in Devon, a great uncle of Charles Symes, served on HMS *L'Aigle* around 1812 (revealed, as we shall see below, by a Trinity House petition). HMS *L'Aigle* was noted in Manning & Walker (734) as having been built in 1801 and having taken part in the capture of the island of Martinique from France in February 1809, in a fleet commanded by

Rear Admiral Cochrane. The muster rolls for HMS *L'Aigle* for 1807 to 1815 are in series ADM 37. Piece ADM 37/3526 is a volume containing monthly musters from September 1811 to December 1812. Each muster lists the ship's crew, including John Simms, number 388 (a unique number on that ship), a gunner's mate, born at Topsham, to whom a bounty of 50 shillings had been paid. There were also details of clothes and tobacco supplied by the navy. The date 8 September 1808 appears in a column headed "date of the parties order for allotting monthly pay". This is the date of John's request that part of his pay be directed to a relative (probably his wife in Topsham). It could well have been when he first joined the navy. The musters note the date, place and reasons for the discharge of many men. For example, Peter Hawkwell is noted as R (run or deserted) on 19 July 1810 at Plymouth. Others are noted as D (discharged) or DD (discharged dead, from illness or action). Some men are noted as promoted (with the name of any ship to which they transferred). Illustration 106 shows an extract from the muster roll for HMS *L'Aigle* for November and December 1812 (some columns are not included). The fourth entry is for John Simms.

Having found John in the 1812 muster rolls for HMS *L'Aigle*, I could work both backwards and forwards in that ship's musters for more information about his naval career. John was recorded as a gunner's mate in muster rolls from May 1809 to April 1810 (in piece ADM 37/1882). The ship was often at sea at the time of these musters, but also sometimes at Portsmouth or Plymouth, and at Flushing in September 1809 (no doubt as part of the Walcheren campaign). The ship usually had some marines on board, or carpenters from dockyards, and a few officers, seamen or shipwrights who were taking passage to another ship or port. Piece ADM 37/5203 contained muster rolls of HMS *L'Aigle* from May 1814 to February 1815. These musters were taken at sea, but also at Genoa, Marseilles, Naples and Gibraltar. John appeared in each muster as a gunner's mate. I reached the muster rolls for July and August 1814, which noted that John was discharged from HMS *L'Aigle*, by promotion, to the ship HMS *Myrmidon*. I could now turn to that ship's musters and continue tracing John's career.

Ships' pay books from 1691 to 1856 (in series ADM 31–35) list the names of all officers and men on ships. They were used by the navy pay office to record the payments actually made to ships' crew. Again, it is essential to know the name of a man's ship in order to use these records. They were copied from the musters (and so duplicate most of the information in those musters) but they are useful for the periods for which no musters survive. They sometimes specify people to whom a man's pay was remitted (perhaps a man's wife or his parents). Furthermore, from about 1765, the pay books for each ship also have alphabets of men's names (indexing them by the first letter of their surnames). There are separate records of men's pay being remitted to their wives, children or other dependants. Allotment registers and declarations of 1795–1812 and 1830–52 are in ADM 27 and remittance registers of 1795–1851 are in ADM 26. They are mostly arranged by ship or date order but some name indexes are noted by Pappalardo (739a).

You may be able to trace a rating's career by finding him in certificates of service that were prepared to support applications to enter Greenwich Hospital or for pensions and medals. The most important of these documents are in ADM 73, reviewed further below, and in ADM 29, noted above. A new index to ADM 29, by B. Pappalardo, was also noted above. It refers to many ratings, such as Henry Leonard, noted as appearing in a register in piece ADM 29/9. The record notes that Henry Leonard was born in Battersea, joined the navy aged 17 in March 1809 (in fact being illegally press-ganged), then served on 10 ships (all named, with relevant dates, in the register) until he was discharged for "neglect of duty" in October 1832.

106. *Extract from the muster roll of HMS L'Aigle for November and December 1812 (TNA, ADM 37/3526)*

The log of the ship upon which a man served will give details of the voyages that he undertook and of actions or campaigns in which he will have taken part. Ships' logs are in ADM 50–55 and are described in TNA military records leaflet 32. Some survive from the 17th century. If a seaman died on active service, this should be noted in a ship's musters and the circumstances of his death (although probably not his name) may be recorded in the ship's log on that date.

The surname index to those on board ships in the 1861 census (# chapter 6) can be used to ascertain an ancestor's ship if he was on board on census night in 1861. The 1881 and 1901 census indexes also make it easy to find most men who were in the navy in those years. Having found an ancestor in a census return for a ship, you can then search the musters of that ship to obtain information about his service. If you do not know the name of your ancestor's ship, but know some details of his service (for example, that he sailed to Sydney in 1845), it may be possible to trace the ship on which he served and its movements. TNA holds list books (in series ADM 8), which were prepared regularly from about 1673 to 1909, recording the location of ships. There are also lists of stations and their ships in ADM 7 (for 1696–1714, 1802–04 and 1812–22). Series ADM 7 and ADM 8 (and station records for 1800–1930 in ADM 121–131, 143–152, 155, 172 and 179) are described by Pappalardo (739a). Ships' stations were also listed, from 1829, in the monthly *United Service Journal and Naval and Military Magazine*. Thus the July 1860 edition (694) lists ships' stations (and commanding officers' names) on 27 May 1860, including:

"Conqueror", 101 [guns] Capt E.S. Sotheby, Channel Fleet
"Renown", 91 [guns] Capt A. Forbes, Mediterranean
"Valorous", 16 [guns] Capt W.C. Aldham, C.B. West Indies
"Wellington", 72 [guns] Capt A.C. Key, C.B. Devonport.

Seamen who joined the navy from 1853 to 1923 are much easier to trace. There are continuous service engagement books (indexed by surname) for these men. Each rating was given a unique continuous service number and these books record the seaman's date and place of birth, his physical description and details of the ships on which he served. Continuous service records for men entering the service from 1853 to 1872 are in series ADM 139 (indexed in ADM 139/1019–1026 in the research enquiries room). From 1873, ratings were also given an official number. Service registers for men entering from 1873 to 1923 are in ADM 188 (indexed in ADM 188/245–267 in the research enquiries room). The records include some men who continued to serve up to 1929 but exclude any whose service continued after that. The entry for Charles Symes in the ADM 139 index was:

Name	Official No	Birth	Entry into service	Birth place
Symes, Charles	59.983 / 16,373B	26 Dec 1854	1871	Stoke, Devon

There are usually two numbers in the index. The continuous service number (in this case 16,373B) is in red ink. The ADM 139 series list showed that piece ADM 139/64 covered continuous service numbers 16,301 to 16,400, thus including the continuous service records (of six pages) for Charles Symes. A copy of the first page appears at illustration 107. The papers revealed that Charles had volunteered for naval service on 22 June 1871 on HMS *Impregnable*. He was born on 26 December 1854 in Stoke Devonport, Devon, and, since he was under 18 when

No. 197.

Continuous Service Engagement: *16373*

B

H.M.S. *Impregnable*
22 June 1871.

When Men or Boys enter for Continuous and General Service, (*C.S.*) Commanding Officers are immediately to fill up this Form and to transmit it to the Accountant-General of the Navy, at the end of the Month, with the List of Engagements executed. (Form, No. 41, *vide* Paymaster's Instructions, Page 40, Article 120, Clause 7.)

Christian and Surname in full .... *Charles Symes*

Where Born.—[If born out of Her Majesty's Dominions, it must be stated whether the parents are British Subjects; Foreigners not being allowed to volunteer for Continuous Service.] *Stoke*

Devon

Date of Birth.—[Great care is to be taken that the date is correctly stated; and a careful examination is to be made of the written Documents produced by Boys in support of their alleged age, in order to ascertain that they have not been tampered with, *Vide*, Foot Note, Chap. ix, Art. 3, Page 78, Admiralty Instructions.] *26 December* 1854

Description .... Height *5.3* Complexion *Sallow*

Weight 114

Hair *Brown* Eyes *Light Blue*

Marks *None*

15a

Ship in which he Volunteers .... *"Impregnable"* and No. on Ship's Books *2*

Date of Entry in Do. ..:.................. *22 June* 1871.

Rating in Do. .... *Boy 2nd Class*

Date of *actually* Volunteering for Continuous Service .... *22 June* 1871.

Commencement of Engagement .... *26 December* 1872.

Period of ditto .... *Ten Years*

Statement of all former Service in the Navy, whether as Seaman or Boy, with names of Ships and dates of Entry and Discharge; and when Men also served in Dockyards, Coastguard, or Revenue Vessels, the names of the Dockyards, Coastguard Stations, and Revenue Vessels, with period of Service, to be stated. If belonging to any Naval Reserve Force, state particulars ....

No. on Ship's Books *26/12/82 - 10*

First Entered

the Man has ever previously been entered for "C.S." the particulars of his former Engagement should be inserted here in Red Ink

Late C.S. No. ____

____ years, from _____ 18 ___.

107. *Extract from the Royal Navy service engagement papers of Charles Symes, 1871 (TNA, ADM 139/964)*

he volunteered, his period of engagement (for 10 years) was only deemed to have commenced on 26 December 1872 (his 18th birthday). He was described as five foot three inches tall, weighing 114 pounds, with a sallow complexion, brown hair and light blue eyes. The papers were signed by Charles and included a certificate signed by his mother, Grace Symes, that she consented to his engagement. The documents included papers for Charles's re-engagement, in March 1883, for another 10 years with effect from December 1882. The first page of those papers is in illustration 108. These noted that he had served on HMS *Impregnable* until December 1872 and was serving on HMS *Royal Adelaide* when he re-engaged. Colledge (712) noted that HMS *Impregnable* was a training ship and that HMS *Royal Adelaide* (a depot ship by 1883) was built at Devonport in 1828. I now had these details of Charles' naval career:

June 1871: volunteered for naval service
June 1871 to December 1872: trained on HMS *Impregnable*
April 1881 (census): serving on HMS *Tenedos*
March 1883: serving on HMS *Royal Adelaide*
May 1893 (marriage certificate): a seaman
November 1894 (daughter's birth certificate): a naval pensioner

I could now turn to each ship's records (such as muster rolls) to obtain more information about Charles's career and reconstruct his voyages (from muster rolls, lists of ships' stations and the *United Service Journal* noted above). Since he was recorded as a naval pensioner in 1894, I could also search for pension records (considered below) for further information.

When a naval rating died (more seamen died from sickness than from enemy action), any pay that was due to him (and any effects that he had left), had to be provided to his next of kin. TNA holds seamen's effects papers from 1800 to 1860 in series ADM 44, which include details of seamen's next of kin (and perhaps evidence of the relationship), some wills and any relevant correspondence. Series ADM 141 contains indexes (in the form of alphabets) to the names of the seamen in ADM 44. Some other seamen's effects papers and registers of dead men's wages are in ADM 80 and 304. Many other seamen's wills from 1786 to 1882 (usually supporting the next of kin's application for a sailor's back pay or a pension) are in ADM 48 and indexed in part by a card index in the research enquiries room and otherwise in registers (on microfilm) in ADM 142.

Naval reserves
From the late 18th century some naval reserve and auxiliary forces were raised to assist the navy. The Sea Fencibles were raised between 1798 and 1813 for home defence. Pay lists of the fencibles and records of their officers' appointments from 1798 to 1813 are in series ADM 28.

The Royal Naval Reserve (RNR) was established in 1859 and consisted of merchant seamen who undertook naval training in case their services were required (20,000 men had enrolled by 1890). TNA holds many records of the RNR. For example, service records of RNR officers of 1862–1920 are in series ADM 240. Pieces ADM 240/37–40 contain the records of those officers who served in the First World War, to which there is a microfiche name index. Some service records of RNR officers are also included in ADM 340, noted above. A few service records of RNR ratings from 1860–1913 survive in BT 164. The service records of the 50,000 ratings who served in the RNR during the First World War (including some who served after 1918) were retained and can be seen in two sequences, on microfiche, in piece BT 377/7. There are two sets

63.—*Revised, January, 1882.*—(5 & 6 Will. IV., Cap. 24, and 16 & 17 Vic., Cap. 69.)
(Article 354 of the Regulations, 1879.)

H. M. S. "*P̶.̶ ̶Adelaide*" *16373*

Continuous Service Engagement, or Re-engagement,

To be forwarded to the Accountant-General of the Navy with Form S.—41.

Christian and Surname in full	Official No., if known
Charles Symes	*59.983*

Date of Birth (*Vide* Arts. 323, 331, & 336 of the Regulations 1879)	Parish, Town, and County where Born (*Vide* Article 329 of the Regulations, 1879)
26th December 1854	*Devonport. Devon*

Personal Description at the date of this Document.

Height	Hair	Eyes	Complexion	Wounds, Scars, or Marks	Trade
ft 3⅝	*Light*	*Grey*	*Fair*		

*Date of actually Volunteering to engage or re-engage	*Commencement of Engagement	Period of Engagement
13th March 83	*26th December 82*	*Ten Years*

Ship in which he Volunteers	Date of Entering present Ship	Rating
Royal Adelaide	*14th December 82*	*Capt Fore Top*

Particulars of former Engagements, if any; but, if none, and the person engaging has had previous Non-Continuous Service, the date of his First Entry should be given. If now a First Entry, to be so stated.   *26th December 7c-10yr*

* If an Engagement is ante-dated for any period, the man's services for such period should be forwarded into Office, with the Engagement, on Form S.—62.

Declaration on Entry from Shore for Continuous Service.

In accordance with Article 12 of the Addenda (1880) to the Admiralty Instructions, the following questions are to be put by the Captain to the person about to engage for C.S., whose answers are to be recorded hereon :—

1.—Are you a British subject? † ....

2.—Have you ever served in the Navy, Army, Army Reserve, Marines, Militia, or in Her Majesty's Indian military forces? ‡ ....

3.—Do you now belong to the Militia or any regiment or corps in Her Majesty's Army, or to any established Naval or Army Reserve force? ....

4.—Have you ever been rejected as unfit for Her Majesty's service, or discharged from it on that account? ..

5.—Have you ever been dismissed with disgrace or with ignominy from the Navy, Marines, or Army? ....

† Foreigners are not to be entered—Article 329 of the Regulations, 1879.
‡ Particulars of service in the Army, Army Reserve, Marines, Militia, or H.M. Indian military forces should be forwarded into Office with this Engagement.

A.G.—22.

G & S [575] 10,000 2/82

108. *Extract from the re-engagement papers of Charles Symes with the Royal Navy, 1883 (TNA, ADM 139/964)*

455

of name indexes, on microfilm in BT 377/1–6 and in BT 377/8–28. Illustration 109 is the service record from BT 377 of Joseph Taylor. It notes Taylor's address, date and place of birth and the names of his father and mother. Taylor enrolled in the RNR in April 1924 and his service record covers the period up to 1934. It notes Taylor's service on merchant vessels, mainly fishing vessels based in Aberdeen and Montrose, as well as his training at naval depots and on the ships *Emperor of India* and the *Iron Duke* (and the payments made to him). Later service records of RNR officers and ratings are held by the MOD.

The Royal Naval Volunteer Reserve (RNVR) was created in 1903. It consisted of men, such as amateur yachtsmen, stokers and firemen, who were not employed at sea but who undertook naval training in their spare time so that they could be called upon to assist the navy in time of war. The RNVR was amalgamated with the RNR in 1958. The First World War service records of RNVR officers and men are in series ADM 337 in the microfilm reading room at TNA. The officers' records (ADM 337/117–128) are used by consulting a card index which notes a man's name, a volume number (1 to 12) corresponding to pieces 117 to 128, and a page number. The ratings' records are arranged by division (for example, London, Mersey or Bristol) and then by a man's service number. A man's service number can be found in the RNVR medal rolls in ADM 171/125–129. Few of these records extend beyond 1919; later service records of RNVR officers and ratings are held by the MOD (but some are being included with RN officers' service records in ADM 340, noted above).

The Royal Naval Division (RND) was formed in 1914 from officers and ratings of the Royal Navy, RNR, RNVR and Royal Marines for whom the navy did not have ships available. The division served as infantry throughout the First World War (in Belgium, at Gallipoli and then in France) and became the army's 63rd (Royal Naval) Division in 1916. The men who died are not included in *Soldiers Died in the Great War* but they are included in the CWGC's *Debt of Honour* register. RND service records are on microfiche in series ADM 339. They are arranged in three alphabetical sequences: for officers (ADM 339/3), deceased ratings (ADM 339/2) and other ratings (ADM 339/1). Records of some RND officers are also included in WO 339. Illustration 110 is the service record of William George Keer with the RNVR and RND from 1914 to 1919. It includes Keer's date of birth, address, physical description, civil employment and religion and the name of his father. Keer joined the RNVR in November 1914. The detailed service record for him notes, for example, his service with Benbow and Drake battalions of the RND, the fact that he was wounded in November 1916 and his successive promotions from Ordinary Seaman to Petty Officer. It also records his commission in August 1918 and transfer to the 1st Reserve Battalion, the Worcestershire Regiment.

Servicewomen

The Women's Royal Naval Service (WRNS) was formed in 1917. Service records of ratings who served up to 1919 are in series ADM 336, arranged by service number but with indexes in ADM 336/1–22. Service records of officers are in ADM 318 (indexed in the series list) and registers of officers' appointments, promotions and resignations are in ADM 321. Some of the files in ADM 318 are lengthy. Illustration 111 is the first page of an application in August 1918 from a teacher, Merle Elizabeth Dawes, for admission as a WRNS officer. This includes her date and place of birth, religion, marital status and education as well as the name, address and occupation of her father. It is worth noting how Dawes' family had moved around the country. She was born in Leytonstone in London, educated in Nottingham (and Liverpool) and lived with her parents in

109. *Service record of Joseph Taylor, a seaman with the Royal Naval Reserve, 1924 to 1934 (TNA, BT 377)*

110. *Service record of William Keer with the Royal Naval Volunteer Reserve and Royal Naval Division, showing successive promotions from ordinary seaman to petty officer, 1914 to 1919 (TNA, ADM 339)*

0722.818

W.S. 4.

FORM OF APPLICATION AND ENROLMENT
FOR ADMISSION AS OFFICER
TO
THE WOMEN'S ROYAL NAVAL SERVICE

The Candidate will complete the following particulars and give names of references as to character:—

1. Name in full { Surname	*Dawes*
{ Christian Names	*Merle Elizabeth*
2. (a) Date and place of birth	*31st July, 1891. "Alcester Villas" Leytonstone. London*
(b) Religion	*Unitarian*
3. Whether married?	*Not married —*
Number and ages of children, if any?	
4. Whether of pure European descent?	*Yes*
5. Whether a British subject of British birth?	*Yes*
6. Nationality by birth of Father	*British*
7. Nationality by birth of Mother	*British*
8. Nationality by birth of Husband (if married)	
9. Occupation of Father	*Passenger & Goods Manager in Liverpool District, Railway Directors Dpt.*
10. Permanent address of candidate	*53 Crescent Rd, Birkdale. Lancashire.*
11. Present address for correspondence	*ditto*
12. Name and address of next of kin or nearest relation resident in the British Isles	*Herbert Dawes (father) 53 Crescent Rd. Birkdale Lancs.*
13. (a) Schools or Colleges at which educated, and any degrees or diplomas obtained	*I Girls High School. Nottingham. College of Domestic Science - Liverpool 1st Class diploma Cookery & Laundry. 2nd Class Diploma Household first aid & Nursing, Hygiene domestic hygiene*
(b) At what age did you leave school?	*15½ yrs.*
14. Occupation or employment in civil life	*Domestic Subject Teacher*
15. Have you any special qualifications or experience which, in your opinion, qualify you for the appointment asked for? If so, describe them	*Experience in controlling adults & children, in teaching & the various experience as Head Cook in Hospital in Catering & Cooking for large numbers able to organise musical & other clubs*

W.R.N.S.
11 SEP 1918

M·O 5/15 x 3 C & S 110

111. *Application of Merle Elizabeth Dawes in 1918 for admission as an officer of the Women's Royal Naval Service (TNA, ADM 318/485)*

459

Birkdale, Lancashire (her father working for W.H. Smith & Son in Liverpool). She was enrolled and served in 1918 and 1919 in Portsmouth and London. Other documents on her file included references from her colleges, a note that she had also worked as a cook at a military hospital in 1917 and 1918 and reports on her work during her period of service.

As with all personnel of the armed forces, you may find more recent service records in your family's own papers. Copies can also be found at markets and ephemera fairs. Illustration 112 is the front page of the certificate of service of Louisa Valentine Waters, who joined the WRNS in June 1941 for the duration of the war. The certificate states that Louisa was born on 14 February 1919, the daughter of G.F. Waters of Surbiton in Surrey. It also notes Louisa's postings from 1941 until her release from the service in November 1946.

Nursing in naval hospitals before 1884 was undertaken by male civilians (usually ex-seamen) assisted by a few women. A female nursing service was established in 1884 (renamed as Queen Alexandra's Royal Naval Nursing Service in 1902). The records of nurses are described in Bourne & Chicken (779) and TNA military records leaflet 56. There are registers of service for nursing staff at the Royal Greenwich Hospital from 1704 to 1864 in ADM 73/83–88 that include much biographical information. Some lists of sisters in the naval nursing service and QARNNS from 1884 to 1927 are in pieces ADM 104/43, 95, 96 and 161–165 (including some indexes). These documents include some biographical information, such as the women's ranks and dates of birth, entry and discharge.

Casualties and honours

Many naval personnel died from wounds or sickness whilst on land. Their burials may be recorded in parish registers or their deaths may be recorded in the GRO registers of deaths (# chapter 5). TNA holds some registers and indexes of the deaths of naval personnel. ADM 106/3017 lists some of the men killed in the period 1742–82. Ratings who were "discharged dead" from 1859 to 1878 are listed in ADM 154. Records of deaths and burials of naval officers and ratings (and some baptisms or births of their children) can be found in ADM 121 for Mediterranean naval stations (1843–1968), in ADM 6/436 and 439 for Bermuda (1848–1946) and in other pieces listed by Pappalardo (739a). Series ADM 104 contains a number of registers, with indexes, listing some casualties from 1854 to 1950.

The burials of those who died on land during the two world wars are listed in GRO registers, in CWGC cemetery registers (# chapter 20) and on the CWGC *Debt of Honour* database. Men who died at sea and have no known grave are also recorded in GRO registers and on six CWGC memorials in Britain (# chapter 8). Their names are included (with service details and next of kin) in the CWGC's published memorial registers, which can also be searched on the *Debt of Honour* database. A typical entry from the Chatham memorial register is:

GOSLING, P.O. [Petty Officer] John Henry, C/K. 61699. R.N. H.M. Submarine *Odin*. 27th June, 1940. Age 36. Son of Frederick William and Kate Gosling; husband of Hilda Gosling of Chertsey, Surrey. 34,2.

Royal Navy, RNR and RNVR officers who were killed in the First World War (on land or at sea) are listed in volume 2 of *The Cross of Sacrifice* by Jarvis & Jarvis (649). Warrant officers and ratings who were killed are listed in volume 4 of the same work. All naval ratings who died in the First World War are listed alphabetically (with a note of their medals, service number, ship

S. 1517 (REVISED MARCH, 1941).

777 45631/D6384 6w 3/41 JP 16/706/1
1003 19834/8098 10M 7/41

WOMEN'S ROYAL NAVAL SERVICE.

Certificate of Service of

NAME ....WATERS, Louisa Valentine..................... Official No. 13774

Date of Birth ...14th February 1919...........

Religious Denomination ......R.C..

Home Address ..22 Herne Road,...........

Surbiton, Surrey..................

National Registration Identity No. ...CHFD 271..

Nearest known Relative or Friend (to be noted in pencil).

Relationship......................

Name ....

Address ....

Date of Enrolment ...~~11th~~ July 1941

17th June 1941.
in acc with ...

Date of Commencing Duty ...4th June 1941

Period of Engagement ..Duration of hostilities

	DESCRIPTION ON ENTRY.				
Height		Colour of			Scars, Marks, etc.
Feet	Ins.	Hair	Eyes	Complexion	

Establishment	Rating	Specialised or Un-specialised	Category (A.F.O. 1587/41)	Mobile or Im-mobile	From	To	Cause of Discharge
H.M.S. VICTORY: W.R.N. S. Depot	Wren	G.	Messenger	M.	4. 6. 41.	15. 6. 41.	Drafted to
H.M.S. VICTORY: C. in C's	Wren	G.	Messenger	M.	16. 6. 41.	24.	
						8.42	Hy ho. Spec Pay
	Wren	Spec		M	25.8.42	3/6/44	Progressive Pay
	Wren	Spec:		M	4/6/44	4/1/4	
H.M.S. Pembroke.	Wren			M.	4/6/44	18 June 45.	
HMS Beaconsfield	Wren		+P op:	M.	19 June 45	30 Nov 45	
HMS Golden Hind P.D.D.	Wren		T, P Op.	M	DEC. 45		
N.M.S. Victory IV	Wren	P.Fd inches	T/P. Op.	M.		7-11-46	Released in Class A.
			T, P. op				

C.E. 51419/41.

112. *Certificate of service with the Women's Royal Naval Service of Louisa Waters from 1941 to 1946*

461

and date and place of birth) in ADM 242/7–10. S. Tamblin has published a roll of honour of about 7,000 men who were killed or wounded at the battle of Jutland in 1916. Some journals kept by naval surgeons between 1795 and 1963 have survived and are held at TNA in series ADM 101. These journals are arranged by ship up to 1915, then by year (but there are indexes to the ships' names). They list the names and rank of men who were wounded or sick, the nature of the wound or sickness and the outcome of treatment (for example "died" or "moved to hospital"). If you discover that your ancestor's ship was involved in a battle, it is worth searching for such a journal in this series. Some other registers or lists of sick or wounded officers and ratings (primarily from naval hospitals) between 1739 and 1945 are listed by Pappalardo (739a).

Pappalardo (739a) lists the pieces in ADM 30, 97, 103 and 105 that record British prisoners of war (sailors, soldiers and civilians) in the period 1793–1815. Many naval personnel who were captured during the two world wars are listed in the sources noted in chapter 20.

Naval medals

Campaign medal rolls for all ranks of naval personnel, from 1793 to 1972, are on microfilm in series ADM 171, mostly arranged by date, then alphabetically by ship's name. In order to find an ancestor you may therefore need to know the name of the ship on which he served. These rolls include awards of the Naval General Service Medal, the Crimea Medal and (for the First World War) the British War Medal and Victory Medal.

Almost 21,000 Naval General Service Medals were issued retrospectively in 1847 (for naval service between 1793 and 1840) to those qualifying seamen who were still alive. The roll for this medal has been published in Douglas-Morris (715). It lists the awards in chronological order of the naval action for which the award was made (and then lists the men in order of surname) but is indexed by ship's name. Thus there is an entry for HMS *Crescent* for its capture of the French frigate *Reunion* off Cherbourg on 20 October 1793, listing the men who received the medal and their ranks. The First World War medals rolls are arranged alphabetically by men's names within these sequences:

ADM 171/89–91	RN, RNVR and RNAS officers
ADM 171/92–93	RNR officers
ADM 171/94–119	RN and RNAS ratings
ADM 171/120–124	RNR ratings
ADM 171/125–129	RNVR ratings

Information about campaign medals since 1939 is still held by the Ministry of Defence, Naval Medal Office, PPPA (Medals), Room 1068, Centurion Building, Grange Road, Gosport, Hampshire PO13 9XA. Men of the Royal Naval Division who fought in France or Belgium from August to November 1914 were awarded the 1914 Star (# chapter 20) and a list of them has been published by NMP.

Series ADM 171 also contains rolls of gallantry medals that were awarded to naval personnel, such as the Conspicuous Gallantry Medal, the Distinguished Service Cross and the Distinguished Service Medal. The CGM was instituted in 1855 and awarded to petty officers and ratings (and NCOs and men of the Royal Marines). Recipients were noted in the *Navy List*. ADM 171/75 is an index to the awards of the CGM from 1914 to 1918. Most citations for the CGM appear in the *London Gazette* and records of annuities to recipients are in series PMG 16. The DSC was instituted in 1901 (originally named the Conspicuous Service Cross) for naval warrant officers (and later commissioned officers below the rank of lieutenant commander). Recipients were listed in the *London Gazette* (about 1,700 from 1901 to 1918 and about 4,500 during the Second World War) and a roll of recipients from 1901 to 1938 has been published in Fevyer (719). The DSC medal rolls for 1942–72 are in ADM 171/164–165. The DSM was instituted in 1914 for petty officers and naval ratings and for NCOs and men of the Royal Marines. Awards were published in the *London Gazette* (about 5,500 during the First World War and about 7,130 during the Second). Rolls of recipients of the DSM during WW1 and WW2 have been published (with the entries from the *London Gazette*) in Fevyer (720) and (721). Some awards of the Distinguished Service Order, Victoria Cross and the Military Medal (# chapter 20) were also made to naval personnel, usually for service ashore.

The "Naval Secretary's Honours and Awards Index", compiled by the Admiralty from 1939 (# chapter 20), included medals and other awards for all personnel in the services controlled by the Admiralty. Much of this information has been published in "Seedie's lists", such as the volume (706) for RN and RNVR personnel serving in coastal forces (for example operating motor torpedo boats). For example, the *London Gazette* of 28 December 1943 announced that the crew of MTB 24, of the Dover Command, had been honoured for attacks on enemy shipping. The DSC was awarded to Lieutenant Victor Clarkson of the RNVR, the DSM was awarded to Master Mechanic Arthur Fox and Leading Seaman Edward Anderson was mentioned in dispatches.

Some other published medal rolls can lead you to the original records for your ancestor. Duckers & Mitchell (717) feature the medal roll from piece ADM 171/25 for naval personnel honoured for their part in the Azoff campaign of 1855 (during the Crimean War). Fevyer & Wilson (722) and (723) list awards from 1900 to 1920 of the Africa General Service Medal to the Royal Navy and Royal Marines and the medals (recorded in piece ADM 171/55) awarded during the Third China War (the Boxer Rebellion) of 1900.

Naval personnel were also entitled to medals for long service and good conduct. There were six separate issues of a Meritorious Service Medal for naval forces between 1848 and 1980 and a list of awards has been published. The long service medals awarded from 1830 to 1990 to the Royal Navy, Royal Marines, RNR and RNVR are at TNA and described in Douglas-Morris (716) with lists of some recipients of each medal. For example, rolls of the RNR Long Service Medal are in pieces ADM 171/70–72, in approximate alphabetical order. The Albert Medal should also be noted at this point. It was instituted in 1866 for those saving lives at sea (extended in 1877 to similar acts on land) and about 530 awards were made up to 1945 (many to seamen, but also to soldiers and civilians). A register of awards from 1866 to 1913 is at TNA in series BT 97 and recipients are listed in Henderson (1042). Recommendations for the award from 1866 to 1950 are in series HO 45.

Pensions for ratings

Until the late 19th century there was no systematic provision of pensions for naval personnel or their dependants. TNA holds records (in series ADM 82) of the Chatham Chest, a fund established in 1590 to provide pensions to sailors who were wounded or to the dependants of sailors killed in action. Administration of the fund was transferred in 1803 to the Royal Greenwich Hospital. There are registers of payments made from the Chatham Chest in 1653–57 and 1675–1799 and also applicants' petitions for pensions. They usually describe how a sailor was killed or injured, the ships on which he served and specify the sailor's (or dependant's) circumstances at the time of the application. There are indexes to pensioners who received payments between 1695 and 1797.

The Royal Greenwich Hospital was founded in 1694 to provide for naval pensioners and their dependants. Registers of baptisms (1720–1856), marriages (1724–54) and burials (1705–1857) are held by TNA in series RG 4 and RG 8 (at the FRC), but many of its other records, of in-pensioners and out-pensioners (that is, those receiving a pension from the hospital but living elsewhere), also survive. They are included in many different series and pieces but listed in Pappalardo (739a), Rodger (740) and in TNA military records leaflet 62. Admissions and discharges of in-pensioners from 1704 to 1869 are recorded in entry books and admission papers (in series ADM 73), including many certificates of service from the navy pay office, dating from 1790, but often dealing with men's service before that year. Applications for admission to Greenwich Hospital, from 1737 to 1859, are in pieces ADM 6/223–266 (with name card indexes to ADM 6/223–247 in the research enquiries room). To support these applications, the Navy Pay Office would prepare certificates of men's naval service, noting the dates served on each ship. The certificates of 1802–94 (for warrant officers and seamen) are in series ADM 29 (noted above).

The papers for Greenwich out-pensioners include registers of applications for 1789 to 1859 in pieces ADM 6/271–320. Thus piece ADM 6/316 is a register for 1855 recording hundreds of men receiving pensions or gratuities, such as:

Name	Pension	Term or duration
Charles Hunt	£9 4s	Life
Richard Hemmett	£21 12s	Life

There are also pay books for pensioners (including many certificates of service) for most of the period 1781–1883, in series ADM 22, ADM 73 and WO 22. As noted above, Greenwich Hospital also had a school for seamen's children and it arranged apprenticeships for them. The school admission papers (1728–1870) and apprenticeship registers (1808–38) are in ADM 73, including many certificates of baptism, details of the parents' marriage and the father's service history.

There were various other pensions or bounties available from the Admiralty or charities, mainly for widows or dependants of commissioned and warrant officers. The relevant pieces (with codes ADM or PMG) and covering dates are listed in Rodger (740) and TNA military records leaflet 62. Some of the records date from the late 17th century and include details of a man's naval service, his marriage, the baptism of his children and the applicant's financial circumstances.

When continuous service for ratings was introduced in 1853, pensions were also offered to men who served for 20 years. Since many men (such as Charles Symes) signed their first engagement at about the age of 18, they could retire from the navy aged about 38, receive a pension and carry on other work. Thus by 1894 Charles, aged 40, was a naval pensioner, but also a merchant seaman. Unfortunately, few records of these pensions have survived.

Courts martial
The records of courts martial of naval officers and seamen for 1680–1910 are in series ADM 1 and for 1911–65 in ADM 156, with further reports and registers in ADM 106, 121, 153, 178 and 194.

These records, mostly arranged by date, are described by Pappalardo (739a), who also describes some indexes and finding-aids, principally the Admiralty digests and indexes in ADM 12.

Miscellaneous naval records

Some other records at TNA may also refer to your naval ancestor. From about 1790, ships' captains had to keep registers (description books) that noted the physical description, age and place of birth of every seaman. A few of these survive. Bounty lists recorded payments to volunteer seamen from the 17th to 19th centuries. Surviving lists for 1695–1708 and 1741/2 are in ADM 30.

Three TNA leaflets describe its enormous holdings of Royal Navy operational records. Records up to 1914 are described in military records leaflet 35 and those for the two world wars are described in military records leaflets 33 and 69. However, you should first refer to the many published histories of naval operations (many available at local libraries) before attempting to use the records at TNA. After each world war official lists of the naval ships that had been lost were published by HMSO. These have been reprinted (with similar lists of merchant ships) in *British Vessels Lost at Sea: 1914–1918 and 1939–1945* (693), recording the name, type and tonnage of each vessel and the date, place and cause of loss. Thus the light cruiser HMS *Pegasus* is noted as having been sunk on 20 September 1914 by the German ship *Konigsberg*. The destroyer HMS *Whirlwind* was sunk on 5 July 1940 by a U-boat torpedo off the coast of Ireland. The official history of naval operations during the First World War (based on Admiralty records) by J.S. Corbett and H. Newbolt, was published in five volumes by HMSO from 1920 to 1931 (and a reprint is available from NMP).

Useful information about the navy, its ships and operations may also be obtained from the National Maritime Museum and the Royal Naval Museum (both considered below), the Society for Nautical Research (which publishes a journal *Mariner's Mirror*), the Britannia Royal Naval College Library (at Dartmouth, Devon) and the Naval History Library (at Central Library, Plymouth, Devon).

Dockyards

Macdougall (732) is a brief history of naval dockyards in Britain and the colonies. The first dockyard was founded in 1496 at Portsmouth, followed by Woolwich (established 1512), Deptford (1513), Chatham (1570), Portsmouth and Sheerness (1665) and Plymouth (1691). By 1770 these dockyards employed about 11,000 artisans, clerks and labourers. The navy also had dockyards abroad (including Gibraltar, Port Royal in Jamaica and Halifax in Nova Scotia). The dockyards were controlled until 1832 by the Navy Board (or the Victualling Board) and after 1832 by the Admiralty. Records of dockyard employees up to the 19th century are at TNA and the piece numbers and covering years of each yard's records are listed in Colwell (242) and TNA military records leaflet 41. Many dockyard officers had previously served in the navy and many shipwrights also served as ships' carpenters (after apprenticeships in the dockyards) so that many dockyard personnel can also be found in ships' records. Examples of the dockyard records are paybooks of the larger yards from 1660 to 1857 (many later records were destroyed) in series ADM 42, and paybooks and musters for smaller yards (in ADM 32, 36 and 37). Description books of artificers for 1748 to 1830 (in ADM 106) note men's physical descriptions. Registers for 1794 to 1815 (in ADM 7) list men who were protected from impressment with the Royal Navy (by reason of their dockyard work). Pension records of officers, artificers and labourers are in various series listed by Colwell (242). There are also photographs of work being carried out in dockyards between 1857 and 1961 in ADM 195.

RECORDS OF THE MERCHANT NAVY

From 1835 merchant shipping was the responsibility of the Register Office of Merchant Seamen and later the Registry General for Shipping and Seamen (RGSS), who reported to the Board of Trade. The Board's archives have department code BT at TNA and detailed information about these records is provided by Watts & Watts (747), Smith, Watts & Watts (742) and TNA domestic records leaflets 89–95 and 111–114. The RGSS is now named the Registry of Shipping and Seamen (RSS). Some very recent records of merchant seamen, such as merchant ships' log books and crew agreements since 1996, are still held by the RSS in Cardiff (PO Box 420, Cardiff CF24 5JW, telephone 02920 448800).

There are detailed records of merchant seamen for 1835 to 1857 and 1918 to 1972 (considered below) which are indexed by surname. However, for other periods you must first ascertain a ship upon which a man served. This may be recorded in parish registers, census records (the 1881 and 1901 census indexes make it easy to find a seaman in these years), wills, letters or (see below) in indexes to crew lists and the Trinity House petitions. The surname index to people on board ships in the 1861 census (# chapter 6) is also very useful. John Symes (an uncle of my great grandfather Charles Symes) was a merchant seaman who was at sea on census night. The index included this entry with the census reference RG 9/4526 folio 71A:

Symes, John 48 M[ar] Able Seaman Topsham, Devon [ship] "Maria"

The census return with this reference, for the ship *Maria*, is at illustration 113. The ship was a schooner of Exeter engaged in the home trade, which had been at Newport river on census night, returning to Topsham (when the master handed in the census schedule) on 25 May 1861. The crew consisted of the master (Thomas Symons), the mate, John Symes, one other seaman and a boy (who appeared to be the master's son).

Civil registration certificates may also assist, but may simply note a man as a merchant seaman, without naming his ship. In addition to the records considered in chapter 5, GRO holds marine registers, which record births and deaths of British nationals on British ships from 1837 up to 1930 for births and 1965 for deaths. The indexes list the names of the children or the deceased (and from 1875 the deceased's age), as well as the name of the ship on which the birth or death took place. Until 1874 the entries are sorted (in groups of 5 or 10 years) by the initial letter of the surname and the first vowel. Thus entries for Brock are under Bo. From 1875, entries are listed by year and then alphabetically. An entry in the index for 1882 is:

Bullworthy, William [Age] 34 [Name of Vessel] *Cornwall* [page] 225

A certificate provides information such as the date of birth (and parents' names) or the date, place and cause of death, the seaman's last place of abode and his birth place (if known). From about 1854 separate registers of births, marriages and deaths at sea were also compiled by the RGSS from ships' log books (considered below) that were filed by ships' masters. These registers (at TNA in series BT 158) extend to 1883 (for marriages), 1887 (for births) and 1890 (for deaths). From

(Form A.)

LIST of the CREW and OTHERS on BOARD of the SHIP or VESSEL called the "_Maria_" on the NIGHT of SUNDAY, APRIL 7th, 1861.

	NAME and SURNAME	CONDITION	AGE OF		RANK or OCCUPATION	WHERE BORN	If Deaf-and-Dumb or Blind
	Write, after the Name of the Master, the Names of the other Officers and Crew: and then the Names of Passengers and Visitors (if any).	Write "_Married_" or "_Unmarried_," "_Widower_" or "_Widow_," against the Names of all Persons except Young Children.	Males	Females	State here the rank of the Officers, and the rating of the Men and Boys of the Crew. The rank or occupation of Passengers and Visitors should be stated as fully and clearly as possible.	Opposite the Names of those born in England, Scotland, Ireland, and the Channel Islands, write the County or Island, and the Town or Parish. If born in the British Colonies including the East Indies, state the Colony. If born in Foreign parts, state the Country; and if also a British Subject add "_British Subject_," or "_Naturalized British Subject_," as the case may be.	Write "_Deaf-and-Dumb_," or "_Blind_," opposite the Name of the Person; and if so from Birth, add "_from Birth._"
1	Thomas Edwards	Married	45		Master	Devon — Topsham	
2	Henry Redman	Unmarried	24		mate	— do —	
3	James Longman	married	39		A.B. seaman	do Beerferris	
4	John Sydnes	married	46		A.B. seaman	do Topsham	
5	Henry Edwards	Unmarried	16		Boy	— do —	
6							
7							
8							
9							
10							
11							
12							
13							
14							
15							

I declare the foregoing to be a true Return.   Witness my Hand,   _(Signature)_   Tho. Edwards

113. _Return for the ship Maria in the 1861 census (TNA, RG 9/4526)_

1874 ships' masters also had to report births and deaths at sea to the RGSS. The RGSS provided this information to the English, Scottish or Irish Registrar Generals (so their registers should include these entries) but the RGSS also prepared his own registers. Those for deaths at sea up to 1888 and births up to 1891 are at TNA in series BT 159 and 160 respectively. Registers (with indexes) of births, marriages and deaths of seamen (and ship passengers) at sea from 1891 to 1972 are in BT 334. Series BT 341 contains 260 files, arranged by year then ship's name, of reports, evidence and correspondence from inquiries into deaths at sea from 1939–46 and 1964.

Crew lists and muster rolls

Merchant ships' masters or owners were required from 1747 to keep muster rolls that listed the crew members of a ship on each voyage. The musters varied in form over the years. Until 1834 they noted a seaman's name, home address, the dates of his engagement and discharge and the name of his previous ship. The musters had to be filed at the ports of arrival or departure. The few that survive are at TNA in series BT 98. Before 1800 they survive only for the ports of Shields (from 1747), Dartmouth (from 1770), Plymouth (from 1761) and Liverpool (from 1772). After 1800 many more rolls have survived but they are arranged by port and year (and are not indexed) and so you need to know a man's home port in order to search for a ship on which he sailed. Due to the number of ships at some ports, this task may be impractical.

From 1835 acts of Parliament required agreements and crew lists to be filed with the Register Office of Merchant Seamen (and later the RGSS). The records up to 1860 are in series BT 98, arranged by port name (or number) and date. They are summarised below but reviewed in detail (with an index of port numbers) in Watts & Watts (747).

(a) *1835–44* The filed documents were:

(i) "Schedule C" filed after each foreign voyage (excluding voyages to northern France, the low countries and parts of Germany) or

(ii) "Schedule D", home or coastal trade (for ships over 80 tons), half yearly returns as at the end of June and December.

These documents include an agreement that describes the voyage that the crew were agreeing to undertake and crew lists which note each man's name, the date he joined the ship, his place of birth, his position (for example mate or ordinary seaman) during the voyage, the date and place that he left the ship and the previous ship on which he had served. The crew lists since 1835 are not indexed, and so the best route into them is through the indexed seamen's registers of 1835 to 1856 (considered below), since they name a man's ship and its home port. Having found the name and port of an ancestor's ship, you can order the pieces in BT 98 (ascertained from the BT 98 series list) that contain the crew lists for ships of that port for the relevant years. The crew lists are in boxes, with the documents in order of the initial letter of the ship's name. Watts & Watts (747) discovered the following information in a crew list for the ship *Minstrel* of Bridlington in 1843:

Name	William Yates	James Watts
Age	21	23
Place of birth	Stroud	Hasbro
Quality	Apprentice	Seaman

Ship in which last served	Minstrel	Lord Wellington
Date of joining ship	2nd December 1842	2nd October 1843
Place where	Hull	Quebec
Time of death or leaving ship	Killed by a fall down the F Hatchway 29th March	Discharged 19th November 1843
Place where	Patras	Hull
How disposed of	Interred in the church yard of St Andrew	Discharged

(b) *1845–56* Series BT 98 also includes further records that had to be filed from 1845. Schedules A and B were, respectively, agreements between master and crew for foreign trade or home trade (that is, the coastal trade or fishing). Schedule G listed the names of crew of a ship that was sailing abroad. These give similar information to the crew lists of 1835–44, but also noted each crew member's wages. Schedule G also noted the numbers of the seamen's register tickets (considered below). There are vast quantities of these crew lists but a few have been transcribed. The crew lists of 1851 for vessels registered in Cornwall have been transcribed and indexed by L. Hore and can be purchased on CD-ROM from Family History Indexes. They contain entries for about 6,000 seamen, with a man's age, ticket number, ship, date and place of joining and his previous ship.

(c) *1857–60* Crew lists for these years are also in BT 98 but arranged by year and by ships' official numbers. These numbers are noted in the *Mercantile Navy List*, published annually from 1850 (copies are at TNA and, from 1857, at Guildhall Library).

(d) *1861–1976* Most agreements and crew lists for this period survive, but they are held in a number of archives. TNA holds a random sample of 10 per cent of them, for each year up to 1938 and for 1951–72, in series BT 99, 100, 144 and 165. The remainder for the years 1861, 1862, 1865, 1875, 1885, 1895, 1905, 1915, 1925, 1935, 1955, 1965 and 1975 are at the National Maritime Museum. Some CROs hold crew lists for local ports for other years up to 1913. For example, Essex Record Office holds crew lists for 1863–1913 for Colchester, Harwich and Maldon. The remainder of the crew lists for 1863–1938 and 1951–76 are held by the Maritime History Group at the University of Newfoundland (considered below). The crew lists for 1939–50 are being transferred from the RSS to TNA (those for 1947–48 are in BT 99, those for 1949–50 are in BT 380 and those for 1939–46 will soon be in BT 380 and 381. The Maritime History Group has produced three indexes to the surviving crew lists of 1863–1938, by reference to each ship's official number (noted in the *Mercantile Navy List*). A microfiche index (698) lists the group's holdings of crew lists for 1863–1913. An index in microfiche or book form (696) lists the group's holdings of crew lists for 1913–38 (noting, for each ship, the types of agreements and crew lists available and whether any of the ships' logs remain with the lists). A third index in book form (695) lists those crew lists of 1863–1913 held at CROs. Guildhall Library has copies of each index and TNA has a copy of the first index. An index to the men and ships recorded in the crew lists and agreements of 1863–1913, held at CROs, is being prepared. The first edition of this index has been released on CD-ROM by S&N Genealogy Supplies and is reviewed in *Family Tree Magazine* (February 2003). This includes transcripts of only a small percentage of the surviving records but lists 270,000 men with their ages, birthplaces, rank, ship and previous ships.

(e) **1977–94**   TNA holds 10% of the crew lists of 1977–94 (in series BT 99 and 100) and the National Maritime Museum holds the others for 1985. The remainder have been destroyed.

Registers of seamen 1835–57

Information from crew lists was used by the Register Office of Merchant Seamen, from 1835 (and later by RGSS), to prepare registers of merchant seamen. The first series of registers, for 1835–36, is at TNA in series BT 120 (available on microfilm). Seamen's names are listed alphabetically with each man's age, place of birth, the name of his ship and his "quality" (his position in the crew). Having found an ancestor, you can then turn to that ship's crew lists.

The second series of registers (for 1835–44) is in series BT 112. This originally consisted of two parts with some name indexes in BT 119. I searched BT 119 for my ancestor Robert Symes of Topsham (father of Charles) and his brother John. There were 12 men named Robert Symes or Sims (none of whom appeared to be my ancestor) but I found John:

Number	Name	Age	Born	Ships served in
6480	Sims, John	22	Topsham	*Mary, Jane Dove, Resolute*

Turning to the registers in BT 112 I found:

No.	Name, age, place of birth	Reference	Reference to voyages	
39441	Sims, John 24	6480	39/204 *Fortitude*	78/326 (?????)
	Topsham		Dec 42	June 43

This example shows two voyages of John Sims (or Symes). The ship's name for one voyage was illegible (and neither voyage appeared to be on any of the three ships noted in BT 119), but the register noted that John sailed on the ship *Fortitude* in the six months ending December 1842. The figure 39 in that voyage reference was the port number. Port numbers are useful for finding a ship's crew lists (in series BT 98) and they are listed in the BT 98 series list and in Watts & Watts (747). Thus 39 is the port number for Exeter. Having found references to John and the ships *Fortitude, Mary, Jane Dove* and *Resolute*, I could now turn to the crew lists to obtain more information about him and his ships. The difficulty that I experienced in using BT 112 and 119 arose because the two parts of the BT 112 registers were, at some point, taken apart and put in approximate alphabetical order by seamen's names. The result is a mess and so researchers should see Watts & Watts (747) and a new finding-aid prepared by them, at TNA, before trying to use the BT 112 registers.

This registration system was replaced in 1845 by a system of seamen's register tickets (which continued until 1853). Each British seaman leaving the country had to have a register ticket (the tickets were held by seamen and so most have been lost). However, the seamen are listed alphabetically (with their birthplace and ticket number) in an index in BT 114. One can then turn to the ticket number in the register of tickets in BT 113. This notes each seaman's date (and place) of birth, residence onshore, physical description, the year he first went to sea, whether he had served in the Royal Navy and whether he was literate. The register also lists, by year, each man's voyages recorded in the crew lists. The codes used in the register are explained by Watts & Watts (747). An example that they give (from piece BT 113/24) for their ancestor James Watts in 1846 is:

OUT (voyage)	1846	HOME (voyage)
1140–75–2		1140–75–2
75–6–4		64–31–7

This shows that in 1846 James Watts was on a ship registered in Newcastle (75 in the top lines) on both outward and inward voyages. The ship is not named, but the entry notes the port rotation number (in this case 1140 in the top lines) given to the ship by its port (Newcastle). The ship's name could be identified by looking through the Newcastle crew lists of 1846 to find the ship with that port rotation number (although this would be a lengthy task). It is also sometimes possible to ascertain a ship's name by comparing the port name and dates of departure and arrival with *Lloyd's List* (see below). The entry notes that Watts' ship left Newcastle (75 in the lower left line) on about 6 April (6–4 in the lower left line) and returned to London (64 in the lower right line) on about 31 July (31–7 in the lower right line). The dates are those of the filing of documents (which may be slightly different from the dates of sailing or arrival). Watts & Watts discovered that ship 1140 of Newcastle was the *Pallas* which sailed from Newcastle to Canada, then back to London. The crew list showed James Watts joining the ship at South Shields on 4 April 1846 and leaving it in London on 31 July, his previous ship having been the *Grantham*.

This ticket system was replaced in 1853, until 1857, by a new register of seamen Series III (in series BT 116). The register lists men alphabetically but also gives a man's age, place of birth and details of his voyages (the ship's name and the date and port of departure). Watts & Watts found the following entry for their ancestor John Watts in the volume (piece BT 116/98) covering surnames that commenced with the letters Wa to Web:

Name	Age	Place of Birth	Voyages
John Watts	25	Norfolk	S 10.2 *Falcon*, London.

From 1857 until 1913 the principal records of merchant seamen are the crew lists for each ship. You therefore need to discover the name of a ship upon which an ancestor sailed in this period in order to search in the crew lists or other records at TNA.

Registers of seamen 1913–41
A Central Index Register of Seamen, in the form of a card index, operated from 1913 to 1941. The cards of 1913–18 have not survived but those for 1918–41 can be seen on microfiche at TNA (the original cards are held by Southampton Archive Service, see appendix VII). They record over 1.25 million seamen.

Seamen of 1918–21 are recorded on CR 10 cards on microfiche in series BT 350. The cards also cover men's service after 1921. They are arranged alphabetically by surname, then forename, and record a man's date and place of birth, his description (with a photograph) and his discharge number. For example, fiche 1399 in the series covers names Kearns, J. to Keating, J. The fiche included a number of men named Keates, one of whom (Richard Oliver Keates) was a nephew of my great grandmother Alice Amelia Keates. Illustration 114 is the front and the reverse of his card, with his photograph. Richard was noted as a steward, born in 1888 in Leytonstone. His next of kin was Mrs Lily Keates, living in Guernsey. The card notes his discharge number, under "Dis. A No.", as 391334 (and this leads you to another card index, in BT 348, noted below). Next to the photograph is a list of the official numbers of ships on which Richard served and his

114. *Card with photograph for the merchant seaman Richard Oliver Keates from the Central Index Register of Seamen 1918–21 (TNA, BT 350)*

dates of signing on (enabling you to turn to crew lists and log books). The ships' names can be found in registers, in BT 336, of changes of ships' masters 1893–1948 (which are arranged by the ships' official numbers but include the ships' names).

Series BT 348 and 349 are also microfiche copies of card indexes. They cover seamen for 1921–41 (excluding those who continued in service after 1941). The cards in BT 349, known as CR 1 cards, are arranged alphabetically, by surname then forename, noting a man's date and place of birth, his description (sometimes with a photograph) and his discharge number, under "Dis. A No.". As with the BT 350 cards, this number leads you to a card index, arranged numerically by men's discharge numbers, in BT 348. These cards (CR 2 cards) note the official numbers (and sometimes names) of ships on which a man sailed and his dates of signing on.

There is yet another card index for the period 1921–41, in BT 364. In some cases, the CR 1, 2 and 10 cards for a man were taken out of the three indexes noted above and placed in this fourth index, arranged by men's discharge numbers. If you cannot find a seaman in the other indexes, he may be recorded in BT 364 but it will be difficult to find him unless you know his discharge number.

Registers of seamen 1942–72

A new Central Register of Seamen operated from 1942, to record all men who had served at sea for at least five years. Men's CR 1 and 2 cards were extracted from the indexes noted above and placed in this new register (known as CRS 10). This register operated until 1972. Forms known as docket books were also prepared for each seaman noting his date and place of birth, qualifications, rank, discharge number and a list of the ships on which he had served. The docket books are in series BT 382, divided into eight groups and then arranged alphabetically. The two main groups are *Series 1, Seamen Mainly of European Origin (1941–46)* and *Series 2, Seamen Mainly of European Origin (1946–72)*. The other groups are listed in Watts & Watts (747) and in TNA domestic records leaflet 90.

A series of "seamen's pouches" (similar to safety deposit boxes) were also created in the period 1913–72 and are in BT 372 but do not survive for all men. Some pouches include cards with men's photographs. They are arranged by men's discharge number but can be searched by a man's name on PROCAT.

Ship's logs

From 1850 masters were required to keep an official log describing the ship's voyages, births or deaths on board and the conduct, illnesses, desertion or punishment of crew. The logs were filed after each foreign voyage (or every six months for home trade ships). Many logs have been destroyed (very few survive for 1880–1901) but most surviving logs up to 1904 are filed with the crew lists held by TNA, the National Maritime Museum and the Maritime History Group. Logs from 1905 to 1919 (with a few from other years) are in series BT 165 at TNA.

Seamen's effects

From 1851 masters of British ships had to surrender to the Board of Trade any wages or effects of seamen who had died during a voyage. A register of seamen's wages and effects for 1852–81 and 1888–89 is in series BT 153 at TNA, noting a seaman's name, the date and place of his engagement, details of his wages, the date (and cause) of death, the name and home port of the ship, the name of the ship's master and (from 1854) the ship's official number. There are indexes to the seamen's names (in BT 154) and to the ships' names (in BT 155). Series BT 156 contains monthly lists of seamen's deaths from 1886 to 1890.

Masters and mates

An alphabetical register of masters' tickets was prepared between 1845 and 1854 (from information in the register of seamen's tickets in series BT 113). This register is in BT 115. Voluntary examinations for masters and mates were introduced in 1845 and made compulsory in 1850. The men who passed were given certificates of competency. Certificates of service were issued to those masters and mates who were exempt from the examinations by reason of their long service. The system also applied to engineers from 1861 and to mates of fishing vessels from 1883. Certificates usually note the year and place of birth of each man and the date and place of his certification as master, mate or engineer. The certificates were copied into registers (which sometimes also note the ships on which a man served and the voyages that he undertook each year). The registers are in series BT 122–6, 128–30, 139–40 and 142–3. For example, BT 125 is the register of competency certificates (1854–1921) for masters and mates of home trade ships. BT 122 is the register of competency certificates (1845–1906) for masters and mates of foreign trade ships. BT 124 and 126 are registers of masters' and mates' certificates of service (up to 1888). Most of these registers extend to around 1913 to 1921 and there are name indexes in BT 127 (for home or foreign trade vessels), BT 138 (for fishing boats) and BT 141 (for engineers). The registers of certificates sometimes include the letters "BB" with a number. This means that disciplinary proceedings were taken against the holder of that certificate. The number is a page in the "Black Books" of 1851–93 in pieces BT 167/33–37 (indexed in BT 167/37).

From 1910 to 1930, RGSS kept a card register as a combined index to competency certificates for masters, mates and engineers. The index is in BT 352. The cards note a man's name, date and place of birth, certificate number, the port in which he was examined and the date he passed his examination. Registers of the issue of certificates to masters, mates and engineers from 1913 are in these series:

BT 317   registers of masters and mates certificates (1917–77)
BT 318   examination registers for masters, mates and engineers (1928–81)
BT 320   registers of engineers' certificates (1913–35).

From 1894 to 1948, a register of changes of ships' masters was also maintained (and is now in BT 336). The register is arranged by ship's number with the date that a master joined the vessel. All these registers are reviewed in detail by Watts & Watts (747) and Smith, Watts & Watts (742). Later records of competency certificates are held by the RSS.

The National Maritime Museum holds many of the masters' and mates' applications for these certificates. You need the certificate number (from TNA documents) and you should give the museum a few days' notice that you wish to see an application. The records generally list the voyages of the applicant from the previous four years (and sometimes longer).

Apprentices

From 1704 parishes could bind pauper boys as apprentices to ships' masters for seven to nine years. Indentures may survive in parish records. Many other boys served as apprentices on ships and they may be recorded in apprenticeship books of 1710–1811 (# chapter 22) at TNA. There is also a register of merchant seamen apprentices at Colchester (1704–57 and 1804–44) at TNA in series BT 167. From 1823 all merchant ships over 80 tons had to carry apprentices. An index of merchant navy apprentices from 1824 to 1953 (giving the date, the apprentice's age, the master's name, the ship's name and its port) is in series BT 150. Surviving indentures (only those for every fifth year) are in BT 151 and 152 (some apprentices' papers are also in the Trinity House records considered below). Before 1880 the index is divided into sections for London and outports, then into groups of years (and into groups by the first letter of boys' surnames). Thus piece BT 150/15 is the outports' index of 1829–36 for surnames commencing A to J. After 1880 each piece of the index covers all ports (for one or more years).

The Marine Society was a charitable society founded in 1756 by Jonas Hanway to train men and boys for maritime service. A biography of Hanway by Taylor (744) contains much information about the society. Men and boys were clothed and trained by the society, then recruited by the navy or by masters or owners of merchant ships. By 1805 the society had recruited 33,000 men and 25,000 boys for service at sea and almost 40,000 men and 65,000 boys by 1906. The National Maritime Museum holds many of the society's records. They are listed on the museum's web site and reviewed by R. Pietsch in *Genealogists' Magazine* (March 2001). There are registers (some indexed) of boys recruited and sent to sea from 1760 to 1958. They record the boys' parents (and their professions) and the ships to which they were sent, enabling researchers to follow a boy's career at sea. The registers of men recruited by the society are incomplete, generally only note a man's age and parish (omitting the name of the ship to which he was recruited) and are not indexed. An article in *Cockney Ancestor* (autumn 1995) by B. Bright shows how the author found his ancestor in the registers of boys. Thomas Warington was born in 1825 in St George in the East in Middlesex. The registers recorded him, aged 12 years, being apprenticed on 12 July 1838 for seven years to Mr Robert Eliot, the master of the ship *Phesdo* which worked in the coal trade from Newcastle.

Apprentices (usually pauper children) also served on fishing boats. An article by P. Horn about fisherboy apprentices at Grimsby appears in *Genealogists' Magazine* (September 1995). Grimsby apprenticeship registers of 1879–1937 list about 6,500 boys being apprenticed to Grimsby boats. An index to the registers has been published. The boys originated from the local area but also from poor law unions across the country, such as those of Dover, Birkenhead and Bethnal Green. Many apprentices also served on fishing boats of ports such as Brixham, Hull and Ramsgate. A register of apprentice fishermen in south-east England from 1639 to 1664 is at TNA (piece HCA 30/897).

The Trinity House petitions

Guilds or fraternities of seamen were formed in medieval times to assist poor or sick mariners and their families, provide pilotage services and build lighthouses. The most famous was the Fraternity of Trinity House, formed at Deptford in Kent in 1514 (which became the Corporation of Trinity House in 1547, with headquarters in London since about 1600). Its history and records are reviewed by A. Camp in *Family Tree Magazine* (December 2002).

The death of a seaman (whether naval or merchant) usually left his widow and children in poverty. From 1514 to 1854 Trinity House dispensed charitable funds (and much of its income from lighthouse dues or property) to seamen, their widows and dependants. By 1815, Trinity House was supporting 144 mariners (or their dependants) in almshouses at Mile End and Deptford and over 7,000 out-pensioners. Guildhall Library holds registers from 1729 to 1946 of the money paid to almspeople and out-pensioners (and registers of 1845–1971) for almspeople only), noting names, ages and the reason for assistance being granted. In order to obtain a pension or a place in an almshouse, people had to submit a petition to Trinity House. These petitions, describing a petitioner's circumstances, were generally on printed forms with supporting documents. They provide useful genealogical information and details of a seaman's career. Many petitions were destroyed but those that survive, for 1787–1854, are at Guildhall Library in 113 volumes (in two roughly alphabetical series). The SoG and LDS Family History Library have microfilm copies. The records also include some apprenticeship indentures (for 1780 and 1818–45), letters from parish priests certifying that baptisms or weddings were recorded in parish registers, and some correspondence about pension or almshouse applications. The records primarily relate to English seamen (and their families), but also to Welsh, Scottish, Irish and Channel Islanders. Camp (710) is an indexed calendar to the Trinity House petitions, from which typical entries are:

Archibald, Ann, 41, wife of John, prisoner of war at Besancon Prison [France], of North Shields, 1813

Syms, Sarah, 38, widow of John, of Topsham, Devon, 1817

The John Syms in the second entry appeared to be a brother of my ancestor Richard Symes (or Syms) of Topsham and an uncle of the John Symes noted in the registers of merchant seamen. The Topsham parish register recorded John's baptism, his marriage to Sally Webber in 1803 (Sally was Sarah Webber's nickname) and the baptism of their three children: Louisa Webber Syms, Charlotte Syms and William Henry Syms. Illustration 115 shows the first page of Sarah's petition, submitted in 1817. It stated that she was aged 38, and was the widow of John Syms of Topsham, who was the mate on the brig *Expedition* for two years (in the trade to Portugal). The petition also stated that Sarah had to look after their three children, Louisa, Charlotte and "Francis" Henry Syms (described correctly later in the petition as William Henry Syms). Sarah was unable to support herself and she requested a widow's pension from Trinity House. Further information was provided on subsequent pages of the petition (and in attached documents). John Williams, the owner of *Expedition*, certified that John Syms had served as the ship's mate on a voyage from Lisbon to Exeter in 1806. Certificates from the curate of Topsham confirmed that Sarah was a lacemaker residing in Topsham, with little income, and confirmed the dates (from the Topsham parish register) of the marriage of John and Sarah (as Sally) and their children's baptisms. The vicar of Otterton confirmed that Sarah Webber had been baptised in that parish in 1779. The papers also included a letter of February 1813 from Sarah (again calling herself Sally) to Mr Lockyer of Plymouth:

My husband John Syms, Gunners' Mate of his Majesty's Ship *Le Aigle* . . . [under] Captain Wolf, having taken a French privateer by the name of *Le Phonix* about two years ago as a prize. I am informed by Elizabeth Brown of the Royal Hospital that you paid the prize money to her. My husband ordered me to receive it. I have sent you my certificate of marriage and beg you pay me as soon as possible . . . Sally Symes (please to direct to me at Mr Howes, Topsham, Devon).

Therefore, John had served as mate on the merchant ship *Expedition* but also as gunner's mate on the warship HMS *L'Aigle*. Surprisingly, the petition gave no information about the date or

the Honourable the Master, Wardens, *and* Assistants
f the CORPORATION of TRINITY-HOUSE, of Deptford-
trond.

The humble Petition of *Sarah Syms*

ut the Name, Age, tion, and Occupa- (any), of the Peti- and her Husband's Name. aged *Thirty eight* Years, Widow of *John Syms* residing at *Topsham in the County of Devon*

Sheweth,

THAT your Petitioner's Husband was bred to the Sea, and served

ete in what Trade band first served there as *Master in the Barg Expedition*

ere the highest in which he ever ed, and in what and particularly in the Station of *Mate* on board the Ship *Expedition* Capt. *Scott & Garante* Master in

the *Portugal* Trade, of which Ship *John Williams* was Owner, and served in that Capacity for *Two Years* Years.

That your Petitioner has *Three* Children unprovided for, and dependent on her for Support, whose Names and Ages

the Ages of are; viz. *Frances Henry Syms born April 1807 10 Years Charlotte Syms Six Years*

That your Petitioner is not now able to support herself and *Children* without the Charity of this Corporation, having

ut Amount of ncome, (if any). no Property or Income to the Amount of more than *One Farthing* Pounds a Year. And no Pension or Relief from any other Public Charity or Company, except

r, what Pension re from any other n, which is re- k particularly

Your Petitioner therefore most humbly prays that she may be admitted a Pensioner of this Corporation, at the usual Allowance.

Your Petitioner will ever pray, &c.

certified and recommended as on the other Side.)

115. *Extract from 1817 petition of Sarah Syms to the Corporation of Trinity House (Guildhall Library)*

circumstances of John's death. He was not recorded as buried at Topsham. Did he die at sea, in action on HMS *L'Aigle* or in the Royal Hospital mentioned in the letter? I could now examine the records of HMS *L'Aigle* and *Expedition* to obtain more information. My research in the records of HMS *L' Aigle* was noted above.

Trinity House also examined and licensed pilots for the port of London, the Thames Estuary and many other British ports. Licensing records are held at Guildhall Library and date back to about 1808. The registers list pilots' ages, residence, qualifications and physical descriptions. There are some 20th-century records of lighthouse keepers (to which access is restricted) and, also at Guildhall Library, court minutes of Trinity House since 1660.

Miscellaneous information about merchant seamen

Watts & Watts (747) describe some further records that refer to merchant seamen:

a. Registers of protection from 1702–1828 (at TNA in series ADM 7) list, chronologically, those merchant seamen, fishermen and others who were exempt from being press-ganged into the navy. These note men's ages or dates of birth.

b. From 1854 a master and seaman had to sign a certificate of discharge and character for that seaman at the end of every voyage. These certificates provide details of the ship, the port (and date) of discharge, the date of the man's recruitment to the ship and his place and date of birth. The documents were provided to the seamen and so copies are rarely held in record offices, but they may be found in private papers. Illustration 117 is the certificate of discharge of John Hall on 25 April 1875 from the ship *South Australian* in the Port of London, signed by Hall and the ship's master, John Bruce. Hall was aged 24. He had been engaged as the second cook and butcher on the *South Australian* in July 1874 for a voyage to Adelaide. His character and conduct were noted on the reverse of the certificate as "very good".

War service of merchant seamen

Many merchant seamen joined the Royal Navy or the reserves (the RNR or RNVR), particularly during the two world wars and so can also be found in Royal Navy records. Other seamen continued to serve in the merchant navy and many were killed or wounded as a result of enemy attacks on British shipping. Rolls of honour for merchant seamen killed in the two world wars are in series BT 339. Officers and men who were killed in the First World War are listed in registers in BT 334 (noting a man's name, age, rank, nationality, birth place, cause of death, ship's name and whether the ship was sunk) and in the database *The Debt of Honour*, on the CWGC web site. They are also listed in volume 5 of Jarvis & Jarvis (649). For example, Daniel Sweeney, a fireman on the SS *Garmoyle* (registered at Glasgow) was drowned on 10 July 1917 and is commemorated on the Tower Hill Memorial in London. The circumstances of losses of merchant ships are noted in *Lloyd's War Losses* (see below).

Records of prisoners of war were reviewed in chapter 20. Many of the 5,000 merchant seamen who were captured during the Second World War are recorded in 359 files (in BT 373/1–359), indexed by ship's name, containing details of a ship's loss or capture. There are also over 3,000 "pouches" (in BT 373/360–3716) for individual seamen with details of their capture, imprisonment and ultimate fate.

Gallantry awards were made to merchant seamen from the mid-19th century and the records of these awards are listed by Watts & Watts (747) and TNA domestic records leaflet 95. For example, a register of awards of the Albert Medal for 1866 to 1913 is in series BT 97 at TNA and awards of Board of Trade medals for gallantry are noted in BT 261. During the First World War, merchant seamen might receive the 1914–1915 Star, the British War Medal and the Victory Medal (# chapter 20) and these awards are listed in ADM 171. The Mercantile Marine War Medal was also instituted in 1919 for those merchant seamen who had sailed in war zones during the war. An alphabetical index to recipients is on microfiche in BT 351. The "Naval Secretary's Honours and Awards Index", compiled by the Admiralty from 1939 (# chapter 20), included medals and other awards for the merchant service during the Second World War. This information has been published in a volume (705) of "Seedie's lists". For example, the cargo ship SS *Empire Purcell* was launched in 1942 but sunk by enemy aircraft in the Barents Sea on 27 May the same year, whilst taking part in North Russian Convoy PQ16. Chief Officer Charles Douthwaite and Third Officer Donald Bedford received commendations. The British Empire Medal was awarded to Able Seaman Joseph Greenwood for damaging an enemy aircraft and Able Seaman William Thomson was awarded the George Medal for rescuing shipmates from a capsized lifeboat.

The Lloyd's marine collection
The historical marine records of the Corporation of Lloyd's of London are held at Guildhall Library. The collection is described in detail in Barriskill (707) to which reference should be made before using the records, but it includes the following documents:

a. The *Mercantile Navy List* (published since 1850) is the official annual list of British-registered merchant vessels. The collection includes the lists from 1857 to 1940 and from 1947 to 1977. They note each vessel's name, official number, port of registry, tonnage (and other technical details), the name and address of the owners (from 1865) and the date and place of a ship's construction (from 1871). The names of men who held masters' or mates' certificates were also listed from 1857 to 1864.

b. *Lloyd's Register* is an annual list of vessels produced for the insurance market. Lists survive from 1764, 1768 and then from 1775 to date. The register contains detailed information about each ship, including its name, previous names, tonnage, date and place of construction, destined voyage, master's and owner's names, port of registry (from 1834) and official number (from 1872). From 1775 the collection's registers were annotated as to casualties (for example wrecked or missing) with dates. Lists of East India Company ships were included from 1778 to 1833.

c. *Lloyd's Captains' Registers*. Each volume, covering a number of years, lists (alphabetically) the holders of masters' certificates from 1869 to 1948, with information such as the date and place of a man's birth (and examination), the names and official numbers of ships on which he served (in some cases since 1851) and general details (using a coding system) about his voyages. Thus the code US means a voyage to the United States (East Coast or Gulf of Mexico ports). The registers and codes are described in a Guildhall Library leaflet and in Barriskill (707). Examples of two entries are noted below.

d. *Lloyd's List* was published weekly (and later daily) from 1741. It recorded ships' arrivals and departures in chronological order for each port, as well as the ship losses that were reported to Lloyd's, and reports of inquiries. Not all ship movements were reported to

Lloyd's but the lists are fairly complete. An entry gives the ship's and master's names and the port from which the vessel had arrived or to which she had sailed. There is a microfilm index to the ships' movements which are recorded in the lists between 1838 and 1927. From 1927 there is a card index, noting all known movements of each vessel. The voyages of an ancestor's ship can therefore be reconstructed. Copies of *Lloyd's List* (but not the indexes) are also held at the National Maritime Museum and the British Newspaper Library.

e. *Lloyd's War Losses* are manuscript volumes for each world war, with chronological entries (but indexed) for ships that were lost through enemy action. They note the ports between which a ship was travelling (and its approximate position) when it was lost and the cargo that it carried. Thus the *Mount Coniston* was noted as lost on 5 August 1916, sunk by a submarine while en route from Port Talbot, carrying coal and machinery to Marseilles. A fascimile of the First World War volume has been reprinted by Lloyds (699). Similar information for both wars is also available in official lists published by HMSO and reprinted (with lists for naval ships) in the volume (693) noted above.

f. There are also lists of missing vessels from 1873 and indexed loss and casualty books for 1837–1972. More details are usually contained in *Lloyd's List*.

Barriskill (707) describes how to search for information in the collection. Thus, the basic sources for a ship are *Lloyd's Register of Shipping* and the *Mercantile Navy List*. A ship's movements can then be traced in *Lloyd's List* and its indexes. Losses in the world wars can be found in *Lloyd's List* or in *Lloyd's War Losses*. In each case Barriskill lists a number of alternative sources in the collection which may assist. If an ancestor obtained a master's certificate, you should turn first to the captains' registers because they provide so much useful information. The registers include an entry for William Field Bulleid, noted as born in London in 1877, who passed his examination at Swansea in 1906. The register records William as master or mate on the ships *Cobequid*, *Chaudiere*, *Tagus*, *Pardo*, *Arzila* and *Mogileff* (between 1913 and 1918) for voyages to the West Indies, South America, the United States and the Mediterranean. Illustration 116 shows an even more detailed entry for Captain James Bullock. This notes the names of 10 ships of which he was master or mate from 1903 to 1927 (one of which was sunk during the war). Bullock was also master of the steamship *Corinthic* which collided with the *Queen Elizabeth*, but he was exonerated from blame by a court of inquiry. The register also notes Bullock's death and refers the researcher to the *Morning Post* newspaper of 28 March 1928.

Information about merchant ships can also be obtained from national or local newspapers (# chapter 17). Many ports had a newspaper that concentrated on shipping news, noting the arrivals and departures of ships and the place from which they had sailed or to which they were bound. Losses of ships may also be reported in detail in national or local papers. Local newspaper articles about losses of ships may list the names of local men who were killed. Hocking (727) lists merchant and naval ships which were lost at sea between 1824 and 1962 (from enemy action or ordinary marine risks). Foreign warships (and large foreign merchant ships) are also included. Typical entries for merchant ships are:

"Aigburth": (owner) A. Rowland & Co; built 1917 [technical details], steamship, was torpedoed and sunk by a German submarine, two miles north east of South Cheek, Robin Hood Bay, on December 5th, 1917. Eleven men, including the captain, were killed.

116. *Lloyd's Captains' Registers 1885–1948; entry for James Bullock, from the Lloyd's Marine collection (Guildhall Library Ms 18569/5)*

"Edmonton": (owner) Watts, Ward & Co; (built) 1879 [technical details] The British cargo ship "Edmonton" was wrecked on Great Bahama Bank on May 30th 1880. She was carrying a cargo of coal on a voyage from Cardiff to Havana.

Registers of ships

Registers of ships provide details of ships and the names of masters and owners. The ownership of a British ship was traditionally divided into 64 shares (and was required to be so from 1825) and someone could own one, two or more shares. Shareholders often included carpenters or other craftsmen (receiving shares in a ship in lieu of payment for their work). At some ports, ships were registered from the 17th century (and some registers survive in CROs), but a national system of registration commenced in 1786. Ships with a burden of more than 15 tons had to be

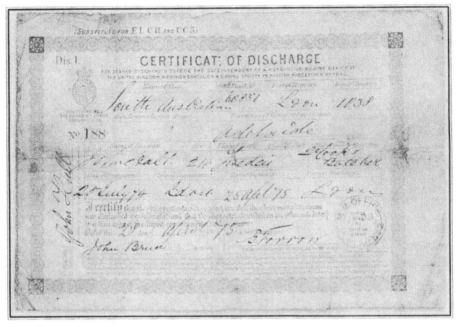

117. Certificate of discharge of John Hall in 1875 from the ship South Australian

registered at the customs' office of their home port. The register noted a ship's name, home port, owners' names (and addresses), the master's name and the date and place of a ship's construction and registration. A certificate of registration was provided (upon which subsequent changes in ownership were noted). The ports' customs officers also copied the information on to a "transcript" which was sent to London. From 1825 any changes in ownership (known as transactions) were marked on the transcripts. The transcripts and transactions for London (from 1786) and for local ports (mostly since 1814) are at TNA in series BT 107. The series list notes the piece numbers for each port. The records for most ports continue up to 1854. An index to the ships' names is in BT 111.

Many ports' registers survive at CROs or in customs houses in ports. The registers of Liverpool for 1786–88, with entries for about 550 ships, have been published in Craig & Jarvis (714). A typical entry is that for the ship *John and Henrietta*, built at Whitby in 1787 and registered at Liverpool on 23 January 1788. The entry notes the ship's tonnage, dimensions and other technical details. From 1788 to 1794 its masters were, in turn, William Dodgson, David Aiken, Joseph Mossop and Thomas Phillips. At the time of registration, the ship was owned by nine men: Thomas Middleton and Richard Downward (Liverpool merchants), William Dodgson (the master) and six merchants of Ulverston (Thomas Sunderland, Samuel Hodgson, George Lowry, John Maychell, William Maychell and Francis Barker). On 14 July 1789 the ship was sold to Andrew Aikin, a Liverpool merchant (probably related to David Aikin, who was appointed master in August 1789). The register notes that the ship was lost off the Spanish coast in 1795.

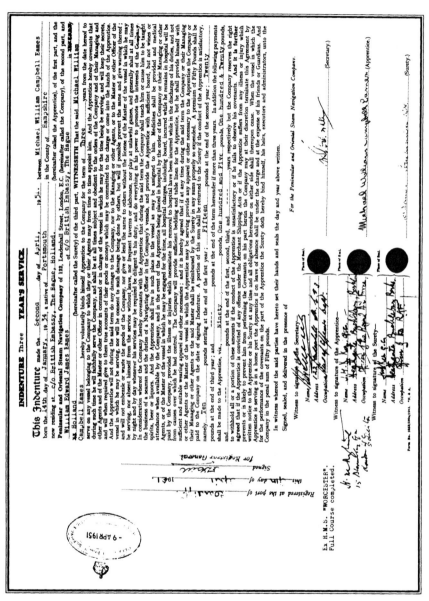

118. *Apprenticeship indenture of 1951: Michael William Campbell Eames becomes an apprentice of the Peninsular and Oriental Steam Navigation Company*

A new registration system was introduced in 1854. Each ship was given an official number and transcripts and transactions were filed separately. Transcripts from 1855 to 1889 are at TNA in series BT 108 (with an index to ships in BT 111) and transactions from 1855 to 1892 are in BT 109. The transcripts refer by number to the transactions. After 1889 all papers for a ship were filed together, but only when the ship was deregistered (lost, scrapped or sold abroad). The documents from 1889 to 1994 are in BT 110, filed by the decade of deregistration (and then alphabetically by ship's name). The date of deregistration can usually be ascertained by studying entries in *Lloyd's Register* or the *Mercantile Navy List*.

Further information about ships

Many books about merchant ships have been published. Some deal with particular types of ships. MacGregor (733) is a detailed study of merchant sailing ships from 1775 to 1875, with many illustrations and an index to names of ships and shipbuilders. Greenhill (725) is a study of merchant schooners in the late 19th and early 20th centuries, naming many ships and shipbuilders. Some published works on merchant ships, held in CROs or local studies libraries, concentrate on the ships of a particular port or area of the country.

Records of some shipping companies and the family papers of shipowners are held in archives and museums (business archives are considered in chapter 22), particularly in port towns or cities. They can be traced through the *National Register of Archives* (# chapters 11 and 27). They may include useful records about a ship and its voyages, perhaps including a ship's accounts. These may note the shareholders of a ship, the master and mate's names, payments to the owners and the expenditure for the ship (for example to local firms for supplies of goods or for repair work). They rarely note ordinary seamen's names.

The information centre of *Lloyd's Register of Shipping*, at 71 Fenchurch Street, London EC3M 4BS (telephone 020 7423 2475), holds some modern records about ships (but not crews) described by B. Jones and E. Taaffe in the 2001 edition of the *FLHH* (5). The centre has copies of *Lloyd's Register* and a small reference library. Lloyd's is also publishing *The Shipwreck Index of the British Isles*. The first volume, with about 7,000 entries, covers the coasts of Cornwall, Devon and Dorset. The second volume covers the coast from Hampshire to the Thames estuary.

Mathias & Pearsall (737) reviewed archives of British shipping companies (and their location) and shipping records in British archives as at 1971. For example, the Ocean Steam Ship Co. Limited of Liverpool was recorded as holding its ledgers, board minutes, crew wage books and ships' logs from about 1860. Exeter City library held archives of J. Holman & Sons, shipowners (including log books, accounts and correspondence). Unfortunately, many shipping companies have moved or gone out of business since 1971 and some research, at business archives or in the *National Register of Archives*, may be necessary to locate their records. However, the records noted as held in archives should still be there (and may have been augmented).

There are some other miscellaneous records, listed below (and held at TNA unless otherwise stated) that record the names of ships and their masters, with details of their voyages and cargos. These will be of interest if you know that an ancestor was an owner or master of a particular ship, or if you know that he was a crew member on a particular voyage. Watts & Watts (747) provide more details of these records and TNA piece numbers.

a. Lloyds assessed ships' seaworthiness and produced surveys (with technical details of a ship and the owner's and master's names). The National Maritime Museum holds the surveys from about 1830, arranged by port and year, but also indexed.

b. Port books since the 13th century record the duty payable on cargoes. The books (listing ships' voyages and masters) are arranged by port and year. Some have been published.

c. Shipping returns (from the 17th to early 19th centuries) provide similar information as port books, but for colonial ports such as those in North America and the West Indies.

d. Customs records include correspondence, from the late 17th to 20th centuries, from local customs officers to the Board of Customs in London. The volumes are arranged by port and date. They include many references to ships and their masters. They may be worth searching if you know the port from which an ancestor (or his ship) worked.

e. Letters of marque were wartime authorisations, from the Admiralty to armed merchant vessels, to attack enemy shipping. They cover the 16th to early 19th centuries and give details of the ship, owner and master.

f. The "receiver of sixpences" levied sixpence a month from merchant seamen's wages to finance Greenwich Hospital (for Royal Navy personnel). Some records survive containing information about a ship, its voyages, home port and the master's name. They are arranged chronologically, but there are some indexes to ships and masters.

g. Records of ships and seamen may also be found in court records, particularly the records of the Court of Admiralty (# chapter 24) at TNA. The disputes considered by this court covered loss of (or damage to) ships and cargo, wrecks, prizes (ships captured during war), seamen's wages as well as piracy and other crimes at sea. The principal files for cases cover the period 1519–1943 and there are depositions and examinations of witnesses (many of them ordinary seamen) from 1536 and prize papers from 1661. However, few of these records are indexed by men's names.

h. Some British railway companies owned ships. Records of the ships and their crews are listed by Richards (854).

Many records of merchant ships and seamen were produced at British ports and retained in the archives of those towns and cities (# chapters 11 and 18 and appendix VII). These included port books with lists of ships, their voyages, cargo and masters. The records of the Court of Admiralty are noted above and in chapter 24, but many ports (such as Ipswich and Southampton) were excluded from that court's jurisdiction until 1835 and so established their own courts to resolve maritime disputes. The records produced in most towns or cities (# chapter 18) also refer, in the cases of ports, to local ships and seamen. Some of these records have been published. For example, volumes of the Southampton Records Series include many transcribed and indexed records of seafarers. The Remembrance books were notebooks of the Corporation of Southampton. Merson (738) is a transcript of the Book of Remembrance for 1514–40. It records that Robert Millett, a ship's master from the Isle of Wight, was made a burgess on 4 July 1520 and that John Abyngton of Southampton, the master of a London ship, was bound over to keep the peace on 20 January 1525. Welch (748) is a transcript of the Admiralty Court book of Southampton for 1566–85. Thomson (745) includes examinations and depositions of 1648–63 before local justices. The litigation included disputes over damage to ships or cargo, payments to seamen and seizures by customs officers. For example, on

15 August 1651, depositions were taken from crew of the ship *John*. William Browne (the boatswain) and John Cherry, John Goulsten and Edward Bristow (mariners) stated that they had been hired by the ship's master (Thomas Earsman) for a voyage from London to Newfoundland. The depositions note the men's ages and the wages they were to receive for the voyage. The ship leaked badly during a storm in the Atlantic and had to return to Southampton. The men were not paid and so sued for their wages. The mariners' claim was supported by the ship's carpenter (Richard Cole of Ratcliffe, Middlesex) who deposed that the *John* had not been seaworthy when she left port.

THE EAST INDIA COMPANY

The East India Company owned or chartered many merchant ships for its maritime trade and also had warships (known as the Bombay Marine, but renamed the Indian Navy in 1830 until its abolition in 1863). An Indian Marine was revived in 1877 and renamed the Royal Indian Navy in 1935.

There are published works listing EIC merchant ships, their voyages, officers and any known crew lists. The merchant ships are also listed in EIC directories and in *Lloyd's Register* from 1778 to 1833. Their movements are recorded in *Lloyd's List*. The *East India Register and Directory* (# chapter 20) included lists of masters and mates of the EIC, usually in sections headed "marine establishment" for each of the Bengal, Bombay and Madras presidencies. The India Office collections, listed by Baxter (1257) and Moir (1306), include some records of the appointment of EIC mercantile officers (including a few baptism certificates) and service records of officers, masters and mates. About 9,700 journals and logs of EIC ships survive, covering the period 1605–1856. These not only describe voyages but often list a ship's crew or are accompanied by pay lists. The collections also include records of the Bombay Marine and Indian Navy from 1613 to 1863. Baxter (1257) lists the published and manuscript sources for these forces, including lists of officers (in directories), records of officers' appointments or service and a few records of sailors. From the mid-19th century there are fairly detailed lists or service records of naval officers but also some service records for European seamen.

MUSEUMS AND OTHER ARCHIVES

The life of seamen is the subject of many published works available at libraries. Marcombe (735) is an illustrated introduction to the life of Victorian sailors. Photographs of life in the Victorian and Edwardian navy are reproduced in Fabb & McGowan (718). Information about maritime history, life at sea and records of local ports and ships can also be found in many archives, libraries and museums. Bryon & Bryon (708) list about 500 British archives, libraries and museums that hold maritime records, with brief summaries of their holdings and notes of any publications that they produce. Some of these archives are small, such as Buckler's Hard Maritime Museum in Hampshire, which holds records of 18th-century shipbuilding at Buckler's Hard. Some archives have large collections, such as the Plymouth branch of Devon Record Office. Its collections cover the maritime history of Plymouth from the late 18th century and include deeds and plans of Devonport dockyard, Plymouth shipping registers from 1824 to 1920 and registers of ship arrivals and departures from 1782 to 1815.

Royal Naval Museum, Portsmouth

The Royal Naval Museum at HM Naval Base, Portsmouth, PO1 3LR (telephone 01705 733060), is open nearly every day of the year although the research collections are generally only open from Monday to Friday (it is advisable to arrange an appointment). The museum holds much useful material, including copies of navy lists for 1797–1992, about 42,000 photographs from the period 1860–1945 and 200 ships' logs, some dating from 1757. It also holds paintings, uniforms, models of ships, diaries of seamen and officers, journals and tape recordings of the recollections of those who served in the navy (and HMS *Victory*, the *Mary Rose* and HMS *Warrior* are all located close to the museum). The King Alfred Library and Reading Room at the museum includes many books relating to the navy. The SoG has a copy of the museum's published guide to its manuscript collections. Specialist collections and material are also held at the Royal Navy Submarine Museum, Gosport, Hampshire, and the Fleet Air Arm Museum, Yeovil, Somerset.

National Maritime Museum

This museum, at Romney Road, Greenwich, London SE10 9NF (telephone 020 8858 4422), is the most important museum and archive in Britain for those interested in maritime history. It is open almost every day of the year. Greenhill (724) is an illustrated guide to the museum's collections, which include photographs, naval uniforms, medals, weapons, models of ships, ships' logs, *Lloyd's List*, *Lloyd's Register*, ships' surveys, the *Mercantile Navy List*, crew lists and business records of shipping companies (including the P&O archive) and shipbuilding yards. A guide to the manuscript collections has been published, in Knight (729), of which volume 2 deals with business records (such as shipping company and dockyard archives), papers of senior naval officers and public records (including much correspondence of the Board of Admiralty). Volume 1 describes the personal collections. These are papers of 300 men, principally senior naval or merchant navy officers and admiralty officials, including ships' logs, letters and photographs. Both volumes are indexed by personal and ship names. The manuscript collection catalogue can also be searched on the museum's web site.

The library holds over 120,000 books or pamphlets and 20,000 periodicals. The catalogue to these (also on the library's web site) can be searched by subject, author and title. The published catalogue includes two volumes (701) that list over 15,000 men (naval officers, merchant seamen, engineers and shipowners) featured in the most important biographical works in the library. The museum is also compiling an index to church, cemetery and public memorials (anywhere in the world) that commemorate seamen (or civilians lost in shipwrecks). The index is described in *Family Tree Magazine* (August 1997) and contains about 2,500 entries. As this index expands, it will become easier to locate information about sea-going ancestors who died away from their home.

The museum has large photographic collections of naval and merchant ships, shipbuilding and ports (with over 250,000 negatives and 500,000 prints) and also about 3,500 paintings and 30,000 prints or drawings, to which there are various catalogues. Copies of photographs can be purchased. Two catalogues, dealing with part of the collections, have been published. One volume (700) catalogues the warship photographs (from the late 19th century up to about 1945) in the Richard Perkins collection. The second volume (702) deals with merchant ships, with the date (and description) of each photograph. The museum also produces an illustrated guide (697) to the negatives in the photographic collections, with 250 photographs to illustrate the range of material available.

Maritime History Group, University of Newfoundland
The group holds large collections of British merchant shipping crew lists for 1863–1938 and 1951–76 and also many other records of British merchant shipping, including copies of archives held elsewhere. It produces a guide to its holdings and an article describing these also appears in *Family History News and Digest* (April 1994). Enquiries about the group's records should be directed to the archivist, Maritime History Archive, Memorial University of Newfoundland, St John's, Newfoundland A1C 5S7. The group provides copies of documents that it holds (for a small fee) in response to written requests.

CHAPTER 22

RECORDS OF TRADES, PROFESSIONS AND BUSINESS

Many sources that refer to tradesmen or professions, such as commercial directories and newspapers, as well as photographs (perhaps of an ancestor's shop or business) have already been noted. Reference has also been made (# chapter 16) to some general published works on trades, such as those of Shire Publications. However, many other records and detailed published sources may be available relating to an ancestor's profession, employment or trade. If a family business still exists, detailed records of that business covering many years may have been retained, while older documents may have been deposited in an archive. Even if the business no longer exists, some of its records may have been archived. Records of an ancestor's profession or occupation may also survive. Members of the professions were generally wealthier than average and more records may have been retained by their families. Many professions and trades also had their own associations, colleges or societies which produced important records and retained archives.

You can establish an ancestor's occupation from some of the records considered above, such as census records or parish registers. He may have been a butcher, shoemaker or agricultural labourer. However, he may be recorded with an occupation that you have never heard of. Waters (875a) is a dictionary of trades and occupations that is particularly useful for discovering old names of trades or the names of occupations that few (if any) people now follow. For example, you will find that a billiter made the moulds used for casting bells; a throster was a silk worker (specifically a silk thrower) and a patten maker made clogs (pattens were wooden clogs with heels) and more recently constructed moulds in a metal works.

You should start by reviewing any published works on your ancestor's trade or profession (perhaps works on gunmakers or goldsmiths), since these not only tell you much about that trade, but also note detailed source material that is available. The number of published works on professions, trades or occupations is enormous and many of these are listed in entries for occupations in Saul & Markwell (27) and in Raymond (851). Raymond (850) provides similar information for London ancestors but also has much information of general interest. Many published works list men who undertook a particular trade (in a city, county or throughout the country). For example, Beard & Gilbert (773) is a biographical dictionary of thousands of English furniture-makers from 1660 to 1840 (including those in allied trades, such as carvers and picture frame makers), based on sources such as directories, newspapers, poll books, fire insurance or apprenticeship records, trade cards, sale catalogues and other published works on furniture. A short entry, for Thomas Eagles of Bedford, is:

Eagles, Thomas. Bedford, turner & chairmaker (1785–1830) recorded [in directories] at Silver Street in 1823 and Old Market Place in 1830.

Many entries refer to other people (such as a man's apprentices or partners) and these people are indexed in a separate work by Evans (794). Thomas Eagles is also noted in a long entry for Henry Clay (of Birmingham and of Covent Garden in London) since Thomas was employed as Clay's agent. Thomas Fewson Eagles (probably a son of Thomas Eagles), succeeded to Clay's premises in London in 1813. An extract from his entry is:

> Eagles, T.F., 18 King Street, Covent Garden, London, manufacturer of paper tea trays to their Majesties and the royal family (1813–1825). Eagles succeeded to the premises and business of Henry Clay . . . he continued to provide for the 6th Duke of Bedford at Woburn . . . trays and teapot stands . . . as his predecessor had done [references to invoices in the Duke of Bedford's archives].

As another example, Baillie (771) is a dictionary of about 35,000 watch and clockmakers (from all countries, but many from Britain) up to about 1825. Most entries are very brief (for example simply noting that James Charnock was apprenticed to a watch or clockmaker in London in 1693), but it is a good starting point for your research.

Some occupations are the subject of many published biographical dictionaries, especially if they were craftsmen who made things that are now sought after by collectors (such as clocks, porcelain, furniture and silverware). Your ancestor may have been a goldsmith (most of whom worked in London). If so, you can consult the records of the Worshipful Company of Goldsmiths of London (the London livery companies' records are considered below) or published histories of that company, such as that covering 1327 to 1509 by Reddaway & Walker (852). However, there are also reference books that should include a biography of your ancestor and information about his work:

a. Grimwade (808) includes biographies of about 3,000 London goldsmiths from 1697 to 1837, with details of their apprenticeships, business addresses and the marks they used on their work, extracted principally from the records of the Worshipful Company of Goldsmiths. This is a typical biography:

> Charnelhouse, William, son of Alexander Charnelhouse of Salford in the County of Oxford, Clerk, apprenticed to Robert Cooper 1 August 1688, [freeman of the Goldsmiths' Company] 27 May 1696. Livery, October 1708. Mark entered 19 June 1703. Address: Gutter Lane . . . Buried in the New Vault, 16 March 1711–12 (register, St Vedast).

b. Heal (818) lists 6,400 goldsmiths who worked in London from 1200 to 1800, with their addresses, marks and the dates between which they are known to have worked, extracted from records of the Goldsmiths' Company, newspapers, directories, wills and trade cards.

c. Culme (788) includes detailed biographies of about 4,000 British gold and silversmiths who were working in the period 1838 to 1914.

d. Chaffers (785) and Jackson (827) are histories of English goldsmiths and their marks with much biographical material. Jackson (827) lists goldsmiths in York, Norwich, Newcastle, Chester, Birmingham and many smaller cities as well as Scottish and Irish goldsmiths.

Some books concentrate on a trade in a particular area. There are many studies of London craftsmen, such as Heal (818) but also many covering other cities, towns or counties. Thus Pickford (845) is a biographical dictionary of about 400 clock or watchmakers in Bedfordshire from 1352 to 1880, compiled from parish registers, directories, newspapers, the census, churchwardens' accounts and apprentice records. Dowler (791), Elliott (793) and Ponsford (846) are similar biographical dictionaries for clock and watchmakers in Gloucestershire, Shropshire and Devon.

Many trades (such as glassmaking or shoemaking) have also been the subject of detailed studies by individuals or organisations and there are some unpublished indexes of people involved in particular professions or trades. Two examples are the shoemakers' index (held at Northampton Central Museum) and the index of gunmakers (which includes over 6,000 surnames). Details of these indexes are contained in Saul & Markwell (27). Gibson & Hampson (158) also note such indexes, for example, that held by Mrs Stage of Twickenham, Middlesex, which has over 70,000 references to coastguards and their families.

The House of Lords Record Office (HLRO) holds a database of the names, occupations and places of residence of about 200,000 witnesses who gave evidence to Parliamentary Committees on private bills from 1771 to 1917. Many of them were engineers, surveyors, other professional people or local tradesmen, giving evidence on bills that concerned the building of railways, roads, docks and canals. HLRO has produced a detailed guide (767) to the database and to private bill procedure and evidence. Searches on the database (for people, companies or places) can be made from a terminal at HLRO or by the HLRO staff in response to a written enquiry.

GUILDS AND LIVERY COMPANIES

Guilds (or gilds) of craftsmen developed in the middle ages for commercial, religious and social reasons and they dominated life in many English towns. West (463) describes them as "chambers of commerce, monopolies, insurance companies, friendly societies, family trustees, religious foundations, burial clubs, institutes of good practice and quality control and, to a very limited extent, trade unions". There were three types of guild. There was the guild merchant (a guild that embraced different trades and crafts) which emerged in towns in the 12th century. Secondly, from the 14th century until Tudor times, there were religious guilds which were founded primarily for charitable purposes, such as the endowment of schools or hospitals. Thirdly, there were the craft guilds (such as those for weavers or tailors), which originated in the 13th and 14th centuries in order to regulate each craft or trade. These soon displaced the guilds merchant.

The craft guilds were originally voluntary associations of craftsmen. They recognised three grades of skill: master craftsman, journeyman (who hired himself to a master on a daily basis) and apprentice (trainee). Apprenticeship is considered in more detail below but, in brief, was a training contract by which a boy learned a trade from his master. The guilds usually controlled their trade or craft by obtaining exclusive rights to practise that trade and imposing limitations on how a man could gain admission to their guild (and therefore practise the trade). Most men had to serve an apprenticeship (usually of seven years) in order to be admitted to the guild. The guilds provided for their members in sickness or old age and for members' widows and children. Some guilds founded their own schools (# chapter 19). Some large towns had many guilds for the different crafts. Newcastle had 46 guilds, including butchers, shipwrights, tanners and weavers. Richmond in Yorkshire had 13 guilds. However, smaller towns which were dependent on only one or two crafts might accordingly have only one or two guilds. Thus Chipping Campden in the Cotswolds was an important centre of the wool industry and the splendid Woolstaplers' Hall (from which the local guild regulated trade and a great part of the town's affairs) still stands in the town centre.

The most famous guilds were those of London, which were known as livery companies because of the distinctive livery that was worn by senior members of each company. There were livery companies for many different trades. By the 19th century there were 77 London livery companies including those for bakers, brewers, butchers, carpenters, clothworkers, coopers, cordwainers, cutlers, drapers, dyers, glaziers, goldsmiths, grocers, mercers, musicians, shipwrights, weavers and wheelwrights. There were also two ancient companies (which had not received a livery): the watermen and lightermen (who operated ferries on the Thames) and the parish clerks. By royal grants and charters (many dating from medieval times), the livery companies obtained monopolies to prevent non-members from practising their trade. The livery companies' monopolies applied in the City of London and its environs, but some companies had wider jurisdictions, sometimes extending miles from the City.

A typical London livery company consisted of a master and two or three wardens (who were elected annually), a court of about 20 assistants, the liverymen (who could be appointed as assistants), freemen and apprentices. Guilds in other towns or cities had a similar structure. The method of obtaining membership (or freedom) of a guild was similar to the procedure for obtaining the freedom of a borough or city (# chapter 17); that is, by servitude, patrimony or redemption. The guilds' powers gradually diminished and most of them had ceased to operate by the late 18th century. London was the main exception, the livery companies remaining important in the regulation of trade until the 19th century (and remaining influential today in city government and charitable works). Some guilds survived in other places, generally as charitable bodies. As the guilds declined, the trade that was actually undertaken by a member became less important, so that a son might follow his father into a particular guild or livery company even though he practised a different trade (so that a baker may not have joined the bakers' company). This can make it difficult to find the records of an ancestor.

Melling (839) is an introduction to the history of guilds, briefly describing each London livery company and listing some published histories of the companies. Hazlitt (817) is more comprehensive, including a detailed history of each company. Raymond (850) also lists many published histories of the livery companies. Some London livery companies still hold their own archives, and applications for access to these records should be made to the clerk of the company. However, the records of most companies are at Guildhall Library and listed in Bullock-Anderson (240) and in Guildhall Library's research guide (750). They include the companies' constitutional, membership, property, financial and charity records. About three quarters of the companies have records that predate 1600. The most useful records are those concerning apprenticeships or admissions to the freedom of a company. These documents generally cover the period since the 17th century but some begin earlier. For example, the records of the Cordwainers' Company include livery lists (1596–1904), freedom admissions (1595–1678 and 1706–1901), apprenticeship bindings (1595–1802), property records (1316–1931) and copies of benefactors' wills. There are similar records for the Bakers' Company. Typical entries from the bakers' registers of admissions of freemen are:

May 7th 1787: George Kennerley who was apprentice to John Francis was admitted a freeman of the Bakers' Company by servitude
July 2nd 1787: Richard Hale was admitted a freeman by redemption
Sept. 3rd 1787: Richard Houlditch was admitted a freeman by patrimony

The apprentice register of the Barber-Surgeons Company, also at Guildhall Library, includes:

6th Dec. 1743: John Davis son of James Davis of Totteridge, Herts., Barber puts himself apprentice to Robert Church, Barber for 7 years.
4th Feb. 1703: Joseph Adams, son of John Adams, late of Lowton or Epping Forest in Essex, cordwainer, deceased, puts himself apprentice to Thomas Stiff of Paternoster Row, London, Barber for 7 years.

Members of livery companies are listed in City of London poll books and electoral registers. If men were admitted to the freedom of the City, they should be included in the admission records at CLRO (# chapter 17). Boyd's *Citizens of London* (# chapter 7) should also be consulted, since this lists many members of the livery companies, particularly in the 17th century, with further information about them that Boyd extracted from parish registers and wills. A great deal of material about the London livery companies has been published. There are many general histories of the companies, some of them with extracts from company records but also many volumes of transcripts of company records such as accounts and court minutes. Researchers should review this published material, available at Guildhall Library (with some volumes at the SoG) before attempting to use the original manuscript material.

Taking the Worshipful Company of Carpenters as an example, there are general histories of the company, such as that by Ridley (855) which includes lists of those men who served as the company's masters, wardens, clerks and beadles. An earlier history, by Jupp and Pocock (830) includes many extracts from the company's records that may refer to your ancestor. Furthermore, seven volumes of transcripts of the company's records have been published in Marsh (835), Marsh & Ainsworth (836) and Millard (840), including the company's Court Book of 1533–94, the Wardens' Accounts of 1438–1614 and some apprenticeship bindings. Those who offended against the rules of a company were brought before its Court and might be fined. Thus, on 17 March 1553, Richard Atkinson was fined 40 shillings for working with a carpenter who was not a member of the company. On 16 July 1568, Thomas Marcam was fined three shillings and four pence for failing to notify the company that he had taken a new apprentice. The Court was also responsible for managing the company's property and so the minutes include information about tenants of the property (members of the company or third parties) and their rents. The Wardens' accounts include receipts for payments from the company's members; gifts, legacies, rent, fines, fees payable on the binding of apprentices and repayments of loans made by the company to its members. The Wardens' payments included the expenses of dinners and pensions or alms paid to poor members of the company, their widows or dependants. Thus the accounts in Marsh (835) note that 2s. 2d. was received in 1553/4 from Thomas Stalker for presenting his apprentice, Thomas Rede, for binding. One year's rent of 20 shillings was received from Richard Logstone and 3s. 4d. was paid as alms to each of Walter Owen, Richard Jonson and Mrs Maxwell.

Many published histories of the livery companies include lists of liverymen and some list a few freemen and apprentices. Webb (460) lists the published works that contain lists of freemen or apprentices, as well as some unpublished indexes of apprentices (many of them held at the SoG). Thus two volumes by McKenzie (837) and (838), list apprentices (and their masters) of the Stationers' Company from 1641 to 1800 (another published volume lists apprentices of 1605–40). The records of the Company of Watermen & Lightermen of the River Thames are particularly important. The river was once London's most important artery and watermen provided a water taxi service whilst the lightermen carried goods in their lighters or barges. R. Cottrell has produced a nine-volume index (on fiche and CD-ROM) to the apprenticeship bindings of the company from 1692 to 1949. The index notes the names of apprentices and masters, the date of the indenture and, if applicable, the date on which an apprentice achieved the freedom of the company.

The SoG is publishing an important series of indexes by Webb (877) of apprenticeship records of other livery companies, up to about 1800, that record the apprentices' parentage. To date, 38 volumes, listing 77,000 apprentices of 53 companies (and about 154,000 of the apprentices' fathers and masters) have been published and the entries are being added to the English Origins web site. For example, volume 1 is an index to almost 1,000 apprentices of the Brewers' Company from 1685 to 1800. A typical entry is:

GREGORY, Thomas (son of) Thomas (of) Enfield, Middlesex, yeoman to Thomas Hendy 24 Aug 1716.

Records of London livery companies do not relate only to the better-off, or only to Londoners. The area over which the companies had jurisdiction varied a great deal, but most had authority for some areas outside the City of London and some for areas up to 10, 20 or even 30 miles from the City. The Company of Watermen had jurisdiction on the Thames as far as Windsor and its records include many people from outside London. Livery company records also refer to many poorer craftsmen, shopkeepers and even some labourers. Apprentices of the companies originated in all parts of Britain (not only in London and its environs). The livery company records can therefore be of interest to all genealogists.

Although most works on guilds and livery companies concentrate on the London companies, it is important to remember the guilds of other cities and towns. The surviving records of these companies, recording the names of many masters and apprentices, can be found in CROs. Some records have been published, such as those of the Company of Shipwrights of Newcastle, in Rowe (857), including company accounts from 1674 (noting many members' names) and the company's orders or resolutions since 1622, including entries such as:

13 July 1818. Alexander Doeg, a free brother of this company, demanded the services of the following apprentices: Thomas Mennam, George Fleck (later left his master), Stoddard Blair, Thomas Doeg, Matthew Grey, who agreed to serve the said Alexander Doeg.

As another example, the register of admissions of the Company of Merchant Tailors in York from 1560 to 1835 has been published in Smith (866). The members' names and dates of admissions have been supplemented by the author with other information from the company's records, such as a member's parentage or details of his apprenticeship and any offices that he held in the company. For example, this is the entry for Richard Crosthwaite:

Son of Thomas Crosthwaite, late of Stoneraise in Threlkeld, Cumberland, Gent. Apprenticed on 17 September 1630 for 8 years to William Allanson of York, Gent, then to George Chater (on 22 March 1633/4) for the rest of his term. Admitted member 31 January 1637/8; searcher in 1641 and warden 1669–71.

Freemasons

Freemasonry developed in Britain in the 17th century, but its origins were earlier, in the craft guilds. Lewis (833) is a guide to tracing ancestors who were Freemasons, describing the history of Freemasonry, the lodge system, Masonic ranks, regalia and their records (with guidance on locating them). Lists of freemasons and the lodges to which they belonged are held by the General Secretary at the United Grand Lodge of England, Freemason's Hall, 60 Great Queen Street, London WC2. The names of current members will not be disclosed. Enquiries about masons in Scotland can be directed to the Grand Secretary at Freemason's Hall, 96 George Street, Edinburgh EH2 3DH, and enquiries about Irish masons may be directed to the Grand Secretary at Freemason's Hall, 17 Molesworth Street, Dublin 2, Eire.

The Seditious Societies Act of 1799 required each freemason's lodge to deposit a certificate, every year, with the Clerk of the Peace for the county. The certificate had to list the names and addresses of the freemasons of that lodge. Quarter Sessions records at CROs (# chapter 25) therefore include lodges' registers and annual certificates (with members' names). More information can be found in lodge membership books, some of which have been deposited in CROs. The library and museum at Freemasons' Hall in London (telephone 020 7395 9257) is open to the public and has a large collection of published and manuscript material on Freemasons. For example, there are annual year books (published since 1908) that list lodges and senior Freemasons, and the *Masonic Year Book Historical Supplement* (759) lists about 35,000 senior Masonic officers from 1717 to 1968. There is an ongoing project to catalogue thousands of manuscript records from the period 1750–1820, including 14,700 annual returns (listing members) made by lodges to Grand Lodge. The catalogue will be available on the Access to Archives web site and the documents will be available in the library at Freemasons' Hall.

Many published lodge histories include lists of a lodge's senior officers (and other members), sometimes back to the 18th century, as well as information on the lodge's activities and meeting places. Fluke (799) is a history of the St George's Chapter of Royal Arch Masons that was founded in 1786 in Deptford. Its first members included T. Williams (a shipwright), R. Bosville (a smith), J. Dixon (a tailor) and J. Woodham (a carpenter). Amherst & Le Strange (768) is a history of Union Lodge in Norwich, established in 1736. The list of members includes a bricklayer, Samuel Blog, who joined in 1786. Those joining in 1794 included William Martin, a merchant of Castleacre aged 32, John Ward, a gentleman of Fakenham aged 23 and Samuel Uthing, a farmer of Horstead aged 24.

APPRENTICESHIP RECORDS

From the 14th century apprenticeship was the system by which a man learned a trade that was controlled by a guild. An act of 1562/3 provided that the apprenticeship term to be served, as a condition of gaining the right to practise a craft, should be at least seven years. Fines could be levied on a man who practised a craft without having served an apprenticeship (or otherwise obtained membership of a guild) and cases appear in Quarter Sessions' records (# chapter 25).

The terms of an apprenticeship were set out in a document known as an indenture, one copy of which was signed by the child's parents (or guardian) and the other by the master. A master would promise to teach the apprentice a trade but also to house, clothe and feed him. The master usually received a payment (a premium) for training the child. Apprenticeship indentures name the apprentice, the master (and his trade), the apprentice's father (and sometimes the father's occupation and residence) and perhaps even the date and place of the apprentice's birth. Many apprenticeships were also recorded in registers (as in the earlier examples from guild records) noting the names of the apprentice, his master and father and specifying the master's trade.

Many apprenticeship records survive in guild, parish and taxation records. Illustration 86 shows the indenture for my ancestor John Bulleid, who was apprenticed to Thomas Bulleid in 1744 by the parish officials of Winkleigh. The records of guilds and livery companies often include registers of masters and their apprentices, but also some indentures. Since the indentures were private contracts between individuals (and held by a master and the apprentice's father), many have been lost or destroyed, but some survive in family papers and business archives. Illustration 118 is an apprenticeship indenture that I found in a market. It records that on 2 April 1951, Michael William Campbell Eames entered into a three-year apprenticeship with the Peninsular and Oriental Steam Navigation Company. The indenture was registered with the Registrar General of Shipping and Seamen. Indentures such as this reveal vital information. Michael Eames was born on 14 January 1934, was originally from Portsmouth and had completed a training course on HMS *Worcester*. The residence of both Michael and his father (William Edward James Eames) is noted as "care of" the British Embassy at The Hague in Holland. After his signature, the father added "Commander, RN". The *Navy List 1951* confirms that he was Naval Attache at The Hague (and that he had been awarded the DSC). On the back of the indenture is an endorsement by the company in April 1954 that Michael Eames had satisfactorily completed his apprenticeship and that one of the vessels on which he served was the *Coromandel*.

The SoG has an indexed collection of over 1,500 indentures from the 17th to 19th centuries, known as *Crisp's Apprentices' Indentures*. The Trinity House petitions and Board of Trade records of merchant seamen (# chapter 21) also contain many apprenticeship indentures. Surviving indentures for poor law apprenticeships (# chapter 18) are usually at CROs. Some charities assisted poor families to pay the premiums required by masters. Most of these charities' records are in CROs. For example, Wiltshire Record Office holds the records of the Wiltshire Society that was founded in London by men from Wiltshire in order to raise funds for apprenticing children of deserving Wiltshire families. Henly (819) is a calendar of over 1,000 apprenticeships arranged by the society from 1817 to 1922, most in London and Wiltshire. In addition to the names of the apprentice and master (and the master's trade) many entries include information about the apprentice's family as in this example:

15 Jan. 1852. ARNOLD, Richard, son of Richard and Sarah of 135 Kent St, Borough: to William Warr Paull, carpenter, builder and undertaker of 106 Great Dover Rd. 7 years, [premium] £20. [Apprentice] aged 14 in Sept. 1851. Mother (formerly Sarah Shipman) from Mildenhall, left a widow 12 years ago. She keeps a small shop in the Borough. Four children in family; the two eldest boys have been apprenticed by the Society. All the children were left dependent on mother.

Indentures or registers of apprentices also survive in city or borough archives and some have been published. Registers for Bristol survive from 1532 and have been published for some years, such as 1552–65 in Ralph (849). A register of Southampton apprentices from 1609 to 1740 has been published in Willis & Merson (880). The register (with about 1,500 entries) of Kingston upon Thames, Surrey, has been published in Daly (789). This covers the four guilds that operated in Kingston; the mercers, woollen drapers, cordwainers and butchers. Registers for Oxford survive from the early 16th century to the 19th century and Graham (804) is a calendar of the registers of 1697–1800, listing over 3,200 apprentices. All these registers include many apprentices who came to the city or borough from other counties (the Kingston register includes four apprentices from Devon and two from Yorkshire). Here are two examples (from Oxford and Kingston):

James Keats son of Thomas Keats of Ampthill, Bedfordshire, yeoman to Edward Pittaway [of Oxford] locksmith for 7 years from 8th February 1741, enrolled 8th March.
Tho. Bronne, son of John Bronne, of York, tailor, to Tho. Blackmore, barber surgeon [of Kingston] for 5 years from Xmas last. 20 Dec 1572.

Stamp duty was imposed, on premiums payable under apprenticeship indentures, from 1710 until 1804. Some payments were made up to 1811 because the duty could be paid up to one year after an apprenticeship term was completed. This tax resulted in most indentures being registered centrally. The registers for England and Wales, known as the *Apprenticeship Books*, are at TNA in series IR 1. They are divided into city registers (generally indentures on which stamp duty was paid in London) and country registers (for payments elsewhere). The registers note the names of the apprentice and his master, the master's trade, the dates of the indenture and payment of duty and (until about 1752) the name of the apprentice's father. Some apprenticeships were exempt from duty (and so not listed), such as those arranged by a parish or those for which the premium was less than one shilling (usually where a boy was apprenticed to his father or another relative).

The registers of 1710–74 are indexed by the typescript *Apprentices of Great Britain*, at the SoG and TNA (in series IR 17). The SoG has published the index on microfiche (749). It is divided into four parts. The apprentices are indexed alphabetically by surname in two series, firstly from 1710 to 1762 (in 33 volumes) and secondly from 1762 to 1774 (in seven volumes). There are about 250,000 entries, giving the year of the indenture, the names of the apprentice, his father and master (and his trade). The parish of the apprentice or master may also be noted. Typical entries are:

1717 Gilman, Jos. Wm. of Southill, Beds. Carp. to Thos. Dilley of Clifton, Beds. tay. £6
1763 Fisher, Wm. to Thos. Gillman of Hockliffe, Beds cordw. £6 6/-
1768 Innard Jos. to Thos. Gillman of Hockliffe, Beds cordw. £6 6/-

The year of the indenture is followed by the apprentice's surname and forename. Any second forename noted (as in the first example) is for the apprentice's father; so that first entry is for "Joseph Gilman, son of William Gilman". Masters' trades are abbreviated (for example, cord is cordwainer and tay is tailor) and the entry notes the premium. Each entry also has a reference such as 45/18, which is the piece number and folio of the entry in the registers in series IR 1. The registers provide little further information except the exact date and term of the indenture (usually seven years), the amount of duty and the date that the tax was collected. There are also two indexes to the masters' names appearing in the apprentices' index, one for 1710–62 and one for 1762–74. The masters' index for 1710–62 is divided into volumes. Volume 1 indexes (alphabetically) the masters named in the first five volumes of the apprentices' index. Volume 2 of the masters' index lists the masters named in volumes 6 to 10 of the apprentices' index and so on. The masters' index for 1762–74 contains the masters' names, in one alphabetical sequence, from the seven volumes of the apprentices' index of 1762–74.

There is no overall index to the apprentices or masters recorded in the registers of 1775–1811 (estimated to contain about 750,000 entries), but some local societies have indexed entries in the registers that relate to their own counties (and they sometimes include this later period).

THE PROFESSIONS

Lawyers
Lawyers are now either solicitors or barristers. Legal proceedings (# chapters 24 and 25) are heard by judges or magistrates (also known as Justices of the Peace). Until the mid-19th century lawyers known as proctors or advocates also acted for the parties in many cases. The sources of biographical information about lawyers are described in detail in Holborn (822) which reviews about 550 books, journals or other sources containing biographical information on lawyers in England, Wales and Ireland. Many lawyers also had another profession or occupation, for example serving as Members of Parliament or civil servants (considered below) and so biographical dictionaries and other sources for those occupations should also be consulted.

Barristers Barristers act as advocates in court and advise on specialist points of law. They are admitted to practise through one of the four Inns of Court (Lincoln's Inn, Middle Temple, Inner Temple or Gray's Inn). Barristers usually attended universities and so can be located in university records (# chapter 19) and were also included in the law lists (reviewed below). Most of the admissions registers of Middle Temple, Gray's Inn and Lincoln's Inn have been published. Those of Middle Temple, in three volumes by Sturgess (871), cover the period 1501–1944 (and two other published volumes cover 1945–75). A typical 17th-century admission entry for Middle Temple is:

15th May 1647: Roger Charnocke, son & heir of George Charnocke of Harwoden, Northants, esq. deceased.

The date upon which a student was subsequently called to the bar is sometimes added. By the 19th century most entries in the Middle Temple registers note a student's age and his father's occupation and address. The admissions registers of Gray's Inn (1521–1889), including marriages in Gray's Inn chapel (1695–1754), have been published in Foster (802). Early entries only give names and dates of admission, but fuller entries appear by the 17th century, such as:

5th August 1620: Saint John Chernock, son & heir of Robert Chernock of Holkett, Bedfordshire, knight.

From about 1830 entries also note a student's age and the university or college that he had attended. Admissions since 1927 (as well as obituaries and other information on members) are included in the Gray's Inn journal *Graya*. Lincoln's Inn has published its admission registers

(1420–1893) in two volumes (763), which include baptisms, marriages and burials in Lincoln's Inn chapel. Early entries provide the student barrister's name and the date of his admission. Most later entries also note the man's age, his university (or college) and his father's name and occupation. Admissions from 1894 to 1973 are listed in two typescript volumes held in Lincoln's Inn library. Inner Temple has published its admissions registers (765) for 1547–1660. Admissions' books for later periods are at the Inner Temple library. Many Inner Temple records (such as accounts and minutes) for 1505–1800 have been calendared and indexed in Inderwick & Roberts (826). These include notes of the admission (and call to the bar) of many students, as well as matters such as payments made by barristers for their chambers.

Other inns were founded (Clement's Inn, Barnard's Inn, Clifford's Inn, Furnival's Inn, New Inn, Staple Inn and Thavie's Inn) and were known as Inns of Chancery. Students who completed studies at these Inns might become solicitors or proctors, but many then entered one of the Inns of Court and trained as barristers. The Inns of Chancery were gradually closed, the last (Clifford's Inn) in 1900. Some admissions registers are available. Thus TNA holds admission books for Clement's Inn (1656–1883). Other useful material about the inn and its members has been published in Carr (784). The admission registers of Barnard's Inn for 1620–1869, with some biographical information about the students, have been published in Brooks (781). A study of Staple Inn by Williams (878) includes a list of students admitted between 1716 and 1884. Admission books of New Inn (1743–1852) are held in Middle Temple library. Holborn (822) notes other sources for members of the Inns of Chancery and Bland (777) is a detailed bibliography of manuscript sources and published books or articles about the Inns of Court and of Chancery which may lead you to further information about an ancestor who was a member.

It is possible, but time-consuming, to discover some of the cases in which a barrister appeared, by reviewing published law reports and original records of civil or criminal trials (# chapters 24 and 25). Holborn (822) considers the best sources and methods of such research.

Proctors and advocates Lawyers who practised in ecclesiastical courts and in the Court of Admiralty (# chapter 24), were civil lawyers and either proctors or advocates (equivalent to barristers and solicitors respectively). The advocates were also doctors of law (having obtained doctors' degrees) and formed an association in the 15th century which developed into the College of Advocates and was based in a building that became known as Doctors' Commons. The college then moved to premises south of St Paul's Cathedral, near to many church courts and registries. The civil lawyers' chambers were located in the same area and the name Doctors' Commons was used for the neighbourhood of the college, chambers and these church courts.

Squibb (868) is a detailed history of the College of Advocates, listing its members (with brief biographical details) from its earliest days up to the 19th century. Most surviving records of the college (including subscription books that contain most advocates' signatures) are at Lambeth Palace Library and described in Squibb (868) and Chapman (926). Appointments of proctors are noted in the Act Books of the Archbishop of Canterbury, which are indexed for 1663–1859 in British Record Society volumes 55 and 63. Civil lawyers are also included in law lists (see below) and in London directories. An article "The Proctor" by J. Titford in *Family Tree Magazine* (January 1991) also provides useful information, including reference to a manuscript list of proctors (with some biographical information) held by Mr Titford. Some records are also held at TNA, for example, proctors' admissions to practice in the Court of Admiralty are noted in that court's records (in series HCA 30).

Solicitors The names of solicitors (also known until 1873 as attorneys at law) are contained in published lists from the late 18th century. Brown's *General Law List* was published in most years from 1775 until 1801 and it was continued as *The New Law List*, then *The Law List* by other publishers until 1976 (and there are various lists since that date). The title page of *The Law List* of 1856 with the first page of its list of solicitors is shown in illustration 119. Entries for solicitors note the name of the firm in which they worked and the town in which the firm was located (or later, the firm's address). Law lists are held at the British Library, or (for most years) at Guildhall Library and (for 1799–1976) at TNA. The SoG also holds most of the lists since 1812. For example, the 1893 *Law List* (757) has alphabetical lists of London solicitors and of country solicitors. These refer to entries for each place (with alphabetical entries for each solicitor). The entry for Glastonbury noted two solicitors surnamed Bulleid, with their dates of qualification and the name of their firm (three other solicitors were also noted for this firm):

Bulleid, George Lawrence	May 1881	Crowders & Vizard
Bulleid, John George Lawrence	Trinity 1848	Crowders & Vizard

By tracing your ancestor in each year's list, the year of his retirement can be ascertained, making it easier to find his death, burial or will. Some solicitors (most of them since the late 19th century) attended universities, so their records (# chapter 19) should also be consulted. At one time solicitors were also members of the Inns of Court but this practice ceased by the 18th century and solicitors then trained at the Inns of Chancery. When these inns closed, the Law Society (see below) became responsible for providing law schools for solicitors. Before being admitted as a solicitor, a man had to serve a period of training, known as articles, with a qualified solicitor. A statute of 1728 prescribed that the period of articles should be five years (now reduced to two years). Articled clerks' names were also entered on rolls. The rolls for 1729–1858 are held by TNA. They are arranged by the date of the articles, but there is a name index.

Until the 19th century a solicitor had to be formally admitted to practise in each court, often by swearing an oath. Records of solicitors can therefore be found in court records (# chapters 24 and 25), such as those of the courts of Common Pleas and King's Bench (at TNA). Bevan (239) and TNA domestic records leaflet 36 list the different courts' records of solicitors and articled clerks. For example, the oaths taken in the Court of King's Bench are on rolls (for 1750–1840 and 1861–74) in series KB 113. From 1749 solicitors had to swear affidavits "of due execution", that they had completed their articles. Registers of these affidavits note the name of the solicitor to whom a clerk was articled. Most registers are indexed. The surviving affidavits often note the names of the clerk's parents. For the Court of Common Pleas, series CP 5 contains registers of articles of clerkship (1758–1867) and admission books (1724–1853). For the Court of King's Bench, there are affidavits of due execution for 1749–1875 (in KB 105–107) which are indexed up to 1845.

A Society of Gentleman Practisers in the Courts of Law and Equity was founded in London in 1739 (but dissolved in 1817). Local law societies were established in the late 18th century and the Law Society was founded in 1831 to regulate the solicitors' profession. It has offices at 110–113 Chancery Lane, London WC2 (with a large library), and at Ipsley Court in Redditch. It holds registers of articles of clerkship from 1860, a register of solicitors' admissions (since 1845) and an unpublished collection made by W. Richards, in 17 volumes, of biographical information on solicitors and attorneys up to 1906. From 1710 to 1811 deeds of articles were also subject to the

CORRECTED TO JAN. 1ST, 1856.

THE LAW LIST;

BEING A LIST OF THE

JUDGES AND OFFICERS

OF THE DIFFERENT

Courts of Justice:

COUNSEL,

WITH THE DATES OF THEIR CALL AND INNS OF COURT:

SPECIAL PLEADERS, CONVEYANCERS;

AND THE

ONLY AUTHENTIC AND COMPLETE LIST OF CERTIFICATED

ATTORNEYS, NOTARIES, &c.,

IN ENGLAND AND WALES,

WITH THE

London Agents to the Country Attorneys,

As printed by Permission of the Commissioners of Inland Revenue.

TO WHICH ARE ADDED,

THE CIRCUITS, JUDGES, CLERKS, AND HIGH BAILIFFS

OF THE

COUNTY COURTS.

LAW AND PUBLIC OFFICERS,	LONDON COMMISSIONERS FOR TAKING
CIRCUITS OF THE JUDGES,	OATHS IN CHANCERY,
TABLE OF SHERIFFS AND AGENTS,	QUARTER SESSIONS, &c., &c.

AND A VARIETY OF OTHER USEFUL MATTERS.

BY WILLIAM POWELL,

OF THE INLAND REVENUE OFFICE, SOMERSET-HOUSE,

REGISTRAR OF CERTIFICATES.

LONDON:

V. & R. STEVENS AND G. S. NORTON,

Law Booksellers and Publishers,

(*Successors to the late J. & W. T. CLARKE, of Portugal Street,*)

26, BELL YARD, LINCOLN'S INN.

1856.

Notice.—*The Law List is made up and closed to the 1st of January in each year.*

Price 6s. 6d. neatly bound.

A NEW, COMPLETE, AND ACCURATE

LIST

OF ALL THE

CERTIFICATED ATTORNEYS

RESIDING IN

LONDON, WESTMINSTER, AND BOROUGH OF SOUTHWARK, AND THEIR ENVIRONS;

PRINTED FROM THE STAMP-OFFICE LISTS.

NOTICE.—Offices, Appointments, &c.—In future all Offices, Appointments and Description, which are inserted in the present year's LAW LIST as held by Attorneys, will be repeated in the next year's LAW LIST, unless they are altered in the slip or ticket delivered at the Stamp Office on renewing the Certificate for the next year.

Those marked thus are Members of the Incorporated Law Society of the United Kingdom, by Charters of Wm. IV. and Victoria;——† the Metropolitan and Provincial Law Association;—— ‡ the Law Association for the Benefit of Widows and Families of Professional Men in the Metropolis and its Vicinity;——‖ the Justices' Clerks' Society.——The "London Commissioners to administer Oaths in Chancery" are thus distinguished : "Com. Oaths in Chy.," and see alphabetical list, post. *⁎* For Perpetual Commissioners in LONDON, see post.*

ABBOT, William, and Wm. Abbot, jun. (firm Abbot & Sons), proctors and notaries, doctors'-commons

*Abbott, Chas. James (firm Jenkins & Abbott), 8, new-inn

Abbott, Francis Geo., com. oaths in chy. (firm Abbott & Wheatly), 22 a, southampton-buildings, chan.-lane, and staines, middlesex (patent agents)

Abbott, George Washington, and Joseph Seymour Salaman (firm Abbott & Salaman), 13, basinghall-street, city

Abell, Francis Gibbs, att. and not., att. of insolvent debtors ct., sol. in bankruptcy, and com. for affidvts. 15, addington-square, camberwell-road, and colchester, essex

Ablett, Isaac, 6, newcastle-st. strand, and 1, christopher-street, hatton-garden

*Abraham, George Frederick, com. oaths in chy., 6, great marlborough-street, westminster, and kentish-town

Abrahams, Michael, 23, southampton-buildings, chancery-lane

Abrahams, Samuel, 4, lincoln's-inn-fields, and 32, aberdeen-place, maida-hill

Abrahams, Samuel Benjamin, 27, bloomsbury-square

Acland, William, 46, upper bedford-place, russell-square

G

119. Extracts from The Law List 1856

stamp duty levied on apprentices' indentures and so many articled clerks appear in the apprenticeship books in IR 1 at TNA, naming the solicitor to whom a clerk was articled and sometimes the clerk's father (and perhaps his profession).

Judges and Justices of the Peace   Most judges are appointed from the ranks of barristers and so can be found in the records noted above. Further information about many judges is contained in the *Dictionary of National Biography* (# chapter 26). Foss (800) is a biographical dictionary of about 1,600 English judges from 1066 to 1870, noting their education, careers (and some biographical details of the judge's family). Simpson (865) includes short biographies of many British (and foreign) judges and lawyers, such as Judge Jeffreys, who contributed to my family history (after Monmouth's rebellion of 1685) by sentencing one of my ancestor's brothers to be transported to Barbados. Lists of judges of each court (# chapters 24 and 25) and senior court officials such as Masters in Chancery, from medieval times to the 1880s, are included in *The Book of Dignities* by Ockerby (843).

Justices of the Peace (also known as magistrates) had no legal training until recent years. They were appointed by the Crown by documents known as commissions. Appointments after 1665 were announced in the *London Gazette*. Records of appointments are also held at TNA, in series listed by Colwell (242). For example, appointments of justices from the 16th to 20th centuries are recorded in C 202 (with indexes). Justices of the Peace are also named in many Quarter and Petty Session records at CROs (# chapter 25) and in directories.

Medicine

Bourne & Chicken (779) review the records of the medical profession and the legislation that has regulated the profession since medieval times. Many sources noted above, such as commercial directories and civil registration, census and apprenticeship records, will record medical ancestors. Furthermore, medical officers of poor law unions can be located in Guardians' records (# chapter 18) and medical officers of the armed forces appear in army lists, the East India or Indian directories, published works on army or EIC medical officers and in the records of the army, navy or East India Company (# chapters 20, 21 and 30).

Until the 19th century the medical profession was divided into physicians (who diagnosed internal disorders), surgeons (who performed operations) and apothecaries (who prepared medicines). By a statute of 1511 the church was empowered to regulate the profession and so medical ancestors can be found in church records. A bishop had power to license those practising medicine or surgery in his diocese (although this system fell into disuse by the late 18th century) and from 1580 to 1775 licences to practise medicine or surgery were also issued by the Archbishop of Canterbury. Licences were provided to applicants (and so have usually been lost), but the issue of a licence was recorded in bishops' registers (# chapter 24), generally held at CROs and noting a man's name, parish, the date of issue and the fee. Thus registers of licences issued by the Bishop of London to physicians or surgeons from the 16th to 18th centuries are at LMA and Guildhall Library. Men licensed from 1529 to 1725 are listed in Bloom & James (778). Records of the licences issued by the Archbishop of Canterbury are at Lambeth Palace Library and its web site includes an index to the physicians and surgeons licensed from 1535 to 1775. Willis (959) includes act book entries for licences issued in the Diocese of Canterbury from 1568 to 1646. Some supporting records, such as testimonials from other practitioners, may also survive at CROs.

Physicians usually had a university degree and this was required by law from 1522. Searches should therefore be made in university records (# chapter 19), especially in those of the medical schools of Scottish universities, which were particularly renowned. The Royal College of Physicians (founded in 1518) licensed physicians who practised in London or within 7 miles of the city. Many country physicians were also granted membership. Records of members (fellows or licenciates) are at the college's library at 11 St Andrews Place, London NW1. Biographies of members up to 1825 (about 1,700 of them) have been published in Munk (841). The entries include the physician's father's name, university education, date of admission to the college and details of his practice. Brown (782) contains detailed biographies of fellows of the college from 1826 to 1925. Licenciates since 1845 are included in the *Medical Directory* and *Medical Register* (considered below) and licenciates from 1826 to 1844 can be found in the college's records. Many physicians outside London were not members of the college, but records of their licences can be found (until the 19th century) in diocesan records. Raach (848) is a directory of over 800 English country physicians of 1603–43 noted in diocesan records or university registers.

Surgeons were closely linked to barbers, and from 1540 to 1745 both professions in London formed the Worshipful Company of Barber-Surgeons. However, the status of surgeons gradually improved and the Barber-Surgeons' Company divided into two in 1745. The Surgeons' Company was replaced in 1800 by the Royal College of Surgeons. Information about members and apprentices is available (by written application) from the college librarian at 35–43 Lincoln's Inn Fields, London WC2. A partial catalogue of the archives held by the college library can be consulted on its web site (# appendix XI). Some records, such as examination registers since 1745, have been deposited at Guildhall Library. Records of the Barber-Surgeons' Company are still held by the Barbers' Company, but copies of the most important registers are on microfilm at Guildhall Library; including apprentice bindings (from 1657), freedom admissions (from 1522) and registers of navy surgeons (1705–45). Other sources for navy surgeons in the 18th and 19th centuries are listed by Bourne & Chicken (779).

In medieval times apothecaries treated most illnesses and were often members of the Grocers' Company (because of the herbs and spices needed to make medicines), but their own London livery company, the Society of Apothecaries, was founded in 1617. Most of the society's records (and the Grocers' Company's records of apothecaries of the 15th to 17th centuries) are at Guildhall Library. The apothecaries' records include freedom admissions and apprentice bindings from 1617 to the 19th century. From 1815 apothecaries had to be licensed by the society (and be apprenticed or later take examinations) in order to practise in England or Wales. Many physicians and surgeons also obtained licences to act as apothecaries. The Society of Apothecaries published annual lists, from 1815 to 1832, of those obtaining licences. A cumulative alphabetical list (of all men obtaining licences from 1815 to 1840) was also published and has been reproduced on microfiche (758) by the SoG, with the date of the apothecary's licence and usually his place of residence. Further records of licentiates of the society up to 1954 are held at Guildhall Library.

Wallis & Wallis (874) list about 80,000 surgeons, physicians, apothecaries, dentists and midwives in the 18th century. The information has been extracted from the apprenticeship registers at TNA, bishops' licences and subscription lists for books and journals. For example, it includes Thomas Charnock (son of Thomas Charnock), who was apprenticed in 1722 to John Metcalfe, an apothecary. Talbot & Hammond (872) is a biographical dictionary of thousands of medical practitioners in England up to about 1518, with information from a wide variety of manuscript and published sources. A sample entry (omitting references) is:

John Maister, surgeon, appears to have practised his craft in Canterbury from 1512 till 1521. Not being a freeman of the city, he paid annual fees of varying amounts (6d to 2s) for the right to carry on his practice.

Apothecaries were replaced by chemists and druggists as the suppliers of medicines and drugs to the public. The Pharmaceutical Society of Great Britain was granted a charter of incorporation in 1843 and registers of its members were published from 1868. The 1910 edition (764) lists the name, residence and date of registration of about 25,000 chemists and druggists who were then practising.

General practitioners developed in the early 19th century. They were usually licenciates of the Society of Apothecaries and some were members of the Royal College of Surgeons or the Royal College of Physicians. The British Medical Association was formed in 1823. The *Medical*

Directory was published from 1845 with the names and addresses of medical practitioners. From 1858 anyone practising medicine or surgery had to register with a new General Council and an official *Medical Register*, listing practitioners' qualifications, commenced publication in 1859. Many copies are held at the SoG. Entries are usually alphabetical, giving a practitioner's name, date of registration, residence and qualification. A typical entry from the 1869 register is:

Registration date	Name	Residence	Qualification
1859 Jan 1.	Bulleid, George.	32, Connaught Terrace, London	Member Royal College of Surgeons England 1852

George Bulleid also appeared in editions up to 1892 (resident at 65 Edgeware Road, London). By 1892 an Edgar George Bulleid also appeared, with the same address, having registered on 3 January 1884. He was a licenciate of the Royal Colleges of Physicians and of Surgeons in Edinburgh. By ascertaining the last entry for a doctor, it is easier to search for his death, will or obituary in other records.

The pulling of teeth was originally carried out by barbers, but modern dentistry was pioneered by surgeons and a registration system for dentists was established in 1878. From the late 19th century dentists were listed in the *Dentists' Register*, such as the 1885 edition (754), which provides dentist's names, addresses, qualifications, and date of registration.

The Wellcome Library for the History and Understanding of Medicine, at 183 Euston Road, London NW1 2BE (telephone 020 8582 7611), has an extensive collection of books and manuscripts, reviewed by C. Hilton in *Genealogists' Magazine* (December 1998 and June 2000). Published sources include directories, biographies and biographical dictionaries of medical men and also medical journals (that include doctors' obituaries). The manuscript collections include transcripts of records of bishops' licences to medical practitioners, private hospitals' records (including patient registers) and doctors' personal papers (such as account books, diaries and notebooks), some including notes on patients. The library's online resources include the Hospital Records Database, maintained jointly with TNA (# chapter 18) and the web site of the Medical Archives and Manuscripts Survey, which catalogues records of medical interest in other archives, for example hospital registers and private asylum records.

Nurses

Useful articles about records of midwives appear in *Family Tree Magazine* (July and August 1990) and Grundy (808a) includes a detailed review of the licensing, registration and work of midwives. Since midwives might have to baptise a sickly child at birth, they were licensed by the church from medieval times until the 18th century. The issue of a licence was noted in bishops' act books and these (with some testimonials) are in diocesan records at CROs. Willis (959) includes entries for midwives' licences (translated from Latin) from act books of the Diocese of Canterbury from 1615 to 1646. An example is:

12th March 1621/2: Ann wife of John Treverse of the parish of Leeds [appeared] and produced a testimonial . . . of various women of Leeds as to her efficiency in the work of a midwife. She humbly petitioned to be admitted to exercise that office within the diocese. Accordingly, when she had taken the oath customary for midwives, the Judge admitted her to exercise the said office . . . and handed her a licence.

Grundy (808a) lists over 300 midwives licensed in Yorkshire in the 17th and 18th centuries as well as hundreds of churchwardens or other people nominating them or witnessing the licence applications. A national registration system was established for midwives in 1902. The Central Midwives' Board issued certificates to midwives and published an annual roll of certified midwives, noting a woman's name, address, qualification and date of enrolment with the board. The 1905 roll (759a) lists over 22,000 midwives such as:

CHARNOCK, Lucie Margaret. 23 Worcester Road, Bootle, Liverpool.
[enrolment] 1905, March 23.
[qualification] L.O.S. [Obstetrical Society of London] Nov 26, 1903.

Records of nurses of poor law unions and military nursing services were reviewed in chapters 18, 20 and 21. Training schools for nurses were established at many hospitals in the late 19th century, and some records of nurses may therefore be found in hospital records (# chapter 18) in hospital archives or at CROs. Thus LMA holds records of nurses at St Thomas' Hospital (1844–1930) and nurses who trained at Guy's Hospital (1880–1937), usually limited to names, dates of training or employment (and sometimes their ages). The Royal College of Nursing was founded in 1916 and a national registration system for civilian nurses was established in 1921. The register of nurses (up to 1973), with indexes, is held by TNA in series DT 10. There is also a roll of nurses since 1944 in DT 11. The register and roll (described in TNA domestic records leaflet 79) give nurses' names, qualifications and address. Some other 20th-century records of nurses at TNA are described in the same leaflet.

Some hospitals issued registers of the nurses they trained. For example, Guy's Hospital issued a handbook for nurses that included a register of nurses trained at the hospital. The 1950 edition (755) listed about 3,000 nurses including:

FINLOW, Ada B., [address] Abbey Fields, near Sandbach, Cheshire. Student nurse, Guy's Hosp., 1910 to 1913. Staff nurse, ditto, to Nov., 1913. Sister, Alexandra Hosp., Queen Square, to Oct., 1914. Member, French Flag Corps, France, 8 months. Staff nurse and sister, Civil Hosp., Reserve, Malta, Salonica and Russia, to 1920. S.R.N. [State Registered Nurse].

Actors and musicians
Actors and other entertainers are difficult to research from original source material because there were no formal training records, most actors moved around the country a great deal and some worked under an alias or stage name. However, there are some useful published sources. *Who's Who in the Theatre*, published since 1912, contains detailed biographies of actors (and other people involved in the theatre). Entries were deleted when an actor died, so it is worth consulting different editions such as the 5th (1926) by Parker (844) and particularly the 16th (1977) by Herbert (820), which lists people whose entries had been deleted, giving the year of the last edition in which they appeared.

Two articles, "Was your ancestor in the theatre?" by S. Fearn in *Family Tree Magazine* (October 1999) and "Family history and the theatre" by A. Ruston in the winter 1988 edition of *Hertfordshire People* (858), provide detailed information on sources for actors held in museums and archives. These include reference books, journals, theatre programmes and playbills (listing actors in a particular play). Information can also be obtained from 19th- and 20th-century theatrical journals such as *The Era* (published weekly from 1838 to 1939), *Theatrical Journal* (weekly from 1839 to 1873), *Theatre* (published from 1877 to 1897), *Theatre World* (published since 1925) and *The Stage* (published since 1881). Copies of these are held at the British Newspaper Library. Many copies are also held at City of Westminster Archives (# appendix VII) or at the Theatre Museum, Tavistock Street, London WC2 (telephone 020 7836 7891), which also holds many photographs and over one million programmes and playbills (although there are no indexes to actors' names).

A 16-volume biographical dictionary by Highfill, Burnim & Langhans (821) includes biographies of 9,000 actors and actresses who performed in London between 1660 and 1800. Most of the biographies include details of a person's birth, marriage and death as well the plays in which he or she took part, with references to thousands of manuscript and printed sources in libraries and archives. Nungezer (842) is a biographical dictionary of English actors before 1642 including William Shakespeare but also many lesser-known actors, such as James Candler, who was leading a company of actors playing in Ipswich in 1569. More information about actors of this period, the plays in which they acted and the places in which they performed can be found in the volumes of *Records of Early English Drama* published by University of Toronto Press.

Circus performers are even more difficult to research because they constantly moved around the country (or abroad) and were even more likely than actors to use stage names. Fortunately, about 3,000 clowns, acrobats, jugglers and other circus performers of the 19th century (of 10,000 estimated to have worked in circuses) are included in a biographical dictionary by Turner (873). Many married other circus performers or were members of families of which a number of generations (and many siblings in each generation) worked in the circus. This is one of the shorter entries:

Palmer, George. Equestrian juggler. Noted at Hengler's Covent Garden circus, 1889–90, where he also performed in dramatic spectacles in the arena, e.g. 'The war in Zululand'. He was assistant equestrian director for that season. Married into the Rancy family and in 1897 was with Rancy's circus, in North Africa. Father of Gaston Palmer [a juggler]. Brother of Sarah Palmer, who married one of the Bourbonnel family.

Biographies of musicians are contained in the various editions of Grove's *Dictionary of Music and Musicians*, first published in four volumes in 1878. Subsequent editions were expanded and Sadie (860) is the sixth edition of 1980, in 20 volumes. Some other directories and biographical dictionaries of musicians, such as *Who's Who in Music*, first published in 1935, are listed in Raymond (851). There was a London livery company of musicians, the records of which are at Guildhall Library.

Architects
There are detailed biographical dictionaries of architects. Colvin (787) includes biographies of English architects from 1600 to 1840, with notes on the buildings they designed. Ware (875) is less comprehensive but includes architects from medieval times (such as Henry Yevele, who died in 1400) up to the 20th century. Harvey (814) is a biographical dictionary of about 1,700 English architects up to 1550 (including master masons and carpenters). Felstead, Franklin & Pinfield

(796) is a detailed work on about 7,000 British architects from 1834 to 1900, recording an architect's birth, death, address, education, training, professional qualifications and noting any obituary. The entry for Thomas Henry Eagles is:

Address: 11 Brunswick Terrace, Windsor, Berkshire (1871) and Royal Indian Engineering College, Cooper's Hill, Staines, Surrey (1881).

Education and training: Articled to Henry Dangerfield of Cheltenham, August 1859, who retired December 1862. Articles transferred to Richard Reynolds Rowe until 1867. Queen's College, Cambridge, October 1867 (graduated 1871). In office of William S. Cross from February 1871 to September 1872. Passed District Surveyor's examination. Date of death: 27 Feb 1892.

Professional qualifications: ARIBA 22 May 1871; FRIBA 23 May 1881.

Practice Information: Lecturer in architecture at Coopers Hill College from September 1872. Works: [List in RIBA Fellows' Nomination Papers]. Honours and Awards: RIBA Medal of Merit 1874.

Obituaries: "Builder" 9 April 1892 and RIBA Proceedings vol. 8 1892.

Who's Who in Architecture by Richards (853) contains biographies of about 600 British and foreign architects. Architects of the 19th and 20th centuries may also be listed in the *Register of Architects*, published in most years since 1885. Records of 40,000 architects are contained in the archives of the Royal Institute of British Architects, at 66 Portland Place, London.

Clergy

Detailed information about clergymen of the Church of England, the Church of Wales and the Episcopal Church of Scotland (and also, until 1985, clergymen of the Church of Ireland) is contained in *Crockford's Clerical Directory*, published since 1858 (originally annually but later every two or three years). The 1858 edition (752) has entries for over 18,500 clergymen. Entries note a clergyman's benefice (or more senior position in the church), any positions or benefices previously held and his education and training.

Anglican clergy before 1858 are listed in the *Clerical Guide* (first published in 1817) and in the *Clergy List* (published from 1841). Thus the 1841 *Clergy List* (751) lists Anglican clergy alphabetically together with details of any benefice that they held. Each benefice is also listed, with information about the incumbent and the benefice. The entry for Winkleigh in Devon notes that it was in the Diocese of Exeter, that the incumbent was Henry Wright, that the population was 1,596 and that the benefice had a value of £215. Many clergy of 1800–40 are also listed in *Index Ecclesiasticus* (unfortunately incomplete) compiled by Foster (801). This notes clergymen's names, their benefices and dates of their institution to those livings. Senior clergy from 1066 to 1857 (and officials at Oxford and Cambridge universities) are listed (with biographical details) in *Fasti Ecclesiae Anglicanae*, originally compiled (up to 1715) by John Le Neve but continued up to 1854 by Hardy (811). This has biographical entries for about 41,000 clergy (arranged by diocese and archdeaconry, but indexed), noting dates of admissions to offices, dates of burial and sometimes the date of a clergyman's will. This work has been expanded (with further source material that has become available) by volumes by Greenway (807) and Horn & others (824) and (825). There are three series (1066–1300, 1300–1541 and 1541–1857), each with entries arranged by diocese and archdeaconry, but indexed.

Some county lists of parish clergy, with biographical information, have been published, for example for Essex (in the journal *Essex Review*) and for Northamptonshire and Rutland (in 16 volumes by H. Longden). Information about a clergyman can also be obtained from parish registers that he prepared (these may include his notes on parish affairs) or from other parish records (illustrating, for example, his role at vestry meetings). Anglican clergy generally studied, until the mid-19th century, at Oxford or Cambridge universities and so those university registers (# chapter 19) should also be consulted since they provide details of education, parentage and subsequent careers. Theological colleges were founded from the mid-19th century, so that not all those who wished to become clergy had to enter Oxford or Cambridge. The SoG holds the Fawcett card index of clergy (and also north country families) prepared from sources such as parish registers, wills, Oxford and Cambridge university registers, *Gentleman's Magazine* and *Musgrave's Obituary*. Thus a card for James Charnock notes that he was a proctor at Oxford University in 1568 and also refers the researcher to an entry in *Musgrave's Obituary*.

The ordination of clergymen as deacons or priests, their appointments to benefices and the appointments of higher clergy are recorded in bishops' registers from the 13th century. They are generally in Latin until the 18th century and held in diocesan records at CROs. Some have been published, especially by county record societies. Related papers may include baptismal or birth certificates, or even testimonials from their colleges or other clergy. Surviving bishops' registers up to 1646, their location (and notes on published copies), are listed in Smith (949). Later diocesan records of clergy are listed in CRO catalogues. Guildhall Library produces a detailed leaflet on records of clergy in the Diocese of London (and some peculiar jurisdictions), including clergy ordination papers since 1674. Clergymen who did not have a benefice might nevertheless preach (with a bishop's licence until the 18th century). Licences might also be granted permitting a clergyman to live away from his benefice or to hold livings in plurality. These are also recorded in bishops' registers. Some records of clerical appointments that are held at TNA are listed in Colwell (242), including returns (in series E 331), from bishops and deans and chapters of London, Salisbury and York, of the institution of incumbents from 1544 to 1912. They are arranged by diocese and date (but indexed).

Searches for ministers of other denominations should be made in the records and archives of the relevant church. There are some published works listing (or providing biographies) of Catholic priests or non-conformist ministers. Four volumes by Anstruther (769) contain biographies of over 3,000 Catholic priests from 1558 to 1800 and Fitzgerald-Lombard (797) lists almost 9,000 Catholic priests of England and Wales from 1801 to 1914, with brief biographies. Ministers of Congregational chapels are listed in *The Congregational Year Book*, for example the edition of 1920 (753), with obituaries of deceased ministers (and some photographs). Unitarian ministers' obituaries appeared in Unitarian year books and other publications and those from 1900 to 1999 have been indexed in Ruston (859). Methodist ministers are listed in various publications, listed in Raymond (851), such as *Hall's Circuits and Ministers* (813), which lists British Methodist circuits and their ministers from 1765 to 1912.

Teachers

Schoolteachers were required by a canon of 1603 to be licensed by bishops. The issue of licences was recorded in Act books that are in diocesan records (usually in CROs). Prosecutions of unlicensed teachers also appear in church courts' records (# chapter 24). From the 19th century, an ancestor may be noted as a teacher in civil registration or census records. Published school and university registers include lists of the teaching staff, sometimes with short biographies or obituaries. Teachers are also noted in published school histories and magazines. Those training to be teachers are listed in the sections for teacher training departments in some university calendars. Many teachers joined the National Union of Teachers and those union members who served or died with the armed forces in the First World War are commemorated in a memorial volume published by the NUT in 1920.

The Teachers' Registration Council was established in 1902. This kept registers of teachers' careers and issued lists of teachers from 1902 to 1907 and from 1912 until 1948 but registration was voluntary and so many teachers are omitted from the records. The registers are now held at the SoG. The 160 volumes (concerning perhaps 50,000 teachers) contain alphabetical entries for teachers registered by the council since 1902, but including details of their earlier careers. Thus Louisa Allison registered with the council in June 1915, having taught at a school in Brighton in 1880 and 1881 and having been headmistress of a school in Exeter from 1899 to 1905 (with subsequent appointments in Deptford, London and Leeds). The volumes are not available to researchers but SoG staff will search for entries.

Members of Parliament
Records and biographical dictionaries of members of Parliament are described in an article "Was your ancestor a Parliamentarian?" by R. Thorne in *Family History News and Digest* (September 1994). Lists of members of Parliament from 1213 are in series C 219 at TNA. Records of proceedings in the House of Commons, described by Bond (922), are held at the House of Lords Record Office. These include journals and minutes of proceedings, lists of members voting (since 1836), and members' papers and diaries. There are published lists and biographical dictionaries of MPs for most periods. Short biographies (and photographs) of MPs are included in *Dod's Parliamentary Companion*, published annually since the mid-19th century. Biographies of MPs who sat in the Commons from 1832 to 1979 are contained in Stenton & Lees (870). MPs for most years between 1386 and 1820 are the subject of detailed biographies in volumes of *The History of Parliament, the House of Commons* published by the History of Parliament Trust. For example, Roskell, Clark and Rawcliffe (856) includes the 3,173 MPs of 1386 to 1421 and Hasler (815) covers the 2,688 MPs who sat from 1558 to 1603. All the volumes refer to many manuscript sources and to other published works in which the MPs appear. Judd (829) is a useful list of the 5,034 MPs who sat in the Commons between 1734 and 1832, with references to other published works which feature those MPs, such as biographical dictionaries, school registers and *Burke's Peerage* (# chapter 26).

Sculptors, artists and authors
Gunnis (809) is a dictionary of British sculptors from 1660 to 1851. It contains about 1,700 detailed biographies, based on church or other monuments and records such as the archives of the Masons' Company of London. One of the shorter entries is for Anthony Goude of Chelmsford:

Goude, who had been assistant to Christopher Cass, set up for himself in Chelmsford before 1726 and was the mason employed on the building of Boreham House, Essex from 1726 until 1731. From 1729 till 1741 he was working for Earl Fitzwalter at Moulsham Hall

[Essex], making the hall chimney-piece in 1732 and a veined-marble chimney-piece. . . . In 1737 he cut the stone capitals for the piers of the stable court, receiving £30. In 1741 he was paid £7 13s. 6d. for the six milestones between Ingatestone and Chelmsford. [Hoare and Fitzwalter archives.]

Biographies of painters are contained in Bryan's *Dictionary of Painters and Engravers*, originally published in 1816 and in revised editions such as the 1853 edition by Stanley (869) and the 1930 edition by Williamson (879). Over 22,000 artists who exhibited works at the principal London exhibitions from 1760 to 1893 are listed in Graves (805), with the exhibition dates and the artists' principal places of work and residence. Johnson & Greutzner (828) list about 41,000 British artists of 1880–1940 with their addresses (in some cases other biographical details) and the exhibitions at which their work was shown.

Kunitz & Haycraft (831) provide about 1,000 biographies of 19th-century authors of Britain and the British Empire, with information about their families, education and works. Kunitz & Haycraft (832) provide biographies of about 650 British authors from before 1800.

Other professions and trades

Published sources for other professions and trades are listed in Raymond (851). For example, lists of members have been published, usually annually, by the Institute of Chartered Accountants (since 1896), the Association of Certified & Corporate Accountants (since 1907), the Stock Exchange (since 1850) and the Institution of Civil Engineers (since 1867). Two works by C. Ramsden contain biographies of about 5,000 bookbinders of 1780 to 1840. There are also biographical dictionaries of printers and booksellers (1641–1775), railway engineers and violin makers.

Sport

An increasing number of people are professional or amateur sportsmen or women. Interest in sport is such that many people would prefer to discover that their great grandfather played cricket or was a professional footballer rather than a noble, lawyer or miner. Researching an ancestor who played sport, whether amateur or professional, is difficult because so many records are held by clubs which do not have facilities (such as an archivist or search room) to allow researchers access to the records. Some club records have been deposited at CROs but family historians can also use many published works.

You may discover that an ancestor played sport from material held by your family. For example, there may be a photograph of grandfather in his football or rugby kit. An ancestor may appear in a team photograph, perhaps taken to celebrate their victory in a league or cup competition. A relative may also hold a medal, badge or cup commemorating an ancestor's sporting success.

National and local newspapers are a very useful source for sporting ancestors. Detailed reports have appeared since the 19th century of sporting events so if you know that an ancestor played cricket for a particular team, it is worth reviewing local newspapers for match reports (in which he may appear by name). If an ancestor commenced his sporting career at school or university, you may find information in a published school register or history (and perhaps even a team photograph that includes him). A school or college may still hold many team photographs that include your ancestor.

There are hundreds of books on sport, including biographical dictionaries and team histories, available at bookshops or libraries, which may refer to an ancestor. For example, Bailey, Thorn & Wynne-Thomas (770) is a biographical dictionary of about 12,000 men, both amateur and professional, who have played first-class cricket in England. Thus, George Banner played for Nottinghamshire in 1885, having been born in Sutton-in-Ashfield on 21 January 1864 (and dying there on 20 March 1890). The annual editions of Wisden's *Cricketers' Almanack* have been the cricket fan's bible since it was first published in 1864. Obituaries of cricketers were included from 1892 and over 5,000 of those have been reprinted in Green (806). There are similar biographical dictionaries and annual handbooks for football, golf, rugby and other sports. Published histories of teams, for example that of York City Football Club by Batters (772), include biographies and photographs of team members and match results.

The first modern Olympiad took place in Athens in 1896 and so competitors in those games may appear in many peoples' family trees. By 1988, over 4,300 men and women had represented Great Britain in Summer or Winter Games, of whom over 400 won an Olympic medal (or title). These competitors are listed in Buchanan (783) with short biographies of those who won medals, such as Arthur Stanley Garton, born in 1889 in Epsom, Surrey who won a gold medal for rowing in 1912.

Alehouses, taverns and inns

From 1552 Justices of the Peace at Quarter Sessions were authorised to select the persons (victuallers) who should be permitted to keep alehouses. Victuallers obtained a licence from the Justices and submitted a bond of surety (or recognizance) for the orderly keeping of such houses. By the early 17th century many sessions required licences to be renewed annually and annual licensing at special licensing sessions was compulsory from 1729. Alehouse keepers had to take out recognizances each year from 1753 and Clerks of the Peace were required to keep registers of the recognizances. Surviving lists of licences and registers of recognizances are usually in Quarter Sessions' records (# chapter 25). Recognizances name the licensee, his parish, the names of those who stood surety for him and (later) the name of the alehouse. Registers of recognizances provide similar information. Quarter Sessions' order books may note the issue of licences or the giving of recognizances. Until the 17th century a tavern was generally a house that sold wine (and an inn was a lodging that often included a tavern). An act of 1553 required taverns to be licensed, usually by the Crown (by Letters Patent) or its agents. Justices of the Peace issued the licences from 1792. Records of wine licences from the 16th to 18th centuries are at TNA.

An act of 1828 replaced most earlier licensing legislation and confirmed annual licensing sessions of Justices, but no records or registers had to be kept (although a few records of licences survive in Justices' papers). An act of 1830 allowed any householder to sell beer, ale or cider with a licence from the Excise authorities (but no records of such licences are known to exist). Accordingly there are few records of licences from 1828 to 1869. The licences provided to the publicans have generally been lost but some survive in family papers or in CROs. Illustration 120 is a licence to sell beer that was granted on 11 October 1841 to Rebecca Hawksworth, who kept the Union in Leek, Staffordshire. A new licensing system for all licensed premises was instituted in 1869. The Justices licensed premises on an annual basis for the sale of beer, ale and wine (and these licences were confirmed, from 1872, by standing committees of Justices). Registers of licences had to be kept from 1872. My ancestor Bernard Herber is noted in commercial directories as the publican at the George Tavern on Cable Street in London just before 1869

Publican's Retail Beer, Cider, and Perry Licence.

No. *862*   No.

L D.

WE, whose Names are hereunto subscribed and Seals set, being the COLLECTOR OF EXCISE OF *Northwich*

COLLECTION,* and the Supervisor of Excise of *Congleton* District within the said Collection, in pursuance of an Act of Parliament made and passed in the Sixth Year of the Reign of His Majesty King George the Fourth, intituled "*An Act to repeal several Duties payable on Excise Licences in Great Britain and Ireland, and to impose other Duties in lieu thereof, and to amend the Laws for granting Excise Licences,*" and of all other Acts and Powers enabling us in this behalf, do hereby license and empower *Rebecca Hawksworth*

residing in a House known by the Sign of *Union* in the Parish of *Leek* in the County of *Stafford* and within the said Collection, (and duly authorized by Justices of the Peace to keep a Common Inn, Ale-house, or Victualling-house,) TO SELL BEER, CIDER, OR PERRY BY RETAIL, to be drank or consumed in the said House or Premises, at† *Leek in the Parish and County afore'd*

(as described by the Entry of the said Trader, dated *10* Day of *Oct'r* 1835 for carrying on therein the said Trade or Business, and as only one separate and distinct Set of Premises, all adjoining or contiguous to each other, and situate in one Place, and held together for the same Trade or Business,) but no where else, from the Day of the Date hereof until and upon the Tenth Day of October next ensuing, the Dwelling-house in which the said *Rebecca Hawksworth* resides, or is to retail Beer, Cider, or Perry as aforesaid,‡ being at the Time of taking out this Licence, together with the Offices, Courts, Yards, and Gardens therewith occupied, rated, rented, or valued *at a Rent of Twenty Pounds per Annum or upwards,*§ and he having paid the Sum of *£3 . 6 . 13¼* for this Licence to the said Collector.

Dated this *11* Day of *Sep'r* in the Year of our Lord 18 *41*

Collector

Supervisor

N. B. The Continuance of this Licence depends upon the Magistrates' Authority to keep the Victualling-house on which it is founded.

Renewal of Licence.

Every Person intending to continue the Trade or Business for which a Licence has been granted, is to give Notice of his Intention to the Collector or Supervisor at least Twenty-one Days before the expiration of his Current Licence. If such Notice be so given, the new Licence must bear Date from the Expiration of his current Licence. If such Notice be not so given, the Licence must bear Date from the Day of the Trader's Application for it, and the Trader will be in the mean while unlicensed.

Penalty for exercising the above Trade without taking out or renewing Licence at the proper Time, £50.

120. *Licence to sell beer granted to Rebecca Hawksworth, 1841*

(unfortunately when licences were not required). The directories record a new publican from 1869 and it is possible that Bernard was unable to obtain a licence when the new licensing system was instituted in that year.

Gibson & Hunter (803) describe the different types of licence and list surviving records (and their location) for each British county. Published guides to Quarter Sessions' records, such as Goodacre & Mercer (978) for Middlesex records, usually provide more detail about local licensing sessions and the surviving records. Gibson & Hunter (803) also describe victuallers' Lenten recognizances, which date from 1572 to 1634. An act of 1562 prohibited inns or taverns from selling meat during Lent and licensees were often required to provide recognizances to ensure that they complied with the act. These are held at TNA in series E 180 and C 203 or in the Palatinates' records (# chapter 24). From 1752 Justices also licensed premises for music and dancing. Surviving records include licence applications, petitions against licences being granted and lists of men who obtained licences.

Quarter Sessions' records may include other references to alehouse keepers. There were many prosecutions for keeping disorderly (or unlicensed) alehouses, or allowing unlawful games to take place. Emmison (975) includes many examples from Elizabethan Quarter Sessions' records in Essex. For example, an innholder in Chatley was presented for receiving persons into his alehouse on Sunday afternoons (and also for not attending church). In 1602 the inhabitants of East Tilbury reported the victualler John Nicolson as "a man of lewd and evil behaviour", who kept an unlicensed alehouse and "compelled" many people to "commit that horrible vice of drunkenness". Nicolson was prohibited from keeping an alehouse and committed to Colchester Gaol until he found sureties for his appearance at his trial.

Some record and family history societies have published licensing records. Wood (881) lists the licensees, inns and public-houses of Banbury, Oxfordshire since the 15th century, with extracts from Quarter Sessions and property records (# chapter 27) and licensees' wills and inventories. Nottinghamshire FHS has published a register (761) of Nottingham alehouse recognizances of 1756–69. This lists approximately 130 alehouses, the name of the landlord and (each year) the names and occupations of the men who acted as the landlord's sureties. These were usually butchers, tailors, frame work knitters or other artisans as in the following example from 1760:

Landlord	John Robinson
Alehouse	The Castle near Chapple Bar
Sureties	George Barker Jr. Butcher and John Carrinton Barber

EMPLOYMENT

There are too many sources for trades or occupations to be listed here, but many are noted in Saul & Markwell (27) and Raymond (850) and (851). Merely as examples, many lists of gamekeepers since the 18th century can be found in Quarter Sessions' records (# chapter 25) and the Seditious Societies Act 1799 required any person having a printing press to file a notice (with his name and address) with the Clerk of the Peace. This provision was repealed in 1869 but many notices survive in Quarter Sessions' records.

Many large businesses have substantial archives and perhaps an archivist. Others have deposited their records at record offices. If a business is still operating, it may be willing to search its archives for information about former employees, or inform you of the record office in which its archives are held. However, even if a business retains its records and can search them for you, this may take some time. My great grandfather William Henry Herber was employed by the company Thomas Tilling as a tram or bus driver. Surviving records of this company are held by London Transport, which has enormous archives. However, the extent of archives held by some organisations makes research more difficult, because the under-staffed archive departments do not have the facilities to deal with millions of documents and the research enquiries that they receive. A gem of information for a genealogist was just another piece of paper for the company at the time and it may not have been retained or properly filed or indexed. Questions of confidentiality also arise, especially with recent records. However, detailed records of some occupations are available to the public and this section deals with some of the most useful.

The Post Office

The Post Office was established in 1635 and has been one of the largest British employers since the 18th century. Post Office archives are at Freeling House, Phoenix Place, London WC1X 0DL (telephone 020 7239 2570) and open to the public Monday to Friday. They are described on the Royal Mail Heritage web site, in Farrugia (795), by A. Parry in the 2001 edition of the *FLHH* (5) and by K. Squelch in *Family History News and Digest* (April 1996).

The archives date from the late 17th century. Senior officials of the Post Office can be traced in accounts, salary lists or correspondence from 1672. Establishment books (periodic lists of senior staff) commence in 1742 (and are in series POST 58 and 59) recording names, ranks, salaries, places of work and dates of appointment. These were also published annually from 1857 to 1975. There are appointment books of 1831 to 1952 (in series POST 58) that record all staff appointments, with their names, date of appointment, grade and place of work. Detailed correspondence files about staff pensions also survive (originally only for senior staff, but for all employees from the 19th century), noting an employee's name, rank, pay, date of birth and past service. These files have name indexes up to 1921. Postmasters staffed local post offices from 1850 and, before that, local tradesmen distributed the mail. They are included in the records noted above but also listed, from 1677, in monthly and annual cash books and account books (POST 2, 3 and 9). There are also lists for some years, with varying amounts of personal information, of postmen, clerks, mail guards and messengers. There is also a large archive of photographs, many featuring individual staff (and copies can be ordered). Some other useful records (many of them indexed) are noted in Farrugia (795), including records of particular post offices, salary lists (from 1793) and recruitment records (from 1861).

Police

Parish constables were considered in chapter 18. Until 1829, London was policed by parish constables, the watch, thief-takers and the Bow Street Foot and Horse Patrols, described by Herber (985), established by the Bow Street Magistrates Henry and Sir John Fielding. Few records of the Bow Street Patrols survive but there is a service register for 1821–29 in MEPO 4/508 at TNA.

The Metropolitan Police Force of London (excluding the City) was formed in 1829. Boroughs and counties were empowered to create local forces from 1835 and 1839 respectively and were required to do so from 1856 (1857 in Scotland). By 1889 there were 231 police forces in England and Wales, but many forces have merged and there are now 43 forces. There are no central police archives. Some forces have their own museum or archive, while others have deposited their records at CROs. Waters (876) is a brief history of the police and a guide to police records, listing police force addresses, museums and archives, with a brief description of the records available. Details of the records in each archive are noted in Bridgeman & Emsley (780) and Shearman (864), the most important being attestation papers, discipline books and personnel books or registers which contain policemen's names, the dates and places of their birth (or their ages) and also some career information.

Detailed records of the City of London Police since 1832 are held at CLRO. Registers list all officers (and their warrant numbers) and there are personnel files for most officers. Records of many Metropolitan Police officers up to about 1933 are held by TNA and described in Cale (964) and TNA domestic records leaflet 52. Enquiries about more recent records should be directed to the Metropolitan Police Archive Service, Wellington House, 67/73 Buckingham Gate, London SW1E 6BE (# appendix XI for its web site). Each Metropolitan officer had a warrant number, beginning with number 1 (in 1829) and reaching 100,000 by 1913. Registers of joiners up to 1933 are at TNA (in series MEPO 4), but the register for 1857 to 1869 (for warrant numbers 35,804–51,491) is missing. Series MEPO 4 also includes registers of leavers from 1889 to 1947 and certificates of service for 1889 to 1909 (for warrant numbers 74,201–97,500) which include a man's date and place of birth, physical description, trade, residence, marital status, number of children, previous employer and details of police service. Series MEPO 21 contains records of police who retired between 1852 and 1932 and who received discretionary pensions (up to 1890) or statutory pensions (from 1890). These records include a man's date and place of birth, physical description, dates of service, marital status and (until 1923) names of his parents and next of kin. Some pension records for 1829–59 are in MEPO 5. Recruits' signatures are included in attestation ledgers of 1869–1958 in MEPO 4.

Information about policemen may also be found in the *Police Gazette*, published from 1828 (and earlier under different names) or *The Police Service Advertiser*, published from 1866 to 1959. Copies of most issues are at the British Newspaper Library. The contents of these (and other journals or almanacs) are reviewed by Waters (876). There is a Police History Society, which publishes an annual journal. Information on uniforms and service conditions can be obtained from the Essex Police Museum, which is reviewed in an article in *Family Tree Magazine* (November 1995). The collections of the Metropolitan Police Historical Museum are presently in store, but it is hoped that the museum will reopen in the near future.

Railways
Hawkings (816), Richards (854) and Edwards (792) are detailed guides to railway company records. Almost 1,000 railway companies existed at some point between the early 19th century and 1923. Some (such as the Midland Railway) had substantial networks but hundreds operated only one or two lines. The larger companies had enormous workforces. The London & North Western Railway employed about 70,000 people in 1897 and (on nationalisation in 1948) British Rail employed about 640,000. Many companies existed for only a few years or merged with other companies. Richardson (25) lists British railway lines (and the companies operating them) and Hawkings (816) lists all railway companies and the dates of their merger into other companies. In 1923 most railway companies were merged into four: the London, Midland & Scottish Railway, the Southern Railway, the Great Western Railway and the London & North Eastern Railway. These were merged into British Rail in 1948 and nationalised.

Records of many railway companies have survived. However, while some companies' records are extensive and detailed, the records of others (particularly staff records) are very limited. Thus the surviving files of the Easingwold Railway Company only contain a list of the employees who were killed in the First World War. However, there are hundreds of registers or other documents recording employees of the Great Western Railway. The records are not centrally indexed, so you need to know the name of the company for which your ancestor worked. Even if you know that he worked as a railwayman in a certain city, there may be three or four companies for which he could have worked. The relevant railways for an area can be ascertained from the lists in Hawkings (816), Richardson (25), Richards (854) or TNA domestic records leaflets 69, 81 and 82. Many surviving railway records are at TNA (mostly with code RAIL) and most other surviving documents are at CROs. Many staff records that are less than 75 years old are not open to the public. Hawkings (816) and Richards (854) list, for each railway company, the surviving records that may be of interest to family historians, their covering dates and their location (with archives' document references). For example, many surviving staff records of the London & North Eastern Railway are at the National Archives of Scotland and TNA, but some are at Aberdeen University Library, Doncaster Central Library and Northampton Record Office.

Each railway had slightly different systems of recording information about its employees, particularly because there were so many types of employee: station managers, porters, ticket clerks, engine drivers, engineers, workshop staff and track maintenance staff. Hawkings (816) is a very detailed analysis of railway company staff records at TNA, CROs and libraries. It lists for each railway the covering dates and types of staff records available, with many examples of staff registers, paylists, appointment lists, rolls of honour and other documents. Many illustrations of the records are also included in Edwards (792). The records may merely note employees' names, grades, places of employment and pay, but they may provide an ancestor's complete service history, the dates and places of his employment, his date of birth, promotions, wages, transfers and retirement. A few extracts from the many examples provided by Hawkings illustrate the importance of these records:

RAIL 264/18 Great Western Railway (*South Devon Railway)
Register of drivers/firemen.
George Webber. Date of birth, 28 July 1833.

Promotion and rates of wages

Date	Rate	Position	Station
7 Jan 1858		Fireman S.D.R★	Falmouth
17 June 1865		Engineman S.D.R★.	
at amalgamation	7/6	Passenger engineman	
11 April 1877	3/6	Chargeman cleaner	Truro

Record of fines

	Locality	Penalty	
15 Feb 1881	Truro	cautioned	Engine thrown off line at turn-table

(Five other events including death of track worker and Webber's disablement by accident.)

RAIL 635/306 South Eastern Railway Company. Staff register, Erith station

Name:	H. Roberts	Number:	1614
Rank:	Porter	Appointed:	17 June 1895
Weekly wage:	£1/-/-	Yearly salary:	£52
Date of birth:	9 June 1869	Remarks:	Resigned
Left service:	19 May 1896	Successor:	G.T. Holland

Rail 684/116 Taff Vale Railway Company
Register of accidents to company's servants (20 events recorded, including)

Date	Place	Name	Grade	Nature of injury and cause
1904 Apr. 27	Aberdare goods yard	Thos. Ed. Brimmell	Guard	Injured finger (slight) placing scotch under wheel of coach and his finger was caught.

Rail 313/4 Hull and Holderness Railway Company, Board of Directors' meetings
31 October 1857. Ordered . . . that John Harmson be appointed Station Master at Burstwick at a salary of 20/- per week.

Great Western Railway Magazine, Vol. 27, No 1, January 1915
G.W.R. men who lost their lives in the war. [twelve men listed, with a photograph of each, including] A.J. Bailey a labourer in the locomotive department at Old Oak Common, was an army reservist, and at the outbreak of war joined his old regiment, the 2nd battalion Highland Light Infantry. He was 30 . . . and had been in the G.W.R. service 8 years. He died in an ambulance hospital on September 23 from wounds received at a place unknown.

Other documents may record a man's apprenticeship or sickness. Many reports of train accidents survive, usually including detailed statements from railway workers. These are in individual company records, but also in detailed reports, dating from 1840, in series RAIL 1053 and MT 29. Surviving railway staff magazines, noting employees' retirements, deaths and service histories (sometimes with photographs) are listed by Richards (854) and Hawkings (816). Trade union records (see below) are also useful and their location and covering dates are listed in Richards (854) which also notes some indexes of railway employees that have been prepared by researchers. Many railway companies built houses for their employees and rent rolls or related documents may also survive. Railway companies' property can often be identified from census records. A railway ancestor may have lived in a street that was almost entirely inhabited by railway workers and their families.

There are hundreds of books of old photographs of railways and steam locomotives (many available at your local library) which may include photographs of the station at which your ancestor worked or the type of locomotive that he drove. Large collections of photographs are held at TNA, described in Edwards (792) and at the National Railway Museum, Leeman Road, York YO2 4XJ. Railway companies also owned a few ships and records of these vessels are listed by Richards (854). Finally, you should note that most men who worked on the construction of railways were not employed by railway companies but by construction companies. The records of these companies are difficult to find and rarely mention labourers.

Civil Servants

Records of many civil servants are held by TNA, often included in the records of the relevant Government department, but also in series such as CSC 10 (examination marks and grades for 1876–1962) and PMG 28 (pension records of 1855–1924). The Civil Service Commission was established in 1855. It needed evidence of a civil servant's age to establish pension entitlement (and applicants' ages before they took examinations). The resulting collection of "evidences of age", extending up to the 1930s, is now held by the SoG. Some mens' records are missing but those that survive (for about 70,000 men born between the early 1800s and 1931) note names, addresses and dates of birth or baptism (with many birth and baptism certificates attached). There is also an incomplete card index that includes some details of civil servants' later careers. The records are not yet available to researchers but they have been indexed (by surname, forename and date and place of birth). Searches in the index will be made, for a fee, by SoG staff (and copies of any relevant documents are then provided).

Senior crown or government ministers and officials, such as Secretaries of State, members of the Board of Trade, Chancellors of the Duchy of Lancaster, Lord Lieutenants, Constables of Dover Castle and many others are listed, in some cases back to medieval times, in *The Book of Dignities* by Ockerby (843). Officials who served in many government departments since the 17th or 18th centuries are listed in volumes of *Office-Holders in Modern Britain*, with appointment and promotion dates extracted from the State Papers Domestic, Patent Rolls, Treasury Books and other records at TNA. Volumes by Sainty (861) list officials of the Treasury, Board of Trade and Admiralty (1660–1870), and of the Secretaries of State (1660–1782), Home Office (1782–1870) and Colonial Office (1794–1870). Volumes by Collinge (786) list officials of the Navy Board (1660–1832) and Foreign Office (1782–1870). Sainty & Bucholz (862) cover the Royal Household (1660–1837). British ambassadors and other diplomatic representatives from 1509 to 1852 are listed, with references to Foreign Office documents at TNA, in Bell (774), Horn (823) and Bindoff, Smith and Webster (776).

Civil servants are listed in directories and almanacs (most of them annual) published since the late 18th century, such as the *Royal British Kalendar*. From 1810, they are listed in the *British Imperial Calendar* (later named the *Civil Service Year Book*). Civil servants of the Foreign, Colonial and Dominion offices are also listed in the *Foreign Office List* (published from 1852) and the *Colonial Office List* (published from 1862), copies of which are at the SoG, TNA and some reference libraries. Many appointments of people who held public or royal offices are noted in the *London Gazette*. Senior civil servants since the late 19th century are also listed in annual guides such as *Whitaker's Almanac* and *Dod's Parliamentary Companion*. TNA also has many records of these officials, the references being listed in Colwell (242) and Bevan (239). For example, records of Royal Household appointments since the 17th century are in the archives of the Lord Steward (code LS), the Lord Chamberlain (code LC) or in Treasury records. These include records of appointments, salaries and pensions. Writs of appointment of Crown servants are on the Fine and Patent rolls. The Patent rolls are reviewed in chapter 27, but entries for royal officials from the HMSO volume (1078) that calendars the Patent rolls of 1476–85 include:

> 1483 April 21. Appointment, during pleasure, of Guy Fairfax, knight, as [a] justice of the King's Bench, receiving the accustomed fee.

There are two series of records at TNA (partially published in calendar form) that contain an enormous amount of information about Crown or government officials and other information of interest to family historians; these are the State Papers Domestic (briefly noted in earlier chapters) and the Treasury Books and Papers. The State Papers Domestic, described in TNA domestic records leaflets 15–20, are papers collected since the reign of Henry VIII by the clerks to the Secretaries of State. They cover all types of government business (including crime, taxes, the navy and property). State Papers of the reign of Henry VIII are in series SP 1, those of the reign of Edward VI are in SP 10, those for George I are in SP 35 and so on. HMSO and the List and Index Society have published indexed calendars of the State Papers up to the reign of George I and for much of the reign of George III. The HMSO volumes are listed in Mullins (260). For example, Daniell (790) is a calendar of the State Papers of 1671. Sample entries are:

March. Grant to Jeremiah Houghton of the office of Keeper of the Armoury at Westminster, in place of James Parker deceased, with the fee of 12d a day to commence from Michaelmas 1666 . . . and grant to Sir George Charnock of the office of Serjeant-at-Arms in reversion after Serjeant Leigh.

October 25th. Warrant for allowance to Sir Thomas Osborne, Baronet, appointed on the 3rd [as] Treasurer of the Navy, of £800 a year for payment of his cashier and other inferior officers, in addition to the £2,000 allowed him as a salary.

Records of the Treasury from the 17th century are at TNA and cover all aspects of central government finance and include a great variety of useful information (for example, payments to ships' masters for the transportation of convicts are reviewed in chapter 25). Treasury Board papers (up to 1920) are in series T 1 and those up to 1745 have been calendared in HMSO volumes, listed in Mullins (260), and continued up to 1775 in volumes 120, 125, 240, 244, 250 and 256 of the List and Index Society. Other treasury papers from 1660 to 1728 are calendared in HMSO volumes entitled *Calendar of Treasury Books*, listed in Mullins (260). Thus volume 12 by Shaw (863), for April to September 1697, calendars records from series such as T 29 (Treasury minute books), T 27 (out letters), T 53 (money books) and T 60 (order books). The following are sample entries:

13 April. Money warrant for £50 to Richard Gregory gent. for one year . . . for keeping the register of loans in the office of the Auditor of Receipt.
30 April. Treasury warrant to the Customs Commissioners to employ Daniel Pitman as a tidesman [at] £35 per annum in London port [in place of] Henry Sincocks deceased.

Customs and Excise
Customs and Excise were separate government departments until they were merged in 1909. Customs officers collected duties on imports and attempted to prevent smuggling. The Excise ensured that duties were paid on home-produced goods. Records of the Boards of Customs and Excise, from 1688 to the late 19th century, are at TNA and contain much information about individual officers. They are described in TNA domestic records leaflet 38, an article by J. Lodey, "Was your ancestor a Customs Officer?" in *Family Tree Magazine* (August 1989) and in "Charles King – Excise officer" by B. Bright in *Cockney Ancestor* (summer 1996).

Customs' records include pay lists for 1675 to 1829 (in series CUST 18 and 19), minute books of 1734 to 1885 which list officers' postings (in CUST 28), staff lists for some years between 1671 and 1922 and pension registers for 1803 to 1922 (in CUST 39). Officers' applications for pensions from 1777 to 1920 are in series T 1 (indexes are in T 2). Customs officers are also recorded in correspondence files of "outports" (that is, ports other than London) in series CUST 50. The material in these files includes much biographical information about officers (including ages and places of birth). Excisemen's postings are recorded in minute books of 1695 to 1867 (in CUST 47). There are a number of volumes for each year, but each volume is indexed. Entry papers for 1820 to 1870 are in series CUST 116, containing letters of recommendation that give a man's name, age, place of birth, marital status and a character reference. There is a card index to the series in the research enquiries room. Pay lists for 1705–1835 are in series T 44. Excisemen's pension records from 1856 are in CUST 39.

Coastguards

The Coastguard service dates from 1822 when three Customs' services, the Preventive Water Guard, the Revenue Cruisers and the Riding Officers were amalgamated. Records of coastguards, including establishment books, musters and pension papers, are at TNA, mostly with department codes CUST and ADM and described in Colwell (242), Bevan (239) and TNA military records leaflet 44. The most important are succession books of 1816–78 in series ADM 175, recording men's service at various stations and noting some personal details. ADM 175 also includes service registers of officers for 1886–1947 and service record cards for ratings, 1900–23. Pension records are in series ADM 23 and PMG 23.

Firemen

Organised groups of men to fight fires were employed in the 18th century by fire insurance companies and subsequently by local civil authorities. Records of these men may be found in local authority archives or in CROs. The National Fire Service (NFS) was formed in 1941 and by 1943 it employed 343,000 men, women and boys (about 116,000 full-time and the others part-time). The responsibility for fire services was returned to local authorities in 1948. The NFS is described in an article by L. Price in *Family Tree Magazine* (July 2003). Surviving personnel records for London are held by the London Fire Brigade Record Centre and records for personnel in other areas may be in local authority archives or CROs. However, all these records are likely to remain confidential (except to those who served as firemen and their next of kin) for some years.

Coalminers

Tonks (872a) reviews the sources available for ancestors who worked in British coal mines (over one million men, women and children in 1900) and includes a short history of the British coal industry and a description of mine operations and of the conditions in which miners worked and lived. This work also lists the archives that hold records of miners, their employers and trade unions and the museums that recreate the miners' living and working conditions. Over 100,000 miners have been killed since 1851, for example 290 at Albion Pit in Glamorgan in 1894 and 204 at New Hartley colliery in Northumberland in 1862 (and many more died as a result of disease caused by the work). The web site of the Coalmining History Resource Centre (# appendix XI) includes a database of coalmining deaths and injuries, with the names of about

90,000 people. The victims of mining disasters in Durham are listed on the web site of Durham Mining Museum. Your ancestor may have been working at a colliery at which a disaster occurred (and was possibly a casualty). Tonks (872a) reviews the sources that evidence such mining disasters, such as official enquiry reports, newspapers, church registers, inquest records, memorials and relief fund accounts.

Ordnance Survey

TNA holds some records of military personnel and civilian employees of the Ordnance Survey, which are described in TNA domestic records leaflet 70.

TRADE AND BUSINESSES

A business can be carried on by a sole trader, by a partnership or through the medium of a company. There are particular records available for companies (considered below) but some sources apply to all businesses. An ancestor's business may be revealed in civil registration, probate or census records. Directories may record the location of that business over a period of time. An ancestor may have advertised his business in a directory (as in illustration 47) or in a local newspaper (as in illustration 79). A local archive may have a photograph of his shop or trading premises. The ancestor may have been a member of a guild and be recorded in apprenticeship or freedom records. He may have printed trade cards. Guildhall Library has an extensive collection of London trade cards (and cards are also held in local record offices). The *London Gazette* contained much information about companies and businesses, such as notices of bankrupts, the winding up of companies and the dissolution of partnerships (as in illustration 75). There is a *London Gazette* index to the notices of partnership dissolutions for 1785 to 1811 but for other years the annual indexes have to be searched. This may be a lengthy task since Probert (847) notes that there are over 1,800 such notices in 1811 alone.

Many business records have not survived and, even if they have, they can be difficult to find. The Business Archives Council, at 101 Whitechapel High Street, London E1 7RE, may be able to help trace the archives of larger businesses. It also has a large library of business history (with over 4,500 printed histories of British businesses) which can be consulted by appointment. Large collections of business records have been deposited in CROs and other archives, so their catalogues and published guides should also be consulted. Thus the records of over 800 businesses that are held at Guildhall Library are listed in Bullock-Anderson (240), including records of many fire insurance companies (# chapter 23) and City of London merchants. As another example, Hackney Archives holds the records, some dating from the 18th century, of many businesses that operated in Hackney and Shoreditch in London, such as Bryant & May (the match makers) and Berger (paint manufacturers).

Probert (847) provides many examples of business records held in local archives, including records of a chemist, a shoemaker and an undertaker. One of the best methods of locating business records is by using the National Register of Archives (NRA) held by RCHM (# chapter 11). The NRA is a database of records deposited in archives and based on more than 43,000 catalogues or lists of manuscript collections. These refer to records of thousands of businesses. The NRA can be searched on terminals at RCHM or through its web site by personal or business name, type of business (for example, brewers) or place name. The NRA briefly describes the types and dates of records, covering dates and refers to any catalogue or list of the archive that holds the documents. In addition, RCHM has produced a catalogue (762), based on information in the NRA, to the records of about 1,200 businesses in the textile and leather trades from 1760 to 1914. Each entry describes the surviving records (such as letter books and accounts), their covering dates and location. Similar RCHM catalogues are proposed for other trades. Habgood (810) is a detailed guide to the records of chartered accountants since the late 18th century. It contains entries for about 180 firms, with similar information to the RCHM catalogue. The records are mostly accounts, or similar business records, but they include partnership agreements, salary books and photographs of partners.

Continuity is an important factor in the progress that you will make in tracing your family tree (# chapter 1). If a number of generations of a family were engaged in the same business or trade, this will assist tracing your ancestors and the research of their lives. My g.g. grandfather, Joseph James Eagles (1843–1918), was a boot and shoe maker. The census returns of 1871 to 1901 recorded that he was living at 118 Tottenham Road in Hackney (a small cottage with his workshop in one room). One of his daughters and two of his sons also worked in the business. Civil registration and census records revealed that his father, Joseph James Eagles (who died in 1857) was also a boot and shoe repairer. His parents were James and Susannah Eagles of Hoxton. Susannah died, a widow, in 1851. Her death certificate stated that her late husband James had been a shoemaker. London directories of 1805 to 1807 also recorded James as a shoemaker in Hoxton Old Town. Susannah's father, Thomas Gillman, was also a shoemaker, living in Hockliffe, Bedfordshire, until his death in 1823. Thomas's father, William, was also recorded in parish registers as a shoemaker. I had therefore discovered six generations of shoemakers.

COMPANIES

For centuries companies have been given their own legal identity by three methods of incorporation: by Royal Charter (such as certain colonial trading companies), by statute (for example railway companies) and since 1844, by registration under the Companies Acts. The Companies Acts provide for the incorporation, in England and Wales, of limited liability companies with shares being issued to the owners. The company was liable for the debts and liabilities of its trade and so many men (wishing to avoid personal liability for business debts) therefore incorporated companies through which to operate their business. If two or more men wished to collaborate in a business, they could incorporate a company, divide the shares between them (perhaps in the proportions in which they contributed capital to the business) and both act as directors. Each company had a unique number and had to file certain administrative records with the Registrar of Companies. The filed records include the names of shareholders and directors, the company's annual accounts (in summary form, without any information of value to genealogists) and a register of mortgages that the company had granted. About 70,000 companies were registered between 1856 and 1900 and a further 1,100,000 companies between 1901 and 1976.

Filed records of surviving companies are held by the Registrar of Companies at Companies House, Crown Way, Maindy, Cardiff CF4 3UZ (telephone 0870 3333636). There is also a London searchroom, at Companies House, 21 Bloomsbury Street, London WC1B 3XD. Most records are available on microfiche (and the fiche can be purchased very cheaply, or copies of particular records can be made from the fiche, using self-service machines). If your ancestor established a company, or acted as director, these records can provide useful information about the business. Probert (847) reviews the indexes available for these records. There is a computer database (available in both London and Cardiff) to existing companies and those dissolved in the last 20 years. TNA also holds an index to the names of the companies that were incorporated between 1856 and 1920 and also to those companies which were on the register in 1930 and in 1937. An index to the names of limited companies (and of directors of companies in recent years) is available (for a fee) on the Companies House web site. Microfiche of companies' filed records can also be ordered through the site. The directors of many companies are also listed in *The Directory of Directors*, published annually from 1880.

The Registrar retains (for 20 years) the filed records of companies that have been dissolved. The records of most dissolved companies are then destroyed, but a sample are passed to TNA and held in series BT 31 and 41. The series lists note the company names and numbers. Brief details of the dissolved companies (the records of which were destroyed) are noted in papers in BT 95 (arranged by the date of the company's incorporation). Companies House in Cardiff also holds a card index to companies dissolved before 1963, with the company's name, number, date of dissolution and a note of whether the company's records were retained by TNA. The index can be searched by application to the archives' department of Companies House in Cardiff, by completing a form at the London searchroom, or sometimes by telephone enquiry.

Separate registration systems applied to companies in Scotland, Ireland, the Channel Islands and the Isle of Man. Research in records of those companies can be made at the relevant registry or record office (and some company records of these jurisdictions are noted in chapter 29). Some other acts of Parliament provided for specialised companies, such as building societies and industrial or provident societies. Certain administrative records of these corporations are held at TNA in the records of the Registrar of Friendly Societies.

Information about companies may be found in other sources. The winding-up and liquidation of companies were generally dealt with by court proceedings (# chapter 24) and advertised in the *London Gazette* and in national or local newspapers. TNA does not generally hold the personnel or other business records of companies (except for some nationalised companies, such as railways). Business records are retained by the companies concerned until they are of no further use and then usually destroyed or (in only a minority of cases) deposited at an archive.

BANK RECORDS

Your ancestor may have had a bank account. Records of the account may still be in a bank's archive, but most information is destroyed and banks owe a duty of confidentiality to their customers and may refuse to provide information to enquirers, even if they prove a descent from the bank's customer. Furthermore, it may be difficult to locate any archives since hundreds of banks have merged over the years and only a few records are in record offices. However, if you do locate them, bank archives can reveal much about your ancestors' prosperity. Probert (847) includes examples of bank records such as signature books that record the opening of accounts (often with a customer's signature, address and occupation) and safe custody registers, noting customers' deposit or withdrawal of items (such as share certificates or jewellery) from the bank. A Business Archives Council booklet notes details (and the location) of deposited records of over 600 banks. For example, Tower Hamlets Local History Library in London holds ledgers of the Limehouse Savings Bank for 1816 to 1896, containing the names and accounts of many local people. The Bank of England has an extensive archive (and museum) in Threadneedle Street, London, which holds staff records, lists of holders of government stock (gilts) and details of some customers' accounts (from its early days as a commercial bank). Appointments must be made for access to the archives.

TRADE UNIONS AND FRIENDLY SOCIETIES

The records of trade unions since the mid-19th century may also include information about your ancestors. For example, registers of members list men's ages, occupations, addresses and dependants. Tracing the records can be difficult. Many branch records (the documents most likely to refer to individual members) have been lost but some are at local record offices or unions' national archives. Many national records of unions are held at the Modern Records Centre, University of Warwick Library, Coventry and briefly described on its web site. Rules of trade unions (but not details of members) are in the records of the Registrar of Friendly Societies (see below) at TNA.

Southall (867) describes trades union records (and the major archives holding union records) and reviews the surviving records of 21 unions, dealing with their foundation, membership and the location (and years covered) of deposited archives. Branch records include minutes of meetings of branch committees (perhaps noting new members' names) and registration books that note members' ages, dates of joining and deaths. There may be records of benefits paid to members or their families, such as funeral benefit (payments to a member or his widow for the cost of a funeral) which can assist the location of a death in civil registration records. Branches often sent annual reports to the national union, listing members (and expenditure on benefits). Records may note a man's transfer to another branch of the union and it is possible to build up a detailed picture of the movement of workers around the county from membership, sick pay, funeral benefit and travel expenditure records of different branches. Southall (867) shows that James Beardpark became a member of the Bolton branch of the Steam Engine Makers' Society in 1835. In 1837 he received funeral benefit for his wife. He is then recorded (for one year) in the branch records of St Helens. He returned to Bolton but was then recorded (from 1840 to 1842) as travelling to Leeds, Preston, Manchester, London, Southampton, Bristol and Derby. Having joined the Derby branch, James received sick pay in August 1842 and the papers then recorded a payment of £8 in June 1844 for his funeral. National union records may also refer to individual members. The 1913 annual report of the National Union of Railwaymen lists the names and addresses of the secretaries of about 1,300 branches of the union in Britain, as well as the recipients of death, disablement and orphans' fund benefits. Thus J. Scott, a driver of the Gateshead branch, received £30 upon his retirement in June 1913 (aged 64), having joined the union on 16 January 1880. Extensive membership records of the Amalgamated Engineering Union from 1850 to 1964, including about 1,000 volumes of admission books, registers of expelled members and branch statements (noting deaths of members and spouses) have been deposited with the SoG. They are being sorted and indexed and so are not yet available to researchers (and some of the more recent records may remain closed for some years).

Bennett, Tough & Storey (775) briefly describes the union records which have been deposited in record offices or libraries and their covering dates. Many smaller unions merged with larger ones, so you should start by finding a published history of the union in which you are interested.

If relevant documents are still held by the union you should first approach that union's national office to ascertain whether the records can be viewed. Union records for particular occupations may also be listed or catalogued with other records relating to that occupation. Thus Richards (854) lists surviving records of British railway companies but also the records of trade unions that were established for railway employees.

Friendly societies are mutual insurance societies in which members subscribe in exchange for old age, sickness and unemployment benefits. The first friendly society was founded in the 16th century but most societies were established in the late 18th or early 19th centuries. The rules of each society and bonds (in the names of the trustees of a society) had to be filed at Quarter Sessions (# chapter 25) from 1793 and later with the Registrar of Friendly Societies (now generally held in the Registrar's records with code FS at TNA). They do not include membership records, but many of these have been deposited at CROs and some are still held by societies (or successor organisations). Logan (834) is a guide to the records of Friendly Societies and of affiliated societies or orders, such as the Independent Order of Oddfellows (Manchester Unity) and the Ancient Order of Foresters, through which Friendly Societies associated with each other. The best way to find Friendly Society records is to search the NRA (described above) and the catalogue of the CRO for the area. Friendly Society records are similar to trade union records. The most useful for family historians are lists of members and registers of sickness or death benefits paid to members or their dependants. Registers of members note names, addresses, occupations and dates of admission, death or leaving the society. Certificates of membership may have been retained in family papers. Further records were generated by the two Orders noted above and many have been deposited in CROs. Their district and local branches were (like freemasons' branches) called lodges, and lists of lodges and their officers were published. The district offices kept registers of officers and of payments made from funeral, widows and orphans funds. Illustrations from all these types of records are included in Logan (834).

PATENTS

The Crown has granted letters patent to inventors since the 16th century, protecting their exclusive right (for a limited period) to manufacture or exploit an invention. Patents (and related records) up to 1853 are at TNA and described in TNA domestic records leaflet 3. Letters patent were enrolled on the Patent Rolls (in series C 66) until 1853 and petitions for the issue of patents from 1661 to 1852 are in series SP 44 and HO 43 (indexed from 1792). Correspondence about petitions from 1782 to 1852 is in HO 42 and 44. Transcripts of the enrolled patents were printed in 1853 and these are in the British Library and some reference libraries. Woodcroft (882) is an index of patentees' names for 1617 to 1852, noting the subject-matter of the patent, the patent number (so that a copy of a patent can be ordered for viewing or purchase) and the date of application. Patents since 1853 are held by the Patent Office and copies can be obtained from the Patent Office sales branch, St Mary Cray, Orpington, Kent BRS 3RD.

ESTATE RECORDS

Many of our ancestors were farm labourers who worked on the estates of yeomen, nobility or gentry. The principal sources noted above that include agricultural labourers are census and parish records. Wills and records of tithes, enclosures and land tax are also good sources for farmers. Further information about farmers and their land (and sometimes labourers) can be found in property records (# chapter 27). On large estates, a farm bailiff or manager was employed to organise the work (and pay the labourers). Account books for estates might record labourers' names, the work they did and their wages. Most of these records have been destroyed, but landowning families still hold some records. Other surviving records are in the CRO for the area of the farm or estate, unless a landowner had estates across the country, in which case the records for all the estates may be at one record office. The names of local landowners can be obtained from parish records, tithe maps, enclosure records, or from tombstones at the parish church. A large collection of farm records, particularly from southern England and the Midlands, is held at the Rural History Centre in Reading (# chapter 11) and listed in its catalogue (756) and on its web site. Documents held for particular farms include title deeds, enclosure records and photographs but also farmers' account books, diaries and correspondence that record the names of many farm labourers. Records in CROs may be indexed by the name of the landowner, farmer or the place where the farm was located. Some landowners and farmers' diaries or account books have been published. Griffiths (807a) is a transcript of an account book of 1673–88 of William Windham, a substantial landowner in Norfolk. This includes details of his management of the estate, the tenants who rented his land (noting their rents and identifying the land) but also referring to some labourers who worked on the properties.

A different type of labourer was employed on farms in the Second World War. The Women's Land Army was formed in 1939 to help increase the amount of food grown in Britain. At its peak, over 80,000 women were serving as "Land girls". The army was disbanded in 1950. Women's service records have not survived but the Imperial War Museum has a card index to them (a week's notice is required in order to see it). A microfiche copy of this index, for 1939 to 1945 only, is at TNA in MAF records. The cards note a woman's name, change of name on marriage, address, date of birth, previous occupation, service number and dates of service (and some include women's photographs).

GYPSY ANCESTRY

The travellers known as Gypsies probably originated in India. They arrived in Britain around 1500 and were referred to as "Egyptians" (from which Gypsy derives). Gypsies were travelling craftsmen and horse-dealers but were treated as vagrants from the mid-16th century. An act of 1563 made it a felony to remain in a company of "vagabonds commonly called Egyptians" and executions did take place:

1592, Aug 8. Simson, Arington, Fetherstone, Fenwicke and Lancaster were hanged for being Egyptians (parish register of St Nicholas, Durham)

The act fell into disuse but was not repealed until 1783. The authorities remained suspicious of Gypsies and so they frequently appear in records of settlement examinations and removal orders (# chapter 18).

Floate (798) is a guide to tracing Gypsy ancestry, particularly how to overcome the hurdles of such research. Because of their itinerant lifestyle, Gypsies may be missing from (or difficult to find in) civil registration, census and parish records. County or national indexes to this material are therefore of vital importance. There are some indexes of Gypsies found in census, parish and legal records (fees may be payable to consult these indexes). Floate (798) also reviews other records that are particularly useful for Gypsy family history such as local newspapers, pedlars' certificates and important archives (of earlier research into Gypsies) held at the libraries of Leeds and Liverpool Universities and at the Rural History Centre, University of Reading. In particular, *The Journal of the Gypsy Lore Society*, first published in 1888, included many family histories and pedigrees. The Romany & Traveller FHS publishes a quarterly journal and has a reference library of Gypsy-related books and material. Useful guidance on tracing Gypsy ancestry is also provided in an article by J. Pateman in *Ancestors* (August/September 2003).

CHAPTER 23

OATHS, TAXATION AND INSURANCE RECORDS

Some records of taxes (death duties, poor law rates and stamp duty) were reviewed in earlier chapters. Our ancestors hated taxes and even rebelled over them, but taxes did produce many helpful records. Perhaps the most famous document relating to taxation is the Domesday Book (# chapter 27). This chapter describes other taxation records, but also records of oaths of allegiance and insurance records, because they all contain useful lists of names.

OATHS

Various statutes required people to take oaths in support of the Crown, Parliament or the Church of England.

The Protestation returns

In 1641 a resolution of Parliament requested all males aged over 18 to take an oath in support of the Crown, Parliament and the Protestant religion, to oppose the "plots and conspiracies of priests and Jesuits" that were allegedly subverting the kingdom. Lists of those taking the oath in each parish were prepared, usually by the parish incumbent or clerk, but some lists consist of men's signatures (or illiterate men's marks). These lists were sent to Parliament in 1642. Most men took the oath and those who refused to sign (mostly Catholics) were sometimes also listed so that for some areas the surviving records constitute an almost complete census of adult males. In a few parishes some women are also listed. The surviving Protestation returns are held in the House of Lords Record Office (HLRO). They are arranged by county, hundred and parish, and listed in Gibson & Dell (891) and in the fifth report of the Royal Commission on Historical Manuscripts published in 1876.

The returns are incomplete, covering only about one third of English parishes (and three Welsh boroughs). For example, there are no surviving returns at HLRO for the City of London, Bedfordshire, Gloucestershire, Herefordshire, Leicestershire, Norfolk, Northamptonshire, Rutland or Suffolk and only incomplete returns survive for many other counties. In contrast, the returns for Cornwall include over 30,000 names from 167 parishes and the returns for Devon list over 63,000 names from 412 parishes. The records can be consulted by appointment and photocopies of entries for parishes can be ordered by post. The returns for some counties (such as Devon, Oxfordshire, Somerset and Cornwall) and individual parishes have been published. Some copies of the returns have also been found in parish records, in some cases where the original returns have not survived (for example for some parishes in Leicestershire, the City of London, Norfolk and Northamptonshire). These parish copies and published transcripts are listed by Gibson & Dell (891). Illustration 121 is part of the return for Sandford in Devon. The list

121. *Extract from the Protestation rolls of 1641/2 for Sandford, Devon (House of Lords Record Office)*

commences with John Davis, Baronet. My ancestor John Bond and his eldest son, Roger Bond, are in the fifth column. The list also includes Lawrence Bond, William Bond and Paul Bond who were probably John's relatives.

Parliament requested two further covenants or declarations to be made in 1643/4. The Vow and Covenant and the Solemn League and Covenant were expressions of loyalty to Parliament to be made by men aged over 18. There are no national collections of lists, but parish records sometimes include lists of those who took the covenants. Surviving lists are catalogued by Gibson & Dell (891), for example for 11 parishes in Essex and six parishes in Suffolk. There are also lists for 20 parishes in Norfolk (most held at HLRO).

Association oath rolls 1695/1696

Following a plot against King William III, the Act of Association of 1695/6 required all those holding public office to take an oath of association, vowing to combine with others for the "preservation of His Majesty's royal person and government". Rolls listing the names of those taking the oath were compiled by county (often divided between hundreds or boroughs) and are at TNA in series C 213 and in some CROs. They include clergymen (Anglican and non-conformist), gentry, army and navy officers, other public office-holders, freemen and many other people. In fact, the rolls were open, in most places, for all adult male householders (and sometimes women) to sign. Coverage varies considerably, but the rolls for some areas are fairly comprehensive lists of adult males. The clergy signed separate rolls (C 213/403–458) which were compiled by diocese and deanery. Surviving Association oath rolls are listed by piece number and place by C. Webb in *Genealogists' Magazine* (December 1983) and in Gibson (890). Some transcripts have been published, for example for Surrey and Wiltshire.

Other oaths of allegiance

The Corporation Act of 1661 and the Test Act of 1672/3 required those accepting military or public office to take oaths of allegiance and supremacy (accepting the king as supreme head of the Church of England) and to lodge at court a certificate, from the parish incumbent and churchwardens, that they had received the sacrament. The acts also required oath-takers to make a declaration against the doctrine of transubstantiation (that consecrated bread and wine changes into Christ's body and blood), so as to exclude Catholics from official posts. Oaths were sworn before Justices at Quarter Sessions or (if an oath-taker lived within 30 miles of Westminster) at the central courts. Many sacrament certificates therefore survive from 1661 to 1828 (when the acts were repealed) in Quarter Sessions' records or at TNA in the courts' records (# chapters 24 and 25). The records at TNA are described in Bevan (239), many being held in series C 224, E 196 and KB 22, while oaths of clergy (1789–1836) and of papists (1778–1829) are in CP 37.

TAXATION RECORDS

Many records of taxation are held at TNA and CROs, in addition to those already considered (such as the apprenticeship books). Jurkowski, Smith & Crook (896) provide a definitive history of English taxes on individuals from 1188 to 1688, including the hearth tax, lay subsidies, feudal aids, poll tax and forced loans, noting the years in which a tax was levied, the methods of collection and the records created. The most important taxes (that resulted in lists of names being produced) are considered in this chapter.

Hearth tax returns

The hearth tax was levied in England and Wales from 1662 to 1689. The legislation is considered in detail by Schurer & Arkell (902). It was a tax of two shillings each year on each fireplace, hearth or stove. Some people, such as paupers, were exempt from paying the tax. The law also exempted householders for whom the local incumbent or parish officers provided a certificate that their houses were worth less than a rent of 20 shillings per year and who owned goods or chattels worth less than £10. Most charitable institutions, such as hospitals and almshouses, were also exempt as were industrial hearths (except smiths' forges and bakers' ovens).

Each year's tax was payable in two equal instalments, on Lady Day (25 March) and Michaelmas (29 September). Tax was payable by the occupier of a property or, if a building was empty, by the owner. After May 1664 landlords had to pay the tax for tenanted property if the occupier was exempt. Furthermore, anyone with more than two hearths became liable to pay the tax even if they would otherwise have been exempt. The tax was levied from Michaelmas 1662 until its abolition after Lady Day 1689. Surviving records, held by TNA or CROs, only cover the periods from Michaelmas 1662 to Lady Day 1666 and from Michaelmas 1669 to Lady Day 1674 since, from Michaelmas 1666 to Lady Day 1669, and from Michaelmas 1674 to Lady Day 1689, the tax was collected by "farmers", or by a commission, and hardly any lists of taxpayers survive for these periods.

The hearth tax records for certain years are almost complete. They consist of assessments, listing taxpayers' names (and the amounts they had to pay, or the number of their hearths), and returns (showing what tax they had paid or the number of their hearths). There are also some schedules of taxpayers who were in arrears and some exemption certificates. The assessments were often marked with the payments made and in those cases there are no separate returns. An assessment was sometimes used for more than one tax collection, but updated in manuscript. The tax was unpopular and widespread evasion resulted in many names being omitted from the records. Although paupers and some other people were not chargeable, the law required them to be listed from 1663 and this makes the returns even more useful. It is unfortunate that this provision of the legislation was often ignored.

The assessments and returns were prepared by parish constables (or, in cities and towns, by sheriffs) then enrolled by clerks at the Quarter Sessions (# chapter 25). Duplicates were sent to the Exchequer. This collection system was inefficient and so from Michaelmas 1664 to Michaelmas 1665 the Crown appointed receivers to collect the tax. Hostility to the tax resulted in continued evasion and low revenue. Collection of the tax was therefore farmed out in 1666. A farmer collected the tax for the government but retained a commission. The Exchequer audited the farmers' records, but lists of taxpayers' names were not provided by farmers to the government and few of the farmers' own records have survived. From Michaelmas 1669 to Lady Day 1674 the tax was again administered by receivers, so that assessments or returns were enrolled at Quarter Sessions and copies sent to the Exchequer. The receivers were belatedly appointed by the Crown in summer 1670, so that three instalments of tax (for Michaelmas 1669 and Lady Day and Michaelmas 1670) had to be collected together at Michaelmas 1670. From Michaelmas 1674 farmers again administered the tax until they were replaced at Michaelmas 1684 (until Lady Day 1689) by a commission which also administered excise duties. The commission did not provide lists of taxpayers' names to the Exchequer and most of the commission's records have not survived.

The Exchequer's accounts and administrative records of the hearth tax are held at TNA in Exchequer Papers and the State Papers Domestic. The rolls listing taxpayers' names are in series

E 179 (with many other taxation records) and the series list for these important documents has been published by the List and Index Society. A database to the records in E 179 has been produced, listing the places covered by each tax (not the names of the taxpayers) so that all the taxes for one place (and then the lists of taxpayers) can be found easily by researchers. The database can be searched on PROCAT. The hearth tax assessments are arranged by county, then by hundred and (within each hundred) by parish. Surviving constables' or Quarter Sessions' copies of hearth tax records are at CROs. The hearth tax papers for some counties have been published. The surviving original records and published transcripts are listed by county in Gibson (890).

Stoate (906) is a transcript of the Devon hearth tax returns for Lady Day 1674. Some of my ancestors lived in Coldridge in the 17th century. In particular, I was looking for Thomas Packer (who married Joane Saunders in 1659) and Joane's family (her parents Zachary and Elizabeth Saunders and her brother Zachary Saunders). My ancestor George Packer (a child of Thomas Packer and Joane Saunders) married Sibilla Reed in Coldridge in 1693, so that any entries for Reed families would also be useful. The entry for Coldridge in Stoate (906) was incomplete (because the original return was damaged) but it nevertheless listed the names of 43 taxpayers and 17 pauper heads of household, and the number of their hearths. The following is an extract:

Mr Rowe, vicar	3	Richard Peperell	1
John Reed	4	Richard Reed	2
Elizabeth Drake	3	Joane Reed	2
Mr Parker	4	John Kingdome	6
Thomas Hellier	2	Thomazin Searle	2
P. Bond	5	Zachary Sanders	1
Thomas Parker	3	John Sanders	1

Paupers

Jane Evans, widow	1	Robert Courtnay	1
William Darke	1	John Saunders	1

Zachary Sanders was undoubtedly Zachary Saunders (either Joane's brother or father). The references to John Saunders and to John Sanders (and the references to three householders surnamed Reed), were useful additions to the information that I was collecting about these families. As to my Packer ancestors, no Thomas Packer was noted, but there was a Thomas Parker (with three hearths) and a Mr Parker (with four hearths). I had to review the original returns to check the spelling of the names, but also check whether there were any families named Parker recorded in the parish registers. If there were no such families, I could be fairly certain that these entries concerned the Packer families for whom I was searching.

The returns for Lady Day 1666 for Norfolk have been published in Seaman (903). I was having some difficulty tracing my ancestors named Pinchin or Pinchen. I had traced the family back to about 1750 in Horstead in Norfolk, but I could not ascertain where the family had come from. However, the 1666 hearth tax return assisted because, as a mini-census, it provided an indication (albeit incomplete) of the location of surnames in Norfolk. The return noted families named Pinchin, Pinching or Pinshin in Norwich and in the parishes of Briston and Barningham

Norwood. There were probably some other Pinchin families in Norfolk that were not listed (because of poverty or missing returns), but it was worth researching the families listed in this tax return to see if there were any links with my ancestors.

Marriage Duty Act 1695

The Stamp Duty Act of 1783 (# chapter 7) levied a tax (until 1794) on the events recorded in parish registers. However, there was also an earlier statute, in similar terms, that resulted in some useful records. The Marriage Duty Act of 1695 imposed a tax from 1 May 1695 (to pay for a war with France), payable on a sliding scale, on the occasion of births (rather than baptisms), marriages and burials. An annual tax was also payable by bachelors (over 25 years old) and by childless widowers. Those people receiving poor relief were exempt from the tax.

Tax collectors produced assessments (based in part on the parish registers) that should have listed all births, marriages and burials and also noted the number of people in each parish in 1695. Anglican clergy were requested to improve the standard of their parish registers (since they were often used by tax collectors). This probably resulted in a reduction in the number of Anglican baptisms, marriages and burials that were omitted from registers. However, the act failed to raise sufficient revenue for the government and was repealed in 1706.

The assessments made under the act's provisions were to be forwarded to commissioners or, later, to Justices of the Peace. Most of these documents have not survived, but there are some lists of inhabitants, catalogued by Gibson & Medlycott (139) and by Gibson (890), such as those for London, Bristol, Leicester, Shrewsbury, Southampton and 16 Wiltshire parishes. Most of the lists are held in CROs. CLRO holds the assessments for 1695 of about 80 parishes in the City of London (which have been published) and 13 London parishes outside the City walls. These list the members of each household, note their relationships to the head of the household and are indexed. The assessments for Bristol have also been published.

Window tax

This unpopular tax was levied from 1696 until 1851, although it was not strictly enforced in the last few years. The form and rates of the tax varied over the years but it consisted of:

a. a flat rate house tax (until 1834 only) with an additional amount (varying with the property's rateable value) from 1778, and

b. a window tax which was charged if a house had 10 or more windows (from 1696 to 1766), seven or more windows (from 1766 to 1825) and eight or more windows (1825 to 1851). Some windows (such as those of business premises attached to a residence) were for some years exempt from tax.

The occupiers of a property (rather than the owners) were liable to pay the tax. Those people who were excused by poverty from paying the church or poor rates were also exempt from the window tax. Many people blocked up some windows to reduce their tax. Returns usually note the name and address of a taxpayer, the number of windows in the house, and the tax paid. Surviving returns for England and Wales are listed in Gibson, Medlycott & Mills (892) and are generally in CROs, although a few are held in the National Library of Wales, TNA or other archives. From 1784 the window tax assessment forms also dealt with other taxes (considered below) such as those for servants, hair powder and horses.

Land tax

Land tax was levied on land with an annual value of more than 20 shillings (and also for a short time upon certain personal property). It was collected from 1693 (on an assessment prepared in 1692) until 1963 although the most extensive surviving records are from 1780 to 1832. Catholics were charged double tax from 1692 to 1831. Collection (and therefore the documentation) was organised by county, hundred and then parish.

Land tax records consist primarily of assessments and returns. They list landowners (proprietors) and from 1772 the occupiers of a property. However, a proprietor might not be a freeholder, but a copyholder or long leaseholder (# chapter 27). An occupier might be a tenant or a sub-tenant. Assessments were produced annually or quarterly, and usually specify the type of land and the amount of tax assessed. Returns note how much tax was actually paid. Most surviving records are in CROs or borough archives, and they are listed by county (with their locations) in Gibson, Medlycott & Mills (892).

Before 1780 the survival of documents varies substantially from place to place, and often only limited records have survived. From 1780 until 1832 (a little before 1780 in some counties), duplicates of the land tax assessments for counties were lodged with the Clerk of the Peace because payment of land tax evidenced a qualification to vote for parliamentary elections, and the Clerk was responsible for producing lists of voters. The Clerk's records usually survive in Quarter Sessions' records (# chapter 25) at CROs. Assessments for boroughs were rarely deposited because borough franchises were different (# chapter 17) and payment of land tax was usually irrelevant to men's entitlement to vote there. From 1832 the introduction of electoral registers made land tax records unnecessary for electoral purposes. Fortunately, many tax commissioners continued to lodge land tax records with the Clerk of the Peace, but their survival for this period is variable. Substantial collections survive for some counties but only limited records for others. Taxpayers were entitled from 1798 to commute their future land tax by a one-off payment (see below). Those taxpayers who commuted their tax were usually still included in lists up to 1832 because the lists evidenced their entitlement to vote. After 1832 the land tax records do not include people who had commuted their tax (since the records were no longer used to prepare voting lists) and so the lists are incomplete and less useful. However, lists of those paying land tax often survive up to 1949, when redemption of future land tax was made compulsory whenever property changed ownership. The tax was finally abolished in 1963.

The records omit many occupiers. For example, an entry for the tax that was levied on cottages owned by a landowner may only specify one or two of the labourers who occupied them. Nevertheless, land tax records can reveal a great deal of information about some families. Devon Record Office holds the land tax returns for the parish of Winkleigh where my Bulleid ancestors lived. One member of this family was Thomas Bulleid, who lived from 1706 to 1791, and was both a churchwarden and an overseer of the poor. Thomas occupied Croft Farm and a typical entry from the land tax records is:

Date	Proprietor	Farm	Occupier	Assessment
18th May 1782	Rev Tremayne	Croft	Thomas Bullied Snr	£2. 3s 10d.

The returns also record some other Bulleid cousins who farmed in Winkleigh. For example, they show that Stabdon Farm was occupied by George Bulleid until 1815 and then by his son Samuel (the parish register records the burial of George in August 1815):

Date	Proprietor	Farm	Occupier	Assessment
18th May 1782	H.A. Fellows	East Collacott	George Bulleid	£4. 0s 3d.
May 1788	H.H. Tremayne	Stabdon	George Bulleid	£5. 16s 10d
1788 to 1815	H.H. Tremayne	Stabdon	George Bulleid	various
1794 to 1805	H.A. Fellows	Middle Collacott	George Bulleid	various
1816 to1832	H.H. Tremayne	Stabdon	Samuel Bulleid	£6. 1s 7d

Land tax assessments often omit a description of the property for which tax was paid. For example, Guildhall Library holds land tax assessments of 1741 to 1824 for the hamlet of Mile End Old Town in the parish of St Dunstan Stepney, Middlesex. Entries for 1796 include:

Proprietors	Rents	Occupiers	Sum assessed
Wm Bowditch	20	John Lacey	£1 3s 4d
Richd Heath	16	Ann Pickering	18s 8d
Wm Snow	10	Mary Clarkson	11s 8d
Francis Ryner	12	John Cope	14s

The land tax statutes themselves also contain useful information. Until 1798 statutes were passed annually, authorising the raising of the tax and specifying the basis for the assessment (land tax became perpetual in 1798, so further annual statutes were unnecessary). Most annual statutes appointed commissioners for each county (and for some cities or boroughs) to administer the levy. For example, the 1731 statute (883) appointed 120 commissioners for Bedfordshire alone, as well as 20 for the town of Bedford. These were obviously the wealthier men of the area but may include your ancestors. Copies of the statutes are held in reference libraries.

Land tax redemption office records
In 1798 property owners were given an option to commute their future land tax by contracting with the tax commissioners to make a single lump sum payment (but often by instalments) that was equivalent to 15 years' tax. The commissioners therefore prepared registers listing those who were liable to tax in 1798. The registers (at TNA in series IR 23) consist of 121 volumes and constitute an almost complete set of land tax assessments for all English and Welsh counties (except Flintshire). They list the names of proprietors and occupiers and also the amount of tax assessed, but they rarely identify properties. The records are arranged topographically, by county, hundred and parish or borough. The IR 23 series list shows that Devon is covered by four volumes (pieces IR 23/16–19). There is also an index to parishes, showing that the returns for Dunsford are in IR 23/16. One page (folio 279) from those returns is at illustration 122. The index also showed that the Winkleigh returns start at folio 193 (which is in piece 16). An extract from the return is:

No.	Proprietor's name	Occupier	Sum Assessed	Contract date
	Revd. H.H. Tremayne	Geo. Bulleid	£6 1s 7d	
24145	do.	Richd. Webber	£3 19s 7d	5 April
	do.	Jn. Bulleid	£4 3s 7d	
	do.	[others]		

COUNTY of *Devon* PARISH of *Dunsford Continued*

An Aſſeſſment made in Purſuance of an Act of Parliament paſſed in the 38th Year of His Majeſty's Reign, for granting an Aid to His Majeſty by a Land Tax to be raiſed in Great Britain, for the Service of the Year 1798.

1215 279

No. of Regiſter.	Names of Proprietors.	Names of Occupiers.	Sums Aſſeſſed.			Date of Contract.
			L.	s.	d.	
	Gold Mrs.	Ann Mortimer	1	14	–	
	Gregory Georg. Ker.	Richd. Seaward	–	11	2	
	Hayne John	John Sercombe	–	13	–	
	Holmes Mr.	Willm. Townsend	–	13	9	
	Hodge Willm.	John Hellyer	–	13	–	
	Hodge Richd.	Himself	1	12	8	
	Harris Mr.	Thos. Norrish	–	19	–	
	Hodge Willm.	John Seaward	–	18	–	
	Harris Mr.	George Connett	–	14	8	
	Hodge John	Richd. Seaward	–	10	11	
	Hemous Thomas	Himself	–	16	4	
	Hawkins Mary	Herself	–	–	8	
	Hellyer Mary	Herself	–	2	10	
	Jerois Mary	Herself	–	0	4	
	Do.	Richd. Warren	–	1	10	
	Lethbridge Oliver	Himself	1	1	4	
	Mortimer Ann	Herself	–	7	7	
	May Jane	Charles Endacott	–	1	6	
	May John	Himself	–	10	–	
	Mortimer George	Himself	–	18	–	
	May John	Himself	–	9	7	
	Do.	Do.	–	4	6	
	May Jane	Willm. Sanford	–	11	4	
	Manning Mr.	Thos. Hemous	1	1	9	
	May George	Himself	–	9	–	
	Do.	Do.	–	6	–	
	Manning Mr.	Willm. Cox	–	9	6	
	May George	Himself	–	6	8	
	Mounsen Simon	Thos. Connett	–	2	5	
	Newbury Mr.	Nicholas Tuckett	1	6	6	
	Forcott Mr.	John White	–	13	9	

122. *A page from the land tax assessments of 1798 for Dunsford in Devon (TNA, IR 23/19)*

George Bulleid (who, as noted above, occupied Stabdon Farm) and John Bulleid were cousins of my ancestor John Bulleid. The number 24145 in the first column is a reference number for the redemption contract by which future tax was commuted by a payment made by Reverend Tremayne, the proprietor. The redemption contracts (dating from 1799 to 1963) are in series IR 24 (with some maps and notes of exemptions) and arranged by number. Many contracts add little to the above details but they may identify a property, note the acreage of land, or record changes in ownership after 1798 (if the land was exonerated from tax by a contract after 1798). The IR 24 series list showed that the contracts numbered 24,000–24,999 are in piece IR 24/36. The contract (dated 5 April 1799) recorded that Henry Hawkins Tremayne redeemed the land tax on many properties in Winkleigh by paying over £2,600 in 16 instalments. Importantly, the contract named each of the farms or other properties (which were not named in the assessments in IR 23). George Bulleid was recorded as the occupier of Stabdon Farm and John Bulleid as the occupier of Heckpen and Popehouse.

Series IR 22 contains the parish books of redemptions, which list, by county and then parish, the redemptioner's name, the name of the occupier, the amount of tax and the contract number.

Lay subsidies

Lay subsidies were taxes that were levied from the 12th to 17th centuries on moveable personal property (such as goods, crops or wages) above a variable minimum value (which effectively exempted the poor from liability). Subsidies were also sometimes levied on land and buildings. The taxes were called lay subsidies because clerical property was exempt, although there were separate clerical subsidies. Most surviving lists, known as the subsidy rolls, are held at TNA in series E 179. A list of the lay subsidies, including poll taxes (discussed below) is contained in Colwell (243) and Jurkowski, Smith & Crook (896). The series list for E 179 (published in five volumes by the List and Index Society) lists the surviving returns by county and by hundred or wapentake (but not by parish). The tax records for a place (for each subsidy or other tax) can be found through the E 179 database on PROCAT noted above. A few documents are also held in CROs.

Early subsidies usually specified a quota that was to be levied, such as a tenth, a fifteenth or a twentieth of the value of a man's property. The subsidies of 1327 and 1332 are the first for which substantial assessments survive. For example, the records of the lay subsidy of 1332 for Devon, published in Erskine (887), contain over 10,000 names. Unfortunately, from 1334 until 1523 the government was not interested in how much each person paid. Townships (# chapter 6) were required to raise a certain amount of tax and so assessments between these years list townships and the total amount of tax payable, but rarely include the names of individual taxpayers (although aliens were often listed).

It is fortunate for genealogists that the Tudor monarchs made great use of subsidies to raise income and also assessed individuals (rather than requiring a certain sum of money from an area). The records since 1523 therefore list taxpayers' names (although Wales was exempt from subsidies until 1543 and Cumberland, Northumberland and Westmorland were exempt until 1603). The subsidies from 1523 taxed a person on the basis of his wages, the value of his goods or his income from land (and sometimes on more than one of these). Some subsidies consisted of a single levy but others consisted of multiple levies that might be spread over a few years. More details are provided in Hoyle (893). The first of these new subsidies, often called the Great Subsidy, was approved by Parliament in 1523 and was levied for four years. The money was collected in

January or February of 1523/4 and in each of the next three years. The subsidy applied to all people over the age of 16 who had income from land (or taxable goods) of £2 per annum, or who had an annual wage of £1 or more. The tax was four pence in the pound. A levy was also made on other interests in land, as described in Colwell (243). Surviving documents, containing many taxpayers' names, are rolls of parchment (in series E 179), usually arranged by hundred, providing the date of assessment, taxpayers' names, the amount of a man's taxable assets or the amount of tax he actually paid. Detailed returns also survive for further subsidies that were levied in 1543, 1544 and 1545 (although not on wage-earners). There were also some later 16th-century subsidies. For example, substantial returns for Devon survive for subsidies in 1571, 1576, 1581 and 1589 and there are some lists for other years. Taxpayers were to be taxed only once in each subsidy. A man who had land or goods in more than one place could therefore obtain a certificate of payment (or of residence) if he paid all his tax in one hundred. He could provide his certificate to tax assessors in another hundred to avoid being taxed there also. Surviving certificates are in series E 115 or E 179 and TNA holds an alphabetical index to the taxpayers to whom they relate.

The returns have been published for some counties or hundreds, the publications being listed in Hoyle (893). Lang (897) is an indexed transcript of the subsidy assessment rolls for London in 1541 (about 4,000 names listed in E 179/144/120) and 1582 (about 7,200 names in E 179/251/16), with a detailed analysis of the legislation and the procedures for collection of the taxes. Stoate (905) contains the returns for Devon for the subsidies of 1524–27, listing over 26,000 men (and a few women) who were liable for the tax. The return for Winkleigh lists 89 names including John Bulhedde who was probably my ancestor. Another published example, for the subsidies of 1543–45 in Devon, is Stoate (904), listing 30,000 taxpayers from nearly all Devon parishes. This lists Nicholas Bulhedd and 76 other taxpayers in Winkleigh in 1545.

Colwell (243) lists the subsidies or similar assessments and levies that were raised at intervals throughout the 17th century. The surviving records of subsidies from 1641 to 1660 are listed, by county and hundred, in Gibson & Dell (891) and those since 1660 are catalogued by Gibson (890). Most of the records are at TNA in series E 179, but some are in other archives. For example, assessments for Middlesex and the City of London for 1693/4 are at CLRO, because the Corporation of London had made loans to the Crown which were repaid by the proceeds of this subsidy being assigned to the Corporation. Some of these later subsidies have been published. Thus Jones (895) contains the names of taxpayers (and the amount of tax assessed) for the assessment for Hammersmith in 1693/4.

During the 16th century the Tudors also relied on the Royal Prerogative to raise taxes such as benevolences (for example that of 1545) or forced loans (many of which were not repaid). Particularly important are the forced loans of 1522 to 1523, which were assessed on the basis of assessments known as military surveys, undertaken in 1522. Commissioners listed the names of all landowners (and all other males aged over 16) with the value of their goods, thus providing the government with records of the wealth and military strength of England. The assessments were then used to calculate the amount which taxpayers should provide to the king by way of a forced loan. Hoyle (893) lists the surviving records (and location) of these military surveys, forced loans and benevolences. Surviving lists of names are mostly in series E 179 or E 351 at TNA and some have been published, such as the military survey of Gloucestershire, in 1522, in Hoyle (894) and the 1545 benevolence for Wiltshire in Ramsay (901).

Charles I also imposed taxes such as Ship money, without recourse to Parliament. Ship money (a major cause of the English Civil War) was levied from 1634 to 1640 in maritime areas (and later elsewhere) to finance the navy. A few lists of taxpayers, arranged by county, survive in series SP 16 and SP 17 of the State Papers Domestic at TNA. Taxes were also levied to pay for the militia following the Militia Acts of 1662 and 1663. Some assessments, listing householders' names, survive and some have been published, such as that for Herefordshire in 1663 by Faraday (888), which also provides a detailed description of the statutes and the assessments.

Poll taxes

Poll taxes were head taxes that were raised in the 14th, 17th and 18th centuries. Men in receipt of poor relief were generally exempt. A levy of four pence per head was imposed in 1377 on those aged over 14. In 1379 it was levied on those aged over 16. The 1381 poll tax of one shilling a head (which resulted in the Peasant's Revolt that year) was levied on those aged over 15. Poll taxes were also collected in 1641, 1660, 1667, 1678, 1689, 1690, 1691, 1692, 1693, 1694, 1697, 1698, 1699, 1702 and 1703 (the statutes authorising the taxes were sometimes a year or more earlier). In addition, a poll tax was levied quarterly from 1 June 1694 to 1 March 1695.

Commissioners were appointed to oversee the tax collection. Local inhabitants drew up assessment lists and acted as tax collectors. Schurer & Arkell (902) reviews poll taxes since 1660, in particular describing the varying bases of assessment and the exemptions. A flat rate tax was usually levied on those aged 16 or over (not receiving poor relief). This tax was of one shilling (reduced to six pence for some taxpayers until 1667), but further tax (of varying percentages) was applied to different forms of income. The poll tax returns of 1377, 1379 and 1381 are at TNA in series E 179. These are in Latin and usually note taxpayers' names (although only rarely in 1379) and the tax paid, but sometimes also note occupations and even relationships between household members. The British Academy is publishing an indexed transcript, by Fenwick (889), of all surviving returns of these poll taxes. The first volume covers counties alphabetically from Bedfordshire to Leicestershire and includes a detailed review of the administration of the taxes and the resulting records. The second volume covers the other English counties. A third volume will include a name index. The records vary in usefulness. For example, lists of taxpayers do not survive for Berkshire for 1377 or 1379 but include about 8,000 people in 1381.

A few assessments survive for the taxes of 1641 to 1703, mostly in series E 179, but some are at CROs. The returns are arranged by county and by hundred. Surviving returns for the 1641 poll tax are listed, by county and hundred, in Gibson & Dell (891) and surviving returns from 1660 onwards are listed by county in Gibson (890).

The free and voluntary present to King Charles II

A statute of 1660 provided for the collection of a "free and voluntary present" for the newly restored monarch, in order to clear his debts. Subscriptions were collected in 1661. Although payment was voluntary, the contributors' names were recorded and so many people no doubt decided to contribute for this reason. In any event, most of the better-off did pay. Fairly complete returns of names survive for about 30 English and Welsh counties (with a few documents for some other counties) containing about 130,000 names in total. Surviving returns, listing individuals (and often their occupations), are held at TNA, in series E 179, arranged by county, then hundred or borough. The piece numbers for each county are listed by Gibson (890). The number of names varies substantially from place to place. For Surrey there are only about half as many names as appear in the hearth tax returns of a year or two later but, for Banbury in Oxfordshire, the numbers are about the same. The records of the voluntary present certainly include some names that do not appear in hearth tax returns.

The collection for distressed Protestants in Ireland, 1642

Civil war broke out in Ireland in late 1641. In 1642 an act of Parliament authorised sheriffs, churchwardens and parish overseers to collect gifts and receive loans, on behalf of the Crown, to be used for the relief of Protestant refugees. The collectors listed the contributors' names (including women). The surviving returns for the collections (at TNA in series SP 28 and E 179) are arranged by county and parish. They list contributors and the amount paid.

There are no surviving records of the collections for many English counties (for example Devon, Herefordshire, Lancashire or Suffolk) and they only survive for three Welsh parishes. In many other English counties, lists survive for only a few parishes (for example eight in Somerset and two in Cheshire). Fortunately, there are substantial records for some counties (for example for 160 Kent parishes). Furthermore, although the collections only list the adults who contributed (whereas the contemporaneous protestation returns should have listed all adult males) the collections sometimes cover areas for which no protestations survive. Thus the protestation returns survive for only one Bedfordshire parish, but the collections survive for 55 parishes. A useful article about the collections by C. Webb appears in *Genealogists' Magazine* (March 1985). Gibson & Dell (891) provide a detailed review of the surviving records, and list them by county and parish. The collections for Surrey, East Sussex and Buckinghamshire have been published.

Other taxes

TNA and CROs hold some other tax records. There was a tax on male servants from 1777 to 1852, with an exemption for male servants engaged in husbandry, trade or manufacture. There was a similar tax on female servants from 1785 to 1792. However, surviving records for both taxes only list the employers. TNA holds assessments for the male servants' tax for 1780 (in series T 47) and the SoG holds an index to these assessments, listing the names of almost 25,000 employers. A horse tax was levied from 1784 to 1874 on people with riding or driving horses (including many used in trade). Taxes were also levied on carriages from 1747 to 1782, silver plate (1756–77), game (1784–1807), coats of arms (1793–1882), dogs (1796–1882), hair powder (1795–1861), sheep (1549/50) and uninhabited houses (1851–1924).

Most records of these taxes have not survived but records for some (for carriages, 1753–66 and silver plate, 1756–62) are at TNA in series E 182 and T 47 and include taxpayers' names. CROs also hold some records of these taxes. Many returns for the horse tax are held in Quarter Sessions' records and note the taxpayer's name, the number of horses and the date the tax was paid. An example from Great Bromley in Essex of 1784 is reproduced in *Essex Family Historian* (August 1992). Quarter Sessions' records include some records of taxes on game. Those men who killed or sold game had to register annually with the Clerk of the Peace and lists of names were kept. The hair powder tax was introduced in 1795. Those who wore a wig (to which white powder was applied) had to pay a duty of a guinea. Army officers, clergy and members of the royal household were exempt. Lists of taxpayers can be found in CROs and the lists for Wiltshire of 1796–97 have been published by Wiltshire FHS (886). The tax helped change fashion and wigs were rarely worn in the 19th century, although the tax was not abolished until 1861. A tax was levied on flocks of sheep from March 1549 to January 1550. Some returns, listing the size of flocks and owners' names, survive at TNA. Chapman (137) recommends the review of the returns for Devon, Huntingdonshire, Oxfordshire, Nottinghamshire and Yorkshire.

Income tax was first introduced in 1789, but was repealed, and then reintroduced in 1803 until 1816. The tax was again reintroduced in 1842 but for many years only affected the wealthier classes. The names of taxpayers were erased from returns up to 1816, but some lists of defaulters and persons in arrears are in series E 182 at TNA.

CONFISCATIONS OF LAND AND COMPOUNDING

The confiscations of Royalists' land during the English Civil War and Commonwealth, as well as the process of compounding, were not strictly taxes, but did result in a very substantial revenue for the government. Other confiscations of property (following the Jacobite rebellions and the dissolution of the monasteries) are considered in chapter 24.

Confiscations of land

During the English Civil War and Commonwealth much land owned by the Crown, the Church and Royalists was confiscated, surveyed and the revenue (such as rent from tenants) was taken for the government's use. The process is described in TNA domestic records leaflet 68. Much of the land was also sold and many deeds of sale were enrolled on the Close Rolls (at TNA in series C 54). Other records, described in the leaflet, are in Exchequer papers or State Papers Domestic. If the land had not been sold by the Restoration, it was usually returned to the owner. Consequently, some records of sequestered church lands are in CROs (in the records of the diocese or other church body that owned the land).

Compounding

In 1643 committees were appointed by Parliament to investigate the part taken by those landowners (known as delinquents) who had supported King Charles I during the civil war. A Committee for the Sequestration of Delinquents' Estates sat from 1643 to 1653 and a Committee for Compounding with Delinquents sat from 1643 to 1660. The committees' work is reviewed in detail by Colwell (243). The Committee for Sequestration confiscated many landowners' property. The property might be returned if a delinquent confessed his delinquency, pledged to support the Commonwealth, then compounded (that is, gave a detailed account of his land and possessions to the Committee for Compounding and paid a fine).

The committees' records of 1643 to 1660 (in series SP 23 of State Papers Domestic at TNA) are known as Royalist composition papers and give detailed information about those men who were investigated, their families and their estates. Indexed calendars of the records of the Committee for Compounding from 1643 to 1660 have been published by HMSO (884). Some entries concern cases against the Charnock family of Lancashire, including:

14 April 1647. Claimants on the estate of Thos. Charnock of Preston, co. Lancaster. Robert Charnock of Astley, his eldest son, compounds for delinquency in deserting his habitation and going into the King's garrisons. He was in Lathom House at its surrender and has since conformed to Parliament. Has taken the National Covenant.
22 May 1649. Begs to amend his particulars, his father having died since his report was drawn up . . . 8 June 1649. Fine £260. 8s. 9d.

18 Dec 1651. Hen. Fleetwood and other trustees of Elizabeth and Ellinor, daughters of Thos. Charnock, petition that in 1631, Thos. Charnock settled on them lands in Astley, Chorley and Charnock Richard . . . in 1634 he granted £60 a year for Elizabeth and Ellinor for 5 years till they were paid £300, but the estate is sequestered for delinquency of Robert, eldest son of Thos. Charnock. Beg the land till the £300 is paid.

Sequestration committees were also established in many counties and some of their records of sequestrations, sales or rentals (or sometimes the papers of committee members) survive in CROs. Thus minutes for 1646–47 of the Bedfordshire Committee of Sequestrations survive in personal papers of Sir William Boteler, are held at Bedford Record Office and have been published by Bedfordshire Historical Record Society.

Advances of money
From 1642 to 1650 there was also a Committee for the Advance of Money. This committee undertook investigations of people's wealth, obtained loans of money for Parliament's use and repaid the money annually with interest. In effect, the advances were forced loans. If people did not subscribe, their goods could be seized although only Royalists had to contribute from August 1646. The records are in State Papers Domestic and they have been calendared in three HMSO volumes (885). A typical entry in the calendar relates to Robert Charnock of Astley (the delinquent noted above), who was assessed on 11 May 1647 to pay £60, but who subsequently obtained a discharge.

INSURANCE

Relatives may hold death certificates or wills which were used to support claims on insurance policies. The policies may also have been kept, perhaps naming the insured's beneficiaries (such as his wife or children). This section reviews two further types of insurance records.

Fire insurance records
Companies were established from the 17th century to insure buildings against fire. Most early fire insurance companies' records have not survived, but some are at CROs or (since many companies were based in London) at Guildhall Library. Fire insurance plans were considered in chapter 15 but other records note details of properties, their use, and names of owners or occupiers.

Hawkings (892a) is a very detailed, illustrated, study of fire insurance records from 1680 to 1920, with lists of those available in archives or still held by some insurance companies. The most useful records for family historians are policy registers. Hawkings reviews (with hundreds of examples from the records) the format of registers of the leading fire insurance companies and the information that they contain. He also describes the important information included in companies' other records, for example registers of losses, claims and endorsements (changes to policies as a result, for example, of an insured building being enlarged), company minutes and staff or agents' registers.

The fire insurance records at Guildhall Library are particularly important and listed in a library leaflet and in Hawkings (892a). For example, they include policy registers of the Hand-in-Hand Fire and Life Insurance Society for 1696 to 1865 (160 volumes), the Sun Fire Office for 1710 to

1863 (1,262 volumes) and the Royal Exchange Assurance Society for 1753 to 1759 and 1773 to 1883 (173 volumes). The Sun Fire Office and Royal Exchange undertook business throughout Britain but the Hand-in-Hand records relate predominantly to London. Unfortunately, many of the registers are not indexed (making it very difficult to find a particular property). There are name indexes to many of the Hand-in-Hand registers and Guildhall Library has a card index to the names of policy holders in some of the Sun registers (1714–31 and 1793–94) and for a few of the Royal Exchange registers (1773–75 and 1792–93). This index is arranged by county, then alphabetically by surname. It notes occupations, the year and the insured's parish. Three typical cards from the Devon section refer to policies for:

Bullhead, Amos	1774	farmer	West Stone, South Molton
Bullhead, John	1726	victualler	The 3 Mariners Inn, Conduit Land, Bideford
Dennis, Jonas	1731	cordwainer	St Mary Arches, Exeter

There is also a microfiche index to the registers of the Sun Fire Office and Royal Exchange for 1775 to 1787. This indexes the register entries by (*inter alia*) the name of the insured, the place and policy number. You can therefore search the indexes for a policy for your ancestor, or search by place name to see which people from an ancestor's village or town took out policies. The index included an entry for my ancestor Thomas Gillman of Hockliffe, Bedfordshire, giving his occupation (shopkeeper and shoemaker), the policy number (375484) and the volume and page of the original register. The index to policy numbers repeated this information and also noted that the policy insured his house and goods for £400. Entry 375484 in the register was:

Michaelmas 1777. Thomas Gillman of Hockliffe in the county of Bedford, shopkeeper and shoemaker. On his new dwelling house only situated as aforesaid, brick pannelled and tiled, not exceeding five hundred pounds   £200

    Household goods therein only not exceeding fifty pounds   £40
    Utensils & stock (not hazardous) therein only, not in excess of
    one hundred and sixty pounds   £160
                                 [total]   £400

Hawkings (892a) includes many examples from policy registers (relating to householders, traders, inns, landowners, tenants, ships and famous people) but also of endorsements to policies, losses and claims. For example, Stephen Round of New Windsor, Berkshire, took out a policy in 1800 with Royal Exchange Assurance in respect of many properties that he owned in Berkshire and neighbouring counties. The policy refers to 22 people (such as Robert Brooker, farmer; Caroline Bartlett, widow and John Rogers, shoemaker) who were tenants of those properties. Two stationers named Robert Armitage and William Roper of St Botolph Bishopsgate, London, made a claim in 1771, to the Sun Fire Office, concerning a fire at their warehouse in Hounsditch. The company records include an affidavit by Armitage and Roper as to their losses (over £163) and a certificate from the minister, churchwardens and leading inhabitants of the parish that they believed that the fire was accidental. Hawkings also shows how company minutes reveal payments to their policy-holders. For example, in July 1810, the Sun Fire Office Committee of Management approved payments of £84 17s to John Wright, yeoman of Tiverton, Devon, and £114 7s 9d to a pawnbroker, Christopher Vickary of Liverpool.

Annuities and tontines

An annuity is an income paid to a beneficiary at regular intervals, for a fixed period or ascertainable period (usually the lifetime of a nominee) in return for a lump sum payment having been previously made into the scheme by a subscriber. A subscriber usually nominated one of his children (or another child) as the nominee to ensure that payment of the annuity continued for as long as possible. The beneficiary might be the subscriber, the nominee, or a third person. The government arranged annuities in the 18th century and thus received money (the lump sums) and repaid it (as annuities), in effect with interest, in later years. Tontines were also used by the government to raise money from the late 17th century, and also took the form of an annuity. Subscribers invested a lump sum of money. The interest from the investment was then shared by the subscribers during their own, or a nominee's, lifetime. As the subscribers or nominees died, the interest paid by the government was shared between a decreasing number of people.

The government organised 11 schemes (in three series) of life annuities and tontines between 1693 and 1789. Registers of the ages, addresses and deaths of beneficiaries and nominees were kept for each scheme. The schemes and surviving records are described by Leeson (898) and Colwell (243). The first tontine commenced in 1693, followed by a series of three life annuities in 1745, 1746 and 1757. A second series consisted of a tontine of 1766, two life annuities (of 1778 and 1779) and a tontine of 1789. A third series consisted of three Irish tontines (although most subscribers were English) in 1773, 1775 and 1777. Most records are at TNA in series NDO 1 to 3 (National Debt Office records) or series E 401, 403, 406 and 407. Records usually include a subscriber's name and address, the nominee's name and perhaps a nominee's age, parents and date of death. The files include documents that were submitted to the authorities, for example certificates of baptism or extracts of wills. The records refer to approximately 15,000 nominees as well as a few thousand subscribers (or assignees of the beneficiaries).

There are published lists in the British Library (and copies at the SoG) of the 1,000 nominees of the tontine of 1693 (and of those nominees who were still alive in 1730 and 1749). The SoG has also published a microfiche index, by Leeson (899), of the 2,559 nominees of the life annuity schemes of 1745, 1746, 1757, 1778 and 1779 and the tontine of 1766. The index gives the names of nominees, their place of residence, their age at entry into the scheme and the year of their death. The SoG also holds indexes of the surnames appearing in the three Irish tontines and in the English tontine of 1789.

The records of public lotteries, for example for the Million Lottery set up in 1694 (at TNA in series C 46), are described in Colwell (243). There are registers of subscribers, lists of nominees (and registers of their deaths) from the late 17th to late 18th centuries.

CHAPTER 24

RECORDS OF THE CIVIL AND ECCLESIASTICAL COURTS

This chapter (and chapter 25) review the English and Welsh courts, the records that were produced in the course of litigation, the location of the records and how to find your ancestors in them. Newspaper reports of court proceedings (# chapter 17) are available from the 18th century onwards, providing details of some civil disputes, criminal trials, witnesses and victims, but more information is contained in surviving court records. They are difficult to use, principally because many of the records are not indexed and many of those before 1733 are in Latin.

Your ancestors may have been involved in a civil or criminal action, in either a secular or ecclesiastical court. This chapter reviews the church courts and those secular courts that dealt predominantly with civil claims, but some of these (for example the Court of King's Bench) also dealt with criminal cases. Both civil and criminal court procedure are therefore reviewed in this chapter. The criminal courts (such as the assizes) and the Justices of the Peace are considered in chapter 25, but they also had some civil jurisdiction. There were also manorial courts that dealt with some criminal and civil actions in medieval times and with the holding of manorial land until the 20th century. These courts are reviewed in chapter 27.

Records of the church courts and of Justices of the Peace are generally held in CROs, and are listed in their catalogues or published guides. Most other civil and criminal court records are at TNA and further assistance with these records can be obtained from Bevan (239) and Hawkings (984). The *Guide to the Contents of the PRO* (228) is also useful, describing each series of the national secular courts' records, but it is out of date in many respects and so should be used in conjunction with the *PRO Current Guide* (234), PROCAT, the series lists at TNA and other finding aids described below.

Some knowledge of legal proceedings and terminology will assist you when examining court records. If someone (Mr Smith) owes me money or damages my goods (or commits some other act that causes me loss), I would have a civil cause of action against him and could take proceedings in the civil courts. I would be the plaintiff or applicant in the litigation and Mr Smith would be the defendant or respondent. The action would be entitled "Herber v. Smith" (the v meaning *versus*). Criminal cases are usually taken by a public body on behalf of the Crown, and a person charged with a crime is also called a defendant, so that an action would be entitled "R v. Smith", the R meaning Rex (the King) or Regina (the Queen). Most courts sat during four terms or sittings each year. The exact dates of these terms varied but Michaelmas term ran from October to December, Hilary term from January to March, Easter term from April to May and Trinity term from June to July.

In civil proceedings a plaintiff started an action by a document known as a writ of summons or bill of complaint. This set out the relevant facts and stated the cause of the action and the amount claimed. More details of a claim might be set out in a plaintiff's statement of claim. A defendant set out his response to the allegations, or his version of events, in a document known as a defence or answer. A plaintiff might then serve a reply and a defendant could respond with a rejoinder. A defendant might also have a claim against a plaintiff. For example, I might sue Mr Smith for a debt, but he might allege that (by a related transaction) I also owe him money. A court usually heard both claims in the same action. Mr Smith would therefore serve a counterclaim. I would answer his allegations in my defence to counterclaim. All these documents are known as pleadings. They set out the parties' formal statements of their cases and the conflicting allegations, so that a court can see the issues that require resolution.

The parties then took interlocutory steps. They disclosed to each other their evidence (for example documents or damaged goods). A party might submit written questions (known as interrogatories) to the other party, which that party might have to answer on oath. Witnesses could give written statements to a party, or be examined on oath by a court official (usually responding to interrogatories posed by one or both parties), the examination being written down to form a deposition. A party or witness might submit an affidavit (that is, a written statement that he swears to be true). The person swearing an affidavit or giving a deposition is a deponent. A deponent might refer, in his affidavit, to documents (for example letters, wills, or title deeds of property) and attach them (or copies) to the affidavit. These are known as exhibits. The parties can agree to compromise a dispute at any time. Mr Smith could therefore agree to pay me half of the amount that I claim in satisfaction of the debt and in settlement of the action. If the parties do not reach a settlement, the parties or their lawyers present their claims and evidence at trial. The court's decision is known as a judgment, order or decree. The court could give judgment in favour of a plaintiff for a monetary amount, or order a defendant to return to a plaintiff some goods that the defendant was found to be wrongfully withholding. One of the parties might wish to challenge the court's decision. This is done by way of an appeal to a higher court. The person appealing is the appellant and the party opposing an appeal is a respondent.

The terminology in criminal cases is very similar. However, a defendant generally never has to say anything or produce any documents. It is up to a prosecutor to prove the case alleged. Criminal cases are commenced by a summons or indictment noting the defendant's name, the crime he is alleged to have committed and when and where the crime took place.

CIVIL COURTS

In medieval times the King, acting through his Council (the Curia Regis), was responsible for the administration of justice. The common law courts such as the Courts of Common Pleas, Exchequer and King's Bench (considered below), grew from the King's Council and applied the common law of England, as supplemented by acts of Parliament. However, the common law had many shortcomings. For example, the common law courts would generally not recognise or enforce trusts (in particular the rights of beneficiaries against trustees), or grant an injunction (a court order that someone should cease certain acts). Furthermore, an action by a wronged person against wrongdoers was only possible if it came within the categories of actions that were recognised by the common law. Procedure was also slow and expensive. Aggrieved subjects therefore often petitioned the King directly for justice to be done and further courts evolved from the King's Council to deal with these petitions. These courts were known as the courts of equity because they applied rules of equity (that is, reflecting conscience or justice) to deal with matters not covered by the common law (or to overcome its injustices). They included the Court of Requests, the Court of Star Chamber, the Court of Exchequer and the Court of Chancery.

The Court of Exchequer developed from the Exchequer, a medieval government department that dealt with financial matters. The Chancery (also known as the Writing Department) was another important government department. It issued charters and letters under the Great Seal, transmitting the king's instructions to his subjects, and also kept records of important matters on rolls in the Chancery (the resulting Charter Rolls, Close Rolls, Fine Rolls and Patent Rolls are considered in later chapters). The Lord Chancellor, who was also Keeper of the Great Seal, headed the Chancery. Petitions for justice were passed to the Lord Chancellor to be dealt with and so, from the Chancery, there developed the principal court of equity; the Lord Chancellor's own court, the Court of Chancery.

The Court of Chancery
This court had jurisdiction in civil disputes throughout England and Wales, although it generally refused to deal with disputes involving less than £10 (or land worth less than 40 shillings per annum) or cases in which the common law could provide a remedy. The Court of Chancery's procedures unfortunately became increasingly complex, slow and expensive, so that a litigant was just as likely to suffer injustice in Chancery as in the common law courts. Appeals from decisions of the Court of Chancery were made to the House of Lords (and there was also a Court of Appeal in Chancery from 1851 to 1875). In 1875 the Court of Chancery became the Chancery Division of the High Court of Justice (considered below).

Chancery Court records are at TNA, date from the late 14th century and are in English. Horwitz (938) is a detailed review of Chancery procedure, records and finding-aids of the 17th and 18th centuries. Chancery records are also described in Gerhold (934), Bevan (239) and TNA legal records leaflets 22 and 42. The indexes and finding-aids for the most important Chancery records are listed in appendix X. Chancery cases were often disputes between members of a family (over land, trusts, marriage settlements or wills). The court's records therefore contain a large amount of genealogical information and the documents produced to the court during litigation included many wills or title deeds. The surviving records are enormous. Horwitz (938) estimates that there were about 750,000 Chancery actions between 1600 and 1800 and about 6,000 bills (by which cases were started) were filed in 1627 alone. Even though the number of cases declined, there were still over 2,300 bills in 1818. There is therefore a good chance that your ancestors appear in the court's records, although they may be difficult to find.

The main pleadings in the Court of Chancery were a plaintiff's bill of complaint (or petition) and a defendant's answer. Witnesses gave evidence before trial by attending for depositions in London (town depositions) or in the provinces (country depositions). Most depositions note a witness's residence, age and occupation. Many applications by the parties were heard by Masters in Chancery, who also reviewed trust or estate accounts (and had custody of many case records) and reported to the court on these matters. The office of Master in Chancery was abolished in 1852 but many case records, from about 1600 to 1852, are filed under the Masters' names and those names are listed by P. Coldham in *Genealogists' Magazine* (December 1981). Much of the Masters' work was later undertaken by Chief Clerks who were allowed to assume the title Master in 1897. Officers known as the Six Clerks received and filed pleadings or other records, and made notes from them in registers so that they could inform the court of the status of an action. The names of the Six Clerks who were in office from the 16th century up to 1842 are listed in Fry (932). Other court officers are described in the *PRO Guide* (228).

Many Chancery Division records since 1875 are archived in the same manner (and classes) as the Court of Chancery records, so they are considered here and in a later section on the High Court. There are three main categories of Chancery records: (a) pleadings (bills of complaint, answers, replications and rejoinders) together known as Chancery proceedings; (b) evidence (affidavits, depositions and exhibits); and (c) court decisions (orders or decrees) and written opinions of Chancery Masters. Unfortunately, the pleadings and other records of a case were not filed together. Records were generally filed by type, so that TNA holds series of pleadings, series of depositions and so on. Records of a particular case will be in various series and may be difficult to find. Indexes cover only some of the records and many of these indexes are alphabets (listing people's names in order only of the first letter of a surname, rather than truly alphabetically). The indexes and alphabets usually refer only to the first plaintiff and the first defendant in each case (other plaintiffs or defendants in a case are rarely noted) and there are very few indexes to the names of witnesses or other people involved in a dispute. For many years, Bernau's index (considered below) was the best starting point for research in the court's records but researchers can now also use PROCAT and the equity pleadings database (reviewed below).

Entry books of court decrees and orders are in series C 33 (for 1544–1875) or J 15 (for 1876–1955). These note the final court judgment but also any interlocutory orders (such as for depositions of witnesses to be taken). There are contemporary alphabets (in series IND 1) for cases from 1544 to 1955, but only to the plaintiffs' names. There are also decree rolls (enrolments of the decrees and orders in C 33) for 1534–1875, in C 78 and 79. Importantly, these note the subject matter of the dispute (taken from the pleadings) as well as the final judgment, but decrees were enrolled for only a minority of Chancery cases (perhaps only 35,000). The decree rolls are being calendared in volumes of the List and Index Society. For example, Hoyle & Norris (942) calendar about 700 decrees (in pieces C 78/86–130) of the late 16th and early 17th centuries. The entries note the parties and the matter in dispute. Typical entries, illustrating the important cases heard in Chancery, are:

C 78/87.10. 26 June 1595. Edmund Argentyne of Colyton, Devon, gent and Margaret his wife, widow of William Westover of Yardbury [Colyton parish], Devon, gent (versus) John Younge the elder of Axminster, Devon, merchant, John Younge the younger of Colyton, merchant, Giles Kensbeare and Richard Westover, all executors of William Westover. Failure to execute the provisions of Westover's will.

C 78/105.8. 16 April 1597. John Huxham of Cornwood, Devon, yeoman, son of John Huxham deceased, who married Eleanor, daughter of Nicholas Fayreweather (versus) Nicholas Fayreweather of Cornwood, yeoman who was the plaintiff's maternal grandfather and who married Thomasine Huxham of Harberton, Devon, widow [plaintiff's grandmother], William Anne of Shaugh Prior, Devon, Mary his wife, the daughter of Nicholas Fayreweather and Walter Heale of Shaugh, yeoman. Possession of lands in Cornwood settled by Nicholas Fayreweather on the marriage of plaintiff's father John, deceased, with Eleanor Fayreweather, daughter of Nicholas Fayreweather; lease of the premises made to Heale.

Having found a relevant case, you can then turn to the pleadings (Chancery proceedings). Most actions did not proceed to judgment, so you should review the Chancery proceedings even if you find nothing relevant in the decrees or orders. TNA legal records leaflets 22 and 42 and the *PRO Guide* (228) describe how the pleadings were filed (and are now archived). Many of the documents are in very poor condition but they are in series C 1–16 and 18 (for the period up to 1875) and subsequently in J 54. Most early proceedings (up to 1558) are in C 1 and most proceedings for 1558–1649 (the reigns of Elizabeth, James I and Charles I) with a few to 1690 are in C 2, 3 and 4. From the 17th century up to 1842, the proceedings are arranged by six divisions, each named after one of the Six Clerks who were in office during the period. For example, for the period 1649–1714, there are Chancery proceedings for the divisions of Bridges, Collins, Hamilton, Mitford, Reynardson and Whittington in series C 5 to C 10 (containing pleadings from about 250,000 actions). The years covered by the other series of Chancery proceedings (in C 11–16 and 18) are noted in appendix X.

The calendars or indexes that will help you find relevant pleadings are also listed in appendix X. Some proceedings are indexed (usually by the first plaintiff's name) in British Record Society volumes, such as Fry (932). Bernau's index and notebooks (considered below) are also useful for finding cases. There are also many calendars of Chancery proceedings. For example, the Record Commissioners published three indexed volumes (908) of calendars of proceedings (mostly in series C 2) from the reign of Elizabeth I (1558–1603). A typical entry is:

Plaintiff	Defendant	Object of suit	Premises
John Ponysforde and Elizabeth his wife	Agnes Norrys widow	Claim by lease	A grist mill called Chappeldown Mill and lands in the parish of Winkleigh, demised to plaintiffs by John Norrys deceased, defendant's husband

There are also published *Public Record Office Lists & Indexes*, or manuscript calendars and indexes to most Chancery pleadings from the 15th to the 18th centuries. For example, most of the pleadings in series C 1 have been calendared (noting the parties and the subject of the dispute) in 10 volumes of the *Lists & Indexes* (# appendix X). Illustration 123 is a page from one of those volumes (*Lists & Indexes volume XXIX*), listing some cases from the early 16th century. The plaintiffs (or complainants), the defendants, the matter in dispute and the county to which the dispute related are noted for each case. The genealogical information from these calendars alone can be substantial. In the fourth action listed, the plaintiff John Jervys is noted as the heir of his cousin Nicholas Jervys but also as the son of Walter Jervys and grandson of John Jervys. There are also four *Lists & Indexes* volumes that calendar (in similar but briefer form) the proceedings in Bridges' division up to 1714 held in series C 5. These are entries from one of the volumes (917):

Bundle/no	Plaintiff	Defendant	Date	Place or subject	County
95/51	Hugh Tucker	Walter, Simon & William Heywood	1690	Winkleigh	Devon
1004/37	Richard Teape	Thomas Payne et al.	1692	Honiton; "the Rose and Crown"	Devon
630/99	Elizabeth Skevington	Godfrey Impey	1667	Personal estate of William Skevington	Bedford

16	Robert Incledene, of Braunton, gentleman, son of John Incledene.	The same	Detention of a silver cup and cover pledged to the said Richard for a debt since paid by Alice, late the wife and executrix of the said John; custom of Braunton town that the son and heir of all persons dwelling in the said town shall have the best jewel that his father had, pleaded in support.	Devon
18	Richard Jakson, of Richmond, scholar.	Miles Seggewyke, John Atkynson, and Richard Bukkyll, administrators of the goods of William Flesshor, clerk.	Proceeds of goods given in trust for complainant when in his nonage by Alice Jacson, widow, to the said William and by him sold. (Inventory with prices annexed.)	York
21	Roger James	Marion Kelway	Detention of deeds relating to messuages and land in the borough of Helston.	[Cornwall]
22	John, son of Walter, son of John Jervys, and cousin and heir of Nicholas Jervys.	Antony, abbot of Hailes	Detention of deeds relating to messuages and land in Winchcombe.	Gloucester
23	William Jakson, citizen and cooper of London, cousin and heir of Lionel, son and heir of Thomas Pirolas, alias Langton.	Christopher Danby, esquire.	Detention of deeds relating to messuages and land in Langton-on-Swale and Scruton in Richmondshire, complainant being son of Agnes, daughter of Robert, son of Margaret, sister of the said Thomas.	York
25	Alice Judde, of St. Clement Danes.	The official of the archdeacon of Surrey.	Breach of promise to marry, against William Plymmoth, of St. Olave's, Southwark, who, notwithstanding previous proceedings herein by his proctor, has obtained prohibitions in Chancery, married one Agnes, and caused complainant to be arrested in an action of debt. Certiorari.	Surrey
26	Thomas Jakes and Elizabeth, his wife, late the wife of Thomas Frowyk, knight, chief justice of the Common Bench.	John Roper, John Pereson, clerk, and Thomas Godeyer, feoffees to uses.	Refusal to make estate of the manor of Finchley and messuages and land in Finchley and Hendon as willed by the said Frowyk.	Middlesex
29	Thomas Janyns, son and heir of Agnes Gardener.	Thomas Wattis and Agnes, his wife.	Detention of deeds relating to a messuage and land in Stretton-on-Dunsmore and Wolston.	Warwick
30	Perys Joye	Philip Dewcarugy and Elizabeth, his wife, administrators of the goods of James Fynche, of London, merchant.	Debt of the said James, for goods bought and money borrowed.	London
31	Margaret Jankyn and Nicholas William, executors of William Jankyn.	Robert Pendeyn, chaplain.	Detention of bonds, writings, and goods, late in the keeping of John Jankyn and others.	--
32	Thomas Jenyn, of London, skinner.	Harman John	Waste and dilapidations upon a messuage in Guildford, in which defendant and Margaret, his wife, have each a different estate, not executed.	Surrey
33	John Isbury, of Letcombe Regis, esquire.	Isabel, executrix and late the wife of John Williames, knight.	Debt of the said Sir John for money lent to him by complainant.	Berks
34	Robert, son and heir of Richard Jenkynson.	Thomas Haitfeld, of Owston.	Detention of deeds relating to a messuage and land in Loversall.	York

123. Calendar of the early Court of Chancery Proceedings in series C 1 at TNA, from PRO Lists & Indexes *volume XXIX*

An important new finding aid to the equity courts' records is the "Equity pleadings database". It is gradually being expanded and linked to the relevant series of records in the PROCAT online catalogue and so is searchable both on terminals at TNA and through the web site of TNA. The database is an index to some records of the Court of Chancery of the 16th to 19th centuries (and will in future also index records of the Courts of Exchequer, Star Chamber and Requests). The Chancery proceedings in series C 6 (Collins division) are the first to be indexed and appear in the database. The records catalogued so far (about 48,000 documents) from pieces C 6/1–419 concern about 30,000 cases between 1606 and 1714. They can be searched by personal name, place, subject or piece reference. The data used in the new index is from two sources. For pieces C 6/1–359, the data were taken from an existing index. This notes the names of the first plaintiff and first defendant (other parties are rarely indexed), the date, county and brief subject matter. The pleadings in pieces C 6/360–419 have been recently examined and so the index to those pieces records the names of all plaintiffs, defendants and most other people mentioned in the pleadings (and their occupation and residence if recorded in the documents), the subject of the dispute and any particular place noted (such as the location of property that was the subject of the dispute). For example, a search for Charnock brings up four results including the case of Charnock-v-Charnock in 1704 in C 6/397/103. Anne Charnock sued Mary Charnock in respect of a relative's will. The database entry is not perfect (it omits the name of the testator) but it does note that the pleadings also refer to William Charnock, Anthony Charnock and Vincent Charnock.

Other finding aids for Chancery proceedings are also being added to PROCAT. The *Lists & Indexes* volumes noted above for pleadings in C 1 (proceedings before 1558) have been added and so can be searched easily if many variations of surnames are used as keywords. The names of the first plaintiff and first defendant in the pleadings in series C 3, 5 and 9–13 can also be searched. The pleadings in C 4 are also being added (by spring 2003, there were entries for about 5,400 records out of about 19,000 in the series). As further documents are added to the Equity pleadings database and the entries on PROCAT are improved, the location of Chancery suits concerning ancestors is going to become much easier.

Some transcripts and abstracts of Chancery pleadings have been published by county record societies. Four volumes of the William Salt Archaelogical Society (909) contain abstracts of many bills of complaint and answers from the reign of Elizabeth relating to Staffordshire people or places. This is one of the shorter abstracts, of a bill of complaint dated 12 April 1559:

> Bundle 76. No. 92 To Sir Nicholas Bacon, knight [then Lord Keeper of the Great Seal, with all the powers of the Lord Chancellor]
>
> Showeth unto your lordship your orator [the plaintiff] William Garmeson of Southwark co. Surrey, ale brewer, that one William Barlowe the elder late of Norton co. Stafford made his will dated 3 August 1543, and left a third of his goods equally between the children of his son Hugh Barlowe. He made Alice his wife and one Richard Edge of Norton executors of his will. Alice Barlowe died, after whose death William Barlowe son of the said Hugh administered her goods. Your orator married Parnell Barlowe, one of the daughters of Hugh, who was entitled to a share of the goods of the late William Barlowe the elder. William Barlowe and Richard Edge offered instead a debt of £5 due from one Thomas Bradwall to William Barlowe the elder, but Thomas Bradwell asserts that the debt has already been paid.

The language is a little difficult to follow but, in brief, William Barlowe the elder (whose wife was named Alice) had a son named Hugh Barlowe. Hugh had children including William Barlowe and a daughter, Parnell, who married the petitioner (William Garmeson). Three generations of an early 16th-century family (predating most parish registers) are therefore revealed in one Chancery complaint.

The journal *The Ancestor* (# chapter 11 and appendix X) edited by O. Barron included abstracts of some Chancery proceedings from the reign of Charles I that were of particular interest to genealogists. Illustration 124 is an example of a page of these abstracts, from volume 2 of *The Ancestor* (July 1902). In one of those cases, there was also sufficient genealogical information to produce a pedigree of three generations.

Some cases ended after a plaintiff filed a bill of complaint (perhaps because a defendant did what the plaintiff required). In some cases the defendant filed an answer but the case did not proceed (perhaps because the plaintiff decided that further action was not worthwhile). In cases such as these (between 60 and 75 per cent of cases in the 17th and 18th centuries) no evidence was taken or submitted to the court. However, if your ancestor's case did proceed, useful information can be found in the surviving records of that evidence. Witnesses in Chancery cases gave depositions by answering the written interrogatories prepared by each party. These lists of questions are usually attached to the depositions. These are often lengthy documents, setting out the date and place of the depositions, before whom they were taken and, for each witness, the answers to those interrogatories that he or she was answering. An example is provided below.

Country depositions from 1558 to 1714 (over 1,800 bundles) are in series C 21 and 22. The names of the first plaintiff and first defendant in each action for which there are depositions (but not the deponents' names) are indexed on PROCAT. Country depositions since 1715 are filed with the pleadings. Town depositions from the 16th century up to 1853 (over 2,500 bundles) are in series C 24, although some 19th-century depositions are in J 17 or filed with pleadings. Illustration 125 is an extract from a deposition (in piece C 24/882) of my ancestor James Charnock, taken in 1663 in a case considered further below. Affidavits (from 1607 to 1875) are in series C 31 and there are registers of affidavits (that is, complete transcripts of originals) for 1615 to 1747 in C 41. Interrogatories from 1598 to 1852 are in C 25. There are a few unpublished indexes or alphabets to these records, described in Horwitz (938), and Gerhold (934) and summarised in appendix X. It is difficult to find evidence from a particular case in the unindexed records. For example, the affidavits in C 31 are in over 3,000 bundles, arranged chronologically until 1819. From 1820 they are arranged by year, then by each of the four annual legal terms, and only then alphabetically by action title (that is, by surname of the first plaintiff).

Masters in Chancery investigated many matters, for example the assessment of damages or disputes about the administration of trust or estate funds. They provided reports or certificates to the court, often attaching accounts or other documents (such as title deeds or wills). Masters' reports and certificates from 1562 to 1875 are in series C 38 and C 39, described in TNA legal records leaflet 39. There are alphabets of the plaintiffs' names, for each year, in series IND 1. These alphabets are listed at the start of the section for C 38 in the Standard set of lists (in the research enquiries room at TNA). For example, the alphabet for C 38/260–262 is IND 1/1967.

Exhibits and Masters' Documents include a wide variety of documents that the court considered during an action (or that Masters used in their investigations), including title deeds, wills, trust documents and marriage settlements. Most exhibits are in series C 103–116 and an index of the cases to which the records relate is attached to the C 103 series list and also

THE ANCESTOR

220

$B\frac{1}{16}$ Bill (12 July 1644) of John Bedwell of Feering, co. Essex, gent.
Answer (14 Oct. 1644) of John Byatt of Sawson, co. Cambridge, gent., and (10 Dec. 1644) of Nicholas Fox of Depden, gent.

> Concerning money matters. John Lyttlebury esq. is named as having married Elizabeth, widow and admix. of Isaac Sutton of London, gent.

$B\frac{1}{17}$ Bill (11 Feb. 1645) of Thomas Bowes of York, grocer.
Answer (   ) of William Trewman of Crake, co. York.

> Concerning a sum of 20*l.* which the compt. alleges to have been delivered by his mother Emott Bowes of York, widow, during her last sickness about six years since, to the defendant, for the setting up in business of the compt., who was then an apprentice. Francis Bowes was her exor., whose widow married one Mr. Musgrave.

$B\frac{1}{28}$ Bill (21 June 1645) of Thomas Browne of Rendham, co. Suffolk, exor. of his father William Browne of Rendham.
Answer (17 Oct. 1645) of William Hurryon the elder and Mary his wife and Mary Hurryon their daughter defendants with Robert Dynington and Elizabeth his wife and John Browne.

> Concerning the estate of William Browne deceased.

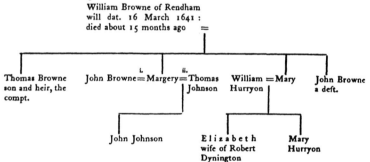

$B\frac{1}{29}$ Bill (25 April 1646) of John Burton of York, draper, and Elizabeth his wife, Beatrix Loftus, Frances Loftus and Mary Loftus (which three are minors and by their guardian James Shoreswood of York.
Answer (4 June 1646) of Henry Collinson and Anne his wife and Percival Levett of York.

> Concerning the alleged concealment of certain evidences by the defendants. The complainants Elizabeth, Beatrix, Frances and Mary are daughters of Edward Loftus of York, deceased, who died seised of a messuage in Fossegate in the city of York, leaving a will dated 2 Aug. 1643, whereof his widow, the defendant Anne, was extrix.

$B\frac{1}{30}$ Bill (27 Nov. 1632) of William Browne, citizen and cordwainer of London.
Answers (7 Dec. 1632) of William Drake and James Drake.

> Concerning the suit of William Drake late of Fincham in Stanley, gent., now deceased, against Charles Saltaston *alias* Saltonstall, for whom the compt. and Thomas Browne, citizen and clothworker, now deceased, became bail in Trinity term 6 Car. I. The defendants are sons and exors. of the said Drake.

124. A page of genealogical abstracts from proceedings of the Court of Chancery in volume 2 of The Ancestor *of July 1902*

searchable on PROCAT (but some of the descriptions are very brief). Exhibits from 1875 (but also many from earlier years) are in series J 90. An indexed calendar of these documents and the cases to which they relate has been published in volumes 197 and 261 of the List and Index Society. Masters' Documents are in series C 117–126, with alphabets in series IND 1. The finding aids are listed in appendix X of this book and Horwitz (938). Series C 101 includes Masters' accounts from about 1700 to about 1850, consisting of some 6,700 volumes of accounts (for example of land rentals, deceased's estates or trading accounts). Alphabets to the first plaintiff's name for each case are in IND 1.

Sacrament certificates for oaths (# chapter 23) sworn in the Court of Chancery from 1673 to 1778 are in series C 224. The oaths taken by lawyers practising in the court are in C 214 and 217. The court's registers of admission of lawyers, with affidavits of due execution of articles, are in C 216. TNA domestic records leaflet 36 describes these documents (and the finding aids) for Chancery and also for the other courts noted below.

C.A. Bernau prepared a card index to the names of over four million parties and witnesses in Chancery and other English court proceedings up to the 18th century. The Bernau index is on microfilm at the SoG and LDS family history centres. It indexes people in alphabetical order of surname and then Christian name (but the index cards are not always in strict alphabetical order). The index covers only a minority of Chancery records but it also covers selected cases in some other courts (considered below) for the following dates: the Court of Star Chamber (1485–1558), the Court of Requests (1485–1546 and 1558–1602) and the Court of Exchequer (1559–1695). Sharpe (952) is a guide to using Bernau's index, explaining the sources used by Bernau and the document references that the index provides. Useful articles on using the index (and finding TNA records to which it refers) appear in *Family Tree Magazine*: by G. Bedingfield (in September 1990) and by G. Lawton (December 1991 to February 1992). Bernau's index only covers certain series of Chancery records, listed in Sharpe (952). For example, Bernau indexed the parties' names in Chancery proceedings from 1714 to 1758 (series C 11), all the deponents of the country depositions from 1558 to 1649 (C 21) and all the deponents up to 1800 of town depositions (that is much of part of series C 24).

I searched Bernau's index for references for the family of Bulleid or Bullhead and found 15 entries for the surnames Bulhead, Bulhed, Bulled, Bulleid, Bullhead or Bullied. One example was a card for Agnes Bullied, involved in a case in 1765. A second example concerned John Bullhead of Marley (or Mariansleigh) in Devon. The cards noted these references:

BULLEID, Agnes   1765   C 12   942/4

BULLHEAD, John of Marley, Devon, yeoman   Aged 27
Eliz to Chas I. 1627. Group 7. Chan Depts.   Bundle P 32 Suit 6

The card for Agnes Bulleid referred to Chancery proceedings in series C 12 (for 1758 to 1800). The piece number was 942/4, so I could then turn to the documents. The card for John Bullhead shows that Bernau's index does not always give a reference that allows you to turn directly to TNA records. It indicates that John provided a deposition in 1627, but you need to refer to Sharpe (952) or the articles by Bedingfield and Lawton in order to link Bernau's references (in this example Chancery Depositions Elizabeth to Charles I) to the series at TNA (this is a country deposition in C 21).

Many cards in Bernau's index refer to "correspondence" and provide a file and page number. These are references to Bernau's genealogical research extracts and pedigrees, prepared during his research, copies of which are on microfilm at the SoG. Bernau also produced 426 volumes of notebooks (with over 100,000 entries) listing the parties and summarising the disputes in the Chancery proceedings from 1714 to 1758 in C 11. Bernau's index refers to these notebooks by stating "Chancery proceedings" and noting a bundle and suit number. The notebooks are on microfilm at the SoG and LDS family history centres. Three articles by G. Lawton in *Family Tree Magazine* (December 1993 to February 1994) describe the notebooks in detail and explain how to link the entries to the court's records. A typical entry describes a case in 1725 as follows (with abbreviations expanded):

Reference 887/25. 1725.
[Plaintiffs] Nicholas Gennys, infant (grandson of Nicholas Gennys) by Mary his mother and also Mary Gennys versus [defendants] Arthur Robinson, clerk; James Yonge and George Ridout, gent; executors in trust of will of Nicholas Gennys, late of Plymouth, grocer, deceased. Depositions taken at Plymouth, Devon.

There are some other important indexes. The most useful Chancery cases are usually those concerning disputes over deceaseds' estates. In addition to the finding aids noted above, there are indexes to disputed estate cases in the Chancery proceedings in series C 5–8 and in C 10, from about 1649 (but sometimes earlier) up to 1714. TNA and the SoG hold an index to the names of testators in about half the bundles in series C 6. P. Coldham has prepared indexes (copies are at TNA and the SoG) to disputed estate cases in C 5, 7, 8 and 10. Entries give the name of the testator (or intestate), his residence, the case title, the year and piece number. A typical entry, from the index to C 8 by Coldham (928), is:

Harris, Philip. Bratton Clovelly, Devon. Turner-v-Horwell, 1702. 598/19

Horwitz & Moreton (940) is another useful finding-aid. It is an indexed calendar of almost 1,000 sample suits in Chancery from 1627, 1685, 1735 and 1785. The work calendars the pleadings but also contains many references, for those suits, to the piece numbers of relevant documents in the series of decrees, depositions, affidavits and Masters' reports.

The importance of Chancery records can be illustrated by three examples: two 18th-century cases in which my ancestor Nicholas Bulleid of Winkleigh (a carpenter) and his brother John Bulleid (a butcher) gave evidence, and a case of 1662 in which my ancestor James Charnock of Eversholt in Bedfordshire was a defendant. Between 1717 and 1720 there was litigation in Chancery over the estate of John Metherell, a farmer of Winkleigh. His daughter Susanna (and her husband William Heywood) sued Samuel Hockaday and Christopher Sheere, who were alleged to have enriched themselves from Metherell's estate (by taking his livestock or collecting rents on property for themselves). Commissioners took depositions in Devon in 1717 and 1720. About 50 people, mostly from Winkleigh, gave evidence about John Metherell's property and family. John Bulleid gave evidence at the Globe Inn in Great Torrington on 1 May, 1717. The plaintiffs' twelfth interrogatory and John's evidence were, in brief:

Were any of the goods of John Metherell sold and for what price, and were such goods sold at a full and fair value or undersold and by and to whom and who received (money) for the same? Did the defendants Hockaday and Sheere take or keep any of the said goods for their own use; if yes, what were the goods and their value?

John Bulleid of Winkleigh, butcher, aged 50 years or thereabouts . . . saith that he was at the survey (with defendant Hockaday) held after the death of John Metherell and that this deponent offered Hockaday six pounds for a dunn mare which was John Metherell's at the time of his death, but Hockaday would not sell the same but kept it, this deponent having seen the said mare in Hockaday's custody several times since . . . and this deponent saith that Hockaday kept a yoke of oxen which were John Metherell's and would not sell them in the survey, which oxen were worth nine pounds and ten shillings in this deponent's judgment, for that is what [he] would have given for them.

Winkleigh residents were also involved in Chancery litigation, between 1726 and 1734, over the estate of Thomas Luxton of Winkleigh who died in 1725/6 (and over two or three wills that he made). There is so much documentation that I have only reviewed a small part of it, but it is a goldmine for descendants of the Luxton family. The main parties were Scipio Luxton, Judith Luxton, Thomas Luxton (the younger), John Stevens (the younger) and Moses Fitch. The depositions dealt with the estate of Thomas Luxton (the elder), but also with the Luxton family (and its property) back to "Old Scipio Luxton" who died in the 17th century. My ancestor Nicholas Bulleid (a carpenter) and his brother John (the butcher noted above) gave evidence. Nicholas told how he helped the defendant Thomas Luxton (the younger) cut down trees from property that Thomas had claimed was his own (but which apparently belonged to the estate of the deceased Thomas). John Bulleid gave evidence that he had rented a house called Chittlehampton in Winkleigh since 1717 from John Stevens the elder. Stevens had been indebted to Thomas Luxton (the deceased) so that Chittlehampton was mortgaged by Stevens to Luxton to secure the debt and John Bulleid had to pay £20 of the annual rent directly to Luxton. The plaintiff Scipio Luxton claimed that Thomas Luxton had, at his death, still been owed money by Stevens and that Luxton's mortgage on Chittlehampton continued in force. However, John Bulleid also stated that Stevens had repaid the debt, that Luxton had returned the property deeds to Stevens and that a deed of release had been executed to confirm the discharge of the mortgage. This is a good example of how Chancery suits can include important information about the witnesses (in this case the residence and rent of John Bulleid) as well as about the parties.

The third example concerns my ancestor James Charnock of Eversholt, who was a son of Robert Charnock and his wife Alice Audley. A complaint and three answers of 1662 are in Chancery proceedings in series C 8 (Mitford division). The complaint was by John Audley, son and heir of Thomas Audley deceased (of Husborne Crawley in Bedfordshire), grandchild of William and Tabitha Audley. John Audley complained that some land in Husborne Crawley (that had been owned by his grandfather William) ought to have descended to him. However, John had been a minor and his guardian (James Charnock) had, on his behalf but allegedly without his authority, sold or mortgaged the premises to Thomas Seabrooke and Abraham Grissell. The answers of Seabrooke and Grissell admitted that the property had been sold to them by James Charnock, but alleged that John Audley consented to the sale. James Charnock alleged that he (as John's guardian) had quite properly sold the property and that the money was received on John's behalf. The Husborne Crawley parish registers included many entries for the Audley family, including an Alice Audley, baptised in 1582/3, who was the sister of William Audley (the grandfather of John Audley). This Alice was probably the mother of James Charnock, who would therefore have been a cousin (as well as guardian) of the plaintiff John Audley. I turned to the series of Chancery evidence, to see if any further records (such as depositions) had survived for this case, perhaps confirming the relationship. I have not yet found any such evidence, but I did find records of a further case brought in 1663 by John Audley against the widow and daughter of Abraham Grissell. The depositions, in series C 24, included one from James Charnock (an extract is shown in illustration 125), and gave further details about the case (but sadly no further information on the relationship of Audley and Charnock).

The Court of Chancery also had a common law jurisdiction. This arose in the 13th century from the practice of lawyers who worked in Chancery (the government department) dealing with claims arising from administrative acts of Chancery officials or disputes between co-owners over the partition of land. In these actions the Chancellor was bound to follow the common law and call in common-law judges to assist him or remit the dispute to the Court of King's Bench. Pleadings are in series C 43–44 (listed in List and Index Society volume 67) and C 206. Orders are in series C 221–222.

As a final point concerning Chancery records, much information can be obtained for a study of local history or one-place genealogy. Gerhold (934) found 79 Chancery suits between 1580 and 1735 relating to the parish of Putney and its residents. Another researcher found 74 Chancery suits up to 1714 concerning the village of Earls Colne. The records of the suits concerning the Luxton and Metherell families, noted above, contain an enormous amount of information about local families and the affairs of Winkleigh. Therefore, anyone researching the history of a particular town or village will find much useful information in Chancery records.

King's Council

After 1066 justice was dispensed by the King's Council (Curia Regis) sitting as a court. The Curia Regis Rolls (in Latin), describing the proceedings of the court and naming the parties and the subject-matter of the dispute, survive for the late 12th and 13th centuries at TNA (in series KB 26) and are described in the *PRO Guide* (228). Indexed transcripts (but not translations) for some years have been published, the volumes being listed by Mullins (260), such as that for 1213–15 by HMSO (911). From the 12th century cases were gradually passed to courts that developed from the Council, such as the Exchequer Court, the Court of Common Pleas and the Court of King's Bench (to which we now turn) and the King's Council developed into the Privy Council (considered below).

The Court of Exchequer

The King's Exchequer was a government department that supervised the collection of tax. It also developed its own court to deal with cases concerning tax or other Crown revenues and this Court of Exchequer gradually took jurisdiction over some disputes between individuals. For example, if John Clark was owed money by James Smith (but was also indebted to the Crown), Clark could sue Smith in the Exchequer Court because he was less able to satisfy the Crown because of the debt owed to him by Smith. By legal fictions it soon became possible for almost anyone to start actions in the Exchequer Court. In addition to this common law jurisdiction, the court began taking jurisdiction in the 1640s over matters of equity, including wills, trusts, mortgages, bonds, tithes and disputes over title to land, and there were about 450 to 650 equity bills of complaint each year in the 17th and 18th centuries. In 1841 the court's equity business

125. *Extract from a deposition, in January 1663, of James Charnock in the Court of Chancery case of John Audley v. Elizabeth Grissell (TNA, C 24/882)*

was transferred to the Court of Chancery. In 1875 the Exchequer Court became the Exchequer Division of the High Court of Justice (discussed below), which was amalgamated in 1880 into the Chancery and Queen's Bench Divisions.

The records of the Court of Exchequer are at TNA. Few survive from before 1558, but many records survive from that year. Records of common law cases are described in the *PRO Guide* (228). For example, bills and writs (sometimes called informations) from the 14th to 19th centuries are in series E 5, order books from the 16th to 19th centuries are in E 12, plea rolls of 1325–1875 are in E 13, docket books of judgments of 1603–1839 are in E 46 (with calendars in E 48 and IND 1) and 19th-century affidavits and depositions are in E 1 and 20. Sacrament certificates filed at court from 1700 to 1827 in support of oaths of allegiance are in E 196.

The procedure and records (and the few finding aids) in equity cases are described in TNA legal records leaflet 19, Horwitz (939), Bryson (925) and Gerhold (934). Most of the records are in English and there are indexes to plaintiffs' surnames. There are three main categories of records: pleadings, evidence, and court opinions or decisions.

The pleadings (principally bills and answers) are filed by monarch's reign, then by county (for example where the disputed land was located) in series E 112 (and E 111 includes bills and answers from various courts, including the Exchequer). Each bill was entered in a bill book (noting all the parties' full names). The 34 bill books covering 1558 to 1841 in pieces IND 1/16820–53 (in Latin until 1733), also arranged by monarch's reign, then county, therefore form indexes to the parties to the bills. Entries were given a suit number (which you need in order to find a bill). If a defendant appeared at court to answer a complaint, this was noted in appearance books, which are in series E 107. These date from 1588 but there are many gaps (such as 1600–32, 1675–1739 and 1756–73). Pleadings that followed answers, called replications and rejoinders are in series E 193 (some are also filed with bills and answers in E 112). Exhibits produced to the court are in series E 140, 214 and 219 or (for cases not complete in 1841 and so transferred to Chancery) in Chancery records (series C 106 and 121).

A party could serve interrogatories for the other party (or witnesses) to answer by depositions taken at Westminster (by the court's judges, known as the Barons of the Exchequer or by their officers, known as examiners) or in the country (by Commissioners appointed by the court). Depositions include a deponent's name, address, age and occupation. They are in series E 133 (Barons' depositions), E 134 (Commissioners' depositions) or E 178 (Special commissions) and date from the 16th to 19th centuries. TNA legal records leaflet 19 lists the finding-aids and indexes for these depositions (and many deponents' names are included in Bernau's index). For example, the 38th to 42nd annual reports of the Deputy Keeper of Public Records (copies are at TNA and the SoG) include calendars of Exchequer actions in which depositions were taken by commission from 1558 to 1760. There are similar (manuscript) calendars at TNA for 1760 to 1841. The calendars of the cases (not the deponents' names) for which there are country depositions in E 134 for 1558–1772 are included in PROCAT. The names of the parties in the cases for which there are depositions in E 133 from 1558 to 1841 are also in PROCAT so that at least the names of the parties to these actions (if not the deponents' names) are now easily searched. Bernau's index remains the best source in which to find a deponent's name.

Minute books containing brief entries for the court's orders during proceedings of 1616–1890 are in 163 volumes in series E 161 (most original orders can also be found in full in series E 131 or in entry books in E 125, 127 and 128). If no settlement was reached, cases proceeded to a trial before all four of the court's judges, the Barons of the Exchequer (trials from 1817 were heard by just one Baron). The court's judgments (decrees) after trial from 1595 to 1841 are briefly set out, in chronological order, in 89 volumes or bundles in series E 162 (or in full in E 128 and 130) and were also copied into entry books in E 126. Records of lawyers practising in the court are in series E 3, 4, 109 and 200.

The importance to family historians of Court of Exchequer equity records can be seen from one sample case identified by Horwitz (939). In 1685, a widow Elianor Biss of Wells in Somerset sued for payment of a bond issued to her late husband, George Biss, by his late brother Edward Biss of Batcombe, Somerset. Elianor sued her nephew James Biss (son of Edward) and a clergyman who was holding the original bond on behalf of the family. The documents located by Horwitz included the bill of complaint, the defendants' answers, depositions from local witnesses (as to the issue of the bond and whether payment had been made) and a court decree setting out the compromise agreed by the parties.

Bernau's index includes a reference to John Bulhead (a common early spelling of Bulleid) as a deponent (the deposition being taken by Commissioners) in an Exchequer case of "12 George II, Easter term no. 10". The calendar for the reign of George II, with actions in order of suit number, is in the 42nd annual report of the Deputy Keeper (916). This does not summarise the depositions, but states where and when they were taken, the names of the parties (and the subject matter) of the action. In fact, the calendar included three entries for this case (depositions being taken at Bideford on three occasions). Illustration 126 is part of the calendar that includes one of the other entries for this case (with reference 8 George II, Trinity term no. 2) as well as three other cases in which depositions were taken at Oxford, Stafford and Northampton. John Bulhead's deposition in 1739 did not in fact really help my research into the Bulleid family but the case and depositions would have been of great assistance to anyone researching the Smith or Marks families. The case concerned the value of the estate of the late John Smith of Bideford in Devon, a tobacco merchant who had traded with Virginia in America. The plaintiffs were Hannah and Mary Smith and the defendants were Sarah Marks, John Marks and John Power. Further examples of entries from the calendars include:

Piece E 178/657. Year 20 Eliz. County Devon. Subject of dispute. Possessions of John Bonivante, traitor, lately hanged, drawn and quartered at Exeter.

Depositions E 134/17 Jas.I/Michaelmas 38
Devon, Exeter (22 Sept). Griffith Rice-v-Alicia Honeywill widow and Mary Symons. Right and title to land and goods of John Honeywill, of Brampford Speke (Devon), late husband of the first defendant, convicted of felony, and (title to) the lands of William Symons and Emmyne, his wife (parents of the defendants) in Brampford Speke.

Webb (955) is a further valuable index, listing 293 Surrey cases in the Court of Exchequer from 1561 to 1835, the parties, deponents (often with a person's age, parish and occupation) and the subject of the dispute.

Court of Common Pleas
This court evolved from the King's Council in the late 12th century. Originally it had almost unlimited jurisdiction but this was gradually restricted to common law disputes (typically concerning debts or land). In 1875 the court became the Common Pleas Division of the High

No. 1.—Exchequer : Depositions by Commission.—Calendar. George 2.—*continued*.

County, &c.	Date.	Term.	No.	Plaintiffs.	Defendants.	SUBJECT-MATTER.
Devon	8 Geo. 2. C. 7 May, 7 Geo. 2. I. D. 19 June, 8 Geo. 2. 1734, at Bideford (pursuant to an order made in the Court of Exchequer, 9 Nov. 1732).	Trin.	2	Thomas Smith, merchant.	Sarah Marks, widow, John Marks, Geo. Strange, John Power, Saml. Smith, Mary Smith, Hannah Smith, and the Attorney-General.	Value and disposition, &c., of the real and personal estate of John Smith, late of Bideford (Devon), merchant, and touching money alleged to be due upon bonds given by him to the custom house at Bideford, for duties payable on tobacco or other duties, &c., &c. [A grant or lease from the Crown of the manor of Aleshatt, and a tenement in Bideford called Stanmeridge, lately belonging to said John Smith are mentioned.] [*See also* 10 Geo. 2, East., Nos. 4 and 7; 12 Geo. 2, East., No. 10.]
London; Oxford.	8 Geo. 2. C. 23 Oct. I. D., the examination of the defendant James Jennings, Esq., taken before Charles Taylor, Deputy Remembrancer of the Court of Exchequer (in execution of a decree of said Court made 20 June 1734), on 15 Nov. 1734.	Mich.	1	Joseph Cane, clerk, vicar of Shiplake.	James Jennings, Esq., and others.	Vicarage and parish of Shiplake (Oxford), and two closes of land in said parish, called Thos. Towers's Close and Robt. Bunce's Close, &c., &c. Tithes. [*See also* 7 Geo. 2, East., No. 2.]
Stafford	8 Geo. 2. C. 11 July. I. D. 30 Aug. 1734, at Mudeley. The forms of the oaths to be taken by the Commissioners and their clerk.	Mich.	2	Sir Edwl. Egerton, Bart. (an infant), by Edmond Holme, clerk, his next friend.	John Crew, Esq.	Rectory and parish of Mudeley *alias* Mawdley, and a capital messuage, &c., called Rhinehill Hall, lately belonging to Sir John Egerton, Bart., and since to Holland Egerton, eldest son of said Sir John and father of plaintiff, &c. Tithes.
Northampton.	8 Geo. 2. C. 3 July, I. D. 22 Oct. 1734, at Northampton. The forms of the oaths to be taken by the Commissioners, and their clerk. First to issue a Commission to examine witnesses in this cause.	Mich.	3	James Underhill	Leland Sprig, Francis Sprig.	Vicarage, prebend, and parish of Bricklesworth *alias* Bricklesworth (Northampton), and a farm and lands in said parish, called Woolfitch Farm. Tithes. [The names and possessions of Dame Susanna D'Anvers, wife of Sir John D'Anvers, Bart., Richard Bringhurst, Sir Wm. Keyt, Bart., Justinian Isham, Esq., Francis Raynsford, and Thos. Bringhurst are mentioned.]

126. *Extract from the calendar of proceedings in the Court of Exchequer, involving depositions taken by commission, in the appendix to the 42nd report of the Deputy Keeper of Public Records*

Court of Justice and it was merged into the Queen's Bench Division in 1880. Records dating from 1194 are at TNA with code CP and described in the *PRO Guide* (228). Early plea rolls of the court, noting the progress of actions, are included in the Curia Regis Rolls noted above. Plea rolls from 1272 to 1874, including most of the court's judgments, are in series CP 40 to which the prothonotaries' (clerks') docket rolls of 1509–1859 in CP 60 act as an index. Other surviving records include entry books of judgments of 1859–74 in CP 64 and affidavits from 1704 to 1875 (in CP 3). The records of property disputes relate not only to true actions for the recovery of property (and include many title deeds), but also fictitious actions (for fines or recoveries), which were designed to record formally a landowner's title to property (# chapter 27). There are also rolls of oaths of Catholics, Quakers and clergy in series CP 10 and 37. Series CP 5, 8, 9, 11 and 69–72 contain records of attorneys practising in the court.

Court of King's Bench

From the 12th century this court (named the Court of Queen's Bench when a queen was monarch) dealt with cases affecting either the monarch in person or the King's Peace. This was extended to most civil (and many criminal) matters, including cases of contract, fraud, abuse of power by public officials and writs of habeus corpus (requesting a man's freedom from allegedly illegal detention). The court's business was divided into two: the Crown side and Plea side. The Crown side dealt with criminal cases, for example claims that a lower court had erred in a conviction. The Plea side dealt with civil actions. The court became the Queen's Bench Division of the High Court of Justice in 1875.

The records (generally in Latin up to 1732) are at TNA. Records of the Crown side are described in the *PRO Guide* (228) and TNA legal records leaflet 34. There are some indexes, noted in the leaflet, such as an index in series IND 1 to London and Middlesex defendants (1673–1845) and provincial defendants (1638–1704 and 1765–1843). There are files of indictments from the 17th century (giving the substance of the allegation against the defendant) in series KB 10–12. Writs of habeus corpus, but also writs of *mandamus* (for example to compel inferior courts to hold hearings) and of *certiorari* (to consider difficult points of law from lower courts) are in writ files in KB 16 and 145. Entries noting the progress of cases from the 14th to 19th centuries are on controlment rolls such as those in KB 29. Depositions and affidavits since the late 17th century are in series KB 1 and 2. Exhibits dating from 1836–86 are in KB 6. Court orders since 1589 are in rule books in KB 21, with drafts in KB 36.

Records of the court's Plea side are described in Colwell (242) and the *PRO Guide* (228). Writs are in series KB 136–138 and some affidavits survive in KB 101. Entries about cases also appear on the Coram Rege rolls in KB 27 (from the 13th century up to 1702) and on the plea rolls in KB 122 (for 1702–1875). Series KB 22 includes sacrament certificates presented in support of oaths of allegiance from about 1728 to 1828. Records of oaths are in KB 24 and 113 and records of lawyers practising in the court are in KB 105–107 and 170–172. It is unfortunate that so few records of this important court have been indexed or published. However, the Selden Society has published some volumes, listed in Mullins (260), of transcripts of lawyers' reports of certain cases heard by the court in medieval times.

Court of Requests

This court (intended particularly for poor litigants or for those cases below the £10 threshold in Chancery) sat from about 1493 to 1642 and could grant equitable remedies. It dealt with civil disputes over land or money, but also some criminal and Admiralty cases. Leadam (945) includes a history of the court and its procedure (similar to that in Chancery), together with extracts of documents from selected cases. The court's records are at TNA in series REQ 1 to 4, described in TNA legal records leaflet 4, including bills, answers, depositions, affidavits and exhibits. There are *Lists & Indexes* calendars, similar to those for Chancery proceedings, and manuscript calendars to the parties to the actions in the pleadings up to 1603 (and about half of those of 1603–25). Webb (957) is an index to the parties in cases relating to Surrey, also listing the names, ages, occupations and place of residence of the deponents in those cases. I located 13 cases in this court, from the calendars at TNA that involved members of the Charnock family. Although I have not yet had the opportunity to look at the original pleadings, the value of these records to genealogists is illustrated by just one entry (from the calendar of pleadings up to 1603 in REQ 2):

Bundle/item	xc 60
Plaintiff	Richard Charnock
Defendant	Thomas Emerye
County	Bedford
Matter	Land in Arlesey to be settled on defendant's daughter on her marriage to plaintiff

Court of Exchequer Chamber

From the 14th century to 1875 this name was used by four different courts that heard appeals from the common law courts. Minute books of decrees and orders of the Court of Exchequer Chamber are in series E 161 and 162 at TNA and some records of appeals from the Court of King's Bench are in KB 122 and 139. Hemmant (937) is a study of the jurisdiction and procedure of the court from 1377 to 1461 with transcripts of reports (prepared by lawyers of the period and held in the British Library and Lincoln's Inn Library) of 37 cases that the court heard in those years.

Court of Star Chamber

The King's Council had a judicial function throughout the medieval period, but Henry VII established separate judicial meetings (or informal committees) of councillors from about 1487, to deal with cases that required the monarch's intervention. The council members sitting in this capacity were named the Court of Star Chamber. Guy (936) is a history of the court and its procedure up to 1603 (and of its surviving records up to 1558). The court was abolished in 1641.

The court originally dealt with civil or criminal actions but from about 1560 it dealt almost exclusively with criminal cases, including those involving allegations of official corruption, abuse of legal procedure, alleged perjury, conspiracy, forgery, fraud, trespass, assault or riot. Most civil cases concerned possession of land (perhaps alleging an armed attack upon the occupier) and many were linked to existing litigation in the common law courts. Star Chamber proceedings were seen as a useful method of bringing pressure on defendants, because they usually had to attend before the Council in person to answer a complaint and this involved travel to London and much expense. Criminal cases were usually commenced by an information which was laid by the Attorney General. A defendant would be interrogated under oath by court officials and there was no jury. Witness evidence was given by affidavit so that a defendant could not examine the deponents. If the defendant was convicted, the court could impose a fine, imprisonment or corporal punishment (such as public floggings, branding or cropping of ears).

Most of the court's surviving records, with code STAC at TNA, are in English. Series STAC 1–4 contain records of cases from the reigns of Henry VII, Henry VIII, Edward VI and Mary respectively. Those in STAC 5–7 concern cases from the reign of Elizabeth and STAC 8–9 hold records of cases from the reigns of James I and Charles I. Series STAC 10 contains various records of 1485 to 1641. The surviving records up to 1558 (in STAC 1–4 and part of STAC 10) are mainly pleadings, depositions, statements of defendants or answers to interrogatories and are reviewed in detail by Guy (936). They survive for less than half of the court's cases in this period. The parties' names are listed in *Lists & Indexes* volumes or in manuscript and typescript indexes at TNA (listed in TNA legal records leaflet 3) and most of these can be searched on PROCAT. The depositions usually include the witnesses' ages and residence. The court's final orders and decrees have not survived, but there are some drafts and copies. Series E 159 contains records of fines paid, from 1596 to 1641, by those convicted by the court. Guy (936) also reviews some records relating to the court that are held at the British Library and the Huntington Library in California.

Some records of this court have been published. Leadam (946) contains indexed transcripts of the surviving records of 68 cases heard by the court from 1477 to 1544. Abstracts of pleadings (and some related documents) for cases relating to Staffordshire people from the reigns of Henry VII, Henry VIII and Edward VI were published in three volumes of the William Salt Archaelogical Society (910). One of those abstracts is this complaint of 1531:

Olcote v. Drayton, Warham, etc
To the King our sovereign Lord . . . Your orators Richard Olcote of Awdeley, co. Stafford, yeoman and Richard Olcote his son. Whereas the said Richard Olcote the father was seised of one cottage and 38 acres of land in the town of Talke, co. Stafford, held [from] Lord Audeley as of his manor of Audeley and about 7 years past granted the same to [Richard Olcote his son] . . . paying therefor yearly to the said Richard his father 40s. Now 18th November last Philip Draykot co. Stafford esquire, John Weldon of Southampton, gentleman, Henry Warham of Byldeways, co. Salop, yeoman, with William Warham, Richard Warham, Thomas Brykkys the elder and Thomas Brykkys of Talke the younger, with others, riotously assembled at Talke, broke [into] the premises of your orator and expelled out of the same . . . Ellen, wife of Richard Olcote the younger and [their] servants and took them to the castle of Heyley . . .

In answer, Henry and William Warham denied riot. They claimed that their family had held the land for three generations, that Richard Olcote the elder had wrongfully obtained possession of the land and that Lord Audeley, the lord of the manor, had directed his steward and bailiffs to expel the Olecote family from the land. In a replication, the Olcotes claimed that the land had been held by two previous generations of their family: John Olcote (father of Richard Olcote the elder) and his father Henry before him. This Star Chamber suit of 1531 thus reveals four generations of the Olecotes, a family of farmers.

Palatinate Courts of Chester, Durham and Lancaster
From medieval times the counties of Cheshire, Durham and Lancashire (with adjacent land of other counties) had separate administrations from the rest of England. They were known as the

Palatinates of Chester, Durham and Lancaster and had their own councils, courts and other administrative bodies. Each palatinate had common law, equity and criminal courts. The Chancery Courts of Durham and Lancaster existed from the 15th century until 1971 and the equity court of Chester, known as the Exchequer Court, existed from the 15th century until 1830. The palatinates and their records are described in the *PRO Guide* (228) and the *Current Guide* (234). For example, bills, answers and depositions from the Chancery Court of Lancaster from the 15th to 19th centuries are at TNA in series PL 6, 7 and 10. Series PL 11 contains registers of the court's decrees and orders (1524–1848), PL 9 contains affidavits (1610–1836) and PL 12 contains exhibits (1653–1864). Depositions in common law cases (1663–1867) are in PL 27. Series CHES 13 and 14 contain decrees, orders and entry books of the Exchequer Court of Chester from the 16th to 19th centuries. Pleadings are in CHES 15–16 and exhibits and depositions are in CHES 11–12. Decrees and orders of the Chancery Court of Durham for 1613 to 1958 are in series DURH 4 and 5, affidavits (1657–1812) are in DURH 1, pleadings (1576–1840) are in DURH 2 and exhibits are in DURH 21. Records of the lawyers practising in the Palatinate courts and records of oaths taken before the courts are in series CHES 35–36, PL 23 and DURH 3 and 9. A few records of the Durham courts are in other archives, such as the University of Durham.

Court of the Duchy of Lancaster
The Duchy of Lancaster has been held by the monarch or a close relative since medieval times. The Duchy's landholdings included much of Lancashire and vast estates in most other counties. A court named the Duchy Chamber of Lancaster sat at Westminster and had equitable jurisdiction over property held by the Duchy. TNA holds many records of the court, from the 13th to 19th centuries, with code DL. For example, there are entry books of decrees and orders (1474–1872) in series DL 5, pleadings (1485–1853) in DL 1, 3 and 49, affidavits and exhibits (1502–1857) in DL 9 and 49 and depositions (1500–1818) in DL 3 and 4. Three volumes, published by the Record Commissioners from 1823 to 1834, include calendars to pleadings (and some depositions) from the Duchy Chamber from 1485 to 1603.

Court of Wards and Liveries
In medieval times all land was held from a monarch by tenants-in-chief in exchange for military or other services (later commuted to money payments). By the 16th century these obligations had been substantially reduced and the most important were the king's rights over minors who were the heirs of deceased tenants-in-chief. The king had custody of such heirs, the right to arrange their marriages, and the right to the profits from their estates during the minority. The king had similar rights over lunatics' estates. The Court of Wards and Liveries was established by Henry VIII in 1541 to supervise these estates. The court was abolished in 1660. Its history and procedure are described in Bell (920). The court's records cover 1541–1650, are at TNA (with code WARD) and are listed in Colwell (242) and List and Index Society volume 18. They include title deeds, inquisitions post mortem (# chapter 27), accounts, surveys, leases and valuations of estates, but also records of court proceedings concerning wards or their lands (in WARD 9 and 13–15).

High Court of Admiralty
The High Court of Admiralty was established in the 14th century. Its jurisdiction extended to most maritime disputes such as piracy, cargo, ship charters, collisions and prize money for the

capture of enemy ships. In 1875 the court became part of the Probate, Divorce and Admiralty Division of the High Court of Justice (considered below) and later part of the Queen's Bench Division. Until 1859 only civil lawyers (advocates and proctors) could act in the court. From 1859 solicitors and barristers were also allowed to practise there.

The records of the Admiralty Court include the files of most cases from the 17th to mid-20th centuries (and some from the 16th century) and mention many merchant seamen. Prize cases were heard in distinct Prize Courts from the late 17th century. A ship had to be confirmed as a prize by the court before it could be sold and prize money paid. Criminal cases in the Admiralty Court concerned matters such as piracy or murder and were heard from the 17th century at Admiralty Sessions at the Old Bailey. Criminal jurisdiction was transferred in 1834 to the Central Criminal Court (# chapter 25). Instance cases were civil disputes concerning matters such as cargo, collisions, salvage or seamen's wage claims. Appeals from instance cases were heard, from 1535 to 1833, by the High Court of Delegates (see below). Appeals from prize cases were heard by a Commission of Appeals in Prize (also known as the High Court of Appeal for Prizes). In 1833 this body and the High Court of Delegates were abolished and appeals were then heard by the Privy Council's Judicial Committee or, from 1876, by the Court of Appeal (both considered below). Vice-Admiralty courts were also established from the 17th century in some English maritime counties and colonies, to deal with admiralty cases. From the 19th century some admiralty cases were also heard in county courts or by Justices of the Peace. Appeals from these courts lay to the Court of Admiralty and later to the Probate, Divorce and Admiralty Division of the High Court, or (for cases abroad) to the Judicial Committee of the Privy Council.

The Admiralty Court's records (including those since it has formed part of the High Court) are at TNA (with code HCA) and described in Watts & Watts (747), the *PRO Guide* (228) and the *Current Guide* (234). Series HCA 3, 5, 6 and 7 contain act books or registers that provide brief summaries of the court's Instance cases from 1524 to 1864. From 1786 each volume has an index to ships' names. The original files of instance cases from 1629 to 1943, with some from as early as 1519 (including pleadings, depositions, affidavits and exhibits), are in series HCA 13, 15–20, 23, 24 and 27. Indexes to the ships' names from many cases since 1772 (invaluable if you know the name of an ancestor's ship) are in HCA 56. Cases about prizes are principally in series HCA 8–11 and 30–32, with records of prize appeals in HCA 41, 42 and 48. Records of criminal cases from 1535 to 1834 (indexed by persons' and ships' names) are in HCA 1. The records of some Vice-Admiralty courts from the 17th to 19th centuries, for example for the Cape of Good Hope (1795–1805) and for Lancashire and Cheshire (1636–39), are in HCA 49. Very few Admiralty Court records have been published, but abstracts of Admiralty examinations for 1637 to 1638 (from HCA 13) are contained in Shilton & Holworthy (741) of which the following is an extract:

John Wardell and others v. John Marston

23 June 1637 witness Dorothy Goodladd of Leigh, Essex, widow, aged 22 [says] that, on 23 October 1635, John Bredcake, master's mate of the *Adventure*, of which plaintiffs were owners, came to [her] and her husband, William Goodladd, since deceased, late master of the ship, at their lodgings at Mr Gardner's house in Tower Wharf, and told them the *Adventure* had arrived at Gravesend, that William Goodladd, her father-in-law, was one of the owners, and Katherine Goodladd of Leigh, widow, deceased, was also a part-owner.

Palace Court

This court sat from 1630 to 1849 and dealt with causes of action that arose within 12 miles of the palace of Westminster (excluding the City of London). In practice it only dealt with small debt claims because defendants could have cases involving £5 or more moved to superior courts. The court records are at TNA in series PALA 1 to 9, including plaint books for 1686 to 1849 in PALA 5, with brief entries for each action brought in the court.

Court for Divorce and Matrimonal Causes

This court (# chapter 14) was established on 1 January 1858 and merged into the Probate, Divorce and Admiralty Division of the High Court in 1875. Files of divorce proceedings (1858–1937) are at TNA (in series J 77) including marriage certificates, court orders and petitions setting out the grounds for divorce, with indexes in J 78.

Supreme Court of Judicature (High Court of Justice and Court of Appeal)

The Supreme Court was established in 1875 by amalgamating the superior civil courts and fusing their common law and equitable jurisdictions (so that any court could apply common law or equitable rules). If there was a conflict between equity and common law, the rules of equity were to apply. The Supreme Court consisted of the High Court of Justice and the Court of Appeal. The Court of Appeal was granted the jurisdiction of the Court of Exchequer Chamber, the Court of Appeal in Chancery and certain appeal courts of the Palatinates. From 1875 it heard all civil appeals from the High Court of Justice (criminal appeals are considered in chapter 25). Few new documents were produced during the course of an appeal, but some records of appeals to the court since 1875 are listed by Colwell (242).

The High Court was granted the jurisdiction of the Courts of King's (or Queen's) Bench, Chancery, Common Pleas, Exchequer, Admiralty, Probate, Bankruptcy, certain Palatinate courts and the Court for Divorce and Matrimonial Causes. The High Court was divided into divisions: the Queen's (or King's) Bench, Chancery, Common Pleas, Exchequer and also the Probate, Divorce and Admiralty Division (for "wills, wives and wrecks"). The Common Pleas and Exchequer Divisions were merged into the Queen's Bench Division in 1880. The High Court was later reorganised into three divisions: Queen's Bench, Chancery and Family. The Chancery Division deals with matters such as land, trusts, mortgages, partnerships and bankruptcy. Queen's Bench deals with contract, commercial and tort cases. There are also specialist courts, such as the Commercial and Admiralty courts (which form part of the Queen's Bench Division) and the Companies Court (part of the Chancery Division).

Most records of the Supreme Court since 1945 have been destroyed rather than passed to TNA; in general only the records of a 2% sample of cases (or of cases of great historical interest) have been retained. This section therefore deals primarily with records before 1945. Records of the Chancery and Queen's Bench Divisions are filed by type rather than by case. The *PRO Guide* (228) contains detailed descriptions of the series. Thus writs of summons from 1880 to 1930 (to 1991 for Queen's Bench) are in series J 59, filed by year and initial letter of the plaintiff's surname. Pleadings from 1880 to 1942 are in J 54 and 55 (with 2% samples since 1942 in J 83 and 84), generally filed by date. Affidavits of 1876–1945 are in series J 4–7 and depositions of 1880–1925 are in J 16 and 17 (to which there are indexes). There are some surviving cause books for each division (for example, those of Chancery for every tenth year from 1880 to 1934 are in J 89) giving the names of parties, their solicitors and the dates of pleadings. The Queen's

Bench cause books note the date of judgments (these judgments are in series J 20–22). Chancery orders from 1876 to 1955 are in entry books in J 15, to which there are indexes. Master's records from the Chancery Division (in J 23–47, 57, 63–4 and 66–8) contain similar material to the Masters' reports and documents of the Court of Chancery. Documents exhibited or deposited at court (principally in Chancery actions) are in J 90 to which there is a calendar in List and Index Society volumes 197 and 261. The records of the Common Pleas and Exchequer Divisions from 1875 to 1880 are listed in the *Current Guide* (234) and Colwell (242). Most of them have code J (such as pleadings in Exchequer cases in series J 55 and Exchequer and Common Pleas judgments in J 20–22) but some are filed with the records of the Courts of Common Pleas and Exchequer (noted above).

Records of contentious probate cases are in the Chancery Division records or in records of the Principal Probate Registry of the Court of Probate (or successor divisions of the High Court). A sample of case files for contentious probates in the Principal Probate Registry, from 1858 to 1960, are in J 121. The series list to J 121 lists almost 5,500 testators (sorted by year, then alphabetically), the year of probate and the action's title. Thus piece J 121/2 concerns the will of William Anderson, proved in 1858, which was the subject of dispute in the case of Laneuville v. Anderson & Guichard. Searches in contentious probate records (and the large amount of genealogical information that they may contain) are considered by Watts & Watts in *Genealogists' Magazine* (June 1981). A probate case (in the Chancery Division) involving their ancestor commenced in 1881 and continued until at least 1926. Watts & Watts show how, by moving between different series of records at TNA, they found the pleadings and 45 decrees or orders, 31 affidavits and 3 Masters' reports (containing information about 150 heirs of their ancestor). This complex action is unusual but it is possible that any researcher could find ancestors involved in similar cases. Even simple cases can provide much genealogical information.

The House of Lords
In addition to its role as one of the Houses of Parliament, the House of Lords is also the final appeal court in Britain. Appeals to the Lords are no longer heard by the whole House, but by a Judicial Committee of Lords (senior judges who have been made peers). Most appeals are now made from the Court of Appeal but this was not always the case. Thus the Lords could hear appeals directly from the Court of Probate or the Court for Divorce and Matrimonial Causes from 1858 to 1875. There are published reports (considered below) of the Lords' judgments in appeals since 1865 and also for some earlier cases. The Lords' judgments in appeals from the Court of Appeal are in series KB 34 at TNA and many records of appeals to the Lords, described in Bond (922), are at the House of Lords Record Office (# chapter 11). These include petitions, orders, judgments and documents that were filed as evidence. Judgments also appear in the House of Lords journal (held at HLRO) and written cases of the parties to many appeals (with transcripts of documents reviewed by the court) were also printed and are at some law libraries.

There are detailed records of legislative proceedings in the House of Lords (such as journals and minutes of proceedings) since about 1500, described in Bond (922). HLRO holds many other important manuscripts relating to the Lords' legislative and judicial functions. These records (from 1498 to 1692) were calendared in appendices to the 1st to 14th reports of the Royal Commission on Historical Manuscripts and those for 1693 to 1718 are calendared in 12 volumes published by HMSO. Many of the records concern defence or other matters of state but they are of interest to genealogists because they also include information (and many abstracts of documents) relating to cases heard by the Lords or to private acts of Parliament. Many of the private acts were naturalisations (# chapter 30) or estate acts, which varied the terms of a trust or settlement (# chapter 27). For example, an act might permit trustees to mortgage land to pay debts of the estate (or to provide money to members of the family who were beneficiaries of the settlement). These documents are full of interesting information about the families whose property was subject to the settlement. For example, the first HMSO volume (918) refers to the appeal to the House of Lords, in 1693, in the case of Zouch v English. James Zouch and his sister Dorothy, widow of Thomas English, were in dispute over a gift of £1,500 made by their father to Dorothy on her marriage. Dorothy alleged that she had been "betrayed" into marriage with Thomas English who had "not allowed her any maintenance and was a man of little or no estate and a prisoner in the King's Bench", a notorious debtors' prison. The estate acts noted in this HMSO volume are also a valuable source for genealogists. For example, Finch's Estate Act, considered by the Lords on 19 January 1694/5, was intended to vest certain land in trustees so that it could be sold by them and the proceeds used to provide for the daughters of the late Joseph Finch. Written consents (necessary to vary an existing trust over the land) were provided by Carolina, Theodora, Judith and Ruth Finch (four of Joseph's daughters), by Thomas Ramsden of Eland, Yorkshire and his wife Elizabeth (another daughter of Joseph) and by Thomas Horton of Barkisland, Yorkshire (the sisters' uncle and guardian).

The Privy Council

The Privy Council was an important legislative, judicial and administrative body that evolved from the King's Council in the 14th century. Its history and role are described in the *Current Guide* (234). It consisted of the king's most important ministers (such as the Chancellor and treasurer) but also some bishops and household officials. It conducted much of its business through committees (one of which developed into the modern Cabinet). The Privy Council was concerned with the king's "business" (that is, public order or foreign affairs), but also with royal grants of land, pardons and tax. It also dealt with local affairs because petitions were received from individuals and communities. Many petitions were referred to the Chancellor (and dealt with in the Court of Chancery) and public order matters (such as cases of treason, rebellion and heresy) were later remitted to the Court of Star Chamber.

The Privy Council's records at TNA have codes PC and PCAP. The most important are the registers in series PC 2 which commence in 1540 and describe the Council's business and decisions, but include much useful information about our ancestors. Fascimiles of the registers for 1631–45 have been published by HMSO and the registers of 1542–1631 have been calendared and indexed in *Acts of the Privy Council of England*, in 46 volumes. Entries from the volume for 1554–56 by Dasent (929) include:

25th May 1554 whereas Thomas Sandesborough, of Stepney labouring man, hath reported certain false and seditious rumours against the Queen's Highness and the quiet state of this realm, the said Sandesborough was by order from the Lords delivered into the hands of the bailiffs of Stepney for the following punishment; tomorrow, 26th May, they shall openly, at Stepney, nail one of his ears to the pillory and cut off his ear to the terror and example of others and then deliver him to the Sheriff of London to be committed to Newgate.

A letter [sent] to the Mayor and Jurates of Dover to make search for one Thomas Burley, who having committed a murder, and condemned for the same, broke [out of] prison and is about to fly over the sea.

Most of the Council's judicial functions were passed to courts such as Star Chamber and Chancery, but it remained a final court of appeal after 1834, acting through its Judicial Committee, from the church courts (considered below). The Committee also heard appeals from the Admiralty Court (from 1833 to 1876) and from the Isle of Man, Channel Islands, Crown colonies, dominions and later Commonwealth countries. Its work is reviewed in the *Current Guide* (234). Records of appeals to the Judicial Committee are in series PCAP 1, 2, 3 and 5. They include cause books, processes and judgments and are described further in the *PRO Guide* (228). There are published reports (considered below) of the Committee's judgments in appeals since 1865 and also of many earlier judgments. The written arguments of the parties to these cases were also printed and can be found at some law libraries.

Bankruptcy

Men could be imprisoned if they fell into debt (considered below). Those who were in trade or business (extended to all debtors in 1861) could also face proceedings in the courts and be declared bankrupt. A court could suspend a debtor's business, call meetings of his creditors and divide his remaining assets between them. Statements of the bankrupt's affairs and affidavits about his debts or business dealings were produced. The Lord Chancellor had authority over bankrupts and bankruptcy actions from 1571 until a Court of Bankruptcy was established in 1831. District bankruptcy courts were established in 1842 to deal with bankruptcies outside London (their jurisdiction was transferred to County Courts in 1861). The Court of Bankruptcy became part of the Supreme Court in 1883, as the High Court of Justice in Bankruptcy. Appeals were originally made to a Court of Review, but later to the Court of Appeal in Chancery, the House of Lords or (from 1875) to the Court of Appeal.

Colwell (243) describes bankruptcy proceedings before the Lord Chancellor and in the Court of Bankruptcy. Creditors petitioned the Lord Chancellor, who issued a Commission of Bankruptcy requiring the debtor to surrender himself and his property to a commissioner. The commission was advertised in the *London Gazette* (see illustration 75), so that creditors could attend meetings and elect an assignee to collect the debtor's goods and value his estate. Creditors gave affidavits or depositions about their claims. A debtor might have sufficient assets to pay his creditors (or he might reach a settlement with them). If not, he could be declared bankrupt. Procedure in the Court of Bankruptcy was similar. From 1875 a creditor's application for a commission was accompanied by a petition for a receiving order, vesting a debtor's estate in the Official Receiver, who examined a debtor (perhaps publicly in court) and called creditors' meetings. Later statutes provided for a trustee in bankruptcy to be appointed (by the court or creditors) to deal with the bankrupt's estate and pay creditors. A typical bankruptcy order was:

In the High Court of Justice in Bankruptcy.   No 389 of 1912
Mr Registrar Brougham
Re JAMES REED ex parte the Official Receiver
Pursuant to a petition dated the 27th day of March 1912 against James Reed lately residing at 262 Kennington Park Road, Kennington and lately carrying on business at 32 Old

Paradise Street, Lambeth . . . (but whose present . . . whereabouts the petitioning creditors are unable to ascertain) property dealer.

On which a Receiving Order was made on the 8th day of May 1912, and on the application of the Official Receiver, and on reading [his] report, the Notice of Motion . . . and the debtor not appearing . . . and hearing the Official Receiver . . . IT IS ORDERED that the debtor James Reed . . . is ADJUDGED BANKRUPT . . . 5th June 1912.

TNA holds the Court of Bankruptcy's and Lord Chancellor's records since the 18th century (in series B 1–12 and 39–40). Series B 1 contains bankruptcy order books for 1710–1877 and B 6 contains some registers of bankruptcy actions from 1733 to the late 19th century. Orders and minute books of the Court of Review and the Court of Appeal in Chancery are in B 1 and 7. Many other registers, files of evidence (such as depositions) and some indexes are listed in Bevan (239), TNA legal records leaflets 5 and 6 and Colwell (242). Many records of bankruptcy actions since 1876 are in the High Court's records, such as entry books of decrees and orders (in series J 15) and cause books (J 12) and some are in Board of Trade records, such as registers of bankruptcy petitions of 1884–1923 in BT 293 and deeds of arrangement in BT 39. Notices about debtors and bankrupts appeared in the *London Gazette* and illustrations 75 and 76 include examples. Notices to creditors were also published in national and local newspapers. There are also some published lists of bankrupts, such as the *Alphabetical List of all the Bankrupts 1774 to 1786* (907) which is also available on microfiche from the SoG. This gives names, town of residence and date of bankruptcy. A register of all bankrupts from 1820 to 1843 has also been published on fiche by the SoG.

Until 1861 insolvent persons who were not engaged in trade or business could not be made bankrupt, but were often imprisoned until the debts were paid. Debtors might therefore remain incarcerated for years unless their family could pay the debts. An imprisoned debtor could petition the Justices of the Peace, from 1670 up to 1812, for discharge and release, if he made oath that his assets did not exceed £10 and if his creditors did not object. Records (such as petitions, schedules of assets, lists of creditors, notices to creditors and orders of discharge) are therefore held in Quarter Sessions' records in CROs. A Court for the Relief of Insolvent Debtors was established in 1813 and the law provided for debtors to be discharged from prison (except in cases of dishonesty) after their assets had been distributed to creditors. Cases outside London could be heard at Quarter Sessions, by commissioners of the Insolvent Debtors Court or, from 1847, by County Courts. In 1861 the distinction between insolvent debtors and bankrupts was abolished and so the jurisdiction of the Insolvent Debtors' Court passed to the Court of Bankruptcy. Only a few records of the Insolvent Debtors' Court survive at TNA (some registers in series B 6 and indexes in B 8). Some records of County Court cases also survive in CROs.

Until 1861 debtors and bankrupts were imprisoned in county gaols or in debtors' prisons. TNA holds records, listed in Hawkings (984) and TNA domestic records leaflet 88, of some of the London debtors' gaols, such as the Fleet Prison, the Prison of the Marshalsea of the King's Household and Palace Court and the King's (or Queen's) Bench Prison (later renamed the Queen's Prison). The Fleet and Marshalsea prisons were closed in 1842 and the Queen's Prison in 1862. Their records are in series PRIS 1 to 11. Thus commitment books of the King's/Queen's Bench Prison from 1719 to 1862 and records of discharges from that prison for 1776 to 1862 are in PRIS 4 and 7. The records of the Fleet Prison include commitment books (1685–1748 and 1778–1842), noting dates of debtors' admissions, in PRIS 1 (indexed from

1725), orders for commitments (1758–1842) in PRIS 2 and warrants for discharges (1775–1842) and many petitions for the release of debtors, in PRIS 3.

Winding up proceedings

Winding up of limited companies (incorporated from 1844 under the Companies Acts) was undertaken by proceedings in the Court of Chancery (or sometimes the Court of Bankruptcy), subsequently in the Chancery Division of the High Court and (from 1890), in the Companies Court of that division. From 1861 winding up actions could also be heard in County Courts. If a winding up order was made, a liquidator would be appointed to sell the company's assets and distribute the proceeds to creditors. Surviving records of these actions are at TNA and listed in Colwell (242). For example, proceedings (usually petitions) and orders from 1849 to 1951 are in series C 26 and J 13 (there is an index to the records of 1891 to 1932). Some examples of the records in J 13 are provided by Probert (847). Liquidators' and receivers' accounts, some dating from 1859, are in series C 30, BT 31 and BT 34. Notices of winding up proceedings also appeared in the *London Gazette*.

County Courts

County Courts were established in 1846 to deal with small debts or other civil claims. As noted above, the county courts also had jurisdiction to hear some admiralty and bankruptcy actions. Their jurisdiction is described in more detail in the *Current Guide* (234). Records of these courts have usually been deposited at CROs (and are therefore described in those archives' catalogues) although records of appeals from county courts (to the High Court or the Court of Appeal) are generally at TNA, mostly with code J.

Commissioners of Forfeited Estates

After the Jacobite rebellion of 1715, commissioners were appointed to ascertain the estates held by traitors. The commissioners' records are at TNA, in series FEC 1 and 2, but also in some classes of records of the Court of King's Bench, the assize courts (# chapter 25) and the Palatinates. The records are described in Shorney (350), TNA domestic records leaflet 21 and in a handbook (1149) which lists the people recorded in the documents. They include returns from Clerks of the Peace (listing traitors' names) and also title deeds and other records of the estates that were forfeited.

Court of Augmentations

Henry VIII dissolved the monasteries in the 16th century and established the Court of Augmentations to administer and sell monasteries' land. Receivers were appointed to take inventories of monastic property, sell assets and administer land that was tenanted (and receive rents). About half of the property was sold during the reign of Henry VIII. The court was dissolved in 1554 and its functions transferred to a department of the Exchequer. Richardson (948) is a detailed history of the court from 1536 to 1554. The court's records are at TNA with code SC (special collections) such as series SC 2, 6, 11 and 12, but also in Exchequer records, such as series E 299, 300, 309 to 315 and 321, the most important of which are the proceedings (in E 321) and "particulars for leases" (in E 310). They are described in the *PRO Guide* (228). The records are incomplete and difficult to use, but some have been published, such as the receivers' accounts for 1536–37 for Bedfordshire monasteries and their properties, in Nicholls

(947). A typical entry for rent received is: "Robt. Charnocke . . . manor of Holcote lying within par[ish] of Holcote . . . 12d". The accounts also record the receivers' expenditure. Abstracts of proceedings and particulars for leases relating to Wales are contained in Lewis & Davies (1192), such as this bill of complaint:

Complainant, John ap David ap Gryffeth ap Llewelin.

Defendant, David ap Gryffeth ap Eynyon, gent.

David ap Griffithe ap Llewelin, complainant's father, seised in fee of certain messuages, lands and tenements in Wysanna, in lordship of Moylde, held of the King as of said lordship, by certain rents and services, who granted same to complainant. Wrongful entry by defendant two years ago into a close of land called Cuttcoyte arlewythe in Wysanna, rent 13s. 4d.

Civic courts

The charters of many boroughs and cities permitted them to have their own courts for civil and administrative (and some criminal) matters. A typical borough had its own Quarter and Petty Sessions (# chapter 25), a court for small debts or other civil claims (arising in the borough's jurisdiction), a coroner's court, a court leet (# chapter 27) and also a piepowder court (which regulated markets and fairs). Procedure in these civic courts was similar to that in other secular courts. Surviving records are usually in CROs or city archives. The work of these local courts is illustrated by the court books from the borough of Witney, Oxfordshire, for 1538–1610, transcribed in Bolton & Maslen (921). The court's business included cases of trespass, property disputes or transactions (# chapter 27), apprenticeships and the activities of local tradesmen but most were actions for small debts, as in these examples from 1578:

23 May. William Elmore of Witney, woollen draper, against Richard Wisedome of Witney, weaver, for 17s. 11d. At the court on 1 Aug. Wisedome promised to pay half at or before 17 Aug and the rest before 23 Nov.

31 Oct. John Butt of Bampton against John Collsburne of Witney, labourer, for 3s. 3d. Paid and discharged at the court on 15 Jan. 1579.

The City of London had a Mayor's Court, the Court of Husting, Sheriffs' courts, a Court of Requests (for small debts) and an Orphan's Court (# chapter 12). The records of these courts are at CLRO and described in Deadman & Scudder (244). Early rolls of the Mayor's Court (for 1298–1307 and 1323–1484) have been published, such as those for 1413–37 in Thomas (953). Sharpe (301) includes a detailed review of the work and powers of the Court of Husting. In addition to proving (from the 13th century) those wills that related to land in the City of London, it acted as the City's County Court and deeds to City property were enrolled there until the 20th century.

Courts were also established to deal with special events. The Great Fire of London in 1666 destroyed or severely damaged large parts of the City. Leases commonly provided for tenants to rebuild after a fire and (since there was no insurance) this was an onerous or impossible burden for many tenants. A Fire Court was therefore established to deal with disputes between landlords and tenants that related to rebuilding. Jones (944) is an indexed calendar of the court's judgments and decrees, which give much information about landlords, tenants and the leases that subsisted at the time of the fire. Some cases note two or more generations of a family inheriting the freehold of a property, or succeeding to the outstanding term of a lease. For example, an abstract of a decree of the court on 13 March 1666 is:

Gilbert Taylor, citizen and woodmonger v. Henry Brewster and Rachell his wife, executrix of Rachell Keynnell, widow
The petitioner was possessed of three messuages and a wharf upon Tower Wharf under a lease of 13 September 1658 from the said Keynnell, which houses were demolished by order of the Privy Council [of] 8 September 1666 for preventing the fire coming to His Majesty's magazine in the Tower . . . the defendants had obtained a verdict for £30 arrears of rent to Michaelmas 1666. Ordered that the petitioner pay the said £30 in full satisfaction of all arrears claimed or to be claimed . . . that the lease be surrendered and that the petitioner be discharged under all covenants [ie to rebuild the premises].

Law reports
Published law reports are the judgments (and sometimes factual summaries) from those civil or criminal cases that decided important points of law. The reports were for reference by lawyers and they therefore concentrate on the legal points at issue rather than the facts, but many reported cases (especially those concerning wills, trusts, property, marriage or divorce) contain much genealogical information. Law reports were only published for a small percentage of cases, but they date from the middle ages. Published reports are held in legal and reference libraries. The surnames of the plaintiff and defendant (the first plaintiff and first defendant if there were more than one), or sometimes the name of a ship or company which was the subject of dispute, are indexed so that it is relatively easy to find a reported case. If you find one in which your ancestor was a party, it is also then easier to find any surviving original court records of the case since the report will note the court and date of judgment. Law reports also introduce you to legal terms and so help you to deal with original manuscript documents that not only use unfamiliar language, but which can be difficult to read or may be in Latin.

There are many different series of law reports, some by a particular reporter and some for cases from a particular court. From 1866 there are official reports for each superior English civil court (or from 1875 for each division of the High Court). Each volume in this official series has its own index of surnames of the first plaintiff and first defendant. In addition, a composite series named the *All England Law Reports* includes not only many reports of cases that appear in the official reports, but also many law reports from earlier periods (many from the period since 1800 and some since 1558). Most of the reports are of civil cases but some cover points of law in criminal cases. Bridgeman (923) indexes the cases in the *All England Law Reports* by the surname of the first plaintiff and first defendant, noting the court, the year (of the volume containing the report) and page number. If you find a case of interest, you can then (from the date of the judgment) also try to find the case in the court records at TNA. A typical index entry is:

Charlesworth and another v. Holt (1873) Ex(chequer) [1861–73] 266

Earlier reports are in many different series, but over 100,000 of these reports, some dating from the 13th century, have been brought together and indexed overall by plaintiffs' and defendants' names in *The English Reports*. This series was published in the early 20th century, but has been reprinted in 176 volumes, including 11 volumes of reported cases in the House of Lords, 27 volumes of Court of Chancery cases, 51 volumes of cases in the Court of King's Bench and so on. A few cases duplicate those in the All England reports. There is an index (914) and (915), arranged in order of the first plaintiffs' surnames. The 11 entries for Charnock include:

Case	Report Series	Volume	Page
Charnock v Corey	2 Brownl & Golds 153	123 (Common Pleas)	868
Charnock v Dewings	3 Car & K 378	175 (Nisi Prius)	597
Charnock v Sherrington	Cro Eliz 364	78 (King's Bench)	543
Charnock v Worsley	1 Leonard 114	74 (King's Bench)	107
Charnock's Case	Holt, 133 (and others)	90 (King's Bench)	972

These reports contained little genealogical information but they concerned two main actions. One was a dispute in 1588 over a sale of land. The other cases concerned points of law that arose from the prosecution for treason in 1695/6 of Robert Charnock for conspiring to assassinate King William III. Brief summaries of two other cases from *The English Reports* are set out below, showing the useful genealogical information often included, but also illustrating the reports' limitations. For example, only a person's surname may be given. There may be no indication of the place where parties came from and there may be few dates apart from the year of the court hearing. The first example is from reports of cases in the Court of Chancery, contained in volume 21 of the reports (912). The second is from reports from the Ecclesiastical, Admiralty, Probate and Divorce courts, in volume 161 (913).

Drury v. Drury [1 Chancery reports 49]. 6 Carolus 1, f.74 [1631–2]
William Smith, seised of the Manor of Coles, made a lease of the demesne thereof to one Clark [also a defendant] for 20 years, and died, leaving the reversion to descend to the plaintiff [Drury] and the defendant, William Drury, his co-heirs. William Drury entered into the whole manor and the defendant Clark is charged to be behind with his rent. The defendant Drury says that he entered [the property of] the defendant Clark for non-payment of rent and [alleges] that he has avoided the lease . . . the court certified that a writ of partition be brought between the said co-heirs . . . and the defendant Drury shall answer to the plaintiff for a moiety of the profits of the premises, from the time of avoiding the defendant Clark's lease.

Grant v. Grant [1 Lee 592]. Court of Peculiars, June 17th 1754.
A suit for restitution of conjugal rights, in the case of a Fleet marriage which was established. Mrs Grant brought suit against her husband for restitution of conjugal rights [in 1753], the husband denying the marriage. Mrs Grant alleged courtship and marriage at the Fleet, on 18th September 1748, co-habitation, birth and baptism of a child, the fact of the marriage being sworn to by two witnesses. Allegation that the plaintiff married Edward Grant at *The Vine and Globe*, in the Fleet market by a clerk named Donaview. The defendant Edward Grant alleges that Mary Bennett, calling herself Grant, pleads a marriage on 18th September 1748. She was with child at that time; a female child delivered in January following. John Grant [brother of Edward] says that Edward declared [at the ceremony] that he would not be married and the parson stopped.

[The evidence of 9 witnesses is then summarised, including:]

Richard Bennett, brother to Mary and has long known Edward Grant. Their child was registered as legitimate. Edward used to lie with [Mary] at her father's house . . . the house in St. Olave's was rated in Edward's name and he behaved to Mary as his wife.

Mary Taylor, sister to Edward Grant and knows Mary well. Edward first began to court Mary about 8 years ago until September or October 1748 when, one night, Edward and John Grant were looking for Mary [Bennett]. Witness believes that Edward, John and Mary then all went out together that night. The next morning, John Grant, her brother, told her that Edward and Mary had been married the evening before. Mary continued to live with her father till he died but Edward went to her when he pleased. Edward has constantly [treated Mary] as his wife and he has now deserted her.

Judgment of Sir George Lee. I give sentence for the marriage and condemn Edward Grant in £30 costs, decree him to be admonished, to take Mary home, co-habit with her and treat her kindly as his wife.

Further reports of criminal trials, contained in pamphlets produced for sale to the public (particularly about crimes that were newsworthy at the time) are considered in chapter 25.

CHURCH COURTS

The organisation of the ecclesiastical courts and their jurisdiction over probate and marriage were considered in chapters 12 and 14. The church courts did not deal with civil claims (such as debts) or truly criminal cases (such as murder or theft) but they had jurisdiction over the clergy and parish officers and over "moral crimes" (that is, the moral conduct of parishioners). The courts' cases concerned the upkeep of church buildings, refusal to pay tithes or church rates, adultery, heresy, witchcraft, prostitution, drunkenness, fornication (sex outside marriage), recusancy, working on Sunday and slander or defamation of a neighbour. The archdeacons' and bishops' courts were often known as the bawdy courts because the cases that they heard frequently involved fornication, adultery and slander. Tarver (951) is a useful analysis of church court procedure and records, with examples of each type of court business. Detailed studies of the church courts include Ingram (943), which reviews the courts in Wiltshire from 1570 to 1640 and Emmison (931), a study of the Essex archdeaconry courts in the reign of Elizabeth I. These works are especially useful since church court records are difficult to use because they were usually written in abbreviated Latin (until 1732) and are rarely indexed.

Church courts were at the height of their powers in the 16th and early 17th centuries. They were abolished in 1642 and, although reinstated in 1661, their powers declined as the Church of England's authority declined with the rise of non-conformist groups and the increasing power assumed by the State over people's behaviour. The church courts lost their jurisdiction over matrimonial causes, probate, defamation and tithes between 1836 and 1858 and now deal with only a few matters, such as marriage licences and clerical discipline.

A parish incumbent was responsible to a rural dean. Deans were responsible for a number of parishes, the work of parish clergy and the upkeep of church buildings, but they did not have courts or dispense ecclesiastical justice. The church court of first instance was usually the archdeacon's court, with appeals being made to a bishop's court. However, there were many exceptions. The bishops' court was often the court of first instance in probate matters. Some archdeacons' courts had limited jurisdictions (and some cases were considered too serious or important for an archdeacon), so that many cases were heard at first instance by the bishop's court. During a bishop's visitation, the archdeacon's court would close and all judicial business took place in the bishop's court. Parishes that were in the jurisdiction of the Dean and Chapters of Cathedrals were subject to the jurisdiction of the Dean and Chapter court (for similar cases as the archdeacon's court). Peculiars also had their own courts.

Bishops and archdeacons rarely sat in their own courts but delegated this task, in the case of an archdeacon to his official and, in the case of a bishop, to a deputy known variously as a Vicar-General, a Chancellor, Commissary General, Auditor or Official Principal. These officials were usually clerics or proctors. A registrar of each court dealt with court administration, the maintenance of records and examination of witnesses. The lawyers who practised in the church courts were proctors and advocates (# chapter 22). Chapman (926) provides more information about court officials and the organisation of church courts.

Church court procedure

There were two types of case. Instance cases were civil suits (for example, defamation, matrimonial or probate cases). They were known, like secular civil actions, by the parties' names, for example "Bulleid v. White". Office cases dealt with moral offences (often described as crimes) and were promoted by the official (that is, a judge) usually as a result of presentments by churchwardens, but sometimes by the court's own motion or because a third party pressed the court to act. Case titles included a defendant's name, for example "Office v. Smith".

Examples of office business included cases against clergymen (for gambling, drunkenness, or ignoring the rules for solemnisation of marriage), against schoolteachers and midwives (for acting without a licence) or against churchwardens (for failure to maintain the church). Parishioners were prosecuted for non-attendance at church, perjury, fornication, adultery or failure to have a child baptised. The courts also dealt with disputes over church seats, church rates or churchwardens' accounts (often a complaint of incoming officers about predecessors' accounts). Tarver (951) includes, as an example of disciplinary action against a clergyman, a deposition of Elizabeth Evans that complains of the cockfighting and violence of the vicar of her parish. Disputes over church seats are particularly useful because evidence may be given of a family's use of a particular seat for many generations. Disputes over payment of church rates or tithes often involved non-conformists, so that a case brought against your ancestor may indicate that he was a non-conformist. In tithe disputes, depositions were often obtained from elderly witnesses (with their ages and place of origin) as to past payments.

Churchwardens could present parishioners to a church court for offences under ecclesiastical law. Presentments were most common during an archdeacon's or bishop's visitation, the purpose of which was to review faith, dissent, morality and administration in the parishes. An archdeacon should have visited each of his deaneries every year and a bishop undertook episcopal visitations around his diocese in his first year of office and then every third year. All clergy, churchwardens, church officials and others (such as teachers) would be summoned to attend the visitation. The diocesan registrar, or archdeacon's clerk, would record proceedings at a visitation and note information about parish affairs (such as the number of recusants or the action taken against unlicensed teachers). Churchwardens' presentments at visitations were noted in books of detections or *libri comperta* (for example listing parishioners who failed to attend church). Many of these records survive in diocesan records. Churchwardens' presentments from about 1660 to

1760 most commonly related to non-attendance at church. The accused were usually non-conformists or Catholics, rather than people who merely missed services now and again.

There were three types of procedure in church courts: plenary, summary and testamentary. Plenary procedure applied in most instance cases. Testamentary procedure was used in probate cases. Office suits might be by either plenary or summary procedure. The procedures are described in detail by Tarver (951) and Chapman (926), but in plenary and testamentary cases, the court relied primarily on documents. Formal pleadings set out the parties' allegations or defences and witnesses gave evidence by statements or depositions rather than orally in court. Many records of these cases survive. Summary procedure was mainly oral so that few records of these actions survive. Court business and decisions were recorded by registrars in act books or court books. The entries might be very short (perhaps just a defendant's name and the court judgment, such as excommunicated) or a lengthy account of a court hearing and decision.

Defendants were called to court by a citation, specifying the defendant, his parish and the date upon which he had to attend. Citations were served by court apparitors who would later swear affidavits that a defendant had been served. If a defendant did not appear at court, a further citation could be served (or read out in church). If the defendant still failed to attend, he could be found in contempt of court and excommunicated. A bishop's court only had jurisdiction over persons in the diocese, so that a defendant or witness from another diocese could only be summoned if the court with jurisdiction over his place of residence issued a citation (following receipt of a letter of request from the first court), requiring him to attend upon the court making the request. If a defendant appeared to answer an instance case, the plaintiff then set out his case in a document called a libel and the defendant could serve an answer. Witnesses gave evidence before a court official who wrote out a deposition (often signed by the witness). These note witnesses' occupations, residences, sometimes their ages or places of birth and often the amount of time they had lived in various places. Some examples from Emmison (931) are noted in chapter 28. A party could submit interrogatories. The answers of a witness or other party may be added to the deposition. The court judgment was given to the parties orally. Both parties prepared a written draft of that judgment (known as the sentence) and the court amended (and approved) the sentence of the party who won the action. Both parties' drafts may appear in court records.

Documents from probate cases included wills, letters of administration, inventories and bonds. Testamentary cases can reveal much information about a testator and his family. One will might be proved but another might then be produced by disappointed relatives. Unpaid beneficiaries might dispute the executors' or administrators' conduct, as in the complaint made against Agnes Bulleid (# chapter 12). Nuncupative wills were especially prone to be disputed by those relatives of a deceased who received nothing (but who would receive part of the estate if the will was rejected and an administration was ordered). Tarver (951) and Cox (364) include many examples of the records from probate disputes. Willis (958) includes an abstract of a deposition (from the Consistory Court of the Bishop of Winchester) that was typical in such cases:

24 March 1592 English v. Bethell (the case of Richard Bethell deceased) Nicholas Smith, yeoman, native of Soke, Winton, aged 50 [states]: Richard Bethell uttered and spoke these words . . . I am desirous to make my will and have sent for Mr Ellys, vicar of Sparsholt, to write it, but if I die before he hath made it I have called you to witness that this is my will. I give all my goods and the lease of my inn to [beneficiaries' names].

A particularly important type of document sometimes found in court records is the probate account. Such accounts could be ordered to be produced when the distribution of an estate was in dispute. Tarver (951) includes an account of 1736 for the estate of a labourer, Thomas Hancock, which was prepared by his widow and named a dozen local traders because debts had been owed to them by Thomas and were paid out of the estate. Over 30,000 surviving English and Welsh probate accounts, most from the 17th century, are listed by name of the deceased, in British Record Society volumes 112–113 by Spufford (950).

The bishops' courts heard most testamentary disputes, usually as instance cases between two parties, over wills proved, or administrations granted, in the bishops', archdeacons' and peculiar courts. The records of these disputes are in CROs. The PCC heard testamentary disputes over wills or administrations that were proved or granted in the PCC, or sometimes over probates granted in lower courts. Extensive records of contentious probate suits in the PCC are at TNA and described by Cox (285) and Scott (300). It may not be easy to find out if there was litigation over a particular will or administration since there is no index to all suits. The indexes to particular types of document are incomplete and some index only the plaintiffs' (rather than the deceased's) name. Indexes to PCC wills and admons may indicate that there was litigation by noting the words "by interlocutory decree" or "by sentence" (that is, by court judgment) against the entry for the deceased. Some other indexes may reveal litigation, such as the Act books for 1536 to 1819 (in series PROB 29) and acts of court for 1740 to 1858 (in PROB 30), which record the dates of cases, the parties' names and various court decisions (for example summoning witnesses). The allegations of plaintiffs for 1665 to 1858 are in PROB 18 and there is a card index to the names of the deceased and plaintiffs. Defendants' answers for 1664 to 1854 are in PROB 25, exhibits (1722–1858) are in PROB 31 (indexed in PROB 33) and depositions (1657–1809 and 1826–57) are in PROB 24 and 26.

Matrimonial causes (such as disputed marriage contracts or claims to a decree of separation) were briefly considered in chapter 14. The church courts' records of these cases can include much information about an ancestor's family and his or her household life. In cases concerning alleged marriage contracts, the parties' parents may be named and the parents or other relatives may have given depositions as to the engagement. In cases concerning separation, details of the marriage of the parties will be recorded and often their ages, place of origin and the names and ages of their children. Defamation cases could be heard in either the secular or church courts. In church courts, defamation could be either an office case (for example if a man defamed a clergyman) or an instance case between parishioners. Most instance cases of defamation in the church courts related to allegations of sexual misconduct and many examples are provided in Cox (364). Surviving records may reveal the parties' occupations, ages, family members and lifestyle.

As noted, the procedure in office cases was usually oral, so few records survive except for citations, some depositions and entries in act books. However, the act books may also list compurgators. Purgation or compurgation was a process whereby a defendant who denied charges had to swear that he was innocent, but also bring up to eight honest neighbours to court to swear that they believed that he was swearing truthfully. If they did so, the case against the defendant was dismissed. If compurgators failed to appear, the defendant was convicted. It was of course possible for a guilty man, with good friends, to evade justice.

Punishments and sentences of the church courts
The church courts imposed various sentences on parishioners. The lightest was a reprimand

(a monition or admonition). More serious was the requirement of a penance (an expression of repentance and confession). The penance might only have to be performed before the priest and churchwardens, but it might have to be performed in public (usually in church or the market place), the guilty party having to wear a white sheet while holding a white wand or rod and confessing his or her sin. Public penance could be commuted by the court into a monetary payment by the guilty person to a charity. Before 1641 fines could be levied, but the money had to be used for charitable purposes (perhaps a payment into the church poor box). Unsuccessful defendants also had to pay substantial court fees. *Suspension ab ingressu ecclesiae* consisted of the church temporarily withdrawing some privileges (such as the ability to attend church) from the guilty. The court could also order a solemn penance (the parishioner being formally turned out of the church for a few days over Lent). A church court might require a certificate from the defendant's parish minister that a penance had been performed. A few of these have survived, or notes of them may be found in correction or *comperta and detecta* books. Punishments are occasionally noted in parish registers:

> 1597. Margaret Sherioux was buried 23 June. She was to stand 3 market days in the town and 3 Sabbath days in the church, in a white sheet, with a paper on her back and bosom, showing her sin . . . she stood one Saturday and one Sunday and died the next (Croydon, Surrey)

> 1677. May 27. Johanna Johnson absolved from the sentence of excommunication and did her penance that day and 29 May for committing fornication with one Robt Knight of Gainsburgh (Scotter, Lincolnshire)

Church courts could also punish laymen by excommunication. Lesser excommunication excluded a guilty person from attending church, while greater excommunication excluded him from the company of all Christians until he was granted absolution. Excommunicates might be refused burial in the parish churchyard and their wills might not be proved by the church courts. A defendant obtained absolution by submitting to the court (if he had been excommunicated for previously failing to appear) or convincing the court that he had been sufficiently punished. Records of excommunications often survive in documents that were read out in church or in court. Statements of absolution, also read out in church, may also survive. Parish registers may record that a person had been excommunicated, perhaps in a burial entry:

> 1615. William Radhouse the elder dying excommunicate was buried by stealth in the night time in the churchyard 29 Jan (Weedon-Beck, Northamptonshire)

The register of Scotter, Lincolnshire includes, in January 1677, a list of 30 people who had been excommunicated. The church courts periodically prepared lists of those who had been excommunicated (in that court session, but also those excommunicated previously who had not yet been granted absolution). There is sometimes a separate excommunications book, noting an excommunicate's offence and parish, such as a register of the Archdeacon of Essex for 1590 to 1602 with about 1,000 names. It should be noted that many people remained excommunicate for years (many were Catholics or non-conformists) and there was little more that the church courts could do. A bishop's court also had certain powers to imprison an offender until 1641. In suitable cases, the court notified the King's Chancery that then issued a writ for the sheriff to arrest the offender. These writs are in series C 85 and C 207 at TNA. From 1641 the church courts were not permitted to fine, imprison or physically punish the guilty parishioners, although in some cases (such as witchcraft) the guilty person would be handed over to the secular courts. The church courts had more power in respect of the clergy, perhaps suspending them from their office and sequestering their income. A clergyman could also be deprived permanently of his office or benefice and even face degradation (that is, ejection from holy orders).

Church court records sometimes include other lists of Catholics or other dissenters. From 1562 those failing to attend church were fined and listed on recusants' rolls (# chapter 13) held at TNA and CROs. The rolls list names, residences, occupations and the fine. Some have been published by the Catholic Record Society, for example in Bowler (314). If a fine was not paid, the recusant could be imprisoned or his property seized. Recusants could also be summoned before the assize courts (# chapter 25) and records of these trials are held by TNA.

Appeals

Appeals in the Province of Canterbury could be made to the Court of Arches (# chapter 12) and appeals in the Province of York were made to the Chancery Court of York. In addition, between about 1580 and 1641 there was a High Commission for Causes Ecclesiastical in the Province of Canterbury and a similar commission in York Province. Until the reign of Henry VIII, final appeals from the church courts could be heard in Rome. As a result of Henry's break with the Pope, the High Court of Delegates was established in 1532. It heard final appeals from the church courts until 1834 (and also heard appeals from instance cases in the Court of Admiralty, the Court of Chivalry and from courts of the Chancellors of Oxford and Cambridge universities). In 1834 jurisdiction over final appeals from church courts was transferred to the Privy Council's Judicial Committee. When probate and matrimonial jurisdiction was transferred from the church courts to civil courts in 1858, final appeals for these cases were heard by the House of Lords.

Licences

People undertaking certain professions, such as apothecaries, midwives and surgeons, originally had to be licensed (# chapter 22) by the bishop or archdeacon. Schoolmasters also had to obtain licences from a church court from 1559. Licences were listed in act books or in separate registers, which often survive with other diocesan records in CROs. Emmison (931) notes many examples, such as the grant of a licence to Jeremiah Cochman, surgeon of Coggeshall, for a fee of 4 shillings. Willis (959) includes entries from 1568 to 1646 from the registers of Canterbury Diocese, for teachers, surgeons, physicians and midwives. Those who acted without a licence could be presented to a church court. Records at Devon Record Office note a complaint by licensed schoolteachers that my ancestor Richard Bond of Sandford was acting as a schoolteacher without a licence in 1706 (I have not yet discovered the result of the complaint):

14 June. Citation of Nathanial Mills, Richard Bury, William Ley of Crediton and Richard Bond of Sandford for teaching school without a licence, at [the] promotion of Samuel Tozer, Samuel Treser and Joseph Mare, licensed schoolmasters.

Location of records

Most church court records are held by CROs, and listed in their catalogues or published guides, such as that for Bedford Record Office (227), which holds the records of the Archdeaconry of Bedford. This extract from its published guide illustrates the types of records available:

Administrative records, etc

Licences; 1706–1807, testimonials supporting applications for schoolmasters', midwifes' and surgeons' licences (5 docs)

Matrimonial business, 1747–1879; bonds and allegations, 1747–1822; allegations, 1823–79 (227 files)

Registration of Dissenters' Meeting Houses; Certificates 1740, 1753–1852 (440 docs)

Court records

Act Books, 1537–45, 1578, 1610–1830 (17 volumes) [such as volume 12, for 1711 to 1713, instance and office business; courts held at Bedford, Gt Barford and Eversholt (93 folios)]

Court Proceedings; 1584–1850 (445 docs) cause papers relating to judicial proceedings in the Archdeacon's court.

The records of the courts of the Diocese of York and of the Province of York are held at the Borthwick Institute in York. Records of the Diocese of Canterbury are held in Canterbury Cathedral Library or in Lambeth Palace Library (which also holds the records of the Province of Canterbury and records of the Court of Arches). Records of the PCC are held at TNA.

The records of the High Court of Delegates are at TNA and described in the *PRO Guide* (228). Cause papers for appeals to the High Court of Delegates from about 1600 to 1834, setting out the basis for the appeal, are in series DEL 2. Importantly, series DEL 1 contains processes, that is 736 volumes of copies of the proceedings from the first instance courts from 1609 to 1834, including depositions, examinations of witnesses and transcribed copies of exhibits (wills, deeds, marriage licences and parish register extracts). Documents in DEL 1 and 2 are indexed in DEL 11. Decrees and orders made during the appeals, with ancillary documents, including further depositions, exhibits and witnesses' responses to interrogatories, are in series DEL 3–10.

Most records of the High Commission for Causes Ecclesiastical in the Province of Canterbury have been lost. The records of the Court of Arches at Lambeth Palace Library were noted in chapter 14 in connection with matrimonial proceedings. Appeals were made in respect of all types of ecclesiastical court business and Houston (941) is an index to surviving records of about 10,400 cases heard by the court since 1660 (earlier records were destroyed). The index notes the names of the first plaintiff and first defendant, the type of case, the court of first instance, the date of judgment (and then provides document references to the courts' records). An example is the case of "Elizabeth Gill (alias Richards) v. Thomas Richards", which concerned a legacy in the will of Jane Richards of Rewe in Devon. The case had been heard in Exeter in 1666 and the Court of Arches gave sentence on 5 July 1667. The index then refers the researcher to volumes and pages of act books, sentences, appeals and process books. For some cases, there are also references to pleadings, depositions and exhibits.

Very few records of the church courts have been published. One exception is Christie (927), containing abstracts of depositions from the Archdeaconry Court of Barnstaple (1570–79). It includes a deposition by Henry Bulhead of Winkleigh, answering allegations that he had contracted to marry Joanna Cornyshe of Ashreigny. Willis (958) includes transcripts or abstracts of depositions from the Bishop of Winchester's Consistory Court (1561–1602). Seven volumes of depositions from the Oxfordshire church courts in the 16th and early 17th centuries have also been published, including Drake (930), which provides abstracts of depositions from about 80 cases from 1542 to 1550. Brinkworth (924) includes abstracts of the act books of the Peculiar Court of Stratford (1590–1625).

Giese (935) and Webb (956) are important indexes to London church court records. They index depositions (and the cases in which they were made) in the Consistory Court of London, 1586–1611 and 1703–13 respectively. They include the deponent's name, age, occupation and place of residence. Webb also records the deponent's place of birth and previous places of residence (which were usually recorded in a deposition). Although most deponents were Londoners, many were born elsewhere. For example, in the action by Henry Burton against his reputed wife Elizabeth Burton, the deposition of Jacob Farlam in January 1707/8 noted that he was a waterman aged 47, who had lived in Rotherhithe for a year but had been born in Hexham, Northumberland.

CHAPTER 25

RECORDS OF THE CRIMINAL COURTS AND CRIMINALS

THE CRIMINAL COURTS AND THEIR RECORDS

Some records of criminals (such as newspaper reports and published law reports) have already been noted. This chapter reviews the records of the Justices of the Peace, the criminal courts and prisons. The Justices and some criminal courts also had jurisdiction over certain civil cases and so the records of those cases are also reviewed below. The documents record criminals, victims, judges and witnesses, so they may evidence your ancestors on each side of the law. Most records of crime and criminals are in Latin up to 1732 and are rarely indexed (the few indexes available are usually limited to defendants' names). Hawkings (984) is therefore an essential reference work to the court and prison records available for criminal ancestors. Cale (964) is also a useful guide to records held at TNA of criminals and the criminal courts since 1800.

Published works on crime or famous criminals may refer to your ancestors. Another advantage of starting with published records of criminal trials is that you quickly become conversant with the legal language and procedure of (and records produced in) criminal investigations and trials. It is then easier to turn to original records of crime and criminals. As noted above, *Devon Murders* by Harrison (983) includes a description of the murder of Jonathan May, a farmer to whom Eliza Rice of Dunsford was apprenticed. Gray (979) is a similar book, dealing with crime in Essex. Many other useful books can be found in libraries or bookshops. Herber (985) is an illustrated history of London crime, including short biographies of notorious criminals and over 400 illustrations of criminals, victims, courts and prisons. *The Chronicles of Newgate* by Griffiths (981) is a history of Newgate Gaol in London, with notes on some prisoners held there or tried in the adjoining Old Bailey Sessions House. Cheney (966) is an account of some prisoners in Newgate in the 19th century.

More detailed published works are the various collections of *State Trials*, the series of volumes *Notable British Trials* and works such as *The Newgate Calendar* and *The Bloody Register*. The *State Trials* are collections of reports of criminal trials from the 12th to 19th centuries. In most of these cases, the defendant was charged with a crime against the state (usually treason) but some were notorious trials of other offences, such as murder, perjury, criminal libel or bigamy. The best series are those by Howell (986), the early volumes of which were edited by William Cobbett, and by MacDonnell (997). Each series has an index volume to the names of the defendants, witnesses and lawyers. The volumes can be seen in reference or law libraries. They have also been published on CD-ROM.

The Newgate Calendar is the name applied to a large number of volumes of differing titles (by different writers or editors), originally published between about 1730 and 1850, containing accounts of hundreds of criminal trials and of the lives of many criminals. They should not be confused with calendars (that is lists) of prisoners at Newgate and other gaols that are described below. Some of the information that these works contain is inaccurate but they are useful. Their titles include *Select Trials at the Sessions House in the Old Bailey*, *The Bloody Register*, *The Tyburn Chronicle*, *The Newgate Calendar* and *The Malefactor's Register*. Many of the volumes have been reprinted (or re-edited, combining accounts of trials from a number of the different works). Examples of the reprints are *The Newgate Calendar* by Wilkinson (1006) and *The Complete Newgate Calendar* by Rayner & Crook (998). One of the early volumes, *The Bloody Register* of 1764, has been reprinted in Groom (982). The trial of Francis Goslin, of Stepney, at the Old Bailey in January 1713 is just one of the many cases in this work. The charge against Goslin was that he (and John Shaw) aided and abetted Robert Furlow to murder John Hutton. Hutton's body was found, in a boat on the Thames near Greenwich, covered in blood. In his pocket was a certificate of apprenticeship, given by a man named Brand, a boatswain on the ship *Nottingham*. This resulted in identification of the corpse as that of John Hutton. The boat had been stolen from John Warren. Goslin was apprehended for another robbery and found to be wearing some of Warren's clothes that had been in the boat. Whilst in custody, Goslin confessed to his involvement in Hutton's death. Goslin said that John Shaw, Robert Furlow and he had stolen the boat and tried to sell it to Hutton but then robbed him. Furlow had cut Hutton's throat. Goslin was convicted of murder and sentenced to death. Goslin told the chaplain at Newgate Gaol that he had been born at Greenwich, was 21 years old, had served an apprenticeship with his father (a waterman) and then served in the Royal Navy and on merchant ships. The report also notes that Shaw was never caught and that Furlow was later tried for murder but acquitted because he had an alibi. This one case will be of great interest to descendants of any of the five men mentioned in it.

The volumes of *Notable British Trials* include detailed reports of famous trials (mostly for murder) and include much of the witnesses' evidence. For example, the trial of Thomas Neill Cream, the Lambeth poisoner, in 1892 is described in Shore (1002). Cream was convicted of murdering a prostitute, Matilda Clover, and executed at Newgate Gaol. He had also killed three other women; Ellen Donworth (alias Ellen Linnell), Alice Marsh, Emma Shrivell (and probably other people in America). Shore includes some genealogical information about Cream and his victims but also the evidence of 37 witnesses (including policemen and doctors as well as the landladies, relatives, friends and neighbours of the deceased). Was your ancestor one of the witnesses? Was one of the victims your ancestor's sister? Was Cream a member of your family?

There are also many published pamphlets or reports on criminal trials. These are held in archives such as the British and Bodleian libraries, but are now more accessible because many of them are being published on microfiche by Chadwyck-Healey as *British Trials 1660–1900* (961). A copy is held at Guildhall Library. The pamphlets reprinted in this series concern thousands of criminal trials, many reporting (almost verbatim) what was said in court. Since the pamphlets were for sale to the public, they tended to deal with the more sensational trials (for murder, highway robbery or treason). They include two particularly important series of pamphlets that are considered below, the *Account of the Ordinary of Newgate* and the *Proceedings*. *British Trials* also includes some interesting civil cases, concerning defamation, criminal conversation and divorce. When complete, the series will consist of almost 5,000 fiche. Cases are indexed (in a separate booklet) by names of defendants, plaintiffs (in civil cases), victims and by location and subject of the trial. Robert Charnock was tried in 1695/6 (noted above) for conspiring to assassinate King

William III. *British Trials* includes a detailed 76-page pamphlet about his trial. Charnock and his co-conspirators (Edward King and Thomas Keyes) were found guilty of treason and hanged, drawn and quartered at Tyburn. Having searched for cases in these published works, you can then turn to the records held in archives.

The Eyre

In the period following the Norman Conquest, many criminals were dealt with in manorial courts held by the Lord of each manor. These courts (and the crimes they dealt with) are considered in chapter 27. Their role was gradually assumed from the 14th century by Justices of the Peace (see below). However, more serious crimes (and some civil cases) were a matter for the King rather than the manorial lords. Accordingly, from the late 12th to 14th centuries, the King's judges were sent out from London every few years to administer justice in the counties, at hearings known as the General Eyre. For example, the visitation of 1198–99 was carried out by groups of justices in five circuits. On the southern circuit, they visited Exeter, Winchester, Wilton and Chichester.

The justices heard civil pleas, crown pleas (trials of people indicted for felonies) and the charges against those held in gaol. Civil (or common) pleas were civil disputes, such as cases of trespass or debt. The justices also heard King's pleas (or Quo warranto proceedings), which were civil suits brought by the Crown, for example to ensure that a person or borough had the right to hold a market or fair. The Eyre also reviewed local administration and presentments made by juries (for example about local wrongdoers). As we shall see below, coroners also presented the justices with their rolls of inquests into suspicious or unnatural deaths.

Crook (974) is a detailed analysis of the General Eyre and its records. They are in Latin, cover the years 1194–1348 (mostly at TNA on the Eyre, Assize or Gaol Delivery Rolls in series JUST 1–4 or the Eyre Rolls of the Palatinate of Chester in CHES 17) and also described in the *PRO Guide* (228). Crook (974) lists the eyres held (and the surviving rolls) for each county. Plea rolls report the eyre's business, listing civil and crown pleas, the amercements (fines), the veredictum (a jury's answers to questions about crimes or administration in a borough or hundred) and schedules from juries naming those suspected of crimes (a procedure later known as indictment). Amercements may also be on separate rolls.

The records are very difficult to use and are really only for experts, but Crook lists those that have been transcribed, translated and published by the Selden Society, the Pipe Roll Society and local record societies. For example, Sutherland (1003) is a transcript (and translation of the parts in Latin or French) of legal reporters' records of the Eyre of Northamptonshire for 1329–30, with further information extracted from the rolls in JUST 1. Some cases include important genealogical information. In one Crown plea, the jury presented that Richard le Saltere had been killed at night in the house of Denise Crabbe in Brackley, by Geoffrey le Saltere of Yorlauston and Agnes (Richard's wife). Agnes and Denise were arrested but Geoffrey fled and was outlawed. The justices at the eyre also heard a case about gruesome events of 13 years before. The jurors of Warden hundred presented that, at Easter 1316, Thomas Murdak, knight, was found dead. The coroner's inquest said that his head had been cut off and his body dismembered. The jury said that he was killed at Stourton, in Kinver Forest near Northampton, by John de Vaus, knight, Elias (John's brother), Gillian (the victim's wife), Robert Sumpter, Robert Purdhome (chaplain), William (the victim's steward), William (his cook) and six others. Gillian Murdak had been convicted in the Court of King's Bench and burned. All the others had fled.

By the time of the 1329 eyre, John de Vaus and his brother Elias had died, but the eyre declared the other men outlaws and their property was seized.

Many Quo warranto and civil cases are also recorded. In one case Nicholas Chanceis was summoned to state by what right he levied a toll on salt and fish in his manor of Upton. His lawyer submitted that the rights had been obtained by Thomas (Nicholas's father) and Hugh (his grandfather). In a more complex case Robert of Hauton (and Agnes his wife) with Lawrence of Buketon (and Rose his wife) sued for rents due from Henry Fitz Robert of Northampton, Walter of Pateshull (and Emma his wife). The rents had originally been due to Philip Fitz Robert of Pisseford, knight (deceased), then to Alice (Philip's daughter) who had married William Fitz Matthew. William and Alice had also died, so the rents were now owed to their daughters Agnes and Rose, the wives of Robert of Hauton and Lawrence of Buketon. Thus one 14th-century case about rents reveals three generations of a family.

The Assize courts

From the 14th century the eyres were replaced by a similar system of visitations to the counties by judges from the courts at Westminster. The hearings were known as assizes. They originally reviewed certain property disputes but the justices' powers were gradually extended to criminal cases and the assizes became the principal English criminal courts until they were replaced by the Crown Courts in 1971.

The assize justices usually worked in pairs and proceeded on circuits. They moved between county towns on royal commissions of the peace or of gaol delivery (to try prisoners), or "oyer and terminer" (to hear and determine) those cases that were not heard by local courts (that is, serious offences such as murder, riot, rape, burglary and treason). The justices also heard some civil cases that originated in the Westminster courts, by writ of nisi prius. This writ ordered a civil trial to be heard in London *unless before then* the justices of assize visited the county (which they usually did). These visitations avoided the need for offenders, litigants, witnesses and jurors to travel to London for trials. The use of judges who worked together in London also provided some uniformity across the country in the application of the law and in sentencing. Unfortunately, the assize system also resulted in an accused being held in prison for many months awaiting trial at the next assizes. The City of London (and later Middlesex) was excluded from the assize circuits but had its own court at Old Bailey. Bristol and the palatinates of Cheshire, Durham and Lancashire also had their own assize courts (or equivalents) until 1832, 1830, 1876 and 1877 respectively. The rest of England was divided between circuits, the number of which (and areas covered) changed at intervals. By 1340 there were six assize circuits:

Circuit	Counties
Home	Essex, Hertfordshire, Kent, Middlesex, Surrey, Sussex
Western	Berkshire, Cornwall, Devon, Dorset, Hampshire, Oxfordshire, Somerset, Wiltshire
Oxford	Gloucestershire, Herefordshire, Shropshire, Staffordshire, Worcestershire
Norfolk	Bedfordshire, Buckinghamshire, Cambridgeshire, Norfolk, Suffolk, Huntingdonshire
Midland	Derbyshire, Rutland, Leicestershire, Lincolnshire, Northamptonshire, Nottinghamshire, Warwickshire
Northern	Cumberland, Northumberland, Westmorland, Yorkshire

In about 1540 Oxfordshire and Berkshire were transferred to the Oxford circuit. Middlesex was detached from the Home circuit and Middlesex cases were heard with City of London cases at sessions (considered below) at Old Bailey. Monmouthshire was added to the Western circuit and the Court of Great Sessions (# chapter 29) was instituted in Wales. In 1830 the Welsh Great Sessions were replaced by a seventh assize circuit (for Wales and Cheshire). Bristol was brought into the assize circuits in 1832. The circuits were reorganised in 1864, 1876 and 1893 (to include Durham and Lancashire) as described in Hawkings (984) and TNA legal records leaflets 13–14.

Assizes were meant to take place three times a year but twice was more usual, generally during the Westminster courts' Lent vacation (late February and March) and long vacation (July and August). Until the early 19th century the three northern counties were only visited once a year. The assizes took place at one or more towns in each county, usually the principal county town, but often in other towns with gaols. Each circuit lasted between two and five weeks depending on the amount of business. However, the number of cases could be very substantial and trials therefore very short. A judge in 1600 might deal with about 10 or 20 cases a day (and on some days up to 50 cases). A trial, in which the accused possibly faced the death penalty, may have taken only 30 minutes. Cockburn (968) is a detailed review of the history and work of the assize courts from the 16th to the early 18th centuries. The introductory volume of Cockburn (970) describes the work of the Home circuit justices during the reigns of Elizabeth and James I, but much of this is also relevant to the other circuits. In particular, Cockburn includes illustrations (with transcripts and translations) of 28 typical documents from 16th- and 17th-century assize files. Hawkings (984) also provides examples of 18th- and 19th-century assize records.

Assize records were kept by the Clerks of the Assize and most are now at TNA. Unfortunately, many have been lost or destroyed, including most records of the Midland circuit and most Elizabethan assize records. Until 1732 most records were also in Latin. Most surviving records up to 1559 are in series JUST 3, with some in JUST 1 or 4 and KB 9. Records since 1559 are in series ASSI 1–54 (for England) and ASSI 57–77 (for Wales since 1830). The records of criminal courts in the Palatinates of Cheshire, Durham and Lancashire (prior to their inclusion in assize circuits) are also at TNA, in series CHES 17–24, DURH 15–19 and PL 15 and 25–28. Details of all these records are contained in the series lists, but brief descriptions, with covering dates, are in the *PRO Guide* (228), Hawkings (984) and TNA legal records leaflets 13–14. Criminal court records of Bristol prior to 1832 are at Bristol Record Office. The records of courts (equivalent to assizes) for the City of London (and Middlesex since 1540) are considered below.

Judges received commissions of assize, of oyer and terminer, or gaol delivery from the Crown Office of Chancery and they informed the county sheriffs of the dates and places for the assizes. A sheriff then prepared calendars, listing prisoners and alleged crimes (with lists of jurors and officials, such as coroners). The Clerk of the Assize would add these to lists of any business outstanding from the last assize. Some assize circuits' minute books list defendants' names, offences, verdicts and sentences, but the most important records of Crown side business (criminal matters) were the indictments. These note an accused's name, description, residence, offence (and date) and the name of any victim. The accused's plea, the verdict and sentence may have been added later. Indictments were drawn up by the staff of the Clerks of Assize, by Clerks of the Peace (for cases referred to assizes by Justices of the Peace) or (in the case of homicides) by an endorsement on the coroner's inquest upon the victim. Unfortunately, few indictments survive from before the mid-17th century (except for the Home circuit). Most Home circuit indictments survive from 1559 and there are published calendars of these (translated and indexed) up to 1625, in 10 volumes by Cockburn (970). There are also further volumes of Kent indictments, by Cockburn (971–973), for 1625 to 1675, including these indictments at Sevenoaks assizes on 5 August 1647 (from piece ASSI 35/88/6):

Indictment of John Sharpe of Bromley, yeoman, for grand larceny. On 1st Aug. 1647 at Bromley he stole a brown gelding (value £7) from Thomas Stevens.

Indictment of Richard Woodman of Headcorn, labourer, for assault. On 21st July 1647 at Headcorn he assaulted Edward Coveney.

Indictment of Edward Dodson of Newington, Surrey, yeoman, for bigamy. On 1st Mar. 1641 at Newington he married Mary Walker while Frances Arnold, whom he had married on 1st July 1628 at Long Eaton in Sawley, Derbyshire was still alive.

The difficulty of using early assize records can be seen from the handwriting, Latin and abbreviations shown in illustration 127. This is an indictment from the Surrey assizes held at Kingston in February 1567. Edward Marche, yeoman, was accused of having broken into the house of a widow, Joan Arnold, in Esher on 16 October and having stolen a hat, a piece of cloth and two pence. Marche was found guilty and sentenced to hang. Assize records also include some files of coroners' inquests (considered below), informations, depositions and recognizances (bonds for defendants or witnesses to attend court). A typical information (in this case from the Northern circuit in 1754) commences as follows:

The information of William Bone of the parish of Sculcotts in the East Riding of the County of York, gardener, taken upon oath this 15th day of March 1754. This informant on his oath saith that . . . [followed by his knowledge of the crime].

Gaol books list those held in prisons and their offences, how they pleaded and sometimes verdicts, as in the following example from the Northern circuit in 1763:

John Hall otherwise Bloom pleads guilty, for stealing a bay mare price £10, property of John Harrison, 4th July last at Beverley.

Gaol delivery calendars record the names of the judges, the place and date of the assizes, the prisoners and their sentences. An example from Cockburn (970) of a gaol delivery calendar for Southwark in Surrey in 1615 includes these entries:

Edward Stocke, John Payne, to be branded.

Thomas Jones remanded on bail to appear at Newgate at the next sessions.

Francis Nethercoate, Thomas Sutton, Blanch Durrant to be whipped.

Thomas Moore, George Browne, Luke Percival, Edward Jennings and Richard Kent to be hanged by the neck.

Many civil matters (perhaps for trespass or breach of contract) were heard at assizes. The assize clerks received papers from the Courts of King's Bench or Common Pleas and, after a trial, they were endorsed with a *postea* (an order or judgment) and returned to the London courts. Records therefore rarely survive in assize papers, except perhaps for a note of an order in a circuit minute

127. *Indictment of Edward Marche for burglary at Kingston assizes, February 1567 (T.N.A, ASSI 35/9/1)*

book, but they may be in King's Bench or Common Pleas records, for example in series KB 20, CP 41 or CP 42. Assize justices also reviewed local administration, for example reviewing the upkeep of bridges or hearing cases about settlement, poor relief and complaints about local tax collectors. There are some published volumes of assize orders. Cockburn (969) includes about 1,200 orders (from series ASSI 24) made on the Western circuit from 1629 to 1648. There was a dispute between the parishes of Tiverton in Devon and Dunster in Somerset as to the place of settlement of Elizabeth Chibbett, a pauper. Tiverton was found liable for her because, although born in Dunster, she had worked as a servant in Tiverton for over one year before falling ill and having to apply for parish relief. Assize courts also dealt with apprenticeships. Cockburn (969) notes an order made at the Devon assizes in Exeter in August 1631:

Order discharging Robert Endicott from his apprenticeship with his father, William Endicott of Exminster, joiner, now a prisoner in the county gaol, and binding him to Edward Cockhill, an Exeter joiner.

Those who ignored licensing requirements could also be brought before the assizes. At the Somerset assizes at Taunton in August 1631 the following order was made:

Robert Brewer of Stogumber, who . . . in contempt of the Justices of the Peace continues to keep an unlicensed alehouse after being several times suppressed, is committed to the house of correction for punishment.

The assize circuits did not include the City of London. Criminal jurisdiction in London, equivalent to the assizes and Quarter Sessions (considered below), was exercised by three commissions: of the peace, of gaol delivery of Newgate and of oyer and terminer. There were a number of sessions of each (for example eight annual sessions of gaol delivery by 1670), usually held at Old Bailey, but sometimes at Guildhall. The Lord Mayor, Recorder and Aldermen of London (and one or more of the King's Bench judges) acted as justices (and also as justices for Southwark). The sessions also dealt with Middlesex cases from 1540. The Old Bailey Sessions ceased in 1834 when the Central Criminal Court was established (also sitting at Old Bailey) with jurisdiction over crimes committed in the City of London, Middlesex and parts of Essex, Kent and Surrey.

Some Old Bailey Sessions' papers survive from 1684 and they are almost complete from 1744. They usually provide details of the defendant, the offence and (from 1791) the verdict and any sentence. The records are at CLRO (for City of London and Southwark cases) and described by Deadman & Scudder (244), or at LMA (for Middlesex cases) and they are all listed in summary in Gibson (976). Most records of the Central Criminal Court since 1834 are at TNA and listed in the *Current Guide* (234) and Colwell (242). Indictments of 1834–1957 are in series CRIM 4, with a calendar in CRIM 5. Some surviving depositions are in CRIM 1. Hawkings (984) includes extracts from these records. Some are very detailed. Thus Hawkings notes that 12 witness depositions survive for a murder trial of 1895. From the late 17th century journalists also prepared detailed reports (for publication) of cases at the Old Bailey Sessions. The reports, entitled *The Proceedings upon the King's Commissions of the Peace, of Oyer and Terminer and Gaol Delivery for the City of London and also the Gaol Delivery for the County of Middlesex* (the *Proceedings*), also came to be known as Old Bailey Sessions papers (they do not, despite their title, include reports on the sessions of the peace). These reports also covered later trials at the Central Criminal Court (from 1834 to 1913). They note the names of the accused, jurors, justices and witnesses. The reports of the crime and the evidence are sometimes very detailed. An almost complete set of the *Proceedings* is held at Guildhall Library. Copies for 1801–1904 are at TNA (in series PCOM 1) and there are also sets at the British and Bodleian libraries. Copies are being included in *British Trials* (961). Transcripts of the *Proceedings* of 1674–1834, featuring about 100,000 trials, are being placed on the excellent Old Bailey web site (# appendix XI for the address) by the universities of Hertfordshire and Sheffield. Transcripts of 45,000 trials for 1714–99 are already available and the remainder should become available online in late 2003 and early 2004. The transcripts can be searched by subject (such as bigamy) or by names of people appearing in them (whether the accused, victims, judges or witnesses). For example, the *Proceedings* for the sessions of 4–9 December 1741 include reports on 100 City of London and Middlesex cases. Some reports are very short:

> Catherine Grice was indicted for stealing a silver stock buckle, value 4s. 6d. and also [cash of] 2s. 6d.; the goods and money of Mary Butler, September 22nd. Guilty. [Goods value decided by jury] 10d.

Juries often decided that stolen goods were less valuable than the prosecution alleged so that a death sentence did not have to be passed. Many reports are more lengthy. At the same sessions, John Runsburgh of Chiswick was convicted of assaulting William Collier on the highway and stealing six pence from him. The report includes evidence of William Collier, but also of Richard Hall, John Wood and George Bridges, who helped Collier arrest Runsburgh. A list of those convicted at the session appears at the end of the report. Seven defendants were sentenced to death (including John Runsburgh), 6 to be burnt in the hand, 8 to be whipped and 52 to be transported (including Catherine Grice). Illustration 128 is a typical page from the *Proceedings*, reporting cases heard at the Old Bailey Sessions that started on 10 May 1780. The judges at the sessions included Brackley Kennet (the Lord Mayor of London), Mr Justice Willes (of the King's Bench) and Serjeant Adair (the Recorder of London). Mary Jones was tried for theft of a watch from Richard Wolfe. Sarah Jones was tried for stealing a watch from Mr Anger Bourn. Mary admitted to being an "unfortunate" (a prostitute) and it is likely that Sarah also followed the oldest profession. It was very common for prostitutes to steal, or attempt to steal, watches or other valuables from their clients, sometimes because a man had refused to pay for his few minutes of pleasure. Both girls were convicted of theft (the all-male juries usually took the men's side in these cases). A later page in the *Proceedings* reported that Mary Jones was sentenced to a whipping and six months imprisonment (Sarah Jones' sentence is not recorded).

Another important series of pamphlets, also included in *British Trials* (961), was *The Ordinary of Newgate, his Account of the Behaviour, Confession, and Dying Words of the Malefactors who were Executed at Tyburn, 1703–72* (the *Ordinary's Account*). Men and women who were to be executed at Tyburn spent their last few days in Newgate Gaol. The Ordinary (the prison chaplain) talked with many of the condemned and these conversations were published (as biographies of the prisoners) in pamphlets at the time of the execution. The pamphlets contain much useful biographical information, but some of it may be untrue.

Records of prisons and prisoners are considered below, but TNA holds some records that relate specifically to prisoners who were tried at assizes. Assize vouchers are lists of the persons

[330]

Saturday the 22d of April about a quarter after eight. The clock ftruck eight as I came over Blackfriars-bridge from Walworth. When I came home, he was at home.

I fuppofe he continued at home till after ten ?——I cannot tell ; I came down about a quarter after ten ; he gave me part of a pot of beer. He had a handkerchief about his head ; he wifhed me a good night and went to bed.

BOTH NOT GUILTY.

Tried by the Firft Middlefex Jury before Mr. Baron PERRYN.

265. MARY JONES was indicted for ftealing a filver watch, value 3l. and a filver watch chain, value 2s. the property of Richard Wolfe, April 17th.

RICHARD WOLFE *fworn.*

I am a tailor. On the 17th of April, as I was going home from a public-boufe between eleven and twelve at night ; the prifoner picked me up. I had been drinking and was a little the worfe for liquor. As I was coming up the Old Jewry, the prifoner took hold of my arm, and faid, *fhe wanted to fpeak with me.* She pulled me down the Old Jewry, till we came to an alley on the right-hand ; there fhe felt about my breeches, and wanted me to feel about her ; I told her I did not underftand that. Then I put my hand to my watch, and felt I had got it. She walked with me out of the alley, up to the beginning of Cheapfide. I was going to crofs the way from her ; I put my hand to my watch and miffed it ; it had a filver chain to it. There was nobody in company with me but the prifoner. I told her fhe had got my watch ; fhe denied it ; I took her to the watch-houfe, and fhe was fearched, and the watch was produced upon the table in the watch-houfe.

(*The watch was produced by the conftable who found it upon her and it was depofed to by the profecutor.*)

PRISONER's DEFENCE.

I am an unfortunate, unhappy girl. As I was coming along Cheapfide, this man afked me to go and drink with him, which I did. Then he faid if I would go with him he would give me fomething. He faid he had nothing to give me then, but I might take his watch to hold. When he was going away he afked me for it again ; I afked him for what he promifed to give me ; he knocked me down like a dog, and faid if I did not give it him he would charge the watch with me, which he did. I did not deny giving it him when I came to the watch-houfe.

Court. Did you give her the watch ?—No.

Did you knock her down ?——No.

GUILTY.

Tried by the London Jury before Mr. Juftice WILLES.

266. SARAH JONES was indicted for ftealing a filver watch, value 4l. the property of Anger Bourn, April 25th.

ANGER BOURN *fworn.*

I am a hair-dreffer. On the 25th of April I had been at a benefit-club ; coming home about a quarter after one o'clock. I was not quite fober, having been drinking. I met the prifoner in St. Paul's church-yard. While I ftood talking with her, I felt her take my watch out of my pocket. She gave it to another woman who ran away ; I took the prifoner to the watch-houfe.

Did any thing indecent pafs between you ? —No. *Something indecent might have paffed perhaps if fhe had not taken my watch.* I faw her give it the other woman who ftood at about four yards diftance.

PRISONER's DEFENCE.

I did not take the watch. I have no witneffes.

GUILTY.

Tried by the London Jury before Mr. Juftice WILLES.

267, 268. THOMAS CARTER and MARY EVANS, otherwife MARY the wife of the faid Thomas Carter, were indicted

128. The trials of Mary Jones and Sarah Jones in 1780, a page from the Old Bailey Proceedings

convicted at assizes and are in series E 370 (for 1714–1832) together with sheriffs' cravings, which are sheriffs' requests for payment of the costs of organising the assizes, holding prisoners in gaol until trial, moving convicts to prison hulks, and the cost of executions. Some cravings are also in series T 64. Sheriffs' payments record the money actually paid to sheriffs for these duties and are in T 90 and 207 (for 1733–1822 and 1832–1959). Treasury warrants record sums paid to sheriffs for the expenses of apprehending criminals. Indexed books of Treasury warrants are in T 53 (1721–1805) and T 54 (1806–27). Hawkings (984) reviews all these records, with many examples, including:

Sheriffs' cravings for Nottingham and Chelmsford gaols (E 370)
Paid for the dieting and maintenance of Paul Hufton, convicted of a burglary, from 1st January 1788 to 12th February, the time of his removal for transportation; . . . 15s.
Thomas Cawkwell, keeper of Chelmsford Gaol in account with the under sheriff . . .
Deborah Lowden convicted Lent Assizes 1822 and remained in gaol from 11th February till 19th May 1823 when she was delivered on board the convict ship off Woolwich . . . £1 15s.

Assize vouchers; Oxfordshire (E 370/49)
At the Assizes and General Delivery of the Gaol (held) at Oxford on [7th March 1821] before Sir James Allan Park [and other justices];
guilty to be hanged . . . William Bolter and John Lee for burglary . . .
guilty of grand larceny, to be kept to hard labour in the House of Correction for three calendar months and during next week to be once well whipped . . . William Larner and Edward Hinder.
guilty of receiving goods knowing the same to have been feloniously stolen, to be transported . . . for 14 years . . . Charlotte Moss.

Treasury warrants (T 53/59)
Arthur Dowel, undersheriff of Montgomery. An order for paying £50, dated 14 March 1789, to Catherine Price for apprehending and convicting John Griffiths, David Morris, Edward Evans, Margaret Webster and Evan Jenks of felony, sheepstealing.

State Papers and the Patent Rolls
The State Papers Domestic (# chapter 22) include much material about crime and legal disputes. Many of the papers since the reign of Henry VIII have been published by HMSO in indexed volumes, listed in Mullins (260). These examples, from the calendar for 1547 to 1580, by Lemon (995), show the important information that the papers contain:

1576. Information against Henry Kanter (alias Kalice), Thomas Cole and others for robbing Robert Fletcher at Helford Haven.
Petition of John Martyn, John Shaplye and other merchants of Totnes and Staverton, Devon to the Council . . . to be a means for the release of their goods which, by order of the French king, had been stayed at Rouen.

The Patent Rolls (# chapter 27) in series C 66 at TNA, date from the 13th century and include information about crime and criminals. The rolls recorded royal pardons to outlaws (reviewed below) but also to others who faced criminal charges or who had been convicted. These examples are from List and Index Society volume 255, which calendars the Patent Rolls of 1588–90:

24 Feb. 1589. Pardon for John Gifford of London, yeoman, indicted for the theft on 27 Dec in St Sepulchre's parish, ward of Farringdon Without, of a mare from Robert Thorne of Sonnynge, co. Oxford, husbandman . . . at the petition of Anne Gifford his wife.

29 May 1590. Pardon for Robert Dawlyn of Swanwiche, Dorset, tayler, for the accidental shooting of Elizabeth Abbott, late wife of Edward Abbott, clerk, rector of Swanwiche, by the discharge of a fowling piece aimed at a mark fixed on an elm, the bullett hitting Elizabeth while she was in her garden out of sight, 21 May [1589], as was found by an inquisition taken at Swanwiche in the hundred of Rowbarrowe, 22 May [1589] before Nicholas Baker, mayor of Warham, coroner of the hundred.

Criminal appeal courts
Convictions at assizes could be appealed or reviewed by a writ of *certiorari* directed to the Court of King's Bench. This court's records (including those relating to its criminal jurisdiction) are at TNA and were reviewed in chapter 24. It had jurisdiction over all criminal cases (its judges sitting at most assizes), supervisory powers over assizes or lesser courts and a particular jurisdiction over criminal matters in Middlesex (because the court's seat was located there). Entries for criminal cases are included on the Plea Rolls (series KB 26–27) up to 1702 and then on the Crown Rolls in KB 28. Files of indictments are in series KB 9 until 1675, then in KB 10 (for London and Middlesex) and KB 11 (for other counties), then in KB 12 for all counties from 1845 until 1875. Bevan (239) refers researchers to indexes of London and Middlesex defendants (1673–1843), and provincial defendants (1638–1704 and 1765–1843).

From 1848 criminal appeals (on points of law) were heard by the Court for Crown Cases Reserved, from 1907 by the Court of Criminal Appeal and from 1966 by the Court of Appeal (Criminal Division). Some of these appeals are recorded in published law reports (# chapter 24). Some records of appeals are held at TNA and listed in Colwell (242). They include registers for 1908–09 and 1914–63 (in series J 81) giving the appellant's name, offence, place and date of conviction, and the nature and result of the appeal. A few case files have also been preserved in J 82.

Justices of the Peace and Quarter Sessions
Justices of the Peace (also known as magistrates) were appointed from the 14th century by commissions of the peace from the king. Their power and jurisdiction gradually increased. They dealt with the less serious criminal cases on behalf of the Crown (although punishments could include death or transportation) and they also took over the criminal jurisdiction of the manorial courts (# chapter 27). Justices had many civil administrative duties (and power to hear some civil disputes), since they inherited much of the jurisdiction of the church and manorial courts (and new duties were given to the Justices by central government). From the 16th and 17th centuries the Justices' responsibilities therefore included:

a. hearing criminal trials (for theft, poaching, assault, vagrancy)
b. supervising the poor law (including settlement and bastardy examinations)

c. enforcing the law against recusants

d. overseeing relationships between apprentices and masters

e. licensing of certain trades (such as alehouse keepers) and ensuring that craftsmen were qualified by guild membership or having served an apprenticeship

f. supervising the administration of taxes, upkeep of highways and local defence

g. the taking of oaths

From 1361 until 1971 the Justices met four times a year, at Easter, Trinity (midsummer), Michaelmas and Epiphany (January). These Quarter Sessions were held for each county except Middlesex, but there were also commissions of the peace for Middlesex and for the City of Westminster. As noted above, sessions were also held at Guildhall or Old Bailey (for the City of London). In addition to Quarter Sessions, certain towns and cities had the right to hold separate borough or city sessions (usually quarterly). Furthermore, there was often too much work to be dealt with at Quarter Sessions and so from the 16th century various statutes empowered the Justices to meet between Quarter Sessions, to deal with minor matters. Thus an act of 1541 required Justices of each county to meet, six weeks before the Quarter Sessions, to make enquiries into vagabonds. An Order in Council of 1605 required Justices to meet to inquire into alehouses. These meetings became known as Petty Sessions and the Justices gradually undertook more types of their work (for example settlement or bastardy examinations, issuing arrest warrants and trying lesser offences) at these sessions. A single Justice also had power to grant warrants or issue a summons (for someone to attend court) and much of this work was dealt with from his home. Most of the Justices' civil responsibilities have now been passed to county councils or other local authorities, but Justices continue to deal with many criminal and some civil matters.

The records of the Justice's work were kept by the Clerk of the Peace who was a lawyer. Surviving records are at CROs or city and borough archives. The records varied in form over time (and from place to place) but there were five main categories:

a. Order books: formal records of Justices' decisions, verdicts and sentences

b. Minute, process or sessions books: the Clerk of the Peace's notes of proceedings (some of the Justices' own notebooks of their work also survive)

c. Indictments: recording criminal charges, with a defendant's name, place of abode, the alleged offence, the date and place of the crime and sometimes the names of victims or witnesses. The verdict and sentence might also be noted

d. Sessions' rolls or files: records used during the sessions, such as petitions, jury lists, depositions, recognizances (sureties or bonds that someone would keep the peace or attend the next sessions), examinations (statements under oath by an accused, a migrant or an unmarried mother) and lists of prisoners. The rolls include estreats of fines (or amercements), that is extracts or copies (made for the Exchequer) listing fines or recognizances that were forfeited

e. Other documents lodged with the Clerk of the Peace (including many already considered) such as poll books, electoral registers, enclosure awards, lists of freemasons, papists or recusants, registers of papists' estates, tax returns (for windows, servants, dogs or horses), alehouse licences and land tax records

Emmison (975) is a detailed analysis of Quarter Sessions (and assize) records of Elizabethan Essex, providing many examples of the wide variety of offences dealt with, but also the Justice's work in respect of the licensing or regulation of alehouses, trades, games and sports. Many records of licences survive in Quarter Sessions' records, such as licences for alehouses (# chapter 22) and for non-conformist meeting houses under the Toleration Act 1689 (# chapter 13). Statutes of 1548 and 1603/4 required butchers to obtain licences to kill or sell meat during Lent. Some licences (and the butchers' recognizances) up to about 1670 survive in Quarter Sessions' records. From 1786 keepers of slaughterhouses also had to obtain a Justices' licence by submitting a certificate from the parish minister and churchwardens approving the applicant. Justices' records may include the certificates and registers of the licences. Justices also granted licences to corn dealers (often known as badgers). The term badger was sometimes applied to itinerant traders (also known as higglers or peddars) and they also had to be licensed by Quarter Sessions. An act of 1710 allowed the Lord of a manor to appoint a gamekeeper (with authority to kill game on the manor) whose name had to be registered with the Clerk of the Peace. Licences to carry guns were also granted at Quarter Sessions, usually to those with the requisite property qualifications. From 1774 private lunatic asylums also had to be licensed by Quarter Sessions.

Many other documents were lodged with the Justices at Quarter Sessions or with the Clerk of the Peace. For example, a man qualified for jury service by possessing land with an annual value of at least 40 shillings (£10 from 1692). From 1696 constables prepared returns (called jurors' or freeholders' lists) of all men aged between 21 and 70 who were liable to serve as jurors. These returns were lodged with the Clerk of the Peace and, until 1832, they note men's ages, occupations and residence (or qualifying property). The Clerk of the Peace used the lists to prepare jurors' or freeholders' books, with jurors' names (arranged by parish), ages, occupations, addresses and the annual value of their property. These books were sent to the county sheriff (but have generally now been filed with Quarter Sessions' records at CROs). An act of 1792 required aliens to be registered (# chapter 30) and so returns of aliens survive in Quarter Sessions' records. Justices' files also include many records of oaths made under statutes such as the Test Act 1673. Middlesex Sessions' records include 164 rolls of oaths and sacrament certificates (# chapter 23). From 1815 Justices received annual or quarterly lists of pauper lunatics from parish officers or poor law Guardians.

Many of the documents issued by Justices, particularly licences, summons, complaints and court orders, are held at CROs or in private collections. Illustration 129 is an information and complaint of Hugh Moore of Checkley, Staffordshire, in 1873, signed by a Justice, calling John Turner of Cheadle to attend court to answer Moore's allegation that Turner had assaulted him. Illustration 130 is a summons for William Gibson of Kingsley to appear at Petty Sessions at Cheadle on 14 October 1870 to answer the complaint of Ann Weaver of Kingsley, Staffordshire, that Gibson was the father of her illegitimate child.

Justices were also empowered, by various statutes from 1601, to levy a county rate from householders to finance expenditure on matters such as the building (and upkeep) of houses of correction, court houses and lunatic asylums, moving prisoners between gaols and court, paying gaolers' fees, prosecution expenses and militia charges. Accounts for these rates with the names of ratepayers (and expenditure books) can be found in Quarter Sessions' records.

Gibson (976) provides for each county a summary list of the Quarter Sessions' records (and their covering dates) held by archives. This should be your first source since the records may be at different branches of a CRO or in borough or city archives. For example, Gibson notes the

THE Information and Complaint of *Hugh Moore*
of the Parish of *Checkley*
of Stafford *farmer* taken this
day of *March* in the year of our Lord One Thousand Eight Hundred and
Seventy *three* before me the undersigned, one of Her Majesty's Justices of
the Peace acting in and for the said County

WHO saith that *John Turner* of the
Parish of *Cheadle in the County* aforesaid *Coal Carrier*
on *Wednesday* the *nineteenth* day of *March instant*
at the Parish of *Checkley* aforesaid did
unlawfully assault *him* the said *Hugh Moore* without any just
cause or provocation contrary to the statute in that case made. AND the said *John Turner*
Moore prayeth that the said *John Turner*
may be summoned to answer the premises.

Taken before me, the day }
and year first aforesaid.

Hugh Moore

129. *Information and complaint of Hugh Moore for assault by John Turner, 1873*

distribution between the branches of Devon Record Office (in Exeter, Barnstaple and Plymouth), of the county's Quarter Sessions records, but also records for the borough sessions of Exeter, Tiverton, Dartmouth, Barnstaple, Bideford, South Molton and Plymouth. The sessions' records of London are also in various archives. Records of sessions of the peace, of gaol delivery and of oyer and terminer for the City of London are at CLRO, but LMA holds records of the Middlesex sessions of the peace (1549–1971), the Westminster sessions' records (1620–1844) and the sessions' records for the administrative county of London since 1889. Most of the earlier sessions' records for those parts of London previously in Essex, Kent or Surrey are in the CROs for those counties. As an example of the variety of Justices' records, it is worth noting (in shortened form) Gibson's entry for the surviving Devon county sessions' records held in Exeter:

a. Order books 1592 to 20th century; process books 1693–1765; writs, indictments and court papers 1592–1940; constable's presentments 1679, 1685, 1726 and 1768; registers of appeals 1730–1876.

b. Recognizance books 1730–65; Estreats 1718–1863; Conviction registers 1753–83. Gaol calendars 1665–1810 and 1824–1953; contracts for transportation of felons 1726–76.

c. Returns of jurymen 1728–1915; jury lists 1730–1876; lists of freeholders 1711–1807.

d. Debtors' papers 1769–1844; register of insolvent debtors 1817–47.

e. Land tax assessments 1747, 1751 and 1780–1832; hearth tax return 1662; registrations of Papists' estates 1717–76.

f. Rolls of oaths of allegiance 1674–1880; sacrament certificates 1688–1828; papists' oaths 1791–1803; dissenting ministers' oaths 1780–1825 and dissenting teachers' oaths 1760–66.

g. Registers of licences for badgers 1729–79; returns of alehouses 1607–1821; registers of alehouse licences 1753–84 and 1822–27.

More detailed listings are available in archives' catalogues, or in their published guides, such as that for Bedfordshire (227) or Hertfordshire, by Le Hardy (994). Some archives have produced guides dealing specifically with Justices' records. Thus Goodacre & Mercer (978) is a detailed list of the Middlesex and Westminster sessions records at LMA. In view of the wealth of information contained in Justices' records, it is unfortunate that so many archives' collections remain unindexed (or even only briefly catalogued), and that only a small proportion of them have been transcribed and published. The number of indexes at CROs, or prepared by family history societies and the amount of published material is increasing, but much remains to be done to make the records easily accessible. Published material from Quarter Sessions' records is listed in Gibson (976), such as nine volumes of Warwickshire Quarter Sessions' records covering 1625–96. A few extracts from the volume for 1682–90 by Johnson (991) illustrate the importance of these records:

Trinity Sessions 1682
Richard Crooke of Solihull, labourer, indicted for extortion in taking 18s. 4d [from] John Woodward and Elizabeth his wife.
Abraham Geydon, yeoman, and John Hancocks, blacksmith, both of Preston Baggott, indicted for assault upon Thomas Newey [fined].

Staffordshire 〔 TO *William Gibson*

to wit. 〕 of *Kingsley* —————————— in the Parish

of *Kingsley* —————————— in the County of Stafford

Labourer

Whereas Application hath been this Day made to me the undersigned one of Her Majesty's Justices of the Peace for the County of Stafford, by *Ann Weaver* —————————— Single Woman, residing at *Kingsley* —————————— in the Petty Sessional Division of the said County for which I act, who hath been delivered of a Bastard Child since the passing of the act of the Eight Year of the Reign of Her present Majesty, intituled " An Act for the further Amendment of the Laws relating to the Poor in England," within Twelve Calendar Months from the Date hereof, and of which Bastard Child she alleges you to be the Father, for a Summons to be served upon you to appear at a Petty Session of the Peace, according to the Form of the Statute in such Case made and provided.

These are therefore to require you to appear at the Petty Session of the Justices holden at *the Police Office in Cheadle* being the Petty Session for the Division in which I usually act, on Friday, the *fourteenth* — day of *October* at Eleven o'Clock in the Forenoon, in the Year of our Lord One Thousand Eight Hundred and *Seventy* — to answer any Complaint which she shall then and there make against you touching the Premises.

Herein fail you not.

Given under my Hand and Seal at *Cheadle* in the County of Stafford this *twenty seventh* — Day of *September* in the Year of our Lord One Thousand Eight Hundred and ~~xxxx~~ *seventy*.

W. S. Allen

130. *Summons for William Gibson of Kingsley, Staffordshire, in 1870 to answer Ann Weaver's application for an affiliation order*

William Sturdy of Wicklesford, yeoman, indicted for keeping a disorderly ale-house; also for not coming to church to hear divine service for three Sundays . . . Elizabeth wife of Richard Pocock of Barston and John Greenwood of Hampton in Arden and Anne his wife presented for not coming to church to hear divine service . . . William Lucas, Samuel Lucas, Richard Lucas, John Field, Thomas Gilbert and William Beavington, all of Eateington, severally presented for not coming to church to hear divine service, being Quakers.

In a dispute between inhabitants of Kenilworth and Offchurch concerning the settlement of Joseph Moreton and Rebecca his wife . . . the court orders them to remain without prejudice at Kenilworth until the next sessions, when both sides are to be heard.

Order for maintenance of a female bastard child begotten on the body of Elizabeth Winge of Pillerton Pryours (spinster), by Richard West and for the indemnification of the parish of Pillerton, where the child was born.

Fines . . . of John Lane, Jonathan Seeley and Edward Eedes, all of Birmingham, for contempt, 5s. each.

Michaelmas Sessions 1682

It appearing . . . that James Harris, James Corry and John Loach are all Scotchmen wandering about as rogues and vagrants . . . and they having declared upon oath their places of birth . . . of Harris at Kirkegwinian (co. Galloway), of Corry in Arnegray Parish (co. Galloway) and of Loach in Onon Parish (co. Annendale), the court orders the constables of Birmingham . . . to cause the said Harris, Corry and Loach to be whipped at Birmingham as rogues and vagabonds and afterwards they are to be conveyed . . . to their places of birth.

Epiphany Sessions 1683

A petition of Catherine wife of Thomas Roberts of Bewsall, labourer . . . a prisoner in the county gaol for the felonious taking away of a quantity of corn. She is unable to maintain herself and her six children . . . the court orders the overseers of the poor of Bewsall to pay her 2s. weekly [for] maintenance and the children unless they show cause to the contrary.

Epiphany Sessions 1685

On the petition of the churchwardens and overseers of Solihull parish stating that they have made a list of poor children in the parish fit to be placed apprentices and also a list of such householders within the parish as are proper to take such poor children as apprentices . . . the court orders the persons hereafter named to take as apprentices the children nominated, that is John Slowe to take John, son of Benedict Slowe . . . Thomas Burton to take John, son of widow Heynes, Clement Newey to take Elizabeth Haywood.

Robert Smith of Nuneaton, turner, bound to appear at the next General Gaol Delivery to be held for this county to answer touching the death of Luke Mortimer, his apprentice.

Many of the Quarter Sessions' records of Hertfordshire have also been published. A volume by Le Hardy (993) calendars the sessions' records of 1752–99, including minute books, presentment books (noting offences and verdicts) and lists of names of over 2,000 men to whom gun licences were issued, including 930 gamekeepers (and the name of the manor). The volume also lists the names of men who took oaths in support of the Crown and filed sacrament certificates in accordance with the Test Act. Works such as these are therefore essential reference for genealogists. Another volume by Le Hardy (993), which calendars the Hertfordshire sessions' records for 1833 to 1843, includes the following entries:

Michaelmas session 1833
Indictments. William Walker of Baldock, labourer, for stealing a tea-kettle value 8s. from Edward Smith, innkeeper [two weeks hard labour then two weeks solitary confinement in the Bridewell and whipped].
Mary Ann, wife of John Dimock of Hoddesdon, for stealing [cutlery] value 13s. from Richard King and £2. 7s. in money from Mary Collins [six weeks in gaol, the last two in solitary confinement].

Easter session 1838
Settlement orders. The adjourned appeal of Enfield, Middlesex, against the removal of Thomas Morris, Amy his wife and Mary Ann, John, Ann and Emma their children from Layston was dismissed.
Maintenance orders. William Kirby of Hornsey Road, Middlesex horsekeeper and Ann Oakman of Standon spinster, for their son born in Ware Union workhouse.
Recognizances entered into . . . witnesses; Daniel Pateman, James Dear and James Dilley, all of Hitchin, labourers [for the case against] James Goddard and John Cooper.

Three entries from a volume (960) of extracts from the Bedfordshire Quarter Sessions' rolls for 1714–1832, illustrate the Justices' powers to control traders, including the grant of a licence to my ancestor Michael Read of Hockliffe to act as a corn dealer:

1758. Indictment of John Bull of the parish of St Paul Bedford, yeoman, for exercising the trade of a tailor, without having been apprenticed thereto for seven years.
7th January 1766. Certificate by the minister, churchwardens and overseers of the poor of Hockliffe, recommending Michael Read to be licensed as a badger or dealer in corn.
1779. 8th July. Certificate of the conviction of Samuel Rose, for selling a half-peck loaf wanting eight ounces; fined 40 shillings.

Family history societies are producing more indexes to Quarter Sessions' records. For example, Shropshire FHS has published a CD-ROM index to over 400,000 people named in the rolls of the county's Quarter Sessions (and Petty Sessions) of 1831 to 1920.

There is little published material from Petty Sessions, but Webb (1005) is a calendar of sessions' minutes (for 1784–93) from Copthorne and Effingham in Surrey, containing similar material to the examples noted above from Quarter Sessions. Some Justices' notebooks of their work have been published and two examples are Bettey (962) and Cirket (967). The latter contains notebooks of 1810–14 of Samuel Whitbread, a Bedfordshire Justice, from which the following are examples in 1811:

July 16. Mary Wilson brought by the constable of Biggleswade to swear a child after birth. Child sworn to Jacob Gayler. Granted a warrant to apprehend Jacob Gayler.
August 2. Sarah Smith of Houghton Conquest complained that the overseers do not make a sufficient allowance for the support of her grandson William Farr, a bastard kept by her.

Wrote to the overseers to attend . . . August 6. The overseer of Houghton [attended] on the complaint of Sarah Smith. I ordered 2s. for the maintenance of the boy.
August 7. Ann Price of Beeston to complain against William Underwood for assaulting her. Granted a warrant.
August 12. Edward George of Tempsford brought his son William George, apprentice to Pearson George of Roxton, wheeler, to complain of his master's ill-usage, particularly for striking him on Friday last. Warrant to appear tomorrow. August 13. [Complaint against] Pearson George for assaulting his apprentice. Dismissed the complaint and ordered the boy to return to his master.

Quarter Sessions' records often lead you to other records concerning your ancestor. Thus these Hertfordshire entries in Le Hardy (993) would lead you to army and navy records:

John Wright of Stevenage, butcher, for assaulting George Warner and Thomas Field . . . guilty and fined £5 for each offence but . . . on 30th April 1757 [he was] discharged, having enlisted into Lord Robert Manners' Regiment of Foot.
James Linsell, committed [in 1796] as a rogue and vagabond to be sent to sea to be employed in his Majesty's service.

However, although these published entries are extremely useful, it is vital to remember that they are not full transcripts. If you find a relevant entry, you should turn to the original records at the CRO for a complete version of the documents referring to your ancestors.

PRISONS AND PRISONERS

The census lists people in prison on census night. Some lists of debtors in prison were also noted in chapter 24. Other records of prisons and prisoners are reviewed in detail in Hawkings (984) and TNA domestic records leaflet 88. Byrne (963) and Herber (985) describe the punishment of criminals, the London prisons (such as Newgate, the Fleet and the Clink) and some of their famous inmates.

From the 13th century most counties had at least one gaol or prison to hold debtors or prisoners awaiting trial. At first, prisons rarely held people as a punishment for crimes (in part because so many crimes carried the death penalty), but sentences of imprisonment became increasingly common. There were also some prisons, known as pledgehouses (or compters in London) that were specifically for debtors. Many parishes also had a cage or lock-up for the temporary imprisonment of offenders. Statutes of 1575/6 and 1603/4 provided for the establishment of Houses of Correction (also known as Bridewells) to hold criminals, beggars and even unmarried mothers. Some prisons were also built by central government, from the early 19th century, to hold convicts (the government also rented cells in county gaols). Convicts were those offenders who had been sentenced to transportation or to imprisonment with hard labour. Other criminals who were imprisoned were known as prisoners. By 1853 there were 12 government prisons in England. Male convicts were held at Chatham, Dartmoor, Leicester, Millbank, Pentonville, Portland, Portsmouth and Woking. Women were held at Brixton and Fulham. Juvenile offenders were held at Parkhurst. Separate asylums were also built by the government for the criminally insane and the records at TNA of these institutions and their inmates are reviewed in Cale (964).

Sheriffs were obliged to provide lists of prisoners (in county gaols or Houses of Correction) to the justices at assizes and it also became customary for sheriffs or gaolers to submit similar lists to the Justices of the Peace. Quarter Sessions' records therefore include many records of county gaols and lists of prisoners. Cities and boroughs had their own gaols and their surviving records are in CROs or in city or borough archives. Thus CLRO holds records, described in Deadman & Scudder (244), for London gaols such as Newgate and Whitecross Street, the compters at Wood Street, Southwark and Giltspur Street, as well as the City House of Correction at Holloway. An act of 1823 made Justices of the Peace responsible for the upkeep of prisons, so Quarter Sessions' records contain reports on prison conditions, with lists of prisoners, their ages and offences. The act also required gaolers to keep journals (and these are usually in CROs or borough archives). Robert Gardner, the gaoler of Banbury, kept a journal from 1829 to 1838, published in Renold (1000), recording the receipt or discharge of prisoners and their crimes. Typical entries are:

1831. Jan 27. Sarah Grey brought by [constable] Claridge on charge of taking tea from Mr J. Dury's shop and cheese from Mr Kirby's.
Jan 28. Sarah Grey taken to Oxford. Committed for trial at the sessions.
Apr 2. Sessions. Sarah Grey (convicted). 7 years transportation.

Criminal registers
Series HO 26 and HO 27 at TNA contain criminal registers for England and Wales from 1805 (or 1791 for London and Middlesex) to 1892, listing all those charged with indictable offences, the date and place of trial, the verdict and the sentence (if convicted). The name of the prison hulk or ship is given for those transported. HO 26 contains the registers of the City of London and Middlesex for 1791–1849. The registers up to 1802 also give prisoners' physical descriptions and places of birth, and sometimes note whether a person could read or write. HO 27 contains similar registers of 1850–92 for London and Middlesex and of 1805–92 for other English and Welsh counties. The registers are arranged annually (thus piece HO 27/11 is a volume for 1815) and then alphabetically by county. Hawkings (984) lists the counties and years covered by each piece and provides many examples of the entries. Thus Alexander Elder, recorded in piece HO 26/2, was a seaman born in London. He was convicted of theft on 25 February 1793, sentenced to death and executed at Newgate on 1 May 1793. Examples from the registers in HO 27 include:

Name	Age	Sentenced	Offence	Sentence
John Locke	20	Devon Q.S, 18 March 1839	Burglary	6 months prison
James Paul	27	Norfolk Assizes 28 March 1835	Poaching	14 years transportation
Jane Beattie	–	Derby Assizes 25 July 1850	Bigamy	Not guilty

S. Tamblin has produced indexes on microfiche and CD-ROM (listed on the web site of Family History Indexes) to the registers of 1805–16 (and some for 1817–40) in HO 27, including about 75,000 names.

Calendars of prisoners and prison registers
Calendars of prisoners were lists of people who were to be tried. From the late 18th century many of these calendars were printed (and copies are at TNA and CROs). Calendars usually note a prisoner's name, crime and perhaps his age, trade and the date when he was committed into

custody. The verdict or sentence may have been noted (after trial) on the calendar. Some post-trial calendars were printed from the early 19th century and these also record the verdict, sentence and perhaps any previous convictions. A few calendars have been published, for example those for Staffordshire assizes 1842–43 in Johnson (990), which includes these entries:

George Harrison, 28 and John Williams, 24. Stealing on the 5th May 1842, at the parish of West Bromwich, one horse, the property of Thomas Turner. Not guilty.

Benjamin Freeth, 25. Assaulting Mary Ann Robinson on the 31st October 1842, at the parish of Harborne, and ravishing and carnally knowing her against her will. Convicted of an assault: to be imprisoned two years and kept to hard labour.

Prisons and gaols kept registers of prisoners' names, ages, crimes, physical descriptions, occupations and marital status. The administration of prisons and gaols was transferred (with some archives) from the counties to the Home Office in 1877, so prison registers may be in CROs or at TNA (although records up to 100 years old may be closed to the public). The calendars and prison (or hulk) registers at TNA are listed in detail by Hawkings (984) and TNA domestic records leaflet 88 but include:

a.   PCOM 2: calendars from 1774 to 1951 of prisoners awaiting trial at various English and Welsh Quarter Sessions and assizes, with many prison registers, such as those of Millbank (1816–71), Bedford (1844–57) and Stafford (1841–76)

b.   HO 23: registers of county prisons, with covering dates 1847 to 1866, such as Bath (1848–55) and Derby (1836–44)

c.   HO 140: county calendars of prisoners, for assizes and Quarter Sessions (1868–1971, but closed for between 30 and 75 years)

d.   HO 8: quarterly prison returns (1848–76), listing prisoners in British prisons or convict hulks (and noting offences, sentences and place and date of conviction)

e.   HO 77: Newgate calendars (lists of prisoners awaiting trial at Newgate Gaol in London). Copies are also at CLRO and LMA. The calendars were subsequently printed and those for 1782 to 1853 are in HO 77. They include names, ages, offences and most verdicts and sentences

f.   HO 24: prison registers and returns for Millbank, Parkhurst and Pentonville, with covering dates of 1838 to 1875

g.   HO 16: lists of prisoners awaiting trial at the Old Bailey, London (1815–49), with names, ages, offences and usually the verdicts and sentences

h.   CRIM 9: Old Bailey post-trial calendars of prisoners (1855–1949)

i.   PCOM 2/404: register of habitual criminals in England and Wales (containing 12,000 names) for 1869–76. From 1869 local prisons were required to compile registers of prisoners who had been convicted of certain crimes, detailing the prisoner's age, trade, offence and sentence, as well as previous convictions, then send them to a central registry (often with a photograph of the prisoner)

j.   MEPO 6: Metropolitan Police registers of habitual criminals (incomplete) for 1881–1959 (closed for 75 years), noting a criminal's physical description, previous convictions and the prison from which he was last released

Illustration 131 is a page from MEPO 6, of December 1916, with photographs of six criminals. The register noted that the man in the top right photograph, numbered 403, was William Pearson (known among criminals as "Boss Pearson"). He was born in London in 1881 and was known to the police for breaking into houses. He had been sentenced to five years imprisonment for burglary at Middlesex Sessions in March 1912 but released on licence in August 1916. He had previously been convicted in London courts of theft, housebreaking or minor offences. It was said that Pearson was a "crafty and persistent criminal" who "would not hesitate to resort to violence to evade arrest".

Hawlings (984) includes many examples from the records listed above, such as:

HO 16/1 Old Bailey Sessions, prisoners committed for trial January 1815

Name	Crime	Verdict	Sentence
Richard James	Larceny above 5s	Guilty	Death
David Kelly	Highway robbery	Guilty of stealing but not violently	Transported 7 years
Thomas Gillham	Obtaining money by false pretences	Guilty	Publicly whipped

PCOM 2/347 Calendar for Yorkshire North Riding Quarter Sessions June 1880

Name/age	Trade	Offence	Verdict	Sentence
Alfred Wright 22	General dealer	Stealing a hen, property of John Ward on 24th April	Guilty	Imprisonment with hard labour for four months at Northallerton Prison
Elizabeth Millington 89	Married woman	Stealing a piece of beef, property of Peter Daniels, at Middlesbrough on 4th May	Guilty	Imprisonment with hard labour for 12 months (previous conviction in April 1878, stealing a chair – 4 months prison)

PCOM 2/206 Newgate prison register

Name: William Lees. Age: 33 [physical description given]. Trade: Hairdresser Address: Hackney Road. When brought into custody: 26th November 1839. Offence: Wilful murder of Elizabeth his wife. Tried: 29th November Verdict: guilty. Sentence: death. How disposed of: 16th December, executed.

TNA also holds lists of convicts in prison hulks (noted below), petitions for pardons or reduction in sentence and correspondence files. The classes are noted in Bevan (239). Three volumes of HMSO calendars of Home Office papers (999, 1001) include the files of the Secretaries of State of 1760–72 (in series SP 37). These list hundreds of criminals and also refer to many documents, such as judges' reports, relating to the criminals' sentences, petitions or pardons. For example, William Fry was sentenced to death at Oxford in 1763 for horse-stealing but his sentence was reduced to transportation to America for 14 years. Nathaniel Rowledge was sentenced to death at Northampton in 1764 for highway robbery. John Croxford then confessed to the robbery and exonerated Rowledge by naming his accomplice as Thomas Seamark, who had already been

SUPPLEMENT "A"

No. 52   Friday, December 29th, 1916.   Vol. III.

131. *Photographs of habitual criminals from registers of the Metropolitan Police, 1916 (TNA, MEPO 6/66)*

executed after a trial at Northampton assizes. Rowledge was granted a temporary respite and Mr Baron Perrott, the judge at Rowledge's trial, was asked to report on the prisoner. He responded that Rowledge was not "an object for mercy, his behaviour on trial was far from that of an innocent man". Rowledge's ultimate fate is not recorded in the calendar. From 1782, the Home Secretary's correspondence concerning pardons, remissions and respites for prisoners was kept in criminal entry books, now in series HO 13 at TNA. Indexes to the names of the prisoners (and the court in which they were convicted) covering 1782–84 and 1798–1805 (about 5,500 prisoners) have been produced by S. Tamblin and are listed on the web site of Family History Indexes. Further reports by judges on criminals' petitions or related papers of 1784–1829 are in HO 47.

From 1819, petitions to the Home Office from criminals, convicted at courts throughout Britain, for pardons or reduction in sentences are in series HO 17 (1819–39) and HO 18 (1839–54). The 6,300 petitions in pieces HO 17/40–79 are indexed in Chambers (965), noting each criminal's name, age (if stated), offence, date and place of trial, sentence, prison (or hulk) and TNA reference. Registers in HO 19 also act as indexes to all the petitions in HO 17 and 18, with each criminal listed alphabetically, his offence, date and place of conviction, sentence, place of imprisonment, remarks on his character and the result of the petition.

Hawkings (984) and TNA domestic records leaflet 88 also describe other prisoners' records at TNA, including:

a. Captions. The court prepared a caption (court order) with the convict's name, crime and sentence. Captions of 1843–71 are in series PCOM 5 and indexed in PCOM 6.
b. Transfer papers. These authorised and recorded a convict's move from one government prison to another, recording the time he spent in prison, any previous sentences, his physical description, any misconduct or punishments and the name and address of his next of kin. Transfer papers for 1856–65 are in PCOM 5/24–52
c. Licences. A licence system was introduced in 1853. Convicts of good behaviour were freed on parole, but were returned to prison if they failed to maintain a respectable way of life. Licences were usually endorsed on captions or transfer papers. Licences for males (1853–87) are in PCOM 3, partly indexed in PCOM 6/1–13. Licences for females (1853–87) are in PCOM 4, indexed in PCOM 6/14–17

CROs hold many prison registers and calendars of prisoners who were tried at assizes or Quarter Sessions. Hawkings (984) lists CRO holdings of prison registers (and many of their calendars of prisoners). Thus Bedford Record Office holds calendars of prisoners tried at Quarter Sessions (1800–1907), assizes (1789–1907) or Bedford borough sessions (1850–70). Devon Record Office holds calendars of prisoners tried at Quarter Sessions between 1665 and 1963 and at assizes for many years between 1791 and 1919. Illustration 132 shows a page from the Bedford prison register, including a photograph of William Doyle of Nottingham, aged 17, who was convicted of arson at Bedford assizes in March 1864 and sentenced to six years' penal servitude.

Somerset Record Office holds gaol returns, registers of prisoners and description books for Wilton Gaol in Taunton. The description books of 1806 to 1825 are indexed in Webb & Parrish (1004). Importantly, they note each prisoner's place of birth, for example:

	Committed	Age	Born	Last residence
Davis, George	16 May 1818	27	St Johns Newfoundland	Goathurst
Day, William	30 March 1816	25	Wedmore	Bath

88.

DATE OF COMMITTAL.	REGISTER NUMBER.	HOW DISPOSED OF.
Sept 22 1863	7335	Remov'd to Pentonville, May 21 1864

Name. William Doyle

Description.

Age — 17 years
Height — 5 ft. 2 in.
Hair — Brown
Eyes — dark grey
Complexion — Pale
Visage — Oval
Weight — 108 lbs
Trade — Frame Work Knitter
Where born — Nottingham
Last residence — Nottingham
Married or Single — Single
Religion — Ch of England
Read and Write — Neither

Marks and Remarks. Small cut mark outside corner of left eye and on left cheek, an anchor in black on left forearm, one outside right arm imperfect

Offence. Setting fire to a stack of wheat, the property of one Jonathan Seymour at the parish of Luton on the 11 Sep 1863

When Tried. Assizes, March 11 1864

Sentence. 6 years P.S.

PREVIOUS CONVICTIONS, &c.

WHERE.	DATE.	OFFENCE.	SENTENCE.	WHERE.	DATE.	OFFENCE.	SENTENCE.
Nottingham	1861	April	Stealing an iron pot	21 Days			
		Attempted housebreaking	Acquitted				
		Suspected of stealing a shovel	supposed				
		to have left Nottingham on that account					

132. *Page from a prison register of Bedford, 1863, concerning William Doyle of Nottingham, aged 17, convicted of arson (Bedford Record Office QGV 10/4)*

Gaol delivery fiats were orders of the court, following a session of gaol delivery, as to what should be done with the prisoners. The lucky ones were delivered (that is released) from gaol. The court might also order that some should continue to be held until trial at the next sessions. The sentence of the court was pronounced upon others, as in these extracts, from Lamoine (992) which contains transcripts of Bristol gaol delivery fiats of 1741–99:

5 April 1746. Gaol delivery of Newgate [Bristol] before William Barnes, Mayor, Sir Michael Foster knight, Justice of the Court of King's Bench, Recorder of Bristol, Joseph Jefferis and Jacob Elton Aldermen.
Timothy James, Henry Slocombe [and 9 others]. Let them remain on their former orders.
Joseph Thornhill. Convicted of petty larceny. Let him be committed to the House of Correction for one month.
Charles Gard, Abigail Williams, Patience Berrow. Convicted of grand larceny. Let them be transported for seven years.
John Barry. Convicted of feloniously forging the will of James Barry deceased . . . Let him be hanged by the neck until he shall be dead.

An imprisoned ancestor may also be found in other records, listed in CRO catalogues, which were produced by gaol officials. Hurley (989) is a transcript of a journal kept by the matron at Fisherton Anger Gaol, Wiltshire from 1849 to 1853. It records the admission, discharge, punishment, conduct and health of the female prisoners. These are entries from 1853:

June 8. Received Dinah Earl and Emma Earl, for a month each, and Ann Green for 21 days.
June 11. The surgeon saw Elizabeth Hilliard and ordered her a dose of house medecine.
June 24. Elizabeth Combs was removed to the Lunatic Asylum, Surrey.
July 19. The governor put Ellen Woods in the dark cell, for misbehaviour at chapel, until locking up time.

Transportation

From the late 16th century some criminals who were sentenced to death were pardoned on condition that they were transported abroad, and the courts' powers to order transportation were extended in the 17th and 18th centuries. Until 1782 transportation was predominantly to the British colonies in America and the West Indies (# chapter 30). The names (and parish) of those transported are listed (in Latin) on the Patent Rolls for 1654–1717 (in series C 66) and for 1661–1782 in the State Papers Domestic (series SP 35–37 and 44). Lists of those transported to America and the West Indies from 1614 to 1775, extracted from records at TNA, are contained in Coldham (1273) and (1273a). The Western assize circuit produced transportation order books from 1629 to 1819 (at TNA in series ASSI 24) listing all persons sentenced to transportation on that circuit and noting the place and date of trial.

After the American War of Independence convicts could no longer be transported to North America and so the courts were therefore empowered to impose an alternative sentence for convicts: hard labour on hulks (the hulls of redundant ships) mostly anchored in the Thames, but also at Chatham, Portsmouth, Plymouth and Sheerness (and at Bermuda and Gibraltar). Hulks were overcrowded and insanitary. The regime was extremely harsh. Byrne (963) notes that, of the 632 prisoners received on the hulk *Justitia* between August 1776 and March 1778, 176 died. Transportation recommenced (to Australia) in 1787 and prisons to house convicts were also built in the 19th century, but the hulks continued to be used in England until 1857, primarily to hold convicts between sentence and transportation. About 162,000 people were transported to Australia between 1787 and 1868 (# chapter 30). The records of transportation at TNA are described in detail by Hawkings (984) and (1292) and summarised below. Having found a record of a convict's transportation, you can then usually work backwards, find the court in which he or she was convicted and locate the trial records.

a. HO 11: convict transportation registers (1787–1867), with chronological entries (by the date of sailing) for all British convicts transported to Australia, noting the ship, the date (and place) of conviction and the sentence. The years covered by each piece (with examples of entries) are noted by Hawkings, such as a list of convicts transported to New South Wales on the *Gorgon* in 1791 including:

Name	Where convicted	When	Term
John Crosby	Chester Great Sessions	3 September 1789	7 years
Thomas Massey	Chester Great Sessions	3 September 1789	Life
James Cam	Norfolk Assizes	12 March 1790	Life
Samuel Marchment	Wilts. Quarter Sessions	13 January 1789	7 years

b. HO 10: lists of convicts in New South Wales and Tasmania, including a census of 1828 with the names of 35,000 persons, both convicts and free settlers

c. TS 18: contracts for the transportation of convicts (1842–67), naming the convicts, with the date and place of their trial and sentence. Hawkings' works list the ships concerned, the year, ports of departure, destination and piece numbers

d. PC 1 and 2: correspondence of the Privy Council, containing some lists of convicts.

e. HO 9, ADM 6/418–23 and PCOM 2/105 and 131–7: prison hulk records (1801–49) listing the name, age and offence of each convict, the place and date of trial and the date of his transfer to a ship for transportation. Hawkings lists the hulks and the years covered in each piece (with many examples from the records)

f. HO 7: records of the prison hulks in Ireland and Bermuda

g. T 38 and HO 8: quarterly lists and returns of prisoners in the hulks. The names of the hulks, dates and piece numbers are listed by Hawkings

h. E 370, T 64, T 90 and T 207: (as noted above) assize vouchers, sheriffs' cravings and payments, often evidencing convicts' moves from prisons to hulks

i. T 1 (Treasury Board papers) and T 53 (Treasury money books) contain ships' lists of criminals who were transported. Hawkings (984) provides examples, such as a list in piece T 1/378, for the Home circuit assizes at Lent 1757. This certified that John Stewart, a London merchant, had custody of 22 convicts for transportation to America, including Thomas Dalton, sentenced in Surrey (to 14 years transportation) and Keziah Little, sentenced in Hertfordshire (seven years).

Executions and outlaws

England was for years a bloodthirsty country. About 72,000 people were executed in the 38 years of the reign of Henry VIII alone. Men were often hanged, drawn and quartered, and women could be burned for treason or murdering their husbands. Executions were a public spectacle: about 40,000 people gathered at Newgate Gaol in 1807 to see the hanging of two murderers. The last public hanging in Britain took place as recently as 1868.

Since so many crimes carried the death penalty (even forgery and sheep stealing until 1832), the privilege of benefit of clergy saved many from the gallows. Benefit of clergy originally allowed those in holy orders to avoid prosecution for certain crimes in the secular courts and be handed over to the church courts (and lesser sentences). The privilege was gradually extended to all first offenders who could read the 51st Psalm, so that many murderers escaped death (although they were usually branded). The privilege was gradually removed from many capital offences and abolished in 1827. The number of offences carrying the death penalty was also reduced and by 1850 most executions were of those convicted of murder.

Linebaugh (996) is an interesting study of those who were executed at Tyburn in London in the 18th century (often for minor crimes), based in part on the pamphlets the *Ordinary's Account* and the *Proceedings* (noted above). Linebaugh notes that the *Proceedings* record that 57 people were tried at the Old Bailey Sessions of 14–17 January 1715, of whom 25 were acquitted and 32 were found guilty. Six were sentenced to hang, 17 to be branded, 8 to be whipped and one to stand in the pillory. Linebaugh also notes that 237 issues of the *Ordinary's Account* describe 1,242 men and women hanged at Tyburn between 1703 and 1772. Of those people, only 39 per cent were born in London (34 per cent were born elsewhere in England and almost 14 per cent in Ireland). For example, William Holloway aged 26, hanged for highway robbery near Hampstead, was born in Berkshire. If your ancestors (or their siblings) seem to disappear, the records of executions may solve the mystery.

From medieval times until 1938 outlaws were those persons declared to be outside the protection of the law, for example because they failed to appear at court despite indictments against them. Their goods and land were forfeited to the Crown. The names of outlaws appear in various court records listed in TNA legal records leaflet 24. Records of escheators from the 13th to 17th centuries (in series E 136) include details of outlaws' property. Pardons to outlaws can be found from the 13th century on the Patent Rolls in series C 66 (# chapter 27). Typical entries from an HMSO volume (1078) that calendars the Patent Rolls of 1476 to 1485 are:

1477 June 17. Pardon of outlawry. Thomas White late of Barnestaple, co. Devon, merchant for not appearing [before the justices] to answer William Coffyn touching a debt of 73s 4d

1477 Feb 14. Pardon to Nicholas Bery, of Toppesham, co. Devon, late of Jersey, merchant, late deputy of Richard Kingesmylle, one of the collectors of customs and subsidies in the ports of Exeter and Dartmouth, of all offences committed by him before Michaelmas last

CORONERS' RECORDS

The office of coroner was established in 1194. Coroners hold inquests into suspicious or sudden deaths and as to whether valuable finds are treasure trove. An inquest jury consisted of between 12 and 23 people (between 7 and 11 people since 1926). Until the 19th century most coroners were elected by freeholders and had jurisdiction over a county, but many boroughs also had the right to have their own coroner. In 1888 counties were divided into districts, listed by Gibson & Rogers (977), each with a coroner appointed by local authorities.

Many coroners' records have been lost or destroyed. Any records surviving from before 1875 are now preserved, but a coroner may destroy any other records more than 15 years old. Coroners' records are generally only open to the public after 75 years (although a coroner may permit earlier access). In view of the loss of many records, it is fortunate that inquest verdicts since the 18th century (and some evidence) were often reported by newspapers. A newspaper reported the verdict of accidental death at the inquest for Charles Symes in 1913 (# chapter 17). Newspaper reports may be the only surviving records of some inquests. Most surviving coroners' records are at TNA or CROs. They are listed, by county, in Gibson & Rogers (977), which also lists some coroners' records that have been published. Coroners originally had to hand their records to the eyre or assize justices. Many coroners' records are therefore in the eyre and assize records at TNA. Furthermore, if an inquest returned a verdict of murder, a criminal trial may have followed, often at the assizes (in which case the coroners' records may survive with the circuit's indictments). From the 16th to 18th centuries the results of coroners' inquests were forwarded to the Court of King's Bench and many coroners' papers are therefore in that court's records at TNA (particularly in series KB 9–12). TNA also holds coroners' records for the Palatinates of Chester (18th and 19th centuries) and for the deaths of prisoners in the King's Bench Prison (1747–50 and 1771–1839) and in Millbank Penitentiary (1848–63).

Surviving coroners' records may include original inquests that summarise the hearing, give details of the deceased, the death and also the names and verdict of the jury. There may be a register of inquests, noting the inquest date, the deceased's name, address and place of death. Files may also include witness depositions and (from 1837) a certificate by which a coroner notified a civil registrar of the cause of death so that the registrar could complete a death certificate. Early coroners' records are generally in Latin and very difficult to use (and rarely calendered). Some early inquests have fortunately been published. Most of these have been extracted from the assize or King's Bench records at TNA. Thus many inquests appear in Cockburn's calendars of assize indictments (noted above) and Hunnisett (988) is a published calendar of the 582 surviving inquests by Sussex coroners from 1558 to 1603 (there are similar volumes by Hunnisett for 1485–1558 and 1603–88) with details of any trials known to have resulted. For example, at Horsham assizes on 27 July 1579, the coroner John Whitinge delivered an inquest taken on 24 July at Henfield:

Jurors; Henry Michell gent, John Bloxson [and 12 others]
On 20 July, when Thomas Symons and Thomas Haucks of Henfield, glover, were playing at dyce at Henfield, abusive words arose . . . by reason of which Haucks, roused to anger, feloniously killed Symons with a dagger . . . giving him several wounds of which he died the same day. [Haucks was charged with murder at the assizes, but convicted only of manslaughter. He pleaded benefit of clergy and was branded and released.]

If an original inquest cannot be found, useful information may be obtained from coroners' bills. Coroners were not paid but from 1752 they could claim expenses (at Quarter Sessions) for attending inquests. Surviving coroner's bills in Quarter Sessions' records usually give a deceased's name, the place and date of the inquest, the expenses claimed and sometimes the verdict. Hunnisett (987) calendars Wiltshire coroners' bills from 1752 to 1796, including:

20 October 1774. St John's parish, Devizes. Richard Palmer; killed by a fracture of his skull falling from his horse near the town £1

26 December 1774. Sutton Veny. Ann Swain, starved and murdered by Stephen Swain, her father, and Tamar his wife . . . 32 miles £2 4s

[Stephen and Tamar Swain were convicted of murder at Salisbury assizes on 18 March 1775 and sentenced to be hanged, with their bodies to be dissected (for anatomy students)]

28 December 1774. All Saints' parish, Chitterne. John White, an old man; found dead in his house; no marks of violence; natural death £1 9s

CHAPTER 26

PEERAGES, THE GENTRY, FAMOUS PEOPLE AND HERALDRY

ROYAL DESCENT

Genealogists are often asked whether they have discovered that any of their ancestors were royalty, nobles or famous people. This is not a silly question. Thousands of people are descended from British monarchs (and many more are descended from nobles or foreign royalty). Camp (6) and Wagner (31) and (32) review the possibility of someone discovering that they are of royal descent (from Saxon kings, the Plantagenets, later English or British monarchs, Irish and Welsh princes or foreign royalty). Wagner (32) includes 93 fascinating pedigrees of Roman emperors, English monarchs and many important English families since the Norman Conquest. Wagner's works are especially interesting because of his study of "gateway" ancestors (those descendants of royalty who, because they had so many children and grandchildren, passed the royal blood to many families). Camp (6) describes the lengths to which some people go (including forging documents) in order to prove their descent from royalty or nobility. An article by Dr P. Cotgreave about forged pedigrees, noting that many were unfortunately published in early genealogical journals or books, appears in *Family Tree Magazine* (July 1995).

Many books describe the lineage of English and British monarchs. Montague-Smith (1050) is a brief description of the royal line of succession of England and Scotland since Saxon times (with some pedigrees of medieval Welsh princes and Irish kings). More detailed pedigrees of English and British monarchs can be found in the various editions of *Burke's Peerage*, other works on peerages noted below and in *Burke's Guide to the Royal Family* (1009). Weir (1067) and Ashley (1020) are also detailed genealogical and biographical guides to the Royal families of Britain. One of the most detailed works of reference for establishing a Royal descent is *The Blood Royal of Britain* (1057) and the four volumes of *The Plantagenet Roll of the Blood Royal* (1058), by the Marquis of Ruvigny and Raineval. These are detailed studies of the legitimate descendants of King Edward III up to the 19th century. They contain family trees, indented pedigrees and name indexes for about 50,000 descendants of Edward III (with information about their births, marriages, deaths, offices and honours). They include people of all classes.

The descendants (living in the 19th century) identified by Ruvigny will have produced children and further generations so that the number of legitimate descendants of Edward III is therefore now much greater than 50,000 (there are also many lines of descent from English kings prior to Edward III). Ruvigny's works were also incomplete. Some legitimate lines of descent from Edward III were not included, although some descendants on these omitted lines are included elsewhere in Ruvigny's work (by reason of marriages to other royal descendants). The volumes also omit illegitimate children and their descendants. It has been estimated that there are about 100,000 descendants of Edward III if illegitimate children and their descendants are included, but this may be an underestimate (because there are so many illegitimate descents). Given-Wilson & Curteis (1039) provide accounts of the lives (and families) of illegitimate children of English monarchs from 1066 to 1485, of whom 41 can be identified fairly certainly. To descendants of these offspring, one must add illegitimate children of later monarchs (such as those of Charles II), the illegitimate offspring of kings' children (such as those of John of Gaunt, son of Edward III) and their descendants' bastards. An article by P. Hall on the illegitimate children of Charles II appears in *Genealogists' Magazine* (September 1987).

It is also worth consulting *The Royal Families of England, Scotland and Wales* by Burke (1026) which was prepared specifically to show the Royal descent of particular families. This work contains over 200 pedigrees of those Royal descendants and the links between particular Victorian families and royal ancestors. Some information in these volumes is incorrect (a warning that unfortunately applies to all early publications by Burke and many other works on peerages or royal ancestry) but the volumes remain useful. Illustration 133 is a typical pedigree, showing the descent from Edward I of Charles Sawyer (born in 1789) of Heywood in Berkshire.

Similar principles apply to foreign royalty. Thousands of people can trace a descent from a royal family somewhere. I have not reviewed the sources for foreign monarchies in this book, but the SoG and reference libraries hold many published works on foreign monarchs and their descendants, to which you can refer if research of your family suggests a link. Louda & MacLagan (1049) is a guide to European royal families since medieval times, including a brief history of the monarchs of each European country and of many smaller kingdoms that once existed, for example in Spain, Germany and Italy. There are pedigrees for each royal house that, although simplified, include the key lines of descent, in some cases to our own royal family, members of the peerage or others. The work also features the coats of arms of many people in each pedigree. Some further information about foreign royalty is noted in chapter 30 below but a CD-ROM entitled "Royal families", produced by British Ceremonial Arts, contains pedigrees (with over 25,000 names) of most European royal families. Many other works on foreign royalty can be purchased from Heraldry Today of Ramsbury in Wiltshire.

Many people claim to have traced their family tree back to a king, a peer or some other notable person, perhaps someone who fought at the Battle of Hastings. These claims may be true but they are often nonsense. I know people who have not traced their ancestry back prior to the 19th century, but who nevertheless claim that their surname originates from some medieval person, whether a king, noble or commoner. Another favourite story is along the lines of "my great grandfather was the illegitimate son of a duke". Many people are descended from kings or the nobility but you should treat any such link as merely theoretical until the line of ancestry is established by working backwards through the records.

THE PEERAGE

An enormous number of people, of all classes and financial status, are descended from noble families, particularly because the wealth and importance of families varied substantially over time. Younger sons of a family were often not as wealthy as their fathers. For example, the youngest son of a duke might join the army but only reach the rank of captain. His youngest son might have been a farmer. His son may have been a shopkeeper and his son only a labourer. Marriages

PEDIGREE XCII.

Charles Sawyer, Esq.

Edward I. King of England.=Margaret, dau. of Philip III. of
France, 2nd wife.

Edmund, of Woodstock, Earl of Kent.=Margaret, dau. of John, and sister and heiress
of Thomas, Lord Wake.

Lady Joan Plantagenet, dau.=Sir Thomas Holland, K.G.,=EDWARD THE BLACK PRINCE,
and heiress, celebrated as the Lord Holland. last husband.
Fair Maid of Kent.

Thomas Holland, 2nd Earl of=Lady Alice Fitzalan, dau. of RICHARD II., King of Eng-
Kent. Richard, Earl of Arundel. land.

The Lady Alianore Holland,=Edward The Lady Eleanor=Thomas Montacute, Earl
dau. and eventual coheir of | Cherlton, Holland, dau. and | of Salisbury.
Thomas, Earl of Kent, and Lord coheir of Thomas,
widow of Roger, Earl of March. | Powis. Earl of Kent.

Joyce Cherlton, dau. and co-=Sir John The Lady Alice =Richard Neville, Earl of
heir of Edward, Lord Powis. de Tiptoft, Montacute, only | Salisbury, eldest son of
  d. in 1443. dau. and heir. | Ralph, Earl of Westmore-
  land, by his second Coun-
Joane Tiptoft, 2nd dau. and in=Sir Edmund tess, Joan de Beaufort,
her issue, coheir of Sir John Inglethorpe. dau. of John of Gaunt, son
de Tiptoft. of King EDWARD III.

Isabel Inglethorpe, dau. and=John Neville, Marquess of Mon- Richard Neville, Earl of
heir. tacute, K.G., 2nd son, d. 1471. Warwick, the renowned
  King Maker.

Lady Anne Neville, dau. and coheir of John,=Sir William Stonor, Knt. of Stonor, co. Ox-
Marquess of Montacute. ford.

Anne, dau. and heir.=Sir Adrian Fortescue.

Margaret, dau. of Sir A. Fortescue.=Thos Lord Wentworth, of Nettlestead, d. 1551.

Anne, dau. of Thomas, Lord Wentworth.=Sir John Poley, of Badley, co. Suffolk.

Margaret, dau. of Sir John Poley, Knt.=Sir Thomas Palmer, Bart. of Wingham, co.
Kent, d. 1625.

Sir James Palmer, Knt. of the Bedchamber=Martha, dau. of Sir William Garrard, of
to King JAMES I., and Chancellor of the Dorney Court, Knt.
Order of the Garter, 3rd son.

Sir Philip Palmer, of Dorney Court, Cup=Phœbe, dau. of Vice-Admiral Sir Henry Pal-
Bearer to King CHARLES II. mer, of Howleech, Kent.

Charles Palmer, Esq. of Dorney, d. 1714,=Jane, dau. of John Jenyns, Esq. of Hayes.
buried at Dorney.

Phœbe, dau. of Charles Palmer, Esq. of Dor-=Richard Harcourt, Esq. of Wigsell, co. Sus-
ney, and sister of Sir Charles Palmer, Bart. sex, M.P., buried in 1777.

Phœbe, elder dau. and coheir of Richard=Anthony Sawyer, Esq. of Heywood, co. Berks.
Harcourt, Esq. of Wigsell. d. in 1813.

John Sawyer, Esq. of Heywood, J.P. and=Sarah, dau. of Anthony Dickins, Esq. of
D.L., b. in 1762, d. in 1845. Cherington, co. Warwick.

Charles Sawyer, Esq. of Heywood, b. in=Henrietta, eldest dau. of Sir George Bowyer,
1789, 19th in a direct descent from King 5th Bart. of Radley, co. Berks.
EDWARD I.

CHARLES SAWYER, Esq., eldest son and heir.

133. A pedigree from Burke's The Royal Families of England, Scotland and Wales *showing the descent of Charles Sawyer from Edward I*

617

also linked one class to another. Thus daughters of kings might marry nobles, daughters of nobles might marry knights, daughters of knights might marry local yeomen and so on. It is therefore possible to trace a family relationship that extends, within only a few generations, from the highest in the land to the lowest. In view of the number of ancestors that you have, it is possible that pedigrees of the nobility will be relevant to your family tree. However, you could trace your ancestors back in time for many generations and still only find farm labourers or shoemakers.

There are five classes of peerage. The first two classes are the peerages of each of England and Scotland, created before the 1707 union of those kingdoms. The third class is of peerages of Great Britain, that is, those created after 1707 but before the union of Britain and Ireland in 1801. The fourth class consists of Irish peers created before 1801 (that is peers in the peerage of Ireland). The fifth category is of peers of England, Scotland and Ireland created since 1801 (that is peers in the peerage of the United Kingdom). There are also five ranks of peer: duke, marquis, earl, viscount and baron. Their origin is described in *Burke's Peerage*. In addition, there is also the hereditary order of baronets (considered below).

There are many published works on peers. These contain a vast amount of genealogical information and are not limited to people who actually had titles, but also concern younger sons or daughters of peers, as well as the families into which they married. The best source of information on men who held peerages is *The Complete Peerage* by Cokayne (1029). The second edition (in 13 volumes) was published from 1910 to 1959 (and later reprinted), including peerages created up to 1938. A 14th volume by Hammond (1041) provides additional material and corrections in respect of peerages recorded in earlier volumes and also includes peerages created up to 1995. *The Complete Peerage* is a historical account of every holder of a peerage, noting the peer's birth, parents, honours, offices, marriage, death and burial, but there is little information about his ancestors or descendants who did not have that title. A typical entry is that for Thomas Arundell who became 4th Baron Arundell of Wardour in 1694:

Thomas (Arundell), Baron Arundell of Wardour, son and heir [of the 3rd Baron], born 1633. He married Margaret, widow of Robert Lucy of Charlecote, county Warwick and daughter of Thomas Spencer, of Ufton in that county. She died 23 Dec 1704 (will dated 12 June 1693). He died 10 Feb 1711/2 at Breamore and was buried at Tisbury, aged about 79 (will dated Jan 1704/5). He went in the suite of the Earl of Castlemaine on the Embassy to Pope Innocent XI in 1686.

Information about other members of noble families can then be obtained from other works on peerages. The best known works on peers (for England, Scotland and Ireland) are *Burke's Peerage* and *Debrett's Peerage*. Although Debrett's is older (first published in 1769 as *The New Peerage* and from 1803 as *Debrett's Peerage*), *Burke's Peerage* (published since 1826) is often more useful because it contains more detailed information about the ancestors of each peer, his family and collateral lines. There are many editions of each work. For example, the 99th edition of *Burke's Peerage* (1008), published in 1949, has over 2,000 pages of information about peers (and baronets), their families and ancestors. There is an illustration of any coat of arms to which a peer or baronet was entitled and a detailed indented pedigree (in similar form to the extract from Burke's *Landed Gentry* in illustration 134), of his lineage and some collateral lines, often extending back to medieval times. For each person in the pedigree, there are dates of birth, marriage and death, with notes of offices they held or noteworthy events in their lives. For example, the entry for

Viscount Torrington (Sir Arthur Stanley Byng) has details of his wife, children and grandchildren, followed by details of his lineage back to Admiral George Byng, 1st Viscount Torrington, who died in 1733. Perhaps 100 descendants of the 1st Viscount are noted, with brief genealogical details for each person and his or her spouse. Entries for some peers are even longer. The lineage of the Earl of Warwick (Charles Guy Fulke Greville) is given back to John Grevill (who died during the reign of Edward III). *Burke's Peerage* ceased publication in 1980 but a new edition (the 106th) by Mosley (1051) was produced in 1999. It includes many illegitimate children of peers and an index to over 106,000 living people featured in the work. This edition is also available in a database, on the Burke's Peerage and Gentry subscription web site. The 107th edition is due to be published in late 2003.

Debrett's Peerage has continued publication for over 230 years with new editions every few years, such as the edition of 1890 (1012), that of 1990 by Kidd & Williamson (1046) and further editions in 1995, 2000 and 2003. *Debrett's Peerage* includes only direct ancestors or children of peers (and baronets) and living relations, as shown in illustration 1. This is the entry from the 1890 edition for the descent and living relations of Edwyn Francis Scudamore-Stanhope, 10th Earl of Chesterfield. Many researchers prefer *Debrett's Peerage* to *Burke's Peerage* because, especially in earlier editions, the information contained in *Debrett's Peerage* may be more reliable. The editors of *Burke's Peerage* included more information on collateral lines and deceased relatives of a peer (or baronet) but relied more heavily on information provided by the families featured in the work. Genealogists should use and compare the entries in both works.

Other works on the descent and families of peers should also be consulted. The SoG has a large collection of volumes on the peerage (and baronets and knights). *Lodge's Peerage*, such as the 1887 edition (1048), contains indented pedigrees but concentrates, like *Debrett's Peerage*, on living relatives of each peer or baronet. *Dod's Peerage*, such as the edition of 1913 (1013), and *Whittaker's Peerage*, such as the edition of 1909 (1015), provide biographies of living peers (and baronets) but only limited information about their ancestors and collateral lines. Older works on the peerage are also useful, for example a nine-volume edition by Brydges of A. Collins' *Peerage of England*, published in 1812, the last volume of which indexes all names appearing in the work.

Since works such as *Burke's Peerage* include the marriages of the younger sons and daughters of peers (and sometimes the names of some of their descendants), the number of people referred to in any volume is enormous, many of them being commoners rather than peers. The chances of being related in some way to at least one noble family must be very great. The problem is ascertaining the link. The peerages are described alphabetically by the title, rather than the surname of the family who held that title. For example, the surnames of the Earls (or Dukes) of Northumberland since 1377 have been Percy, Nevill, Dudley, Fitzroy and Seymour. The peers' surnames are indexed in *Burke's Family Index* (1007) and in Leeson (1047), which also refers to other works on the peerage for each surname. However, an entry for a peerage in *Burke's* or *Debrett's Peerage* may refer to 10, 20 (or more) other families with whom that titled family intermarried, and those other family names are rarely indexed. You should therefore concentrate on research of your own family tree and only turn to works on peerages when you have established a link with a particular family.

If you do find a link, you should not simply accept a published entry as correct. The information contained in works such as *Burke's* or *Debrett's Peerage* is usually correct but as noted above, there are some errors, especially in the earlier editions. You should therefore verify the material yourself. The source material for the entries is usually not specified, but since the entries record names and the dates (and many places) of relevant events, it is usually not too difficult to find the parish registers, wills, civil registration records, county histories, Herald's visitations (noted below) or other material that should corroborate the published information.

If you are researching a family that held a peerage that is now extinct or dormant, you should consult one of the earlier editions of *Burke's* or *Debrett's Peerage*, or works on extinct peerages. Burke's *Genealogical History of the Dormant, Forfeited and Extinct Peerages of the British Empire* was first published in 1831. The 1883 edition (1024), notes the lineage of holders of peerages that became dormant or extinct up to 1883 and (although not indexed) refers to about 40,000 people. A similar work by Pine (1056) records the lineage of familes with titles that became dormant from 1884 to 1971 (and a few that Burke omitted).

Many records of peers are held at the House of Lords Record Office and described in Bond (922), including charters or Letters Patent of creation, pedigrees and records of proceedings of the House (which list the Lords present at sittings). There are records of some trials of peers by the House (such as Lord Mohun's trial for murder in 1693). There are also records of peerage claims (including pedigrees and documents evidencing the claimant's ancestry).

BARONETS

The title of baronet was created by King James I in 1611. Most early baronets were drawn from landowning families but, in later years, the title was also conferred on men distinguished in commerce, science, the arts or the military. Baronetcies were created by Letters Patent (at TNA in series C 66) and also announced in the *London Gazette*. *The Complete Baronetage* by Cokayne (1030) describes the lineage of men who were created baronets up to 1800, with details of the birth, marriage and death of each baronet and information such as the public offices that he held or the university that he attended. *Burke's* and *Debrett's Peerage* also include pedigrees of baronets. The lineage of men who held baronetcies that became extinct are set out in Burke (1027). The Charnock (or Chernock) family lived at Hulcot in Bedfordshire in the 16th and 17th centuries (descended from the Charnock family of Lancashire). Sir John Charnock of the Hulcot family was created a baronet in 1661, but the title became extinct in 1779. Burke (1027) provides detailed information about four generations of the family from 1661 to 1779, but also notes the lineage of the family back to the early 16th century (and some descendants up to the 19th century).

THE GENTRY

Burke's *Landed Gentry of Great Britain and Ireland* provides pedigrees of the gentry, that is those county families without hereditary title (whom Burke calls the "untitled aristocracy"). This work was first published (in four volumes from 1833 to 1837) as *A Genealogical and Heraldic History of the Commoners of Great Britain and Ireland* (presently available as a paperback reprint from GPC and also on CD-ROM). A second edition was published between 1842 and 1848 and there have been many editions since, such as the 18th edition (of 1965), by Townend (1063). The featured families are indexed in *Burke's Family Index* (1007). A new edition, the 19th, has been published for Scotland (and volumes for England and Wales should be published soon).

The information for each family is presented in the form of indented pedigrees. Illustration 134 shows the entry from the second edition for the Fanshawe family of Fanshawe Gate in

FAN

FANSHAWE OF FANSHAWE GATE.

FANSHAWE, HENRY, Esq. of Dengy Hall, co. Essex, capt. R. N., *b.* 9 Dec. 1778, *m.* 1st, 1 May, 1810, Anna-Maria, dau. of Lieut.-Gen. Jenkinson, and 2ndly, 20 Jan. 1823, Caroline, dau. of F.-F. Luttrell, Esq., second son of J.-F. Luttrell, Esq. of Dunster Castle, co. Somerset.

Lineage.

ROBERT FANSHAWE, Esq. of Fanshawe Gate, in the parish of Dronfield, co. Derby, had two sons, I. JOHN, of whom presently, and II. Henry, Remembrancer of the Exchequer, *temp.* Queen ELIZABETH, *d.* 1568, leaving, by Dorothy, his wife, dau. of Sir George Stonerd, two daus., his co-heirs, Anne, wife of William Fuller; and Susanna, *m.* to Timothy Lucy, Esq. The elder son, JOHN FANSHAWE, Esq. of Fanshawe Gate, who *d.* in 1578, left, by Margaret, his wife, dau. of Eyre, of Hassop, four sons and two daus.; of the former, the eldest,

THOMAS FANSHAWE, Esq. of Ware Park, *s.* his uncle, the Remembrancer of the Exchequer. He *m.* 1st, Mary, dau. of Anthony Bouchier, and had by her a son,

HENRY (Sir), K.B., Remembrancer of the Exchequer, who *m.* Elizabeth, sixth dau. of Thomas Smyth, Esq. of Ostenhanger, and by her was father, *inter alios*, of two sons,

THOMAS, K.B., created VISCOUNT FANSHAWE, of Donamore, in the kingdom of Ireland, in 1661. His lordship, who fought under the royal banner at Edgehill, *d.* in 1665, leaving (with four daughters, of whom the youngest, Elizabeth, *m.* Sir Thomas Fanshawe, of Jenkins,) three sons, 1. THOMAS, second Viscount Fanshawe, K.B., father of EVELYN, third Viscount, who died under age; 2. Charles, fourth Viscount Fanshawe, *d. s. p.* in 1710; and 3. Simon, fifth Viscount, who also *d. s. p.* in 1716.

RICHARD (Sir), created a baronet in 1650, who left (with a dau., Margaret, *m.* to Vincent Grantham, Esq. of Goltho', co. Lincoln,) a son and successor, SIR RICHARD FANSHAWE, second baronet, who *d. unm.* in 1695, when the title became extinct.

Mr. Fanshawe *m.*, 2ndly, Joan Smyth, sister of Thomas, Viscount Strangford, and had by her two sons and five daus.

Thomas (Sir), of Jenkins, co. Essex, K.B., supervisor-general, and clerk of the Crown, who *d.* in 1631, leaving by Anne, his wife, dau. of Urian Babington, of London, a son, Thomas Fanshawe, Esq. of Jenkins, whose son, Sir Thomas Fanshawe of Jenkins, knighted in 1660, left an only dau. and heiress, Susan, *m.* to Baptist Noel, fourth son of Baptist, Viscount Camden.

WILLIAM, of whom presently.

Alice, *m.* to Sir Christopher Hatton, K.B.

Elizabeth, ⎫ both *d. s. p.*
Mary, ⎭

Catharine, *m.* to John Bullock, Esq. of Darley and Norton, co. Derby.

Margaret, *m.* to Sir Benjamin Ayloff, Bart. of Braxstead.

Thomas Fanshawe, of Ware, *d.* 19 Feb. 1600; his youngest son,

WILLIAM FANSHAWE, Esq. of Passelews, in the parish of Dagenham, Essex, one of the auditors of the Duchy of Lancaster, *m.* Catharine, dau. of Sir John Wolstenholm, of London, and dying 4 March, 1634, was *s.* by his son,

JOHN FANSHAWE, Esq. of Passelews, *b.* in 1619, who *m.*, 1st, a dau. of Kingsmill, Esq. of Sidmanton, Hants, by whom he had a son, WILLIAM, and he *m.* 2ndly, Alice, dau. of Thomas Fanshawe, Esq. of Jenkins, by whom he had a son,

John, of Passelews, who *m.* a dau. of John Coke, Esq. of Melbourne, co. Derby, and dying about the year 1700, left issue,

1. Thomas, of Passelews, who had (with two daus., Susan, *m.* to the Rev. Dr. Blackburne; and Frances, *m.* to Massingberd, Esq.,) a son, Thomas, of Passelews, who *m.* Anne, dau. of Sir Crisp Gascoyne, lord mayor of London, and had, with two daus., a son, John-Gascoyne Fanshawe, Esq., who *m.* Miss Partington, and had issue, John, *b.* in 1773; Henry, *b.* in 1775; Charles-Gascoyne, *b.* in 1778; Thomas-Lewis, *b.* in 1792; and Mary.

2. John.

3. Charles, who *m.* Elizabeth, dau. of Sir John Rogers, Bart., and had three sons, 1. John Fanshawe, Esq., who by Penelope, his wife, dau. of Dredge, Esq. of Reading, had, (with three daus., Penelope, Catherine-Maria, and Elizabeth-Christiana,) two sons, John, *b.* 1763, and Robert-Charles, *b.* 1780; 2. Robert Fan-

396

FAR

shawe, who *m.* Christiana, dau. of Ginnis, Esq., and by her had (with nine daus., Christiana, *m.* to the Rev. Francis Haggit; Elizabeth, *m.* to Francis Glanville, Esq. of Catchfrench; Susan, *m.* to Vice-Admiral Bedford; Catherine, *m.* to Admiral Sir T.-Byam Martin; Cordelia, *m.* to Admiral Sir T.-Chambers White; Anne; Penelope, *m.* to Col. Duckworth; Mary, *m.* to Admiral Sir Robert Stopford, G.C.B.; and Henrietta) three sons, Robert, captain R.N., *d.* in 1804; Edward, C.B., colonel R.E., *m.* in 1811, Frances-Mary, sister of Sir Adolphus-John Dalrymple, Bart.; Arthur, captain R.N., *m.* a dau. of Admiral Colpoys; and 3. Charles Fanshawe, Esq., Recorder of Exeter, who *m.* Elizabeth, dau. of John Seale, Esq. of Mount Boone, co. Devon, and had a son, Charles-John, *b.* 1780.

1. Susanna.

The eldest son,

WILLIAM FANSHAWE, Esq. of St. Martin's-in-the-Fields, co. Middlesex, sometime Master of the Requests to King CHARLES II., *m.* Mary, dau. of Mrs. Lucy Walters, and sister of James, Duke of Monmouth, relict of William Sarsfield, of Lucan, Ireland, elder brother of Patrick, Earl of Lucan, and *d.* in the year 1707, leaving (with three daus., Ann-Dorothy, *m.* to Mathews, Esq., barrister-at-law; Lucy-Catherine, *d. unm.*; and Ann-Mary, *m.* to Mark Newdigate, of Ireland) an only son,

THOMAS-EDWARD FANSHAWE, Esq. of Great Singleton, co. Lancaster, who was next heir male of Simon, last Viscount Fanshawe, of Dengy Hall, Essex. He *m.* Elizabeth, dau. of William Snelling, Esq. of Bromley, co. Middlesex, and by her had (with three daus., Elizabeth, *m.* in 1719, to Corbyn Morris, Esq.; Anne; and Mary) an only son,

SIMON FANSHAWE, Esq., of Fanshawe Gate, *b.* 4 March, 1715-16, who *m.* Althea, second dau. of William Snelling, Esq., and had, with daus., of whom Frances *m.* John Jenkinson, Esq., an only son and heir,

HENRY FANSHAWE, Esq., *b.* 5 May, 1756, colonel in the British Guards, and subsequently a general officer in the Russian service, under the Empress CATHERINE II. He was governor of Kioo, and subsequently of the Crimea, and served with distinction under the Duke of Wurtemburg. He *d.* a Russian senator, at Warsaw, in 1828. By his wife, Susanna-Frances (whom he *m.* 26 Feb. 1778), dau. of Charles le Grys, Esq. of Norwich, he had issue,

I. HENRY, his heir, the present Captain Fanshawe, R.N., of Dengy Hall.

II. Charles-Robert, of Fanshawe Gate, co. Derby, in holy orders, vicar of Coaley, co. Gloucester, *b.* 4 April, 1786, *m.* 1st, Patty, dau. of the Rev. Mr. Faithful; and 2ndly, Jane, dau. of the Rev. Mr. Williams, by the former of whom only, who *d.* in 1823, he has issue,
1. Charles-Simon, *b.* 9 Oct. 1806, *m.* in May, 1833, Rosa, third dau. of Charles Ricketts, Esq.
2. John, *m.* in Aug. 1842, Elizabeth, dau. of Upton, Esq.
3. Robert, *b.* 11 April, 1814, *m.* 1st, Pamela, dau. of Gen. Boye, E. I. Co.'s service; and 2ndly, the dau. of Col. Wrottesley.
1. Althea, *m.* in 1835, to John-C. Badeley, M.D., of Chelmsford.
2. Ellen, *d.* in 1818.   3. Susanna-Frances-Faithful.
4. Emily, *m.* in 1841, to Henry-Gorges Moysey, Esq., lieut. 11th hussars, son and heir of the Ven. Charles-Abel Moysey, D.D., Archdeacon of Bath.
5. Maria.

III. Thomas-Edward, *d. unm.*

IV. William-Simon, *b.* 25 January, 1784, general in the Russian service, *m.* the dau. of a Polish gentleman named Maisner, and *d.* in Russia, in 1829, leaving issue.

V. Frederick, chamberlain to the Emperors ALEXANDER and NICHOLAS. He was murdered by the Poles, in 1830. He married and left issue.

VI. George, lieutenant-general in the Russian service, and aide-de-camp to the Emperor NICHOLAS, *m.* Mademoiselle Bonet, and has issue.

I. Sophia, *d. unm.*

Arms—Or, a chev. between three fleurs-de-lis, sa.
Crest—A dragon's head, erased, or, flames of fire issuing from the mouth, ppr.
Seat—Dengy Hall, co. Essex.

FARDELL OF LINCOLN.

FARDELL, JOHN, Esq. of Holbeck Lodge, co. Lincoln, barrister-at-law, F.S.A. and F.A.S., *b.* 4 May, 1784, *m.* 26 Sept. 1809, Mary, youngest dau. of John Tunnard, Esq. of Frampton House, in the same shire, and has issue,

---

134. *Extract from* Burke's Landed Gentry *(1843 edition) showing an indented pedigree for the family of Fanshawe of Fanshawe Gate, Derbyshire*

Derbyshire. The lineage provided for this family dates back to the 16th century and also includes the names of 53 men and women who married into the Fanshawe family (and usually the names of a woman's father). It is difficult to find entries for families that married into the gentry since few editions of *Burke's Landed Gentry* are indexed (exceptions include the second edition of 1842–48). The 18th and 19th editions of Burke's *Landed Gentry* are included in a database on the Burke's Peerage and Gentry subscription web site (and can be searched for any name appearing in them).

Genealogical information about untitled families is also included in *Armorial Families* by Fox-Davies, first published in 1895. The best edition is probably the fifth of 1929 (1035). It contains biographical information about men who were entitled to a coat of arms (considered below) as well as information about his family and a description (or illustration) of his coat of arms.

The heads of titled and untitled families are also featured in *The County Families of the United Kingdom*, by Walford (1066) published at intervals from 1860 to 1920. A typical entry gives the name (and family seat) of a landowner and a brief biography with details of his birth, marriage, parents and the name of his heir. Another useful reference is *Handbook to the Titled, Landed and Official Classes* by Kelly (1014) published annually since 1874. This provides brief biographies of the heads of those families with titles or large estates (and also of other noteworthy people).

The works noted above for peers, baronets and the landed gentry can be seen in libraries but are becoming increasingly difficult to find in secondhand bookshops. An alternative in respect of some volumes is to buy the CD-ROM *Notable British Families* produced by Broderbund and GPC. This includes scanned versions, searchable by name, of 11 works on titled or armigerous families of Britain, America and the British colonies, including Burke's *History of the Commoners*, Burke's *Dormant Peerages*, Burke's *Dormant Baronetcies* and (see below) Burke's *General Armory*.

FAMOUS PEOPLE

If any of your family owned a property or were prominent in a particular place, then the Victoria county histories (# chapter 16) or similar works should be consulted. Other famous people may be found in the *Dictionary of National Biography* (*DNB*), by Stephen & Lee (1061). Publication of the original edition (of 63 volumes) of the *DNB* commenced in 1885. It was reissued in 21 volumes in 1908 and 1909 with biographical entries up to 1901. Supplemental volumes for the 20th century have also been produced at periodic intervals. The complete work is also available on CD-ROM. The *DNB* contains detailed biographies of noteworthy persons from all walks of life (such as judges, poets, politicians, painters, authors, military officers and clergymen), recording information on their births, marriages or deaths, as well as information on their careers and references to source material. A useful version (in three volumes) to keep at home for quick reference is *The Concise Dictionary of National Biography* (1011) which contains summaries of all the biographies that appear in the main work up to 1985. This is supplemented by *The Dictionary of National Biography: Missing Persons* by Nicholls (1051a) which includes biographies for over 1,000 men and women who were omitted from the original *DNB*, such as the poet Wilfred Owen and Alice Keppel (a mistress of Edward VII). *Modern English Biography* by Boase (1022) deals with about 30,000 prominent people who died between 1851 and 1900. Six volumes were published between 1892 and 1921. Entries record a person's birth, marriage, death, education and career.

Information about prominent people can also be obtained from the annual editions of *Who's Who* (published since 1849); for example the 1916 edition (1016) contains almost 2,500 pages with thousands of entries. If a person died after 1896, it is easier to find relevant entries by first consulting the volumes of *Who Was Who*, which contain the entries for those people who had appeared in *Who's Who* but subsequently died. Thus, *Who Was Who 1897–1916* (1018) contains the biographies, extracted from *Who's Who*, of people who appeared in *Who's Who* but who died between 1897 and 1916. All the entries in *Who Was Who* from 1897 to 1995 and in *Who's Who 1998* (about 110,000 biographies) are also available together on CD-ROM, published by Oxford University Press. Entries in *Who's Who* and *Who Was Who* provide genealogical details (such as births, parentage, marriages and deaths) and information about people's education and careers that lead you to many other sources. For example, *Who Was Who 1951–1960* (1019) includes an entry for Professor C.H. Bulleid, a shortened version of which is set out below. His descendants can turn to school and university registers and also attempt to locate details about his employers.

Bulleid, Prof C. H. OBE. 1918; M.A; Assoc. M. Inst. C.E, M.I.Mech.E; Prof of Engineering, Nottingham University since 1949; born Hatherleigh, Devon, 10 January 1883, son of S.J. Bulleid; married 1912, Dorothy daughter of Neville Cox of Derby; two sons;
Educated; Exeter School; Trinity College, Cambridge. Employed Midland Railway, Derby (1908–10) . . . Parsons Marine Steam Turbine Co (1911–1912). Professor of Engineering, University College, Nottingham (1912–1949);
During war (1914–1918), General Manager Nottingham National Shell Factory and subsequently Chief Engineer Admiralty School of Mines, Portsmouth. Died 29 June 1956.

Similar information about noteworthy people is contained in the annual *Kelly's Handbook* (1014) noted above. For example, the 1965 edition includes army and navy officers, senior civil servants, MPs, peers, judges and distinguished people in drama, literature, art and commerce. Lists of peers, MPs and senior civil servants, judges, policemen, clergy, military officers (and senior officers of organisations such as the BBC, the Post Office and the Charity Commission) are also included in *Whitaker's Almanack*, published annually since 1868. If your ancestor was a peer, politician, judge, senior military officer or otherwise noteworthy, his portrait may have been painted (# chapter 11). Other publications, in the style of *Who's Who*, have been produced as commercial ventures, funded principally by those people featured in each volume. For example *Who's Who in Norfolk* (1017), published in 1935, includes biographies of clergymen, lawyers, army officers, other professionals and businessmen, such as the following:

Palmer, Edward Ernest, J.P. Retired draper. South Dene Lodge, King's Road, Great Yarmouth. Born 1858 in Yarmouth. Son of the late N.B. Palmer.
Educated at The College, Great Yarmouth.
Married 1885, Laura Sarah, daughter of the late Thomas Ashford of Badingham.
Member of Great Yarmouth Education Committee; Chairman of the Juvenile Employment Committee; Senior Deacon of Congregational Church, Great Yarmouth.
Recreations; golf, books and pictures. Eldest son; Donald Ashford.

Similar volumes were published for other counties. Another useful series of biographical dictionaries is that published by W.T. Pike in the period 1898 to 1912, subtitled *Contemporary*

Biographies, which were reviewed by J. Titford in *Family Tree Magazine* (April 2001). These 33 volumes, each covering a British or Irish city or county, were edited by W.T. Pike and a co-editor or by Pike alone, as in the case of his volume for London (1054). Each volume included photographs of the city or county and biographies (with photographs) of hundreds of men, arranged in sections for professions such as doctors, barristers, solicitors, engineers, architects, surveyors and accountants. A typical page from the London volume, including portraits and biographies of the accountants Edmund Burton, Howard Button and Ebenezer Carr is at illustration 135. The biographies include information about a man's career and important genealogical information. The entry for Edmund Hamilton Burton records his birth at Lee Park Lodge, Blackheath, his father's name (Dr. John Moulden Burton), his education at Winchester College, his marriage to Florence (daughter of Richard Miles of Edinburgh), his home address in Putney and his business address in the City of London.

The grant by the Crown of hereditary titles, such as earldoms, was reviewed above. However, many other people were honoured. From medieval times, men were created knights as an integral part of the feudal system (# chapter 27) and obligations of military service accompanied the honour. As the feudal system decayed, the Crown continued to create knights, as a reward for their service to the Crown, but without the burden of the military obligations of knight service. These knights came to be known as Knights Bachelor. Various orders of knights of chivalry were also founded as part of the Crown's system of honours. The most famous orders are the Knights of the Garter (instituted in 1348), the Knights of the Thistle (instituted for Scotland in 1687), the Knights of St. Patrick (instituted for Ireland in 1783) and the Knights of the Bath (instituted in 1725). Shaw (1059) lists the men who were created knights of these orders (or Knights Bachelor) up to 1905, based on the records of each order, the *London Gazette* and manuscripts at the College of Arms and British Library. For example, Robert Charnock was created a Knight Bachelor on 29 July 1619 by King James I (who was renowned for selling honours). Francis Carew of Devon, Charles I's servant of the Privy Chamber, was created a Knight at Charles' coronation on 1 February 1625/6. The most recent order of knights is that of the Royal Victorian Order, which dates from 1896 and recognises service to the monarch or members of the Royal Family.

The Harleian Society has published some biographical dictionaries of knights, principally from medieval times, in volumes listed by Mullins (260). The names (and sometimes biographies) of knights then living also appear in many editions of *Burke's Peerage* and similar works. There are also some published biographical dictionaries for each order of knights, such as Holmes (1043) for the Order of the Garter and Wollaston (1069) for Knights Bachelor living in 1946. Galloway, Stanley & Martin (1038) list recipients of the Royal Victorian Order.

Other orders and medals have been introduced over the years in order to honour both men and women. The Order of the British Empire was instituted in 1917 to recognise important services to the Empire. By 1921, the OBE had been awarded to about 26,000 people who are listed, with biographies, in Thorpe (1062). Announcements of later awards of the OBE can be found in the *London Gazette*. There are also published lists (some with biographies) of recipients of other awards for gallantry (other than in battle) or services. One example is the register of the George Cross (1014a), which contains photographs of most people who were decorated. Fevyer (1031) contains biographies of recipients of the George Medal. Galloway, Stanley & Martin (1038), list recipients of the Royal Victorian Medal and Henderson (1042) lists recipients of the Albert and Edward Medals.

London

Burton.—EDMUND HAMILTON BURTON, 47, Spencer Road, Putney, and 16, St. Helen's Place, E.C.; son of Dr. John Moulden Burton; born at Lee Park Lodge, Blackheath; educated at Winchester College. Articled to J. and J. Sawyer, accountants, of Adelaide Place, London Bridge; remained with them about two years after articles, and then commenced to practise for himself as Hamilton Burton and Company; Fellow of the Institute of Chartered Accountants; has been fond of cricket, football, racquets, and fives. Married Florence Lillie, daughter of Richard Miles, of Edinburgh.

Mr. E. H. Burton.

Button.—HOWARD BUTTON, 37, Marlborough Crescent, Bedford Park, W.; 40, Queen Victoria Street, E.C.; and 75, New Street, Birmingham; son of John J. Button; born at Birmingham, in 1875; educated at King Edward's Grammar School, Birmingham, of which he became a Foundation Scholar; articled to Howard Smith, Slocombe and Co.; became an Associate of the Institute of Chartered Accountants in 1898; commenced to practise in 1899 in partnership with Howard W. Brettell, A.C.A.; came to London in 1901, and manages the London business of the firm; Fellow of the Chartered Institute of Secretaries; fond of athletics, and is a member of the Mounted Infantry Company of the 1st Middlesex V.R.C.

Mr. Howard Button.

Carr.—EBENEZER CARR, 24, Coleman Street, E.C., and 3, Montrell Road, Streatham Hill; son of the late John Carr, city merchant; born at Cranbrook, Kent, June 30th, 1851; educated privately. Has been in practice as a professional accountant in London for over twenty years, and has been retained on many occasions by the L. and N.W. Railway Company as investigating accountant in compensation cases; was one of the original members of the Incorporated Society of Accountants and Auditors, and elected one of the first members of the Council of the Society; is a Fellow of the same, and was its President for four years, from July, 1890, to July, 1894; was presented with an address in recognition of his services to the Society in 1894; author of "A Complete System of Practical Book-keeping" (three editions), and "Investors' Book-keeping," published as one of Effingham, Wilson and Company's "Series of Useful Handy Books," and at the request of the *Drapers' Record*, has written special articles on "Drapers' Book-keeping"; in January, 1889, lectured before the Society on Book-keeping and Auditing, and at the Society's Autumnal Conference held at Glasgow in 1901, contributed a paper on "The Duties and Responsibilities of Auditors"; Fellow of the Royal Statistical Society; member of the London

135. Portraits and biographies from Pike's London at the Opening of the Twentieth Century: Contemporary Biographies *of 1905*

HERALDRY

Heraldry is a complex subject which is only briefly summarised here since many detailed studies are available. Williamson (1068) is a good general guide to heraldry. Woodcock & Robinson (1070) is a more detailed work with a useful bibliography. Other detailed and well illustrated works on heraldry include Friar (1036) and (1037), *Boutell's Heraldry* revised by Brooke-Little (1023) and, possibly the best, *A Complete Guide to Heraldry* by Fox-Davies (1034), which was revised in 1969 by J.P. Brooke-Little. The Heraldry Society, founded in 1947, publishes a quarterly journal, *The Coat of Arms*, and has an extensive library. Further information can be obtained from the society's secretary at PO Box 32, Maidenhead, Berkshire SL6 3FT.

In brief, heraldry is a system of identification that uses hereditary personal devices portrayed on shields. Heraldry developed in Europe in the 12th and 13th centuries (possibly for military purposes but also as a display of status and vanity). Distinctive devices, marks and colours on flags, shields or on tunics worn over armour (coats of arms) assisted the identification of knights in battle. The arms were also used in tournaments and for ceremonial purposes. Coats of arms were passed down from father to son (and often varied through the generations) and were used to decorate manuscripts, stained glass windows and funeral monuments.

The right to bear a coat of arms in England was granted to a man and his descendants (usually only his descendants in the male line). Consequently, each of the grantee's sons (and each of their sons and so on) had a right to the arms, so long as they differentiated their arms (by marks of cadency considered below) from the original grantee (or from the man to whom that original right had descended). The right to a coat of arms only passed to a daughter if there were no male heirs, in which case any sons of that daughter could later inherit her right to the arms. Wives, widows and daughters had a courtesy right to display their husbands' or fathers' arms, usually on a lozenge (that is the shape of a diamond).

Heraldry is important to genealogists because the descent of coats of arms through families evidences relationships. Thus the records of the Heralds' visitations (noted below) included many pedigrees since this was how entitlement to ancient coats of arms was proved. One should not underestimate the number of people who are descended from men entitled to a coat of arms. However, it is most unlikely that you will find that you have a right to a coat of arms. It is more likely that your descent from such a family is through one or more female lines. It is improbable that you are entitled to bear a coat of arms if that right is not already known by your immediate family (it would be very unlikely for a family to "forget" that it had a right to arms). Unfortunately, the existence of businesses offering to reveal to you a coat of arms that allegedly belongs to your family has become even more widespread in recent years.

The right to bear arms in England and Wales (heraldry in Scotland and Ireland is considered in chapter 29) is controlled by the Earl Marshal (on behalf of the Queen), assisted by the Corporation of the Kings, Heralds and Pursuivants of Arms (known as the College of Arms), who were granted a charter of incorporation by Richard III in 1484. The hundreds of men who have held the offices of Kings, Heralds or Pursuivants of Arms from medieval times to the 1880s are listed in *The Book of Dignities* by Ockerby (843). Heralds originally carried messages in battle and officiated at tournaments and ceremonies. At first, men displayed coats of arms without authority from anyone, but the use of arms gradually became controlled by the Crown through the Heralds. The Heralds had two principal tasks. Firstly, they undertook visitations (described below) to regulate rights to use coats of arms. Men who could prove (at a visitation) an ancient use of the arms by their family were granted permission to continue using them. The Heralds also made new grants of arms to people, particularly men who were raised to the peerage or knighted. Grants of arms are still made to individuals and organisations (such as colleges, schools and societies). Anyone can apply for a grant of arms and they will generally be granted if the person is deemed worthy, perhaps a public figure, military officer or a professional such as a doctor, lawyer or teacher.

The College of Arms, in Queen Victoria Street, London EC4, has extensive archives, described by Woodcock & Robinson (1070) and Wagner (1065). They include original grants of arms (a list of grantees, extracted from various records, has been published by the Harleian Society), medieval rolls of arms, manuscript records of visitations, many other manuscript pedigrees, a register of baptisms (# chapter 7), copy extracts from wills, parish registers and many other public records, as well as some records of the Court of Chivalry. The archives are not open to the public but searches in the records are undertaken by the Heralds for a fee.

It is useful to know some heraldic language (which is mostly Norman French) and some details of heraldic design. More information can be obtained from the detailed works on heraldry noted above. Although commonly called a coat of arms, the shield together with all its accessories is truly named an achievement. This usually consists of a shield, helmet, crest and perhaps two supporters, that is, a figure on each side of the shield (such as the lion and unicorn supporters to the arms of the Queen). A family motto might appear on a scroll drawn under the shield. It is the shield alone that is now called the coat of arms. Coats of arms often appear as illustrations, but you may also come across a blason, which is a written description of the shield, using the heraldic terms for its design and colours. For example, the shield can be divided in a number of ways. A shield divided by a vertical line up the middle is known as *per pale*. The right side of a shield, as the wearer would view it, is known as *dexter*, and the left side is *sinister*. A shield divided by a horizontal line across the centre is *per fess*. The lower half of a shield is the *base* and the top half is the *chief*. If the shield is divided into four quarters, it is described as *quarterly* and if it is divided by a diagonal line, it is *per bend*. The colours used on a shield are classified as metals: gold (or) and silver (argent), "colours": black (sable), blue (azure), green (vert), purple (purpure) and red (gules), and nine "furs" including ermine (depicted by black spots on a white background) and vair (depicted by shield-shaped pieces in blue and white). A *charge* was anything displayed on the shield, such as bands (horizontal, diagonal or vertical), crosses, chevrons, stars, circles, animals (such as lions or swans) or objects (perhaps flowers or stars).

The placing of two people's arms side by side on one shield (if both a man and his wife had the right to bear a coat of arms) was known as impalement. Compounding was the mingling together of two coats of arms to form new arms (to permit more differentiation of arms), perhaps by quartering, in which the shield was divided into four quarters. For example, if a man had no sons, his daughter or daughters inherited his right to the coat of arms. If such a daughter married a man with a coat of arms, her arms could be impaled with his or they could appear on a small shield in the centre of her husband's arms. The sons of that couple could obtain the Heralds' permission to bear a coat of arms that combined both, their father's arms in two of the quarters and the arms of their mother's family in the other two quarters. Coats of arms could, in time, include the arms of many families. The rules were complex, but are explained in detail in works such as Woodcock & Robinson (1070).

The male head of a family would bear his coat of arms, but his sons added marks of cadency to their shield in order to distinguish their arms from his. For example, a second son should have added a crescent and a third son should have added a five-pointed star. In turn, the sons of those sons should have applied a second set of cadency marks to distinguish their arms from those of their fathers, uncles and cousins. When a man died, his eldest son had the right to bear his father's arms (without marks of differentiation). That son's children would then apply only one set of marks of cadency rather than two. The system became very complex.

If you want to know whether a particular family had a coat of arms, you should refer to Burke's *General Armory of England, Scotland, Ireland and Wales* (1025), first published in 1842, which describes families' coats of arms from sources such as Heralds' visitations and grants. For each surname listed, the county (or sometimes town or parish) of the family is noted and a blason (description in heraldic language) of the arms is then provided. Thus the coat of arms of the Charnock family of Hulcot, Bedfordshire was described as "Ar. on a bend sa, three crosses crosslet of the first". Detailed books on heraldry will assist you to decipher such a blason and produce a picture of the arms. Unfortunately, some entries were incorrect or based upon sources of doubtful veracity (it includes an entry for the Bullhead family which appears unfounded). The 1884 edition of Burke's *General Armory* contains references to about 60,000 coats of arms. Many corrections and additions to the work, prepared by Alfred Morant, are contained in Humphery-Smith (1044).

As noted above, *Armorial Families* by Fox-Davies, such as the fifth edition of 1929 (1035), is a directory of men in the late 19th and early 20th centuries who were entitled to a coat of arms. The work includes a description or illustration of a man's coat of arms and genealogical information about his family. Illustrations of the coats of arms of all English monarchs and many of their relations are contained in Pinches & Pinches (1055).

During your research, you may come across a coat of arms with no indication of the name of the family entitled to those arms. In order to identify the family entitled to a certain coat of arms, you should refer to the *Ordinary of British Armorials* by Papworth & Morant (1053), which lists British coats of arms in alphabetical order of the charges that are featured on the shields. For example, if the arms that you are researching feature an axe, you can find (listed and described) all those coats of arms that featured axes. However, in order to find an entry, it is necessary to search for the charge that appears first in the blason of the coat of arms, and then (within that section) for the second charge that appears in the blason. You must therefore blason a shield (explained in the works noted above) before you can find it in the ordinary. Woodcock (1071) is another detailed work on arms used before 1530, with an index of names. It can be used to find a particular coat of arms or to find a family (and its arms).

The crest was originally an ornament on the helmet included in a family's achievement. Generally, a family cannot have a crest without a coat of arms, but crests became very popular and were often used separately by a family, as decoration on letterheads, plates or cutlery. Fairbairn's *Book of Crests of the Families of Great Britain*, published in various editions from 1859 to 1904 and revised in 1986 by Butters (1028), lists family surnames and describes (with an illustration) the crest used by that family.

HERALD'S VISITATIONS

A man originally obtained the right to bear a coat of arms because that right was granted to him or because his ancestors had used the arms before the system of grants was introduced. Visitations were undertaken by heralds in each English county (at intervals of approximately 20 or 30 years) between about 1530 and 1686, in order to record the use of coats of arms. The Heralds therefore recorded, as part of their work, the pedigrees of the families using coats of arms. For each county, the sheriffs compiled lists of nobles, gentry, knights and gentlemen, who were then called before the Heralds to show the arms that they were using and prove their entitlement (by grant or long use) to those arms. These submissions included much genealogical information. Much of the information submitted to the Heralds was oral tradition of the family (sometimes unreliable) backed up by monuments in the local church or documents in family archives.

The original records of visitations are at the College of Arms and listed in Wagner (1065). Some of these were copied (and additions made to the copies) by heralds or antiquaries and most of these are in the British Library but some are in other archives. Humphery-Smith (1044) includes a catalogue of the manuscript records of the visitations at the College of Arms, the British Library and other archives and also lists published versions. The Harleian Society has published many visitations, for example the visitation of Nottinghamshire 1662–64 in Squibb

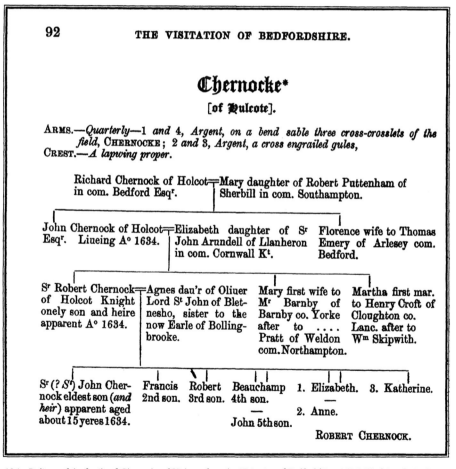

136. Pedigree of the family of Chernocke of Hulcote, from the Visitation of Bedfordshire, 1634 (Harleian Society)

(1060) and the visitations of Bedfordshire 1566, 1582 and 1634 in Blaydes (1021). Some visitations have been privately printed and others have been published by county record societies, for example that of Lincolnshire 1666, published by Lincoln Record Society in Green (1040) and the visitations of Yorkshire 1584–5 and 1612, published by the Surtees Society in Foster (1033).

Many published visitations do not rely on the original Heralds' records at the College of Arms but on later copies, particularly those in the British Library. They describe a family's coat of arms and include a pedigree of three or more generations, showing the descent of the right to arms. They usually include some genealogical information (such as details of marriages) of brothers and sisters of members of the main branch of the family, or other collateral lines. Published visitations are generally well indexed, including the names of all people appearing in the visitations, not just the principal families featured in the pedigrees. People marrying into these families can therefore be easily found. A similar form of index, for the manuscript copy visitations held in the British Library, was produced by R. Sims in 1849 as *Index of Pedigrees Contained in the Heralds' Visitations and Other Manuscripts in the British Museum*. This has been reprinted and is also reproduced in Humphery-Smith (1044).

Even if you do not find your ancestors in the visitations, they may include families which are worth noting because they may feature in your later research. I traced my ancestry on one line to the Charnock (or Chernock) family of Eversholt in Bedfordshire, who were fairly prosperous with some landholdings. Three generations of this family, James, Robert and James, lived in Eversholt from the late 16th to the mid-17th century. The visitations of Bedfordshire did not include this family (since it had no coat of arms) but did include, in the visitations of 1566 and 1634, in Blaydes (1021), five generations (from the 16th and 17th centuries) of the Chernocke (or Charnock) family of Hulcot (or Holcot) which did have a coat of arms. This family originated in Lancashire and had extensive property (as noted above, a member of the family was created a Baronet in 1661). Illustration 136 is the Chernocke pedigree from the published visitation of 1634. Chernocke and Charnock are not common names and the parishes of Eversholt and Hulcot were only about five miles apart. It was therefore worth researching the Chernocke family at Hulcot because they were possibly related to my ancestors at Eversholt.

If your ancestor did bear a coat of arms, you should extend your research to medieval rolls of arms (most of which are actually books) that were compiled by the Heralds from the 14th century. They include illustrations of coats of arms of lords and knights, perhaps those at a particular battle or tournament. These rolls are held by the British Library, the College of Arms, the Society of Antiquaries or the Bodleian Library and listed (with references to published copies) in Wagner (1064).

CHAPTER 27

FURTHER PROPERTY RECORDS

It is very difficult to trace your ancestors in the period before the commencement of parish registers in the mid-16th century. Before then, you may locate sporadic references to your ancestors (or to people who could be your ancestors) in wills, tax records or court documents. However, you are unlikely to be able to trace a line of descent in this period (and in particular find documents that evidence that one man was related to another) unless you find your ancestors in property records. These do not only refer to men who owned a substantial amount of land. They also refer to yeomen, tenant farmers and even to men who worked as labourers. In order to use property records, it is necessary to understand the English law of property. Property law has always been complex and, in order to understand property law, it is necessary to start in about 1066, with a description of the manorial system.

MANORIAL RECORDS

The manorial system was established throughout England by the time of Domesday book. It developed from a fusion of the Saxon system of agricultural estates and a feudal system of military tenures (introduced to England by the Normans) by which each man owed faith (or fealty) and military service to his lord. A lord owed fealty and service directly to the king or to another lord (who in turn owed allegiance to the king or another lord). The manorial system featured a feudal relationship between men and their lord centred around a manor, that is, a large area of land held by the lord, which included the lord's house, tenants' and labourers' cottages (perhaps in a village or hamlet), farmland, woods and perhaps a church. The lord kept some land (the "demesne") for his own use, but granted the remainder (and his protection) to men who worked the land and provided him with services or rent.

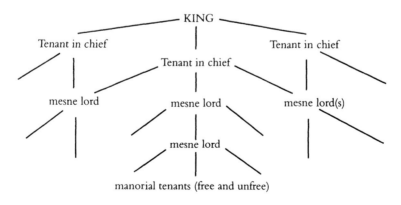

Since 1066 only the monarch has, as a matter of law, owned land. All other men could only hold land (for a period of time) from another man. If a man held land directly from the king, he was known as a tenant-in-chief of the Crown. Tenants-in-chief held their land (say 50 manors) from the king in return for services, perhaps to provide the king with a number of knights. By a process known as sub-infeudation, a tenant-in-chief provided land (perhaps 45 of those manors) to his retainers in return for their military services (so that the tenant-in-chief could provide knights for the king). These retainers were lords of their manors and known as mesne lords since they owed allegiance to a superior lord. A mesne lord might in turn, by sub-infeudation, provide one or more of his manors to his own retainers (who held them as mesne lords) in return for their services. Below the mesne lords were the tenants of each manor who actually worked the land. The terms upon which a man held the land (that is, the services or payment which he provided to his lord) constituted his "tenure" and he was a tenant. The period for which a man held land (the duration of his tenancy) was his "estate" in the land. Further sub-infeudation was prohibited by the statute Quia Emptores in 1290. From that year, a new tenant replaced his predecessor in the tree (by purchase, or by forfeiture of the predecessor's tenancy and a grant to the new tenant). The tree was not extended by the insertion of new tenures and new tenants. A new tenant took the land as well as the service obligations owed by his predecessor to the superior feudal tenant.

Tenures

Tenures soon came to be classified according to the kind of service rendered to the lord. There were two types of tenure, free and unfree. There were different forms of free tenure. There were tenures in chivalry, for example requiring a tenant to provide a number of armed horsemen for his lord (known as tenure of knight service). This tenure was soon commuted to a money payment (or scutage). There were spiritual tenures, for example those of divine service or frankelmoign by which a clergyman who held land would provide spiritual services to his lord (for example praying for the lord's family once a week). There were socage tenures, such as common socage by which a tenant provided agricultural services to his lord, of a fixed amount and type. Thus a man might hold land from his lord in exchange for ploughing the lord's retained land 20 days a year.

In cases of unfree (or villein) tenure, men known variously as villeins, serfs or bondmen held land from their lord in exchange for providing a fixed amount of work for the lord (for example four days a week), but the nature of the work could vary. Tenures (and most aspects of manorial affairs) depended primarily on local custom, so that any description of manorial life is a generalisation. This is particularly true of the classification of manorial tenants. Some authors use the terms villein or serf interchangeably. Some consider that there were substantial differences between their status, with serfs being almost indistinguishable from slaves. However, it is generally the case that unfree tenants were not free to leave a manor without the lord's permission and they were also subject (as we shall see below) to many other obligations (or incidents) of tenure, many of them onerous.

The incidents of tenure gradually faded away during the later middle ages, most being replaced by monetary payments. Military tenures were abolished in 1660, and all forms of tenure were converted to common socage by statute in 1922. Almost all land is now held by freehold owners directly from the monarch (rather than from intermediate lords), which is why land reverts to the Crown when landowners die without any legal heirs.

Life on the manor

There were between 25,000 and 65,000 manors in England (compared to about 12,000 parishes). Manors varied greatly in size. A parish might include one, two or more manors, but some manors extended over more than one parish. A manor might consist of little more than a farm with some tenants' cottages, but it might be a substantial estate that included one or more villages and hamlets, extensive farmlands, common land and forests. The village of Cottenham in Cambridgeshire was divided between six manors while the manor of Wakefield in Yorkshire covered over 150 square miles. In medieval times, the manorial lords were not only landlords but also local judicial and administrative authorities, acting through their manorial courts (considered below) that dealt with manorial affairs, property dealings and local justice. Some manorial lords also claimed to have testamentary jurisdiction over their tenants' wills or administrations. From the 14th century, the work of manorial courts was gradually transferred to the church or secular courts and to the ecclesiastical parishes (and later to secular local authorities). However, some manorial courts continued to operate in England until the 19th century, dealing principally with transfers of property on the manor.

Hone (1110) is a detailed description of the manorial system, life on the manor, the work of manorial officials, manorial courts and their records (with many examples and illustrations), the cultivation of manorial land, tenants' services and the role of the church. Ellis (1103) is an illustrated guide to manorial records and Emmison (1104) includes a detailed study, from surviving records of 74 Essex manors, of life on the manor and the role of manorial officials and courts. Bennett (1091) and Overton (1123) are also useful guides to the manorial system. Although manors varied in size, an average manor consisted of a village and the surrounding farmland and woods. The lord lived in the manor house (with its own grounds) near to the village and church. The free tenants and villeins lived in, or near, the village. Their houses or cottages might have small, adjoining, enclosed, plots of land (closes) upon which they could grow some food or keep animals. Free tenants were usually more prosperous than villeins, farming the land that they held from their lord but sometimes also working at trades (perhaps as blacksmiths or carpenters). Around the village was the manorial land, consisting of the lord's demesne, large open arable fields (usually three of them), meadows, wasteland, commons and woodland. The open fields were divided into strips. Each freeman and villein held strips in each field (so that each tenant had a share in the best and worst land) and worked upon those and upon the lord's demesne. Manorial tenants also had rights of common and so could graze their animals on the common pasture or heath (or even on the manor's arable land when it lay fallow). Tenants had other rights, such as a right to take wood from the forest for fire, building or making tools.

Responsibility for running the manor was divided between officials known as the steward (or seneschal), bailiff, reeve, hayward and constable. The lord appointed a steward as his agent to manage one or more of his manors and preside over his manorial courts. The lord also appointed a bailiff, who assisted the steward in managing the estate and ensuring that tenants undertook their labour obligations and paid their rents. Other manorial officials, often elected by the manorial court, ensured that farming was carried out in accordance with the manor's customs, in particular that a tenant did not overstep his rights of common to the detriment of other tenants. The reeve arranged the tenants' duties for the lord, summoned tenants to court and collected the fines, heriots and quit-rents (considered below) due to the lord. The hayward supervised the repair of the manor's fences and looked after any common stock of animals. The constable maintained the peace, expelled vagrants from the manor and ensured that vermin, such as crows, were controlled.

The development of tenancies

The lord of a manor granted land to tenants in return for military or agricultural services. The terms (or incidents) of tenure varied by custom from manor to manor and are well illustrated by the examples from Essex manors noted in Emmison (1104). The lord was entitled to an oath of fealty, rents and labour services from his tenants. He might be entitled to require tenants to grind their corn at his mill and they generally had to attend the manorial court. Until the abolition of most incidents of tenure in 1660, a payment (or heriot) such as the tenant's best beast, might be due to the lord on a tenant's death. The tenant's heir often had to pay a fixed sum of money to the lord (known as a relief) before he could take possession of his father's landholding. Free tenants (or freeholders) could freely dispose of their land and leave the manor (without the lord's consent). Their labour obligations were gradually commuted to fixed periodic rental payments (known as quit-rents). By the 16th century almost all freehold land was held by tenants for fixed rents and these soon became worthless because of inflation.

Until the mid-14th century the majority of English people were unfree (that is serfs or villeins). However, many people obtained their freedom during the 14th to 16th centuries, so that serfdom (or villeinage) disappeared by about 1600. At the time of the Norman conquest, there were also many slaves in England, but slavery generally disappeared by about 1200. The term villein covered a wide range of people, such as a man holding 30 acres, or a man with a cottage and perhaps only 5 acres. Most villeins had a house or cottage, with one or more crofts (a term that usually denoted a plot of meadow) and strips in the open fields. They worked on the lord's demesne (the amount and type of work varying, by custom, from manor to manor). Villeins were bound to their lord and were unable to leave the manor without his permission. They might obtain permission to live away from the manor but have to pay the lord a chevage. They might also need the lord's permission for their daughters to marry, and this entailed payment of a merchet. Villeins gradually came to be called customary tenants because the terms by which they held land from the lord depended upon the customs of the manor.

Villeins' labour obligations were gradually commuted to rents, although they remained bound to their lord. However, a villein was sometimes able to buy his freedom from the lord (a procedure known as manumission) and he might then continue to farm some land as a free tenant, or set himself up in a trade or move elsewhere. Many lords were willing to grant freedom for money since they could then pay for hired labourers who worked more efficiently than unpaid villeins. Many villeins also absconded from the manor, usually to a nearby town or city, since they could claim their freedom if they avoided recapture (and being returned to the manor) for a year and a day. In the 14th century when many villeins' labour services were already being commuted to money payments, England was devastated by the Black Death. The resulting labour shortage improved the bargaining power and position of all tenants. Restrictions on villeins' movements declined, principally because it became easier for a villein to abscond and then present himself at another manor as a free man. Lords who were in need of labourers were willing to hire such men, or grant them free tenancies of land, without asking questions. Villeins who remained on their own lord's manor were able to ignore many of the old customs of the manor and obtain better terms of tenancy (most surviving labour obligations were commuted to money payments).

The rights and obligations of villeins (or customary tenants) were often set out in documents such as the manorial court rolls. Unlike freeholders, they could not simply transfer their land to their heirs or to third parties, since any transactions relating to customary land were subject to the lord's consent, dealt with by a surrender or admission in the manorial court. If a tenant died, his death might be recorded in the court rolls. His heir would attend court to seek admission as the new tenant of the holding and pay a sum of money (a fine) to the lord. A fine was not a penalty payable for an offence or incorrect behaviour; it was a monetary charge (similar to a tax) payable to the lord of the manor. The new tenant's admission was also noted on the court roll. There was a similar process (with a fine payable by the tenant and a record made in the court rolls) if the lord of the manor died or if a customary tenant wished to dispose of his land to a third party. The surrender took place in court (by the tenant handing over a rod as a symbol of surrender) and was recorded (with the new tenant's admission) in the court rolls. New tenants (whether heirs or third parties) were given a copy of the court roll entry to prove their title to the land. Customary tenancies therefore also became known as copyhold tenancies (that is, land held by copy of the court roll). The rolls usually note the relationship (if any) between the old and new tenant and perhaps their ages. Customary and copyhold tenants might have the right to let their land to a sub-tenant and (later) to mortgage their property to raise money. The lord's permission was usually required for these transactions and so they are also recorded in the court rolls. Surviving court rolls, or the tenants' copies of the entries, may therefore note a number of generations of a family holding a property, whether a large farm, a cottage or a small plot.

In many places the court records for copyhold land continue up to 1925 (when all remaining copyhold land was converted to freehold). Illustration 137 shows a tenant's copy of an entry in the court rolls of the manor of Great Samford in Essex. This notes the admission, on 18 June 1747, of Thomas Smith on the surrender of Thomas Turpin. In summary:

Manor of Great Samford . . . At a general Court Baron for the Manor on Thursday 18th June 1747, before William Kirby, Deputy Steward . . .

At this court cometh Thomas Turpin eldest son and heir of Thomas Turpin deceased and in open court surrendreth by the Rod out of his hands unto the hands of the Lord by the hand of his Deputy Steward all the copyhold lands descended to him on the death of Thomas his father . . . to the absolute use of Thomas Smith of Great Samford, draper and of his heirs and assigns forever

Whereupon cometh unto court the said Thomas Smith and humbly prayeth to be admitted to the premises [described] to which premises Thomas Turpin deceased was admitted at a court holden for this manor on 19th April 1708 on the surrender of Samuel Rowton

To which Thomas Smith the Lord of the Manor granteth seizin of the premises by the Rod to hold according to the custom of the Manor.

By the late 18th century, many manorial documents were in much simpler form. Illustration 138 records the admission in 1793 of William Hodgson as a customary tenant of a property, Stub Place, in the manor of Corney and Middleton. The Court Baron of the lord of the manor, Sir John Pennington, Lord Muncaster, was presided over by his steward Cuthbert Atkinson. William Hodgson was admitted upon paying annual rent of 11 shillings and a fine of £11, due upon the death of the previous lord, Sir Joseph Pennington (Cokayne's *Complete Baronetage* records that Sir Joseph had died in February 1793).

There were two types of copyhold or customary land. The first was heritable copyhold. This land passed, on a copyholder's death, to his heir. The identity of a man's heir depended on local

Manor of   At a general Court Baron there holden for the Manor aforesaid on Thursday the 18th day of June

Great Samford   in the year of our Lord 1747 Before William Bishop Deputy Steward of Thomas Thruston Esquire Chief Steward there

to witt—   (Amongst other things it is thus recorded)

At this Court cometh Thomas Turpin Eldest Son and Heir of Thomas Turpin lately deceased and in open Court surrendereth by the Rod out of two hands into the hands of the Lord of the said Manor by the hands of the said Deputy Steward All and singular the Rights Members and appurtenances to the absolute Use and Behoof of Thomas Smith of great Samford aforesaid Draper and of his heirs & assigns for ever Whereupon cometh into Court the said Thomas Smith and humbly prayeth to be admitted to the premisses so to him surrendered as aforesaid (that is to say) To one piece of inclosed Land adjoining to the down of the said Thomas deceased in great Samford aforesaid containing in &c. Which premisses the said Thomas Turpin deceased was admitted to at a Court Baron six feet more or less And in length thirty feet more or less Which premisses the said Thomas Smith the Lord holden for this Manor on the 15th day of April in the year of our Lord 1708 on the surrender of Samuel Newton To which said Thomas Smith the Lord by the said Deputy Steward granteth Seizin of the said premisses by the Rod To hold the same to him the said Thomas Smith and his heirs of the Lord at the Will of the Lord according to the custom of the said Manor by the Rents and Services therefore due and of Right accustomed and hath Pay his fine to the Lord and is admitted Tenant.

Mem: At the same time the said Thomas Smith surrendereth the said premisses to the Use of his Wife

                                       Ext by me W. Bishop Deputy Steward there

137. *Manor of Great Samford, Essex: admission at a Court Baron of Thomas Smith on the surrender of Thomas Turpin, 18 June 1747*

custom. The principle of primogeniture was followed on most manors (the heir being the eldest son). On other manors, the custom was borough English (the heir was the youngest son) or gavelkind (all sons were joint heirs and shared the property between them). A copyholder who wished to pass on his copyhold land in accordance with the terms of his will rather than allow it to pass automatically to his heir, could do this by surrendering the land to the use of his will. This surrender was recorded in the court rolls. When the tenant died, his will was produced in court and the designated recipient of the land could be admitted. My ancestor Edward Hannell, a yeoman of Hockliffe, died in 1737. In his will, he declared that:

> I give to Elizabeth my wife my customary or copyhold land held of the manor of Leighton Buzzard, otherwise [known as] Grovebury, which I have surrendered to the use of this my will, for the term of her life.

The second type of copyhold land was copyhold for lives, that is, a copyhold interest that subsisted during the lives of one or more people (usually for three lives, for example the copyholder, his wife and his heir). The land then reverted to the lord, who could grant it to a new tenant. The manorial custom of free bench should also be noted; this was the right of a widow to retain her husband's tenement after his death (until she remarried). In the case of a copyhold for lives, the death of a man (perhaps the third life) could result in his children losing the land since it would revert to the lord. In some cases, ageing tenants (who were widowers and the last of the three lives) took a new, younger, wife and entered into a secret agreement with her and his sons that, upon his death, she would assert her right of free bench and retain the property, but allow her stepsons to continue farming the land (she would continue living at the property or receive financial support from her stepsons). Examples of such marriages and arrangements in 17th-century Dorset are described in an article "New Wives for Old Men" by J.H. Bettey in the journal (1088) of Bristol & Avon FHS (spring 1979).

Copyhold land that was held for lives was gradually converted into leasehold land (considered below). Legislation in the 19th century also provided for copyhold land to be enfranchised (that is, converted to freehold) by agreement of lord and tenant. The lord received compensation (an amount agreed between lord and tenant, or awarded by government officials). Enfranchisement documents from 1841 to 1925 are at TNA in series MAF 9, arranged by county and manor. Registers are in MAF 76 and some files containing evidence of titles are in MAF 20. Copyhold tenure was finally abolished by a statute of 1922, with all remaining copyhold land being compulsorily enfranchised with effect from 1 January 1926.

The manorial courts
There were three types of manorial court: the Court Leet, the Court Customary and the Court Baron. Many manorial lords were franchised by royal charter or warrant to hold a Court Leet with view of frankpledge. The view of frankpledge (dating from Saxon times) was a court that reviewed the working of the system of frankpledge, by which communities were divided into groups (known as tithings) of about 12 households. Men were responsible for the good behaviour of the other men of their tithing and if a man committed an offence, he and his tithing could be brought before the court. As time passed, the tithing system became obsolete and was replaced in part by the king's courts but in part by the Court Leet which tried certain offences (assaults, breaches of the peace, poaching, trade offences and nuisances) that were

MANOR
OF
{Corney & Middleton} placeable

THE COURT BARON, and Court of DEMISSIONS of the Right Honourable Sir JOHN PENNINGTON, Baronet, LORD MUNCASTER, of the Kingdom of Ireland, Lord of the faid Manor, holden in and for the faid Manor the *Twenty feventh* Day of *November* - in the Thirty-fourth Year of the Reign of our Sovereign Lord GEORGE the THIRD, King of Great Britain, &c. and in the Year of our Lord, 1793 by CUTHBERT ATKINSON, Gentleman, Steward.

At this Court came *William Hodgson Gentleman* and prayed to be admitted Tenant to a Cuftomary *Meffuage & Tenement* - - - .with the Appurtenances, called *Stub-place* - - ———— fituate, lying, and being within the Manor aforefaid, of the yearly Cuftomary Fineable Rent of *feven fhillings* - - — - - - ———— upon the Death of Sir JOSEPH PENNINGTON, Baronet, the laft General Admitting Lord, and having paid his Fine of *feven pounds* - - - - - (as in the Margin) he is thereupon admitted Tenant, *To hold* to *him, his* Heirs and Affigns, according to the Cuftom of the faid Manor, yielding, paying, and performing the Rents, Fines, Herriots, Town Terms, Boons, ~~Turns,~~ Dues, Duties, Suits, and Services therefore due and as Right accuftomed, at the ufual Days and Times.

Cuthbert Athinson
Steward

N°. (10)

138. *Manor of Corney and Middleton: the Court Baron of Lord Muncaster admits William Hodgson as a customary tenant, 1793*

committed within the manorial boundaries. The court sometimes also appointed constables. The Court Leet declined in importance and is rarely mentioned after the 17th century, most of its functions being undertaken by the Justices of the Peace. However, the Court Leet survived in some areas, such as Manchester, until the 1840s.

The Court Baron had jurisdiction over disputes between tenants or between a lord and his tenants. The lord could hold both a Court Baron (for freehold tenants) and a Court Customary (for customary tenants) but their sessions were usually combined and called the Court Baron. It sat at variable times, perhaps every three weeks or monthly. The Court Baron's functions varied from place to place and over time, but it generally dealt with the transfer of land, performance of the tenants' services, management of common land and breaches of manorial custom. The Court Baron also gradually declined in importance. By the late 18th century, it was rarely concerned with matters other than dealings in copyhold land. As the amount of copyhold land was reduced (by conversion into freehold or leasehold property), the court's role declined even further but some Courts Baron continued their work of conveying copyhold land until 1925.

Manorial records

The majority of surviving manorial records are the manorial court rolls (or books) which contain the minutes of the manorial courts. Court rolls survive from the early 13th century and are fairly abundant from the 14th century. Until about 1732 (except for 1653–60), most manorial records were kept in Latin (often very abbreviated) and the earlier records are therefore very difficult to use. Stuart (1130) is of great assistance in transcribing, translating and using manorial records, with many examples and a useful dictionary of terms. Palgrave-Moore (1124) also provides useful examples of entries in court rolls with translations. Other works that assist researchers with handwriting and Latin were noted in chapter 4.

A typical manorial court roll notes the date, the type of court being held (for example a Court Baron, a Court Leet, or sometimes both combined) and the names of the lord of the manor and the steward. This is usually followed by a list of the tenants who had asked to be excused from attending court, but who had to pay a small sum of money for their non-attendance. These excuses were known as essoins. Those who did not offer excuses for their absence could be fined as "default of tenants" (the fines were called amercements or misericorda). Some tenants were then sworn in, by an oath of allegiance to the lord, to form a jury that adjudicated on disputes and acted as accusers, informing the court of offenders or of disputes that had arisen. The first task of the court was to appoint men as manorial officials (if posts had become vacant). The court then considered the jury's presentments of tenants who were in dispute or who had allegedly committed offences. For example, a tenant may have failed to pay his rent or have grazed more animals than he was allowed on the common land. A tenant who claimed to have been unjustly dispossessed of his land by another tenant might take action in the manorial court for its recovery. The offences dealt with by manorial courts are described by A. Travers in *Genealogists' Magazine* (March 1983). Many offences, such as assault, were punishable by fines or by the offenders being put in the stocks. Finally, the court dealt with property transactions, reporting the deaths of tenants, admitting heirs, or recording the lord's consent to a tenant transferring his land to another man.

Some manorial court rolls have been published and many are listed in West (462). For example, Baber (1090) contains a calendar of the manorial court rolls of 1494 to 1504 for the manor of Bromsgrove and King's Norton, with entries concerning the election of officials, jurors, heriots, land pleas, personal actions or tenants who were presented for offences. Many entries note personal relationships; such as "Robert Ryle and Alice his wife" or "the tenants present the death of Richard Hille . . . Thomas Hille is son and heir". Importantly, Baber notes that, in the court rolls for one year from October 1503, a total of 228 individuals are recorded in some capacity. As another example, Gomme (1107) is a translation of the manorial court rolls for 1394 to 1422 for Tooting Beck (in Surrey), referring to hundreds of people living on the manor. If there are surviving court rolls for the manor on which your ancestors lived, there is a good chance that your ancestors will be recorded. The following extracts from manorial court rolls, noted by West (462), illustrate the importance of these records:

17th June 1281. Robert Wodecock pays 6d for licence to transfer his land to . . . Henry Fulfen.
23rd March 1294. William de Yieldingtree pays the lord 3s as fine and relief for John his son to receive the inheritance of his mother, Matilda's land.
24th July 1301. Thomas Squire is accused of having cut turf from the lord's wasteland and turfed his own with it, without the lord's permission.

Hone (1110) also includes many examples from manorial court rolls, including the following entries from the rolls (held at TNA) of the manor of Winterborne in Berkshire:

The suitors come and are sworn, and present that Thomas Hatt hath overburdened the common pasture with his sheep, and (he) is commanded for the future not to do so under penalty of 10 shillings . . .
Also they present that William Barcoll, freeholder, hath closed his last day [i.e. died], who held of the lord certain lands by knight service. And they say that Alice [aged five] and Sibell [aged three] are daughters and next heirs of the said William and upon this comes William Webbe and gives to the lord a fine for the minority of the aforesaid heirs [that is he sought wardship of the daughters until they came of age] of 3s 4d . . .
To the same court comes John Brown, and takes of the lord a cottage in Blackemer, late in the tenure of John Bradeley, to have and to hold to him, for the term of his life, according to the custom of the manor, by rent and other services . . . and he does fealty to the lord, and so is admitted tenant thereof . . .

You are fortunate if your ancestors lived in Manchester because records of the Court Leet of the manor of Manchester have survived and been published for 1552–1686 and 1731–1846, in Earwaker (1101). The records deal primarily with the relationships between the manorial tenants and between the tenants and their lord. Thus on 2nd October 1560, George Pendilton was ordered to move a dung hill in the "marketstede lane" before the "feast of Symon and Jude [Oct 28]". Many entries contain important genealogical information. The jury presented, in September 1556 and March 1570 respectively, that:

George Hulton is son and heire to Willm Hulton late of Donyngtoun and is at lawfull age and is burgesse and coheere to Robart Laborerr in the right of Elisabethe his mother and owethe to doe his [service] and feoltye and paye [heriot] and relief to the Lord

Robarte Cloughe [has] married Margaret Pilkintone, daughter and heire unto Thomas Pilkintone and payeth unto the lorde, for such landes as they holde of hym, 10d by [the] yere and is therefore to be entered burgess and to doe such servys as other tenants owe

Many Courts Leet ceased to operate by the 17th century, but the Manchester court continued to work until 1846 (dealing predominantly with public nuisances), when its powers were transferred to the Corporation of Manchester. These are later entries from the court's records:

[April 1760] We the jurors do present the following persons for the following offences and they are amerced in the several sums over against their respective names: [11 people named including] Elizabeth Fenton of Manchester spinster for exposing fish to sale within this manor on the fifth day of November 1759 which were not marketable . . . £1.
[April 1845] The jurors . . . present that Robert Brooks and John Wilson being . . . inhabitants of and in the said manor on the 14th day of February last in a slaughter house in Cotton Street in this manor and within the jurisdiction of this court had in their possession large quantities of flesh meat to wit the carcase of a cow in a diseased and unwholesome state and unfit for the food of man with intent . . . to expose the same to sale contrary to the laws and customs of this manor and to the common nuisance of the liege subjects of our said Lady the Queen . . . Robert Brooks and John Wilson be amerced in the sum of £10.

Many researchers believe that they will never trace their ancestors back far enough to use manorial records. However, the latter example shows how some of these records are not even as old as the introduction of civil registration. Anyone's ancestors may be found in these records.

Vital genealogical information can be found in the manorial court rolls. My ancestor Edward Hannell, of Hockliffe in Bedfordshire, held some copyhold land from the manor of Grovebury (at Leighton Buzzard). No trace of Edward's baptism could be found although it appeared likely that he was a son of Abraham Hannell. The surviving manorial court rolls for Grovebury were at Bedford Record Office. They recorded, in 1719, the admission of Edward Hannell to the land in succession to Abraham Hannell. The entry recorded Edward as Abraham's eldest son and referred to Abraham's will (which has not survived in church probate records). As a further example, Steel (29) notes many entries, in rolls of the Court Leet of the manor of Calstock in Cornwall, concerning the Honeycombe family, including an entry for 1559 recording that Philip Honeycomb had hanged himself and that his widow Margaret had inherited his tenancy.

There are some other surviving court records. Estreat rolls record the amercements imposed by a court, with names of tenants, their offence and the amount paid. These rolls may also record the heriots or fines levied upon the admission of a new tenant. Many other manorial documents survive, such as accounts, surveys or extents, maps, rent rolls and relief rolls. Surveys were written descriptions of property (only rarely was a map or drawing attached), the purpose of which was to record for the lord the landholdings on the manor and the attendant rights and obligations. Some surveys deal only with the lord's demesne (and are usually called extents) but many deal with all, or large parts, of the manor. They indicate boundaries, perhaps naming tenants or fields, or describe the rights and obligations of tenants, listing the rents or specifying rights of common. Surveys therefore also protected tenants, preventing a lord from secretly increasing rent or labour services over a period of time. Surveys were produced increasingly during the 13th and 14th centuries and are relatively common for the mid-16th century (when

Henry VIII dissolved the monasteries and sold many of their manors) and for the period following the English Civil War (when parliamentary commissions sold many of the Crown's manors). The purchasers were keen to establish, by detailed surveys, the extent of their new properties and the rent or other obligations owed to them by tenants. A custumal was similar to a survey, setting out the customs of the manor, the classes of tenants (and sometimes their names), details of the land, the services or rents owed to the lord and also the lord's obligations. Surveys, extents and custumals are in CROs or listed in published catalogues of maps, such as that for Essex Record Office by Emmison (385). Published examples of surveys include those of the manor of Leeds in 1612 and 1628 in Kirby (1112), for Walsham le Willows, Suffolk in 1577 in Dodd (1100), and for the manor of Wensleydale, Yorkshire in 1613 in Willan & Crossley (1134). The latter includes this entry:

> The tenants of Dale Grange . . . Roger Metcalfe holdeth one dwellinge house with a stable
> & turfehouse and garden plot adjoyninge; value per annum. 13s 4d.

Some custumals have been published, such as 13 custumals of Sussex manors of the 13th and 14th centuries in Peckham (1126). Examples of extents and custumals are also provided by Hone (1110), for example an extent of the manor of Nonnesplace, in Bicester, Oxfordshire in 1325 (held by a Benedictine priory at Caddington, Bedfordshire) of which extracts are:

> Free tenants of inheritance
> John le Veche and Agnes his wife hold a messuage and curtilage (courtyard) which is between Emma Bartlett's land and John Baker's land. They hold also an acre of land whereof half an acre lies in the land called Grasscroftfurlong and extends towards Chesterton between Walter Langley's land and William Hamond's land and they pay for the same one half-penny at Easter . . .
> Rents and services of customary tenants
> Robert son of Nicholas Germeyn holds a messuage and half a virgate of land in bondage at the will of the lady, and owes one [day] ploughing in winter and one hoeing . . .

Relief rolls record a tenant giving up a property and a new tenant relieving him of his obligations (these rolls sometimes record the commutation of labour services to rent). As labour services were replaced by rent, the surveys and custumals noted above were replaced by rent rolls (or rentals) which list the names of tenants and their rents. It also became increasingly common for maps of the manorial land to be prepared in order to establish boundaries or to assess the amount and use of tenants' land (to fix suitable rents). Many of these maps note tenants' and fields' names, the land use, the rent or other rights and obligations. Examples of such maps appear as illustrations in Ellis (1103). The demesne land was originally farmed for the lord by villeins and (later) by paid labour. Manorial accounts or compoti were therefore produced, recording money received for the produce that was sold and noting expenditure on tools, seeds or other expenses. The labour shortages after the Black Death in the 14th century caused many lords to cease cultivating their demesne land. Some leased this land to tenants for rent, usually a market rent because demesne land was not subject to the restrictions of manorial customs. Any new land brought into cultivation (extent land), perhaps by clearing forest on the manor, could also be leased out in this way. Leasehold land is considered below, but as lords rented out demesne land, so the manorial accounts became ledgers of the tenants' names and rents (and the lord might employ a receiver to collect the revenue). Many manorial accounts have been published, such as those for the 14th to 17th centuries for the manor of Leeds in Kirby (1112) and Le Patourel (1113). Examples of manorial accounts are also provided by Hone (1110), including:

> Manors of Bicester Priory: £13 6s 8d received from John Donesmore for the farm of Bemount . . . and 4s received for 21 lambs sold to John Deye of Wrechwyke . . . and for John Leseby, making fences at the sheepfolds of Wrechwyke . . . 13d.

Locating manorial documents

The Victoria county histories and similar works are a good starting point for research in manorial records. They list many manors and the names (and pedigrees) of many manorial lords. Manorial documents are held in many archives, particularly CROs, TNA, the British and Bodleian libraries, Oxford and Cambridge University libraries and Lambeth Palace Library. Many records are also in private collections. The first places to search for records are the Manorial Documents Register (considered below) and the CRO for the county in which the manor was located. That CRO may also be able to tell you where other surviving records are held.

The records of one manor may be located in a number of places: one or more CROs, TNA, the British or Bodleian libraries or in private collections. Thus manorial documents for the manor of Leighton Buzzard (alias Grovebury) are in at least two archives. The manor had been held by the Dean and Canons of St George's Chapel at Windsor, but was later sold. Bedford Record Office holds the manor's court rolls (1393–1558 and 1627–1727) and other manorial documents (in archives deposited by Sir Michael Kroyer Kielberg). Some court rolls for the manor, for the reigns of James I and Charles I, are also held in the records of the Ecclesiastical Commissioners at TNA.

However, although many manorial records survive from as early as the 13th century, it is important to note that many have been lost. An article by A. Travers in *Genealogists' Magazine* (March 1983) reviews a sample of manors in Huntingdonshire, Oxfordshire, Sussex, Wiltshire and Westmorland. For one-third of those manors, only the name of the manor is known (there are no known surviving records). Records survive from the 18th and 19th centuries for about half the manors. There are good runs of records from the 16th and 17th centuries for less than one fifth of the manors. There are substantial records since before the 16th century for only about 5 per cent of the manors.

Manorial records are often deposited with the papers of the family who held the lordship (at the time of archiving) or with the archives of an organisation (such as the Church) that held the manor at any time. Thus the Bodleian Library holds about 1,000 manorial court rolls (for manors that were held by Oxford University colleges). CLRO holds the records of manors that were held by the Corporation of the City of London (mostly in Middlesex and Surrey but also in Oxfordshire and Buckinghamshire). Guildhall Library holds records of many manors of the Diocese of London, the Dean and Chapter of St Pauls and London livery companies. Most of these manors were in Middlesex or southern England, but some were in other counties, such as Norfolk and Staffordshire. Hone (1110) lists the manorial court rolls in archives such as the British, Bodleian and Cambridge University libraries. Sayers (1129) lists the manorial court rolls and other manorial records at Lambeth Palace Library, relating to manors that were held by the Archbishop of Canterbury, the Bishops of Bath and Wells, Ely, Chichester, Winchester and

Worcester (or by various Deans and Chapters). The manors were located throughout England but particularly in Kent, Surrey and Sussex.

Many manorial records are held at TNA. Some (such as those in series CRES 5 and 34) relate to the Crown's substantial estates throughout the country. Others relate to estates of the Duchy of Lancaster. For example, series DL 30 contains many court rolls for manors of the Duchy from the 13th century to 1925. Series SC 2 contains over 500 bundles of manorial court rolls and related records from the 13th to 19th centuries, over half relating to property of the Duchy of Lancaster but many others from the Court of Augmentations or from the Palatinates. Many other manorial documents are held in court records (usually because they were submitted as evidence in litigation), particularly in Chancery exhibits, in Masters' documents or in the Court of Wards' records. Some manorial court rolls at TNA are also held in series of the records of the Ecclesiastical Commissioners, who were appointed in 1835 to administer land held by the church. Ellis (1103) describes how to find these manorial records at TNA and lists the available indexes and finding aids.

There are detailed catalogues to the manuscripts (including manorial records) held in the British Library. You can search for a place-name in the 10 volume *Index of Manuscripts in the British Library* (1087). This incorporates, in alphabetical order, the entries from various catalogues, such as *Index to the Charters and Rolls in the British Museum* by Ellis & Bickley (1102) and volumes of the *Catalogue of Additions to the Manuscripts in the British Museum*, for example that for 1861–75 (1079). These tell you that, for Upminster in Essex, the British Library holds a manorial court roll for Upminster Hall manor in 1652 (and notes its reference to enable the document to be found in the library's collections). For Hoath in Kent, the library holds court rolls of Shelvingford Manor in 1405 and 1457–96, a 15th century rental and various grants of land (also from the 15th century).

There are some published guides to the location of surviving manorial records. For example, Webb (1132) deals with Surrey manors and Webb (1133) deals with manors in London and Middlesex. If you cannot find records of a particular manor in published lists or in the catalogues of the CRO for the county in which the manor lay, the best method of locating them is to consult the Manorial Documents Register. Although copyhold tenure was converted to freehold by a statute of 1922, the manorial court records were still necessary to prove a landowner's title. It was provided that the location of surviving court records should be noted in a Manorial Documents Register (so that landowners could obtain access to them). The register is a card index, held by the Royal Commission on Historical Manuscripts (# chapter 11). There is a card for each parish in England and Wales (arranged by county, then alphabetically) which lists the manors which are known to have existed within that parish. For example, the card for Winkleigh in Devon notes five manors (Winkleigh, Winkleigh Keynes, Winkleigh Tracy, Southcote and Hollocombe). There is another series of cards for all known manors, arranged by county, then alphabetically. These cards list the known surviving types of records for each manor and their covering dates and locations. There are seven cards for the manor of Winkleigh. These do not record any surviving court rolls, but refer to surveys of 1653 (at the Duchy of Cornwall office) and of 1844 (at North Devon Record Office), rentals of 1817 and 1857 and a schedule of rents of 1646 (at Devon Record Office). The cards also refer to the archives' catalogues (if copies are held by the RCHM) and sometimes the relevant archive's own document reference.

The sections of the register for manorial records of Wales, Norfolk, Hampshire (including the Isle of Wight) and the three ridings of Yorkshire have been converted into a database that can be consulted on the RCHM web site. Searches can be made for records of a particular manor, for records of the manors within a parish, or for particular types of documents (such as court rolls) for all manors in a county. Searches produce the same information as the card index including the dates and type of records, their location and reference numbers for archives' catalogues that describe them.

Inquisitions post mortem

Inquisitions post mortem were Crown inquests, concerning the Crown's tenants-in-chief who had died. They were held from the early 13th century until military tenures were abolished in 1660. Inquests (with juries) were held by crown officials named escheators to discover what property the deceased had held from the Crown, ascertain the services to which it was subject, take temporary possession of it, identify the tenant's heir and ensure that he then took possession of the land and swore fealty to the king. Inquisitions therefore identify a man's family and his property. If the heir was a minor, the king was entitled to hold the property and retain any rents until the heir came of age. If there was no heir, the land reverted to the Crown. A report of the inquest was made to the Chancery. Two important types of documents survive (in Latin), the inquisitions themselves and entries on the Fine Rolls.

The Fine Rolls originally recorded fines (payments to the Crown), but also the appointments of Crown officers, including orders given to escheators in each county to conduct inquisitions in respect of deceased tenants-in-chief. The rolls at TNA extend from 1199 to the 17th century and HMSO has published 22 volumes of calendars for 1272 to 1509. Typical entries of orders to escheators from the volume (1076) for 1485 to 1509 are set out below. They indicate the date of Crown tenants' deaths. Some include important genealogical information.

1493 Sept 2. Writ of diem clausit extremum to the escheator in the counties of Warwick and Leicester after the death of Gerard Dodynsell, who held [land] of the King in chief.

Writs of diem clausit extremum, after the death of the following persons, directed to the escheators in the counties named: Sept 16. John Eyland. Nottingham. Oct 30. Isabel Sapcote, widow, late the wife of Richard Sapcote Knight; Northampton and Rutland.

1501 February 13. Order to the escheator [of] Southampton and Wiltshire to take the fealty of George Forster, son and heir of Humphrey Forster esquire and Alice, late his wife, and cause him to have full seisin of all the lands, which the said Humphrey held . . . after the death of the said Alice, of the inheritance of the said George, whose homage the King has respited until midsummer next.

Inquisitions post mortem are at TNA, date from 1235 to 1649 and describe landowners' property and name their heirs. The main collection of inquisitions is in series C 132–142. For example, inquisitions from the reign of Henry III are in series C 132 and those of the reign of Edward I are in C 133. Inquisitions were also filed at the Exchequer (and are now in series E 149–150), in the Palatinate courts of Chester (in series CHES 3), Durham (in DURH 3) and Lancaster (PL 4) and in the courts of the Duchy of Lancaster (in DL 7). From the reign of Henry VIII, inquisitions were also filed at the Court of Wards (and now in WARD 7). The documents are in Latin and difficult to read. Illustration 139 is an inquisition from 1283 in respect of the

139. Inquisition post mortem held in 1283 upon the decease of Philip de Baunville

lands of Philip de Baunville in Cheshire. Hugh of Barlestone and 11 other jurors stated, on oath, that Philip had held land in Scorton and Macclesfield and that his heirs were his three daughters, Joan aged 20, Ellen aged nine and Agnes aged eight.

Indexed calendars of the inquisitions (but omitting the jurors' names) have been published by HMSO for 1235–1422 and 1485–1509 and are listed in Mullins (260). For example, Volume 2 (1072) includes inquisitions from part of the reign of Edward I, including an inquisition of 1288 upon William de Ferariis, who held over 20 manors in Lancashire, Essex, Northamptonshire and Leicestershire. The inquisition refers to 30 or 40 of William's tenants, for example, William Gogard on the manor of Hetchernok (Heath Charnock). An extract from this inquisition is:

> William de Ferariis. Writ, 20 December 16 Edward I [1288]
> Northampton [The manor of] Neubotle. The manor . . . [extent given] held of the King in chief by socage.
> Lancaster [The manor of] Hetchernok. A third part held by Thomas Banaster by service of 21d yearly and two parts held by William son of Hugh Gogard by homage and service of 3s 9d yearly. [The manor of] Chernok Ricard. A moiety held by Henry de Lee by homage and service of 5s and the other moiety held by Henry de Chernok by homage and service of 2s yearly.

The names of the deceased in the Chancery, Exchequer and Court of Wards' inquisitions of 1509–1649 are indexed in volumes of *Public Record Office Lists & Indexes* (at TNA and the SoG) and the deceased in the inquisitions of 1413–83 in series C 138–141 are indexed in List and Index Society volumes 268–269.

Some indexed abstracts of inquisitions have also been published by record societies. Abstracts for Gloucestershire (1236–1413 and 1625–42), Wiltshire (1242–1377 and 1625–42) and London (1509–1603) have been published in British Record Society volumes listed in Mullins (260). Fry (1106) is a calendar of Cornwall and Devon inquisitions (from the 13th century to 1649), published by Devon & Cornwall Record Society, and Brown (1093), published by the Yorkshire

Archaeological and Topographical Association, contains Yorkshire inquisitions (with jurors' names) from 1241 to 1283, of which the following is an example:

William de Feugers. Writ directed to Thomas de Normanville and dated at Westminster 10th July 1281. Inquisition made by Geoffrey de Toccotes, Walter de Thorpe, Peter Ragott, Robert, son of Weila, Alan de Manteby [and seven other jurors], who say upon their oath that: William de Feugers held of the king in chief the town of Castelleuigton [Castle Levington] by the service of half of one knight's fee. The capital messuage there is worth by the year one mark. There are in demesne, 41 bovates, each worth by the year with meadow 12s, 11 cottages, each worth yearly 16d. Demesne wood, about 20 acres worth half a mark yearly. Two water mills are worth by the year five marks. Andrew, son of the said William de Feugers, is his next heir and aged fifty years . . . Done at Stokesley . . . 19 August 1281.

TITLE DEEDS AND OTHER PROPERTY RECORDS

As the manorial system declined, property transactions (whether freehold or leasehold) were increasingly private contracts between a seller (a vendor) and a buyer, or between a landlord and tenant. Since registration of land titles was only introduced relatively recently, most transactions were therefore only recorded in documents that belonged to the parties.

Title deeds

If Mr Smith buys a property from Mr Jones, he needs to be sure that Mr Jones is the true owner (otherwise Mr Smith will not obtain good title to the property). If the registers of title at land registries record someone as the owner, a purchaser may rely upon that. However, in the case of land that is not registered (or any land before registration was introduced), the seller's title to the property is evidenced by title deeds. Many documents record that people had an interest in land (for example, wills, tithe maps and land tax records). However, it is title deeds that reveal exactly what interest a person had in the land (freehold, leasehold or copyhold) and describe the land's location and area.

If your ancestor owned or leased a property, you should attempt to locate any documents relating to it, since they can provide much useful information. For example, Thomas Bulleid of Croft Farm in Winkleigh, in Devon, was a farmer, apprentice master and churchwarden in the 18th century but, after his death, his children lived in poverty, working as agricultural labourers (and many of their children were apprenticed by the parish to local farmers). The reason for this was the nature of Thomas's interest in Croft Farm. He only inherited a leasehold interest from his uncle. This was a three life lease (that is, lasting until the death of the last of three named people). On Thomas's death, the farm reverted to the freehold owner and Thomas's family (with no further rights in the farm) became landless labourers.

An enormous number of property deeds survive in record offices but they are underused for a number of reasons. They are rarely indexed (and sometimes poorly catalogued) and can be difficult to understand at first, because they contain many legal terms and are often in Latin. Some understanding of property law is also necessary in order to use deeds. The genealogical information that one deed contains may be extremely limited (and one deed is often difficult to understand without reference to other deeds) and so the effort involved in finding and using title deeds can be out of all proportion to the useful information that is obtained.

However, deeds are easier to use after a little study and the assistance of books such as Alcock (1089) or briefer guides such as Cornwall (1096) or Dibben (1099). Once you understand the different types of deeds and can separate the legal and repetitious text from the important information, the benefit obtainable from deeds is substantial. Fortunately, since deeds were kept so as to prove title to land (and usually had to be handed to the new owner when land was sold), those people dealing with deeds (principally lawyers) kept them in bundles relating to a particular property. Archived title deeds are therefore usually in their original bundles and if a catalogue refers you to a deed for an ancestor's property, it is likely that there will be a series of deeds for the same property. It is unfortunate that so many deeds have not been archived, but destroyed or sold at markets or in antique shops. In those cases, the bundles have usually been broken up and the documents sold separately. Deeds lose much of their value when separated and it is now impossible to reconstitute the original bundles.

Estates in land

As noted above, the duration of a man's tenancy or possession of land is an estate. The four types of estates are: fee simple, fee tail, for life (all of which were freehold estates and of unknown duration), and a term of years (also called a lease). Fee means an estate in land that can be inherited. The fee simple absolute is the greatest estate possible, simple meaning that it could be transferred to anyone by will, gift or sale and absolute meaning that it is not subject to any contingencies. This estate was granted by the words "to Thomas Read and his heirs and his assigns". Most people who now own land have a fee simple absolute. In practice, they are the absolute owners of land and can freely dispose of it.

A life estate (for example a grant of land by S to X for life) continued until X died. X could transfer the land to Y, but Y's interest only continued while X was alive. A grant could be made *pour autre vie* (for the life of another), perhaps to X during the life of Y. When Y died, the interest of X came to an end. At the expiry of a life estate, the land reverted to the holder of the fee simple. While the life estate subsisted, the holder of the fee simple (S) had a fee simple in reversion, because he had the right to the return of the land at the expiry of the life estate. On the death of the life tenant, the interest of S reverted to a fee simple in possession. As another example, S could grant the land to X for life, then to Y for life, then to Z and his heirs. X would take possession. When X died, Y took possession (if he was still alive). During the lives of X and Y, the interest of Z was a fee simple in reversion. When Y died, Z (or his heirs) could take possession and thus hold the fee simple in possession.

The fee tail was an interest that lasted as long as there were living lineal descendants of the person to whom the land was originally granted. S could grant the land to X and the heirs of his body. If all X's heirs died out, the land reverted to S (or to his heirs). X (and each of his heirs to whom the land subsequently descended) only had a life interest and this limited their rights over the land. The fee tail kept the land within a family because, whatever X did, the land went to his heir (Y) on X's death. Y was similarly restricted. He could lease out the land during his lifetime but could not give a third party any greater interest than his own, since the land would devolve upon Y's own son (Z) upon Y's death. A purchaser could only buy an interest limited to the life of the tenant in possession. That was an uncertain period – it could be one year or 50 years. In the 13th century it became possible to destroy (or bar) a fee tail (converting it into a fee simple) by a legal action known as the levy of a fine. A similar process (a common recovery) developed in the late 15th century (and both are considered further below). A tenant in tail and an intending purchaser collaborated with a man of straw in court proceedings (about a fictitious dispute) to obtain a court judgment confirming that the intending purchaser was entitled to a fee simple in possession of the land. From 1833 statutes provided alternative methods of barring entails. The statutes and resulting documents are described in detail in Colwell (243).

Leaseholds were noted above. A landowner granted a right of occupation (called a tenancy or lease) to a third party for a period of time (perhaps six months or 99 years). A leaseholder (or tenant) could sub-let the property (for part of the term) to another person (a sub-tenant).

Proving title

A vendor of land now has to prove his ownership (or that of preceding owners) for at least the previous 15 years. Until 1925 this period was 30 years. Deeds were therefore retained showing a succession of owners, perhaps A selling to B, then B selling to C. Deeds might be retained for much longer, perhaps hundreds of years (especially if they evidenced important rights that attached to the land). If D wished to purchase the property from C, he could review the deeds to ensure that C had the right to sell it. In many cases A and B (or earlier owners) might have been related to each other and the land might have been inherited rather than purchased. The title deeds may therefore include wills, sometimes wills that were not proved (and so not in court records) since probate was unnecessary if a will only dealt with real property. Bundles of title deeds may also include civil registration certificates or copy entries from parish registers of baptisms, marriages or burials (certified by parish officials). There may be letters of administration (if a landowner died without having made a will) and deeds evidencing the land passing to the deceased's widow or children. The land may be noted as having been held previously by copyhold tenure and lead you to manorial court rolls that record surrenders and admissions, perhaps through many generations.

Title deeds (and related papers) name not only the landowners but many other people, such as tenants (of houses or farmland), trustees, mortgagees and owners of adjoining land. If your ancestors farmed land in a certain parish, it may be worthwhile consulting any deeds relating to that parish since they may refer to your ancestor's property or mention your ancestors in other capacities. It is not easy to locate these records. It is a time-consuming task and (unless the deeds have been calendared or indexed) your chances of finding a reference are small.

The form of title deeds

Cornwall (1096) is a useful guide to title deeds from the 16th to 19th centuries. Alcock (1089) is a more detailed examination of title deeds since medieval times, dealing particularly with the language used in deeds and explaining how to abstract the important information. The first problem is the deed itself. It is likely to be old (therefore requiring careful handling), dirty and folded (perhaps difficult to unfold without damaging it). However, the lawyers who used these records faced the same problems and so a deed usually has an endorsement or title upon the back (appearing on the outside of the folded document) that briefly identifies it. For example, an endorsement might state that it is a lease of a named farm in a certain parish and give the date and the names of the landlord and tenant. If a deed has been catalogued, it is usually this endorsement which has been used for the catalogue entry. You should also check whether the back of a title deed contains any further information. For example, there may be a note of the receipt of a purchase price or repayments of a mortgage on the property.

The second difficulty is handwriting (# chapter 4). You should always have alphabets of old handwriting to hand when you review title deeds. The third difficulty is that most deeds were in Latin until the 16th century. You should therefore also have a Latin dictionary available. Even if deeds are in English, they include many obsolete legal words. Some of these words (for example copyhold, freehold, fee simple, life estate or fee tail) have already been explained. Some other commonly used words and their meanings are:

appurtenance :	something that belongs to something else (appurtenances of land may include buildings, rights of way or fences)
attorney :	someone authorised to act for another, thus Mr Smith could sign a document as the attorney for Mr Jones
curtilage :	the area of land surrounding a house and used for domestic purposes
messuage :	a dwelling house

Bundles of deeds often contain an abstract of title. This document summarises a series of title deeds, perhaps covering many years, and is therefore extremely useful. An abstract was usually required if a property was being split. A farmer might own five fields and hold title deeds stretching back for many years. If the farmer sold one field, he could not pass the deeds to the purchaser since he would still require them for the other four fields. A lawyer therefore prepared an abstract of title, summarising the deeds that gave his client good title to the fifth field. This abstract (certified by the lawyer as a true summary of the deeds) was given to the purchaser. I have an abstract of title for some copyhold land of the manor of Hedingham Upland in Essex dating from about 1800, when the property was purchased by Osgood Gee from Henry Spurling. These are some extracts:

26th October 1656. John Sparrow was admitted upon the surrender of Richard Alston to one garden with two crofts of land, by estimation five acres, called "Albins" lying in Great Maplested, to one croft of land called Castle Croft, by estimation two acres, lying in Great Maplested, also to Collins Garden with one croft of land adjoining, called Collins Croft, containing by estimation one acre.
19th April 1666. John Sparrow, son and heir of John Sparrow deceased was admitted [to the same lands].
19th April 1669. Mark Guyon was admitted upon the surrender of John Sparrow son of John Sparrow [to the same lands] and Mark Guyon was also admitted, on the surrender of Henry Alston and Elizabeth his wife, to one parcel of meadow called Collins, by estimation one acre, and one parcel of land called Nether Croft, by estimation two acres, lying in Great Maplested which she [Elizabeth, wife of Henry] took up by the name of Elizabeth Easterford at a court held on 24th September [in the sixth year of the reign of Charles I].
18th April 1693. Rachel the wife of Thomas Bullock, sister and heir of William Guyon deceased, who was the son and heir of the said Mark Guyon deceased, was admitted to the same parcels as the said Mark.
5th April 1711. John Bullock, son and heir of Rachel Bullock deceased (formerly Guyon) was admitted to [the same lands].
1st October 1719. Rachel Bullock spinster was admitted as sister and heir of the said John Bullock then deceased, to the same lands.

The information contained in an abstract of title may be sufficient for your purposes, but it is worthwhile enquiring as to the location of the original deeds since they will contain more detailed information than the abstract. In medieval times, title deeds and related records might also be copied into a cartulary, that is, a compilation of records of land held by a body (such as an abbey) or an individual. A cartulary might cover the landowner's property throughout the country and therefore constitute an easily accessible reference for the owner as to his land (and its rights, privileges and tenants). Surviving cartularies are catalogued in Davis (1098). Many have been published, such as cartularies of John Pyel and Adam Frounceys (two wealthy London merchants of the 14th century) in O'Connor (1122), and the cartulary of Bradenstoke Priory in Wiltshire (covering the priory's lands from the 12th to 14th centuries) in London (1115).

A deed was often also called an indenture. The same wording was written out twice upon the paper or parchment and the document was then cut in two, by an indented (or wavy) cut so that the two pieces (and only those two pieces) fitted together. Each party kept one part and if one party tried to subsequently change his copy, that alteration could be evidenced by reviewing the matching document held by the other party.

Most title deeds recorded the transfer of an interest in property from one person to another. Their format was therefore similar, whether the transaction was a transfer of a freehold or a leasehold, the grant of a mortgage or the transfer of property to trustees of a settlement. The important legal parts of a typical deed (in this case a lease) excluding the identity of the property and the names of the parties, would therefore be:

This Indenture dated the [date] between [names and descriptions of the parties] witnesseth that whereas [a recital followed, noting the purpose of the transaction or describing earlier relevant transactions] . . . now the [name of landlord] in consideration of [a sum of money or other consideration] . . . does demise [or lease or grant] unto [name of the tenant] all that [description of the property] . . . to have and to hold the said property . . . for the term of [number of years, or life, or lives of named person or persons].

This would be followed by detailed provisions for the amount and payment of rent and for the obligations of the landlord and tenant (for example for repair of the property) during the term of the lease. The terms of a transfer (or conveyance) of a freehold were similar, although there would usually be one capital payment (rather than periodic payments of rent) and it would usually be a transfer for all time (rather than for a limited period) and so there was usually no need for any continuing obligations between the parties. The recitals (usually contained in a clause starting with the word whereas) can be extremely important, because they often summarise earlier relevant transactions. Thus a deed can record a sale of property from Mr Smith to Mr Jones. The recital may record that Mr Smith had inherited the property from his father or purchased it from Mr Brown. The sale may be by trustees or executors, in which case the recitals usually refer to a will or deed of settlement (and the relevant dates, parties and terms) by which those trustees or executors became entitled to sell the property. A title deed was completed by the signatures and seals of the parties (although it was not always necessary for all the parties to sign the document) and the signatures of witnesses.

Leases
A lease is a grant by a landlord to a tenant of the right to occupy property for a period of time. The tenant would periodically pay rent to the landlord, or pay a capital sum (a fine or

This Indenture

premium), or pay both rent and a premium. Two copies of a lease were usually prepared. The original lease was signed by the landlord and kept by the tenant. The other copy (the counterpart) was signed by the tenant and kept by the landlord. A lease might be stated to continue year by year until one of the parties gave notice of termination, or be for a term of years, perhaps 1, 21, 50 or 99 years. If a leaseholder died, he could bequeath the unexpired term of the lease to someone else (leasehold land was personalty) so references to leasehold property appear in many wills.

The term of a lease might, alternatively, be for the life of the tenant or another person. The three-life lease was also very common (developing from the copyholds for three lives noted above). The lease was stated to continue for 99 years or (if earlier) until the death of the last of three named people. The lease would therefore last for 99 years if one of the three named people lived that long. This reference to a 99 year lease was inserted in order to convert a lease of uncertain duration (no one knew when the last person would die) and therefore a freehold estate that required livery of seisin (discussed below), into a fixed term lease of 99 years (albeit liable to end earlier if all three named people died) which could be granted by a simple deed. Illustration 140 shows an extract from a three-life lease dated 19 June 1837 by which Revd Rogers leased fields at Helston in Cornwall to Thomas Sleeman for a premium of £210 and an annual rent of £1. The lease was for 99 years and the three lives named in the lease were Henry Sleeman, William Sleeman (both sons of Thomas) and John Read. An endorsement on the back of the lease noted their ages, at the time of grant, as 27, 26 and 12 respectively. The lease continued until all three people died and there is a note, "expired October 1884", below the endorsement, so it appears that all three men had died by October 1884. The three named people were not necessarily subsequent tenants of the property. If the first tenant died and one or more of the lives was still alive, that first tenant could bequeath his interest in the lease to another person (who could hold the property during the continuance of the lives). However, a tenant farmer might name one or more of his sons or grandsons as the lives (as Thomas Sleeman named his sons Henry and William) and he may also have bequeathed his interest in the leasehold property to one of those descendants.

Families (and landlords) desired settled arrangements and certainty for the future. It was therefore common for the parties to prevent such leases expiring. After the death of the first or second named lives, the then tenant (perhaps a son or grandson of the original tenant) might agree to surrender the remaining term of the lease to the landlord and pay him another premium, in exchange for the landlord granting a further three-life lease, in which the tenant could name three more lives (his own wife, sons or grandsons). The new lease might also recite the terms (and the lives) of the lease being surrendered. Thus Dibben (1099) includes an example of such a lease of 1751 (between the landlord William Ashburnham, Dean of Chichester and the tenant Mary Hasler, a widow of Aldingbourne in Sussex) reciting that:

> . . . the said Dean, in consideration that Mary Hasler hath surrendered up one Indenture of Lease bearing date 4th March 1747 made by the said Dean unto Mary Hasler of [the property] for the natural lives of Henry Hollist (since deceased), John Hasler and Richard Hasler . . . which said surrender was made to the intent that the said Dean might grant a new lease (to) Mary Hasler . . . for the natural lives of John Hasler, Richard Hasler and William Faulkner, aged fourteen . . .

Three-life leases are therefore very useful to genealogists. They were particularly common in counties such as Devon, Cornwall and Somerset. Because a tenant often named members of his family (particularly sons and grandsons) as the lives, the survival of such leases compensates in part for the loss of Devon, Cornwall and Somerset wills in the Second World War.

If a tenant decided to sub-let the property, or part of it, to a third party, this was known as a sub-lease. The third party became a sub-tenant, paying rent to the tenant, who continued paying rent to the landlord. If a tenant transferred all his rights in the lease to a third party, this was done by way of an assignment and the third party became the new tenant (for the remaining term of the original lease), paying rent directly to his landlord. Dibben (1099) includes typical wording of an assignment. Information on leases may also have been recorded in a landowner's estate papers, perhaps lists of his tenants, their property and rents.

The location of title deeds
CROs hold vast collections of title deeds, most of which concern property located in the county that the CRO serves. You should start a search at a CRO by consulting its catalogues and indexes, searching for records by family name, the name of the property or by the parish in which it was located. CROs hold collections of deeds by reason of:

a. the deposit of records relating to local property
b. the deposit of deeds (relating to anywhere in the country) belonging to particular people or organisations
c. enrolment of deeds (considered below) with the Clerk of the Peace, to ensure their survival for the future

Record offices may hold deeds relating to a property because the land was owned at some point by the church or by a charity. Many deeds remain in private collections of the family that owned the land, but many families have deposited their papers at a record office. They may be in record offices for counties (or even countries) other than that in which the land was located because they form part of a family's (or organisation's) collection, relating to property in many places. A landowning family may have leased a property to your ancestors and the lease may have been retained by the landlord's family but not by your family. It is therefore important to ascertain the names of the owners of any land that your ancestors occupied. This can be done by studying church monuments, directories, parish registers or tithe and land tax records. You can then ascertain whether any estate documents of that family survive and where they are held. For example, the Russell family (Dukes of Bedford) had many large estates in Bedfordshire, Devon, Buckinghamshire, London, Middlesex, Cornwall, Hertfordshire, Northamptonshire and Huntingdonshire. Thousands of deeds, manorial rolls and rentals survive for the family's property, many of them catalogued in a Bedfordshire County Council booklet (1085). Deeds of the Devon and Cornwall properties are at Devon Record Office in Exeter, but those for most other counties are at Bedford Record Office. The Duchy of Cornwall has always had large landholdings, particularly in south-west England. The majority of the Duchy's records are at its offices in London and many older records can be inspected by the public. It is estimated that the Bodleian Library holds about 50,000 deeds, including many families' collections.

Many municipal corporations had large landholdings in the city or town and records may survive in borough archives or CROs. The church, charities and businesses also held large amounts of property (also in CROs). Guildhall Library holds many records of properties owned by the Diocese of London and the London livery companies. The India Office collections (# chapter 30) at the British Library include many deeds for the English property of the East India Company. CLRO holds records (some dating back to the 13th century) of the Corporation of London's substantial landholdings, such as the Royal Contract estates, which were obtained from King Charles I in repayment of money loaned to him by the corporation. You should also remember that many of the largest property holders are modern organisations. Thus the Ministry of Defence and local authorities are large landowners and they may have title deeds (covering many centuries) in their archives or deposited at CROs.

Records of land held by the church are in many archives, particularly CROs and Lambeth Palace Library. The records include title deeds, surveys, leases and rent rolls. For example, Parliament sequestered much church land between 1645 and 1660 (# chapter 23), surveyed it, then sold it or rented it to tenants in order to raise money. The land that was not sold was returned to the church in 1660. The Dean and Chapter of Norwich had many properties in Norwich and this land was sequestered and surveyed in 1649. Much of it was restored to the church in 1660 and the parliamentary surveys survive at Norwich Record Office and Lambeth Palace Library. Each property or building is described, but also the terms of any lease and the tenant's name.

National archives, such as the British Library, TNA and the National Library of Wales, also hold many title deeds, but deeds for a particular area can be difficult to find. The vast collections of deeds at TNA are in many different series and most are not indexed. The holdings of TNA are considered in more detail below but, by way of example, it holds the records of Crown estates, some private collections and (in the law courts' records) many title deeds of properties that were the subject of a dispute. Title deeds and other property records relating to a particular place that are held in the British Library can be found using the same catalogues as noted above for the location of manorial documents, principally the 10-volume *Index of Manuscripts in the British Library* (1087). This does not index the names of people recorded in the deeds but tells you, for example, that the library holds various deeds of 1364 and 1586–1832 from Wath-upon-Dearne in Yorkshire (and provides references for finding the documents).

Many property records are in courts' records at CROs or borough archives, particularly in records of courts such as the Court of Husting or the Fire Court in the City of London (# chapter 24). The National Register of Archives held by RCHM (# chapter 11) is very useful if you are searching for property records. You can search the database for the name of a particular family or organisation. The register notes the archive that holds any such collection and also refers to any relevant catalogue or list that is held by RCHM. Many deeds of English property are held abroad (particularly in North America). For example, the Huntington Library in California holds a large collection of deeds from the archive of the Dukes of Buckingham (fortunately described and indexed in detail in a published guide). Many other collections are sadly uncatalogued or even unknown to English archivists and researchers. However, the position should improve as computers assist the study, abstraction and cataloguing of these records.

RCHM and record societies have transcribed, calendared and published many collections of deeds and other manuscripts. You should check these published sources before attempting to use the original records. For example, many collections are calendared in hundreds of RCHM reports, which are listed (with descriptions of the collections covered by each volume) in Mullins (260). Copies of the reports are held at TNA and many other libraries and archives. For example, the 1907 report (1086) calendars the manuscript collections of the Bishop of Salisbury, the Bishop of Exeter, the Dean and Chapter of Exeter, the Earl of Leicester, Sir William Clayton, Major Money-Kyrle, Mr F.H.T. Jervoise and the Corporations of Salisbury, Orford and Aldeburgh. These collections include many title deeds or other property records, some dating back to the 12th century. The calendars published in the first 81 reports (those volumes published up to 1942) are indexed by persons' names in Bickley (1092) and Hall (1108). There are also published indexes of place names so that you can find documents in the calendars that relate to a particular town, village or manor. The location of many of the collections calendared in the RCHM reports (particularly private collections) has changed, but many of these moves are noted in an HMSO booklet (1084).

County record societies' publications may also assist. For example, the parliamentary surveys of 1649 for property of the Dean and Chapter of Norwich (noted above) have been calendared in a Norfolk Record Society volume by Metters (1118). The transcripts include descriptions of many properties, the names of tenants, their rents and other terms of their leases.

Medieval deeds
Having considered title deeds and their location in general terms, we can now review certain deeds (and the methods of finding them) in more detail.

The formal methods of transferring property varied over time, as have the records of those transfers. There were two types of property or interests in property. Land and buildings (that is tangible property) were known as corporeal hereditaments. Intangible rights, such as a right of way or the right to possess land in the future, were incorporeal hereditaments. In early medieval times incorporeal hereditaments could be transferred by the execution of a document known as a deed of grant. However, the transfer of corporeal hereditaments had to take place not by a document but by an act representing the passing of possession. Thus a key or part of the property (such as a turf from the land) was handed to the new owner by the vendor in the presence of witnesses. This was an act of enfeoffment (delivery of possession of the fee) which was called livery of seisin. It was soon realised that it would be useful to have a document that recorded that seisin had been given (in case people forgot) and so a document known as a feoffment would be prepared. This would record that, on a certain date, a person had given and delivered seisin of a particular property to another person in the presence of named witnesses. The feoffment did not transfer title to the property, but evidenced that the transfer, by livery of seisin, had taken place. Cornwall (1096) provides some typical wording of a feoffment:

Know all present and future men that I Thomas de Deyuile have given granted and by this my present charter confirmed to Robert de la Mersche one virgate of land with its appurtenances in the town of Great Kenebelle . . . To have and to hold the aforesaid virgate to the said Robert his heirs and assigns of the chief lord of that fee for the services thence due and accustomed for ever . . . and I the said Thomas and my heirs will warrant the aforesaid virgate to the said Robert his heirs and assigns for ever In witness of which thing I have affixed my seal to this my present charter with these men as witnesses . . .

The document was authenticated by Thomas fixing his seal to it in the presence of witnesses (although a signature gradually became more usual). Alcock (1089) analyses other medieval title deeds (and particularly the Latin wording that was generally used). The main terms of such deeds were similar to the documents noted above but there were differences, many of them resulting from ancient provisions of property law, and so you should study Alcock's work before you attempt to use such deeds.

Fines and recoveries

From the 12th century an alternative method of recording that a transfer of land had taken place was by a fine or, from the 15th century, a recovery. These were both judgments in court actions about fictitious disputes.

The levying of a fine was a legal action which originated in the 12th century to record the transfer of property. It was also used to bar an entail of land. The vendor and purchaser cooperated in legal proceedings (about a fictitious dispute over possession of land) to obtain a court judgment that recorded the purchaser's rights to the property. The purchaser (as plaintiff or querient) started proceedings against the vendor (the deforciant) by a writ of covenant, alleging (falsely) that the vendor had deprived the purchaser of the land. The parties then agreed to settle the action. In return for the querient (purchaser) paying the deforciant (vendor) a sum of money (that is, the value of the property), the deforciant accepted by a "final agreement" that the querient was entitled to the land by his gift and the deforciant renounced all rights that he or his heirs had to the land. The court gave leave for the settlement to be effected and the land was then passed to the purchaser.

The "finalis concordia" (final concord) or fine was a brief record of the court judgment, the wording of which usually commenced "this is the final agreement" and was recorded in triplicate on the same document. The document was then cut into three pieces by indented (or wavy) cuts. The left and right-hand sides were kept by the two parties. The lower part (or foot) of the document was retained by the court and enrolled, usually on the rolls of the feet of fines of the Court of Common Pleas now at TNA in series CP 25, with related documents in CP 24 and 26–30. Fines are also held in the Palatinates' records, in series CHES 31–32, DURH 11–12 and PL 17–18. Fines date from 1195 to 1839 (are in Latin until 1733) and the calendars and indexes (in series IND 1) are described in the *PRO Guide* (228). Typical wording of fines of the 16th and 19th centuries is set out in TNA legal records leaflet 2 and Cornwall (1096) respectively. Many calendars of the feet of fines have been published by HMSO and county record societies. Thus Reichel & Prideaux (1128) is a calendar of Devon feet of fines for 1196–1369, Lewis (1114) and Meekings (1117) are calendars of the feet of fines for Surrey of 1196–1558, and Yorkshire entries in the feet of fines of the Tudor period have been published by the Yorkshire Archaeological and Topographical Association. Two typical entries from one of those Yorkshire volumes (1083), covering 1571–82, are set out below. In addition to details of the land that was the subject of the fine, many fines include (as in these examples) the names of landowners' wives. Some entries (such as the second example) include more than one generation of a family.

1580 Michaelmas Term

Plaintiff	Deforciant (Defendants)	Property
William Charnock, gent	William Worseley, gent and Katherine his wife	The moiety of the manor of Kyghley and 200 messuages, 100 cottages, 4 watermills and 4 windmills with lands in Kyghley.

1582 Michaelmas Term

Plaintiff	Deforciant (Defendant)	Property
John Sunderland	Henry Aikroide & Ann his wife & John Aikroide, son & heir apparent of Henry and Ann	5 messuages with lands in Airingden, alias Airingden Park and Sowerby.

The use of fines to bar entails was prohibited by statute in 1285 (although they continued to be used to record transfers of land). This led to the development by the late 15th century of the common recovery, which was also a fictitious legal action by colluding parties to convey property. It was used until 1834 to bar entails, but also for general conveyancing. In the latter case, an intending purchaser (known as the demandant) issued proceedings that claimed the property from the freehold owner. The freeholder did not defend the proceedings but, at court, requested a third party (the vouchee) to warrant that he had good title. This third party was usually the court crier or another man of straw, who then left the court and failed to return. Consequently, the court then granted judgment to the demandant, for possession of the property. In order to convey entailed property (and bar the entail) a more complex process was used. In brief, a purchaser (the demandant) started proceedings in which he falsely claimed that he owned the land but had been ejected by a fictional person. The tenant in tail and one or more men of straw (such as the court crier) would not defend the action (or vouch for each other's title) and so judgment for possession of the property was granted to the demandant. Examples of the wording of recoveries (in Latin until 1733) are provided in Cornwall (1096) and Dibben (1099). The recoveries were enrolled at court, on the Plea Rolls (now in series CP 40 at TNA) until 1583 then on the Recovery Rolls (now in series CP 43) of the Court of Common Pleas. There are indexes at TNA in CP 60 and IND 1. Recoveries were also enrolled on rolls of the Palatinate courts in CHES 29–32, DURH 13 and PL 15.

Uses

Marriage settlements were reviewed in chapter 14. The groom or the father of one of the spouses settled property (land, shares or money) upon the couple to provide them with land and income during the marriage. A landowner could also use a settlement (or trust) to designate the ownership of property, within the family, for the next few generations. Trusts and settlements had their origin in the middle ages, when (as noted above) landowners could not devise their real estate by will. To avoid this restriction, lawyers created the "feoffment to uses", which divided the legal estate (or tenure) in land from the right to use the property (the beneficial interest). A conveyed his land in fee simple to X and Y (the feoffees to uses), who held it to the use of A, or to the use of his son, or another person B. A (or B) was the *cestui que use* (that is, "he who uses") or the beneficiary. A had a beneficial interest in the land (to use and profit from it) which was personal property and so could be devised in his will to whomever he wished.

X and Y were the owners in law and liable to perform any feudal services to which the land was subject, but they were not in actual possession so they could not perform the services. A (or B) was not the legal owner so was not liable for the service obligations. Uses also avoided payment of fines to lords. If the owner A had died, a fine would be payable to the lord in order that A's heir (B) could take possession. If A conveyed the land to X and Y as feoffees, they could continue to hold the land when A died (and was succeeded as beneficiary by his heir B), so that no fine was payable. If X or Y died, another feoffee could be appointed so that there was always one or more feoffees and so no fine was payable to the lord. The king and other manorial lords therefore lost revenue from the creation of uses. This resulted in the Statute of Uses of 1535/6 which provided that whoever had the use or profit of land (A or B in the example above) should be treated as seised of (that is, holding) the legal estate, and so liable for any services. Men were again enabled to devise their land by will by the Statute of Wills of 1540 and the use later developed into the trust (considered below).

Bargain and sale

From 1535 property could also be transferred by a bargain and sale which recorded that property had been bargained and sold by one person to another. This constituted an effective transfer of property, without seisin taking place (for the reasons explained below). A deed of bargain and sale recorded that one person agreed to convey his property (or an interest in a property) to another in consideration of a payment. A deed of bargain and sale records the parties' names, the date, the consideration and the property. It usually includes the words "doth bargain and sell" and is signed and sealed by both parties. Cornwall (1096) includes typical wording of these deeds, such as this extract:

THIS INDENTURE made the seventh day of March in the twelfth yeare of the Reigne of our Sovereigne Lord George by the Grace of God of Great Britain France and Ireland King Defender of the Faith, etc, . . . 1725 BETWEEN John Brinckhurst junior of the Moor in the parish of Great Marlow, Bucks, gentleman of the one part and Jeremiah Oakeley of White Waltham, Berks esquire of the other part WITNESSETH that as well for and in consideration of the summe of [£1,100] paid by the said Jeremiah Oakeley in such manner and for such uses as are mentioned to be paid in certain indentures of release bearing even date with these presents and made between Jonathan Wilson of Fetter Lane London gentleman of the first part the said John Brinckhurst the younger of the second part and the said Jeremiah Oakeley of the third party . . . and in consideration of the summe of five shillings . . . paid by the said Jeremiah Oakeley to the said John Brinckhurst the younger . . . the receipt whereof is hereby acnowledged and for diverse other good causes and considerations . . . HE the said John Brinckhurst the younger HATH Granted Bargained and Sold and by these presents DOTH Grant Bargain and Sell unto the said Jeremiah Oakeley his heires and assigns ALL THAT [property described] . . . TO HAVE AND TO HOLD the said messuage or tenement farm lands hereditaments and all the singular other premises with the appurtenances before in and by these presents Granted Bargained and Sold and every part and parcell thereof unto the said Jeremiah Oakeley his heires and assignes to the onely proper use and behoofe of him the said Jeremiah Oakeley his heires and assignes for ever and to and for no other use intent or purpose whatsoever IN WITNESS whereof the said partyes to these presents have hereunto sett their hands and seales the day and yeare first above written.

The payment by a purchaser to the vendor of the agreed value of the land raised a use in favour of the purchaser who, by the Statute of Uses, was therefore treated as the legal owner. There was no livery of seisin, but the effect of the Statute of Uses allowed the conveyance of a legal estate by a simple deed. Uses could therefore be established by bargains and sales (which could be kept secret), without feoffments and the true ownership of land could also be kept secret. The Statute of Enrolments of 1535/6 therefore provided that no transfer of freehold land was valid (if livery of seisin did not take place) unless the transfer was both evidenced by a deed and that deed was enrolled within six months (with a court at Westminster, certain city or borough courts or with a Clerk of the Peace). This requirement also applied in the Palatinates from 1563. The enrolment of deeds (considered below) published the transfer (or terms of the use) and therefore disclosed the true owner's identity (as intended by the Statute of Uses).

The 16th-century courts also decided that a deed of bargain and sale could not, by itself, operate to enfeoff the purchaser since there was no livery of seisin. The giving of physical possession was still required and a separate feoffment was therefore often also prepared, confirming livery of seisin to the purchaser. Cornwall (1096) also provides the wording of a longer form of bargain and sale, incorporating the feoffment, that included the vendor's assurance to the purchaser that he had a valid title to the land and that the purchaser would enjoy peaceable possession of it.

Lease and Release

Lawyers soon found a method of avoiding the publicity and inconvenience of either livery of seisin or the enrolment of a deed of bargain and sale. A Lease and Release were two interdependent documents, used together as the most important method of conveying land in England between the mid-17th century and 1845. Alcock (1089), Cornwall (1096) and Dibben (1099) review these documents in detail, with examples of the wording typically used. The two documents were executed with consecutive dates. By the first, the vendor (A) bargained and sold a lease of the land (for six months or a year) for a nominal rent, to the purchaser (B) who was thus brought into actual possession of the property. A was seised of the property to the use of B for that six months or year. The Statute of Uses therefore vested the land in B, but no enrolment was necessary because the freehold was not transferred (there was only a lease). The next day, by the second document (the release), the vendor A released his freehold reversion of the property (that is, his entitlement to the return of the property at the end of the lease term) to the purchaser B, for payment of the property's value. By the release (the most important document and sometimes very complex), any third parties with an interest in the property would also release those rights to the purchaser so that he became the new beneficial owner. As the release was not a transfer of the unencumbered freehold, it did not have to be enrolled. Livery of seisin was unnecessary since a reversionary interest in land was an incorporeal hereditament which could be transferred by a deed. Cornwall (1096) includes, as examples of a Lease and Release, two documents, of 7 August 1701 and 8 August 1701 respectively, that transfer land from William Hanney to John Welch. The important parts of these documents are:

LEASE. witnesseth that . . . William Hanney for and in consideration of the sum of five shillings . . . HATH demised granted bargained & sold and by these presents doth demise grant bargaine & sell unto the said John Welch . . . TO HAVE & TO HOLD the said [property] and appurtenances unto the said John Welch his executors administrators & assignes from the day next before the day of the date hereof unto the end & terms of one whole yeare from thence next ensuing fully to be compleate & ended YIELDING and paying therfore unto the said William Hanney his heires or assignes the rente of one peppercorne on the feast day of St Michael the Archangell next ensueing the date hereof if the same shall be lawfully demanded TO the intent and purpose that the said John Welch may be in the actuall possession of all and singular the said premises and may thereby & by force of the statute for transferring uses into possession be enabled to accept of a grant & release of the reversion & inheritance therof to him his Heires & Assignes for ever IN WITNESS . . .

RELEASE. witnesseth that . . . William Hanney for & in consideration of the summe of [£73] . . . and for diverse other goods causes & valuable considerations . . . HATH granted bargained sold remised released quitclaimed and confirmed and by these presents doth grant . . . unto the said John Welch (in his actuall possession & seizin now being by virtue of a bargaine & sale for a yeare to him thereof made by the said William Hanney beareing date the day next before the date hereof and by vertue of the statute for transferring of uses into possession) . . . TO HAVE & TO HOLD the said [property] intended to be hereby granted & released & every part thereof with the appurtenances to the said John Welch his heires & assignes for ever to & for the only proper use & behoofe of the said John Welch his heires & assignes for evermore . . .

The two documents taken together conveyed the property from William Hanney to John Welch. No livery of seisin or enrolment was required. The lawyers had by-passed the Statute of Uses and the Statute of Enrolments. In 1841 a statute provided that a release in certain terms would be sufficient by itself as a conveyance and so a prior lease was no longer needed. In 1845 a release also became unnecessary when a statute provided that corporeal hereditaments could (like incorporeal hereditaments) be conveyed by a simple deed.

Trusts and settlements
Before the Statute of Uses a landowner could transfer land to feoffees to hold for the use of family members, perhaps to X for life, then Y for life, then to Z in fee tail. The use ensured that a family estate remained intact for later generations. At any time someone would only have a life interest and others would have contingent interests (contingent upon the death of the life tenant). Such a settlement could only be broken by agreement of all those with an interest in the property. The life tenant was subject to strict controls as to what he could, or could not, do with the property. He was generally entitled to any income from the property but he could not sell or mortgage it (unless all those with an interest in the property agreed). The estate therefore passed down the generations because it was protected from profligate heirs.

The Statute of Uses rendered uses ineffective, because a life tenant (X) was treated by the statute as the legal owner of the property (because he had the use of it) and was therefore able to ignore the interests of those (Y and Z) with future rights. However, it was equitable (or just) that the future rights of Y and Z should be protected. From the 17th century the Court of Chancery was willing to protect their rights (as against X). Lawyers therefore drew up instruments of settlement that the courts would enforce. Alcock (1089) and Cornwall (1096) give examples of the complex terms of the documents creating settlements. A landowner (the settlor) directed (by will or deed) that land should pass to a succession of family members, usually the landowner for the remainder of his life, then his widow (if she survived him) for the remainder of her life, then their eldest son (for his life) and then his eldest (usually unborn) son, as a tenant in tail (that is, entitled to the remainder). If the eldest son had no children, the settlement provided for the property to pass to the settlor's second son (and then his children) and so on. A settlement might also provide dowries for daughters or pin money for widowed relatives. The property thus stayed in the family. Although settlements usually operated behind a trust (trust meant the same as use), by a transfer of the legal estate to trustees (to hold for the benefit of beneficiaries), this was not necessary until 1925.

Before the tenant in tail came into possession (and was able to bar the entail and sell the fee simple to a third party) a new settlement would be entered into, tying up the family estate for another few generations. For example, a father might be the life tenant. His son was the tenant in tail who would come into possession on the father's death. When the son came of age, the father would persuade the son (perhaps in exchange for an immediate income or capital payment) to join with him in a resettlement, with a new succession of life interests and appointing a future grandson or great grandson as the tenant in tail. The documents evidencing settlements were often very long and detailed (and usually kept with the title deeds to a property). Consequently, if you are fortunate enough to be descended from a family which had property that was subject to such settlements, you may obtain an enormous amount of genealogical information.

Charitable settlements and endowments
Property might be settled on trust for a charity so that rents from the property could be used to help the poor, or fund a school or hospital. A charity might also purchase property (perhaps farmland or houses) as an investment. Information about these properties (and the tenants), can be found in parochial charity records, in reports of the *Commissioners for Inquiring Concerning Charities* (502) or in reprinted sections of those reports (# chapter 18). Thus, *The Endowed Charities of London* (498) includes the parish of St Michael Bassishaw. The entry notes a charity established by William Leman and Cornelius Fish, as follows:

From an indenture dated 30th April 1638, made between William Leman of the one part, and Humphrey Burre and others, parishioners of the parish of St Michael Bassishaw, of the other; it appears that King James I, by letters patent dated 2nd October in the 17th year of his reign, had granted to [Sir John] Leman, knight and alderman of London, and to Cornelius Fish, chamberlain of the City, and their heirs, five messuages in the respective possession of Alice Cobb, John Humphrey, Lady Anne Egerton, Peter Muffet and John Gifford . . . and by the said indenture, William Leman, as heir of Sir John Leman, who survived Cornelius Fish . . . to the intent that the premises and the rents and profits thereof should be employed according to the discretion of the churchwardens in works of charity, and for the use, benefit and relief of the parishioners . . . granted the said premises to Humphrey Burre and others . . . the rents of the premises were then received by the parish . . . the messuage in the occupation of Alice Cobb . . . formerly one house, known by the sign of the Cock, and still called the Cock Estate, consists now of six houses, three at the end of Basinghall Street and three in London Wall, respectively let for 21 years, from midsummer 1818 to the following tenants:

	£	s.	d.
James Prior at a rent of	38	0	0
Hugh Wilson	25	0	0
Joseph (now Elizabeth) Stewardson	52	10	0
William Hudswell	20	0	0

Jane Hunter	24	0	0
John (now Martha) Woodall	52	10	0

Making a total rent of £212 0s 0d. The other houses mentioned in the indenture . . . were burnt in the great fire [of 1666].

Mortgages

If a landowner wanted to borrow money and a lender wanted security for repayment, this could be dealt with by the landowner granting a mortgage over the property to the person or organisation (now normally a bank or building society) that lent the money (a mortgagee). Most mortgages took the form of a long lease of the property by the landowner to the lender (but the lender allowed the landowner to remain in occupation). If the debt was repaid, the mortgage was discharged and the lease came to an end. If the landowner defaulted in payment of capital or interest, the lender could take actual possession of the property in accordance with the terms of the lease. In some cases a mortgage was effected by the landowner (X) conveying his fee simple to the lender (but the lender permitted X to remain in possession), with a provision for reconveyance of the property when the loan was repaid. If a lender required repayment, but the borrower did not have sufficient funds, the borrower had to find someone else to lend the money. If he did so, the original mortgage was discharged and a new mortgage was granted by the owner to the new mortgagee. Alternatively, the subsisting mortgage could be assigned by a deed of assignment to the new mortgagee in consideration of the new mortgagee paying funds to the original mortgagee. Typical examples of the wording of mortgages and assignments are provided by Alcock (1089), Dibben (1099) and Cornwall (1096).

Enrolment of deeds

Registration of title to land in England and Wales was considered above. However, there were earlier methods of registering ownership of land. Some boroughs had courts which recorded land ownership by enrolling deeds (that is, by copying the deeds on to rolls). One example is the Court of Husting in London, the records of which date from about 1250. As noted above, from the Statute of Enrolments of 1535, feoffments were only valid (without livery of seisin) if they were enrolled at the courts at Westminster (usually on the Close Rolls) or in the records of the Clerk of the Peace (now at CROs). For example, the collection at Devon Record Office dates from 1536 to about 1760, with about 1,300 deeds from the 16th century. Furthermore, many deeds were voluntarily enrolled at the Westminster courts from as early as the 13th century, to ensure that a record of a transaction survived.

The Close Rolls, covering the period from about 1200 up to 1903, are particularly important and are described in the *PRO Guide* (228). The rolls, in series C 54 at TNA, originally recorded royal instructions to officials about a wide range of subjects, but they were also used to enrol documents for preservation, including grants of land by the Crown and deeds recording the sale of private property. Alcock (1089) estimates that there are about 75,000 deeds from the reign of Queen Elizabeth I alone. The enrolled documents include deeds of bargain and sale (particularly after the Statute of Enrolments), disentailing deeds, conveyances on trust for schools (or other charitable purposes), deeds poll (for changes of name), patents and naturalization certificates. From the late 16th century the Close Rolls were also used to enroll conveyances of the estates of bankrupts and (from 1717) to enroll deeds and wills of papists. HMSO has published indexed transcripts of the Close Rolls for 1204–72 (in 14 volumes), and indexed calendars of the rolls from 1272 to 1509 (in about 50 volumes). The volumes are listed in Mullins (260). TNA holds annual name indexes in series C 275 to the grantees (buyers), or to the places in the later rolls up to 1837 and indexes to grantors from 1573 to 1902. These are two examples of the useful material contained on the Close Rolls, these entries of 1317 and 1487 being taken from the HMSO calendars for 1313–18 (1074) and 1485–1500 (1075):

1317 Oct. 28. To Master John Walewayn, escheator of this side [of] Trent. Order to deliver to Joan, wife of Walter de Shelvestrode, daughter of William le Coynte, a moiety of the manor of Wardon, co. Bedford, to have for her maintenance until further orders . . . her husband, who is staying in Ireland in the King's service . . . as appears by an inquisition taken by the said escheator that William held in chief at his death a moiety of the said manor by the service of a quarter of a knight's fee, and that Joan and Margery his daughters are his nearest heirs and that Joan was aged 30 years and more and Margery six weeks and three days on 8 June last.

1487. William Askham, fishmonger of London, son of William Askham, gentleman of Berkyng, co. Essex, to Hugh Hunt gentleman and Joan his wife, widow of William Askham, senior, James Smyth fishmonger, Robert Yarom mercer, each of London, their heirs and assigns. Gift with warranty of all his lands and tenements . . . in the parish of St Dunstan's in the East, London: and appointment of John Wheteley, grocer of London, as his attorney to convey seisin of the same, under the seals of Sir Henry Colet, Mayor of London [and three others]. Witnesses: Thomas Raven, John Heron [and seven others] Dated London 19 May.

The Patent Rolls, also at TNA (in series C 66), were a record made in Chancery of matters such as correspondence with foreign princes, treaties, but also (up to the 17th century) royal grants of lands, offices and pardons. The rolls are in Latin up to 1733. The rolls for 1201–32 have been transcribed and indexed. Calendars (with name indexes) have been published by HMSO for 1216–1582, the volumes being listed in Mullins (260), and for 1584–90 by the List and Index Society (volumes 241–243, 247 and 255). TNA holds manuscript alphabets (by initial letter of grantees' surnames), by regnal year, for the rolls of 1583 and for those from 1590 to 1946 in series C 274. As an example, the HMSO volume (1078) calendars the Patent Rolls of 1476–85. A typical grant is:

1484 March 9. Grant to Robert Brakenbury, esquire of the body and the heirs male of his body, for his good services against the rebels, of the manors or lordships of Mote, Merden, Detlyng and Newenton, co. Kent and all lands, rents and services in [those] towns, hamlets.

Typical grants from the Patent Rolls of 1589 (from List and Index Society volume 255) are:

12 June. Grant to Robert Drewrye of the wardship and marriage of Fleetwood Dormer, son and heir of Peter Dormer, with an annuity of £5 from 3 Dec., 26 Eliz., when Peter died.

21 March. Grant for lives in succession to John Cowper, the present tenant, Manner Cowper and Thomas Cowper, his sons, of Knighton Farm, co. Wilts., late of Henry, Earl of

Arundel; from Michaelmas last; with reservations; yearly rent £6; heriot the best beast. For a fine of £6 paid to the Exchequer.

The Palatinates of Durham and Lancaster had their own chanceries, the patent rolls of which are at TNA in series DURH 3 and PL 1 and include grants in similar terms to those noted above.

Deeds were also enrolled by other courts, such as the Exchequer, Common Pleas and King's Bench. The series at TNA that contain these rolls (and some available calendars and indexes) are listed below and in Alcock (1089) and Bevan (239).

Other deeds and property records at TNA

The Charter Rolls (in series C 53) record the granting by royal charter, from 1199 to 1516, of land, honours or privileges in perpetuity to individuals and corporations. Transcripts up to 1226, and then calendars up to 1516, have been published by HMSO, the volumes being listed in Mullins (260). The following example is taken from the volume (1073) for 1427–1516:

> Feb 28. 1448. Westminster. Grant, of special grace, to William Dawbeney, king's squire and his heirs of a yearly fair at their manor or lordship of Southpederton, Somerset on the vigil, the day and morrow of the Nativity of St John the Baptist and the three days following.

Grants of land were also recorded in the State Papers Domestic (# chapter 22). Thus the calendar for 1671 by Daniell (790) includes entries such as:

> 1671 June 30. Grant to John Ferrars of the reversion of the manor of Walton, co. Derby and the advowson of the parish church of Walton.

The Treasury books and papers (# chapter 22) also include information about property. Thus the HMSO calendar for April–September 1697 by Shaw (863), includes entries such as:

> 12 April: Treasury warrant to the Clerk of the Pipe for a lease to John Thatcher of a tenement in Shippon, co. Berks, for 99 years terminable on 3 lives on the ancient rents of 8s and 4d . . . a fine of £20 . . . all payable to the Receiver General of the Duchy of Cornwall.

Extents for Debts are descriptions and valuations of the land and goods of debtors which were prepared to enable creditors to recover the money owed to them. The procedure is described in Conyers (1095). In brief, registration and acknowledgement of debts (a recognizance) took place before the mayors of certain cities and towns, such as London, York, Bristol and Salisbury (and later before justices of the King's Bench or Common Pleas). If a debtor defaulted, a writ was issued out of Chancery to the county sheriff for an extent to be taken. The debtor could be imprisoned and his lands and goods seized, assessed (the extent) by the sheriff and a jury and then sold. The writs and extents are mostly in series C 131, 228 and 239 at TNA and cover the 14th to 18th centuries. Carlin (1094) is a list of over 1,900 extents for debts from 1316 to 1650 of debtors who held property in London or Southwark including, in 1632/3, Robert Charnock, knight, of Holcot in Bedfordshire. Conyers (1095) includes 171 abstracts of Wiltshire extents from 1306 to 1603. A shortened version of one of the less detailed abstracts is:

C 131/100. Thomas Marmyon, esquire, of Kyngesdon

16 Feb. 1514. Capias returnable 30 April, sued out by William Botrie, citizen and mercer of London, to whom Thomas acknowledged £100 on 18 March 1513 before William Broun . . . mayor of the Staple of Westminster, payable [on] 1 Nov. Endorsed; the lands were delivered to the king on 20 March 1514. Thomas has not been found.

18 March 1514. Inquisition at Wilton before John Danvers, knight by William Mondye, Christopher Payne, [14 other jurors named]. [Thomas Marmyon] seised . . . in the right of his wife Anne for her life of the manor of Kevell and 10 messuages, 300 acres of land, 400 acres of pasture, a watermill and 6s. in rents in Calston, Chesylden, Lyddington, Wanborowe, Walcott, Rodburne and Heydon, worth 20 marks yearly.

The PRO Guide (228) and Alcock (1089) contain more detailed information about the series of records at TNA that include property deeds (and any indexes and calendars for them). One example is ADM 75 which consists of 236 bundles of deeds to property owned by Greenwich Hospital, in various counties, dating from the 13th century to 1931. Here are further examples (some briefly mentioned above).

a. Ancient Deeds (series E 326–329) consist of thousands of deeds up to the death of Elizabeth I. Modern Deeds (E 330) cover the period since the reign of James I. Most of the deeds relate to the vast estates of religious houses dissolved by Henry VIII. Series E 305 contains deeds by which the Crown then sold or granted that confiscated property and E 309–311 contain leases of the property. Most of these records were held by the Court of Augmentations and the Exchequer Augmentations Office (# chapter 24).

b. Deeds of the Exchequer (series E 40–44 and 210–214) contain thousands of deeds from medieval times to the 19th century.

c. Records of the Court of Chancery: (a) Ancient Deeds (up to 1603) in series C 146–148 and Modern Deeds from the 17th to 19th centuries in C 149, (b) deeds produced as exhibits to the court (from the 13th to 19th centuries) in series C 116, (c) the Duchess of Norfolk's deeds (about 9,000 title deeds) dating from about 1150 to 1850 in C 115 and (d) deeds produced as exhibits in actions in the Chancery Division of the High Court in series J 90.

d. Records of the Duchy of Lancaster, including deeds from the 12th to 17th centuries in series DL 25–27 and leases in DL 14–15.

e. Records of the Palatinate of Chester, including enrolled deeds from the 14th to 19th centuries in series CHES 2, and feet of fines and common recoveries from the 13th to 19th centuries in CHES 29, 31 and 32.

f. Records of the Palatinate of Durham, including leases and enrolled deeds in series DURH 3, feet of fines from 1535 to 1834 in DURH 12 and deeds from about 1600 to about 1800 in DURH 21.

g. Records of the Palatinate of Lancaster, such as plea rolls (including deeds of bargain and sale, feet of fines and common recoveries) from the 15th to 19th centuries in series PL 15 and enrolled deeds for the same period in PL 14.

h. Records of Crown estates include sales, purchases, leases and grants (1802–1912) and copyhold enfranchisements (1851–1919) in series CRES 9; grants, leases and surveys

(1570–1961) in CRES 40, title deeds of the 13th to 20th centuries in CRES 38; ancient and modern deeds in the records of the Exchequer Auditors of Land Revenue in series LR 14–16 and estate deeds of attainted persons after the Jacobite rebellion of 1715 in series FEC 1. Manors and other properties held by the Crown were often leased out and copies of these Crown leases were enrolled in the Exchequer. Crown leases also appear, *inter alia*, in series E 365, 367 and 381.

i.   The Memoranda Rolls of the Exchequer (considered further below) in series E 159 and 368 include many private deeds that were enrolled to ensure that a permanent record survived. The rolls also include records of lands forfeited to the Crown.

j.   Licences to alienate and pardons. The tenure of knight service, that is, land held in return for providing knights to the Crown, was noted above. A tenant could not sell land held by this form of tenure without a Crown licence. If a tenant made an application, an inquisition might be held to establish whether the transaction would prejudice the Crown. A licence might then be granted. A Crown pardon might be issued if the land was sold without a licence. Licences to alienate and pardons were enrolled from 1216 to 1660 on the Patent Rolls (in series C 66) and payments for the licences are recorded on the Fine Rolls (in series C 60) from 1272 to 1648. Inquisitions *ad quod damnum* (in series C 142–143 and E 150–151) contain details of the enquiries by local juries before escheators of the Crown, undertaken before a licence was granted. A typical entry for a licence, from the Patent Rolls of 1589 (calendared in List and Index Society volume 255) is:

2 April. Licence for Thomas Wroughton, knight, and Henry Unton, knight, and Dorothy his wife, and for Edward Unton and Katherine his wife, Edmund Braye and Christopher Lytcott to alienate the manor of Cadmerend, co. Oxford and Buckingham, to Basil Fetiplace; for 40 shillings paid to the Queen's farmer.

HMSO has published six volumes of calendars containing (in four series: A to D) many of the Ancient Deeds noted in a, b and c above. These are from the Exchequer (series A and D), the Court of Augmentations (series B) and Chancery (series C). For example, the first HMSO volume (1080) calendars about 1,800 deeds from each of series A, B and C and the sixth volume (1081) calendars about 4,300 Chancery deeds. An example from the latter, dated 31 May 1523, is:

C.7371. Indenture, being a demise by Robert Thorne, prior, and the convent of Barnstaple, to William Downe and Robert and Alexander, his sons, for their lives in survivorship, of the reversion of three closes called "Newparkes" in the parish of Barnstaple now held by John Palmer, Wilmota his wife and Joan their daughter, for their lives in survivorship; rent 26s.8d and a heriot of 21s . . . the tenants to do suit of court yearly and suit of the prior's mills.

The List and Index Society has also published some calendars of the Ancient Deeds (for example in its volumes 95, 158 and 200).

The Pipe Rolls and Memoranda Rolls
The Pipe Rolls recorded the auditing of the annual accounts submitted to the Exchequer by sheriffs, the king's agents in the shires, whose functions included collecting money owed to the

Crown. The earliest roll is that of 1131 and they survive in an almost unbroken series from 1155 to 1832. They are held at TNA in series E 372. The most important function of the rolls was to record money that the sheriff had collected, note how much remained owing and record the sheriff's expenses. The debts included fees for administrative acts in the Exchequer or Chancery, fees for legal action in the courts, and the "Farm" (payments to the Crown from tenants of certain lands). The sheriff also collected amercements, reliefs, scutages, aids and fines. The rolls record the names of landowners (and other debtors), the location of their land and sometimes the names of their wives, heirs or other relatives. The rolls for some years have been transcribed and published by the Pipe Roll Society, in volumes listed in Mullins (260) and the rolls for some counties and years have been published by county record societies. For example, the Pipe Roll of 1295 for Surrey, in Mills (1119), includes these entries:

Fulk de Archiak and Mabel his wife, one of the daughters of William de Fortibus – £100 9s 2d for the debts of the same William.
Edward Lovekyn, bailiff of the liberty of the vill of Kingston owes half a mark for Isabella, daughter of Walter de Moleseye, for disseisin.
The account of Andrew le Constable and John Nichole, executors of the will of Walter Hereman, deceased, of the issues of the vill and castle of Guildford for the same deceased . . . [dates and rents noted].

The Memoranda Rolls at TNA survive from 1217. They originated as notes arising during the auditing of the sheriff's annual accounts, for example recording action to be taken in the future, but soon became notes of daily business of the Exchequer. They deal with the collection of money owed to the Crown and so record recognizances, bonds, the seizure of goods or land and also decrees and orders of the Court of Exchequer. The rolls also include commissions, grants and letters patent issued from the Exchequer, and private deeds that were acknowledged before one of the Barons of the Exchequer. Two sets of these notes were prepared (increasingly different from the 14th century) and so the Memoranda Rolls are in two series, that of the King's Remembrancer in series E 159 (up to 1926) and that of the Lord Treasurer's Remembrancer in series E 368 (up to 1835). The Pipe Roll Society has published transcripts of the Memoranda Rolls for a few years and an indexed calendar of the rolls for 1326–27 has been published by HMSO (1077). TNA also has transcripts of the rolls for a few years (from the reigns of Henry III and John). These examples of entries from 1326–27, from the HMSO calendar (1077), illustrate the importance of the Memoranda Rolls (and the need for further calendars to be produced):

Assignment of Richard de Ty and John de Wytelesbury to inquire as to lands in Rutland held by John Basset, late a collector of the tenth and sixth there [Basset had probably not accounted to the Exchequer for all the tax he had collected].

William, son of William de Burton in the Clay, 6 Feb., quitclaim dated London 2 Feb. 1326/7 to Henry de Edenstowe, clerk, Robert his brother, Sarah their sister and the heirs of Henry and Robert of all lands which they hold by his feoffment in Burton and Stretton in the Clay, Notts and an acre of meadow in Lee, Lincs, and also of a messuage in Burton in the Clay which they hold by gift of William's brother, Robert.

Kent. Walter de Pateshull and Joan his wife, eldest daughter and coheir of Richard de Rokesle and Joan his wife, were attached to answer for relief from the younger Joan's pourparty of the lands held by Richard and his wife. [Walter attends but not Joan, who appoints attorneys].

Acknowledgements of debts: Yorks. John Braban, son and heir of Giles Braban, merchant of York; 100L. to Luke Colleville, clerk. 16 Jan.

MORE SURVEYS AND MAPS

Various surveys of property have already been noted but there are some further types of surveys that may include references to your ancestors.

Glebe terriers

Glebe terriers were surveys of church property in a parish, listing houses, fields and sometimes the tithes payable. Many terriers date from the 16th or 17th centuries and note the names of tenants of church land or names of neighbouring landowners. Surviving terriers are in parish, archdeaconry or diocesan records (mostly in CROs) and some have been published, for example 122 terriers of 1634 from Berkshire in Mortimer (1121) and 146 terriers of 1578 to 1640 from Buckinghamshire in Reed (1127). The descriptions of properties include parishioners' homes, farms or businesses as in these extracts from Abingdon St Helen, Berkshire in 1634:

Three howses in Abingdon . . . a howse in Ock Street divided into three tenementes set lying & being in the southsid of the said street, on the westsid a tenement free land to Mr Edmond Bostock now in the tenure of Francis Payne, and in the eastsid free land somtyme the sign of the Bear now in the tenure of Thomas Wild
Another tenement in West St Hellens Street in the westsid . . . now in the tenur and occupacion of Joan Coxeter widow lying next to freland of Robert Morris alias Hall.

Modern surveys

A great deal of work has been undertaken by historians and archaeologists resulting in the publication of modern surveys, principally of London and other cities, that review the history, economy and architecture of those places. These studies may include photographs, engravings and plans of properties but also details of the ownership, leases and use of buildings gathered from many of the sources noted earlier in this chapter. If such a survey includes a property that was occupied at some point by your ancestor, useful information about them and their property may be quickly obtained. The best series of such works are the volumes of *The Survey of London*, such as volume 25 by Darlington (1097). This covers the parishes of St George the Martyr in Southwark and St Mary Newington. It describes, for example, how the manor house (and some surrounding fields) of Walworth were leased to Henry Penton in 1686. He died in 1715 and the property passed to his nephew John Penton, from whom it passed to his son Henry in 1725 and then to his son, another Henry, in 1762.

Similar information can be found in studies of other towns and cities, for example the *Survey of Medieval Winchester* by Keene (1111). One of the properties examined in this work, a house in Kingsgate Street, is recorded in the Patent Rolls and Chancery records (and records in

Winchester Cathedral Library). These note the occupiers (and rent) of the property at various dates between 1352 and 1649, including Richard Hether, yeoman (with his wife Alice), who took a 50-year lease of the property in 1542 from the Dean and Chapter of Winchester Cathedral. A subsequent occupier was John Chernock, butler of Winchester College, who was living in the property in 1546 and 1562.

Estate maps and records

Maps were reviewed in chapter 15, but maps of landowners' estates are reviewed here because they normally survive with other records of a landowner's property. From the late 16th century many landowners commissioned surveys and maps of their estates, particularly to value their property or to establish rents. The production of large-scale Ordnance Survey maps in the late 19th century replaced the need for specially commissioned estate maps, but from the 16th to 19th centuries estate maps are an important source, used in conjunction with tithe or enclosure maps. Estate maps may be very detailed, showing each field (and perhaps naming them), woods, roads, paths, marshland and ponds. The acreage and land use may be noted and buildings (such as barns or workers' cottages) may be described. Some examples of estate maps appear as illustrations in Hindle (389). Estate maps may show only one farm, but may record a farmer's fields throughout a parish, or even in a number of parishes. They may record the names of adjoining landowners. A number of surveys may survive for the same property. For example, at the parish of Laxton in Nottinghamshire, surveys were carried out in 1635, on several dates between 1730 and 1740 and also in 1789, 1812, 1820 and 1862.

Rentals or rent rolls are schedules (sometimes attached to estate maps) that list the tenants, the rent paid (or due) and describe tenants' land and cottages. If a good run of them can be located, they become even more useful since they may note a number of generations of the same family renting a farm or cottage (even though the exact relationship between succeeding tenants is rarely noted). For example, CLRO holds rentals of the Bridge House estates of the Corporation of London in an almost continuous series from 1404 to the 20th century. Many other rent rolls survive in archives or family papers. Illustration 141 shows an example of a rent roll of March 1790, recording rents payable to Theophilus Jones for lands and tenements on the estate of Monaghan in Ireland. The roll lists eight tenants, the most interesting entry being the first. The tenant is recorded as "the heirs of John Hamilton" and the lease is noted to be for three lives and 31 years, having commenced on 25 March 1744. John, Robert and Hugh Hamilton are noted as "the heirs of John Hamilton" and it is recorded that "the only life in being is Hugh Hamilton".

Estate maps and rent rolls were private documents and are not easy to find. Many remain in private hands (perhaps in estate or solicitors' offices) with other documents, including leases, rent registers and correspondence files. Many estate records have fortunately been deposited at CROs. Emmison (246) estimates that, as at 1974, over 20,000 estate maps from before 1850 had been deposited at archives, on average almost two for each ancient parish. Hindle (389) estimates that about 30,000 private estate maps have survived. However, estate records are usually catalogued under the name of the family that deposited them (or the name of the firm of solicitors by which they were deposited). You therefore need to ascertain the names of the landowners at the time that your ancestors worked on (or rented land from) an estate or the names of subsequent landowners, who may have inherited (and subsequently deposited) the estate's archives. Furthermore, if a landowner held property in many counties, all papers may have been lodged at one CRO. The National Register of Archives at the RCHM lists many estate records in archives

141. Rent roll of March 1790, recording rents due to Theophilus Jones from lands on the estate of Monaghan, Ireland

and private collections. There are also some published lists of CROs' holdings of maps and some published county bibliographies of estate and other maps.

Extensive estates were owned by the Crown, the Church, charities, borough corporations and livery companies. CROs or RCHM can advise as to the location of their estate records for a particular place. For example, as noted above, Guildhall Library has a large collection of records relating to the estates held throughout the country by the Diocese of London and by the London livery companies. Examples of the manorial records, deeds and family estate papers that can be found in family and solicitors' collections at CROs are shown by these two shortened entries from the published guide to the Bedford Record Office (227):

HOW (Mrs E. How White)
Deeds. Aspley Guise, 1619–1840 (409 deeds); Houghton Conquest, 1621–1751 (10); Woburn and district, 1641–1878 (10) . . . Ilford (Essex) 1760–64 (2);
Estate. Accounts, 1728–74 (3 volumes); surveys 1641–1751; correspondence (1760–94)
Family. Wills and settlements, 1717–1828; inventories, papers

WILLIS (solicitors) Leighton Buzzard
Founded before 1785 by D. Willis . . . the firm is now Simpson & Co
Deeds. Leighton Buzzard, 1620–1887 (389 deeds); Billington, Eggington and Stanbridge, 1591–1850 (68); Chalgrave, 1586–1845 (48), Eaton Bray and Totternhoe, 1622–1825 (58); Toddington, 1689–1901 (111) and 1,107 deeds for other Bedfordshire parishes. Deeds concerning seven parishes in Buckinghamshire (and Northamptonshire and London).
Estate. Court papers, Leighton Buzzard, 1803–71 (157), various terriers.
Enclosure. Various papers concerning Leighton Buzzard, Billington, Eggington and Heath and Reach.

DOMESDAY BOOK

Domesday book (originally known as the Book of Winchester) is the oldest survey of land, owners and occupiers in Britain. It is described in TNA domestic records leaflet 1. Domesday was a valuation survey for William the Conqueror of his new kingdom. It became known as Domesday, or day of judgement, because no appeals were possible from the assessors' findings. One volume, known as Little Domesday, dealt with Norfolk, Suffolk and Essex. Great Domesday dealt with the rest of England except London, Northumberland, Cumberland, Durham, Northern Westmoreland and Winchester (which were omitted). Parts of Northumberland and Durham were covered in the 12th century by the Boldon book. The survey, written in Latin, named the tenants-in-chief and their immediate sub-tenants as at 1086 and at the time of the conquest in 1066. Most of the survey deals with the use and value of land.

The Victoria county histories include a translation of the section of Domesday dealing with that county. Facsimiles of sections of Domesday are also available at most CROs. However, the most convenient method of reviewing Domesday book (or the Boldon book) is by obtaining the relevant volume of a series edited by J. Morris and published by Phillimore in 35 volumes. Each volume has a facsimile of the survey, with a translation on the facing page, and indexes of names and places (the complete series is also available on CD-ROM). The survey of Devon, in Volume

9, by Thorn & Thorn (1131), contains references to villages in Devon in which my ancestors lived. The translation for an entry for Dunsford is:

> Saewulf holds DUNSFORD. He held it himself before 1066. It paid tax for 1 virgate of land. Land for 1 plough. 3 smallholders, pasture, 20 acres. Value 40d.

As another example, Hockliffe is mentioned in Volume 20, for Bedfordshire, by Morris (1120):

> Land of Ralph Tallboys' wife . . . in Manshead Hundred . . . Azelina [wife of Ralph] holds Hockliffe herself . . . land for 8 ploughs . . . 13 villagers and 11 smallholders with 6 ploughs; meadow for 4 ploughs; woodland, 100 pigs. In total the value is. £8; before 1066, £12. Askell held this manor before 1066.

Finn (1105) is a detailed introduction to Domesday book, describing how it was compiled and reviewing the entries and their meaning. You are most unlikely to trace your ancestry to persons named in Domesday, unless you find a link with nobility, but it is fun to read entries, over 900 years old, about places in which your ancestors later lived.

CHAPTER 28

TRACING MIGRANTS
AND LIVING RELATIVES

MIGRANTS

Migration of your ancestors between different places in Britain in the 19th century makes your research more difficult. However, some records evidence an ancestor's movement during this period and also note his place of origin. In particular, the census records of 1851 to 1901 note people's birthplaces. You may find your ancestor in London in the 1881 census with his birthplace recorded as Exeter. You can then turn to the earlier census records of both London and Exeter (as well as civil registration and parish records) in order to find the ancestor and his family and so continue tracing that ancestral line. In those cases in which the census records do not solve the problem of an ancestor's origin, there are many other 19th-century records which may help (such as some army records that note a soldier's place of birth). These were reviewed in earlier chapters and they are summarised below.

However, ancestors' movements between parishes, counties or even countries cause more difficulties when you research your family tree prior to 1851. For example, an ancestor may first appear in a London parish register upon his marriage in 1792. He may have had a number of children baptised, but then died before the 1851 census recorded his place of birth. How can you discover his place of origin? As another example, if your ancestor's baptism was recorded in the register of a rural parish in the 17th or 18th centuries, yet that register does not record the marriage (or place of origin) of his parents, how can you ascertain the parents' places of birth? This chapter summarises those sources that may assist you to solve such problems.

The problems caused by migrant ancestors can occur at any period and in respect of people in any place, but most difficulties arise in relation to ancestors who moved to cities (particularly to London). Some of the problems of ancestral research in London and the sources available to researchers are reviewed in Webb (1138) and many lists and finding-aids for Londoners are listed in Gibson & Creaton (1136). London has always been a magnet for people from all over the country, even before the industrial revolution which is often (incorrectly) considered as the first period of substantial movement of British people. The population of London has grown dramatically over the centuries (despite the high mortality rate caused by London's insanitary conditions) and most of this population increase has occurred because of migration of people into London. The 17th century was perhaps the most unhealthy period to live in London. It is estimated that the plague killed about 33,000 people in 1603 alone, over 41,000 in 1625 and almost 69,000 in 1665. Despite this, London's population continued to grow, reaching about 575,000 by 1700. Camp (6) estimates that during the 17th century (when the total English population was only about five million), the average number of migrants into London each year, minus those who left, was approximately

8,000. Those of us with London ancestors (or ancestors in any large city which attracted people from the surrounding countryside) therefore face a particular difficulty. Each time you step back a generation, you find more ancestors living in that city who were not born there, and there may be no indication of their place of origin.

Many people also moved to London temporarily (for business, education or pleasure). Rich families spent time at their London residences as well as at their country homes, so that their children may have been baptised in either a country parish or in a London church. There were always many people who were travelling through London on their way elsewhere, and many of these trips were interrupted by unexpected deaths, by a sudden marriage or by the birth of a child. London parish registers therefore include many baptisms, marriages and burials relating to families who generally lived outside London (and perhaps far away). In particular, the records of London should be searched when you are having difficulty finding an ancestor's marriage. The anonymity of London (and to an extent any city) has always been one of its attractions. For the period before 1754 the Fleet registers (and the registers of other London marriage centres) are a particularly useful source for migrant ancestors.

The answers to the problems caused by ancestors' movements may be found in the records that we have already considered. Reference should also be made to Camp (1135), which is a useful study of the sources that may reveal the origins of an ancestor who moved within England and Wales. Those sources can be summarised as follows:

1. Marriage certificates since 1837 record the address or place of residence of a spouse. The place of origin of a spouse from outside the parish may be noted, although he or she might have given an address of convenience within the parish of marriage.

2. The first entry for a person in a parish register may indicate his origin. For example, the registers of Winkleigh in Devon recorded Robert and Grace Stanlake "of Ashreigney". Marriage entries since 1754 should record the place of residence of each spouse (in the same manner as marriage certificates) and this may be another parish, county or even country. Some marriage entries before 1754 may also include this information. Unfortunately, it is common for a migrant into a parish to be noted as a sojourner or even "of this parish" (despite being a recent arrival).

3. Banns registers and allegations or bonds for marriage licences often reveal the place of origin of one or both spouses.

4. If your ancestor arrived in a parish as a single person, it can be very difficult to locate his baptism. If your ancestor's marriage is the first entry for him in a parish register, you should search that marriage register for other contemporaneous marriages of people with his surname. They may be siblings who arrived at the same time as your ancestor. If you can find any such marriages (and if they are truly your ancestor's siblings), you will find it easier to discover their place of origin. For example, your ancestor, William Watson, may have arrived in a parish and got married at about the same time that Mary Watson and Thomas Watson also arrived and got married. It is very likely that William, Mary and Thomas are related (and possibly siblings). Finding a parish in which all three were baptised is much easier then finding the baptism of just your ancestor William. Similar considerations apply to any burials of people surnamed Watson, in the receiving parish, in the few years following William's arrival. They could be William's parents or siblings.

5. The IGI, Boyd's, or county marriage or baptism indexes may reveal families of your ancestor's surname (or even entries that are possibly his baptism), in another parish. The records of that possible home parish can then be reviewed. If you find one or more baptism entries that could relate to your ancestor, there are some important points that you must consider. Let us say that you are researching the origin of your ancestor George Potter, who married in the parish of Coldhill in 1748. You search the registers of surrounding parishes and the IGI for the county but only find one possible baptism, that of a George Potter in the parish of Deepvale in 1723. You must check whether there is a burial or marriage of a George Potter in Deepvale or nearby parishes. If so, that George Potter is unlikely to be your ancestor who turned up in Coldhill in 1748. If there are no marriage or burial entries for him in Deepvale, it is likely that he moved away from Deepvale and so he could be your George Potter who appeared in Coldhill (and you can then search for corroborative evidence). However, you must remember that the IGI or other indexes may only include some of the baptisms that could be that of your ancestor. The baptisms of others may been recorded in registers that have been lost, or which have been omitted from any index that you consult. You may be searching for a baptism in Devon around 1750 and find five possible entries. However, a few other candidates were perhaps also born in those parts of Cornwall, Dorset and Somerset that adjoin Devon. Other children may have been born but not baptised, or no baptism may have been recorded. Your ancestor may have been born elsewhere in Britain or even abroad. You must not assume that the baptism entries that you locate are the only children who could be your ancestor, particularly if you are considering (unwisely) choosing one of them as your ancestor by way of a process of elimination. There is always the possibility of other candidates. You cannot safely identify an ancestor by eliminating others (for example by finding their marriages or burials). You must look for corroborative evidence to prove that a particular entry is your ancestor.

6. A man's will may disclose his place of origin. He may refer to his previous places of residence, although this is uncommon. He may leave money or gifts to institutions, relatives or other people in a place other than that in which he lived at the time of his death. This place often turns out to be his place of origin. Wills may also refer to land held by a testator in a place other than his place of residence. The location of this land may be his place of origin (or the place of origin of his parents). For example, my ancestor Edward Hannell, of Hockliffe in Bedfordshire, died in 1737. His will referred to his land at Leighton Buzzard and I found the burial of a woman (later established to be his mother) in the Leighton Buzzard registers. A will can also prove the migration of the deceased's children. The 1823 will of Thomas Gillman of Hockliffe (# chapter 12) proved that my ancestors, James and Susannah Eagles of Hoxton, Middlesex had moved to Hoxton from Hockliffe and that Susannah was the daughter of Thomas. You should therefore review the wills of those people who might be your ancestors (or other relatives of your migrant ancestor), to see if those wills disclose any link.

7. Apprentice records at TNA, or in livery company or borough records often indicate an apprentice's place of origin. In chapter 22, examples were noted of apprentices in Kingston upon Thames coming from Devon and Yorkshire. Parish or workhouse apprentice records may also evidence migration. The parish records of Dunsford in Devon include an apprenticeship indenture by which my ancestor William Rice was

apprenticed by the overseers of Dunsford to a farmer in the neighbouring parish of Holcombe Burnell.

8. Other parish records may note an ancestor's movement between parishes. Removal orders and settlement examinations or certificates may record a pauper's place of origin. Disputes over settlement rights, heard by the Justices of the Peace or at the assizes, may also reveal the place from which an ancestor moved. Overseers' records of payments of the poor or other parish rates may indicate the approximate date of a man's arrival in a parish. The records of Boards of Guardians since 1834 may also reveal a pauper's birthplace or a place in which he previously lived.

9. Directories are particularly useful for tracing the movements of craftsmen, shopkeepers and tradesmen within a city or county.

10. Monumental inscriptions sometimes record the deceased's place of origin, particularly if that person had lived, or been born, far away from his place of burial.

11. Newspaper obituaries or reports of crimes may note the place of origin or birthplace of the deceased, a criminal or a victim of crime. Shopkeepers and tradesmen often advertised a proposal to move their business, or advertised the opening of their business (and noted any previous place in which they had carried on the trade).

12. Many professional records note a man's place of birth (perhaps attaching certificates of baptism), for example clergy ordination papers, lawyers' admission papers or articles of clerkship, excise entry papers and licences for the medical profession.

13. Employment and military records may record a man's place of origin. Metropolitan (and later county) police records usually note a man's place of birth. Many records of the army, navy and merchant service also reveal birthplaces. The naval muster rolls (# chapter 21) recorded that John Simms (or Syms) was born in Topsham in Devon. Army records noted the birthplace of John Radford as Whitestone in Devon.

14. Records of freemen, guilds or London livery companies often note places in which a man traded and his place of birth. Their apprenticeship registers were noted above.

15. Court records, particularly depositions in civil cases, may record someone's place of birth or previous places of residence. Criminal or prison registers also record the place of birth of a prisoner or places in which he or she previously lived.

16. School or university records may note the place of birth of a child or the place of residence of his parents.

17. Title deeds to property, settlements and manorial court records may evidence your ancestor owning land in more than one parish. You should review the records of all those parishes in which the land was situated, because the ancestor and his family could have originated in any of them.

18. Indexes of strays may also assist and are considered below.

Names can indicate origins (# chapter 1) either generally (for example a Welsh name or a surname commencing Tre, indicating a Cornish origin) or because a study of the surname reveals that it was particularly common (or originated in) a particular part of the country. For example, my Bulleid ancestors came from North Devon. Until the late 19th century this surname rarely appears in records for any other part of Britain.

Locating the birthplace of migrant ancestors is often made more difficult because they had names that were difficult to spell, or which could be spelt in many ways (and still sound similar).

You may have located your ancestor's marriage in a parish, but find no record of his baptism. You should not immediately assume that he originated elsewhere. Search back in the registers first. Had the family lived in the parish and only temporarily moved away? If so, the move was probably of only a short distance, perhaps to an adjoining parish. Had the family remained in the parish but temporarily worshipped at a non-conformist chapel, and so been recorded in that chapel's registers? Had there been a change in the name by which the family was recorded? I noted above that my ancestor Ann Voisey (and two other people surnamed Voisey) were married in Sandford in Devon around 1793. There were no Voisey baptisms at earlier dates, but the family had in fact been in Sandford for many years (a previous incumbent had recorded the family in the registers with the surname Vesey).

If the IGI or county indexes of parish registers do not assist in locating an ancestor's baptism, you may have to search the registers of parishes that are near to the receiving parish, in order to find baptism entries that possibly relate to your ancestor. You can then search parishes that are further away, in ever expanding circles. You should concentrate on parishes in and around market towns, or further along a main road from the parish in which you have already found your ancestors. Unfortunately, people moved more often (and further) in the 16th to 19th centuries than is commonly believed. Emmison (931) includes extracts from church court records of Essex of the late 16th and early 17th centuries. These note the places of residence (and earlier places of residence) of plaintiffs, defendants and witnesses. Many of these people had moved since their birth (and some had moved great distances). Some examples from 1584 are:

Agnes Warde of West Ham (resident 23 years) previously of Canborne, Isle of Wight;
Roger Carter aged 43 of West Ham (resident 28 years) previously of Queenhithe, London (for 3 years); before that Kirkaynton, Derbyshire;
Thomas Betson aged 71 of Wanstead (resident 2 years), previously Bulphan and Brentwood, Essex (for about 32 years) and before that Rotherham, Yorkshire.

In view of these examples of the extensive movement of people in the 16th century, you should not limit your search for an elusive ancestor (at any time) to a particular county. An ancestor might have moved from anywhere in Britain and so you may have to undertake a long search to discover his place of origin. Furthermore, we shall see in chapter 30 that millions of British people emigrated, or moved abroad temporarily (and millions of people came to Britain from abroad), so that a genealogist often has to review the records of British people elsewhere in the world, or commence research in the archives of foreign countries.

Strays

A stray is a record of an event in one place that names a person from another place (and names that place). What is "another place"? Some people consider this to be a parish (of origin) other than the parish in which the event is recorded, but the term is usually used for out of county origins. Consequently, a man is considered to be a stray if he is noted, when married in Devon, as being from outside Devon (perhaps from Wiltshire). Particularly large numbers of strays are found in London and other cities, but many are also found in ports, in expanding towns, or in other places that had some particular attraction. Thus many strays are found in Oxford and Cambridge because men (often from far away) attended the universities and many then settled permanently in those cities.

It can be very difficult to trace ancestors who moved between counties, or who moved temporarily to another county and perhaps married, died or had children there. Many researchers therefore note entries in records that refer to strays. Indexes of these strays are available, but they cover only a small minority of strays, and strays can of course only be recorded if the document itself notes a person as being from outside the county. Despite this, indexes of strays may include your elusive ancestor who moved between counties. Many family history societies hold indexes of strays (particularly those extracted from census records) and many of these indexes are listed in Gibson & Hampson (158).

The National Strays Index (NSI) is administered by the FFHS. Searches in the NSI cannot be made but the complete NSI can be purchased on microfiche from the FFHS administrator for a small charge and details of the index can be obtained by sending an SAE. Supplemental fiche are produced at regular intervals. The NSI includes strays who have been found in records such as parish registers, the census returns or poor law records. Member societies of the FFHS send records of the strays that they have found to the FFHS "strays' clearing house". These are included in the NSI, but also copied to the FHS for the county or area of the stray's origin. An entry in a Suffolk marriage register involving a man from Devon will be sent from the FHS in Suffolk to the clearing house, which then sends the entry to both the NSI and to the Devon FHS (for inclusion in its own strays' index). Searches can be made by researchers in the relevant county FHS index. These county strays' indexes include some material that is not in the NSI. For example, some records of Devon people found in London records, may have been sent directly to Devon FHS by researchers who were reviewing London records.

COLLATERAL LINES

Many researchers try to trace other descendants of their ancestors. You might wish to do the same in order to discover the names and occupations of all descendants of a particular ancestor, or because other living descendants of your ancestors might have photographs, medals, a family bible, wills or other documents that relate to your common ancestors.

Tracing family lines forward in time can be difficult, particularly because of the frequency and distance of families' movements (within Britain or to other countries) especially in the 19th and 20th centuries. Consequently, the task of tracing your ancestors' descendants is, in some respects, similar to the task of tracing missing people. Rogers (1137) describes the methods of locating lost relatives, neighbours or old friends, principally for welfare and medical reasons, or because they are beneficiaries of a will, but also for family history. Rogers describes the agencies involved in this work, but agencies such as the police and Salvation Army do not exist in order to help a genealogist who is trying to find descendants of his great uncle Tom. Rogers also notes that many useful modern records are not available to genealogists, such as recent criminal, passport and bank account records or the archives and data held by DVLC, the Inland Revenue or the National Health Service. However, the service undertaken by Traceline, to pass on letters to those appearing in NHS records (if you give their last known address), was noted above.

The records described in earlier chapters of this book can be used to trace other descendants of your ancestors. The census records may help you to trace a family up to 1901. I was able to trace forward and find the families of William and John Rice, two brothers of my ancestor Richard Rice (# chapter 6). Electoral registers, commercial, trade and telephone directories or rates books of the 19th and 20th centuries note a family living in one place for a period of time and reveal the approximate date when the family moved on. Civil registration records include the marriages and deaths of ancestors' relatives and give addresses of the spouses, the deceased or the person (perhaps the deceased's child) who informed a registrar of the death. Medical and law directories, other professional lists (such as modern directories of chartered accountants or surveyors) or army and navy lists, will help you to trace a professional person throughout his career. The calendars of wills and administrations since 1858 can be searched to find entries for family members. These may note names and addresses of a deceased's children and you can then find them in directories, electoral registers or civil registration records.

The task of working forward in time to locate other descendants of your ancestors has become easier because of the publication of many county or national indexes of entries from parish registers, census returns, directories and monumental inscriptions. The 1881 census index and the 1901 census online service are particularly useful for locating ancestors' siblings (and their descendants) in the late 19th and early 20th centuries. Identifying relatives and their addresses in 1881 and 1901 brings you forward to a time when there are probate records for a greater proportion of the population (and these may note their children's names and addresses). At this time, directories were increasing their coverage of private residents and the number of directories for particular trades and occupations or lists of members of professional societies was also increasing. You can move forward through such directories to find your relatives in successive years.

You may also locate relatives by advertising your research in *Family Tree Magazine*, the GRD, the *Big R* or FHS journals. Other descendants of your ancestors may also be tracing their family tree and they may (in turn) be in contact with other cousins who can assist you. You can also advertise for relatives in national or local newspapers. This can produce useful responses, but may fail because the descendants of your ancestors may have moved away from the area. My mother and father (and their nine brothers and sisters) were born and brought up in London (in Stoke Newington and Westminster respectively), but none of them remain in London. If someone advertised in London newspapers, requesting members of my parents' families to contact them, they would not receive any response.

Tracing collateral lines can be difficult and time-consuming (and is perhaps less interesting than the search for ancestors). You may make little progress on collateral lines unless you make a concerted effort and dedicate substantial time to the task. The following section is a brief account of my research into the descendants of my ancestor George Keates. Much work remains to be done, but this account may help you to undertake similar research.

The Keates family
My g.g.g. grandfather George Keates died in 1870, at Wallwood Farmhouse on Hainault Road in Leyton, Essex. He was survived by his son John Josiah Keates (my ancestor), four other sons (George, William, Ebenezer and Jesse), his widowed second wife Anna (née Unwin) and three daughters by that second marriage (Emma, Flora and Alice). I had already located many descendants of John Josiah Keates, but I wanted to find any other photographs or records of George Keates and his family, and so I commenced searching for the descendants of John Josiah's brothers and sisters.

(1) Anna, Emma, Flora and Alice Keates At the time of the 1871 census (a few months after George's death), his widow Anna and their three daughters (and a servant) were still living at

Wallwood Farmhouse. The rates records for Leyton, Leytonstone and Walthamstow revealed that, until at least 1880, Anna was the owner (in succession to her deceased husband, George) of many houses and shops that were rented to tenants. In the 1881 census Anna and the three girls (and a servant) were living at Goldsmith Lodge on Church Road in Leyton. The three daughters were still unmarried. I searched the 1891 census of Leyton, but I could not find Anna or her daughters. I then checked the GRO indexes, looking for the death or remarriage of Anna and the marriages (or deaths) of the daughters. I searched up to about 1920, but found nothing. This search was very time-consuming, so I tried a different approach. The 1881 census recorded Anna as a widow aged 52 and the rates' records suggested that she had been quite wealthy. I therefore worked on the basis that she had not remarried and that it was likely that she would have left a will (or that there would have been letters of administration for her estate). I searched the National Probate Calendar and was successful. An entry in the calendar of 1913 recorded that Anna had died in 1911 in Selby Road, Anerley, in Kent. Anna's unmarried daughter, Emma Keates (then aged 55), was appointed as Anna's administratrix "with will annexed". Anna executed her will in 1890 (when living in Selby Road), dividing her estate equally between her three daughters (Emma, Alice and Flora). However, she had not appointed an executor and this was the reason for the appointment of Emma as administratrix. The estate was small, but this may have been because Anna had passed on much of her property before her death, or because her wealth had gradually diminished because she had lived off her capital since her husband's death in 1870. Emma was appointed as administratrix about two years after Anna's death. The papers did not disclose the reason for the delay.

I had already searched the GRO indexes up to 1920 for Anna's death (but without success). The administration papers recorded that Anna had died in 1911. I reviewed the entries for 1910 to 1913 again but could not find any entry. This may be one of those few cases in which a death is included in a superintendent registrar's records, but not in the Registrar General's records. That is a point that I must check in the future. However, I had the address (in Selby Road, Anerley) at which Anna had lived in 1890 (when she executed her will) and died in 1911. I therefore turned back to the 1891 census records. The return recorded Anna and her three daughters living at Selby Road. All three daughters were unmarried. Emma was a schoolteacher and Alice and Flora (as well as their mother) were recorded as "living on their own means" (thus explaining why Anna's estate was depleted when she died 20 years later). The unmarried daughters were aged between 28 and 33 (and the eldest, Emma, was still a spinster when she was appointed as administratrix in 1913). It was therefore possible that none of them had ever married, and so I turned back to the National Probate Calendar, hoping that one or more of the sisters had left a will. I started in 1911 and worked forwards. This was much quicker than searching the GRO death indexes. I found a will for each sister. Alice and Flora both died in 1936 at 2 Maple Road, Anerley, and Emma died in 1948 aged 90 (at a house nearby). None of the sisters had married (and they do not appear to have had any children). Alice and Flora's wills directed that their property be divided between their surviving sisters. Following their deaths, Emma had executed a will leaving gifts to the church and some charities, but also to many relatives on her mother's side (the Unwin and Westrope families). Many addresses were given for those relatives. I checked local telephone books and found a member of the Westrope family still living nearby (she was a child when Emma died). She kindly sent me two photographs. One was of Emma Keates in old age and the other was a photograph of one of the other sisters (we do not know whether it is Alice or Flora). Anna and her three daughters were buried in two graves in Beckenham cemetery.

Although I had obtained two photographs, four wills and more information about members of the Keates family, I had unfortunately not found any more living descendants of George Keates. Since there were no descendants of these three half-sisters of John Josiah Keates, I decided to investigate whether I could find any living descendants of his four brothers, all of whom I had already located in the census records up to 1861. I have not yet located any descendants who are still alive (principally because of the limited time that I have been able to spend on this research), but I have already made encouraging progress.

(2) William Thomas Keates William was born in 1838 and is recorded as a mast and block maker in the 1861 census. I have not found him in the 1871 census, nor found a record of his marriage but the 1881 census included William (a carpenter) with his wife Sarah and a baby named Thomas, living at Pine Cottages in Capworth Street, Leyton. In the 1891 census William was recorded as a builder, living at 1 Keates Cottages on Esther Road, Leyton, with Sarah, his son Thomas, a daughter Louisa and a son Frank. William died in 1899 and his death certificate recorded that he was a carpenter journeyman of 12 Gladstone Street, Leytonstone. I have not found any will or administration for William. His widow Sarah reported his death to the registrar. In the 1901 census, I found the widowed Sarah, living at 83 Sophia Road, Leyton and working as a charwoman. Four children lived with her: Thomas (a house painter), Louisa (a dressmaker), Frank (aged 11) and Florence (aged 9). Florence was noted as born in Tooting, in south-west London. This was a surprise because I was not previously aware of any link between the Keates family and south-west London. No further information about Sarah (or the children) has yet been found and much work therefore remains to be done in order to find any living descendants of William.

(3) Ebenezer James Keates Ebenezer was born in 1842 and was recorded as a mast and block maker in the 1861 census. He married Isabel Ashton in Stepney in 1868. The 1871 census included Ebenezer (a blockmaker), Isabel and two children (George and Priscilla Anna) living in Leyton High Street. Leyton ratebooks recorded that from 1877 to 1880 Ebenezer and his family had occupied a house and shop in Leyton (both owned by his stepmother, Anna Keates). In the 1881 census Ebenezer and Isabel were again recorded in Leyton High Street, with five children (George, Anna, Charles, John and Frank). Ebenezer was a builder employing six men. Surprisingly, the children Charles and John (aged 8 and 6 respectively) were recorded as born in Canada, so that it appeared that the family had lived in Canada at least during the period 1873–75. I have not yet discovered why (or exactly when) Ebenezer and his family went to Canada, nor why (or exactly when) they returned to England.

Ebenezer and most of his family were also living in Leyton (at 1 Claremont Road) at the time of the 1891 census. A further son (Archibald) was recorded (born in Leyton in 1882). Ebenezer's eldest son, George Keates, was not with the family in the census. He had married Leah Hart in Holborn in 1890. His occupation was recorded as clerk and his address was given as Saint John Street. I have not found him in the 1891 or 1901 censuses.

Ebenezer continued living at 1 Claremont Road, Leyton (he appears in a Leyton directory of 1894/5). By the time of the 1901 census, Ebenezer was a widower, living at 26 Pretoria Road, Romford and working from home on his own account as a carpenter. Four of Ebenezer's children lived with him: Anna, John (a carpenter), Frank (a storekeeper in an aluminium warehouse) and Archibald (a clerk for an oil wholesaler). I have not been able to find Ebenezer's will or administration. I did find a death certificate of 1913, for an Ebenezer James Keates (of about the correct age) who died at 521 Chiswick High Road. However, this Ebenezer was a coffeehouse keeper and I have not yet found any evidence to confirm whether or not this record does relate to the death of my ancestor's brother.

(4) George Albert Keates George was born in 1840 and is recorded in the 1861 census as a mast and block maker. The GRO records revealed that George married Fanny Tyler in 1869 in Somers Town in London and that in 1870 they had a son (also named George Albert Keates) at their home on Hainault Road in Leyton. The 1871 census recorded George, Fanny and their son as living on Hainault Road (a few houses away from John Josiah Keates).

I could not find George or his family in the 1881 census, but did find them in the 1891 census, living at 8 Forest Road in Leytonstone. There was no mention of their son George but the census recorded five other children (Mary, Frederick, Blanche, Richard and James). Two of the children (Mary aged 11 and Frederick aged 9) were noted as born in St Catherines, Ontario, in Canada. George and his family had therefore also lived in Canada, at least during 1880–82 (that is, a few years after his brother Ebenezer). This explained why I had not found George in the 1881 census. I had no idea why George had gone to Canada (or why he returned). I did not know where Ebenezer had lived in Canada (and my searches of Canadian directories for 1870 to 1890 did not reveal any members of the Keates family). It is particularly odd that Ebenezer should go to Canada in about 1872 and return in or about 1876, to be followed by his brother George in or about 1880. One possibility is that the opportunities for carpenters or mast and block makers were diminishing in England in this period and so the brothers went to Canada to find work or set up their own business.

I consulted the 1881 census of Canada (# chapter 30) on *FamilySearch* and found George and Fanny Keates in Port Dalhousie, Ontario. George was noted as a block maker. The relationships of people in a household are not recorded in this census but there were four children, all born in Ontario, living with George and Fanny: Clarissa (aged 9), Herbert (aged 7), Edith (aged 5) and Mary (aged 2). There was no sign of the son George (born in 1870). Perhaps he had died in either England or Canada. The two-year old Mary was undoubtedly the same girl who appeared (aged 11) in the 1891 census noted above. However, if (as appeared likely) Clarissa, Herbert and Edith were children of George and Fanny, what had become of them by the time of the 1891 census, noted above? It was unlikely that they remained in Canada, without their parents, in view of their tender ages. Had they died? As so often in family history research, my discovery of this census entry raised more questions than it answered. I will have to undertake research in Canada to ascertain whether the children died there and to find out more about the work and life there of George and his brother Ebenezer.

The 1901 census recorded George at 8 Forest Road, Leytonstone, working on his own account, as a carpenter and ships' block maker. His wife Fanny was not at home on census night and there was no sign of the children, Clarissa, Herbert and Edith, who had been recorded in Canada in 1881. However, three of George's children were there: Mary (a dressmaker), Frederick (a carpenter), Blanche, Richard but also a further son, Alfred (aged 7).

I searched for a will for George. I found an entry for him in the 1921 National Probate Calendar. George executed his will in 1885. He was then living at 5 Forest Road, Leytonstone and he appointed his wife Fanny (or, if she should die, his brothers John Josiah and Jesse) as his executors. George died on 26 December 1921 at 13 Forest Road, Leytonstone. This was the third address in Forest Road that had been recorded for him. I do not yet know whether he had moved between different houses in the same street or whether he lived in the same house that was renumbered twice. George's widow Fanny obtained a grant of probate in February 1922. I then searched the National Probate Calendar since 1922 for a will or administration for Fanny (hoping that this would identify her children and their addresses) and found a grant of letters of administration for her estate. Fanny was still living in Leytonstone at her death in 1937. The court appointed her daughter, Mary Julia Prockter (the wife of Arthur Harold Prockter) as administratrix. The letters of administration gave Mary and Arthur's address as 1 Yoxley Approach, Ilford, Essex.

I had brought this line of the Keates family tree forward to 1937 and I hope to find further information about them, especially about Mary Prockter, in the near future. I have not yet found any further trace of the other children of George and Fanny, but I know their names and years of birth and so with luck should be able to locate them in other records in due course. While there remains a large amount of research to undertake on this family, it is encouraging that I had found records of a descendant who was alive in 1937.

(5) Jesse Keates   Jesse Keates was born in 1846 and was living with his father George and his stepmother Anna in Walthamstow in the 1861 census. I have not yet located him in the 1871 census but in the 1881 census he is recorded as a carpenter, lodging with a widow Morris in Capworth Street, Leyton. In 1885 he was appointed, in the will of his brother George, as an executor if George's wife should predecease him. A Post Office directory of 1888 recorded Jesse Keates as a builder at Argyle Cottage, on Church Road in Leyton. In the 1901 census, Jesse (an unmarried, employed carpenter aged 54) was one of two lodgers of a widow Harriet Thorpe at 103 Church Road, Leyton. No information about Jesse for later years (particularly a marriage, will or administration) has yet been found.

(6) Summary   Much work remains to be done. Tracing a family tree forward in time can be very difficult and time-consuming. In some ways, it is more difficult than tracing the family tree back in time. You do not know if a person stayed in an area, moved down the road, emigrated, died young, got married or had any children (or where any of those events took place). Furthermore, it is difficult to concentrate on working forwards when there is so much research to be undertaken in respect of your ancestors.

There are many other sources in which I can continue my search for George Keates' descendants. The GRO indexes of births, marriages and deaths must be consulted further in order to find the marriages and deaths of the children that I have identified of each of William, Ebenezer and George. I must locate records of the marriage of Mary Keates to Arthur Prockter, their deaths and the births of any children. I should also use electoral registers and directories since 1937 to ascertain how long Mary and Arthur lived in Yoxley Approach in Ilford. The National Probate Calendar may also have entries for their wills or administrations and thus bring me further forward from 1937. Ratebooks, electoral registers and directories should allow me to trace the occupants at the other properties that I have identified. George and Anna Keates owned a large amount of property in Leyton and Walthamstow. I must check whether local archives have any title deeds for these properties. I will continue my search for living descendants of the brothers of John Josiah Keates and I hope that this section has shown how it is possible to trace a family tree forward in time, and that the research can be worthwhile.

CHAPTER 29

SCOTLAND, WALES, IRELAND, THE ISLE OF MAN AND THE CHANNEL ISLANDS

The information and advice in preceding chapters concentrates on genealogical research in England and Wales, but much of it also applies to ancestral research elsewhere in the British Isles. This chapter reviews the records that relate specifically to other parts of the British Isles and how to undertake research in those places. If you live in England, this may entail travelling to archives far away, but much research can also be undertaken on the Internet, at local reference libraries, LDS family history centres or in the large collections of material at the SoG.

SCOTLAND

Scotland was united in the 9th century by Kenneth MacAlpin. The lineage of Scottish kings is set out in works such as Montague-Smith (1050). Scotland and England have had the same monarchs since 1603, when James VI of Scotland succeeded to the English throne. Scotland and England have had the same government and Parliament since the Treaty of Union of 1707. However, Scottish law and administration (and therefore Scottish records) have always remained slightly different to those in England. Scotland also adopted the Gregorian calendar (so that 1 January was the first day of the year) in 1600, 152 years before England. Most of the records that you review will therefore have dates in the new style.

Anyone researching Scottish ancestry should study Scottish history (particularly of the 16th and 17th centuries) since this is of great help when using Scottish records. The wars and religious ferment of the 17th century are described in volume 12 of the *NIPR* (151), including the abolition of Episcopacy in 1638, the temporary predominance of the Presbyterians, the restoration of the bishops in 1661 and the persecution of Presbyterians until the Declaration of Indulgence in 1687. Presbyterianism then became the established form of the Church (with Episcopalians as non-conformists). Some knowledge of the Jacobite rebellions of 1715 and 1745 is also useful, particularly because of the changes imposed on the Highlands following the battle of Culloden.

Sinclair's works (1223) and (1224) provide a detailed analysis of research in Scotland, particularly in the records held at the National Archives of Scotland (NAS), formerly named the Scottish Record Office, which is located in two buildings: General Register House, Princes Street, Edinburgh EH1 3YY (telephone 0131 535 1334) and New Register House, Charlotte Square, Edinburgh EH2 4DJ (telephone 0131 535 1413). Opening times are noted on the NAS web site (# appendix XI). Documents at NAS are coded in a similar manner to those at TNA.

These codes and the procedure for ordering documents are described by Sinclair (1223) and (1224). These works also contain a detailed review of Scottish source material, names, the clan system and emigration, useful bibliographies and a summary of Scottish history and religious affairs. Volume 12 of the *NIPR* (151) reviews Scottish genealogical records, religion, government, language and names, and contains a detailed bibliography. Simpson (1222) is an illustrated work on Scottish handwriting from 1150 to 1650, dealing not only with Latin and English but also with French, Gaelic and Scots (which was used in records from the late 14th century). Moody (1205) is a good introduction to historical sources for Scottish towns and Adam (1152) and Way & Squire (1232) describe research of Highland ancestry.

The SoG has published a booklet listing the Scottish genealogical sources that it holds (such as copy parish registers, census indexes, MIs, directories and local history books). Internet sources for Scotland are listed in Raymond (1214) and the web site of the Scottish Archives Network will soon feature an online database of the catalogues of 49 Scottish archives. The Scottish Genealogy Society has a library at 15 Victoria Terrace, Edinburgh (telephone 0131 220 3677, see appendix XI for its web site) and publishes *The Scottish Genealogist*. There are also many Scottish family history societies, contact details for which are contained in the *FLHH* (5), most of which are members of the Scottish Association of Family History Societies.

The National Library of Scotland (NLS) at George IV Bridge, Edinburgh EH1 1EW (telephone 0131 226 4531) is Scotland's largest library and, like the British Library, has the right to receive all UK and Irish publications. The opening times of NLS are noted on its web site (# appendix XI). It holds about 7 million books or pamphlets, about 1.6 million maps and 120,000 volumes of manuscripts, including publications of the Scottish history and genealogical societies.

Names and family histories
Published Scottish genealogies (in family or local histories and works on the peerage) are catalogued by surname in Stuart (1227). Ferguson (1169) lists about 2,000 published Scottish family histories that are held in 76 libraries (and the revised edition of 1986 also includes the extensive holdings of published family histories at NAS). NAS also holds some manuscript genealogies, to which there is an index.

The development of Scottish surnames, their meaning and early evidence of their use are reviewed by Black (1156). In Lowland Scotland hereditary surnames developed in similar manner as in England. In the Highlands surnames developed in the 16th and 17th centuries. Some clan members already had the surname of their chief, but others gradually adopted that name. Christian names can be very important in Scottish research because children were often named in a particular order after their relatives. There were many exceptions and regional variations, but the first son was often given the Christian name of his father's father, a second son was given the Christian name of his mother's father and a third son was named after his father. The first daughter was usually given the Christian name of her mother's mother, a second daughter was named after her father's mother and a third daughter was given the name of her mother. This tradition may alert you to look out for the baptism or birth of a child whose name appears to have been missed, especially if you have a gap of a few years between two children of a family.

Civil registration
Civil registration only commenced in Scotland on 1 January 1855 but the system was (and remains) superior to that in England and Wales. Births, marriages and deaths were recorded by

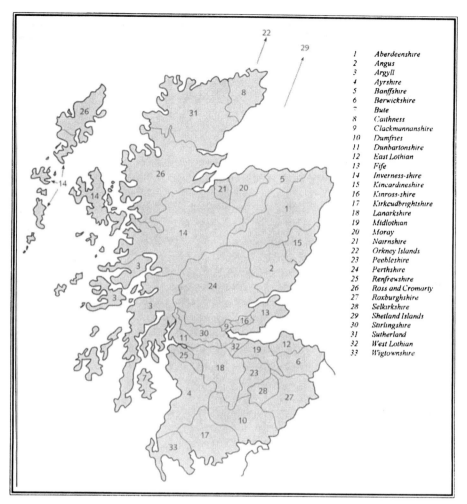

1	Aberdeenshire
2	Angus
3	Argyll
4	Ayrshire
5	Banffshire
6	Berwickshire
7	Bute
8	Caithness
9	Clackmannanshire
10	Dumfries
11	Dunbartonshire
12	East Lothian
13	Fife
14	Inverness-shire
15	Kincardineshire
16	Kinross-shire
17	Kirkcudbrightshire
18	Lanarkshire
19	Midlothian
20	Moray
21	Nairnshire
22	Orkney Islands
23	Peeblesshire
24	Perthshire
25	Renfrewshire
26	Ross and Cromarty
27	Roxburghshire
28	Selkirkshire
29	Shetland Islands
30	Stirlingshire
31	Sutherland
32	West Lothian
33	Wigtownshire

142. *The counties of Scotland before 1975*

district registrars but copies of all records are held centrally by the General Register Office for Scotland (GROS) at New Register House, Edinburgh EH1 3YT (telephone 0131 334 0380). A search fee is charged for a day, week or longer periods but this also permits access to the census records and many parish registers. Researchers' seats are limited, so you should reserve a place (in writing or by telephoning) in advance. Importantly, researchers can see microfiche copies of the registers and not just the indexes. Searching the indexes is much easier, and the register entries contain more information, than in England. An enormous amount of information was included when the system started in 1855, but the requirements were reduced in 1856, although increased again in 1861. Birth entries of 1855 and since 1861 contain (in addition to the information noted in England) the date and place of a child's parents' marriage. Birth entries of 1855 note the age and birthplace of the child's parents, and details of their other children. Marriage entries since 1855 record the names of each spouse's mother (including her maiden name). Marriage entries of 1855 note the birthplace and number of former marriages of each spouse (and the number of children by those marriages). Death entries of 1855 and since 1861 give the names and occupation of the deceased's parents (including the mother's maiden name) and the name of the deceased's spouse. In 1855 the deceased's place of birth and the names of any children were included. The deceased's place of burial was noted from 1855 to 1860.

Before viewing the registers, you must still find the correct index entry but there is a computerised index covering the whole of Scotland from 1855 to date for each of births, marriages and deaths. Searches on the computer terminals at GROS can be made by year or a period of years. Relevant entries appear on the screen and you note the year, registration district, the district reference number and entry numbers (so that you can then view microfiche copies of the registers). The birth indexes from 1929 and the death indexes since 1974 note the mother's maiden surname. The death indexes include ages at death from 1868 and dates of birth from 1969. Deaths of married women are also indexed by their maiden name since 1866. It is vital to remember the same rules (as to searching for different spellings of names) that you would observe if searching book indexes. Searches for names commencing Mc or Mac must be undertaken very carefully. All possibilities must be researched. Mistakes, or different spellings of a name, could be the fault of the ancestor or of a registrar or clerk. An ancestor may not have known or cared how his name was spelt. James (1186) found four signatures of his ancestor Alexander Macfarlane, spelling his own name in three different ways.

Because the registers are viewed on microfiche, information can be obtained from them without buying certificates, although certificates can also be purchased. These cost £11 and are available within a few working days, but cheaper, uncertified photocopies of register entries are available for certain years, to researchers visiting GROS. The possibility of seeing register entries before paying for copies or certificates assists location of the correct entry and avoids the need for the checking system.

The indexes from 1855 of births (up to 1902), marriages (up to 1927) and deaths (up to 1952) can also be consulted on the ScotlandsPeople web site (# appendix XI) accessed on terminals at GROS or from any computer. Digital images of the original register entries for those events and years have also been added to the site except that the marriage registers presently extend only up to 1898 (those for 1899–1927 will be available soon). The site also includes indexes (described below) to parish registers and to the 1891 and 1901 censuses. A password is issued to researchers registering at the site. Access to the indexes for 48 hours costs £6 (which includes a credit for up to 30 pages of search results). Searches are made by surname, forename, type of event, year (or range of years), registration district or (for parish registers) by county. Having found a relevant index entry, you can order an extract from the records, such as a birth certificate or census entry, for £10.

Microfilm copies of the Scottish indexes of births, marriages and deaths from 1855 to 1920 (and in some cases later) are also held at LDS family history centres and the SoG, which also holds copies of the actual Scottish registers of 1855. A terminal that gives access to the computer indexes of Scottish civil registration records is also available at the FRC in London (for an hourly fee) although it is still necessary to send an application and fee to Edinburgh to obtain entries from the registers. Index searches are also undertaken, for a fee, by GROS staff. Leaflets S2 and SU/3 (available at GROS) describe the procedure and fees. Part of the fee is refunded if a search is unsuccessful.

Some other registers are also held by GROS, listed in leaflet S1 and indexes to these registers are also on computer terminals at GROS. The registers cover:

a. children adopted since 1930
b. Consular returns of births and deaths (since 1914) and marriages (since 1917) of those of Scottish birth or descent
c. divorces since 1984
d. some births, marriages and deaths abroad since 1860
e. deaths of Scottish servicemen in the Boer War and the two world wars
f. births and deaths since 1855 on British registered vessels at sea (if the deceased, or the father of the child, was Scottish)
g. births and deaths since 1948 on UK registered aircraft (if the deceased, or the father of the child, was Scottish)
h. army records of births, marriages and deaths of Scots at military bases at home and abroad since 1881

Census records

The Scottish censuses of 1841 to 1901 are public records and held by the Registrar General. The daily pass fee at GROS noted above includes access to these records. The census records are in similar form to those of England, except that from 1861 they also noted how many of the rooms occupied by a household had one or more windows, and also whether people were employers and (if so) how many people they employed. Indexes to the 1891 and 1901 census returns are available on computer at GROS. Digital images of the 1891 and 1901 census returns of Scotland, with indexes, are on the ScotlandsPeople web site (the cost of using this site is noted above). The LDS census index for 1881 (# chapter 6) includes Scotland. The fiche-version of the index is arranged by Scottish county and notes the same information as the index for England and Wales. Both the fiche and CD-ROM versions are held at NAS, the SoG and LDS family history centres. The 1881 index is also available on terminals at GROS and will soon be added to the ScotlandsPeople web site (and images of the actual returns will be added in the future). Images of the census records of 1841–71 will also be added to the site, enabling them to be browsed online, with indexes to those returns being added later. GROS, NAS and the SoG hold some census indexes for other years. Some census listings before 1841 also survive and are listed by Gibson & Medlycott (139).

Parish registers

There were over 900 ancient parishes of the Church of Scotland. Various 16th- and 17th-century enactments required parish incumbents to keep registers, but they were often ignored. The keeping of registers was also hindered by struggles between Presbyterians and Episcopalians for dominance in the established Church in the 17th century. A few registers commence as early as 1553, but most start after 1600 and some registers only commence much later, particularly around 1689, when Presbyterianism was restored as the established form of the Scottish Church. A few registers only commence in the 18th century (the register for Stornoway dates from 1780). Many registers have been lost or have gaps of some years. The registers include very few burials and in some parishes there are no records of burials until 1855, when civil registration commenced. There are also no bishops' transcripts to fill the gaps.

Many people, especially in the 18th and early 19th centuries, failed to have baptisms of their children registered. However, there is a register of neglected entries, listing some births, marriages or deaths which are known to have taken place in Scotland from 1801 to 1854, but for which there are no entries in parish registers. Further omissions in parish registers (and the loss of registers) were caused by what is called the "Disruption" of the Church of Scotland in 1843. Theological differences resulted in many ministers leaving the Church of Scotland to establish the Free Church of Scotland. Some registers were probably lost at this time and families of those following the Free Church ministers also cease to appear in Scottish parish registers (but may be recorded in Free Church registers, see below).

Most surviving parish registers of the Church of Scotland of 1553–1854 (known as the Old Parochial Registers or OPRs) are held by the Registrar General at New Register House and are available in microform. They can also be seen on microfilm at LDS family history centres. Some registers (and many copies) are at Scottish regional record offices, listed in appendix VII. Copies of registers held by the SoG are listed in its catalogue; those in the collection as at 1995 are listed in the SoG booklet (152). Many copies are also held at the Scottish Genealogy Society's library. A booklet by the Scottish Association of Family History Societies (1148) contains maps showing the parishes in each county with lists, for each parish, of the dates of surviving pre-1855 registers. The pre-1975 counties of Scotland are shown on the map in illustration 142. The IHGS publishes 10 maps (each covering one or more Scottish counties) showing approximate parish boundaries and probate jurisdictions. These are included in the *Phillimore Atlas* (165).

Entries for baptisms usually note a mother's maiden name. This assists you to identify the baptisms of your ancestors' siblings and to find the parents' marriage. The names of godparents (or sponsors) of a child are often noted and they were normally relatives or the parents' friends. Scottish laws on marriage (and the prohibited degrees) are set out in Chapman & Litton (362). Parish registers usually record only the proclamations of marriage (similar to the reading of banns) and rarely record a marriage itself. Proclamations were usually recorded in each spouse's parish. An entry of proclamations does not prove that a marriage took place (although it usually did so). A couple could also marry without proclamations (analogous to an English marriage by licence) and in those cases the marriage itself is usually noted in the registers. It was also possible in Scotland to marry without a church service (the irregular border marriages, for example at Gretna Green, were noted in chapter 14). A marriage could be effected by public promises between a couple (followed by consummation) or even by simply referring in public to the other person as one's spouse. Marriages could also be effected by cohabitation and repute. In these cases, there is usually no official record of a marriage.

GROS and the LDS have produced an index to the approximately 10 million entries of baptisms and marriages in the OPRs and the register of neglected entries. The index is on microfiche, arranged by county, with an addendum containing about 31,000 corrections and entries omitted from the main index. It can be seen at GROS, NAS, NLS, the SoG or LDS family history centres and can also be purchased. The OPR index is also included in the computerised indexes at GROS, in *FamilySearch* (online and on CD-ROM) and on the ScotlandsPeople web site.

The web site of Scots Origins (which previously operated an online service for GROS) also features useful indexes: civil registration indexes from 1855, census indexes for 1861 and 1871, the OPR index (for 1700–1855 only) and the IGI for Scotland (see below). Transcripts of some of the original records can also be ordered online through the site.

Entries from some Scottish parish registers are included (with entries from non-conformist registers and entries submitted by researchers) in the Scottish section of the IGI. This contains about 15 million entries in the same format as English entries. It is available on fiche (with a section for each pre-1974 Scottish county) and in *FamilySearch* (online and on CD-ROM). It is worth consulting both the IGI and the OPR index. Some parish registers were indexed in full for the OPR index but not for the IGI (and the IGI includes some material that is not in the OPRs).

Neither the OPR index nor the IGI include burials or deaths. However, a National Burial Index for Scotland (1553–1855) is being prepared.

The registers of Scottish churches in England are also important sources. Many Scots (merchants, soldiers or those attached to the Stuart kings' households) lived temporarily in England. Volume 12 of the *NIPR* (151) lists the surviving registers of Scottish churches in England (and their covering dates), including nine in London alone. The registers of Scots' churches in Berwick upon Tweed and Durham may also include entries for your Scottish ancestors. The registers of English parishes should also not be overlooked.

Non-conformist registers

A 1560 act of the Scottish Parliament abolished Catholic forms of worship in the Scottish Church. Catholics were persecuted throughout the 16th, 17th and 18th centuries. Catholic support for the 1745 rebellion resulted in all Catholics being declared rebels and outlaws. Their priests were banished or imprisoned. A Catholic Relief Act was passed in 1793 and it is only from then that substantial Catholic records survive. Catholic missions in Scotland are listed in Gandy (324) and (325) and many published books and articles on Scottish Catholics are listed in Gandy (1172). Copies of Catholic registers up to 1855 have been deposited at NAS but few commence before the 19th century.

Volume 12 of the *NIPR* (151) provides detailed information on Scottish non-conformism, including the struggle between the Presbyterians and the Episcopalians in the 16th and 17th centuries, as to the form of government within the Church of Scotland. At different periods either the Presbyterians or the Episcopalians could be deemed as non-conformist although the Presbyterians were ultimately successful in controlling the Church. Presbyterianism became the established form of the Scottish church in 1689. From that time, the Episcopalians (who were generally loyal to the Stuart cause and desired a church that was ruled by bishops) were persecuted by the authorities, particularly after the failure of the 1715 and 1745 rebellions. Most Episcopalian clergy were ejected from their parishes, at first in the south of Scotland but later also in the north. It was not until the late 18th century that penal laws were relaxed, the Episcopal Church was able to organise itself properly and its congregations could meet without fear. Some original registers of the Episcopal Church are held at NAS but there are also microfilm copies of other surviving registers.

The other principal non-conformist groups in Scotland were Quakers, Methodists and Congregationalists. Some of their registers and other records are held locally, but many are at NAS. Many records of Quaker meetings in Scotland are at Friends House in London or at meeting houses in Edinburgh, Glasgow or Aberdeen. There were also some Scottish Baptist congregations, the first being founded in 1652. By the mid-19th century there were about 100 Congregational chapels in Scotland. Most of their registers are at NAS. The first Methodist chapel was founded in 1764 (in Aberdeen). Four circuits were established in 1765 and the movement gradually gathered strength. Most of their records are held at chapels. Some registers of the Free Church from 1843 are held by NAS but others are still held by the churches and some have been lost.

Monumental inscriptions, directories and maps
Many transcripts of MIs are held by regional record offices and family history societies. The collection at the SoG is listed in its catalogue or, as at 1997, in Collins & Morton (186). Scottish directories from 1773 to 1950 (such as those by Pigot, Slater or Kelly) and the archives holding copies, are listed in Shaw & Tipper (212). Early city directories include Williamson's Edinburgh directory of 1773 and Tait's Glasgow directory of 1783. Many Scottish directories are included in parts 2 and 3 of the *Biography Database* on CD-ROM. Lewis' *Topographical Dictionary of Scotland* was published in 1846 and has been reprinted by GPC and also produced on CD-ROM.

Maps of Scotland are briefly described in an essay by J. Stone in Wallis (407), which also summarises the map collections at 36 Scottish archives and libraries. The Ordnance Survey mapped all of Scotland at a scale of six inches to the mile (1:10,560) and also (except for uncultivated areas) at 25 inches to the mile (1:2,500) in the late 19th century. Urban areas were also mapped at larger scales. These maps are held at NAS and at regional record offices. The Register House plans at NAS are a collection of about 90,000 maps and plans, extracted from other classes of records. These include plans of parishes, estates, towns and farms. A topographical card index and other finding aids are described by Sinclair (1224). The best collection of Scottish maps is at NLS, also described by Sinclair (1224). The NLS web site features hundreds of maps of Scotland and its counties, Ordnance Survey town plans as well as 400 military plans and maps, most from the 18th and 19th centuries.

Wills
Scottish law provided, until 1868, that real property (land and buildings) should descend to the eldest son or, if there was no son, to any daughters equally, then to the surviving spouse. Therefore, until 1868, only movable property (such as money, furniture or livestock) could be the subject of a testamentary disposition. From 1868 all property could be devised or bequeathed. Probate consisted of the grant of a confirmation (of the appointment of executors). If a deceased left no testament, the court could appoint an executor by a testament dative, the equivalent of an English administration. Testaments were thus of two types: a testament testamentar if the deceased left a testament, and a testament dative if the deceased was intestate but left property to be distributed. An inventory of the deceased's goods may also survive.

Until the 16th century testaments were proved in church courts but from about 1560 until 1823 all testaments were proved in secular commissary courts (commissariots). The Principal Commissariot of Edinburgh had jurisdiction throughout Scotland and over the testaments of Scots dying abroad (but with property in Scotland). There were also 22 provincial commissariots. Their areas of jurisdiction are noted in Gibson & Churchill (291) and on the IHGS maps for Scotland. Surviving testaments up to 1823 are at NAS and have been indexed, by commissariot, by the Scottish Record Society. Copies of these indexes are at NAS and the SoG. Probate jurisdiction was transferred on 1 January 1824 to civil sheriff courts, listed in Sinclair (1223), although the transfer did not in practice occur in some areas until a few years later. The sheriff courts' jurisdiction approximated to the county boundaries at that time. The Edinburgh Sheriff

Court had jurisdiction over Scots dying abroad. Most of the older sheriff court records are at NAS. More recent records are still at sheriffs' courts. Various indexes for the period 1824–75 are at NAS. For the period 1876–1959, there are annual volumes at NAS, entitled *Calendar of Confirmations and Inventories*, listing (alphabetically) all confirmations granted in Scotland each year. The easiest method of finding testaments at NAS from the period 1500–1901 is to consult an overall index to them (520,000 documents) on the ScottishDocuments web site. The index notes the testator's name, occupation, place of residence and the date the will was registered. The index is also linked to digital copies of the wills which can be downloaded from the web site for £5 per will (payable by credit or debit card). NAS also holds estate duty registers of the Inland Revenue dating from 1804. These provide similar information to the records in England (# chapter 12) and are described in Sinclair (1223). The SoG has a large collection of Scottish probate indexes and abstracts, listed in Newington-Irving (297).

Newspapers and journals
The *Edinburgh Gazette*, containing similar information for Scotland as the *London Gazette*, was published from 1680. The *Scots Magazine* (named the *Edinburgh Magazine* from 1817) was published from 1739 to 1826 and was similar in content to the English *Gentleman's Magazine*. There are annual indexes to the notices of births, marriages, deaths and appointments.

Newspapers were first published in Scotland in the 17th century, but the first regularly published Scottish paper (three times a week) was the *Edinburgh Evening Courant*, founded in 1718. Later local newspapers included the *Glasgow Journal* and the *Aberdeen Journal*, founded in 1741 and 1748 respectively. Many more newspapers were established in the early 19th century. In Edinburgh, for example, the *Edinburgh Weekly Chronicle*, the *Edinburgh Star* and the *Edinburgh News* were founded in 1808 and the *Evening Post* was established in 1827. Many papers were also founded in places such as Glasgow, Ayr, Aberdeen and Dundee. The first Scottish daily newspaper was *The Conservative*, founded in 1837, followed by the *North British Daily Mail* in 1847. The holdings of NLS and other Scottish libraries of Scottish newspapers are listed in Ferguson (1170) and in a published report of the British Library "Newsplan" project (# chapter 17) by Mackenzie (1194).

Elections
Scotland shared a common parliament with England and Wales from 1707. Until 1832 the franchise was very restricted because burgh representatives were elected by burgh councils and the voting qualification in the counties (originally freehold land with a value of 40 shillings) was increased to take account of inflation. Gibson & Rogers (485) list the few surviving poll books and note that only 2,662 men could vote in Scotland in 1788. The franchise was extended from 1832 and Gibson & Rogers (483) list surviving Scottish electoral registers since 1832 (most held at NAS or NLS) except for those held at the British Library, which are listed in Cheffins (474).

Parish records
The English poor law and settlement acts did not apply to Scotland but Scottish paupers could obtain relief from charities or from their parishes (if they were old, infirm, orphans or destitute children under 14). The parishes were not obliged to assist able-bodied paupers. Money was raised by assessments on heritors (the principal parish landowners). Rates and payments may be recorded in Kirk minutes. NAS holds many records, described in Sinclair (1223), of the Kirk

sessions of parishes (and some microfilms of these records are at local archives). They consist mainly of accounts, listing payments to the poor, or minutes dealing with matters such as the parishioners' behaviour. Other parish and borough records are in regional record offices or libraries. The Poor Law (Scotland) Act of 1845 established parochial boards to administer poor relief in each parish. Many records of parochial boards are at NAS and described in Sinclair (1223), or at regional record offices. They include detailed information on the people who received assistance. Sheriff court records (considered below) include many appeals of parishioners from the refusal of boards to grant relief. They also include applications by officials for orders that men should support their illegitimate children or wives whom they had deserted.

Schools and universities
The development of education in Scotland (and its records) is described in Chapman (551). Four universities (Aberdeen, Glasgow, St Andrews and Edinburgh) were founded in Scotland by 1500. The original university records are described in detail by Hamilton-Edwards (1178). An article in *Family Tree Magazine* (October 1998) by J. Titford describes published registers of Scottish universities, such as those of King's College, Aberdeen (1495–1860), Aberdeen University (1860–1970), St Andrews University (1413–1579 and 1747–1897) and Glasgow University (1727–1897). Many Scottish men studied abroad, for example before the foundation of Scottish universities or during the periods of discrimination against Catholics. Watt (1231) is a biographical dictionary of Scots who graduated in England or Europe up to 1410 and Halloran (1177) is a history of the Scots College at Paris up to 1792, listing the known students.

Many school registers have been published and are listed in Torrance (1228). Some examples are the Fettes College register for 1870–1932 (1142), the register of Trinity College, Glenalmond, 1847–1929 (1143) and the register of Edinburgh Academy, 1824–1914 (1141). Some school registers and other records date back to the 18th century but the names of pupils at most schools are not recorded until registers of leaving certificates, with names, subjects and grades, commence around 1908. Sinclair (1223) describes records of schoolteachers. Until 1872 most schools were maintained by the parish or burgh and so some teachers are noted in heritors' or council minutes. In the 18th and 19th centuries many schools were founded in the Highlands and Islands by the Society in Scotland for Propagating Christian Knowledge and so many teachers are noted in the society's records (including a register of schools and salary books) at NAS. School boards were founded in 1872. Their records are held by local councils, regional record offices or NAS, including minute books that note teachers' appointments.

Tax
A hearth tax was levied in Scotland from 1691 to 1695 and poll taxes were levied from 1693 to 1699. Surviving records are at NAS and listed in Gibson (890). Many window tax records have survived, particularly for 1748 to 1798, naming occupiers of property. A few surviving land tax records are at NAS and listed in Gibson, Medlycott & Mills (892). Surviving records of servants' tax and other assessed taxes are at NAS and described by Sinclair (1223). Scottish apprenticeship indentures were liable to duty and are therefore included in the apprenticeship registers at TNA. From 1910 surveys and valuations of land were undertaken in Scotland in similar manner to those in England and Wales (# chapter 15). NAS holds valuation maps (noting numbers for each property) and fieldbooks which specify the property, owners and tenants (and record the rent and duration of a tenancy).

Military records

Records of Scottish regiments and soldiers since the union of 1707 are at TNA and many published works on Scottish regiments, particularly regimental histories and rolls of honour, are listed in Torrance (1228). There was no standing army in Scotland before 1707 and troops were raised when needed. Some early records, such as some 17th-century muster rolls and officers' commissions, are at NAS and described in Hamilton-Edwards (1178). Muster rolls of the Scots army in England in 1646 are held at TNA in piece SP 41/2. Much useful information is also contained in *The Scots Army 1661–1688* by C. Dalton. NAS holds 17th- and 18th-century militia muster lists, catalogued in Gibson & Dell (631). Dobson (1165) lists many Jacobites who were involved in the 1715 rebellion and notes their fate (with references to original documents and published works), for example:

Dalziel, John, brother of the Earl of Carnwath, Captain, prisoner at Preston, transported to Virginia or Carolina.
Robertson, Donald, Captain in Murray's battalion, at Preston, prisoner, executed at Lancaster, 18 Feb 1716.

Livingstone (1193) is a muster roll of the Young Pretender's army in 1745 and 1746, including some English and Irishmen. The soldier's fate (whether killed, taken prisoner, executed, or escaped) is noted in most cases. Thus, George Robertson of Badro fought in the Atholl brigade and was killed at Culloden. Alexander Fraser of Moray fought in the Duke of Perth's regiment and was captured and transported.

The Scottish militia was re-established in 1797 and its records are listed in Gibson & Medlycott (632) and held at NAS or TNA (such as the militia regimental returns in series WO 13). The Scottish National War Memorial, at Edinburgh Castle, displays the names of Scots who were killed in the two world wars. The memorial's officers provide details of entries to next of kin or close relatives (other applicants have to pay a fee and may have a long wait for their enquiries to be dealt with). The University of Edinburgh roll of honour (1150) contains short biographies of almost 8,000 staff and students, or former students, who served in the First World War as well as photographs of about 850 of the 944 men who died.

Scotland had only a small navy before union. Scottish sailors since 1707 may be found in Royal Navy records at TNA. Merchant seamen are recorded in a few agreements or crew lists held at NAS, or in those at TNA and other archives noted in chapter 21.

The professions

Torrance (1228) is a detailed list of published books, articles and directories for Scottish professions, trades and occupations. Men who have held senior offices in Scotland, such as crown and government ministers, lord lieutenants, judges and bishops, from medieval times to the 1880s are listed in Ockerby (843). Records of the legal profession are reviewed in Hamilton-Edwards (1178). The Scottish equivalent of an English barrister is an advocate and Scottish solicitors were previously known as writers. Information on Scottish advocates from 1532 to 1943 (such as births, parentage, marriages and deaths) are provided in Grant (1175). The *Scottish Law List* commenced publication in 1848 and information about Scottish solicitors may also be obtained from the Law Society of Scotland (in Edinburgh).

Ministers of the Church of Scotland since the Reformation are listed in *Fasti Ecclesiae Scoticanae* (published in 10 volumes) which is based on the records of Kirk sessions, Synods and General

Assemblies. The entries are arranged by Synod, then Presbytery, then parish. The details of a minister's career (and other biographical information about him and sometimes his family) are given under his last incumbency. However, each entry gives details of any parish to which a minister transferred so that you can easily trace a minister's career through to the final, detailed entry. Volume I by Scott (1219) deals with the ministers of the Synod of Lothian and Tweeddale and volumes II–VII, also by Scott, deal with the other synods up to the dates of publication (between 1915 and 1928). Volume VIII by Scott (1220) includes later entries for all synods up to 1929 (and an addendum to earlier volumes). Volume IX by Lamb (1189) covers ministers from 1929 to 1954. Biographies of clergy from medieval times up to 1638 are contained in Watt (1230). Bertie (1157) is a biographical dictionary of clergy of the Episcopal Church from 1689 to 2000. Episcopalian clergy who managed to avoid ejection from their parishes in the years following 1689 are also listed in *Fasti Ecclesiae Scoticanae*, noted above. Information about Catholic clergy can be found in the annual *Catholic Directory for Scotland* and in Johnson (1187), a biographical dictionary of Catholic parish clergy from 1879 to 1989. Torrance (1228) lists published works about other non-conformist ministers and many useful sources at NAS are described in Sinclair (1223).

The names, addresses and qualifications of medical practitioners since 1858 are listed in medical registers and directories (# chapter 22). Information about physicians and surgeons in Scotland can also be obtained from Scottish university records or by writing to the librarians of the three Scottish colleges. The Royal College of Physicians of Edinburgh is located at 9 Queen Street, Edinburgh EH2 1JQ. A list of the college fellows from 1681 to 1925 has been published. The college also has lists and other records of those licensed by it to practise in and around Edinburgh. The Royal College of Surgeons of Edinburgh is located at Nicholson Street, Edinburgh EH8 9DW. A list of its fellows from 1581 to 1873 has been published and minutes of the college, since 1581, record the names of candidates who were examined by the college and those surgeons who were licensed to practise by the college. The Royal College of Physicians and Surgeons of Glasgow, at 234–242 St Vincent Street, Glasgow G2 5RJ, also has a large library that includes some lists and other records of members and licentiates of the college. NAS holds registers of nurses in Scotland for the period 1885–1930, but nurses, midwives, dentists and chemists can also be found in the published lists noted in chapter 22.

Records of trades, occupations and business
Scotland had many guilds, such as the Edinburgh Company of Merchants founded in 1505, the Guild of Bakers of Aberdeen (founded in the 16th century) and the companies of tailors, weavers and bakers of Dundee (all incorporated in 1575). Some information about Scottish guilds is contained in Melling (839) and the records held at NAS are listed in Sinclair's works. The Scottish equivalent of freemen were burgesses and records of them can be found in burgh records (at NAS or local archives) or in guild records. Some lists of burgesses have been published and are listed in Torrance (1228).

Detailed records survive for customs and excise officers. There were separate Boards of Customs and of Excise for Scotland from 1707 to 1829 and their records are at NAS. For example, the Customs' establishment books are quarterly lists, arranged by port, of all customs officers. There are also accounts that record the payment of officers' salaries. NAS also holds records of the Post Office of Scotland, including establishment books that list all salaried staff from 1803 to 1911.

Scotland has had its own registration system for limited companies since 1856. Most records are held by the Registrar of Companies at 102 George Street, Edinburgh, but a list of all registered companies is at NAS, with files of some dissolved companies. Reports on surviving business records are included in the National Register of Archives (Scotland), which is a department of NAS and located at General Register House. The NAS gifts and deposits series includes some business archives, for example those of the Sun Alliance Insurance Company. Sinclair (1224) describes many other business records at NAS, such as those of local authorities and canal companies.

NAS also holds the records of many Scottish railway companies, listed in Richards (854), including staff records that are similar to the English and Welsh records described in chapter 22. Archives holding records of Scottish coal mines and miners are listed by Tonks (872a).

Property records

The extensive records of Scottish property (many in Latin until the 19th century) are described in detail in Sinclair (1223) and (1224) and in Hamilton-Edwards (1178). Some of the documents are similar to English records (# chapter 27) but Scotland had a different legal system so there were many differences in the form of records and the legal terms used. Some types of Scottish property documents are not found in English records, such as retours of services of heirs, the registers of sasines and the registers of deeds.

Scottish property was subject to feudal systems of tenure and held ultimately by the Crown. A vassal of the Crown received a grant (or feu) of land for a period of time (as in England, termed an estate) in return for military or agricultural services. Crown grants, by charters under the Great Seal, are described by Sinclair (1224). Many have been published or indexed. Vassals could, in turn, sub-feu an estate in the land (or part of it) to others. A grant was recorded in a deed known as a feu charter or feu disposition. Services were later commuted to a monetary sum (a grassum) and annual payments (feu duty), that were abolished only in the 20th century. When a tenant of the Crown died, his heir had to prove his right to inherit the land. An inquest was held by a sheriff to ascertain what land was held by the tenant. A retour (or return) of the jury's decision was made to the Chancery. Retours of services of heirs are held at NAS, date from about 1530 and are generally in Latin until 1847. Retours name the heir and the deceased (sometimes the date of death) and their relationship. There are published, indexed, summaries of the records up to 1699 and indexes from 1700 to 1859, all of which have also been reproduced on CD-ROM by the Scottish Genealogy Society. NAS also holds records of Crown grants of land, such as Crown charters, Great Seal charters, Privy Seal charters and signatures. These documents (and indexes to them or published calendars) are described by Sinclair (1223).

Possession of land had to be transferred to a new tenant in a public ceremony of sasine (the equivalent of English livery of seisin). The process was known as infefment (the equivalent of English enfeoffment). The ceremony was public so that people could witness it (in case of a subsequent dispute as to title to the property). From the late middle ages, an independent notary was also employed to record the proceedings of sasine and infefment. Transactions were recorded in protocol books. NAS holds some notaries' protocol books, mostly from the 16th and 17th centuries, and others are held in regional record offices. The important information contained in these books can be illustrated by an extract from the protocol book of John Foular, for 1528 to 1534, published by the Scottish Record Society in Durkan (1166). Six entries (of 31 August and 5 September 1528) referred to the decease of both John Napier and his son John and noted the names of the widow of John the elder and five of his daughters (and some of their husbands). An extract from one entry is:

1528 Aug 31. Sasine to Jonet Napier, on her cognition by William Lander, baillie, as daughter and one of the heirs of the late John Napier, burgess, and as sister and one of the heirs of the late John Napier her brother, of her portion, viz. the seventh part of [property described] which Jonet Napier immediately resigned (into) the hands of the baillie, who gave sasine of the same to William Adamson, burgess and Jonet Napier his spouse.

Registers of sasines were also introduced in the late 16th century, in order to record lifetime transfers of title to land (whether by sale, gift or mortgage). The document that effected a change in ownership, or the grant of security for a loan, was copied into a sasine register. The Secretary's register was used from 1599 until it was closed in 1609. It was arranged in divisions for each part of Scotland. A General register of sasines was introduced in 1617, in which documents could be recorded for property anywhere in Scotland and there were also Particular registers (for particular areas of Scotland). From 1681 there were also separate registers of sasines for about 70 Royal Burghs, such as Aberdeen, Edinburgh, Glasgow and Dundee. The General register of sasines was divided into separate divisions for different areas of Scotland in 1868 and so the Particular registers were then closed. The registers of Royal Burghs were gradually closed in the 20th century and property transfers were then recorded in the General register. The General register now amounts to about 50,000 volumes (although Scottish property is now subject, as in England, to land registration). NAS holds the General and Particular registers (and most of the Royal Burgh registers). The Royal Burgh registers, the areas covered by the Particular registers and the archives holding them are listed in Sinclair (1223). NAS holds volumes of abridgements, which abstract the important information from the General and Particular registers since 1781. This extract is from the Sasine abridgements for Elgin and Forres in 1812:

Jan. 3. Joseph Cook, shoemaker, College of Elgin, seised, Dec. 31, 1811, in lands called Spynie Manse in the College of Elgin; on Disp. by John Harral, gardener, College of Elgin, to Isobel Adam, his spouse, in liferent, and Margaret, Katharine, Janet, Christian and Isobel Mathew, daughters of Alexander Mathew in Cloves, in fee, Jun. 27, 1786; and Disp. & Assig. by them, Dec. 26, 27, 1811. P.R. 10. 49.

There are name indexes to the abridgements and also place-name indexes for most years. Searches for transactions can be made in the search sheet for a property, which notes every reference to that property in the General register since 1871. For searches in the period 1781–1870, you must use the abridgements (and indexes). For the period prior to 1781, you should search the Particular or Royal Burgh register for the area in which your ancestor lived. Some of these registers are indexed. If you have no luck, you can try the General registers (which are indexed up to 1720). If you know where your ancestors lived (whether in a small cottage or in large house) you should be able to trace who owned the land over a period of years. If your ancestor owned the property, details of his purchase and sale can also be obtained.

From the 16th century Scottish courts also kept registers of deeds into which landowners or businessmen could have their important documents copied to ensure their preservation. The deeds cover matters such as property transfers, trusts, marriage contracts or business transactions and some registers have been indexed. Sinclair (1223) describes the registers in detail and examples of the registered documents are included in Hamilton-Edwards (1178). Relevant documents are difficult to find because they may be in registers of a number of courts. From 1804 registers were operated by the Court of Session, sheriff courts and Royal Burgh courts, but any court had power to register deeds until 1804. Searches are also difficult because the registers include deeds in order of their date of registration (often very different from the date of the document). Thus many deeds relating to a particular piece of land or trust, dated over many years, might have been registered at the same time. The Court of Session's register commences in 1554. Sinclair (1223) describes its arrangement and the available calendars and indexes. NAS also holds many deeds registers of the sheriff courts, Royal Burghs and commissary courts (described below) for the period up to 1804.

A *Return of Owners of Land of One Acre and Upwards* for Scotland was published by HMSO in 1872/3 and can be purchased on microfiche or CD-ROM. Property valuations were also undertaken in order to assess tax liabilities. NAS holds a few valuation and land tax records for properties prior to 1855. A statute of 1854 provided for all land in Scotland to be valued annually. Valuation rolls were prepared for each county or burgh, listing the value of each property, the owner, tenant and (if it was rented for more than £4 per year) the occupier. There are some place indexes. Land was leased to tenants by a document known as a tack (these sometimes survive in estate papers). Some rentals listing tenants and rents also survive, but to start a search you need to find any deposited archives of the family that owned the property. Many families' archives are at NAS in the gifts and deposits series, indexed by family and estate names. Some calendars of the collections have been published and collections in other Scottish archives are noted in the National Register of Archives (Scotland). Records of the Jacobite risings and the subsequent forfeiture of Jacobites' estates (considered below) also include many property documents.

Scottish civil courts

Scottish court records are difficult to use because of the number of courts and the lack of indexes. Volume 12 of the *NIPR* (151) describes the Scottish court system in detail. Cases from throughout Scotland could be heard by the Court of Session, the Privy Council, the Court of Exchequer and the Court of Admiralty, while commissary courts, burgh courts, sheriff courts and Justices of the Peace heard cases in particular areas. Most records are at NAS. They are reviewed in detail by Sinclair (1223) and therefore only summarised below.

Civil and criminal jurisdiction was originally exercised by the King's Council but was gradually delegated. The highest civil court was the Court of Session, established in 1532. Its records are extensive and described in the *Annual Report of the Keeper of the Records of Scotland 1972* but they are difficult to use because of their complicated arrangement. Examples of searches in the court's records are described in Sinclair (1223). Chronological minute books, noting brief details of all cases before the court, commence in 1557 (and are reasonably complete from 1576). The books were printed annually from 1782 and have indexes to the parties' names. Having found a relevant entry, you can search for the case records and any decree. Registers of acts and decrees commence in 1542. Up to about 1810 these note orders made by the court and provide an almost verbatim record of the proceedings but from 1810 (although indexed) they only provide summaries of the claim and the judgment.

The Privy Council in Scotland acted in a judicial capacity until 1707. Its registers up to 1691 have been published. The Court of Exchequer dealt with revenue cases from 1708 to 1856. The parties to actions are listed in minute books and there are also some books of orders and affidavits. The Admiralty Court dealt with maritime matters (although civil cases were transferred to the Court of Session in 1830). Its records are at NAS. Other civil cases, such as contract or debt disputes (but also criminal cases), were heard by the sheriff courts. Sinclair's works list these courts, the counties in which they had jurisdiction and the NAS classes in which records are held. Sheriffs' act books record the proceedings and trials but they are very incomplete until the late 18th century and there are very few indexes. Of particular interest are the 1,289 volumes of the registers of hornings (covering 1610–1902), which record the parties in debt actions. There is a general register and particular registers for each county but no indexes.

Commissary courts dealt with probate matters and, until 1823, some other civil matters (principally debt actions). Cases are recorded in act books and there are also minute books and registers of decrees, but very few indexes. Marriages could be annulled by the church courts and they could also grant separation *a mensa et thoro*, on similar grounds as the English courts. However, divorces could also be granted by the church courts (in the early 16th century), the Commissary Court of Edinburgh (1563–1830) and the Court of Session (since 1830). Divorce was available in cases of adultery and desertion (of four years) and from 1938 for cruelty. Surviving records are held at NAS.

NAS also holds a few records of Justices of the Peace, burgh courts and franchise courts (courts of local landowners held by a franchise from the Crown) but the records are incomplete and unindexed. By 1707 there were 66 burghs and the records of their courts, known as Bailies, are described in detail in the *NIPR* (151). They had both civil and criminal jurisdiction but their jurisdiction gradually declined since many litigants preferred the Court of Session for civil cases and the commissary courts for registration of deeds. From 1756 the Justices of the Peace or burgh courts granted licences for alehouses and NAS holds some surviving records. The different types of franchise courts (such as Regality courts and Barony courts), their jurisdiction, procedure and records are described in detail in the *NIPR* (151). Their jurisdiction was substantially reduced in 1747. Many of the cases concern disputes between tenants, including assault, theft, debt, damage to property and also defamation. A few of these courts' records have been published, such as those of the regality court of Melrose.

Until the Reformation the church courts had jurisdiction over marriage, legitimacy, defamation, testaments and the discipline of clergy, but also certain debts and contracts. Bishops usually delegated their judicial functions to officials or commissaries. The church courts were split in the 16th century into the Presbyterian or Reformed church courts (or Kirk session courts) and the secularised commissary courts (noted above). From the mid-16th century, supervision of the clergy and congregations was undertaken by senior church officials in meetings known as synods. Further details of the courts and their records are provided in the *NIPR* (151).

Scottish criminal court records

In the middle ages the King's Justiciar dealt with criminal matters (and other justiciars were appointed to assist him). The justiciars also had some civil jurisdiction until the 16th century. NAS holds the records of the justiciars and of the High Court of Justiciary, which was established in 1672 as the highest Scottish criminal court. It sat in Edinburgh and (from 1708) on circuit elsewhere in Scotland. It dealt with serious cases (murder, rape, robbery and arson), appeals from lower courts and, increasingly, business from the jurisdiction of the sheriff courts. Trials before the High Court of Justiciary (and justiciars) are reported in books of adjournal or in minute books (dating from 1576) for both Edinburgh and circuit cases. There are chronological lists of cases and some indexes. The most useful records are precognitions (a written report of the witnesses' evidence). Sinclair (1223) describes all these records and indexes, as well as records (such as lists of 19th- and 20th-century indictments) of the Lord Advocate who prosecuted serious crimes.

As in England, executions in Scotland were carried out in public until 1868 and from then inside prisons. Young (1235) is an illustrated encyclopaedia of executions in Scotland from 1750 to 1963, based primarily on newspaper accounts. It includes a biographical dictionary of the 464 men and women who were executed (and their executioners). It also describes the places of execution. You can therefore easily find information about an ancestor or relative who was executed, his offence and place of execution. For example, James Miller was executed at Gallow Hill in Aberdeen on 16 November 1753 for burglary. Miller had been whipped through the streets as a reputed thief and banished from Aberdeenshire but he was caught stealing from a house a few days later. He was convicted and condemned. After hanging, his body was saved from the surgeons (who were permitted to use bodies of criminals for dissection) by some sailors who were said to have buried Miller at sea.

Crimes such as assault or theft were usually dealt with by the sheriff courts. Their records are at NAS but a particular case can be difficult to find because of the lack of indexes. Registers or rolls note the name of an accused, the offence and the sentence. Some evidence from witnesses has also been preserved. Minor offences might also be tried in burgh or franchise courts or (from 1609) by Justices of the Peace. The NAS holdings of these records are briefly described in Sinclair (1223) but most are unindexed. Prisoners (whether guilty of crimes or debtors) may be found in surviving prison registers, many at NAS, but few commence before the mid-19th century. Prisoners who were transported to Australia were placed on ships sailing from England, so they may be recorded in English prison or hulk records at TNA.

Many records of the Jacobite rebellions of 1715 and 1745 are at TNA and reviewed in TNA domestic records leaflet 21. The State Papers Domestic of the reign of George I (series SP 35), George II (SP 36) and State Papers Scotland (SP 54) include correspondence about the rebellions, papers about the trials of Jacobites and also lists of prisoners. Records of trials are in series KB 8 of the records of the Court of King's Bench, but also in some assize, Treasury and Palatinate records. After the 1715 rebellion the government established a Forfeited Estates Commission for England. This worked until 1723, taking control of English estates forfeited by rebels' or Jacobite supporters, then surveying and selling them. The commission's records are at TNA in series FEC 1 and 2 (# chapter 24) and described in detail in a handbook (1149). The government also appointed Forfeited Estates commissioners for Scotland. The commissioners' records (and many other records of the 1715 and 1745 rebellions) are at NAS and described in Sinclair (1224).

Scottish Record Office texts and calendars and local record societies
The SRO (now NAS) texts and calendars are an important series of published transcripts and abstracts of public records concerning Scotland, mostly held at NAS but some (such as the State Papers) at TNA. The volumes are listed by Mullins (260) but include registers of the Privy

Council for Scotland from 1545 to 1691, the State Papers relating to Scotland for 1547 to 1603 and the Exchequer Rolls of Scotland (including accounts and rentals of Crown lands) from 1264 to 1600. There are also many other history and record societies in Scotland. Their publications are listed in Stevenson & Stevenson (1226).

Peerages and heraldry

Balfour-Paul (1154) describes the lineage of Scottish monarchs, each Scottish peer and also many collateral branches. The entries are indented pedigrees, in alphabetical order of titles, providing much biographical information, including each peer's education and official posts. Scots' peerages are also included in *Burke's* and *Debrett's Peerage* and similar works (# chapter 26). Some other works on Scottish peers are listed in Torrance (1228).

The use of coats of arms in Scotland has been controlled since medieval times by the Lord Lyon King of Arms and the heralds (now at New Register House). The principal difference between Scottish and English grants of arms is that a Scottish grant is only made to a man and the heirs of his body, not to all his descendants. Younger sons of an original grantee (or his heirs) cannot use their father's arms, but must apply to the Lord Lyon for the grant of a version of those arms, suitably differentiated. All persons using Scottish coats of arms have been required since 1672 to register them at the Lyon Court, in the *Public Register of all Arms and Bearings in Scotland*. Two ordinaries of Scottish arms, noting all arms registered up to 1973, have been published. More information on Scottish heraldry can be obtained from general works on heraldry (# chapter 26), from the Heraldry Society of Scotland in Edinburgh or from the detailed *Scots Heraldry* by Sir Thomas Innes of Learney (1185). This includes notes on Scottish armorial manuscripts from medieval times and on the Lord Lyon's *Public Register of Genealogies* (pedigrees, with documentary evidence, registered with the Lord Lyon). It also includes many illustrations of Scottish coats of arms, from various manuscripts, bookplates and buildings.

The clans

Adam (1152) is an essential source for information on Scottish clans. It provides a detailed description of the history, organisation and laws of the clan system as well as a map showing the homelands of the clans and lowland families. The clan system was the product of kinship, but also local defence and feudalism. The word clan was the Gaelic equivalent of family and a Scottish clan has been described as a social group of families descended (or accepting themselves as descended) from a common ancestor. Clans lived on the lands of their chief's family, owed fealty to the chief and were under his protection. A sept was a part of a clan, being a "house within a house", a family branch which retained a separate identity within the clan. Thus, clan Buchanan included the septs of Colman and Donleavy. Adam briefly describes each clan: its history, tartan, lands, culture, the origin of its name, the part it took in historical events and the armorial bearings and noteworthy members of the chief family. Different tartans for each clan probably only arose in the 18th century, as Scottish regiments in the British army adopted a particular tartan pattern to differentiate themselves from other regiments. This led to the clans from which each regiment was recruited adopting those tartans, and then other clans consequently adopting their own tartans in the late 18th or early 19th centuries. Way & Squire (1232) is another detailed work on about 300 Scottish clans, with illustrations of their tartans. Information on tartans can also be obtained from the Scottish Tartan Society which has a museum.

Museums

Scottish museums are listed and described in an HMSO booklet and in James (1186). These include the Highland Folk Museum (near Aviemore) and museums illustrating particular aspects of life, such as agricultural museums, the Scottish Fisheries Museum or the Glasgow Museum of Transport. There are also many museums of clans and Scottish army regiments, listed by Wise (692) and James (1186), such as the Royal Scots' Museum in Edinburgh Castle and the Black Watch Museum in Perth.

The Scots abroad

Emigration and records of the British abroad are reviewed in chapter 30. The Scots emigrated to all parts of the world, particularly to the Protestant plantations in Ireland (in the 17th century), to North America (in the 18th and 19th centuries) and to New Zealand and Canada (in the 19th century). Whyte (1233) is a bibliography of hundreds of works dealing with the Scots overseas.

WALES

In the early medieval period much of south and east Wales was ruled by Anglo-Norman lords (the Marcher lords) who were nominally subject to the English crown. The north and west of Wales was ruled by independent Welsh princes until it was conquered in 1282 by Edward I, formed into the Principality of Wales and divided into the shires of Anglesey, Caernarvon, Merioneth, Cardigan and Carmarthen. The administration of Wales from the 13th century to 1536, particularly by the Marcher lordships and the Council in the Marches of Wales (which had much administrative and judicial power until the 17th century), is described in detail in the *Current Guide* (234). Wales was formally united with England in 1536. The March was abolished in 1540 and seven new counties were created from it. The counties of Wales until 1974 are shown in illustration 67. From 1284, but especially after 1536, most Welsh records are very similar to English records, but ancestral research in Wales can be more difficult than in England. Rowlands (1216) is a useful collection of essays dealing with the problems. Contact details of the six principal Welsh FHS (of Dyfed, Clwyd, Gwynedd, Gwent, Powys and South Wales) are listed in the *FLHH* (5).

Names

Hereditary surnames only came into general use in Wales in the 16th and 17th centuries (even later in some areas). Before this, the Welsh used a patronymic system, whereby a son had a given name to which was added the word *mab, map, ab* or *ap* (meaning son of) and his father's given name. A man's name might also include earlier generations so that the name Thomas ab Owen might continue ab William, and so on. Girl's names incorporated *verch* (meaning daughter of), *ferch* or *ach* before the father's name. Ancestral research is difficult without a settled surname, particularly because some given names (such as John, David, Evan, Thomas and William) were so common. These given names developed into surnames (Jones, Davies, Evans, Thomas and Williams) and so research remains difficult, even in the period since surnames became commonly used, because of the prevalence of those surnames. Morgan (1206) and Rowlands (1217) review the development of Welsh surnames and explain the patronymic system, the meaning of names, their origin and the sources evidencing their earliest known use. Although church and court records were written in Latin or English, many other documents were in Welsh, or may include either Welsh or English words or names. Thus a document may refer to David or William, but alternatively record them in Welsh (as Dafydd or Gwilym). The English and Welsh names for places may be very different. Thus Newport in Pembrokeshire is Trefdraeth and Holyhead in Anglesey is Caergybi. Rowlands (1216) has chapters on place names and basic Welsh for family historians, and refers to more detailed works on these subjects.

Civil registration and census records

Wales was subject to the same civil registration system as England, but research of Welsh families is more difficult because there are so many entries for some names. The checking system is therefore more important for Welsh research. Certificates of births, marriages and deaths in Wales since 1963 have been produced in both English and Welsh. The GRO records are at the FRC in London and at district registries in Wales. A copy of the GRO indexes can also be seen at the National Library of Wales (NLW), Penglais, Aberystwyth, Dyfed SY23 3BU (telephone 01970 632800, see appendix XI for its web site).

Welsh census returns are on microfilm at the FRC, NLW and at the Welsh area record offices in Clwyd, Dyfed, Glamorgan, Gwent, Gwynedd and Powys (their addresses are listed in appendix VII). The SoG holds microfilms of the 1851 and parts of the 1841 and 1861 censuses (and various census indexes) as listed in Churchill (138). Glamorgan FHS has transcribed, indexed and published all of the censuses for the whole of the old county of Glamorgan (the indexes for 1841 and 1851 are available on CD-ROM) and some other county indexes are also available (for example Radnorshire 1841 and Montgomeryshire 1851). The 1881 and 1901 census transcriptions and indexes (# chapter 7) include the whole of Wales. The 1891 and 1901 censuses note whether people spoke Welsh. Some census returns from 1801 to 1831 that include names are listed in Gibson & Medlycott (139).

Parish registers

There were about 1,000 Anglican parishes or chapelries in Wales by 1812. These are shown on four IHGS maps which are included in the *Phillimore Atlas* (165). Welsh parish registers are similar to English registers, but a greater proportion of the older registers have been lost (only about one third of Welsh parishes have registers surviving before 1700). The English and Welsh names for each parish (including about 200 founded after 1812), their surviving registers (and their locations) are listed in volume 13 of the *NIPR* (151). Very few bishops' transcripts commence before 1660 (and only a minority before 1700). Many of the surviving registers and transcripts are at NLW and most others are at area record offices. The copy registers held by the SoG are listed in its catalogue and those held as at 1995 are listed in the SoG booklet (152).

The IGI on microfiche for Wales is divided between the pre-1974 counties. Each county section has two indexes, one for surnames and one for given names. However, entries can be difficult to find, particularly before 1813, because a person's surname may not be clear in the original source. For example, if a parish register records the baptism of William, son of John Thomas and his wife Mary, it is unclear whether William was later known as William Thomas or William John (that is William son of John). In most cases, the IGI includes such an entry, in the given names index, as William (a "son of John Thomas/Mary") and in the surname index under the surname John (as William John son of John Thomas and Mary). If you search for the baptism of a William Thomas, you will not find an entry under Thomas in the surname index. The data in the IGI in *FamilySearch* (on CD-ROM or online) is an updated version of that on microfiche and the same considerations apply to searches. You search by surname or given name (and by baptism/birth or marriage). If you search by surname, a parent search (# chapter 7) can also be made. Boyd's marriage index does not cover Wales, but there are some Welsh marriage indexes, listed in Gibson & Hampson (141). For example, Glamorgan FHS has published a microfiche index to marriages from all surviving Glamorgan parish registers and bishops' transcripts from 1538 to 1837. R. James has produced a CD-ROM of indexes of Welsh genealogical material that includes marriage indexes for Cardiganshire and Pembrokeshire (1813–37) and Carmarthenshire (1754–1837) with an index to 39,000 wills proved in St David's Diocese (1564–1858). The disk was reviewed in *Family Tree Magazine* (April 1998). The National Burial Index includes some entries for Wales and indexes to some marriages and burials in Wales are also included in databases on the FFHS web site *FamilyHistoryOnline*. A few other transcripts and indexes of Welsh parish registers that are available online are listed in Raymond (167a).

Non-conformists
Non-conformity was widespread in Wales, particularly from the late 18th century. The Welsh Calvinistic Methodists (later the Presbyterian Church of Wales), the Congregationalists (who had about 500 chapels by 1850) and the Countess of Huntingdon's Connection were especially popular. Most non-conformist registers are at NLW or at TNA and the FRC (and NLW also has microfilm copies of those registers). Welsh non-conformist registers in series RG 4 and 8 at TNA are listed in List and Index Society volume 266, with the name of the chapel, the type of event recorded (baptisms, births, marriages or burials) and the years covered. Ifans (1184) lists the covering years (and location) of surviving registers of about 1,350 Welsh non-conformist chapels (out of the 5,500 known to have existed), with entries arranged by pre-1974 county and then alphabetically by the Welsh name of the chapel's location (English names for these places are also noted). Clifford (319) lists Congregational chapels, surviving registers and their location. Leary (336) lists the registers of Welsh Methodist chapels that are held by TNA and the copy registers held by the SoG. Catholic missions in Wales and surviving registers are listed in Volume 3 of Gandy (324) and published works on Welsh Catholics are listed in Gandy (1171). Records of Welsh Quakers are at the FRC or Friends House in London. In addition to preparative and monthly meetings, there were three quarterly meetings in Wales (for North Wales, South Wales and for Monmouthshire) and a Welsh yearly meeting from 1688.

Probate records
Wills and administrations of Welsh people since 1858 are at First Avenue House (# chapter 12), but NLW has copies for all Welsh counties except Montgomeryshire (copies of which are at Shropshire Record Office). Wales was in the province of Canterbury and so wills of Welsh people could be proved in the PCC before 1858. There were four Welsh dioceses (St Asaph, Bangor, St Davids and Llandaff), each of which had a consistory court. There were also some archdeaconry courts (such as that for the Archdeaconry of Brecon) and one peculiar, that of Hawarden. Camp (280) and Gibson (291) list the church courts, their surviving records and indexes. Wills proved in the church courts in Wales before 1858 are at NLW or, for some border areas, at the CRO of adjoining English counties, because some English dioceses included parts of Wales. The Diocese of Chester included parts of Denbighshire and Flintshire, Lichfield Diocese included part of Flintshire and Hereford Diocese included parts of Montgomeryshire, Radnorshire and Monmouthshire. Most wills at NLW have been indexed. The Mormons have

also produced a microfiche *Abstracts and Indexes of Wills* proved until 1858 in the Welsh consistory courts, indexing the names of testators, witnesses and legatees. The indexes and other probate material for Wales held at the SoG are listed in Newington-Irving (297). Other records of the church courts are at NLW and listed, by diocese, in NLW's published guide (1144). These include bishops' registers, marriage bonds and allegations, act books and ordination papers.

Directories, newspapers, maps and tax records

Directories of Wales before 1856 are listed with their locations in Norton (211) and those from 1850 to 1950 are listed in Shaw & Tipper (212). Six directories and all known Welsh book subscription lists up to 1830 are included on part 3 of the *Biography database* on CD-ROM. Weekly newspapers were founded in Swansea and Carmarthen in 1804 and 1810 respectively. English language local newspapers are held at the British Newspaper Library at Colindale, NLW, area record offices or libraries, and are listed (with covering dates and locations) in Gibson, Langston & Smith (484). Those newspapers in Welsh are catalogued at each archive.

Surviving poll books and their location are listed in Gibson & Rogers (485) and surviving electoral registers since 1832 are listed in Gibson & Rogers (483), most being held in area record offices or at NLW. Lewis produced a topographical dictionary of Wales in 1833, in similar form to his work for England (# chapter 16). Maps of Wales are described in an essay (with detailed bibliography) by R. Davies in Wallis (407), which also summarises the holdings of maps in Welsh archives and libraries. Hearth tax, marriage tax, other tax records and association oath rolls are at TNA, NLW or area record offices. The records since 1660 (and published copies) are noted in Gibson (890). Land tax records and tithe apportionments are held by NLW or area record offices and listed in Gibson, Medlycott & Mills (892).

Education

Records of education in Wales are described by D. Pretty in Rowlands (1216). Many grammar schools were founded in Wales in the 16th and 17th centuries but few records of pupils at these schools survive from before the late 18th century. Later records of these schools (and of church, charity and state schools founded in later centuries) can be found using the finding aids noted in chapter 19. One should also search for the children of Welsh families at English schools and universities. One published source of particular importance is the calendar (published annually) of the University of Wales, founded in 1893. For example, the calendar for 1939–40 (1151) lists the students then attending the University of Wales, examination results of previous years, and those students (still living) who had graduated from the university since its foundation.

Military and occupational records

Welsh soldiers will be found in army records at TNA, particularly in the records of Welsh regiments. Gibson & Dell (631) list surviving Tudor and Stuart muster rolls for Wales (mostly at TNA but some at the British Library or NLW). Militia records from 1757 to 1876 are at TNA, area record offices or NLW and listed in Gibson & Medlycott (632). A series of detailed books on the Welsh militia from 1757 to 1908 is being produced. Thus Owen (1211) is a history and list of archives for each militia or volunteer unit of Anglesey and Caernarvonshire during this period, with photographs, details of units' uniforms, some lists of officers and muster rolls or militia lists. Military museums in Wales are listed in Wise (692) and an HMSO booklet describes all Welsh museums.

Welsh occupational records can generally be found in the sources noted in chapter 22. Coalmining was particularly important in Wales and the archives that hold records of Welsh coal mines and miners are listed by Tonks (872a). The South Wales Coalfield Collection at the University of Swansea, described in the 2002 edition of the *FLHH* (5), preserves oral and written evidence of coal miners and mining in South Wales, including photographs, interview tapes, records of trade unions, mine inspectors and of a few collieries, as well as an indexed register of fatal accidents 1934–41.

Law and order

Following the conquest of Wales in 1282, justice in the Principality was administered by royal governors through Great Sessions in each county. In the rest of Wales, the Marcher lords had their own courts. The monarch was represented in the Marches by the Council in the Marches, which also had its own court, dealing with some civil cases as well as criminal cases, particularly those relating to public order. This court's operations were suspended from 1642 to 1660 and it was abolished in 1689. The few surviving records of these Sessions or March courts at TNA are described in the *Current Guide* (234). Following the union of England and Wales in 1536, the March was abolished (in 1540) and a new system of justice was established. Justices of the Peace were appointed to deal with minor criminal cases at Quarter Sessions. Surviving records (similar to those in England) are in area record offices or at NLW (for example, order books of 1647–75 for Denbighshire). A Court of Great Sessions was also established for the whole of Wales except Monmouthshire (which was added to an English assize circuit). The Court of Great Sessions applied English law and operated until 1830 on four circuits: Brecon (covering Brecon, Glamorgan and Radnor), Carmarthen (for Cardigan, Carmarthen and Pembroke), Chester (Flint, Denbigh and Montgomery) and North Wales (Anglesey, Caernarvon and Merioneth). Sessions took place twice a year in each county. The court had jurisdiction over all criminal offences and could hear those civil cases that, in England, were dealt with by the courts of King's Bench and Common Pleas. It also had an equity jurisdiction although few equity cases were heard because the Court of the Council in the Marches and the English Chancery and Exchequer Courts also had jurisdiction in Wales and they were considered better courts for important cases. The Court of King's Bench also began to take jurisdiction in Wales in the late 18th century. Civil business in the Court of Great Sessions then diminished and Welsh litigants increasingly used London courts. Appeals from the Court of Great Sessions lay to the Court of King's Bench (for actions concerning real property) and to the Court of the Council in the Marches and later to the House of Lords (in personal actions).

Many records of the Court of Great Sessions have been lost but those that survive are at NLW. They are similar in form to English legal records and generally in Latin until 1732. They are listed (with covering dates) in Hawkings (984) and reviewed in detail, with class lists, in Parry (1212). The most important records of criminal cases are the gaol files. These include indictments (with details of the accused and the alleged offence), lists of jurors, calendars of prisoners (some including verdicts and sentences), recognizances (binding victims or witnesses to appear at court or forfeit a sum of money), coroners' inquests, examinations of the accused and depositions of victims and witnesses.

Many pleadings in civil actions (and some judgments) were recorded on the plea rolls. Docket rolls contain entries for civil cases tried or pending at each session, with some judgments, and so can be used as indexes to those civil cases. Writs, pleas and other documents from civil cases are also in the papers of the Prothonotary (chief clerk). Pleadings in equity cases are listed in bill books and filed with any affidavits, interrogatories and depositions for the same case. The outcome of equity cases is noted in order, minute and decree books. Docket books also act as indexes to actions for fines and recoveries (property transactions dressed up as civil disputes). The court's files include feet of fines, enrolments of fines and recoveries and final concords (agreements that brought actions for fines to an end). In the case of recoveries, pleadings and judgments were enrolled on the plea rolls. The Court of Great Sessions also heard petitions for release from imprisoned insolvent debtors. Some petitions, inventories and notices to creditors are in the gaol files and the Prothonotary papers. The records also include admissions of lawyers to practise in the court (admission and oath rolls, articles of clerkship and affidavits).

As noted, many Welsh litigants used the English courts before 1830 and so Welsh ancestors should also be sought in the records of those courts, particularly Chancery, Exchequer and King's Bench (# chapter 24). Four published finding aids for Welsh cases in English civil courts should be noted. Jones (1188) contains abstracts of pleadings of 1542–1603 concerning Wales in the Court of Exchequer (abstracts for 1603–25 have also been published). Lewis (1191) summarises Chancery pleadings concerning Wales up to 1558 and Davies (1163) lists the parties in Chancery actions of 1558–1714 that concern Montgomeryshire. Lewis & Davies (1192) describe the records of the Court of Augmentations (that administered and sold monasteries' land from 1536 to 1554) relating to Wales and Monmouthshire and include abstracts of proceedings and property leases.

The Court of Great Sessions was abolished in 1830. From that date, most civil actions involving Welsh litigants will be found in the records of the English courts (# chapter 24). Welsh counties were also included in the English assize system as the North and South Wales circuit (but split into two divisions in 1876). Welsh assize records since 1830 are at TNA (in series ASSI 57–77) and described by Hawkings (984).

Most Quarter Sessions' records (a few as early as 1541) and borough courts' records are in area record offices. They also hold some prison registers, listed in Hawkings (984) and coroners' records, listed in Gibson & Rogers (977).

Family records
NLW also holds large collections of title deeds, estate records and family papers. These are briefly described (but with references to more detailed catalogues and lists at NLW) in the NLW guide (1144), with entries arranged by family name or place. Early manuscript records, especially many medieval pedigrees, are in Welsh, but many have been published by the University of Wales Press. Detailed articles by F. Jones in the 1948 volume of *Transactions of the Honourable Society of Cymmrodorion* and by M. Siddons in Rowlands (1216) describe many manuscripts, dating from between 1100 and 1700, containing pedigrees of Welsh princes and gentry. More recent ancestors who were noteworthy may also be found in *The Dictionary of Welsh Biography* or in editions (published in 1921, 1933 and 1937) of *Who's Who in Wales*.

IRELAND

In medieval times Ireland was divided into five kingdoms. The English invaded in the 12th century and gained full control of Ireland in the reign of Henry VIII. English monarchs then styled themselves Kings of Ireland. Substantial Protestant settlements were established in the 17th century and Ireland was formally united to Great Britain by the Act of Union of 1801. The six counties of Northern Ireland (Antrim, Armagh, Down, Fermanagh, Londonderry and Tyrone), shown in the map at illustration 143, remain part of the United Kingdom and the other 26 counties have since 1922 formed Eire or the Republic of Ireland. Research in Ireland is difficult because of the loss of many records in 1922 (at the Four Courts in Dublin, then the location of the Irish Public Record Office), but most sources remain available for researchers.

Irish records are generally similar to those of England. British administration in Ireland up to 1922, described in the *Current Guide* (234) and Prochaska (1213), was the responsibility of both the Lord Lieutenant and his officials in Dublin (headed by a Chief Secretary) and, from 1801, the British cabinet and civil service. Many records of Irish ancestors are therefore held in Britain, particularly at TNA. Those at TNA are described by Prochaska (1213) and many of these have been considered in earlier chapters. Researchers with Irish ancestors will find useful material in the records of the army (particularly of Irish regiments and militia), naval or merchant seamen, PCC wills and administrations, death duty registers, Crown estates (for property in Ireland), the Irish tontines, registers of the Privy Council and the records of the Chancery (particularly the Close, Charter and Patent Rolls). From the early 16th century, the State Papers included much material about Irish affairs (for example those in series SP 60–63, 65 and 67). They are described in TNA domestic records leaflet 25. Calendars of State Papers relating to Ireland have been published in HMSO volumes listed by Mullins (260). TNA holds a few series of particular relevance to Irish ancestors and these are considered below. There are also important manuscript collections relating to Irish genealogy at the British, Bodleian and Lambeth Palace libraries, described by C.R. Humphery-Smith in *Family Tree Magazine* (April 1990).

There are many excellent guides to Irish genealogical records. Grenham (1176) and Ryan (1218) are the best modern guides. They provide detailed lists of sources such as census returns, estate records, directories, MIs and local history books. Ryan (1218) also includes illustrations of many important Irish records, lists of family history societies and many maps of assistance to researchers. Falley (1168) is also a very detailed work which, although out of date in some respects, provides an excellent analysis of many records that are only briefly noted in most books (for example manuscript collections and published or unpublished family histories). Falley also includes detailed bibliographies of published works containing genealogical material, such as biographical dictionaries, local histories, school registers, directories and publications of the Irish Manuscripts Commission. Maxwell (1200) is a detailed guide to research in Northern Ireland. Camp (1161) lists the SoG's holdings of Irish records and transcripts, particularly its extensive collection of published works. Raymond (1215) and an article by J. Grenham in *Ancestors* (February/March 2003) list Internet sources for Ireland and researchers should also search the extensive pages for Irish counties and parishes on GENUKI (# chapter 11). Yurdan (1236) includes background to the 19th-century famines and Irish emigration. Helferty & Refausse (1181) provide brief descriptions of the holdings of 249 Irish archives and museums (and their addresses, telephone numbers, web sites and opening hours). An HMSO booklet describes the museums in Ireland.

People and places
Sexton (1221) contains almost 200 photographs of Irish people (and of houses your Irish ancestors would have lived in) between 1840 and 1930. Useful lists and studies of Irish surnames are contained in MacLysaght (1195–1197), which also provide biographical information on

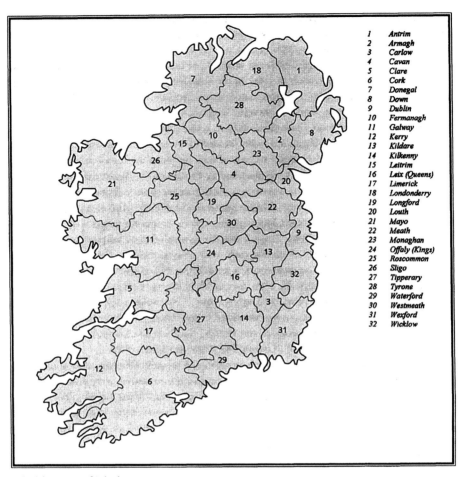

1	*Antrim*
2	*Armagh*
3	*Carlow*
4	*Cavan*
5	*Clare*
6	*Cork*
7	*Donegal*
8	*Down*
9	*Dublin*
10	*Fermanagh*
11	*Galway*
12	*Kerry*
13	*Kildare*
14	*Kilkenny*
15	*Leitrim*
16	*Leix (Queens)*
17	*Limerick*
18	*Londonderry*
19	*Longford*
20	*Louth*
21	*Mayo*
22	*Meath*
23	*Monaghan*
24	*Offaly (Kings)*
25	*Roscommon*
26	*Sligo*
27	*Tipperary*
28	*Tyrone*
29	*Waterford*
30	*Westmeath*
31	*Wexford*
32	*Wicklow*

143. The counties of Ireland

famous people with the surnames listed. The CD-ROM entitled *Grenham's Irish Surnames*, by J. Grenham, includes information on 27,000 Irish surnames, including their geographical distribution. The biographical works such as the *DNB* reviewed in chapter 26 include many Irish people. In addition, Boylan (1158) contains biographies of about 1,000 distinguished Irish men and women. Clare (1162) is a useful list of published family histories.

The four Irish provinces (Ulster, Connaught, Leinster and Munster) were divided into 32 counties, which were subdivided into 325 baronies. These were sub-divided into about 2,450 (Anglican) parishes. These parishes were sub-divided into about 64,000 townlands (a parish might contain 25 to 30 townlands). A townland originated from a family's holding of land and might vary in size from ten to thousands of acres. A townland did not necessarily contain a town (and sometimes had no population at all). Some names were used for many different places and so it may be difficult to find where an ancestor lived even if you know the name of the place. An important reference work for Irish research is therefore the *Alphabetical Index to the Townlands and Towns, Parishes and Baronies of Ireland* (also known as the Townland Index) a number of editions of which were compiled in the late 19th century. This lists all townlands or towns and gives the county, barony, parish and poor law union in which they were situated. The Townland Index is held at many archives and the 1861 version has been reprinted by GPC (and a copy has also been published on the Internet). GPC also publishes *A New Genealogical Atlas of Ireland* by B. Mitchell which contains maps showing the location of counties, dioceses, baronies and civil parishes and the areas of jurisdiction of civil probate registries and poor law unions.

Civil registration

Civil registration commenced on 1 April 1845 for Protestant marriages and on 1 January 1864 for all births, marriages and deaths. Registration districts in Ireland were based, as in England, on the poor law unions. Civil registration entries are in similar form to England and Wales. Records are held by the Registrar General at Joyce House, 8–11 Lombard Street East, Dublin 2 (telephone Dublin (00 353 1) 6354000), except for birth, marriage and death records for Northern Ireland since 1 January 1922, which are held by the Registrar General of Northern Ireland at Oxford House, 49–55 Chichester Street, Belfast BT1 4HL (telephone 02890 252000). The Registrar General in Belfast also holds copies of the indexes for births (in what is now Northern Ireland) since 1864. Certificates can be ordered online from the Registrar's web site but you need the full references from the indexes. The FRC in London has a computer link to the index of births (only) in Northern Ireland, 1922–92 but an application form (and fee) must still be sent to Belfast to obtain a certificate. In both Dublin and Belfast a daily fee is payable to search the indexes and further fees are charged for certificates. In Dublin one can order a certificate of a register entry or (at far less cost) a print from a microfiche copy of the registers. Postal applications for index searches or certificates can be made to both Dublin and Belfast. The index volumes each cover one year from 1864 to 1877, but are quarterly thereafter, except for births which revert to annual volumes from 1903, when the mother's maiden surname is also listed. Special care is required if you are researching names with a number of variations (such as Reilly, Riley and O'Reilly), since prefixes such as O or Mac may have been omitted. The BVRI (# chapter 7) includes births of 1865–74 and Protestant marriages of 1847–64 from the Irish civil registration indexes. Copies of the Irish indexes to births, marriages and deaths 1864 to 1959 can also be seen at the LDS Hyde Park Family History Centre in London.

The Registrar General in Dublin holds other useful registers, such as those for adopted children (since 1953); births at sea to Irish parents (since 1864), deaths at sea of Irish-born persons (1864–1921) and British Consulate records of Irish births and deaths abroad (1864–1921). The Registrar General in Belfast also holds registers of marine births and deaths (since 1922); adopted children (since 1931); war deaths (1939–48) and British Consulate records of births, marriages and deaths abroad (since 1922).

Census records

A census was taken in Ireland every 10 years from 1821 until 1911. A census was also taken in 1926 and will hopefully become available to the public in the near future. All census records for 1861 to 1891 were destroyed by the government. Only a few sections of the census returns for 1821 to 1851 survived the 1922 fire. They are held at the National Archives (the new name for the Public Record Office) at Bishop Street, Dublin (telephone Dublin (00 353 1) 4072300).

These sections (and abstracts or transcripts of the lost records) are listed in Grenham (1176) and Gibson & Medlycott (139). They include some lists of inhabitants' names in 1821 and 1831 since (in contrast to England and Wales at that time) the authorities required all names to be listed.

The census records of 1901 and 1911, covering what is now Eire and Northern Ireland are also open to the public at the National Archives. The returns are arranged by poor law union, then district electoral division, parish and townland. Indexes at the National Archives list the district electoral divisions (and the townlands in each division). The returns that the public view are the household schedules (completed by the head of household or the enumerator) since they were not copied into enumerators' books. They do not record people's exact birthplace, but only the city, county or country (other than Ireland) of birth. The schedules do, however, provide people's names, age, sex, religion, marital status and relationship to the head of the household. They also note whether a person could read or write. The 1911 census required married women to state how long they had been married, the number of children born to them (and the number still living). An index to the 1901 census is being prepared by Largy Books of Canada and the volumes for Fermanagh and Tyrone are held at the National Archives and the SoG.

The National Archives and the Public Record Office of Northern Ireland (PRONI) at 66 Balmoral Avenue, Belfast BT9 6NY (telephone 02890 255905), hold records of applications for old age pensions made from 1908 to 1922. The applicants were born before civil registration of births commenced (in 1864) and so were allowed to use abstracts of searches (undertaken by government officials) from the census records of 1841 and 1851 in order to prove their age. If your ancestor applied for a pension in this period, it is possible that an extract from the lost census records concerning his family has survived with the application. The abstracts include 29,000 people and have been transcribed and indexed in Masterson (1199).

Church registers
Although the majority of people were Catholic, the Anglican Church of Ireland was the official church in Ireland until 1869. Its parishes were organised into 31 dioceses. Its ministers were only required to record baptisms and burials from 1634 and most surviving registers only commence in the late 18th century. Furthermore, over half of the Church of Ireland registers were deposited by 1922 at the PRO in Dublin and most of them were destroyed in the 1922 fire. Fortunately, some Anglican registers, as well as many Catholic and non-conformist registers, had not been deposited (and some transcripts survive for those that were lost). Most surviving Anglican registers (for parishes now in Eire) are in the Representative Church Body Library, Braemor Park, Churchtown, Dublin (telephone Dublin (00 353 1) 4923979, see appendix XI for its web site), and listed, with covering dates, in Neill (1209). The registers of Ulster are held in a number of locations but copies of all surviving registers are available on microfilm at PRONI. Mitchell (1203) lists the surviving registers (for all religious denominations) for each parish, with commencement dates and locations. Thus, for the civil parish of St Mary's, Kilkenny, the Anglican and Catholic registers commence in 1729 and 1754 respectively and there are also Presbyterian, Methodist and Quaker registers. The copy registers held by the SoG are listed in Camp (1161). An Irish FHS booklet (1140) lists the available indexes to Irish parish registers. The Irish section of the IGI contains about two million entries from surviving registers (or copies).

Although incumbents should have sent transcripts of registers to the bishop, this requirement was rarely observed (and most of the returns were destroyed in 1922). The few surviving transcripts are reviewed in an article in *Irish Roots* (1995, number 3).

Catholic and Anglican parishes often had different names. Catholic parishes (there were about 1,040) were also generally larger than Anglican parishes and many new Catholic parishes were founded in the early 19th century. Grenham (1176) includes maps of each county in Ireland, showing the Catholic dioceses and parishes as at about 1800 with lists of the dates and locations of surviving Catholic registers. Catholic registers were not so badly depleted by the 1922 fire as the Anglican registers but they are also very incomplete since Catholic priests were not required to keep registers. Persecution of Catholics for many years also dissuaded many priests from recording their parishioners' names. Although some Catholic registers date from the late 17th century, most do not commence until about 1830 and only about 20% of Catholic parishes kept burial registers. Catholic baptismal registers often include the mother's maiden name. Most Catholic registers are still held by the church, but most surviving registers up to 1880 are on microfilm at the National Library of Ireland, Kildare Street, Dublin (telephone Dublin (00 353 1) 6030200).

Many Presbyterian, Methodist, Quaker and other non-conformist records have also survived. The Presbyterian Church in Ireland was established in the 17th century, principally by Scots arriving as settlers, but faced legal restrictions until the 19th century (Presbyterian ministers were prohibited from performing marriages until 1782). Registers were unfortunately not kept by many congregations until about 1820. Surviving registers are held by the congregations or by the Presbyterian Historical Society at Church House, Fisherwick Place, Belfast BT1 6DW (telephone 02890 322284) which also holds church minute books and records of Presbyterian clergy. Microfilm copies of many Presbyterian registers are also at PRONI. Falley (1168) provides a detailed review of Presbyterian records and lists surviving Presbyterian registers, manuscript records and published works on the church and its ministers. A useful article on the Presbyterian Church also appears in *Family Tree Magazine* (March 1988). The Presbyterian Historical Society publishes a directory of the names and addresses of Presbyterian clergy.

The Methodist church established chapels from about 1820 and still holds most of its records. The earliest register dates from 1816 but there are few burial registers since Methodists were generally buried in Anglican churchyards and recorded in Anglican burial registers. Falley (1168) provides a detailed review of Irish Methodists, their records and published sources. There were also a few Baptist and Congregational chapels in Ireland and most of their records remain in their ministers' custody (some are at PRONI). Many Huguenots arrived in Ireland in the 17th century and much material about Huguenots in Ireland has been published by the Huguenot Society (# chapter 13). The first Quaker meeting in Ireland was established in 1654. Goodbody (1174) describes Irish Quaker records (which are similar to those in England). Most are held at the library of the Society of Friends, Swanbrook House, Morehampton Road, Donnybrook, Dublin, but PRONI holds many Quaker records for those areas now in Northern Ireland. Quaker registers of births, marriages and burials date from the 17th century although they are incomplete. There are detailed records of meetings, membership, finance, property and schools. Goodbody (1174) also describes the manuscript collections, diaries, pedigrees and abstracts of wills in the Quaker archives. Harrison (1180a) is a biographical dictionary of about 300 noteworthy Irish Quakers. Irish Quaker births and marriages 1850–75 are included in the BVRI.

Directories

Directories of Dublin were published from the mid-18th century and a directory for Limerick was published in 1769. The number of town or city directories then increased rapidly. Directories for Ireland as a whole commenced with Pigot's commercial directory in 1820, followed by Slater's and Thom's directories. Falley (1168) lists the surviving directories for Northern Ireland (and the archives holding them) and also lists many directories for the rest of Ireland. The largest collection is at the National Library but the SoG also has a large collection, listed in Camp (1161).

Monumental inscriptions
The loss of many parish registers has resulted in Irish MIs (and the birth, marriage and death notices in newspapers) becoming of greater importance. Many transcripts of MIs have been published and are listed in Grenham (1176), most importantly in the *Journal of the Association for the Preservation of the Memorials of the Dead in Ireland* (published 1888–1934) and in *Gravestone Inscriptions* for Ulster (in 28 volumes published by the Ulster Historical Foundation). Catholics were sometimes buried in Protestant graveyards, so you should check the records of all local burial grounds.

Probate records
Until 1858 probate was dealt with by the Church of Ireland's courts, that is, in a consistory court for each diocese or, if there was property in more than one diocese, in the Prerogative Court of the Diocese of Armagh. There were no archdeaconry courts and only a few peculiar courts. Many wealthier testators also had property in England, Wales or Scotland and the probate records in those jurisdictions, especially the PCC records, should be consulted. Most wills (and other probate records) of the Irish church courts up to 1857 were lost in the 1922 fire. In 1858 testamentary jurisdiction was transferred to civil courts, consisting of the Probate Court (and a central Principal Registry) in Dublin and 11 district registries. Since 1922 the district registry in Belfast has been the Principal Registry for Northern Ireland. Clerks at district registries made transcripts of wills and letters of administration in will books, and then sent the original wills and admons to the Principal Registry in Dublin. Most of the latter's records were destroyed in 1922, but wills proved since 1922 are available and calendars of all wills proved (and admons granted) since 1858 survive at the National Archives and PRONI. These note a deceased's name, address and occupation, the date and place of death, the estate's value and the executors' or administrators' names and addresses.

Copies or abstracts of up to one-third of the lost wills may have survived. The district registry transcripts of wills and administrations (for 1858 to 1922) are at the National Archives, except for those from the district registries of areas now in Northern Ireland (that is, the registries of Belfast, Armagh and Londonderry), which are at PRONI. Many surviving indexes of wills and of administration bonds (for the period prior to 1858) are listed in Falley (1168) and Gibson & Churchill (291). One important survival is the series of abstracts of about 37,500 Prerogative Court wills up to 1800 made by Sir William Betham, Ulster King of Arms, which are held by the National Archives. About 7,500 wills also survive in the manuscript collections of the Genealogical Office (described below) and an index to these wills has been published by the Irish Manuscripts Commission.

The National Archives and PRONI have also tried to replace some of the lost probate records by collecting (from family or solicitors' archives) many wills, grants of probate and letters of administration for the period up to 1922 (including many wills that were not proved) and many abstracts or transcripts made before 1922. The National Archives hold over 20,000 items (in addition to the Betham abstracts) to which there is an index. PRONI holds about 5,000 wills which have also been indexed. There are some other collections. A few medieval wills and inventories survive, from the Consistory Court of Dublin, in the library of Trinity College, Dublin. Friends House in Dublin also holds copies of many Quakers' wills from the 17th and 18th centuries. The English Inland Revenue made transcripts or abstracts of many Irish wills and administrations from 1828 to 1839 and indexes are held by the National Archives. Because of their importance in proving ownership of land, copies of wills were also lodged, until about 1832, at a Registry of Deeds (considered below). Indexed abstracts of about 2,100 wills deposited at this registry from 1708 to 1832 are included in Eustace (1167). Estate papers were deposited with the Land Commission (the records of which are at the National Archives) for land that was being sold pursuant to various Land Acts since 1870. These papers contain about 10,000 wills dating from before 1858 and an index to them is available at the National Archives, the National Library and at PRONI. An index to the testamentary records of 1484–1858 held at the National Archives can be consulted on the web site of Irish Origins (# appendix XI). Further details of surviving probate records and abstracts or transcripts of the lost records are provided by Grenham (1176). The large collection of Irish will indexes, abstracts and other probate material at the SoG is listed in Newington-Irving (297) and Camp (1161).

Marriage and divorce
Many marriage licence records were destroyed in 1922. However, indexes survive at the National Archives for the Prerogative Court and for all dioceses (except Derry). These usually note the date of the bond and the names of the bride and groom. There are also abstracts (made before 1922) of many marriage licence bonds. The surviving records are listed in Gibson (367) and the indexes held at the SoG are listed in its booklet (356). The civil form of divorce introduced in England and Wales in 1858 did not extend to Ireland. Those in Ireland who wanted a divorce (or the right to separate from a spouse) could only continue to apply to the church courts or obtain a private Act of Parliament. Civil divorce was introduced in Northern Ireland in 1939.

Maps, newspapers and elections
Lewis produced a topographical dictionary for Ireland in 1837, in similar form to that for England (# chapter 16) and this has been reprinted by GPC (and has also been produced on CD-ROM). An essay by Andrews & Ferguson, in Wallis (407), briefly describes the maps of Ireland and provides a detailed bibliography. Ordnance Survey maps were produced in the 19th century, including those at a scale of six inches to the mile between 1841 and 1855. Wallis (407) also briefly describes the maps held at over 30 Irish archives or libraries.

The *Dublin Gazette*, containing similar information for Ireland as the *London Gazette*, was published from 1705. Birth, marriage and death notices (as well as business advertisements and court reports) appear in national and local newspapers. Large collections of Irish newspapers are held at the National Library, the British Newspaper Library and at PRONI (and are listed on their web sites). A few newsletters or journals were published in the late 17th century and there were six newspapers in Dublin by 1710; provincial papers soon followed in places such as Limerick (in 1716) and Waterford (1729). Belfast had its own newspapers in the late 17th century but the earliest surviving copies are for the *Belfast Newsletter* (first published in 1737). Munter (1207) describes the early Irish press and lists 172 Irish newspapers up to 1750, with the location of surviving copies. Libraries' holdings of Irish newspapers are listed in a report for Ireland of the British Library's Newsplan project (# chapter 17) by Smyth (1225) and a useful list of indexes to Irish newspapers is provided by Grenham (1176). The newspapers of Northern Ireland since 1737 are listed in a booklet (1147) published by PRONI and the Library Association. Most 18th- and 19th-century poll books for Ireland were destroyed in 1922, but those surviving for Ulster, Leinster, Munster and Connacht for 1832–72 are listed in Walker & Hoppen (1229). Surviving poll books of the 18th and 19th centuries that are held at PRONI are listed in Maxwell (1200). Electoral registers since 1872 are held at PRONI and the National Library. Lists of freemen in the 18th century survive for many boroughs or cities such as Dublin. The records at Dublin City Archives, at City Assembly House, 58 South William Street, Dublin 2 (telephone Dublin (00 353 1) 6775877), are described in the 2002 edition of the *FLHH* (5). They include the city's freedom records, property deeds, accounts, court records and charity petitions.

Records of the poor
Irish parish records are not as extensive as those of England but some records survive at the National Archives and PRONI. For example, vestry records survive for some towns and cities (and a few rural parishes) and these list parish officials and those who contributed money for relief of the poor. Those for the parish of St John the Evangelist, Dublin, 1595–1658 have been published. Some minutes of Presbyterian Church sessions refer to baptisms, marriages, deaths, emigrants, pew rents or mention the crimes or sins of church members.

Ireland suffered heavily from poverty and food shortages from the 17th to 19th centuries. Famines occurred regularly but the worst was the Great Famine of 1845–49 when about one million people died. Many records survive concerning poor relief granted by the Boards of Guardians of the 137 poor law unions and the operation of workhouses (established by the Irish Poor Law Act of 1838). As a result of the poverty and distress suffered in Ireland in the mid-19th century, these records cover a much greater proportion of the population than in England. The extent of the Great Famine was such that workhouses could not cope and so much outdoor relief was granted in the form of money or food. Union records at PRONI and the National Archives include admission and discharge registers, indoor relief lists and punishment books.

Education
Education in Ireland is reviewed by Chapman (551). The registers of students at Trinity College, Dublin (founded in 1593) up to 1860 have been published in *Alumni Dublinenses* by Burtchaell & Sadleir (1160). Annual calendars of Queen's University, Belfast have been published since 1851. Other published registers and calendars of Irish universities are reviewed by J. Titford in *Family Tree Magazine* (December 1998). There are some published registers of schools dating from as early as the 17th century, such as Londonderry Free Grammar School and Kilkenny School. There are also some published registers of independent and charity schools dating from the 18th century. A national primary education system was established in 1831 and many registers of these schools survive, listing the names and ages of pupils, fathers' addresses, occupations and religions. In most of Eire, these registers are still held by the schools, but many from schools in Northern Ireland are held at PRONI.

Military and occupational records
Many Irishmen served in British army regiments and so army records (particularly for Irish regiments) at TNA at Kew should be consulted. The Royal Kilmainham Hospital for army pensioners was opened in 1684. Its records are at TNA in series WO 118 and 119 (and indexed).

There are admission books (1759–1863) and discharge records (1783–1822) for in-pensioners, with personal details and information on a soldier's service. The responsibility for paying Kilmainham's out-pensioners was transferred in 1922 to the Royal Hospital at Chelsea and records of pensions paid in Irish districts are in the district pension returns in WO 22. TNA also holds (with code AP) the records of a trust founded in 1922 to provide cottages or land in Ireland for men who had served in the armed forces in the First World War. These records are described in Prochaska (1213) and contain correspondence, minutes, registers of properties and accounts. Many records of the Irish militia (from 1793 to 1876) are at TNA in series WO 13. A few are in the National Archives in Dublin or at PRONI. Surviving Tudor and Stuart muster rolls for Ireland, mostly held at the British Library but some at PRONI, are listed in Gibson & Dell (631). Many Irishmen can also be found in the records of the Royal Navy and merchant marine (# chapter 21).

The Irish Constabulary (renamed the Royal Irish Constabulary in 1867) was created in 1836 from groups of part-time policemen. Almost 84,000 men served in the force until it was disbanded in 1922. Records of the constabulary are at TNA at Kew and described in TNA domestic records leaflet 54 and in Herlihy (1183), which also lists about 3,000 of those men (with brief biographies) who were awarded medals, wounded or killed in the course of their service. There are detailed service records in series HO 184, with registers containing names, ages, religion, trade, native county, dates of appointment, promotions, retirement or death. The registers are arranged by service number but there are surname indexes. Copies of the registers and indexes can also be seen at the National Archives and LDS family history centres. Lists of RIC officers were published from 1840 to 1921, noting where they were stationed. Copies are held at the National Library and the British Library. Pension records are at TNA in series PMG 48. TNA also has detailed records of customs officers in Ireland, particularly in series CUST 20 and 39, including salary books or establishment lists from the 17th century up to 1922.

Men who have held senior offices in Ireland, such as lord lieutenants, governors, other crown and government ministers, judges, bishops and deans, from medieval times to the 1880s are listed in Ockerby (843). R. Refausse described the sources for Church of Ireland clergy in *Genealogists' Magazine* (June 2002). Particularly important are succession lists for most dioceses with biographies of the clergy in each parish, many of which have been published (unpublished manuscripts for other volumes are in the Representative Church Body Library). Most of these clergy attended Trinity College, Dublin and so are noted in its published registers. Information about clergymen can also be obtained from *The Catholic Directory, Almanack and Registry*, issued annually since 1836 or the *Irish Church Directory*, listing Anglican clergymen, published annually since 1862. Grenham (1176) lists detailed sources of information on the other professions. Ball (1154a) is a biographical dictionary of the judges who served in Ireland from 1221 to 1921, many of whom trained at the Inns of Court in London (and many were from English families). Records of limited companies registered in Ireland are at the Companies Registration Office of Northern Ireland, at IDB House, 64 Chichester Street, Belfast, or at the National Archives in Dublin. Railway company archives for Northern Ireland are held at PRONI, the companies being listed by Richards (854). TNA also holds records of some Irish railway companies in series RAIL 131 and 162.

Records of land and property
An act of 1823 provided for the conversion of tithes (which were payable to Anglican clergy) from payments in kind into monetary payments. Valuations of the land that was subject to tithes

are contained in Tithe Applotment books. They list (by parish then township) the heads of households who were occupiers of agricultural land at the time of the survey (which varies, from parish to parish, between 1823 and 1837). The books, at the National Archives and PRONI, note the area of land, the tithe payable and sometimes the name of any landlord of the property. Surnames in these books are included (with the names from Griffith's Valuation, noted below) in a general index of surnames (the Householders' Index) for each county, barony and parish, which has been produced by the National Library. An index to the books has also been produced on CD-ROM.

A survey (known as the Primary or Griffith's Valuation) to assess liability for poor rates was carried out from 1847 to 1865. There is a valuation book for each poor law union, naming the occupiers of buildings or land, their landlords and noting each property's size, rateable value and description. The books are held at the National Archives, on microfilm at the National Library and are also available, with a surname index, on a CD-ROM. The index can also be searched on the web site of Irish Origins (# appendix XI). Illustration 144 is an example of a page from this valuation. Maps showing the location of the properties listed in Griffith's Valuation (and those listed in later valuation lists of 1855 to 1968) are at the Valuation Office at the Irish Life Centre, Abbey Street Lower, Dublin 1. Indexes to the names of people appearing in Griffith's Valuation are included in the Householders' Index, noted above. The Valuation Office holds the notebooks used by surveyors when undertaking Griffith's Valuation, which provide further information about some properties. There are also books (at the Valuation Office or PRONI) recording changes in the property, ownership or occupation (so that valuations could be updated). A *Return of Owners of Land of One Acre and Upwards* for Ireland was published by HMSO in 1876, listing over 32,000 landowners (alphabetically by county). Copies are at the National Archives and at PRONI (and can be purchased on microfiche).

The Register of Deeds, held at the Deeds Registry, Henrietta Street, Dublin (telephone Dublin (00 353 1) 6707500) records transfers of land, or tenancies (of 21 years or more) since 1708. Registration was voluntary and designed to avoid disputes over title to land. Copies of the deeds were lodged at the registry and transcribed into registers. They are indexed (on computer) by place and by names of the transferors, grantors or lessors (but not the transferees, grantees or lessees). Microfilm copies of old manuscript indexes are also held at the National Library, PRONI and LDS family history centres. The register does not only include land transfers. There are other records of land ownership (such as mortgages, marriage settlements and wills) and business agreements, such as deeds for the establishment or dissolution of partnerships. The documents only concern a minority of the population but Falley (1168) provides abstracts of sample documents from the register, illustrating the useful information that can be obtained.

Many other categories of records suffered losses in the fire of 1922. The surviving records (now held at the National Archives) are listed in the 55th to 58th reports of the Deputy Keeper of the Public Records in Ireland, published from 1928 to 1951 and most are also reviewed in Falley (1168). Families' estate records often remain in private collections but many are in the National Archives, National Library or PRONI. Estate records located up to 1976 are listed in a published catalogue and many of these collections have been calendared in reports of the Deputy Keeper of the Public Records and are briefly described in Falley (1168). Thus the estate papers of the Dukes of Abercorn (calendared in the Deputy Keeper's reports) contain over 1,500 documents (such as conveyances, leases, rent rolls and family settlements) from about 1610 to 1900 relating to the family's estates in the counties of Tyrone and Donegal. Other important

PRIMARY VALUATION OF TENEMENTS.

PARISH OF KILLAVINOGE.

No. and Letters of Reference to Map.	Townlands and Occupiers.	Immediate Lessors.	Description of Tenement.	Area.			Net Annual Value. Land.			Buildings.			Total.		
				A.	R.	P.	£	s.	d.	£	s.	d.	£	s.	d.
	BALLYSORRELL, BIG.														
	(Ord. Ss. 29 & 30.)														
1	John Maher,	Frederick Lidwell, Esq.	Moory pasture,	11	1	26	4	15	0	—			4	15	0
2	John Maher,	Frederick Lidwell, Esq.	Land,	94	0	2	59	5	0	—			59	5	0
—	a Michael Treby,	John Maher,	House, offices, & garden,	0	2	24	0	10	0	1	0	0	1	10	0
3	A a Thomas Bennett,	Frederick Lidwell, Esq.	House, offices, and land,	20	1	27	11	10	0	1	15	0	13	5	0
—	B Thomas Bennett,	Frederick Lidwell, Esq.	Land,	32	1	33	8	10	0	—			8	10	0
—	A b John Cormack,	Thomas Bennett,	House,				—			0	15	0	0	15	0
—	c Margaret Russell,	Thomas Bennett,	House and garden,	0	0	18	0	1	0	0	14	0	0	15	0
4	Frederick Lidwell, Esq.	In fee,	Land,	37	2	5	13	15	0	—			13	15	0
—	d Margaret Henley,	Frederick Lidwell, Esq.	House,				—			0	10	0	0	10	0
—	b Margaret Ahern,	Frederick Lidwell, Esq.	House,				—			0	5	0	0	5	0
—	c Catherine Fogarty,	Frederick Lidwell, Esq.	House and garden,	0	1	31	0	5	0	0	10	0	0	15	0
5	Martin Carroll,	Frederick Lidwell, Esq.	Land,	62	1	30	30	15	0	—			30	15	0
—	a Vacant,	Martin Carroll,	House and offices,				—			1	0	0	1	0	0
6	a Michael Kerin,	Fredk. Lidwell, Esq.	House, offices, & land,	31	3	13	6	10	0	1	0	0	7	10	0
	b Patrick Carey,		House and land,				6	10	0	0	10	0	7	0	0
7	William Ryan,	Frederick Lidwell, Esq.	House and land,	20	2	27	11	10	0	0	15	0	12	5	0
8	a Patrick Healy,	Frederick Lidwell, Esq.	House, offices, & land,	79	1	27	15	0	0	1	0	0	16	0	0
	b Michael Maher,	Frederick Lidwell, Esq.	House and land,				3	15	0	0	5	0	4	0	0
	c Daniel Lahy,	Frederick Lidwell, Esq.	House and land,				3	15	0	0	10	0	4	5	0
	Fredk. Lidwell, Esq.	In fee,	Land,				7	10	0	—			7	10	0
—	Patrick Healy & parts.	Frederick Lidwell, Esq.	Bog,	122	0	38	0	10	0	—			0	10	0
—	d Thomas Carroll,	Frederick Lidwell, Esq.	House and garden,	0	0	12	0	1	0	0	14	0	0	15	0
9	Gt. S. & W. Railway Co.	In fee,	Land and railway,	9	2	3	6	5	0	—			6	5	0
			Total,	523	0	36	190	12	0	11	3	0	201	15	0
	BALLYSORRELL, LITTLE.														
	(Ord. Ss. 23, 24, 29, & 30.)														
1	William Bennett,	Dudley Byrne, Esq.	House and land,	1	0	0	0	10	0	0	15	0	1	5	0
2	A a Dudley Byrne, Esq.	Philip Gowan, Esq.	House, offices, and land,	133	0	19	70	5	0	16	10	0	86	15	0
—	B Dudley Byrne, Esq.	Philip Gowan, Esq.	Land,	113	3	26	52	5	0	—			52	5	0
—	Dudley Byrne, Esq.	Philip Gowan, Esq.	Bog,	107	3	20	0	10	0	—			0	10	0
—	A b William Kirwan,	Dudley Byrne, Esq.	House and garden,	0	0	30	0	2	0	0	5	0	0	7	0
3	Daniel Dwyer,	Dudley Byrne, Esq.	House and land,	7	2	24	3	10	0	0	5	0	3	15	0
4	Gt. S. & W. Railway Co.	In fee,	Railway,	5	1	24	4	0	0	—			4	0	0
			Total,	369	0	23	131	2	0	17	15	0	148	17	0
	BOGGAUN.														
	(Ord. S. 23).														
1	James Ryan,	George Goold, Esq.	Land,	29	0	7	15	10	0	—			15	10	0
2	Jeremiah Commerford,	George Goold, Esq.	House and land,	38	1	27	18	0	0	0	15	0	18	15	0
3	Michael Quinlan,	George Goold, Esq.	Land,	12	3	29	5	15	0	—			5	15	0
—	Michael Quinlan,	George Goold, Esq.	Bog,	4	0	12	0	1	0	—			0	1	0
4	George Redding,	George Goold, Esq.	House and land,	18	0	4	7	15	0	0	15	0	8	10	0
			Total,	102	1	39	47	1	0	1	10	0	48	11	0
	CLONBUOGH.														
	(Ord. Ss. 24 & 30.)														
1	Earl of Carrick,	In fee,	Bog,	88	3	10	0	10	0	—			0	10	0
2	A a William Rorke,	Earl of Carrick,	House, offices, and land,	70	1	29	31	10	0	4	10	0	36	0	0
—	B William Rorke,	Earl of Carrick,	Land,	41	2	1	31	10	0	—			31	10	0
—	A b Vacant,	William Rorke,	House and offices,				—			2	0	0	2	0	0
—	A c Mary Flynn,	William Rorke,	House,				—			0	10	0	0	10	0
—	B a Mary Flynn,	William Rorke,	House,				—			0	5	0	0	5	0
—	b Edward Long,	William Rorke,	House and garden,	0	1	33	0	5	0	0	5	0	0	10	0
—	c Catherine Neale,	William Rorke,	House and garden,	0	1	16	0	5	0	0	5	0	0	10	0
3	A William Rorke,	Earl of Carrick,	Land,	24	3	34	11	10	0	—			11	10	0
—	B William Rorke,	Earl of Carrick,	Land,	6	3	35	3	5	0	—			3	5	0
—	A a Patrick Burke,	William Rorke,	House,				—			0	5	0	0	5	0
—	A b Henry Doyle,	William Rorke,	House,				—			0	5	0	0	5	0
4	Patrick Cahill,	Earl of Carrick,	Land,	6	2	14	3	10	0	—			3	10	0
5	Patrick Doolan,	Earl of Carrick,	House and land,	1	3	34	1	5	0	0	5	0	1	10	0
6	Patrick Brennan,	Earl of Carrick,	Land,	3	3	7	2	5	0	—			2	5	0

144. A page from Griffith's Valuation, *carried out between 1847 and 1865*

manuscript collections concerning property are described in Falley (1168). For example, the National Library has microfilm copies of the Annesley collection, including records of plantation (the Protestant settlement of Ulster), such as books of survey and distributions. These are land surveys, for most of Ireland, from 1636 to 1641 and 1689 to 1703, describing estates and the changes in ownership following rebellions in Ireland. They list the landowners' names (particularly many Catholics whose land was forfeited around 1641 or 1689 and the names of the new owners). Armagh Public Library holds Armagh manor rolls for 1625 to 1627 and rent rolls for property of the Diocese of Armagh from 1615 to 1746. Donegal County Library holds a manuscript register of freeholders in Donegal for 1767 to 1768. Solicitors' collections also include many title deeds. Thus the collection of Alexander Bell & Son at the National Archives includes over 2,000 deeds dating from 1703 to 1901.

Tax records

Most hearth tax records were destroyed in 1922 but a few surviving rolls and transcripts are listed in Gibson (890). Some subsidy rolls and poll tax records also survive. For example, subsidy rolls for Antrim (of 1666), Down (1663) and Tyrone (1664) and poll tax lists for Armagh, Down and Fermanagh (for 1660) are at PRONI. Some other surviving lists of names are noted in Grenham (1176) such as the Irish tontines (# chapter 23).

Law and order

Many Irish court records were destroyed in 1922 but surviving records are described in the 55th to 58th reports of the Deputy Keeper of the Public Records of Ireland and by Falley (1168). Calendars of some of the lost court records were included in the 5th to 54th reports of the Deputy Keeper. Examples of the surviving records (at the National Archives) include Exchequer decrees (1624–1804), abstracts (from the Patent and Close Rolls) of enrolled deeds, leases, decrees, depositions and inquisitions (12th–18th centuries), insolvency petition books (1790–1872), indexes to fines in the Court of Common Pleas (1705–1835), indexes to recoveries in the same court (1590–1834) and judgment books of Exchequer and King's Bench (1851–99). Large collections of court records of Ulster are at PRONI, some listed in Neill (1209) and Maxwell (1200), such as presentments of Grand Juries and records of Quarter Sessions and County courts. Many decrees and orders of the Court of Chancery of Ireland and certain other courts are in Chancery records (particularly in series C 79) at TNA at Kew. Some other legal records are in libraries' manuscript collections and listed in Falley (1168). Thus Donegal County Library holds Donegal grand jurors' books of presentments for 1768–83 and 1815–56. The library of Trinity College in Dublin holds volumes of depositions of Protestant settlers concerning the damage to their property during the rebellion of 1641. Manuscript collections deposited by solicitors include many records of litigation. Examples are the papers of Alexander Bell & Son and of E.J. French deposited at the National Archives, containing hundreds of documents from their clients' cases in the courts of Chancery, Exchequer, King's Bench, Bankruptcy or Common Pleas.

M. Coffey reviews a series of Ejectment Books at the National Archives in *Family Tree Magazine* (May 1998). These include summaries of cases before the Irish Circuit Court in which landlords applied for court orders to evict tenants for non-payment of rent. Many of the records have been destroyed but most of those for County Clare survive for 1816–1914 and less extensive collections survive for other counties. The books are arranged by county and by year. Each book notes the names of hundreds of landlords and tenants (and details of their properties and rents) but they are unfortunately not indexed.

Information about court cases is also available from secondary sources, such as newspapers, journals and published law reports. *The Irish Reports*, published by Butterworth Ireland Limited, consist of 176 volumes of law reports from 1838 to 1925 (with further volumes to the present date). Henry (1182) is a useful study of crime in Dublin from 1780 to 1795 (and particularly of criminals who were hanged) with detailed information (often from the *Hibernian Journal*) on cases heard by commissions of oyer and terminer or by the Dublin and Kilmainham Quarter Sessions. Over 200 executions are listed with a note of the date, the court and the crime (and the names of many victims, witnesses and those accused of crimes). Wanted criminals and escaped convicts (and their crimes) were described from 1822 in the weekly journal *Hue and Cry*, later named the *Police Gazette*, copies of which can be seen at the National Library.

Heraldry and family records

The heraldic authority in Ireland from the 16th century was the Ulster King of Arms. The functions of this office in respect of Northern Ireland were transferred to the College of Arms in London in 1943. The Office of Arms in Ireland, Eire's equivalent to the College of Arms, is now known as the Genealogical Office and located at 2 Kildare Street, Dublin (telephone Dublin (00 353 1) 6621062). It holds about 700 manuscript volumes of grants of arms, visitations, pedigrees, wills, inquisitions post mortem and funeral certificates. Much of this material is available on microfilm at the National Library and at LDS family history centres. Detailed lists of the records and indexes available at the Genealogical Office are included in Falley (1168), the first (1992) edition of Grenham (1176) and in *The Genealogical Office, Dublin* by Grenham, published by the Irish Manuscripts Commission.

The families of Irish peers are included in some of the works on peerages noted in chapter 26. In addition, Irish families were included in the earlier editions of *Burke's Landed Gentry*, then in separate works entitled *Burke's Landed Gentry of Ireland* and most recently in *Burke's Irish Family Records* (1159). This provides indented pedigrees of 514 Irish families from medieval times. Many of those families originated in England. For example, the lineage of Leslie Daunt is traced back (with much information on collateral lines) to Thomas Daunt who had moved to Ireland from Gloucestershire (and died in 1620). The line is then traced back to a Simon Daunt living in Gloucestershire in about 1380.

Emigration

Millions of people emigrated from Ireland, particularly in the 19th century. Perhaps 3,900,000 went to America between 1820 and 1900; about 1,700,000 emigrating as a result of the Great Famine. As in England, information on emigrants in this period is sparse, but information on convicts and settlers in Australia in the late 18th and early 19th centuries is included in Colonial Office files at TNA at Kew. The National Archives and PRONI have some lists of emigrants to the United States and Canada in the 19th century. A few ships' lists of passengers leaving Ireland for America (listing about 4,500 emigrants between 1803 and 1806 and about 27,500 between 1847 and 1871) have been published in Mitchell (1201) and (1202). Records of people arriving at their destinations, especially in North America and Australia, are far superior. These records (and other published lists of emigrants) are considered in chapter 30. Grenham (1176) provides a detailed list of sources which include Irish emigrants. Of particular assistance are published lists

(# chapter 30) of Irish emigrants to America from 1846 to 1851 in Glazier & Tepper (1288) and also of assisted emigrants to New South Wales between 1840 and 1870. The National Archives also hold records (with a surname index) of about 40,000 Irish convicts who were transported to Australia between 1791 and 1868. The index can be consulted on the National Archives' web site.

Family history societies

The SoG has an extensive collection of published records for Ireland but you should also consider joining an Irish family history society, such as the Genealogical Society of Ireland (11 Desmond Avenue, Dun Laoghaire, Co. Dublin) or the Irish FHS, of PO Box 36, Naas, County Kildare, which publishes *Irish Family History*. The Irish Genealogical Research Society has an Irish branch (41 Evora Crescent, Howth, Co. Dublin) and a London branch (although its library is temporarily closed) and publishes *The Irish Genealogist*, which includes transcripts of many original records. A quarterly journal, *Irish Roots* (1146), is also available. Enquiries about genealogical research in Northern Ireland can be directed to the Ulster Historical Foundation, of Balmoral Buildings, 12 College Square East, Belfast BT1 6DD (# appendix XI for its web site), which publishes genealogical material and undertakes paid research, or the North of Ireland FHS which publishes a journal *North Irish Roots*. There are two Irish associations of professional researchers: the Association of Professional Genealogists in Ireland (correspondence should be addressed to the Honorary Secretary, 30 Harlech Crescent, Clonskeagh, Dublin 4) and the Association of Ulster Genealogists and Record Agents (Glen Cottage, Glenmachan Road, Belfast BT4 2NP). Family history and genealogy societies from all over Ireland are involved in the "Irish genealogical project", which aims to transcribe and computerise Irish genealogical records (and provide a research service at 34 genealogical centres throughout Ireland). Articles in the 2000 edition of the *FLHH* (5) and in *Family History Monthly* (October 2003) describe the progress of the project, the societies taking part and the addresses of the genealogical centres.

THE ISLE OF MAN

The Isle of Man is a dependency of the British Crown but has its own parliament and laws. Manx genealogical records are similar to English records and described in Narasimham (1208). This work also includes a glossary of Manx Gaelic words that are commonly contained in wills, property deeds and other records. Much genealogical material from the Isle of Man, for example registers of baptisms and marriages, can be seen on microfilm at LDS family history centres. The SoG also holds much information.

Civil registration was compulsory for births and deaths from 1878 and for marriages from 1884. There was also a voluntary registration system for births and marriages from 1849. The registers are held at the Civil Registry, Registries Building, Deemster's Walk, Bucks Road, Douglas, Isle of Man IM1 3AR (telephone 01624 687039). The public can inspect the original registers and buy certified copies. The SoG has microfilm copies of the indexes up to 1964 and copies of some 19th-century registers. Parish registers, some dating from the early 17th century, are similar in form to English registers. A list of the registers and a map of parishes is included in volume 15 part 1 of the *NIPR* (151). From 1849 incumbents had to make copies of the entries and these are now held at the Civil Registry. The government also copied all earlier registers. Therefore, although many original registers remain with incumbents, microfilm copies of all registers can be seen at the Manx National Heritage Library, Manx Museum and National

Trust ("Manx Museum") at Kingswood Grove, Douglas, IM1 3LY (telephone 01624 648000). Bishop's transcripts were also required from 1734 and those up to 1799 are also on microfilm at the Manx Museum. The SoG holds copies of some Manx parish registers, listed in Taylor (171) and the Isle of Man section of the IGI includes all recorded marriages and many baptisms. The Civil Registry also holds indexes to the baptisms in each parish. Microfilm copies of these indexes are at the Manx Musuem. There are also indexes to the marriage registers of each church up to 1883. The Manx Museum holds some non-conformist registers of baptism, whilst non-conformist marriage registers from 1849 are at the Civil Registry. These registers are listed in volume 15 of the *NIPR* (151).

Census records for 1841 to 1901 are at TNA, the FRC and the Manx Museum. The Isle of Man FHS has indexed the census records of 1841, 1851, 1861, 1881 and 1891 (and published that of 1851). The Isle of Man is also included in the LDS 1881 census index and in the 1901 census online service. Monumental inscriptions were recorded in 1797 and the Isle of Man FHS is recording surviving MIs. Transcripts are at the Manx Museum and an index can be purchased. Wills survive from the early 17th century. Manx wills and administrations were proved in the church courts (the Consistory Court of Sodor and Man or the Archdeaconry Court of the Isle of Man) until 1884 and since then in the Manx High Court of Justice. The Manx Museum now holds wills and administrations up to 1910, with a number of indexes. Wills proved since 1911 are held in the Deeds and Probate Office at the Civil Registry in Douglas. The Isle of Man was in the province of York and so wills could also be proved, up to 1858, in the PCY or PCC. Some wills since 1858 have been proved at the Principal Probate Registry in London. Other records of the Manx ecclesiastical courts are similar to English records and described by Narasimham (1208), who also briefly describes surviving Manx directories, periodicals and manuscript collections of genealogical interest. Newspapers and their locations are listed in Gibson, Langston & Smith (484), with some indexes noted in volume 15 of the *NIPR* (151). Militia documents, for the Manx Fencibles, are in the Manx Museum.

Manx property records are described in Narasimham (1208). At intervals from 1511 to the late 19th century, the landowners in each parish were listed in *Liber Assedationis*. Changes in land ownership (whether by sale, gift or inheritance) were recorded from 1511 to 1916 in the *Liber vastarum*, which was compiled twice a year. Occupiers of land owned by the Bishop of Sodor and Man are recorded from 1511 in the *Liber Episcopi*. All these records can be seen on microfilm at the Manx Museum. In addition, many title deeds of property survive from as early as the 17th century. Those surviving from the period up to 1910 are at the Manx Museum and documents since that date can be viewed at the Civil Registry.

THE CHANNEL ISLANDS

The Channel Islands are not part of the United Kingdom, but are dependencies of the Crown. Jersey, Alderney and Guernsey each have their own parliaments (and are self-governing on internal matters). The other inhabited islands are Sark, Herm, Jethou and Brechou. Some knowledge of French will assist your research in the Channel Islands, since many records are in French, some parish records only being in English since the Second World War. Le Poidevin (1190) and Backhurst (1153) provide detailed information on research in Guernsey and Jersey respectively. The Channel Islands FHS and the Société Jersiaise can undertake paid research for those people who are unable to visit the islands. The principal archives and libraries are:

Jersey

The Jersey Archive, Clarence Road, St Helier, JE2 4JY (telephone 01534 833300) which has a catalogue on its web site

Judicial Greffe (also Superintendent Registrar), Morier House, Halkett Place, St Helier, JE1 1DD (01534 502300)

Société Jersiaise, Lord Coutanche Library, 7 Pier Road, St Helier, JE2 4XW (01534 730538)

Guernsey

Guernsey Archives Service, 29 Victoria Road, St Peter Port, GY1 1HU (01481 724512)

HM Greffier (also Registrar General), The Royal Court House, St Peter Port, GY1 2PB (01481 725277)

The Priaulx Library, Candie Road, St Peter Port, GY1 1UG (01481 721998)

Civil registration of births and deaths commenced in Guernsey in 1840, in Jersey in 1842, on Alderney in 1850 and on Sark in 1915 (deaths) and 1925 (births). Civil registration of marriages commenced in 1842 in Jersey but only in 1886 on Alderney, in 1919 on Guernsey and 1925 on Sark. Jersey registers are held by the Superintendent Registrar, who is also the Judicial Greffe. Guernsey registers are held by the Registrar General (also known as HM Greffier). Enquiries about civil registration records of Alderney should be directed to the Greffier at the Registry for Births, Deaths, Companies, Land and Marriages in St Anne, Alderney GY9 3AA and (for Sark) to HM Greffier in Guernsey.

The civil registration records of Jersey are not open to the public. Applications for searches and certificates must therefore be made by post and a fee is payable. A microfiche index for Jersey births, marriages and deaths from 1842 to 1900 is held by the Société Jersiaise and by the Channel Islands FHS, who will search this index for a fee. Jersey marriage certificates usually state the spouses' birthplaces. Because of the small number of Christian names and surnames used in Jersey, special care is necessary in order to identify your ancestors in Jersey records. The Guernsey indexes of civil registration and the registers themselves are open to public inspection. Until 1949 deaths of married women on Guernsey were recorded under their maiden names. Some Guernsey death certificates also note the maiden name of the deceased's mother. The SoG has copies of the Guernsey registers of births and deaths (1840–1907) and marriages (1840–1901) with indexes up to 1963 for deaths and 1966 for births and marriages. Copies of the 19th-century civil registration records of births, marriages and deaths in Guernsey are also held at the Priaulx Library, to which free access is available.

During the Second World War, many people left Guernsey for England, or were interned in Germany, and separate registers were kept of births, marriages and deaths from 1940 to 1945. These are held by the Guernsey Registrar and copies are held by the SoG. Harris (1180) is a useful book about Channel Islanders who were deported to Germany during the war, including lists of deportees and descriptions of life in the internment camps. Piece HO 144/22920 at TNA is a list, prepared by the Germans, of those deported. Jersey and Guernsey residents had to carry identity cards during the German occupation. Forms submitted for the issue of the cards, with duplicates of the photographs used on them, are in Jersey and Guernsey archives. The forms include a person's place and date of birth, address and occupation. The Jersey records are reviewed by A. Glendinning in Channel Islands' FHS journal (spring 1995).

Census records for Jersey and Guernsey are at the FRC and TNA. Microfilm copies of the Jersey returns are also held by the Jersey Archive, St Helier Public Library and the Société Jersiaise. Copies of the Guernsey returns of 1841–91 are at the Priaulx Library, with indexes for 1841, 1851 and 1891. The 1881 census index (on fiche, CD-ROM and on *FamilySearch*) and the 1901 census online service include Jersey and Guernsey. The other censuses of Jersey have also been indexed. Those for 1851, 1871 and 1891 have been published. Those for 1841 and 1861 are held by the Société Jersiaise and Channel Islands FHS, which also hold copies of censuses of Jersey for 1806 and 1815, known as General Don's muster lists or rolls. The 1806 roll lists over 4,000 heads of household (with the numbers of household members). The 1815 roll lists those men in the militia, their rank and age, but also gives the names (and sometimes occupations) of all other men aged 17 to 80, with the numbers of women, boys and girls in each household. TNA holds the Association Oath rolls for Jersey and Guernsey of 1696 which include most adult males (pieces C 213/462–463). Glendinning (1173) is a transcript of the Jersey roll with biographical material on many signatories.

Balleine (1155) is a biographical dictionary of about 300 men and women of Jersey. Marr (1198) is a biographical dictionary of about 200 noteworthy residents of Guernsey since medieval times. It also lists about 550 people who were recorded in assize or other documents of the 13th to 15th centuries.

Many parish registers of baptisms, marriages and burials on Jersey, Guernsey, Sark and Alderney are still held at the parish churches. Lists of the registers (and maps of parishes of Jersey and Guernsey) are included in volume 15 part 1 of the *NIPR* (151). No bishops' transcripts appear to survive for any of the islands. Some original Jersey registers are at the Jersey Archive but almost all Jersey registers up to 1842 have been transcribed and indexed by the Channel Islands FHS (and some are held by the SoG). Many records of baptisms in Jersey give the mother's maiden name and the names of godparents (who were often relatives). Fathers' occupations are rarely stated. Some original Guernsey registers (and copies of most of the others) are at the Priaulx Library. The SoG has copies of a few registers. The IGI includes a section for the Channel Islands, although the Jersey entries also include Land Registry records (considered below) and researchers' submitted entries, with only a few entries from the parish registers. Catholic registers for the Channel Islands are listed in Gandy (324). There were also some Methodist and other non-conformist groups on Jersey, Guernsey, Sark and Alderney and they are listed in the *NIPR* (151).

Wills and administrations in Guernsey are proved (and the records held) by the Ecclesiastical Court of the Bailiwick of Guernsey in St Peter Port, except for wills of realty since 1841 which are held by HM Greffier. Probate jurisdiction in Jersey was exercised by the Ecclesiastical Court of the Dean of Jersey until 1949. Real property in Jersey was inherited in accordance with rules of law and so could not be devised by will until 1851. Wills of realty since 1851 are held at the Land Registry (noted below). Jersey wills of personalty and administrations from 1660 are held by the Jersey Archive. Since the 16th century the Channel Islands have been part of the Diocese of Winchester and the Province of Canterbury. Wills of Jersey and Guernsey inhabitants could therefore also be proved (up to 1858) in the PCC and (from 1858) in the Principal Probate Registry.

TNA holds Guernsey and Jersey militia regiments' returns for 1843 to 1852 in series WO 13. Some 17th- and 18th-century Jersey muster lists are held by the Société Jersiaise and listed by Gibson & Dell (631). About 3,000 men from Guernsey served in the First World War. They are listed (with details of casualties and a history of the Guernsey units' service) in *Diex Aix, God Help Us, the Guernseymen who Marched Away 1914–1918* by E. Parks, available from NMP. A roll of honour has also been published for the men of Jersey who died in the war.

Most Jersey and Guernsey newspapers can be seen at St Helier Public Library and the Priaulx Library respectively. They are listed in Gibson, Langston & Smith (484). Newspapers commenced publication in Jersey (some in English and some in French) in the late 18th century and there is a large collection at the Société Jersiaise.

Much genealogical material, for example of property and the courts, is held at the Guernsey Archives Service. The various Jersey civil courts are described by Backhurst (1153). The records are held by the Judicial Greffier to whom an application must be made for access. Jersey's ecclesiastical court records are held at the Jersey Archive. Jersey criminal records are not available to the public. A Land Registry was established in Jersey in 1602 to record the sale, lease or mortgage of land. From the early 19th century the registers also record the division of land between the children of a deceased landowner (the eldest received most) and any subsequent sales by younger children to the main beneficiary. The Land Registry registers and indexes have been microfilmed by the Mormons.

CHAPTER 30

IMMIGRATION, EMIGRATION AND INVESTIGATION ABROAD

This chapter considers research in the rest of the world. The first section deals with records of immigrants to the British Isles; the second section reviews records of British emigrants; the third section describes records held in Britain (such as church registers) that document the British abroad; the fourth section deals, very briefly, with research in some foreign countries, and the last section lists, for a few countries, some books or articles that provide a useful starting point for research. The up to date addresses, telephone numbers and web sites of record offices, libraries and family history societies around the world (and lists of some researchers who undertake work abroad) are included in the annual editions of the *FLHH* (5).

You may wish to undertake genealogical research in foreign countries for a number of reasons. An ancestor may have come to Britain from abroad, or spent some time abroad. Relatives may have emigrated and you may wish to trace them so as to include them on the family tree, or because they may possess records about your mutual ancestors. There are many foreign links in my family tree. My g.g. grandfather, Bernard Herber, was born in Germany in 1823 but had emigrated to England by 1851. My grandfather Henry John Herber had a brother who emigrated to Australia and another brother who emigrated to Canada with his sister and their widowed mother, Alice Amelia Keates. Three of Alice's brothers emigrated to Australia in the early 20th century and two of her uncles (George and Ebenezer Keates) spent some time in Canada with their families, but returned to England.

Research of immigrants and emigrants can be difficult and time-consuming. For example, many countries did not commence civil registration of births, marriages and deaths until long after Britain. The language, form and organisation of some foreign genealogical records may also be very different to British records. If you are undertaking research in Europe, the problems caused by historical changes in national boundaries, the destruction of records (due to war or revolution) and people's migration (due to war or economic conditions), are far greater than in Britain and may make your search very difficult. In some countries the records of family history are quite limited compared to the extensive records available in Britain. A detailed analysis of how to undertake research in foreign countries is beyond the scope of this book, but the purpose of this chapter is to assist you to start that research.

Foreign research does not necessarily require you to travel abroad. Your own research in the original records is always best, but factors of language, time and finance may prevent this. The best way to start your research is to use the resources of the SoG, TNA and LDS family history centres, or undertake research by correspondence with a local researcher or genealogical society. Published material about the British abroad, or about foreign records, is particularly important (and many examples are given below) since it is usually easily accessible in this country. Starting in this manner will assist you later in progressing research in a foreign archive much more quickly (and give you a proper understanding of the records).

The SoG has very large collections of material for most areas of the world. The collections for countries such as the United States, Canada and Australia are particularly large, so it might take you some time to exhaust these before you have to turn to other sources. Yeo (1342) includes lists for many foreign countries of copy registers (or indexes) of births, baptisms, marriages, deaths and burials held at the SoG, TNA or Guildhall Library. The SoG's holdings of census records and indexes are listed in Churchill (138). Newington-Irving (297) lists the SoG's collection of foreign will indexes, abstracts and other probate material. The wills of British people dying abroad, but holding property in England or Wales, were proved in England in the PCC until 1858 and later at the Principal Probate Registry (# chapter 12). The worldwide IGI should also be consulted. The sections of the IGI for foreign countries are very similar to the British sections and are quite extensive for countries such as the United States, Canada and Germany. The BVRI (a supplement to the IGI for the British Isles) was reviewed in chapter 7. The Mormons have a produced a similar Vital Records Index, on CD-ROM, for Western Europe. This contains entries for over 12 million baptisms, births and marriages from the 16th century up to 1905 extracted from records in Austria, Belgium, France, Germany, Italy, Luxembourg, the Netherlands, Spain and Switzerland. Both the worldwide IGI and the Western Europe Vital Records Index can be consulted at LDS family history centres and at the SoG.

LDS family history centres can also be used to call upon the Mormons' enormous microfilmed collections of genealogical material from around the world. Ordering a film of a German parish register or American census records for viewing at LDS family history centres is much easier, quicker and cheaper than travelling to German or American archives that hold the original records. Before commencing research in any foreign place, you should consult the LDS Family History Library Catalog (# appendix XI) to ascertain what resources are held by the LDS for that place. If you live near London, you should also consult the catalogue of films held permanently at the Hyde Park Family History Centre, since this may avoid your having to order the films from Salt Lake City. The centre has over 43,000 microfilms and microfiche and holds the largest collection, in Britain, of material from the Caribbean (particularly Jamaica and Barbados) and Eastern Europe (particularly Jewish records). For example, for the parish of St Elizabeth in Jamaica, the centre holds microfilm copies of the registers of births (1878–1930), marriages (1880–1950) and deaths (1878–1995) as well as some indexes.

There are two books that provide introductions to research in a selection of countries. Currer-Briggs (1276) includes chapters on British and German emigration to America, the settlement of Canada, Australia and New Zealand and brief descriptions of the genealogical sources in Australia, South Africa, New Zealand and most European countries. Baxter (1252) is an introduction to research in Europe, including a review of some of the general problems of European research, such as the shifting of national borders. For example, the land within the German Empire of 1918 is now mostly within Germany and Poland, but also in the Baltic states, France and Belgium. The Austro-Hungarian Empire collapsed in 1918 and records of the empire's inhabitants can therefore now be found in Austria, Poland, Hungary, Italy, the Czech Republic, Slovakia, Romania, Slovenia, Croatia and Serbia. Baxter (1252) also includes useful sections on the genealogical records of each European country. In a few cases (such as Albania and Bulgaria) the section may be the only English text that is available on research in that country. In many cases the sections are relatively detailed (such as 18 pages on research in Holland). Later in this chapter, a number of more detailed books are also listed in respect of different countries of the world. Most of these can be consulted at the SoG. Your local library may also have copies or be able to obtain them for you on inter-library loan.

Some published sources for foreign royal families were noted in chapter 26. The SoG and reference libraries hold many other published works on foreign royalty, in particular the *Almanach de Gotha*, first published in 1763. It records living members of each European sovereign house (including many houses no longer reigning) as well as indented pedigrees of those families. A new edition (the 182nd) of *Almanach de Gotha* (the first since 1944) was published in 1998 and the 183rd edition (1237) was published in 1999.

Genealogical societies in Britain (in addition to the SoG) can also assist. Researchers with German or French ancestry should join the Anglo-German FHS or the Anglo-French FHS. You could also employ a researcher abroad (although the fees may be substantial) and you should consider joining a family history society in the country in which your ancestors or relatives lived. Many overseas societies are listed, with contact details, in the *FLHH* (5). Some societies are also members of the FFHS and their publications are listed in Hampson (249) and Perkins (263).

Another key starting point for research abroad is to see what information is available on the Internet. The best place to start is on the web site of Cyndi's List (# chapter 11). There you will find at least basic information on research in most countries (and sometimes very detailed guidance), contact details for archives and family history societies, catalogues of some of the material held at archives as well as transcripts or indexes of much source material. The resources available on the Internet for research abroad are too extensive to list in this book but you should review them before you plan any foreign trips.

IMMIGRATION

It is important to obtain as much information as possible about immigrants from British records before starting research abroad. The census reveals many immigrants' places of birth and many of the records reviewed in earlier chapters note the place of origin of immigrants, in the same way as they indicate the origins of a migrant (# chapter 28). The registers of foreign churches in England (# chapter 13) may also include your immigrant ancestors. The web site Moving Here (# appendix XI) is dedicated to immigration to Britain since 1800. Material is being contributed from many archives and libraries and includes historical images and personal accounts of immigration as well as databases of source material. For example, the site includes admission and discharge registers of the Jew's Free School in London for 1869–1900 (with about 20,000 names and an index). There are also transcripts of a few passenger ships' lists of immigrants. Some other sources on this site are noted below.

Immigrants have been arriving in the British Isles for centuries, such as the Huguenots and other foreign Protestant groups who were fleeing from persecution in Europe (# chapter 13). Other important groups of immigrants followed. Many French nobles fled to England from the French Revolution. The Irish migrated to Britain in large numbers and this process was increased by famine in Ireland in the 19th century. In the 1861 census about 520,000 residents of England (and 207,000 people in Scotland) were stated to have been born in Ireland. In the 19th century Germans arrived in Britain in increasing numbers and from the late 19th century there were substantial influxes of Polish and Jewish people. Immigration has continued in the 20th century, mainly from British colonies or Commonwealth countries such as India, Pakistan, Hong Kong and Jamaica, but also from Czechoslovakia, Germany and Poland in the 1930s and 1940s (particularly Jewish people escaping from Nazi atrocities) and Hungary in 1956–57.

Many people think that it is only since the Second World War that people from Africa and the Caribbean have arrived in Britain. However, this is incorrect. African men were first brought to England in 1555 and many black slaves worked in England until slavery was abolished here in the 18th century. Linebaugh (996) suggests that the black community in London in the late 18th century amounted to between 10,000 and 20,000 people (perhaps 3 per cent of London's population). Articles about the black community in England since the 16th century appear in *Family Tree Magazine* (October 1995) by S. Pearl and in *Family History Monthly* (October 2003) by A. Adolph. File & Power (1284) is an illustrated guide to black settlers in Britain since 1555. The Black Genealogical Society has been formed to encourage interest in black genealogy. Black people were very poorly recorded (often without surnames) until civil registration started in 1837. Many were baptised or married in the Fleet in the early 18th century, but burials often appear in Anglican registers. This is a fairly typical entry, from the burial register of St Leonards, Shoreditch in London:

26 June 1805. Betty, a black woman servant to the Reverend Mr Stancourt of Hoxton Square. Aged 17 years.

There is some published material on immigrants, such as the Huguenots (# chapter 13) but also on other communities. For example, Catsyannis (1264) is a detailed study, including pedigrees, documents and photographs, of Greek families, their churches and businesses in London from the 17th to 19th centuries.

Some records of immigrants are held at TNA. Lists of passengers on ships arriving in Britain from outside Europe survive from 1890 to 1960 (with a few from 1878 to 1888) in series BT 26. They were prepared by ships' masters and note a passenger's name, age, occupation, date of entry and proposed place of residence. They are arranged by port, then year and then ship, but they are not indexed, so you need to know an immigrant's port of entry and approximate date of arrival. Registers in BT 32 list, for each port, the names of ships and their dates of arrival since 1906. Some lists have been transcribed, particularly for 1948–60, and are searchable by person's name on the web site of Moving Here.

Some other records of immigrants at TNA are described in TNA domestic records leaflet 50. There are records of aliens becoming British subjects, by the processes of denization or naturalisation. Many of these note an immigrant's date of arrival or place of birth. A person who was a subject of the British Crown (with the rights which that status conferred) was known as a denizen, whether he obtained that status by birth or by grant. A formal grant of that status was known as denization. Aliens in Britain (particularly merchants) were subject to various disabilities, so denization was advantageous and could be granted by the Crown (by Royal Charter or by Letters Patent under the Great Seal). From the 16th century the rights of a denizen could also be granted by a private act of Parliament, but these parliamentary grants became known as naturalisation because the person was then deemed to have always been a subject of the Crown (although the practical effect was much the same). Parliamentary naturalisation required the applicant to receive the Sacrament of the Lord's Supper and take oaths of supremacy and allegiance (# chapter 23). Some people (for example Jews and Catholics) were therefore unable to use this process and instead relied on the denization procedure until the requirements for the oaths were withdrawn in the 19th century. These procedures were expensive and so only a minority of aliens used them. A cheaper procedure was introduced in 1844 when the Home Secretary was empowered to grant naturalisation to aliens by a certificate.

Letters Patent of denization were published in the *London Gazette* and enrolled on the Patent Rolls (in series C 66 and 67) up to 1844. Private acts of Parliament are at the House of Lords Record Office. Naturalisation certificates granted by the Home Secretary are at TNA in series HO 1 (for 1844–71) and HO 334 (for 1870–1969). Certificates of 1844–73 were also enrolled on the Close Rolls (C 54). Petitions for, and correspondence relating to, applications for denizations and naturalisations are in HO 1 (for 1789–1871), HO 45 (1872–78), HO 144 (1879–1933, but presently open only up to 1922) and HO 405 (1934–48, presently closed). There are various indexes to these documents. The Huguenot Society has published indexes to letters of denization and naturalisations by act of Parliament for 1509–1603 and 1603–1800. Indexes are attached to the series list of HO 1 in the research enquiries room at TNA (and also available on microfilm at the SoG) to denizations of 1801–73, naturalisations by act of Parliament of 1801–1900 and naturalisation certificates of 1844–1961. Illustration 145 shows a page from the index of naturalisation certificates. Naturalisations by act of Parliament of 1900–47 are included in an index to local and personal acts of Parliament, published by HMSO in 1949. Kershaw & Pearsall (1299) provide more information about all these documents and indexes (and about applications to the Home Office for the opening of those files that are presently closed). From 1886, the names of those receiving naturalisation certificates were also listed in the *London Gazette* (but not included in the *Gazette* indexes). Only a small minority of immigrants ever bothered with matters such as naturalisation, especially since their children, by a British wife, acquired British nationality. I have not found any naturalisation or denization records for my ancestor Bernard Herber who arrived from Germany in the 19th century, but his employer Jacob Safran, who was possibly a brother of Bernard's mother, did obtain a naturalisation certificate. He is listed in the index to series HO 1 (on the page at illustration 145) as having emigrated from Germany (and having received a naturalisation certificate on 14 December 1857).

All foreigners arriving in England should have registered, under the Aliens Act 1792, with a Justice of the Peace, providing their name, rank, address and occupation. Landlords of lodging houses were also required to give notice to the parish constable or overseers (who informed the Clerk of the Peace) of any aliens who resided in their lodgings. A few of these registration records are in CROs and listed in Kershaw & Pearsall (1299). An example from records held at LMA, of the registration of a Monsieur Lemire in 1797 (who had fled the French Revolution) appears as an illustration in Colwell (11). Some passes issued to aliens from 1793 to 1836, with their names, port of entry, nationality, religious denomination, occupation, most recent place of residence and intended destination, are in series HO 1 at TNA. The Aliens Act of 1836 required aliens to sign and file certificates of arrival, specifying their name, port of entry (and date of arrival), nationality and profession. Certificates for 1836 to 1852 are in 236 volumes in series HO 2, arranged by port of arrival. An index for 1836–49 is in pieces HO 5/25–32 and an index for 1850–52 has been produced by L. Metzner. Series HO 5 also contains entry books of 1794 to 1909, containing correspondence relating to many aliens during that period.

280	CERTIFICATES OF NATURALIZATION.					
Name.	Country.	Date of Certificate.	Place of Residence.	Number of Certificate.	Number of Home Office Paper.	Remarks.

S.

Name.	Country.	Date of Certificate.	Place of Residence.	Number of Certificate.	Number of Home Office Paper.	Remarks.
Saado, Shaoul ...	Aleppo ...	24 September 1866	... ...	5199	—	
Saalfeld, Adolphe ...	Germany ...	18 July 1896 ...	Manchester ...	A 9120	B 20848	
Saalfeld, Albert ...	Hamburg ...	22 February 1847	... ...	544	—	
Saalfeld, Heinrich ...	Prussia ...	30 September 1870	... ...	A 60	—	
Saam, Carl	Germany ...	12 February 1885	London	A 4249	A 38358	
Saatweber, Gustav Adolf.	Germany ...	28 April 1886 ...	Manchester ...	A 4552	A 43029	
Sabag, Abraham ...	Morocco ...	26 March 1852 ...	... ...	1366	—	
Sabbatella, Gianovaria	Italy... ...	1 January 1887...	Cheltenham ...	A 5136	A 45508	
Sabbatella, Guiseppe	Italy... ...	16 June 1897 ...	Swindon ...	A 9690	B 23946	
Sabel, Ephraim ...	Nassau ...	3 October 1850...	... ...	1195	—	
Sabel, Ernest Eugene	Prussia ...	6 February 1869	... ...	6078	—	
Sabel, Frederic ...	Weisbaden ...	2 December 1852	... ...	1480	—	
Sabol, Friedrich Jacob	Germany ...	14 May 1888 ...	London ...	A 5769	B 3013	
Sabol, Max	Germany ...	29 November 1876	... ...	A 2073	59794	
Sabol, Paul Ferdinand	Germany ...	30 November 1875	... ...	A 1763	49708	
Sabol, Robert ...	Germany ...	27 July 1892 ...	Nottingham ...	A 7173	B 12749	
Sabela, Hermann Joseph.	Germany ...	31 March 1890 ...	Hadfield ...	A 6355	B 8159	
Sabela, Peter Joseph	Germany ...	28 September 1893	Grantham ...	A 7666	B 14996	
Saber, Lewis ...	Prussia ...	18 May 1866 ...	... ...	5047	—	
Sabit, Edouard Jules Armand.	France ...	28 May 1894 ...	London	A 7892	B 16189	
Sablovski, Joseph ...	Russia ...	16 February 1887	Leeds	A 5277	A 45172	
Sacazan, Joseph ...	Turkey ...	10 September 1890	Salo	A 6484	B 8746	
Sacher, Jacob ...	Russia ...	11 November 1896	London	A 9326	B 22050	
Sachs, Albert ...	Germany ...	13 September 1878	London	A 2712	76934	
Sachs, Charles ...	Russia ...	18 April 1882 ...	Bradford... ...	A 3672	A 15215	
Sachs, Charles Frederick.	Prussia ...	16 June 1871 ...	... ...	A 380	4258	
Sachs, Georges Paul	France ...	... ...	... ...	—	—	See des Renaudes, Georges Paul
Sachs, Gustav	Prussia ...	12 July 1866 ...	... ...	5117	—	
Sachs, Henry William	Wesenberg...	11 June 1862 ...	... ...	3857	—	
Sachs, Hermann ...	Prussia ...	10 January 1859...	... ...	2830	—	
Sachs, Ludwig Hugo	Germany ...	11 November 1897	Croydon	A 9948	B 25277	
Sachs, Marcus ...	Prussia ...	12 July 1854 ...	... ...	1838	—	
Sachs, Marcus ...	Prussia ...	30 April 1857 ...	... ...	2426	—	
Sachs, Sigismund ...	Prussia ...	18 September 1858	... ...	2742	—	
Sachse, Friedrich Albert Emil.	Prussia ...	20 May 1867 ...	... ...	5481	—	
Sack, August Frederick Henry.	Brunswick ...	23 October 1889...	London	A 6246	B 7262	
Sack, Hermann Ludwig Theodor.	Prussia ...	14 August 1865...	... ...	4785.	—	
Sacke, Simon ...	Russia ...	9 April 1873 ...	... ...	A 970	21180	
Sackier, Lazarus ...	Russia ...	16 November 1891	Manchester ...	A 6908	B 11528	
Sacks, Solomon ...	Prussia ...	27 January 1845...	... ...	30	—	
Sacrong, Nicholas ...	Egypt ...	18 May 1866 ...	... ...	5036	—	
Sadie, Jacob... ...	Russia ...	4 March 1898 ...	London	A 10111	B 25557	
Sadkie, Hyman ...	Russia ...	21 February 1898	Birmingham ...	A 10087	R 25864	
Sadokierski, Salomon	Russia ...	5 January 1895...	London	A 8174	B 17483	
Sadoun, Roubin Ben	France ...	18 January 1878...	... ...	A 2491	69665	
Saegert, Wilhelm Peter Theodor.	Russia ...	17 October 1856...	... ...	2336	—	
Saetah, Lazarus ...	Russia ...	29 December 1896	.London	A 9398	B 22841	
Safar ...	Russia ...	19 September 1895	Mashed	AAA 42	B 17269	
Saffenreuter, Gustavus Willibrord.	Germany ...	13 December 1882	Pendleton ...	A 3824	A 21730	
Saffer, Joseph ...	Russia ...	24 November 1894	Leeds	A 8117	B 16736	
Saffer, Marks ...	Russia ...	14 November 1894	Leeds	A 8079	B 16739	
Saffer, Nathan ...	Russia ...	14 January 1887...	Leeds	A 5182	A 45717	
Safier, Maks... ...	Russia ...	10 April 1897 ...	London	A 9584	B 23354	
Safran, Jakob ...	Germany ...	14 December 1857	... ...	2570	—	
Sagar, Michael ...	Russian Poland.	1 May 1861 ...	... ...	3528	—	
Sagianos, Nicolas ...	Greece ...	15 January 1891...	Manchester ...	A 6588	B 9848	
Sagovitz, Solomon ...	Russia ...	5 June 1900 ...	London	A 11531	B 31474	
Sagrandi, John Pandeli. }	Greece ...{	31 January 1866... / 26 October 1870...	} ... ...{	4950 / B 12	—	
Sagrandi, Pandeli John.	Greece ...	31 March 1873 ...	... ...	A 965	21094	
Sagrandi, Pandia Eustratio.	Scio	3 February 1854	... ...	1732	—	
Sagrini, Louis Perret	Piedmont ...	30 July 1845 ...	... ...	198	—	

145. Index to naturalisation certificates, 1844–71, in series HO 1 (TNA)

Series HO 3 also contains some lists of immigrants that were submitted by ships' masters in the periods 1836–61 and 1866–69. Colwell (243) includes an illustration of such a list, recording seven aliens (including Karl Marx) submitted by the master of the ship *City of Boulogne* when it arrived in London in 1849. The Anglo-German FHS has an index to about 36,000 Germans recorded in the lists of 1853 to 1869. For other years, if you can find the date and place of your ancestor's arrival, you can refer to *Lloyd's Register* to discover which ships arrived at that port on that date and from where they had sailed. This can narrow down your area of search to perhaps two or three ships.

Records of aliens in the 20th century are also available. About 60,000 Germans were living in Britain at the outbreak of the First World War. An Aliens Registration Act required all aliens to register with the police and the authorities interned many of them (about 30,000 Germans, Austrians and Turks in 1914 and 1915). Some lists of the internees are at TNA in series HO 144. A few registration cards of aliens also survive. Series MEPO 35 includes about 1,000 from the London area and Bedford Record Office holds about 25,000 cards, from 1919–80, featuring the person's photograph, address, occupation and last address outside Britain. Similar documents at other CROs are listed in Kershaw & Pearsall (1299). From 1905, aliens might be deported (for example, if they were convicted of certain crimes). Series HO 372 at TNA contains registers of those ordered to be deported from 1906 to 1963, listing each person's name, nationality, offence, date of conviction and the place to which he or she was deported.

The registration system for aliens living in Britain continued during the Second World War and thousands of aliens were interned or deported. Many of the records have been destroyed, but index cards survive covering most aliens, including the internees. The index cards for about 200,000 people are on microfilm in series HO 396 (arranged alphabetically in 307 sets) noting aliens' dates and places of birth, occupations and places of residence. If the tribunal decided that a person should be interned, the reasons were noted on the back of the card (these are not included on the films). Digital images of some cards are being made available on the web site of Moving Here. Approximately 28,000 Germans and Italians were interned. Some were deported to camps in Canada and Australia and others were gradually released, but about 8,000 were brought before an Alien Internment Tribunal. About 75 sample files for interned aliens survive in series HO 214. Some internment camp records, including lists of internees, are in HO 215 and other records of aliens and internees survive in CROs, listed in Kershaw & Pearsall (1299).

Records of some Czech refugees who arrived in Britain in the 1930s are at TNA, especially in series HO 294. There are also records in WO 315, described by Kershaw & Pearsall (1299), of Polish soldiers who served with the British armed forces in the Second World War and then settled in Britain.

EMIGRATION

People emigrated for many reasons. Some fled from religious persecution, some were convicts who were transported and some went abroad with the armed forces or for business reasons (but decided to settle abroad permanently). However, most emigrants left for economic reasons, especially poverty at home and the inducement of a new life abroad. Records of emigrants can be found in the archives of Britain and the country of destination.

Permanent colonisation by the British commenced in North America in 1607 and in the West Indies in 1612. In the late 18th and early 19th centuries large-scale emigration also took place to

Australia and Africa. British emigrants travelled almost everywhere in the world but the Americas were the most popular destination. It is estimated that about 540,000 people left England between 1630 and 1700 of whom about 380,000 went to the Americas. Some estimates are even higher. Rogers & Smith (452) note estimates that about 850,000 people emigrated from England to America or the West Indies between 1630 and 1699, with a similar number following in the 18th century. It is also estimated that almost 2.4 million people emigrated from England between 1551 and 1851. Over 200,000 people emigrated from Ireland to the United States between 1820 and 1840 alone. The number of British and Irish emigrants has always been substantial, but the numbers were especially high in the 19th century. Hey (23) estimates that 10 million people emigrated from the British Isles in the 19th century, about 2.7 million (many from Ireland) between 1846 and 1855 alone. Hey (22) notes that, between 1837 and 1867, about 3.5 million people emigrated to the United States, about a million to Australia or New Zealand and about 750,000 to Canada. Between 1870 and 1920 another three million British people emigrated to the United States. Although many emigrants (perhaps up to 25 per cent) returned to Britain (because their new life was a failure, or because they never intended to emigrate permanently), millions never returned home. It is very likely that these emigrants include some of your ancestors' brothers and sisters.

Records of emigrants at TNA are described in TNA domestic records leaflet 107. The main sources for emigrants are contained in the records of the Colonial Office, the Board of Trade, the Treasury and the Home Office. Thus Treasury Board papers for 1557 to 1920 (in series T 1) consist of the board's correspondence, reports and related documents, with many references to people in (or going to) the colonies. Calendars of these documents for 1557 to 1775 have been published by HMSO and the List and Index Society. Passenger lists of vessels leaving British ports were generally only retained from 1890. Those for the period up to 1960, for destinations outside Europe, are at TNA in series BT 27. The lists note a passenger's name, occupation, age and destination, but they are arranged by year, by port and then chronologically by the vessel's date of sailing. You therefore need to know the name of the ship or the approximate date of sailing in order to find a person. Registers of the names of ships leaving each port between 1906 and 1951 are in series BT 32. Prior to 1890 only a few passenger lists have survived in Britain (and are held at TNA) but these give similar details.

Passport records are described in TNA domestic records leaflet 60. Passports were not required until 1914 (so most people did not apply for one) but some were issued as early as 1794, principally to diplomats or merchants. They included photographs (from 1914) and, since 1921, were in similar form to those we use today. A register of passport applications and of the passports issued from 1794 to 1948 is at TNA in series FO 610, noting applicants' names and destinations. The entries are in date order, but there are name indexes for 1851–62 and 1874–1916 (on microfilm) in series FO 611. A few sample passports have been retained in series FO 96 and 655 and there are correspondence files for 1815–1905 in series FO 612–614. Furthermore, in the late 16th and early 17th centuries, a "licence to pass beyond the seas" was sometimes issued and a few surviving records (mainly listing soldiers going to Holland or civilians travelling to New England, Barbados or other colonies) are at TNA in series E 157 and CO 1. The names of those people receiving licences, who were going to America or the West Indies between 1600 and 1700, are listed in Hotten (1295). There are some other published lists of British emigrants, the most important of which is Coldham's *Complete Book of Emigrants* (1274). This work (also available on CD-ROM from GPC) consists of chronological (but indexed) abstracts of documents in English archives, such as transportation and apprentice records, licences to pass beyond the seas and port books (from ports such as Bristol, Liverpool and Plymouth), with entries for about 140,000 emigrants to America from 1607 to 1776. Coldham's works on transportees and some other works on emigrants to America are noted below.

Many records of the British colonies are at TNA. Some useful records of colonists, particularly in North America and the West Indies in the 17th and 18th centuries, are noted in Bevan (239) and TNA overseas records leaflet 51. The Colonial Office records include correspondence, orders, land grants and reports from colonial officials. They refer to many emigrants (particularly government officials, army or naval officers, merchants and landowners) but it is difficult to find information on a particular person, since few of the records are indexed. HMSO has published indexed calendars of some of the series of Colonial Papers, such as the general series (in series CO 1) and the Board of Trade minutes for 1675 to 1704 (in series CO 391) in volumes entitled *Calendar of State Papers Colonial, America and West Indies 1574–1739*. For example, the volume for 1737 by Davies (1277) calendars and indexes about 1,000 documents from those Colonial Office files, of which the following are extracts:

> January 17. Antigua. Governor William Mathew of Antigua reports to the Council of Trade and Plantations enclosing affidavits and reports; affidavit of William Fisher of Antigua, sworn before Governor Mathew in Antigua on 13th November 1736. Deponent was sailing in the ship *Fanny* of Antigua (Thomas Nanton, master) to St. Vincent, but . . . was taken about 4th September by a Spanish sloop . . . the six white men aboard the *Fanny* were stripped naked by the Spaniards and severely whipped. One, Timothy Nibbs, was wounded with cutlasses.
>
> November 23. Grants by the Trustees for Georgia to Lieutenant Colonel James Cochran of 500 acres of land in Georgia; grants of 500 acres of land also to Major William Cook and to George Preston junior of Valyfield in the county of Perth.

More information can be found in HMSO published calendars of *Acts of the Privy Council of England: Colonial Series* for 1613–1783 (in six volumes) and *Journals of the Commissioners for Trade and Plantations* for 1704–82 (14 volumes). You can then turn to original records, particularly those of the Colonial and Dominions offices, at TNA. The files are extensive and most have no name indexes but you may find material about your ancestor, perhaps a merchant or civil servant in Hong Kong. A search on PROCAT would tell you that the holdings at TNA for Hong Kong include 590 volumes of correspondence of 1841–1943 (in series CO 129) and 86 volumes of government gazettes, described below, of 1846–1940 in CO 132.

Assisted emigration

Thousands of people were assisted to emigrate. Many people emigrated to work as indentured servants in the colonies, especially in America and the West Indies. They agreed to work for masters, usually on a plantation, for a stipulated number of years in exchange for payment of their passage and board and (after completion of their term of service) a grant of land and a cash payment. Many indentures are held at TNA and Guildhall Library.

Assisted passage was also granted to the poor. Some parishes sponsored the emigration of paupers in order to reduce the number of poor that would have to be supported by the parish in the future. A parish would pay for a poor family's passage and food (and perhaps supply clothing and some cash) from the poor rate or by borrowing money from local landowners and repaying it, with interest, over a number of years. The vestry minutes or overseers' records may record this assistance. For example, volume 2 of *Sussex Family Historian* (237) notes resolutions in the vestry minutes of Battle in Sussex for 1841, including:

11 Feb 1841 . . . to pay the expense of James Eldridge, wife and 3 children to Australia not exceeding twenty pounds.
18 Mar 1841 . . . to advance William Gibbs and family of 5 children, twenty five pounds to assist him to emigrate to Canada.

The Poor Law (Amendment) Act of 1834 permitted poor law unions to supply money, clothing or goods to poor families for their passage to the colonies. This assistance continued until 1890. Hey (22) notes that, from 1836 to 1846, Boards of Guardians assisted about 14,000 English and Welsh people to emigrate, especially to Canada. The Poor Law Commissioners' records of the administration of this system are at TNA (in series MH 12), including correspondence and lists of pauper emigrants (arranged by county and poor law union), often specifying the emigrants' occupations and destinations.

Assistance was also granted by the Colonial Land and Emigration Office (later the Colonial Commission of Land and Emigration), which was established in 1833 to aid emigration by making land grants and providing free passage to the colonies (funded by the sale of Crown lands in the colonies). By 1869 it had assisted about 300,000 British and Irish people to emigrate. The Colonial Office's Emigration Original Correspondence for 1817 to 1896, in series CO 384 at TNA, contains correspondence from settlers or intending settlers in North America, the West Indies and Australia. There are also registers for North America for 1850–68 (in series CO 327 and 328), emigration entry books for 1814–71 (in CO 385) and papers of the Commission of Land and Emigration for 1833–94 (in CO 386), all containing the names of many emigrants. TNA also holds petitions by settlers for land grants in Australia, New Zealand and Canada (and many grants survive in the archives of those countries). Many former soldiers settled in the colonies and they can often be found in War Office pension records in series WO 22 (# chapter 20).

Emigration of children
In the second half of the 19th century many organisations arranged the emigration of poor children or orphans to Australia, Canada, New Zealand or other parts of the Empire, to start a new life (and to help pioneers in those places who needed cheap labour). Child migration schemes originated in the early 17th century. In 1617 the Virginia Company in America asked for children to be sent from England to join the fledgling colony and the City of London sent over 100 poor or orphaned children from Christ's Hospital School (established in 1553 to provide free schooling for children of freemen of the City of London). Guildhall Library holds the school's registers from 1554. The registers of 1605 to 1775 contain about 30,000 entries, of which about 1,000 relate to children sent to America. The children are listed in Coldham (1272); for example Joseph Wells, born on 7 November 1662 (a son of Richard Wells, a carman) who was admitted to the school from the parish of St Andrew Wardrobe on 27 February 1671 and bound as an apprentice in September 1677 to serve John Munford in Virginia.

The Poor Law Amendment Act of 1850 permitted Boards of Guardians to send children under the age of 16 overseas. Philanthropic organisations, such as Dr Barnardo's, also began organising the migration of pauper children or orphans (particularly from workhouses or from the streets of Britain's insanitary cities) to a new life abroad. Bean & Melville (1258) describes child emigration from the 17th century up to 1965, particularly the work of philanthropic organisations which took part in the child emigration movement. Between 1869 and 1948 at least 100,000 children were sent from Britain to new homes in Canada. About 50,000 children were also sent to Australia, New Zealand and South Africa, including a few thousand after the Second World War. Harrison (1291) contains the personal stories of over 100 of these children. Useful information about the organisations that arranged child emigration (and their records) is also provided in Harrison's article "Off to a new life", in *Family Tree Magazine* (September/October 1986). An article by P. Horn in *Genealogists' Magazine* (June 1997) provides useful background on the emigration of pauper children to Canada and some records of the emigrants. The web site of the National Archives of Canada features a database, prepared from ships' passenger lists, of about 100,000 children sent to Canada between 1869 and the 1930s.

Transportation

Many other people were forced to leave Britain. Convicts were transported from England from the early 17th century (# chapter 25). About 50,000 were transported to the West Indies to work on the sugar plantations, or to America (especially Virginia and Maryland) between 1615 and 1775. Perhaps 100,000 Irish people were transported to America in the 17th century. Following the Duke of Monmouth's rebellion in England in 1685, many of the rebels were transported as indentured servants for 10 years (although the survivors were generally freed in 1690 or 1691). Lists of those transported are included in Hotten (1295). Wigfield (1341) is a detailed study of Monmouth's rebels, compiled principally from assize records, listing about 4,000 men involved in the rebellion (and noting whether they died, escaped, were executed or transported). Samuel Bond of Sandford, aged 20, the brother of my ancestor Richard Bond, was transported to Barbados on the ship *Jamaica Merchant* and sold to a plantation owner named Daniel Parsons.

There are many other published lists of those transported from Britain to the colonies in North America and the West Indies. Thus Coldham (1269), compiled from Treasury papers and rolls of gaol delivery sessions or other court records at TNA (# chapter 25), lists English convicts who were transported to colonial America. Volume I lists thousands of people who were convicted in Middlesex and who were transported between 1617 and 1775. The entries note the sessions at which a person was convicted, the ship's name (if known), the destination and date of embarkation. Thus Mary Earley was sentenced to transportation at Middlesex sessions of gaol delivery in April 1773 and transported the same month on the ship *Patapscoe*, bound for Maryland. Volume II of Coldham's work lists thousands of people convicted in London between 1656 and 1775. Thus James Charnock was sentenced to transportation at sessions of gaol delivery in January 1724 and transported to the Carolinas in February 1724 on the ship *Anne* under Captain Thomas Wrangham. These two volumes have been superseded by further work by Coldham. *The Complete Book of Emigrants in Bondage 1614–1775* by Coldham (1273), with a supplement published in 1992, includes the information from the Middlesex and London volumes noted above (but also much information from assize records and the records of about 50 Quarter Sessions) so that about 53,000 convicts are listed (with similar information as that noted above for Mary Warley and James Charnock). The CD-ROM noted above, of Coldham's *Complete Book of Emigrants* (1274), includes this work (and the supplement) but does not include the most recent volume by Coldham (1273a), which contains abstracts of records of a further 9,000 transported criminals.

The American War of Independence put an end to transportation to North America. However, convicts were then sent to hulks in the Bahamas or at Gibraltar and in 1788 the first convicts were transported to Australia. It is estimated that between 1788 and 1868 about 162,000 men and women were transported from Britain to Australia. Transportation records held in Britain and Ireland were noted in chapters 25 and 29 (and Australian records are considered below), but Colonial Office correspondence files at TNA (in series CO 201, 202, 207, 360 and 369) refer to many convicts (as well as free settlers) in New South Wales from 1789.

Miscellaneous records of immigrants and emigrants
The records held abroad that include information on British people living abroad (whether as temporary visitors or permanent settlers) are too vast and detailed to be adequately covered here. However, as an example, an article by B. Meringo in *Genealogists' Magazine* (March 1987) reviews detailed records for 1822 to 1858 that are held at the town hall in Boulogne, France, concerning people travelling between Britain and the port of Boulogne. The records include about 300,000 people: many British people moving to and from the continent, but also many French, Italians and other nationalities emigrating to Britain.

The amount of published material on emigrants in their new homes is so vast that only the most important works can be noted in this chapter. However, one important type of published work should be noted here, since it is relevant to colonists in many parts of the world. Many towns or communities (particularly in the United States, Canada and Australia) are of recent origin. For example, large parts of the Canadian provinces of Alberta and Saskatchewan were only settled by Europeans (displacing Indian tribes) in the late 19th or early 20th centuries, so their history may start only one generation before living memory. A popular type of book about such communities is what I call the "pioneer" study; that is, a work describing the community's history and noting each family of settlers (and their descendants). A good example concerns the town of Richmound in Saskatchewan (1251), which was established in 1910. It includes an account of the town's history, maps, photographs, extracts from records and a section on each family of settlers and their descendants from 1910 to 1978. Richmound's settlers came from other parts of Canada, the United States and many European countries (including Poland, Russia, Norway, Britain, Germany and Austria). If there is such a book for the place in which your relatives settled, it is likely to include valuable genealogical information (although much will have been provided by the families and so you should try to corroborate it by documentary evidence).

THE BRITISH ABROAD

British people who lived abroad were subject to foreign civil registration systems from the late 19th century and some of these are considered below. The baptisms, marriages and burials of the British abroad were also recorded in many local church registers (and perhaps in the IGI). The SoG has copies of many church registers from around the world, particularly Canada, the United States, India and the West Indies, listed in its booklet (152).

In addition, Anglican churches were established (and maintained their own registers) in many places in which the British settled. For example, the registers of the Anglican church in

Hamburg, Germany, commence in 1617. From the 17th century Anglican churches were also founded in British colonies. Many of their registers are held locally but some, or copies, have been brought back to Britain. The Bishop of London was responsible for many years for certain Anglican churches abroad and therefore received many original registers, bishops' transcripts or copies. These are held at Guildhall Library or TNA and many of them are listed in Yeo (1342). The registers at Guildhall Library relate particularly to Anglican congregations in Western Europe (for example those of Lisbon in Portugal) but also in China, South America and Africa. Examples of these registers are:

Italy: Turin, baptisms and burials 1866–67	MS 11,830
France: Dieppe, baptisms 1825–29 & burials 1825–28	MS 10,891B

Guildhall Library also holds registers (called the International memoranda) of baptisms, marriages and burials conducted by chaplains at British diplomatic missions or by other diplomatic representatives, who had been licensed by the Bishop of London, and who sent records to the London Diocesan registry. The memoranda cover the period from 1816 to 1924 in 13 volumes (Guildhall Library MS 10,926/1–13) and are indexed. The memoranda are listed by country (with covering dates) in Yeo (1342), for example entries for Ascension Island (baptisms in 1846 and marriages from 1847 to 1856) and the Philippines (baptisms in 1872). A typical entry in the memoranda is:

I hereby certify that Edward John Bury, son of Edward Bury of Newton Saintloe . . . Somerset and Mary his wife, and Charlotte Maria, daughter of John, Duke of Argyle of Inverary Castle . . . Argyleshire and Elizabeth his wife, were joined together in Holy Matrimony, according to the rites of the Church of England, in my presence, this 23rd day of March 1819; G. Dawkins, H.M. Charge d'affaires at Florence . . . This marriage was solemnized between us; Edward John Bury and Charlotte Maria Campbell; by me Samuel Oliver, chaplain on half pay to the 22nd regiment of Dragoons
In the presence of: J. Russell . . . Thos. Fras. Fremantle.

There are many other records in Britain documenting the birth, baptism, marriage, burial or death of the British abroad. Certain registers held by the Registrar General in London (such as those of the armed forces) were noted in chapters 5, 20 and 21. The Registrar General also holds registers from 1849 of births and deaths of British nationals in foreign countries (other than in the British Empire and Commonwealth) which were recorded by British Consuls and also records of marriages attended or conducted by consuls. TNA also holds some further records of the Registrar General and these can be seen on microfilm at the FRC or TNA. They include registers of some Anglican communities abroad which had been sent to the Bishop of London and are now held in the following series:

RG 32: Miscellaneous foreign returns, 1831–1968
RG 33: Miscellaneous foreign registers and returns, 1627–1960
RG 34: Miscellaneous foreign marriages, 1826–1921
RG 35: Miscellaneous foreign deaths, 1830–1921
RG 36: Births, marriages and deaths in protectorates of Africa and Asia, 1895–1965

Some indexes are in series RG 43 (and copies of these are also at the FRC). Bevan (239) lists the country and covering dates of most of the registers and some are listed in Yeo (1342). A few examples are:

Belgium: Brussels, marriages 1816–90	RG 33/3–8
China: Shanghai, marriages 1852–1951	RG 33/12–20
France: Paris, deaths 1846–52	RG 35/11
Holland: Rotterdam, baptisms and marriages 1708–94	RG 33/89

The Foreign Office records at TNA include various registers (from which the consular returns at the GRO were compiled) and some that are not included in the GRO records. The countries and covering years are listed in Bevan (239) and Yeo (1342). There is also some correspondence, in series FO 83 and 97, about consular marriages abroad from 1814 to 1915 (indexed up to 1893 in FO 802/239). Examples of the registers include:

Taiwan: deaths 1873–1901	FO 721/1
Germany: Berlin, births 1944–54 & deaths 1944–45	FO 601/2–6
Russia: St Petersburg, births 1856–1938, marriages 1892–1917 and	
deaths 1897–1927	FO 378/3–9

Some registers of Anglican communities abroad, which were returned to the Archbishop of Canterbury, are at Lambeth Palace Library and listed by Yeo (1342). Registers of Anglican churches in India, Pakistan, Bangladesh and Burma are in the India Office collections at the British Library (with other records of the British in India) and considered below. In summary, if you are searching for the birth, baptism, marriage, death or burial of a British ancestor abroad, you should consult (in addition to the IGI) the following sources:

a. GRO foreign, military and marine registers
b. registers at TNA in series RG 32–36 and 43
c. Foreign Office registers at TNA
d. registers and memoranda at Guildhall Library
e. India Office collections at the British Library
f. local records

It is also worth reviewing, for any country, the entry in Colwell (242), since TNA has many records relating to other countries, particularly those in the British Empire. These may concern your ancestors or evidence their life in those countries. For example, TNA holds registers of slaves in Bermuda (1821–34) and Ceylon (1818–32) and, among other records for British Guiana, newspapers (1835–56) and poll tax returns (1765–94). During most of the 19th and 20th centuries, the government of each British colony or dominion published its own government gazette, in similar format to the *London Gazette* (# chapter 17). Copies of these gazettes were sent to London from 1837 (and in some cases earlier) and are now held in the Colonial Office records at TNA. They can be found by searching PROCAT by the name of the colony or dominion. These gazettes provide invaluable information about the British abroad in the notices of government, military and clerical appointments, deceased's estates, bankruptcies, civil and criminal court cases, as well as land grants or claims in the colony.

Records are also available of about 18,000 British civilians, who were living in Hong Kong, Shanghai, Singapore, Malaysia or elsewhere in the Far East and who were interned by the Japanese during the Second World War. Most of these records are held at TNA and the Imperial War Museum, and are reviewed by R. Bridge in *Genealogists' Magazine* (December 2002).

Information about the life of the British abroad can also be obtained at the British Empire & Commonwealth Museum in Bristol. The museum has many exhibits, a library as well as film, sound and manuscript archives about the history of the Empire and Commonwealth. In particular, there are over 1,000 recordings of the reminiscences of people who lived or worked in the Empire as administrators, soldiers, businessmen, farmers and housewives.

INVESTIGATIONS ABROAD

This section summarises the genealogical records available in a number of countries and refers to detailed works on those records. Reference can also be made to the general works on research in foreign countries, such as Baxter (1252) and Currer-Briggs (1276), noted above.

United States of America

Drake (1279) is a concise guide to research in the United States, but Greenwood (1290) and *The Source* by Eakle & Cerny (1280) (updated by L. Szucs and S. Luebking) are works that provide detailed information on all the sources noted below (with many illustrations and examples) as well as bibliographies on each aspect of American research. Anyone intending to research in American records should refer to one of these works.

The United States has a federal system of government. It is far less centralised than Great Britain and individual states have retained many legislative powers and therefore their own records. Many records can also be found at the "county" level (into which each state is divided). These three levels of government (federal, state and county), result in genealogical records being held in many more archives. Despite this, the National Archives in Washington DC (holding principally federal records) is probably the most important archive for genealogical material. Its holdings, which include passenger arrival lists, censuses, military, property and court records, are reviewed in its published guide (1245). Many of the records at the National Archives have been microfilmed and can also be seen at 11 branches of the National Archives (for example in Boston, New York, Chicago and Los Angeles).

Genealogy is very popular in North America and there are many family history societies which can assist you with the records of a particular state or city. A vast amount of material has also been published, particularly by the Genealogical Publishing Co. Inc. (GPC) of 1001 North Calvert Street, Baltimore, Maryland 2102–3897 (# appendix XI for its web site), and Clearfield Company of 200 East Eager Street, Baltimore, Maryland 21202. Researchers should review the GPC and Clearfield catalogues for material such as family histories, pedigrees of colonial families, lists of immigrants and catalogues of manuscript collections. There are also many published works, listed in Greenwood (1290) or the GPC or Clearfield catalogues, on genealogical research in (or transcribed records of) particular states. The LDS collections of American material (both original sources and published works) in the Family History Library in Salt Lake City are particularly large so that much research can be undertaken at family history centres in Britain by ordering microfilms. Furthermore, *FamilySearch* (# chapter 11) includes the US social security death index. This lists the names of about 64 million people who died between 1960 (but sometimes earlier) and 1999 and whose deaths were reported to the US Social Security administration. The information for each person usually includes dates of birth and death and the place of residence at the time of death. No information about relatives is included. *FamilySearch* also includes the Military Index of about 100,000 American servicemen who died in the Korean or Vietnam wars. These indexes are described in Nichols (167).

One particular problem of American research is the number of places, even within the same state, which have the same name. This is principally because settlers named the counties, cities, towns or villages where they settled after their places of origin (often places in Britain). Detailed maps and gazetteers are therefore essential. There were also frequent boundary changes, particularly for counties. Greenwood (1290) notes that a family living in the same house in Jefferson in North Carolina from 1700 to 1800 could be found in the records of seven different counties (mainly because of boundary changes).

The European powers established colonies in America in the early 17th century and so records until the American revolution are similar to those of Britain or the other colonial powers. Churches registered baptisms, marriages and burials but there were many different religious groups and no established Church. Many non-conformists emigrated to America (for example from England, Holland and Germany) and so a great number of Protestant churches were established, such as the Congregational Church, the Protestant Episcopal Church, the Lutheran Church, the Baptist Church and the Society of Friends (the state of Pennsylvania was established as a Quaker state). It can therefore be very difficult to determine your ancestors' church, or find a family in the records of one church over a period of time (or locate any surviving records). Most records are held by the church (or its central archive or historical society) and many have been microfilmed by the Mormons. Greenwood (1290) provides a useful schedule, for each state, noting the principal locations of each religious group's records. Eakle & Cerny (1280) and Greenwood (1290) provide many examples from church records. The church registers are similar to English parish registers (and they also produced records such as vestry minutes). The Quakers held Preparative, Weekly, Monthly, Quarterly and Yearly Meetings (as in England) and produced minutes of the meetings and records of births, marriages and deaths.

Civil registration of births and deaths was a state responsibility, so the systems and commencement dates vary accordingly. The first state to introduce centralised civil registration was Massachusetts (1842), followed by New Jersey (1848), New Hampshire (1850) and Rhode Island (1852). Many states did not introduce civil registration until the late 19th or early 20th century (for example, Alabama in 1908 and Georgia in 1919). Some cities introduced civil registration much earlier, for example New Orleans (from 1790 for births and 1803 for deaths). The principal records of marriages are registers of churches (or Justices of the Peace) and licences issued by county clerks. Centralised state records of marriages only commence in the late 19th or early 20th centuries. Eakle & Cerny (1280) list the addresses to which you should write to obtain records of births, marriages and deaths. There are also a number of state-wide indexes to births, marriages and deaths, most of which are listed by Eakle & Cerny (1280) and are held by the LDS Family History Library.

Federal censuses were taken in 1790 and then every 10 years (although many areas were not settled, or constituted as states, until much later) and records are open to the public at the National Archives after about 72 years. The Mormons have microfilm copies of all the public census records. Greenwood (1290) and Eakle & Cerny (1280) provide details of the available records and the information contained in each census. The names of heads of families were recorded from

1790 and names of all people in a household from 1850. The records from 1850 include a person's age, sex, occupation and place of birth (and relationship to the head of the family from 1880). Most of the census of 1890 was destroyed, but surviving schedules list about 6,200 people. There are indexes to each of the censuses of 1790 to 1920 and most of these indexes have been published in books or on CD-ROM. An index to the 1880 census is included in *FamilySearch*. Information from restricted census records can be supplied to the person to whom the information relates, the next of kin or (in certain instances) to other relatives. The 1840 census notes those men who were Revolutionary War pensioners of the federal government and the 1890 census notes veterans of the Union Army of the Civil War (or widows of deceased veterans). The 1900 returns specify the number of years each person had been in the United States and the 1910 returns note the year of immigration. In 1910 people also had to indicate whether they had fought in the Union or Confederate armies. There were also many special censuses (of counties, cities or states) taken by state or federal governments (such as that of 1857 in Minnesota). These censuses (and any published versions or indexes) are listed by Eakle & Cerny (1280).

Directories of some American cities date from the late 18th century and many that are available on microform are listed by Eakle & Cerny (1280). A selection of directories from cities such as Baltimore, Boston, Charleston and New York are included on *The Biography Database 1680–1830* (# chapter 9). Eakle & Cerny (1280) provide guidance to research in business and professional directories and in newspapers (with lists of many newspaper indexes, especially of marriage and obituary notices, that are available).

Greenwood (1290) lists many American biographical dictionaries. Perhaps the best is Johnson (1297), which is a 20-volume dictionary of American biography published from 1928 to 1936, with various supplemental and index volumes published since then. The United States does not have earls, knights or similar titles but many descendants of British noble or landed families have emigrated to America. The 1939 edition of *Burke's Landed Gentry* included 1,600 pedigrees of American families (including over 50,000 people) that had such a descent. This section has been reprinted by GPC (1240) and is included on the CD-ROM *Notable British Families* (# chapter 26). *American Presidential Families* by Brogan & Mosley (1260) is in similar format to *Burke's Peerage*, but features the ancestors and descendants of all American Presidents from George Washington 1789 to Bill Clinton in 1993.

The number of immigrants arriving in the United States was enormous, particularly in the 19th and early 20th centuries. In 1905 alone, almost one million immigrants arrived from Europe. Tepper (1328) and Greenwood (1290) provide detailed reviews of American records, since the colonial period, of passengers arriving in America by ship. The most useful are customs' and immigration passenger lists, most of which are in the National Archives (microfilm copies are at LDS family history centres). Only a few records of passengers' names survive from before 1820. For example, records of the port of Philadelphia include almost 5,000 ships' baggage lists (used to calculate duty on immigrants' belongings), naming about 40,000 passengers, from the period 1800–19. An official system of listing immigrants commenced in 1820. Masters of vessels arriving in the United States had to file lists (with customs officers) of all passengers' names, ages, sex, occupations and country of origin. These customs' passenger lists also provide details of the ship and its voyage and were copied to the Secretary of State. Detailed records survive for most of the important ports and are held at an archive in Philadelphia and at the National Archives in Washington. There are also immigration passenger lists since 1882 (but later for some ports) which provide similar information, but also note a person's last place of residence and (if they were meeting a relative in America) the name and address of that relative. Information from these records can usually only be obtained if you know the port of entry or the ship's name. The customs and immigration lists for each port, their covering dates (and any published lists and indexes) are reviewed by Tepper (1328).

There are many published works on immigrants to America since the 17th century (based on American, British and other countries' records). Many of these works are listed by Eakle & Cerny (1280) and Greenwood (1290), such as *Immigrants to New England, 1700–1775* by E. Bolton, published by GPC in 1931. Published works such as these should be used (at the SoG, reference libraries or LDS family history centres) before attempting to use the original records. Many of the published works on the early settlers of North America are also available on CD-ROM. Three examples are *Genealogies of Mayflower Families, 1500s–1800s, A Genealogical Dictionary of New England 1600s–1700s* and Coldham's *The Complete Book of Emigrants 1607–1776* and *The Complete Book of Emigrants in Bondage 1614–1775*. You should in particular refer to Filby & Meyer (1282) and Filby (1283). The original three volumes of *Passenger and Immigration Lists Index* by Filby & Meyer (1282) list about 480,000 passengers (from published passenger and immigration records) who arrived in the United States and Canada in the 17th, 18th and 19th centuries. Annual supplements from 1982 to 2003 bring the number of people listed in this work to over 4 million. Entries typically give a passenger's name and age, year of arrival and port of entry. Any accompanying passengers (such as wife and children) are also listed, as well as the source of the information. The original three volumes and 17 supplements up to 1999 of Filby & Meyer's work (containing about 2,987,000 entries) can also be purchased on CD-ROM. The immigrants' names are taken from about 2,550 published passenger or immigration lists, dating from 1538 to 1900, and listed in Filby (1283). This guide supersedes the bibliography of ship passenger lists by Lancour & Wolfe (1301).

Some published lists concentrate on British emigrants to America. The works by Coldham and Hotten were noted above. Some other examples of the published material that deals predominantly with British emigrants are:

a. H. Newman: *To Maryland from Overseas, a Complete Digest of the Jacobite Loyalists Sold into White Slavery in Maryland and the British and Continental Background of Approximately 1,400 Maryland Settlers from 1634 to the Early Federal Period with Source Documentation*, GPC (1986)

b. Coldham (1271) contains hundreds of abstracts of wills of people living in America (or other wills concerning America) that were proved from 1610 to 1857 in the Prerogative Court of Canterbury. The PCC had jurisdiction over English estates of those dying abroad, so this source is particularly useful for families with land in England and America

c. J. Savage: *A Genealogical Dictionary of the First Settlers of New England* (1860–1862), reprinted by GPC (1994) lists all known settlers in New England up to 1692 with details of their children and grandchildren

d. Virkus (1336) provides pedigrees of about 54,000 Americans living in the late 19th or early 20th centuries back to their earliest known ancestors in America (recording about 425,000 people from the 17th to 19th centuries). Thus the ancestry of Charles Gilman (born 1861) is noted back to Edward Gilman (died 1681) who sailed from England in 1638 in the ship *Diligent* with his wife Mary Clark, five children and three servants, settling in Dorchester, Massachusetts and later at Exeter, New Hampshire

e. Dobson (1278) is a biographical directory of many Scottish people who settled in North America from 1625 to 1825, with information extracted from records such as wills, land grants and the Scottish registers of deeds

f. Glazier & Tepper (1288) provides transcripts of passenger lists of ships arriving in New York from 1846 to 1851 (from the US Customs' passenger lists noted above). About 460,000 people are listed (primarily Irish people escaping from the famine), with their age, sex, occupation, ship's name, date of arrival and port of departure.

Many of these (and similar works on immigrants to America) have also been issued on CD-ROM, such as *Irish Immigrants to North America 1803–1871*, *Huguenot Settlers in America 1600s–1900s*, *Germans to America 1875–1888* and *Passenger and Immigration Lists: Boston 1821–1850*.

There was little control by US authorities over immigration until 1891 when all aliens entering the country were required to report to Federal immigration officers for vetting as to their health, place of origin and destination. Between 1892 and 1954, about 75% of immigrants arriving in America landed at Ellis Island in New York harbour. The number of arrivals there between 1892 and 1924 alone was over 17 million. The American Family Immigration History Center at Ellis Island has a database to the immigrants of 1892–1924, prepared from passenger lists and shipping manifests, which can also be searched on the Ellis Island web site. A "wall of honour" at the museum on Ellis Island lists 500,000 immigrants who landed there (also listed on an Ellis Island wall of honour web site) to which further names, submitted by immigrants' descendants, are being added.

Naturalisation or citizenship was originally a state responsibility and there are some state naturalisation records. From 1868 people were citizens of the United States, rather than of a particular state, and detailed federal naturalisation records date from 1906 (but are confidential for 75 years). Naturalisation proceedings took place in federal courts and the records are held at the National Archives. Details of the system and records are provided by Greenwood (1290). Schaefer (1319) is a guide to US naturalisation records, which usually include an immigrant's date and place of birth. The Mormons hold microfilm copies of US passport applications (at the National Archives) from 1795 to 1919 and US citizenship applications from 1906 to 1941.

There are both federal and state court systems (for each of civil and criminal matters). There are federal district courts, Courts of Appeal and a Supreme Court. Each state has a Supreme Court at the top of a hierarchy of courts (of varying names and jurisdictions). American court records can therefore be even more difficult to use than English court records and researchers should review the detailed section on court records in Eakle & Cerny (1280) before attempting to use the records. Wills and probate developed as a state responsibility, so that the records and archives in each state are slightly different. In most states there were county probate courts (but sometimes state probate courts) and the relevant courts are listed in Greenwood (1290). In most cases those courts still have custody of the probate records but many have been microfilmed by the Mormons. Divorce was also within states' jurisdiction and the state courts' records since the 18th or early 19th centuries should be consulted.

American land records, especially from the colonial period, are particularly useful because so much land was available that most settlers up to the 19th century were able to own land and therefore appear in the records. All land was originally claimed by the British Crown and granted to the 13 colonies, which provided land to settlers. After the American Revolution the federal government claimed all land (other than that in the first 13 states) and gradually transferred it, either directly to settlers or to new territories or states (which in turn granted land to individuals). The principal colonial record of land is the land grant. The grant process and surviving records (such as land surveys, petitions and grants) are reviewed in detail by Greenwood (1290) and Eakle & Cerny (1280). The law of property in America was very similar to English law and so records of land transactions (following the initial grants) are also very similar. Counties generally had jurisdiction over land transactions and so most surviving records are held by county clerks, registries or courts. Many land records in archives are indexed and Greenwood (1290) is a good starting point for research, whilst Eakle & Cerny (1280) describe the legislation and published material for each state. In addition, land has always been a basis for taxation in America and many detailed tax lists (recording the landowners) survive from the early 19th century. Eakle & Cerny (1280) also provide a detailed list of business archives (many of large US corporations) and sections on the records of prisons, coroners, schools and hospitals.

TNA at Kew holds many records of the British colonies in North America, although names of individual colonists are very difficult to find. The documents, principally in Colonial Office records, are described in TNA overseas records leaflet 51. TNA also holds records of some land grants in the 17th and 18th centuries and of compensation claims by loyalists after the American War of Independence (for example in series FO 4, AO 3, AO 12, AO 13 and T 79). These are described in TNA overseas records leaflet 35 and abstracts of some of the documents are contained in Coldham (1270).

American genealogists are very interested in the colonial, revolutionary and American civil wars. Records of the colonial wars are not extensive but there are many published works about the conflict (and some soldiers). Records of the revolutionary war are more substantial, including records of pensions awarded to men who served in the American army. Most are held at the National Archives and reviewed by Eakle & Cerny (1280) and Greenwood (1290), who also lists the published works on the war and those men who fought in it. Reports of Congress between 1792 and 1841 listed about 120,000 revolutionary war pensioners, noting their rank, regiment, date of enlistment, place of residence, nature of wounds or date of death (and some references to widows and orphans). These reports are available on a CD-ROM. There are fairly detailed records for army and navy personnel since 1784, including records of men's service during the American Civil War. Detailed records for both Union and Confederate armies are at the National Archives and reviewed by Greenwood (1290). Records for both armies are arranged by State, then unit (and indexed by surname). There are also 27 volumes of a roll of honour to 200,000 Union soldiers who died in the war, with each soldier's rank, regiment, date of death and place of burial. The volumes have been reprinted by GPC and also issued on a CD-ROM.

FamilySearch, on CD-ROM or online includes not only the IGI and *Ancestral File*, but also the US Social Security Death Index and the US Military Deaths Index. The Social Security Index includes 64 million people for whom a death benefit was claimed from the US Government. Most entries are for deaths since 1960 but some are as early as 1936. Entries typically include a name, dates of death and birth, social security number (SSN) and the deceased's last place of residence. If you find a person's SSN in the index, the Social Security administration in Baltimore can, on receipt of a written application and a fee, disclose certain information such as that person's place of birth and parent's names as listed on the person's application for the SSN. The Military Deaths Index lists the men who died in the Korean and Vietnam wars, with their date of birth, place of residence, marital status, date (and place) of death, army rank and number.

Australia

Captain Cook discovered Australia in 1770. European settlement commenced in New South Wales, originally as a penal colony for convicts, in 1788. Until 1901 there were six separate colonies in Australia but in that year, these colonies became states and a federal capital (now Canberra) was founded. Vine Hall (1334) is an extremely detailed guide to genealogical sources in Australia, which anyone researching in Australian records should obtain. It describes the archives holding genealogical material, the published guides to those archives and lists local and family history societies (and many of their publications). For each state Vine Hall lists the types of records available (such as civil registration records, census returns, directories, land records and newspapers), describes them in detail, notes the archives holding the records and lists any published copies or transcripts. An accompanying volume by Vine Hall (1334a) lists the most important published transcripts of records and indexes that are available for genealogists.

Although European settlement of Australia commenced with the foundation of a penal colony, free settlers, soldiers, administrators (and their descendants) soon outnumbered convict arrivals. As Vine Hall (1334) notes, about 63,000 convicts and 14,000 free settlers arrived between 1788 and 1830 but the numbers were 51,000 and 65,000 respectively in the period 1831–40, 32,000 and 108,000 in the period 1841–50, 14,000 and 587,000 in the period 1851–60 and 2,000 and 167,000 in the period 1861–70. About 162,000 convicts had been sent to Australia by the time transportation ended in 1868 but over 900,000 free settlers had also arrived. Therefore, although many Australians are descended from convicts (it is estimated that about 250,000 Australians have ancestors who sailed on the First Fleet), most Australian ancestors located by genealogists will in fact be free settlers.

Lists of those on the First, Second and Third Fleets, whether convicts or soldiers, have been published. The First Fleet arrived in January 1788, having left England on 13 May 1787. The Second and Third Fleets followed in 1790 and 1791. Transportation to New South Wales continued until 1840 and to other parts of Australia until 1868. Gillen (1287) and Flynn (1285) are detailed biographical dictionaries for the First and Second Fleets, recounting the story of these fleets and providing biographies of each crew member, convict, their families or other passengers (about 1,500 people in each fleet) extracted from Australian and British records (including trial records, ships' musters and Admiralty, Colonial Office and Treasury papers at TNA). Conditions on the fleets were harsh, particularly on the Second Fleet (known as the Death Fleet) – 26 per cent of the convicts on the Second Fleet died during the voyage and another 14 per cent died within eight months of landing in Australia. Two of the shorter entries concerning convicts, one (for Jane Marriott) from Gillen (1287), and one (for Daniel Miller) from Flynn (1285) show how useful these biographical dictionaries can be:

Jane Marriott (? to 1793) . . . stole a black silk cloak from her mistress and was sentenced to transportation at the Old Bailey on 18 April 1787 after the garment had been found on her. On the 20th, with a group of women from Newgate, she was sent by wagon to Portsmouth to embark on the *Prince of Wales* on 3 May. She made no impact on the colony and was probably the Jane Merrit buried at Parramatta on 30 April 1793.

Daniel Miller (1755–1790) . . . was sentenced to seven years transportation at the 30 June 1788 Aylesbury (Buckinghamshire) assizes for the theft of fish from a garden pond . . . He was held in Aylesbury Gaol until just before 20 October 1788 when he was sent on board the Thames hulk *Censor*, age given as 32. On 12 November 1789, he embarked on the *Neptune* transport. He was buried at Sydney Cove on 11 July 1790, within days of landing.

Cobley (1268) provides further detail about the crimes, trials and sentences of the First Fleet convicts, with detailed reference to the source material including newspaper reports of the trial and references to the Old Bailey Sessions Papers or to assize records at TNA. Ryan (1315) lists the convicts on the Third Fleet, noting each convict's date and place of conviction, the length of sentence and the ship of transportation. Smee (1323) includes details of many of those convicts' children and grandchildren.

The State Archives of New South Wales have published many of the records concerning convicts on microfiche, including convict indents (lists of convicts on the transport ships), pardons and musters. An indent notes the trial court, date and sentence (and sometimes the convict's age, physical description, marital status, number of children, occupation and offence). Indexes to over 120,000 convicts who arrived in New South Wales and Tasmania up to 1842 are available on fiche and CD-ROM. Some convicts are omitted from these indexes. However, a CD-ROM index, published by the Society of Australian Genealogists, lists all the convicts (and their ship and crime) known to have arrived in New South Wales from 1788 to 1812. The Archives Office of Tasmania has produced a CD-ROM index of convicts transported to Tasmania. A microfiche index to convict indents, produced by the Genealogical Society of Victoria (1248), is another useful finding aid since it lists convicts sent to New South Wales and Tasmania (and also 10,000 transported to Western Australia, 1850–53), the ship upon which they arrived, the date and the indent reference. There is a vast amount of other published and unpublished material about convicts in Australia, such as records of courts and prisons, correspondence, applications to marry, death registers, freedom certificates, pardons and tickets of leave. All of these are listed and described by Vine Hall (1334).

English court records of the trials and transportation of convicts were reviewed in chapter 25. Hawkings (1292) is a detailed study, with many illustrations of records from TNA and other English archives, which shows how to trace a convict from his trial in England to his new life in Australia. It reviews the records of convicts at TNA but also the records of ships' crews and free emigrants from 1788 to 1868. Some convicts' families applied to join them. Wives' petitions (in series PC 1 and HO 12) include details of convicts, their families and their travel. Many convicts also appear in TNA holdings of the colony's early records, for example, pardons or correspondence in Colonial Office records, such as New South Wales Original Correspondence 1801–21 (in series CO 201) and entry books of convicts for 1788 to 1825 (series CO 207).

There were also many free settlers and these, together with convicts who had completed their sentence, received free grants of land (convicts were available to work the land in exchange for the settlers feeding and clothing them). Colonial Office records at TNA include many petitions (and related correspondence) for grants of land in, or free passage to, Australia. Flynn (1285) includes a detailed bibliography of manuscript and published sources for the early colonists in New South Wales, and Vine Hall (1334) reviews the land records of each state. The Crown made free grants of land in New South Wales until 1831, from which date the land had to be purchased. The different types of land title (and the resulting records) are described by Vine Hall (1334), together with the location of records of grants, indexes and abstracts of the records. Records of land grants and later transactions are held in state archive offices or land title offices. A collection of about 400,000 books, 60,000 manuscripts, and over one million prints, maps and pictures of the early years of settlement in Australia are held in the Mitchell Library in Sydney and described in a guide (1250).

Between 1788 and 1900 about one million immigrants arrived in Australia, the vast majority from Europe. Although passenger lists in Britain from before 1890 have generally not survived, extensive lists up to about 1960 are available in Australia, usually sorted by port, date and ship's name (but many are indexed). A ship's list may note an immigrant's age, country or place of birth, occupation, port (and date) of departure and date of arrival in Australia. Peake (1312) describes the surviving lists of passengers, settlers, convicts and soldiers (for Australia and New Zealand) and the archives in which they are held. There are a large number of indexes to the passengers, many of them listed in Vine Hall (1334), such as 64 indexes that include people arriving in New South Wales alone.

As noted above many people were assisted to emigrate from Britain by Boards of Guardians. There were also other forms of assistance in Australia, for example the payment of government bounties to settlers (or to agents who in turn paid for immigrants' expenses). Australian archives hold many records of the assisted emigration of British people to Australia and many of these are indexed. Thus there is a microfiche index (1239) to British assisted immigrants to Victoria from 1839 to 1871, providing the immigrant's and ship's name, the month and year of arrival and references to the original arrival registers (which are also reproduced in the microfiche). An index to immigrants to Victoria 1852–89 is on the web site of the Victoria Public Record Office. The New South Wales State Archives Office holds many records (such as agents' immigrant lists, wage agreements and passenger lists) and has produced an index (1247) to the assisted immigrants named in these records from 1844 to 1859. There are similar indexes for 1860 to 1896. Each index notes the immigrant's name, age, ship, year of arrival (with references to the source documents). The Western Australian Genealogical Society is also producing an index to all the passengers (about 900,000) who arrived in Australia from 1880 to 1925.

The 1828 census of New South Wales and Tasmania includes about 35,000 people (settlers or convicts) and gives ages, occupations, residences, their year of arrival (and name of the ship) or whether they were born in the colony. For example, it includes Richard Eagles, aged 34, a convict who arrived in New South Wales in 1816 on the ship *Neptune*, working as a servant to Mrs Broughton in Appin. TNA has a microfilm copy of this census (in series HO 10) and Sainty & Johnson (1318), also available on CD-ROM, is an alphabetical transcript. Other musters of population in New South Wales and Tasmania were taken between 1788 and 1859. Many are at TNA in series HO 10 and listed by Hawkings (1292). Some of these musters have been published, such as those of New South Wales and Norfolk Island in 1805/6 and 1811 in Baxter (1255) and (1256). A few other musters or householder lists of the early 19th century for South Australia, Victoria and Western Australia are listed in Vine Hall (1334). Censuses for the whole of Australia commenced in 1881 but most returns were destroyed once they had been used for statistical analysis.

Volumes of the *Australian Biographical and Genealogical Record* are an indispensable source for 19th century Australians. This is a project to research and publish biographies of every person who was born or arrived in eastern Australia from 1788 to 1841 and also to publish as many biographies as possible of other Australians who were alive prior to 1899. The first four volumes, including Spurway (1325), contain detailed biographies of 6,000 people (1,700 of them with photographs) which also refer to over 80,000 of their relatives.

Each Australian state (and the Capital Territory) has its own system of civil registration of births, marriages and deaths. The systems commenced at different dates: Tasmania (1838); Western Australia (1841); South Australia (1842); Victoria (1842); New South Wales (1856); Queensland (1856); Northern Territory (1870); and ACT (1930). Some records about living people are only released to that person (or with his or her authority), as noted by Vine Hall (1334). However, many indexes to the records are available on fiche, CD-ROM and on the Internet. For example, indexes of the civil registration records of New South Wales (up to 1905 for births and up to 1945 for marriages and deaths) are on the web site of the NSW Registrar General. Indexes to many early civil registration records, some including parish register entries for the period before civil registration commenced, have also been published on CD-ROM and can be reviewed at the SoG or purchased. Thus the *Queensland Pioneers Index* is an index to births, marriages and deaths (and some baptisms) in Queensland for 1829–89. The *Victorian Pioneers Index* is an index to similar material from Victoria for 1837–88 and there are similar "Pioneer" indexes for New South Wales (1788–1918), Western Australia (1841–1905) and Tasmania (1803–99). The SoG also has a microfiche index to deaths in Victoria from 1914–40 and a CD-ROM of deaths in South Australia from 1842–1915 (there are also published indexes to South Australia births 1842–1906 and marriages 1842–1916).

The registered information is sometimes more detailed than in England. In 1923 in Queensland, William Edward Keates (the brother of my great grandmother Alice Amelia Keates) had to register the death of his wife Daisy. In addition to the information that would have been included on an English certificate, William also had to give the names and ages of their living and deceased children, Daisy's father's name and occupation and her mother's maiden surname. He also had to state when and where Daisy had been buried, when and where their marriage had taken place and how long they had been in Australia, specifying the states in which they lived. A birth certificate usually identifies the date and place of the parents' marriage and the names and ages of any elder siblings. A marriage certificate usually identifies the mothers of the spouses as well as their fathers.

Vine Hall (1335) is a list of originals, transcripts, microforms and indexes of Australian parish and non-conformist registers (and their locations). It is not complete, but includes most surviving registers, many of them up to the period after the Second World War. Many early church registers are held by the state civil registrars. Entries from many of these registers are included in the "Pioneer" indexes noted above and some entries up to about 1875 are included in the Australian section of the IGI. Cemeteries in each state and many published memorial inscriptions are listed in Vine Hall (1334). Wills and administrations since 1788 have been dealt with by state probate courts and registries. The courts of each state, their records, indexes and finding aids are described in Vine Hall (1334). For example, the Queensland State Archives have an online index to Queensland wills 1857–1900 and the Archives Office of Tasmania has an online index to Tasmanian wills 1824–1938. The SoG holds indexes of wills proved in New South Wales (1800–1985) and in Victoria (1841–99).

Commercial directories appeared in the early 19th century and are listed in Vine Hall (1334) with the location of surviving copies. Newspapers first appeared in Sydney in 1803 and in the State of Victoria in 1838. They include notices of births, marriages and deaths and lists of arrivals of ships (whether with convicts or free settlers). These arrival notices often given brief accounts of the ship's voyage. A number of libraries and archives hold indexes to the *Sydney Gazette* for 1803–29 and the *Australian* for 1824–42. The *Sydney Herald* (now the *Sydney*

Morning Herald) also commenced publication in 1831. Many indexes to the birth, marriage and death notices in 19th-century Australian newspapers are listed by Vine Hall (1334). There are also official journals similar to the *London Gazette* such as the *New South Wales Gazette* (first published in 1832). Electoral rolls were prepared in Victoria from 1841, New South Wales from 1842 and a little later in other states. Surviving rolls for each year (and their location) are listed by Vine Hall (1334).

Ritchie (1314) is a 12-volume dictionary of Australian biography for 1788 to 1939 with a separate index volume and subsequent supplement volumes. *Who's Who in Australia* (under a number of titles) has been published every two or three years, but sometimes annually, since 1906.

Perkins (665) is a detailed bibliography that includes histories of the Australian armed forces and Vine Hall (1334) describes the original records available concerning those who served in the Australian army, navy and merchant marine. Service records of about 420,000 Australian men who served in the army in the First World War are held by the First World War Personnel Records Service at the National Archives of Australia in Canberra. There is also a published roll of approximately 374,000 of them who served outside Australia, recording a man's name, rank, unit and dates of his enlistment, death or return to Australia. Records of about 1.3 million men and women who served in the Australian army, navy or air force in the Second World War are also being made available at the National Archives. About one million of them (including many who served in the merchant navy) are listed in an online database (# appendix XI). The Australian War Memorial (AWM), PO Box 21, Woden 2606, ACT, keeps cemetery and memorial registers (similar to those of the CWGC) for about 60,000 Australians who were killed in the First World War and over 34,000 in the Second. The AWM web site includes databases of the First World War soldiers who died and those who served abroad.

There are many genealogical societies in Australia (74 in New South Wales alone) and these are listed by Vine Hall (1334). Some of these societies are members of the FFHS and their publications are listed in Hampson (249) and Perkins (263). In particular, the Society of Australian Genealogists has a large library and publishes *The Australian Genealogist* and now *Descent*.

Canada

Baxter (1254) is a detailed guide to genealogy in Canada. St-Louis-Harrison & Munk (1317) is a briefer guide, published by the National Archives of Canada (NAC). *Family Tree Magazine* (May to August and December 1992) contains articles by A. Douglas reviewing genealogical research in the different provinces of Canada.

European settlement was commenced by the French in "New France" (Quebec), by the British in Newfoundland and by trading posts of the Hudson's Bay Company (founded in England in 1670). By the end of the Seven Years' War in 1763, all of eastern Canada was controlled by the British and settlement then spread westwards. Perhaps 70,000 Americans (the United Empire Loyalists) entered Canada after the American War of Independence. Confederation of Upper Canada (now Ontario), Lower Canada (now Quebec), Nova Scotia and New Brunswick took place in 1867. Manitoba was created in 1870 and territories of the Hudson's Bay Company were acquired in 1871. British Columbia and Prince Edward Island joined the Confederation in 1871 and 1873 respectively. Saskatchewan and Alberta were established as provinces in 1905 and the Yukon and Northwest Territories were subsequently established. Finally, the British colonies of Newfoundland and Labrador joined Canada in 1949. Canada therefore has ten provinces and two territories. When you commence research, you first need to ascertain in which province your ancestors lived.

As in the United States, place names can be a problem because many places (or areas) were given the same or similar names. Thus, there is a Saint John in New Brunswick and a St John's in Newfoundland. There is a Waterloo in Quebec and another in Ontario. Good maps and a gazetteer are therefore essential for research. It is important to remember that the majority of records in Quebec are in French. Baxter (1254) has a good general chapter about migration to Canada, particularly of Scots, Irish, Germans, United Empire Loyalists and Ukrainians. The NAC has many ship's passenger lists from 1865 for arrivals in Quebec, from 1881 for Halifax (in Nova Scotia) and later for many other ports. A few earlier lists are also at the NAC or provincial archives. It is necessary to know the date and port of an immigrant's arrival in order to find a person, but a consolidated index to these records is being prepared. GPC publishes some volumes listing thousands of people arriving in Nova Scotia before 1867. Immigration records since 1920 can only be consulted with the immigrant's permission or proof of his or her death. It is important to remember that many immigrants to Canada arrived via the United States so that US shipping lists may also have to be searched.

Civil registration of births, marriages and deaths was the responsibility of a Registrar General (or equivalent officer) in each province or territory. The addresses for enquiries are listed in Baxter (1254) and St-Louis-Harrison & Munk (1317). Registration commenced in 1864 in Nova Scotia (but did not cover births and deaths from 1876 to 1908), in 1869 in Ontario, 1872 in British Columbia, 1878 in Saskatchewan, 1882 in Manitoba, 1888 in New Brunswick, 1891 in Newfoundland, 1897 in Alberta, 1906 in Prince Edward Island and in the early 20th century in Yukon and Northwest Territories. Civil registration in Quebec only commenced in 1926. Even after civil registration commenced, records were often incomplete until the early 20th century. Records in Quebec are open to public searches, as are some records over 100 years old in other provinces. The indexes for Ontario (from 1869) are now open to the public up to 1899 (births), 1914 (marriages) and 1924 (deaths). The British Columbia indexes and registers (on microfilm) are open up to 1896 (births), 1921 (marriages) and 1976 (deaths) and the indexes can be searched on the British Columbia Archives web site. The SoG holds a copy of the Alberta Genealogical Society's index of Alberta births, marriages and deaths from 1870 to 1905, giving full names, type, place and date of event, names of parents or spouse, sex, age and reference number. Most of the open indexes of civil registration records are available on microfilm through LDS family history centres. Most other records are closed, so that only officials can search (in response to applications for a certificate for a particular birth, marriage or death) and you must provide information that assists the officials to undertake a search. You may also have to pay a fee and prove a family link with the person whose entry is being searched.

Church registers commenced in about 1812 in what is now Ontario. In Quebec, church registers were kept from about 1620, and copies of the registers were sent by clergymen to a local court official. Those for before 1926 are mostly in the Quebec archives (divided between nine regional centres). In New Brunswick clergymen reported marriages from the late 18th century to county clerks and these marriage registers run up to 1888 and are held at the Provincial archives. Baxter (1254) lists the archives of each of the Anglican, Baptist, Catholic, Lutheran, Presbyterian, United and Mennonite churches and the Quakers. Microfilm copies of many of these registers are at the NAC.

A census was taken over the whole dominion in 1871, 1881, 1891, 1901 and 1911. Census records up to 1901 (and a census of 1906 of Alberta, Manitoba and Saskatchewan) are available to the public at the NAC and at LDS family history centres. The 1911 census is due to be released soon. Each census is arranged by province, then county, then township, but some indexes are available and the SoG has a copy of an index to heads of households in the 1871 census of Ontario. This is also available on the NAC web site with images of the whole 1901 census. An index to the 1881 census is available on CD-ROM and online in *FamilySearch*, although this census does not record the relationships of people in the household. There are also censuses for 1851 and 1861 for large parts of the maritime provinces, Quebec and Ontario. Before this, there are a few local censuses (mostly held at the NAC). For example, there are census returns of heads of households for Quebec in 1825, 1831 and 1842 and for Ontario in 1842, 1848 and 1850. The SoG holds a census index for Nova Scotia in 1770. Directories for cities in eastern Canada generally begin around 1850 (but exist for as early as 1819 for Montreal) and for cities in western Canada around 1900. Some Canadian biographical dictionaries are held by the SoG including *Who's Who in Canada* and the *Dictionary of Canadian Biography* (1241).

The archives held by NAC are described in Baxter (1254) and St-Louis-Harrison & Munk (1317). In addition to census records, some church registers and passenger lists, there are naturalisation and passport records, published and unpublished family histories, newspapers and some land, military and school records. Baxter (1254) also has a chapter on each province or territory, listing archives, libraries and genealogical societies and also noting the covering dates and location of census records, wills, newspapers, directories, church registers, electoral registers and land records. The provincial archives also publish leaflets describing the records that they hold. Most provinces have a family history society (most of which are members of the FFHS) and produce various guides to research. Thus Merriman (1304) is a detailed guide to Ontario records, including civil registration records, church registers, wills, census returns and immigration, court, military, land, cemetery and educational records. Publications by many Canadian societies are listed in Hampson (249) and Perkins (263). Most Canadian FHS journals are held by the SoG, such as *Families*, published since 1962 by the Ontario Genealogical Society. Reference to publications such as these is essential because genealogical records (and the availability of indexes or finding aids) vary so much from province to province.

The Hudson's Bay Company received its Royal Charter in 1670. The company's original archives are held at the Provincial Archives of Manitoba in Winnipeg and those before 1904 can be seen on microfilm. TNA at Kew also holds copies of these films in series BH 1. The records are briefly described in Baxter (1254) and a useful article on the company (and the North West Company), "Gentlemen adventurers and remittance men" by A. Douglas appears in *Genealogists' Magazine* (June 1992). Many of the company's records have been published.

In what is now Ontario, land grants were made by the colonial government from the 18th century and by the province from 1867. Surviving records include settlers' petitions for grants (sometimes including family details) dating from 1764, and records of various land and settlement companies (such as the Canada Company). The Ontario Archives hold a computerised index to land grants which can be searched by the grantee's surname or the township in which the land was located. The index notes the date and type of grant, the property's location (a lot or concession number) and a reference to the original records (such as land petitions, township papers or Canada Company registers). These records are described in detail by Merriman (1304). Land ownership since the initial grant can be traced in land registry records (dating from 1797) since transactions were registered at county land registries and there is an abstract index for each district. The original abstract indexes are at registry offices but many are on microfilm at the Ontario Archives. Entries are generally arranged by township, then concession and lot, so you need to know where the property was located, but the records should refer to each piece of land and record all transactions. The system and surviving records are described in Merriman (1304) and in a guide (1246) published by the Ontario Genealogical Society. You can then attend at a district registry to obtain further information about a property or copies of the records (copies of some records are on microfilm at the Ontario archives). There are also detailed land records for Quebec, dating from the 17th century, which were maintained by notaries. They are held in many Quebec registry offices, but there are indexes for 1637 to 1841 (and microfilm copies at NAC). Detailed land records also survive for other provinces and are described in Baxter (1254).

Service records for the Canadian armed forces are held by NAC. Some musters and pay lists of militia forces survive from the 19th century and lists of officers were published in *Militia Lists* from the 1850s. Muster rolls, pension records, medal registers and service records are held at NAC for servicemen of the war of 1812, rebellions in 1837/8, 1870 and 1885, and the Fenian Raids of 1866 and 1870. An index to the 600,000 men who served in the First World War is on the NAC web site (with scanned images of some men's attestation papers). About 110,000 Canadians were killed in the two world wars. Official lists of all Canadian casualties (killed, wounded, missing and prisoners) for 1914–18 have been published with entries arranged by time period, then by unit. Morton (1309) is a useful study of the Canadian forces in the war and the SoG holds some other works on the Canadians in the war, including lists of medal awards. Histories of units of the Canadian armed forces are listed in Perkins (665).

South Africa
The Dutch established a colony at Cape Town in the 17th century and many Germans also settled there in the 18th century. The colony was occupied by the British from 1795 to 1803 and again in 1806 when it was annexed. Organised parties of British settlers began arriving in Southern Africa in 1820. Many of the settlers of Dutch descent moved north and established new settlements in what are now the Transvaal and Orange Free State. British settlement continued in the 19th century, resulting in wars with the Zulus in Natal and with the Boers of Transvaal and Orange Free State. By 1902 the British controlled all these areas and the Union of South Africa was created in 1910.

Detailed guidance to research in South Africa (and Zimbabwe and Namibia) is provided by Lombard (1302) and in his article in *Genealogists' Magazine* (December 1978). A briefer work, *Family History: A South African Beginner's Guide* by E. Harrison was published in 1996. Most South African genealogical material is held in government archives (in Pretoria) or in provincial archive depots in Pretoria, Cape Town, Pietermaritzburg, Bloemfontein and Johannesburg.

Some biographical dictionaries of early British settlers in South Africa have been published. Philip (1312a) provides biographies for 4,800 British people known to have lived at the Cape between 1795 and 1819, including settlers, soldiers, merchants and seamen. Thus John Howard, a shopkeeper aged 32, arrived at the Cape in 1799. He was recorded, in 1800, as having a (British) servant named Thomas Goodsire. Hockly (1294a) lists the settlers of 1820 and their families and Morse Jones (1308) is a biographical dictionary of about 2,000 British people who settled in South Africa between 1820 and 1826.

Registration of births, marriages and deaths for the whole of South Africa commenced in 1923. The registers and indexes are not open to the public, so that information must be provided to the Department of Home Affairs for a search to be made. Registration also took place earlier in each province, in Cape of Good Hope (from 1895, with incomplete registers since 1820 for marriages), Natal (from 1868), Transvaal (from 1901) and Orange Free State (from 1902). These records are held in provincial archives. For the period before civil registration, one must turn to church records. From 1665 to 1778 the Dutch Reformed Church (DRC) was the only officially recognised Church and in some places it remained the only church for many more years (and so most whites were members of it) until other churches were established. Thus the first Anglican church in South Africa was founded in the Cape in 1814. Presbyterian, Congregationalist and Methodist churches were also established in the following years. The various churches in South Africa (and their records) are described by Lombard (1302). The DRC registers are usually held by parishes, or in DRC archives in each province. Copies of many church registers are also held by the government archives in Pretoria. Most Methodist archives are held in archives in Cape Town and Johannesburg.

Census records of the Cape of Good Hope commenced in 1865 and for the remainder of the country in 1904, but they were destroyed after extracting statistics. South African probate records are described in an article by S. Hayes in *Family Tree Magazine* (September 1989). Wills and death notices (including information on the deceased's date and place of birth and death, his parents, spouse and children) are lodged at registries of the Supreme Court in each province. The estate files for a deceased often include estate accounts, lists of beneficiaries and correspondence. Many older wills (and estate files) have been transferred to the government or state archives.

As an example of the records held in provincial archives, the Cape Town archives also hold tax rolls and land grants (from the late 17th century), notarial archives (including wills, marriage contracts, leases and deeds of partnerships) and magistrates' records (including records of civil and criminal court cases, tax lists and muster rolls). Contracts and deeds relating to real property are registered with the Registrar of Deeds at deeds' offices in each province. Searches can be made but you must know the location of the property concerned.

The National Library of South Africa consists of the State Library in Pretoria and the South African Library (SAL) in Cape Town. SAL holds Cape directories and newspapers as well as about 20,000 maps and 500,000 photographs. The *Cape Government Gazette* was established in 1800 and contains similar information to the *London Gazette*, including notices of births, marriages and deaths. Colonial Office records at TNA at Kew include many files of correspondence from, or relating to, settlers at the Cape of Good Hope 1795–1910 in series CO 48, 49, 336 and 462. Service records of men who fought in the First World War are held at the National Archives. About 14,000 South Africans died in the First World War and about 12,000 in the Second. Rolls of honour for these men have been published. The Genealogical Society of South Africa is a member of the FFHS.

New Zealand

Bromell (1261) is a detailed, illustrated guide to tracing ancestry in New Zealand, including a chapter on Maori genealogy. European settlement, principally by traders, commenced in about 1790. New Zealand was at first governed from New South Wales but it became a Crown colony in 1840. Settlement of the country (by free settlers and assisted emigrants) was encouraged by organisations such as the New Zealand Company and was boosted by the discovery of gold.

Many settlers came via New South Wales, the records of which should also be consulted. The new colony was divided into provinces until 1875 (when provincial government was abolished). Early settlement in New Zealand is described in articles by V. Parker in *They Came in Waves* (1251a). In the early days of the colony, many people lived far from churches and so church ministers travelled great distances in their parishes, conducting baptism and marriage ceremonies at settlers' homes and burials at a settlement's cemetery.

The New Zealand Society of Genealogists is a member of the FFHS, publishes the journal *New Zealand Genealogist*, and has transcribed and published many records, including church registers, MIs and ships' passenger lists. Many important New Zealand records and indexes have also been published, on microfiche, by BAB Microfilming (BAB), of 6 Kathryn Avenue, Mt Roskill, Auckland 1004. The microfiche resources available to assist genealogical research in New Zealand are described in an article by A. Bromell in *They Came in Waves* (1251a).

Archives New Zealand holds extensive resources for genealogists. The most important are noted below, but many others are described in Bromell (1261) and by S. Hamilton in *They Came in Waves* (1251a). The Alexander Turnbull Library in Wellington also has a large collection of reference material on New Zealand's history, including directories, electoral rolls, jury lists, photographs, rate assessments, local histories and maps.

Many passenger arrival lists have survived and are listed by Peake (1312). Most official passenger lists are held at Archives New Zealand but many other lists are held locally. Morris & Hafslund (1307) is a microfiche index of assisted immigrants to New Zealand from Britain and Ireland from 1855 to 1871, listing the ships, the names and ages of passengers (with a surname index) and usually their occupations and place of origin. Archives New Zealand also holds further lists of assisted immigrants (1871–88) and most passenger ship arrivals from 1883 to 1973, and these are indexed up to 1910. The arrivals of many ships and passengers were reported in local newspapers, sometimes with detailed accounts of the immigrants and their voyage. Some libraries have prepared indexes to these shipping reports (sometimes indexing ships, but often the passengers' names). The Colonial Office records at TNA (noted above) contain many records of emigrants to New Zealand. In particular, series C 208 contains records of the New Zealand Company for 1839 to 1858, including applications for land and registers of passengers.

Civil registration of births, marriages and deaths of Europeans started in 1848 and became compulsory in 1856. Maori births, marriages and deaths were also recorded (but only voluntarily until 1911 for marriages and 1913 for births and deaths). Records are held by district registrars, churches (in the case of most marriages) and by the Registrar General (at the Central Registry in Lower Hutt). Microfiche copies of the indexes up to 1991 are available through LDS family history centres and other libraries and archives (for example, the SoG holds the indexes up to 1920). The registers provide more information than in England. From 1876 birth entries give the parents' ages, places of birth and the date and place of their marriage. From 1916 the entries also record any previous children of the couple. From 1876 death entries note the names of the deceased's parents, the maiden name of the mother, the father's occupation, when and where the deceased was buried, where he or she had been born and how long he or she had lived in New Zealand. If the deceased was married, the entry noted the place of marriage and the name and age of the deceased's widow or widower. The age and sex of any living issue were also recorded. The extra information in marriage entries was (from 1867, when divorce became available in New Zealand) the date of any subsequent divorce and (from 1881) each spouse's birth place, parents' names (including mother's maiden name) and the addresses of witnesses. You can obtain certified copies of register entries but, as noted by Bromell (1261), these do not contain all the information noted in the registers. Alternatively, for many years, you can obtain photocopies (made from microfilm copies of the registers). You can also inspect the registers and transcribe the entries.

Anglican parish registers were compiled from about 1820 and many are still held by the churches as are a few early registers of Methodists, Baptists, Presbyterians and Catholics. Other registers are held in diocesan archives, listed by Bromell (1261), who also includes illustrations of typical register entries. The SoG holds a list of New Zealand parish registers, transcripts and indexes prepared in 2000 by B. Garner.

Most census records were destroyed once statistics had been compiled, but a few early lists have survived and most of these are held by Archives New Zealand. Many commercial directories are available for the whole of New Zealand, or particular cities, dating from the 1850s. A large number of these have been reproduced on microfiche by BAB. Newspapers also recorded births, marriages, deaths and obituaries. There is a published list of New Zealand newspapers from before 1940, specifying the libraries and archives that hold copies. Many newspaper indexes have been prepared and some of these are listed by Bromell (1261). Some electoral rolls up to 1900 are at Archives New Zealand and those since 1928 are held by the Registrar General. BAB has published most surviving rolls of 1853 to 1981 on microfiche and also reproduced Jury lists of 1842–63, listing those men eligible to sit on a jury. Scholefield (1321) is a biographical dictionary of New Zealanders that can also be consulted online.

Many school records are held by the archives of each religious denomination. State school records from the late 19th century include admission registers noting details of the child and its parents (including names, address, child's age or date of birth and the child's previous or subsequent school). Some of these records are held at Archives New Zealand.

Archives New Zealand and local Land and Deeds Registry offices hold extensive land records. Since the offer of land was an incentive for immigrants, a large percentage of early immigrants are recorded as landowners in these records. Archives New Zealand holds many early title deeds, land claims, surveys and maps. Deeds register offices were established in 1841 and these registered Crown grants of land as well as documents evidencing subsequent transactions concerning that land. Land registration was introduced in 1870 (becoming compulsory in 1924). Certificates of title describe the land and its present and previous owners. Bromell (1261) describes the records and indexes that are available. The SoG holds a copy of the return of freeholders of 1882.

Wills were proved in courts of New South Wales until 1842 when the Supreme Court of New Zealand (now named the High Court) was founded. Wills and administrations since that date are at the registry of the High Court (for example, in Wellington, Christchurch or Auckland) that was nearest to the deceased's place of residence. Each registry has an index to the records that it holds but an index by M. Corser to probates up to 1900 is available on microfiche (for example, at the SoG). If someone died without leaving a will or without appointing executors, the estate was administered by the Public Trust and the estate accounts were published in the *Provincial Gazette* (later the *New Zealand Gazette*), for example, recording the money obtained from sales of assets or naming beneficiaries. Archives New Zealand holds other records of the Supreme Court since 1842, such as calendars of criminal cases from 1840 to 1948, records of magistrates' courts since 1846 and coroners' reports from about 1845 (although these are closed for 50 years after creation).

Some militia returns listing able-bodied men and records of the Royal New Zealand Fencibles survive from the 19th century and are held at Archives New Zealand. The following important records of military service by New Zealanders are also held there:

a. Boer War: nominal rolls, casualty lists and medal rolls.
b. First World War: embarkation rolls, medal rolls and casualty lists (17,000 New Zealanders were killed). Embarkation rolls of the New Zealand Expeditionary Force 1914–18 have been published, listing men's names, regiment, number, occupation and address (and their next of kin's name and address). A roll of honour of those killed has also been published.
c. Second World War: embarkation rolls, medal rolls and casualty lists. A roll of the New Zealand Expeditionary Force 1939–45 has been published, listing each man's name, unit, rank, number, and address (and his next of kin's name and address).

BAB has also reproduced the three published rolls noted above on microfiche. Many other published works on the armed forces of New Zealand are listed by Perkins (665).

India and Asia

Much of India, as well as the territories that now form Pakistan, Bangladesh and Burma was controlled from about 1600 by the East India Company (EIC) and later by the British Government, firstly through a Board of Control (which regulated the affairs of the EIC from 1784 to 1858) and then through the India Office until 1947. A separate Burma Office also existed from 1937 until 1948. The EIC also controlled land around the forts and trading posts that it established in places such as China, Malaysia, Afghanistan, St Helena, Aden and the Gulf. Excellent records of the EIC and the India Office (concerning government, commerce and military affairs), consisting of about a quarter of a million files or volumes, are held in the India Office collections at the British Library at 96 Euston Road, London NW1 2DB (telephone 020 7412 7873). Most of the records relate to the period up to about 1947 when independence was granted to India, Pakistan and Burma but some records post-date these events. There are also some miscellaneous records, such as those relating to colleges established by the EIC in England.

The EIC was established by Royal Charter on 31 December 1600, giving the company the exclusive right to trade in India and other parts of Asia. The EIC became a very substantial trading company and most of its records deal with commerce and trade, but its records are important because they concern the administration of territories controlled by the company and the many British people who served in the organisation. The EIC also had large military forces (# chapters 20 and 21) that protected its trade and extended its influence throughout Asia. As the power of the EIC increased, its records covered a wider range of subject matter, including records of baptisms, marriages and burials of the British in India and much other genealogical and biographical material. Moir (1306) is a detailed review (with a lengthy bibliography) of the history, administration and records of the EIC, the Board of Control and the India Office. Baxter (1257) is a briefer guide to the genealogical and biographical sources in the India Office collections (the British Library also produces a number of leaflets about its most important collections). Many records, particularly copy registers of baptisms, marriages and burials, directories, monumental inscriptions and wills of the British in India are held by the SoG and listed in Taylor (1327). Hamilton-Edwards (19) also includes a useful chapter on the EIC.

The EIC established trading stations (or factories) in India in the 17th century, purchasing goods such as textiles and spices for export to England. It gradually extended its commercial and political influence and soon controlled much of India through three presidencies of Bengal, Madras and Bombay. It also established factories elsewhere in Asia, including Singapore and Canton. However, as its power increased, there was growing concern in England about the company's activities and corruption. The government therefore established a Board of Control in 1784 to supervise the company's business and its civil and military government. The Board's control over the company gradually increased, with a Governor-General being based in Calcutta, until 1858 when, following the Indian mutiny, the Crown became directly responsible for the government and administration of India (and the other EIC territories) and the remaining powers of the EIC and the Board of Control were transferred to the India Office. The Crown was represented in India by the governor-general (with the title Viceroy) and from 1858 to 1947 the India Office was responsible for the direct government of most of India and British possessions in Burma and Malaysia (all forming part of British India). In addition, some parts of India continued to be ruled by Indian princes but in practice they remained to a great extent under the control of the India Office.

Moir (1306) describes the administrative departments of the EIC and the administrative records that were produced, from Court Minutes of the directors' meetings to factories' correspondence files. The company also had establishments in Britain. There was a military seminary at Addiscombe to train officers for the EIC army. The East India College was founded in Hertford in 1806 (to train the company's clerks) and transferred to Haileybury in 1809 until 1858. The company had warehouses in the City of London from the early 18th century and established almshouses in London in 1627, a lunatic asylum in 1818, and barracks for soldiers that it recruited.

The army, navy and merchant marine records of the EIC and India Office were considered in chapters 20 and 21. The other records in the India Office collections are summarised below, but more detailed information about them can be obtained from Baxter (1257) or Moir (1306). In particular, there are thousands of administrative and correspondence files and also many dealing with accounts and other commercial records. If you locate an ancestor working for the EIC or in the administration of the India Office, these files are worthy of further study. Importantly, class Z consists of about 2,500 volumes of indexes to many of the files in the India Office collections. Although many of the indexes are to the records' subject matter, there are also many name indexes. Examples are 24 volumes of indexes (in class Z/L/AG/34) to wills, administrations and inventories from 1618 to 1909 and the indexes to the ecclesiastical returns of births, baptisms, marriages, deaths and burials (noted below). The single most important source in the India Office collections is the biographical index, compiled from many sources but particularly the records of births, baptisms, marriages, deaths and burials in British India and other territories. It contains almost 300,000 entries for both civil and military servants of the EIC and the India Office, but also their families and other Europeans living in India.

The collections include lists of stockholders of the EIC from 1600 and many published biographical dictionaries relating to the British in India, all listed in Baxter (1257). From about 1803 published directories are an important source. The *East India Register* was published from 1803 to 1858. From 1860 there is the *Indian Army and Civil Service List* (until 1876), the *India List* (until 1906), the *India Office List* (until 1937) and the *India and Burma Office List* (until 1947). Some copies of the *East India Register* and the Indian army and civil service lists have been reproduced on microfiche by MM Publications and on CD-ROM by Archive CD Books. These directories contain an enormous amount of information about those serving in the armies, marine services or civil administration of India up to 1947. For example, the *East India Register and Directory for 1821* (1243) includes indexed lists of civil and military personnel and notices of births, marriages and deaths in each EIC presidency, such as these from Madras:

Marriages: July 1. Capt Sidney Cotton 22nd Dragoons, to Miss M. Hackett
Deaths: January 20. Mrs Eliza Vanderputt.

The register includes lists of directors of the EIC (with dates of election) and of proprietors of EIC stock, in Britain and in India, with addresses, for example:

Champion, Mrs Ann, widow, Old Street Road
Chapman, Mr Aaron, Highbury Park, Middlesex
Davidson, Walter, esq. Calcutta

The register includes lists of EIC civil servants stationed in Britain, India or at the other factories, as well as lists of those training at the East India College. Illustration 146 is an extract from the list of civil servants on the Bengal establishment. For example, John Cheap is noted as the commercial resident at Soonamooky and Robert Grant as the collector of government customs at Cawnpore. These published EIC registers and directories also include lists of EIC army officers, in similar form to the British army lists (# chapter 20), cadets at the Military Seminary and retired officers. Illustration 147 shows a list of officers of the 7th Regiment of Native Infantry of Bengal from the 1819 *East India Register* (1242). There are lists of EIC ships (and masters) and lists of ships licensed by the EIC for the East Indies' trade. Thus the 1821 register (1243) records the issue of a licence to G.H. Gibbons of Finch Lane, London for the ship *Andromeda* of Sunderland, the master being F.G. Stewart, for a voyage from London to Bombay. Lists of European inhabitants in each presidency are also useful. The Bengal list includes:

Bailey, Abraham. indigo-manufacturer, Dulnagur
Burn, Alexander. carpenter
Carey, Felix. missionary, Serampore
Franks, John C. mariner

Anglican churches were established in British India from the late 17th century. Church ministers' or chaplains' registers (the ecclesiastical returns) of baptisms, marriages and burials (and sometimes births and deaths) were sent to the EIC offices in London and later to the India Office. Indexes are in class Z/N of the India Office collections. There are three main series of registers, for the presidencies of Bengal (1713–1947), Madras (1698–1947) and Bombay (1709–1947), which include returns of Burma up to 1936 and of Singapore (1830–68). In addition, there are returns for St Helena (1767–1835), Aden (1840–1969), Whampoa (that is, Canton) and Macao (1820–33), settlements in Malaysia (from the mid-18th century), Burma (from 1937), Kuwait (1937–61), Roman Catholic returns for each presidency (1835–54), registrar marriages in India and Burma (1852–1911) and post-independence returns for India and Pakistan (from 1947). Most of the registers are indexed, either in the biographical index or in

SUDDER DEWANNEE and NIZAMUT ADAWLUT.

, chief judge

John Fendall,
William E. Rees, } puisne judges
Samuel Thos. Goad,
William Dorin, Register
Paul M. Wynch, deputy, and translator of the regulations

BOARD of TRADE.

John Adam, president
George Udny,
John Pascal Larkins, } members
John Trotter, import warehouse keeper
George Udny, export warehouse keeper
Chas. Bayley, sub-export warehouse-keeper
Chas. C. Hyde, assistant
R. C. Plowden, secretary
Walter Nisbet, sub-secretary
James King, secretary in the salt and opium departments
Henry Sargent, acting ditto
Henry M. Thacker, first assistant,   do
Charles Morley, accountant
T. J. C. Plowden, superintendent of the western salt chokies
John Ewer,   ditto   of the eastern   ditto
G. R. B. Berney, ditto   of the midland   ditto

BOARD of REVENUE.

James Stuart, president
Richard Rocke, } members
Wm. O. Salmon, } members
Samuel Swinton, officiating
George Warde, secretary
John P. Ward, sub-secretary

SENIOR MERCHANTS.

Seaton of Apt.
1765 Shearman Bird, (at home)
1768 William Augustus Brooke, senior judge of the court of appeal at Benares, and agent to the governor general there
1769 Joseph Burnard Smith
1771 Robert Bathurst, collector of government customs and town duties at Mirzapore
1772 Henry Chicheley Plowden, salt agent for the division of Chittagong, and Bullcah
1775 John Addison, commercial resident at Buxleah.
1776 John Hall, postmaster general, and his Majesty's deputy postmaster general in Bengal

Seaton of Apt.
1775 Richard Rocke, senior member of the board of revenue
Sir James Edward Colebrooke, Bart. senior member of the board of commissioners in the ceded and conquered provinces, and agent to the governor general at Bareilly
1777 Samuel Middleton
George Udny, senior member of the board of trade and president of the marine board, and export warehouse-keeper
1775 Thomas Brooke
John Fendall, a puisne judge of the courts of the sudder dewannee and nizamut adawluts
Robert Grant, collector of government customs at Cawnpore
1780 Charles Rusel Crommelin, salt agent at Hidgellee and collector of land revenue there
John Herbert Harrington, (at home)
Henry Douglas, senior judge of the provincial courts of appeal and circuit for the division of Patna
Charles Sweedland, commercial resident at Benares, Goruckpore, Mow, and Azimghur, and agent for the provision of opium at Benares
1780 James Wynte, (at home)
Richard Becher, (at home)
1782 John Cheap, commercial resident at Soonamooky
Sir Harry Verelat Darell, Bart. (at home)
Neil Benjamin Edmonstone, (at home)
Francis Hawkins, senior judge of the provincial courts of appeal and circuit for the division of Bareilly
George Dowdeswell, first member of council
William Towers Smith, senior judge of the provincial courts of appeal and circuit for the division of Moorshedabad
Alexander Wright
Pellegrin Treves
1789 James Money, commercial resident at Etawah and Culpee
William Leycester, second judge of the provincial courts of appeal and circuit for the division of Bareilly
John Ahmuty, senior judge of the provincial courts of appeal and circuit for the division of Dacca
William Cowell, second judge of the provincial courts of appeal and circuit for the division of Benares
Honble. James R. Elphinstone, second judge of the provincial courts of appeal and circuit for the division of Patna
Duncan Campbell, opium agent in Behar
Colin Shakespear, superintendent of stamps
1790 James Patle, senior judge of the provincial courts of appeal and circuit for the division of Calcutta

B 2

146. Extract from the list of covenanted civil servants on the Bengal establishment of the East India Company; from the East India Register and Directory, 1819

147. List of officers of the 7th Regiment of Native Infantry of the army of the Presidency of Bengal; from the East India Register and Directory, *1819*

separate indexes for each series. The information in the registers is similar to that contained in English parish registers and civil registration records.

Over 860 files of registers, accounts and MIs from cemeteries in India are held in the India Office collections in class R/4. There are also many wills of British people dating from 1618 to 1948 (proved in local courts, usually staffed by British judges and lawyers), grants of letters of administration from 1774 to 1948 and some inventories. The classes are listed in Moir (1306). There are also many English language Indian newspapers dating from 1780.

EIC and India Office civil servants are listed in the EIC and India Office directories noted above, but the India Office collections also include many records of civil servants, including notices of appointments, staff lists, salary books and pension records. The relevant classes are listed by Baxter (1257). There were two types of EIC civil servant. Covenanted civil servants (or writers) filled the more senior posts and entered into bonds or covenants to faithfully perform their duties. Posts were often filled by the EIC directors' nominees (friends, relatives or others) and this patronage system continued until the mid-19th century. Writers had to submit petitions for employment, with birth or baptism certificates and educational and personal references. These writers' petitions cover 1749 to 1805. From 1806 most of those training to be civil servants attended the East India College. Candidates' application papers cover the period 1806–56 and contain much biographical information. The relevant India Office collections class references, and many published lists of civil servants, are noted in Baxter (1257) and Moir (1306). Uncovenanted civil servants took lesser positions and were generally recruited in India (they were either resident Anglo-Indians or Eurasians). Records of these civil servants include appointment and establishment lists, such as 252 volumes of records of service from 1702 to 1928 (which are mostly annual establishment lists). There are also records of bonds, agreements and appointments of both types of civil servant from the mid-18th century up to 1947. Civil servants and their families are also recorded in the ecclesiastical returns of baptisms, marriages and burials and the records of wills noted above.

Both the EIC and the India Office administered some pension funds for civil servants, army and navy officers and other ranks. These funds and the records are described in Moir (1306). For example, the Poplar Pension Fund provided pensions for officers and seamen of the EIC mercantile marine and their families. The Bengal, Madras and Bombay Civil Funds provided pensions for widows and children of civil servants of the EIC and India Office. The Lord Clive Military Fund provided pensions for officers and other ranks of the EIC armies (and their widows) and there were separate pension funds for the Bengal and Madras armies.

The India Office collections contain many ships' logs (# chapter 21) and lists of passengers to and from India. Until 1833 a British subject required the permission of the EIC in order to enter India and a licence was necessary to trade there. Notes of applications and permissions appear in the EIC Court minutes and correspondence files. The lists of passengers are described in Baxter (1257) and in more detail in Moir (1306). Baxter (1257) also includes detailed references to the classes of documents recording judges, lawyers and railway staff in British India. The records of railway companies in India include many staff lists, noted by Richards (854). The Indian police service was formed in 1861 and senior officers were listed in the India Office directories. A roll of over 1,700 senior police officers, extracted from these directories, is held at the SoG and an article about the police and this roll appears in *Genealogists' Magazine* (September 1985). Baxter (1257) describes the particular records of personnel and the settlements or trading posts in Malaysia, China, St Helena, Ceylon, Aden and the Gulf. J. Titford reviewed the genealogical records and published sources for St Helena in *Family Tree Magazine* (July 1998). The records of Singapore (particularly of British people) are reviewed by S. Barnard in *Family Tree Magazine* (November 2002) and by A. Glendinning in *Genealogists' Magazine* (December 1997). The latter article also considers records of British people in Malaya.

The India Office collections include enormous collections of maps, prints, drawings and photographs. The map collections of India and other parts of Asia include about 50,000 items. The collections of prints, drawings and photographs, described in a booklet by Losty (1303), consist of many thousands of prints, paintings and drawings but also over 250,000 photographs (from official and private collections) from the period of British rule in India. They are being catalogued on to a computer database.

The SoG has large collections of material for Anglo-Indian genealogy, described in Taylor (1327), including published biographies and gazetteers, but also many copies of registers of baptisms, marriages or burials and MIs from Indian cemeteries, listed in Collins & Morton (186).

The SoG holds many copies of the *East India Register* and later directories, listed in Taylor (1327), which also describes the Percy-Smith or *India Index*, a slip index (sorted alphabetically by name) which can be seen on microfilm. This includes baptisms, births, marriages, burials and deaths of the British in India (primarily from 1790 to 1857) but also many references to other material such as the *East India Register*, Indian army lists, MIs and other published and manuscript works. The British Ancestors in India Society has been formed for those people researching their British ancestors in India.

The Caribbean

The British, French, Spanish and Dutch were the principal European settlers of the Caribbean islands. There were free settlers, indentured servants, convicts and many African slaves. The surviving British records of emigrants prior to the late 19th century were considered above (many of the surviving passenger lists have been published, for example in the works by Coldham and Hotten). Indentured servants received free passage to the American and West Indies' plantations, but then served seven to ten years on the plantations, after which they were granted a few acres of land. Lists of indentured servants may be found in archive offices for the ports (such as Bristol) where they were recruited. Records of transportation of convicts were noted above (and in chapter 25). From the mid-17th century the plantations' need for cheap labour was satisfied by slaves brought from Africa. It is estimated that over 1.5 million slaves were transported to the British West Indies from 1640 until the slave trade was abolished in 1808. There are few early records of slaves, since they were treated as chattels and (like other property) they could be bought, sold or inherited. They are rarely recorded in parish registers.

Most genealogical records (such as church registers and wills) are held on the islands, but many original documents (and copies) are also located in Britain (or in the archives of the other colonial powers). Grannum (1289) lists the addresses of archive offices on many of the Caribbean islands and includes a detailed bibliography of finding aids and published genealogical or historical works. The Mormons have microfilmed some Caribbean parish registers and these can be seen at LDS family history centres. Articles by J. Titford in *Family Tree Magazine* (November 1998 and January 1999) reviewed general manuscript and published sources for the British colonies in the West Indies and an article "West Indian Sources in England" by A.J. Camp, in *Family Tree Magazine* (November 1987), notes English holdings of copy parish registers, wills, MIs, indexes and history books for Antigua, Bahamas, Barbados, Cuba, Dominica, Grenada, Guadeloupe, Haiti, Jamaica, Montserrat, Nevis, St Kitts, Tobago and Trinidad.

The records of the West Indies at TNA are reviewed in detail, with many illustrations, in Grannum (1289). TNA has many records of settlers in the West Indies, particularly in the files of the Colonial Office (and other government departments that were responsible for colonial affairs, such as the Board of Trade, Privy Council, Foreign Office and the Lords of Trade and Plantations). The files consist primarily of correspondence between government officials in London and the local governors and their administrations. Calendars of the earlier files have been published by HMSO in 40 volumes of *Calendar of State Papers Colonial: America and West Indies 1574–1739*. Although the correspondence is mainly of an administrative nature, much useful information can be found since the papers include lists of inhabitants, land grants, tax lists and reports on local affairs. An example for Antigua, from Colonial Office papers, was noted above. The most important are those of births, baptisms, marriages and deaths, which are also considered in the section "The British Abroad" above and in Yeo (1342) and Bevan (239). For example, TNA holds registers of some baptisms, burials and marriages from 1726 to 1745 in Antigua. Other records are held locally, so that a baptism of 1730 could be in either TNA records or locally held registers. Wills of most West Indies' residents were proved in local church courts (or later, civil courts) but the wills of British subjects, dying abroad (or at sea) with estates in England or Wales, were proved in the PCC or in the Principal Probate Registry in London. Lists of West Indians' wills of 1628–1816 in the PCC are included in *Caribbeana* by V. L. Oliver.

The series of Colonial Office records at TNA for each British Caribbean island are listed in Grannum (1289). Thus, for Barbados, correspondence (1689–1951) is in series CO 28, registers of correspondence (1850–1948) are in series CO 376 and 565, session papers (1660–1965) are in CO 31 and government gazettes (1867–1975) are in CO 32. Gazettes were similar in form to the *London Gazette* (# chapter 17), containing official announcements, notices of births, marriages and deaths, lists of jurors and notices of land sales or court hearings. A researcher should also review the general classes of Colonial Office records since many of these refer to Barbados. Thus, colonial papers (of 1574 to 1757) are in series CO 1 and correspondence (1689–1952) is in CO 323. Colonial Office papers include some lists of people for each island and many of these are identified by Grannum (1289). Thus, for Barbados, Grannum notes a list of most white inhabitants in 1715 (piece CO 28/16), returns of paupers and pensioners for 1821 to 1825 (piece CO 28/97) and an electoral register of 1951 (piece CO 32/124). Records of land grants are important for West Indies' genealogy. Most are in local archives but some records survive in Colonial Office records at TNA and are listed for each island by Grannum (1289). Many maps and plans also survive at TNA in Colonial Office and War Office records.

Most people in the West Indies are descended from slaves. TNA holds some records of slaves and slave-owners, particularly of surveys, undertaken in each island from 1813 to 1834, to compensate slave owners for the abolition of the slave trade. The documents are in series T 71, described in Grannum (1289) and give the names of owners, plantations and (sometimes) the slaves (and perhaps their ages or country of origin). Manumissions (grants of freedom) are generally in the deeds registry or court records on each island.

Some colonial regiments were raised in the West Indies for the British army (# chapter 20) and some records of these units are held at TNA, in musters and pay lists (mostly in series WO 12), soldiers' documents (in WO 97), description books and casualty returns (WO 25), war diaries (WO 95 and 169), First World War campaign medals (WO 329) and pension registers (WO 22). The regiments and relevant pieces are listed by Grannum (1289).

Hundreds of monumental inscriptions from the British West Indies are recorded in Oliver (1310). The SoG holds the Smith collection, consisting of 43 volumes of notes by a professional genealogist who worked mainly on West Indies genealogy. A colonists index for North America and the Caribbean Islands, mainly for the 17th century, has been prepared by Mrs Williamson of Horley, Surrey. This includes information from parish registers, wills and monumental inscriptions and can be consulted for a fee. The immigration of West Indians into Britain is principally evidenced by ships' passenger lists for the period up to 1960 in series BT 26 at TNA. However, passengers are difficult to find in these lists because they are arranged by date of arrival and by port and very few are indexed.

An article "Family History in the Bahamas" by E.H. Whittleton in *Genealogists' Magazine* (December 1975) provides useful background material on the Bahamas. Chandler (1266) is a guide to the records of Barbados (including government, court, church and military records) and useful articles on genealogical sources in Barbados, by J. Titford, appear in *Family Tree Magazine*

(May and June 1997). Although some parish registers have been lost, there are published transcripts by J.M. Saunders of the surviving records of baptisms and marriages up to 1800 in the 11 parishes of Barbados and abstracts (also by Saunders) of wills and administrations from 1639 to 1725 (also available from GPC on a CD-ROM). A 1715 census of the white inhabitants of Barbados was noted above. Civil registration of births commenced in 1890 and registration of deaths in 1925. There are extensive records of property, although many deed books of the 17th and 18th centuries are missing.

Civil registration records of Bermuda commence in 1866 and are held by the Registrar General of Bermuda at Government Administration Building, 30 Parliament Street, Hamilton, Bermuda. Many early Bermuda parish registers and lists of population for 1619 to 1826 have been transcribed and published in Hallett (1293). Abstracts of wills from 1629 to 1835 have also been published, with indexes to all the names recorded in them, in Hallett (1294).

The English captured Jamaica from the Spanish in 1655 and it remained a British colony until after the Second World War. The population in the 17th and 18th centuries consisted primarily of slaves brought from Africa until slavery was abolished (the population was about 20,000 whites and 300,000 slaves in 1800). Mitchell (1305) is a detailed guide to Jamaican genealogical resources, indexes and published material, including those at LDS family history centres and other libraries or archives outside Jamaica. A useful article on Jamaican sources in Britain by C. Soares appears in *Family Tree Magazine* (April 1991). Civil registration began in Jamaica in 1880, recording similar information as in England. The records and indexes are held by the Registrar General's Office, Twickenham Park, Spanish Town and many have been filmed by the Mormons. From 1655, baptisms, marriages and burials were recorded in Anglican parish registers. Most of the registers up to at least 1880 have been deposited with the Registrar General. Copies and some indexes are at the National Archives in Spanish Town and available on microfilm through LDS family history centres but very few entries appear in the IGI. Entries for slaves or former slaves begin to appear in the registers from the early 1800s. There were some Catholic, Jewish and non-conformist congregations in Jamaica and their records are described in Mitchell (1305).

Wills and administrations were dealt with by courts in Jamaica (and are now held by the Registrar General) but can also be found in the records of the PCC and the Principal Probate Registry. Following the English conquest, land in Jamaica belonged to the Crown and was granted to individuals by patent. Deeds for the subsequent sale of property might also be enrolled. The patents and over 1,200 volumes of deeds (with some indexes to the parties) are held by the Registrar General. Extensive court records from the late 17th to the late 19th century are held by the National Archives and the Registrar General. Mitchell (1305) also reviews the sources for slaves in Jamaica, such as estate records and manumissions, some early lists of inhabitants or landholders and the sources for Jewish, German, French, Indian and Chinese immigrants.

J. Titford has reviewed genealogical records and published sources for some other Caribbean islands in *Family Tree Magazine*. The articles covered St Kitts (May and July 1999), Nevis (September and November 1999, January and March 2000), Anguilla (June 2000), British Virgin Islands (September 2000), Montserrat (December 2000, March 2001), Antigua (June and September 2001), Grenada (December 2001, March 2002) and St Lucia (June 2002).

The South Atlantic Islands
Records of St Helena were noted with EIC records considered above. Genealogical records and published sources for the Falkland Islands, Ascension and Tristan da Cunha are reviewed by

J. Titford in *Family Tree Magazine* (February, March, May and September 1998) and Cannan (1263) includes useful information about these islands, their churches and some noteworthy inhabitants.

France

Pontet (1313) is a general guide to genealogical research in France. A useful chapter is also contained in Baxter (1252). The Anglo-French FHS is a member of the FFHS and produces publications on research in France and a journal *French Ancestor*. The December 1996 edition includes a useful summary, by P. Pontet, of research in French parish registers and civil registration records. France has been divided into *départements* (almost 100 of them) since the French Revolution and each has its own archives. Genealogical records are also held at local town halls (a *mairie* or *Hôtel de Ville*), at libraries (in larger towns or cities) or at the National Archives. Large towns and cities are divided into *arondissements*, each with its own town hall and archives.

Records of civil registration, which date from 1792, are held at registries in local town halls. Copies are deposited at the local magistrates court and, when they are 100 years old, these copies are placed in the Departmental archives, usually in the most important town of that Department. Only records over 100 years old can be consulted by the public. The lack of national indexes makes searches extremely difficult. At each town hall (or Departmental archive) the entries are indexed by tables covering ten-year periods but only tables for events more than 100 years ago are available to the public. Staff at town halls or archives may undertake searches in the closed records in response to written requests but in some cases they may refuse and you will have to request a local genealogist (or society) to search for you and then order the document. Pontet (1313) provides detailed guidance as to applications for civil records.

In general, birth entries in the registers note the parents' names and sometimes (and usually since 1922) their address, profession and ages. Marriage entries note the parents, the profession and date (and place) of birth of each spouse. Death entries often include the deceased's date (and place) of birth and names of parents and spouse. Importantly, women retain their maiden name despite marriage. Death or burial records therefore note women by this name. From 1897 birth entries have margins for a note of the person's later marriage but also (from 1939) divorce and (from 1945) death. A certificate of the complete entry for a birth or marriage within the last 100 years will only be issued to the person recorded by the entry, to direct descendants or to people authorised by them. Some authorities refuse to provide full certificates for earlier births or marriages and for some or all deaths. Anyone can obtain an extract (for any event of any period) but these usually just give names, date, place and the type of event.

Some Catholic parish registers are still held at churches but most for the period up to 1792 are in Departmental archives. Some records of baptisms date back to the 13th century and some records of marriages and burials date from the 14th century. The keeping of registers was made compulsory in 1539 (for baptisms) and in 1579 (for marriages and burials). Many Protestants fled from France in the 16th and 17th centuries (# chapter 13) and persecution discouraged the keeping of registers, but Protestant registers from the 16th century may be found at a church, *mairie*, departmental archive or in the library of the Protestant Historical Society in Paris. Many records for Paris were destroyed in 1871 so researchers should review an article on research before this date in *Family Tree Magazine* (July/August 1985). Censuses were taken with people's names and occupations every five years from 1926 and are held at departmental archives. Before 1926 most census records only noted numbers of people (but sometimes also the names of heads of household or family members). A department's archives may also hold local census records (with names) for some earlier years. Voting lists from 1848 (listing only men until 1945) note names, addresses, occupations and places of birth. They are held in *mairies* or Departmental archives. French men have been liable to conscription since about 1800. Recruitment lists usually survive from about 1870, listing the names of men in their twentieth year (and so eligible to be called up), their occupations, date and place of birth, address, physical description and parents.

Notarial records are extremely important in France. The documents prepared by notaries include property transfers, marriage settlements, wills, inventories and records of meetings of creditors. Notaries retain documents that are less than 125 years old but many older records have been deposited in Departmental archives. Other land or property records (and those of the courts) are held in the National Archives, *mairies* or Departmental archives. An important source of genealogical information is contained in military records held by the Army and Navy Historical Services, both located in Vincennes, near Paris. Records of servicemen survive from the 17th century and often record the names of a man's wife and children, his date of marriage, the name (and address) of any other next of kin, a physical description of the man and details of his service (including wounds or death). There are many genealogical societies in France (at least one for each department) and details of these can be obtained from the Fédération des Sociétés Françaises de Généalogie, d'Heraldique et de Sigillographie, 11 Boulevard Pershing, 78000 Versailles.

Germany

German records are described in detail by Baxter (1253) and more briefly by Smelser (1324), Towey (1333) and Bernard (1259). The Anglo-German FHS publishes a journal *Mitteilungsblatt* and useful indexes (of records of Germans in England) have been produced for the society by L. Metzner and P. Freeman. They include indexes to registers of German churches in London, records of aliens in series HO 2 and HO 3 at TNA (see above) and to records of German troops in the British army, particularly regiments of Hessians during the American War of Independence and the King's German Legion during the Napoleonic Wars. The society also has an index, linked to their other indexes, of people of German descent who appear in British records, intended principally to assist researchers find recorded birthplaces for German ancestors.

Germany was not united until 1871. Before that it was divided between hundreds of kingdoms, duchies, electorates, free cities and principalities, varying in size from large kingdoms such as Prussia, Saxony and Bavaria to small states or free cities, such as Saxe-Coburg-Gotha and Bremen, with just a few thousand people. Many of the archives of these small states were passed to archives of the post-unification German states, but many remain in the hands of the old ruling families and access may be restricted or impossible. In 1945 a large part of Germany was transferred to Poland (and smaller areas were transferred to the Soviet Union, Belgium, Czechoslovakia, France and Denmark). Baxter (1253) notes that perhaps 15 million Germans left their homes in the ceded territories (or elsewhere in Europe). While many records from the ceded territories (including most church registers of Pomerania, Posen, Prussia and Silesia) are in German archives, some are held by archives in the country now incorporating the area concerned. Details of these areas and archives are listed in Baxter (1253). Germany was also divided into the Federal Republic of Germany (West Germany) and the German Democratic Republic (East Germany) and only recently reunited. Baxter (1253) lists the states in each of these and in the reunited country. This historical background helps explain the lack of unity in

German records until the late 19th century and the loss of many records. It should also be noted that the Thirty Years War (1618–48) resulted in the death of about one third of the German population and the destruction of many records.

Civil registration commenced in 1876 in the German Empire, but earlier in certain states: 1798 in Rhineland, 1810 in Baden, 1850 in Frankfurt, and 1864 in Prussia. Unfortunately, records are not held or indexed centrally but held in local civil registry offices so you need to know an ancestor's approximate place of birth or marriage in order to approach the correct registry. Some registries permit access to 20th century records only to proven descendants of the individual concerned. The various German churches (predominantly Roman Catholic, Lutheran or Presbyterian) prepared registers of baptisms, marriages and burials from the 16th century. Lists of archives for each of the present German states and for each of the Evangelical, Catholic and Lutheran churches are contained in Baxter (1253) and Smelser (1324). Until the mid-19th century many registers were in Latin (and older German scripts can also be very difficult to read). The Mormons hold about 100,000 microfilms of German church registers, listed by Cerny (1265) and in the *Family History Library Catalog*. The IGI for Germany is divided into four sections: Prussia, Hesse-Darmstadt, Saxony and Germany, and each section should be checked for relevant entries.

There are no national German census returns until 1871 but there are some earlier 19th-century censuses for particular states. The census years for each part of Germany (and the location of the records) are noted by Baxter (1253). Wills are held in district courthouses or in state archives. There are registers of citizens of larger towns, some dating from the 16th century, often including dates of baptism and details of the parents and grandparents of a newcomer to the town who applied for the right to reside there. Police registration was introduced in most states around 1840 (in order to control people's movements). The records are generally in state or local archives and include people's names, residence, dates and places of birth and occupation. The large independent cities, such as Hamburg, Danzig and Bremen, had substantial archives dating from medieval times, including guild records, citizen lists, muster rolls and property records. Lists of guild members may also name a man's trade, wife, children and place and date of his marriage and birth.

Many Germans emigrated to other parts of Europe and to the Americas from the 17th century. Between about 1750 and 1850 perhaps 150,000 Germans settled in Russia alone. Baxter (1253) suggests that about 200,000 Germans emigrated to North America in the 18th century and over three million emigrated to America in the 19th century. Many Germans settled in England, and the German churches in London are described in Towey (1333). Many Germans (and other Europeans) emigrating to North America left from the ports of Hamburg and Bremen, often travelling via England. Millions of people from Germany and eastern Europe left from Hamburg between 1850 and 1914 including, according to Clapsaddle (318), about 730,000 Jews. Bremen passenger lists have been lost but Hamburg passenger lists for 1850–1914 and 1919–34 have survived and name over five million emigrants. Baxter (1253) describes the lists, the available indexes and where to consult them. The Mormons have microfilm copies of the lists and some indexes. Towey (1333) describes another useful source for Germans who were emigrating. In many states, they needed permission to leave and had to prove that, for example, they were not leaving dependants who would later be a burden on the state. Some files include detailed genealogical and biographical information about an emigrant and his family and some of the records have been indexed. Other useful sources in Germany include:

a. Funeral sermons: a memorial of the deceased's life read out by a clergyman at a funeral. Thousands of sermons (mainly for wealthy people) survive from the 16th to 19th centuries

b. Lineage books: Germans' interest in the family and heritage resulted in the production of hundreds of pedigrees of families (mainly middle class people), many dating from the late 18th century. Over 200 volumes of these pedigrees have been published

c. Local family books: containing more recent family trees and histories (prepared by genealogists and genealogical societies) of the families in particular areas

d. Genealogical dictionaries of the nobility: the *Almanach de Gotha*, noted above, contains pedigrees of German royal or princely families. Pedigrees of noble or landed families are included in over 120 published volumes of *Genealogisches Handbuch des Adels* and coats of arms are recorded in the *Wappenbuch*, published regularly since the 17th century

e. Army records: those for Germany since 1871 and for Prussia and many other states before 1871 were destroyed in 1945 but those that survive, for example for Bavaria (and published lists of officers) are described in Towey (1333)

f. Confirmation records: kept by both Catholic and Lutheran churches recording the name of the child who was confirmed (usually aged between 12 and 20) the date and place of birth and the father's name and occupation

Baxter (1253) also lists many city, parish and family archives, as well as the addresses of German genealogical associations. Those researchers interested in more recent family history should note the enormous collection of files (about 30 million documents) of the Nazi party from 1933 to 1945, including files on about 10 million members of the party during that period. The original files are in the German Federal archives and microfilm copies are held in the United States; all are open to the public.

Gibraltar
Gibraltar became a British possession in 1704. Civil registration records date from 1848 for births, 1862 for marriages and 1869 for deaths, although registration was only compulsory from later dates. The registers and indexes are open to the public at the registrar's office at 277 Main Street, Gibraltar and microfilm copies of the registers are available at LDS family history centres. Census records and other population lists are available for 1777, 1791, 1834, 1868/71, 1878/81, 1891, 1901, 1911, 1921 and 1931 at Gibraltar Government Archives, 6 Convent place, Gibraltar. Microfilms of most of these are held by the LDS. Catholic, Anglican and Methodist registers of baptisms, marriages and burials are available (some have been filmed by the LDS) and wills are held at the archives of the Supreme Court of Gibraltar. The *Gibraltar Chronicle* has been published since 1801 and includes local news, obituaries and notices of births, marriages and deaths. Further details and useful addresses are noted by P. Blake in *Practical Family History* (August/ September 2000) and by L.R. Burness and J.A. Bryden in *Genealogists' Magazine* (March 1983 and September 1993 respectively). Howes (1296) is a detailed study of the population of Gibraltar in the 18th and 19th centuries with transcripts of some 18th century lists of inhabitants.

OTHER COUNTRIES

This section lists some books or articles, mostly held at the SoG, that provide information upon research in particular countries. The bibliographies in these works usually note some further published material. It is also important to remember the other sources already described: the records available through LDS family history centres, the works by Currer-Briggs (1276) and Baxter (1252), and the worldwide IGI.

Austria

Senekovic (1322) is a good beginner's guide to research of Austrian ancestors, providing a brief history of Austria and the Austro-Hungarian empire, a gazetteer, a list of Austrian genealogical societies and a directory of Austrian church registers and covering dates.

The Czech and Slovak republics

Wellauer (1338) is a brief guide to Czechoslovakian genealogical research dealing mainly with records in the United States (and the Czech language). Schlyter (1320) is a more detailed guide to Czechoslovak names, language, archives, church records and civil registration.

Finland

Choquette (1267) reviews Finnish names, places, archives, church and emigration records.

Hungary

Suess (1326) is a good basic guide to Hungarian genealogical research and a useful article by A.M. Glendinning appears in *Genealogists' Magazine* (September 1994).

Italy

Konrad (1300) is a good beginner's guide to research of Italian ancestors, considering records of Italians in the United States but also reviewing Italian records such as wills, censuses and registers of births, marriages and deaths. Colletta (1275) and *Italian Genealogical Records* by T. Cole, published by Ancestry (1995) include more detailed guidance to Italian records.

Malta

J. Cole lists the key genealogical records of Malta in *Family Tree Magazine* (January 2002).

Mexico

A CD-ROM index to vital records of Mexico has been published.

Netherlands

Franklin (1286) is a good basic guide to Dutch history and genealogical research, including sections on records in Holland, names, heraldry and emigration to the United States. Useful articles on genealogical sources in Holland also appear in *Ancestors* (August/September 2003), *Family Tree Magazine* (August 1987) and *Genealogists' Magazine* (December 1961 and March 1962).

Norway and Denmark

Wellauer (1340) includes notes on Norwegian history and records, with illustrations of the records available and lists of sources held by the Mormons. Thomsen (1331) reviews Danish and Norwegian names, language, handwriting, genealogical resources (such as church registers, wills, census and land records) and notes the sources available at LDS family history centres. Thomsen (1330) lists the Norwegian church registers available on LDS microfilms.

Poland
Wellauer (1339) is primarily intended for Americans of Polish descent who are searching for information in US archives about their immigrant ancestors, but information is also provided about Polish history and genealogical sources in Poland. An article on Polish genealogy by B. Klec-Pilewski appears in *Genealogists' Magazine* (December 1969). A more detailed guide to research in Poland, *Polish Roots* by R.A. Chorzempa, has been published by GPC.

Portugal
A useful article by C.R. Humphery-Smith on genealogy in Portugal appears in *Family Tree Magazine* (September 1996).

Russia
Until the Russian revolutions of 1917 many British subjects were resident in Russia, perhaps 30,000 of them in 1917. Registers of baptisms, marriages and deaths of these British residents are in the collections at TNA and Guildhall Library noted above. Records of the British army units that served in Russia during the civil war are held at TNA. Many other records of the British community in Russia are contained in the Leeds Russian archive at the Brotherton Library, University of Leeds. A useful article about this archive, with a helpful bibliography, appears in *Family Tree Magazine* (February 1988). *A Handbook of Archival Research in the USSR* by P. Grimstead is available at some reference libraries.

Spain
Ryskamp (1316) is a detailed, illustrated guide to genealogical research in Spain, Mexico and other Spanish-speaking countries of Central and South America.

Sweden
Olsson (1311) is a short introductory booklet on genealogical records and research in Sweden. Thomsen (1329) provides maps of Sweden and lists of parishes with the covering dates of parish registers held by the Mormons on microfilm.

Switzerland
Wellauer (1337) provides notes on Swiss history and religion, and records of births, marriages, deaths and the census, sources held by the Mormons and many illustrations of Swiss records.

Zimbabwe
Zimbabwe was formerly the British colony of Rhodesia. Many of the country's archives are described in *Guide to the Historical Manuscripts in the National Archives of Rhodesia* by T. Baxter and E. Burke and in *Guide to the Public Archives of Rhodesia, 1890–1923* by T. Baxter.

SOME USEFUL ADDRESSES

Australia
Society of Australian Genealogists, Richmond Villa, 120 Kent Street, Observatory Hill, Sydney, NSW 2000
State Library of New South Wales, Macquarrie Street, Sydney, NSW 2000

National Archives of Australia, Queen Victoria Terrace, Parkes Place, Canberra, ACT 2610 (branch offices are also located in Sydney, Hobart and other cities)

National Library of Australia, Parkes Place, Canberra, ACT 2600

New South Wales State Archives Office, 2 Globe Street, Sydney, NSW 2000

Northern Territory Archives Service, corner of McMinn and Kerry Streets, Darwin NT 5790

Queensland State Archives, PO Box 1397, Sunnybanks Hills, Brisbane, Queensland 4109

State Library of South Australia, North Terrace, Adelaide SA 5001

South Australia State Archives, PO Box 1056, Blair Athol West, South Australia 5084

Tasmania State Archives, 77 Murray Street, Hobart, Tasmania 7000

State Library of Victoria, Archives Division, Swanston Street, Melbourne, Victoria 3000

Western Australia State Library, State Archives and Public Record Office, Alexander Library Building, Perth Cultural Centre, James Street, Perth WA 6000

The Registrar Generals

of New South Wales, Prince Albert Road, Sydney, NSW 2000

of Northern Territory, PO Box 3021, Darwin NT 5794

of Queensland, Old Treasury Buildings, Queen Street, Brisbane, Queensland 4000

of South Australia, Edmund Wright House, 59 King William Street, Adelaide SA 5000

of Tasmania, Law Department, 81 Murray Street, Hobart, Tasmania 7000

of Victoria, Law Department, 233 William Street, Melbourne, Victoria 3000

of Western Australia, Oakleigh Building, 22 St George's Terrace, Perth WA 6000

Canada

National Archives of Canada, 395 Wellington Street, Ottawa, Ontario K1A 0N3

Provincial Archives of British Columbia, 865 Yates Street, Victoria, BC. V8V 1X4

Provincial Archives of Manitoba, 200 Vaughan Street, Winnipeg, Manitoba R3C 1T5

Provincial Archives of Alberta, 12845–102nd Avenue, Edmonton, Alberta T5N 0M6

Public Archives of Nova Scotia, 6016 University Avenue Halifax, Nova Scotia B3H 1W4

Provincial Archives of New Brunswick, PO Box 6000, Fredericton, New Brunswick E3B 5H1

Public Archives of Prince Edward Island, Coles Building, Richmond Street, Charlottetown, Prince Edward Island C1A 7M4

Archives of Ontario, 77 Grenville Street West, Toronto, Ontario M5S 1BS

Saskatchewan Archives Board, Regina Office, 3303 Hillsdale Street, Regina, Saskatchewan S4S 0A2 and Saskatoon Office, Murray Building, University of Saskatchewan, Saskatoon, Saskatchewan S7N 5A4

Newfoundland and Labrador Archives, Colonial Building, Military Road, St John's, Newfoundland A1C 2C9

Archives Nationales du Quebec, PO Box 10450, Sainte-Foy, Quebec G1V 4N1 (this is the central administration which can direct you to the relevant regional archive centre)

Yukon Archives, PO Box 2703, Whitehorse, Yukon Territories, Y1A 2C6

Archives of the Northwest Territories, Prince of Wales Northern Heritage Centre, Yellowknife, NWT. X1A 2L9

South Africa

National Archives, Union Building, Private Bag X236, Pretoria

The Genealogical Society of South Africa, Suite 143, Postnet, X2600, Houghton 2041

South African Library, National Reference and Preservation, PO Box 496, Cape Town 8000

USA

National Archives & Records Administration, 700 Pennsylvania Avenue NW, Washington D.C. 20408

Genealogical Society of Utah, Family History Library, 35 North West Temple Street, Salt Lake City, Utah 84150

National Genealogical Society, 4527 17th Street North, Arlington, Virginia 22207–2399

Virginia State Archives, 11th Street at Capitol Square, Richmond, Virginia 23219–3491; other state archives are listed in the *FLHH* (5) and in Eakle & Cerny (1280)

New Zealand

Alexander Turnbull Library, 70 Molesworth Street, Wellington

Archives New Zealand, P.O. Box 12–050, 10 Mulgrave Street, Wellington 6001 (with regional offices in Auckland, Christchurch and Dunedin)

Central Registry of Births, Deaths & Marriages, PO Box 31–115, 191 High Street, Lower Hutt (registry offices also in Auckland, Wellington and Christchurch)

New Zealand Society of Genealogists Inc. P.O. Box 8795, Symonds Street, Auckland 1035

APPENDIX I

CODES FOR AREAS AND VOLUMES IN THE GRO INDEXES

Roman Numerals (1837 to 1851)

I–III	London & Middlesex
IV	London & Surrey
V	Kent
VI	Beds, Berks, Bucks and Herts
VII	Hants and Sussex
VIII	Dorset, Hants and Wilts
IX	Cornwall and Devon
X	Devon and Somerset
XI	Glos and Somerset
XII	Essex and Suffolk
XIII	Norfolk and Suffolk
XIV	Cambs, Hants and Lincs
XV	Leics, Northants, Notts & Rutland
XVI	Oxon, Staffs, Warwicks & Berkshire
XVII	Staffordshire
XVIII	Glos, Shropshire, Staffs, Warwicks and Worcs
XIX	Cheshire, Derbyshire and Flints
XX	Lancashire
XXI	Lancashire and Yorkshire
XXII	Yorkshire
XXIII	Yorkshire
XXIV	Durham and Yorkshire
XXV	Cumberland, Lancs, Northumberland & Westmorland
XXVI	Brecknocks, Carmarthens, Glams, Herefords, Mons, Pembs, Radnors & Shropshire
XXVII	Anglesey, Caernarvons, Cardigans, Denbighs, Flints, Merioneths, and Montgomeryshire

Arabic Numerals and Letters (1852 to 1946)

1a–1c	London & Middlesex
1d	London, Kent & Surrey
2a	Kent and Surrey
2b	Hants and Sussex
2c–2d	Berks and Hants
3a	Berks, Bucks, Herts, Middx and Oxon
3b	Beds, Cambs, Hunts, Northants & Suffolk
4a	Essex and Suffolk
4b	Norfolk
5a	Dorset and Wiltshire
5b	Devonshire
5c	Cornwall and Somerset
6a	Glos, Herefords and Shropshire
6b	Staffs, Warwicks and Worcs
6c	Warwicks and Worcestershire
6d	Warwickshire
7a	Leics, Lincs and Rutland
7b	Derbyshire and Notts
8a	Cheshire
8b–8e	Lancashire
9a–9d	Yorkshire
10a	Durham
10b	Cumberland, Northumberland & Westmorland
11a	Glamorgan, Monmouth and Pembrokeshire
11b	Anglesey, Brecknocks, Denbighs, Montgomeryshire, Flints and Radnorshire

APPENDIX II

INDEXES TO OTHER GRO RECORDS

Chapter 5 reviewed civil registration records. In addition to the indexes of births, marriages and deaths since 1837, the GRO holds indexes to the following records:

1. Army chaplains' registers of births, marriages and deaths from 1796 to 1880
2. Regimental registers of births in the United Kingdom (from 1761) and abroad (from 1790) up to 1924 (and also unindexed regimental registers of marriages)
3. Army returns of births, marriages and deaths abroad (1881–1955) and RAF returns from 1920
4. Consular records of births, marriages and deaths 1849–1965
5. Adopted children's register (from 1927)
6. Marine registers of births (1837–1965) and deaths (1837–1950) on British merchant or naval ships
7. Deaths; Natal and South Africa Forces (Boer War) 1899 to 1902
8. First World War deaths (army) 1914–1921 – officers
9. First World War deaths (army) 1914–1921 – other ranks
10. First World War deaths (navy) 1914–1921
11. Second World War deaths (RAF) 1939–1948 – all ranks
12. Second World War deaths (army) 1939–1948 – other ranks
13. Second World War deaths (army) 1939–1948 – officers
14. Second World War deaths (navy) 1939–1948
15. Indian Services war deaths 1939–1948
16. UK High Commission records of births, marriages and deaths abroad 1950–1965
17. Army, navy and RAF registers of births, deaths and marriages (abroad) 1956–1965
18. Births and deaths in British civil aircraft from 1947–1965
19. Births, marriages and deaths (military, civil and chaplains' registers) in the Ionian Isles (1818–64)
20. Births, marriages and deaths in Protectorates of Africa and Asia 1941–1965
21. Miscellaneous foreign registers of births, marriages and deaths 1956–1965
22. Registers of births, marriages and deaths abroad since 1966
23. Registers of stillbirths from 1 July 1927 (only available with consent of the Registrar General)

APPENDIX III

CHAPMAN COUNTY CODES

England (ENG)

BDF	Bedfordshire	HEF	Herefordshire	OXF	Oxfordshire
BRK	Berkshire	HRT	Hertfordshire	RUT	Rutland
BKM	Buckinghamshire	HUN	Huntingdonshire	SAL	Shropshire
CAM	Cambridgeshire	KEN	Kent	SOM	Somerset
CHS	Cheshire	LAN	Lancashire	STS	Staffordshire
CON	Cornwall	LEI	Leicestershire	SFK	Suffolk
CUL	Cumberland	LIN	Lincolnshire	SSX	Sussex
DBY	Derbyshire	LND	London	WAR	Warwickshire
DEV	Devon	MDX	Middlesex	WES	Westmoreland
DUR	Durham	NFK	Norfolk	WIL	Wiltshire
ESS	Essex	NTH	Northamptonshire	WOR	Worcestershire
GLS	Gloucestershire	NBL	Northumberland	YKS	Yorkshire
HAM	Hampshire	NTT	Nottinghamshire		

Channel Isles (CHI)

ALD	Alderney	GSY	Guernsey	JSY	Jersey	SRK	Sark

Wales (WLS)

AGY	Anglesey	DEN	Denbighshire	MGY	Montgomeryshire
BRE	Breconshire	FLN	Flintshire	PEM	Pembrokeshire
CAE	Caenarvonshire	GLA	Glamorgan	RAD	Radnorshire
CGN	Cardiganshire	MER	Merionethshire		
CMN	Carmarthenshire	MON	Monmouthshire		

Scotland (SCT)

ABD	Aberdeenshire	ELN	East Lothian	PEE	Peebleshire
ANS	Angus	FIF	Fifeshire	PER	Perthshire
ARL	Argyllshire	INV	Inverness-shire	RFW	Renfrewshire
AYR	Ayrshire	KCD	Kincardineshire	ROC	Ross & Cromarty
BAN	Banffshire	KRS	Kinross-shire	ROX	Roxburghshire
BEW	Berwickshire	KKD	Kirkudbrightshire	SEL	Selkirk
BUT	Bute	LKS	Lanarkshire	SHI	Shetland Isles
CAI	Caithness	MLN	Midlothian	STI	Stirlingshire
CLK	Clackmannanshire	MOR	Moray	SUT	Sutherland
DFS	Dumfries	NAI	Nairn	WLN	West Lothian
DUN	Dunbartonshire	OKI	Orkney Isles	WIG	Wigtownshire

Ireland (IRE)

ANT	Antrim	DUB	Dublin	LIM	Limerick	ROS	Roscommon
ARM	Armagh	FER	Fermanagh	LDY	Londonderry	SLI	Sligo
CAR	Carlow	GAL	Galway	LOG	Longford	TIP	Tipperary
CAV	Cavan	KER	Kerry	LOU	Louth	TYR	Tyrone
CLA	Clare	KID	Kildare	MAY	Mayo	WAT	Waterford
COR	Cork	KIK	Kilkenny	MEA	Meath	WEM	Westmeath
DON	Donegal	LET	Leitrim	MOG	Monaghan	WEX	Wexford
DOW	Down	LEX	Leix	OFF	Offaly	WIC	Wicklow

APPENDIX IV

SEIZE QUARTIERS OF BESSIE MAUD SYMES

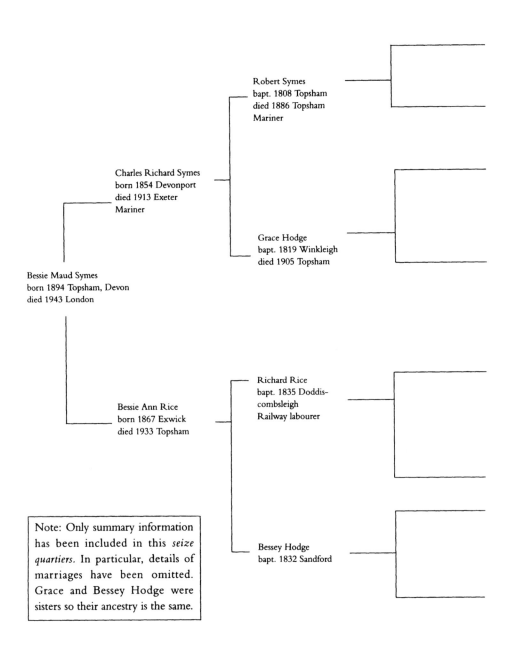

Robert Symes
bapt. 1808 Topsham
died 1886 Topsham
Mariner

Charles Richard Symes
born 1854 Devonport
died 1913 Exeter
Mariner

Grace Hodge
bapt. 1819 Winkleigh
died 1905 Topsham

Bessie Maud Symes
born 1894 Topsham, Devon
died 1943 London

Richard Rice
bapt. 1835 Doddis-
combsleigh
Railway labourer

Bessie Ann Rice
born 1867 Exwick
died 1933 Topsham

Bessey Hodge
bapt. 1832 Sandford

Note: Only summary information has been included in this *seize quartiers*. In particular, details of marriages have been omitted. Grace and Bessey Hodge were sisters so their ancestry is the same.

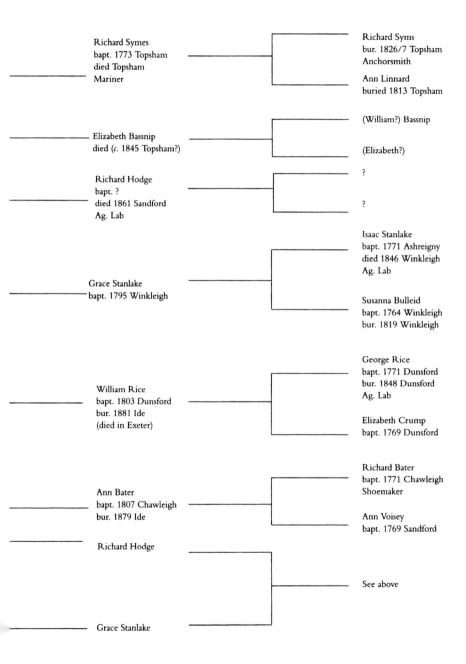

Richard Symes
bapt. 1773 Topsham
died Topsham
Mariner

Richard Syms
bur. 1826/7 Topsham
Anchorsmith

Ann Linnard
buried 1813 Topsham

Elizabeth Bassnip
died (c. 1845 Topsham?)

(William?) Bassnip

(Elizabeth?)

Richard Hodge
bapt. ?
died 1861 Sandford
Ag. Lab

?

?

Grace Stanlake
bapt. 1795 Winkleigh

Isaac Stanlake
bapt. 1771 Ashreigny
died 1846 Winkleigh
Ag. Lab

Susanna Bulleid
bapt. 1764 Winkleigh
bur. 1819 Winkleigh

William Rice
bapt. 1803 Dunsford
bur. 1881 Ide
(died in Exeter)

George Rice
bapt. 1771 Dunsford
bur. 1848 Dunsford
Ag. Lab

Elizabeth Crump
bapt. 1769 Dunsford

Ann Bater
bapt. 1807 Chawleigh
bur. 1879 Ide

Richard Bater
bapt. 1771 Chawleigh
Shoemaker

Ann Voisey
bapt. 1769 Sandford

Richard Hodge

See above

Grace Stanlake

APPENDIX V

(A) EXTRACTS FROM THE BULLEID FAMILY TREE

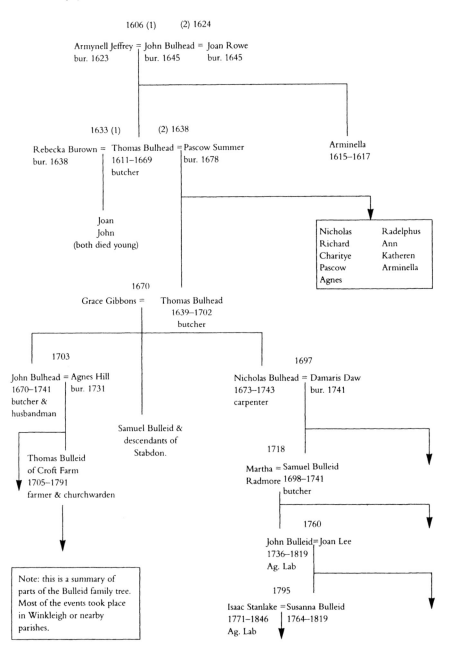

1606 (1)   (2) 1624

Armynell Jeffrey = John Bulhead = Joan Rowe
bur. 1623   bur. 1645   bur. 1645

1633 (1)   (2) 1638

Rebecka Burown = Thomas Bulhead = Pascow Summer
bur. 1638   1611–1669   bur. 1678
butcher

Arminella
1615–1617

Joan
John
(both died young)

Nicholas   Radelphus
Richard   Ann
Charitye   Katheren
Pascow   Arminella
Agnes

1670

Grace Gibbons = Thomas Bulhead
1639–1702
butcher

1703

John Bulhead = Agnes Hill
1670–1741   bur. 1731
butcher &
husbandman

1697

Nicholas Bulhead = Damaris Daw
1673–1743   bur. 1741
carpenter

Samuel Bulleid &
descendants of
Stabdon.

Thomas Bulleid
of Croft Farm
1705–1791
farmer & churchwarden

1718

Martha = Samuel Bulleid
Radmore 1698–1741
butcher

1760

John Bulleid = Joan Lee
1736–1819
Ag. Lab

Note: this is a summary of
parts of the Bulleid family tree.
Most of the events took place
in Winkleigh or nearby
parishes.

1795

Isaac Stanlake = Susanna Bulleid
1771–1846   1764–1819
Ag. Lab

(B) EXTRACTS FROM THE KEATES FAMILY TREE

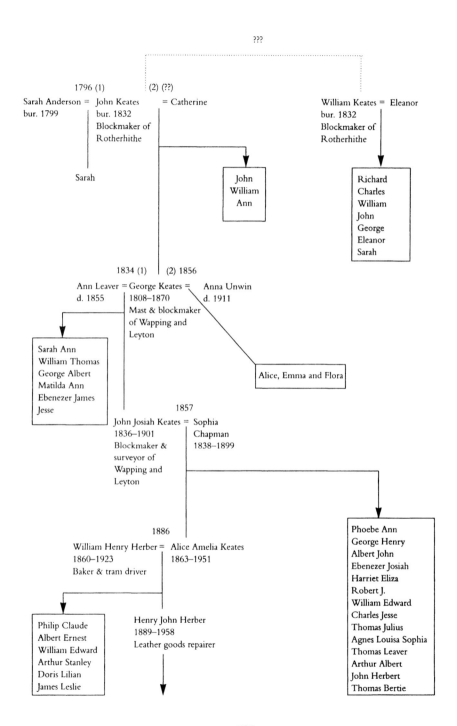

APPENDIX VI

THE NATIONAL ARCHIVES' INFORMATION LEAFLETS

The leaflets produced by TNA to assist researchers at Kew and the FRC are listed below. The FRC leaflets can be obtained in the search room of TNA at the FRC and TNA leaflets can be obtained at Kew. All the leaflets can be viewed on (and printed out from) the web site of TNA. Many of the leaflets have not yet been amended to take account of the change of the name of the Public Record Office to The National Archives. The necessary amendments will presumably be made in the near future.

Family Records Centre leaflets

Census leaflets
Census returns
How to use the 1841 census
How to use the 1851 census
How to use the 1861 census
How to use the 1871 census
How to use the 1881 census
How to use 1881 surname index
How to use the 1891 census
How to use additional census finding aids

Wills and probate leaflets
Probate records from 1858
Wills and probate records – where to find them
How to use PCC wills before 1700
How to use PCC wills after 1700
How to use Death Duty records 1796–1903
How to use Death Duty records – how to interpret them
How to use PCC administrations before 1700
How to use PCC administrations after 1700

Tracing missing persons leaflets
Tracing missing persons
Tracing missing persons: useful addresses

Other Family Records Centre leaflets
How to use: non-conformist registers
How to use: the International Genealogical Index (IGI)
How to use: Family Search
How to use: microform services
How to use: self-service photocopier

The National Archives' leaflets
Some numbers are not presently used in each series of the leaflets listed below.

General information leaflets

14. Access to public records
15. Copyright
18. List annotation
19. Reprographic copies of records in the Public Record Office
21. Suggestions for groups visiting the Public Record Office
25. How to cite documents in the Public Record Office
34. The constitutional place of the Public Record Office
35. Public Record Office: aims and structures
36. Photographs held by the PRO
38. Public Record Office: acquisition policy

Legal records information leaflets

1. Manorial records in the Public Record Office
2. Land conveyances: feet of fines, 1182–1833
3. The Court of Star Chamber, 1485–1642
4. Court of Requests, 1485–1642: a court for the 'poor'
5. Bankrupts and insolvent debtors: 1710–1869
6. Bankruptcy records after 1869
7. Land conveyances: enrolment of deeds, and registration of title
8. Land conveyances: trust deeds (land for charitable uses) 1736–1925
9. Manor and other local court rolls, 13th century–1922
10. Inquisitions post mortem, Henry III–Charles I: landholders and their heirs
11. Court of Wards and Liveries, 1540–1645: land inheritance
12. English assizes, 1656–1971: key to series for civil trials
13. Criminal trials at the assizes
14. English assizes: key for criminal trials, 1559–1971
15. Welsh assizes, 1831–1971: key to classes for criminal and civil trials
16. Transportation to America and the West Indies, 1615–1776
17. Transportation to Australia 1787–1868
19. Equity proceedings in the Court of Exchequer
20. The General Eyres, 1194–1294
21. Money (funds) in court
22. Chancery proceedings: equity suits from 1558
23. Probate records
24. Outlawry in medieval and early modern England
27. Old Bailey and the Central Criminal Court: criminal trials
28. Supreme Court, Chancery Division: cases after 1875
29. Supreme Court: appeal cases after 1875
30. Coroners' inquests
31. The Treasury Solicitor
32. Change of name
33. Chancel repairs
34. King's Bench (Crown Side) 1675–1875
39. Chancery: Masters reports and certificates
41. Chancery Masters' and other exhibits: sources for social and economic history
42. Early Chancery proceedings: equity suits before 1558
43. Divorce records before 1858
44. Divorce records after 1858
45. Wills and death duty records after 1858
46. Wills before 1858: where to start

Domestic records information leaflets

1. Domesday Book
2. Royal grants: Letters Patent and charters, 1199–present day
3. Inventions: patents and specifications
4. Oath rolls and sacrament certificates after 1660

5. Medieval and early modern sources for family history
6. Parliamentary records after 1500
7. Printed Parliamentary papers
8. Medieval customs' accounts
9. Port books, 1565–1799
10. Taxation records before 1660
11. Family history in England and Wales
12. Sources for the history of religious houses and their lands, c. 1000–1530
13. Civilian gallantry medals
14. The dissolution of the monasteries
15. Letters and papers of Henry VIII
16. State Papers Domestic: Edward VI–Charles I, 1547–1649
17. State Papers Domestic: The Commonwealth, 1642–1660
18. State Papers Domestic: Charles II–Anne 1660–1714
19. State Papers Domestic: George I to George III, 1714–1782
20. State Papers Domestic: miscellaneous classes
21. Jacobite risings, 1715 and 1745
22. Cabinet Office records
23. Education: records of special services
24. Records relating to technical and further education
25. State Papers Ireland, 1509–1782
26. The Royal Household and wardrobe before 1660
27. Royal Warrant holders and household servants
28. Privy Council: registers 1540 onwards
29. Privy Council correspondence, from c. 1481
30. Seals
31. Pipe rolls, 1129–1835
32. The hearth tax 1662–1688
33. Markets and fairs
34. The Titanic
35. Coal mining records in the PRO
36. Lawyers: records of attorneys and solicitors
37. Privy Council: proclamations, Orders in Council, and Statutory Instruments
38. Customs, excise, tax collectors and civil servants
39. Treasury Board: letters and papers, 1557–1920
40. Registration of companies and businesses
41. Tithe records: a detailed examination
42. English local history: a note for beginners
43. Second World War, 1939–1945: the War Cabinet
44. How to read Roman numerals
45. Stationers' Hall copyright records
46. Valuation Office records: The Finance (1909–1910) Act
47. Home Office correspondence: 1839–1949
48. World War Two: the home front
49. Grants of British nationality
50. Immigrants
51. Internees: First and Second World Wars
52. Metropolitan Police (London): Records of service
53. The census, 1801–1901: statistical reports
54. Records of the Royal Irish Constabulary
55. How to use LAB 2
56. Ships' passenger lists, 1878–1960
57. Death Duty records, from 1796
58. How to interpret Death Duty registers
59. Agricultural statistics, from 1866 onwards: parish summaries
60. Passport records
61. Births, marriages and deaths at sea
62. League of Nations
63. Education: records of teachers

64. Sources for the history of mines and quarries
65. Education: elementary and secondary schools
66. Catholic recusants
67. Elementary (primary) schools
68. Crown, church and royalist land: 1642–1660
69. Records relating to railways
70. Records of the Ordnance Survey
71. Poor law records, 1834–1871
72. Maps in the PRO
73. Nineteenth century public health and epidemics: some PRO sources
74. Common Lands
75. Public rights of way
76. Anglo-Jewish history: sources in the PRO, 18th–20th centuries
77. Architectural drawings in the PRO
78. Tracing a 19th century criminal in the PRO
79. Civilian nurses and nursing services
80. Apprenticeship records as sources for genealogy
81. Railways: administrative and other records
82. Railways: staff records
83. Canals: administrative and other records
84. Byelaws
85. Ecclesiastical census of 1851
86. Enclosure awards
87. Enclosure records (an example)
88. Sources for convicts and prisoners 1100–1986
89. Merchant seamen: registers of service, 1835–1857
90. Merchant seamen: registers of service 1913–1972
91. Merchant shipping: crew lists and agreements after 1861
92. Merchant shipping: crew lists and agreements, 1747–1860
93. Merchant seamen: officers' service records 1845–1965
94. Merchant shipping: registration of ships, 1786–1994
95. Merchant seamen: medals and honours
98. Royal Warrant holders, and suppliers of goods, from 1660
99. Census of England and Wales: read this first
100. Registered designs and trade marks
101. Registered designs: diamond marks
102. Labour Ministry records
103. The poor and the poor laws
104. Lunatic asylums, 18th–20th centuries
105. Lunacy and the state
106. National farm surveys of England and Wales, 1940–1943
107. Emigrants
109. Health between the wars: 1919–1939
110. Merchant seamen: records of the RGSS, a guide to leaflets
111. Merchant seamen: interpreting voyage details in the registers of officer's services
112. Merchant seamen: abbreviations found in the RGSS registers
113. Merchant seamen: interpreting voyage details in the registers of seamen, series II
114. Merchant seamen: interpreting the voyages in the registers of seamen's tickets and the alphabetical registers of masters

Military records information leaflets
1. Medieval and early modern soldiers
2. Tudor and Stuart local soldiery: militia muster rolls
3. Civil war soldiers 1642–1660
4. Army: officers' records 1660–1913
5. British army: soldiers' discharge papers, 1760–1913
6. British army: soldiers' pensions, 1702–1913
7. Army: muster rolls and pay lists, *c.* 1730–1898

8. First World War, 1914–1918: the conduct of the war
9. British army soldiers' papers: First World War 1914–1918
10. British army officers' records: First World War 1914–1918
11. First World War, 1914–1918: army war diaries
12. British prisoners of war, c. 1760–1919
13. War dead: First and Second World Wars
14. British army: useful sources for tracing soldiers
15. First World War: disability and dependants' pensions
16. First World War: conscientious objectors & exemptions from service
17. British army lists
18. The militia, 1757–1914
19. Prisoners of war and displaced persons 1939–1953
20. British prisoners of war, 1939–1953
21. Army: operations after 1945
22. Army: Courts Martial, 17th–20th Centuries
23. Army: campaign records, 1660–1714
24. British army: campaign records, 1714–1815
25. Army: operational records 1816–1913
26. Intelligence records in the Public Record Office
27. War crimes of the Second World War
28. Records of the Royal Air Force: research and development records
30. Royal Navy: officers' service records
31. Royal Navy: ratings' service records 1667–1923
32. Royal Navy: log books and reports of proceedings
33. Royal Navy: operational records, First World War, 1914–1918
35. Royal Navy: operational records 1660–1914
36. Admiralty charts (maps)
37. Royal Naval Reserve
38. Royal Naval research and development
41. Naval dockyards
43. Ships wrecked or sunk
44. The Coastguard
45. Royal Marines: other ranks' service records
46. Royal Marines: how to find a division
47. Royal Marines: officers' service records
48. Royal Marines: further areas of research
49. RAF, RFC and RNAS: First World War, 1914–1918: service records
50. Royal Air Force: Second World War, 1939–1945: service records
54. First World War, 1914–1918: military maps
55. British army: nurses and nursing services
56. Royal Navy: nurses and nursing services
57. Royal Air Force: nurses and nursing services
60. Royal Navy: pay and pension records: commissioned officers
61. Royal Navy: pension records: warrant officers
62. Royal Navy: pension records: ratings
66. Records of the Board of Ordnance
68. Second World War: British army operations
69. Royal Navy: operational records Second World War, 1939–1945
70. Operational records of the Royal Air Force
71. The Royal Naval Volunteer Reserve
72. Auxiliary army forces: volunteers, Yeomanry, Territorials & Home Guard 1769–1945
73. Army officers' commissions
74. Records of women's services, First World War
75. Army: Courts Martial: First World War, 1914–1918
76. Armed services: campaign medals, and other service medals
77. Armed services: gallantry medals
78. Armed services: gallantry medals, further information
79. Royal Navy: officers' service records, First World War, and confidential reports, 1893–1942

Overseas records information leaflets

1. Diplomatic sources before 1509
2. State Papers, Foreign
3. The Privy Council and the colonies
4. Captured enemy documents: films of German Foreign Ministry (GFM) archive and other sources
5. The French lands of the English kings
6. Maps and plans: foreign, colonial and dominions
7. Great Britain and the French Revolution
8. Indonesia since 1945
9. Irish genealogy
10. Colonial Office: Advisory Committees
11. Ireland: the Easter rising 1916
12. Foreign Office: card index, 1906–1910
13. Foreign Office: card index, 1910–1919
14. The records of the Foreign Office from 1782
15. Ireland: Roger Casement
16. Refugees and minorities
17. Embassy and consular archives
19. Treaties
25. International organisations: 20th century Europe
29. British propaganda in the 20th century
30. Researching British colonies and dominions
31. Dominions Office
32. Calender of State Papers Colonial, America and West Indies
33. Colonial Office: registers of correspondence, 1849–1926
34. Colonial Office: registers of correspondence, 1926–1951
35. Land grants in America and American loyalists' claims
36. Government gazettes of the British Empire and Commonwealth
51. The American and West Indian colonies before 1782
52. The American Revolution
53. Emigrants to North America after 1776

APPENDIX VII

COUNTY RECORD OFFICES AND OTHER ARCHIVES

England
Bedfordshire   Bedfordshire and Luton Archives and Record Service, County Hall, Cauldwell Street, Bedford MK42 9AP

Berkshire   Berkshire Record Office, 9 Coley Avenue, Reading RG1 6AF
Museum of English Rural Life, Rural History Centre, University of Reading, Whiteknights, Reading RG6 2AG

Buckinghamshire   Buckinghamshire Record Office, County Hall, Walton Street, Aylesbury HP20 1UA

Cambridgeshire   Cambridgeshire Archives Service, County Record Office, Shire Hall, Castle Hill, Cambridge CB3 0AP
Cambridgeshire Archives Service, Huntingdon branch, Grammar School Walk, Huntingdon PE29 3LF
Cambridge University Library, Archives & MS department, West Road, Cambridge CB3 9DR

Cheshire   Cheshire & Chester Archives and Local Studies, Duke Street, Chester CH1 1RL
Stockport Archive Service, Central Library, Wellington Road South, Stockport SK1 3RS

Cleveland   Teesside Archives, Exchange House, 6 Marton Road, Middlesbrough TS1 1DB

Cornwall   Cornwall Record Office, County Hall, Truro TR1 3AY
Royal Institution of Cornwall, Royal Cornwall Museum, River Street, Truro TR1 2SJ

Cumbria   Cumbria Record Office, The Castle, Carlisle CA3 8UR
Cumbria Record Office, 140 Duke Street, Barrow in Furness LA14 1XW
Cumbria Record Office, County Offices, Strickland Gate, Kendal LA9 4RQ

Derbyshire   Derbyshire Record Office, Ernest Bailey Building, New Street, Matlock (address correspondence to County Hall, Matlock DE4 3AG)

Devon   Devon Record Office, Castle Street, Exeter EX4 3PQ
Westcountry Studies Library, Castle Street, Exeter EX4 3PQ
Exeter Cathedral Library, Bishop's Palace, Exeter EX1 1HX
Plymouth & West Devon Area Record Office, Unit 3, Clare Place, Coxside, Plymouth PL4 0JW
North Devon Record Office, North Devon Library, Tuly Street, Barnstaple EX31 1EL

Dorset   Dorset Archives Service, 9 Bridport Road, Dorchester DT1 1RP

Durham   Durham County Record Office, County Hall, Durham DH1 5UL
Centre for Local Studies, Darlington Library, Crown Street, Darlington DL1 1ND
Durham University Library, Archives & Special Collections, Palace Green, Durham DH1 3RN

Essex   Essex Record Office, Wharf Road, Chelmsford CM2 6YT (branches at Southend-on-Sea, Colchester, and Saffron Walden)

Gloucestershire   Gloucestershire Record Office, Clarence Row, Alvin Street, Gloucester GL1 3DW
Bristol Record Office, "B" Bond Warehouse, Smeaton Road, Bristol BS1 6XN

Hampshire   Hampshire Record Office, Sussex Street, Winchester SO23 8TH
Portsmouth City Records Office, 3 Museum Road, Portsmouth PO1 2LJ
Southampton Archives, Civic Centre, Southampton SO14 7LY
Isle of Wight Record Office, 26 Hillside, Newport PO30 2EB

Herefordshire   Herefordshire Record Office, Harold Street, Hereford HR1 2QX
Hereford Cathedral Archives & Library, 5 College Cloisters, Cathedral Close, Hereford HR1 2NG

Hertfordshire   Hertfordshire Archives and Local Studies, County Hall, Pegs Lane, Hertford SG13 8EJ

Huntingdonshire (see Cambridgeshire)

Kent   Centre for Kentish Studies, County Hall, Maidstone ME4 1XQ (branches in Folkestone, Ramsgate and Sevenoaks)
Canterbury Cathedral Archives, The Precincts, Canterbury CT1 2EH
East Kent Archives Centre, Enterprise Zone, Honeywood Road, Whitfield, Dover CT16 3EH

Lancashire   Lancashire Record Office, Bow Lane, Preston PR1 2RE

Leicestershire (including Rutland)   The Record Office for Leicestershire, Leicester and Rutland, Long Street, Wigston Magna, Leicester LE18 2AH

Lincolnshire   Lincolnshire Archives Office, St Rumbold Street, Lincoln LN2 5AB
North East Lincolnshire Archives, Town Hall Square, Grimsby DN31 1HX
Lincolnshire County Library, Local Studies Section, Lincoln Central Library, Free School Lane, Lincoln LN1 1EZ

London   London Metropolitan Archives, 40 Northampton Road, London EC1R 0HB
Guildhall Library, Aldermanbury, London EC2P 2EJ
Corporation of London Records Office, Guildhall, London EC2P 2EJ
City of Westminster Archives Centre, 10 St Ann's Street, London SW1P 2DE
[See chapter 11 and bibliography for lists of borough archive offices and local studies centres]

Manchester (Lancashire and Cheshire)   Greater Manchester Record Office, 56 Marshall Street, New Cross, Manchester M4 5FU
Methodist Archives and Research Centre, John Rylands University Library, 150 Deansgate, Manchester M3 3EH
Manchester Archives & Local Studies, Manchester Central Library, St Peter's Square, Manchester M2 5PD
[See chapter 11 and bibliography for lists of other archives, such as those in Bolton, Bury, Wigan, Salford and Stockport]

Merseyside   Liverpool Record Office and Local History Department, William Brown Street, Liverpool L3 8EW
Merseyside Record Office, Liverpool Central Library, William Brown Street, Liverpool L3 8EW

Norfolk   Norfolk Record Office, Gildengate House, Anglia Square, Upper Green Lane, Norwich NR3 1AX

Northamptonshire   Northamptonshire Record Office, Wootton Hall Park, Northampton NN4 9BQ
Northamptonshire Central Library, Abington Street, Northampton NN1 2BA

Northumberland   Northumberland Record Office, Melton Park, North Gosforth, Newcastle upon Tyne NE3 5QX
Berwick-upon-Tweed Record Office, Council Offices, Wallace Green, Berwick-upon-Tweed TD15 1ED

Nottinghamshire   Nottinghamshire Archives, Castle Meadow Road, Nottingham NG1 1AG
Nottingham Central Library, Local Studies Centre, Angel Row, Nottingham NG1 6HP

Oxfordshire   Oxfordshire Archives, St Luke's Church, Temple Road, Cowley, Oxford OX4 2EN
Bodleian Library, Broad Street, Oxford OX1 3BG

Rutland (see Leicestershire)

Shropshire   Shropshire Records and Research Centre, Castle Gates, Shrewsbury SY1 2AQ

Somerset   Somerset Archive and Record Service, Obridge Road, Taunton TA2 7PU
Bath & North East Somerset Record Office, Guildhall, High Street, Bath BA1 5AW

Staffordshire   Lichfield Joint Record Office, The Friary, Lichfield WS13 6QG
Staffordshire Record Office, Eastgate Street, Stafford ST16 2LZ

Suffolk   Suffolk Record Office, Gatacre Road, Ipswich IP1 2LQ (branches at Bury St Edmunds and Lowestoft)

Surrey   Surrey History Centre, 130 Goldsworth Road, Woking, Surrey GU21 1ND

Sussex   East Sussex Record Office, The Maltings, Castle Precincts, Lewes BN7 1YT
West Sussex Record Office, Sherburne House, 3 Orchard Street, Chichester (address correspondence to County Hall, West Street, Chichester PO19 1RN)

Tyne and Wear   Tyne and Wear Archives Service, Blandford House, Blandford Square, Newcastle NE1 4JA

Warwickshire   Warwickshire County Record Office, Priory Park, Cape Road, Warwick CV34 4JS

West Midlands   Birmingham Central Library, Archives Division, Chamberlain Square, Birmingham B3 3HQ
Coventry City Archives, Mandela House, Bayley Lane, Coventry CV1 5RG
Wolverhampton Archives & Local Studies, 42–50 Snow Hill, Wolverhampton WV2 4AG

Wiltshire   Wiltshire Record Office, County Hall, Bythesea Road, Trowbridge BA14 8BS

Worcestershire   Worcestershire Record Office, History Centre, Trinity Street, Spetchley Road, Worcester WR1 2PW
St Helens Record Office-Worcestershire, Fish Street, Worcester WR1 2HN

Yorkshire   North Yorkshire County Record Office, Malpas Road, Northallerton DL7 8SG
Borthwick Institute of Historical Research, St Anthony's Hall, Peasholme Green, York YO1 2PW
Sheffield Archives, 52 Shoreham Street, Sheffield S1 4SP
East Riding of Yorkshire Archives Service, The Chapel, Lord Roberts' Road, Beverley (address correspondence to the Archives Service at County Hall, Beverley HU17 9BA)
York City Archives, Exhibition Square, Bootham, York YO1 7EW
West Yorkshire Archive Service, Newstead Road, Wakefield WF1 2DE (branches at Bradford, Halifax, Huddersfield and Leeds)

Wales (pre-1996 authorities)
Clwyd (Denbigh and Flintshire)   Denbighshire Record Office, 46 Clwyd Street, Ruthin LL15 1HP
Flintshire Record Office, The Old Rectory, Rectory Lane, Hawarden, Deeside CH5 3NR

Dyfed (Cardigan, Carmarthen, Pembroke)   Pembrokeshire Record Office, The Castle, Haverfordwest SA61 2EF
Carmarthenshire Archive Service, Parc Myrddin, Richmond Terrace, Carmarthen SA31 1DS
Cardiganshire (Ceredigion) Archives, Swyddfa'r Sir, Marine Terrace, Aberystwyth SY23 2DE

Glamorgan   Glamorgan Record Office, Glamorgan Building, King Edward VII Avenue, Cathays park, Cardiff CF10 3NE
West Glamorgan Archive Service, County Hall, Oystermouth Road, Swansea SA1 3SN

Gwent (Monmouthshire)   Gwent Record Office, County Hall, Cwmbran, Gwent NP44 2XH

Gwynedd (Anglesey, Caernarfon, Merionoth)   Caernarfon Area Record Office, Victoria Dock, Caernarfon LL54 1SH (address correspondence to County Offices, Shirehall Street, Caernarfon LL55 1SH)
Archifdy Meirion Archives, Cae Penarlag, Dolgellau LL40 2YB
Llangefni Area Record Office, Shire Hall, Llangefni LL77 7TW
Department of Manuscripts, University College of North Wales, Bangor LL57 2DG

Powys (Brecon, Montgomery, Radnor) Powys County Archives Office, County Hall, Llandrindod Wells LD1 5LD

Scotland (pre-1996 authorities)

Borders   Scottish Borders Archive & Local History Centre, Library Headquarters, St Mary's Mill, Selkirk TD7 5EW

Central   Central Region Archives, Unit 6, Burghmuir Industrial Estate, Stirling FK7 7PY

Dumfries and Galloway   Dumfries and Galloway Archive Centre, 33 Burns Street, Dumfries DG1 2PS

Grampian   Aberdeen City Archives, Old Aberdeen House, Dunbar Street, Aberdeen AB24 1UL and The Town House, Broad Street, Aberdeen AB10 1AQ
Moray Council Record Office, The Tolbooth, High Street, Forres IV36 0AB

Highland   Highland Region Archives, The Library, Farraline Park, Inverness IV1 1NH

Lothian   Edinburgh City Archives, City Chambers, High Street, Edinburgh EH1 1YJ

Orkney   Orkney Archives, Orkney Library, Laing Street, Kirkwall KW15 1NW

Shetland   Shetland Archives, 44 King Harald Street, Lerwick ZE1 0EQ

Strathclyde   Ayrshire Archives Centre, Craigie Estate, Ayr KA8 0SS
Argyll and Bute District Archives, Manse Brae, Lochgilphead, Argyll PA31 8QU
Strathclyde Regional Archives and Glasgow City Archives, Mitchell Library, North Street, Glasgow G3 7DN

Tayside   Dundee City Archives, 21 City Square, Dundee DD1 3BY
Perth and Kinross Council Archives, A.K. Bell Library, 2–8 York Place, Perth PH2 8EP

APPENDIX VIII

COMMENCEMENT DATES OF THE REIGNS OF ENGLISH AND BRITISH MONARCHS

William I	25 December 1066	Henry VIII	22 April 1509
William II	26 September 1087	Edward VI	28 January 1547
Henry I	5 August 1100	Lady Jane Grey	6 July 1553
Stephen	25 December 1135	Mary I	19 July 1553
Henry II	19 December 1154	Philip and Mary	25 July 1554
Richard I	3 September 1189	Elizabeth I	17 November 1558
John	27 May 1199	James I	24 March 1603
Henry III	28 October 1216	Charles I	27 March 1625
Edward I	20 November 1272	Charles II	30 January 1649
Edward II	8 July 1307	James II	6 February 1685
Edward III	25 January 1327	William and Mary	13 February 1689
Richard II	22 June 1377	William III	28 December 1694
Henry IV	30 September 1399	Anne	8 March 1702
Henry V	21 March 1413	George I	1 August 1714
Henry VI	1 September 1422	George II	11 June 1727
Edward IV	4 March 1461	George III	25 October 1760
Edward V	9 April 1483	George IV	29 January 1820
Richard III	26 June 1483	William IV	26 June 1830
Henry VII	22 August 1485	Victoria	20 June 1837

There were interregnums from 30 January 1649 to 29 May 1660 (the Commonwealth) and from 12 December 1688 to 16 February 1689. Regnal years were little used after the reign of Queen Victoria but the years of the commencement of the reigns of later monarchs were as follows: Edward VIII (1901), George V (1910), Edward VIII (1936), George VI (1936) and Elizabeth II (1952).

APPENDIX IX

WILLS AND ADMINISTRATIONS IN THE PREROGATIVE COURT
OF CANTERBURY: A SUMMARY OF FINDING-AIDS

The easiest method of finding a PCC registered will is to use DocumentsOnline through the web site of TNA. However, you may choose to use the other indexes, noted below. Administrations are not included in DocumentsOnline and so it is still necessary to follow the traditional methods of searching, including use of these published indexes.

There are also many published volumes of abstracts or transcripts of PCC wills. A few of these are listed below but there are many others that may assist your search for a PCC will, especially if you are searching for wills in which your ancestor is recorded as a beneficiary or executor. For example, P. Coldham has produced abstracts (published by GPC) of many PCC wills from 1610 to 1857 of testators in America or of wills that otherwise relate to America. Abstracts of some PCC wills can also be found in county record society volumes and in many published family histories. Bank of England abstracts of wills from 1717 to 1845, the majority from the PCC, are held at the SoG (# chapter 12). Indexes to these abstracts are available on microfiche and on the web site of English Origins.

In the following list BRS refers to volumes of the British Record Society, Index Library, full details of which are contained in Mullins (260). As noted in chapter 12, many wills and administrations since 1796 (including a large number from the PCC) are also recorded in the death duty registers.

Wills

1383–1558	BRS vols 10 and 11
1558–1583	BRS vol. 18
1584–1604	BRS vol. 25
1605–1619	BRS vol. 43
1620–1629	BRS vol. 44
1620	*Register Soame*, abstracts by J.H. Lea (1904)
1620–1624	*Year book of probates, abstracts of probates and sentences* by J. Matthews & G.F. Matthews (1911)
1630–1655	*Year books of probates* by J. & G.F. Matthews, 8 vols (1903–27)
1630–1639	*Sentences and Index Nominum* by J. Matthews & G.F. Matthews (1907)
1630	*Register Scroope* abstracts by J.H. Morrison (1934)
1653–1656	BRS vol. 54
1657–1660	BRS vol. 61
1657–8 (part)	*Register Wootton* abstracts by W. Brigg, 7 vols
1661–1670	*Wills, Sentences and Probate Acts* by J.H. Morrison (1935)
1671–1675	BRS vol. 67
1676–1685	BRS vol. 71
1686–1693	BRS vol. 77
1694–1700	BRS vol. 80
1701–1749	An index (including administrations) is at the FRC. It can be purchased on fiche.
1750–1800	*Index to wills proved in the PCC* by A.J. Camp, 6 vols (1976–92)
1750	*Register Greenly* abstracts by G. Sherwood (1918)
1801–1852	M/S calendars (alphabets) at the FRC
1853–1858	HMSO index (including admons) *Calendar of the grants of probate and letters of administration made in the PCC*, 16 vols, at the FRC and the SoG (also on microfiche of post-1858 probate calendars)

Administrations

1559–1580	*Administrations in the PCC* by R. Glencross, 2 vols (1912–17); T/S addenda & corrigenda by B. Lloyd (1979) at the FRC and Guildhall Library
1581–1595	BRS vol. 76
1596–1608	BRS vol. 81

1609–1619	BRS vol. 83
1620–1630	*Letters of administration in the PCC* by J.H. Morrison (1934)
1631–1648	BRS vol. 100 (T/S index at the FRC to some grants omitted from 1643–44)
1649–1654	BRS vol. 68
1655–1660	BRS vols 72, 74 and 75
1661–1662	M/S calendars (alphabets) at the FRC
1663–1664	T/S index at the FRC
1665–1700	M/S calendars at the FRC
1701–1749	Included in wills' index for this period, see above
1750–1852	M/S calendars (alphabets) at the FRC (and card index for 1750–1800 at the SoG)
1853–1858	HMSO index (as for wills 1853–58)

APPENDIX X

Chapter 24 noted some of the finding-aids available for researchers who are attempting to find their ancestors in the records of the Court of Chancery; for example, the Bernau index, PROCAT, the Equity Pleadings Database and certain volumes of *PRO Lists & Indexes*.

This appendix lists many other finding-aids that are available for the most useful records of the Court of Chancery (and some records of the Chancery Division of the High Court of Justice). Published finding-aids for each class are noted, in the following table, by a star and number in square brackets, for example [*1], and the works to which these numbers refer are listed in a bibliography at the end of the appendix. References to series IND 1 are to the alphabets and indexes in that series at TNA. Their piece numbers are listed in PROCAT, Bevan (239) and in a catalogue of indexes (published by the List and Index Society).

Where it is noted below that a series can be searched by the parties' names on PROCAT, it is usually only the names of the first plaintiff and first defendant that have been indexed, even if the case was between three plaintiffs and nine defendants.

Abbreviations

BRS:	British Record Society, Index Library
LIS:	List and Index Society
PROLI:	PRO Lists & Indexes

Series	Description of documents and finding-aids
C 1	Early Chancery Proceedings 1386–1558
	*Transcripts of cases in bundles 1 & 2 in [*1] and cases in bundle 3 in [*7].*
	*Bundles 3–37 calendared in volume XII of [*9], with parties' names indexed in [*12] and in Bernau Index. Bundles 38 to 1519 calendared in other 9 volumes of [*9]; the parties' names in volumes XVI, XX, XXIX and XXXVIII being included in Bernau Index (T/S index to parties' names in volume XXXVIII also at TNA) and the parties names in volume LV in T/S index at SoG. Most of these finding-aids have been added to PROCAT, permitting searches by the parties' names.*
C 2/Eliz	Chancery Proceedings, Series I 1558–1603
	*Most calendared in three indexed volumes of [*1]. Those omitted are calendared in an indexed T/S at TNA, published in part in [*2] and [*13].*
C 2/Jas I	Chancery Proceedings, Series I 1603–1625
	*Cases with first plaintiff's surnames beginning with A to K, calendared in [*11] (and some parties' names in Bernau Index). Cases with first plaintiff's surname beginning L to Z, calendared in 4 M/S vols at TNA. Three-volume index to places at TNA.*
C 2/Chas I	Chancery Proceedings, Series I 1625–1649
	*Surnames of first plaintiffs and first defendants published in [*4] and [*5] and indexed in two T/S vols by P.W. Coldham at TNA. First defendants' names in Bernau Index. About 440 cases calendared in [*3]*
C 3	Chancery Proceedings, Series II 1558–1660
	*Boxes 1 to 469 calendared in [*8] and parties' names in Bernau Index. T/S alphabet at TNA of first plaintiffs' names for boxes 470–485. Searchable on PROCAT by the names of the first plaintiff, first defendant and the county most relevant to the dispute.*
C 4	Chancery Proceedings, Answers (supplement C 1–3) medieval to 17th century

Calendar (with index) at TNA to plaintiffs' and defendants' names but only for bundles 1–34 and 36–48. Bundles 49 to 173 are not calendared or indexed. The names of the first plaintiff, first defendant and the county most relevant to the dispute are being added to PROCAT.

C 5   Chancery Proceedings 1613–1714, Bridges Division

Calendared in [*10]. Parties names in Bernau Index. T/S index by P.W. Coldham to deceased individuals, in disputed estate cases, at TNA (with suit title). Searchable on PROCAT by the names of the first plaintiff, first defendant and the county most relevant to the dispute.

C 6   Chancery Proceedings, c. 1625–1714, Collins Division

M/S calendars of suit names at TNA. Pieces 1–419 are searchable by the parties' names (first plaintiff and first defendant only for pieces 1–359), date, place and subject of the dispute on the Equity Pleadings Database. Incomplete T/S index (about 50% of bundles only) at TNA and the SoG to parties to disputed estate cases.

C 7   Chancery Proceedings, c. 1620–1714, Hamilton Division

M/S calendars of suit names at TNA. T/S index by P.W. Coldham to deceased individuals, in disputed estate cases, at TNA (with title of suit).

C 8   Chancery Proceedings, c. 1570–1714, Mitford Division

M/S calendars of suit names at TNA. T/S index by P.W. Coldham to deceased individuals, in disputed estate cases, at TNA (with title of suit).

C 9   Chancery Proceedings 1649–1714, Reynardson Division

Alphabetical list of names of first plaintiffs (with first defendants' names) in series list and published in [*6], but not indexed and excludes depositions. First defendants' names in Bernau index. Searchable on PROCAT by the names of the first plaintiff, first defendant and the county most relevant to the dispute.

C 10   Chancery Proceedings, c. 1640–1714, Whittington Division

M/S calendars of suit names at TNA. T/S index by P.W. Coldham to deceased individuals, in disputed estate cases, at TNA (with title of suit). Searchable on PROCAT by the names of the first plaintiff, first defendant and the county most relevant to the dispute.

C 11   Chancery Proceedings, Various Six Clerks, Series I 1714–1758 (these and later Chancery Proceedings include Country Depositions 1715–1880)

List of suits at TNA. Searchable on PROCAT by the names of the first plaintiff, first defendant and the county most relevant to the dispute. Calendared (with all parties' names) in Bernau's Notebooks and parties' names in Bernau Index. For depositions taken in Devon, the names of the parties and the deponents are listed in a T/S volume by J.H. Mann at the SoG.

C 12   Chancery Proceedings, Various Six Clerks, Series II 1758–1800 (some earlier)

Alphabetical list of suits at TNA. Searchable on PROCAT by the names of the first plaintiff, first defendant and the county most relevant to the dispute. Some parties' names in Bernau index.

C 13   Chancery Proceedings 1800–1842, Various Six Clerks, Series III

Alphabetical lists of suits (for each Six Clerks' Division) at TNA. Searchable on PROCAT by the names of the first plaintiff, first defendant and the county most relevant to the dispute.

C 14   Chancery Proceedings 1842–1852

Alphabetical lists of suits at TNA.

C 15   Chancery Proceedings 1853–1860 (include Town Depositions from 1854)

Series list refers to 27 volumes of alphabetical lists of suits in IND 1.

C 16   Chancery Proceedings 1861–1875 (include Town Depositions)

Series list and alphabetical lists of suits at TNA.

C 18   Miscellaneous Proceedings from the Six Clerks' office; 17th to 19th centuries

T/S list of suits at TNA.

C 21   Country Depositions 1558–1649

List of of titles of suits at TNA. Searchable on PROCAT by the names of the first plaintiff and first defendant. Deponents' names in Bernau index.

C 22   Country Depositions 1649–1714

List of titles of suits at TNA. Searchable on PROCAT by the names of the first plaintiff and first defendant. Parties' (and some deponents') names in Bernau index. Printed calendar with index "Chancery depositions before 1714-Snell" at TNA and SoG (for suits 1 to 495), giving case title, date and place of depositions and the names, ages and residence of the deponents. Similar M/S calendar at SoG for suits 496 to 601. T/S index at SoG to parties' and deponents' names for many Norfolk depositions.

C 23   Sealed or unpublished Depositions; Elizabeth I to Victoria

List of suits in IND 1.

C 24   Town Depositions 1534–1853

Alphabets of suit names in IND 1. Deponents' names up to about 1800 in Bernau index.

C 25   Interrogatories 1598–1852

Series list of suits at TNA.

C 31	Affidavits 1607–1875
	Indexes in IND 1.
C 32	Cause Books 1842–80 (names of parties & references to all decrees and orders)
C 33	Entry books of decrees and orders 1544–1875
	In two series: "A" and "B". Alphabets to first plaintiffs' names, arranged by year and legal term, in IND 1 (IND volumes for each year listed in series list).
C 36	Ordinary and Appeal Petitions, 1774–1875 (petitions for winding-up, appeals etc)
	Arranged alphabetically by petitioners' surname. Index by suit title in IND 1.
C 37	Minute Books of decrees and orders 1639–1875 (chronological orders, etc which were then written up in the entry books in C 33)
C 38 & C 39	Masters' reports and certificates 1562–1875
	Alphabets (by plaintiffs' surnames) to the suit titles, in IND 1.
C 41	Registers of affidavits 1615–1747 (include many affidavits that are now lost)
	See C 31.
C 42	Awards and Agreements 1694–1844 (results of cases decided by arbitration)
	Series list.
C 78 & C 79.	Decree rolls for 1534–1903
	*T/S calendars for C 78/1–1250 (circa 1700). Published for C 78/1–130, with indexes, in [*14] to [*17]. Alphabets (by year and plaintiffs' surnames) for later rolls in IND 1.*
C 101	Masters' accounts 1700–1850
	Alphabets (by plaintiffs' surnames) to the suit titles, in IND 1.
C 103–114	Exhibits 13th to 19th centuries, arranged by Masters' names; C 103 Blunt, C 104 Tinney, C 105 Lynch, C 106 Richards, C 107 Senior, C 108 Farrar, C 109 Humphrey, C 110 Horne, C 111 Brougham, C 112 Rose, C 113 Kindersley, C 114 (unknown)
	Series lists include case titles. Searchable on PROCAT by the case titles (but usually just the names of the first plaintiff and first defendant). Old versions of some of these lists published by LIS (vols 13 and 14). Card index at TNA to some wills in these classes.
C 115	Exhibits; Duchess of Norfolk's Deeds, 12th to 19th centuries
C 117–126	Masters' documents (include affidavits, estate accounts, wills & other documents), arranged by Masters' names; C 117 Brougham, C 118 Horne, C 119 Rose, C 120 Tinney, C 121 Richards, C 122 Farrar, C 123 Humphrey, C 124 Blunt, C 125 Senior and C 126 Kindersley
	Alphabets (by plaintiffs' surnames) to the suit titles, in IND 1.
C 171	Exhibits; Six Clerks' Office, 14th to 19th centuries

Bibliography

[*1]   J. Bayley; *Calendars of the proceedings in Chancery in the reign of Queen Elizabeth, to which are prefixed examples of earlier proceedings . . . from the reign of Richard II to Elizabeth*; Record Commissioners, 3 vols (1827–32)

[*2]   R. Holworthy; *Calendar of Chancery Proceedings, Elizabeth . . . those suits omitted from the printed Calendar published in 1827/30 by the Record Commissioners*; SoG (1913)

[*3]   O. Barron (ed.); *The Ancestor*, vols 1–5, 7, 9, 11 and 12, Archibald Constable (1902–05)

[*4]   W.P.W. Phillimore; *A Calendar of Chancery Proceedings, bills and answers, temp. Charles I*, vols i to iii (plaintiffs A to R), BRS vols 3, 5 & 6 (1889–91)

[*5]   E.A. Fry; *A Calendar of Chancery Proceedings, bills and answers, temp. Charles I, vol. iv (plaintiffs S to W)*, BRS vol. 14 (1896)

[*6]   E.A. Fry; *Index of Chancery Proceedings (Reynardson's Division)*, vols i & ii, BRS vols 29 & 32 (1903–04)

[*7]   W.P. Baildon; *Select cases in Chancery 1364–1471*, Selden Society (1896)

[*8]   *Index of Chancery Proceedings*, PROLI, 1558–79 vol. VII (1896), 1579–1621 vol. XXIV (1908) and 1621–60 vol. XXX (1909).

[*9]   *Lists of Early Chancery Proceedings*, PROLI, 9 Ric. II to Edw. IV vol. XII (1901), 1467–85 vol. XVI (1903), 1485–1500 vol. XX (1906), 1500–15 vol. XXIX (1908), 1515–29 vol. XXXVIII (1912), 1529–38 vol. XLVII (1922), 1533–38 vol. L (1927), 1538–44 vol. LI (1929), 1544–53 vol. LIV (1933), 1553–58 vol. LV (1936).

[*10]   *Index of Chancery Proceedings, Bridges' division 1613–1714*, PROLI, vol. XXXIX (1913), vol. XLII (1914), vol. XLIV (1915) and vol. XLV (1917).

[*11]   *Index of Chancery Proceedings, James I, A–K*, PROLI, vol. XLVII (1922),

[*12]   C.A. Walmisley; *An index of persons named in early Chancery Proceedings Richard II (1385) to Edward IV (1467)*; Harleian Society vols 78–9 (1927–28)

[★13]   *Chancery Proceedings: supplement, Elizabeth I (C 2/A1–C10)*; LIS, vol. 202 (1983)
[★14]   *Calendar of Chancery Decree Rolls, C 78/1–14*; LIS, vol. 160 (1978)
[★15]   *Calendar of Chancery Decree Rolls, C 78/15–45*; LIS, vol. 198 (1983)
[★16]   K. Wyndham; *Calendar of Chancery Decree Rolls, C 78/46–85*; LIS, vol. 253 (1994)
[★17]   R.W. Hoyle & M.M. Norris; *Calendar of Chancery Decree Rolls, C 78/86–130*; LIS, vol. 254 (1994)

APPENDIX XI

WEB SITES FOR FAMILY HISTORIANS

The first part of this appendix lists the address, or Uniform Resource Locator (URL), of the most important web sites for family historians. The resources available at those sites have been briefly described in this book. The second part lists some other sites that may be of interest to those researching particular topics or those researching in particular areas of the country. The prefix http:// should be prefixed to all the URLs listed below.

A greater selection of sites is listed in Christian (9), Raymond (167a), (196a), (268), (668a), (1214) and (1215) and in the annual editions of the *FLHH* (5) or can be found through the gateway web sites of GENUKI or Cyndi's List, maintained by Cyndi Howell. The following list does not include the web sites of family history societies, museums, CROs or other local archives since they are listed in the *FLHH* and in Raymond's works. Links to most FHS web sites are also included on the web sites of GENUKI and the FFHS.

The URLs of web sites do change frequently. Many of these changes are reported in *Family Tree Magazine*, *Ancestors* and in other journals, but reference should also be made to the latest editions of the *FLHH* and Raymond's works.

1901 census online service: www.census.pro.gov.uk
Access to Archives (A2A): www.a2a.pro.gov.uk
Ancestry.com: www.ancestry.co.uk (UK and Irish records only) or www.ancestry.com
Archive CD Books: www.archivecdbooks.com
Archives New Zealand: www.archives.govt.nz
Association of Genealogists and Researchers in Archives: www.agra.org.uk
Association of Scottish Genealogists and Record Agents: www.asgra.co.uk
Australian War Memorial: www.awm.gov.au
Back to Roots: www.backtoroots.co.uk
Baptist Historical Society: www.baptisthistory.org.uk
Bodleian Library: www.bodley.ox.ac.uk
Borthwick Institute of Historical Research: www.york.ac.uk/inst/bihr
British Columbia Archives: www.bcarchives.gov.bc.ca
British Library: www.bl.uk
British Library (book catalogue): blpc.bl.uk
British Library (manuscripts catalogue): molcat.bl.uk
British Library Newspaper Library: www.bl.uk/collections/newspaper
British Library Oriental and India Office Collections: www.bl.uk/collections/oriental
British Telecom archives: www.bt.com/Archives
British Telecom telephone listings: www.bt.com/phonenetuk
Burke's Peerage & Gentry online database: www.burkes-peerage.net
Cambridge University Library: www.lib.cam.ac.uk
Catholic Central Library: www.catholiclibrary.demon.co.uk
Catholic Record Society: www.catholic-history.org.uk/crs
Church of Jesus Christ of Latter-Day Saints (family history centres): www.lds.org.uk/genealogy/fhc
College of Arms: www.college-of-arms.gov.uk
Commonwealth War Graves Commission: www.cwgc.org
Companies House: www.companieshouse.gov.uk
Corporation of London Record Office: www.cityoflondon.gov.uk/archives/clro
The Digital Library of Historical Directories: www.historicaldirectories.org
Durham University Library (Archives): www.dur.ac.uk/Library
Ellis Island (Family Immigration History Center): www.ellisislandrecords.org
Ellis Island (wall of honour): www.wallofhonour.com

English Origins: www.englishorigins.com
FAMILIA: www.familia.org.uk
Family History Indexes: www.fhindexes.co.uk
Family History Online: www.familyhistoryonline.net
Family Records Centre: www.familyrecords.gov.uk
Family Research Link (GRO indexes): www.1837online.com
FamilySearch (LDS): www.familysearch.org
Federation of Family History Societies: www.ffhs.org.uk
FFHS Publications and online bookshop (incorporating GENfair): www.familyhistorybooks.co.uk
Francis Boutle Publishers: www.francisboutle.demon.co.uk
Francis Frith collection: www.francisfrith.com
FreeBMD: FreeBMD.rootsweb.com
FreeCEN: FreeCEN.rootsweb.com
Genealogical Publishing Co: www.genealogical.com
The Genealogist (census indexes): www.TheGenealogist.co.uk
General Register Office (Southport): www.statistics.gov.uk/registration
General Register Office for Scotland: www.gro-scotland.gov.uk
General Register Office (Dublin): www.groireland.ie
General Register Office (Northern Ireland): www.groni.gov.uk
GENUKI: www.genuki.org.uk
Alan Godfrey Maps: www.alangodfreymaps.co.uk
Guildhall Library (manuscripts collection): ihr.sas.ac.uk/ihr/ghmnu
Guildhall Library (Collage): collage.nhil.com
Guild of One-Name Studies: www.one-name.org
House of Lords Record Office: www.parliament.uk
Cyndi Howell: www.cyndislist.com
Huguenot Library catalogue: www.ucl.ac.uk/ucl-info/divisions/library/huguenot
Huguenot Society: www.huguenotsociety.org.uk
Imperial War Museum: www.iwm.org.uk
Institute of Heraldic & Genealogical Studies: www.ihgs.ac.uk
Internet Library of Early Journals: www.bodley.ox.ac.uk/ilej
Irish Origins: www.irishorigins.com
Jersey Archive: www.jerseyheritagetrust.org
Jewish Genealogical Society of Great Britain: www.ort.org/jgsgb
Lambeth Palace Library: www.lambethpalacelibrary.org
London Gazette online: www. gazettes-online.co.uk
London Metropolitan Archives: www.cityoflondon.gov.uk/archives/lma
London School of Economics: www.lse.ac.uk
Metropolitan Police Archive Service: www.met.police.uk/history/archives
MM Publications: www.mmpublications.co.uk
Modern Records Centre: www.warwick.ac.uk/services/library/mrc
Moving Here: www.movinghere.org.uk
The National Archives (United Kingdom): www.nationalarchives.gov.uk (see also the Public Record Office, PRO online catalogue, PRO DocumentsOnline and the 1901 census online service)
National Archives & Records Administration (USA): www.archives.gov
National Archives of Australia: www.naa/gov.au
National Archives of Canada: www.archives.ca
National Archives of Ireland: www.nationalarchives.ie
National Archives of Scotland: www.nas.gov.uk
National Archivist: www.nationalarchivist.com
National Army Museum: www.national-army-museum.ac.uk
National Library of Australia: www.nla/gov.au
National Library of Ireland: www.nli.ie
National Library of Scotland: www.nls.uk
National Library of Wales: www.llgc.org.uk
National Maritime Museum: www.nmm.ac.uk
National Maritime Museum (manuscripts catalogue): www.manuscripts.nmm.ac.uk/frank/htm
National Monuments Record (England): www.english-heritage.org.uk
National Monuments Record (English listed buildings): www.imagesofengland.org.uk

National Register of Archives: www.hmc.gov.uk/nra
Naval & Military Press: www.naval-military-press.com
New South Wales Registrar General: www.bdm.nsw.gov.au
New Zealand Registrar General: www.bdm.govt.nz
New Zealand Society of Genealogists: www.genealogy.org.nz
Newspaper Detectives: www.newspaperdetectives.co.uk
Office for National Statistics: www.ons.gov.uk
Old Bailey Proceedings: www.OldBaileyOnline.org
Original Indexes: www.original-indexes.demon.co.uk
Phillimore & Co: www.phillimore.co.uk
Probate Service: www.courtservice.gov.uk
PRO DocumentsOnline: www.pro.gov.uk/online/docsonline
PRO-Online: www.pro-online.pro.gov.uk
PRO online catalogue (PROCAT): www.pro.gov.uk/online
Public Record Office: www.pro.gov.uk (see also 1901 census service above)
Public Record Office of Northern Ireland: proni.nics.gov.uk
Registry of Deeds, Dublin: www.irlgov.ie/landreg
Representative Church Body Library: www.ireland.anglican.org/library
Roll of honour: www.roll-of-honour.com
Royal Air Force Museum: www.rafmuseum.org.uk
Royal College of Surgeons: www.rcseng.ac.uk/services/library
Royal Commission on Historical Manuscripts: www.hmc.gov.uk
Royal Mail Heritage: www.royalmail.com/heritage
Rural History Centre: www.rdg.ac.uk/instits/im/rural
S&N Genealogy Supplies: www.genealogysupplies.com
S&N Genealogy Supplies (census indexes): www.BritishDataArchive.com
ScotlandsPeople: www.scotlandspeople.gov.uk
Scots Origins: www.scotsorigins.com
Scottish Archives Network: www.scan.org.uk
Scottish Association of Family History Societies: www.safhs.org.uk
Scottish Documents (wills index): www.ScottishDocuments.com
Scottish Genealogy Society: www.scotsgenealogy.com
Shire Publications: www.shirebooks.co.uk
Society of Friends' Library (London): www.quaker.org.uk
Society of Genealogists: www.sog.org.uk (see also the English Origins site above)
Stepping Stones: www.stepping-stones.co.uk
Strict Baptist Historical Society: www.strictbaptisthistory.org.uk
Sutton Publishing: www.sutton-publishing.co.uk
Stuart Tamblin: (see the Family History Indexes' site above)
The Times Digital Archive: www.galegroup.com/Times
TWR Computing: www.twrcomputing.freeserve.co.uk
Ulster Historical Foundation: www.ancestryireland.com
Valuation Office of Ireland: www.vaoff.ie
Victoria (Australia) Public Record Office: www.vic.gov.au/prov
Nick Vine Hall: www.vinehall.com.au
West Country Studies Library: www.devon-cc.gov.uk/library/locstudy
WorldConnect (pedigree database): www.worldconnect.genealogy.rootsweb.com

Some miscellaneous sources on the Internet
In addition to the general sources noted above, the following web sites may assist your research.

Civil registration
Cheshire births, marriages and deaths (about one million entries from superintendent registrar indexes): CheshireBMD.org.uk

Census records
Cambridgeshire FHS 1841 census index: www. cfhs.org.uk

Parish register transcripts and indexes and cemetery records
Wirksworth, Derbyshire: www.lds.co.uk/wirksworth
Joiner marriage index (County Durham, Northumberland and the North riding of Yorkshire): Website.lineone.net/~jjoiner
Index to about 45,000 marriages in Middlesex: www.enol.com/~infobase/gen/parish
Abney Park Cemetery (London) burials 1840–1936: Freepages.genealogy.rootsweb.com/~abneypark

Directories
Pigot's directories of Herefordshire 1830 and 1840: freepages.genealogy.rootsweb.com/~nmfa/genealogy
Pigot's commercial directory for Derbyshire 1835: www.genuki org.uk/big/eng/DBY/Pigot1835

Wills
Cheshire Record Office index to wills proved at Chester 1492–1940 (in ecclesiastical courts and at the District Probate Registry): www.cheshire.gov.uk/Recoff
Index to wills proved at Gloucester 1541–1858 (on Gloucestershire Record Office genealogical database): www.gloscc.gov.uk/pubserv/gcc/corpserv/archives/genealogy

Non-conformist and Jewish records
Jewish consolidated surname index (database of over 2 million people in 30 sources): www.avotaynu.com/csi

Maps and gazetteers
Modern Ordnance Survey maps:www.ordsvy.gov.uk
First edition 1:10,560 County Series Ordnance Survey maps (1846–99): www.oldmaps.co.uk
Gazetteer of 50,000 British place names (and noting the administrative areas in which they are located): www.gazetteer.co.uk

Poor law records
West Sussex Record Office database of about 6,000 settlement examinations, removal orders and other poor law records from 1662–1835: www.westsussex.gov.uk/RO/DB/poorlaw.asp
Guide to the workhouses of Britain and Ireland, by P. Higginbotham, with maps, photographs and historical notes (and maps of poor law unions): www.workhouses.org.uk

Military records
Searchable database of 50,000 soldiers, sailors and airmen, compiled from Absent Voter Lists of Leeds, 1918–19: www.leeds.gov.uk/warvoters
The Fleet Air Arm Archive (includes biographical material for commanding officers of FAA squadrons 1939–45): www.fleetairarmarchive.net

Ships and seamen
The Titanic: biographies of 2,000 passengers and crew: www.encyclopedia-titannica.org

Professions and occupations
Index of Methodist ministers, 18th to 20th centuries, with some biographies (Methodist Archives and Research Centre, John Rylands Library): rylibweb.man.ac.uk/data1/dg/methodist/bio
Biographical database of British chemists: www5.open.ac.uk/Arts/chemists
Coalmining History Resource Centre (lists of mines and database of 90,000 names relating to mining deaths): www.cmhrc.co.uk
Database of sugar bakers and sugar refiners: www.mawer.clara.net
Durham Mining Museum: www.dmm.org.uk/mindex.htm

Criminal records
Ilchester Gaol registers 1821–44 (Somerset Archive and Record Service):www.somerset.gov.uk/archives

Database of 1,000 prisoners in Bedford Gaol 1801–77 (including photographs and gaol register entries for about 100 prisoners): www.schools.bedfordshire.gov.uk/gaol

Lincolnshire Archives' index of convicts transported 1788–1840: www.demon.co.uk/lins-archives/con_a_txt

Some executions in England since 1606: www.fred.net/jefalvey/execute

Index of prisoners in Gloucester Gaol 1815–79 (on Gloucestershire Record Office database noted above)

Heraldry

Database compiled from some of the published visitations of Devon, Dorset and Somerset: web.ukonline.co.uk/nigel.battysmith/visitations

Scotland

Angus Roll of Honour (First World War): Vzone.virgin.net/ian.edwards2

Caithness Roll of Honour (First World War): www.internet-promotions.co.uk/archives/caithness/roll/index.htm

Corstorphine (Midlothian) war dead, 1914–18 and 1939–45: www.angelfire.com/ct2/corstorphine

Indexes to records of Dundee and Forfar Sheriffs Courts: www.dundee.ac.uk/archives/genuki/ANS/Topics

Royal College of Surgeons of Edinburgh: www.rcsed.ac.uk

Scots at war (roll of honour with biographical information on Scottish servicemen): www.saw.arts.ed.ac.uk

Many more sites are listed in Raymond (1214).

Wales

Monmouthshire records (including marriages 1725–1812, pedigrees, wills and marriage bonds): Freepages.genealogy.rootsweb.com/~monfamilies/myfamily-history

Ireland

Database of births, marriages and census entries: www.irishfamiltrecords.com

The General alphabetical index to the townlands and towns, parishes and baronies of Ireland 1851: Scripts.ireland.com/ancestor/placenames

Database of counties, townlands, parishes and baronies: www.seanruad.com

Directories (Pigot 1824 and Slater 1846), index of wills and Griffiths' valuation of 1857 for Donegal: freepages.genealogy.rootsweb.com/~donegal

National School registers for Lawrencetown, Co. Down: www.lawrencetown.com

King James's Irish Army list: www.irishroots.com/KJames

Many more sites are listed in Raymond (1215).

Channel Islands

Registers of Victoria College, Jersey: www.societe-jersiaise.org/whitsco/VCIndex1

United States

Immigrant Ships Transcribers' Guild (transcripts of 3,500 passenger lists): istg.rootsweb.com

Australia

Second World War service rolls: www.ww2roll.gov.au

Canada

Index of awards to 8,000 Royal Canadian Air Force personnel (Second World War): www.airforce.ca/citations/wwii

New Zealand

Dictionary of New Zealand biography: www.dnzb.govt.nz

BIBLIOGRAPHY

Some of the books that I consulted when preparing this book have been superseded by new editions. Those new editions are noted in square brackets following the entry. The changes between editions are not necessarily substantial.

Abbreviations
ABGR: Australian Biographical & Genealogical Record
BALH: British Association for Local History
BBC: British Broadcasting Corporation
BHRS: Bedfordshire Historical Record Society
BRA: British Records Association
BRS; British Record Society
CUP: Cambridge University Press
DCRS: Devon & Cornwall Record Society
FFHS: Federation of Family History Societies
GPC: Genealogical Publishing Co. Inc.
HMSO: Her Majesty's Stationery Office
IHR: Institute of Historical Research, University of London
LIS: List and Index Society
LSE: The London Stamp Exchange Ltd (now NMP)
MUP: Manchester University Press
NMP: Naval & Military Press Ltd
OUP: Oxford University Press
PRO: Public Record Office (now The National Archives)
RHS: Royal Historical Society
RKP: Routledge & Kegan Paul Ltd
SAFHS: Scottish Association of Family History Societies
SBC: Spottiswoode Ballantyne & Co. Ltd
SoG: Society of Genealogists
YAS: Yorkshire Archaeological Society

General
(1) *Explore your family's past*, Reader's Digest (2000)
(2) *Family Tree Magazine*, J.M. & M. Armstrong & partners
(3) *Genealogists' Magazine*, SoG
(4) *Practical family history*, ABM Publishing Limited
(5) Blatchford, R. *The family and local history handbook*, GR Specialist Information Services, 7th edn (2003)
(6) Camp, A.J. *Everyone has roots; an introduction to English genealogy*, GPC (1978)
(7) Chapman, C.R. *Tracing your British ancestors*, Lochin Publishing (1993)
(8) Christian, P. *Finding genealogy on the Internet*, D. Hawgood, 2nd edn (2002)
(9) Christian, P. *The genealogist's Internet*, PRO, 2nd edn (2003)
(10) Cole, J.A. & Titford, J. *Tracing your family tree*, Thorsons, 4th edn (2002)
(11) Colwell, S. *The family history book: a guide to tracing your ancestors*, Phaidon (1980)
(12) Colwell, S. *Tracing your family tree*, Faber & Faber (1984)
(13) Currer-Briggs, N. & Gambier, R. *Debrett's guide to tracing your ancestry*, Webb & Bower (1981) 3rd impression (1990)
(14) Drake, M. & Finnegan, R. *Sources and methods for family and community historians, a handbook*, CUP (1994)
(15) Fitzhugh, T.V.H. *The dictionary of genealogy*, A&C Black, 5th edn (1998) revised by S. Lumas for the SoG
(16) Friar, S. *The local history companion*, Sutton (2001)

(17) Gandy, M. *An introduction to planning research: short cuts in family history*, FFHS (1993)

(18) Gardner, D.E. & Smith, F. *Genealogical research in England & Wales*, Bookcraft, 3 vols (1956–64)

(19) Hamilton-Edwards, G. *In search of ancestry*, Phillimore, 4th edn (1983)

(20) Harvey, R. *Genealogy for librarians*, Library Association Publishing, 2nd edn (1992)

(21) Hawgood, D. *Internet for genealogy*, D. Hawgood, 2nd edn (1999)

(22) Hey, D. *The Oxford guide to family history*, OUP (1993)

(23) Hey, D. *Family history and local history in England*, Longman (1987)

(24) Hey, D. *The Oxford companion to local and family history*, OUP (1996)

(25) Richardson, J. *The local historian's encyclopaedia*, Historical Publications, 3rd edn (2003)

(26) Rogers, C.D. *The family tree detective: a manual for analysing and solving genealogical problems in England and Wales, 1538 to the present day*, MUP, 3rd edn (1998)

(27) Saul, P. & Markwell, F.C. *The family historian's enquire within*, FFHS, 5th edn (1995)

(28) Steel, D. & Taylor, L. *Family history in focus*, Lutterworth (1984)

(29) Steel, D. *Discovering your family history*, BBC, revd edn (1986)

(30) Titford, J. *Succeeding in family history, helpful hints and time-saving tips*, Countryside Books (2001)

(31) Wagner, A. *English genealogy*, Phillimore, 3rd edn (1983) and a condensed version, *English ancestry*, OUP (1961)

(32) Wagner, A. *Pedigree and progress, essays in the genealogical interpretation of history*, Phillimore (1975)

(33) Yurdan, M. *Tracing your ancestors*, David & Charles (1988)

Chapter 1

(34) Bardsley, C.W. *A dictionary of English and Welsh surnames with special American instances* (1901), GPC reprint (1980)

(35) Barrow, G.B. *The genealogist's guide, an index to printed British pedigrees and family histories 1950–75*, Research Publishing Co. (1977)

(36) Berry, W. *County genealogies, pedigrees of the families of the county of Sussex collected from the heraldic visitations and other authentic manuscripts in the British Museum . . . and from the information of the present resident families*, Sherwood, Gilbert & Piper (1830)

(37) Bowerman. A.L. *The Bater book and allied families*, Gateway Press (1987)

(38) Cass, F.C. *East Barnet*, London and Middlesex Archaeological Society (1885–92)

(39) Cresswell, J. *Bloomsbury dictionary of first names*, Bloomsbury (1990)

(40) Crisp, F.A. *Visitation of England and Wales*; 18 vols (some with J.J. Howard), and *Visitation of England and Wales, notes*, 10 vols F.A. Crisp (1893–1914)

(41) Crisp, F.A. *Visitation of Ireland*, 6 vols (some with J.J. Howard), F.A. Crisp (1897–1918)

(42) Foster, J. *Pedigrees of the county families of England, vol. I Lancashire*, J. Foster (1873)

(43) Hanks, P. & Hodges, F. *A dictionary of surnames*, OUP (1988)

(44) Hanks, P. & Hodges, F. *A dictionary of first names*, OUP (1990)

(45) Marshall, G.W. *The genealogists' guide*, 4th edn (1903) GPC reprint (1973)

(46) McKinley, R.A. *A history of British surnames*, Longman (1990)

(47) Reaney, P.H. *The origin of English surnames*, RKP (1967)

(48) Reaney, P.H. & Wilson, R.M. *A dictionary of English surnames*, RKP, 3rd edn (1991)

(49) Smith, E.F. *Baptism and confirmation names containing . . . the names of Saints with Latin and modern language equivalents*, Benziger Brothers (1935)

(50) Thomson, T.R. *A catalogue of British family histories*, Research Publishing Co. in association with the SoG, 3rd edn (1980)

(51) Titford, J. *Searching for surnames, a practical guide to their meanings and origins*, Countryside Books (2002)

(52) Whitmore, J.B. *A genealogical guide; an index to British pedigrees in continuation of Marshall's genealogists' guide*, parts 1–4, Harleian Society, vols 99, 101, 102, 104 (1947–52) reprinted with further addenda, J.B. Whitmore (1953)

(53) Withycombe, E. *The Oxford dictionary of English Christian names*, OUP, 3rd edn (1977)

Chapter 2

(54) Betjeman, J. *Victorian and Edwardian London from old photographs*, Batsford (1969)

(55) Betjeman, J. & Rowse, A.L. *Victorian and Edwardian Cornwall from old photographs*, Batsford (1974)

(56) Chugg, B. *Victorian and Edwardian Devon from old photographs*, Batsford (1975)

(57) Clark, K.D. *Greenwich and Woolwich in old photographs*, Sutton (1990)

(58) Denney, M. *Historic waterways scenes; London & South-East England*, Moorland (1993)

(59) Donnachie, I. & Macleod, I. *Victorian and Edwardian Scottish lowlands from historic photographs*, Batsford (1979)

(60) Evans, B. *Bygone Walthamstow*, Phillimore (1995)

(61) Farrell, J. & Bayliss, C. *Hammersmith and Shepherds Bush in old photographs*, Sutton (1995)

(62) Gladwin, D.D. *Victorian and Edwardian canals from old photographs*, Batsford, 2nd edn (1992)

(63) Goff, M. *Victorian and Edwardian Surrey from old photographs*, Batsford (1972)

(64) Gray, J.S. *Victorian and Edwardian Sussex from old photographs*, Batsford (1973)

(65) Howarth, K. *Oral history, a handbook*, Sutton (1998)

(66) Howgego, J.L. *Victorian and Edwardian City of London from old photographs*, Batsford (1977)

(67) Jarvis, S. *Victorian and Edwardian Essex from old photographs*, Batsford (1973)

(68) Jay, B. *Victorian cameraman; Francis Frith's views of rural England 1850–1898*, David & Charles (1973)

(69) Jubb, I. *Exeter collection*, Obelisk Publications (1993)

(70) Keen, N.H. *Faces of Britain, a picture of Britain 1880–1919*, Bookmart (1993)

(71) Labbett, A. *Crediton collection*, Obelisk Publications (1987)

(72) Labbett, A. *Crediton collection II*, Obelisk Publications (1993)

(73) Lloyd, D. *The archive photographs series: Ludlow*, Chalford (1995)

(74) Lutt, N. *Bedfordshire at work in old photographs*, Sutton (1994)

(75) Mander, D. & Golden, J. *The London borough of Hackney in old photographs, 1890–1960*, Sutton (1991)

(76) McLaughlin, E. *Interviewing elderly relatives*, FFHS, 4th edn (1999)

(77) McCulla, D.H. & Hampson, M. *Victorian and Edwardian Warwickshire from old photographs*, Batsford (1983)

(78) Oliver, G. *Photographs and local history*, Batsford (1989)

(79) Pols, R. *Dating old photographs*, FFHS, 2nd edn (1995)

(80) Pols, R. *Family photographs 1860–1945*, PRO (2002)

(81) Reeve, F.A. *Victorian and Edwardian Cambridge from old photographs*, Batsford (1978)

(82) Shaw, B.E. *Frank Meadow Sutcliffe; photographer; a selection of his work*, The Sutcliffe Gallery (1985)

(83) Shaw, B.E. *Frank Meadow Sutcliffe; photographer; a second selection*, The Sutcliffe Gallery (1989)

(84) Shaw, M. *Frank Meadow Sutcliffe; photographer; a third selection*, The Sutcliffe Gallery (1990)

(85) Smith, G. *The archive photographs series: Islington*, Chalford (1995)

(86) Smith, G. *The archive photographs series: Stoke Newington*, Chalford (1995)

(87) Spence, J. *Victorian and Edwardian railway travel from old photographs*, Batsford (1977)

(88) Thomas, P. *Exeter in old photographs*, Sutton (1988)

(89) Thompson, P. *The voice of the past: oral history*, OUP (1978)

(90) Weightman, G. *Pictures from the past: London past*, Collins & Brown (1991)

(91) Wilson, D. *Francis Frith's travels – a photographic journey through Britain*, J.M. Dent & Sons in collaboration with the Francis Frith collection (1985)

(92) Winter, G. *A country camera 1844–1914*, Penguin (1973)

(93) Winter, G. *A cockney camera; London's social history recorded in photographs*, Penguin Books (1975)

(94) Yates, B. *North Devon coast in old photographs*, Sutton (1989)

Chapter 3

(95) *Computers in genealogy*, SoG

(96) Christian, P. *Web publishing for genealogy*, D. Hawgood, 2nd edn (1999)

(97) Fitzhugh, T.V.H. *How to write a family history*, Alphabooks (1988)

(98) Hawgood, D. *Computer genealogy update*, D. Hawgood (1997)

(99) Hawgood, D. *An introduction to using computers for genealogy*, FFHS, 3rd edn (2002)

(100) Hunnisett, R.F. *Indexing for editors*, BRA (1972)

(101) Lynskey, M. *Family trees: a manual for their design, layout and display*, Phillimore (1996)

(102) McLaughlin, E. *Laying out a pedigree*, FFHS (1988)

(103) Meadley, D. *Writing a family history*, Meadley Family History Services, 2nd edn (1990)

(104) Palgrave-Moore, P. *How to record your family tree*, Elvery Dowers, 5th edn (1991)

(105) Titford, J. *Writing and publishing your family history*, FFHS (1996)

(106) Titford, J. *The Titford family 1547–1947*, Phillimore (1989)

Chapter 4

(107) Barrett, J. & Iredale, D. *Discovering old handwriting*, Shire (1995)

(108) Buck, W.S.B. *Examples of handwriting 1550–1650*, SoG reprint (1996)

(109) Chapman, C.R. *How heavy, how much and how long? Weights, money and other measures used by our ancestors*, Lochin Publishing (1995)

(110) Cheney, C.R. *Handbook of dates for students of English history*, RHS (1945)

(111) Gooder, E.A. *Latin for local history, an introduction*, Longman, 2nd edn (1978)

(112) Grieve, H.E.P. *Examples of English handwriting 1150–1750*, Essex Record Office, 5th impression (1981)

(113) Hector, L.C. *The handwriting of English documents*, Edward Arnold, 2nd edn (1966)

(114) Latham, R.E. *Revised mediaeval Latin word-list from British and Irish sources*, OUP (1965)

(115) Martin, C.T. *The record interpreter*, Stevens & Sons, 2nd edn (1910) reprint by Phillimore (1982)

(116) McLaughlin, E. *Reading old handwriting*, FFHS, 3rd edn (1995)

(117) McLaughlin, E. *Simple Latin for family historians*, FFHS, 5th edn (1994)

(118) Morris, J. *A Latin glossary for family and local historians*, FFHS, revd edn (2002)

(119) Munby, L. *How much is that worth?*, Phillimore for BALH (1989) [revd edn 1996]

(120) Munby, L. *Reading Tudor and Stuart handwriting*, Phillimore for BALH (1988)

(121) Saunders, J.B. *Mozley & Whiteley's law dictionary*, Butterworths, 9th edn (1977) [11th edn 1993 by E.R. Hardy Ivamy]

(122) Thoyts, E.E. *How to read old documents* (1893), Dolphin Press reprint (1972)

(123) Webb, C. *Dates and calendars for the genealogist*, SoG, revd edn (1994)

(124) Wright, A. *Court hand restored or the students assistant in reading old deeds . . . describing the old law hands . . .*, Reeves & Turner, 9th edn by C.T. Martin (1879)

Chapter 5

(125) Colwell, S. *The Family Records Centre*, PRO (2002)

(126) Fogg, N. *General Register Office one-name lists in the library of the SoG*, SoG, 2nd edn (1997)

(127) Foster, M.W. *A comedy of errors or the marriage records of England and Wales 1837–1899*, M.W. Foster (1999)

(128) Gibson, J. *General Register Office and international genealogical indexes; where to find them*, FFHS (1988)

(129) Newport, J.A. *An index to the civil registration districts of England & Wales, 1837 to date*, P. Pledger (1989)

(130) Nissel, M. *People count; a history of the General Register Office*, HMSO (1987) 2nd impression (1989)

(131) Phillimore, W.P. & Fry, E.A. *An index to changes of name under authority of act of Parliament or royal licence and including irregular changes from . . . 1760 to 1901* (1905), reprinted by GPC (1968)

(132) Rogers, C.D. *Tracing the natural parents of adopted persons in England and Wales, notes for guidance*, FFHS, 2nd edn (1992)

(133) Stafford, G. *Where to find adoption records, a guide for counsellors*, British Agencies for Adoption and Fostering, 2nd edn (1992)

(134) Wiggins, R. *St. Catherine's House districts*, R. Wiggins (1994)

(135) Wood, T. *An introduction to civil registration*, FFHS (1994)

Chapter 6

(136) *Devon FHS 1851 census surname index*, vol. 21, Devon FHS (1991)

(137) Chapman, C.R. *Pre-1841 censuses and population listings in the British Isles*, Lochin Publishing, 3rd edn (1992)

(138) Churchill, E. *Census indexes in the library of the SoG*, SoG, 3rd edn (1997)

(139) Gibson J. & Medlycott, M. *Local census listings 1522–1930, holdings in the British Isles*, FFHS, 3rd edn (1999)

(140) Gibson, J. & Hampson, E. *Census returns 1841–1891 in microform; a directory to local holdings in Great Britain, Channel Islands, Isle of Man*, FFHS, 6th edn reprint (2001)

(141) Gibson, J. & Hampson, E. *Marriage, census and other indexes for the family historian*, FFHS, 8th edn (2000)

(142) Higgs, E. *Making sense of the census; the manuscript returns for England and Wales, 1801–1901*, HMSO (1989)

(143) Higgs, E. *A clearer sense of the census; the Victorian censuses and historical research*, HMSO (1996)

(144) Lumas, S. *Making use of the census*, PRO, 4th edn (2002)

(145) Mathias, P. *The first industrial nation; an economic history of Britain, 1700–1914*, Methuen (1969)

(146) McLaughlin, E. *The censuses 1841–91, use and interpretation*, FFHS, 5th edn (1992)

(147) Rosier, M.E.B. *Index to census registration districts, 1841–1891*, M. Rosier, 6th edn (1998)

Chapter 7

(148) *A handlist of parish registers, register transcripts and related records at Guildhall Library, Part I, City of London*, Guildhall Library, 7th edn (1999)

(149) *A handlist of parish registers, register transcripts and related records at Guildhall Library, Part II, Greater London*, Guildhall Library, 8th edn (2001)

(150) *A list of parishes in Boyd's marriage index*, SoG, 6th edn (1994)

(151) *National index of parish registers; a guide to Anglican, Roman Catholic and non-conformist registers together with information on bishop's transcripts, modern copies and marriage licences*, SoG (1970 to date). Individual volumes and the authors or editors are as follows:

    Vol. 1: General sources of births, marriages and death before 1837 by D.J. Steel (1976)

    Vol. 2: Sources for nonconformist genealogy and family history by D.J. Steel (1973)

    Vol. 3: Sources for Roman Catholic and Jewish genealogy and family history by D.J. Steel & E.R. Samuel (1973)

    Vol. 4: South East England; Kent, Surrey and Sussex by P. Palgrave-Moore (1980)

Vol. 4 Part 1: Surrey by C. Webb (1990)

Vol. 5: South Midlands and Welsh border counties comprising the counties of Gloucestershire, Herefordshire, Oxfordshire, Shropshire, Warwickshire and Worcestershire by D.J. Steel, A.E.F. Steel & C.W. Field (1976)

Vol. 5 Part 1: Shropshire by S. Watts (2002)

Vol. 6 Part 1: Staffordshire by P.D. Bloore, 2nd edn (1992)

Vol. 6 Part 2: Nottinghamshire by W.T. Stott, 2nd edn (1993)

Vol. 6 Part 3: Leicestershire and Rutland by C. Webb (1995)

Vol. 6 Part 4: Lincolnshire by A. Wilcox (1995)

Vol. 6 Part 5: Derbyshire by C. Webb (1995)

Vol. 7 Part 1: Suffolk by A. Wilcox (2001)

Vol. 7 Part 2: Cambridgeshire by A. Wilcox (2001)

Vol. 7 Part 3: Norfolk by A. Wilcox (2002)

Vol. 8 Part 1: Berkshire by A. Wilcox, 2nd edn (2002)

Vol. 8 Part 2: Wiltshire by C. Webb (1992)

Vol. 8 Part 3: Somerset by C. Webb (1998)

Vol. 8 Part 4: Cornwall by A. Wilcox (1999)

Vol. 8 Part 5: Devon by A. Wilcox (1999)

Vol. 8 Part 6: Hampshire and Isle of Wight by A. McGowan (2001)

Vol. 8 Part 6 (sic): Dorset by A. Wilcox (2002)

Vol. 9 Part 1: Bedfordshire and Huntingdonshire by C. Webb (1991)

Vol. 9 Part 2: Northamptonshire by C. Webb (1991)

Vol. 9 Part 3: Buckinghamshire by C. Webb (1992)

Vol. 9 Part 4: Essex by A. Wilcox (1993)

Vol. 9 Part 5: London and Middlesex by C. Webb, 2nd edn (2002)

Vol. 9 Part 6: Hertfordshire by F.J. Parker (1999)

Vol. 10 Part 1: Cheshire by C. Webb (1995)

Vol. 10 Part 2: Lancashire by P.B. Park (1998)

Vol. 10 Part 3: Cumberland & Westmorland by P.B. Park & J. Arnison (1999)

Vol. 11 Part 1: Durham and Northumberland by C.P. Neat (1979)

Vol. 11 Part 2: Yorkshire (North and East Ridings and York) by A. Wilcox (1998)

Vol. 11 Part 3: Yorkshire (West Riding) by A. Wilcox (1998)

Vol. 12: Sources for Scottish genealogy and family history by D.J. Steel & A.E.F. Steel (1970)

Vol. 13: Parish registers of Wales by C.J. Williams & J. Watts-Williams, National Library of Wales, Welsh County Archivists' Group & SoG, 2nd edn (2000)

Vol. 14: [The SoG has adopted, as vol. 14, *Non-conformist registers of Wales* by D. Ifans (1184), noted in the bibliography to chapter 29 below]

Vol. 15 Part 1: Channel Islands and the Isle of Man by C. Webb (2000)

(152) *Parish register copies in the library of the SoG*, SoG, 11th edn (1995)

(153) *West Kent sources; a guide to family and local history research in the Diocese of Rochester*, North West Kent FHS, 3rd edn (1998)

(154) Burn, J.S. *The history of parish registers in England, also of the registers of Scotland, Ireland, the East and West Indies, the dissenters, and the episcopal chapels in and about London, with observations on bishops' transcripts*, 2nd edn (1862) EP Publishing reprint (1976)

(155) Chapman, J.H. *The register book of marriages belonging to the parish of St George, Hanover Square, in the county of Middlesex, vol. 1 1725 to 1787*, Harleian Society (1886)

(156) Cox, J.C. *The parish registers of England*, Methuen (1910)

(157) Finlay, R. *Parish registers: an introduction*, Historical Geography Research Series (1981)

(158) Gibson, J. & Hampson, E. *Specialist indexes for family historians*, FFHS, 2nd edn (2000)

(159) Hanson, J. & Stevens, M. *City of London burial index 1813–1853 part 3*, John Hanson (1997)

(160) Harnden, J. *The parish registers of Herefordshire*, Friends of Hereford Record Office, 2nd edn (1988)

(161) Harris, C.G. *Oxfordshire parish registers and bishops' transcripts*, Oxfordshire FHS, 5th edn (1997)

(162) Harris, T.C. *Guide to parish registers deposited in the Greater London Record Office*, GLRO, 2nd edn (1991)

(163) Hawgood, D. *IGI on computer*, D. Hawgood (1998)

(164) Hawgood, D. *FamilySearch on the Internet*, FFHS & D. Hawgood (1999)

(165) Humphery-Smith, C. *The Phillimore atlas and index of parish registers*, Phillimore, 3rd edn (2003)

(166) McIntyre, P. *Parish register typescripts prepared by W.H. Challen from parishes in London, midland and southern counties in 87 volumes* (1984)

(167) Nichols, E.L. *Genealogy in the computer age: understanding FamilySearch (Ancestral File, International Genealogical Index and Social Security Index)*, Family History Educators, revd edn (1993)

(167a) Raymond, S.A. *Births, marriages and deaths on the web, part 1 General, Southern England, the Marches and Wales, part 2 The Midlands, Northern England and East Anglia*, FFHS (2002)

(168) Rosier, M.E. *Index to parishes in Phillimore's marriages*, Family Tree Magazine, 2nd edn (1991)

(169) Smith, F. *A genealogical gazetteer of England, an alphabetical dictionary of places with their location, ecclesiastical jurisdiction, population . . . of every ancient parish in England*, GPC (1968)

(170) Taylor, N. *County sources at the Society of Genealogists, Cornwall, Devon, parish registers, nonconformist registers, marriage licences, monumental inscriptions*, SoG (2001)

(171) Taylor, N. *County sources at the Society of Genealogists, Cheshire, Lancashire and the Isle of Man, parish registers, nonconformist registers, marriage licences, monumental inscriptions*, SoG (2001)

(171a) Taylor, N. *County sources at the Society of Genealogists, the City of London & Middlesex, parish registers, nonconformist registers, marriage licences, monumental inscriptions*, SoG (2002)

(172) Wainwright, T. *Barnstaple parish register of baptisms, marriages and burials 1538 to 1812*, J.G. Commin (1903)

(173) Watkins, J. & Saul, P. *Tracing your ancestors in Warwickshire (excluding Birmingham)*, Birmingham and Midland Society for Genealogy and Heraldry, 4th edn (1996)

(174) Webb, C. *City of London burials 1813–1853, parts 1 and 2*, West Surrey FHS, microfiche no.6 (1991)

(175) Webb, C. *A guide to Middlesex parish documents (including poor law records)*, West Surrey FHS, 2nd edn (1993)

(176) White, W.S.W. *The register book of christenings, weddings and burials within the parish of Leyland in the county of Lancaster 1653 to 1710, with a few earlier transcripts 1622–1641*, Record Society of Lancashire and Cheshire (1890)

(177) Winchester, A. *Discovering parish boundaries*, Shire (1990)

(178) Wright, D. *East Kent parishes: a guide for genealogists, local historians & other researchers in the Diocese of Canterbury*, D. Wright, 2nd edn (2002)

Chapter 8

(179) *The monumental inscriptions of the church & churchyard of St Margaret's, Worthing, Norfolk*, RAF Swanton Morley FHS (1994?)

(180) *Monumental inscriptions in the churchyards of St Helen & St Giles, Rainham and St Mary & St Peter, Wennington*, East of London FHS (1992)

(181) Brooks, C. *Mortal remains, the history and present state of the Victorian and Edwardian cemetery*, Wheaton (1989)

(182) Cansick, F.T. *A collection of curious and interesting epitaphs copied from the existing monuments of distinguished and noted characters in the cemeteries and churches of Saint Pancras, Middlesex*, J. Russell Smith, 3 vols (1869–73)

(183) Chapman, L. *Church memorial brasses and brass rubbing*, Shire (1987)

(184) Clayton, M. *Victoria and Albert Museum, catalogue of rubbings of brasses and incised slabs*, HMSO, 2nd edn (1929)

(185) Collins, L. *Monumental inscriptions in the library of the SoG, part 1, Southern England*, SoG (1984)

(186) Collins, L. & Morton M. *Monumental inscriptions in the library of the SoG; part II, Northern England, Wales, Scotland, Ireland and overseas*, SoG, revd edn (1997)

(187) Davis, C.T. *The monumental brasses of Gloucestershire* (1899), Kingsmead reprints (1969)

(188) Guiseppi, M.S. & Griffin, R. *Appendix to a list of monumental brasses in the British Isles by Mill Stephenson 1926*, Headley Brothers (1938)

(189) Hamlin, P.E. *Rosary cemetery, monumental inscriptions 1819–1986 & burials 1821–1837*, Norfolk & Norwich Genealogical Society (1986)

(190) Hibbert, C. *London's churches*, Macdonald (1988)

(191) Joyce, P. *A guide to Abney Park cemetery*, Abney Park Cemetery Trust, 2nd edn (1994)

(192) Lack, W., Stuchfield, M. & Whittemore, P. *The monumental brasses of Bedfordshire*, Monumental Brass Society (1992)

(193) Le Strange, R. *A complete descriptive guide to British monumental brasses*, Thames & Hudson (1972)

(194) Macklin, H.W. *Monumental brasses*, George Allen & Unwin, 7th edn (1953)

(195) Ormerod, G. *The history of the County Palatine and city of Chester . . .*, 2nd edn by T. Helsby; Routledge (1882)

(196) Pattinson, P. *Rayment's notes on recording monumental inscriptions*, FFHS, 4th edn (1992)

(196a) Raymond, S.A. *Monumental inscriptions on the web*, FFHS (2002)

(197) Sherlock, P. *Monumental inscriptions of Wiltshire; an edition in fascimile of 'Monumental inscriptions in the county of Wilton' by Sir Thomas Phillipps 1822*, Wiltshire Record Society (2000)

(198) Stephenson, M. *A list of monumental brasses in the British Isles*, Headley Brothers (1926)

(199) Stephenson, M. *A list of monumental brasses in Surrey* (1921), Kingsmead Reprints (1970)

(200) White, H.L. *Monuments and their inscriptions*, SoG (1987)

(201) Wolfston, P.S. *Greater London cemeteries and crematoria*, SoG, 4th edn by C. Webb (1997)

Chapter 9

(202) *Pigot's directory 1830; Devonshire* (microfiche), SOG (1992)

(203) *Pigot's directory 1830; Norfolk* (microfiche), SOG (1992)

(204) *Pigot and Co's national commercial directory, comprising the merchants, bankers, professional gentlemen, manufacturers and traders in . . . Bedfordshire, Cambridgeshire, Huntingdonshire, Lincolnshire and Northamptonshire . . .*, J. Pigot & Co. (1830) reprinted by M. Winton (1992)

(205) *The Post Office London directory, 1848, comprising . . . official directory, commercial directory, court directory . . .*, 49th edn W. Kelly & Co (1848)

(206) *Royal Blue Book, court and parliamentary guide 1939*, Kelly's Directories Ltd (1939)

(207) *Webster's Royal Red Book, incorporating Boyle's court guide and fashionable register for January 1928*, A. Webster, 271st edn (1928)

(208) Atkins, P.J. *The directories of London 1677–1977*, Mansell (1990)

(209) Kelly, E.R. *The Post Office directory for Buckinghamshire*, Kelly & Co. (1864)

(210) Newington-Irving, N.J.N. *Directories and poll books (including almanacs and electoral rolls) in the library of the SoG*, SoG, 6th edn (1995)

(211) Norton, J.E. *Guide to the national and provincial directories of England and Wales, excluding London, published before 1856*, RHS (1950)

(212) Shaw, G. & Tipper, A. *British directories, a bibliography and guide to directories published in England & Wales (1850–1950) & Scotland (1773–1950)*, Leicester University Press, 2nd edn (1997)

(213) Thomas, D. St J. *Three Victorian telephone directories*, David & Charles (1970)

(214) White, W. *History, gazetteer and directory of Norfolk and the city and county of Norwich*, William White, 2nd edn (1845)

Chapter 11

(215) *Ancestors*, The National Archives and Wharncliffe Publishing

(216) *British Isles genealogical register 1994, Devon*, FFHS (1994)

(217) *Catalogue of additions to the manuscripts in the British Museum 1854–75, vol. II (1861–75)*, Trustees of the British Museum (1877)

(218) *Cockney ancestor*, East of London FHS

(219) *The Devon family historian*, Devon FHS

(220) *Devon Record Office, brief guide, part I: official and ecclesiastical* (1968?)

(221) *The Essex family historian*, Essex Society for Family History

(222) *Essex family history; a genealogist's guide to the Essex Record Office*, Essex Record Office, 4th edn (1995)

(223) *Family history*, IHGS

(224) *Family history monthly*, Diamond Publishing

(225) *Family history news and digest*, FFHS

(226) *Guide to genealogical sources*, Norfolk Record Office, 3rd edn (1993)

(227) *Guide to the Bedfordshire Record Office*, Bedfordshire County Council (1957)

(228) *Guide to the contents of the Public Record Office*, HMSO, 3 vols (1963–68)

(229) *Journal of Bedfordshire FHS*

(230) *Journal of West Middlesex FHS*

(231) *Maps and plans in the PRO, vol. 1 British Isles c. 1410 to 1860*, HMSO (1967)

(232) *Metropolitan*, London & North Middlesex FHS

(233) *The Norfolk ancestor*, Norfolk & Norwich Genealogical Society/Norfolk FHS

(234) *Public Record Office, current guide (microfiche)*, PRO (1998)

(235) *Register of one name studies 2000*, The Guild of One Name Studies; 16th edn (2000)

(236) *Root and branch*, West Surrey FHS

(237) *Sussex family historian*, Sussex Family History Group

(238) *Using the library of the Society of Genealogists*, SoG (1994)

(239) Bevan, A. *Tracing your ancestors in the Public Record Office*, PRO, 6th edn (2002)

(240) Bullock-Anderson, J., Chubb, C. & Cox, J. *A guide to archives & manuscripts at Guildhall Library*, Guildhall Library, 2nd edn (1990)

(241) Cole, J. & Church, R. *In and around record repositories in Great Britain and Ireland*, Family Tree Magazine, 4th edn (1998)

(242) Colwell, S. *Dictionary of genealogical sources in the PRO*, Weidenfeld & Nicolson (1992)

(243) Colwell, S. *Family roots; discovering the past in the PRO*, Weidenfeld & Nicolson (1991)

(244) Deadman, H. & Scudder, E. *An introductory guide to the Corporation of London Record Office*, Corporation of London (1994)

(245) Eakins, R. *Picture sources UK*, Macdonald (1985)

(246) Emmison, F.G. *Archives and local history*, Phillimore, 2nd edn (1974)

(247) Gardiner, L. *Pictures from the past, the peoples' war*, Selecta Book (1993)

(248) Gibson, J. & Peskett, P. *Record offices and how to find them*, FFHS, 9th edn (2002)

(249) Hampson, E. *Current publications by member societies*, FFHS, 10th edn (1999)

(250) Harvey, R. *A guide to genealogical sources in Guildhall Library*, Guildhall Library, 4th edn (1997)

(251) Hawgood, D. *Internet for genealogy*, D. Hawgood (1996)

(252) Hawgood, D. *GENUKI, U.K. & Ireland genealogy on the Internet*, D. Hawgood & FFHS (2000)

(253) Howells, C. *Cyndi's list, a comprehensive list of 70,000 genealogy sites on the Internet*, GPC, 2nd edn (2002)

(254) Hull, F. *Guide to the Kent County Archives Office*, Kent County Council (1958)

(255) Iredale, D. *Enjoying archives, what they are, where to find them, how to use them*, David & Charles (1973)

(256) Johnson, K.A. & Sainty, M.R. *Genealogical research directory, national & international, 2003*, Johnson & Sainty (2003)

(257) Marcan, P. *Greater London local history directory*, Marcan Publications, 2nd edn (1993)

(258) McLaughlin, E. *No time for family history?*, FFHS, 2nd edn (1992)

(259) Mortimer, I. *Record repositories in Great Britain; a geographical directory*, PRO (1999)

(260) Mullins, E.L.C. *Texts and calendars, an analytical guide to serial publications* and *Texts and calendars II, an analytical guide to serial publications 1957–1982*, RHS (1958 and 1983) supplemented by pages, on the web site of RCHM (# appendix XI), entitled *Texts and calendars since 1982: a survey* by I. Mortimer and C. Kitching

(261) Olding, S. *Exploring museums, London*; HMSO (1989) ·

(262) Owen, D.B. *Guide to genealogical resources in the British Isles*, Scarecrow Press (1989)

(263) Perkins, J. *Current publications on microfiche by member societies*, FFHS, 5th edn (2002)

(264) Raymond, S. *British genealogical periodicals, a bibliography of their contents*, FFHS vol. 1, *Collectanea topographica et genealogica, Topographer and genealogist and The ancestor* (1991); vol. 2, *The genealogist*, part 1 sources; part 2 family histories (1991); vol. 3, *Miscellanea genealogica et heraldica*, part 1 sources; part 2 families (1993)

(265) Raymond, S.A. *British genealogical books in print*, FFHS (1999)

(266) Raymond, S.A. *British genealogical microfiche*, FFHS (1999)

(267) Raymond, S.A. *British family history on CD*, FFHS (2001)

(268) Raymond, S.A. *Family history on the web, an Internet directory for England and Wales*, FFHS, 2nd edn (2002)

(269) Sackett, T. *London*, Waterton Press (1998)

(270) Silverthorne, E. *London local archives; a directory of local authority record offices and libraries*, Guildhall Library & Greater London Archives Network, 3rd edn (1994)

(271) Smith, D.M. *A guide to the archive collections in the Borthwick Institute of Historical Research*, University of York (1973)

(272) Wall, J. *Directory of British photographic collections*, Heinemann for the Royal Photographic Society (1977)

(273) Webb, C.C. *A guide to genealogical sources in the Borthwick Institute of Historical Research*, University of York, 2nd edn (1988)

(274) West, W.J. *The maritime photographs of Francis Frith*, Waterfront Publications (1993)

(275) Wilson, A. *Exploring museums: South West England*, HMSO (1989)

(276) Yung, K.K. *National Portrait Gallery: complete illustrated catalogue 1856–1979*, National Portrait Gallery (1981)

Chapter 12

(277) *An index to the Bank of England wills extracts 1807–1845*, SoG (1991)

(278) *The Guildhall miscellany*; Corporation of London, vol. IV, no. 1 (October 1971)

(279) *Wills and other probate records proved in the Chester Diocesan Consistory Court 1492–1857*, Cheshire County Council (1997)

(280) Camp, A.J. *Wills and their whereabouts*, A.J. Camp, 4th edn (1974)

(281) Camp, A.J. *An index to the wills proved in the Prerogative Court of Canterbury, 1750–1800*, SoG, 6 vols (1976–93)

(282) Carlton, C. *The Court of Orphans*, Leicester University Press (1974)

(283) Cirket, A.F. *Archdeaconry of Bedford wills (1450–1857) and administrations (1670–1857); part I 'A-Kimnot'*, BRS, vol. 104 (1993)

(284) Cirket, A.F. *Archdeaconry of Bedford wills (1450–1857) and administrations (1670–1857); part II 'Kimpton-Z'*, BRS, vol. 105 (1994)

(285) Cox, J. *Wills, inventories and death duties, the records of the Prerogative Court of Canterbury and Estate Duty Office, a provisional guide*, PRO (1988)

(286) Cox, J. *An introduction to . . . affection defying the power of death; wills, probate and death duty records*, FFHS (1993)

(287) Emmison, F.G. *Essex wills; the archdeaconry courts 1597–1603*, Essex Record Office (1990)

(288) Evans, N. *Wills of the Archdeaconry of Sudbury 1630–1635*, Suffolk Record Society, vol. 29 (1987)

(289) Fry, E.A. *Calendars of wills and administrations relating to the counties of Devon & Cornwall proved in the Court of the Principal Registry of the Bishop of Exeter 1559 to 1799 and of Devon only proved in the Court of the Archdeaconry of Exeter 1540 to 1799 preserved in the Probate Registry at Exeter*, BRS, vol. 35 (1908)

(290) Fry, E.A. *Calendars of wills and administrations relating to the counties of Devon & Cornwall proved in the Consistory Court of the Bishop of Exeter 1532 to 1800, preserved in the Probate Registry at Exeter*, BRS, vol. 46 (1914)

(291) Gibson, J. & Churchill, E. *Probate jurisdictions, where to look for wills*, FFHS, 5th edn (2002)

(292) Gibson, J. *Wills and where to find them*, Phillimore for BRS (1974)

(293) Havinden, M.A. *Household and farm inventories in Oxfordshire, 1550–1590*, HMSO (1965)

(294) Holman, J. & Herridge, M. *Index of Surrey probate inventories 16th–19th centuries*, Domestic Buildings Research Group (1986)

(295) McGregor, M. *Bedfordshire wills proved in the Prerogative Court of Canterbury 1383–1548*, BHRS, vol. 58 (1979)

(296) McLaughlin, E. *Wills before 1858*, FFHS, 5th edn (1995)

(297) Newington-Irving, N. *Will indexes and other probate material in the library of the SoG*, SoG (1996)

(298) Nicholson, G. & Readdie, J.A. *Personal names in wills proved at Durham 1787–1791*, Northumberland & Durham FHS (1994)

(299) Rubinstein, W. & Duman, D.H. 'Probate valuations, a tool for the historian', article in *The Local Historian*, vol. 11, no. 2 (1974–75)

(300) Scott, M. *Prerogative Court of Canterbury wills and other probate records*, PRO Publications (1997)

(301) Sharpe, R. *Calendar of wills proved and enrolled in the Court of Husting, London 1258 to 1688*, 2 vols CLRO (1889–90)

(302) Steer, F.W. *Farm and cottage inventories of mid-Essex 1635–1749*, Essex County Council (1950)

(303) Webb, C. *Index of Surrey wills proved in the Archdeaconry Court 1752–1858*, West Surrey FHS, 2nd edn (1994)

(303a) Webb, C. *An index of wills proved in the Archdeaconry Court of London 1700–1807*, SoG (1996)

Chapter 13

(304) *Avotaynu; the international review of Jewish genealogy*, G. Mokotoff, Avotaynu

(305) *Catholic archives*, The Catholic Archives Society

(306) *Catholic Record Society miscellanea*, Catholic Record Society, vol. 35 (1936)

(307) *Non-conformist, Roman Catholic, Jewish and burial ground registers*, Guildhall Library research guide, 3rd edn (2002)

(308) *Recusant history, a journal of research in post-reformation Catholic history in the British Isles*, Catholic Record Society

(309) *Shemot*, The Jewish Genealogical Society of Great Britain

(310) *Transactions, sessions 1968–1969*, The Jewish Historical Society of England

(311) *Wesley's Chapel, the museum of Methodism*, Wesley's House, Pitkin Pictorials (1994)

(312) Ackers, J.S. & Ackers, L.M.C. *Surname index, Bishop Leyburn's confirmation register 1687*, J.S. & L.M.C. Ackers (n.d)

(313) Barton, D.A. *Discovering chapels and meeting houses*, Shire, 2nd edn (1990)

(314) Bowler, H. *Recusant roll no 3 (1594–1595) and recusant roll no 4 (1595–1596), an abstract in English*, Catholic Record Society, vol. 61 (1970)

(315) Brace, H.W. *The first minute book of the Gainsborough Monthly Meeting of the Society of Friends 1669–1719*, Lincolnshire Record Society, vols 38, 40 & 44 (1948–51)

(316) Breed, G.R. *My ancestors were Baptists, how can I find out more about them?*, SoG, 4th edn (2002)

(317) Chandler, J.H. *Wiltshire dissenters' meeting house certificates and registrations 1689–1852*, Wiltshire Record Society (1985)

(318) Clapsaddle, C. *Tracing your Jewish roots in London; a personal experience*, Society for the Jewish Family Heritage (1988)

(319) Clifford, D.J.H. *My ancestors were Congregationalists in England and Wales, how can I find out more about them?*, SoG, 2nd edn (1997)

(320) Cooper, W.D. *Lists of foreign Protestants and aliens resident in England 1618–1688 from returns in the State Paper Office*, Camden Society (1862)

(321) Currer Briggs, N. & Gambier, R. *Huguenot ancestry*, Phillimore (1985)

(322) Ede, J. & Virgoe, N. *Religious worship in Norfolk; the 1851 census of accommodation and attendance at worship*, Norfolk Record Society (1998)

(323) Egan, J. *The Bishops' register of confirmations in the Midland district of the Catholic Church in England 1768–1811 and 1816*, Catholic FHS (1999)

(324) Gandy, M. *Catholic missions and registers 1700–1880, vol. 1 London & the Home Counties, vol. 2 The Midlands & East Anglia, vol. 3 Wales & the West of England, vol. 4 North East England, vol. 5 North West England, vol. 6 Scotland*, M. Gandy (1993)

(325) Gandy, M. *Catholic parishes in England, Wales & Scotland; an atlas*, M. Gandy (1993)

(326) Gandy, M. *Catholic family history; a bibliography of local sources*, M. Gandy (1996)

(327) Gillow, J. *A literary and biographical history, or bibliographical dictionary of the English Catholics from the breach with Rome in 1534 to the present time*, 5 vols Burns & Oates (1885)

(328) Gooch, L. & Allison, M. *A descriptive catalogue of the publications of the Catholic Record Society 1904–1989*, Catholic Record Society (1990)

(329) Green, J.J. *Quaker records, being an index to 'The annual monitor' 1813–1892*, Edward Hicks (1894)

(330) Gwynn, R.D. *Huguenot heritage, the history & contribution of the Huguenots in Britain*, RKP, 2nd edn (2001)

(331) Hilton, J.A., Mitchinson, A.J., Murray, B. & Wells, P. *Bishop Leyburn's confirmation register of 1687*, North West Catholic History Society (1997)

(332) Hudleston, C.R. *Durham recusants' estates 1717–1778*, Surtees Society (1962)

(332a) Joseph, A. *My ancestors were Jewish, how can I find out more about them?*, SoG, 3rd edn (2002)

(333) Kaganoff, B.C. *A dictionary of Jewish names and their history*, RKP (1978)

(334) Kelly, B.W. *Historical notes on English Catholic missions* (1907), reprint by M. Gandy (1995)

(335) Kirk, J. *Biographies of English Catholics in the eighteenth century*, Burns & Oates (1909)

(335a) Lart, C.E. *Huguenot pedigrees*, 2 vols (1924–28)

(336) Leary, W. *My ancestors were Methodists; how can I find out more about them?*, SOG, revd edn (1999)

(337) Leimdorfer, V. *Quakers at Sidcot 1690–1990*, Sidcot Preparative Meeting (1990)

(338) Lindsay, P. *The synagogues of London*, Valentine Mitchell & Co. (1993)

(339) McLaughlin, E. *Non-conformist ancestors*, FFHS (1995)

(340) Milligan, E.H. & Thomas, M.J. *My ancestors were Quakers; how can I find out more about them?*, SOG, revd edn (1999)

(341) Mordy, I. *My ancestors were Jewish, how can I find out more about them?*, SOG, 2nd edn (1995)

(342) Mortimer, R. *Minute book of the men's meeting of the Society of Friends in Bristol 1686–1704*, Bristol Record Society vol. 30 (1977)

(343) Mullett, M. *Sources for the history of English non-conformity 1660–1830*, BRA (1991)

(343a) Oates, P.J. *My ancestors were Inghamites*, SoG (2003)

(344) Palgrave-Moore, P. *Understanding the history and records of non-conformity*, Elvery Dowers, 2nd edn (1988)

(345) Ramsay-Sharp, C. *Huguenot surname index quarto series volumes 1–40*, Society of Australian Genealogists microfiche (1996)

(346) Rigg, J.M. *Calendar of the plea rolls of the Exchequer of the Jews . . . vol. I Henry III 1218–72, vol. II Edward I 1273–1275*, Jewish Historical Society; Dawson reprints (1971)

(347) Ross, J.M. *Naturalisation of Jews in England*; Transactions of the Jewish Historical Society of England, vol. 24 (1975)

(348) Ruston, A. *My ancestors were English Presbyterians/Unitarians; how can I find out more about them?*, SOG, 2nd edn (2001)

(349) Scouloudi, I. *Returns of strangers in the metropolis 1593, 1627, 1635, 1639, being a study of an active minority*, Huguenot Society, vol. 57 (1985)

(350) Shorney, D. *Protestant nonconformity and Roman Catholicism; a guide to sources in the PRO*, PRO Publications (1996)

(351) Smith, J.P. *Lancashire registers I, The Fylde I*, Catholic Record Society, vol. 15 (1913)

(352) Trappes-Lomax, R. *Lancashire registers VI*, Catholic Record Society, vol. 36 (1936)

(353) Twinn, K. et al. *Nonconformist congregations in Great Britain; a list of histories and other material in Dr. Williams' Library*, Dr. Williams' Trust (1973)

(354) Wiggins, R. *My ancestors were in the Salvation Army; how can I find out more about them?*, SoG, 2nd edn (1999)

Chapter 14

(355) *Index to divorces as listed in Palmer's indexes to 'The Times' newspaper London, 1788–1910*, About Archives (n.d.)

(356) *Marriage licences: abstracts & indexes in the library of the SoG*, SoG, 4th edn (1991)

(357) *Vicar-General marriage licences 1751–1775 & corrigendum*, SOG (1996) and further volumes for 1694–1725, SoG (1998), 1726–50, SoG (1997), 1776–1800, SoG (1996), 1801–25, SoG (1997) and 1826–50, SoG (1997)

(358) Armytage, G.J. *The register of baptisms and marriages at St George's Chapel, May Fair*, Harleian Society registers, vol. XV (1889)

(359) Bannerman, W.B. & Bannerman, G.G.B. *Allegations for marriage licences in the Archdeaconry of Sudbury in the county of Suffolk, part I 1684–1754, part II 1755–81, part III 1782–1814, part IV 1815–39*, Harleian Society vols 69–72 (1918–20)

(360) Benton, T. *Irregular marriage in London before 1754*, SoG, 2nd edn (2000)

(361) Burn, J.S. *History of the Fleet marriages with some account of the wardens of the prison, the parsons and their registers to which are added notices of the May Fair, Mint and Savoy chapels and numerous extracts from the registers*, Rivington, 2nd edn (1834)

(362) Chapman, C.R. & Litton, P.M. *Marriage laws, rites, records and customs*, Lochin Publishing (1996)

(362a) Chilman, P.W.G. *An index to the Archbishop of York's marriage bonds and allegations* [various dates but covering 1660–1734], Borthwick Institute Lists & Indexes vols 23, 29 and 33 (1999–2003)

(363) "Claverhouse", *Irregular border marriages*, Moray Press (1934)

(364) Cox, J. *Hatred pursued beyond the grave*, HMSO (1993)

(365) Crisp, F.A. *Fragmenta genealogica, vol. XI, marriage settlements*, F.A. Crisp (1906)

(366) Foster, J. *London marriage licences 1521–1869*, Quaritch (1887)

(367) Gibson, J. *Bishops' transcripts and marriage licences, bonds and allegations; a guide to their location and indexes*; FFHS, 5th edn (2001)

(368) Hale, S. *Fleet marriage entries relating to S.W. Kent, S.E. Surrey and Sussex from the register books numbered 1 to 273 in class RG 7 at the PRO*, 3 vols typescript (1983–85) and *Fleet marriage index*, 3 vols typescript (1992)

(369) Herber, M.D. *Clandestine marriages in the chapel and rules of the Fleet Prison 1680–1754, vols 1–3*, Francis Boutle Publishers (1998–2001)

(370) Horstman, A. *Victorian divorce*, Croom Helm (1985)

(371) Lloyd, B. *The Fleet forgeries, a study of the crime and carelessness of the clerical classes in the days of yore*, typescript (1987)

(372) Menefee, S.P. *Wives for sale, an ethnographic study of British popular divorce*, Blackwell (1981)

(373) Moens, W.J.C. *Hampshire allegations for marriage licences granted by the Bishop of Winchester 1689–1837*, Harleian Society vols 35–36 (1893)

(374) Newsome, E.B. & Newsome, W.R. *An index of marriage bonds & allegations in the peculiar jurisdiction of the Dean & Chapter of York 1613–1839*, Borthwick Institute Lists & Indexes vol. 1 (1985)

(375) Newsome, E.B. & Newsome, W.R. *An index to the Archbishop of York's marriage bonds and allegations* [various dates but covering 1735–1839], Borthwick Institute Lists & Indexes vols 3–7, 9, 10, 13 and 15 (1986–96)

(376) Outhwaite, R.B. *Clandestine marriage in England 1500–1850*, Hambledon Press (1995)

(377) Singleton, C. *Diocese of Carlisle marriage licence/bonds, vol. I 1668–1739, vol. II 1740–1752*, Cumbria FHS & Cumbria Archive Service (1994–98)

(378) Stone, L. *Uncertain unions & broken lives; marriage and divorce in England 1660–1857*, OUP (1995)

(379) Stone, L. *Road to divorce, England 1530–1987*, OUP (1992)

Chapter 15

(380) *Guildhall studies in London history*, Guildhall Library, vol. II, no. 2, April 1976

(381) *The old series Ordnance Survey, vol. 1 Kent, vol. 2 Devon, Cornwall & West Somerset, vol. 3 South-Central England, vol. 4 Central England, vol. 5 Lincolnshire, Rutland & East Anglia, vol. 6 Wales, vol. 7 North-Central England, vol. 8 Northern England & Isle of Man*, Harry Margary (1977–92)

(382) *The return of owners of land 1873; Devon* (microfiche); R. Cleaver, V. Palmer and T. Wilcock (1992)

(383) *The return of owners of land 1873; Middlesex (excluding the metropolis)*, West Surrey FHS (1991)

(384) Barker, F. & Jackson, P. *The history of London in maps*, Barrie & Jackson (1990)

(385) Emmison, F.G. *Catalogue of maps in the Essex Record Office 1566–1855*, Essex County Council, revd edn (1969)

(386) Evans, E.J. *Tithes; maps, apportionments & the 1836 Act*, Phillimore for BALH, revd edn (1993)

(387) Foot, W. *Maps for family history; a guide to the records of the tithe, valuation office & national farm surveys of England and Wales, 1836–1943*, PRO Publications (1994)

(388) Harley, J.B. *Maps for the local historian, a guide to the British sources*, Bedford Square Press (1972)

(389) Hindle, B.P. *Maps for local history*, Batsford (1988)

(390) Hollowell, S. *Enclosure records for historians*, Phillimore (2000)

(391) Howgego, J. *Printed maps of London, c.1553–1850*, Dawson, 2nd edn (1978)

(392) Hyde, R. *Printed maps of Victorian London, 1851–1900*, Dawson (1975)

(393) Kain, R.J.P. & Prince, H.C. *Tithe surveys for historians*, Phillimore (2000)

(394) Margary, H. *The A to Z of Victorian London*, Harry Margary & Guildhall Library (1987)

(395) Margary, H. *The A to Z of Regency London*, Harry Margary & Guildhall Library (1985)

(396) Moule, T. *The county maps of old England*, Studio Editions (1990)

(397) Oliver, R. *Ordnance Survey maps, a concise guide for historians*, Charles Close Society (1993)

(398) Ravenhill, W. *Christopher Saxton's 16th century maps; the counties of England and Wales*, Chatsworth Library (1992)

(399) Ravenhill, W. *Benjamin Donn; a map of the county of Devon, 1765*, DCRS and the University of Exeter (1965).

(400) Sandell, R.E. *Abstracts of Wiltshire inclosure awards and agreements*, Wiltshire Record Society (1971)

(401) Sheppard, F. & Belcher, V. 'The deeds registries of Yorkshire and Middlesex', *Journal of the Society of Archivists*, vol. 6 no. 5 (April 1980)

(402) Short, B. *The geography of England and Wales in 1910; an evaluation of Lloyd George's domesday of landownership*, Historical Geography Research Group No.22 (1989)

(403) Stuart, E. *Lost landscapes of Plymouth, maps, charts & plans to 1800*, Sutton (1991)

(404) Tate, W.E. *A domesday of English enclosure acts and awards* (edited by M.E. Turner), University of Reading Library (1978)

(405) Tate, W.E. *The English village community & the enclosure movements*, Gollancz (1967)

(406) Turner, M. *English parliamentary enclosure, its historical geography and economic history*, Dawson (1980)

(407) Wallis, H. *Historian's guide to early British maps; a guide to the location of pre-1900 maps of the British Isles preserved in the United Kingdom and Ireland*, RHS (1994)

(408) Wright, G.N. *Turnpike roads*, Shire (1992)

Chapter 16

(409) *East London record*, East London History Society

(410) *The Victoria history of the counties of England: Bedfordshire*, 3 vols & index (1904–14), Dawson reprint for IHR (1972)

(411) Anderson, J.P. *The book of British topography, a classified catalogue of the topographical works in the library of the British Museum relating to Great Britain and Ireland*, W. Satchell & Co. (1881)

(412) Baker, M. *Discovering Christmas customs and folklore*, Shire, 3rd edn (1992)

(413) Barratt, N. *Tracing the history of your house, a guide to sources*, PRO (2001)

(414) Batts, J.S. *British manuscript diaries of the 19th century; an annotated listing*, Rowman & Littlefield (1976)

(415) Beresford, J. *The diary of a country parson 1758–1802*, OUP (1935, reprinted 1979)

(416) Bettey, J.H. *Church and parish; a guide for local historians*, Batsford (1987)

(417) Bishop, G. *A parish album of St. Ive*, Columbian Press (1988)

(418) Blythe, R. *Akenfield; portrait of an English village*, The Literary Guild (1969)

(419) Borer, M.C. *An illustrated guide to London*, Robert Hale (1988)

(420) Calder, J. *The Victorian and Edwardian home from old photographs*, Batsford (1984)

(421) Dunning, R. *Local history for beginners*, Phillimore, revd edn (1980)

(422) Edwards, P. *Farming, sources for local historians*, Batsford (1991)

(423) Edwards, P. *Rural life: guide to local records*, Batsford (1993)

(424) Ekwall, E. *The concise Oxford dictionary of English placenames*, OUP, 4th edn (1960)

(425) Elton, A., Harrison, B. & Wark, K. *Researching the country house; a guide for local historians*, Batsford (1992)

(426) Eveleigh, D.J. *The Victorian farmer*, Shire (1991)

(427) Farrar, C.F. *Old Bedford*, Simpkin, Marshall & Co (1926)

(428) Girouard, M. *Life in the English country house*, Penguin Books (1980)

(429) Godber, J. *History of Bedfordshire*, Bedfordshire County Council (1969)

(430) Harvey, J.H. *Sources for the history of houses*, BRA (1974)

(431) Hawgood, D. *One-place genealogy*, D. Hawgood (2001)

(432) Hayter-Hames, J. *A history of Chagford*, Phillimore (1981)

(433) Hey, D. (ed.) *The history of Myddle, by Richard Gough*, Penguin Books (1981)

(434) Hoskins, W.G. *Local history in England*, Longman, 3rd edn (1984)

(435) Laslett, P. *The world we have lost; further explored*, Methuen, 3rd edn (1983)

(436) Latham, R.C. & Matthews, W. *The diary of Samuel Pepys*, vols 1–11; Bell & Hyman (1971)

(437) Lewis, S. *Lewis' topographical dictionary of England*, S. Lewis & Co, 5th edn (1844)

(438) Lysons, D. & Lysons, S. *Magna Brittania, being a concise topographical account of the several counties of Great Britain, vol. VI, Devon*, Thomas Cadell (1822)

(439) Lysons, D. *An historical account of those parishes in the county of Middlesex, which are not described in the 'Environs of London'*, T. Cadell, 3 vols (1795–1800)

(440) May, T. *The Victorian domestic servant*, Shire (1999)

(441) Muller, H.G. *Baking and bakeries*, Shire (1986)

(442) Porter, S. *Exploring urban history, sources for local historians*, Batsford (1990)

(443) Raymond, S. *Norfolk, a genealogical bibliography*, FFHS (1993)

(444) Raymond, S. *London and Middlesex, a genealogical bibliography*, FFHS, 2nd edn (1994)

(445) Raymond, S. *Buckinghamshire, a genealogical bibliography*, FFHS (1993)

(446) Raymond, S. *Devon; a genealogical bibliography; vol.1 Genealogical sources, vol. 2 Devon family histories and pedigrees*, FFHS, 2nd edn (1994)

(447) Raymond, S.A. *Lancashire, a genealogical bibliography, vol. 1 Lancashire genealogical sources, vol. 2 Registers, inscriptions and wills, vol. 3 Lancashire family histories and pedigrees*, FFHS (1996–97)

(448) Reaney, P.H. *The Church of St Mary, Walthamstow*, Walthamstow Antiquarian Society (1969)

(449) Reaney, P.H. *The origin of English placenames*, RKP (1960)

(450) Richardson, J. *Islington past*, Historical Publications (1988)

(451) Riden, P. *Record sources for local history*, Batsford (1987)

(452) Rogers, C.D. & Smith, J.H. *Local family history in England 1538–1914*, MUP (1991)

(453) Rowland, B. *Ide*, Obelisk Publications (1985)

(454) Shepherd, T. *London & its environs in the 19th century*, Jones (1829) Bracken Books reprint (1983)

(455) Stanier, P. *Shire county guide 27: Devon*, Shire (1989)

(456) Stow, J. *A survey of London . . .*, J.M. Dent & Sons (1912)

(457) Swann, J. *Shoemaking*, Shire (1986)

(458) Tames, R. *Soho past*, Historical Publications (1994)

(459) Trump, H.J. *Teignmouth, a maritime history*, Phillimore, 2nd edn (1986)

(460) Webb, C. *A guide to London & Middlesex genealogy & records*, West Surrey FHS (1994)

(461) Weinreb, B & Hibbert, C. *The London encyclopaedia*, Pan Macmillan, revd edn (1993)

(462) West, J. *Village records*, Phillimore, revd edn (1997)

(463) West, J. *Town records*, Phillimore (1983)

Chapter 17

(464) *The Corporation of London, its origin, constitution, powers and duties,* OUP (1950)

(465) *A handlist of poll books and registers of electors in Guildhall Library,* Corporation of London (1970)

(466) *The Illustrated London News,* vol. 25, July to December 1854, William Little (1854)

(467) *The official index to The Times January to March 1915,* J.P. Bland (1915)

(468) *Palmer's index to The Times newspaper (London) 1790–95,* S. Palmer (1925) Kraus reprint (1978)

(469) *Tercentenary handlist of English & Welsh newspapers, magazines & reviews, 1620–1919,* Times Publishing Co. (1920) Dawson reprint (1966)

(470) Aldous, V.E. *My ancestors were freemen of the City of London,* SoG (1999)

(471) Armytage, G.J. *Obituary prior to 1800 (as far as relates to England, Scotland & Ireland) compiled by Sir William Musgrave,* Harleian Society vols 44–49 (1899–1901)

(472) Bergess, W.F., Riddell, B.R.M. & Whyman, J. *Bibliography of British newspapers; Kent,* British Library (1982)

(473) Chapman, C.R. *An introduction to using newspapers and periodicals,* FFHS (1993)

(474) Cheffins, R.H.A. *Parliamentary constituencies and their registers since 1832,* The British Library (1998)

(475) Collins, F. *Register of the freemen of the city of York from the city records, vol. I 1272–1558,* Surtees Society (1896)

(476) Collins, F. *Register of the freemen of the city of York from the city records, vol. II 1559–1759,* Surtees Society (1899)

(477) Crane, R.S. & Kaye, F.B. *A census of British newspapers and periodicals 1620–1800,* Holland Press (1979)

(478) Cranfield, G.A. *A handlist of English provincial newspapers and periodicals 1700–1760,* Bowes & Bowes (1952)

(479) Davies, J.B. *The freemen and ancient borough of Llantrisant,* Llantrisant & District Local History Society (1989)

(480) Doolittle, I.G. *The City of London and its livery companies,* Gavin Press (1982)

(481) Farrar, R.H. *An index to the biographical and obituary notices in the Gentleman's Magazine 1731–1780,* BRS (1891)

(482) Fry, E.A. *An index to the marriages in the Gentleman's Magazine 1731–1768,* William Pollard & Co (1922)

(483) Gibson, J. & Rogers, C. *Electoral registers since 1832 and burgess rolls,* FFHS, 2nd edn (1990)

(484) Gibson, J., Langston, B. & Smith, B.W. *Local newspapers 1750–1920, England and Wales, Channel Islands and the Isle of Man, a select location list,* FFHS, 2nd edn (2002)

(485) Gibson, J. & Rogers, C. *Poll books c.1696–1872; a directory to holdings in Great Britain,* FFHS, 3rd edn (1994)

(486) Gordon, R. *Report of the Newsplan project in the East Midlands April 1987–July 1988,* British Library (1989)

(487) Hope Dodds, M. *The register of freemen of Newcastle upon Tyne from the corporation guild and admission books, chiefly of the seventeenth century,* Newcastle upon Tyne Records Committee (1923)

(488) Hunter Blair, L. *The register of freemen of Newcastle upon Tyne from the corporation guild and admission books, chiefly of the eighteenth century,* Newcastle upon Tyne Records Committee (1926)

(489) Jurica, A.R.J. *A calendar of the registers of freemen of the city of Gloucester 1641–1838,* Bristol and Gloucestershire Archaeological Society (1991)

(490) Lake, B. *British newspapers; a history and guide for collectors,* Sheppard Press (1984)

(491) McLaughlin, E. *Family history from newspapers,* FFHS, 3rd edn (1994)

(492) Murphy, M. *Newspapers and local history,* Phillimore for BALH (1991)

(493) Nangle, B. *The Gentleman's Magazine, biographical and obituary notices 1781–1819, an index,* Garland Publishing (1980)

(494) Rowe, M. M. & Jackson, A.M. *Exeter freemen 1266–1967,* DCRS (1973)

(495) Smith, L. *Devon newspapers: a finding list,* Standing Conference on Devon history (1973)

(496) Ward, H. *Freemen in England,* H. Ward (1975)

(497) Woodman, J. *The freedom of the City of London, some notes on its history, customs and privileges,* Journal of the Honourable Company of Master Mariners (1960)

Chapter 18

(498) *The endowed charities of the City of London; reprinted . . . from 17 reports of the commissioners for inquiring concerning charities,* M. Sherwood (1829)

(499) *Nottingham Union workhouse admissions and discharges register 1st November 1856 to 11th December 1858,* Nottinghamshire FHS (1995)

(500) *Parish poor law records in Devon,* Devon Record Office (1993)

(501) *Radford St Peter's church rate books, Old & New Radford 1823–1824, Old Radford 1825–1828,* Nottinghamshire FHS (1995)

(502) *Reports of the commission for inquiring concerning charities,* HMSO; 32 volumes and index (1819–40)

(503) *St. James Clerkenwall, settlement examinations 1778–1851, index of examinants,* London & North Middlesex FHS (1993)

(504) *Wiltshire pew rents, vol. I, Calne, Devizes St John, Melksham,* Wiltshire FHS (1995)

(505) Albert, W. & Harvey, P.D.A. *Portsmouth and Sheet Turnpike commissioners' minute book 1711–1754,* Portsmouth Record Series (1973)

(506)   Attreed, L.C. *The York House books 1461–1490*, Sutton (1991)

(507)   Berryman, B. *Mitcham settlement examinations 1784–1814*, Surrey Record Society (1973)

(507a) Bewes, W.A. *Church briefs or royal warrants for collections for charitable objects*, A&C Black (1896)

(508)   Bishop, L. *The general accounts of the churchwardens of Chipping Campden 1626 to 1907*, Campden Record Series (1991)

(509)   Castle, E. & Wishart, B. *Foleshill Union workhouse punishment book 1864–1900*, Coventry FHS (1995)

(510)   Cole, A. *An introduction to poor law documents before 1834*, FFHS (1993)

(511)   Cowe, F.M. *Wimbledon vestry minutes 1736, 1743–1788*, Surrey Record Society (1964)

(512)   Cox, J.C. *Churchwardens' accounts from the fourteenth century to the close of the seventeenth century*, Methuen (1913)

(513)   Earwaker, J.P. *The constables' accounts of the Manor of Manchester . . . 1612–1647 and 1743–1776*, Corporation of Manchester (1891–92)

(514)   Farmiloe, J.E. & Nixseamen, R. *Elizabethan churchwardens' accounts*, BHRS (1952)

(515)   Gibson, J., Rogers, C. & Webb, C. *Poor law union records, 1. South East England and East Anglia*, FFHS, 2nd edn (1997)

(516)   Gibson, J. & Rogers, C. *Poor law union records, 2. The Midlands and Northern England*, FFHS, 2nd edn (1997)

(517)   Gibson, J. & Rogers, C. *Poor law union records, 3. South West England, the Marches and Wales*, FFHS, 2nd edn (2000)

(518)   Gibson, J. & Youngs, F.A. *Poor law union records, 4. Gazetteer of England and Wales*, FFHS, 2nd edn (1993)

(519)   Hobson, M.G. & Salter, H.E. *Oxford Council acts 1626–1665*, OUP (1933)

(520)   Holdsworth, W. *The handy book of parish law*, George Routledge & Sons, 3rd edn (1872) Wiltshire FHS reprint (1995)

(521)   Holland, J. *Surrey poor law index & calendar*, West Surrey FHS CD-ROM (2001)

(522)   McLaughlin, E. *Annals of the poor*, FFHS, 5th edn (1994)

(523)   McLaughlin, E. *Illegitimacy*, FFHS, 5th edn (1992)

(524)   McLaughlin, E. *The poor are always with us*, FFHS (1994)

(525)   McLaughlin, E. *Iver, Bucks, settlement papers*, Bucks Genealogical Society (1994)

(526)   Pennington, D.H. & Roots, I.A. *The committee at Stafford 1643–1645, the order book of the Staffordshire County Committee*, MUP (1957)

(527)   Prescott, E. *The English medieval hospital 1050–1640*, B.A. Seaby (1992)

(528)   Price, F.D. *The Wigginton constables' book 1691–1836*, Phillimore (1971)

(529)   Rowe, M.M. & Draisey, J.M. *The receivers' accounts of the City of Exeter 1304–1353*, DCRS (1989)

(530)   Rumbelow, D. *The complete Jack the Ripper*, Penguin, revd edn (1988)

(531)   Sutton, D. *York civic records vol. IX (1588–90)*, YAS vol. 138 (1978)

(532)   Tate, W.E. *The parish chest; a study of the records of parochial administration in England*, CUP, 3rd edn (1969)

(533)   Watkin, H.R. *Parochial histories of Devonshire, no. 5; Dartmouth, vol. I Pre-reformation*, Devonshire Association (1935)

(533a) Webb, C. *An index of London hospitals and their records*, SoG (2002)

(534)   Weinstock, M. *Weymouth & Melcombe Regis minute book 1625–1660*, Dorset Record Society (1964)

(535)   Whiting, C.E. *The accounts of the churchwardens, constables, overseers of the poor and overseers of the highways of the parish of Hooton Pagnell 1767–1820*, YAS, vol. 97 (1938)

(536)   Wright, S.J. 'A guide to Easter books and related parish listings'; articles in *Local Population Studies*, no. 42 (Spring 1989) and no. 43 (Autumn 1989)

Chapter 19

(537)   *Brasenose College register*, Oxford Historical Society vol. 55; Blackwell (1909)

(538)   *The Cambridge University calendar for the year 1928–1929*, CUP (1928)

(539)   *Exeter Bishop Blackall Episcopal Charity School admission register 1839–1855*, Devon FHS (2000)

(540)   *Exeter University register 1893–1962, a register of officers, officials, staff, graduates and holders of diplomas, certificates and testamurs*, University of Exeter (1970)

(541)   *The Oxford University calendar 1847*, J.H. Parker & H. Slatter (1847)

(542)   *The Oxford University calendar for 1947*, Clarendon Press (1947)

(543)   *School, university & college registers & histories in the library of the SoG*, SoG, 2nd edn (1996)

(544)   *University of London, the calendar for the year 1927–28*, University of London Press (1927)

(545)   Austen-Leigh, R.A. *The Eton College register 1698–1752*, SBC (1927)

(546)   Austen-Leigh, R.A. *The Eton College register 1753–1790*, SBC (1921)

(547)   Baty, D. & Gedye, N.G.E. *Durham School register, fifth edition to March 1991* (1991)

(548)   Boreham, J.Y. *Highgate School register 1838–1938*, Langley & Sons (1938)

(549)   Brannigan, Y. & Brannigan, J. *Hawkesbury School 1860–1968, school log book 1885–1908*, Coventry FHS (1996)

(550)   Burbridge, T.H. *Durham School register, third edition to December 1939*, CUP (1940)

(551)   Chapman, C.R. *The growth of British education and its records*, Lochin Publishing, 2nd edn (1992)

(552) Darch, O.W. & Tween, A.S. *Chigwell register together with a historical account of the school by the Rev. Canon Swallow*, Governors of Chigwell School (1907)

(553) Emden, A.B. *A biographical register of the University of Oxford to AD 1500*, OUP (1957)

(554) Emden, A.B. *A biographical register of the University of Oxford 1501 to 1540*, OUP (1974)

(555) Emden, A.B. *A biographical register of the University of Cambridge to 1500*, CUP (1963)

(556) Foster, J. *Alumni Oxoniensis, the members of the University of Oxford 1500–1714; their parentage, birthplace and year of birth, with a record of their degrees, being the matriculation register of the university* . . ., James Parker & Co., 4 vols (1891)

(557) Foster, J. *Alumni Oxoniensis, the members of the University of Oxford 1715–1886*, James Parker & Co., 4 vols (1888–91)

(558) Foster, J. *Oxford men 1880–1892 with a record of their schools, honours and degrees*, James Parker & Co. (1893)

(559) Foster, J. *Oxford men and their colleges*, James Parker & Co. (1893)

(560) Horn, P. *The Victorian and Edwardian schoolchild*, Sutton (1989)

(561) Horn, P. *Village education in nineteenth-century Oxfordshire, the Whitchurch School log book (1868–93) and other documents*, Oxfordshire Record Society (1979)

(562) Innes Smith, R.W. *English-speaking students of medicine at the University of Leyden*, Oliver & Boyd (1932)

(563) Jacobs, P.M. *Registers of the universities, colleges and schools of Great Britain and Ireland*, Athlone Press for the IHR (1964)

(564) May, T. *The Victorian schoolroom*, Shire (1994)

(565) Mayor, J.E.B. *Admissions to the college of St John the Evangelist in the University of Cambridge, parts I & II, January 1629/30–July 1715*, CUP (1893)

(566) Morton, A. *Education and the state from 1833*, PRO Publications (1997)

(567) Robinson, C.J. *A register of the scholars admitted into Merchant Taylors' School from 1562 to 1874, compiled from authentic sources and edited with biographical notices*, Farncombe & Co. (1882)

(568) Rouse Ball, W.W. & Venn, J.A. *Admissions to Trinity College, Cambridge 1546–1900*, 5 vols, Macmillan (1911–16)

(569) Scott, R.F. *Admissions to the college of St John the Evangelist in the University of Cambridge, part III July 1715–November 1767 and part IV July 1767–July 1802*, CUP (1903 and 1931)

(570) Stapylton, H.E. *The Eton School lists from 1791 to 1877*, Simpkin, Marshall & Co (1885)

(571) Sterry, Sir W. *The Eton College register 1441–1698*, SBC (1943)

(572) Venn, J & Venn, J.A. *Alumni Cantabrigiensis, a biographical list of all known students, graduates and holders of office at the University of Cambridge from the earliest times to 1900*, CUP, part I, to 1751, 4 vols (1922–27); part 2, from 1752 to 1900, 6 vols (1940–54)

(573) Webb, C. *An index of London schools and their records*, SoG, 2nd edn (2000)

Chapter 20

(574) *The Air Force list, April 1936*, HMSO (1936)

(575) *The Army list for January 1858*, MM Publications microfiche reprint (1995)

(576) *Bid them rest in peace, a register of Royal Marines deaths 1939–45*, Royal Marines Historical Society, 2nd edn (1992)

(577) *The Distinguished Conduct Medal 1914–1920, citations, the King's (Shropshire Light Infantry)*, LSE (1985)

(578) *List of British officers taken prisoner in the various theatres of war between August 1914 and November 1918* . . ., compiled from records kept by Messrs. Cox & Co's enquiry office, Cox & Co. (1919) LSE reprint (1988)

(579) *A memorial record of Watsonians who served in the Great War 1914–1918*, War Memorial Executive (1920)

(580) *National roll of the Great War 1914–1918*, National Publishing Company, 14 vols (1918–22)

(581) *Officers died in the Great War*, HMSO (1919)

(582) *Prisoners of war British army 1939–1945*, HMSO (1945), Hayward reprint in association with the Imperial War Museum (1990)

(583) *Prisoners of war, naval and air forces of Great Britain and the Empire*, HMSO (1945), Hayward reprint (1990)

(584) *Record of service of solicitors and articled clerks with His Majesty's forces 1914–1919*, Solicitors' War Memorial Fund (1920), NMP reprint (2001)

(585) *The register of the Victoria Cross*, This England (1981)

(586) *Seedie's list of Fleet Air Arm awards 1939–1969*, Ripley Registers (1990)

(587) *Service of military officers arranged alphabetically, corrected to December 1920*, HMSO (1920), Hayward reprint for LSE (1986)

(588) *Soldiers died in the Great War*, HMSO, 80 volumes (1919–21) Hayward reprint (1989)

(589) *The South African war casualty roll, the Natal Field Force, 20th Oct. 1899–26th Oct. 1900*, Hayward (1980)

(590) *The South African war casualty roll, the 'South African Field Force', 11th Oct. 1899–June 1902*, Hayward (1982)

(591) *The war graves of the British Empire, France, vol. 12, cemeteries Fr. 176 to Fr. 202*, Imperial War Graves Commission (1925)

(592) *War service record 1939–1945, The Commercial Bank of Scotland Limited* (1952)

(593) *With full and grateful hearts, a register of Royal Marines deaths 1914–19*, Royal Marines Historical Society (1991)

(594) Abbott, P.E. & Tamplin, J.M. *British gallantry awards*, Nimrod Dix, 2nd edn (1981)

(595) Abbott, P.E. *Recipients of the Distinguished Conduct Medal 1855–1909*, Hayward, 2nd edn (1987)

(596) Adler, M. *British Jewry book of honour*, Caxton (1922)

(597) Anderson, T.C. *War services of all the officers of H.M.'s Bengal Army . . .* (1863), Hayward reprint (1985)

(598) Askwith, W.H. *List of officers of the Royal Regiment of Artillery from the year 1716 to the year 1899 to which are added notes on officers' services*, Royal Artillery Institution, 4th edn (1900)

(599) Becke, A.F. *History of the Great War, order of battle of divisions*, HMSO (1935–45)

(599a) Beckett, I.F.W. *The First World War, the essential guide to sources in the UK National Archives*, PRO (2002)

(600) Beckett, J.D. *An index to the regimental registers of the Royal Hospital Chelsea 1806–1838*, Manchester & Lancashire FHS (1993)

(601) Brereton, J.M. *A guide to the regiments and corps of the British army on the regular establishment*, Bodley Head (1985)

(602) Brett-James, N.G. *The book of remembrance and war record of Mill Hill School 1939–1945*, Stannard (n.d.)

(603) Brough, R. *White Russian awards to British & Commonwealth servicemen during the allied intervention in Russia 1918–20 with a roll of honour*, Tom Donovan Publishing (1991)

(604) Brown, G.A. *For distinguished conduct in the field, the register of the Distinguished Conduct Medal 1939–1992*, Western Canadian Distributors (1993)

(605) Brown, M. *The Imperial War Museum book of the Western Front*, Sidgwick & Jackson in association with the Imperial War Museum (1993)

(606) Brown, M. *The Imperial War Museum book of the First World War*, Sidgwick & Jackson in association with the Imperial War Museum (1991)

(607) Cantwell, J.D. *The Second World War, a guide to documents in the PRO*, HMSO, 3rd edn (1998)

(608) Chambers, B. *Indexes to Army of Reserve 1803, vol. 1 Berkshire, Dorset, Gloucestershire, Hampshire/Isle of Wight and Wiltshire*, B. Chambers (1999)

(609) Chambers, B. *Regimental indexes 1806, vol. 1 WO 25/909–911, vol. 2 WO 25/912–916, vol. 3 WO 25/871–873 & 877–879*, B. Chambers (1998)

(610) Chorley, W.R. *Royal Air Force Bomber Command losses of the Second World War; vol. 1 aircraft and crews lost during 1939–40, vols 2–6 aircraft and crew losses 1941, 1942, 1943, 1944, 1945*, Midland Counties Publications (1992–98)

(611) Clutterbuck, L.A. *The bond of sacrifice, a biographical record of all British officers who fell in the Great War, vol. I August to December 1914, vol. II January to June 1915*, Anglo-African Publishing Contractors (1914–15), NMP reprint (2001)

(612) Cole, C. *Royal Flying Corps communiques 1915–1916*, Tom Donovan (1990)

(613) Connolly, T.W. & Edwards, R.F. *Roll of officers of the corps of Royal Engineers from 1660 to 1898*, The Royal Engineers Institute (1898)

(614) Cook, F. & Cook, A. *Casualty roll for the Crimea 1854–1856*, Hayward (1976)

(615) Creagh, O'Moore & Humphris, E.M. *The VC and DSO, a complete record of all those officers, non-commissioned officers and men of His Majesty's . . . forces who have been awarded these decorations from . . . their institution*, Standard Art Book Co., 3 vols (1924)

(616) Dalton, C. *English army lists and commission registers 1661–1714*, Eyre & Spottiswoode, 6 vols (1892–1904), Francis Edwards reprint (1960)

(617) Dalton, C. *George the First's army 1714–1727*, Eyre & Spottiswoode, 2 vols (1910–12)

(618) Devereux, J. & Sacker, G. *Roll of honour land forces World War 2 (vols 1–4)*, Promenade Publications (1999–2001)

(619) Dooner, M.G. *The 'Last Post', being a roll of all officers (naval, military or colonial) who gave their lives for their Queen, King and country, in the South African war 1899–1902* (1903), Hayward reprint (1980)

(620) Drew, R. *Medical officers in the British army, vol. II, 1898–1960*, Wellcome Historical Medical Library (1968)

(621) Enser, A.G.S. *A subject bibliography of the First World War, books in English 1914–1978*, Andre Deutsch (1979)

(622) Enser, A.G.S. *A subject bibliography of the Second World War, books in English 1939–1975*, Andre Deutsch (1977)

(623) Enser, A.G.S. *A subject bibliography of the Second World War, books in English 1975–1983*, Gower Publishing (1979)

(624) Everson, G.R. *The South Africa 1853 medal, being the roll of the recipients & the story of the campaign medal issued for the frontier wars between 1834 and 1853*, Samson Books (1978)

(625) Fabb, J. *The Victorian & Edwardian army from old photographs*, Batsford (1975)

(626) Farrington, A. *The second Afghan war 1878–1880 casualty roll*, LSE (1986)

(627) Fowler, S. & Spencer, W. *Army records for family historians*, PRO, 2nd edn (1998)

(629) Fowler, S., Elliott, P., Conyers Nesbit, R. & Goulter, C. *RAF records in the PRO*, PRO Publications (1994)

(630) Franks, N.L.R. *Royal Air Force Fighter Command losses of the Second World War, vol. 1 operational losses: aircraft and crews 1939–41, vol. 2 losses 1942–43, vol. 3 losses 1944–45*, Midland Publishing (1997–99)

(631) Gibson, J. & Dell, A. *Tudor and Stuart muster rolls, a directory of holdings in the British Isles*, FFHS (1991)

(632) Gibson, J. & Medlycott, M. *Militia lists and musters 1757–1876, a directory of holdings in the British Isles*, FFHS, 4th edn (2000)

(633) Gliddon, G. *VCs of the First World War, The Somme*, Sutton (1994)

(634) Gliddon, G. *VCs of the First World War, The road to victory 1918*, Sutton (2000)

(635) Gould, R.W. & Douglas-Morris, K.J. *The Army of India Medal roll 1799–1826*, Hayward (1974)

(636) Gould, R.W. *Locations of British cavalry, infantry and machine gun units 1914–1924*, Heraldene (1977)

(637) Hall, J.A. *A history of the Peninsular War, volume VIII, The biographical dictionary of British officers killed and wounded*, Greenhill Books (1998)

(638) Halley, J.J. *The squadrons of the Royal Air Force and Commonwealth, 1918–1988*, Air Britain (Historians), revd edn (1988)

(639) Hallows, I. *Regiments and corps of the British army*, Arms & Armour Press (1991)

(640) Hamilton-Edwards, G. *In search of army ancestry*, Phillimore (1977)

(641) Hart, H.G. *The new annual army list and militia list for 1863, containing dates of commissions and a statement of the war services and wounds of nearly every officer in the army, ordnance, marines and Bengal Staff Corps, corrected to the 29th December 1862, with an index*, John Murray (1863)

(642) Hodson, V.C. *List of the officers of the Bengal Army 1758–1834*, vols I–II (surnames A to K), Constable (1927–28); vols III–IV (surnames L to Z), Phillimore (1946–47)

(643) Holding, N. *World War I army ancestry*, FFHS, 3rd edn (1997)

(644) Holding, N. *More sources of World War I army ancestry*, FFHS, 3rd edn (1998)

(645) Holding, N. *The location of British army records, a national directory of World War I sources*, FFHS, 4th edn (1999) revised by I. Swinnerton

(646) Hoskins, W.G. *Exeter militia list 1803*, Phillimore (1972)

(647) Howard, A.J. & Stoate, T.L. *The Devon muster roll for 1569*, T.L. Stoate (1977)

(648) James, E.A. *British regiments 1914–1918*, Samson Books (1978) NMP and Liverpool Company reprint (1993), new version of *British cavalry and yeomanry regiments in the Great War* and *British infantry regiments in the Great War* (1969–76)

(649) Jarvis, S.D. & Jarvis, D.B. *The cross of sacrifice*, vol. 1 *Officers who died in the service of British, Indian and East African regiments and corps 1914–1919*, vol. 2 *Officers who died in the service of the Royal Navy, Royal Naval Reserve, Royal Naval Volunteer Reserve, Royal Marines, Royal Naval Air Service and Royal Air Force 1914–1919*, vol. 3 *Officers who died in the service of the Commonwealth and Colonial regiments and corps 1914–1919*, vol. 4 *Non-commissioned officers and men of the Royal Navy, Royal Flying Corps and Royal Air Force 1914–1919*, vol. 5 *The officers, men and women of the Merchant Navy and Mercantile Fleet Auxiliary 1914–1919*, Roberts Medals/NMP (1993–2000)

(650) Joslin, E.C., Litherland, A.R. & Simpkin, B.T. *British battles & medals*, Spink & Son, 6th edn (1988)

(651) Laffin, J. *British VCs of World War 2, a study in heroism*, Sutton (1997)

(652) Liddell Hart, B. *History of the Second World War*, Macdonald (1989)

(653) Lummis, W.M. & Wynn, K.G. *Honour the Light Brigade, a record of the services of officers, non-commissioned officers and men of the five light cavalry regiments, which made up the Light Brigade at Balaclava on October 25th 1854 and saw service in the Crimea from September 1854 to the end of the war*, Hayward (1973)

(654) Lutt, N. *Bedfordshire muster lists 1539–1831*, BHRS (1992)

(655) Mackinnon, J.P. & Shadbolt, S.H. *The South African campaign of 1879*, Sampson Low (1880), reprinted by Greenhill Books with index by J. Young (1995)

(656) Maddocks, G. *Liverpool Pals, a history of the 17th, 18th, 19th and 20th (Service) battalions, The King's (Liverpool Regiment) 1914–1919*, Leo Cooper (1991)

(657) McInnes, I. *The Meritorious Service Medal, the immediate awards 1916–1928*, NMP (1992)

(658) McInnes, I. *The Meritorious Service Medal to aerial forces*, Picton Publishing (1984)

(659) McInnes, I. & Fraser, M. *Ashanti 1895–96, a roll of British and West Indian recipients of the Ashanti Star . . .*, Picton Publishing (1987)

(660) McInnes, I. & Webb, J.V. *A contemptible little flying corps*, LSE (1991)

(661) Morgan, F.C. *List of officers of the Royal Regiment of Artillery, vol. II, June 1862 to June 1914*, Royal Artillery Institution (1914)

(662) Mullen, A.L.T. *The Military General Service Medal roll 1793–1814*, LSE (1990)

(663) Oram, G. *Death sentences passed by military courts of the British Army 1914–1924*, Francis Boutle Publishers (1998)

(664) Peacock, E. *The army lists of the roundheads and cavaliers . . . the names of the officers in the Royal and Parliamentary armies of 1642*, Chatto & Windus, 2nd edn (1874)

(665) Perkins, R. *Regiments & corps of the British Empire & Commonwealth 1758–1913, a critical bibliography of their published histories*, R. Perkins (1994)

(666) Peterkin, A. & Johnston, W. *Medical officers in the British army, vol. I, 1660–1898*, Wellcome Historical Medical Library (1968)

(667) Purves, A.A. *Ribbons and medals*, Osprey Publishing (1983)

(668) Putkowski, J. *British Army mutineers*, Francis Boutle Publishers (1998)

(668a) Raymond, S.A. *War memorials on the web, part 1 Southern England, the Marches and Wales, part 2 The Midlands, Northern England and East Anglia*, FFHS (2003)

(669) Richards, D. & Saunders, H. St G. *Royal Air Force 1939–1945; vol. I, The fight at odds* (by Richards); *vol. II, The fight avails* (by Richards & Saunders), *vol. III, The fight is won* (by Saunders); HMSO (1953–54)

(670) Roper, M. *The records of the War Office and related departments 1660–1964*, PRO Publications (1998)

(671) Ruvigny & Raineval, Marquis of. *The roll of honour, a biographical record of members of His Majesty's naval and military forces who fell in the Great War 1914–1918*, Standard Art Book Co. (1919?), LSE reprint (1987)

(672) Samways, R. *We think you ought to go; an account of the evacuation of children from London during the Second World War based on the original records of the London County Council*, Corporation of London (1995)

(673) Slocombe, I. *First World War tribunals in Wiltshire*, Wiltshire FHS (1997)

(674) Spencer, W. *Air force records for family historians*, PRO (2000)

(675) Spencer, W. *Records of the militia & volunteer forces 1757–1945, including records of the Volunteers, Rifle Volunteers, Yeomanry, Imperial Yeomanry, Fencibles, Territorials and the Home Guard*, PRO Publications (1997)

(676) Spencer, W. *Army service records of the First World War*, PRO, 3rd edn (2001)

(676a) Steppler, G.A. *Britons, to arms!, the story of the British volunteer soldier*, Sutton (1992)

(677) Swinnerton, I. *Identifying your World War I soldier from badges and photographs*, FFHS (2001)

(678) Swinson, A. *A register of the regiments and corps of the British army; the ancestry of the regiments and corps of the regular establishment*, Archive Press (1972)

(679) Tavender, I.T. *Casualty roll for the Indian Mutiny 1857–59*, Hayward (1983)

(680) Tavender, I.T. *Casualty roll for the Zulu and Basuto wars, South Africa 1877–79*, Hayward (1985)

(681) Tavender, I.T. *The Distinguished Flying Medal, a record of courage 1918–1982*, Hayward (1990)

(682) Thomas, G. *Records of the Royal Marines*, PRO Publications (1994)

(683) Thorpe, B. *The men of the Wooburn war memorial – their stories*, The Thames Valley Hospice (1993)

(684) Walker, R.W. *Recipients of the Distinguished Conduct Medal 1914–1920*, Midland Medals (1981)

(685) Watts, M.J. & Watts, C. *My ancestor was in the British army; how can I find out more about him?*, SoG, revd edn (1995)

(686) Webb, J.V. *Recipients of bars to the Military Cross 1916–1920 to which is added MCs awarded to warrant officers 1915–1919*, J.V. Webb (1988)

(687) Westlake, R. *The Rifle Volunteers, the history of the Rifle Volunteers 1859–1908*, Picton Publishing (1982)

(688) White, A.S. *A bibliography of regimental histories of the British Army*, Society for Army Historical Research and the Army Museums Ogilby Trust (1965), LSE reprint (1988) and NMP CD-ROM (2001)

(689) Whittaker, L.B. *Stand down: Orders of battle for the units of the Home Guard of the United Kingdom, November 1944*, Westlake Military Books (1990)

(690) Williamson, H.J. *The roll of honour, Royal Flying Corps & Royal Air Force for the Great War*, NMP (1992)

(691) Wilson, E. *The records of the Royal Air Force, how to find the few*, FFHS (1991)

(692) Wise, T. & Wise, S. *A guide to military museums and other places of military interest*, T.Wise, 10th edn (2001)

(692a) Wynn, K.G. *Men of the Battle of Britain, a biographical directory of 'The Few'*, CCB Associates, 2nd edn (1999)

Chapter 21

(693) *British vessels lost at sea 1914–18 and 1939–45*, Patrick Stephens reprint (1988) of HMSO publications: *Navy losses* (1919), *Merchant shipping losses* (1919), *Ships of the Royal Navy, statement of losses during the Second World War* (1947) and *British merchant vessels lost or damaged by enemy action during the Second World War* (1947)

(694) *Colburn's united service magazine and naval and military journal*, Hurst & Blackett (July 1860)

(695) *A guide to the crew agreements and official logbooks, 1863–1913, held at the county record offices of the British Isles*, Maritime History Archive, Memorial University of Newfoundland (1991)

(696) *A guide to the agreements and crew lists, series II (BT 99), 1913–1938*, Maritime History Archive, Memorial University of Newfoundland (1987)

(697) *Historic photographs at the National Maritime Museum, an illustrated guide*, National Maritime Museum (1995)

(698) *Index to crew lists, 1863–1913*, Maritime History Group, microfiche (1974)

(699) *Lloyd's war losses, the First World War, casualties to shipping through enemy causes 1914–1918*, Lloyd's of London Press (1990)

(700) *National Maritime Museum catalogue of warship photographs*, Richard Perkins collection, HMSO (1968)

(701) *National Maritime Museum, catalogue of the library, vol. 2 parts 1 and 2, biography*, HMSO (1969)

(702) *National Maritime Museum general catalogue of historic photographs, vol. 2, merchant sailing ships*, National Maritime Museum (1976)

(703) *The naval who's who 1917*, Hayward reprint (1981)

(704) *The Navy list, corrected to 20th September 1851*, John Murray (1851), MM Publications microfiche reprint (1995)

(705) *Seedie's list of awards to the Merchant Navy for World War II*, Ripley Registers (1997)

(706) *Seedie's list of coastal forces awards for World War II*, Ripley Registers (1992)

(707) Barriskill, D.T. *A guide to the Lloyd's marine collection and related marine sources at Guildhall Library*, Guildhall Library, 2nd edn (1994)

(708) Bryon, R.V. & Bryon, T.N. *Maritime information, a guide to libraries & other sources of information in the United Kingdom*, Maritime Information Association, 3rd edn (1993)

(709) Campbell, J. *Lives of the British admirals, containing a new and accurate naval history from the earliest periods . . . down to the year 1779*, G. & J. Robinson (1785)

(710) Camp, A.J. *The Trinity House petitions; a calendar of the records of the Corporation of Trinity House, London in the library of the SoG*; SoG (1987)

(711) Charnock, J. *Biographia Navalis, or impartial memoirs of the lives and characters of officers of the navy of Great Britain from . . . 1660 to the present time . . .*, vols I–IV and supplemental vols I–II; R. Faulder (1794–98)

(712) Colledge, J.J. *Ships of the Royal Navy; the complete record of all fighting ships of the Royal Navy from the 15th century to the present*, Greenhill (1987)

(713) Colledge, J.J. *Ships of the Royal Navy; an historical index; vol.2, navy-built trawlers, drifters, tugs and requisitioned ships*, Augustus Kelley (1970)

(714) Craig, R. & Jarvis, R. *Liverpool registry of merchant ships*, Chetham Society (1967)

(715) Douglas-Morris, K.J. *The Naval General Service Medal 1793–1840*, NMP (n.d.)

(716) Douglas-Morris, K.J. *Naval Long Service medals 1830–1990*, K. Douglas-Morris (1991)

(717) Duckers, P. & Mitchell, N. *The Azoff campaign 1855, dispatches, medal rolls, awards*, Kingswood Books (1996)

(718) Fabb, J. & McGowan, A.C. *The Victorian and Edwardian navy from old photographs*, Batsford (1976)

(719) Fevyer, W.H. *The Distinguished Service Cross 1901–1938*, LSE (1991)

(720) Fevyer, W.H. *The Distinguished Service Medal 1914–1920*, Hayward (1982)

(721) Fevyer, W.H. *The Distinguished Service Medal 1939–1946*, Hayward (1981)

(722) Fevyer, W.H. & Wilson, J.W. *The Africa General Service Medal to the Royal Navy & Royal Marines*, LSE (1990)

(723) Fevyer, W.H. & Wilson, J.W. *The China War Medal 1900 to the Royal Navy & Royal Marines*, LSE (1985)

(724) Greenhill, B. *The National Maritime Museum*, Scala Books (1982)

(725) Greenhill, B. *The merchant schooners, a portrait of a vanished industry, . . . a survey . . . of the history of the small fore-and-aft rigged sailing ships of England & Wales in the years 1870–1940 with something of their previous history and subsequent fate*, David & Charles, revd edn (1968)

(726) Hailey, J. *Maritime sources in the library of the SoG*, SoG (1997)

(727) Hocking, C. *Dictionary of disasters at sea during the age of steam, including sailing ships and ships of war lost in action 1824–1962*, Lloyds' Register of Shipping, 2 vols (1969)

(728) Hurst, N. *Naval chronicle 1799–1818, index to births, marriages and deaths*, N. Hurst (1989)

(729) Knight, R.J.B. *Guide to the manuscripts in the National Maritime Museum, vol. 1, the personal collections, vol. 2, public records, business records and artificial collections*, Mansell Publishing (1977–80)

(730) Lavery, B. *Shipboard life and organisation 1731–1815*, Navy Records Society vol. 138 (1998)

(731) Lyon, D. *The sailing list: all the ships of the Royal Navy-built, purchased and captured 1688–1860*, Conway Maritime Press (1993)

(732) Macdougall, P. *Royal dockyards*, Shire (1989)

(733) MacGregor, D.R. *Merchant sailing ships, vol. 1, 1775–1815, their design and construction*, Argus Books (1980); *vol. 2, 1815–1850, supremacy of sail*, Conway (1984) and *vol. 3, 1850–1875, heyday of sail*, Conway Maritime (1984?)

(734) Manning, T.D. & Walker, C.F. *British warship names*, Putnam (1959)

(735) Marcombe, D. *The Victorian sailor*, Shire, revd edn (1995)

(736) Marshall, J. *Royal Naval biography, or memoirs of the services of all the flag officers . . . captains, and commanders whose names appeared on the Admiralty list of sea officers at the commencement of (1823) or who have since been promoted*, Longman, Hurst, Rees, Orme & Brown, 4 vols & supplements (1823–35)

(737) Mathias, P. & Pearsall, A.W.H. *Shipping: a survey of historical records*, David & Charles (1971)

(738) Merson, A.L. *The third book of remembrance of Southampton 1514–1602, vol. I 1514–1540*, Southampton Records Series vol. 2 (1952)

(739) O'Byrne, W.R. *A naval biographical dictionary . . . the life & services of every living officer in Her Majesty's navy from the rank of Admiral . . . to that of lieutenant*, John Murray (1849)

(739a) Pappalardo, B. *Tracing your naval ancestors*, PRO (2003)

(740) Rodger, N.A.M. *Naval records for genealogists*, PRO Publications, 3rd edn (1998)

(741) Shilton, D.O. & Holworthy, R. *High Court of Admiralty examinations 1637–1638*, Anglo-American Records Foundation (1932)

(742) Smith, K., Watts, C. & Watts, M. *Records of merchant shipping and seamen*, PRO Publications (1998)

(743) Syrett, D. & DiNardo, R.L. *The commissioned sea officers of the Royal Navy 1660–1815*, Scolar Press for the Navy Records Society, revd edn (1994)

(744) Taylor, J.S. *Jonas Hanway, founder of the Marine Society, charity and policy in 18th century Britain*, Scolar Press (1985)

(745) Thomson, S.D. *The book of examinations and depositions before the Mayor and Justices of Southampton 1648–1663*, Southampton Records Series vol. 37 (1994)

(746) Toogood, C.G. & Brassey, T.A. *Index to James' naval history, edition 1886*, Navy Records Society vol. 4 (1895)

(747) Watts, C.T. & Watts, M.J. *My ancestor was a merchant seaman; how can I find out more about him?*, SoG; 2nd edn (2002)

(748) Welch, E. *The Admiralty Court book of Southampton 1566–1585*, Southampton Records Series vol. 13 (1968)

Chapter 22

(749) *Apprentices of Great Britain, series I 1710–1762 and series II 1762–1774*, SoG microfiche (1994–98)

(750) *City livery companies and related organisations; a guide to their archives in Guildhall Library*, Guildhall Library, 3rd edn (1989)

(751) *The clergy list for 1841*, C. Cox (1841)

(752) *The clerical directory 1858*, John Crockford (1858)

(753) *The Congregational year book 1920*, Congregational Union of England and Wales (1920)

(754) *The dentists' register 1885*, Spottiswoode (1885)

(755) *Guy's Hospital; nursing guide, handbook of Nurses' League, and register of nurses trained at Guy's Hospital who are members of the Nurses' League*, Guy's Hospital, 13th edn (1950)

(756) *Historical farm records, a summary guide to manuscripts and other material in the university library collected by the Institute of Agricultural History and the Museum of English Rural Life*, University of Reading (1973)

(757) *The law list 1893*, Stevens & Sons (1893)

(758) *A list of persons who have obtained certificates of their fitness and qualification to practise as apothecaries from August 1, 1815 to July 31, 1840*, SoG microfiche (1990)

(759) *Masonic year book historical supplement*, United Grand Lodge of England, 2nd edn (1969)

(759a) *The midwives roll 1905*; Central Midwives Board (1905)

(760) *The medical register 1869*, The General Council of Medicine (1869)

(761) *Nottingham alehouse recognizances 1756–1769*, Nottinghamshire FHS records series, vol. 94 (1994)

(762) *Records of British business and industry 1760–1914, textiles and leather*, HMSO (1990)

(763) *The records of the Honourable Society of Lincoln's Inn; vol. I from 1420 to 1799, vol. II admissions from 1800 to 1893 and chapel registers*, Lincoln's Inn (1896)

(764) *The registers of pharmaceutical chemists, chemists and druggists . . . 1910*, The Pharmaceutical Society of Great Britain (1910)

(765) *Students admitted to the Inner Temple 1547–1660*, Inner Temple (1877)

(766) 'Was your ancestor on the stage?' *Journal of Cambridgeshire FHS*, vol. 9 no. 5 (February 1994)

(767) *Witnesses before Parliament, a guide to the database of witnesses in committees on opposed private bills 1771–1917*, House of Lords Record Office (1997)

(768) Amherst, Lord & Le Strange, H. *History of Union Lodge, Norwich No. 52* (1898)

(769) Anstruther, G. *The seminary priests; vol. I Elizabethan, vol. II Early Stuarts 1603–1659, vol. III 1660–1715, vol. IV 1716–1800*, Mayhew-McCrimmon (1968–77)

(770) Bailey, P., Thorn, P. & Wynne-Thomas, P. *Who's who of cricketers, a complete who's who of all cricketers who have played first-class cricket in England, with full career records*, Guild Publishing (1984)

(771) Baillie, G.H. *Watchmakers and clockmakers of the world*, NAG Press, 3rd edn (1976)

(772) Batters, D. *York City, a complete record 1922–1990*, Breedon Books (1990)

(773) Beard, G. & Gilbert, C. *Dictionary of English furniture makers 1660–1840*, Furniture History Society and W.S. Murray & Son (1986)

(774) Bell, G.M. *A handlist of British diplomatic representatives 1509–1688*, RHS (1990)

(775) Bennett, J., Tough, A. & Storey, R. *Trade unions & related records*, University of Warwick, 6th edn (1991)

(776) Bindoff, S.T., Malcolm Smith, E.F. & Webster, C.K. *British diplomatic representatives 1789–1852*, RHS (1934)

(777) Bland, D.S. *A bibliography of the Inns of Court and Chancery*, Selden Society (1965)

(778) Bloom, J.H. & James, R.R. *Medical practitioners in the Diocese of London, licensed under the Act of 3 Henry VIII, c. 11, an annotated list 1529–1725*, CUP (1935)

(779) Bourne, S. & Chicken, A.H. *Records of the medical professions; a practical guide for the family historian*, Bourne & Chicken (1994)

(780) Bridgeman, I. & Emsley, C. *A guide to the archives of the police forces of England & Wales*, Police Historical Society (1990)

(781) Brooks, C.W. *The admissions registers of Barnards Inn 1620–1869*, Selden Society (1995)

(782) Brown, G.H. *Lives of the fellows of the Royal College of Physicians of London 1826–1925*, Royal College of Physicians (1955)

(783) Buchanan, I. *British Olympians, a hundred years of gold medallists*, Guinness (1991)

(784) Carr, C. *Pension book of Clement's Inn*, Selden Society (1960)

(785) Chaffers, W. *Gilda aurifabrorum, a history of English goldsmiths and plateworkers and their marks stamped on plate*, W.H. Allen (1883)

(786) Collinge, J.M. *Office-holders in modern Britain; vol. 7 Navy Board officials 1660–1832, vol. 8 Foreign Office officials 1782–1870, vol. 9 Officials of Royal Commissions of Inquiry 1815–1870*, IHR (1978–84)

(787) Colvin, H. *A biographical dictionary of British architects 1600–1840*, Yale University Press, 3rd edn (1995)

(788) Culme, J. *The directory of gold & silversmiths, jewellers and allied trades 1838–1914*, Antique Collectors' Club (1987)

(789) Daly, A. *Kingston upon Thames register of apprentices 1563–1713*, Surrey Record Society (1974)

(790) Daniell, F.H.B. *Calendar of State papers, domestic series, January to November 1671*, HMSO (1895)

(791) Dowler, G. *Gloucestershire clock and watchmakers*, Phillimore (1984)

(792) Edwards, C. *Railway records, a guide to sources*, PRO (2001)

(793) Elliott, D.J. *Shropshire clock and watchmakers*, Phillimore (1979)

(794) Evans, A. *Index to the dictionary of English furniture makers 1660–1840*, Furniture History Society (1990)

(795) Farrugia, J. *A guide to Post Office archives*, Post Office (1986) [revd edn 1996]

(796) Felstead, A., Franklin, J & Pinfield, L. *Directory of British architects 1834–1900*, Mansell Publishing (1993)

(797) Fitzgerald-Lombard, C. *English and Welsh priests 1801–1914, a working list*, Downside Abbey (1993)

(798) Floate, S.S. *My ancestors were gypsies*, SoG (1999)

(799) Fluke, B.F. *History of the St George's Chapter of Royal Arch Masons of England, No. 140, formerly called the Chapter of Hope, No. 49, 1786–1936*, Blackheath Press (1936)

(800) Foss, E. *A biographical dictionary of the judges of England . . . 1066–1870*, John Murray (1870)

(801) Foster, J. *Index ecclesiasticus*, Parker & Co (1890)

(802) Foster, J. *The register of admissions to Gray's Inn 1521–1889 together with the marriages in Gray's Inn chapel 1695–1754*, Hansard Publishing Union Ltd (1889)

(803) Gibson, J. & Hunter, J. *Victuallers' licences, records for family & local historians*, FFHS, 2nd edn amended reprint (2000)

(804) Graham, M. *Oxford City apprentices 1697–1800*, Oxford Historical Society (1987)

(805) Graves, A. *A dictionary of artists who have exhibited works in the principal London exhibitions from 1760 to 1893*, Henry Graves & Co., 2nd edn (1895)

(806) Green, B. *The Wisden book of cricketers' lives, obituaries from Wisden Cricketers' Almanack*, Macdonald (1986)

(807) Greenway, D.E. *John Le Neve Fasti ecclesiae anglicanae 1066–1300, vol. I St Paul's London, vol. II Monastic cathedrals (Northern & Southern provinces), vol. III Lincoln diocese, vol. IV Salisbury*, IHR (1968–91)

(807a) Griffiths, E. *William Windham's green book 1673–1688*, Norfolk Record Society (2002)

(808) Grimwade, A.G. *London goldsmiths 1697–1837; their marks and lives*, Faber & Faber (1976)

(808a) Grundy, J.E. *History's midwives including a C17th and C18th Yorkshire midwives nominations index*, FFHS (2003)

(809) Gunnis, R. *Dictionary of British sculptors 1660–1851*, Abbey Library, revd edn (1964)

(810) Habgood, W. *Chartered accountants in England and Wales: a guide to historical records*, MUP (1994)

(811) Hardy, T.D. *Fasti ecclesiae anglicanae or a calendar of the principal ecclesiastical dignitaries in England & Wales and of the chief officers in the universities of Oxford and Cambridge from the earliest time to the year 1715 compiled by John Le Neve, corrected and continued from 1715 to the present time*, OUP, 3 vols (1854)

(812) Harrison, E. *Office-holders in modern Britain; vol. 10 Officials of Royal Commissions of Inquiry 1870–1939*, IHR (1995)

(813) Hartley, T.G. *Hall's circuits and ministers; an alphabetical list of the circuits in Great Britain with the names of the ministers stationed in each circuit*, Methodist Publishing House, revd edn (n.d.)

(814) Harvey, J. *English medieval architects; a biographical dictionary down to 1550*, Sutton, revd edn (1984)

(815) Hasler, P.W. *The history of Parliament, the House of Commons 1558–1603*, History of Parliament Trust & HMSO (1981)

(816) Hawkings, D.T. *Railway ancestors, a guide to the staff records of the railway companies of England and Wales 1822–1947*, Sutton (1995)

(817) Hazlitt, W.C. *The livery companies of the City of London, their origin, character, development and social and political importance*, Swan Sonnenschein & Co (1892)

(818) Heal, A. *The London Goldsmiths, 1200–1800, a record of the names and addresses of the craftsmen, their shop-signs and trade cards*, CUP (1935) David & Charles reprint (1972)

(819) Henly, H.R. *The apprentice registers of the Wiltshire Society 1817–1922*, Wiltshire Record Society vol. 51 (1997)

(820) Herbert, I. *Who's who in the theatre, a biographical record of the contemporary stage*, Pitman Publishing, 16th edn (1977)

(821) Highfill, P.H., Burnim, K.A. & Langhans, E.A. *A biographical dictionary of actors, actresses, musicians, dancers, managers and other stage personnel in London 1660–1800*, 16 volumes, Southern Illinois University Press (1973–93)

(822) Holborn, G. *Sources of biographical information on past lawyers*, British and Irish Association of Law Librarians (1999)

(823) Horn, D.B. *British diplomatic representatives 1689–1789*, RHS (1932)

(824) Horn, J.M. et al. *John Le Neve Fasti ecclesiae anglicanae 1300–1541, vol. I Lincoln, vol. II Hereford, vol. III Salisbury, vol. IV Monastic cathedrals, vol. V St Paul's London, vol. VI Northern province (York, Carlisle & Durham), vol. VII Chichester, vol. VIII Bath & Wells, vol. IX Exeter, vol. X Coventry & Lichfield, vol. XI Welsh dioceses (Bangor, Llandaff, St Asaph, St Davids), vol. XII introduction and index*, compiled by J.M. Horn (vols II–V, VII, IX and XII), B. Jones (vols VI, VIII, X and XI) and H.P.F. King (vol. I); IHR (1962–67)

(825) Horn, J.M. *John Le Neve Fasti ecclesiae anglicanae 1541–1857; vol. I St Paul's London, vol. II Chichester, vol. III*

Canterbury, Rochester and Winchester, vol. IV York (with D.M. Smith), *vol. V Bath and Wells* (with D.S. Bailey), *vol. VI Salisbury, vol. VII Ely, Norwich, Westminster and Worcester, vol. VIII Bristol, Gloucester, Oxford and Peterborough, vol. IX Lincoln,* IHR (1969–99)

(826) Inderwick, F.A. & Roberts, R.A. *A calendar of the Inner Temple records 1505–1800,* vols I–V (early volumes edited by Inderwick, later volumes by Roberts), Inner Temple (1896–1936)

(827) Jackson, C.J. *English goldsmiths and their marks, a history of the goldsmiths and plate workers of England, Scotland and Ireland . . .,* Macmillan, 2nd edn (1921)

(828) Johnson, J. & Greutzner, A. *Dictionary of British art, vol. V British artists 1880–1940,* Antique Collectors' Club (1976)

(829) Judd, G.P. *Members of Parliament 1734–1832,* Yale University Press (1955)

(830) Jupp, E.B. & Pocock, W.W. *An historical account of the Worshipful Company of Carpenters of the City of London,* Pickering & Chatto, 2nd edn (1887)

(831) Kunitz, S.J. & Haycraft, H. *British authors of the nineteenth century,* H.W. Wilson (1936)

(832) Kunitz, S.J. & Haycraft, H. *British authors before 1800, a biographical dictionary,* H.W. Wilson (1952)

(833) Lewis, P. *My ancestor was a Freemason,* SoG (1999)

(834) Logan, R. *An introduction to Friendly Society records,* FFHS (2000)

(835) Marsh, B. *Records of the Worshipful Company of Carpenters, vol. I Apprentices' entry books 1654–1694, vol. II Warden's account book 1438–1516, vol. III Court book 1533–1573, vol. IV Warden's account book 1546–1571,* The Carpenters' Company (1913–16)

(836) Marsh, B. & Ainsworth, J. *Records of the Worshipful Company of Carpenters, vol. V Warden's account book 1571–1591, vol. VI Court book 1573–1594,* The Carpenters' Company (1937–39)

(837) McKenzie, D.F. *Stationer's Company apprentices 1641–1700,* Oxford Bibliographical Society (1974)

(838) McKenzie, D.F. *Stationer's Company apprentices 1701–1800,* Oxford Bibliographical Society (1978)

(839) Melling, J.K. *Discovering London's guilds and liveries,* Shire, 5th edn (1995)

(840) Millard, A.M. *Records of the Worshipful Company of Carpenters, vol. VII Warden's account book 1592–1614,* The Carpenters' Company (1968)

(841) Munk, W. *The roll of the Royal College of Physicians of London . . . biographical sketches of all the eminent physicians from the foundation of the college in 1518 to 1825,* The Royal College of Physicians; 3 vols 2nd edn (1878)

(842) Nungezer, E. *A dictionary of actors and of other persons associated with the public representation of plays in England before 1642* (1929), AMS reprint (1971)

(843) Ockerby, H. *The book of dignities containing lists of the official personages of the British Empire, civil, diplomatic, heraldic, judicial, ecclesiastical, municipal, naval and military, from the earliest periods to the present time . . .,* 3rd edn W.H. Allen (1894)

(844) Parker, J. *Who's who in the theatre, a biographical record of the contemporary stage,* Pitman, 5th edn (1926)

(845) Pickford, C. *Bedfordshire clock & watchmakers 1352–1880,* BHRS (1991)

(846) Ponsford, C.N. *Devon clocks and clockmakers,* David & Charles (1985)

(847) Probert, E.D. *Company and business records for family historians,* FFHS (1994)

(848) Raach, J.H. *A directory of English country physicians 1603–1643,* Dawsons (1962)

(849) Ralph, E. *Calendar of the Bristol apprentice book, pt III 1552–1565,* Bristol Record Society (1992)

(850) Raymond, S.A. *Londoners' occupations, a genealogical guide,* FFHS (1994)

(851) Raymond, S.A. *Occupational sources for genealogists,* FFHS, 2nd edn (1996)

(852) Reddaway, T.F. & Walker, L.E.M. *The early history of the Goldsmiths' Company 1327–1509 and the book of ordinances 1478–83,* Edward Arnold (1975)

(853) Richards, J.M. *Who's who in architecture . . . 1400 to the present day,* Weidenfeld & Nicolson (1977)

(854) Richards, T. *Was your grandfather a railwayman?, a directory of railway archive sources for family historians,* FFHS, 4th edn (2002)

(855) Ridley, J. *A history of the Carpenters' Company,* The Carpenters' Company (1995)

(856) Roskell, J.S., Clark, L. & Rawcliffe, C. *The history of Parliament, the House of Commons 1386–1421,* History of Parliament Trust & Sutton (1992)

(857) Rowe, D.J. *The records of the Company of Shipwrights of Newcastle upon Tyne 1622–1967, vol. I,* Surtees Society (1970)

(858) Ruston, A. 'Family history and the theatre'; *Hertfordshire people,* Journal of the Hertfordshire Family and Population History Society, no. 35 (Winter 1988)

(859) Ruston, A. *Transactions of the Unitarian Historical Society supplement; obituaries of Unitarian ministers 1900–1999, index and synopsis,* Unitarian Historical Society (2000)

(860) Sadie, S. *The new Grove dictionary of music & musicians,* Macmillan, 6th edn (1980)

(861) Sainty, J.C. *Office-holders in modern Britain; vol. 1 Treasury officials 1660–1870, vol. 2 Officials of the Secretaries of State 1660–1782, vol. 3 Officials of the Board of Trade 1660–1870, vol. 4 Admiralty officials 1660–1870, vol. 5 Home Office officials 1782–1870, vol. 6 Colonial Office officials 1794–1870,* IHR (1973–76)

(862) Sainty, J.C. & Bucholz, R.O. *Office-holders in modern Britain; vols 11–12 Officials of the Royal Household 1660–1837, part I Department of the Lord Chamberlain, part II Departments of the Lord Steward and Master of the Horse,* IHR (1997–98)

(863) Shaw, W.A. *Calendar of Treasury books, vol. XII April–September 1697*, HMSO (1933)

(864) Shearman, A. *My ancestor was a policeman, how can I find out more about him?*, SoG (2000)

(865) Simpson, A.W. *Biographical dictionary of the common law*, Butterworth (1984)

(866) Smith, D.M. *The Company of Merchant Taylors in the City of York, register of admissions 1560–1835*, University of York (1996)

(867) Southall, H., Gilbert, D. & Bryce, C. *Nineteenth century trade union records, an introduction and select guide*, Historical Geography Research Series (1994)

(868) Squibb, G.D. *Doctors' Commons, a history of the College of Advocates and Doctors of Law*, Clarendon Press (1977)

(869) Stanley, G. *A biographical and critical dictionary of painters and engravers by M. Bryan*, H.G. Bohn, revd edn (1853)

(870) Stenton, M. & Lees, S. *Who's who of British Members of Parliament, a biographical dictionary of the House of Commons, vol. I 1832–1885, vol. II 1886–1918, vol. III 1919–1945 vol. IV 1945–1979*, Harvester Press (1976–81)

(871) Sturgess, H.A.C. *Register of admissions to the Honourable Society of the Middle Temple from the 15th century to 1944*, Butterworth, 3 vols (1949)

(872) Talbot, C.H. & Hammond, E.A. *The medical practitioners in medieval England; a biographical register*, Wellcome Historical Medical Library (1965)

(872a) Tonks, D. *My ancestor was a coalminer*, SoG (2003)

(873) Turner, J. *Victorian arena, the performers, a dictionary of British circus biography*, 2 vols Lingdales Press (1995–2000)

(874) Wallis, P.J. & Wallis, R.V. *Eighteenth century medics (subscriptions, licences, apprenticeships)*, Project for Historical Bibliography, 2nd edn (1988)

(875) Ware, D. *A short dictionary of British architects*, Allen & Unwin (1967)

(875a) Waters, C. *A dictionary of old trades, titles and occupations*, Countryside Books, revd edn (2002)

(876) Waters, L.A. *Notes for family historians*, Police History Society (1987)

(877) Webb, C. *London apprentices, vol. 1 Brewer's Company 1685–1800, vol. 2 Tyler's and Bricklayer's Company 1612–44 & 1668–1800*, and 35 other volumes, for the following companies, from various dates up to circa 1800 in most cases; *vol. 3 Bowyers, Fletchers, Longbowstringmakers, vol. 4 Glovers, vol. 5 Glass-sellers, Woolmen, vol. 6 Broderers, Combmakers, Fanmakers, Frameworkknitters, Fruiterers, Gardeners, Horners, vol. 7 Glaziers, vol. 8 Gunmakers, vol. 9 Needlemakers, Pinmakers, vol. 10 Basketmakers, vol. 11 Distillers, vol. 12 Makers of Playing Cards, Musicians, Saddlers, Tobaccopipemakers, vol. 13 Pattenmakers, vol. 14 Spectaclemakers, Loriners, vol. 15 Gold and Silver Wyre Drawers, vol. 16 Tinplateworkers, vol. 17 Innholders, vol. 18 Poulters, vol. 19 Upholders, vol. 20 Paviors, vol. 21 Founders, vol. 22 Armourers and Brasiers, vol. 23 Coachmakers and Coach Harness Makers, vol. 24 Ironmongers, vol. 25 Dyers, vol. 26 Cooks, vol. 27 Masons, vol. 28 Farriers, vol. 29 Carmen, vol. 30 Curriers, vol. 31 Wax Chandlers, Brown Bakers, vol. 32 Apothecaries, vol. 33 Plumbers, vol. 34 Plaisterers, vol. 35 Cutlers, vol. 36 Brewers, vol. 37 Feltmakers, vol. 38 Painter-Stainers*, SoG (1996–2003)

(878) Williams, E. *Staple Inn, Customs House, Wool Court and Inn of Chancery; its medieval surroundings and associations*, Constable & Co. (1906)

(879) Williamson, G. *Bryan's dictionary of painters and engravers*, G. Bell & Sons, revd edn (1930)

(880) Willis, A.J. & Merson, A.L. *A calendar of Southampton apprenticeship registers 1609–1740*, Southampton University Press (1968)

(881) Wood, V. *The licensees of the inns, taverns and beerhouses of Banbury, Oxfordshire from the fifteenth century to today*, Oxfordshire FHS (1998)

(882) Woodcroft, B. *Alphabetical index of patentees of inventions 1617–1852* (1854), Evelyn, Adams & Mackay revd edn (1969)

Chapter 23

(883) *An act for granting an aid to His Majesty by a land tax to be raised in Great Britain for service of the year 1731*, His Majesty's Printer (1731)

(884) *Calendar of the proceedings of the Committee for Compounding 1643–1660, vol. I general proceedings, vol. II cases 1643–6, vol. III cases 1647–June 1650, vol. IV cases 1650–3, vol. V cases January 1654–December 1659*, HMSO (1889–92)

(885) *Calendar of the proceedings of the Committee for the Advance of Money 1642–1656 preserved in the State Paper Department of the PRO, parts 1–3*, HMSO (1888)

(886) *The hair powder tax, Wiltshire*, Wiltshire FHS (1997)

(887) Erskine, A.M. *The Devonshire lay subsidy of 1332*, DCRS (1969)

(888) Faraday, M.A. *Herefordshire militia assessments of 1663*, RHS (1972)

(889) Fenwick, C.C. *The poll taxes of 1377, 1379 and 1381*, OUP for the British Academy, 2 vols (1998–2001)

(890) Gibson, J. *The hearth tax, other later Stuart tax lists and the association oath rolls*, FFHS, 2nd edn (1996)

(891) Gibson, J. & Dell, A. *The protestation returns 1641–42 and other contemporary listings; collection in aid of distressed Protestants in Ireland, subsidies, poll tax, assessments or grants, vow and covenant, solemn league and covenant*, FFHS (1995)

(892) Gibson, J., Medlycott, M. & Mills, D. *Land and window tax assessments*, FFHS, 2nd edn (1998)

(892a) Hawkings, D. *Fire insurance records for family and local historians*, Francis Boutle Publishers (2003)

(893) Hoyle, R. *Tudor taxation records, a guide for users*, PRO Publications (1994)

(894) Hoyle, R. *The military survey of Gloucestershire 1522*, Bristol and Gloucestershire Archaeological Society (1993)

(895) Jones, P.E. *17th century taxation in Hammersmith*, Hammersmith Local History Group (1970)

(896) Jurkowski, M., Smith, C. & Crook, D. *Lay taxes in England and Wales 1188–1688*, PRO Publications (1998)

(897) Lang, R.G. *Two Tudor subsidy rolls for the City of London: 1541 and 1582*, London Record Society, vol. 29 (1993)

(898) Leeson, F. *A guide to the records of the British state tontines and life annuities of the 17th & 18th centuries*, Pinhorns (1968)

(899) Leeson, F. *Index to the British state tontine and annuities 1745–1779*, SoG microfiche (1994)

(900) Meekings, C.A. *The hearth tax 1662–1689, exhibition of records*, PRO (1962)

(901) Ramsay, G.D. *Two sixteenth century taxation lists 1545 and 1576*, Wiltshire Archaeological & Natural History Society, records branch vol. X (1954)

(902) Schurer, K. & Arkell, T. *Surveying the people; the interpretation and use of document sources for the study of population in the later 17th century*, Leopard's Head Press (1992)

(903) Seaman, P. *Norfolk and Norwich hearth tax assessment, Lady Day 1666*, Norfolk & Norwich Genealogical Society (1988)

(904) Stoate, T.L. *Devon lay subsidy rolls, 1543–5*, T.L. Stoate (1986)

(905) Stoate, T.L. *Devon lay subsidy rolls, 1524–7*, T.L. Stoate (1979)

(906) Stoate, T.L. *Devon hearth tax return, Lady Day 1674*, T.L. Stoate (1982)

Chapter 24

(907) *An alphabetical list of all the bankrupts 1774 to 1786*, J. Jarvis (1786) SoG microfiche reprint

(908) *Calendars of the proceedings in Chancery in the reign of Queen Elizabeth*, 3 vols The Record Commission (1827–32)

(909) *Collections for a history of Staffordshire*, N.S. vol. VII and 3rd series, volumes for 1926, 1931 and 1938, William Salt Archaeological Society (1904–38)

(910) *Collections for a history of Staffordshire*, N.S. vol. X and 3rd series, volumes for 1910 and 1912, William Salt Archaeological Society (1907–12)

(911) *Curia Regis rolls of the reigns of Richard I and John preserved in the PRO, vol. VII 15–16 John, appendix 7 Richard I – 1 John*, HMSO (1935)

(912) *The English reports, vol. XXI, Chancery I, containing Cary, Choyce cases in Chancery, Tothill, Dickens, reports in Chancery vols I to III, Nelson and equity cases abridged, vol. I*, Stevens & Sons (1902) Professional Books reprint (1987)

(913) *The English reports, vol. CLXI, Ecclesiastical, Admiralty, Probate & Divorce I, containing Lee, vols 1 and 2, Haggard (Consistory) vols 1 and 2, Phillimore, vols 1 and 2*, Stevens & Sons (1902) reprint by Professional Books (1986)

(914) *The English reports, index of cases A to K*, William Green & Sons (1932) reprint by Professional Books (1986)

(915) *The English reports, index of cases L to Z*, William Green & Sons (1932) reprint by Professional Books (1986)

(916) *The 42nd annual report of the Deputy Keeper of the Public Records*, HMSO (1881)

(917) *Index of Chancery proceedings, Bridges division 1613–1714, R-Z*, PRO Lists & Indexes, HMSO (1917)

(918) *The manuscripts of the House of Lords, vol. I (new series)*, HMSO (1964)

(919) Addy, J. *Death, money and the vultures*, Routledge (1992)

(920) Bell, H.E. *An introduction to the history and records of the Court of Wards and Liveries*, CUP (1953)

(921) Bolton, J.L. & Maslen, M.M. *Calendar of the court books of the borough of Witney 1538–1610*, Oxfordshire Record Society vol. 54 (1985)

(922) Bond, M.F. *Guide to the records of Parliament*, HMSO (1971)

(923) Bridgeman, G. *The all England law reports reprint, index & table of cases 1558–1935*, Butterworth (1968)

(924) Brinkworth, E.R.C. *Shakespeare and the bawdy court of Stratford*, Phillimore (1972)

(925) Bryson, W.H. *The equity side of the Exchequer, its jurisdiction, administration, procedures and records*, CUP (1975)

(926) Chapman, C.R. *Sin, sex and probate, ecclesiastical courts, their officials and their records*, Lochin Publishing, 2nd edn (1997)

(927) Christie, P. *Of chirche-reeves and of testamentes; the church, sex and slander in Elizabethan north Devon*, Devon FHS (1994)

(928) Coldham, P.W. *Index to disputed estates in Chancery, Mitford division C 8 1575–1714*, transcript P.W. Coldham (1978)

(929) Dasent, J.R. *Acts of the Privy Council of England; new series, vol. V. 1554–1556*, HMSO (1892)

(930) Drake, J.H. *Oxford church courts, depositions 1542–1550*, Oxfordshire County Council (1991)

(931) Emmison, F.G. *Elizabethan life; morals & the church courts*, Essex County Council (1973)

(932) Fry, E.A. *Index of Chancery proceedings (Reynardson's division), 1649–1714, vol. I A to K*, BRS vol. 29 (1903)

(933) Garrett, R.E.F. *Chancery and other legal proceedings*, Pinhorns (1968)

(934) Gerhold, D. *Courts of equity, guide to Chancery & other legal records for local and family historians*, Pinhorns (1994)

(935) Giese, L.L. *London Consistory Court depositions, 1586–1611: list and indexes*, London Record Society (1995)

(936) Guy, J.A. *The Court of Star Chamber & its records to the reign of Elizabeth I*, HMSO (1985)

(937) Hemmant, M. *Select cases in the Exchequer Chamber before all the Justices of England 1377–1461*, Selden Society vol. 51 (1933)

(938) Horwitz, H. *Chancery equity records and proceedings 1600–1800*, PRO Publications, 2nd edn (1998)

(939) Horwitz, H. *Exchequer equity records and proceedings 1649–1841*, PRO (2001)

(940) Horwitz, H. & Moreton, C. *Samples of Chancery pleadings and suits, 1627, 1685, 1735 and 1785*, LIS, vol. 257 (1995)

(941) Houston, J. *Cases in the Court of Arches 1660–1913*, BRS, vol. 85 (1972)

(942) Hoyle, R.W. & Norris, M.M. *Calendar of Chancery decree rolls C 78/86–130*, LIS, vol. 254 (1994)

(943) Ingram, M. *Church courts, sex and marriage in England, 1570–1640*, CUP (1990)

(944) Jones, P.E. *The Fire Court, calendar to the judgments and decrees of the court of judicature appointed to determine differences between landlords and tenants as to rebuilding after the Great Fire, vols I & II*, William Clowes & Sons (1966–70)

(945) Leadam, I.S. *Select cases in the Court of Requests 1497–1569*, Selden Society, vol. 12 (1898)

(946) Leadam, I.S. *Select cases before the King's Council in the Star Chamber, commonly called the Court of Star Chamber, vol. I 1477–1509, vol. II 1509–44*, Selden Society vols 16 and 25 (1903–11)

(947) Nicholls, Y. *Court of Augmentations accounts for Bedfordshire*, BHRS, vols 63 and 64 (1984–85)

(948) Richardson, W. *History of the Court of Augmentations 1536–1554*, Louisiana State University Press (1961)

(949) Smith, D.M. *Guide to bishops' registers of England and Wales, a survey from the middle ages to the abolition of the Episcopacy in 1646*, RHS (1981)

(950) Spufford, P. *Index to the probate accounts of England and Wales*, BRS vols 112–113 (1998–99)

(951) Tarver, A. *Church court records, an introduction for family historians*, Phillimore (1995)

(952) Sharpe, H. *How to use the Bernau index*, SoG, 2nd edn (2000)

(953) Thomas, A.H. *Calendar of plea and memoranda rolls of the City of London 1413–37*, CUP (1943)

(954) Warne, A. *Church and society in 18th-century Devon*, Augustus Kelley (1969)

(955) Webb, C. *Surrey cases & deponents in the Court of Exchequer 1561–1835*, West Surrey FHS (1994)

(956) Webb, C. *London's bawdy courts, volume 1 1703–1713, Consistory Court of London, index to cases and depositions (with birthplaces)*, SoG (1999)

(957) Webb, C. *Handlist and index to Surrey cases and depositions in the Court of Requests c.1500–1624*, West Surrey FHS (1999)

(958) Willis, A.J. *Winchester Consistory Court depositions 1561–1602*, A.J. Willis (1960)

(959) Willis, A.J. *Canterbury licences (general) 1568–1646 (Diocese of Canterbury)*, Phillimore (1972)

Chapter 25

(960) *Bedfordshire county records, notes and extracts from the county records comprised in the Quarter Sessions rolls from 1714 to 1832*, Bedfordshire County Council (1907?)

(961) *British trials 1660–1900*, Chadwyck Healey (1990 and continuing)

(962) Bettey, J.H. *The casebook of Sir Francis Ashley JP, recorder of Dorchester 1614–35*, Dorset Record Society (1981)

(963) Byrne, R. *Prisons and punishments of London*, Grafton (1989)

(964) Cale, M. *Law and society; an introduction to sources for criminal and legal history from 1800*, PRO Publications (1996)

(965) Chambers, J. *Criminal petitions index, 1819–39, parts 1–4 pieces HO 17/40–79*, J. Chambers (n.d.)

(966) Cheney, M. *Chronicles of the damned; the crimes and punishments of the condemned felons of Newgate Gaol*, Marston House (1992)

(967) Cirket, A.F. *Samuel Whitbread's notebooks 1810–1811, 1813–1814*, BHRS, vol. 50 (1971)

(968) Cockburn, J.S. *A history of English assizes 1558–1714*, CUP (1972)

(969) Cockburn, J.S. *Western circuit assize orders 1629–1648, a calendar*, RHS (1976)

(970) Cockburn, J.S. *Calendar of assize records, home circuit indictments*, 11 vols Elizabeth I: Essex, Hertfordshire, Kent, Surrey and Sussex, James I: Essex, Hertfordshire, Kent, Surrey and Sussex, & introduction volume, HMSO (1975–85)

(971) Cockburn, J.S. *Calendar of assize records, Kent indictments Charles I*, HMSO (1995)

(972) Cockburn, J.S. *Calendar of assize records, Kent indictments 1649–1659*, HMSO (1989)

(973) Cockburn, J.S. *Calendar of assize records, Kent indictments Charles II 1660–1675*, HMSO (1995)

(974) Crook, D. *Records of the General Eyre*, HMSO (1982)

(975) Emmison, F.G. *Elizabethan life; disorder*, Essex County Council (1970)

(976) Gibson, J. *Quarter Sessions records for family historians, a select list*, FFHS, 4th edn (1995)

(977) Gibson, J. & Rogers, C. *Coroners' records in England and Wales*, FFHS, 2nd edn amended reprint (2000)

(978) Goodacre, K. & Mercer, E.D. *Guide to the Middlesex Sessions records 1549–1889*, GLRO (1965)

(979) Gray, A. *Crime and criminals in Victorian Essex*, Countryside Books (1988)

(980) Gray, I.E. & Gaydon, A.T. *Gloucestershire Quarter Sessions archives 1660–1889 and other official records*, Gloucestershire County Council (1958)

(981) Griffiths, A. *The chronicles of Newgate* (1883) reprinted Dorset Press (1987)

(982) Groom, N. *The Bloody Register. A select and judicious collection of the most remarkable trials for murder, treason, rape, sodomy, highway robbery, piracy . . . and other high crimes and misdemeanours from the year 1700 to the year 1764 inclusive*, E. & M. Viney (1764) reprinted RKP/Thoemmes Press (1999)

(983) Harrison, P. *Devon murders*, Countryside Books (1992)

(984) Hawkings, D.T. *Criminal ancestors; a guide to historical criminal records in England & Wales*, Sutton (1992)

(985) Herber, M.D. *Criminal London, a pictorial history from medieval times to 1939*, Phillimore (2002)

(986) Howell, T.B. (continued by T.J. Howell) *A complete collection of state trials and proceedings for high treason and other crimes and misdemeanours from the earliest period to the present time*, 34 vols, the first 10 volumes edited by W. Cobbett as *Cobbett's complete collection of state trials*, R. Bagshaw et al. (1809–28)

(987) Hunnisett, R.F. *Wiltshire coroners' bills 1752–1796*, Wiltshire Record Society (1981)

(988) Hunnisett, R.F. *Sussex coroners' inquests 1558–1603*, PRO Publications (1996)

(989) Hurley, B. *Fisherton Anger gaol matron's journal*, Wiltshire FHS (1997)

(990) Johnson, D.A. *Staffordshire assize calendars 1842–1843*, Collections for a history of Staffordshire, 4th series, vol. 15, Staffordshire Record Society (1992)

(991) Johnson, H.C. *Warwick county records vol. VIII, Quarter Sessions records, Trinity 1682 to Epiphany 1690*; L. Edgar Stephens (1953)

(992) Lamoine, G. *Bristol gaol delivery fiats 1741–1799*, Bristol Record Society vol. 40 (1989)

(993) Le Hardy, W. *Hertfordshire county records, calendar to the sessions books, sessions minute books and other sessions records, with appendices; vol. VIII 1752 to 1799; vol. X, 1833 to 1843*, Hertfordshire County Council (1935 and 1957)

(994) Le Hardy, W. *Guide to the Hertfordshire record office, part I, Quarter Sessions and other records . . .*, N. Moon (1961)

(995) Lemon, R. *Calendar of State Papers, domestic series of the reigns of Edward VI, Mary and Elizabeth, 1547–1580*, HMSO (1856)

(996) Linebaugh, P. *The London hanged; crime & civil society in the 18th century*, Verso, 2nd edn (2003)

(997) MacDonnell, J. *Reports of state trials, new series*, 8 vols, HMSO (1888–1898)

(998) Rayner, J.L. & Crook, G.T. *The complete Newgate calendar*, The Navarre Society (1926)

(999) Reddington, J. *Calendar of Home Office papers of the reign of George III, vol. I 1760 (25 Oct.) to 1765, vol. II 1766–1769*, HMSO (1878–79)

(1000) Renold, P. *Banbury gaol records*, Banbury Historical Society, vol. 18 (1987)

(1001) Roberts, R.A. *Calendar of Home Office papers of the reign of George III 1770–1772*, HMSO (1881)

(1002) Shore, W.T. *Notable British trials, trial of Thomas Neill Cream*, William Hodge (1923)

(1003) Sutherland, D. *The eyre of Northamptonshire 3–4 Edward III, 1329–30, vol. I*, Selden Society (1983)

(1004) Webb, A.J. & Parrish, P. *The Wilton gaol description register 1806–1818*, and *The Wilton gaol description register 1818–1825*, Harry Galloway Publishing (1994–97)

(1005) Webb, C. *Petty session minutes; Copthorne and Effingham hundreds 1784–93*, West Surrey FHS (1989)

(1006) Wilkinson, G.T. *The Newgate calendar*, Sphere Books (1991)

Chapter 26

(1007) *Burke's family index*, Burke's Peerage (1976)

(1008) *Burke's genealogical and heraldic history of the peerage, baronetage and knightage*, Burke's Peerage, 99th edn (1949)

(1009) *Burke's guide to the Royal family*, Burke's Peerage (1973)

(1010) *The coat of arms*, The Heraldry Society, no. 161 (Spring 1993) and no. 165 (Spring 1994)

(1011) *The concise dictionary of national biography, from earliest times to 1985*, OUP (1992)

(1012) *Debrett's peerage, baronetage, knightage and companionage 1890*, Debrett's (1890)

(1013) *Dod's peerage, baronetage & knightage of Great Britain and Ireland for 1913*, Simpkin Marshall (1913)

(1014) *Kelly's handbook to the titled, landed and official classes*, Kelly & Co, 7th edn (1881)

(1014a) *The register of the George Cross*, This England, revd edn (1990)

(1015) *Whitaker's peerage, baronetage, knightage and companionage for the year 1910*, Whitaker's Peerage (1913)

(1016) *Who's who 1916; an annual biographical dictionary*, A&C Black (1916)

(1017) *Who's who in Norfolk*, Baylis (1935)

(1018) *Who was who, a companion to 'Who's who' containing the biographies of those who died during the period 1897–1916*, A&C Black (1920)

(1019) *Who was who, a companion to 'Who's who' containing the biographies of those who died during the period 1951–1960*, A&C Black (1961)

(1020) Ashley, M. *British monarchs, the complete genealogy, gazetteer and biographical encyclopedia of the Kings and Queens of Great Britain*, Robinson (1998)

(1021) Blaydes, F.A. *The visitations of Bedfordshire, 1566, 1582 and 1634*, Harleian Society, vol. 19 (1884)

(1022) Boase, F. *Modern English biography containing many thousand concise memoirs of persons who died between the years 1851–1900*, Frank Cass & Co. (1965)

(1023) Brooke-Little, J. *Boutell's heraldry*, Frederick Warne, revd edn (1983)

(1024) Burke, B. *A genealogical history of the dormant, abeyant, forfeited and extinct peerages of the British Empire*, Burke's Peerage (1883)

(1025) Burke, B. *The general armory of England, Scotland, Ireland and Wales comprising a registry of armorial bearings from the earliest to the present time*, Harrison & Sons (1884), Burke's Peerage reprint (1961)

(1026) Burke, B. *The Royal families of England, Scotland and Wales with pedigrees of royal descents in illustration*, Harrison 2nd edn (1876)

(1027) Burke, J.B. *A genealogical and heraldic history of the extinct & dormant baronetcies of England, Ireland & Scotland*, J.R. Smith, 2nd edn (1884), Burke's Peerage reprint (1964)

(1028) Butters, L. *Fairbairn's crests of the families of Great Britain & Ireland*, 4th edn (1905) reprint by Heraldry Today (1996)

(1029) Cokayne, G.E. *The complete peerage*, St. Catherine's Press, 2nd edn by V. Gibbs, H.A. Doubleday et al., 13 vols (1910–59)

(1030) Cokayne, G.E. *The complete baronetage*, W. Pollard & Co. (1900–06), Sutton reprint (1983)

(1031) Fevyer, W.H. *The George Medal*, Spink (1980)

(1032) Foster, J. *The dictionary of heraldry; feudal coats of arms & pedigrees*, Studio Editions (1994)

(1033) Foster, J. *The visitation of Yorkshire made in the years 1584/5 by Robert Glover, Somerset Herald, to which is added the subsequent visitation made in 1612 by Richard St George, Norroy King of Arms, with several additional pedigrees*, Surtees Society (1875)

(1034) Fox-Davies, A. *A complete guide to heraldry*, T. Nelson & Sons, revised by J. P. Brooke-Little (1969)

(1035) Fox-Davies, A.C. *Armorial families, a directory of gentlemen of coat-armour*, T. & E. Jack (1929) David & Charles reprint (1970)

(1036) Friar, S. *A new dictionary of heraldry*, Alphabooks (1987)

(1037) Friar, S. *Heraldry for the local historian and genealogist*, Sutton revd edn (1996)

(1038) Galloway, P., Stanley, D. & Martin, S. *Royal service vol. I, The Royal Victorian Order, The Royal Victorian Medal, The Royal Victorian Chain*, Victorian Publishing (1996)

(1039) Given-Wilson, C. & Curteis, A. *The royal bastards of mediaeval England*, RKP (1984)

(1040) Green, E. *The visitation of the county of Lincoln made by Sir Edward Bysshe, knight, Clarenceux King of Arms 1666*, Lincoln Record Society (1917)

(1041) Hammond, P.W. *The complete peerage, volume XIV addenda & corrigenda*, Sutton (1998)

(1042) Henderson, D.V. *Heroic endeavour, a complete register of the Albert, Edward and Empire gallantry medals and how they were won*, Hayward (1988)

(1043) Holmes, G. *The Order of the Garter: its knights and stall plates 1348 to 1984* (1984)

(1044) Humphery-Smith, C.R. *General armory two, Alfred Morant's additions & corrections to Burke's general armory*, Tabard Press (1973)

(1045) Humphery-Smith, C.R. *Armigerous ancestors and those who weren't; a catalogue of visitation records together with an index of pedigrees, arms and disclaimers*, IHGS (1997)

(1046) Kidd, C. & Williamson, D. *Debrett's peerage and baronetage 1990*, Debrett's Peerage (1990)

(1047) Leeson, F. *A directory of British peerages*, SoG, revd edn (2002)

(1048) Lodge, E. *The peerage and baronetage of the British Empire as at present existing*, Hurst & Blackett, 56th edn (1890)

(1049) Louda, J. & MacLagan, M. *Lines of succession, heraldry of the Royal families of Europe*, Little, Brown & Company, revd edn (1999)

(1050) Montague-Smith, P. *The Royal line of succession*, Pitkin Pictorials (1974)

(1051) Mosley, C. *Burke's peerage and baronetage*, Burke's Peerage (Genealogical Books) Ltd, 106th edn (1999)

(1051a) Nicholls, C.S. *The dictionary of national biography: missing persons*, OUP (1993)

(1052) Ormond, R. & Rogers, M. (eds) *Dictionary of British portraiture*, vols 1 and 4 compiled by A. Davies, vols 2 and 3 compiled by E. Kilmurray, Batsford (1979–81)

(1053) Papworth, J.W. & Morant, A.W. *An alphabetical dictionary of coats of arms belonging to families in Great Britain and Ireland forming an extensive ordinary of British armorials*, T. Richards (1874); reprint by Tabard Publications as *Papworth's ordinary of British armorials* with an introduction by G.D. Squibb & A.R. Wagner (1961)

(1054) Pike, W.T. *London at the opening of the twentieth century; contemporary biographies*, W.T. Pike & Co (1905)

(1055) Pinches, J.H. & Pinches, R.V. *The Royal heraldry of England*, Heraldry Today (1974)

(1056) Pine, L.G. *The new extinct peerage 1884–1971*, Heraldry Today (1972)

(1057) Ruvigny & Raineval, Marquis of. *The blood royal of Britain, being a roll of the living descendants of Edward IV and Henry VII . . .* (also known as *The Tudor roll of the blood royal of Britain*); T. & E. Jack (1903)

(1058) Ruvigny & Raineval, Marquis of. *The Plantagenet roll of the blood royal, being a complete table of all the descendants now living of Edward III, King of England*, 4 vols, the *Clarence volume* (descendants of George, Duke of Clarence); the *Anne of Exeter volume* (descendants of Anne Plantagenet, Duchess of Exeter); the *Isabel of Essex volume* (descendants of Isabel Plantagenet Countess of Essex and Eu) and the *Mortimer-Percy volume* (descendants of Lady Elizabeth Percy née Mortimer; T.C & E.C Jack (1907–11)

(1059) Shaw, W.A. *The knights of England, a complete record from the earliest time to the present day of the knights of all the orders of chivalry in England, Scotland and Ireland, and of Knights Bachelor*, Sherratt & Hughes (1906)

(1060) Squibb, G.D. *The visitation of Nottinghamshire, 1662–4*, Harleian Society, N.S. vol. 5 (1986)

(1061) Stephen, L. & Lee, S. *Dictionary of national biography*, Smith, Elder & Co (1885 and continuing)

(1062) Thorpe, A.W. *Burke's handbook to the most excellent Order of the British Empire*, The Burke Publishing Co. (1921), LSE reprint (1988)

(1063) Townend, P. *Burke's genealogical and heraldic history of the landed gentry*; Burke's Peerage, 18th edn 3 vols (1965–72)

(1064) Wagner, A.R. *A catalogue of English mediaeval rolls of arms*, Harleian Society (1948)

(1065) Wagner, A.R. *The records & collections of the College of Arms*, Burke's Peerage (1952)

(1066) Walford, E. *The county families of the United Kingdom*, Robert Hardwicke, 1st edn (1860)

(1067) Weir, A. *Britain's Royal families, the complete genealogy*, Random House, revd edn (1996)

(1068) Williamson, D. *Debrett's guide to heraldry and regalia*, Headline (1992)

(1069) Wollaston, G.W. *Knights Bachelor 1939–1946*, a list of the existing recipients of the honour of knighthood, together with a short account of the origin, objects, and work of the Imperial Society of Knights Bachelor, 20th edn (1946)

(1070) Woodcock, T. & Robinson, J. M. *The Oxford guide to heraldry*, OUP (1988)

(1071) Woodcock, T. et al. *Dictionary of British arms; medieval ordinary*, vol. I (with H. Chesshyre), vol. II (with J. Grant and I. Graham); Heraldry Today (1996)

Chapter 27

(1072) *Calendar of inquisitions post mortem and other analogous documents; vol. II, Edward I*, HMSO (1906)

(1073) *Calendar of the Charter Rolls preserved in the Public Record Office, vol. VI 5 Henry VI to 8 Henry VIII 1427–1516*, HMSO (1927)

(1074) *Calendar of the Close Rolls preserved in the Public Record Office, Edward II 1313–1318*, HMSO (1893)

(1075) *Calendar of the Close Rolls preserved in the Public Record Office, Henry VII, vol. I 1485–1500*, HMSO (1893)

(1076) *Calendar of the Fine Rolls; vol. XXII, Henry VII, 1485–1509*, HMSO (1962)

(1077) *Calendar of the Memoranda Rolls (Exchequer) preserved in the Public Record Office, Michaelmas 1326–Michaelmas 1327*, HMSO (1968)

(1078) *Calendar of the Patent Rolls, Edward IV, Edward V, Richard III, 1476–1485*, HMSO (1901)

(1079) *Catalogue of additions to the manuscripts in the British Museum 1861–1875*, Trustees of the British Museum (1877) reprinted (1967)

(1080) *A descriptive catalogue of ancient deeds in the PRO, vol. I*, HMSO (1890)

(1081) *A descriptive catalogue of ancient deeds in the PRO, vol. VI*, HMSO (1915)

(1082) *Facsimiles of national manuscripts from William the Conqueror to Queen Anne . . . part I*, Ordnance Survey Office (1865)

(1083) *Feet of fines of the Tudor period, part II, 1571–1582*, Yorkshire Archaeological and Topographical Association (1888)

(1084) *Guide to the location of collections described in the reports and calendars series 1870–1980*, HMSO (1982)

(1085) *Guide to the Russell estate collections for Bedfordshire and Devon to 1910 deposited in the county record offices at Bedford and Exeter*, Bedfordshire County Council (1966)

(1086) *Historical Manuscripts Commission; report on manuscripts in various collections, vol. IV; the manuscripts of the Bishop of Salisbury, Bishop of Exeter, etc . . .*, HMSO (1907)

(1087) *Index of manuscripts in the British Library*, 10 vols Chadwyck-Healey (1986)

(1088) *Journal of the Bristol & Avon FHS*, no. 15 (Spring 1979)

(1089) Alcock, N.W. *Old title deeds, a guide for local and family historians*, Phillimore, revd edn (2001)

(1090) Baber, A.F.C. *The court rolls of the manor of Bromsgrove and King's Norton 1494–1504*, Wiltshire Historical Society (1963)

(1091) Bennett, H.S. *Life on the English manor 1150–1400, a study of peasant conditions*, CUP (1938)

(1092) Bickley, F. *Guide to the reports of the Royal Commission on Historical Manuscripts 1870–1911, part II, index of persons*, HMSO (1935)

(1093) Brown, W. *Yorkshire inquisitions of the reigns of Henry III and Edward I, vol. I*, Yorkshire Archaeological and Topographical Association (1892)

(1094) Carlin, M. *London and Southwark inventories 1316–1650, a handlist of extents for debts*, University of London (1997)

(1095) Conyers, A. *Wiltshire extents for debts Edward I–Elizabeth I*, Wiltshire Record Society (1973)

(1096) Cornwall, J. *An introduction to reading old title deeds*, FFHS (1993)

(1097) Darlington, I. *Survey of London, vol. XXV, St George's Fields, the parishes of St George the Martyr, Southwark and St Mary Newington*, London County Council (1955)

(1098) Davis, G.R.C. *Medieval cartularies of Great Britain, a short catalogue*, Longmans (1958)

(1099) Dibben, A.A. *Title deeds*, Historical Association, revd edn (1990)

(1100) Dodd, K.M. *The field book of Walsham-le-willows 1577*, Suffolk Record Society (1974)
(1101) Earwaker, J.P. *The Court Leet records of the manor of Manchester . . . 1552 to 1686 and . . . 1731 to 1846*, City of Manchester, 12 vols (1884–90)
(1102) Ellis, H.J. & Bickley, F.B. *Index to the charters and rolls in the Department of Manuscripts, British Museum, vol. I Index locorum, vol. II Religious houses and other corporations and index locorum for acquisitions from 1882 to 1900*, Trustees of the British Museum (1900–12)
(1103) Ellis, M. *Using manorial records*, PRO Publications (1994)
(1104) Emmison, F.G. *Elizabethan life; home, work & land from Essex wills and sessions and manorial records*, Essex Record Office (1991)
(1105) Finn, R.W. *Domesday Book; a guide*, Phillimore (1986)
(1106) Fry, E.A. *A calendar of inquisitions post mortem for Cornwall and Devon from Henry III to Charles I, 1216–1649*, DCRS (1906)
(1107) Gomme, G.L. *Court rolls of Tooting Beck manor, vol. I*, London County Council (1909)
(1108) Hall, E.C.S. *Guide to the reports of the Royal Commission on Historical Manuscripts 1911–1957, part II, index of persons, vol. I, A-Foullon*, HMSO (1966)
(1109) Harvey, P.D.A. *Manorial records*, Sutton for the BRA (1984)
(1110) Hone, N.J. *The manor and manorial records*, Methuen, 2nd edn (1912)
(1111) Keene, D. *Winchester studies 2: Survey of medieval Winchester*, Clarendon Press (1985)
(1112) Kirby, J.W. *The manor and borough of Leeds, 1425–1662, an edition of documents*, Thoresby Society (1983)
(1113) Le Patourel, J. *Documents relating to the manor and borough of Leeds, 1066–1400*, Thoresby Society (1956)
(1114) Lewis, F.B. *Pedes finium, or fines relating to the county of Surrey . . . 7 Richard I to the end of the reign of Henry VII*, Surrey Archaeological Society (1894)
(1115) London, V.C.M. *The cartulary of Bradenstoke Priory*, Wiltshire Record Society (1979)
(1116) McLaughlin, E. *Manorial records*, E. McLaughlin (1996)
(1117) Meekings, C.A.F. *Abstracts of Surrey feet of fines 1509–1558*, Surrey Record Society, vol. XIX (1946)
(1118) Metters, G.A. *The parliamentary survey of Dean & Chapter properties in and around Norwich in 1649*, Norfolk Record Society, vol. 51 (1985)
(1119) Mills, M.H. *The Pipe Roll for 1295, Surrey membrane*, Surrey Record Society, vol. VII (1924)
(1120) Morris, J. *Domesday Book, vol. 20, Bedfordshire*, Phillimore (1977)
(1121) Mortimer, I. *Berkshire glebe terriers*, Berkshire Record Society, vol. 2 (1995)
(1122) O'Connor, S.J. *A calendar of the cartularies of John Pyel and Adam Fraunceys*, RHS (1993)
(1123) Overton, E. *A guide to the medieval manor*, Local History Publications (1994)
(1124) Palgrave-Moore, P. *How to locate and use manorial records*, Elvery Dowers (1985?)
(1125) Park, P.B. *My ancestors were manorial tenants; how can I find out more about them?*, SoG, revd edn (2002)
(1126) Peckham, W.D. *Thirteen custumals of the Sussex manors of the Bishop of Chichester and other documents*, Sussex Record Society (1925)
(1127) Reed, M. *Buckinghamshire glebe terriers*, Buckinghamshire Record Society, vol. 30 (1997)
(1128) Reichel, O.J. & Prideaux, F.B. *Devon feet of fines, vol. I 1196 to 1272 and vol. II 1272 to 1369*, DCRS (1912 and 1939)
(1129) Sayers, J. *Estate documents at Lambeth Palace Library, a short catalogue*, Leicester University Press (1965)
(1130) Stuart, D. *Manorial records; an introduction to their transcription and translation*, Phillimore (1992)
(1131) Thorn, C. & Thorn, F. (eds) *Domesday Book, vol. 9 Devon (part I)*, Phillimore (1985)
(1132) Webb, C. *A guide to Surrey manorial records*, West Surrey FHS (1993)
(1133) Webb, C. *A guide to London & Middlesex manorial records*, West Surrey FHS (1995)
(1134) Willan, T.S. & Crossley, E.W. *Three 17th century Yorkshire surveys*, YAS (1941)

Chapter 28

(1135) Camp, A.J. *My ancestors moved in England and Wales; how can I trace where they came from?*, SoG (1994)
(1136) Gibson, J. & Creaton, H. *Lists of Londoners*, FFHS, 3rd edn (1999)
(1137) Rogers, C. *Tracing missing persons; an introduction to agencies, methods & sources in England and Wales*, MUP, 2nd edn (1985)
(1138) Webb, C. *My ancestors were Londoners; how can I find out more about them?*, SoG, 3rd edn (1999)

Chapter 29

(1139) *Channel Islands FHS journal*, no. 66 (Spring 1995)
(1140) *Directory of parish registers indexed in Ireland*, Irish FHS 3rd edn (1997)
(1141) *The Edinburgh Academy register, a record of all those who have entered the school since its foundation in 1824*, Edinburgh Academical Club (1914)

(1142) *The Fettes College register 1870 to 1932*, Edinburgh University Press (1933)

(1143) *The Glenalmond register, a record of all those who have entered Trinity College, Glenalmond 1847–1929*, Old Glenalmond Club (1929)

(1144) *Guide to the manuscripts and records, the National Library of Wales*, NLW (1994)

(1145) *Guide to the National Archives of Scotland, Scottish Record Office*, The Stair Society & The Stationery Office (1996)

(1146) *Irish roots*, Belgrave Publications, 1995, no. 3 (1995)

(1147) *Northern Ireland newspapers 1737–1987, a checklist with locations*, Library Association (Northern Ireland branch) and PRONI, 2nd revd edn (1987)

(1148) *The parishes, registers and registrars of Scotland*, SAFHS (1993)

(1149) *The records of the Forfeited Estates Commission*, HMSO (1968)

(1150) *University of Edinburgh roll of honour 1914–1919*, Oliver and Boyd (1921)

(1151) *University of Wales, the calendar for the academic year 1939–1940*, University of Wales Press Board (1939)

(1152) Adam, F. *The clans, septs and regiments of the Scottish highlands*, revised by Sir Thomas Innes of Learney; Johnson & Bacon, 8th edn (1970), reprint (1984)

(1153) Backhurst, M. *Family history in Jersey*, Channel Islands FHS (1991)

(1154) Balfour-Paul, Sir J. *The Scots peerage*, David Douglas, 9 vols (1904–14)

(1154a) Ball, F.E. *The judges in Ireland, 1221–1921*, John Murray (1926) reprint by Round Hall Press (1993)

(1155) Balleine, G.R. *A biographical dictionary of Jersey*, Staples Press, reprinted by La Haule Books (1993)

(1156) Black, G.F. *The surnames of Scotland: their origin, meaning & history*, New York Public Library (1946)

(1157) Bertie, D.M. *Scottish episcopal clergy 1689–2000*, T&T Clark (2000)

(1158) Boylan, H. *A dictionary of Irish biography*, Gill and Macmillan (1978)

(1159) Burke, B. *Burke's Irish family records*; Burke's Peerage, 5th edn (1976) previously published as *Burke's landed gentry of Ireland* in 1899, 1904, 1912 and 1958

(1160) Burtchaell, G.D. & Sadleir, T. *Alumni Dublinenses: a register of the students, graduates, professors and provosts of Trinity College, in the University of Dublin*, Williams & Norgate (1924)

(1161) Camp, A.J. *Sources for Irish genealogy in the library of the Society of Genealogists*, SoG, 2nd edn (1998)

(1162) Clare, W. *A simple guide to Irish genealogy, first compiled by the Rev. Wallace Clare*, Irish Genealogical Research Society, 3rd edn revised by R. Ffolliott (1966)

(1163) Davies, J.W. *Montgomeryshire pleadings in the Court of Chancery 1558–1714*, NLW & The Powysland Club (1991)

(1164) Davis, B. *Irish ancestry; a beginner's guide*, FFHS, 3rd edn (2001)

(1165) Dobson, D. *Jacobites of the '15*, D. Dobson & Scottish Association of Family History Societies (1993)

(1166) Durkan, J. *Protocol book of John Foular 1528–34*, Scottish Record Society (1985)

(1167) Eustace, P.B. *Registry of Deeds, Dublin, abstracts of wills, vol. I 1708–45, vol. II 1746–85 and vol. III* (with E. Ellis) *1785–1832*, Irish Manuscripts Commission (1954–84)

(1168) Falley, M.D. *Irish and Scottish-Irish ancestral research, a guide to the genealogical records, methods and sources in Ireland, vol. I repositories and records, vol. II bibliography and family index*, M.D. Falley (1962), GPC reprint (1989)

(1169) Ferguson, J.P.S. *Scottish family histories held in Scottish libraries*, National Library of Scotland, revd edn (1986)

(1170) Ferguson, J.P.S. *Scottish newspapers held in Scottish libraries*, National Library of Scotland, revd edn (1984)

(1171) Gandy, M. *Catholic family history, a bibliography for Wales*, M. Gandy (1996)

(1172) Gandy, M. *Catholic family history, a bibliography for Scotland*, M. Gandy (1996)

(1173) Glendinning, A. *Did your ancestors sign the Jersey Oath of Association roll of 1696?*, Channel Islands FHS (1995)

(1174) Goodbody, O.C. *Guide to Irish Quaker records 1654–1860*, Irish Manuscripts Commission (1967)

(1175) Grant, F.J. *The Faculty of Advocates in Scotland, 1532–1943*, with genealogical notes, Scottish Record Society (1944)

(1176) Grenham, J. *Tracing your Irish ancestors; the complete guide*, Gill & Macmillan, 2nd edn (1992)

(1177) Halloran, B.M. *The Scots College Paris 1603–1792*, John Donald Publishers (1997)

(1178) Hamilton-Edwards, G. *In search of Scottish ancestry*, Phillimore, 2nd edn (1983)

(1179) Hamilton- Edwards, G. *In search of Welsh ancestry*, Phillimore (1986)

(1180) Harris, R.E. *Islanders deported; part 1, the complete history of those British subjects who were deported from the Channel Islands during the German occupation of 1940–1945 and imprisoned in Europe*, CISS Publishing (1979)

(1180a) Harrison, R.S. *A biographical dictionary of Irish Quakers*, Four Courts Press (1997)

(1181) Helferty, S. & Refausse, R. *Directory of Irish archives*, Four Courts Press, 3rd edn (1999)

(1182) Henry, B. *Dublin hanged; crime, law enforcement and punishment in 18th century Dublin*, Irish Academic Press (1994)

(1183) Herlihy, J. *The Royal Irish Constabulary, a short history and genealogical guide with a select list of medal awards and casualties*, Four Courts Press (1997)

(1184) Ifans, D. *Nonconformist registers of Wales*, National Library of Wales and the Welsh County Archivists' Group (1994)

(1185) Innes, Sir T. *Scots heraldry, a practical handbook . . .*, Oliver & Boyd, 2nd edn (1956)

(1186) James, A. *Scottish roots; a step by step guide for ancestor hunters in Scotland and overseas*; Macdonald, 6th reprint (1988)

(1187) Johnson, C. *Scottish Catholic secular clergy 1879–1989*, John Donald Publishers (1991)

(1188) Jones, E.G. *Exchequer proceedings (equity) concerning Wales Henry VIII–Elizabeth, abstracts of bills and inventory of further proceedings*, University of Wales Press Board (1939)

(1189) Lamb, J.A. *Fasti ecclesiae Scoticanae; vol. IX, ministers of the church from the union of the churches, 2nd October 1929 to 31st December 1954*, Oliver & Boyd (1961)

(1190) Le Poidevin, D. *How to trace your ancestors in Guernsey*, Quality Service Printers (1978)

(1191) Lewis, E.A. *An inventory of early Chancery proceedings concerning Wales*, University of Wales Press (1937)

(1192) Lewis, E.A. & Conway Davies, J. *Records of the Court of Augmentations relating to Wales and Monmouthshire*, University of Wales Press (1954)

(1193) Livingstone, A., Aikman, C. & Hart, B. *Muster roll of Prince Charles Edward Stuart's army 1745–6*, Aberdeen University Press (1984)

(1194) Mackenzie, A. *Report of the Newsplan project in Scotland, September 1994*, British Library Board (1994)

(1195) MacLysaght, E. *The surnames of Ireland*, Irish Academic Press, 6th edn (1985)

(1196) MacLysaght, E. *Irish families*, Allen Figgis & Co Ltd, 1957, Irish Academic Press reprint, 4th edn (1985)

(1197) MacLysaght, E. *More Irish families*, Irish Academic Press, 2nd edn (1982), revised and enlarged edition of *More Irish families* incorporating *Supplement to Irish families*

(1198) Marr, L.J. *Guernsey people*, Phillimore (1984)

(1199) Masterson, J. *Ireland: 1841/1851 census abstracts (Northern Ireland and Republic of Ireland)*, GPC (1998)

(1200) Maxwell, I. *Tracing your ancestors in Northern Ireland*, The Stationery Office (1997)

(1201) Mitchell, B. *Irish passenger lists, 1847–1871, lists of passengers sailing from Londonderry to America on ships of the J. & J. Cooke Line & the McCorkell Line*, GPC (1988)

(1202) Mitchell, B. *Irish passenger lists, 1803–1806, lists of passengers sailing from Ireland to America extracted from the Hardwick papers*, GPC (1995)

(1203) Mitchell, B. *A guide to Irish parish registers*, GPC (1988)

(1204) Moody, D. *Scottish family history*, Batsford (1988)

(1205) Moody, D. *Scottish towns; sources for local historians*, Batsford (1992)

(1206) Morgan, T. & Morgan, P. *Welsh surnames*, University of Wales Press (1985)

(1207) Munter, R. *A handlist of Irish newspapers, 1685–1750*, Bowes & Bowes (1960)

(1208) Narasimham, J. *The Manx family tree, a beginner's guide to records in the Isle of Man*, Isle of Man FHS 3rd edn (2000) by N. Crowe and P. Lewthwaite

(1209) Neill, K. *How to trace family history in Northern Ireland*, Irish Heritage Association and BQ Publications (1986)

(1210) O'Connor, M.H. *A guide to tracing your Kerry ancestors*, Flyleaf Press (1990)

(1211) Owen, B. *The history of the Welsh militia and volunteer corps, vol. 1 Anglesey and Caernarfonshire*, Palace Books (1989)

(1212) Parry, G. *A guide to the records of Great Sessions in Wales*, NLW (1995)

(1213) Prochaska, A. *Irish history from 1700, a guide to sources in the PRO*, BRA (1986)

(1214) Raymond, S.A. *Scottish family history on the web, a directory*, FFHS (2002)

(1215) Raymond, S.A. *Irish family history on the web, a directory*, FFHS (2001)

(1216) Rowlands, J. & Rowlands, S. *Welsh family history; a guide to research*, Association of Family History Societies for Wales, 2nd edn (1998)

(1217) Rowlands, J. & Rowlands, S. *The surnames of Wales*, FFHS (1996)

(1218) Ryan, J.G. *Irish records; sources for family and local history*, Ancestry Publishing, revd edn (1997)

(1219) Scott, H. *Fasti ecclesiae Scoticanae, the succession of ministers in the Church of Scotland from the reformation, revised and continued to the present time; vol. I Synod of Lothian and Tweeddale*, Oliver & Boyd (1915) (vols II–VII published 1917–28)

(1220) Scott, H. *Fasti ecclesiae Scoticanae, vol. VIII, Ministers of the church from the date of publication of volumes I to VII to the union of the churches, 2nd October 1929 and addenda & corrigenda 1560–1949*; Oliver & Boyd (1950)

(1221) Sexton, S. *Ireland, photographs 1840–1930*, Laurence King Publishing (1994)

(1222) Simpson, G.G. *Scottish handwriting 1150–1650; an introduction to the reading of documents*, Tuckwell Press, revd edn (1998)

(1223) Sinclair, C. *Tracing your Scottish ancestors: a guide to ancestry research in the Scottish Record Office*, HMSO, revd edn (1997)

(1224) Sinclair, C. *Tracing Scottish local history; a guide to local history research in the Scottish Record Office*, HMSO (1994)

(1225) Smyth, S. *Report of the Newsplan Project in Ireland*, British Library & National Library of Ireland, revd edn (1998)

(1226) Stevenson, D. & Stevenson, W. *Scottish texts and calendars; an analytical guide to serial publications*, RHS (1987)

(1227) Stuart, M. *Scottish family history, a guide to works of reference on the history and genealogy of Scottish families*, Oliver & Boyd (1930) GPC reprint (1994)

(1228) Torrance, D.R. *Scottish trades and professions, a selected bibliography*, SAFHS (1991)

(1229) Walker, B.M. & Hoppen, K.T. 'Irish election pollbooks 1832–1872', from *Irish booklore*, vol. 3, no 1 & vol. 4, no 2; Blackstaff Press (1976–77)

(1230) Watt, D.E.R. *Fasti ecclesiae Scoticanae medii aevi ad annum 1638*, Fasti Committee department of mediaeval history, St Salvator's College, St Andrews & Scottish Record Society; 2nd draft edn (1969)

(1231) Watt, D.E.R. *A biographical dictionary of Scottish graduates to 1410*, Clarendon Press (1977)

(1232) Way, G. & Squire, R. *Collins Scottish clan & family encyclopedia*, HarperCollins (1994)

(1233) Whyte, D. *The Scots overseas, a selected bibliography*, SAFHS, 2nd edn (1995)

(1234) Whyte, D. *Introducing Scottish genealogical research*, Scottish Genealogy Society, 5th edn (1984)

(1235) Young, A.F. *The encyclopaedia of Scottish executions 1750 to 1963*, Eric Dobby Publishing (1998)

(1236) Yurdan, M. *Irish family history*, Batsford (1990)

Chapter 30

(1237) *Almanach de Gotha, genealogy 1999, vol. I part I, Reigning and formerly reigning Royal houses of Europe and South America, part II Mediatized sovereign houses of the Holy Roman Empire*, Almanach de Gotha, 183rd edn (1999)

(1238) *Ancestry, the family history source from ancestry.com*, MyFamily.com, Inc.

(1239) *British immigration to Victoria resource kit, assisted immigrants from UK 1839–1871*, Public Record Office of Victoria (n.d.)

(1240) *Burke's American families with British ancestry, the lineages of 1,600 families of British origin now resident in the United States of America*, GPC reprint (1996) from *Burke's genealogical and heraldic history of the landed gentry, 16th edn* (1939)

(1241) *Dictionary of Canadian biography*, University of Toronto Press/OUP, 13 vols (1966–91)

(1242) *The East India register & directory for 1819*, East India Company (1819)

(1243) *The East India register & directory for 1821*, MM Publications microfiche reprint (1995)

(1244) *The East India register & directory for 1825*, East India Company (1825)

(1245) *Guide to genealogical research in the National Archives*, National Archives & Records Service (1982)

(1246) *A guide to Ontario land registry records*, Ontario Genealogical Society (1994)

(1247) *Immigration, index to assisted immigrants arriving Sydney and Newcastle 1844–1859*, Archives Authority of New South Wales, 3 vols (1987)

(1248) *Index of New South Wales convict indents 1788 to 1842*, Genealogical Society of Victoria (1986)

(1249) *The Indian army list, January 1931*, Government of India (1931)

(1250) *The Mitchell Library, Sydney, historical and descriptive notes*, Trustees of the Public Library of New South Wales (1936)

(1251) *Richmound's heritage, a history of Richmound and district 1910–1978*, Richmound Historical Society (1978)

(1251a) *They came in waves; conference proceedings 2003*, New Zealand Society of Genealogists (2003)

(1252) Baxter, A. *In search of your European roots, a complete guide to tracing your ancestors in every country in Europe*, GPC (1986)

(1253) Baxter, A. *In search of your German roots, a complete guide to tracing your ancestors in the Germanic areas of Europe*, GPC, 3rd edn (1994)

(1254) Baxter, A. *In search of your Canadian roots; tracing your family tree in Canada*, GPC, 3rd edn (2000)

(1255) Baxter, C.J. *Musters of New South Wales and Norfolk Island 1805–1806*, ABGR (1989)

(1256) Baxter, C.J. *General musters of New South Wales, Norfolk Island and Van Diemen's Land 1811*, ABGR (1987)

(1257) Baxter, I.A. *India Office Library and records; a brief guide to biographical sources*, British Library, 2nd edn (1990)

(1258) Bean, P. & Melville, J. *Lost children of the Empire*, Unwin Hyman (1989)

(1259) Bernard, R. *Tracing your German ancestors*; Anglo-German FHS, 2nd revd edn (1992)

(1260) Brogan, H. & Mosley, C. *American presidential families*, Sutton & Morris Genealogical Books (1993)

(1261) Bromell, A. *Tracing family history in New Zealand*, Godwit Publishing, 3rd edn (1996)

(1262) Cable, K.J. & Marchant, J.C. *Australian biographical and genealogical record, series 2 1842–1899 volume 2*, ABGR in association with the Society of Australian Genealogists (1987)

(1263) Cannan, E. *Churches of the South Atlantic Islands 1502–1991*, A. Nelson (1992)

(1264) Catsyannis, T. *The Greek community of London*, T. Catsyannis (1993)

(1265) Cerny, J. *A guide to German parish registers in the Family History Library of the Church of Jesus Christ of Latter-Day Saints*, GPC (1988)

(1266) Chandler, M. *A guide to records in Barbados*, Blackwalls for the University of the West Indies (1965)

(1267) Choquette, M. & others. *The beginner's guide to Finnish genealogical research*, Thomsen's Genealogical Center (1985)

(1268) Cobley, J. *The crimes of the First Fleet convicts*, Angus and Robertson (1970)

(1269) Coldham, P.W. *English convicts in colonial America, vol. I Middlesex 1617–1775, vol. II London 1656–1775*, Polyanthos (1974–76)

(1270) Coldham, P.W. *American loyalist claims, abstracted from the PRO Audit Office series 13, bundles 1–35 & 37*, National Genealogical Society (1980)

(1271) Coldham, P.W. *American wills & administrations in the Prerogative Court of Canterbury 1610–1857*, GPC (1989)

(1272) Coldham, P.W. *Child apprentices in America from Christ's Hospital, London 1617–1778*, GPC (1990)

(1273) Coldham, P.W. *The complete book of emigrants in bondage 1614–1775*, GPC (1988)

(1273a) Coldham, P.W. *More emigrants in bondage 1614–1775*, GPC (2002)

(1274) Coldham, P.W. *The complete book of emigrants, vol. I 1607–60, vol. II 1661–99, vol. III 1700–50, vol. IV 1751–76*, GPC (1987–93)

(1275) Colletta, J.P. *Finding Italian roots, the complete guide for Americans*, GPC revd edn (1996)

(1276) Currer-Briggs, N. *Worldwide family history*, RKP (1982)

(1277) Davies, K.G. *Calendars of State Papers, colonial series, America and West Indies, vol. XLIII, 1737*, HMSO (1963)

(1278) Dobson, D. *Directory of Scottish settlers in North America 1625–1825*, GPC, 6 vols (1984–86)

(1279) Drake, P. *In search of family history, a starting place*, Heritage Books Inc, 2nd edn (1992)

(1280) Eakle, A. & Cerny, J. *The source; a guidebook of American genealogy*, Ancestry Publishing Co. (1984), 3rd edn by L. Szucs & S. Luebking (2001)

(1281) Farrington, A. *Guide to the records of the India Office military department*, India Office Library (1982)

(1282) Filby, P.W. & Meyer, M.K. *Passenger and immigration lists index*, Gale Research Co., 3 vols (1981) with annual supplements (1982–2003)

(1283) Filby, P.W. *Passenger and immigration lists bibliography 1538–1900, being a guide to published lists of arrivals in the United States and Canada*, Gale Research Co., 2nd edn (1988)

(1284) File, N. & Power, C. *Black settlers in Britain 1555–1958*, Heinemann (1981)

(1285) Flynn, M. *The Second Fleet; Britain's grim convict armada of 1790*, Library of Australian History, revd edn (2001)

(1286) Franklin, C.M. *Dutch genealogical research*, C.M. Franklin (1982)

(1287) Gillen, M. *The founders of Australia, a biographical dictionary of the First Fleet*, Library of Australian History (1989)

(1288) Glazier, I.A. & Tepper, M. *The famine immigrants, lists of Irish immigrants arriving at the port of New York 1846–1851*, GPC, 7 vols (1983–86)

(1289) Grannum, G. *Tracing your West Indian ancestors; sources in the PRO*, PRO, 2nd edn (2002)

(1290) Greenwood, V. *The researcher's guide to American genealogy*, GPC, 3rd edn (1999)

(1291) Harrison, P. *The home children*, Watson & Dwyer Publishing, 3rd edn (1979)

(1292) Hawkings, D.T. *Bound for Australia*, Phillimore (1987)

(1293) Hallett, A.C.H. *Early Bermuda records 1619–1826*, Juniperhill Press (1991)

(1294) Hallett, A.C.H. *Early Bermuda wills 1629–1835*, Juniperhill Press (1993)

(1294a) Hockly, H.E. *The story of the British settlers of 1820 in South Africa*, Juta, 2nd edn (1957)

(1295) Hotten, J.C. *The original lists of persons of quality, emigrants, religious exiles, political rebels, serving men sold for a term of years, apprentices, children stolen, maidens pressed and others who went from Great Britain to the American plantations 1600–1700 . . . from MSS preserved in the State Paper department at the PRO*, GPC (1962)

(1296) Howes, H.W. *The Gibralterian, the origin and development of the population of Gibralter from 1704*, Mediterranean Sun Publishing, 3rd edn (1991)

(1297) Johnson, A. et al. *Dictionary of American biography*, OUP, 20 vols (1928–36)

(1298) Kershaw, R. *Emigrants and expats, a guide to sources on UK emigration and residents overseas*, PRO (2002)

(1299) Kershaw, R. & Pearsall, M. *Immigrants and aliens, a guide to sources on UK immigration and citizenship*, PRO (2000)

(1300) Konrad, J. *Italian family research*, Summit Publications, 2nd revd edn (1990)

(1301) Lancour, H. & Wolfe, R.J. *A bibliography of ship passenger lists 1538–1825, being a guide to published lists of early immigrants to North America; compiled by H. Lancour*, New York Public Library, 3rd edn revised by R.J. Wolfe (1969)

(1302) Lombard, R.T. *Handbook for genealogical research in South Africa*, Institute for Historical Research, Human Sciences Council; 2nd edn (1984)

(1303) Losty, J.P. *Prints, drawings and photographs in the India Office Library*, British Library (n.d.)

(1304) Merriman, B.D. *Genealogy in Ontario, searching the records*, Ontario Genealogical Society, 3rd edn (1996)

(1305) Mitchell, M.E. *Jamaican ancestry: how to find out more*, Heritage Books (1998)

(1306) Moir, M. *A general guide to the India Office records*, British Library (1988)

(1307) Morris, H. & Hafslund, B. *New Zealand assisted passenger list 1855–1871, from here to there*, W. & F. Pascoe Pty (1994)

(1308) Morse Jones, E. *Roll of the British settlers in South Africa, part I, up to 1826*, 1820 Settlers Monument Committee (1969)

(1309) Morton, D. *When your number's up; the Canadian soldier in the First World War*, Random House (1993)

(1310) Oliver, V.L. *The monumental inscriptions of the British West Indies*, F.G. Longman (1927)

(1311) Olsson, N.W. *Tracing your Swedish ancestry*, Ministry of Foreign Affairs (1982)

(1312) Peake, A.G. *National register of shipping arrivals, Australia and New Zealand*, Australian Federation of Family History Organisations, 3rd edn (1993)

(1312a) Philip, P. *British residents at the Cape 1795–1819, biographical records of 4,800 pioneers*, David Philip (1981)

(1313) Pontet, P. *Ancestral research in France*, P. Pontet (1998)

(1314) Ritchie, J. & others. *Australian dictionary of biography*; Melbourne University Press, vols I to XII 1788 to 1939 and index vol. (1966–91)

(1315) Ryan, R.J. *The Third Fleet convicts*, Horwitz Grahame (1983)

(1316) Ryskamp, A. *Finding your Hispanic roots*, GPC (1997)

(1317) St-Louis-Harrison, L. & Munk, M. *Tracing your ancestors in Canada*, National Archives of Canada, 12th edn (1997)

(1318) Sainty, M.R. & Johnson, K.A. *Census of New South Wales November 1828*, Library of Australian History (1985)

(1319) Schaefer, C.K. *Guide to naturalization records in the United States*, GPC (1997)

(1320) Schlyter, D.M. *A handbook of Czechoslovak genealogical research*, Genun Publishers (1990)

(1321) Scholefield, G. *Dictionary of New Zealand biography*, Department of Internal Affairs, 2 vols (1940)

(1322) Senekovic, D. *Handy guide to Austrian genealogical records*, Everton Publishers (1979)

(1323) Smee, C.J. *Third Fleet families of Australia, containing genealogical details of three hundred & eleven Third Fleeters, their children and grandchildren*, C.J. Smee (1991)

(1324) Smelser, R.M. *Finding your German ancestors*, Ancestry (1991)

(1325) Spurway, J.T. *Australian biographical and genealogical record, series I 1788–1841 with series 2 supplement 1842–1899*, ABGR in association with the Society of Australian Genealogists (1992)

(1326) Suess, J.H. *Handy guide to Hungarian genealogical records*, Everton Publishers (1980)

(1327) Taylor, N.C. *Sources for Anglo-Indian genealogy in the library of the SoG*, SoG (1990)

(1328) Tepper, M. *American passenger arrival records, a guide to the records of immigrants arriving at American ports by sail and steam*, GPC (1988) [revd edn (1993)]

(1329) Thomsen, F.A. *Genealogical guidebook & atlas of Sweden*, Thomsen's Genealogical Center (1981)

(1330) Thomsen, F.A. *Genealogical maps & guide to the Norwegian parish registers*, Thomsen's Genealogical Center (1981)

(1331) Thomsen, F.A. *Scandinavian genealogical research manual, vol. I Danish-Norwegian language guide and dictionary; vol. II the old handwriting and names of Denmark and Norway; vol. III Danish-Norwegian genealogical research sources*, Thomsen's Genealogical Center (1980)

(1332) Thurston, A. *Sources for colonial studies in the PRO, vol. I Records of the Colonial Office, Dominions Office, Commonwealth Relations Office and Commonwealth Office*, PRO (1999)

(1333) Towey, P. *An introduction to tracing your German ancestors*, FFHS, 2nd edn (2002)

(1334) Vine Hall, N. *Tracing your family history in Australia, a national guide to sources*, N. Vine Hall, 3rd edn (2002)

(1334a) Vine Hall, N. *Tracing your family history in Australia, a bibliography*, N. Vine Hall (2002)

(1335) Vine Hall, N. *Parish registers in Australia; a list of originals, transcripts, microforms & indexes of Australian parish registers*, N. Vine Hall, 2nd edn (1990)

(1336) Virkus, F.A. *The abridged compendium of American genealogy, first families of America, a genealogical encyclopedia of the United States*, 7 vols (1925–42) GPC reprint (1987)

(1337) Wellauer, M. *Tracing your Swiss roots*, M.A. Wellauer (1988)

(1338) Wellauer, M. *Tracing your Czech & Slovak roots*, M.A. Wellauer (1980)

(1339) Wellauer, M. *Tracing your Polish roots*, M.A. Wellauer, revd edn (1991)

(1340) Wellauer, M. *Tracing your Norwegian roots*, M.A. Wellauer (1979)

(1341) Wigfield, W.M. *The Monmouth rebels 1685*, Somerset Record Society (1985)

(1342) Yeo, G. *The British overseas; a guide to records of their baptisms, births, marriages, deaths and burials available in the United Kingdom*, Guildhall Library 3rd edn (1994) by P. White & others

INDEX

CPSIA information can be obtained at www.ICGtesting.com
Printed in the USA
269901BV00004B/102/P